Encyclopedia of Sociology

Editorial Board

Encyclopedia of Sociology

VOLUME 3

Edgar F. Borgatta
Editor-in-Chief
University of Washington, Seattle

Marie L. Borgatta
Managing Editor
University of Washington, Seattle

MACMILLAN PUBLISHING COMPANY
New York

MAXWELL MACMILLAN CANADA
Toronto

MAXWELL MACMILLAN INTERNATIONAL
New York · Oxford · Singapore · Sydney

Macmillan Publishing Company
866 Third Avenue, New York, NY 10022

Maxwell Macmillan Canada, Inc.
1200 Eglinton Avenue East, Suite 200
Don Mills, Ontario M3C 3N1

Printed in the United States of America

Library of Congress Catalog Card No.: 91-37827

printing number
3 4 5 6 7 8 9 10

Macmillan, Inc., is part of the Maxwell Communication Group of Companies.

Library of Congress Catalog in Publication Data
Encyclopedia of sociology / Edgar F. Borgatta, editor-in-chief, Marie L. Borgatta, managing editor.
p. cm.
Includes bibliographical references and index.
ISBN 0-02-897051-9 (set).—ISBN 0-02-897052-7 (v. 1) : $90.00
1. Sociology—Encyclopedias. I. Borgatta, Marie L.
HM17.E5 1991
301'.03—dc20 91-37827
CIP

EDITORIAL AND PRODUCTION STAFF

Philip Friedman, *Publisher*
Elly Dickason, *Editor in Chief*
Martha Goldstein, *Senior Project Editor*
Lynn Constantinou, *Production Manager*
Karin K. Vanderveer, *Assistant Editor*

The paper used in this publication meets the minimum requirements of American National Standard for Information Sciences—Permanence of Paper for Printed Library Materials. ANSI Z39.48–1984.

Encyclopedia of Sociology

L

LABELING THEORY *See* Deviance.

LABOR FORCE Although labor force concepts were originally designed to study economic activity and guide government policies, economic activities are a form of *social* behavior, with numerous social determinants and consequences. Hence labor force behavior has been the subject of a substantial body of sociological research.

MEASUREMENT

The U.S. Bureau of the Census developed the labor force concept to measure the number of working-age people who were economically active during a particular time: the calendar week preceding the sample interview (Cain 1979; U.S. Department of Labor 1982). It has two components: (1) *the employed,* those who, during the reference week, did any work at all as paid employees, self-employed, or unpaid family workers working at least fifteen hours in a family-operated enterprise. Included also are those who were employed but on vacation, home sick, or not on the job for various other reasons, and (2) *the unemployed:* those who were not employed during the reference week but were available for work and had actively sought employment sometime within the preceding four-week period. All those who are neither employed or unemployed are defined as being out of the labor force and primarily include students, housewives, the retired, and the disabled. Since the size of the population affects the number of people who work, labor force measures are usually expressed in ratio form. The *labor force participation rate* is the percentage of the total working-age *population* that is in the labor force, whereas the *unemployment rate* is the percentage of the *labor force* that is unemployed. To compare particular subgroups in the population, analysts compute group-specific measures such as the percentage of all women, versus men, who are in the labor force or the percentage of black, versus white, labor force members who are unemployed.

The Census Bureau developed the labor force concepts during the Great Depression of the 1930s in response to the government's difficulty in charting the severity of unemployment during that crisis. Prior to 1940, measures of economic activity were only collected at the time of the decennial censuses, making it impossible to track business-cycle fluctuations in unemployment; for example, most of the Great Depression came between the 1930 and 1940 censuses. Hence, to provide ongoing unemployment data, the Census Bureau initiated the monthly Current Population Survey in the 1940s.

A second problem was the ambiguity of the previously used measure of economic activity, the *gainful worker concept,* which was designed to ascertain individuals' usual occupations, if they had them, rather than whether they were actually working at any given time (Durand 1948; Hauser 1949). In fact, census enumerators were often specifically instructed to record an occupation, even if the individual were currently unemployed, thus *over*stating the number employed. On the other hand, some kinds of employment were often *under*estimated because people who considered their market work to be secondary to their other activities, such as taking care of the home and children or going to school, were less likely to report themselves as employed in response to a question on their usual occupation. Such misreporting was unlikely with the labor force measure, since most people could remember whether they had worked at all the previous week or, if not, whether they had been looking for a job. Information on occupation and on other important characteristics of their employment, such as hours worked, was then obtained separately in response to additional questions.

While labor force concepts are relatively unambiguous measures of economic activity, they too exhibit problems. A general concern is the adequacy of the unemployment measure. The extent of unemployment may be understated if persistently unemployed persons eventually give up trying and drop out of the labor force. The Census Bureau has therefore included additional questions to try to ascertain the number of such "discouraged workers" (Cain 1979). The work of Clifford Clogg and Teresa Sullivan extends this approach to address the larger question of "*under*-employment" (Sullivan 1978; Clogg and Sullivan 1983). They have developed and applied a variety of indicators of underemployment, in order to achieve a more extensive assessment of the problem. In addition to the usual unemployment rate and estimates of discouraged workers, they use three other indicators: a measure of involuntary part-time work (due to economic factors); low work-related income relative to the poverty level, and a measure of the proportion of workers who are "overeducated" ("mismatched") for the jobs they hold. The "adequately employed" are all those who are not underemployed in any one of these five categories. Their results indicate that underemployment is more common among the young and the old and appears to have increased in recent years. While several of the indices, particularly the mismatch measure, are somewhat controversial (Keyfitz 1981), their work represents an important innovation in the multidimensional measurement of underemployment.

A major characteristic of the labor force concept is that it is a measure of market-oriented economic activities. People are only considered employed if they work for pay (or in the production of goods or services for sale). Yet there is a considerable amount of economic production for home consumption. Hence, labor force status per se is an imperfect indicator of whether an individual is economically productive; for example, full-time homemakers are never counted as employed, although they usually put in long hours producing goods and services for their families. However, if the market-oriented nature of the measure is kept in mind, this limitation is not too serious in a modern industrial society. Increases in married women's labor force participation can then be interpreted as indicating their growing participation in the market sector of the economy, usually in addition to their home productive activities, although working wives do less housework than nonworking (Vanek 1974; Berardo, Shihan, and Leslie 1987).

More serious problems arise in comparing societies at different levels of economic development (Moore 1953). Preindustrial subsistence economies produce few goods or services for a market. As societies develop economically, an increasing proportion of labor is sold in the marketplace, and the goods and services families consume are also increasingly purchased, rather than home-produced. It is often difficult to undertake a meaningful comparison of labor force or unemployment rates among such different economies. The measurement of agricultural employment, especially that of women and youth, can be particularly problematic in countries with a large subsistence sector, and measurement inconsistencies are common (Dixon 1982). Moreover, *unemployment*, especially in rural areas, is often manifested as *under*-employment, and its extensiveness is difficult to determine.

DETERMINANTS AND CONSEQUENCES OF LABOR FORCE CHANGES

The size and rate of growth of the labor force is dependent on three factors.

1. *The size and rate of population growth.* A large and/or rapidly growing population produces a large and/or growing labor force.

2. *The propensity of the population to enter the labor force and how this varies among population subgroups.* Age and sex, and what these signify biologically and socially, are the major reasons for varying propensities. Infants and young children do not work but, generally starting in adolescence, labor force participation increases with age, peaking for those in their late thirties and early forties and starting an accelerating decline thereafter. Married women, particularly mothers of young children, have historically had lower labor force participation rates than adult males, although this is much less so now than in the past (U.S. Department of Labor 1988).

3. *The composition of the population.* Since different population segments have different work propensities, the composition of the population affects the overall proportions in the labor force. Sharp *short*-run fluctuations in the U.S. birth rate have led to corresponding variations in the relative size of the working-age population. After sixteen–eighteen years, baby booms greatly increase the number of new labor force entrants, while baby busts reduce it. However, the overall *long*-run declines in U.S. fertility, combined with declines in mortality among the elderly, have increased the relative number of elderly in the population, an age group with low work propensities. On the other hand, foreign migration to the United States somewhat counteracts the effects of an aging population, since it has historically been disproportionately composed of young working-age adults drawn to the United States by job opportunities.

One long-term trend in labor force participation in the United States has been the decline in employment of older males, primarily due to the earlier retirement made possible by the institution and spread of the social security system, combined with the greater availability of disability benefits and pensions. The employment of young males has also decreased, due to more extended schooling, although offset somewhat by a rise in student employment (U.S. Department of Labor 1988). However, the most substantial postwar change in employment behavior has been the enormous increase in married-women's labor force participation. While paid employment used to be generally limited to the period between school and marriage, since the 1940s married women's employment has become so prevalent that, by 1988, between 65 percent and 73 percent of those in the 20–44 age groups were in the labor force. Moreover, almost 60 percent of married mothers of children under age six were also in the labor force (Oppenheimer 1970; U.S. Department of Commerce 1989b).

There are several reasons for this rapid rise in women's employment in addition to the impetus provided by rapid economic growth. The bureaucratization of government and industry has raised the demand for clerical workers. Population growth, prosperity, and rising living standards have greatly expanded the consumption of services. This, in turn, has raised the demand for salespeople, or those in the helping professions such as teachers and social workers, and nurses and others in health-related occupations. Since the great majority of young, single, out-of-school women work, the result of this increasing demand has been a strong and continuing demand for a previously underutilized source of female labor: married women (Oppenheimer 1970).

For their part, married women often had several major reasons for wanting to work: the need, early in marriage, to help set up a new household and perhaps save money for a down payment on a house; the desire to save for the children's schooling; the couple's desire to achieve a high level of living. In addition, a woman's desire for greater personal economic security has also probably been an important factor. Trends in the cost of living have also increased the need to raise family income to achieve and maintain a high living standard (Oppenheimer 1982).

The effects of changing labor force behavior are not limited to the economic realm. A number of sociologists, as well as economists, have argued that it has also had an important impact on marriage and the family. Since the late 1960s the average age at marriage has risen substantially, after having declined through most of the twentieth century; nonmarital cohabitation has become increasingly prevalent; and marital instability has accelerated its long-term upward trend, after a sharp reversal in the early post–World War II period. Two competing employment-related explanations for these trends are currently under debate. In one, the argument is that married women's rapidly rising labor force participation has increased their economic independence from males (Becker 1981; Espenshade 1985; Goldscheider and Waite 1986; Farley 1988). The result is a decreasing desire on the part of women to remain in an unhappy marriage or even to marry at all. In addition, since women's traditional time- and energy-consuming familial roles of childbearing and child rearing compete with the pursuit of individual career goals, more women are either forgoing childbearing entirely or settling for one or two children at most.

The extensiveness of the changes in women's employment qualifies this factor as one potentially important reason for the recent trends in marriage and family behavior. However, it is well known that marriage formation and marital stability are also related to *men's* employment characteristics (Goldscheider and Waite 1986; Teachman, Polonko, and Leigh 1987; Ross and Sawhill 1975; Cherlin 1979). Moreover, research in both sociology and economics indicates that men's labor market position, especially *young* men's, has also changed substantially since the late 1960s. Particularly important has been the marked decline in the earnings position of young men relative to that of prime working-age males (Easterlin 1987; Oppenheimer 1988). The reason for this, Richard Easterlin hypothesizes, is that the prolonged postwar baby boom led to a lengthy period during which relatively large birth cohorts were crowding the labor market, and the resulting increase in competition for good jobs reduced the relative economic position of the young, at least temporarily. This led, in turn, Easterlin argues, to delayed marriage, lower fertility, and more unstable marriages. However, the small baby-bust cohorts (the result of the long-term declines in fertility since the late 1950s) have only recently started entering the labor market and, according to Easterlin, their small size should lead to an improvement in the relative economic position of the young, facilitating earlier marriage and providing greater economic security to marriages already formed.

Tests of Easterlin's hypothesis have had mixed results, some positive and some negative (MacDonald and Rindfuss 1981; Devaney 1983). One important problem is that marriage and fertility behavior seem to fluctuate more in response to historical factors such as wars, business cycles, and social changes than to a cohort phenomenon such as group size (Rodgers and Thornton 1985; Smith 1981). For example, marriage delays increased during the 1980s, even though the relative size of cohorts entering the labor market had started to decline (U.S. Department of Commerce 1989a). There are also reasons to believe that the poor relative economic position of young males may never entirely reverse itself, despite shifts in relative cohort size. Rising educational attainment postpones young men's transition to their adult occupational careers, reducing their relative economic position in youth, although it may improve in maturity (Oppenheimer 1982). In addition, there is evidence that the structure of the American economy has been shifting in recent years. There has been a decline in manufacturing employment, particularly in the well-paid, durable-goods industries, accompanied by a substantial rise in the absolute and relative importance of employment in service industries (Urquhart 1984). Part of this reflects an expansion of jobs in low-paying service industries such as fast food and other retail trade industries, but there has also been an expansion in technical service jobs at various levels, most of which require a relatively well-educated labor supply. The result seems to be a worsening of the relative economic position of less-educated workers, particularly those who have not completed high school (Markey 1988).

William Julius Wilson (1987) has elaborated this argument to explain the particularly sharp decline in marriage formation among blacks, combined with the rapid increase in marital instability and the resultant rise in female-headed families. His hypothesis is that, because of the suburbanization of manufacturing and the growth of information-processing industries in large central cities, less educated, central-city blacks are increasingly isolated from good blue-collar jobs, resulting in a sharp rise in black unemployment rates and a decline in labor force participation, as well as the growth of criminal behavior. In short, an urban ghetto underclass with poor long-term economic prospects has been created. The consequence, Wilson argues, is a decline in the relative supply of "eligible" (i.e., nonincarcerated and employed) males for black women to marry.

Critics of Wilson's thesis, have argued, however, that central-city labor markets are not really isolated and that the black labor market disadvantage exists regardless of location (Ellwood 1986). Moreover, the work of Robert Mare and Christopher Winship (1984) indicates that at least some of the decline in black youth employment is the result of an increase in delayed labor force entry by more employable black males, due to rising school enrollment and military service. In addition, whatever the reasons for the shifts in these males' relative economic position, two back-to-back recessions in the 1980s exacerbated these problems, especially since recessions selectively affect the young and minorities most heavily, that is, those with less job security. Other critics have argued that increases in delayed marriage and marital instability are not limited to the "underclass" populations Wilson is describing (Farley 1988). However, this may simply reflect the fact that young men *in general* have recently experienced a deterioration in their labor market position, a deterioration that has been, however, particularly acute among blacks.

This article has reviewed the history of labor force measures, as well as several important current issues in labor force analysis. First, the study of the labor force reveals the changing significance of work in the lives of different segments of the population. Second, since economic behavior affects other social systems such as the family and stratification systems, labor force analysis will continue to be an essential field for sociological analysis.

(SEE ALSO: *Occupational and Career Mobility; Work and Occupations*)

REFERENCES

Becker, Gary S. 1981 *A Treatise on the Family.* Cambridge, Mass.: Harvard University Press.

Berardo, Donna Hodgkins, Constance L. Shehan, and Gerald R. Leslie 1987 "A Residue of Tradition: Jobs, Careers, and Spouses' Time in Housework." *Journal of Marriage and the Family* 49:381–390.

Cain, Glenn C. 1979 "Labor Force Concepts and Definitions in View of Their Purposes." *Concepts and Data Needs—Appendix Vol. 1.* Washington, D.C.: National Commission on Employment and Unemployment Statistics.

Cherlin, Andrew J. 1979 "Work Life and Marital Dissolution." In George Levinger and Oliver C. Moles, eds., *Divorce and Separation: Contexts, Causes and Consequences.* New York: Basic Books.

Clogg, Clifford C., and Teresa A. Sullivan 1983 "Labor Force Composition and Underemployment Trends, 1969–1980." *Social Indicators Research* 12:117–152.

Devaney, Barbara 1983 "An Analysis of Variations in U.S. Fertility and Female Labor Force Participation Trends." *Demography* 20:147–142.

Dixon, Ruth B. 1982 "Women in Agriculture: Counting the Labor Force in Developing Countries." *Population and Development Review* 8:539–561.

Durand, John D. 1948 *The Labor Force in the United States, 1890–1960.* New York: Social Science Research Council.

Easterlin, Richard A. 1987 *Birth and Fortune.* Chicago: University of Chicago Press.

Ellwood, David T. 1986 "The Spatial Mismatch Hypothesis: Are There Teenage Jobs Missing in the Ghetto?" In Richard B. Freeman and Harry J. Holzer, eds., *The Black Youth Employment Crisis.* Chicago: University of Chicago Press.

Espenshade, Thomas J. 1985 "Marriage Trends in America: Estimates, Implications, and Underlying Causes." *Population and Development Review* 11:193–245.

Farley, Reynolds 1988 "After the Starting Line: Blacks and Women in an Uphill Race." *Demography* 25: 477–495.

Goldscheider, Frances Kobrin, and Linda J. Waite 1986 "Sex Differences in the Entry into Marriage." *American Journal of Sociology* 92:91–109.

Hauser, Philip M. 1949 "The Labor Force and Gainful Workers: Concept, Measurement and Comparability." *American Journal of Sociology* 54:338–355.

Keyfitz, Nathan 1981 "Review of Measuring Underemployment, by C. C. Clogg." *American Journal of Sociology* 86:1163–1165.

MacDonald, Maurice M., and Ronald R. Rindfuss 1981 "Earnings, Relative Income, and Family Formation." *Demography* 18:123–136.

Mare, Robert D., and Christopher Winship 1984 "The Paradox of Lessening Racial Inequality and Joblessness among Black Youth: Enrollment, Enlistment, and Employment, 1964–1981." *American Sociological Review* 49:39–55.

Markey, James P. 1988 "The Labor Market Problems of Today's High School Dropouts." *Monthly Labor Review* 111:36–43.

Moore, Wilbert E. 1953 "The Exportability of the Labor Force Concept." *American Sociological Review* 18:68–72.

Oppenheimer, Valerie Kincade 1970 *The Female Labor Force in the United States: Demographic and Economic Factors Governing Its Growth and Changing Composition* (Population Monograph Series, No. 5). Berkeley, Calif.: University of California, Institute of International Studies.

Oppenheimer, Valerie Kincade 1982 *Work and the Family: A Study in Social Demography.* New York: Academic Press.

Oppenheimer, Valerie Kincade 1988 "A Theory of Marriage Timing." *American Journal of Sociology* 94:563–591.

Rodgers, Willard, and Arland Thornton 1985 "Changing Patterns of First Marriage in the United States." *Demography* 22:265–279.

Ross, Heather L., and Isabel V. Sawhill 1975 *Time of Transition: The Growth of Families Headed by Women.* Washington, D.C.: Urban Institute.

Smith, D. P. 1981 "A Reconsideration of Easterlin Cycles." *Population Studies* 35:247–264.

Sullivan, Teresa A. 1978 *Marginal Workers, Marginal Jobs: The Underutilization of American Workers.* Austin, Tex.: University of Texas Press.

Teachman, Jay D., Karen A. Polonko, and Geoffrey K. Leigh 1987 "Marital Timing: Race and Sex Comparisons." *Social Forces* 66:239–268.

U.S. Department of Commerce, Bureau of the Census 1989a "Marital Status and Living Arrangements: March 1989." *Current Population Reports* (P-20, No. 445).

U.S. Department of Commerce, Bureau of the Census 1989b *Statistical Abstract of the United States: 1989.* Washington, D.C.: U.S. Government Printing Office.

U.S. Department of Labor, Bureau of Labor Statistics 1982 *BLS Handbook of Methods,* Vol 1. Washington, D.C.: U.S. Government Printing Office.

U.S. Department of Labor, Bureau of Labor Statistics 1988 *Labor Force Statistics Derived from the Current Population Survey* (Bulletin 2307). Washington: U.S. Government Printing Office.

Urquhart, Michael 1984 "The Employment Shift to Services: Where Did It Come From?" *Monthly Labor Review* 107:15–22.

Vanek, Joan 1974 "Time Spent in Housework." *Scientific American* 231:116–120.

Wilson, William Julius 1987 *The Truly Disadvantaged.* Chicago: University of Chicago Press.

VALERIE KINCADE OPPENHEIMER

LABOR MOVEMENTS AND UNIONS

Broadly defined, labor movements consist of collective actions, mainly on the part of wage workers in market societies, to improve their economic, social, and political positions in society. The main organizational forms of movements are labor unions and political parties. Others include producer and consumer cooperatives, credit unions, newspapers, and educational, welfare, cultural, and recreational facilities.

From the inception of the discipline, sociologists have studied labor movements and unions, but their scholarly production has been modest. The *American Journal of Sociology, American Sociological Review,* and *Social Forces,* in 195 accumulated years of publication, offered only fifty articles whose titles reveal a focus on labor movements and unions. Although Europeans produced more studies than American sociologists, labor economists and social historians have contributed even more. Sociologists have conspicuously neglected collective bargaining, mediation, and arbitration. Yet they have contributed to knowledge about labor movements and unions while attacking related problems in such central areas of the discipline as social stratification (e.g., working-class formation, income inequality), organizations (union leadership turnover), race and gender relations (discrimination in unions), politics (party preferences of unionists), and industry (shop–floor life, the labor process). Students of social movements, with some notable exceptions (Lipset 1971; Tilly 1978; Jenkins 1985), have also neglected labor movements and unions. Yet when sociological contributions are added to the sociologically oriented work of labor economists and historians, a sizable literature becomes available.

SOCIAL ORIGINS OF THE LABOR MOVEMENT

The labor movement and unions began to emerge with the Industrial Revolution and free labor markets in eighteenth-century England. Scholars agree that labor unions do not trace their origins to medieval guilds. Master-owners dominated guilds, which were status groups, while propertyless journeymen created mutual aid and protective societies to buffer the vicissitudes of a free market. Later, workers created temporary organizations to withhold their labor from employers, control production, and protect their wages. Eventually the organizations became permanent. They sought to control the supply of local labor, the training of workers, and the conditions of work in local factories (Jackson 1984). As product markets grew and spread and unions responded by creating new local unions, the movement became larger, more formalized, and more diversified. Thus, individual unions organized themselves around occupational, industrial, regional, religious, and other lines (Sturmthal 1974).

Since this organizational fragmentation exposed unions to changing business strategies, labor leaders realized that they needed a united movement to respond to threats wherever they might occur. However, the vision of a united movement always remained difficult to realize because individual unions and sets of unions hesitated to sacrifice their special interests for the undefined well-being of the movement. Many scholars have mistakenly confused the growth of the labor movement with the formation of the working class, or proletariat. Although the two phenomena are related, they vary enormously in time and place. When labor movements first emerged, they were not class movements. Rather, they were efforts on the part of the minority of skilled workers to protect their traditional privileges (Calhoun 1982). When unions later expanded to include all workers, then wage, status, and influence distinctions based on skill typically persisted (Form 1985, p. 96). In contrast, the appearance of a cohesive class movement involved a much more complex process; the building of ties between a stratified labor movement, nonunionized workers, and parties (Tilly 1978; Katznelson and Zolberg 1986).

Both the character and strength of labor movements must be understood in the context of the societies in which they arise and especially in the context of labor's relationship to capital and the state. Some scholars maintain that autonomous labor movements and unions survive only in capitalist democratic industrial societies. When membership is compulsory, when unions embrace the entire labor force, and when unions are subsumed under totalitarian political institutions, they lack the strength and independence to pursue the special interests of workers (Sturmthal 1968).

TYPES OF LABOR MOVEMENTS

Labor movements can be subsumed under five types, according to their relationships to government and the broader society. Three types include the majority of movements. In the first, or independent, type such as the United States, the labor movement and its unions are independent of all major institutions, economic, political, and religious. Although American labor seeks political influence, it is a voluntary part of a multiclass coalition in the Democratic party and, as a special interest group, has limited representation in government. In the second, or social, democratic type such as European capitalistic democracies, the labor movement has formal social legitimacy and, being a dominant player in a socialist, labor, or social democratic party, it sometimes shares in the control of the government. In the third, or party-incorporated, type, found in some developing societies with mixed economies such as Mexico, labor movements are formally part of a coalition of a permanent ruling party. This incorporation places some restrictions on labor's economic, political, and governmental independence. The fourth and fifth types of labor movements have even less independence. In the enterprise unions of Japan and Korea, the labor movement consists mainly of unions that have consultative roles in individual enterprises. The national bonds of these unions are weak and loose. Finally, in totalitarian and soviet countries, labor movements and their unions have displayed the least independence because they have been subjected to strong party and governmental controls.

In the first, or independent, type, labor unions most closely conform to the characteristics of genuine social movements because they exist in a turbulent economic and political environment, must mobilize resources, and adapt creatively or decline or die (Tilly 1978). In the second, or social democratic, type, as in Britain, the labor movement is institutionally tied to a dominant party and to a political program that attracts other segments of society. Here labor shares some attributes of a social movement because it must adapt to a changing economy and constantly seek the support of other interests in its quest for a party majority and a share of governmental power (Bauman 1972). Enterprise-based labor movements and movements embedded in permanent ruling parties and governments display very few attributes of social movements.

AMERICAN EXCEPTIONALISM

Scholars have long tried to explain why labor movements in most of the advanced industrial democracies became attached to labor or socialist parties and why the United States is an exception (Sombart 1906). Despite some irreconcilable theories, some consensus has emerged. Most scholars agree that European societies have longer and stronger links to past institutions. Where landed aristocrats, business, military, and religious elites cohesively resisted the incorporation of workers in the polity, class-oriented parties tended to appear. They sought to obtain voting rights for workers with the eventual aim of securing governmental protection for unions and providing them with benefits that could not be wrested from employers through collective bargaining. Moreover, in such exclusionary class environments, unions not only supported class parties but also developed separate institutions tuned to their interests such as intellectual elites, cooperatives, newspapers, banks, schools, and recreational clubs. In Europe, in response to a threatening, all-embracing, Marxist labor movement, churches created Christian labor unions and parties and extended their schools, hospitals, newspapers, and clubs to envelop workers in a class-inclusive organizational system (Knapp 1976).

The labor movement in the United States faced a different environment. The absence of traditional exclusionary aristocratic, military, and religious elites had the effect of dampening the class sentiments of workers. Early extension of suffrage to all adult males removed that objective as a rallying goal of unions. The rapid expansion of industry into new areas, high rates of immigration and internal migration, and ethnic and religious diversity in the labor force undermined workplace bonds. Moreover, an aggressive capitalist class, not bound by traditions of obligation toward subordinates, successfully convinced legislatures to erect a legal and judicial framework that favored property rights over organizational rights. Labor movements did develop in the late nineteenth and early twentieth centuries that sought to organize workers politically (Knights of Labor, International Workers of the World) and, for a few years, the Socialist party won notable local victories. But the American presidential system, the decentralized state structure, the constitutional barriers to the federal government's making national economic policy, and the electoral college system undermined third-party movements (Lipset 1977).

These circumstances created an American labor movement that has traditionally focused on wage bargaining and working conditions. Without the leverage of a strong pro-labor party in office, the movement's fortunes were exposed to economic vicissitudes and business onslaughts. Thus, American unions experienced membership growth before and during World Wars I and II, periods of relative prosperity and governmental tolerance. Membership, as a percentage of the labor force, declined rapidly in the depressions after World War I, slowly after World War II, and rapidly during the economic recessions of the 1970s and 1980s. The slower pace of the post–World War II decline reflected changes in labor's political environment during the Great Depression.

POSSIBLE CONVERGENCE OF LABOR MOVEMENTS

A combination of events moved American unions toward the European social democratic pattern, and events in Europe moved its labor movements toward the American pattern. During the crisis of the Great Depression in the United States, the Democratic party came to power with the backing of urban industrial workers. It quickly designed a program whose purpose was to increase labor's purchasing power, to reduce price competition, and to restore economic order. The National Industrial Recovery Act (1934) and the subsequent National Labor Relations Act (1935) gave unions legal protection to grow (Skocpol 1980). Meanwhile, a militant union drive greatly augmented the membership. Eager to protect and extend its gains, a split but grateful labor movement, swollen with new unskilled members in the Committee for Industrial Organization, abandoned its traditional nonpartisan political stand and backed the Democratic party. After World War II, both the Congress of Industrial Organizations and the American Federation of Labor formed political units to mobilize voters to keep the Democratic party in power. To most intents and purposes, these units became part of the Democratic electoral machine. This marriage of Labor and the Party and the commitment of both to the welfare state led some scholars to conclude that the American labor movement was no longer exceptional because it had helped create a welfare state similar to those forged by the social democratic parties in Europe (Greenstone 1977).

This claim appears farfetched because neither the American labor movement nor the Democratic party ever embraced socialism. Yet it is possible for nations to achieve some socialist reforms without adopting socialism. Also, it is possible for social democratic parties to avoid nationalizing industries once they are in office. Zygmunt Bauman (1972) early pointed out that the Labour Party in Britain and social democratic parties elsewhere had to deemphasize their socialist programs in order to come to power. And, where they did, nationalization of the economy was partial or tentative. Parties had to compromise on public ownership of industry in order to secure the votes of middle-class groups that embraced some social welfare goals of labor parties but not socialism. Once in power, social democratic parties had to make many concessions to intellectuals and legislators, as well as to business, military, religious, and other groups. Moreover, even in cases where the majority of the labor force was unionized, large minorities of workers and their unions also opposed socialization. In short, the conservative forces in social democratic parties and the associated labor movements pushed both of them toward the American pattern.

Recent evidence suggests that the third type of labor movement, those part of a coalition of a permanent ruling party (Mexico, Yugoslavia, Poland) are beginning to show signs of independence. They are carrying out strikes, forming independent partylike structures, and searching for coalitions with other interest groups. And even enterprise unions in Japan and party-submerged unions in the Soviet Union show signs of independence.

If present trends continue, perhaps the long-term evolutionary trend of labor movements will be toward parallel convergence. Sufficient research is not available to uncover all of the causes of this plausible trend, but at least three conditions seem to be involved. First, if governments create organizations that have the appearance of labor movements and expect workers to participate in elections, conferences, and other union-like activities, appearances of independence eventually become actualized under turbulent conditions. Thus, in Japan, enterprise bargaining and the participation of workers in union affairs are beginning to show Western patterns of independence and conflict (Okochi, Karsh, and Levine 1974; Kuruvilla et al. 1990). Second, this process is speeded up when external political and economic crises destabilize traditional authority patterns in industry. Thus, during the economic and political turbulence in Mexico and the Soviet Union of the late 1980s, party unions usurped the authority of management over working conditions, wage determination, and political choice. Third, as economies develop more complex industrial and occupational systems, managers find it increasingly difficult to exert overall control. Bodies that resemble labor unions then begin to confront authorities and press for worker rights. In situations such as existed in Poland in the late 1980s, unions, with the help of clergy, intellectuals, farmers, and others, defied central authority, formed independent parties, and pushed for a decentralized social order. This may produce a labor relations system akin to those in Western capitalist democracies.

DEMOCRACY OR OLIGARCHY IN THE LABOR MOVEMENT

Unlike most institutions, the labor movement everywhere claims to be democratic in its ideology and structure. Union officers are leaders of the membership and, whether elected or appointed, should represent its interests. Sociologists have long pondered whether democratic movements that develop large and complex organizations can avoid the rigid bureaucracy and stratification so characteristic of other institutions.

The most famous exponent of the position that democratic organizations evolve into oligarchies was Robert Michels (1911), who studied the socialist party in pre-World War I Germany. He held that its officers became a self-perpetuating elite. They controlled communication with the membership, appointed their staffs and successors, and pursued their self-interests. Subsequent case studies of labor unions challenged Michels's thesis. In a detailed analysis of the International Typographical Unions, Seymour Martin Lipset, Martin A. Trow, and James A. Coleman (1956) found that its party system fostered electoral competition, officer turnover, and member involvement in union affairs. J. David Edelstein and Malcolm Warner's (1979) study of fifty-one international unions showed that the extent of officer turnover varied with certain constitutional provisions such as frequency of elections, percentage of officers elected, and frequency of conventions. Daniel B. Cornfield (1989) found that substantial ethnic turnover among officers of the United Furniture Workers of America resulted from the external changes in the economy, the regional dispersal of the industry, political disputes among the officers, ethnic tolerance among the members, and a tradition of membership union involvement. Most of these case studies focused on relatively small unions whose members were rather homogeneous in their skills and earnings.

These challenges to Michels reveal some conditions that facilitate leadership turnover. Importantly, they do not reveal the extent to which these conditions prevail in the universe of unions and in labor movements as a whole. Nor do they reveal the conditions that strengthen oligarchy. Compared with other organizations, turnover among top officers of most large unions is low. It is probably even lower in the national and international associations of unions. And when the labor movement is defined to include labor political parties, oligarchic tendencies may be even larger.

Unfortunately, very few scholars have examined organizational cleavages and stratification tendencies within labor movements over their entire histories. In a rare study, Bauman (1972) demonstrated that cleavages along skill lines persisted during the entire growth of the British labor movement. Skilled workers formed societies at the beginning of the Industrial Revolution. From 1850 to 1890, they formed craft unions that sought and obtained legitimacy, and between 1890 and 1924, they became an elite sector of a mass union movement. They still maintained their identity in the large industrial unions that appeared. With the development of the Liberal, and later the Labour parties, trade union leaders gradually became subordinated to university-trained, middle-class intellectuals who dominated the Party, its seats in Parliament, and its government positions. Herman Bensen (1986) argues that this pattern applies equally well to the American labor movement. Finally, Alain Touraine (1986) notes that everywhere labor union involvement in political parties and governments increases occupational stratification, magnifies the distance between unions and their parties, and subordinates union interests to workers' goals. Apparently, increasing size and organizational complexity of the labor movement is accompanied by increasing stratification and an increasingly unresponsive bureaucracy. This kind of evidence supports Michels's original argument.

CONCLUSIONS

American sociological research has fluctuated with the fortunes of the labor movement. As union membership and power grew, research increased, hitting its apogee in the 1950s and 1960s. As membership began to fall, research slackened. Yet labor's problems always offered new research opportunities. Today, scholars should analyze why some labor movements decline while others stabilize or grow. Most current explanations of labor's decline in the United States are inadequate. Thus, the economy's shift from manufacturing to services does not account for the decline because Lipset (1986, p. 426), dean of sociological research on American labor, shows that in eleven capitalist democracies industrial shifts do not vary with level of unionization. Michael Goldfield's (1987) study of labor's decline in the United States supports Lipset's position. After Goldfield eliminated changes in the economy and changes in industrial and occupational composition of the labor force as possible causes, he demonstrated that a sustained employer drive slowly succeeded in shifting the decisions of the National Labor Relations Board against organized labor. He and Richard B. Freeman and James L. Medoff (1984) also show that the impressive growth of white-collar unions demonstrates that unions can grow despite employer resistance. Moreover, some of the membership decline also results from spending less money on organizing drives.

Sociologists have neglected other research areas such as collective bargaining, perhaps because these areas call for an intimate understanding of labor–management interaction. While sociologists have improved their theory and statistics, they have neglected field studies on how unions actually work (see Freeman and Medoff 1984). For example, the surge in statistical studies on income discrimination in the 1970s (see Berg 1981) has provided many data on the amount of discrimination but little on the informal bargaining processes that protect or eradicate it. The tradition of case studies that characterized the 1950s (e.g., Seidman et al. 1958) needs to be revived. Nowhere is this need more urgent than in the study of union politics at the local, state, and national levels. Field studies should examine labor's relations with the Democratic party and state legislatures.

The changing world economy also raises challenging research questions. Movement toward a global economy and large tariff-free trade zones, such as the European Economic Community, eventually will force unions of different nations to coordinate their collective bargaining and political strategies, lest they be weakened by the flexible investment strategies of multinational firms. How will this be done and what will be the effects? The movement of soviet economies, as well as some managed economies of underdeveloped nations, toward freer markets suggests that their unions will have to engage in true collective bargaining. And they will have to consider how their behavior will affect prices, profits, and societal stability. How will this transition be made? The global trend toward greater union participation in economic decisions at the enterprise level calls for comparative analysis. Paradoxically, collective bargaining will become increasingly complex and politicized as more of the world moves toward a freer market economy. This will increase the organizational complexity and internal stratification of labor, reviving Michels's concern about oligarchy.

If the labor movement is going to survive, especially in the United States, it must increase the loyalty and involvement of its members, as well as its societal political influence. These mandates will pull labor leadership in two directions. First, at the level of the workplace, members measure union performance in terms of their earnings improvements and the quality of work life. Although the two goals are related, American unions have traditionally handled them separately. To make progress on these two fronts, labor must press for greater participation in the economic and organizational management of the enterprise. Fierce resistence is inevitable. Second, to regain political influence, as it must or continue to decline, labor must forge stronger and more lasting bonds with Hispanics, African-Americans, women, the elderly, and other nonunionized groups. Again, paradoxically, the labor movement will become stronger the more it stresses the well-being of other less fortunate groups in society (Form 1990). The labor movement will surely survive, but, in so doing, it will have to create innovative solutions to two evolutionary dilemmas: increasing membership loyalty in the face of increasing organizational complexity, and increasing public acceptance while improving the well-being of its members.

(SEE ALSO: *Labor Force; Social Movements*)

REFERENCES

Bauman, Zygmunt 1972 *Between Class and Elite.* Manchester, England: Manchester University Press.

Benson, Herman 1986 "The Fight for Union Democracy." In Seymour Martin Lipset, ed., *Unions in Transition.* San Francisco: Institute for Contemporary Studies.

Berg, Ivar (ed.) 1981 *Sociological Perspectives on Labor Markets.* New York: Academic Press.

Calhoun, Craig 1982 *The Question of Class Struggle.* Chicago: University of Chicago Press.

Cornfield, Daniel B. 1989 *Becoming a Mighty Voice: Conflict and Change in the United Furniture Workers of America.* New York: Russell Sage Foundation.

Edelstein, J. David, and Malcolm Warner 1979 *Comparative Union Democracy.* New Brunswick, N.J.: Transaction Press.

Form, William 1985 *Divided We Stand: Working-Class Stratification in America.* Urbana: University of Illinois Press.

——— 1990 "Organized Labor and the Welfare State." In Kai Erikson and Stephen P. Vallas, eds., *The Nature of Work.* New Haven, Conn.: Yale University Press.

Freeman, Richard B., and James L. Medoff 1984 *What Do Unions Do?* New York: Basic Books.

Goldfield, Michael 1987 *The Decline of Organized Labor in the United States.* Chicago: University of Chicago Press.

Greenstone, J. David 1977 *Labor in American Politics.* Chicago: University of Chicago Press.

Jackson, Kenneth Robert 1984 *The Formation of Craft Markets.* Orlando, Fla.: Academic Press.

Jenkins, J. Craig 1985 *The Politics of Insurgency: The Farm Worker Movement in the 1960s.* New York: Columbia University Press.

Katznelson, Ira, and Aristide R. Zolberg (eds.) 1986 *Working-Class Formation: Nineteenth Century Patterns in Europe and the United States.* Princeton, N.J.: Princeton University Press.

Knapp, Vincent J. 1976 *Europe in the Era of Social Transformation: 1700–Present.* Englewood Cliffs, N.J.: Prentice-Hall.

Kuruvilla, Sarosh, Daniel G. Gallagher, Jack Fiorito, and Mitsuru Wakabayashi 1990 "Union Participation in Japan: Do Western Theories Apply?" *Industrial and Labor Relations Review* 43:366–373.

Lipset, Seymour Martin 1971 *Agrarian Socialism: The Cooperative Commonwealth Movement in Saskatchewan.* Berkeley: University of California Press.

——— 1977. "Why No Socialism in the United States." In Seweryn Bialer and Sophis Sluzar, eds., *Sources of Contemporary Radicalism.* Boulder, Colo.: Westview Press.

——— 1986 "North American Labor Movements: A Comparative Perspective." In Seymour Martin Lipset, ed., *Unions in Transition: Entering the Second Century.*" San Francisco: Institute for Contemporary Studies.

———, Martin A. Trow, and James A. Coleman 1956 *Union Democracy.* New York: Free Press.

Michels, Robert (1911) 1959 *Political Parties.* New York: Dover.

Okochi, Kazuo, Bernard Karsh, and Solomon B. Levine, eds. 1974 *Workers and Employers in Japan: The Japanese Employment Relations System.* Princeton, N.J.: Princeton University Press.

Seidman, Joel, Jack London, Bernard Karsh, and Daisy L. Tagliacozzo 1958 *The Worker Views His Union.* Chicago: University of Chicago Press.

Skocpol, Theda 1980 "Political Response to Capitalist Crisis." *Politics and Society* 10:155–201.

Sombart, Werner 1906 *Warum gibt es in den Vereinigten Staaten keinen Socialismus.* Tübingen: Mohr.

Sturmthel, Adolph F. 1968 "Labor Unions: Labor Movements and Collective Bargaining in Europe." In David L. Sills, ed., *International Encyclopedia of the Social Sciences,* Vol. 8. New York: Macmillan and Free Press.

——— 1974 "Trade Unionism." In *Encyclopedia Britannica,* Vol. 5. Chicago: William Benton.

Tilly, Charles 1978 *From Moblization to Revolution.* Reading, Mass.: Addison-Wesley.

Touraine, Alain 1987 "Unionism as a Social Movement." In Seymour Martin Lipset, ed., *Unions in Transition.* San Francisco: Institute for Contemporary Studies.

WILLIAM FORM

LABOR THEORY OF VALUE *See* Marxist Sociology.

LATIN AMERICAN STUDIES Sociological research on Latin American societies has focused on the understanding of the causes and consequences of different patterns of development. Since the 1950s, this research has been guided by the counterpoint between two different theoretical approaches and the findings generated with their help. In the 1950s and 1960s, the field was dominated by what came to be known as the modernization approach. In the 1970s and 1980s, dependency and world system theories became prevalent (Klaren and Bossert 1986; Valenzuela and Valenzuela 1978). Each of these paradigms spawned useful lines of research, but eventually they became unsatisfactory, either because some of their assumptions were inconsistent with the facts or because they were incapable of encompassing important areas of social reality. The field is now ripe for a new conceptual framework, which could incorporate useful aspects of the previous ones. In the past few years, there has been a shift toward a state-centered approach, but it is still unclear whether it will develop into a synthetic paradigm.

THE REGION

The study of Latin American societies is complicated by the heterogeneous nature of the region. The nations that compose Latin America (in the usual definition of the region, the successor states to the Spanish and Portuguese empires in the New World, plus Haiti), share some common traits, but they also have important differences.

Countries vary in terms of their economy and social structure, their ethnic composition, and their political institutions. The economic differentials are substantial. The region includes Argentina and Uruguay (whose per capita Gross Domestic Products [GDP] are $2,520 and $2,470, about the same as Yugoslavia and Hungary), as well as Venezuela, an oil exporter, with a per capita GDP of $3,250, similar to that of Portugal. At the other extreme, there are countries like Haiti and Bolivia, with per capita GDPs of $380 and $570, which are comparable to those of the Central African Republic and the Philippines, respectively (World Bank 1990). Social structures vary accordingly: About 85 percent of the Argentine and Uruguayan population is urban, but the percentages in Haiti and Guatemala are 26 and 34 (Inter-American Development Bank 1989); manufacturing accounts for about 30 percent of the GDP of Argentina, Brazil, or Mexico (about the same as in France, Italy, or Sweden), but the proportion is only 13 percent in Honduras and 18 percent in El Salvador, whose levels of industrialization are comparable to those of Egypt and Morocco, respectively; and enrollment ratios in postsecondary education vary from about 40 percent of the twenty- to twenty-four-year-olds in Argentina and Uruguay to about 9 percent in Honduras or Guatemala (World Bank 1990).

Latin American countries differ widely in their ethnic composition. The three basic components, Iberian settlers and other European immigrants, American Indians, and blacks, are found in varying proportions in the different countries. Some are relatively homogeneous: Most of the Argentine and Uruguayan populations are of European origin (the greater part, the product of transatlantic immigration at the turn of the century), and the population of Haiti is basically African. Other nations, like Mexico, Peru, and Guatemala, have maintained the colonial pattern of ethnic stratification, with mostly "white" elites ruling over largely Indian citizenries. Most of the population in countries like Chile, Colombia, Venezuela, the Dominican Republic, El Salvador, and Honduras is the product of miscegenation. And Brazil has a heterogeneous population, with large contingents of all the ethnic groups and their various mixes (Ribeiro 1971; Lambert 1967).

With respect to their political institutions, countries in the region vary as well. Some, like Costa Rica, Chile, and Uruguay, have had long histories of constitutional rule (punctuated by authoritarian episodes), while others, like Argentina, Brazil, or Peru, have wavered between instability and authoritarianism for much of the postwar period. All over South America, military dictatorships gave way to constitutional governments in the 1980s (O'Donnell and Schmitter 1986). The legitimacy and overall potential for institutionalization of these new governments vary according to the strength of liberal democratic traditions, the presence of revolutionary organizations, the subordination of the state apparatus to the government, the vitality of the party system, and the dynamism of the economy. Authoritarian rule still endures, the most notable being the state-corporatist regime in Mexico, and high levels of insurgency exist in El Salvador and Peru. Finally, Cuba is one of the few remaining state-socialist polities in the world.

Nevertheless, there are economic, social, and political commonalities, besides the obvious cultural and religious ones. As far as the economy is concerned, and in spite of the variability noted above, Latin American countries share four important traits. First, all these societies belong, in terms of their per capita product, to the low or lower-middle ranks in the world system. Second, all Latin American nations have basically been, and most still are, in spite of the considerable industrialization that took place in the most advanced countries, exporters of raw materials or foodstuffs and importers of manufacturing and/or manufacturered products. Third, industrialization, especially after the Great Depression of the 1930s, has been based on import-substitution policies. These policies have led to low growth rates and even outright stagnation once the domestic markets were saturated, a stage that the most advanced countries in the region reached in the 1970s and 1980s. As a consequence, all these countries are facing the crisis associated with the need to restructure their economies to switch to export-led industrialization. Fourth, Latin American societies are highly dependent, in most instances because large segments of their economies are under the control of external actors (multinational corporations, in particular) and in practically all cases because of their high level of indebtedness to governments and banks in the advanced industrial countries.

There are many differences among Latin American social structures and political institutions, but all these countries, except Haiti, originated as Spanish and Portuguese colonies. The pillars of the original institutional matrix were the organization of the economy around the large agrarian property; a highly centralized political system, in which representative features were weak; and a cultural system centered in the Catholic church, in which the toleration of pluralism was extremely low (Lambert 1967; Veliz 1980). This institutional core disintegrated as a consequence of the economic and social changes of the nineteenth and twentieth centuries: New social actors were formed, and old ones were transformed by urbanization, industrialization, and the expansion of education and also by the irruption of external economic, political, and cultural forces. Further, in some societies there were substantial changes in the composition of the population. However, the common origins still account for important similarities in the historical trajectories of the countries of the region.

In the realm of politics, commonalities are also evident in the post independence period, especially after the Great Depression. At that time, liberal democratic regimes, most of which had not integrated the lower classes into the political system, collapsed throughout the region. In the following decades, most Latin American countries wavered between unstable democracy and nondemocratic forms of rule. South America has been especially prone to two of these: populist-corporatist regimes, and bureaucratic military dictatorships (Malloy 1977; Pike and Stritch 1974; Stepan 1978; O'Donnell 1973; 1988). Many South American polities evolved cyclically in that period: Populist-corporatist regimes (such as those headed by Juan Peron in Argentina and Getulio Vargas in Brazil) were frequent from World War II to the 1960s; military regimes and their coercive counterparts in the society, guerrilla warfare or terrorism, predominated in the 1960s and 1970s (Argentina, Brazil, Chile, Uruguay, Peru); and democratization has swept the area in the 1980s.

MODERNIZATION THEORY

Modernization perspectives shared two core assumptions that distinguished them from dependency and world system theories. The first of these assumptions was that the central variables for understanding the development of a society are internal to the society; the second was that development is an evolutionary process, whose main characteristics are common to all societies. These commonalities have underlied different approaches, which can be classified in terms of the variables they have considered central for the analysis of development, because of their primary causal weight, and of the nature of the evolutionary process societies were supposed to undergo.

A first type of approach, sometimes of Parsonian or anthropological inspiration, privileged the value system, or culture, as the basic part of society, in the sense that values were expected to determine the basic traits of the economy or the polity. Change in values or culture appeared then as a key dimension in the process of transition from "traditionality" to "modernity." Examples of this approach were Lipset's (1967) analysis of entrepreneurship in Latin America, or Wiarda's (1973) argument about the influence of the corporatist Iberian tradition on the political evolution of Latin American societies.

The second approach was structural, in the sense that it viewed the social or economic structures as the determining part of society and that it saw changes in these structures as the central aspect of the process of development. The most elaborate versions of this perspective were inspired in Durkheim and the most structural version of Parsonian theory: They regarded the degree of integration of society as the key characteristic of the social order, and they focused on the processes of differentiation and integration as the keys for the understanding of development, still conceptualized in terms of the "traditionality –modernity" continuum. Germani's (1962; 1981) model of Latin American modernization in terms of the counterpoint between mobilization and integration is a good example of this perspective (see also Kahl 1976). Assumptions of this type also underlied the typology of stages of economic development made popular by ECLA, the influential Economic Commission for Latin America of the United Nations (Rodriguez 1980).

These approaches spawned important types of sociological research in the 1950s and 1960s, but reality showed that the assumptions behind the evolutionary paradigm were problematic. Toward the end of the 1960s, it became clear that the predictions derived from the model of the traditionality–modernity continuum in relation to the social structure and the political system were inconsistent with the facts. In the social structure, the expansion of capitalist agriculture and the development of industry in societies with large peasantries did not lead to the dissolution of "traditional," or precapitalist, rural social relations. Its survival (Stavenhagen 1970; Cotler 1970), and the emergence of what came to be known as "dualistic" or structurally heterogeneous societies, meant that the patterns of social development of Latin America were not replicating those of the Western European countries that were considered the universally valid models of modernization.

Political processes in the 1960s and early 1970s were also paradoxical in relation to this theory: Lipset's (1981, pp. 27–63) thesis that liberal democracy was a correlate of development (as measured by variables such as income, urbanization, industrialization, and education) seemed to be contradicted by the fact that it was precisely the most "modern" countries (Argentina, Uruguay, Chile) that were the most prone to instability and authoritarianism. On the basis of this propensity, O'Donnell (1973) formulated the thesis that, in the peculiar situation of Latin American industrialization, countries of this type were the most likely candidates for bureaucratic authoritarianism. This thesis was itself questioned from different perspectives (Collier 1979), but the lack of correlation between development and democracy seemed nevertheless obvious at that time. Later, the wave of democratization that swept Latin America in the 1980s, and the revolutions of 1989–90 in Eastern Europe, would indicate that the relationship proposed by Lipset does exist, even though it does not seem to be linear.

DEPENDENCY AND WORLD SYSTEM THEORIES

Dependency and world system theories were the contemporary elaboration of themes found in Marxism, the theory of imperialism in particular (Lenin 1968; Luxemburg 1968). They were based on two propositions that sharply contradicted the assumptions of modernization theory. The first was that internal characteristics of societies, such as their level of development or the nature of their political system, are determined by their position in the international system. The second assumption was a corollary of the first: Since the main causes of development are external, there is no reason to expect that all societies will follow the same evolutionary trajectory. On the contrary, the world system is organized into a more dynamic, developed, and powerful core and a more passive, backward, and dependent periphery. Beyond these commonalities, there were differences between the dependency and world system approaches.

Dependency theory, which in itself was a Latin American product, emphasized the radical distinction between core and periphery, and it took dependent societies as its unit of analysis. Its focus was on the mechanisms it claimed were responsible for the preservation of underdevelopment, in particular the transfer of economic surplus to the core via trade and investment (Cardoso and Faletto 1979; Frank 1969; 1972). Wallerstein's (1974) world system approach, on the other hand, singled out the world economy as the unit of analysis, and it explored the functions of different types of societies (core, semiperiphery, and periphery) in that system.

Since the late 1960s, these theories have generated important pieces of research. Cardoso and

Faletto's (1979) comparative analysis of Latin American societies showed how different positions in the world economy generated different class structures and different patterns of development (see also Kahl 1976). Evans's (1979) study of Brazil showed how the peculiarities of the country's development were shaped by the interaction among the state, foreign capital, and the domestic bourgeoisie. Gereffi (1983) explored the consequences of dependency in a key industry. From a world system perspective, Alejandro Portes and his colleagues (1981; 1985; 1989) conducted important studies of the labor flows in the world economy and of the articulation between the formal and informal economies.

These approaches improved our understanding of Latin American development in two ways. First, by focusing on the effects of external factors and processes (those in the economy in particular, but the political and cultural ones as well), dependency and world system perspectives corrected the assumption characteristic of modernization theory that societies could be studied in relative isolation. Second, since these theories constructed models of the world economy that were either pericentric (Doyle 1986), as in dependency theory, or that emphasized the analysis of peripheral and semiperipheral social structures alongside that of the core, as in world system theory, they balanced the emphasis on core structures and processes characteristic of most preexisting studies of imperialism, which tended to ignore the institutions and dynamism of the periphery.

However, the basic tenets of dependency and world system theories have also led in some cases (but not in the best research spawned by these perspectives) to simplistic assumptions, in particular to a tendency to consider internal structures and processes, especially the political and cultural ones, as transmission belts for external economic and political forces. The pendulum swang to the other extreme: from the neglect of external economic and political determinants of social change, characteristic of modernization theory, to a disregard for internal factors.

TOWARD A NEW PARADIGM

In the late 1980s, the basic assumptions of dependency and world system theories also became problematic. In the first place, research on the role of the state in the development process led to its reconceptualization as an autonomous actor (see Evans, Rueschemeyer, and Skocpol 1985 and Waisman 1987 for a Latin American case). This challenged the conceptions characteristic of most approaches close to the Marxist tradition, dependency and world system theories included, that tended to see the state, claims of "relative autonomy" notwithstanding, as basically an instrument of either domestic ruling classes or foreign forces. Secondly, there was a rediscovery of social movements in the region (a consequence that the redemocratization processes of the 1980s could not fail to produce). More often than in the past, agency came to be seen as relatively independent in relation to its structural and institutional context (see the essays in Eckstein 1989, for instance), a conceptualization that differs sharply from the structuralist assumption inherent in dependency and world system perspectives. Finally, the proposition according to which the central determinants of the development of Latin American countries are external has also been challenged (Waisman 1987; Zeitlin 1984). Now, as in the 1970s, there is a growing consensus that existing paradigms do not encompass our current understanding of Latin American development.

A new theoretical synthesis should integrate the valid components of the modernization, dependency, and world system approaches and also allow for the autonomy of the state and the role of agency. A point of departure should be the recognition of three facts. The first is that the division of the world into core, periphery, and semiperiphery is not sufficient to encompass the diversity of developmental situations and trajectories relevant for the study of the countries of Latin America. It is necessary to construct a typology of more specific kinds of peripheral societies (and of core societies as well; the core–

periphery distinction is still too abstract), and to describe more systematically the structural "tracks" that have crystallized in the region at different stages of development of the world economy.

The second is that the different developmental paths followed by Latin American societies have been determined by empirically variable constellations of external and internal processes and of economic, political, and ideological-cognitive ones. Few propositions that privilege the causal role of specific factors are likely to be generally valid. Rather than seeking propositions of this type, as modernization, dependency, and world system approaches have tried to do, it would be more productive to map the specific bundles of factors that have influenced developmental outcomes in critical situations. Third, development is a discontinuous process (an instance of punctuated equilibrium, in Krasner's [1984] words), but we lack a theory of the transition points, that is, of the crossroads where acceleration, stagnation, retrogression, and changes of developmental tracks have taken place. The Latin American experience indicates that these are the points in which major changes in the world system, such as depressions, wars, important technological developments, organizational changes in production or trade, and restructuring of the economic or military balance of power, have interacted with domestic economic, political, and cultural processes. Comparative analysis would permit a systematic examination of these critical junctures and of their possible consequences for the developmental trajectory of different societies in the region. This suggests a potentially fruitful empirical focus for research: the analysis of the relationship between group choices (including those made by the state elites) and changes in the social structure at the transition points mentioned above. This would involve the study of the structural and cultural processes through which different strategic groups (state elite included) have generated their ideological and political preferences as well as the process of institutionalization, that is, the set of mechanisms through which group behavior and state policies have affected the social structure and produced different developmental outcomes.

(SEE ALSO: *Hispanic-American Studies; Mexican Studies)*

REFERENCES

Cardoso, Fernando H., and Enzo Faletto 1979 *Dependency and Development in Latin America.* Berkeley: University of California Press.

Collier, David (ed.) 1979 *The New Authoritarianism in Latin America.* Princeton: Princeton University Press.

Cotler, Julio 1970 "The Mechanisms of Internal Domination and Social Change in Peru." In Irving L. Horowitz, ed., *Masses in Latin America.* New York: Oxford University Press.

Doyle, Michael W. 1986 *Empires.* Ithaca, N.Y.: Cornell University Press.

Eckstein, Susan 1989 *Power and Popular Protest: The Latin American Social Movements.* Berkeley: University of California Press.

Evans, Peter B. 1979 *Dependent Development: The Alliance of Multinational, State, and Local Capital in Brazil.* Princeton: Princeton University Press.

———, Dietrich Rueschemeyer, and Theda Skocpol (eds.) 1985 *Bringing the State Back In.* Cambridge: Cambridge University Press.

Frank, Andre G. 1969 *Capitalism and Underdevelopment in Latin America.* New York: Monthly Review Press.

———1972 *Lumpenbourgeoisie–Lumpendevelopment.* New York: Monthly Review Press.

Gereffi, Gary 1983 *The Pharmaceutical Industry and Dependency in the Third World.* Princeton: Princeton University Press.

Germani, Gino 1962 *Politica y sociedad en una epoca de transicion.* Buenos Aires: Paidos.

———1981 *The Sociology of Modernization: Studies of Its Historical and Theoretical Aspects with Special Regard to the Latin American Case.* New Brunswick, N.J.: Transaction Books.

Horowitz, Irving L. (ed.) 1970 *Masses in Latin America.* New York: Oxford University Press.

Inter-American Development Bank 1989 *Economic and Social Progress in Latin America: 1989 Report.* Washington, D.C.: Inter-American Development Bank.

Kahl, J. A. 1976 *Modernization, Exploitation, and Dependency in Latin America.* New Brunswick, N.J.: Transaction Books.

Klaren, Peter F., and Thomas J. Bossert (eds.) 1986

Promise of Development. Boulder, Colo.: Westview Press.
Krasner, Stephen D. 1984 "Approaches to the State: Alternative Conceptions and Historical Dynamics." *Comparative Politics* 16:223–246.
Lambert, Jacques 1967 *Latin America: Social Structures and Political Institutions.* Berkeley: University of California Press.
Lenin, V. I. 1968 *Imperialism: The Highest Stage of Capitalism.* Moscow: Progress Publishers.
Lipset, Seymour Martin 1967 "Values, Education, and Entrepreneurship." In Seymour M. Lipset and Aldo Solari, eds., *Elites in Latin America.* New York: Oxford University Press.
———(1960) 1981. *Political Man: The Social Bases of Politics.* Baltimore: Johns Hopkins University Press.
Luxemburg, Rosa 1968 *The Accumulation of Capital.* New York: Monthly Review Press.
Malloy, James M. (ed.) 1977 *Authoritarianism and Corporatism in Latin America.* Pittsburgh: University of Pittsburgh Press.
O'Donnell, Guillermo A. 1973 *Modernization and Bureaucratic-Authoritarianism: Studies in South American Politics.* Berkeley: Institute of International Studies.
———1988 *Bureaucratic Authoritarianism: Argentina, 1966–73 in Comparative Perspective.* Berkeley: University of California Press.
———, and Phillippe C. Schmitter 1986 *Transitions from Authoritarian Rule: Tentative Conclusions about Uncertain Democracies.* Baltimore: Johns Hopkins University Press.
Pike, Frederick B., and Thomas Stritch (eds.) 1974 *The New Corporatism.* Notre Dame: University of Notre Dame Press.
Portes, Alejandro, and Robert L. Bach 1985 *Latin Journey: Cuban and Mexican Immigrants in the United States.* Berkeley: University of California Press.
Portes, Alejandro, Manuel Castells, and Lauren A. Benton (eds.) 1989 *The Informal Economy: Studies in Advanced and Less Developed Countries.* Baltimore: Johns Hopkins University Press.
Portes, Alejandro, and John Walton 1981 *Labor, Class, and the International System.* New York: Academic Press.
Ribeiro, Darcy 1971 *The Americas and Civilization.* New York: Dutton.
Rodriguez, Octavio 1980 *La teoria del subdesarrollo de la CEPAL.* Mexico City: Siglo XXI.
Stavenhagen, Rodolfo 1970 "Classes, Colonialism, and Acculturation." In Irving L. Horowitz, ed., *Masses in Latin America.* New York: Oxford University Press.
Stepan, Alfred 1978 *The State and Society: Peru in a Comparative Perspective.* Princeton: Princeton University Press.
Valenzuela, J. Samuel, and Arturo Valenzuela 1978 "Modernization and Dependency: Alternative Approaches in the Study of Latin American Underdevelopment." *Comparative Politics* 10(2): 535–557.
Veliz, Claudio 1980 *The Centralist Tradition in Latin America.* Princeton: Princeton University Press.
Waisman, Carlos H. 1987 *Reversal of Development in Argentina: Postwar Counter-Revolutionary Politics and Their Structural Consequences.* Princeton: Princeton University Press.
Wallerstein, Immanuel 1974 *The Modern World System: Capitalist Agriculture and the Origins of the European World-Economy in the Sixteenth Century.* New York: Academic Press.
Wiarda, Howard J. (ed.) 1973 "Toward a Framework for the Study of Political Change in the Iberic-Latin Tradition: The Corporative Model." *World Politics* 25:206–235.
World Bank 1990 *World Development Report 1990.* New York: Oxford University Press.
Zeitlin, Maurice 1984 *The Civil Wars in Chile.* Princeton: Princeton University Press.

CARLOS H. WAISMAN

LAW AND LEGAL SYSTEMS Law is surprisingly difficult to define. Perhaps the best-known definition within the sociology of law community is that of Max Weber. "An order will be called *law* if it is externally guaranteed by the probability that coercion (physical or psychological), to bring about conformity or avenge violation, will be applied by a *staff* of people holding themselves specially ready for that purpose" (1954, p. 5). Similar definitions include Donald Black's terse statement that "Law is governmental social control" (Black, 1976, p. 2). While these types of definitions have sometimes been attacked as employing a Westernized conception, appropriate for developed states but inappropriate for other societies, Hoebel advances a similar definition of law in all societies: "The really fundamental *sine qua non* of law in any society—primitive or civilized—is the legitimate use of physical coercion by a socially authorized agent" (Hoebel 1954, p. 26).

Definitions such as these are perhaps more interesting for what they exclude than for what they include. Weber and Hoebel attempt to draw a line where the boundary between law and something else is fuzziest. By including the term *legitimate,* Hoebel's definition is intended to distinguish law from the brute exercise of force. The leader of a criminal gang who forces people to give him money may be doing many things, but he is not enforcing the law. He is not a socially authorized agent, and his use of force is not legitimate. Legitimacy itself is a slippery concept, and disagreements about when it is present give rise to questions such as whether the Nazis governed under the rule of law.

The inclusion of coercion and specialized agents of enforcement in both Weber's and Hoebel's definitions is meant to distinguish law from customs or norms, the breach of which either is not sanctioned or is sanctioned only by members of the group against which the breach occurred. The internal rules (norms and customs) governing a family's life or an organization's life are not law unless they are reinstitutionalized, that is, unless they are "restated in such a way that they can be applied by an institution designed (or at very least, utilized) specifically for that purpose" (Bohannan 1965, p. 36).

The boundary maintenance functions of definitions such as those of Weber, Hoebel, and Bohannan undoubtedly have their place, but law's empire is so large that the border skirmishes occurring out on its frontiers have limited influence on our shared understanding of the words *law* and *legal system.* Wherever it occurs, law is a body of rules that speak to how people should behave in society (substantive law) and how the legal system itself should proceed (adjective law). The volume and complexity of rules may be expected to parallel the size and complexity of the society of which they are a part. But broad categories of substantive law—tort, property, criminal law—apparently exist in all legal orders, as do the fundamentals of adjective law—procedure and evidence.

Moreover, by restricting the term *law* to rules enforced by specialized legal staffs, these definitions exclude much of what the legal sociologist will find interesting. There is "law-stuff" everywhere. Families and organizations do generate rules and do coerce or induce compliance. These groups constitute what Moore (1973) calls "semi-autonomous fields." Not only are the rules of these organizations interesting in their own right, the interaction of these rules and the state rules we call law helps to shape the fundamental choice between avoidance and compliance that is faced by all to whom rules are addressed. We will be well served if we follow Griffiths' (1984) advice and view "legalness" as a variable rather than thinking of "law" as a special, definable species of social control. The complex body of substantive and adjective rules at different levels comprise a legal system.

LEGAL SYSTEMS

The comparative study of law might trace its roots to Aristotle's comparison of Greek city-state constitutions. A more recent example is Montesquieu, who, in *The Spirit of the Laws* (1748 [1962]), attempted to explain legal diversity in terms of various factors in the social setting. Interspersed between these efforts were comparisons of canon law with Roman law in Europe and with the common law in England. Despite these precursors, the modern study of comparative legal systems became a topic of sustained academic interest only during the last 100 to 150 years.

The history of comparative law is set forth in a number of works, including Zweigert and Kotz (1987) and David and Brierley (1985). The present essay discusses a small part of this history, focusing on what Zweigert and Kotz call scientific or theoretical comparative law rather than legislative comparative law, in which foreign laws are examined and invoked in the process of drafting new nation-state laws.

Early theoretical efforts, exemplified by Maine's *Ancient Law* ([1861] 1963), adopted evolutionary theories of legal development. In Maine's famous formulation, legal systems, following changes in social arrangements, move from *status* wherein one's rights and duties were determined by one's social niche (the law of feudalism) to *contract,* wherein ones rights and duties were determined by oneself and the contracts one entered into (eventually the law of capitalism).

A second well-known developmental theory of changes in legal systems is that of Durkheim ([1893] 1964). A societal movement from mechanical to organic solidarity is accompanied by a movement from repressive law (law that punishes those who violate a shared moral understanding) to restitutive law (law that attempts to facilitate cooperation and to return people to a status quo ante when rule violations occur).

From the sociological point of view, perhaps the most important contributor to the early development of comparative law was that preeminent lawyer-social scientist, Max Weber. Weber's contribution was in three parts. First, he developed the device of an ideal type, a stylized construct that represents the perfect example of a phenomenon. The ideal type acts as a yardstick against which we might measure actual legal systems. Second, using ideal types, he provided a typology of legal systems classified by the formality and the rationality of their decision-making processes. Ideally, legal systems could be thought of as formal or substantive, rational or irrational. A legal system is formal to the extent that the norms it applies are intrinsic to the system itself. Substantive law, as the term was used earlier, should not be confused with the substantive dimension of Weber's typology. A legal system is substantive in Weber's sense to the extent that the source of the norms it applies is extrinsic to the legal system. For example, a legal system would be substantive if a court resolved disputes by reference to a religious rather than a legal code.

A legal system is rational if it yields results that are predictable from the facts of cases; that is, case outcomes are determined by the reasoned analysis of action in light of a given set of norms. A legal system is irrational when outcomes are not predictable in this way. Basically, a legal system is rational to the extent that similar cases are decided similarly.

A formally irrational system exists when the legal order produces results unconstrained by reason. Classic examples are judgments following consultation of an oracle or trial by ordeal. Substantive irrationality exists when lawmakers and finders do not resort to some dominant general norms but, instead, act arbitrarily or decide upon the basis of an emotional evaluation of a particular case. Weber apparently had in mind the justice dispensed by the Khadi, a Moslem judge who, at least as Weber saw him, sat in the marketplace and rendered judgment by making a free and idiosyncratic evaluation of the particular merits of each case.

A substantively rational legal system exists when lawmakers and finders follow a consistent set of principles derived from some source other than the legal system itself. Again, Weber thought that Moslem law tended toward this type insofar as it tried to implement the thoughts and commands of the Prophet.

Western legal systems, especially those of civil law countries such as France and Germany, most nearly approximated the formally rational ideal, a legal system where the generality of legal rules is high and where the legal rules are highly differentiated from other social norms.

The relationship between formal and substantive law is obviously more complex than can be reflected in these four Weberian types. For example, legal systems may be procedurally quite formal while incorporating substantive norms rooted in nonlegal institutions. Moreover, rational systems may incorporate potentially irrational components, as when the final judgment in a case is left to a lay jury. Nevertheless, as ideal types Weber's categories help to locate idealized Western law in a wider universe of possible legal systems.

The importance of Weber's categories, like those of Maine, reside in large part in his efforts to link types of rationality with different types of societies and different ways of organizing legal systems. He associated an irrational legal order with domination by a charismatic leader. Formal rationality, on the other hand, accompanies the rise of the bureaucratic style of organization. Weber regarded logically formal rationality as the most "advanced" kind of legal ordering and as particularly hospitable to the growth of the capitalist state.

Weber's third contribution to comparative legal studies was his insight that the nature of a society's legal system is shaped by the kinds of individuals who dominate it. On the European continent, in the absence of a powerful central court, domination fell into the hands of the university law faculties who strove, through the promulgation and interpretation of authoritative texts, to create and understand the legal system as a general and autonomous set of rules. The common law in England, on the other hand, grew under the tutelage of a small elite judiciary and accompanying centralized bar, more concerned with pronouncing rules for the settlement of disputes than in developing generalized rules of law (Weber 1954). In time, the differences in the legal systems created by these different sets of *honoratiores* helped to spur interest in comparative legal systems.

Overall, Weber's contribution was part of a general movement away from comparing the legal codes of various societies and toward a comparison of the legal solutions that "are given to the same actual problems by the legal systems of different countries seen as a complete whole" (Zweigert and Kotz 1987, p. 60, quoting Rabel). From this perspective, legal systems confront similar problems, and if we examine the whole system we will uncover fundamental differences and similarities in their various solutions. The effort to uncover these similarities and differences has taken several different paths.

Macrocomparisons. One path has involved attempts to develop macrocomparisons of entire legal systems. This effort has resulted in a number of taxonomies of legal systems in which the laws of nations are grouped by what are commonly called "legal families." The criteria for classification and the ultimate categories of family types have varied from scholar to scholar. Among the factors that have been used are historical tradition, the sources of law, the conceptual structure of law, and the social objectives of law. Socialist writers have traditionally focused on the relationship of law to underlying economic relations and a society's history of class conflict (Szabo and Peteri 1977; Eorsi 1979), although more recent efforts paint a much more complex picture that threatens some of the presumed differences between socialist and "capitalist" law (Sypnowich 1990). David (1950) and David and Brierley (1985) base their classification on ideology (resulting from philosophical, political, and economic factors) and legal technique. Zweigert and Kotz (1987, p. 69) base their classification on a multiple set of criteria they call the "style" of law. Legal style includes: historical background and development, predominant modes of thought in legal matters (contrasting the use of abstract legal norms in civil law versus the narrow, reasoning by analogy typical of the common law), distinctive concepts (such as the trust in the common law and the abuse of right in civil law), the source of law (statutory or case law), and ideology (e.g., the ideology of socialist and Western legal families).

Given the wide variety of criteria used by various scholars, perhaps it is surprising that the resulting "families" tend to be quite similar. To provide but one example, Zweigert and Kotz (1987) divide the world into the following eight families: (1) Romanistic family (e.g., France); (2) Germanic family (e.g., Germany); (3) Nordic family (e.g., Sweden); (4) common law family (e.g., England); (5) socialist family (e.g., Soviet Union); (6) Far Eastern family (e.g., China); (7) Islamic systems; and (8) Hindu law. While some taxonomies may have fewer civil law divisions, this set of categories shares with many others a Eurocentric emphasis and a resulting inability easily to fit non-European legal systems into the taxonomy (see Ehrmann 1976; David and Brierley 1985), although the rise of non-Western societies such as Japan should help to redress this imbalance in time (see Institute of Comparative Law, Waseda University 1988).

The Eurocentric and Western emphasis is not

simply a matter of greater particularity in describing differences between the legal traditions of Europe. It is also reflected in the concepts used to make distinctions. The categories of the various typologies are based primarily on a comparison of private law rather than on public or constitutional law and on substantive law rather than on adjective law. A different focus may lead to different family configurations. For example, American and German constitutional law are in some ways more similar to each other than to French or English constitutional law. The focus on private substantive law has the additional result that it overemphasizes legal doctrine while underemphasizing the degree to which legal systems are a product of the surrounding society. The consequence is to understate similarities in Western legal arrangements that may be captured by the idea of a legal culture.

One alternative designed to avoid this tendency is found in Merryman's (1969) concept of legal traditions. Legal traditions are

> *a set of deeply rooted, historically conditioned attitudes about the nature of law, about the role of law in the society and the polity, about the proper organization and operation of a legal system, and about the way law is or should be made, applied, studied, perfected, and taught. The legal tradition relates the legal system to the culture of which it is a partial expression.* (Merryman 1969, p. 2)

From this perspective the Western legal tradition usefully may be compared and contrasted to legal systems in other cultures (Barton et al. 1983).

A second alternative to the "legal families" approach are taxonomies that are not based on differences in substantive law. One recent example, closer to the Weberian heritage, is that of Damaska (1986). Like Weber, Damaska uses two dimensions to develop ideal-typical legal orders. The first dimension divides legal orders into activist and reactive systems of justice. Activist states attempt to use law to manage society, whereas reactive states attempt only to provide a legal framework for social interaction. At the heart of the image of law of the activist state is the state decree, spelling out programs, assigning tasks, and distributing welfare to citizens. At the heart of the reactive state are devices facilitating agreement, contracts, and pacts. While it might be thought that this dimension is designed primarily to distinguish capitalist and socialist legal orders, Damaska observes that not all types of socialist models follow the state socialism that has dominated the Soviet Union and Eastern Europe. Yugoslavian self-management concepts speak to this reactive tradition in socialism. Likewise, capitalist societies exhibit considerable differences in their commitment to an activist state.

Damaska's second dimension divides legal orders into hierarchical and coordinate systems of judicial organization. In the hierarchical ideal officials are professionals who are arranged in a strict hierarchy and who employ special, technical standards of decision making. The coordinate ideal describes a more amorphous machine in which legal functionaries are amateurs who are arranged in relationships of relatively equal authority and who do justice based on prevailing ethical, political, or religious norms. Weber's vision of the Moslem Khadi applying substantive (religious) law would appear to describe this type of legal order.

There are other strong parallels between Damaska's and Weber's ideal types. Their categories are less obviously Eurocentric and, more important, employ a set of concepts that facilitate an understanding of ways in which the relationship between the state and society is mediated through law. Both analyses are inclined toward a functional approach. Rather than beginning with individual legal histories and doctrines and grouping them into families, this approach begins with a set of problems—how to mediate the relationship of the state and society and how to organize the structure of the legal honoratiores—and arranges legal systems according to how they address these problems.

Damaska's distinction between the hierarchical and coordinate ideal and Weber's distinction between formal and substantive rationality direct our attention to a central issue concerning law—

the degree to which different legal systems are autonomous. An autonomous legal system is independent of other sources of power and authority in social life; its legal outcomes are influenced only by preestablished, status-neutral rules of the legal system; the actions and actors brought to the legal system are dealt with only after their dispute is translated into a set of legal categories (debtor–unsecured creditor, lessor–lessee); parties come to law with equal competence. An extreme version of legal autonomy is a legal system that is autopoietic. An autopoietic system, like a living organism, produces and reproduces its own elements by the interaction of its elements (Teubner 1988). Legal autonomy and even legal autopoiesis are best thought of as variables, other important ways in which we may distinguish legal systems. Using Damaska's typology, we might expect that legal systems that reflect the hierarchical ideal will be more likely to exhibit some of the features of greater autonomy.

Microcomparisons. Microcomparisons of legal systems are concerned with the details of specific legal rules and institutions rather than with entire legal systems (Rheinstein 1968). The functional approach is even more pronounced at this level. Scholars often begin with a specific social problem and seek to discover the various ways in which legal systems solve it, or they begin with a specific legal institution and examine how it operates in various systems. For example, Shapiro (1981) makes a comparative analysis of the court as an institution in common law, civil law, imperial Chinese, and Islamic legal systems.

The most valuable work done at this level has been that of legal anthropologists. By examining the dispute-processing activities of African, Latin American, and Asian legal tribunals they have provided new insights into the connection between a society's social relationships and the way in which it processes disputes. Ethnographies by Gluckman (1967), Gulliver (1963), Nader (1969) and others exposed a general pattern wherein tribunals confronted with disputes among individuals who are in multiplex and enduring relationships are more likely to widen the range of relevant evidence and to search for outcomes that allow flexibility, compromise, and integration. Tribunals confronted with disputes among individuals who are in one-dimensional and episodic relationships are more likely to narrow the range of relevant evidence and to provide binary outcomes where one side clearly wins and the other loses.

Legal ethnographies have also supported the earlier observation based on macrocomparisons that the organization of courts and judges plays a role in determining styles of dispute processing. Fallers (1969), for instance, found that the Soga, a society in many ways very similar to the Barotse studied by Gluckman, tended to craft decisions that were narrower and that resulted in "legalistic" rulings. His explanation was that the "judiciary" in the two societies differed in at least one key respect. The Soga courts were more purely "judicial" bodies without administrative and executive functions. A specialized legal staff was more likely to issue narrower opinions. Moreover, because binary outcomes result in a judgment to be enforced against a losing party, the availability of a coercive judicial apparatus may facilitate this type of dispute resolution (Lempert and Sanders 1986).

Perhaps because of the seminal work by Llewellyn and Hoebel (1941) on the Cheyenne, the work of legal anthropologists, more than most macro approaches to the study of legal systems, builds on the sociological jurisprudence and the legal realist traditions (Pound 1911–12; Oliphant 1928; Llewellyn 1930; Arnold 1935). It is concerned with the law in action, with the actual experience of the legal staff and the disputants. As a consequence, legal anthropology has had a substantial influence on the sociological study of disputing and what has come to be called alternative dispute resolution in Western societies (Greenhouse 1986; Abel 1981).

Recently, anthropologists have come to appreciate the degree to which African and other consensual legal systems are themselves partly the outgrowth of colonial experience and of the distribution of power in society (Starr and Collier

1989). This observation underlines a more general point that has been noted by macro and micro scholars alike. Nearly all existing legal systems are, to a greater or lesser extent, externally imposed, and therefore all legal systems are layered. In many societies layering occurs because of the existence of a federal system creating an internal hierarchy of rules, some of which are imposed from above. Layered legal systems also occur when nations such as Turkey (the Swiss code) or Japan (the German code) shop abroad and adopt the laws of another nation as the basic framework for substantial parts of their own legal system. In some situations the imposition is done wholesale and involuntarily, as when colonial powers impose a legal system. The result can be considerable social dislocation (Burman and Harrell-Bond 1979). In time, multiple layers may exist, as in Japan, where indigenous law has been overlaid by both the adopted German code and American constitutional law concepts imposed after World War II.

In each of these situations a society's legal system is unlikely to fit easily within any of the legal families. For instance, a society may borrow another's substantive and adjective law for commercial law purposes but retain the existing law of domestic relations. Frequently, such societies are said to have a "dual legal system." However, to the degree that this phrase describes a situation where two equal systems stand side by side and rarely interact, it fails to capture the rich variety of hierarchical structures in layered systems. An important task for the students of legal systems is to understand the process by which individuals and groups use law at different levels and in so doing transform both.

At the uppermost layer of legal systems are legal arrangements that are multinational or transnational in scope. Within the European Economic Community, following the Treaty of Rome in 1957 and the Single European Act in 1987, the adoption/imposition of a multinational regime is proceeding rapidly. The process requires the harmonization of a large body of law including corporate, intellectual property, environmental, tax, products liability, banking, transportation, product regulation (e.g., food and pharmaceuticals), and antitrust law. Member states must conform their national laws to comply with community directives, inevitably leading to the homogenization of European law. This process, along with the substantial alterations in property and contract law accompanying the economic changes in the Soviet Union and Eastern Europe, suggests that the differences among legal systems of European origin will diminish over the next few decades, especially differences among laws governing commercial and economic transactions.

Indeed, the existence of a global economic order promotes some similarities in all laws governing economic transactions. Islamic law has been compelled to create a number of legal devices and fictions designed to avoid direct confrontation with several teachings of the Koran, such as the prohibition against charging interest that would make participation in a modern economic order difficult (David and Brierley 1985, p. 469).

A number of additional global issues also create pressures toward the creation of transnational legal arrangements. These include transnational crime, ethnic and racial conflict, world population and migration patterns, labor flows, and, perhaps most significant, environmental regulation. Common legal structures created to address these issues and demands that nation-state legal systems enact and enforce appropriate compliance mechanisms may lead to the rebirth of the ideal of international legal unification that was popular at the beginning of the century. As can be seen in the European example, such unification inevitably involves some imposition of law.

Because pressures to build a more complex body of transnational law coincide with the diminution of differences in Western legal systems, over the next few decades one of the most interesting issues in the study of legal systems will involve movements toward and resistance to a transnational legal order premised on the hegemony of Western legal systems and Western legal concepts. The future task of comparative law is to understand the processes of borrowing, imposition, and resistance, both among nations and between levels of legal systems.

(SEE ALSO: *Court Systems of the United States; Social Control; Law and Society; Sociology of Law*)

REFERENCES

Abel, Richard 1981 *The Politics of Informal Justice, 2 vols.* New York: Academic Press.

Arnold, Thurmond 1935 *The Symbols of Government.* New Haven, Conn.: Yale University Press.

Barton, John, James Gibbs, Victor Li, and John Merryman 1983 *Law in Radically Different Cultures.* St. Paul, Minn.: West Publishing Co.

Black, Donald 1976 *The Behavior of Law.* New York: Academic Press.

Bohannan, Paul 1965 "The Differing Realms of the Law." *American Anthropologist* 67 (6, pt. 2): 133–142.

Burman, Sandra, and Barbara Harrell-Bond, eds. 1979 *The Imposition of Law.* New York: Academic Press.

Damaska, Mirjan 1986 *The Faces of Justice and State Authority: A Comparative Approach to the Legal Process.* New Haven, Conn.: Yale University Press.

David, René 1950 *Traité élémentaire de droit civil comparé.* Paris: Librairie Générale de Droit et de Juris prudence.

———, and John Brierley 1985 *Major Legal Systems in the World Today.* London: Stevens and Sons.

Durkheim, Emile (1893) 1964 *The Division of Labor in Society.* New York: Free Press.

Ehrmann, Henry 1976 *Comparative Legal Cultures.* Englewood Cliffs, N. J.: Prentice-Hall.

Eorsi, Gy 1979 *Comparative Civil Law.* Budapest: Akademiai Kiado.

Fallers, Lloyd 1969 *Law Without Precedent: Legal Ideas in Action in the Courts of Colonial Busoga.* Chicago: University of Chicago Press.

Gluckman, Max 1967 *The Judicial Process among the Barotse of Northern Rhodesia.* Manchester, England: Manchester University Press.

Greenhouse, Carol 1986 *Praying for Justice.* Ithaca, N.Y.: Cornell University Press.

Griffiths, John 1984 "The Division of Labor in Social Control." In Donald Black, ed., *Toward a General Theory of Social Control.* New York: Academic Press.

Gulliver, P. M. 1963 *Social Control in an African Society: A Study of the Arusha.* London: Routledge and Kegan Paul.

Hoebel, E. Adamson 1954 *The Law of Primitive Man.* Cambridge, Mass.: Harvard University Press.

Institute of Comparative Law, Waseda University, ed. 1988 *Law in East and West.* Tokyo: Waseda University Press.

Lempert, Richard, and Joseph Sanders 1986 *An Invitation to Law and Social Science.* Philadelphia: University of Pennsylvania Press.

Llewellyn, Karl 1930 "A Realistic Jurisprudence: The Next Step." *Columbia Law Review* 30:431–465.

———, and E. Adamson Hoebel 1941 *The Cheyenne Way: Conflict and Case Law in Primitive Society.* Norman: University of Oklahoma Press.

Maine, Henry (1861) 1963 *Ancient Law: Its Connection with the Early History of Society and Its Relation to Modern Ideas.* Boston: Beacon Press.

Merryman, John Henry 1969 *The Civil Law Tradition: An Introduction to the Legal Systems of Western Europe and Latin America.* Stanford, Calif.: Stanford University Press.

Montesquieu (1748) 1962 *The Spirit of the Laws,* 2 vols. New York: Hafner.

Moore, Sally Falk 1973 "Law and Social Change: The Semi-Autonomous Social Field as an Appropriate Subject of Study." *Law and Society Review* 7:719–746.

Nader, Laura 1969 "Styles of Court Procedure: To Make the Balance." In Laura Nader, ed., *Law in Culture and Society.* Chicago: Aldine.

Oliphant, Herman 1928 "A Return to *Stare Decisis.*" *American Bar Association Journal* 14:71, 159.

Pound, Roscoe 1911–12 "The Scope and Purpose of Sociological Jurisprudence." Parts 1, 2, and 3. *Harvard Law Review* 24:591–619; 25:140–168; 25: 489–516.

Rheinstein, Max 1968 "Legal Systems." In David L. Sills, ed., *International Encyclopedia of the Social Sciences,* Vol. 9. pp. 204–210. New York: Macmillan.

Shapiro, Martin 1981 *Courts: A Comparative and Political Analysis.* Chicago: University of Chicago Press.

Starr, June, and Jane Collier (eds). 1989 *History and Power in the Study of Law: New Directions in Legal Anthropology.* Ithaca, N.Y.: Cornell University Press.

Sypnowich, Christine 1990 *The Concept of Socialist Law.* Oxford: Clarendon Press.

Szabo, I., and Z. Peteri (eds.) 1977 *A Socialist Approach to Comparative Law.* Leyden, The Netherlands: A. W. Sijthoff.

Teubner, Gunther (ed.) 1988 *Autopoietic Law: A New Approach to Law and Society.* Berlin: Walter de Gruyter.

Weber, Max 1954 *On Law in Economy and Society.* New York: Simon and Schuster.

Zweigert, Konrad, and Hein Kotz 1987 *Introduction to Comparative Law.* Vol. 1, *The Framework.* Oxford: Clarendon Press.

JOSEPH SANDERS

LAW AND SOCIETY The concepts of *law* and *society* refer to macrostructural phenomena. Is there a macro-oriented theory of law and society or a macro sociolegal theory to guide this field? As an interdisciplinary endeavor, the sociology of law relies upon, or is influenced by, the intellectual assumptions and propositions of general sociology and legal theory. This article will therefore consider the relationship of this field to both parent disciplines.

RELATIONSHIP TO GENERAL SOCIOLOGY

It is no exaggeration to state that the field of sociology lacks a systematically developed and precise theory of society. Although interest in macrosociological theory building has been in evidence for the past two decades, particularly among those concerned with comparative sociology (Eisenstadt and Curelaru 1977), no such theory has yet been developed in sufficient detail and precision to guide empirical research. This is not to deny the fact that such macrotheorists as Marx, Durkheim, Weber, and Parsons have exerted a pervasive influence on various specialties within sociology, including the relationship between law and society.

Marx. Marx conceived of law as a component of the "superstructure" of a capitalist society. As an epiphenomenon of the superstructure, it provides a rationale or ideology for preserving the existing class relations in a capitalist economy. Concepts of property and contract, for example, become instrumentalities for maintaining and reproducing class hegemony. In other words, legal concepts and doctrines reinforce the position of the ruling class and, at the same time, become the constituents of the "false consciousness" from which the working class suffers. Implicit in this theory of law as a weapon wielded by the state in a capitalist society against the working class is the assumption that if private property were abolished and a classless socialist society were ushered in, the state would "wither away" and, with it, law would "wither away" as well.

As usually formulated, the Marxian theory of law and society is not empirically verifiable. It does not follow, however, that this theory is devoid of any empirical implications. Questions can be raised—and have been raised—concerning class bias in the adjudication of civil and criminal cases, in the emergence of significant legal norms—for example, those regarding inheritance—and in the recurrent failure of agrarian reform laws. Likewise, it is possible to investigate a proposition counter to the Marxian thesis, namely, that the passage of laws in a capitalist state can potentially diminish the power of the ruling class vis-a-vis the working class. A case in point is the enactment of the National Labor Relations Act of 1935 in the United States, which institutionalized the rights of employees to unionize and to engage in collective bargaining with employers. Research questions such as those cited above would test the validity of some propositions derivable from the Marxian theory of law and society.

Durkheim. Turning to Durkheim's contribution to this field, one of necessity reverts to his *Division of Labor in Society* (1933), in which he argued that in societies characterized by "mechanical solidarity" there is a predominance of repressive laws, whereas in societies characterized by "organic solidarity" there is a predominance of restitutive laws. A number of social scientists have subjected Durkheim's thesis to empirical tests and have found it wanting (Schwartz and Miller 1964). It is a testament, however, to the intriguing character of Durkheim's thesis that it continues to evoke the interest of researchers (Baxi 1974; Schwartz 1974; Sheleff 1975). A more general formulation of Durkheim's thesis would be that societies differing along various dimensions of societal development—of which the division of labor is but one—will exhibit systematic differences in their legal systems (Evan 1968).

In the course of developing his thesis that the division of labor is the principal source of social solidarity, Durkheim formulated his seminal idea of an "index" (Durkheim 1933, pp. 64–65). Apart from his fame as the "father of modern sociology," Durkheim is the originator of the concept of an "index", that is, an indirect and "external" measure of a complex dimension of social structure such as social solidarity. That he developed the concept of an index in connection with "juridical rules" and types of laws is of particular interest to sociologists of law and legal scholars. Under the circumstances, it is indeed surprising that to date, with few exceptions (Evan 1965, 1968, 1980; Merryman, Clark, and Friedman 1979; Lidz 1979), this facet of Durkheim's work has been neglected. The concept of a "legal index" or a "legal indicator" merits systematic attention if we are to become more precise in our understanding of the role of law in social change.

Weber. In comparison with the work of Durkheim and Marx, Weber's contributions to the sociology of law are appreciably more diverse and complex. Embedded in an intricate mosaic of ideal types and comparative and historical data on the emergence of legal rationality in Western civilization and on the role of law in the origins of capitalism (Weber 1950; Rheinstein 1954; Trubek 1972; Collins 1980), Weber's welter of legal conceptualizations poses a difficult challenge to the empirically oriented researcher. For example, his famous typology of lawmaking and lawfinding suggests possible research leads for comparative and historical analysis. Rheinstein, who edited and translated Weber's work on the sociology of law, lucidly summarizes his typology in the following manner:

1. *irrational, i.e., not guided by general rules*
   a. *formal: guided by means which are beyond the control of reason (ordeal, oracle, etc.)*
   b. *substantive: guided by reaction to the individual case*
2. *rational, i.e., guided by general rules*
   a. *substantive: guided by the principles of an ideological system other than that of the law itself (ethics, religion, power, politics, etc.)*
   b. *formal:*
      (1) *extrinsically, i.e., ascribing significance to external acts observable by the senses*
      (2) *logically, i.e., expressing its rules by the use of abstract concepts created by legal thought itself and conceived of as constituting a complete system.*

(Rheinstein 1954, p. l)

Assuming that the meaning of each of these ideal type categories can be clarified and that legal indicators can be developed for each of the types, a comparative study could be undertaken to explore differences in lawmaking and in lawfinding of such major legal systems as common law, civil law, socialist law, and Moslem law. Equally challenging would be a study of long-term trends within each of these legal systems. The findings of such an inquiry would shed light on the occurrence of the evolutionary stages postulated by Weber:

> *The general development of law and procedure may be viewed as passing through the following stages: first, charismatic legal revelation through "law prophets"; second, empirical creation and finding of law by legal honoratiores; . . . third, imposition of law by secular or theocratic powers; fourth and finally, systematic elaboration of law and professionalized administration of justice by persons who have received their legal training in a learned and formally logical manner.* (Rheinstein 1954, p. 303)

Another significant thesis in Weber's corpus of writings on law is the innovative role he attributes to "legal honoratiores" or "legal notables" (Bendix 1960). Is Weber's thesis more valid for civil law systems, with its heavy immersion in Roman law, than it is for common law, let alone for socialist law or Moslem law? Once again it would be necessary to develop appropriate legal indicators to measure the degree to which legal notables—lawyers, judges, and high-level civil servants—introduce new rules and new interpretations of existing legal norms in the course of administering justice.

Parsons. For decades, Parsons was the leading macrosociological theorist in the United States, making singular contributions to structural functionalism and to a general theory of action. Focusing on the action of social systems, Parsons developed a "four-function paradigm." According to Parsons, every society faces four subsystem problems: adaptation, goal attainment, integration, and pattern maintenance or latency (AGIL). The societal subsystems associated with these four functional problems are, respectively, the economy, the polity, law, and religion and education.

Following Weber, Parsons treats law as a rational-legal system consisting of a set of prescriptions, proscriptions, and permissions. The legal system, especially in highly differentiated modern societies, performs the functions of a "generalized mechanism of social control" (Parsons 1962). This function is performed vis-à-vis the economy, the polity, and pattern maintenance or latency. The net effect of the pervasive normative regulation is the integration of society. As Parsons puts it: "The legal system . . . broadly constitutes what is probably the single most important institutional key to understanding . . . problems of societal integration" (Parsons 1978, p. 52).

With his four-function paradigm, Parsons addresses the nexus between law and society with the aid of "generalized media of interchange." The economy in a developed and differentiated society uses the medium of money for transactions. Functionally analogous media of exchange operate in each of the other subsystems—power in the polity, value commitment in pattern maintenance, and influence in law.

Suggestive as Parsons's framework is for understanding interinstitutional relations, the generalized media of interchange have not, as yet, been operationalized so as to explain how the legal system interacts with other societal subsystems. In other words, since Parsons has not explicated specific linkages between the legal and nonlegal subsystems, it is difficult to discern what hypotheses can be tested against any body of data. Hence, a reasonable conclusion is that Parsons's macrosociological theory, in its present form, is actually a metatheory.

The foregoing review of some sociological theories of law and society raises two common themes: (1) each of the theorists endeavored to comprehend the macrostructural relationships between law and other institutional systems of a society, and (2) if the hypotheses implicit in these theories are to be empirically tested, systematic attention would have to be devoted to the development of a body of legal indicators. The current generation of sociologists of law has yet to face up to the problems engendered by both of these themes.

RELATIONSHIP TO LEGAL THEORY

Is the relationship between the sociology of law and the field of legal theory any less problematic than it is with general sociology? On its face, the question should be answered in the affirmative because the sociologist of law must take some of the legal scholars' subjects as objects of inquiry. In actuality, because of the traditions of legal scholarship, legal scholars do not generally provide an analytical basis for sociological research. Legal scholarship tends to be preoccupied with legal rules, legal principles, and their application to a multitude of specific conflict situations. As a consequence, the scholarly literature—apart from being intellectually insular—is almost entirely verbal and idiographic, with virtually no interest in a *nomothetic,* let alone *quantitative,* analysis of legal phenomena. Furthermore, there is a high degree of specialization within legal scholarship such that most scholars tend to devote their entire careers to a particular body of law, be it labor law, criminal law, contract law, family law, and so forth, in their own country. Those scholars specializing in comparative law are inclined to study a particular specialty, for example, family law, by comparing case studies from two or more countries (Glendon 1975). Relatively few legal scholars seek to study the legal system of an entire society, such as the work of Hazard (1977) and Berman (1963) on the Soviet legal system. And fewer still have had the temerity to undertake systematic comparisons of total legal systems or families of legal systems, as exemplified in the work of David and Brierly (1968) and Wigmore (1928); and those who do make no effort to relate characteristics of total legal systems to the social-structural attributes of the societies in which they are embedded.

Surveying current legal theory, three distinct theoretical perspectives can be discerned: the theory of legal autonomy, critical legal studies, and autopoietic law. Each of these perspectives will be briefly reviewed and appraised for their implications for a theory of law and society.

Legal Autonomy. Traditional conceptions of the legal order and "sources of law" are based on two assumptions, the first being that the law is a "seamless web," a relatively "closed system." Whatever processes of change occur in the law are generated from within the legal system, not from without. In other words, processes of change are immanent or endogenous and are not externally induced. The second assumption is that the legal system is, by definition, autonomous from other systems or institutions of a society. Therefore, it is unnecessary to inquire into how the legal system interacts with other subsystems of a society or into what degree of autonomy a given legal system actually has from other societal subsystems.

Perhaps the most quintessential articulation of the theory of legal autonomy in recent years can be found in the work of Watson, a renowned legal historian and comparative law scholar. Watson has repeated his thesis of legal autonomy in a number of monographs and articles (Watson 1974, 1978, 1981, 1983, 1985, 1987). He contends that the growth and evolution of the law is determined largely by an autonomous legal tradition, which exists and operates outside the sphere of societal needs.

> *To a large extent law possesses a life and vitality of its own; that is, no extremely close, natural or inevitable relationship exists between law, legal structures, institutions and rules on the one hand and the needs and desires and political economy of the ruling elite or of the members of the particular society on the other hand. If there was such a close relationship, legal rules, institutions and structures would transplant only with great difficulty, and their power of survival would be severely limited.* (Watson 1978, pp. 314–315)

> *Law is largely autonomous and not shaped by societal needs; though legal institutions will not exist without corresponding social institutions, law evolves from the legal tradition.* (Watson 1985, p. 119).

Unlike the Marxist view of law, Watson's is that the law does not advance the interests of the ruling class; instead, it reflects the "culture" of the legal elite. He bolsters his provocative thesis with a study of legal borrowing, which he refers to as "legal transplants" (1974). The fact that the individual statutes, legal doctrines, and entire codes have been borrowed by countries differing in cultural, political, economic, and other respects provides evidence, according to Watson, in support of his thesis of legal autonomy.

The concept of "legal transplant" has a naturalistic ring to it as though it occurs independent of any human agency. In point of fact, however, elites—legal and nonlegal—often act as "culture carriers" or intermediaries between societies involved in a legal transplant. Legal scholars who are associated with political elites may be instrumental in effecting a legal transplant. Moreover, many instances of legal borrowing involve the "imposition" of a foreign body of law by a colonial power (Burman and Harrell-Bond 1979). Hence, it is a mistake to describe and analyze the diffusion of law as if it were devoid of human agency. If human volition is involved, it is indeed questionable whether the borrowed legal elements do not perform a societal function—at the very least on behalf of the legal elite.

Critical Legal Studies Unlike Watson's internalist focus on the legal system and its autonomous development, the critical legal studies (CLS) movement appears to pursue a dual strategy: externalist as well as internalist. CLS is externalist in its critique of the social order and of the values dominating judicial decision making. It is internalist in its fundamental critique of traditional jurisprudence and legal reasoning.

The CLS movement emerged in the late 1970s in American law schools. It brought together a diverse group of scholars with a left-of-center ideology concerned about inequality and injustice in American society. Although lacking any consensus regarding societal transformation, CLS scholars sought to identify the impact of society's dominant interests on the legal process and the impact of social and political values on legal decision making.

In his introduction to a volume of essays by CLS authors, David Kairys discusses the "basic elements" of the legal theory of this movement. Three of these elements are externalist in nature:

> *We place fundamental importance on democracy, by which we mean popular participation in the decisions that shape our society and affect our lives. . . . We reject the common characterization of the law and the state as neutral, value-free arbiters, independent of and unaffected by social and economic relations, political forces, and cultural phenomena. The law's ultimate mechanism for control and enforcement is institutional violence, but it protects the dominant system of social and power relations against political and ideological as well as physical challenges.* (Kairys 1982, pp. 3–5)

These three externalist principles of the CLS movement have a familiar ring to them; namely, they are reminiscent of criticisms leveled by Marxists and neo-Marxists against the legal order of capitalist societies.

By far the most distinctive contribution of the CLS movement has been its elaborate internalist critique of legal reasoning and legal process. As Kairys puts it:

> *We reject . . . the notion that a distinctly legal mode of reasoning or analysis characterizes the legal process or even exists. . . . There is no legal reasoning in the sense of a legal methodology or process for reaching particular, correct results. There is a distinctly legal and quite elaborate system of discourse and body of knowledge, replete with its own language and conventions of argumentation, logic, and even manners. In some ways these aspects of the law are so distinct and all-embracing as to amount to a separate culture; and for many lawyers the courthouse, the law firm, the language, the style, become a way of life. But in terms of a method or process for decision making—for determining correct rules, facts, or results—the law provides only a wide and conflicting variety of stylized rationalizations from which courts pick and choose. Social and political judgments about the substance, parties, and context of a case guide such choices, even when they are not the explicit or conscious basis of decision.* (Kairys 1982, p. 3)

Not only do critical legal scholars reject the notion of legal reasoning, they also reject other idealized components constituting a "legal system," in particular, that law is a body of doctrine, that the doctrine reflects a coherent view of relations between persons and the nature of society, and that social behavior reflects norms generated by the legal system (Trubek 1984, p. 577).

The general conclusion CLS writers draw from "unmasking" the legal system, "trashing" mainstream jurisprudence, and "deconstructing" legal scholarship (Barkan 1987) is that "law is simply politics by other means" (Kairys 1982, p. 17). Such a conclusion, on its face, does not hold out any promise for developing a new, let alone heuristic, approach to a theory of law and society. On the contrary, its antipositivism combined with its search for a transformative political agenda has prompted CLS writers to view with increasing skepticism the sociology of law and research into the relationship between law and society (Trubek and Esser 1989).

Autopoietic Law. Similar in some respects to Watson's theory of legal autonomy, but fundamentally different from the theory of the CLS movement, autopoietic law claims to be a challenging new theory of law and society (Teubner 1988a). For the past few years several continental social theorists, who are also legal scholars, have enthusiastically developed and propagated the theory of autopoietic law. A complex cluster of ideas, this theory is derived from the work of two biologists, Maturana and Varela (Varela 1979; Maturana and Varela 1980).

In the course of their biological research, Maturana and Varela arrived at some methodological realizations that led them to generalize about the nature of living systems. Maturana coined the term *autopoiesis* to capture this new "scientific epistemology" (Maturana and Varela 1980, p. xvii). "This was a word without a history, a word that could directly mean what takes place in the dynamics of the autonomy proper to living systems." Conceptualizing living systems as machines, Maturana and Varela present the following rather complex and abstract definition:

> *Autopoietic machines are homeostatic machines. Their peculiarity, however, does not lie in this but in the fundamental variable which they maintain constant . . . an autopoietic machine continuously generates and specifies its own organization through its operation as a system of production of its own components, and does this in an endless turnover of components under conditions of continuous perturbations and compensation of perturbations.* (Maturana and Varela 1980, pp. 78–79)

Another definition of autopoiesis is presented by Zeleny, one of the early advocates of this new theory:

> *An* autopoietic system *is a distinguishable complex of component-producing processes and their resulting components, bounded as an autonomous unity within its environment, and characterized by a particular kind of relation among its components, and component-producing processes: the components, through their interaction, recursively generate, maintain, and recover* the same *complex of processes which produced them.* (Zeleny 1980, p. 4)

Clearly, these definitions and postulates are rather obscure and high-level generalizations that, from a general systems theory perspective (Bertalanffy 1968), are questionable. Especially suspect is the assertion that autopoietic systems do not have inputs and outputs. The authors introduce further complexity by postulating second- and third-order autopoietic systems, which occur when autopoietic systems interact with one another and, in turn, generate a new autopoietic system (Maturana and Varela 1980, pp. 107–111). Toward the end of their provocative monograph, Maturana and Varela raise the question of whether the dynamics of human societies are determined by the autopoiesis of its components. Failing to agree on the answer to this question, the authors postpone further discussion (Maturana and Varela 1980, p. 118). Zeleny, however, hastens to answer this question and introduces the notion of "social autopoiesis" to convey that human societies are autopoietic (Zeleny 1980, p. 3).

Luhmann, an outstanding German theorist and jurist, has also gravitated to the theory of autopoiesis. According to Luhmann, "social systems can be regarded as special kinds of autopoietic systems" (1988b, p. 15). Influenced in part by Parsons and general systems theory, Luhmann applied some systems concepts in analyzing social structures (1982). In the conclusion to the second edition of his book *A Sociological Theory of Law* (1985), Luhmann briefly refers to new developments in general systems theory that warrant the application of autopoiesis to the legal system. Instead of maintaining the dichotomy between closed and open systems theory, articulated by Bertalanffy, Boulding, and Rapoport (Buckley 1968), Luhmann seeks to integrate the open and closed system perspectives. In the process he conceptualizes the legal system as self-referential, self-reproducing, "normatively closed," and "cognitively open"—a theme he has pursued in a number of essays (1985, 1986, 1988c).

This formulation is, to say the least, ambiguous. Given normative closure, how does the learning of the system's environmental changes, expectations, or demands get transmitted to the legal system? Further complicating the problem is Luhmann's theory of a functionally differentiated modern society in which all subsystems—including the legal system—tend to be differentiated as self-referential systems, thereby reaching high levels of autonomy (Luhmann 1982). Although Luhmann has explicitly addressed the issue of integrating the closed and open system perspectives of general systems theory, it is by no means evident from his many publications how this is achieved.

Another prominent contributor to autopoietic law is the jurist and sociologist of law Gunther Teubner. In numerous publications, Teubner discusses the theory of autopoiesis and its implications for reflexive law, legal autonomy, and evolutionary theory (Teubner 1983a, 1983b, 1988a, 1988b). One essay, "Evolution of Autopoietic Law" (1988a), raises two general issues: the prerequisites of autopoietic closure of a legal system, and legal evolution after a legal system achieves autopoietic closure. With respect to the first issue, Teubner applies the concept of *hypercycle,* which he has borrowed from others but which he does not explicitly define. Another of his essays (Teubner 1988b) reveals how Teubner is using this concept. For Teubner, all self-referential systems involve, by definition, "circularity" or "recursivity" (1988b, p. 57). Legal systems are preeminently self-referential in the course of producing legal acts or legal decisions. However, if they are to achieve autopoietic autonomy their cyclically constituted system components must become interlinked in a "hypercycle," "i.e., the additional cyclical linkage of cyclically constituted units" (Teubner 1988b, p. 55). The legal system components—as conceptualized by Teubner, "element, structure, process, identity boundary, environment, performance, function" (1988b, p. 55)—are general terms not readily susceptible to the construction of legal indicators.

The second question Teubner addresses, legal evolution after a legal system has attained autopoietic closure, poses a similar problem. The universal evolutionary functions of variation, selection, and retention manifest themselves in the form of legal mechanisms.

> *In the legal system, normative structures take over variation, institutional structures (especially procedures) take over selection and doctrinal structures take over retention.* (Teubner 1988a, p. 228)

Since Teubner subscribes to Luhmann's theory of a functionally differentiated social system, with each subsystem undergoing autopoietic development, he confronts the problem of intersubsystem relations as regards evolution. This leads him to introduce the intriguing concept of *co-evolution.*

> *The environmental reference in evolution however is produced not in the direct, causal production of legal developments, but in processes of co-evolution. The thesis is as follows: In co-evolutionary processes it is not only the autopoiesis of the legal system which has a selective effect on the development of its own structures; the autopoiesis of other subsystems and that of society also affects—in any case in a much more mediatory and indirect way—the selection of legal changes.* (Teubner 1988a, pp. 235–236)

Given the postulate of "autopoietic closure," it is not clear by what mechanisms nonlegal subsystems of a society affect the evolution of the legal system and how they "co-evolve." Once again, we confront the unsolved problem in the theory of autopiesis of integrating the closed and open systems perspectives. Nevertheless, Teubner, with the help of the concept of co-evolution, has drawn our attention to a critical problem even if one remains skeptical of his proposition that "the historical relationship of 'law and society' must, in my view, be defined as a co-evolution of structurally coupled autopoietic systems" (Teubner 1988a, p. 218).

At least three additional questions about autopoietic law can be raised. Luhmann's theory of a functionally differentiated society in which all subsystems are autopoietic raises anew Durkheim's problem of social integration. The centrifugal forces in such a society would very likely threaten its viability. Such a societal theory implies a highly decentralized social system with a weak state and a passive legal system. Does Luhmann really think any modern society approximates his model of a functionally differentiated society?

A related problem is the implicit ethnocentrism of social scientists writing against the background of highly developed Western societies where law enjoys a substantial level of functional autonomy, which, however, is by no means equivalent to autopoietic closure. In developing societies and in socialist countries, many of which are developing societies as well, this is hardly the case. In these types of societies legal systems tend to be subordinated to political, economic, or military institutions. In other words, the legal systems are decidedly *allopoietic.* To characterize the subsystems of such societies as *autopoietic* is to distort social reality.

A third problem with the theory of autopoietic law is its reliance on the "positivity" of law. This fails to consider a secular legal trend of great import for the future of humankind, namely, the faltering efforts—initiated by Grotius in the seventeenth century—to develop a body of international law. By what mechanisms can autopoietic legal systems incorporate international legal norms? Because of the focus on "positivized" law untainted by political, religious, and other institutional values, autopoietic legal systems would have a difficult time accommodating themselves to the growing corpus of international law.

Stimulating as is the development of the theory of legal autopoiesis, it does not appear to fulfill the requirements for a fruitful theory of law and society (Blankenburg 1983). In its present formulation, autopoietic law is a provocative metatheory. If any of its adherents succeed in deriving empirical propositions from this metatheory (Blankenburg 1983), subject them to an empirical test, and confirm them, they will be instrumental in bringing about a paradigm shift in the sociology of law.

The classical and contemporary theories of law and society, reviewed above, all fall short in providing precise and operational guidelines for uncovering the linkages over time between legal and nonlegal institutions in different societies. Thus, the search for a scientific macro sociolegal theory will continue. To further the search for such a theory, a social-structural model will now be outlined.

A SOCIAL-STRUCTURAL MODEL

A social-structural model begins with a theoretical amalgam of concepts from systems theory with Parsons' four structural components of social systems: values, norms, roles, and collectivities (Parsons 1961, pp. 41–44; Evan 1975, pp. 387–388). Any subsystem or institution of a societal system, whether it be a legal system, a family system, an economic system, a religious system, or any other system, can be decomposed into four structural elements: values, norms, roles, and organizations. The first two elements relate to a cultural or normative level of analysis and the last two to a social-structural level of analysis. Interactions between two or more subsystems of a society are mediated by cultural as well as by social-structural elements. As Parsons has observed, law is a generalized mechanism for regulating behavior in the several subsystems of a society (Parsons 1962, p. 57). At the normative level of analysis, law entails a "double institutionalization" of the values and norms embedded in other subsystems of a society (Bohannan 1968). In performing this reinforcement function, law develops "cultural linkages" with other subsystems, thus contributing to the degree of normative integration that exists in a society. As disputes are adjudicated and new legal norms are enacted, a value from one or more of the nonlegal subsystems is tapped. These values provide an implicit or explicit justification for legal decision making.

Parsons's constituents of social structure (values, norms, roles, and organizations) are nested elements, as in a Chinese box, with values incorporated in norms, both of these elements contained in roles, and all three elements constituting organizations. When values, norms, roles, and organizations are aggregated we have a new formulation, different from Parsons's AGIL paradigm, of the sociological concept of an institution. An institution of a society is composed of a configuration of values, norms, roles, and organizations. This definition is applicable to all social institutions, whether economic, political, religious, familial, educational, scientific, technological, or legal. In turn, the social structure of a society is a composite of these and other institutions.

Of fundamental importance to the field of the sociology of law is the question of how the legal institution is related to each of the nonlegal institutions. A preliminary answer to this question will be set forth in a model diagramming eight types of interactions or linkages between legal and nonlegal institutions (see Figure 1).

On the left-hand side of the diagram are a set of six nonlegal institutions, each of which is composed of values, norms, roles, and organizations. If the norms comprising the nonlegal institutions are sufficiently institutionalized, they can have a direct regulatory impact on legal personnel as well on the citizenry (interaction 4, "Single institutionalization"). On the other hand, according to Bohannan (1968), if the norms of the nonlegal institutions are not sufficiently strong to regulate the behavior of the citizenry, a process of "double institutionalization" (interaction 1) occurs whereby the legal system converts nonlegal

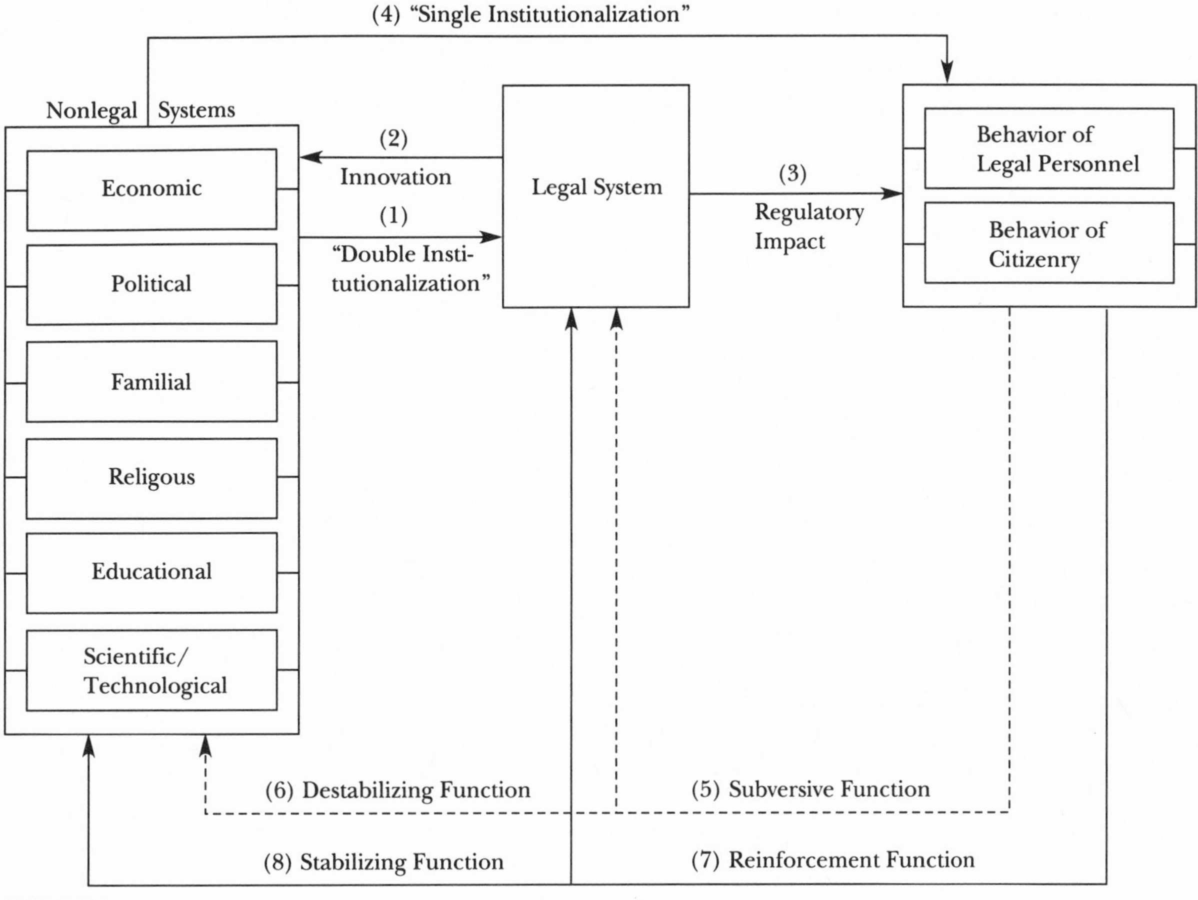

FIGURE 1
A Social-Structural Model of the Interactions of Legal and Nonlegal Institutions

institutional norms into legal norms. This effect can be seen in the rise in the Colonial period of "blue laws," which were needed to give legal reinforcement to the religious norms that held the Sabbath to be sacred (Evan 1980, pp. 517–518, 530–532). In addition, the legal system can introduce a norm that is not a component of any of the nonlegal institutions. In other words, the legal system can introduce an innovative norm (interaction 2) that does not have a counterpart in any of the nonlegal institutions (Bohannan 1968). An example of such an innovation is "no-fault" divorce (Weitzman 1985; Jacob 1988).

The legal system's regulatory impact (interaction 3) may succeed or fail with legal personnel, with the citizenry, or with both. Depending on whether legal personnel faithfully implement the law, and the citizenry faithfully complies with the law, the effect on the legal system can be reinforcing (interaction 7) or subversive (interaction 5), and the effect on nonlegal institutions can be stabilizing (interaction 9) or destabilizing (interaction 6).

In systems-theoretic terms, the values of a society may be viewed as goal parameters in comparison with which the performance of a legal system may be objectively assessed. The inability of a legal system to develop "feedback loops" and "closed loop systems" to monitor and assess the efficacy of its outputs makes the legal system vulnerable to various types of failures. Instead of generating "negative feedback," that is, self-corrective measures, when legal personnel or rank-and-file citizens fail to comply with the law, the system generates detrimental "positive feedback" (Laszlo, Levine, and Milsum 1974).

CONCLUSION

What are some implications of this social-structural model? In the first place, the legal system is not viewed as only an immanently developing set of legal rules, principles, or doctrines insulated from other subsystems of society, as expressed by Watson and to some extent by Luhmann and Teubner. Second, the personnel of the legal system, whether judges, lawyers, prosecutors, or administrative agency officials, activate legal rules, principles, or doctrines in the course of performing their roles within the legal system. Third, formally organized collectivities, be they courts, legislatures, law-enforcement organizations, or administrative agencies, perform the various functions of a legal system. Fourth, in performing these functions, the formally organized collectivities comprising a legal system interact with individuals and organizations representing interests embedded in the nonlegal subsystems of a society. In other words, each of the society's institutions or subsystems—legal and nonlegal—has the same structural elements: values, norms, roles, and organizations. Interinstitutional interactions involve an effort at coupling these structural elements across institutional boundaries. A major challenge to the sociologists of law is to discover the diverse couplings or linkages—cultural and social-structural—between the legal system and the nonlegal systems in terms of the four constituent structural elements. Another challenge is to ascertain the impact of these linkages on the behavior of legal personnel and on the behavior of the citizenry, on the one hand, and to measure the impact of "double institutionalization" on societal goals, on the other.

A serendipitous outcome of this model is that it suggests a definition of law and society or the sociology of law, that is, that the sociology of law deals primarily with at least eight interactions or linkages identified in Figure 1. Whether researchers accept this definition will be determined by its heuristic value, namely, whether it generates empirical research concerning the eight linkages.

(SEE ALSO: *Law and Legal Systems; Social Control; Sociology of Law*)

REFERENCES

Barkan, Steven M. 1987 "Deconstructing Legal Research: A Law Librarian's Commentary on Critical Legal Studies." *Law Library Journal* 79:617–637.

Baxi, U. 1974 "Comment—Durkheim and Legal Evolution: Some Problems of Disproof." *Law and Society Review* 8:645–651.

Bendix, Reinhard 1960 *Max Weber: An Intellectual Portrait.* New York: Doubleday.

Berman, Harold J. 1963 *Justice in the U.S.S.R: An Interpretation of the Soviet Law.* Cambridge, Mass.: Harvard University Press.

Bertalanffy, Ludwig von 1968 *General System Theory.* New York: G. Braziller.

Blankenburg, Erhard 1983 "The Poverty of Evolutionism: A Critique of Teubner's Case for 'Reflexive Law.'" *Law and Society Review* 18:273–289.

Bohannan, Paul 1968 "Law and Legal Institutions." In David L. Sills, ed. *International Encyclopedia of the Social Sciences.* New York: Macmillan and Free Press.

Buckley, Walter (ed.) 1968 *Modern Systems Research for the Behavioral Scientist.* Chicago: Aldine.

Burman, Sandra, and Barbara E. Harrell-Bond (eds.) 1979 *The Imposition of Law.* New York: Academic Press.

Collins, Randall 1980 "Weber's Last Theory of Capitalism: A Systemization." *American Sociological Review* 45:925–942.

David, Rene, and John E. C. Brierley 1968 *Major Legal Systems in the World Today.* London: Free Press and Collier-Macmillan Ltd.

Durkheim, Emile 1933 *The Division of Labor in Society.* New York: Free Press.

Eisenstadt, S. N., and M. Curelaru 1977 "Macro-Sociology: Theory, Analysis and Comparative Studies." *Current Sociology* 25:1–112.

Evan, William M. 1965 "Toward A Sociological Almanac of Legal Systems." *International Social Science Journal* 17:335–338.

——— 1968 "A Data Archive of Legal Systems: A Cross-National Analysis of Sample Data." *European Journal of Sociology* 9:113–125.

———1975 "The International Sociological Association and the Internationalization of Sociology." *International Social Science Journal* 27:385–393.

———1980 *The Sociology of Law.* New York: Free Press.

Glendon, Mary Ann 1975 "Power and Authority in the Family: New Legal Patterns as Reflections of Changing Ideologies." *American Journal of Comparative Law* 23:1–33.

Hazard, John N. 1977 *Soviet Legal System: Fundamental Principles and Historical Commentary.* 3rd ed. Dobbs Ferry, N.Y.: Oceana Press.

Jacob, Herbert 1988 *Silent Revolution: The Transformation of Divorce Law in the United States.* Chicago: University of Chicago Press.

Kairys, David, ed. 1982 *The Politics of Law.* New York: Pantheon.

Laszlo, C. A., M. D. Levine, and J. H. Milsum 1974 "A General Systems Framework for Social Systems." *Behavioral Science* 19:79–92.

Lidz, Victor 1979 "The Law as Index, Phenomenon, and Element: Conceptual Steps Towards a General Sociology of Law." *Sociological Inquiry* 49:5–25.

Luhmann, Niklas 1982 *The Differentiation of Society.* New York: Columbia University Press.

———1985 *A Sociological Theory of Law.* Elizabeth King and Martin Albrow, trans. London: Routledge and Kegan Paul.

———1986 "The Self-Reproduction of Law and Its Limits." In Gunther Teubner, ed., *Dilemmas of Law in the Welfare State.* Berlin: Walter de Gruyter.

———1988a "The Sociological Observation of the Theory and Practice of Law." In Alberto Febrajo, ed., *European Yearbook in the Sociology of Law.* Milan: Giuffre Publisher.

———1988b "The Unity of Legal Systems." In Gunther Teubner, ed., *Autopoietic Law: A New Approach to Law and Society.* Berlin: Walter de Gruyter.

———1988c "Closure and Openness: On Reality in the World of Law." In Gunther Teubner, ed., *Autopoietic Law: A New Approach to Law and Society.* Berlin: Walter de Gruyter.

Maturana, Humberto R., and Francisco J. Varela 1980 *Autopoiesis and Cognition.* Dordrecht, The Netherlands: D. Reidel Publishing Co.

Merryman, John Henry, David S. Clark, and Lawrence M. Friedman 1979 *Law and Social Change in Mediterranean Europe and Latin America.* Stanford, Calif.: Stanford Law School.

Parsons, Talcott 1961 "An Outline of the Social System." In Talcott Parsons, Edward Shils, Kasper D. Naegele, and Jesse R. Pitts, eds., *Theories of Society.* New York: Free Press.

———1962 "The Law and Social Control." In William M. Evan, ed., *Law and Sociology.* New York: Free Press.

———1978 "Law as an Intellectual Stepchild." In Harry M. Johnson, ed., *Social System and Legal Process.* San Francisco: Jossey-Bass.

Rheinstein, Max (ed.) 1954 *Max Weber on Law in Economy and Society.* Cambridge, Mass.: Harvard University Press.

Schwartz, R. D. 1974 "Legal Evolution and the Durkheim Hypothesis: A Reply to Professor Baxi." *Law and Society Review* 8:653–668.

Schwartz, R. D., and J. C. Miller 1964 "Legal Evolution and Social Complexity." *American Journal of Sociology* 70:159–169.

Sheleff, L. S. 1975 "From Restitutive Law to Repressive Law: Durkheim's *The Division of Labor in Society* Revisited." *European Journal of Sociology* 16:16–45.

Teubner, Gunther 1983a "Substantive and Reflexive Elements in Modern Law." *Law and Society Review* 17:239–285.

———1983b "Autopoiesis in Law and Society: A Rejoinder to Blankenburg." *Law and Society Review* 18:291–301.

———1988a *Autopoietic Law: A New Approach to Law and Society.* Berlin: Walter de Gruyter.

———1988b "Hypercycle in Law and Organization: The Relationship Between Self-Observation, Self-Constitution, and Autopoiesis." In Alberto Febrajo, ed., *European Yearbook in the Sociology of Law.* Milan: Giuffre Publisher.

Trubek, David M. 1972 "Max Weber on Law and the Rise of Capitalism." *Wisconsin Law Review* 730: 720–753.

———1984 "Where the Action Is: Critical Legal Studies of Empiricism." *Stanford Law Review* 36:575.

———, and John Esser 1989 " 'Critical Empiricism' in American Legal Studies: Paradox, Program, or Pandora's Box?" *Law and Social Inquiry* 14:3–52.

Varela, Francisco J. 1979 *The Principle of Autonomy.* New York: North-Holland.

Watson, Alan 1974 *Legal Transplants: An Approach to Comparative Law.* Charlottesville: University of Virginia Press.

———1978 "Comparative Law and Legal Change." *Cambridge Law Journal* 37:313–336.

———1981 *The Making of the Civil Law.* Cambridge, Mass.: Harvard University Press.

——— 1983 "Legal Change, Sources of Law, and Legal Culture." *University of Pennsylvania Law Review* 131:1,121–1,157.

——— 1985 *The Evolution of Law.* Baltimore: Johns Hopkins University Press.

——— 1987 "Legal Evolution and Legislation." *Brigham Young University Law Review* 1987: 353–379.

Weber, Max 1950 *General Economic History.* New York: Free Press.

Weitzman, Lenore J. 1985 *The Divorce Revolution: The Unexpected Social and Economic Consequences for Women and Children in America.* New York: Free Press.

Wigmore, John Henry 1928 *A Panorama of the World's Legal Systems.* 3 vols. St. Paul, Minn.: West Publishing Co.

Zeleny, Milan 1980 *Autopoiesis, Dissipative Structures, and Spontaneous Social Orders.* Boulder, Colo.: Westview Press, for the American Association for the Advancement of Sciences.

WILLIAM M. EVAN

LAW ENFORCEMENT *See* Police.

LEADERSHIP Leadership is a concept most often used in the study of small groups or complex organizations. It refers to a set of social processes: directing the productive activities of a group, defending the group against external threat, maintaining group cohesion, and so forth. It may also refer to individuals performing leadership roles, as when reference is made to "the leadership" of a group or organization. There are often multiple leadership roles within a single group, and different situations often make different types of leaders more effective.

Max Weber noted that there are three types of "legitimate authority" in social and economic organizations. The first rests on charismatic qualities of the leader as an individual, the second involves patriarchal or traditional principles, and the third is leadership by formal rules, or bureaucratic authority. Many sociologists agree with Weber's hypothesis that modern societies stress bureaucratic leadership.

Small group theory and research suggests strongly that all social groups have two distinctive leadership positions. The task leader is responsible for organization and direction. The social leader deals with group solidarity or morale.

This distinction between the task leader and the social leader is based on functionalist theory. Most empirical studies show this pattern of dual leadership. Research also supports the principle that the two roles are incompatible: Different individuals usually occupy the two roles.

Contrary to popular belief, most leaders are not all-powerful individuals with the freedom to do whatever they like. They are subject to stronger expectations than other group members. They are often considered role models, and if leaders fail in their roles, they are subject to serious sanctions by the group or organization. If the group does not succeed in attaining its goals, the leader is blamed or replaced. Thus, leadership is clearly a two-way social process.

LEADERSHIP IN SMALL GROUPS

Much of the current theory and research on leadership in small groups is based on the work by Robert F. Bales and Philip E. Slater (1955), who hypothesized that all social systems have functional needs for two types of leadership roles: a task leader and a social–emotional leader.

The task (or instrumental) leadership role deals with problems of defining the task, suggesting solutions, and moving the group toward achievement of the goals of production, efficiency, and so forth. The person occupying this role dominates the group's activity, especially in the early stages of the problem-solving process. A strong correlation has been found between how much an individual talks and that individual's ratings as a task leader by observers or group members.

The social–emotional (or expressive) leader occupies a less visible role in most groups, but this role seems equally essential to the effective functioning of the group. When the task leader dominates the group discussion, suggests solutions, and criticizes others' contributions, the social–emotional leader acts as a buffer and helps to maintain group cohesion. This function is most obvious in the later stages of the problem-solving process: When a solution has been reached, the social–emotional leader often wraps up the discussion by making jokes, complimenting the task leader, and so forth.

INDIVIDUAL CHARACTERISTICS AND LEADERSHIP

Most individuals occupying leadership roles exhibit traits such as intelligence, dominance, extroversion, and talkativeness. However, the sociological perspective argues that leaders are made, not born. This approach downplays the impact of personality traits on the emergence of leadership. Situational factors, the type of task, and social characteristics appear to have more significant effects on the selection of specific individuals for leadership roles.

Studies of informal groups with no designated leader reveal that socially significant factors such as gender, age, race, education, and occupation all affect the choice of leader by group members. *Expectation states theory* calls these factors "diffuse status characteristics" because they are associated with very general expectations about abilities and status. When the wider society gives lower status to females, the young, nonwhites, and those with lower levels of education and occupation, such statuses will usually be carried into the group's structure and result in those types of persons being chosen less often as leaders. However, there are usually some "task-relevant characteristics" that are equally important in leadership emergence: For example, a group member who is an experienced computer programmer will naturally receive more votes as leader if the task is something related to computers.

LEADERSHIP STYLES AND SITUATIONAL FACTORS

Leadership roles are heavily influenced by the type of task, by the communication patterns imposed by spatial or technological factors, and by group size.

Generalizations about leadership are made risky by the diversity of tasks groups face. Another way to put this is that different types of groups give rise to different types of leadership structures. For example, when a task is simple and can be divided among all group members, the leader will act as a coordinator or chair rather than as an active director or "head."

Fiedler (1967) proposed a "contingency model of leadership effectiveness," which has received considerable support from empirical research. Fiedler argues that leaders who stress task completion rather than group morale will be most effective in situations when the task is complex and leader–follower relationships are strained. In other words, authoritarian task leaders and democratic social–emotional leaders will be successful in different situations.

Many studies show that leaders, formal and informal, are the center of group attention. Laboratory research on seating arrangements and communication networks reveal that task leaders emerge from more visible or central positions (e.g., at the head of the table). Naturalistic studies also show that leaders actively choose to take prominent positions within the group.

The size of the group has a pronounced effect on leadership structures. Georg Simmel (1950, pp. 87–104) noted the "significance of numbers for social life" long ago, pointing out the increased need for coordination as group size increases. Large informal groups, and all complex organizations, exhibit multiple levels of leadership.

LEADERSHIP IN FORMAL ORGANIZATIONS

Bureaucracies and formal organizations require effective leadership, in part because of their sheer size and diversity. Sociologists such as Max Weber and Simmel both wrote about this need for a hierarchy of authority.

Early empirical research tested the differences between "human relations" and "scientific management" styles of leadership. In the former, the social–emotional needs of individuals are considered by supervisors in an attempt to encourage productivity and lessen turnover. The latter approach stresses tasks, efficiency, and authority. Subsequent theory and research on management styles has generally paralleled the work on small groups, showing that the nature of the task, the characteristics of the group members, and the type of leadership are all important factors in determining effectiveness.

There is a continuing concern for the important question: How much impact do leaders actually have on their organization? The best conclusion at this stage of knowledge is that some factors create more favorable opportunities for leaders. When the environment is supportive, and the organization is not already highly structured, effective leadership may emerge. Of course, because of the great difficulty in conducting experimental research on complex organizations, much of the evidence for this conclusion remains anecdotal.

Decision making is another facet of leadership. Executives are hired to make decisions for the organization, but sociologists have found that effective organizations usually require some degree of participative decision making. It appears that even if no objective criterion of success is available, when members of an organization are involved in the process, they tend to evaluate the decision (and the formal leader) as being satisfactory. However, as noted above, when the group clearly fails to achieve its goals, the leader is often replaced.

LEADERSHIP IN SOCIAL MOVEMENTS

The sociological study of social movements and politics seems a natural arena for the analysis of leadership, but in fact research is quite sparse.

Conflict-oriented sociologists consider leadership as essential to political mobilization. Without effective leadership, social movements may remain nothing more than mobs. At the same time, authoritarian leadership is often viewed as a damaging source of within-group inequality and divisiveness in democratic movements. Robert Michels's (1959) "iron law of oligarchy" captures this dilemma and argues that every human organization will create its own potentially oppressive leaders.

This makes the legitimation of leadership essential in democracies. One way to limit the concentration of power, or its abuse, is to establish a set of written rules that apply to any individual who occupies an influential position. Frequent changes in leadership are not usually desirable or possible, and so the group must follow this bureaucratic route.

Weber pointed out that the followers of charismatic leaders who want to perpetuate the movement when the leader dies face the opposite problem. The charisma of the individual must be transformed into a combination of traditional and legitimate authority. He called this the "routinization of charisma."

(SEE ALSO: *Decision-Making Theory and Research; Small Groups*)

REFERENCES

Bales, Robert F., and Philip E. Slater 1955 "Role Differentiation." In T. Parsons and R. F. Bales, eds., *Family, Socialization, and Interaction Process.* Glencoe, Ill.: Free Press.

Bass, Bernard M. 1960 *Leadership, Psychology, and Organizational Behavior.* New York: Harper.

Borgatta, Edgar F., Carl S. Couch, and Robert F. Bales 1954 "Some Findings Relevant to the Great Man Theory of Leadership." *American Sociological Review* 19:755–759.

Fiedler, Fred E. 1967 *A Theory of Leadership Effectiveness.* New York: McGraw-Hill.

Gibb, Cecil A. 1969 *Leadership: Selected Readings.* Baltimore: Penguin.

Hare, A. P. 1976 "Leadership." In A. Paul Hare, ed., *Handbook of Small Group Research.* 2d ed. New York: Free Press.

Michels, Robert 1959 *Political Parties: A Sociological Study of the Oligarchical Tendencies of Modern Democracy.* New York: Dover.

Simmel, Georg 1950 "Quantitative Aspects of the Group." In *The Sociology of Georg Simmel,* trans. Kurt H. Wolff. New York: Free Press.

Stogdill, R. 1974 *Handbook of Leadership.* New York: Free Press.

Tannenbaum, Arnold S. 1968 "Leadership: Sociological Aspects." In David L. Sills, ed., *International Encyclopedia of the Social Sciences.* New York: Macmillan and Free Press.

Weber, Max 1962 "The Three Types of Legitimate Rule." In Amitai Etzioni, ed., *Complex Organizations: A Sociological Reader.* New York: Holt, Rinehart, and Winston.

PAUL MORGAN BAKER

LEARNING THEORIES *See* Behaviorism; Socialization.

LEGISLATION OF MORALITY In *The Division of Labor in Society* ([1893] 1984), Emile Durkheim advanced the idea that the distinctive sociological feature of crime is society's reaction to it. Durkheim was writing at a time when Lombroso's view on the heritability of criminality dominated scientific and popular opinion. Science sought the etiology of crime in the biology of the criminal, in *atavism*—crime viewed as a reversion to primitive, ancestral characteristics. From this perspective, the harmfulness of criminality was taken for granted. Given his more comparative and anthropological outlook, Durkheim rejected the idea that crime was condemned by society because of its harmful consequences or because the deviant act was in itself evil. For Durkheim, many things that attracted the severest reprimands of society were objectively quite harmless, such as the neglect of the food taboos or the neglect of religious observance. In his view, the major issue was the integrative function of law, not the individual sources of deviance. Indeed, in *Suicide* ([1897] 1951) he characterized individual acts of despair as expressions of social structural pathologies. He also noted that the integrative function of law extracted far more from the condemnation of the lower class thief than from the middle class embezzler—even though the latter's financial gain was greater and the social consequences of his acts much more adverse. From these observations Durkheim concluded that the societal reactions to crime and deviance were not based on rational models of the incapacitation or deterrence of the offender. In contrast to such utilitarian thinking, the societal reaction to crime was marked by an impassioned moral condemnation. This common feeling of moral outrage was a mark of the collective consciousness of society, particularly in highly cohesive, simple, or "tribal" societies. The condemnation of crime exercised the collective outlook, and it reinforced the group's collective beliefs and values. In short, the criminal was a scapegoat, and if he did not exist in fact, given his functional importance, he could be invented.

With the advance of more competitive and technologically sophisticated societies, the division of labor resulted in a partitioning of the collective consciousness across various elements of society and resulted in the rise of legal codes with less appetite for vengeance and with a greater investment in the reconciliation of competing interests. Hence, for Durkheim, punitive criminal law was the hallmark of primitive societies, which enjoyed a "mechanical" division of labor (i.e., a homogeneity of work functions), while reconciliatory civil law characterized advanced societies with an "organic" division of labor (i.e., a diverse but mutually dependent specialization of tasks). The former societies were characterized by brutal executions, the latter by written contracts.

Other nineteenth-century authorities tackled the role of law in society. Marx and Engels shared Durkheim's insight that the thing that needed explaining was not why people break laws—the problem of criminology—but why people make laws—the problem of the sociology of law (Cain and Hunt 1979). In their view, law was primarily an instrument of control and a source of both mystification and legitimation. As the urban merchant classes expanded their private estates into the countryside, these classes employed laws to transform the existing common rights of the rural peasants to the harvest of the forest—to deer, fish, pasture, firewood, and so forth—into crimes of theft from private property (Thompson 1975). In addition, the rise of capitalist agriculture, which was associated with the international trade in wool, cleared the British and European common lands of subsistent peasant farmers. Under contract law, the disenfranchised peasants became independent juridical subjects, able to engage in agreements to sell their labor for wages in the cities, although the urban working classes, having been displaced from subsistence on rural estates, had little choice, aside from starvation, but to work in factories.

Durkheim's position on law as an expression of the collective consciousness and Marx and Engel's views on law as an instrument of control continue to exert influence on contemporary thinking about law and morality. Where Durkheim treated the law as an expression of general social consciousness, Marx and Engels viewed it as an expression of a class consciousness, although, to be fair, Durkheim's model of collective consciousness held for a sort of mythic primitive society—akin to Hobbes on the "natural" state of man confronting the war of all against all or akin to Veblen or Freud's primal horde. In each case, the ideal type was an imaginative, indeed a fictional, reconstruction of human origins. The division of consciousness by class would have been possible for Durkheim in advanced societies—even if it constituted a state that he classified in *The Division of Labor in Society* as "abnormal" and even if it was the sort of awareness he wanted to overcome through the "corporations" that cut across class divisions and that Durkheim speculated might form the political nucleus of a future society.

In North America, sociological theories about the legislation of morality took a distinctive turn with investigations of "moral panics," "victimless crimes," and "moral entrepreneurs"—all of which figured importantly in the labeling theories of the 1960s. The studies investigated distinctively morally charged issues and stressed the influence of both social movements and the mass media in the construction of the criminal law. By way of example, Sutherland (1950) examined the role of "moral crusaders" in the context of the sexual psychopathy laws that were enacted in 1937 and thereafter in eleven northern states, California, and the District of Columbia. These laws provided for indefinite incarceration in hospitals for the criminally insane for anyone pronounced by a psychiatrist to be a sexual psychopath. Retrospectively, this diagnosis is not based on a discernible medical disease. In fact, many psychiatric categories are only labels for things we do not like. Nonetheless, a wide series of jurisdictions, with one eye to reforming sexual deviants, enacted laws based on this "disease."

There was a threefold process underlying the creation of these laws. First, the laws were enacted after a state of fear and hysteria following newspaper accounts of several sex crimes committed coincidentally in quick succession. In these states there was a rush to buy guns, guard dogs, and locks and chains, reflecting widespread evidence of public fears. Second, these fears were fueled by news coverage of related sex crimes in other areas and other times in history and of sex-related behaviors and morality (including questions regarding striptease) and by letters to newspaper editors and statements made by public figures. The third phase was the creation of committees to study "the facts" of the sex crimes and "the facts" of sexual psychopathology. These committees, though initially struck on the basis of collective terror, persisted long after the fear and news stories subsided. They resulted in a presentation of briefs to legislative bodies, particularly by a new class of medical experts—psychiatrists. The community hysteria was legitimated by the identification of the crimes as a form of disease by the psychiatric professionals. The legislatures responded to public fears by passing laws to control the offending parties, in this instance by making sexual psychopaths subject to incarceration under psychiatric supervision.

A second important illustration is the history of the American prohibition movement, reported in the classic sociological study by Joseph Gusfield—*Symbolic Crusade* (1963). From 1919 to 1933 an amendment to the American Constitution outlawed the manufacture and sale of alcoholic beverages. The law was passed after decades of lobbying by members of the numerous "temperance movements," who originated predominantly from fundamentalist Protestant stock, largely from rural areas, and initially of middle class background.

They were the upholders of the Protestant ethic and valued hard work, self-reliance, and sobriety.

Gusfield argues that as America industrialized during the nineteenth century, the traditional rural settlers experienced a loss of social status compared to the new urban classes and experienced a challenge to their traditional values as urban development introduced increasingly nontraditional immigrants. The temperance movements were a form of status politics designed to reaffirm the prestige of a life-style. In the early period (1825–1875) the temperance movements pursued their objective through education, persuasion, and the reform of social conditions that caused excessive drinking. With increasing urbanization and greater European immigration, however, the tactics changed from a policy of socialization to one of coercive reform. The temperance movement became a prohibition movement. And when conservative forces came to dominate the political scene in America following World War I, the value of sobriety was to be achieved coercively —by outlawing booze. In Canada prohibition was approved in a national plebiscite in 1898 and enabled by federal law in 1916. The federal law allowed provinces to implement their own legislation, and all but Quebec outlawed booze, although booze continued to be manufactured for export—usually illicitly to the United States—and was available in Canada by prescription in pharmacies. The Canadian experiment in forced temperance ended in the mid-1920s, and the United States repealed prohibition in 1933.

Gusfield's work is important for several reasons. It stressed the idea that legislation was "symbolic"—that it reflected the values of distinctive social groups and that such groups struggled to have their views insinuated into state legislation. Unlike Marx, who viewed political struggle as class politics, Gusfield stressed "status" politics—the advancement of group respectability or status by seeking to have the group values enshrined in law. Gusfield further implied that laws, particularly in the field of "victimless crimes," were symbolic in another sense. Instrumentally, prohibition was a terrible failure. It created huge markets for organized crime, and liquor consumption appears to have proceeded in spite of the law. Hence, the condemnation of insobriety was merely ritualistic (i.e., symbolic) because it did not extirpate drunkenness nor seriously inhibit liquor consumption. Similar arguments have been raised regarding the criminalization of narcotics, prostitution, and pornography—classical "victimless crimes," the markets for which thrive on a demand that seems little impeded by legal proscription.

The labeling theories of the 1960s developed the Durkheimian emphasis on the importance of societal reaction to crime (Kitsuse 1962; Lemert 1967) and identified some of the processes by which conduct was successfully labeled as criminal or how it successfully evaded such a label (Becker 1963). Theorists explored the self-fulfilling prophecies of deviant labels and the role of stigma in stabilizing rejected identities (Goffman 1961, 1963). The role of moral entrepreneurs was identified; these Weberian charismatics personified the struggle against evil and expedited legal change by campaigning in the media on the dire consequences of everything from dance halls to crime comics to television violence and marijuana use. Research on societal reaction proliferated. Studies focused on the manufacture of mental illness (Scheff 1966; Szasz 1961, 1970), the creation of witchcraft as a form of labeling (Erikson 1966; Currie 1968), the selective policing and the resulting social construction of delinquents (Cicourel 1968), the political hysteria that underlay political show trials (O'Connor 1972), the role of hysterical stereotypes in the criminalization of narcotics (Cook 1969; Lindesmith 1965), and the mythification of the Hell's Angels in the popular press (Thompson 1966).

The studies of this period had an insurgent flavor and a barely concealed contempt for legal structures and institutions that drew the line between conformity and deviance in an arbitrary fashion. This was particularly true in the context of legislation outlawing "victimless crimes." John Stuart Mill had established the ideological pedigree of this critique when he suggested that the democratic state's sole justification for limiting the freedom of an individual was that the person's behavior was harmful to others. Legal critics in the 1960s and 1970s objected to the extension of the law to cover vices and immoral activities since the participants in these acts, it was argued, were autonomous beings who had chosen them voluntarily and so were mischaracterized as either criminals or victims. The argument was that participants were not criminals since their behavior was not harmful to others, and they were not victims since their fates were chosen voluntarily (Schur 1965). Since these activities flowed from free choice in democratic states, how could they have been made unlawful? The answer lay in the fact that conservative forces led by moral entrepreneurs had stampeded democratic governments through wild allegations that the activities in question were so harmful that they struck at the very fabric of society and that however voluntary or self-inflicted the corruption, its control and eradication was justified for the sake of society itself. More recent studies have taken a different turn. Studies of the law-and-order campaigns associated with the resurgency of political conservatism have led sociologists to ask different sorts of questions.

Where Gusfield stressed that legislation might take on a symbolic aspect that reflects the interests of discrete social groups, recent work suggests that laws may *mystify* the social conditions that give rise to them and consequently may result in social control that is sought for altogether different reasons than the ones identified in the legislation. Taylor (1982) argues that many crime waves, moral panics, and anticrime campaigns are orchestrated in response to basic social conflicts and shifting economic realities and that they function to misdirect our attention away from social contradictions. Three noted British investigations lend support to this view. Hall et al. (1978) argue that the moral panic in British papers over street mugging in the early 1970s that resulted in calls for tougher jail sentences and more law and order in England mystified a basic structural shift in employment patterns that occurred during attempts to dismantle the British welfare state. In the late 1960s and early 1970s there was a conservative political movement in both America and Great Britain to curb state investments in public welfare—to "downsize" governments and to privatize public institutions. There was a certain amount of conscious political resistance in the labor movement and in socialist political quarters. However, the control culture succeeded in redefining the political resistance into an issue of individual lawlessness that required tougher policing, particularly of those persons who experienced the greatest amount of social dislocation as a result of fiscal restraint—poor youth, minority groups, and immigrants. The reports of street "muggings" imparted to England the imagery of lawlessness from the American ghetto, creating the impression that there were dramatic increases in street crime, that the crimes were disturbingly "un-British," and that they were symptomatic of a wider threat to Great Britain's collective security as witnessed by violence in industrial disputes (fights at picket lines) and misconduct among soccer fans.

Having defined the problem as individual lawlessness, the conservative solution of more law and order, greater investment in policing, longer jail sentences, and so forth, occluded the problem of youthful unemployment that *resulted* from conservative fiscal policies and that contributed to theft and other petty rackets in the first place. In this interpretation, moral panics have a material foundation in everyday experience, but where the earlier labeling theorists viewed the panics as *causes* of legal change, the British theorists suggest that panic was the *result* of social change. Sensationalism over crime in the popular media legitimates the introduction of coercive legislation that frequently suspends normal democratic liberties and replaces parsimonious forms of control with more punitive measures. In the case reported by Hall et al. (1978), penalties for petty street crimes increased dramatically as the public, the judiciary, and the politicians were treated to hysterical excesses in the popular press of violent youth running amok.

A similar structural argument is advanced by Stanley Cohen in *Folk Devils and Moral Panics* (1972). This study examines the role of the media in the re-creation of the "mods" and "rockers." There have been a series of distinct trends in youth culture in both America and Great Britain over the last four or five decades—the zoot suiters, the Teddy Boys, the beats, the skin heads and punks, the soccer hooligans, and the motorcycle rebels—all of whom expressed antiauthoritarianism and youthful rebellion. What seems to have set off the postwar youth cultures was society's relative affluence, which created conditions for distinctive consumption patterns supporting unique fashion styles, musical tastes, and recreational opportunities. The mods and rockers were motorcycle-riding youth groups who appeared in the British seaside resorts in the middle 1960s. As Hunter Thompson discovered in his study (1966) of the California Hell's Angels, the British newspapers made a feast of the mods' antics, typically exaggerating and reporting spuriously on their activities. Cohen (1972) stresses that the function of the news hysteria was to create a kind of rogue's gallery of folk devils—vivid, even fearsome images that registered collective fears about the youth, their mobility, and their independence, which served as collective reminders of what youth should not be.

In this approach, moral panics are an ongoing, recurrent, and predictable aspect of the popular culture. From this perspective, they are not considered the handiwork of individual moralists who may or may not decide for personal reasons to pursue a moral campaign. Moral panics are orchestrated when individuals feel compelled by their sense of the collective consciousness to repair a breach in the ideological fabric of society. Typically, such persons are affiliated with institutions that have a long-standing investment in moral control—church organizations, community groups, political parties, and so forth—or who occupy roles as self-appointed arbiters in democratic societies—academic experts, professional journalists, and publishers.

Also, moral panics and the legislative changes they engender track important shifts in social structure fairly closely. This is the conclusion of Pearson's *Hooligan: A History of Respectable Fears* (1983). Pearson reports that the current "public" appetite for law and order, for stiffer justice, and for a return to the past are recurrent themes in Western history. The historical perspective suggests that the feelings that, from the perspective of crime and delinquency, things are at an unprecedented nadir, that the present conduct of society compares poorly with the way things were in a previous golden age, that the family is falling apart, and that the popular entertainments of the lower classes are criminogenic, are recurrent in every major period of British history from the 1750s to the present. Over time, the rhetoric of decline has an uncanny similarity. Pearson's point is that crime fears or moral panics occur when the legitimacy of state control over the working-class is somehow challenged or brought into question. In the nineteenth century the British working class was only partially integrated into the political process. Consequently, their consent to government—which was dominated by the propertied classes—was usually testy. In the 1840s in particular, there is an apprehension in philanthropical writings about the working class "dodgers," bold, independent delinquents viewed as potential revolutionaries who might fuel the Chartist movement and overthrow the private ownership of property. In this context, philanthropists prescribed education and policing to create internal restraints in the interest of protecting property.

From this perspective, class tensions were misinterpreted in the public press and by middle class politicians as "rising crime and delinquency," and the middle class solutions were recurrently more "law and order" on the one hand and education on the other—that is, more police repression and control, a return to birching, a removal of the un-British elements of the population, a repudiation of meretricious American culture, and a return to the tranquility of the golden age when people knew their place.

It is difficult to give an overall assessment of how the processes of legislating morality discovered in the labeling period in America can be integrated with the class conflict approaches stressed in the recent British studies. Certainly, there is no reason to believe that the class antagonisms that characterize British society are as developed in North America, nor that these would be a monolithic source of legal change. On the other hand, there is also no reason that the search for systematic sources of moral panics as effects of social change could not be undertaken in North American studies. Since the early 1980s it has become clear that the preoccupation with abortion, pornography, the funding of AIDS research, gay bashing, and the Equal Rights Amendment in U.S. public discourses is related to important trends in family composition and female labor force participation. For the traditionally minded, the suppression of access to abortion, pornography, and the ERA, as well as lethargy in dealing with AIDS, all seems to be an attempt to turn the clock back toward patriarchal families. For more progressive feminists, access to abortion on demand, suppression of degrading pornography, and the confrontation of the epidemics of sexual and physical violence against women and children are essential ideological matters for the insurance of greater female social and economic advancement. In both cases, the public imagery of epidemics of fetal massacres on the one hand, and epidemics of incest and female abuse on the other, are not the products of idiosyncratic moral campaigns but arise in the context of profound social structural transformations—suggesting the need to develop a convergence of theories of symbolic interests and structural shifts that have developed independently to date.

(SEE ALSO: *Deviance; Social Control*)

REFERENCES

Becker, Howard S. 1963 *Outsiders.* New York: Free Press.

Cain, M., and A. Hunt 1979 *Marx and Engels on Law.* New York: Academic Press.

Cicourel, Aaron 1968 *The Social Organization of Juvenile Justice.* London: Heinemann.

Cohen, Stanley 1972 *Folk Devils and Moral Panics.* Oxford: Basil Blackwell.

Cook, S. 1969 "Canadian Narcotics Legislation 1908–1923: A Conflict Approach." *Canadian Review of Sociology and Anthropology* 6:36–46.

Currie, Elliott P. 1968 "Crimes Without Criminals: Witchcraft and Its Control in Renaissance Europe." *Law and Society Review* 3(1):7–32.

Durkheim, Emile (1893) 1984 *The Division of Labor in Society.* New York: Free Press.

——— (1897) 1951 *Suicide.* New York: Free Press.

Erikson, Kai T. 1966 *Wayward Puritans.* New York: Wiley.

Goffman, Erving 1961 *Asylums.* New York: Doubleday/Anchor.

——— 1963 *Stigma.* Englewood Cliffs, N.J.: Prentice-Hall.

Gusfield, Joseph R. 1963 *Symbolic Crusade: Status Politics and the American Temperance Movement.* Urbana: University of Illinois Press.

Hall, S., C. Critcher, T. Jefferson, J. Clarke, and B. Roberts 1978 *Policing the Crisis: Mugging, the State, and Law and Order.* London: Macmillan.

Kitsuse, John I. 1962 "Societal Response to Deviance: Social Problems of Theory and Method." *Social Problems* 9:247–256.

Lemert, Edwin 1967 "The Concept of Secondary Deviation." In E. Lemert, ed., *Human Deviance, Social Problems, and Social Control.* Englewood Cliffs, N.J.: Prentice-Hall.

Lindesmith, A. 1965 *The Addict and the Law.* Bloomington: Indiana University Press.

O'Connor, Walter D. 1972 "The Manufacture of Deviance: The Case of the Soviet Purge, 1936–1938." *American Sociological Review* 37:403–413.

Pearson, Geoffrey 1983 *Hooligan: A History of Respectable Fears.* London: Macmillan.

Scheff, Thomas 1966 *Being Mentally Ill.* Chicago: AVC.

Schur, Edwin 1965 *Crimes without Victims.* Englewood Cliffs, N.J.: Prentice-Hall.

Sutherland, Edwin 1950 "The Diffusion of Sexual Psychopath Laws." *American Journal of Sociology* 56:142–148.

Szasz, Thomas 1961 *The Myth of Mental Illness.* New York: Heuber-Harper.

——— 1970 *The Manufacture of Madness.* New York: Harper and Row.

Taylor, Ian 1982 "Moral Enterprise, Moral Panic, and Law-and-Order Campaigns." In M. M. Rosenberg, R. A. Stebbins, and A. Turowitz, eds., *The Sociology of Deviance.* New York: St. Martin's Press.

Thompson, E. P. 1975 *Whigs and Hunters.* Harmondsworth, England: Penguin.

Thompson, Hunter S. 1966 *Hell's Angels.* New York: Random House.

AUGUSTINE BRANNIGAN

LEGITIMACY The concept of legitimacy was initially applied to governments. In particular, apologists for monarchy argued that kings had a divine right to govern, and supporters of each pretender to the throne argued that their candidate was the legitimate monarch, sanctioned by God (Bendix 1980). Later, sociologists adopted a secularized standard according to which a government or other system of dominance is legitimate, provided those subject to it believe it deserves obedience. The subjects' belief can reflect a variety of standards of judgment and values, and can apply both to the regime as a whole and to particular role occupants. In particular, Weber (1978, pp. 212–301) proposed that governments can be justified by charisma, tradition, or conformity to enacted rules. By extension, nongovernmental institutions have been identified as legitimate if people who could do better in the short run by flouting the institutional pattern nevertheless willingly support the institution.

LEGITIMACY AND STABILITY

Sociological interest in legitimacy stems primarily from Weber's conjecture that legitimacy plays a crucial role in stabilizing social organization. Even if everyone had exactly the same interests, individual judgments about the best course of action would undoubtedly differ. Moreover, at least in the short run, individual interests typically dictate varied courses of action. Consequently, if all members of a collectivity continually pursue their short-run interests as vigorously as possible, there will be continual turmoil.

In practice this extremely undesirable situation rarely arises, because every ongoing collective endeavor institutionalizes the submission of some members to others' decisions. This submission rests on a combination of force, side payments, affection, and legitimacy. As considerations other than norms become important in regulating social relations, those relations tend to become unstable and turbulent. Rule that depends directly and visibly on the application of force encourages jousting over who is strongest, and direct payment for compliance can lead to endless bargaining over how much that compliance is worth. Contrariwise, social relations will run smoothly to the extent that they appear natural, morally correct, and inevitable (that is, legitimate). Consequently, Weber (1978, p. 213) argued that "every system [of domination] attempts to . . . cultivate . . . belief in its legitimacy."

Policing in the contemporary United States illustrates the problems that low legitimacy can induce. Although most people accept police authority without question, substantial segments of the population do not, particularly during periods of turmoil and civil violence. In communities where the legitimacy of policing is questioned, police can be drawn into what Heirich (1971) described as a "spiral of conflict." Unable to rely on voluntary compliance, the police increasingly resort to force, further undermining popular acceptance and occasionally provoking collective mobilization against themselves (Waddington, Jones, and Crichter 1989). As popular endorsement of policing declines, moreover, the risks facing individual policemen rise dramatically and police morale suffers, making it hard to staff the police force. Unless this spiral is interrupted, the result can be disastrous, with ever lower quality of policing and increasing disorder.

ENDORSEMENT, AUTHORIZATION, AND HABITUAL OBEDIENCE

During the 1960s and 1970s growing civil violence and disaffection were viewed as precursors to government instability, because institutional stability was supposed to depend on widespread popular acceptance of fundamental values justifying institutions (Eckstein and Gurr 1975; Kaase 1980). This interpretation of legitimacy probably reflected the dominance of democratic institutions and ideologies, as did Lipset's (1981, p. 64) advocacy of a stringent criterion for legitimacy that required most of those subjected to a system of domination to accept it as optimal. The emphasis on consensus fostered discussions emphasizing support from those whose immediate interests would have been furthered by different arrangements. Thus, free elections were defined as legitimate in societies where the losers as well as the winners respect the authority of those who are elected. Similarly, where capitalist institutions of private property are legitimated, employees submit to private proprietors' authority because they regard it as just, even when this submission impoverishes them and undermines their sense of personal worth (Sennett 1981; Sennett and Cobb 1972).

In fact, popular consent is only one basis for institutional legitimacy, and "nothing like a nationwide consensus is either necessary or possible" (Bendix 1977, p. 26). Instead, much of the limited empirical evidence available supports Stinchcombe's conjecture (1968, p. 150) that in modern societies, "the person *over whom power is exercised* is not usually as important as *other power-holders* in establishing legitimacy." One factor that reduces the likelihood that most people will sanction institutions on the basis of whether they support their personal values is their limited understanding of how institutions work (Lipset 1981, pp. 196–199; Prothro and Grigg 1960; McClosky 1964). In most communities a small segment of the population is relatively well informed and politically active, and members of this political elite are more likely than other people to endorse the political regime (Dahl 1961; Lipset 1981, pp. 207–209; Kaase 1980), although some critics doubt that even elite individuals can effectively evaluate which social values concrete procedures and organizations support (Kolko 1984). An even more important reason for the relative unimportance of popular legitimacy is that few people have the cultural and material resources to devise plausible alternatives, organize themselves into a coherent opposition (Tilly 1978), or even articulate criticisms of existing arrangements (Harding 1984).

The recognition that the masses can rarely rebel, because they are "organizationally outflanked" (Mann 1986, p. 7; Barker 1990, p. 114f; Mills 1963, pp. 353–355), has encouraged a reinterpretation of how governments and other institutions mobilize support in "modern societies" like the contemporary United States. If explicitly justified popular support is taken as the criterion, many governments are clearly not legitimate and "legitimacy" probably has little to do with stability. In fact, as the discussion of policing suggests, although frank illegitimacy will tend to destabilize organizations, disaffection alone will not. Stable police authority clearly could be maintained even when substantial segments of the population were disaffected.

One reason that governments can thrive without active popular support is that conscious "endorsement" of an institution by those subjected to it is only one basis for legitimacy (Dornbusch and Scott 1975). "Authorization" from those who are not immediately implicated in an institution or from the institutional environment provides a distinct basis for legitimacy (Meyer and Scott 1983; Meyer and Rowan 1977); and police power continues to be authorized by other state agencies and by bystander publics when those subjected to policing withdraw their endorsement (Gamson 1990).

In addition, where power is concentrated, the key problem is enlisting the support of the powerful groups or individuals. Weber (1978, p. 214) noted that adequate administration could make popular endorsement unnecessary. Nevertheless, although he recognized that governments could rely primarily on economic incentives to mobilize support within their administration, he assumed that most of these governments would seek endorsement from the elite staff. The tendency of organizational development, however, has been to concentrate considerations of value at the top and focus attention among most of the staff on means. Since most mobilization in societies like the contemporary United States occurs through bureaucratized, standing organizations, individual judgments of institutions are rarely called into play. The immediate problem for governmental agencies—and for other associations as well—is maintaining sufficient institutional legitimacy to enlist other organizations' support. Even national governments—or at least the weaker ones—need to conform to the norms articulated within the United Nations and other international associations in order to gain these agencies' support.

Finally, except when crises open up debates about legitimacy, "interlocking . . . political, economic, social, and cultural forces . . . sustain public definition[s]" of institutions that make challenges not merely illegitimate but practically unthinkable (Harding 1984, pp. 379f.). Analysts, as well as theorists (Barker 1990; Mann 1986; Mills 1963), differ as to whether systems that rest primarily on this type of organized or institutionalized support and the "habitual obedience" it encourages should be described as legitimate, but agree that social mobilization is organized into most ongoing social arrangements. Established governments typically obtain the compliance they need without resorting directly either to side payments or to force, and also without invoking direct appeals to values.

EFFICACY AND LEGITIMACY

In theory, effectiveness and legitimacy might form distinct sources of organizational stability. In practice they are intimately commingled (Lipset 1981, pp. 64–70). Those whose expectations are met have little occasion to consider whether there are better approaches (Mills 1963, pp. 579–580), and organizations can rely on habitual obedience so long as the established procedures work. This is important, because active mobilization tends to open up the question of possible alternatives.

When expectations are thwarted, however, the presence or absence of principled bases for supporting current arrangements becomes critical. Although most of the recent research on noninstitutionalized collective mobilization has focused on the need for material and organizational resources, new movements clearly require active legitimation as well (Gamson 1990). Dissatisfaction is not an adequate basis for mobilization: the dissatisfaction needs to be transformed into a grievance (Tilly 1978). In other words, the dissatisfied need to identify some party as being at fault. Minimally, mobilization against the government or any authority requires questioning the legitimacy of current policies and practices (Piven and Cloward 1979, pp. 3–4). Massive rebellion is particularly likely if the rebels succeed in identifying an alternative standard of what is right with a convincing basis of authorization (Coleman 1990, pp. 487–489; Goldstone 1982, pp. 203–204).

If an authority is thoroughly legitimated, the disaffected will tend to interpret their problems in terms of temporary aberrations and will continue to support the system even if they disapprove of how it is working. Those who mobilize to change the system will tend to choose limited targets and to frame their objective as correcting rather than as overthrowing or remaking the current system. Moreover, challenges will generate countermobilization if a system is legitimated.

Contrariwise, if legitimacy is low, attacks on the system will tend to become increasingly radical. Moreover, narrowly based legitimacy may be relatively brittle. In particular, depending exclusively on authorization or elite endorsement—at least in a democratic society—leaves organizations in an exposed position once the question of appropriateness is opened.

The ramifications of the policing crisis discussed earlier illustrate the fragility of systems that depend primarily on external authorization. Once the situation was defined as a crisis, extraordinary measures were adopted. In some instances, the visible systemic support for the police sufficed to quell the disturbances. In other contexts, however, the novel use of force to maintain order encouraged those who were disaffected to reframe the situation as one in which policing was illegitimate or only contingently legitimate (Barker 1990, pp. 166–171). Consequently, the disaffected population openly defied the authorities. This defiance was problematic, both because it revealed the distance between the official position and the popular position and because it provided an occasion for articulating that defiance (Bendix 1977, p. 26; Fantasia 1988, pp. 9–14).

CURRENT RESEARCH: NOVELTY AND LEGITIMACY

The tangled interconnections between legitimacy and efficacy exacerbate the difficulty of studying legitimacy in stable systems. Consequently, empirical research on legitimacy primarily concentrates on periods of crisis, experimentation, and innovation, when active mobilization and appeals for legitimacy become important. One major strand of current research focuses on the elaboration of legitimating accounts (Hobsbawm and Ranger 1983; Gamson 1988; Snow and Benford 1988). A second strand focuses on the links between organizational age and legitimacy (Hannan and Freeman 1989). The emphasis of current research also reflects the recognition that active construction of accounts is most important when recruiting new resources.

(SEE ALSO: *Interpersonal Power; Organizational Structure)*

REFERENCES

Barker, Rodney 1990 *Political Legitimacy and the State.* New York: Oxford University Press.

Bendix, Reinhard 1977 *Nation-Building and Citizenship,* new, enl. ed. Berkeley: University of California Press.

——— 1980 *Kings or People: Power and the Mandate to Rule.* Berkeley: University of California Press.

Coleman, James S. 1990 *Foundations of Social Theory.* Cambridge, Mass.: Belknap.

Dahl, Robert 1961 *Who Governs?* New Haven: Yale University Press.

Dornbusch, Sanford M., and W. Richard Scott 1975 *Evaluation and the Exercise of Authority.* San Francisco: Jossey-Bass.

Eckstein, Harry, and Ted R. Gurr 1975 *Patterns of Authority: A Structural Basis for Political Inquiry.* New York: Wiley.

Fantasia, Rick 1988 *Cultures of Solidarity: Consciousness, Action, and Contemporary American Workers.* Berkeley: University of California Press.

Gamson, William A. 1988 "Political Discourse and Collective Action." In Bert Klandermans, Hanspeter Kriesi, and Sidney Tarrow, eds., *From Structure to Action.* Greenwich, Conn.: JAI Press.

——— 1990 *The Strategy of Social Protest,* 2nd ed. Belmont, Calif.: Wadsworth.

Goldstone, Jack A. 1982 "The Comparative and Historical Study of Revolutions." *Annual Review of Sociology* 8:187–207.

Hannan, Michael T., and John Freeman 1989 *Organizational Ecology.* Cambridge, Mass.: Harvard University Press.

Harding, Susan 1984 "Reconstructing Order Through Action: Jim Crow and the Southern Civil Rights Movement." In Charles Bright and Susan Harding, eds., *State-Making and Social Movements.* Ann Arbor: University of Michigan Press.

Heirich, Max 1971 *The Spiral of Conflict: Berkeley, 1964.* New York: Columbia University Press.

Hobsbawm, Eric, and Terence Ranger (eds.) 1983 *The Invention of Tradition.* New York: Cambridge University Press.

Kaase, Max 1980 "The Crisis of Authority: Myth and Reality." In Richard Rose, ed., *Challenge to Governance: Studies in Overloaded Polities.* Beverly Hills, Calif.: Sage.

Kolko, Gabriel 1984 *Main Currents in Modern American History.* New York: Pantheon.

Lipset, Seymour Martin 1981 *Political Man.* Baltimore: Johns Hopkins University Press.

Mann, Michael 1986 *The Sources of Social Power: A History of Power from the Beginning to A.D. 1760.* New York: Cambridge University Press.

McClosky, Herbert 1964 "Consensus and Ideology in American Politics." *American Political Science Review* 58:361–382.

Meyer, John W., and Brian Rowan 1977 "Institutionalized Organizations: Formal Structure as Myth and Ceremony." *American Journal of Sociology* 83:340–363.

Meyer, John W., and W. Richard Scott 1983 *Organizational Environments: Ritual and Rationality.* Beverly Hills, Calif.: Sage.

Mills, C. Wright 1963 *Power, Politics, and People: The Collected Essays of C. Wright Mills,* Irving Louis Horowitz, ed. New York: Oxford University Press.

Piven, Frances Fox, and Richard A. Cloward 1979 *Poor People's Movements: Why They Succeed, How They Fail.* New York: Vintage.

Prothro, James W., and Charles M. Grigg 1960 "Fundamental Principles of Democracy: Bases of Agreement and Disagreement." *Journal of Politics* 22:276–294.

Sennett, Richard 1981 *Authority.* New York: Vintage.

———, and Jonathan Cobb 1972 *The Hidden Injuries of Class.* New York: Vintage.

Snow, David A., and Robert D. Benford 1988 "Ideology, Frame Resonance, and Participant Mobilization." In Bert Klandermans, Hanspeter Kriesi, and Sidney Tarrow, eds., *From Structure to Action*. Greenwich, Conn.: JAI Press.

Stinchcombe, Arthur L. 1968 *Constructing Social Theories*. New York: Harcourt.

Tilly, Charles 1978 *From Mobilization to Revolution*. Menlo Park, Calif.: Addison-Wesley.

Waddington, David, Karen Jones, and Chas Critcher 1989 *Flashpoints*. New York: Routledge.

Weber, Max 1978 *Economy and Society: An Outline of Interpretive Sociology*, Guenther Roth and Claus Wittich, trans. Berkeley: University of California Press.

CAROL CONELL

LEISURE Since 1930 the sociology of leisure in North America and Europe has not developed in a linear or cumulative fashion. Rather, research agendas, the accepted premises for research and theory, and the "common wisdom" of the field have been revised and challenged. Change did not come in one great overturning but in a sequence of revisions. A dialectical model seems to be most appropriate for following the sequence. Through the 1950s, there was an accepted consensus as to both issues and premises. This consensus was eroded as well as challenged by new research. The "revised consensus" expanded agendas for both research and theory without completely overturning earlier developments.

Currently, a more critical antithesis has emerged to subject the second consensus to a more thoroughgoing revision. The sources of this antithesis have included conflict or neo-Marxist theory, gender-focused critiques, non-Western perspectives, and various poststructural analytical approaches. Critiques are associated with concepts such as hegemony and power, commodification, gender and patriarchical structures, imperialism, world views, ideologies, and existential action. Now a central question concerns the kind of synthesis that will be developed in the ongoing process.

The dialectical sequence provides a dynamic framework for a review of central areas in the study of leisure. Although many issues and lines of research can be identified, four have consistently been most salient. In a highly abbreviated form, we will summarize the dialectics of theory and research in relation to (1) work and time, (2) family and community, (3) aging and the life course, and (4) the nature of leisure.

WORK AND TIME

Leisure and Work Domains. When sociologists turned their attention to leisure in the 1960s, three perspectives were adopted. The first, based on earlier community studies, approached leisure as a dimension of the social organization of the community (Lundberg, Komarovsky, and McInerney 1934; Dumazedier 1967). The second, exemplified by work that David Riesman initiated at the University of Chicago, viewed leisure as social action that created its own worlds of meaning. The third, the one that came to shape domain assumption and research agendas, emerged from the sociology of work. Its fundamental premise was that economic institutions are central to the society and that economic roles are the primary determinants of other roles. Leisure was assumed especially to be secondary and derivative. As a consequence, various theorists proposed models of how leisure's role was determined by work. Some modeled leisure as similar to work ("spillover" or identity), others as contrasting with work (compensation), and still others as separate from work (Wilensky 1960; Parker 1971). The bias, however, was clearly toward some kind of determination rather than toward segmentation.

As research proceeded, the "long arm of the job" was found to be both shorter and less powerful than expected as only limited, modest, and sometimes inconsistent relationships were found between leisure styles and occupational level and type (Wilson 1980). In a fuller perspective, on the other hand, it was evident that economic roles are determinative of the social context of adult lives—schedules, control of resources, autonomy, and other basic conditions (Blauner 1964). Leisure is part of the reward structure of a social system with differential access to resources based largely on socioeconomic position.

A second revision of the common wisdom concerned time available for leisure. The long-term reduction in the average number of hours in the work week from as high as eighty in the early days of the Industrial Revolution to about forty in the post–World War II period, along with the five-day work week and paid vacations for many workers, had led to an unquestioned assurance that more and more leisure time would be the product of increased economic productivity. In the 1970s, however, the declining rate of the decrease in hours worked per week, moving toward stability, produced a revised consensus suggesting segmented time scarcity and a variety of social timetables.

A next challenge to the early common wisdom was a recognition of leisure as a dimension of life with its own meaning and integrity. Leisure is more than leftover and derivative time; it has its own place in the rhythm and flow of life. First, leisure came to be defined more as activity than as empty time. Among the themes emerging were relative freedom of choice, distinction from the obligations of other roles, and the variety of meanings and aims that might be sought in such activity. Just as important as the revised definition, however, was the identification of leisure as something more than a derivation of work. Social life could not be characterized as work versus leisure but consisted of multiple sets of intersecting roles. Leisure, although having a particular relationship with the bonding of family and other immediate communities (Cheek and Burch 1976), had multiple contexts, connections, and meanings (Kelly 1981).

The Challenge of Critical Theory. The domain assumptions of functional sociology have been challenged by critical analyses with roots in neo-Marxist cultural studies (Clarke and Critcher 1985), by historical study that focuses on power and the struggles of the working class, and by social construction approaches that take into account the interpretive activity of social actors (Rojek 1985).

The central theme of the critical challenge is social control by ruling elites. Leisure is seen as a critical element in the hegemony of ruling elites in a capitalist society. In order to assure compliance in the workplace, the political arena, and in the marketplace, leisure has emerged as central to the capitalist reward and control system. Leisure is, from this critical perspective, a market-mediated instrument that binds workers to the production process and to roles that support the reproduction of the capital-dominated social system. Leisure is defined as a commodity that must be earned and is indissolubly connected to what can be purchased and possessed.

A number of themes are gathered in this critique. The power to enforce compliance is masked behind an ideology in which "freedom" comes to be defined as purchasing power in the marketplace of leisure. Such "commodity fetishism" (Marx 1970) of attachment to things defines life and leisure in terms of possessions. Social status is symbolized by leisure display (Veblen [1899] 1953). Absorption in mass media legitimates consumption-oriented values and world views (Habermas 1975). What appear to be varying styles of leisure reflect the profoundly different conditions of work, family, and leisure assigned by class, gender, and race (Clarke and Critcher 1985).

A Prospective Synthesis. The fundamental presupposition of any sociology of leisure is that leisure is a thoroughly social phenomenon, a product of the social system, and a phenomenon of the culture. Leisure is not separate and secondary but embedded in the institutional structures, social times, and power allocations of the society. In a complex social system, both individual self-determination and institutional control differ by economic and social position. Leisure is not segmented but woven into the system. Out of the current dialectic between the original consensus and the critique, a number of issues call for attention.

The first agenda is to move beyond ideologies to examine the lived conditions of poor, excluded, and disinherited children, women, and men. Their struggles for life in the present and for a future are reflected in what they do to express themselves, create community, fill ordinary hours and days, and seek new possibilities.

The second issue is to identify the ways in which economic roles provide contexts, resources, limitations, and orientations for other areas of life—family and community as well as leisure. The question is not the simple determination of life and leisure by work but how determinative definitions of both the self and society are learned in a power-differentiated social context.

The third issue is one of meanings. Purchasing is not necessarily commodification, and owning is not fetishism. What are the commitments, symbols, meanings, self-definitions, and world views that are the cognitive context of decisions and actions? What are the meanings and outcomes of leisure-related spending, media use, packaged entertainment, and images of pleasure? Possession may be a way of life or an instrument of activity. Does leisure, in fact, reflect a culture of possession? Or is there a deep paradox between alienation and creation that permeates the entire society?

The fourth issue concerns time. If we discard misleading models about average work weeks, what are the actual patterns and varieties of time structure and allocation? How do these patterns and possibilities vary by economic role, gender, life course, family conditions, ethnicity and race, location, and other placement factors? Time remains a basic resource for leisure, one that not only varies widely but is one index of the possibility of self-determination.

FAMILY AND COMMUNITY

Leisure as a Context for Family Bonding. If leisure is not just activity determined by and complementary to work, does leisure have some other critical relationship to the social system? The evident connection is, of course, to family and other immediate communities (Roberts 1970). Most leisure is in or around the home. The most common leisure companions are family and other close friends and intimates.

The basis of the first consensus was the series of community studies beginning in the 1930s (Lundberg, Komarovsky, and McInerney 1934; Lynd and Lynd 1956). Leisure was found to be a web of ordinary activity, mostly social interaction and tied to the institutions of the community, from the family outward to status-based organizations. From this perspective, the later work of Cheek and Burch (1976) argued that the primary function of leisure is to provide a context for social bonding, especially that of family and ethnic community.

An anomaly in family leisure began a revision to the first consensus. The family context was reaffirmed and the centrality of the family to leisure supported (Kelly 1983). However, despite the traditional focus on freedom as the primary defining theme of leisure, activity with major components of obligation was found to be most important to most adults. The major theme was that leisure was closely tied to central roles, not separate from them.

Leisure, then, is bound to both the roles and the developmental requirements of life (Rapoport and Rapoport 1976). In fact, from this perspective it may be quite central to life, not residual or secondary at all. It is a primary setting for social bonding and expression as well as for human development. The implied issue, on the other hand, is the consequences for the nature of freedom and choice in leisure. No activity embedded in primary role relationships can ever be free of accompanying obligations and responsibilities (Kelly 1987a, Chapter 6). Leisure might be more central, but it is also less pure and simple.

Power and Self-Determination in Leisure Roles. First, there is the challenge posed by changing family patterns now that an unbroken marriage and family through the life course has become a minority probability. The most radical response and antithesis, however, begins with the suggestion that leisure, like other areas of life, has roles. That is, the expectations and power differentials that characterize family, work, and community roles are found in leisure as well. Currently the most salient source of this challenging antithesis is the focus on gender, especially from a feminist perspective (Henderson et al. 1989).

The critique calls for sociologists to go beneath the rhetoric of freedom and self-expression to the realities of lives with limited power of self-determination. From this perspective, the history of the culture is characterized by male domination of women in profound and multifaceted ways that permeate every aspect of life (Deem 1986). Not only have women been repressed in where they are permitted to go and what they are allowed to do in leisure, but even in the home women's leisure is fundamentally different from that of men. It is usually women who are expected to do the work that makes "family leisure" possible. It is the "hidden work" of women that offers relative freedom to much of the leisure of men and children.

What, then, is the meaning of freedom and self-determination for any subordinate population segment? What about the poor, the racially and ethnically excluded, those cut off from opportunity in abandoned urban areas, and even many of the old? The resources of time, money, access, and autonomy are evidently unevenly distributed in any society.

In this antithesis, the connections of leisure to nonwork roles and resources, especially family and community, and the positive evaluation of how leisure contributes to development through the life course are brought up against a critical model of society. Leisure may indeed be indissolubly tied to family and community, but in ways that reflect social divisions and dominations as well as expressive action.

Leisure's Immediate Context: The New Agenda. Leisure takes place in its small worlds but also in the larger scale of the society. Further, its actualization is in the midst of real life. Research may be based on premises of systemic integration and the benefits of leisure as well as challenged by critiques reflecting ideologies of subjugation and alienation. A new agenda for research, however informed, should be directed toward the actual lived conditions of decisions, actions, relationships, and roles. In such an agenda related to community and family, several themes are highlighted by critiques of the common wisdom.

First, the realities of leisure as a struggle for action and self-determination in the midst of acute differences in power and access to resources will receive more attention. Especially gender, race, and poverty will reconstitute research strategies and frames past the easy assumptions that leisure is equally free and beneficial for all. The realities of family instability and crisis as well as of community divisions and conflicts will be taken into account as the immediate communities of leisure are reformulated.

Second, underlying the new agenda is the theme of differential power, not only power to command resources but to determine the course of one's life and what is required of others. In the action of leisure, there is both a relative openness for action and modes of repression that stimulate submission *and* resistance.

Third, the danger of leisure becoming increasingly privatized, bound only to immediate communities and the small worlds of personal life construction, is a perspective that runs counter to the functional view of leisure as a context for social bonding. There may be a negative side to a focus on the family basis of leisure activity and meanings. As technologies increasingly make the home a center of varied entertainment, leisure could become more and more cut off from larger communities.

In general, leisure is surely not peripheral to the central concerns and relationships of life. That, however, does not lead simply to bonding without domination, to development without alienation, or to intimacy without conflict.

AGING AND THE LIFE COURSE

Continuity and Change in the Life Course. The earliest consensus was simply that age indexed many kinds of leisure engagement. In a simple model, age was even referred to as a cause of decreased rates of participation. It was assumed that something decremental happened to people as they aged. The rates of decline varied according to activity: rapid for sports, especially team sports; more gradual for travel and community involvement. Attention given to those in their later years, generally in their sixties and seventies but sometimes fifties as well, suggested that such "disengagement" might even be functional. Perhaps older people needed to consolidate their activity and recognize their limitations.

The revised consensus began by recasting age as an index of multiple related changes rather than as an independent variable. Further, the revised framework became the life course rather than linear age (Neugarten 1968). A number of themes emerged.

First, in the Kansas City study of adult life, normative disengagement was replaced with activity (Havighurst 1961). Rather than needing or wishing to withdraw from activity, older people were found to revise their patterns and commitments in ways that fit their later life roles and opportunities. Leisure was conceptualized as multidimensional in meaning as well as in forms. More recently, this approach has led to a discovery of the "active old," those before and in retirement who adopt life styles of engagement in a variety of leisure activities and relationships. Further, such engagement has been found consistently to be a major factor in life satisfaction (Cutler and Hendricks 1990).

Second, the model of inevitable decrement was challenged by research that failed to measure high correlations between age and functional ability. Rather, a model of aging that stressed *continuity* rather than loss and change was applied to leisure as well as to other aspects of life (Atchley 1989). A return to earlier socialization studies provided a base for a revised model that identified lines of commitment rather than age-graded discontinuity. The "core" of daily accessible activity and interaction remains especially central to time allocation through the life course (Kelly 1983).

Third, the life course also provided a perspective in which intersecting work, leisure, and family roles and opportunities were related to developmental changes (Rapoport and Rapoport 1976). Leisure is not a list of activities dwindling with age but a social environment in which many critical issues of life may be worked out. Developing sexual identity for teens, expressing intimacy for those exploring and consolidating family commitments, reconstituting social contexts after mid-life disruptions, and ensuring social integration in later years are all central requirements of the life course that are developed in leisure. Not only interests but also significant identities are often found in leisure as well as in family and work (Gordon, Gaitz, and Scott 1976).

In the revised consensus, then, the life course with its interwoven work, family, and community roles was accepted as a valuable framework for analyzing both the continuities and changes of leisure. Leisure was seen as tied not only to role sequences but also to developmental preoccupations. The life course was found to incorporate revisions and reorientations rather than to consist of an inevitable downhill slide measured by participation rates in selected recreational pursuits.

An Integrated View of Life and Leisure. The regular and predictable transitions of the life course model, however, seem to gloss over many of the realities of contemporary life. A majority of adults in their middle or later years have experienced at least one disrupting trauma in health, work, or family that has required a fundamental reconstituting of roles and orientations (Kelly 1987b). Further, conditions are not the same for all persons in a social system. Race, gender, class, and ethnicity designate different life chances.

In this perspective of continuity and change in a metaphor of life as journey, a number of issues call for attention. First, salient differences in life conditions are more than variations in starting points for the journey. Rather, deprivation and denial are cumulative in ways that affect every dimension of life. Second, individuals come to define themselves in the actual circumstances of life, not in an abstracted concept. Identities, the concepts of the self that are central to what we believe is possible and probable in our lives, are developed in the realities of the life course. And, third, the structures of the society, including access to institutional power, provide forceful contexts of opportunity and denial that shape both direction and resources for the journey.

In this revised life course approach, leisure remains as a significant dimension, tied to family, work, education, community, and other elements of life. Changes in one may affect all the others. Leisure, then, is distinct from the product orientation of work and the intimate bonding of the family and yet connected to both.

Leisure and the Life Course: New Agendas. From the perspective of the life course, research focusing on leisure now requires several revised issues, and among the most significant are the following.

First, leisure is woven through the life course. It is existential in a developmental sense. That is, leisure is action that involves *becoming,* action in which the actor becomes something more than before.

Second, the developmental orientation of some leisure is highlighted by this perspective that recognizes lines of action as well as singular events and episodes. What has been termed "serious leisure" by Stebbins (1979) is activity in which there is considerable personal investment in skills and often in equipment and organization. Such investment places serious leisure in a central position in identity formation and expression. Leisure identities may provide continuity through the transitions and traumas of the life course. Yet, how women and men define themselves and take action toward redefinition has been a subject of speculation more than research.

Third, what is the place of leisure in the schema of life investments and commitments? Further, how do those investments differ according to the life conditions of men and women as they make their way through the shifting expectations and possibilities of the life course? Gallier (1988) presents a model of the life course that emphasizes disruptions rather than linear progress. In an irregular life journey, work, family, and leisure may rise and fall both in salience and in the "chunks" of time they are allocated. Gallier proposes that education, production, and leisure become themes woven through life rather than discrete sequential periods.

THE NATURE OF LEISURE

As already suggested, perspectives on the nature of leisure have changed in the modern period of scholarly attention from the 1930s to the present. The change is not self-contained but reflects shifts in theoretical paradigms and draws from other disciplines, especially that of social psychology.

Leisure as Free Time and Meaning. Despite repeated references to Greek roots and especially Aristotle, the first accepted operational definition of leisure was that of time. Leisure did not require that all other role obligations be completed but that the use of the time be more by choice than requirement. How choice was to be measured was seldom addressed. Concurrently, international "time-budget" research quantified leisure as one type of activity that could be identified by its form (Szalai 1974). Leisure was assumed to be clearly distinguished from work, required maintenance, and family responsibilities.

The first consensus, although persisting in many research designs, did not endure long without amendment. To begin with, it was obvious that any activity might be required, an extension of work or other roles. Further, even terms as simple as *choice* or *discretionary* implied that the actor's definition of the situation might be crucial.

In the 1970s, the field claimed more attention from psychologists who focused on attitudes rather than activities. Leisure was said to be defined by attitudes or a "state of mind" that included elements such as perceived freedom, intrinsic motivation, and a concentration on the experience rather than external ends (Neulinger 1974). Attention was directed toward meanings, but wholly in the actor rather than in definitions of the social context. Such psychological approaches were one salient influence on sociologists who added at least three dimensions to the earlier consensus regarding time and activity.

First, in the 1950s, the Kansas City research (Havighurst 1961) and the community studies tied leisure to social roles. The satisfactions one anticipated in an activity involved meanings and relationships one brought to the action context as well as what occurred in the time frame.

Second, the immediate experience might be the critical focus for leisure, but it occurs in particular environments that involve social learning, acquired skills and orientations (Csikszentmihalyi 1981), and interaction with components imported from other role relationships (Cheek and Burch 1976). Freedom is or is not perceived in actual circumstances.

Third, although the dimension of freedom recurs in the literature, studies of experiences and activity engagements found that leisure seldom is monodimensional. The meanings, outcomes, motivations, and experiences themselves are multifaceted (Havighurst 1961; Kelly 1978).

In the revised approaches, then, leisure is a more complex phenomenon than either the earlier sociologists or psychologists proposed. In fact, the consensus broke down under the weight of multiple approaches that ranged from individualistic psychology to functional sociology, from presumably self-evident quantities of time to interpretive self-definitions and lines of action, and from discrete self-presentations (Goffman 1967) to actions embedded in life course role sequences (Rapoport and Rapoport 1976).

Revolt against the Abstract. Antithetical themes came from several directions. First, which is fundamental to accounting for life in society, the interpretive acts of the individual or the social context in which the action takes place (Giddens 1979)? Further, since the forms and symbols by which action is directed are learned and reinforced in the society, can action be prior to the context? The nature of leisure, then, is neither a contextual act nor a determined social role. Rather, it is actualized in processual action (Rojek 1990). And this process has continuities that extend beyond the immediate to personal development and the creation of significant communities (Kelly 1981).

Second, a number of critical analysts have raised questions about the positive cast usually given to leisure. Such positive approaches seem to presuppose resources, options, perspectives, and self-determination that are in fact unequally distributed in societies (Clarke and Critcher 1986). Do the unemployed and the poor have enough resources for discretion and choice to be meaningful concepts? Do histories of subjugation and life-defining limits for women in male-dominated societies make assumptions of self-determining action a sham? Such opportunity differences are most substantive in a market system of buying, renting, or otherwise acquiring resources. The real contexts of leisure are not voids of time and space but are extensions of the structures of the society and ideologies of the culture.

Third, a consequence of this distorted and constricted context of leisure is alienation. Leisure is not entirely a free, creative, authentic, and community-building activity. It may also be, perhaps at the same time, stultifying and alienating. It may separate rather than unite, narrow rather than expand, and entrap rather than free. It may, in short, be negative as well as positive. It is not a rarefied ideal or a perfect experience. It is real life, often involving struggle and conflict as well as development and expression.

The dialectic between expression and oppression that characterizes the rest of life in society is the reality of leisure as well. Being role-based in a stratified society means being limited, directed, and excluded. The contexts of any experience, however free and exhilerating, are the real culture and social system. The multiple meanings of leisure include separation as well as community, determination as well as creation, and routine as well as expression. The former simplicity of leisure as essentially a "good thing" becomes alloyed by situating it in the real society with all its forces, pressures, and conflicts.

Leisure as a Dimension of Life. The question is, then, what does such extension and critique do to any conceptualization of the nature of leisure? Leisure encompasses both the existential and the social. It has myriad forms, locales, social settings, and outcomes. Leisure is neither separated from social roles nor wholly determined by them. Leisure has developed amid conflict as well as amid social consensus, in division as well as in integration, with control as well as with freedom. It may involve acquiescence as well as resistance, alienation as well as authenticity, and preoccupation with self as well as commitment to community. Leisure, then, is multidimensional and cannot be characterized by any single or simple element.

A further issue is whether leisure is really a domain of life at all. Is leisure clearly distinguished from work, family, community, church, and school, or is it a dimension of action and interaction within them all? In the childhood and adolescent periods, leisure is a social space for the exploration and development of sexual identities as well as for working out the issues of peer identification and independence from parents and the past. It also stresses the theme of expression that is central to developing a sense of selfhood, of personal identity among emerging social roles. In the early adult period, leisure adds the dimension of bonding to intimate others, especially in the formation and consolidation of the family. In later years, leisure has meanings tied to integration with significant other persons and to maintaining a sense of ability when some work and community roles are lost. Leisure, then, might be conceptualized as being woven into the intersecting role sequences of the life course rather than being a segregated realm of activity. Productivity is not limited to work, bonding to the family, learning and development to education, or expression to leisure. Production, bonding and community, learning and development, and relative freedom and self-authenticating experience may all be found in any domain of life.

Yet, there must also be distinguishing elements of leisure, or it disappears into the ongoing round of life. Further, those elements should be significant in relation to central issues of life such as production and work, love and community, sexuality and gender, learning and development, emotion and involvement. It should connect with the lived conditions of ordinary life rather than be an esoteric and precious idea to be actualized only in rare and elite conditions.

Leisure, then, may be more a dimension than a domain, more a theme than an identifiable realm (Kelly 1987a). That dimension is characterized by three elements: First, it is action in the inclusive sense of doing something, of intentioned and deliberate act. Such action is existential in producing an outcome with meaning to the actor. Second, this action is focused on the experience more than on the result. It is done primarily because of what occurs in the defined time and space. And, third, leisure as a dimension of life is characterized by freedom more than by necessity. It is not required by any role, coercive power, or repressive ideology. Leisure is not detached from its social and cultural contexts but is a dimension of relatively self-determined act within such contexts. Its meaning is not in its products as much as in the experience, not in its forms as much as in its expression.

The sociology of leisure, then, is not a closed book or a finalized product. Rather, central issues are currently being raised that promise to reform the field in its premises as well as conclusions. No common wisdom will go unchallenged, no consensus remain unchanged, and no theoretical formulation be above conflict. Yet every challenge, conflict, and developing synthesis provides a new basis for at least one conclusion: Leisure is a significant dimension of life that calls for both disciplined and innovative attention.

(SEE ALSO: *Life Course)*

REFERENCES

Atchley, Robert 1989 "A Continuity Theory of Normal Aging." *Gerontologist* 29:183–190.

Blauner, Robert 1964 *Alienation and Freedom: The Factory Worker and His Industry.* Chicago: University of Chicago Press.

Cheek, Neil, and William Burch 1976 *The Social Organization of Leisure in Human Society.* New York: Harper and Row.

Clarke, John, and Charles Critcher 1985 *The Devil Makes Work: Leisure in Capitalist Britain.* Champaign: University of Illinois Press.

Csikszentmihalyi, Mihaly 1981 "Leisure and Socialization." *Social Forces* 60:332–340.

Cutler, Stephen, and Jon Hendricks 1990 "Leisure and Time Use across the Life Course." In R. Binstock and L. George, eds., *Handbook of Aging and the Social Sciences.* 3rd ed. New York: Academic Press.

Deem, Rosemary 1986 *All Work and No Play: The Sociology of Women and Leisure.* Milton Keynes, UK: Open University Press.

Dumazedier, Joffre 1967 *Toward a Society of Leisure.* New York: Free Press.

Gallier, Xavier 1988 *La deuxieme carrière: Âges, emplois, retraite.* Paris: Éditions du Seuil.

Giddens, Anthony 1979 *Central Problems in Social Theory: Action, Structure, and Contradiction in Social Analysis.* Berkeley: University of California Press.

Goffman, Erving 1967 *Interaction Ritual.* New York: Anchor Books.

Gordon, Chad, C. Gaitz, and J. Scott 1976 "Leisure and Lives: Personal Expressivity across the Life Span." In R. Binstock and E. Shanas, *Handbook of Aging and the Social Sciences.* New York: Van Nostrand Reinhold.

Habermas, Jurgen 1975 *Legitimation Crisis.* Boston: Beacon Press.

Havighurst, Robert 1961 "The Nature and Values of Meaningful Free-Time Activity." In R. Kleemeier, ed., *Aging and Leisure.* New York: Oxford University Press.

Henderson, Karla, M. Deborah Bialeschki, Susan M. Shaw, and Valeria J. Freysinger 1989 *A Leisure of One's Own.* State College, Pa.: Venture Publishing.

Kelly, John R. 1978 "Situational and Social Factors in Leisure Decisions." *Pacific Sociological Review* 21:313–330.

——— 1981 "Leisure Interaction and the Social Dialectic." *Social Forces* 60:304–322.

——— 1983 *Leisure Identities and Interactions.* London: Allen and Unwin.

——— 1987a *Freedom to Be: A New Sociology of Leisure.* New York: Macmillan.

——— 1987b *Peoria Winter: Styles and Resources in Later Life.* Lexington, Mass.: Lexington Books.

Lundberg, George, Mirra Komarovsky, and M. McInerney 1934 *Leisure: a Suburban Study.* New York: Columbia University Press.

Lynd, Helen, and Robert Lynd 1956 *Middletown.* New York: Harcourt Brace.

Marx, Karl 1970 *The Economic and Philosophical Manuscripts of 1844.* M. Milligan, trans. London: Lawrence and Wishart.

Neugarten, Bernice 1968 *Middle Age and Aging.* Chicago: University of Chicago Press.

Neulinger, John 1974 *The Psychology of Leisure.* Springfield, Ill.: C. C. Thomas.

Parker, Stanley 1971 *The Future of Work and Leisure.* New York: Praeger.

Rapoport, Rhona, and Robert Rapoport 1976 *Leisure and the Family Life Cycle.* London: Routledge and Kegan Paul.

Roberts, Kenneth 1970 *Leisure.* London: Longmans.

Rojek, Chris 1985 *Capitalism and Leisure Theory.* London: Tavistock.

——— 1990 "Leisure and Recreation Theory." In E. Jackson and T. Burton, eds., *Understanding Leisure and Recreation.* State College, Pa.: Venture Publishing.

Stebbins, Robert 1979 *Amateurs: On the Margin between Work and Leisure.* Beverly Hills, Calif.: Sage.

Szalai, Alexander 1974 *The Use of Time: Daily Activities of Urban and Suburban Populations in Twelve Countries.* The Hague: Mouton.

Veblen, Thorstein [1899] 1953 *The Theory of the Leisure Class.* New York: New American Library.

Wilensky, Harold 1960 "Work, Careers, and Social Integration." *International Social Science Journal* 12:543–560.

Wilson, John 1980 "Sociology of Leisure." *Annual Review of Sociology* 6:21–40.

JOHN R. KELLY

LESBIANISM *See* Sexual Orientation.

LEVELS OF ANALYSIS The cases used as the units in an analysis determine the level of analysis. These cases may be quite varied, for example, countries, political parties, advertisements, families, or individuals. Thus, analysis may occur at the individual level, family level, advertisement level, and so forth.

The types of variables used at any one level of analysis, however, may be quite different. As an example, in studying the determinants of individuals' attitudes toward public education, the individuals (the units of analysis) may be described in terms of their sex and race (measures of individual properties), whether they attended a public or private college, and the region of the country in which they reside (measures of the collectives to which they belong). The analysis in this example is at the individual level because the cases used are individuals who are described in terms of individual properties and the properties of the collectives to which they belong.

This article focuses on (1) some types of variables used to describe the properties of collectives and members and their use at different levels of analysis; (2) some problems that arise in using relationships at one level of analysis to make inferences about relationships at another level of analysis; (3) a brief discussion of a statistical model that explicates some of these problems; and (4) some proposed solutions or partial solutions to the problem of cross-level inference.

TYPES OF VARIABLES USED TO DESCRIBE COLLECTIVES AND MEMBERS

Lazarsfeld and Menzel (1969) propose a typology of the kinds of properties (variables) that describe "collectives" and "members." For example, in discussing the properties of collectives, Lazarsfeld and Menzel distinguish between analytical, structural, and global properties.

Analytical properties are obtained by performing some mathematical operation upon some property of each *single* member. These properties are typically referred to as aggregate variables. Examples are the percentage of blacks in cities, the sex ratio for different counties, and the standard deviation as a measure of heterogeneity of incomes in organizations.

Structural properties of collectives are obtained by performing some operation on data about the relations of each member to some or all of the others. Such measures are common in network analysis. For example, friendship density could be defined as the relative number of pairs of members of a collective who are directly connected by friendship ties. Since the total number of potential ties in a group with N members is $N(N-1)/2$, density is the total number of ties divided by this number.

Global properties of collectives are not based on information about the properties of individual members either singly or in relationship to one another. Having a democratic or nondemocratic form of government is a global property of collectives. Being a private rather than a public school is a global property of a school. The proportion of GNP spent on education is a global property of countries.

Thus, variables that describe collectives can be based on summary data concerning single members of those collectives, the relationships of members to other members, or some global characteristic of the collective itself.

Turning to variables that describe the properties of members of collectives, there are four major types: absolute, relational, comparative, and contextual.

Absolute properties are obtained without making use either of information about the characteristics of the collective or of information about the relationships of the member being described to other members. Thus, sex, level of education, and income are absolute properties of individuals.

Relational properties of members are computed from information about the substantive relationships between them and other members. For example, the number of friends an individual has at school is a property of the individual based on other members in the collective. The number of family members is another such measure.

Comparative properties characterize a member by a comparison between their value on some (absolute or relational) property and the distribution of this property over the entire collective of which they are a member. A person's class rank or birth order are comparative properties.

Contextual properties describe members by a property of the collective to which they belong. For example, being from a densely populated census tract or a school with a certain percentage of nonwhite students is a contextual property describing the context in which the member acts. Contextual properties are characteristics of collectives that are applied to members.

Contextual variables remind us that the level of analysis is determined by the cases used as the units of analysis, not by the level of the phenomena described by a particular variable. Thus, all of the variables that describe a collective may be used at the individual level of analysis as well as those that describe individual properties; for example, a person's attitude may be predicted on the basis of the percentage of blacks in the person's school (contextual/analytic), whether or not the school is private or public (contextual/global), the density of friendships at the school (contextual/structural), the person's sex (absolute), his or her class standing (comparative), and the number of friendship choices he or she receives (relational).

INFERENCES FROM ONE LEVEL TO ANOTHER

The section above described two different levels analysis, the collective (or aggregate) and the member (or individual). Sociologists typically distinguish other levels depending on the units of analysis; for example, the units may be schools, advertisements, children's stories, or riots. To make inferences from relationships discovered at one level of analysis to relationships at another level is not logically valid, and sociologists have labeled such inferences "fallacies." Still, at times one may be able to argue for the reasonableness of such inferences. These arguments can be based on statistical considerations (Duncan and Davis 1953; Goodman 1953; 1959) or on rationales that closely tie relationships at one level with those at another (Durkheim [1897] 1966; Dornbusch and Hickman 1959).

Disaggregative fallacies (often called ecological fallacies) are the classic case of cross-level fallacies. They were brought to the attention of sociologists by Robinson (1950). He cites two cases of cross-level inferences, both of which involve making inferences about relationships at the individual level based on relationships discovered at the aggregate level. Robinson noted that the Pearson product moment correlation between the percent black and the percent illiterate in 1930 for the Census Bureau's nine geographical divisions was 0.95 and for states it was 0.77, while the correlation (measured by phi) on the individual level between being illiterate or not and being black or not was only 0.20. The relationship between percent illiterate and percent foreign-born was −0.62 for regions and −0.53 for states, while the correlation between being illiterate or not and being foreign-born or not at the individual level was positive (0.12).

Robinson demonstrated that relationships at one level of analysis do not have to be the same as those at another level. To assume that they must be the same or even that they must be quite similar is a logical fallacy.

Aggregative fallacies occur in the opposite direction, that is, when one assumes that relationships existing at the individual level must exist at the aggregate level. Robinson's results show that it cannot be assumed that the negative relationship between being foreign born and being illiterate at the individual level will be mirrored at the state level.

Universal fallacies (Alker 1969) occur when researchers assume that relationships based on the total population must be true for subsamples of the whole. It may be true, for example, that the relationship between population density and the crime rates of cities for all cities in the United States is not the same for southern cities or for cities with a population of over one million. Here, the fallacy is to assume that a relationship based on the total population must hold for selected subpopulations.

Similarly, one might commit a *selective fallacy* (Alker 1969) by assuming that relationships based on a particular sample of cities must hold for all cities. If the selected cities are a random sample of cities, this is a problem of statistical inference, but if they are selected on some other basis (e.g., size), then making inferences to cities of other sizes is a selective fallacy.

Cross-modality fallacies occur when the inference is from one distinct type of unit to another distinct type of unit. A cross-modality fallacy has occurred when trends in advertisement content are used to make inferences about trends in the attitudes of individuals, or designs on pottery are used to infer the level of need for achievement in different cultures. (Aggregative and disaggregative fallacies are cross-modality fallacies because groups and individuals are distinct units. But these fallacies have traditionally been classified separately.)

Cross-sectional fallacies occur when one makes inferences from cross-sectional relationships (relationships based on units of analysis from a single point in time) to longitudinal relationships. *Longitudinal fallacies* occur when one makes inferences from longitudinal relationships (relationships based on units of analysis across time units) to cross-sectional ones.

In all of their many manifestations, cross-level inferences are not logically valid inferences

(Skyrms 1975). That is, relationships on one level of analysis are not necessarily the same as those on another level. They may not even be similar.

STATISTICAL ANALYSIS OF DISAGGREGATIVE AND AGGREGATIVE INFERENCES

This section presents the results of a mathematical demonstration of why disaggregative and aggregative inferences are fallacies, that is, why results at the aggregate level are not necessarily mirrored at the individual level. The derivation of this model is not shown here but may be found in several sources (Duncan, Cuzzort, and Duncan 1961, Alker 1969, Hannan 1971, and Robinson 1950). Readers who prefer not to investigate these formulas can skip to the next section.

The individual-level or total correlation (r_{xyt}) between two variables (X and Y) can be written as a function of the correlation between group means (the aggregate-level correlation: r_{xyb}), the correlation of individual scores within groups (a weighted average of the correlations within each of the groups: r_{xyw}), and the correlation ratios for the two variables, X and Y. The correlation ratio is the ratio of the variance between groups (the variance of the group means: V_{xb}) to the total variance (variance of the individual scores: V_{xt}). Thus, the individual-level or total correlation can be written as in equation 1.

$$r_{xyt} = r_{xyw}\sqrt{1-\left(\frac{V_{xb}}{V_{xt}}\right)^2}\sqrt{1-\left(\frac{V_{yb}}{V_{yt}}\right)^2} + r_{xyb}\left(\frac{V_{xb}}{V_{xt}}\right)\left(\frac{V_{xb}}{V_{yt}}\right) \qquad (1)$$

Similarly, the individual level regression coefficient can be written as a function of the within-group regression coefficient, the group level (between group) regression coefficient, and the correlation ratio for variable X (equation 2).

$$b_{yxt} = b_{yxw} + \left(\frac{V_{xb}}{V_{xt}}\right)^2 (b_{yxb} - b_{yxw}) \qquad (2)$$

It is a simple algebraic exercise to derive formulas for r_{xyb} and b_{yxb} (the aggregate-level correlation and regression coefficients) in terms of correlation ratios, and correlation and regression coefficients at other levels.

These formulas clearly demonstrate why one cannot use the ecological or group-level correlation or regression coefficients to estimate individual-level relationships: The individual level relationships are a function of group level relationships, within-group-level relationships, and correlation ratios. This approach can be extended to include other levels of analysis, for example, individuals on one level, counties on another, states on another, and time as yet another level (see, e.g., Alker 1969; Duncan, Cuzzort, and Duncan 1961).

SEPARATING AGGREGATE-LEVEL AND INDIVIDUAL-LEVEL EFFECTS

In some situations one may want to argue that the best measures of individual-level "effects" are provided by analyses at the individual level that include as predictors relevant individual properties and the properties of the collective to which the individuals belong (contextual variables). Estimates of these individual-level relationships are then "controlled" for group-level effects (Alwin and Otto 1977).

Since the relationship between group-level means may reflect nothing more than the relationship between variables at the individual level, it has been suggested that the best estimate of group level effects compares the regression coefficient for the group means and for the individual scores. Lincoln and Zeitz (1980) show how this may be done in a single regression equation while at the same time controlling for other relevant variables. For both of these techniques to work, some stringent assumptions must be met, including assumptions of no measurement error in the independent variables and of a common within-group regression coefficient.

SOLUTIONS TO THE PROBLEM OF INFERENCES FROM ONE LEVEL TO ANOTHER

Cross-level inferences can and often are made by sociologists. There is no absolute stricture against making such inferences, but when researchers make them, they need to do so with some awareness of their limitations.

While both Duncan and Davis (1953) and Goodman (1953, 1959) maintain that it is in general inappropriate to use aggregate level (ecological) relationships to make inferences about individual level relationships, they each propose strategies to set bounds on the possible relationships that could exist at one level of analysis given relationships that exist at the other. The bounds are designed for use with aggregated data (analytic measures), and in some circumstances these techniques are useful.

"Theory" may also allow one to make cross-level inferences. For example, Dornbusch and Hickman (1959) tested Riesman, Glazer, and Denney's (1950) contention that other-directedness in individuals declined in the United States during the first half of the twentieth century. They obviously could not interview individuals throughout the first half of the century, so they turned to advertisements in a women's magazine (*Ladies Home Journal* from 1890 to 1956) to examine whether these ads increasingly used themes of other-directedness. Their units of analysis were advertisements, but they explicitly stated that they wanted to make inferences about changes in the other-directedness of individuals. Is this justified? The answer is No, on strictly logical grounds. That is, changes in the contents of advertisements do not demonstrate changes in individuals' personalities. But Dornbusch and Hickman (1959) convincingly argue that advertisements (in this case) are likely to reflect aspects of other-directedness in the targets of the advertisements (individuals). They recognize the need for other tests of this hypothesis, using other types of data.

Perhaps the classic case in sociology of an analysis built on the ecological fallacy is Emile Durkheim's ([1897] 1966) analysis of suicide. One factor that Durkheim sees as "protecting" individuals from suicide is social integration. When individuals are married, have children, are members of a church that provides a high degree of social integration (e.g., Catholic rather than Protestant), or live at a time when their countries are in crisis (e.g., a war or electoral crisis), they are seen as more integrated into social, religious, and political society and less likely to commit suicide. Much of the data available to Durkheim did not allow an analysis on the individual level. There was no "suicide registry" with detailed data on the sex, religion, family status, and so forth of those committing suicide. There were, however, census data on the proportion of Catholics, the proportion married, and the average family size in different regions. Other sources could be used to ascertain the rate of suicide for different regions. Using these data, Durkheim showed that Catholic countries had lower suicide rates than Protestant countries, that within France and Germany Catholic cantons had much lower suicide rates than Protestant cantons, that departments in France with larger average family sizes had lower suicide rates, and that the suicide rate was lower during the months of electoral crises in France than during comparable months of the previous or following year. He combined this evidence with other evidence dealing with individuals (e.g., suicide rates for married versus unmarried men), and it was all consistent with his theory of suicide and social integration.

One could dismiss these aggregate-level relationships by arguing that perhaps in Protestant countries those of other religions kill themselves at such a high rate that the suicide rates are higher in Protestant countries than in Catholic countries (and similarly in Protestant cantons in France and Germany). Isn't it possible that in departments with relatively small average family sizes there is a tendency for those in large-size families to kill themselves relatively more often? This would create a relationship at the aggregate level (department level) in which smaller average family size is associated with higher rates of suicide. It is possible, because relationships at one level of analysis are not necessarily mirrored at another level of analysis. But Durkheim's results are not easily dismissed.

Strict logic does not justify cross-level inferences. But logic is not the only rational way to justify inferences. If a series of diverse relationships that are predicted to hold at the individual level are found at the aggregate level, they do not prove that the same relationships would be found at the individual level, but they are not irrelevant. It is incumbent on the critic of a study such as Durkheim's to give a series of alternative explanations explaining why the relationships at the aggregate level should differ from those at the individual level. If the alternative explanation is not very convincing or parsimonious, researchers are likely to find Durkheim's evidence persuasive. To the extent that social scientists are convinced that a set of advertisements are designed to appeal to motivations in their target population, that the target population of the magazine in which the advertisements appears represents the population of interest, and so on, they will find Dornbusch and Hickman's cross-level inference persuasive.

Persuasion is a matter of degree and is subject to change. Sociologists would want to examine additional studies based on, for instance, other populations, modalities, and periods. These data might strengthen cross-level inferences.

(SEE ALSO: *Measurement; Scientific Explanation*)

REFERENCES

Alker, Hayward R. 1969 "A Typology of Ecological Fallacies." In Mattei Dogan and Stein Rokkan, eds., *Quantitative Ecological Analysis in the Social Sciences.* Cambridge, Mass.: MIT Press.

Alwin, Duane F., and Luther B. Otto 1977 "High School Context Effects on Aspirations." *Sociology of Education* 50:259–272.

Dornbusch, Sanford M., and Lauren C. Hickman 1959 "Other-Directedness in Consumer-Goods Advertising: A Test of Riesman's Historical Theory." *Social Forces* 38:99–102.

Duncan, Otis D., Ray P. Cuzzort, and Beverly Duncan 1961 *Statistical Geography: Problems in Analyzing Areal Data.* Glencoe, Ill.: Free Press.

Duncan, Otis D., and Beverly Davis 1953 "An Alternative to Ecological Correlation." *American Sociological Review* 18:665–666.

Durkheim, Emile [1897] 1966 *Suicide.* New York: Free Press.

Goodman, Leo A. 1953 "Ecological Regression and Behavior of Individuals." *American Sociological Review* 18:663–664.

——— 1959 "Some Alternatives to Ecological Correlation." *American Journal of Sociology* 64:610–625.

Hannan, Michael T. 1971 *Aggregation and Disaggregation in Sociology.* Lexington, Mass.: Lexington Books.

———, and Leigh Burstein 1974 "Estimation from Grouped Observations." *American Sociological Review* 39:374–392.

Lazarsfeld, Paul F., and Herbert Menzel 1969 "On the Relation between Individual and Collective Properties." In Amitai Etzioni, ed., *A Sociological Reader on Complex Organizations.* New York: Holt, Rinehart, and Winston.

Lincoln, James R., and Gerald Zeitz 1980 "Organizational Properties from Aggregate Data: Separating Individual and Structural Effects." *American Sociological Review* 45:391–408.

Reisman, David, Nathan Glazer, and Reuel Denney 1950 *The Lonely Crowd.* New Haven: Yale University Press.

Robinson, William S. 1950 "Ecological Correlations and the Behavior of Individuals." *American Sociological Review* 15:351–357.

Skyrms, Brian 1975 *Choice and Chance.* Encino, Calif.: Dickenson.

ROBERT M. O'BRIEN

LIBERALISM/CONSERVATISM "Is (or was) Blank a liberal?" The precise reply to this question inevitably begins with a throat-clearing preface such as, "It all depends on the period you have in mind—and the place. Are you speaking of someone in nineteenth-century England, the United States during the Franklin Roosevelt New Deal days, contemporary Great Britain, continental Europe, or contemporary U.S.A.?"

For Americans nurtured on the "liberal" tradition of Franklin Delano Roosevelt and the Democratic party, the significance of the *L* word was quite clear. The private business establishment, left to its own devices, had brought about the economic collapse of 1929. "Rugged individualism" had demonstrated its inadequacies even for many rugged individualists themselves. Almost two-thirds of a century after that collapse, the Great American Depression still retains the power to evoke terrifying memories of mass unemployment, bank failures, small business bankruptcies, soup kitchens, and popular ditties like "Brother can you spare a dime?" These were all nostalgic but chilling reminiscences of the desolation to which "nonliberal," or "conservative," social, economic, and political policies had led. There seems to persist an enormous reluctance to release this era and its memories to the historians as just another noteworthy episode in American history like the War of 1812 or the Panic of 1873.

For other Americans, some of whom matured perhaps too rapidly during the late 1960s and whose memories were filled with visions of the war in Vietnam, the battles for Civil Rights, and the turmoil in urban ghettos, things were much less clear. Stalwarts of liberalism like Hubert Humphrey (senator, vice president, and unsuccessful Democratic candidate for President) seemed to become part of the very establishment toward which hostility was directed. Government, instead of representing a liberating force, increasingly was seen as the source of existing difficulties. Liberalism, for many, was no longer the solution; it had become part of the problem.

Liberalism has often been identified with the struggle to free individuals from the confining embraces of other persons, institutions, or even habitual ways of behaving. It is seen by its advocates as a liberating orientation. Thoughts that, in various times and places, have been called liberal, all seem to have as their common denominator this fundamental notion of freedom for individual human beings.

It was during the period between the Reformation and the French Revolution that a new social class emerged. Political control by a landowning aristocracy was challenged by this new class whose power lay only in the control of movable capital. It consisted of such people as bankers, traders, and manufacturers. Science began to replace religion as the source of ultimate authority; contract replaced status as the legal foundation of society. The ideas of individual initiative and individual control became the basis for a new philosophy: liberalism (Laski 1962, p. 11).

Liberalism began as the champion of freedom and the foe of privilege derived from inherited class position. But freedom was not fought for on behalf of everyone in society. The constituency of liberalism consisted of those who had property to defend. Its supporters sought to limit the range of political authority and tried to develop a system of fundamental rights not subject to invasion by the state (Laski 1962, p. 13). Most of the population (e.g., factory and agricultural workers) were not initially included in the concerns of liberalism. But redefinitions of governmental concerns and authority inevitably had consequences for all members of society. Thoughtful economists and others soon realized this.

Thus, from the perspective of the closing years of twentieth-century America, it is easy to forget that classical economists like Adam Smith and David Ricardo, far from being simply reflex ideologists for the business establishment, were deeply concerned about liberty for individuals and saw their classical economic doctrines as the best way to insure it. In this sense, many contemporary Americans could legitimately view them as representatives of the liberal, rather than the conservative, genre. The *free enterprise* game was originally a liberal game.

For many participants in this great game of free enterprise, it became increasingly more obvious that the game was "fixed," that somehow participants did not emerge with either their liberty or their pocketbooks intact. To insure even a modicum of freedom and liberty for individuals, it became necessary to provide them with a helping hand from a source outside the marketplace. This source, a powerful and beneficent outsider, the national government, could help monitor the rules and to some extent the play of the economic game. It *could* provide, for heavy losers or potential losers, social benefits in the form of such consolations as unemployment insurance, old age pensions, insured bank accounts, and coordinated measures to combat environmental pollution. It *could* help protect consumers from the harmful effects of adulterated food and drug products; it *could* protect workers from the hazards of unregulated workplaces. In short the liberal ethos in twentieth-century America incorporated as one of its tenets reliance on government action to protect the liberty of individuals.

The conservative ethos, on the other hand, during the same period has been characterized by a hands-off posture with respect to many aspects of government policy. This constitutes a fascinating reversal of traditional conservatism. The shades of Edmund Burke and other historical conservative spirits might well cringe at the characterization of their philosophy as "less government."

For some observers, this liberal–conservative contrast seems to be based on different psychological sets, or frames, of mind. Thus, we have been told that liberals are more hospitable to change, more willing to reexamine institutions and established practices in the light of new problems and needs. From this perspective, conservatives are those who appeal to the experience of the past but do not learn from it. Liberals are presented as being less reverent of the status quo, more venturesome in the realm of ideas, and much more optimistic about the possibilities available through exploration and discovery (Girvetz 1966).

Willingness to change becomes meaningful only when viewed against the nature of the status quo. When "liberal" governments adopt measures to provide for persons who are aged, ill, unemployed, or handicapped (as they have in some Scandinavian countries), to be "liberal" may mean to *retain* the status quo. To eliminate the measures —to engage in change—may be precisely what Western conservatives might demand.

For many observers of the dramatic events occurring at the end of the 1980s and in the early 1990s in Eastern Europe, members of communist parties who struggled to maintain their power in government were labeled "conservatives." Those fighting for *free enterprise* and other capitalist-like changes were called "liberal reformers." Communists for many years had been viewed by Western conservatives as the ultimate enemy; liberals were characteristically referred to by many of these conservatives as thinly disguised "Reds." In a dramatic and even comic reversal, dedicated Stalinists were now described as "conservatives."

At one time or another a wide variety of ideas have been called conservative. There have been efforts, however, to reduce the essence of these ideas to a limited number of more or less well defined notions. Clinton Rossiter and Russell Kirk, two ardent defenders of the conservative faith, once prepared a summary that received widespread approval. Although not all conservatives would necessarily agree with everything appearing in their summary, "it would be exceedingly difficult to find a conservative who did not agree with a good deal of what Professors Kirk and Rossiter impute to their tradition" (Witonski 1971, pp. 34–35).

The imputation begins with an assumption about the more or less immutable character of human nature. Behind the curtain of civilized behavior there exists, in human beings, wickedness, unreason, and an urge to engage in violence. In addition, a great deal of emphasis is placed upon the conviction that people are not naturally equal in most qualities of mind, body, and spirit. Liberty is more important than social equality. This leads to the conclusion that society must always have its classes. It is futile to level or eliminate them. Accordingly, societies will always require ruling aristocracies; efforts to have majority rule will lead to errors and potential tyranny.

Human beings, this conservative ethos insists, are not born with rights. These are earned as a result of duties performed. Service, effort, obedience, cultivation of virtue and self-restraint are the price of rights. Of primary importance to liberty, order, and progress, is the institution of private property. Inherited institutions, values, symbols, and rituals are indispensable and even sacred. Human reason is subject to error and severely limited; the surest guide to wisdom and virtue is historical experience.

Beyond this, fundamental to conservatism is the belief that all political problems are fundamentally religious in nature. Narrow rationality cannot, in itself, satisfy human needs. Both society and conscience are ruled by divine intent. Conservatives, it is asserted, have an affection for the traditional life; others (presumably liberals) favor narrow uniformity, egalitarianism, and pursuit of utilitarian goals. The only true equality is moral equality; civilized society requires orders and classes. Property and freedom are inseparable. If property is separated from private possession, liberty disappears.

This basic conservative creed goes on to say that human beings have anarchic impulses and are governed more by emotion than by reason. It therefore becomes necessary to place controls on human appetite. The correct method of accomplishing this is through tradition and sound "prejudice."

Finally, the proper instrument for social change is Providence. Some change is necessary from time to time to conserve society. It is like the perpetual renewal of the human body. But this change must always be accomplished slowly and with an awareness of the direction in which Providence is moving social forces (Witonski 1971, pp. 32–34).

Undergirding the entire structure of this conservative doctrine is a more or less explicit version of the *chain of being*. This metaphor is designed to express the enormous extent, variety, order, and unity of "God's Creation." The chain stretches from the foot of God's throne to the meanest of inanimate objects. Every speck of creation is a link in this chain, and every link except those at the two extremities is simultaneously bigger and smaller than another; there can be no gap (Tillyard 1959). The classic examination of the history of this idea was written by Arthur S. Lovejoy (1960).

Every category of things excels at *something*. Plants are higher than stones, but stones are stronger and more durable. Animals ("Beasts") are above plants, but plants can assimilate nourishment better. Human beings are above beasts but inferior to them in physical energy and desires.

All this suggests a sort of interdependency among all objects and living creatures. Central to the idea of the chain is the concept that every object, animal or person, is part of an all-encompassing whole. Basic to the metaphor is an implicit, if not always explicit, view of the universe as an organism (strong traces of this continue to be found in some formulations of contemporary systems theory).

Pushed to its logical conclusion, this suggests that all creatures and objects are equally important. Every existing part of the cosmic organism might well be seen as necessary (perhaps in some unknown way) for the survival of the whole. This, in turn implies that, although they do different things, all human beings, for example, are equally necessary. This logic could lead to dangerous subversive doctrines about social equality. Another feature was required to make the chain-of-being notion acceptable to those searching for reasons to justify existing inequalities in human societies. This was found in the *primacy doctrine*, the idea that, within each category of objects and creatures, there is one above the others, a *primate*. The eagle is first among birds; the whale or dolphin, among "fishes"; the rose, among flowers; the fire, among elements; the lion or elephant, among beasts; and, naturally, the emperor, among men (Tillyard 1959, pp. 29–30).

More recently, the distinguished conservative sociologist Robert Nisbet has insisted that conservatism is simply one of three major political ideologies of the eighteenth and nineteenth centuries. The other two are *liberalism* and *socialism*. Interestingly, an ideology for him, in addition to having a "reasonably" coherent body of ideas, has a *power base* that makes possible a victory for the body of ideas. It extends over a period of time and has "major" advocates or spokespersons as well as a "respectable" degree of institutionalization and charismatic figures. For conservatism, these figures would include people like Edmund Burke, Benjamin Disraeli, and Winston Churchill. Liberals have their own counterparts to these. The philosophical substance of conservatism dates from 1790 with the publication of Edmund Burke's *Reflections on the Revolution in France* (Nisbet 1986; Burke 1855).

There is a fascinating contradiction to be found in conservative doctrine. Methodologically, Nisbet offers it as a champion of historical method. This he approves of as an alternative to the liberal utilitarianism of Jeremy Bentham that is "soulless," "mechanical," and even "inhuman." Bentham's doctrine idolizes pure reason, but human beings require a different mode of thought, one based on feelings, emotions, and long experience, as well as on pure logic.

In attacking liberal utilitarianism, Nisbet is attacking a doctrine essentially abandoned by twentieth-century American liberals. Sociologist L. T. Hobhouse must be credited with having made the most serious effort to reformulate liberal doctrine.

Utilitarianism, as fashioned by Jeremy Bentham and his followers, was the visible core of nineteenth-century liberalism. It has been defined as "nothing but an attempt to apply the principles of Newton to the affairs of politics and morals" (Halevy 1972, p. 6). The principle of utility, the notion that every possible action of human beings is either taken or not depending upon whether it is seen as resulting in either pleasure or pain, was the basis for an "objective science" of behavior modeled on the physical sciences. As such, in common with other alleged sciences, it was perhaps congenitally soulless, somewhat mechanical, and potentially inhuman. Using a "rational" (but not empirically derived) model, it announced that, by pursuing his or her own pleasure and avoiding pain, each person would maximize happiness for everyone. Society was simply a collection of separate individuals operating in their individual self-interests. Government action, or "interference," constituted a disservice to these individuals and should be rejected on "scientific" grounds.

Hobhouse took issue with this view but modestly presented John Stuart Mill as the transition figure between the old and new liberalisms. Mill, reared on Benthamite doctrine, continually brought it into contact with fresh experience and new trains of thought. As a result, Mill is, "the easiest person in the world to convict of inconsistency, incompleteness, and lack of rounded system. Hence also his work will survive the death of many consistent, complete, and perfectly rounded systems" (Hobhouse 1964, p. 58).

Hobhouse noted that, although the life of society is, ultimately, the life of individuals as they act upon each other, the lives of individuals would be quite different if they were separated from society. He stressed the fact that collective social action does not necessarily involve coercion or restraint. The state is simply one of many forms of human association, a form to which individuals owe much more of their personal security and freedom than most people recognize. "The value of a site in London," he pointed out, "is something due essentially to London, not to the landlord. More accurately, a part of it is due to London, a part to the British empire, a part, perhaps we should say, to Western civilization" (Hobhouse 1964, p. 100). "Democracy," he tells us, "is not founded merely on the right or the private interest of the individual. . . . It is founded equally on the function of the individual as a member of the community" (Hobhouse 1964, p. 116).

In sum, Hobhouse helped provide a theoretic basis for a twentieth-century liberalism severed from the constricted framework of its origins and aimed at the liberation of *all* members of society. It continues to be very much concerned with feelings, emotions, and historical experience. Twentieth-century *conservatism* assumed the mantle of rigid utilitarianism shorn of its humanistic aspirations.

The contradictions in conservative doctrine become even more apparent when the matter of prejudice is considered. As Nisbet explains it, prejudice has its own intrinsic wisdom anterior to intellect. It can be readily applied in emergencies and does not leave one indecisive at the moment of decision. It sums up in an individual mind tradition's authority and wisdom (Nisbet 1986, p. 29).

This seems to epitomize the "mechanical" thought attributed to utilitarian or enlightenment liberals. Prejudice, in these terms, is, in effect, a mode of preprogrammed decision making. It insists upon shackling the human mind when confronted with new or unforeseen situations. It demands that such situations be dealt with through the use of what may well be outdated modes of thought, with strategies that were perhaps once useful but have lost their relevance. It denies a role for human creativity.

It is but a step from this doctrine to the

prejudice castigated by civil rights activists and others. We meet a man whose skin is black or yellow; we meet a woman whose features tell us she is Jewish. We have preprogrammed responses to each of these, based on the "wisdom" of tradition, informing us that they, in various ways, are inferior creatures who must be dealt with accordingly.

The feudal origins of conservative doctrine are seen most clearly in its adamant stand on the issue of inheritance and property. Not only does it fight all efforts to loosen property from family groups by means of taxation, it fights all other efforts to redistribute wealth, ranging from special entitlements to affirmative action programs. It insists upon the indestructability of existing hierarchical structures in society, seeing all efforts to modify them as attacks on cultural and psychological diversity.

Further complicating the distinction between liberalism and conservatism has been what some might refer to as a fringe movement within conservatism, called *neoconservatism.*

One explanation for the emergence of this phenomenon begins by noting that in the mid-1960s American universities, as well as literature and art in general, had become increasingly radicalized. Some cold war liberals, others who were uncomfortable with black power politics, and some critics of the counterculture disengaged themselves from liberalism. Prominent names in this group include Irving Kristol, Norman Podhoretz, and sociologists Seymour Martin Lipset, Nathan Glazer, Daniel Bell, and James Coleman. Some of these continue to reject the label but "it is as though by some invisible hand their writings and lectures gave help to the conservative cause when it was needed" (Nisbet 1986, p. 101).

Periodicals most strongly identified with neoconservatism are *The Public Interest* and *Commentary.* Neoconservatives have had close ties with the Scaife, Smith Richardson, John M. Olin, and other foundations. They have appeared as resident scholars and trustees of think tanks like the Hoover Institution, The Heritage Foundation, and the American Enterprise Institute (Gottfried and Fleming 1988, p. 73).

Unlike more traditional conservatives, neoconservatives are not irrevocably opposed to some possible versions of a welfare state. They do not depend upon historical methodology; on the contrary, they seem to show a marked preference for quantification.

Thus, the difference between contemporary liberalism and conservatism is apparently not to be found in issues of methodology, personality, or individual items of public policy. Yet there seems to remain an ineradicable core of difference. Ultimately this must be sought in the structure of material interests on the one hand and values on the other.

Historically, conservative doctrine was formulated as an intellectual defense of feudal property rights against the onslaughts of an emerging, business-oriented, industrializing bourgeoisie. Liberalism, with its early defense of individualism, championed the enemies of conservative doctrine and properly (from its perspective) fought against dominance by a central governing authority. Subsequently (as in the case of New Deal liberalism), it discovered that the logic of unhampered individualism led to serious economic difficulties for large numbers of the population. Experiments with varieties of the welfare state since the days of Bismarck probably can all be traced in considerable measure to the fear of more drastic consequences that might follow any effort to persist in an uncontrolled laissez-faire economy.

In the contemporary world complexity has become compounded. It has probably always been the case that some people refuse to act in accordance with their own more or less self-evident material interests. These days, however, the arts of propaganda and advertising have been raised to a level of effective applied science. It is difficult for many to recognize exactly where their own self-interest lies. Beyond this, numerous techniques have been developed with the practical effect of inducing many to adopt positions in marked contrast to their own existing material interests. Government-sponsored lotteries hold out the hope of dramatic changes in class position. Tales of fabulous profits to be made in real estate or the stock market induce many to identify with the interests toward which they aspire rather than with those they hold and are likely to retain.

This is not the only source of confusion. Although many intellectuals, as well as others, having "made it," subsequently become concerned with the maintenance of an order that has been good to them (Coser 1977), there are many others who, despite coming from very well-to-do backgrounds, maintain values consistent with economic deprivation. There are indeed generous souls as well as villains to be found among adherents of both liberalism and conservatism.

The shape of values is by no means always coterminous with the shape of existing material interests. Labels like liberalism and conservatism are uncertain predictors of specific actions, as are existing material interests. A variety of social forms, or structures, can be used to serve either selfish or communally oriented values. It is these values that are ultimately more reliable auguries.

In recent years there have been efforts to develop more useful theoretical frameworks for conceptualizing value configurations and more empirically based social policy alternatives. For example, Amitai Etzioni has elaborated an "I–We" paradigm as a substitute for both "unfettered" individualism and organismic views of society (Etzioni 1988). S. M. Miller and his colleagues eschew the *liberal* label in favor of *progressive,* a term less saddled with conflicting conceptual baggage. They have provided an agenda for social policy issues requiring considerable rethinking by those unwilling to accept either contemporary conservative and neoconservative doctrine or traditional socialist formulations (Ansara and Miller 1986).

It is clear that serious linguistic difficulties serve to exacerbate the problem of distinguishing clearly between liberalism and conservatism. Each term tends to represent a generic symbol for a range of widely diversified issues, values, and interests. Surrogate expressions are used extensively in popular speech to convey either finer shades of meaning or degrees of opprobrium.

For conservatives these expressions may include "right-wing crazies," "extreme right," "right-wing," "supply-siders," "libertarians," "filthy rich," "Republicans," and others. In contemporary America, portions of the conservative spectrum voice strong opinions not only on economic issues but also on such "social" issues as pornography, abortion, and affirmative action, although opinion on these issues is by no means unanimous. Traditional conservatism would, of course, back state-supported cultural standards in speech, art, literature, and entertainment. Nineteenth-century liberalism would oppose these in the name of individual "rights." Is abortion a woman's "right" or is it an "offense" against society? Many conservatives might define it as an offense; others might well define it as a right—a traditional liberal position.

Among liberals, surrogate expressions in use include "Red," "parlor-pink," "left-liberal," "bleeding heart," "tax and spender," "Democrat," and "Progressive." The liberal spectrum tends to support rights of women to have abortions or, more generally, to maintain control over their own bodies. It opposes abrogation of rights of self-expression through pornography legislation, censorship, or other efforts to monitor art, literature, theatre, and other communication vehicles. On the other hand, American liberals favor limitations on the asserted "rights" of corporations or individual business persons to discriminate in employment, housing, and other areas on the basis of skin color, age, religion, or physical disability—property rights that many conservatives insist are inviolable.

As one might expect, survey researchers have made and continue to make strong efforts to detect empirical differences between persons who are called or who call themselves liberal or conservative. Data from a variety of survey research studies indicate that, despite the existence of important philosophical differences between liberals and conservatives, changing social and economic conditions have at times compelled them to alter their positions on certain economic, social, and political issues without altering their underlying philosophies (McCloskey and Zaller 1984, p. 191). In general, these studies seem to confirm stereotypical images of both liberals and conservatives.

Liberals show a marked preference for social progress and human betterment, especially for the poor and powerless. Some believe personal happiness and success depend heavily upon institutional arrangements. Most liberals are "inveterate reformers"; they continually look for ways to improve the human condition by remodeling social, economic, and political institutions. Underlying this pursuit of change, social reform, and benevolence is faith in the potential perfectability of human beings and their capacity to manage their own affairs in a responsible and reasoned fashion.

Conservatives have a different notion of what constitutes the good society and how it can be achieved. Survey research data show that they have a more pessimistic view of human nature and its perfectability. They feel that people need strong leaders, firm laws and institutions, and strict moral codes to keep their appetites under control. Firm adherence to conventional norms and practices is essential for human well-being. They believe that those who fail in life must bear primary responsibility for its consequences. They are far less likely than liberals to support movements that have as their objectives the eradication of poverty, the better treatment of oppressed minorities, or the alleviation of social distress generally. They maintain that these movements, by disrupting existing institutions, do more harm than good (McCloskey and Zaller 1984, pp. 190–191).

Conventional public opinion polling techniques encounter increasing difficulties in this area. Thus, one study examined a hypothesized inverse relationship between socioeconomic status and conservatism on a wide range of so-called social issues. (Many observers felt that, during the 1970s and 1980s, as well as during the late 1960s, the main support for liberal and left political parties in the United States and other Western industrialized countries came from youthful members of the upper or middle strata.) It found that, in practice, many issues defied a neat separation of interests and values or of economic versus social arenas. Many social issues such as environmental protection, nuclear power, defense spending, and race or gender problems have an economic dimension, to the extent that they influence opportunities for jobs or profits. Conversely, government domestic spending, a classic economic issue, may have a social dimension if it is seen as involving welfare or aid to minorities. No consistent relationship between socioeconomic status and conservatism was found, with one exception. Liberalism on social issues tends to increase with education, but even here the relationship varies considerably from issue to issue. The authors suggest that lack of a consistent relationship reflects both the diversity of social issues and the fuzziness of the social/economic distinction (Himmelstein and McCrae 1988).

Another study examined what appeared to be an anomaly in this area. It postulated that high socioeconomic status remains one of the best predictors of Republican party support and conservative attitudes in the United States, that Republicans are wealthier, more educated, and hold higher status jobs than Democrats and independents. Jewish liberalism, however, confounds this general relationship. American Jews are generally wealthier, better educated, and hold higher status jobs than average Americans but continue to be the most liberal white ethnic group in the United States (Lerner, Nagai, and Rothman 1989, p. 330).

The emergence of a small cadre of Jewish neoconservative intellectuals has raised questions about Jewish liberalism. A sample of Jewish elites was compared with their Gentile counterparts. The study found that Jewish elites continue to be more liberal. Despite a plethora of competing explanations, the study concludes that Jewish liberalism is a product of a family tradition of liberalism that developed in response to European conditions. Specifically, the authors suggest that the Jewish elites inherited a tradition of responding in particular ways to felt marginality. This raises the question as to whether a realignment might occur when this cohort of American Jews loses its prominence and is replaced by a cohort with different patterns of socialization. In a concluding footnote, the authors raise the open question of whether events in the Middle East and the emergence in the Democratic party of an increasingly powerful African-American presence less supportive of Israel can transform the liberalism of American Jews (Lerner, Nagai, and Rothman 1989).

A study of public opinion on nuclear power concludes that assessing public opinion through responses to survey questions with fixed categories presents serious difficulties. It compares these difficulties with those arising from the effort to "impose elite dichotomies such as 'liberal' and 'conservative' on a mass public whose beliefs are not organized by such dimensions" (Gamson and Modligani 1989, p. 36).

Perhaps the more general difficulty is not to be found solely in the insufficiency of measuring instruments but in the increasingly more truncated vistas of the "mass publics." Fundamental philosophical positions and value orientations seem to have become increasingly more obscured by the exigencies of short-range decision making.

In societies where immediate job opportunities, social pressures, and short-range profits have serious implications not only for the quality of life but also for existence itself, it is scarcely surprising to find that many public issues and even individual values are filtered through the prisms of short-run individual economic concerns and ethnic identification. Manipulating perceptions of vital interests through sophisticated media technology does much to resolve the recurrent riddle, "Is Blank a liberal—or a conservative?"

(SEE ALSO: *Attitudes; Individualism; Public Opinion; Value Theory and Research; Voting Behavior)*

REFERENCES

Ansara, Michael, and S. M. Miller 1986 "Opening Up of Progressive Thought." *Social Policy* 17:3–10.

Burke, Edmund 1855 "Reflections on the Revolution in France." In *Works,* Vol. 1. New York: Harper.

Coser, Lewis A. "Introduction." In Coser, Lewis A., and Irving Howe, eds. 1977 *The New Conservatives: A Critique from the Left.* New York: Meridian.

Etzioni, Amatai 1988 *The Moral Dimension: Toward a New Economics.* New York: Free Press.

Gamson, William A., and Andre Modigliani 1989 "Media Discourse and Public Opinion on Nuclear Power: A Constructionist Approach." *American Journal of Sociology* 95:1–37.

Girvetz, Harry K. 1966 *The Evolution of Liberalism.* New York: Collier.

Gottfried, Paul, and Thomas Fleming 1988 *The Conservative Movement.* Boston: Twayne.

Halevy, Elie (1928) 1972 *The Growth of Philosophic Radicalism,* trans. Mary Morris. London: Faber and Faber.

Himmelstein, Jerome L., and James A. McRae, Jr. 1988 "Social Issues and Socioeconomic status." *Public Opinion Quarterly* 52:492–512.

Hobhouse, L. T. (1911) 1964 *Liberalism.* New York: Oxford University Press.

Laski, Harold J. (1936) 1962 *The Rise of European Liberalism.* New York: Barnes & Noble.

Lerner, Robert, Althea K. Nagai, and Stanley Rothman 1989 "Marginality and Liberalism Among Jewish Elites." *Public Opinion Quarterly* 53:330–352.

Lovejoy, Arthur 1960 *The Great Chain of Being: A Study of the History of an Idea.* New York: Meridian.

McCloskey, Herbert, and John Zaller 1984 *The American Ethos: Public Attitudes Toward Capitalism and Democracy.* (A Twentieth Century Fund Report) Cambridge, Mass.: Harvard University Press.

Nisbet, Robert 1986 *Conservatism.* Minneapolis: University of Minnesota Press.

Tillyard, E. M. W. 1959 *The Elizabethan World Picture.* New York: Vintage.

Witonski, Peter (ed.) 1971 *The Wisdom of Conservatives,* vol. 1. New York: Arlington.

ROBERT BOGUSLAW

LIFE COURSE The study of lives represents an enduring interest of the social sciences and reflects important social changes over the twentieth century. Most notably, developments after World War II called for new ways of thinking about lives, society, and their connection. Launched in the 1920s and 1930s, pioneering longitudinal studies of children in the United States became studies of the young adult in postwar America, thereby focusing attention on trajectories that extend across specific life stages. In addition, the changing demography of society assigned greater significance to problems of aging and study of them. Insights regarding old age directed inquiry to earlier phases of life and to the process by which life patterns are shaped by a changing society.

The life course represents a concept and a theoretical perspective. As a concept, it refers to age-graded life patterns embedded in social institutions and subject to historical change. The life course consists of interlocking trajectories or pathways across the lifespan that are marked by sequences of social transitions. As a theoretical orientation, the life course has established a common field of inquiry by providing a framework that guides research in terms of problem identification and formulation, variable selection and rationales, and strategies of design and analysis.

CONCEPTUAL DISTINCTIONS

A number of concepts have been applied interchangeably to studies of life patterns (life course, life cycle, lifespan, and life history), but each makes a distinctive contribution that deserves notice in mapping the conceptual domain. The *life course* is defined by trajectories that extend across much of the life course, such as family and work; and by short-term changes or transitions, such as leaving home, getting a full-time job, and marrying (Elder 1985). Transitions are always embedded in trajectories and social arrangements that give them distinctive meaning, such as loss of a job for the young adult and the middle-aged. Interlocking trajectories and their transitions structure the individual life course, since movement across life stages entails the concurrent assumption of multiple roles. Major transitions in the life course typically involve multiple life changes, from entry into the diverse roles of adulthood (Modell 1989) to later-life changes in work, residence, and family (Hareven 1978). These transitions may also entail a sequence of phases or choice points. The transition to unwed motherhood thus involves premarital sexual experience followed by decisions not to have an abortion, not to give the child up for adoption, and not to marry the father (Furstenberg 1976). Causal influences vary across the choice points.

The social meanings of age give structure to the life course through age norms and sanctions, social timetables for the occurrence and order of events, generalized age grades (childhood, adolescence, etc.), and age hierarchies in organizational settings. In theory, a normative concept of social time specifies an appropriate time or age for marriage, childbearing, and retirement (Neugarten and Datan 1973; Lawrence 1984). Differential timing orders events (as when marriage occurs before the first child's birth) and determines the duration of waiting time between one event and the next. Empirical findings are beginning to cumulate on event timing, sequences, and durations, although the knowledge base is thin on causal mechanisms (Hogan and Astone 1986). Beyond these social distinctions, age has historical significance for the life course by locating people in historical context according to birth cohorts.

Family transitions invariably place the life course in a broader matrix of kinship relationships, one that extends beyond the boundaries of the immediate family to in-laws, parents, and grandparents. Within the life course of each generation, unexpected and involuntary events occur through life changes in related generations. Thus a fifty-year-old woman becomes a grandmother when her daughter has a first baby, and parents lose their status as son and daughter when their own parents die. Among dual-earner couples, the timing of retirement has become a family contingency as couples work out an appropriate course of action for each partner and their relationship (O'Rand, Henretta, and Krecker 1991). Synchronization of lives is central to life-course planning in families. As in the case of social age, the road map of marriage, kinship, and the generations tells family members where they have been, are, and will be.

The *life-cycle* concept is frequently used to describe a sequence of life events from birth to death, though its more precise meaning refers to a sequence of parenthood stages over the life course, from birth of the children through their departure from the home to their own childbearing (O'Rand and Krecker 1990). This sequence, it should be noted, refers to a reproductive process in human populations. Within a life cycle of generational succession, newborns are socialized to maturity, give birth to the next generation, grow old, and die. The cycle is repeated from one generation to the next, though *only* within the framework of a population. Some people do not have children and consequently are not part of an intergenerational life cycle.

The life cycle is commonly known in terms of the family cycle, a set of ordered stages of parenthood defined primarily by variations in family composition and size (Hill 1970; Elder 1977). Major transition points include marriage, birth of the first and last child, the children's transitions in school, departure of the eldest and youngest child from the home, and marital dissolution through the death of one spouse. The stages are not defined in terms of age, as a rule, and typically follow a preferred script of a marriage that bears children and survives to old age, an increasingly rare specimen in contemporary society. Moreover, as Rindfuss, Swicegood, and Rosenfeld (1987, p. 27) conclude, "understanding the nature and importance of sequence in the life course requires analyzing what the roles themselves mean and how they are causally linked." This meaning derives in large measure from knowledge of the duration and timing of events. Thus, a rapid sequence of births produces a very different family dynamic in terms of demands and pressures from that of widely dispersed births. A mother's life stage, whether she is in late adolescence or her mid-thirties, also has obvious relevance to the meaning of a birth sequence.

Lifespan specifies the temporal scope of inquiry and specialization, as in lifespan sociology or psychology. A lifespan study extends across a substantial period of life and generally links behavior in two or more life stages. Instead of limiting research to social and developmental processes within a specific life stage, a lifespan design favors studies of antecedents and consequences. Any coverage of lifespan issues necessarily brings up the meaning of *life stage.* Sociologists tend to focus on the social life course, in which life stage refers to either socially defined positions, such as the age of adolescence, or to analytically defined positions, such as the career stage of men or women at age forty. Thus, men who differ in age when they encounter work-life misfortune may be said to occupy different life stages at the time.

Developmental stages and trajectories are the foci of lifespan psychology. Examples include Erik Erikson's (1963) psychosocial stages, such as the stage of generativity. Lifespan psychology gained coherence and visibility through a series of conferences at the University of West Virginia beginning in the late 1960s (Baltes and Reese 1984). The approach is defined by a concern with the description and explanation of age-related biological and behavioral changes from birth to death. In terms of stage and rate of advance, social and developmental trajectories may show varying degrees of correspondence, such as a physical rate of maturation that does not match the athletic demands of a student's role.

Life history commonly refers to a lifetime chronology of events and activities that typically and variably combine data records on education, work life, family, and residence. These records may be generated by obtaining information from archival materials or from interviews with a respondent, as in the use of a life calendar or age–event matrix (Freedman et al. 1988). Life calendars record the age (year and month) at which transitions occur in each activity domain, and thus depict an unfolding life course in ways uniquely suited to event-history analyses and the assessment of time-varying causal influences (Featherman 1986; Mayer and Tuma 1990). Life history also refers to self-reported narrations of life, as in Thomas and Znaniecki's famous life history of Wladek in *The Polish Peasant in Europe and America* (1918–1920). Whether self-reported or collected by a research staff, life histories are products of data collection in the form of time-ordered events or accounts.

All the concepts above have a place in studies of the life course. Contemporary inquiry extends across the lifespan and frequently draws upon the life records and life cycles of successive generations. The life course takes the form of a multidimensional and intergenerational concept; a moving set of interlocking trajectories and transitions, such as work, marriage, and being parents. Within this context, misfortune and opportunity are *intergenerational* as well as life problems. Failed marriages and work lives frequently lead adult offspring back to the parental household and alter the parents' life plans for their later years. Conversely, economic setbacks and marital dissolution among the parents of adolescents may impede the children's transition to adulthood by postponing higher education and marriage. Each generation is bound to fateful decisions and events in the other's life course.

As implied by relations among these concepts, age and kinship distinctions inform a common theoretical orientation on the life course, one that defines this topic as a field of inquiry, identifies key problems, and structures research through concepts and models. The age-graded life course, timetables, and birth cohorts are central to the sociology of age and the life course. From the field of kinship comes life cycle, generation or generational position, lineage, and family time (Hagestad 1990).

In a family timetable of four generations, the number and configuration of the generations can vary sharply across a single lifespan. Consider a person born during World War I who became one of several great-grandchildren of a woman in her nineties. Three higher stations in the generational series are occupied: the parent, grandparent, and great-grandparent generations. This hierarchy continues until the great-grandmother dies, in the child's sixth year. By the time the child enters middle school, both grandparents on both sides of the family have died, producing a two-generation structure. Changes of this sort in generational position have consequences for self-identity, intergenerational obligations, and social support, but the full significance depends on the individual's historical context and life stage.

The recent convergence of age and kinship distinctions is most readily seen by describing an early phase of life study, before World War II, and comparing developments at that time with those observed since the 1960s.

LIFE COURSE STUDY IN HISTORICAL CONTEXT

The study of lives has known two eras of distinctive vitality: the phase before 1940, which is most closely identified with the early Chicago school of sociology (1915–1935), and the decades since 1960. The first era viewed lives from a kinship perspective and neglected variations in life patterns. At a time of rapid demographic and social change, studies in the second era discovered the complexity of lives and articulated for the first time a framework linking social history and social structure in the life course.

Era I: The Generations and Lives. The first wave of research interest in the life course accompanied the sociological study of problems in a rapidly changing society—waves of immigrants to cities, high rates of delinquency, and other forms of social pathology. Following the example set by Thomas and Znaniecki ([1918–1920] 1974), researchers began to use life records to study lives in changing times. Thomas (Volkart 1951, p. 593) urged that research take full advantage of the "longitudinal approach to life history." Studies, he argued, should investigate "many types of individuals with regard to their experiences and various past periods of life in different situations" and follow "groups of individuals into the future, getting a continuous record of experiences as they occur."

Thomas's approach to this record of experience had much to do with kinship and the generations and very little to do with the meanings of age, whether social or historical. The sequence of generations in *The Polish Peasant* is only loosely placed in historical time and context. Indeed, the age range of members of a particular generation may exceed thirty years. People of similar age frequently occupy very different generational positions, such as parent and grandparent. Moreover, the ages and years of emigration are not reported so that we do not know precisely when people left their homes and communities for urban destinations. From the standpoint of this study and others from that period, the sociology of age had not as yet informed the conceptual framework of life-course research.

A number of longitudinal studies launched with children born in the 1920s or earlier seemed to follow Thomas's recommendation for this type of research design. Most prominent in this effort are the Lewis Terman study of gifted Californians born between 1904 and 1920, the Oakland Growth Study of persons born in 1920 and 1921, and the Berkeley Guidance and Growth Studies of children who were born in 1928 and 1929 (see Eichorn et al. 1981). These studies were not designed to track the developmental course of children into the adult years, but they eventually did so, with data collection continuing well into the 1980s and thus capturing the later years of the respondents' lives. However, it is notable that early uses of the data did not examine the age-graded life course and its developmental effects, nor did this research explore the implications of historical change in this rapidly changing part of the twentieth century. These emphases emerged after 1960 and soon encouraged uses of the archival data that linked human development and lives to aspects of a changing society. Life patterns and the historical record were no longer unrelated fields of inquiry.

Era II: The Discovery of Variability in Lives. A major advance in life-course theory came from the generalized recognition of variability in lives by social scientists—notably Bernice Neugarten, Norman Ryder, and Matilda Riley—who were studying development, aging, and cohorts during the 1960s. There are three dimensions of this new consciousness. First, research began to report a wide variability of *age patterns* in lives. Contrary to modal views of age patterns in cultures (Eisenstadt 1956; cf. Kertzer and Keith 1984), people of the same age do not march in concert across major events of the life course; rather, they vary in pace and sequencing, and this variation has real consequences for people and society (Hogan 1981). Second, *kinship and family* emerged as a primary source of variation and regulation in life trajectories. Lives are lived interdependently among members of family and kin units. Third, the new work on aging underscored the role of *historical change* as a source of life-course variation (Baltes and Reese 1984). Important methodological issues stemmed from this recognition. If social change and aging are interrelated, then research must disentangle the different sources of age-related behavior change over the life course.

Social timing and life-course variations. During the late 1950s and early 1960s, a research program led by Bernice Neugarten (Neugarten and Datan 1973) developed a normative perspective on the life course that featured the concept of normative timetables and individual deviations from such expectations. The timetable of the life course refers to social age, as defined by people's expectations of norms regarding events. In theory, age expectations specify appropriate times for major transitions. There is an appropriate time for entering school, leaving home, getting married, having children, and retiring. Generally, departures from the usual timetable entail social and psychological consequences, from informal sanctions to lost opportunities and life-course disorder. Ever since this pioneering work and the growth of social demography, the study of differential timing and order among events has been one of the most active domains in life-course research. However, we still lack knowledge of age expectations in large populations concerning events in the life course. Study of the *normative* foundation of the life course deserves far more attention than it has received to date.

Neugarten addressed her work on the normative timetable to the individual life course, though her thinking prompted consideration of the interlocking transitions of family members. One of the clearest examples of this phenomenon comes from a study of female lineages in a black community of Los Angeles (Burton and Bengtson 1985). The birth of a child to the teenage daughter of a young mother created a large disparity between age and kinship status, between being young and facing the prospects of grandparental obligations. Four out of five mothers of young mothers actually refused to accept these new child-care obligations, shifting the burden up the generational ladder to the great-grandmother, who in many cases was carrying a heavy load. By comparison, the women who became grandmothers in their late forties or so were eager for the new role; in this lineage, a timely transition to motherhood by the daughter meant her own mother's timely transition to grandmotherhood.

The most significant integration of age and kinship distinctions among contemporary studies of the life course is found in *Of Human Bonding* (Rossi and Rossi 1990). Using a three-generation sample in the Boston region, the study investigates the interlocking nature of the life course within family systems, with particular focus on the relation between individual aging and kin-defined relationships across the lifespan. Most of the study centers on the formation, maintenance, and expression of parent–child ties, as indexed by affective closeness, association, and value consensus. Using contemporaneous and retrospective data, the study first charts patterns of aging, expressed in age concepts of self, level of energy, and goals; then examines types of kin obligations over the life course and their correlates; and concludes with a thorough study of developmental and social factors in parent–child solidarity. Among their numerous results, the authors find that affective closeness between adult children and their parents varies according to the quality of family life in childhood, the degree of shared values in adulthood, and the aging experience of the parents (good health, etc.).

Clearly, much has been achieved in conceptual models of the life course since the 1960s, but these models refer mainly to the life course worked out by the individual *within* a social system of institutionalized pathways—the life course as constructed by the individual in terms established by the larger society. Mayer (1986, p. 166) had these terms in mind when he identified key societal mechanisms "which impose order and constraints on lives," including institutional careers, the cumulative effects of delayed transitions, the collective conditions associated with particular cohorts (historical circumstances, etc.), and state intervention and regulation. The growth of the state in social regulation counters the potential fragmentation of increasing institutional differentiation. At the individual level "the state legalizes, defines, and standardizes most points of entry and exit: into and out of employment, into and out of marital status, into and out of sickness and disability, into and out of formal education. In doing so, the state turns these transitions into strongly demarcated public events and acts as a gatekeeper and sorter" (Mayer 1986, p. 167). These are elements of what Buchmann (1989, p. 28) properly calls "the public life course."

Social change and lives. Though studies of social change and life patterns had been conducted up to the 1960s as if they had little in common, this assumption was challenged by Norman Ryder's (1965) concept of the interaction of social and life history. He proposed the term *cohort* as a concept for studying the life course. With its "life stage principle," Ryder's essay provided a useful point of departure toward understanding the interplay between social change and the life patterns of age cohorts: The impact of a historical event on the life course reflects the life stage at which the change was experienced. Differences in life stage offer insight into the adaptive resources, options, and meanings that become potential elements in relating social change and life outcomes.

Ryder's essay on the bond between age and time brought more sophisticated awareness to connections between historical and individual life time and, in doing so, generated fresh insights concerning the temporal aspects of lives. Once individuals are placed in historical context, the personal impact of historical conditions must be considered. The publication of *Aging and Society* (Riley, Johnson, and Foner 1972) strengthened this sensitivity to the historical setting of birth cohorts and brought historical differentiation to notions of the age-graded life course. By relating birth cohorts and age divisions in the social structure, this volume highlights important differences between these modes of age differentiation. For example, birth cohorts do not possess the social and cultural meanings of normatively defined age divisions, and their age spans (from one year to fifteen or more) vary greatly according to historical conditions and the requirements of research. These variations raise unexplored questions concerning the interaction of historical change, cohorts, and prescribed age divisions in life patterns.

Genuine empirical study of historical influences on life patterns gained encouragement from a vigorous new wave of research that used archival data to construct life courses and life-styles in past time. For example, a sociological study of historical influences on the life course tested Ryder's life-stage principle by tracing the effects of drastic income loss in the Great Depression on the family and individual experience of two birth cohorts, one with birthdates at the beginning of the 1920s and the other with birthdates between 1928 and 1929 (Elder 1974; 1979). Consistent with the life-stage hypothesis, the younger children were more strongly influenced by family hardship than the older children, with impairment most evident in the lives of the younger boys. Though diminishing in strength over time, the difference persisted up to the middle years in work life, family relationships, and psychological functioning.

This depression study illustrates one of the ways lives can be influenced by social change: a *cohort effect.* Historical influence takes the form of a cohort effect when social change differentiates the life patterns of successive cohorts, such as the older and younger children from the 1920s. History also takes the form of a *period effect* when the influence of a social change is relatively uniform across successive birth cohorts. Secular trends in the scheduling of marriages and first births across the twentieth century are largely an expression of massive period effects. A third type of effect occurs through *maturation* or *aging.*

Unfortunately, efforts to partition the variance according to these effects have not advanced knowledge on social change in lives. Too often research does not address questions that specify a type of social change or the process by which it alters the life course. Instead, questions assign environmental change to an error term or compare multiple cohorts as a test of the generalization boundaries of behavioral outcomes. Even when history is substantively important, it may be operationalized as a period or cohort effect that provides no clue as to the precise nature of the influence. In addition, cohort comparisons restrict what is learned about the effects of social change by obscuring variations within successive cohorts. As the Great Depression study makes clear, the economic decline was not uniformly experienced by families, and not all subgroups of children were affected by family hardship in the same way. Experiential variations by subgroups within specific cohorts represent a significant conceptual distinction, as Mannheim's writings (1928) on generation units imply.

By the 1990s, the life course had become a general theoretical framework for the study of lives, human development, and aging *in a changing society.* Rapid change drew attention to historical influences and prompted the new sociological literatures on age and kinship to fashion concepts of a life course embedded in social institutions and subject to historical changes and the choices-cum-actions of individuals. This development is coupled with the continued growth of longitudinal studies and the emergence of new methodologies for the collection and analysis of the life-history data that represent time, process, and context (Freedman et al. 1988; Mayer and Tuma 1990). However, much work remains in relating lives to their changing society, a point stressed by the central themes of promising research in life-course study.

PROMISE AND CHALLENGE: CENTRAL THEMES

Despite promising cross-level developments in life-course research, most studies continue to follow one of two tracks, the macroscopic or microscopic. Explanations for life-course change often draw upon a mix of cultural, demographic, and economic factors at the macro level, but they seldom relate these structures to patterns of individual behavior. This limitation may reflect the task of linking social change and lives—a challenging venture because so little theory extends across levels and provides guidelines for causal chains. Theories are available on the macro and micro level, but one finds little guidance of this kind in connecting levels. The major challenges for life-course studies are to account for the process by which social structures and changes make a difference in life patterns, and to explain continuity and change in observed effects across the life course. Both types of accounts or explanations entail linkages in the overlapping regions of different conceptual systems, such as the individual and the interactional context and the relation between this setting and the large-scale social organization.

Empirical research has identified five mechanisms that portray some ways in which changing times affect life patterns: control cycles, situational imperatives, the accentuation principle, the life-stage distinction, and a concept of interdependent lives (Elder and Caspi 1990). The first three concern the relative fit between a changing environment and the life course, whether compatible or not. The life-stage notion, from the work of Norman Ryder (1965), refers to the individual's location within the life course when major social change occurs, such as childhood, late adolescence, or old age. The concept of interdependent lives relates all people to significant others who mediate the influence of social change.

An account of historical influence at a point in time does not explain why the effect persists in some cases and fades in others over the individual life course, as in the case of American children who grew up in the Great Depression (Elder 1974). Keeping this distinction in mind, the following discussion begins with mechanisms linking social change and life patterns, then turns to processes that account for continuity and change of influences across the life course.

Rapid social change produces a disparity between claims and the resources to achieve them, resulting in a corresponding loss of control, followed by efforts to regain control, through adaptations of one kind or another. *Control cycles,* then, refer to equilibrating processes in which losing control prompts efforts to restore control. Families in the Great Depression regained a measure of control over their situations through expenditure reductions and multiple earners (Elder 1974). Families and individuals constructed and reworked their life course through adaptations of this kind.

The influence of a social change depends in part on the behavioral requirements or demands of the new situation, called the *situational imperatives.* A long-term research program directed by Kohn and Schooler (Kohn 1969; Kohn and Schooler 1983) shows that the behavioral imperatives of work shape how men and women think and function. The most powerful imperative is occupational self-direction or autonomy; the greater the self-direction, the more workers deal with substantively complex, nonroutinized tasks that entail minimal supervision. Self-directed workers also seek out jobs that allow them substantial control. Demotions or de-skilling would lower such control and could initiate efforts to regain it through exploration of other job possibilities.

Life-course choices and behavioral adaptations are shaped by the imperatives of the new situation, and by the resources or dispositions people bring to it. *Accentuation* refers to the process by which the new situation heightens selected attributes. Explosive men become more explosive, and weak family relationships shatter under stress. To illustrate this dynamic, consider a study of personality under social catastrophe (Allport, Bruner, and Jandorf 1941). After analyzing personal documents on ninety individuals who experienced the Nazi revolution of the 1930s, the investigators observe that "very rarely does catastrophic social change produce catastrophic alterations in personality" (p. 7). On the contrary, the basic structure of personality persists despite the upset and upheaval in the total life space. Moreover, "where change does take place, it seems invariably to accentuate trends clearly present in the pre-crisis personality" (p. 8).

The *life-stage principle* supplements the accentuation dynamic by claiming that an individual's life stage at the point of social change determines whether and how the person will be influenced by the change. Children born in 1920 and 1928–1929 are cases in point. On the basis of the life-stage principle, there is reason to expect more adverse effects of family hardship among the younger children, and the results generally affirm this conclusion for boys (Elder 1979).

From a general perspective, social change is

expressed in lives through the experience of others, and this experience of *interdependent lives* (as in families, etc.) represents a primary means by which large-scale social changes affect the life course. For example, McAdam's (1989) study of adults who participated in a civil rights project during the Mississippi summer of 1964 found that organizational and social ties helped to sustain activist politics and its influence on their marital and occupational choices. This interpretation leads to questions concerning the mechanisms through which such ties facilitate continuity in political behavior. What is it about friendship continuity that sustains political continuity from adolescence to the middle years?

Caspi and Bem (1990) identify three types of interaction between person and environment over the life span—proactive, reactive, and evocative—that have particular relevance to the likelihood and nature of life-course continuity and change. *Proactive* interaction applies most directly to McAdam's finding and refers to the process by which people select rewarding or compatible environments, as in mate selection. Studies suggest that the personal stability of men and women across the life course is partly due to the stabilizing influences of marital partners and friends with whom they have much in common (Caspi and Bem 1990). This dynamic applies to the remarkable political stability of women who attended Bennington College in the 1930s and were studied by Theodore Newcomb (Alwin, Cohen, and Newcomb 1991). Conversely, social discontinuity between childhood and adult friends is a potential factor in behavioral change over this part of the life course. Sampson and Laub's (1990) follow-up of a low-income sample of delinquents and controls provides some evidence along this line. They found that adult bonds to conventional figures and lines of activity defined a route of escape from delinquency for a substantial number of the men. The puzzle is how such bonds are formed among young men with a history of antisocial behavior.

Reactive interaction refers to a situation in which different individuals encounter the same objective environment but interpret and respond to it differently. Different adaptations thereby construct different life trajectories and entail the possibility of increasing individual differences up to old age.

Evocative interaction refers to the reciprocal intermingling of behavior and personal attributes in social relationships. An individual's personality elicits distinctive responses from others, a process exemplified by affirmative responses to personal competence (Clausen 1991) and the destabilizing effects of personal irritability and explosiveness. When ill-tempered, hostile adults evoke similar behavior from others, they may learn this definition of the other (reactive interaction) and in turn become more inclined to respond explosively to any evidence of personal threat.

In summary, the flourishing area of life-course studies owes much to the general recognition that any effort to make sense of individual behavior should be informed by knowledge of (1) how lives and societal change are reciprocally linked and (2) how early events and influences persist and fade across the life course in a changing world. These lines of inquiry are interrelated in a number of respects. The impact of an ever-changing environment is central to an understanding of life-course continuity and change, whereas knowledge of such continuity enables us to interpret the full meaning of historical effects in human lives.

The two tasks also have in common the challenge of building conceptual bridges in largely uncharted territory that extends across multiple levels of analysis. At present, the wealth of theories on the macro and micro levels is not matched by theories that specify chains of influence between different levels. Little is known about the downward causation process in connecting macro change in social institutions and environments to the micro experience of individuals. Most studies of human lives continue to follow one of two tracks, the individual or the macroscopic level, although the most important future advances will be made by research that takes seriously the multiple-level, embedded, and dynamic features of the life course.

(SEE ALSO: *Health and the Life Course; Social Gerontology*)

REFERENCES

Allport, Gordon W., J. S. Bruner, and E. M. Jandorf 1941 "Personality under Social Catastrophe: Ninety Life-Histories of the Nazi Revolution." *Character and Personality* 10:1–22.

Alwin, Duane F., Ronald L. Cohen, and Theodore M. Newcomb 1991 *Aging, Personality, and Social Change: Attitude Persistence and Change over the Life-Span.* Madison: University of Wisconsin Press.

Baltes, Paul B., and Hayne W. Reese 1984 "The Life-Span Perspective in Developmental Psychology." In Marc H. Bornstein and Michael E. Lamb, eds., *Developmental Psychology: An Advanced Textbook.* Hillsdale, N.J.: Erlbaum.

Buchmann, Marlis 1989 *The Script of Life in Modern Society: Entry into Adulthood in a Changing World.* Chicago: University of Chicago Press.

Burton, Linda M., and Vern L. Bengtson 1985 "Black Grandmothers: Issues of Timing and Continuity of Roles." In Vern L. Bengtson and Joan F. Robertson, eds., *Grandparenthood.* Beverly Hills, Calif.: Sage.

Caspi, Avshalom, and Daryl J. Bem 1990 "Personality Continuity and Change across the Life Course." In Lawrence A. Pervin, ed., *Handbook of Personality: Theory and Research.* New York: Guilford Press.

Clausen, John A 1991 "Adolescent Competence and the Shaping of the Life Course." *The American Journal of Sociology* 96:805–842.

Eichorn, Dorothy H., John A. Clausen, Norma Haan, Marjorie Honzik, and Paul H. Mussen (eds.) 1981 *Present and Past in Middle Life.* New York: Academic Press.

Eisenstadt, S. N. 1956 *From Generation to Generation: Age Groups and Social Structure.* Glencoe, Ill.: Free Press.

Elder, Glen H., Jr. 1974 *Children of the Great Depression: Social Change in Life Experience.* Chicago: University of Chicago Press.

——— 1977 "Family History and the Life Course." *Journal of Family History* 2:279–304.

——— 1979 "Historical Changes in Life Patterns and Personality." In Paul B. Baltes and Otis G. Brim, Jr., eds., *Life-Span Development and Behavior,* Vol. 2. New York: Academic Press.

——— 1985 "Perspectives on the Life Course." In Glen H. Elder, Jr., ed., *Life Course Dynamics: Trajectories and Transitions, 1968–1980.* Ithaca, N.Y.: Cornell University Press.

———, and Avshalom Caspi 1990 "Studying Lives in a Changing Society: Sociological and Personological Explorations." In A. I. Rabin, Robert A. Zucker, R. Emmons, and Susan Frank, eds., *Studying Persons and Lives.* New York: Springer.

Erikson, Erik H. (1950) 1963 *Childhood and Society,* 2d ed., rev. and enl. New York: Norton.

Featherman, David L. 1986 "Biography, Society, and History: Individual Development as a Population Process." In Aage B. Sorensen, Franz E. Weinert, and Lonnie R. Sherrod, eds., *Human Development and the Life Course: Multidisciplinary Perspectives.* Hillsdale, N.J.: Erlbaum.

Freedman, Deborah, Arland Thornton, Donald Camburn, Duane Alwin, and Linda Young-DeMarco 1988 "The Life History Calendar: A Technique for Collecting Retrospective Data." *Sociological Methodology* 18:37–68.

Furstenberg, Frank F., Jr. 1976 *Unplanned Parenthood: The Social Consequences of Childbearing.* New York: Free Press.

Hagestad, Gunhild O. 1990 "Social Perspectives on the Life Course." In Robert H. Binstock and Linda K. George, eds., *Handbook of Aging and the Social Sciences,* 3d ed. New York: Academic Press.

Hareven, Tamara K. (ed.) 1978 *Transitions: The Family and the Life Course in Historical Perspective.* New York: Academic Press.

Hill, Reuben 1970 *Family Development in Three Generations.* Cambridge, Mass: Schenkman.

Hogan, Dennis P. 1981 *Transitions and Social Change: The Early Lives of American Men.* New York: Academic Press.

———, and Astone, Nan Marie 1986. "The Transition to Adulthood." *Annual Review of Sociology* 12:109–130.

Kertzer, David I., and Jennie Keith (eds.) 1984 *Age and Anthropological Theory.* Ithaca, N.Y.: Cornell University Press.

Kohn, Melvin L. (1969) 1977 *Class and Conformity: A Study in Values, with a Reassessment.,* 2d ed. Chicago: University of Chicago Press.

———, and Carmi Schooler. 1983. *Work and Personality: An Inquiry into the Impact of Social Stratification.* Norwood, N.J.: Ablex.

Lawrence, Barbara S. 1984 "Age Grading: The Implicit Organizational Timetable." *Journal of Occupational Behavior* 5:23–35.

Mannheim, Karl [1928] 1952 "The Problem of Generations." In *Essays on the Sociology of Knowledge,* trans. Paul Kecskemeti. London: Routledge and Kegan Paul.

Mayer, Karl Ulrich 1986 "Structural Constraints on the Life Course." *Human Development* 29:163–170.

——— and Nancy Brandon Tuma (eds.) 1990 *Event History Analysis in Life Course Research.* Madison: University of Wisconsin Press.

McAdam, Doug 1989 "The Biographical Consequences of Activism." *American Sociological Review* 54: 744–760.

Modell, John 1989 *Into One's Own: From Youth to Adulthood in the United States, 1920–1975.* Berkeley: University of California Press.

Neugarten, Bernice L., and Nancy Datan 1973 "Sociological Perspectives on the Life Cycle." In Paul B. Baltes and K. Warner Schaie, eds., *Life-Span Developmental Psychology: Personality and Socialization.* New York: Academic Press.

O'Rand, Angela M., John C. Henretta, and Margaret L. Krecker 1991 "Family Pathways to Retirement: Early and Late Life Family Effects on Couples' Work Exit Patterns." In Maximiliane Szinovacz, D. Ekerdt, and Barbara H. Vinick, eds., *Families and Retirement: Conceptual and Methodological Issues.* Newbury Park, Calif.: Sage.

———, and Margaret L. Krecker 1990 "Concepts of the Life Cycle: Their History, Meanings, and Uses in the Social Sciences." *Annual Review of Sociology* 16:241–262.

Riley, Matilda W., Marilyn Johnson, and Anne Foner 1972 *Aging and Society.* Vol. 3, *A Sociology of Age Stratification.* New York: Russell Sage Foundation.

Rindfuss, Ronald R., C. Gray Swicegood, and Rachel A. Rosenfeld 1987 "Disorder in the Life Course: How Common and Does It Matter?" *American Sociological Review* 52:785–801.

Rossi, Alice S., and Peter H. Rossi. 1990. *Of Human Bonding: Parent-Child Relations across the Life Course.* New York: A. de Gruyter.

Ryder, Norman B. 1965 "The Cohort as a Concept in the Study of Social Change." *American Sociological Review* 30:843–861.

Sampson, Robert J., and John H. Laub 1990 "Crime and Deviance over the Life Course: The Salience of Adult Social Bonds." *American Sociological Review* 55:609–627.

Thomas, William I., and Florian Znaniecki [1918–1920] 1974 *The Polish Peasant in Europe and America.* 2 vols. New York: Octagon.

Volkart, Edmund Howell 1951 *Social Behavior and Personality: Contributions of W. I. Thomas to Theory and Social Research.* New York: Social Science Research Council.

GLEN H. ELDER, JR.

LIFE EXPECTANCY Life expectancy (or the expectation of life) is the average length of life remaining to be lived by a population at a given age. It is computed in the process of building a life table and can be computed for any age in the life table. Life expectancy at birth is the most commonly presented value because it provides a succinct indicator of mortality that reflects mortality conditions across the age range and is unaffected by the age structure of the actual population and thus can be compared across populations. The symbol used to represent life expectancy is $\mathring{e}_x$ where x represents an exact age.

LIFE EXPECTANCY IN THE UNITED STATES

In 1989, life expectancy at birth, $\mathring{e}_0$, in the United States was 75.2 years; at age 65, $\mathring{e}_{65}$ was 17.2 years; and at age 85, $\mathring{e}_{85}$ was 6.2 years (National Center for Health Statistics 1990a). These figures can be interpreted to mean that if a baby born in 1989 were exposed to the mortality conditions existing at each age of the life span in 1989, the baby with an average length life would live 75.2 years.

PERIOD AND COHORT VALUES

The 1989 U.S. life table is a period life table, based on cross-sectional data collected over a year; thus, this life table indicates the mortality experience of a hypothetical cohort. No actual cohort ever experiences the mortality in a period or cross-sectional life table; rather, the table indicates mortality conditions if the mortality levels of each age group at the period of time used as a reference were experienced by the hypothetical cohort. Because mortality has been falling over time, period life tables for a cohort's year of birth have indicated an average expected length of life that is lower than that actually achieved by the cohort. For instance, in 1900 the cross-sectional life table for the United States showed expectations of life of forty-six for males and forty-nine for females. On the basis of actual experience to date, the 1900 birth cohort is expected to average a length of life of fifty-two years for males and fifty-eight years for females (Faber and Wade 1983).

Generation or cohort life tables, like that described for the 1900 birth cohort, based on the experience of an actual cohort, are sometimes constructed, and these indicate the average length of life actually lived after specific ages for a real cohort. The major difficulty in building cohort life tables is obtaining population and death data for a cohort from birth until the last survivors have died—over a 100-year period.

A mistaken notion held by many people is that life expectancy at birth is a good indicator of the age at which an older individual will die. This notion has undoubtedly led to some poor planning for old age because a person who has already reached older adulthood on average will die at an age that exceeds life expectancy at birth by a significant amount. Expectation of life in 1989 was 17.2 years for sixty-five-year-olds, 10.9 for seventy-five-year-olds, and 6.2 for eighty-five-year-olds. With this number of years remaining to be lived on average, sixty-five-year-olds should expect to live to eighty-two on average. Those who live to seventy-five should expect to live to almost eighty-six, and those who live to eighty-five can expect to live to ninety-one on average. While expectation of life decreases as age increases, the expected age at death increases for those who survive.

CHANGES IN LIFE EXPECTANCY OVER TIME

As noted above, life expectancy has been increasing over time. This has probably been going on since some time in the last half of the nineteenth century, although reliable data for large sections of the country are not available to track the increase before 1900. In 1900, life expectancy at birth for both sexes was 47.3 years (U.S. Bureau of the Census 1975). This indicates an increase in life expectancy between 1900 and 1989 of 27.9 years. Most of this increase in life expectancy since 1900 is due to declines in mortality among infants and children. These mortality declines were due primarily to the diminishing force of infectious and parasitic diseases, which were the most important causes of death among children.

Because life expectancy was low in the past, people often hold the mistaken notion that very few people ever reached old age under high mortality conditions. Yin and Shine (1985) have demonstrated that this mistaken notion is so prevalent that it has been commonly incorporated into gerontology textbooks. The fact is that even under conditions of low life expectancy, once childhood is survived, the chances of living to old age are quite high. This is indicated by the fact that life expectancy at the older years has not increased over time nearly as much as life expectancy at birth. For instance, while life expectancy at birth has increased almost thirty years since 1900, life expectancy for white males at age forty has increased only seven years between 1900 and 1987, from 27.7 years to 35.1 years; at age seventy, the increase for males has been slightly less than three years, from 9.0 to 11.8 (U.S. Bureau of the Census 1975; National Center for Health Statistics 1990b).

It should be noted, however, that in recent years the pace of improvement in life expectancy at the oldest ages has increased. In 1970 expectation of life for white males at age seventy was 10.5 years, indicating an improvement of 1.5 years in the seventy years between 1900 and 1970. Between 1970 and 1987, the increase was 1.3 years —almost as great as the improvement during the first seven decades of the century. This reflects the new era of mortality decline where decreases in mortality are due to decreased mortality from chronic conditions and are concentrated among the old.

CALCULATION OF LIFE EXPECTANCY

These observations about changes in life expectancy should make clear that life expectancy at birth is heavily weighted by mortality conditions at the youngest ages. A brief explanation of how life expectancy is calculated demonstrates why this is the case.

Life expectancy, or $\mathring{e}_x$, is computed from the T_x and l_x columns of the life table: $\mathring{e}_x = T_x / l_x$. T_x is the total number of years lived by the life table population after reaching age x, and l_x is the number of people surviving to exact age x in the life table population. To use a simplistic illustration, if mortality is reduced by a child surviving death early in the first year of life and then living to be seventy-five, approximately seventy-five years would be added to the total number of years lived by the population. On the other hand, if mortality declines because a person survives death at age seventy-five and then dies at eighty, only five years will be added to the total number of years lived. Thus, changes in mortality at the youngest ages have added the most to life expectancy in the past.

A number of authors have studied the relationships between changes in age-specific mortality and life expectancy. Vaupel (1986) concludes that a reduction in the force of mortality of 1 percent at all ages would not produce as much gain in life expectancy today as it did in 1900. This is because we have already made so much progress in lowering infant and child mortality. Vaupel also shows that as mortality moves to lower levels, more progress is made in increasing life expectancy from mortality declines at older ages rather than at younger ages. At the level of mortality now experienced in the United States, much of the future increase in life expectancy will come from mortality declines occurring at ages over sixty-five. This is true because of previous success in reducing mortality at earlier ages to such low levels.

DIFFERENTIALS IN LIFE EXPECTANCY

There are large differentials in life expectancy among demographic and socioeconomic groups in the United States. Males have lower life expectancies than females throughout the age range. Males' lower chances for a longer life are thought to result from a combination of biological differences and life-style factors. In 1987, $\mathring{e}_0$ was 71.5 for males and 78.4 for females (National Center for Health Statistics 1990b). By age fifty, the difference is narrowed to five years with a life expectancy of 26.0 for men and 31.0 for women. At age eighty-five, men can expect to live another 5.2 years, while women can expect to live 6.4 years.

There is also a significant difference in life expectancy between whites and blacks in the United States. This is assumed to result from the differences in socioeconomic status and accompanying life circumstances that exist between blacks and whites. In 1987, life expectancy at birth was 75.6 for whites and only 69.4 for blacks. At age sixty-five, white life expectancy was 17.0 years; while for blacks of that age, it was 15.4 years. At the oldest ages, a crossover in mortality occurs, and black life expectancy exceeds white life expectancy. In 1987 this was true at ages above eighty-three. The crossover shows up repeatedly in comparisons of black and white mortality in the United States and has been attributed to the "survival of the fittest" among the black population (Manton and Stallard 1981). Recently, however, some doubt has been raised as to whether the crossover is real or is a statistical artifact resulting from age misstatement by older blacks in both the census and vital records of deaths (Coale and Kisker 1986). Interestingly, Hispanics appear to have life expectancy values that are similar to non-Hispanic whites (Schoen and Nelson 1981).

INTERNATIONAL DIFFERENCES

The life expectancy of a country is related to its level of socioeconomic development. Most countries that are classified as "more developed" have higher levels of life expectancy at birth than most of the countries classified as "developing"; however, within each of these groups of countries there is quite a bit of variability in life expectancy. While the United States has a high level of life expectancy compared to that of the developing countries of the world, the United States ranks quite low in life expectancy among developed countries and relative to its income level. A recent United Nations listing of the developed countries by level of life expectancy at birth ranks U.S. males as fifteenth and U.S. females as eighth (United Nations 1982). The countries with higher life expectancy for women include Japan and the Scandinavian countries. For men, most European countries including some in southern Europe have higher life expectancies at birth than the United States. The low ranking of the United States is attributed, in part, to the inequities in mortality among subgroups of the population, especially the high level among blacks, and also to the high level of violent deaths. In recent years Japan has become the world leader in life expectancy at birth, with values of $\mathring{e}_0$ of 75.6 for men and 81.4 for women in 1987 (Ogawa 1989). These values exceed 1987 U.S. values by 4.1 years for men and 3.0 years for women. The success of the Japanese in raising their levels of life expectancy has been due to large declines in mortality from cerebrovascular disease and maintenance of low levels of heart disease relative to other developed countries (Yanagishita and Guralnik 1988).

RELATED CONCEPTS

There are some concepts that are related to life expectancy and sometimes confused with life expectancy. One is *lifespan.* The lifespan of a species is the age to which the longest-lived members survive. The lifespan of humans is thought to be approximately 115 years. Reports of longer-lived humans, while widely circulated, have not been documented. Current thinking is that while life expectancy has increased dramatically over the last century, the lifespan of humans has not changed over time; however, this does not mean it will never change. If future discoveries enable us to retard the aging process, it may be possible to lengthen the human lifespan in the future.

Life endurancy is another related concept that is computed from the life table. This is the age at which a specified proportion of the life table entry cohort is still alive. For instance, in 1990 the age at which ten percent of the life table population remains alive is expected to be ninety years for men and ninety-six years for women. Life endurancy has been increasing over time and is expected to continue to change with changes in survival rates. In 1900 the 10-percent survival age was eighty-one for men and eighty-two for women (Faber and Wade 1983).

Finally, *total life expectancy* at any age is the sum of two parts: *active life expectancy* and *inactive life expectancy.* Active life expectancy has been interpreted by some to mean average length of life free of dependency on others for the performance of basic activities necessary to living, such as eating, bathing, getting in and out of bed, and so forth (Katz et al. 1985; Rogers, Rogers, and Belanger 1989). Others have interpreted active life expectancy as average length of life free from a disability that causes a person to alter his or her normal activity (Wilkins and Adams 1983; Bebbington 1988; Crimmins, Saito, and Ingegneri 1989; Colvez et al. 1986). Crimmins, Saito, and Ingegneri (1989) estimated that active life expectancy or disability-free life expectancy at birth in the United States in 1980 was 55.5 years for men and 60.4 years for women. The difference between blacks and whites in disability-free life expectancy at birth was even greater than the difference in total life expectancy. In 1980 black disability-free life expectancy was 49.1 years, while that for whites was 56.2 years.

Interest in active life expectancy has grown recently as people have recognized that gains in total life expectancy today may not mean the same thing as in the past. Past gains in life expectancy came about largely because fewer people died of infectious diseases, either because they did not get the diseases or they received treatment that prevented death. People thus saved from death were generally free of the disease. Under these circumstances gains in life expectancy were accompanied by better health in the population surviving. Now, with gains in life expectancy being made because of declining death rates from chronic diseases especially among the old, it is not clear that the surviving population is a healthier population. This is because generally there is no cure for the chronic diseases, and their development has not been prevented. People are being saved from death, but they live with disease. This is the basis for questioning whether the additions to life expectancy are healthy or unhealthy years. Studies that have addressed the issue of changes in active life expectancy over time have reported that while life expectancy has definitely increased in recent years, active life expectancy has not increased (Wilkins and Adams 1983; Crimmins, Saito, and Ingegneri 1989).

(SEE ALSO: *Birth and Death Rates; Demography*)

REFERENCES

Bebbington, A. C. 1988 "The Expectation of Life Without Disability in England and Wales." *Social Science and Medicine* 27:321–326.

Coale, A. J., and E. E. Kisker 1986 "Mortality Crossovers: Reality or Bad Data?" *Population Studies* 40:389–401.

Colvez, A., J. M. Robine, D. Bucquet, F. Hatton, B. Morel, and S. Lelaidier. "L'espérance de vie sans incapacité en France en 1982." *Population* 41: 1,025–1,042.

Crimmins, E. M., Y. Saito, and D. Ingegneri 1989 "Changes in Life Expectancy and Disability-Free Life Expectancy in the United States." *Population and Development Review* 15:235–267.

Faber, J., and A. Wade 1983 *Life Tables for the United States: 1900–2050.* Actuarial Study No. 89. Baltimore: U.S. Department of Health and Human Services, Social Security Administration, Office of the Actuary.

Katz, S., L. Branch, M. Branson, J. Papsidero, J. Beck, and D. S. Greer 1985 "Active Life Expectancy." *New England Journal of Medicine* 309:1,218–1,224.

Manton, K. G., and E. Stallard 1981 "Methods for Evaluating the Heterogeneity of Aging Processes in Human Populations Using Vital Statistics Data: Explaining the Black/White Mortality Crossover by a Model of Mortality Selection." *Human Biology* 53:47–67.

National Center for Health Statistics 1990a "Annual Summary of Births, Marriages, Divorces, and Deaths: United States, 1989." *Monthly Vital Statistics Report.* 38(13). Hyattsville, Md.: U.S. Public Health Service.

——— 1990b *Vital Statistics of the United States, 1987.* Vol. 2, *Mortality,* Part A. Washington, D.C.: U.S. Public Health Service.

Ogawa, N. 1989 "Population Aging and Its Impact Upon Health Resource Requirements at Government and Familial Levels in Japan," *Ageing and Society* 9:383–405.

Rogers, R., A. Rogers, and A. Belanger 1989 "Active Life among the Elderly in the United States: Multistate Life Table Estimates and Population Projections." *The Milbank Quarterly* 67:370–411.

Schoen, R., and V. Nelson 1981 "Mortality by Cause among Spanish Surnamed Californians, 1969–1971." *Social Science Quarterly* 62:259–274.

United Nations 1982 *Levels and Trends of Mortality since 1950.* New York: United Nations.

U.S. Bureau of the Census 1975 *Historical Statistics of the U.S., Colonial Times to 1970, Bicentennial Edition,* Part 2. Washington, D.C.: U.S. Government Printing Office.

Vaupel, J. 1986 "How Change in Age-Specific Mortality Affects Life Expectancy." *Population Studies* 40:147–157.

Wilkins, R. and O. Adams 1983 "Health Expectancy in Canada, Late 1970's: Demographic, Regional, and Social Dimensions." *American Journal of Public Health* 73:1073–1080.

Yanagishita, M. and J. Guralnik 1988 "Changing Mortality Patterns That Led Life Expectancy in Japan to Surpass Sweden's: 1972–1982." *Demography* 25:611–624.

Yin, P., and M. Shine 1985 "Misinterpretations of Increases in Life Expectancy in Gerontology Textbooks." *The Gerontologist* 25:78–82.

EILEEN M. CRIMMINS

LIFE HISTORIES The life history approach to social research and theory subsumes several methodological techniques and types of data. These include case studies, interviews, use of documents (letters, diaries, archival records), oral histories, and various kinds of narratives. The popularity of this approach has waxed and waned since the early 1900s. It was used extensively in the 1920s and 1930s and was identified with the Chicago sociology of W. I. Thomas, Robert Park, Clifford Shaw, and others. The succeeding generation witnessed the solidification of quantitative measurement techniques coupled with survey data collection, and the increased use of those approaches paralleled a relative decrease in life history research. In the 1970s, however, there began a resurgence of interest in life history research not only in the United States but in Europe. The work of some sociologists, such as Howard S. Becker and Anselm Strauss, has maintained the early Chicago tradition, while newer generations of scholars such as Norman Denzin and Michal McCall (United States), Ken Plummer (England), Daniel Bertaux (France), and Fritz Schütze (Germany) have augmented life history research. This resurgence has been accompanied by the creation of Research Committee 38 (Biography and Society) of the International Sociological Association in the late 1970s and has included a broadened interdisciplinary base through the incorporation of narrative theory and methods from other disciplines. In that broadened use there has been a transition from the approach as purely a methodological device to one of both method and substance. It is that transition that frames this essay.

The main assumptions of this approach are that the actions of individuals and groups are simultaneously emergent and structured and that individual and group perspectives must be included in the data used for analysis. Accordingly, any materials that reveal those perspectives can and should be regarded as essential to the empirical study of human social life. Life history materials, as described above (see Denzin 1989a, chap. 8; Plummer 1983, chap. 2; Gottschalk, Kluckhohn, and Angell 1945), contain first-, second-, and third-order accounts of past actions as well as plans and expectations regarding future actions. Those materials will reveal significant information concerning the author's (writer or speaker) meanings. Invariably, those materials pertain also to the processual character of social life, and thus there is a major emphasis on temporal properties such as sequence, duration, and tempo. These assumptions and emphases have been characteristic of the vast majority of life history studies.

The first major empirical study in American sociology that systematically combined explicit theory and method was Thomas and Znaniecki's *The Polish Peasant in Europe and America* (1918–20). Their purpose was to investigate Polish immigrants in America, especially their problems in adjusting to American urban life, and they used their famous attitude–value scheme as an explanatory framework. Attitudes referred to individual subjective meanings and values to objective societal conditions, and they proposed a set of causal explanations based on how the relations of attitudes and values were interpreted by individuals and groups. In their five-volume, 2,200-page book, they presented almost 800 pages of life history data in support of their conclusions and generalizations. Those data included newspaper articles, letters to family members, records from courts and social work agencies, and a 300-page biography of one person that was presented as a representative case (Blumer 1939).

This research, which the Social Science Research Council in 1938 voted as the most outstanding in sociology to that date, depended solely on life history data. Because of its systematic incorporation of theory and method, it stimulated and became an examplar for a long series of similar studies. These included research on race relations, delinquency, housing, mass media, migration, occupations, and other issues centered primarily in the areas of ethnic and urban studies (Bulmer 1984). The emphasis during this period was on the contributions of life history methods to sociology as an empirical and scientific discipline. Accordingly, researchers using this approach focused on methodological problems such as reliability, validity, hypothesis formation, and making generalizations, although comparatively less concern was given to sampling (Gottschalk, Kluckhohn, and Angell 1945). Reflecting the major issue of pre–World War II sociological work, the focus was on the adequacy of this approach for discovering law-like behavior or empirically valid generalizations. The emphasis, in short, was on the approach as a research tool.

The developments in this approach since the early 1970s, perhaps stimulated in part by the increased interest in historical sociology and in part by the articulation of insoluble problems in statistical approaches, have been more interdisciplinary, international, and sophisticated than the early works (McCall and Wittner 1990; Jones 1983; Roth 1987). It is increasingly recognized that all social science data, whether represented in discursive or numeric forms, are interpretations (Denzin 1989b; Gephart 1988). That recognition is one of the central tenets of the narrative approach to social research (Fisher 1987; Reed 1989; Richardson 1990), which makes the ontological claim that human beings inherently are storytellers. This shift in emphasis concerning the subject matter of sociology, in which human behavior is conceptualized as significantly communicative and narrative in nature, is precisely what has reframed the utility and potential of the life history approach.

Current uses of life history research display considerable variation as well as more precise conceptual distinctions. Terms such as *life story, biography, discourse, history, oral history, personal experience narratives, collective narratives,* and *sagas* are now distinguished from one another (Denzin 1989a, pp. 184–187), and frameworks for linking types of verbal accounts to types of generalizations have been developed (Sperber 1985, pp. 9–34). Moreover, these developments have occurred within and across different theoretical approaches and disciplines.

It is now common to regard life histories as a legitimate form of data in which their currency are established through the propositions contained in narrative theory. Some of the uses found in contemporary work include the following. Schütze (1983) has developed what he calls the narrative interview. This approach focuses on establishing event sequences across the life course on the basis of interview data. These sequences are derived from detailed analyses of biographical materials with special attention to the structural factors that have shaped the person's life. Analytical summaries are developed and, through analytical inductive procedures, are compared to subsequently developed summaries. The goal is to produce theoretical interpretations centering on various analytical interests such as life course transitions, career models, or natural histories. Riemann and Schütze (1991) provide a substantive application of this method in the area of chronic illness.

Bertaux (1981; Bertaux and Kohli 1984) has long been an advocate of life history research and has been the primary organizer of the Biography and Society Section of the International Sociological Association. He has conducted a number of projects that have goals similar to those of Schütze. His collaborative research on social movements (1990), for example, used life history data from members of students movements in the United States, England, Ireland, Italy, West Germany, and France. There he shows the application of the method in large-scale comparative research projects. The epistemological approach was to gather data on lived, biographical experiences of the activists but to analyze those data in collective, generic terms. That is, his strategy was to focus on similarities rather than differences across nations, to ground empirically theoretical statements about, for example, processes of commitment to social-movement ideologies. The contention of this research is that biographical and life history data from ordinary people will reveal those similarities and thus make contributions to cross-national research.

Dolby-Stahl (1989), a folklorist, has developed a variation of the life history approach she calls "literary folkloristics," which focuses on personal narrative data. She uses reader response theory to develop an interpretive method for studying the interdependence of personal narratives (stories) and collective narratives (e.g., ethnic group folklore). Her procedures entail locating the respondent (storyteller) in large collectivities (e.g., single parents), identifying salient themes (e.g., day care), and connecting personal to collective narratives (e.g., the respondent's accounts of day care and media or community accounts). The assumption of this approach is that personal and collective narratives are inherently connected, and thus a personal story is always in some way a collective story. Further, the assumption that the researcher in varying ways is part of the collective story requires facing the interpretive nature of data collection. In this respect, the researcher draws on her own shared cultural experiences to analyze the life history or narrative data provided by the respondent. These procedures locate the life history approach squarely in interpretive social theory, in which credible interpretation is the goal as opposed to, say, producing explanations justified by measures of reliability and validity.

Similarily, Denzin (1989b) has developed an interpretive approach that draws conceptually from postmodernism and phenomenology and methodologically from Clifford Geertz's advocacy of thick description. He calls his method "interpretive biography," which is designed to study the turning points or problematic situations people find themselves in during transition periods. Data include documents, obituaries, life histories, and personal experience stories, with the emphasis on how such information is read and used. The basic question he asks concerns how people live and give meaning to their lives and capture those meanings in written, narrative, and oral forms. His approach thus addresses an enduring problem in sociology, which C. Wright Mills located at the intersection of biography and history, and the newer problem articulated by interpretive theories regarding the interpretations of texts, cultural forms, and personal acts.

All social science data are made up of human interpretations, and nearly all such data are reconstructions or representations of past events and experiences. Through developing techniques for gathering, coding, and analyzing explicitly reconstructive data, the life history approach is not only suitable for studying the subjective phases of social life but the historical and structural aspects as well. It can be used for a wide variety of topics and purposes, ranging from research on the trajectories of personal biographies to organizational functioning to migration patterns. It invariably leads to theories emphasizing social processes. Life history research is complemented by the newer statistical methods of event history analysis (Allison 1984) but has the advantage of a close linking of methodological procedures to a theory of action. That link is the most clearly and explicitly seen in the recent work on narrative and society. That work represents a revival of life history research among American and European social scientists and has contributed to the interdisciplinary nature of sociology.

(SEE ALSO: *Case Studies; Qualitative Methods*)

REFERENCES

Allison, Paul 1984 *Event History Analysis: Regression for Longitudinal Event Data.* Newbury Park, Calif.: Sage.

Bertaux, Daniel (ed.) 1981 *Biography and Society: The Life-History Approach in the Social Sciences.* London: Sage.

——— 1990 "Oral History Approaches to an International Social Movement." In Else Øyen, ed., *Comparative Methodology: Theory and Practice in International Social Research.* London: Sage.

———, and Martin Kohli 1984 "The Life-Story Approach: A Continental View." *Annual Review of Sociology* 10:149–167.

Blumer, Herbert 1939 *An Appraisal of Thomas and Znaniecki's "The Polish Peasant in Europe and America."* New York: Social Science Research Council.

Bulmer, Martin 1984 *The Chicago School of Sociology.* Chicago: University of Chicago Press.

Denzin, Norman 1989a *The Research Act.* Englewood Cliffs, N.J.: Prentice-Hall.

——— 1989b *Interpretive Biography.* Newbury Park, Calif.: Sage.

Dolby-Stahl, Sandra 1989 *Literary Folkloristics and the Personal Narrative.* Bloomington: Indiana University Press.

Fisher, Walter 1987 *Human Communication as Narrative.* Columbia: University of South Carolina Press.

Gephart, Robert 1988 *Ethnostatistics: Qualitative Foundations for Quantitative Research.* Newbury Park, Calif.: Sage.

Gottschalk, Louis, Clyde Kluckhohn, and Robert Angell 1945 *The Use of Personal Documents in History, Anthropology, and Sociology.* New York: Social Science Research Council.

Jones, Gareth 1983 "Life History Methodology." In Gareth Morgan, ed., *Beyond Method: Strategies for Social Research.* Beverely Hills, Calif.: Sage.

McCall, Michal, and Judith Wittner 1990 "The Good News About Life History." In Howard S. Becker and Michal McCall, eds., *Symbolic Interaction and Cultural Studies.* Chicago: University of Chicago Press.

Plummer, Ken 1983 *Documents of Life.* London: Allen and Unwin.

Reed, John Sheldon 1989 "On Narrative and Sociology." *Social Forces* 68:1–14.

Richardson, Laurel 1990 "Narrative and Sociology." *Journal of Contemporary Ethnography* 19:116–135.

Riemann, Gerhard, and Fritz Schütze 1991 "Trajectory as a Basic Theoretical Concept for Analyzing Suffering and Disorderly Social Processes." In David R.

Maines, ed., *Social Organization and Social Processes: Essays in Honor of Anselm Strauss.* Hawthorne, N.Y.: Aldine de Gruyter.

Roth, Paul 1987 *Meaning and Method in the Social Sciences.* Ithaca, N.Y.: Cornell University Press.

Schütze, Fritz 1983 "Biographieforschung und narratives Interview." *Neue Praxis* 3:283–293.

Sperber, Dan 1985 *On Anthropological Knowledge.* Cambridge: Cambridge University Press.

Thomas, W. I., and Florian Znaniecki 1918–20 *The Polish Peasant in Europe and America,* 5 vols. Chicago: University of Chicago Press.

DAVID R. MAINES

LIFE-STYLES AND HEALTH Life-styles are a major determinant of who shall live and who shall die (Fuchs 1974). Mechanic (1978, p. 164) argues that the concept of life-styles refers to a diverse set of variables, including nutrition, housing, health attitudes and beliefs, risk-taking behavior, health behavior and habits, and preventive health behavior.

Establishing the causal linkage between life-styles and health is not a simple task. Variables included in life-styles interact with each other (Mechanic 1978), making it difficult to separate out their unique contributions to health and illness. There is a need to adjust for confounding variables such as race, gender, education, and psychological distress.

In addition, there are problems in specifying the nature of the etiological relationship between life-styles and disease. Not every person who engages in an unhealthy life-style will die prematurely. For example, some heavy smokers do not develop lung cancer. Genetic predisposition, comorbidities, other health habits, and access to adequate medical care are factors that may intervene in the relationship between host and disease.

The most convincing models of the relationship between life-styles and health are those built on triangulated evidence from animal, clinical, and epidemiological studies. As an example, consider the link between tobacco use and cancer. In experimental animal studies, one group of animals is exposed to tobacco smoke while the control group is not. If the experimental group has a higher incidence of cancer than the control group, the study provides evidence to link smoking with cancer. Another strategy involves clinical studies. Lung tissue of smokers is compared with lung tissue of nonsmokers. If more smokers than nonsmokers show cancerous cells in the lung tissue, this provides additional data to confirm that smoking causes lung cancer. A final strategy uses epidemiological methods. In prospective studies, separate groups of smokers and nonsmokers are followed over time to establish the risk of developing cancer. If, all else being equal, members of the smoking group develop more cases of cancer, the causal relationship between smoking and cancer is confirmed.

With these methodological issues in mind, three behaviors are selected to illustrate how life-styles impact on health: tobacco use, alcohol consumption, and diet. For these three variables there are extensive animal, clinical, and epidemiological data to support the causal relationship between each agent and disease. Illustrations are provided to indicate how healthy habits can reduce mortality rates.

TOBACCO USE

Tobacco use has been defined as the most important single preventable cause of disease and death in society. It is responsible for more than one of every six deaths in the United States. Tobacco use kills more than 390,000 Americans annually (Office of Smoking and Health 1989). According to Warner, "Thirty percent of all cancer deaths are attributable to smoking, as are 21% of all coronary heart disease deaths, 18% of stroke deaths, and 82% of deaths from chronic obstructive pulmonary disease" (1989, p. 142).

Careful epidemiological studies have determined that tobacco use causes lung, laryngeal, lip, and esophageal cancer. Tobacco use is also associated with coronary artery disease, chronic bronchitis, cerebrovascular disease, emphysema, and low birth weight (Office of Smoking and Health 1989). In addition, smoking has been linked to cancer of the cervix, pancreas, and liver. There is new evidence that women who smoke at the time of conception have an increased risk for an ectopic pregnancy (Chow et al. 1988; Coste, Job-Spira, and Fernandez 1991).

Passive smoking is also associated with increased rates of illness (Center for Disease Control 1988). Increased risks for lung cancer and heart disease are reported for nonsmokers who live with smokers (Sandler et al. 1989). Children exposed to parental smoking have a greater risk for wheezy bronchitis (Neuspiel et al. 1989).

ALCOHOL

The National Institute on Alcohol Abuse and Alcoholism (1990) estimates that alcohol use is responsible for 100,000 deaths each year in this country. Half of the motor vehicle fatalities in 1987 were alcohol related (National Highway Traffic Safety Administration 1988). Alcohol has frequently been implicated in suicides, falls, drownings, and fires and burns (NIAAA 1990).

From 10 to 20 percent of heavy drinkers develop cirrhosis of the liver, which was the ninth leading cause of death in the United States in 1987 (Grant, Dufour, and Harford 1988). The liver is the primary site of alcohol metabolism, and drinkers are at risk for other forms of liver disease, including alcoholic hepatitis and cancer.

Chronic alcohol consumption may cause damage to the heart muscle, heart arrhythmias, and hypertension. There is suggestive evidence that alcohol may relate to ischemic heart disease and cerebrovascular illness (Moore and Pearson 1986). Alcohol abuse is also a risk factor for cancer of the liver, breast, esophagus, nasopharynx, and larynx (Driver and Swann 1987; Freudenheim and Graham 1989). NIAAA concludes: "The range of medical consequences of alcohol abuse is both immense and complex—virtually no part of the body is spared the effects of excessive alcohol consumption" (1990, p. 127).

Alcohol also functions as a teratogen, producing defects in the human fetus in utero. The possible effects of alcohol on the fetus include gross morphological defects and cognitive/behavioral dysfunctions. Fetal alcohol syndrome is the most severe consequence of the mother's heavy drinking during pregnancy and is characterized by craniofacial anomalies, mental retardation, central nervous system dysfunction, and growth retardation (Jones and Smith 1973; Rosett 1980; Abel and Sokol 1986). Fetal alcohol syndrome is one of the leading preventable causes of birth defects.

DIET

Dietary factors have been linked to mortality from cardiovascular disease and cancer. It is estimated that diet contributes to up to one-third of cardiovascular deaths (Milio 1986) and up to 35 percent of all deaths from cancer (Doll and Peto 1981).

Among men, diet-related cancer occurs in the colon or rectum and the prostate. Among women, cancer of the breast, colon/rectum, and uterine corpus have been found to be related to diet (Schatzkin, Baranovsky, and Kessler 1988). Diets with high levels of saturated fats are related to cancer of the colon and rectum. Further, there is evidence that a high-vegetable-fiber diet may help to prevent colon cancer. Fat intake may be related to breast cancer, although the evidence is conflicting. There are some data to support the hypothesis that fat intake increases the risk of lung cancer (controlling for smoking levels), prostate cancer, and bladder cancer (Freudenheim and Graham 1989).

The relationship between diet and coronary heart disease is well established (Fraser 1968). Dietary practices that increase the levels of serum lipids and lipoproteins increase the rate of coronary heart disease. Individuals whose diets are high in saturated fats and cholesterol have a higher risk for myocardial infarction. There is some recent evidence that oatmeal and oat bran may reduce cholesterol levels, which in turn may lower the risk of heart disease (Humble 1991).

HEALTHY HABITS

The Alameda County Study (Berkman and Breslow 1983) illustrates how healthy habits may increase life expectancy. The authors followed 4,700 persons for nine years and found that five health practices prolonged life expectancy: never smoking, exercising regularly, drinking alcohol in moderation, being of average weight for height, and sleeping seven or eight hours a day. Women who engaged in all these healthy practices had an adjusted mortality rate of 3.9/100 compared with 11.9/100 for women who engaged in none to two of these practices. The comparable rates for men were 5.8/100 and 16.0/100. These differences persisted after controlling for perceived health status, socioeconomic factors, and psychological characteristics. These healthy practices lowered the mortality rate for heart disease, cancer, and cerebrovascular disease.

Three examples were selected to illustrate the role of life-styles in health. There are other life-style components that are related to health which are beyond the scope of this chapter. For example, stressful life-styles have been linked to mental illness, gastrointestinal disorders, and heart disease. Regular use of seat belts reduces the likelihood of death or injury in automobile accidents. Proper dental hygiene decreases the rate of dental caries. Childhood immunizations prevent measles, mumps, and polio.

It must be emphasized that while a healthy life-style may be a necessary condition for longevity, it is not a sufficient condition. Many variables interact with life-styles to protect against disease and death. For example, evidence is mounting that genetics has a very important role in the risk for heart disease and cancer. Thus, the models predicting who shall live and who shall die involve complicated interactions of health practices, genetic risk, sociodemographic characteristics, and so on. Nonetheless, individuals who abstain from smoking, drink alcohol in moderation, and watch dietary fat and cholesterol intake have a better chance of survival than those who do not.

(SEE ALSO: *Alcohol; Drug Abuse; Health and the Life Course; Health Promotion*)

REFERENCES

Abel, Ernest L., and Robert J. Sokol 1986 "Fetal Alcohol Syndrome Is Now Leading Cause of Mental Retardation." *Lancet* ii:1222.

Berkman, Lisa F., and Lester Breslow 1983 *Health and Ways of Living: The Alameda County Study.* New York: Oxford University Press.

Center for Disease Control 1988 "Passive Smoking: Beliefs, Attitudes, and Exposures, United States, 1986." *Morbidity Mortality Weekly Review* 37:239–241.

Chow, W. H., J. R. Daling, N. S. Weiss, and L. F. Voigt 1988 "Smoking and Tubal Pregnancy." *Obstetrics and Gynecology* 71:167–170.

Coste, Joel, Nadine Job-Spira, and Herve Fernandez 1991 "Increased Risk of Ectopic Pregnancy with Maternal Cigarette Smoking." *American Journal of Public Health* 81:199–201.

Doll, R., and R. Peto 1981 "The Causes of Cancer: Quantitative Estimates of Avoidable Risks of Cancer in the U.S. Today." *Journal of the National Cancer Institute* 66:1193–1308.

Driver, H. E., and P. F. Swann 1987 "Alcohol and Cancer (Review)." *Anticancer Research* 7:309–320.

Fraser, G. 1968 *Preventive Cardiology.* New York: Oxford University Press.

Freudenheim, Jo L., and Saxon Graham 1989 "Toward a Dietary Prevention of Cancer." *Epidemiologic Reviews* 11:229–235.

Fuchs, Victor 1974 *Who Shall Live? Health Economics and Social Change.* New York: Basic Books.

Grant, B. F., M. C. Dufour, and T. C. Harford 1988 "Epidemiology of Alcoholic Liver Disease." *Seminars in Liver Disease* 8:12–25.

Humble, Charles G. 1991 "Oats and Cholesterol: The Prospects for Prevention of Heart Disease." *American Journal of Public Health* 81:159–160.

Jones, K. L., and A. W. Smith 1973 "Recognition of the Fetal Alcohol Syndrome in Early Infancy." *Lancet* i:1267–1271.

Mechanic, David 1978 *Medical Sociology,* 2nd ed. New York: Free Press.

Milio, N. 1986 *Promoting Health Through Public Policy.* Ottawa: Canadian Public Health Association.

Moore, R. D., and T. A. Pearson 1986 "Moderate Alcohol Consumption and Coronary Artery Disease: A Review." *Medicine* 65:242–267.

National Highway Traffic Safety Administration, National Center for Statistics 1988 *Drunk Driving Facts.* Washington, D.C.: NHTSA.

National Institute on Alcohol Abuse and Alcoholism 1990 *Seventh Special Report to the U.S. Congress on Alcohol and Health.* DHHS Pub. no. (ADM) 90–1656. Rockville, Md.: U.S. Department of Health and Human Services.

Neuspiel, Daniel R., David Rush, Neville R. Butler, Jean Golding, Polly Bijur, and Matthew Kurzon 1989 "Parental Smoking and Post-Infancy Wheezing in Children: A Prospective Cohort Study." *American Journal of Public Health* 79:168–171.

Office of Smoking and Health 1989 *Reducing the Health Consequences of Smoking: 25 Years of Progress. A Report to the Surgeon General.* DHHS Pub. no. (CDC) 89-8411. Washington, D.C.: U.S. Department of Health and Human Services.

Rosett, Henry L. 1980 "A Clinical Perspective of the Fetal Alcohol Syndrome." *Alcoholism* (New York) 4:119–122.

Sandler, Dale P., George W. Comstock, Knud J. Helsing, and David L. Shore 1989 "Deaths from All Causes in Non-Smokers Who Lived with Smokers." *American Journal of Public Health* 79:163–167.

Schatzkin, Arthur, Anne Baranovsky, and Larry G. Kessler 1988 "Diet and Cancer: Evidence from Associations of Multiple Primary Cancers in the SEER Program." *Cancer* 62:1451–1457.

Warner, Kenneth E. 1989 "Smoking and Health: A 25-Year Perspective." *American Journal of Public Health* 79:141–143.

JANET HANKIN

LINGUISTICS *See* Sociolinguistics.

LITERATURE In everyday usage literature is the telling, writing, and acting out of stories. In all-encompassing terms, it includes essays, biographies, memoirs, and the many varieties of oral or written expression that use language to represent fact or fantasy. These forms are created through mutual acts of individuals and groups who are the "authors" or initiators, the "agents" or facilitators, and "audiences" or responders. Literature is embedded in the basic process of communication and thus serves pervasive social needs. No human society exists without some form of it. For that reason the conscious practice and study of literature has been evident in ancient as well as modern societies, although the sociology of literature as a social scientific specialty has had difficulty in acquiring a firm place among the dominant fields of sociological enterprise.

As one of the major arts such as music, painting, and dance—all of them creative forms of symbolic expression inherent in the cultural patterning of human groups—literature has not been the subject of intensive theoretical or empirical scrutiny as have been the so-called primary social institutions of the family, religion, and education. Such invidious disregard of literature has been more typical of American than of British and European sociology. However, in recent years the parochial boundaries have been breached, and the publication of review articles, theoretical and pragmatic studies, and experimental research have proliferated on both sides of the Atlantic.

The sociology of literature derives from several deceptively simple assumptions: Literature reflects the values and experiences of society and implicitly functions to control and generate social action. A vast body of information and controversy has developed from these basic formulations since some shrewd and naive extraliterary connections were made around 1800 by Madame de Stael between climate and melancholia, religion and national character, and women's status and the novel (Swingewood 1972, p. 27). However, classical Greek philosophers had established the grounds for relationships between social and aesthetic domains. On the one hand was Plato's hostility to poets and their artifices because he saw them as the corrupters of truth by emotional arousal. That view of poets and other artists in *The Republic* has carried over into contemporary battles between the guardians of law and propriety and the irreverent or imaginative writers who may be imprisoned or condemned to death for offending holy writ. On the other hand, Aristotle devised rules for judging the nature and value of tragedy in *The Poetics* without invoking such drastic sanctions.

That ancient quarrel between poets and philosophers still reverberates in contemporary clashes between "the two cultures" (Snow 1959)—the sciences and the humanities: Literature is often regarded as too value-laden for the natural scientist, and science is seen as too pragmatic for the artist. Although there has been "some degree of convergence" between the physical and cultural sciences (Wolff 1977, p. 18), many partisans still are unreconciled. These conflicts have to do with the protean qualities of literature, whose essence is defended as inviolable by poets and their aesthetic cohorts.

DEFINITIONS AND AMERICAN APPROACHES

Most studies have focused on those novels, poetry, plays, and other imaginative works that have endured passing fame. The label of "literature" generally is not applied to books produced for mass audiences or to nonfiction such as biography, history, memoirs, or essays. However, the ecumenical ideal in sociology or in other value-neutral disciplines does not exclude lowbrow or personal forms of writing. More interdisciplinary groups, conferences, and journals concerned with popular culture, science and the arts, and literature and politics have broken through the taste-leaders' barriers. Herbert Gans's support for vernacular culture (1985), Harold Wilensky's evidence of how mass culture has penetrated into high and middle class behavior (1964), and Ariel Dorfman's uncovering of American culture traits through analysis of Babar and the Lone Ranger (1983) are illustrative of the growing attention being given to the profane as well as the sacred arts.

The forms of factual or fanciful literature that are interwoven with their intrinsic qualities usually have enduring and often unanticipated consequences. These qualities and effects are the most elusive elements for sociological as well as philosophical-critical analysis. Most of the intra- and interdisciplinary quarrels about what literature is or means and whether or not it is an orthodox subject stem from its linguistic properties. In that respect, writing is uniquely different from all of the nonverbal arts. Music, dance, and painting communicate visually and aurally, relying on distinctive cultural cues other than words. All symbolic expressions are potentially ambiguous; gestures and signs, as well as words are full of connotations. These conventional forms of language, spoken or written, in the context of fiction, in legal or scientific discourse, or just in informal conversation are no guarantee that the initiator and the responder are in perfect communion. Some of the dangers in making language the medium for artistic expression arise because the conventional symbols are loaded with semantic content and organized syntactically by rules valid only for a given community (Escarpit 1968, p. 419). This basic principle has been understood by some anthropologists who have experienced the frustration of using linguistic codes that are alien to foreigners. Laura Bohannan's assumption that *Hamlet* could be universally understood in all cultures (1966) was thwarted by the reaction of African Tiv elders who considered murder and incest conventional practices and for whom ghosts were familiar zombies.

Sociological concern for the essential product —the writing in itself—has not been as evident in American scholarship as in British and European studies. James Barnett thought otherwise, claiming that sociologists should abandon their "exclusive concentration on works of art" (1959, p. 210). However, he was referring to the social and cultural sources of such works and not to their intrinsic qualities. His classification of arts and stress on the importance of popular arts (p. 197) nevertheless enlarged the base for more innovative sociological research in the arts.

His own early studies of the American divorce novel (Barnett 1939; Barnett and Gruen 1948) suggesting how such fiction mirrored marital discord in American society was inspired by Pitirim Sorokin's coding of thousands of art works (1937) to test theories of social-cultural fluctuations. Barnett considered such content analyses and other studies of the arts a primary justification for studying the arts (1959, p. 198). Application of scientific methods to aesthetic phenomena and to producers, disseminators, and consumers has had a strong grip on American research. It has also served implicitly as a way of proving the *bona fides* of sociologists interested in the arts (see Inglis 1938; Albrecht 1956; Coser 1963; and Griswold 1981).

Additional reasons for past neglect of the arts by sociologists and more recent incorporation of this marginal specialty are described by Zolberg (1990, pp. 42–61). Howard Becker's lead article in *The American Sociological Review* in 1974, which became the core of his *Art Worlds* (1982) testified to the second (or third) coming of age of the sociology of literature and of the other arts. Sorokin's study of the fluctuations of the forms of art might be considered the first of such advents, although such claims are not readily verifiable. Another sign of the modern courtship of literature and sociology was Robert Escarpit's monograph ([1958] 1971) that described the world of writers just as Becker's focused more generally on galleries, critics, publishers, printers, and other agents. Becker explicitly disavowed that his study of art worlds was the sociology of art: "(It is) rather the sociology of occupations applied to artistic work" (1982, p. xi). Such empirical analyses of the collective support structures have encouraged more research on government and corporate patronage, on the book publishing industry, and the role of academic support systems. In recent years this examination of mainstream sources of artistic productivity has revealed how the role of the poet is shaped by social forces, the career development of novelists, the decision making process of book publishers, the characteristics of best-sellers, and the functions of agents and critics. These studies have supplemented the voluminous, eclectic bibliography compiled by Hugh Duncan of historical, sociological, and critical works produced prior to World War II (1953, pp. 143–213).

In addition to defining what literature is and means—the first theme described in this section—and identifying the social-biographical characteristics of the writer in the second, the agencies that help the production and consumption of literature constitute the third major element in sociological analysis. All three are blended in the macroscopic approaches by Escarpit and Becker and also in Zolberg's more theoretical reassessment (1990). Lerner and Mims (1933) summarized some historical roots and social consequences of literature, especially with references to the impact on mass audiences. Escarpit (1968) followed that general scheme, but Barnett touched only briefly on the need for more quantitative study of publics (1959, p. 210). Dornbusch (1964) suggested more empirical research, calling for the use of experimental and control groups and comparisons among elite evaluators (1964). Relatively few sociologists, but more psychologists, have pursued these methods. However, with electronic advances in book printing and distribution, new possibilities have opened for research into media effects. To characterize books as part of the mass media might once have been anathema to elite critics, but the book culture—the idea of a distinctively literary object—has lagged behind technology. Malcolm Bradbury and Bryan Wilson claim that the book has increasingly become one of the media and has "lost its scarcity value" ([1958] 1971, p. 17). By the mid-1980s, for example, the six largest producers of books—USSR, West Germany, United States, United Kingdom, Japan, and Canada—were printing nearly 340,000 new titles each year (*Bowker Annual Library and Book Trade Almanac* 1990, p. 499). Such magnitudes combined with new developments in computer technology suggest the increasing likelihood of utilizing mass media research techniques. Reader-interpreter responses to "texts" may or may not depend on quantitative analysis. Yet, even in the hermeneutic domain where French and British philosopher-critics excel, there are rich possibilities in such analysis.

EUROPEAN AND BRITISH INFLUENCES

Empirical "peopled" research in the arts as described by Blau (1988) is less evident in Europe and Great Britain. There sociological tradition has been more concerned with global theories, particularly those of Marx and Weber. Class and social structure have been the mother lode of critical analysis of literature and aesthetics. George Lukács and Lucien Goldmann, the dominant figures of the early twentieth century in these fields, concentrated almost exclusively on the classical pantheon—Shakespeare, Cervantes,

Goethe, Pascal, Racine, and Tolstoy—as the sources for defining epochs and class hierarchies. Lukács's theories of historical process, literary forms, and their impact on the transformation of social reality rely on the familiar formulation: literature reflects and influences society. His reliance on deduction and insight in the fashion of Enlightenment philosophers distinguishes his methods from those of the more empirically centered data gatherers and interpreters. Lukács was more concerned with literature as a "utilitarian aesthetic," according to Swingewood (1977, p. 36), than with its "literary" character. Despite the ideological pressures of the Stalinist era, he remained dedicated to intellectual ideals. His exposition of historical realism radiated among many literary scholars such as Jean-Paul Sartre and members of the Frankfurt School who transported his ideas to America. Leo Lowenthal, for one, modeled his *Literature and the Image of Man* (1957) after Lukács's methods. In the eclectic manner of Georg Simmel, Lowenthal examined popular literature as commodity and art. His study of changing culture heroes as reflected in magazine biographies blended European abstraction with American fascination with numbers (1961, pp. 103–136).

Goldmann's influence has not been as wide but has been central for French and some British writers. His generalizations about how literature arises out of the social milieu are based less on Marxian views than on application of group consciousness. According to Jane Routh, Goldmann's focus is not in the work itself but in the relationship between the "day to day consciousness of a social group and the imaginary universe created by the writer" (1977, p. 151). The French structuralists have adopted this perspective and elaborated on it with Claude Lévi-Strauss's unique applications of myth. Deconstructionism and postmodern interpretation proliferated from these sources. Roland Barthes is a leading structuralist whose stress on linguistic competence has stimulated new definitions of "text"—something akin to the context of writer, reader, and community. Although his vocabulary has been criticized as being too idiosyncratic (Sammons 1977, p. 12), his vivid imagery follows the traditions of Simmel and Weber. Two of his essays on La Rochefoucauld and Flaubert, for instance, are models of analytic precision ([1972] 1980, pp. 3–22, 69–78).

Although the "literary sociology" of continental writers seems remote from American sociological methods, a reconciliation of these divergent schools is evident in the work of Janet Wolff and her British colleagues. Her hermeneutic approach to aesthetics and sociology (1977; 1983; 1984) and that of Elizabeth Bird's suggest that the question of literature's virtual nature transcends any one discipline (1987, pp. 47–48). Vera Zolberg has some doubts regarding Wolff's vacillation about a value-free approach (1990, pp. 200–201). However, Zolberg is optimistic that recent trends in the work of Judith Balfe and Jeffrey Goldfarb, for example, will encourage more sociological focus on aesthetic issues and evaluative judgments. Bradbury and Wilson had offered a principle twenty years earlier that comports with current theoretical developments: "to explore the 'specificity of the literary fact' " ([1958] 1971, p. 7). That suggestion resonates with the concept of "social facts" as Durkheim outlined it in his Rules of Sociological Method.

Poetry, novels, and other forms of literature tend to acquire lives of their own. What is valued or disvalued in different times and places change in unanticipated ways. However, identifying the sources of alterations in the standards of taste is filled with risks. L. L. Schucking's attempts in 1923 encountered R. L. Leavis's hostile attack (1962, pp. 195–203). Since the 1980s, Pierre Bourdieu's research on taste cultures ([1979] 1984) seems to have gained substantial support among American sociologists and holds promise for a synthesis of approaches. The explosion of experimental forms of the novel, the impact of racial and feminist movements in fiction and historical documentary, and the violent reactions of Islamic audiences to the imaginative blend of fact, fiction, and magic in Salman Rushdie's *Satanic Verses* (1989) presage unending challenges.

These events and prospects should continue to offend, entertain, and enlighten readers—as literature always has done—and to open up more fields, broad and deep enough to compel rich collaborative engagement by philosophers, literary critics, and all variant types of social scientists.

REFERENCES

Albrecht, Milton C. 1956 "Does Literature Reflect Common Values?" *American Sociological Review* 21:722–728.

Barnett, James H. 1939 "Divorce and the American Novel: 1858–1937." Ph.D. diss. University of Pennsylvania, Philadelphia.

———1959 "The Sociology of Art." In R. K. Merton, Leonard Broom, and L. S. Cottrell, Jr., eds., *Sociology Today.* Vol. 1. New York: Harper and Row.

———, and Rhoda Gruen 1948 "Recent American Divorce Novels: 1938–1945." *Social Forces* 26:322–328.

Barthes, Roland (1972) 1980 *New Critical Essays.* New York: Hill and Wang.

Becker, Howard 1982 *Art Worlds.* Berkeley: University of California Press.

Bird, Elizabeth 1987 "Aesthetic Neutrality and the Sociology of Art." In Michelle Barrett, Philip Corrigan, Annette Kuhn, and Janet Wolff, *Ideology and Cultural Production.* New York: St. Martin's Press.

Blau, Judith 1988 "Study of the Arts: A Reappraisal." In W. Richard Scott and Judith Blake, eds., *Annual Review of Sociology,* vol. 14.

Bohannan, Laura 1966 "Shakespeare in the Bush." *Natural History* 75:28–33.

Bourdieu, Pierre (1979) 1984 *Distinction: A Social Critique of Taste.* Cambridge, Mass.: Harvard University Press.

Bowker Annual Library and Book Trade Almanac 1990 New York: R. R. Bowker.

Bradbury, Malcolm, and Bryan Wilson [1958] 1971 "Introduction." In Robert Escarpit, *The Sociology of Literature,* 2nd ed. London: Frank Cass.

Coser, Lewis 1963 *Sociology Through Literature.* Englewood Cliffs, N.J.: Prentice-Hall.

Dorfman, Ariel 1983 *The Empire's Old Clothes: What the Lone Ranger, Babar, and Other Innocent Heroes Do to Our Minds.* New York: Pantheon.

Dornbusch, Sanford 1964 "Content and Method in the Study of the Higher Arts." In R. N. Wilson, ed., *The Arts in Society.* Englewood Cliffs, N.J.: Prentice-Hall.

Duncan, Hugh D. 1953 *Language and Literature in Society.* Chicago: University of Chicago Press.

Escarpit, Robert (1958) 1971 *Sociology of Literature,* 2nd ed. London: Frank Cass.

———1968 "The Sociology of Literature." In David L. Sills, ed., *International Encyclopedia of the Social Sciences.* New York: Macmillan and Free Press.

Gans, Herbert J. 1985 "American Popular Culture and High Culture in a Changing Class Structure." In Judith H. Balfe and Margaret Wysomirski, eds., *Art, Ideology, and Politics.* New York: Praeger.

Griswold, Wendy 1981 "American Character and the American Novel: An Expansion of Reflection Theory." *American Journal of Sociology* 86:740–765.

Inglis, Ruth A. 1938 "An Objective Approach to the Relationship Between Fiction and Society." *American Sociological Review* 3:526–536.

Leavis, F. R. 1962 *The Common Pursuit.* London: Chatto and Windus.

Lerner, Max, and Edward Mims 1933 "Literature." In E. B. A. Seligman and Alvin Johnson, eds., *Encyclopedia of the Social Sciences.* New York: Macmillan.

Lowenthal, Leo 1957 *Literature and the Image of Man.* Boston: Beacon Press.

———1961 *Literature, Popular Culture, and Society.* Englewood Cliffs, N.J.: Prentice-Hall.

Routh, Jane 1977 "A Reputation Made: Lucien Goldmann." In Jane Routh and Janet Wolff, eds., *The Sociology of Literature: Theoretical Approaches.* Sociological Review Monograph 25. Keele, Staffordshire: University of Keele.

Rushdie, Salman 1989 *The Satanic Verses.* New York: Viking Penguin.

Sammons, Jeffrey L. 1977 *Literary Sociology and Practical Criticism.* Bloomington: Indiana University Press.

Snow, C. P. (1959) 1964 *The Two Cultures and a Second Look.* London: Cambridge University Press.

Sorokin, Pitirim (1937) 1957 *Social and Cultural Dynamics,* Vol. 1. Boston: Porter Sargent.

Staele-Holstein, Germaine de (1800) 1959 *De la literature considérée dans ses rapports avec les institutions sociales.* Geneva: Droz.

Swingewood, Alan 1972 "The Social Theories of Literature." In Diane T. Laurenson and Alan Swingewood, *The Sociology of Literature,* New York: Schocken Books.

———1977 "Marxist Approaches to the Study of Literature." In Jane Routh and Janet Wolff, eds.,

The Sociology of Literature: Theoretical Approaches. Sociological Review Monograph 25. Keele, Staffordshire: University of Keele.

Wilensky, Harold L. 1964 "Mass Society and Mass Culture: Interdependence or Independence?" *American Sociological Review* 29:173–197.

Wolff, Janet 1977 "The Interpretation of Literature in Society: The Hermeneutic Approach." In Jane Routh and Janet Wolff, eds., *The Sociology of Literature: Theoretical Approaches.* Sociological Review Monograph 25. Keele: Staffordshire: University of Keele.

———1984 *The Social Production of Art.* London: Allen and Unwin.

Zolberg, Vera L. 1990 *Constructing a Sociology of the Arts.* Cambridge: Cambridge University Press.

HYMAN A. ENZER

LONGITUDINAL RESEARCH According to Heckman and Singer, "Longitudinal data are widely and uncritically regarded as a panacea. . . . The conventional wisdom in social science equates 'longitudinal' with 'good' and discussion of the issue rarely rises above that level" (1985, p. ix).

There is probably no methodological maxim in sociology more often repeated than the call for longitudinal data. From the work of David Hume more than 250 years ago, to the exhortations for a "radical reformation" in the work of Stanley Lieberson (1985, p. xiii), the importance of longitudinal data has been emphasized and reemphasized. Yet it is doubtful that there is an area of sociological method in which more disagreement exists both as to rationale and as to method. Until relatively recently, it has been possible to ignore the problem because longitudinal data have been relatively rare, and methods for their analysis quite sparse. Since 1965, however, there has been a virtual flood of new longitudinal data and a concomitant increase in sophisticated methods of analysis. In large part the computer has made both developments possible, permitting the management of data sets of enormous complexity along with analyses undreamed of only a short while ago.

At the micro level, numerous longitudinal studies have tracked individuals over a good share of their lifetimes. For example, some participants in the Oakland and Berkeley studies of growth and development have been sporadically studied from birth until well into their seventies (Elder, this volume). On a more systematic basis, the Panel Study of Income Dynamics (PSID) has interviewed a panel based on an original sample of five thousand families (households) on an annual basis since the mid 1960s, supplementing the sample with new households formed as split-offs from the original families (Duncan and Morgan 1985). Many other large-scale panel studies, some extending over periods of thirty years and longer, are in progress (Migdal et al. 1981).

At the macro level, extended time series on various social and economic indicators such as GNP, fertility, mortality, and education are gradually becoming available in machine-readable form from virtually all industrialized societies and from many that are less developed. In some cases, data series, particularly for vital statistics, go back for decades. In other cases, such as China and the Soviet Union, modern-era data are gradually being accumulated and linked to earlier series. Descriptions of many such data sets can be found in the annual guide published by the Inter-University Consortium for Political and Social Research (ICPSR 1991).

Perhaps the most exciting developments are at the nexus of macro- and micro-level analysis. In the United States, for example, the General Social Survey (GSS) has obtained data on repeated cross-sectional samples of the population (that is, the population is followed longitudinally but specific individuals are not) on an annual basis (with two exceptions) since 1972. More recently, annual surveys modeled on the GSS have been started in a number of other countries (Smith 1986). Because of the careful replication, these surveys permit one to track aggregate responses of the changing population on a wide variety of issues (such as on attitudes toward abortion or capital punishment) over time. As the time series becomes ever longer, it is possible to carry out a multilevel analysis, linking micro and macro variables. For example, using the GSS, DiPrete and Grusky (1990) attempt to link short-term changes in rates of social mobility to macro-level changes in the U.S. economy.

Although the size and complexity of the longitudinal data base has expanded rapidly, so have the statistical tools with which to analyze it. Perhaps the most exciting development is in the area of "event history models," which permit one to relate an underlying rate of transition in continuous time to a set of "covariates" or independent variables. However, event models are by no means the only development. New and powerful approaches to the analysis of means over time, to structural equation models, and to various forms of categorical data analysis have given the researchers unprecedented power. Standard computer packages now make routine what was impossible in the 1980s.

THE RATIONALE FOR LONGITUDINAL RESEARCH

Longitudinal studies are carried out in virtually every area of the social sciences. Although studies of infant development and national development share certain similarities, it is not likely that a single rationale, design, or approach to analysis will simultaneously apply to every area in which longitudinal data might be collected. At the most abstract level, there are three basic reasons for conducting a longitudinal study.

First, in any area in which development and change over time are at issue, there is, almost by definition, a necessity to obtain time-ordered data. Questions pertaining to rate and sequence of change, and to variability in rates and sequences are at the heart of longitudinal research. At one level, these questions are essentially descriptive, and getting an adequate descriptive handle on time-ordered data is an essential first step in coming to any understanding of change.

A second reason involves the role of temporal priority in causal analysis. There are few things on which philosophers of science agree when it comes to causation (see Marini and Singer 1988 for a superb review), but one is that A must precede B in time if A is to be taken as a cause of B. It is natural to assume that observing A before B means that A precedes B. Unfortunately, designs that actually allow one to establish temporal, let alone causal, priority are not as easily arrived at as one might think.

Related to the issue of temporal priority is the cross-sectional fallacy. Lieberson (1985, pp. 179–183) argues that assertions of causality based on cross-sectional data must necessarily imply a longitudinal relationship. To show that city size "leads to crime" based on cross-sectional data implies a dynamic relationship that may or may not be true. The problem is particularly acute in cross-sectional age comparisons that are necessarily confounded with cohort differences. All cross-sectional attempts to ascertain the "effect" of age on income confound cohort differences in average income with age differences.

A third reason, particularly relevant to sociologists, is the necessity to distinguish gross change from net change. A census taken at two points in time shows changes in the distribution of a variable, say occupation, at the macro level. We might find that the proportion of the population in service-oriented occupations increases over the period of a decade. That indicator of net change conceals myriad patterns of gross change at the individual level. The count of persons in service occupations at two points in time consists of persons who were occupationally stable over the interval and persons who changed in various ways. Of course the population itself changed over the interval due to age-related changes in the labor force, migration, and differing levels of labor-force participation. All of this is masked by repeated cross-sectional samples.

Finally, although not really a "rationale" for longitudinal research, observation plans with repeated measures on the same individuals can offer certain statistical advantages. Cook and Ware (1983) discuss these in detail.

TYPES OF LONGITUDINAL DATA

For many sociologists, the term *longitudinal* connotes a particular design, usually referred to as a panel study, in which individual subjects are measured repeatedly over time. A more general definition is desirable. Longitudinal data consist of information that can be ordered in time. Such data can be obtained in a variety of ways: by measuring the subject prospectively at repeated intervals, by obtaining a retrospective history in one or more interviews, from institutional records, or various combinations of these approaches. "Strong" longitudinal data preserve exact time intervals, while "weak" data provide sequence and order but lose interval. The distinction is parallel to that between interval and ordinal measurement.

As Featherman (1977) notes, under some circumstances, retrospective data collection may have substantial advantages of time and cost. Most surveys collect retrospective data of one kind or another, such as educational attainment, family background, and marital histories. Using structured interviewing methods in which the respondent is provided with a time-oriented matrix, it is possible to collect quite accurate information on many aspects of the life course. For example, as part of an ongoing panel, Freedman et al. (1988) obtained retrospective reports of family structure and other demographic variables that had previously been measured contemporaneously. The results are highly encouraging; when retrospective questions of this kind are asked carefully and interviewers are well trained, respondents can provide accurate and detailed information.

Of course not all variables can be measured retrospectively. Most researchers would argue that any attempt to measure past psychological states is invalid on its face. Reporting of the timing and frequency of events, even those which are quite salient, such as hospitalization, appears to suffer from serious recall problems. Subjects tend to forget them or to telescope them in time. Reports of exact earnings, hours worked, and other economic variables may suffer from similar problems. The truth is that we don't have much information on what can and cannot be measured retrospectively. A systematic research program on these issues is becoming more and more necessary as new methods of data analysis that depend on the exact timing of events continue to evolve.

Another serious weakness of the retrospective design is that it represents the population that survives to the point of data collection and not the original population. In some situations this kind of selection bias can be quite serious—for example, in intervention studies that are subject to high levels of attrition.

Prospective studies in which a subject is measured at some baseline and then at repeated intervals are usually referred to as panel studies. Panel designs have a number of strengths along with several significant weaknesses. The primary strength, at least in principle, is accuracy of measurement and correct temporal referents. Depending on the exact design of data collection, subjects are measured at a point close enough in time to the event or status in question to permit reliable and valid assessment. Under certain circumstances temporal priority may be more firmly established.

Second, the prospective design provides greater leverage on attrition. Besides measuring a population defined at baseline, preattrition information can be used to determine the extent to which attrition is "random" and perhaps can be used to correct estimates for selection bias. There is a trade-off, however. Frequent measurement has two potentially undesirable side effects. First, subjects may tire of repeated requests for cooperation and drop out of the study. Second, "panel conditioning" may result in stereotypic responses to repeated questions. Thus, relative to the retrospective design, there may actually be a net *decrease* in data quality.

On the surface, prospective designs that extend in time are far more costly than retrospective designs. There is a clear cost/quality trade-off, however, that cannot be easily evaluated without consideration of the purposes of the survey. In obtaining population estimates over time, the panel may actually be less expensive to maintain than resampling the population repeatedly. On the other hand, using a panel for this purpose brings problems of its own in the form of attrition and panel conditioning.

QUASI-EXPERIMENTAL AND DESCRIPTIVE APPROACHES

The large-scale, multiwave surveys so common now have rather diffuse origins. Paul Lazarsfeld introduced the panel design (Lazarsfeld and Fiske 1938). In his hands, the panel study was basically a *quasi-experimental design.* A panel of subjects was recruited and measured repeatedly, with the foreknowledge that a particular event would occur at a particular time. The most famous application is to election campaigns. As such, the design is a simple example of an interrupted time series.

A second source of current designs is the child development tradition. Baltes and Nesselroade (1979) cite examples going back to the late eighteenth century, but systematic studies date to the 1920s (Wall and Williams 1970). The best of these studies emphasized cohort-based sampling of newborns and systematic assessment of development at carefully determined intervals. In the tradition of experimental psychology, investigators paid attention to careful control of the measurement process, including the physical environment, the raters and observers, and the measurement instruments. The development of age-specific norms in the form of averages and variation about them was seen as a primary goal of the study. Unanticipated events, such as an illness of either mother or child or factors affecting the family, were seen as undesirable threats to the validity of measurement rather than as opportunities to assess quasi-experimental effects.

Large-scale multiwave panel studies of the kind described above combine aspects of both traditions, often in somewhat inchoate and potentially conflicting ways. On the one hand, investigators are interested in describing a population as it evolves. Often basic descriptive information on rates, variability, and sequence is unknown, calling for frequent measurement at fixed intervals. On the other hand, there is also interest in evaluating the impact of specific transitions and events, such as childbearing, retirement, and loss of spouse. Meeting these two objectives within the constraints of a single design is often difficult.

DESIGN ISSUES

Although it might be argued that the ideal longitudinal study should take a huge sample of the population without age restriction, measure it constantly, and follow it in perpetuity with systematic supplements to the original sample, cost and logistics intervene. Although there is an infinite range of potential designs, longitudinal studies can be classified on various dimensions including (a) the consistency of the sample over time, (b) population coverage, particularly with regard to age, and (c) measurement protocols, including not only choice of variables but also timing, interval, and frequency. These factors will influence the extent to which the study can be used for descriptive purposes, relating information to a well-defined population, and/or drawing causal inferences on temporal and quasi-experimental aspects of the design.

Consistency of the Sample. The following classification is based on Duncan and Kalton (1987) and on Menard (1991).

1. *Repeated Cross-Sectional Surveys.* A new sample is drawn at each measurement point. The GSS, described above, is an example. This is a longitudinal study at the macro level. It describes a dynamic population.
2. *Fixed-Sample Panel.* A sample is drawn at baseline and measured repeatedly over time. No new subjects enter the sample after baseline. Several examples are described above. The sample refers only to the cohorts from which it was drawn. It may continue to represent them adequately if panel attrition is completely at random.
3. *Dynamic Sample Panel.* After baseline, subjects are added to the panel in an attempt to compensate for panel attrition and represent changes in the underlying population. The PSID is a major example.
4. *Rotating Panels.* A sample is drawn and interviewed for a fixed number of waves and then dropped. At each measurement point a new sample is also drawn so that samples enter and leave on a staggered basis. The best-known

example is the Current Population Survey carried out by the U.S. Bureau of the Census. At any given time, the sample consists of subjects who have been in the panel from one to four months.

5. *Split Panels.* In addition to a basic panel survey, a coordinated cross-sectional survey is drawn at each measurement point. In effect, this is a quasi-experimental design in which comparisons between samples permit tests of panel conditioning, among other things. This design is rare.

Population Definition. The broader the population sampled, the wider the potential generalization. On the other hand, homogeneity provides greater leverage for some kinds of causal inference. The following rough classification is useful. See Campbell (1988) for elaboration.

1. *Unrestricted Age Range.* A sample of the entire (adult) population is selected and followed.
2. *Restricted Age Range.* A sample of persons in a narrow age band, such as adolescents in developing nations, is selected, with resulting homogeneity of developmental process.
3. *Event-Based.* A sample is selected on the basis of a particular event. Birth is the prime example; others are motherhood, school completion, business start-up, and administrative reorganization. Subjects can be members of a cohort experiencing the event at a fixed time or can be drawn on a floating baseline, as is the case when each new patient in a given clinic is followed prospectively.
4. *Population at Risk.* A sample is selected on the likelihood (but not the certainty) that it will experience a particular event. Although similar to an event-based sample, it is less controlled. Age-restricted samples are usually at risk for certain events, which is one reason for restricting age in the first place. An interesting example at the macro level is a sample of cities likely to experience a disaster such as an earthquake or a hurricane.

Measurement Protocols. What variables should one measure with what frequency at what time intervals? Answering such a question requires a clear appreciation of the linkage between the substantive purpose of an investigation and the mode of data analysis. For example, if one's intent is to study labor-force participation using event history models, then frequency of measurement would be dictated primarily by (a) the frequency of change of labor-force status among subjects, (b) the amount of variability in individual rates of change, (c) the necessity to obtain exact dates of transitions for the analysis, and (d) the maximum time interval at which subjects can provide reliable and valid recall data. If the investigators have explanatory models in mind, then the measurement protocol will have to deal with similar issues for the regressors.

If one is, however, interested in the effects of widowhood, which might be studied either descriptively or as a quasi-experiment using an interrupted time series approach, very different measurement strategies would be optimal. At the very least, one would try to schedule measurements at fixed intervals *preceding and following* the event. If economic effects were the primary focus, annual measurement might be sufficient; but if the grief process was the focus, more frequent measurement would be required.

The more undifferentiated the sample, and the more multipurpose the study, the more difficult it is to achieve an effective measurement strategy. Many of the large-scale longitudinal studies carried out since the 1960s have one or more of the following characteristics that tend to interfere with analysis:

1. Multiple substantive foci that result in attempts to measure scores, if not hundreds, of variables.
2. Nonoptimal measurement intervals because of conflicting demands of different kinds of variables and topics. A secondary problem is that intervals are often determined by administrative and funding criteria rather than by substantive intent.
3. Measurement strategies that are chosen without regard to statistical analysis. The problem is acute for event history models that require dated transitions rather than reports of status

at fixed intervals. Other examples are failure to acquire multiple indicators of constructs for LISREL models and intersubject variation in measurement intervals that interferes with growth curve estimation.

4. Weak identification of temporal sequence. This problem is most often a result of a "snapshot" orientation to measurement in which the subject's status is ascertained at a sequence of fixed measurement points. Knowing that at time 1 someone is married and prosperous and that at time 2 that person is single and poverty-stricken doesn't tell us much about causal order or effect.

CAUSAL INFERENCE AND LONGITUDINAL DESIGN

As noted, the extent to which longitudinal studies allow one to establish causal effects is the subject of some controversy. Indeed, the whole issue of causal inference from nonexperimental data is extremely controversial (Berk 1988; Freedman 1991), with some taking the position that it is impossible in any circumstance other than a randomized design involving an experimentally manipulated stimulus. Although that may be an extreme position, the assumption that one can use time-ordered observational data to establish causal order is difficult to defend.

Cross-sectional analyses and retrospective designs suffer from the fact that variables which are supposed to have time-ordered causal effects are measured simultaneously. As a result, various competing explanations of observed associations, particularly contaminated measurement, cannot be ruled out. Asking about educational aspirations after completion of schooling is an example. Panel designs at least have the advantage of measuring presumed causes prior to their effects. Even in that case, establishing temporal order is not as easy as it might appear. This is particularly true when one attempts to relate intentions, attitudes, and similar cognitive variables to behaviors. Marini and Singer (1988) give an example based on education and marriage. Consider two women who leave school and get married. One may have decided to terminate her education in light of a planned marriage, and the other may have decided to marry following a decision to terminate education. The observed sequence of events tells us nothing. They note:

> *Because human beings can anticipate and plan for the future, much human behavior follows from goals, intentions and motives, i.e., it is teleologically determined. As a result, causal priority is established in the mind in a way that is not reflected in the temporal sequences of behavior or even in the temporal sequence of the formation of behavioral intentions. (Marini and Singer 1988, p. 377)*

Because of the many varieties of longitudinal research design and the many controversies in the field, it is difficult to give hard-and-fast rules about when causal inference may be justified. Dwyer (1991), writing for epidemiologists, provides a useful way to approach the problem based on whether there is variance in presumed causes and effects at baseline.

Variation in Independent Variable

		NO	YES
Variation in Dependent Variable	NO	I	II
	YES	III	IV

Examples include the following:

I. Follow crime-free baseline sample through possible arrest, incarceration, and later recidivism.
II. Relate aspirations of eighth graders to eventual level of educational attainment.
III. Carry out an experimental intervention, such as a job training program, that attempts to increase existing skill levels.
IV. Relate organizational characteristics at baseline to later levels of productivity.

Cases I and III can be observational or (quasi-) experimental. Cases II and IV are strictly observational. In each case, although variation may not exist in the variable of direct interest, there may be variation in closely related variables. In the experimental case, this corresponds to lack of randomization and, thus, uncontrolled variation in potential causal variables. The same is true in purely observational studies. In case II, although there is no variation in the direct outcome of interest, there is often variation in related variables at baseline. In the example given, although there is no variation in educational attainment in terms of years of schooling completed, aspirations are certainly based in part on the child's prior academic success in the grade school environment. Case IV presents the most difficult situation because it picks up data in the middle of an ongoing causal sequence. This is precisely the situation where many researchers believe that panel data can untangle causal sequence, but neither temporal-sequenced observations nor complex analysis is likely to do so.

To reiterate an important point about design, in large-scale longitudinal research each of these four cases is typically embedded in a complex design, and the degree of causal inference depends on many factors ranging from the timing of measurement to attrition processes.

COMMON PROBLEMS IN LONGITUDINAL DATA ANALYSIS

Those who collect and analyze longitudinal data face certain generic problems. Virtually any researcher will face some or all of the following difficulties.

Conceptualizing Change. James Coleman notes that the concept of change is "a second order abstraction . . . based on a comparison, or difference, between two sense impressions, and, simultaneously, a comparison of the times at which the impressions occurred" (1968, pp. 428–429). It is particularly difficult to think about the *causes* of change, and this difficulty has been reflected in arguments about how to model it. In particular, there has been a running debate about the use of change scores, computed as a simple difference ($\Delta Y = Y_2 - Y_1$) versus a regression approach in which the time 2 variable is regressed on time 1 plus other variables. In an influential paper, Bohrnstedt (1970) showed that simple gain scores tended to have very low reliability relative to either variable composing them. In light of that and other problems, Cronbach and Furby (1969) argued that the best way to model change was to treat "residualized gain scores" as dependent variables in regression analysis. The basic equation is

$$Y_2 = \alpha + \beta_1 Y_1 + \beta_2 X_1 \cdots + \beta_k X_k + \epsilon$$

where Y_1 is the baseline measure and the X's are any set of independent variables. Hence the effect of X is net of the baseline score. This method has become standard in many fields of inquiry.

More recently, a number of papers have appeared that question the use of residualized gain scores. Liker, Augustyniak, and Duncan (1985) argue that equations in which one takes differences on both sides of the model ($\Delta_Y = \alpha + \beta(\Delta X) + \epsilon$) have strong advantages, particularly when one wants to "difference out" unchanging characteristics of subjects. Allison (1990) argues that in some cases the difference score as a dependent variable is not only acceptable but necessary. The issue is not purely statistical; it depends in large part on exactly what process one is attempting to model. Suffice it to say here that an issue which was once thought to be resolved has been reopened for serious examination.

Related to the issue of change scores and their reliability is the problem of regression toward the mean. Whenever a variable is positively correlated over time, subjects with high scores at time 1 will tend to have somewhat lower scores at time 2, while those with lower time 1 scores will tend to have higher scores at time 2. As a result, gain scores will be negatively correlated with initial values. This problem is exacerbated by random measurement error and was a primary reason for the predominance of residualized gain models in the past. Again, however, the issue is one of the underlying model. There are cases where feedback processes do indeed result in regression to the mean (Dwyer 1991) and the regression is by no means an "artifact." There is no question that one always needs to correct for measurement error, but regression to the mean should not necessarily be treated as an annoyance to be gotten rid of by statistical manipulation.

Lack of Independence. A standard assumption in elementary statistical models such as least squares regression is that errors are independent across observations. In the equation

$$Y_i = a + \beta X_i + \epsilon_i, \text{ where } i \text{ indexes the subject,}$$

we typically assume $\text{cov}(\epsilon_i \epsilon_j) = 0$. If the same subject is observed at two or more points in time, the independence assumption is almost certain to be violated due to omitted variables, correlated errors of measurement, or other problems. This difficulty permeates virtually all statistical approaches to longitudinal data and requires complex methods of estimation.

Articulating Analysis with Observation Plan. Ideally, one should have in mind a model for how the underlying process of change in a variable articulates with the observation plan. In part, this requires some knowledge of causal lag or how long it takes for changes in X to result in changes in Y. The data analysis method chosen should be congruent with both the underlying process of change and the observation plan. Observation plans may obtain exact dates of transitions (when did you quit your job?), locate the subject's state at time t (are you currently working?), or obtain retrospective information relative to some other time point (were you working as of June 30?). Studies that have multiple goals are difficult to optimize in this respect.

Construct Validity. In long-term longitudinal studies, the validity of constructs may degrade over time, sometimes through changes in the subjects themselves, sometimes through measurement problems such as conditioning, and sometimes through changes in the environment. For example, the meaning of terms used in political research such as *liberal* may change with time, or references to specific issues such as abortion may become more or less salient. In growth studies, subjects may "age out" of certain variables. This issue is quite understudied, at least by sociologists.

Measurement Error. Measurement error is a serious problem for statistical analysis, particularly regression, because it results in biased estimates. The problem is particularly acute when independent variables are subject to error. In the longitudinal case, errors of measurement tend to be correlated across subjects over time, causing even greater difficulty. A major reason for the popularity of structural equation packages like LISREL (Jöreskog and Sörbom 1988; Bollen 1989) is that they permit one to model correlated error structures. This is not to say that LISREL is an all-purpose solution; indeed, its error-handling capabilities probably lead to its use in situations where other approaches would be better.

Time-varying Independent Variables. In a typical situation one is faced with a set of fixed independent variables such as age, sex, and race, and a set of variables whose values may change over the course of a study. In studies of income, for example, educational levels and family structure may change between observations. Although work on this problem has been going on in economics for some years (Hsiao 1986), sociologists have been slow to respond. The problem always leads to great statistical and computational complexity.

Missing Data, Attrition, Censoring, and Selection Bias. Attrition in panel studies is inevitable. In rare cases attrition is completely random, but more commonly it is associated with other variables. Standard listwise and pairwise missing data "solutions" are rarely appropriate in this situation. Three types of solutions are available. First, one can develop weights to correct for attrition. Second, one can model the attrition process directly, using "selection bias" models (Heckman 1979; Berk 1983). Finally, one can impute estimates of missing data (Little and Rubin 1987). This entire area is controversial and under rapid development. A special case of attrition occurs when observations are *censored* in such a way that measurement stops before a transition of interest, such as ending a panel study of fertility before all subjects have completed childbearing.

APPROACHES TO DATA ANALYSIS

The period since 1975 or 1980 has seen enormous increases in the power and sophistication of longitudinal data analysis. Singer (1985) is a useful overview; Dwyer and Feinleib (1991), especially chapter 1, provides a comprehensive review, as does Von Eye (1990). This material is much too complex to cover in this brief review. A more reasonable goal is to provide a few examples of the kinds of substantive questions that one can ask with longitudinal data and appropriate methods for answering them.

Outcomes at Fixed Points in Time. Example: "predicting" a person's savings at age sixty-five. This is the simplest longitudinal question; indeed, in one sense it is not longitudinal at all. The dependent variable involves change over time very indirectly, and the independent variables usually involve life cycle variables like the nature of labor-force participation. These data can often be collected retrospectively, and the only advantage of a *repeated measures* approach is control over measurement error.

It is not uncommon to see models for fixed outcomes at arbitrary time points—for example, level of education attainment as of the last available wave of an ongoing panel study. This is a particular problem when the sample consists of subjects who vary in age or is not defined on the basis of some reasonable baseline. When the outcome is a discrete transition, such as marriage, censoring is often a problem.

Means over Time. Example: Comparison of aspiration levels of boys and girls over the middle school years. With a sequence of independent samples, this is a straightforward analysis-of-variance problem. If the same individuals are measured repeatedly, a number of problems arise. First, the observations are not independent over time; we have to assume that the usual statistical assumption of independence in the error terms will be violated. Within the ANOVA tradition, this problem can be approached via multivariate analysis of variance or as a classic univariate design. Hertzog and Rovine (1985) compare the two approaches. Sociologists have tended to ignore mean comparisons, preferring to work with structural equations; however, analyses of means are often far more direct and informative. See Fox (1984) for an interesting application to an interrupted time series.

Classic ANOVA ignores individual-level heterogeneity. Over the course of five observation points, students vary about the group means. The description of change at the individual level rather than at the group level may be of some interest. A simple approach is to use "blocking variables" such as race to account for additional heterogeneity. Adding covariates to the model is another. A more sophisticated approach is to model the individual-level growth curve directly. Conceptually, analysis begins by estimating an equation to describe each respondent's score with respect to time, often using a polynomial model. The coefficients of these equations are then treated as dependent variables in a second-stage analysis. There are a number of different statistical approaches to this kind of analysis. Rogosa (1988) has argued forcefully in favor of approaching longitudinal analysis in this way. Dwyer (1991) provides an interesting example. McCardle and Aber (1990) deal with such models in a LISREL context.

Structural Equation Systems. Figure 1, based on Blau and Duncan's classic path model of occupational mobility, is a longitudinal analysis, although it is not often thought of in those terms. For our purposes, the important point is that the exact timing of variables was not assumed to be of great import, although the sequence was. Education was taken to intervene between measures of family background and occupational attainment, and its timing was not specified. The latter variable was assumed to reach some plateau relatively early in the occupational career; again, timing was

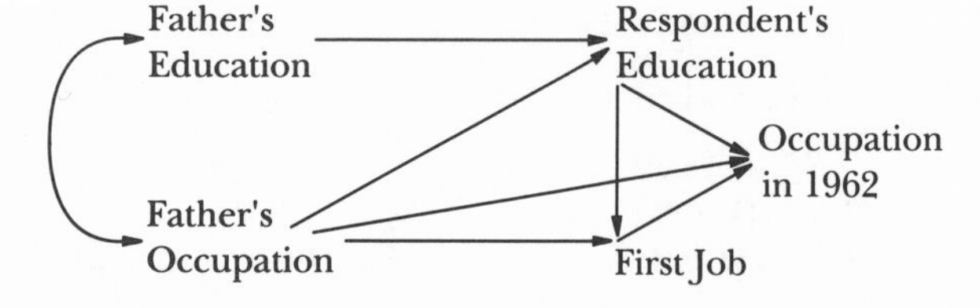

FIGURE 1
A Basic Model of Attainment (Adapted from Blau and Duncan 1967)

not important. Models of this kind, with rather vague time referents and in which it is assumed that the order of events does not vary across subjects, have played an important role in sociology for some time, adding great clarity to the notion of intervening variables. It is natural to assume that structural equation models are a natural way to analyze multiwave panel data.

Kessler and Greenberg (1981) deal at length with the application of structural equation models to panel data, particularly to cross-lagged structures where both variables vary at baseline. They show that attempting to estimate relative causal effects must be handled in the context of a formal model rather than by comparing cross-lagged partial correlations. Figure 2, based on Campbell and Mutran (1982), is a multiwave panel model with intervening variables. Here, a number of statistical and conceptual difficulties become obvious. First, what is the lag time for the effect of health on income satisfaction and vice versa? Second, how does one deal with the potentially complex error structure of observed variables? Third, if illnesses intervene (as measured by times in hospital), how does the timing of events relative to the timing of observations affect the results? Fourth, how does one deal with discrete intervening variables that fail to meet standard distributional assumptions? Finally, how does one handle correlated errors in equations over time? These are by no means the only questions that could be raised, and it is not clear that models of this kind are the most effective way to approach multiwave panel data.

Event History Models. This class of models treats the underlying rate of change in a discrete variable as the dependent variable in a regression-like framework. Typically, the dependent variable is conceived of as the instantaneous risk of transition at time *t* conditional on prior history. The formulation is dynamic rather than static, and time enters the analysis explicitly. Allison (this volume) discusses a number of such models in detail. At first glance, the model may seem mathematically esoteric, but the basic ideas are straightforward. The underlying concepts are closely re-

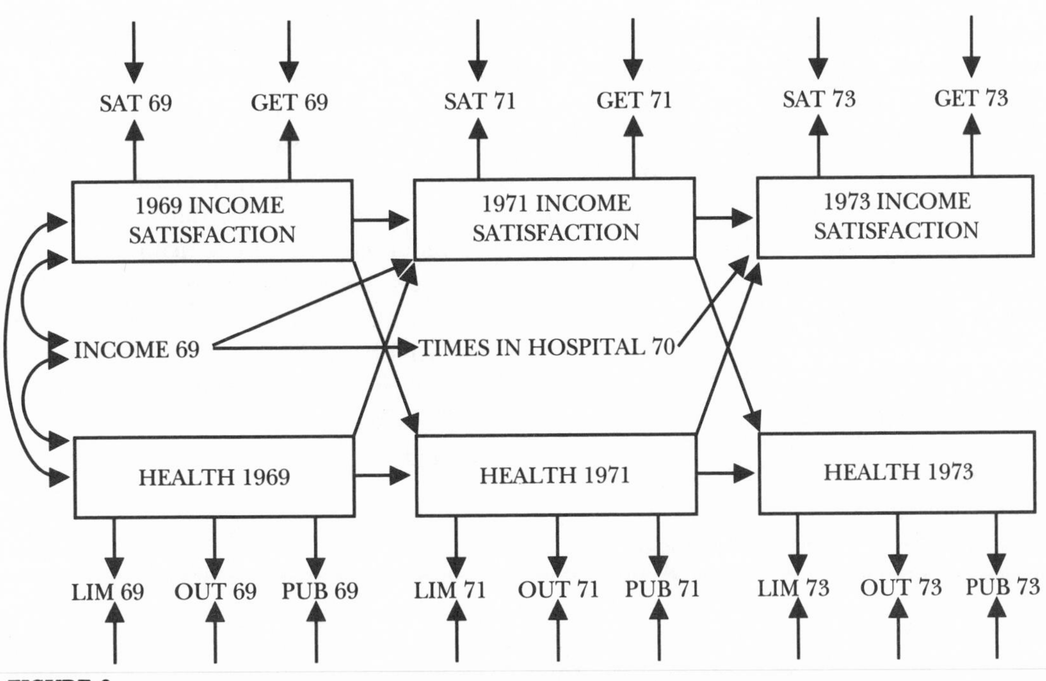

FIGURE 2
A Model for Health and Income Satisfaction (Adapted from Campbell and Mutran 1982)

lated to the life table and to Markov models. The Markov model, as applied in the classic labor-force studies of Blumen, Kogen, and McCarthy (1955), assumes a transition process that is constant over time and invariant across subjects. Event history models allow one to relax both assumptions, specifying a time-dependent rate of change and a set of individual-level "covariates" that allow transition processes to vary with characteristics of the subjects. Covariates can be allowed to change with time as well, at the cost of substantial computational complexity.

In one of the first applications in sociology, Tuma, Hannon, and Groeneveld (1979) showed that the rate of marital dissolution among subjects in an income-maintenance experiment depended on the treatment condition, thus demonstrating that event models could be used for causal analysis. Event models are inherently dynamic and take the timing of transitions explicitly into account. They are having enormous impact not only on how sociologists analyze data but also on how they conceptualize problems and design data collection.

Differential Equation Models. Coleman (1964, 1968, 1981), among others, has argued that the appropriate way to study change in continuous variables is via differential equation models. A simple differential equation relating Y to its own level and to an exogenous variable takes the form

$$\frac{dY}{dt} = a + b_1 Y + b_2 X_1$$

where dY/dt is the rate of change in Y with respect to time, that is, the derivative. The rate of change is not directly observed, of course; and to estimate the coefficients of the model, it is necessary to integrate the equation. Coleman (1968) shows that for this particular model, it is possible to obtain estimates of a, b_1, and b_2 by first estimating a regression equation of the form

$$Y_t = a^* + b_1^* Y_{(t-1)} + b_2^* X_1$$

using ordinary regression and then transforming the regression coefficients to obtain the coefficients of the differential equation model. In this particular case the coefficients of the differential equation model are

$$a = \frac{a^* C^*}{\Delta t}$$

$$b_1 = \frac{\ln b_1^*}{\Delta t}$$

$$b_2 = \frac{b_2^* C^*}{\Delta t}$$

where

$$C^* = \frac{\ln b_1^*}{(b_l^* - 1)}$$

The resulting coefficients describe the time path of Y as a function of its initial value and the value of X. Note that this model assumes that X is not changing over time. One implication of this model is that if one wishes to assume that Y at time t does not depend on its initial value, then residualized gain score models of the kind described above are inappropriate.

Applications of differential equation models in sociology have been relatively rare, although they would seem to be a natural way to approach the analysis of change. Many of the seemingly endless arguments about the representation of change in regression models stems from the application of static methods to dynamic processes. The difficulty is that it is not easy or always possible to transform the differential equations in such a way that they can be estimated by simple regression. Doing so requires considerable mathematical sophistication on the part of the researcher. Tuma and Hannon (1984) discuss these and related models at length. Arminger (1986) provides an example of how to recast a standard three-wave LISREL-based panel analysis into a differential equation model.

CONCLUSION

It is no accident that words like *controversial* and *under discussion* recur frequently in this review. Many important issues regarding the collection, analysis, and interpretation of longitudinal data remain to be resolved. Frequently, what are in fact conceptual issues are argued in statistical terms. The literature is technical and mathematically demanding. But important progress is being made and will continue as new methods of research continue to emerge.

(SEE ALSO: *Causal Inference Models; Cohort Analysis; Event History Analysis; Time Series Analysis; Quasi-Experimental Research Designs)*

REFERENCES

Allison, Paul D. 1984 *Event History Analysis: Regression for Longitudinal Event Data.* Newbury Park, Calif.: Sage.

———1990 "Change Scores as Dependent Variables in Regression Analysis." In Clifford C. Clogg, ed., *Sociological Methodology,* Vol. 20. London: Basil Blackwell.

Arminger, Gerhard 1986 "Linear Stochastic Differential Equation Models for Panel Data with Unobserved Variables." In Nancy B. Tuma, ed., *Sociological Methodology,* Vol. 16. Washington, D.C.: American Sociological Association.

Baltes, Paul B., and John R. Nesselroade 1977 "History and Rationale of Longitudinal Research." In John R. Nesselroade and Paul B. Baltes, eds. *Longitudinal Research in the Study of Behavior and Development.* New York: Academic Press.

Berk, Richard A. 1983 "An Introduction to Sample Selection Bias in Sociological Research." *American Sociological Review* 48:386–398.

———1988 "Causal Inference in Social Science." In Neil J. Smelser, ed., *Handbook of Sociology.* Newbury Park, Calif.: Sage.

Blau, Peter M., and Otis Dudley Duncan 1967 *The American Occupational Structure.* New York: Wiley.

Blumen, Isadore, M. Kogan, and P. J. McCarthy 1955 *The Industrial Mobility of Labor as a Probability Process.* Ithaca, N.Y.: Cornell University Press.

Bohrnstedt, George W. 1969 "Observations on the Measurement of Change." In Edgar F. Borgatta, ed., *Sociological Methodology,* Vol. 2. San Francisco: Jossey-Bass.

Bollen, Kenneth A. 1989 *Structural Equations with Latent Variables.* New York: Wiley.

Campbell, Richard T. 1988 "Integrating Conceptualization, Design, and Analysis in Panel Studies of the Life Course." In K. W. Schaie, R. T. Campbell, W. Meredith, and S. C. Rawlings, eds., *Methodological Issues in Aging Research.* New York: Springer.

Campbell, Richard T., and Elizabeth Mutran 1982 "Analyzing Panel Data in Studies of Aging." *Research on Aging* 4:3–41.

Coleman, James S. 1964 *Introduction to Mathematical Sociology.* New York: Free Press.

———1968 "The Mathematical Study of Change." In Hubert M. Blalock, Jr., and Ann B. Blalock, eds., *Methodology in Social Research.* New York: McGraw-Hill.

———1981 *Longitudinal Data Analysis.* New York: Basic Books.

Cook, Nancy R., and James H. Ware 1983 "Design and Analysis Methods for Longitudinal Research." *Annual Review of Public Health* 4:1–23.

Cronbach, Lee J., and Leta Furby 1970 "How We Should Measure Change—Or Should We?" *Psychological Bulletin* 74:32–49.

DiPrete, Thomas A., and David B. Grusky 1990 "Structure and Trend in the Process of Stratification for American Men and Women." *American Journal of Sociology* 96:107–143.

Duncan, Greg J., and Graham Kalton 1987 "Issues of Design and Analysis of Surveys Across Time." *International Statistical Review* 55:97–117.

Duncan, Greg J., and James Morgan 1985 "The Panel Study of Income Dynamics." In Glen H. Elder, ed., *Life Course Dynamics: Trajectories and Transitions, 1968–1980.* Cambridge: Cambridge University Press.

Dwyer, James 1991 "Overview of Models for Longitudinal Data." In James Dwyer and Manning Feinleib, eds., *Statistical Models for Longitudinal Studies of Health.* Oxford: Oxford University Press.

———, and Manning Feinleib (eds.) 1991 *Statistical Models for Longitudinal Studies of Health.* Oxford: Oxford University Press.

Featherman, David L. 1977 "Retrospective Longitudinal Research: Methodological Considerations." *Journal of Economics and Business* 32:152–169.

Fox, John 1984 "Detecting Change in Level and Slope in Repeated Measures Analysis." *Sociological Methods and Research* 12:263–278.

Freedman, David A. 1991 "Statistical Models and Shoe Leather." In Peter V. Marsden, ed., *Sociological Methodology.* Oxford: Basil Blackwell.

Freedman, Deborah, Arland Thornton, Donald Camburn, Duane Alwin, and Linda Young-DeMarco 1988 "The Life History Calendar: A Technique for Collection of Retrospective Data." In Clifford C. Clogg, ed., *Sociological Methodology,* Vol. 18. Washington D.C.: American Sociological Association.

Heckman, James J. 1979 "Sample Selection Bias as a Specification Error." *Econometrica* 47:153–161.

———, and Burton Singer 1985 *Longitudinal Analysis of Labor Market Data.* Cambridge: Cambridge University Press.

Hertzog, Christopher, and Michael Rovine 1985 "Repeated-Measures Analysis of Variance in Developmental Research: Selected Issues." *Child Development* 56:787–809.

Hsiao, Cheng 1986 *Analysis of Panel Data.* Cambridge: Cambridge University Press.

Inter-University Consortium for Political and Social Research 1991 *Guide to Resources and Services.* Ann Arbor, Mich.: Institute for Social Research.

Jöreskog, Karl G., and Dag Sörbom 1988 *LISREL 7: A Guide to the Program and Applications.* Chicago: SPSS.

Kessler, Ronald C., and David F. Greenberg 1981 *Linear Panel Analysis: Models of Quantitative Change.* New York: Academic Press.

Lazarsfeld, Paul R., and M. Fiske 1938 "The 'Panel' as a New Tool for Measuring Opinion." *Public Opinion Quarterly* 2:596–612.

Lieberson, Stanley 1985 *Making It Count.* Berkeley: University of California Press.

Liker, Jeffrey, Susan Augustyniak, and Greg J. Duncan 1985 "Panel Data and Models of Change: A Comparison of First Order Difference and Conventional Two-Wave Models." *Social Science Research* 14:80–101.

Little, Roderick J. A., and Donald B. Rubin 1987 *Statistical Analysis with Missing Data.* New York: Wiley.

Marini, Margaret M., and Burton F. Singer 1988 "Causality in the Social Sciences." In Clifford C. Clogg, ed., *Sociological Methodology,* Vol. 18. Washington, D.C.: American Sociological Association.

McArdle, J. J., and Mark S. Aber 1990 "Patterns of Change within Latent Variable Structural Equation Models." In Alexander von Eye, ed., *Statistical Methods in Longitudinal Research,* Vol 1. San Diego, Calif.: Academic Press.

Menard, Scott 1991 *Longitudinal Research.* Newbury Park, Calif.: Sage.

Migdal, Susan, Ronald P. Abeles, and Lonnie R. Sherrod 1981 *An Inventory of Longitudinal Studies of Middle and Old Age.* New York: Social Science Research Council.

Nielson, Francois, and Rachel A. Rosenfeld 1981 "Substantive Interpretations of Differential Equation Models." *American Sociological Review* 46:159–174.

Rogosa, David 1988 "Myths About Longitudinal Research." In K. W. Schaie, R. T. Campbell, W. Meredith, and S. C. Rawlings, eds., *Methodological Issues in Aging Research.* New York: Springer.

Singer, Burton 1988 "Longitudinal Data Analysis." In Samuel Kotz and Norman Johnson, eds., *Encyclopedia of Statistical Sciences,* Vol. 5. New York: Wiley.

Smith, Tom W. 1986 "The International Social Survey Program." *Journal of Official Statistics* 2:337–338.

Tuma, Nancy Brandon, and Michael T. Hannan 1984 *Social Dynamics: Methods and Models.* Orlando, Fla.: Academic Press.

von Eye, Alexander 1990 *Statistical Methods in Longitudinal Research.* San Diego: Academic Press.

Wall, W. D., and H. L. Williams 1970 *Longitudinal Studies and the Social Sciences.* London: Heinemann.

RICHARD T. CAMPBELL

LONG-TERM CARE Long-term care consists of a range of health, supportive personal care, and social services delivered over a sustained period to individuals who lack some capacity for self-care (Kane and Kane 1987). It includes services for persons with chronic physical or mental illness, mental retardation, or other severe disabling conditions. Long-term care is distinct from acute care in that its purpose is maintenance and custodial rather than curative. It entails, primarily, low-level technology that is provided by low-paid paraprofessionals or family members; and, notably, its costs are paid for by individuals or welfare programs, rather than by traditional insurance mechanisms.

NEED FOR LONG-TERM CARE

Major demographic, social, and health changes resulting in large and growing numbers of older, disabled persons have led to a corresponding increase in the need for long-term care. Improved standards of living and medical advances in the prevention and control of infectious diseases have enabled increasing proportions of the population to live longer. The elderly population as a whole has grown twice as fast as the total population since the 1970s, and this growth has been most rapid for the group over the age of eighty-five (Ferraro and Wan 1990; Longino 1990). Because the incidence of chronic illness increases with age, this growth in the aged population has resulted in a significant increase in the number of persons with chronic disabilities that are the primary determinants of need for long-term care (Senate Committee on Aging 1988). The extent of an individual's disability is most often measured by assessing functional ability, using one of a variety of measures of activities of daily living (ADL) or instrumental activities of daily living (IADL) (see Kane and Kane 1981). According to the 1982 National Long Term Care Survey, 11.7 percent of males and 13.3 percent of females age sixty-five to seventy-four have some type of limitation; the percentages are 40.8 percent for males and 48.2 percent for females age eighty-five and older (Soldo and Manton 1985). However, it is important to note that while the prevalence of functional disability is higher among the oldest old, the actual number of disabled persons is largest among the younger old (Macken 1986).

Recent research suggests that the chances of going through life without disability may be declining in measurable ways (McKinlay et al. 1989). Despite some debate about the compression of morbidity (Fries 1980; Schneider and Brody 1983), some researchers present an overall picture of increasing disability that counters the hopeful view of increased life expectancy and the compression of morbidity (Brody et al. 1987). Together, these trends have led to large and increasing numbers of elderly needing long-term care.

Despite frequent references to the long-term care "system," there is little systematic about long-term care. It varies from state to state and from community to community in composition, organization, eligibility criteria, and financing mechanisms. Among the formal services that have been included are nursing homes, home care, adult day care, respite care, a variety of sheltered housing options, senior centers, congregate dining, and home-delivered meals.

LONG-TERM CARE PROVIDERS AND SERVICES

Nursing Homes. Although the majority of long-term care is provided by informal sources, nursing homes are the bulwark of the current formal long-term care system and the service that has the highest costs. It has been estimated that at any one time about 5 percent of the population age sixty-five and older resides in a nursing home; however, estimates of lifetime risk of institutionalization can range from 25 percent to 35 percent for current-cohort older persons (Liang & Tu 1986; Vincente et al. 1979). Factors associated with nursing home placement include age, sex, and marital status. The need for nursing home care increases with age. The percentage of nursing home residents per thousand is thirteen times higher for men eighty-five and over than for men sixty-five to seventy-four, and eighteen times higher for women eighty-five and over than for women sixty-five to seventy-four (Ferraro and Wan 1990). The large majority of nursing home patients are female and unmarried.

Family Care. The majority of long-term care takes place within the home, and the bulk of this care comes from relatives, friends, and neighbors. According to data from the 1979 and 1980 Home Care Supplement to the National Health Interview Survey, 3.7 million persons of all ages who are living in the community either use equipment or need help from other persons in at least one basic physical activity; about 60 percent of this group are over the age of sixty-five (LaPlante 1989). And as is true with the nursing home population, age is associated with functional dependencies among the elderly living in the community. The oldest old are much more likely to be living in the community with functional dependencies than are the younger old, and they are more likely to have multiple assistance needs.

Estimates of the amount of long-term care provided by informal sources range from 70 percent to 80 percent. Soldo (1984) estimated that 73 percent of care provided for elderly dependent persons in the community came from informal sources; only 16 percent of these persons also received care from formal services. Informal sources provide assistance with a wide range of tasks, including help with banking and legal matters, help with transportation, and assistance with household tasks and personal care. A sizable literature has developed which indicates that the type, intensity, and duration of caregiving varies by the relationship and proximity of the potential caregiver to the receiver (Stone et al. 1987; Montgomery 1991b).

There is a consensus within the literature that a hierarchy exists for designating the informal source of care and for types of care provided (Cantor 1980). When they are available, spouses provide care. When there is no spouse, daughters step in, followed by daughters-in-law, sons, and then more distant relatives. Spouses are likely to provide all types of care when care is needed, including personal care. Daughters and daughters-in-law also provide personal care, although less frequently than do spouses. In contrast, sons, more distant relatives, and friends are more likely to play a backup role, helping with emergencies and limited-time tasks (Gurland et al. 1978; Montgomery 1991b).

A huge literature has emerged that has documented the social, psychological, and physical costs of this informal care (Montgomery 1985; George and Gwyther 1986), and has contributed to the focus on formal support services as a means to augment or replace informal support. The most commonly used community formal support services are home care and adult day care (Benjamin 1991).

Home Care. Home care, like long-term care, is difficult to define because it encompasses a wide range of specific services. Home care is used to refer to in-home health and supportive services that include professional, paraprofessional, post-acute, and long-term care in a recipient's home (Benjamin 1991; Kane and Kane 1987). At one end of the continuum of cost and skills, these include physician and nursing services, and at the other end of the continuum, they include housekeeper and chore services (Kane and Kane 1987).

Using data from the 1984 Supplement on Aging, Stone (1986) reports that 21.5 percent of older Americans used one or more community social and health services in a six-month period. Three-fourths of this user group had used senior centers only. Utilization of home-based services was not widespread. Only 2.9 percent of all elderly persons reported use of visiting nurse care; 1.6 percent used home health aide services; 1.4 percent used homemaker services; and 1.9 percent used home-delivered meals. Nearly 80 percent of the elderly used no community services during this period, and more than half of those who did (11.4 percent), utilized only one service. The receipt of home care services by an older person is a relatively rare event among the general population of older cohorts.

As would be expected, analysis of data on service utilization by impaired older persons reveals greater use of home care services by this subpopulation. Using data from the 1979 Home Care Supplement, Soldo (1985) reported that one out of four older persons with functional limitations (25.1 percent) had received formal "community home care" services, and nearly half of these (10 percent overall) were totally dependent upon formal services. Analysis of data from the 1982 National Long Term Care Survey indicated that the use of formal community care services was even higher (31 percent) among persons with severe functional and cognitive impairments (Stone et al. 1987).

Adult Day Care. Although nursing home care, informal care, and home care are the most common sources of long-term care, three other types of services are often considered to be part of long-term care. These are sheltered care, adult day care, and respite services. Adult day care is a community-based, therapeutically oriented program that provides health, social, and rehabilitative services to frail older persons in a congregate setting during daytime hours. Day care centers vary in emphasis from those that focus on rehabilitation and follow a medical model to those that focus on maintenance and follow a social model. A wide range of services can be offered through such programs, including physical therapy, health maintenance programs, assistance with daily activities, and social and recreational activities.

During the 1980s the number of day care centers expanded greatly; according to one study there are currently 1,347 day care centers throughout the country with an average daily enrollment of 24 persons (Conrad et al. 1990). Unfortunately, many day care centers struggle to keep their census up and their doors open because there are few sources of third-party payment for adult day care and many potential clients cannot afford it. In the design and delivery of their services, adult day care centers focus on the impaired older person. Their goals include the maintenance of maximum functioning in their clients and the improvement of their quality of life. One of the main purposes of day care centers, however, is to benefit family members who are providing the majority of care for these impaired elders, by providing family members a break from their daily caregiving tasks. As such, adult day care has become one of the primary sources of respite care.

Respite Care. Like most other long-term care services, respite care can entail a wide range of services. In addition to adult day care, respite services have included nursing home services, home care services, and stays in hospitals. The unique aspect of respite is not the specific service that is offered but the purpose for which the service is offered, which is to provide a break for the primary caregiver of an impaired elder. Research focused on long-term care and families has consistently reported that respite services, particularly in-home services, have emerged as the type of support most frequently desired by family members (Montgomery 1991a). However, due to lack of funding by third-party sources, it remains a service that is not widely available. More troubling is the past research which shows that respite services frequently go unused when they are available, a fact that has prompted researchers to begin investigating factors affecting utilization (Montgomery 1991a; Lawton 1989).

Sheltered Care. Although the bricks-and-mortar part of housing falls outside long-term care per se, Kane and Kane (1987) argue that housing policy can provide a framework for effective long-term care delivery and that many housing arrangements can directly or indirectly provide services, such as congregate meals and social programs, which can be considered aspects of long-term care. Federal housing for the elderly, congregate care settings, board and care housing, shared housing, and life care communities have been developed as means to ensure long-term care. Although there has been evidence that such housing improves the ability of functionally impaired persons to live independently, these housing options are not widely available nor is there a consistent means of financing such housing for low-income, impaired older persons.

LONG-TERM CARE AS A PUBLIC ISSUE

Long-term care has become a salient and publicly debated issue primarily because the growing numbers of persons needing care and the rapidly rising costs of health care have created a burden for both the public purse and individual resources (Kane and Kane 1987; Estes and Lee 1985). Because funding of long-term care has been limited, decentralized, categorical, and linked with welfare programs, the heavy burdens of long-term care have touched not only the poor but also millions of middle-income families and individuals. For these persons the high cost of caring for a chronically or acutely ill elderly person can lead to impoverishment and the necessity of relying on public resources (Estes and Lee 1985). Hence, the focus of public debate has been the primary dilemma of long-term care—to identify an affordable and equitable means to provide care.

Biomedical Bias. To a large extent, the long-term care dilemma has emerged as a consequence of three distinct but related value conflicts. First, long-term care has suffered because there is a biomedical bias among providers and policymakers (Estes and Lee 1985). In accord with the medical model, legitimate health care needs are those which require technical and medical care that will lead to cures or rehabilitations. The social and custodial needs of patients are given low priority. This bias toward medical care in the allocation of resources has resulted in the "medicalization" of services, as exemplified in the high proportion of publicly financed health expenditures allocated to hospital and physician coverage, as opposed to community, in-home, and other social services (Estes and Lee 1985).

This bias toward medical care in the allocation of public resources is also reflected in the two separate mechanisms that currently finance the majority of care for the elderly (Meyer and Quadagno 1990). Medicare, which is the primary source for financing acute medical care, is a universal health program; Medicaid, which is the primary source for financing long-term care, is a means-tested program for the impoverished. Furthermore, Medicare is a centralized federal mechanism for paying for acute care needs, while Medicaid is a decentralized, federal/state mechanism that varies across states in terms of eligibility, coverage, and benefits (Ferraro and Wan 1990). These differences in funding mechanisms have contributed to the low priority given to long-term care by physicians and hospitals because it is not economically rewarding for health care professionals to provide services to Medicaid beneficiaries.

Criteria for Eligibility. The dual basis for financing long-term care versus acute care reflects the second conflict that underlies the long-term care policy dilemma, the criteria of eligibility for benefits. Specifically, long-term care policy reflects an ambivalence toward the belief that age is a legitimate criterion for defining need (Meyers and Quadagno 1990). A historical review of policy development indicates that both the Medicare Act and the Medicaid legislation are grounded in welfare policy that has been strongly influenced by the Elizabethan poor laws, which were created to assist only the deserving poor and to discourage the undeserving poor from seeking help (Meyer and Quadagno 1990). The difference between the two programs rests in the definition of *deserving.* The Medicare program, with its emphasis on acute care, treats age as a legitimate criterion for determining *deserving.* Marmor (1970, p. 15) notes that the Medicare Act of 1965 defined the aged as both "needy and deserving through no fault of their own because they had less income and greater medical needs." However, the deep ambivalence that Americans have long felt about poverty is reflected in the fact that the Medicare Act provides for universal entitlement for the elderly only for acute care needs. The long-term care needs of disabled elderly, which are primarily social service needs, are financed through Medicaid, a means-tested program that defines need based on income and disability rather than on age. As such, long-term care policy is the stepchild of traditional welfare policy, which has been developed and instituted by state and local government to deal with the poor. The goal of this public policy has been to manage the care of the poor in the most efficient and least costly way, rather than to redress the underlying social causes of dependency (Estes and Lee 1985).

Family Responsibility. The third value conflict that contributes to policy debates and the dilemma of providing adequate long-term care also has its roots in the Elizabethan poor laws. This conflict concerns the appropriate role of family members in providing long-term care. At issue is the relative responsibility of the state versus that of the family. Although social historians have documented the economic basis for family responsibility in the past, there is a widely held public belief that family responsibility for the care of the elderly is a moral obligation (Schorr 1980). In part, this belief has emerged because the Elizabethan poor laws, which specifically designated the family members as the parties having the first line of responsibility for the care of dependent members, have been the model for modern welfare laws. These laws were created to protect the public purse after industrialization freed individuals to earn a living apart from family-owned land and businesses, creating the possibility that older persons could become dependent on the community for care.

Despite this economic basis for the creation of the Elizabethan poor laws and modern derivatives in welfare and long-term care legislation, the reasons for enacting them have often been couched in moral language, creating and reinforcing a common belief about the moral basis of family responsibility (Schorr 1980). The presence of this belief, combined with the reality that the majority of long-term care is provided by family members, has led to policy debates about the appropriate role of the family, and to the implementation of programs and practices aimed at retaining and/or supporting families as the primary sources of long-term care (Borgatta and Montgomery 1987).

Together these three value conflicts have created the context within which long-term care policy and practices have been debated and legislation has been formulated and reformulated. As a result, long-term care policy has evolved in a piecemeal, crisis-oriented manner that has perpetuated an uncoordinated set of services with fragmented funding. The three value conflicts have also been the context within which research and demonstration programs have been implemented to address the long-term care dilemma. These demonstrations and policy changes have usually been aimed at constraining costs of long-term care for the public purse by substituting low-cost services for higher-cost services, restricting access to services, and/or shifting responsibility for care to the family. The most notable experiments have been the national channeling demonstration of the 1980s, the establishment of social/health maintenance organizations; the imposition of a prospective payment system (diagnostic-related groups) in 1983; and the passage (1988) and repeal (1989) of the Medicare catastrophic coverage. Additionally, numerous programs introducing respite care, support groups, and education programs for family caregivers have been designed and tested (Montgomery 1991a). Unfortunately, none of these experiments has led to a solution of the long-term care dilemma, which will continue to be a major policy issue until the basic value conflicts are addressed more directly.

(SEE ALSO: *Death and Dying; Health and the Life Course; Nursing Homes; Social Gerontology*)

REFERENCES

Benjamin, A. E. 1991 (Forthcoming) "In-Home Health and Supportive Services for Older Persons: Background and Perspective." In M. Ory and A. Duncker, eds., *In-Home Health and Supportive Services for Older People.* Newbury Park, Calif.: Sage.

Borgatta, E. F., and R. J. V. Montgomery 1987 "Aging Policy and Societal Values." In E. F. Borgatta and R. J. V. Montgomery, eds., *Critical Issues in Aging Policy: Linking Research and Values.* Newbury Park, Calif.: Sage.

Brody, J., D. Brock, and T. F. Williams 1987 "Trends in the Health of the Elderly Population." *Annual Review of Public Health* 8:211–234.

Cantor, M. H. 1980 "The Informal Support System: Its Relevance in the Lives of the Elderly." In E. F. Borgatta and N. G. McCluskey, eds., *Aging and Society: Current Research and Policy Perspectives.* Beverly Hills, Calif.: Sage.

Conrad, K. J., P. Hanrahan, and S. L. Hughes 1990 "Survey of Adult Day Care in the United States." *Research on Aging* 12, no. 1:36–56.

Estes, C. L., and P. R. Lee 1985 "Social, Political, and Economic Background of Long Term Care Policy." In C. Harrington, R. J. Newcomer, and C. L. Estes, eds., *Long Term Care of the Elderly: Public Policy Issues.* Beverly Hills, Calif.: Sage.

Ferraro, K. F., and T. T. H. Wan 1990 "Health Needs and Services for Older Adults: Evaluating Policies for an Aging Society." In S. M. Stahl, ed., *The Legacy of Longevity.* Newbury Park, Calif.: Sage.

Fries, J. F. 1980 "Aging, Natural Death, and the Compression of Morbidity." *New England Journal of Medicine* 303:130–135.

George, L. K., and L. P. Gwyther 1986 "Caregiver Well-being: A Multidimensional Examination of Family Caregivers." *The Gerontologist* 26, no. 3:253–259.

Gurland, B., L. Dean, R. Guland, and D. Cook 1978 "Personal Time Dependency in the Elderly of New York City: Findings from the U.S.-U.K. Cross-National Geriatric Community Study." New York: Community Council of Greater New York.

Kane, R. A., and R. L. Kane 1981 *Assessing the Elderly: A Practical Guide to Measurement.* Lexington, Mass.: D. C. Health.

——— 1987 *Long-Term Care: Principles, Programs and Policies.* New York: Springer.

LaPlante, M. P. 1989 "Disability in Basic Life Activities

Across the Life Span." *Disability Statistics Report* 1:1–42.

Lawton, M. P. 1989 "A Controlled Study of Respite Service for Caregivers of Alzheimer's Patients." *The Gerontologist* 29, no. 1:8–16.

Liang, J., and E. J. Tu 1986 "Estimating Lifetime Risk of Nursing Home Residency: A Further Note." *The Gerontologist* 26, no. 5:560–563.

Longino, C. 1990 "The Relative Contributions of Gender, Social Class, and Advancing Age to Health. In S. M. Stahl, ed., *The Legacy of Longevity.* Newbury Park, Calif.: Sage.

Macken, C. L. 1986 "A Profile of Functionally Impaired Elderly Persons Living in the Community." *Health Care Financing Review* 7:33–49.

Marmor, T. 1970 *The Politics of Medicare.* New York: Aldine.

McAuley, W. J., S. S. Travis, and M. Safewright 1990 "The Relationship Between Formal and Informal Health Care Services for the Elderly." In S. M. Stahl, ed., *The Legacy of Longevity.* Newbury Park, Calif.: Sage.

McKinlay, J., S. McKinlay, and R. Beaglehole 1989 "Trends in Death and Disease in the Contribution of Medical Measures." In H. Freeman and S. Levin, eds., *Handbook of Medical Sociology.* Englewood Cliffs., N.J.: Prentice-Hall.

Meyer, M. H., and J. Quadagno 1990 "The Dilemma of Poverty-Based Long-Term Care." In S. M. Stahl, ed., *The Legacy of Longevity.* Newbury Park, Calif.: Sage.

Montgomery, R. J. V. 1984 "Barriers to the Design and Delivery of Family Support Services." Paper presented to Conference on Families at Interage, September.

———1985 "Measurement and the Analysis of Burden." *Research on Aging* 7, no. 1:137–152.

———1991a "Examining Respite: Its Promise and Limits." In M. Ory and A. Duncker, eds., *In-Home Health and Supportive Services for Older People.* Newbury Park, Calif.: Sage.

———1991b "Gender Differences in Patterns of Child-Parent Caregiving Relationships." In J. W. Dwyer and R. T. Coward, eds., *Gender and Family Care of the Elderly.* Newbury Park, Calif.: Sage.

Schneider, E. L., and Jacob A. Brody 1983 "Aging, Natural Death, and the Compression of Morbidity: Another View." *New England Journal of Medicine* 309, no. 14:854–856.

Schorr, A. L. 1980 *Thy Father and Thy Mother . . . a Second Look at Filial Responsibility and Family Policy.* No. 13-11953. Social Security Administration. Washington, D.C.: U.S. Government Printing Office.

Senate Committee on Aging 1988 *Developments in Aging, 1987,* Vol. III, *Long Term Care Challenge.* Washington, D.C.: U.S. Government Printing Office.

Soldo, B. J. 1982 "Effects of Number and Sex of Adult Children on LTC Service Use Patterns." Paper prepared for the annual meeting of the Gerontological Society of America, November.

———1984 "Supply of Informal Care Services: Variation and Effects on Service Utilization Patterns." In W. Scanlon, ed., *Project to Analyze Existing Long-Term Care Data,* vol. 3. Washington, D.C.: The Urban Institute.

———1985 "In-Home Services for the Dependent Elderly: Determinants of Current Use and Implications for Future Demand." *Research on Aging* 7, no. 2:281–304.

Soldo, B., and K. Manton 1985 "Health Status and Service Needs of the Oldest Old: Current Patterns and Future Trends." *Milbank Memorial Fund Quarterly* 63:286–319.

Stone, R. 1986 "Aging in the Eighties, Age 65 Years and Over—Use of Community Services." NCHS Advance Data, no. 124. Hyattsville, Md.: National Center for Health Statistics.

———, G. Cafferata, and J. Sangl 1987 "Caregivers of the Frail Elderly: A National Profile." *The Gerontologist* 27:616–626.

Vincente, L. 1979 "The Risk of Institutionalization Before Death." *The Gerontologist* 19:361–367.

Weissert, W. G., T. Wan, B. Livieratos, and S. Katz 1980 "Effects and Costs of Day-Care Services for the Chronically Ill." *Medical Care* 18:567–584.

RHONDA J. V. MONTGOMERY

LOVE

LOVE Sociologists agree that love is one of the most elusive concepts to deal with from a scientific point of view. Indeed, they often point out that poets, novelists, and musical composers are much more adept at producing eloquent expressions about this pervasive sentiment. Dictionary definitions are of limited use in categorizing the essential ingredients of love, except to connote its many variations as an attitude, an emotion, or a behavior. No one definition can capture all the dimensions of love, which can involve a wide range of elements such as romantic obsession, sexuality, caring, even irrationality. Part of the difficulty is that individuals and their cultures define love very differently, depending on particular relationships and circumstances. The love of an infant, for example, is not the same as that felt toward a parent, a spouse, a relative, a friend, or a lover.

Conceptions of love have varied from one culture to another, from one historical era to another (Murstein 1974; Hunt 1959). The range of psychological, social, and cultural meanings attached to love would, therefore, appear to be limitless. However, we experience and express love mostly according to the culture and subcultures in which we have formed our sentiments. The formation of these sentiments begins very early and evolves through the physical and emotional attachments that characterize the parent–child relationship. While idiosyncratic patterns exist, love scripts by and large reflect the influence of cultural conditioning. In short, love is largely a learned response.

Cultural norms are internalized and program us to fall in love with specific types of people, within certain social contexts, to the exclusion of others. However, love is not necessarily related to marriage. There is a saying, for example, that in the West one falls in love and then gets married, whereas in the East one marries and then falls in love. In some societies arranged marriages were and still are contracted. The emotional intensity a couple feels toward each other is given little or no consideration. Instead, emphasis is given to the sociopolitical implications of the marital alliance for the families and kinship groups involved.

In the United States, on the other hand, love is viewed as an important condition to marriage. We are generally suspicious of anyone who would marry for any other reason. We are not comfortable with the idea that in some cultures a man marries his mother's brother's daughter because that is the prescribed pattern. Even among our upper classes, where concern over protecting family resources leads to a greater emphasis on such practical considerations in mate selection, couples are expected to espouse mutual love as the basis for their marriage, else their motives become suspect. Marital alliances concocted primarily to preserve or enhance family wealth often receive a cynical response from the public at large.

Families recognize that courtship and mate selection merge not only two individuals but also two different kinship lines, which in turn may affect their socioeconomic and political stature. Consequently, families invest considerable energy and resources to control love (Goode 1959). Several mechanisms to accomplish this have been identified, including the direct control provided by (1) child marriages, in which betrothal may occur before puberty or even before the child is born; (2) defining the pool of eligibles, that is, delineating whom one can and cannot marry; (3) physical or social isolation to limit the probabilities of contact; and (4) various indirect controls such as moving to preferred residential neighborhoods, enrolling children in appropriate schools, joining select organizations, or attending certain churches. The latter mechanism is most characteristic of Western societies.

In American society a *romantic love complex* exists, and this complex posits love as a central prerequisite to marriage. The basic components of this complex are assimilated through the mass media—through romantic stories in novels, magazines, television, and movies. In this way we are psychologically prepared to fall in love. The major characteristics of romantic love include romantic democracy; that is, cultural differences between couples are minimized or ignored because "love and love alone" is sufficient. Indeed, it involves the notion that romantic love thrives on such differences. Romantic love also includes romantic intensity; that is, people are expected to fall in love instantly (love at first sight) and deeply, with great emotional attachment. Finally, romantic love includes romantic monopoly in that once the "bolt from the blue" strikes, the couple presume exclusive emotional and social rights to each other, in perpetuity (Merrill 1959). A person experiencing the full thrust of this complex is supposedly consumed by constant thoughts about the beloved, a longing to spend all one's time with that person, a sad pining in the beloved's absence, and a feeling that life would not be worth living without him or her (Tennov 1980).

There is disagreement as to the extent to which people adhere to the tenets of the romantic love complex and whether it actually influences mate selection. Sociologists have generally viewed it as a poor basis for the establishment of permanent unions inasmuch as it involves an element of capricious choice based upon an unpredictable emotion. Moreover, romantic love is not completely rational. Part of its credo is that there is one and only one true love or ideal mate. Yet we know that people fall in and out of love several times in a lifetime.

People caught up in the romantic complex often idealize their partners. Some argue that this process of idealization, in which a distorted positive picture of the love partner is constructed, results from the blockage of sexual impulses by cultural prohibitions. If this were true, then one would expect a liberalization of our sexual mores to be accompanied by a decline in romanticism. However, this does not appear to have happened, at least in Western societies. What does happen is that the elements of the romantic love complex, including the idealized picture of the partner, are modified to fit the reality of that person that emerges through close and intimate interaction over time. Couples unable to make this accommodation are apt to suffer disillusionment, and their marriages may encounter persistent difficulties. For marriage to succeed, the overromanticized notions and idealizations of romantic love must eventually be replaced by *conjugal love,* which is based upon habits, common interests, mutual acceptance, and mature companionship derived from a shared history.

Sexual impulses and romantic love are often directed at the same person, but they are not the same. People are known to pursue sexual encounters in the absence of any romantic feelings. One is derived from our biological heritage, and the other is a learned cultural pattern. They bear a relationship to one another, however, in that romance often encompasses sexually motivated behavior plus a cluster of cultural expectations (Merrill 1959).

There appear to be gender differences with respect to love and loving. It is generally assumed that such differences reflect culturally defined sex roles. Women have been stereotypically portrayed as starry-eyed romantics, while men are viewed as exploitative realists. However, research shows that men fall in love more quickly than women do and with less deliberation, score higher on scales of romanticism, express stronger romantic attitudes, and suffer greater emotional stress when relationships are terminated. Because women may have potentially more to lose from a social and economic standpoint, they tend to be more prudent or discriminating in establishing and maintaining love relationships (Hochschild 1983). They are more apt to take into account practical considerations regarding mate selection. Hence, in comparison to men, women are more likely to terminate relationships and more easily to disengage emotionally when couples break up (Rubin 1973).

Social scientists have explored the sequences through which the dimensions of love relationships develop and have constructed numerous typologies of love. They have also detected and described a number of styles of loving (Kemper 1988; Lasswell and Lasswell 1980). Love is said to begin typically with physical symptoms—palpitations of the heart, rapid breathing, sweating, and so on. At this stage the symptoms are essentially similar to those associated with other emotions such as fear. Next the person proceeds to label this arousal as a love response. This labeling process gains impetus from social pressures and cultural dictates, which prod one to define the experience as love and to follow its ritualistic patterns.

The optimum conditions for love to flourish require that the couple be equally involved in and committed to each other and the relationship. Where there is unequal involvement, the person with the strongest commitment may be vulnerable to exploitation. This is known as the *principle of least interest,* in which the partner with the least interest has the most control. Few relationships that are based on this principle can endure.

(SEE ALSO: *Courtship; Interpersonal Attraction; Mate Selection, Theories)*

REFERENCES

Goode, William J. 1959 "The Theoretical Importance of Love." *American Sociological Review* 24:38–47.

Hochschild, Arlie R. 1983 *The Managed Heart.* Berkeley: University of California Press.

Hunt, Morton 1959 *The Natural History of Love.* New York: Alfred A. Knopf.

Kemper, Theodore 1988 "Love and Like and Love and *Love.*" In David Franks, ed., *The Sociology of Emotions.* Greenwich, Conn.: JAI Press.

Lasswell, Marcia, and Norman M. Lasswell 1980 *Styles of Loving.* New York: Doubleday.

Merrill, Francis E. 1959 *Courtship and Marriage.* New York: Holt-Dryden.

Murstein, Bernard I. 1974 *Love, Sex, and Marriage Through the Ages.* New York: Springer.

Rubin, Zick 1973 *Loving and Liking.* New York: Holt, Rinehart and Winston.

Schwartz, Gary, Don Mertem, Fran Beham, and Allyne Rosenthal 1980 *Love and Commitment.* Beverly Hills, Calif.: Sage.

Tennov, Dorothy 1980 *Love and Limerence: The Experience of Being in Love.* New York: Stein and Day.

FELIX M. BERARDO

M

MACROSOCIOLOGY The term *macro* denotes large; thus macrosociology refers to the study of large-scale social phenomena. This covers a very broad range of topics that includes groups and collectivities of varying sizes, the major organizations and institutions of one or more societies, cross-sectional or historical studies of a single society, and both comparative and historical analyses of multiple societies. At the grandest level it may cover all of human society and history.

Sociologists distinguish macrosociology from microsociology, which focuses on the social activities of individuals and small groups. The micro-macro distinction forms one of the central dualisms characterizing divergent sociological perspectives. Seemingly polar opposites such as conflict-consensus, stability-change, structure-action, subjective-objective, and materialist-idealist, as well as micro-macro, provide a shorthand for denoting differences in central assumptions, subjects, and models. As with many other oppositional concepts, however, the boundary between micro- and macrosociology is not clearly distinguished, and at the margins there is much room for overlap.

Typically, micro-level studies examine individual thought, action, and interaction, often coinciding with social-psychological theories and models, whereas macro-level investigations target social structures. Nevertheless, in defining these terms there is a major conceptual ambiguity that can be formulated in the form of a question: Should the distinction be based on substantive (specialty and subdisciplinary areas within sociology such as social change and development), theoretical (e.g., functionalist, Marxist, neo-Marxist), metatheoretical (type of paradigm, epistemology) or methodological (type of research design and analysis techniques) criteria? Since sociologists often use the terms micro and macro quite casually as convenient devices for categorizing broad areas of theory and research, each of these criteria can be found in the literature, and quite often they are seriously confounded.

A useful means of distinguishing between the two approaches is based on the concept of "units of analysis." Macrosociology uses as its subjects structural-level units of analysis or cases that are larger than observations of individual action and interaction. Even here, however, there is room for slippage, since it is quite possible to make observations on smaller units (e.g., individuals) with the intention of analyzing (making inferences about) larger entities (e.g., groups, classes). Also, the issue of where to draw the line remains. Rather than attempting to draw any hard-and-fast line delineating macro- from micro-level phenomena, it is helpful to conceptualize a continuum of the subject matter of sociology, with micro and macro defining two end points and with societal-level phenomena clearly placed at the macro pole. George Ritzer, for example, describes one "level of social reality" as a micro-macro continuum moving from individual thought and action through interaction, groups, organizations, and societies to culminate in world systems (Ritzer 1988, pp. 512–518).

Since the macro end of the continuum focuses on social structure, it is important to clarify the use of this term. In a review essay, Neil Smelser (1988, pp. 103–129) describes structure as patterned relationships that emerge from the interaction of individuals or groups over time and space. Institutions and identifiable collectivities are the outcomes of systematically related structures of activities. Structure is dually defined as located in collective actors and in their interaction. Thus social class is an example of social structure, as are the relationships between classes whose locus is the economy. The study of both social class and the economy are examples of macrosociology.

HISTORICAL BACKGROUND

The concern with macro-level phenomena is as old as the discipline of sociology and arguably is the primary motivation for the creation of classical sociological theory and research. The men generally accorded honored places in the pantheon of sociology's founders (e.g., Auguste Comte, Herbert Spencer, Karl Marx, Emile Durkheim, and Max Weber) all included macro-level phenomena among their dominant concerns. The traditions they established retain their definitive role for the central issues of sociology in general and macrosociology in particular.

The themes pursued by these and other classical theorists are found in current theory and research. For example, the evolutionary perspective on the development of human society advanced in crude forms by Comte, Spencer, and to a lesser extent Marx have been updated, refined, and in conjunction with much subsequent anthropological work, given current voice by Gerhard Lenski (1966). Marx's historical materialist explanation of the unfolding of capitalism has spawned numerous offspring, including dependency and world systems theories. Similarly, Weber's comparative and historical studies of the development of modern states are reflected in the work of Barrington Moore (1966) and Theda Skocpol (1979). Durkheim's analyses of the division of labor in modern societies as well as the sources of societal integration underlie all functional analysis and modernization theory as well as most contemporary studies of the occupational structure. In short, the macrosociological problems defined early in the history of sociology remain major foci of current sociological research.

Also located in these early works but often overlooked in subsequent interpretations is an issue that is the current central project of many social theorists: the links between macro- and micro-level phenomena. At least in the writings of Marx, Weber, and Durkheim, to a greater or lesser degree, efforts are made to connect individual- and structural-level activities in some coherent fashion. For example, Marx is often considered the quintessential macrosociologist, providing the foundation for much current macrosociology. Yet as Bertell Ollman (1976) and others point out, there is a distinct social psychology anchored in Marx's concept of alienation that in turn motivates and is motivated by his macro-level models of productive relations and class conflict. This concern with linkage has often been ignored or forgotten in the distinctive development of different schools of sociological thought. After years of separate development and sometimes acrimonious debate, efforts to build unified social theories that include both ends of the micro-macro continuum now constitute a major agenda for many sociologists. Examples of some of these efforts will be reviewed after a discussion of more traditional themes found in contemporary macrosociological theory and research.

THEMES IN MACROSOCIOLOGICAL THEORY AND RESEARCH

Macrosociological studies focus on large-scale structural arrangements dealing with social institutions, social change, conflict, and development. Studies vary in both subject and theoretical orientation, but the two are closely related. For example, large-scale studies of single total societies or particular societal institutions often work from a functionalist perspective in which the effort is to understand how the complexity of component parts fit together and serve larger social goals. On the other hand, studies of social change, either within a single society or across cultures, more often use one of the many variants of conflict, Marxist, and neo-Marxist perspectives. They do so because such theories are better equipped to explain conflict and change than the relatively static models promoted by functionalism, and because functionalism no longer dominates sociology. These are broad generalizations, however, which invite counterexample.

Given the sweeping scope of macrosociology, it is not possible to provide comprehensive coverage of all the topics and theories subsumed under this approach. The next section will illustrate key concerns of macrosociologists by describing exemplary theory and research in the areas of societal and social change and selected social institutions.

Societal Change. The numerous approaches to the study of societal change illustrate the diversity of sociological perspectives. At the most sweeping level, evolutionary theories take all of human history and society as their subject. Evolutionary theory has gone hand in hand with functionalism, as in Talcott Parsons' later work (1966), and with critical theory as exemplified by Jurgen Habermas (1979), who uses an evolutionary model to explain the development of normative structures and forms of rationality. It has also taken a materialist form, as developed by anthropologists (Harris 1977) and a few sociologists (Lenski and Lenski 1987). While there are relatively few sociologists who currently operate on this scale or who find it useful for analyzing more confined periods of historical change, current theories of human evolution have been influential in providing comparative evidence for the material and normative bases of different forms of social organization and for describing the broadest patterns of societal change. These include the distribution of societal goods and services, the more enduring forms of inequality (e.g., patriarchy), and normative systems.

The Emergence of the Modern World. Sociologists more often limit their study of change to the emergence of modern industrial society, either to trace the paths taken by mature industrialized societies to reach their current stage of development or to investigate the problems of developing nations. Here, too, different approaches emerge from different theoretical perspectives. Modernization theory, which until not too long ago dominated accounts of development and change, grew out of functionalism and evolutionary perspectives. In the version articulated by economist W. W. Rostow (1960), nonindustrial societies, through diffusion and a natural developmental sequence, were expected to follow a series of stages previously traversed by fully industrialized nations to attain the significant characteristics of modern societies considered prerequisites for development. This process required breaking from traditional social norms and values to build institutions based on "modern" values such as universalism, rationalization, and achievement orientation.

Although today largely abandoned in favor of more historically and materially grounded theories, modernization theory was highly influential among both scholars and policymakers of the post-World War II era. In fact, it can be argued that its influence in part explains its repudiation, since students of and from emerging developing nations viewed it as an instrument of continued colonial and capitalist domination. Their search for tools to provide a better explanation for their disadvantaged and subordinate position in the international arena led to the adoption of Marxist-based models of dependency, underdevelopment, and world systems to replace modernization as the dominant approach to change and development within the modern era. As summarized by Peter Evans and John Stephens (1988, p. 740), these "approaches turned the modernization theorists' emphasis on diffusion . . . on its head, arguing instead that ties to 'core' countries were a principal impediment to development."

In an influential early formulation, dependency theorist André Gunder Frank (1967) maintained that the experience of most nonindustrial nations is explained by the "development of underdevelopment." In other words, the exploitation of peripheral Third World nations by capital in the core, developed world increased the economic, social, and political misery experienced by the majority populations of those Third World countries. Alliances between local and international elites actively worked to defend the status quo distribution of power and privilege at the expense of peasant- and working-class majorities. Later versions refined the models of class conflict and competition or, as in the writings of Samir Amin (1976), elaborated the model of the relationships between center and periphery economies to show how underdevelopment grows out of the exploitive links between the two types of systems. All versions contribute to a refutation of the trajectory of development described by modernization theory.

A more global approach to development issues was formulated by Immanuel Wallerstein (1974, 1980, 1988) and his followers. World systems theory elaborates the Marxist model of economic domination into a system in which exploitation occurs worldwide. Wallerstein broadens the focus on class relations among and across nations to examine the development of an international division of labor in the capitalist world economy where core industrial nations exploit peripheral regions as sources of raw materials and labor. This approach has been both enormously influential and controversial, generating massive amounts of research on the model itself, particular spatial and historical portions of the world system, and particular subsectors and groups. A helpful overview that charts the intricacies of this perspective can be found in a text by Thomas Shannon (1989).

The emphasis on First World as well as Third World development found in world systems theory provides a bridge to a slightly different tradition, which focuses on the emergence of the core industrial nations and their political systems. Much of this literature is concerned with the development of modern political as well as economic systems. For example, while Barrington Moore's (1966) study of the transformation of agrarian societies into modern industrial states remains firmly anchored in a Marxist emphasis on class relations and productive systems, it is also concerned with the political roles played by antagonistic classes and the political outcomes of their confrontation. Numerous other studies pursue a similar comparative perspective on the upheavals that accompanied the emergence of modern Western industrial nations (cf. Tilly, Tilly, and Tilly 1975).

Some studies move toward a Weberian approach by focusing on the emergence of modern states. The extent to which the state and the economy operate as autonomous systems or are subsumed by one or the other forms an ongoing theme in much current debate. For example, Theda Skocpol (1979) begins with a class-based approach to explain the social revolutions that ushered in modern states in France, Russia, and China but ends by adopting a more state-centered model in which the state and its administrative apparatus may be relatively autonomous actors in the emergence of modern society.

One other type of study in this tradition deserves mention. These are studies of social and political change that occur within a particular society at various stages in the industrialization process. John Walton (1987) provides a convenient typology based on cross-classifying epochs and processes of industrialization. The resulting types range from protoindustrialization through deindustrialization. Studies from early periods focus on the emergence of particular classes, class conflict, and their influence on the historical development of modern nations, as in E. P. Thompson's (1963) and John Foster's (1974) influential accounts of English class formation, Ron Aminzade's (1984) analysis of nineteenth-century France, and Herbert Gutman's (1966) studies of American class culture and conflict. Works on later periods examine the consolidation of control of the labor process (Burawoy 1979; Edwards 1979), deindustrialization (Bluestone and Harrison 1982), and informalization of labor markets (Portes et al. 1989).

Finally, while beyond the scope of this review, there are also other important traditions that either fall under the topic of social change or have strong links to one or the other approaches described above. One of these is found in a vast literature on social movements that has many points of intersection with the work on comparative and historical social and political change discussed here. Another is work that applies theories of dependency and uneven development to regional development problems internal to particular societies. Finally, there are structural and poststructural approaches to the development of major social institutions and forms of repression, as found in the complex but increasingly influential work of Michel Foucault (1979, 1980, 1985). While this last example could as easily be classified under studies of social institutions and processes, it is included here because of its focus on changes in historical times that have produced modern social forms.

Social Structures, Processes, and Institutions. The type of work discussed under societal and social change incorporates investigation of many of the major social structures, processes, and institutions that form the core subject matter of sociology. Studying change in economic and political systems requires scrutiny of economies, polities, and other social institutions and their major organizational manifestations and constituencies. However, other theoretical and substantive approaches subsumed under macrosociology either have fallen outside the scope of these large-scale studies of social change and development or are at their periphery. Theoretical perspectives include relatively recent developments such as structural, poststructural, and feminist theories. Important substantive areas are defined by a cumulating empirical base of knowledge about power structures, work structures, social stratification and mobility, labor markets, and household and family arrangements. Virtually all theoretical perspectives discussed so far are represented in this empirical work.

While it is impossible to survey each of these areas, the burgeoning literature using feminist theories to investigate gender stratification provides a prime example of new approaches to macrosociology. There have been at least two major contributions of feminist theory to macrosociology. One has been to show how theories of social reproduction must be joined to theories of economic production to understand social life fully. Another contribution has been to delineate the ways patriarchy coexists with particular economic systems to explain the position of women in society. Feminist theorists argue that analyses that ignore the system of gender relations embedded in patriarchy are incomplete. A variety of social arrangements, including the subordination of women, are predicated on how tasks that exist outside the labor market (household labor, childbearing and child rearing, consumption activities, etc.) are allocated. An influential example is found in Heidi Hartmann's (1981) socialist feminist analysis of the intersection of capitalism and patriarchy, which explains women's disadvantaged status in both the labor market and in the household in late capitalism as the outcome of an uneasy alliance between the two systems. With increasing demand for women's labor in the second half of the twentieth century, the intersection of the two systems has taken the form of the "double day"—i.e., women burdened by responsibility for both formal labor market activity and household work.

Similar insights from feminist perspectives have informed studies of both developing nations and industrialization. For example, Ester Boserup's (1970) critique of conventional development theories demonstrates the pitfalls for development projects resulting from ignoring women as well as the ways women have been marginalized by this approach. Kathryn Ward (1985) shows how analyzing gender in conjunction with a world systems approach expands knowledge of the social consequences of core nation exploitation of the periphery. This approach explains the declining status of Third World women relative to men as well as anomalies in fertility patterns in these nations. Finally, the historical research of Louise Tilly and Joan Scott (1978), among others, has been important in understanding how the shift from household economies to wage labor affected working-class women and their families.

THE FUTURE OF MACROSOCIOLOGY: MICRO-MACRO LINKS

One of the perennial debates that surfaces among sociologists is whether macro or micro processes have primacy in explaining social life. A variant revolves around the issue of whether micro processes can be derived from the macro or vice versa. Those who believe that that the macro has causal priority risk being labeled structural determinists. Those who think that macro phenomena can be derived from micro processes are dismissed as reductionists. Quite often an uneasy truce prevails in which practitioners of the two types of sociology go their own ways, with little interaction or mutual influence.

Recently, however, there have been renewed efforts to construct theory and conduct research built on genuine principles of micro-macro linkage. These have come from a variety of theoretical traditions and perspectives, including those with both macro and micro foundations. While many of these efforts ultimately result in de facto claims for theoretical primacy of one or the other approach, they nonetheless represent an interesting effort to create uniform and widely applicable sociological theory.

One large class of models builds on rational-choice theory. Although this approach begins with assumptions of methodological individualism and purposive action (i.e., social phenomena must be explained in terms of intentional human action), sociologists from widely varying perspectives have adopted this approach as the means to link individual action with structural-level phenomena systematically (Friedman and Hechter 1988). Even some fairly orthodox Marxist sociologists have adopted this approach, as described in a manifesto of analytical Marxism by Erik Olin Wright (1989).

Ultimately, most of the efforts to integrate micro and macro levels reflect the initial concerns of the theorist. For example, Randall Collins's efforts begin with a micro focus on interaction to derive macro phenomena, while neofunctionalist Jeffrey Alexander (1985) gives primacy to subjective forms of macro phenomena. Perhaps the most highly developed integrative effort is found in Anthony Giddens's (1984) theory of structuration, in which social structure is defined as both constraining and enabling of human activity as well as both internal and external to the actor.

The efforts to link micro and macro phenomena are mirrored in a growing body of empirical research. Such work appears to follow Giddens's view of the constraining and enabling nature of social structure for human activity and the need to link structure and action. It appears safe to say that while macrosociology will always remain a central component of sociological theory and research, increasing effort will be devoted to creating workable models that link it with its micro counterpart.

(SEE ALSO: *Global Systems Analysis; Modernization Theory; Social Change; Social Movements*)

REFERENCES

Alexander, Jeffrey (ed.) 1985 *Neofunctionalism.* Beverly Hills, Calif.: Sage Publications.

Amin, Samir 1976 *Unequal Development: An Essay on the Social Formations of Peripheral Capitalism.* New York: Monthly Review Press.

Aminzade, Ron 1984 "Capitalist Industrialization and Patterns of Industrial Protest: A Comparative Urban Study of Nineteenth-Century France." *American Sociological Review* 49:437–453.

Bluestone, Barry, and Bennett Harrison 1982 *The Deindustrialization of America: Plant Closings, Community Abandonment, and the Dismantling of Basic Industry.* New York: Basic Books.

Boserup, Ester 1970 *Women's Role in Economic Development.* New York: St. Martin's Press.

Burawoy, Michael 1979 *Manufacturing Consent: Changes in the Labor Process Under Monopoly Capital.* Chicago: University of Chicago Press.

Collins, Randall 1988 "The Micro Contribution to Macro Sociology." *Sociological Theory* 6:242–253.

Edwards, Richard 1979 *Contested Terrain: The Transformation of the Workplace in the Twentieth Century.* New York: Basic Books.

Evans, Peter, and John Stephens 1988 "Development and the World Economy." In Neil Smelser, ed., *Handbook of Sociology.* Newbury Park, Calif.: Sage Publications.

Foster, John 1974 *Class Struggle and the Industrial Revolution: Early Industrial Capitalism in Three English Towns.* London: Weidenfeld and Nicholson.

Foucault, Michel 1979 *Discipline and Punish: The Birth of the Prison.* New York: Vintage.

———1980 *The History of Sexuality, vol. 1: An Introduction.* New York: Vintage.

———1985 *The Uses of Pleasure,* Vol. 2, *The History of Sexuality.* New York: Pantheon.

Frank, André Gunder 1967 *Capitalism and Underdevelopment in Latin America.* New York: Monthly Review Press.

Friedman, Debra, and Michael Hechter 1988 "The Contribution of Rational Choice Theory to Macrosociological Research." *Sociological Theory* 6:201–218.

Giddens, Anthony 1984 *The Constitution of Society: Outline of the Theory of Structuration.* Berkeley: University of California Press.

Gutman, Herbert G. (1966) 1977 *Work, Culture, and Society in Industrializing America.* New York: Vintage Books.

Habermas, Jurgen 1979 *Communication and the Evolution of Society.* Boston: Beacon Press.

Harris, Marvin 1977 *Cannibals and Kings: The Origins of Cultures.* New York: Random House.

Hartmann, Heidi 1981 "The Family as the Locus of Gender, Class, and Political Struggle: The Example of Housework." *Signs* 6:366–394.

Lenski, Gerhard 1966 *Power and Privilege: A Theory of Social Stratification.* New York: McGraw-Hill.

———, and Jean Lenski 1987 *Human Societies: An Introduction to Macrosociology,* 5th ed. New York: McGraw-Hill.

Moore, Barrington, Jr. 1966 *Social Origins of Dictatorship and Democracy: Lord and Peasant in the Making of the Modern World.* Boston: Beacon Press.

Ollman, Bertell 1976 *Alienation,* 2nd ed. Cambridge: Cambridge University Press.

Parsons, Talcott 1966 *Societies: Evolutionary and Comparative Perspectives.* Englewood Cliffs, N.J.: Prentice-Hall.

Portes, Alejandro, Manuel Castells, and Lauren Benton (eds.) 1989 *The Informal Economy: Studies in Advanced and Less Developed Countries.* Baltimore: Johns Hopkins University Press.

Ritzer, George 1988 *Sociological Theory,* 2nd ed. New York: Alfred A. Knopf.

Rostow, W. W. 1960 *The Stages of Economic Growth.* Cambridge: Cambridge University Press.

Shannon, Thomas Richard 1988 *An Introduction to the World System Perspective.* Boulder, Colo.: Westview Press.

Skocpol, Theda 1979 *States and Social Revolutions.* Cambridge: Cambridge University Press.

Smelser, Neil 1988 "Social Structure." In Neil Smelser, ed., *Handbook of Sociology.* Newbury Park, Calif.: Sage Publications.

Thompson, E. P. 1963 *The Making of the English Working Class.* New York: Vintage.

Tilly, Charles, Louise Tilly, and Richard Tilly 1975 *The Rebellious Century, 1830–1930.* Cambridge, Mass.: Harvard University Press.

Tilly, Louise, and Joan Scott 1978 *Women, Work, and Family.* New York: Holt, Rinehart, and Winston.

Wallerstein, Immanuel 1974 *The Modern World-System: Capitalist Agriculture and the Origins of the European World-Economy in the Sixteenth Century.* New York: Academic Press.

———1980 *The Modern World-System II: Mercantilism and the Consolidation of the European World-Economy, 1600–1750.* New York: Academic Press.

———1988 *The Modern World System III: The Second Era of Great Expansion of the Capitalist World-Economy 1730–1840.* San Diego, Calif.: Academic Press.

Walton, John 1987 "Theory and Research on Industrialization." *Annual Review of Sociology* 13:89–108.

Ward, Kathryn 1985 *Women in the World-System: Its Impact on Status and Fertility.* New York: Praeger.

Wright, Erik Olin 1989 "What Is Analytical Marxism?" *Socialist Review* 19:35–56.

ANN R. TICKAMYER

MALTHUSIAN THEORY *See* Demographic Transition; Human Ecology and the Environment.

MARITAL ADJUSTMENT Marital adjustment has long been a popular topic in studies of the family, probably because the concept is believed to be closely related to the stability of a given marriage. Well-adjusted marriages are expected to last for a long time, while poorly adjusted ones end in divorce. Simple as it seems, the notion of marital adjustment is difficult to conceptualize and difficult to measure through empirical research. After more than half a century of conceptualization about and research on marital adjustment, the best that can be said may be that there is disagreement among scholars about the concept, the term, and its value. In fact, several scientists have proposed abandoning entirely the concept of marital adjustment and its etymological relatives (Lively 1969; Donohue and Ryder 1982; Trost 1985).

CONCEPTUAL ISSUES

Scientists have long been interested in understanding which factors contribute to success in marriage and which to failure. As early as the 1920s, Gilbert Hamilton (1929) conducted research on marital satisfaction by using thirteen clusters of questions. In 1939, Ernest Burgess and Leonard Cottrell published *Predicting Success or Failure in Marriage,* in which they systematically discussed marital adjustment. They defined the adjustment as "the integration of the couple in a union in which the two personalities are not merely merged, or submerged, but interact to complement each other for mutual satisfaction and the achievement of common objectives" (p. 10).

Researchers have not agreed upon the use of the term itself. To describe the seemingly same phenomenon, some have used the terms *marital quality, marital satisfaction,* and *marital happiness.* Robert Lewis and Graham Spanier, for example, have defined marital quality as "a subjective evaluation of a married couple's relationship" (Lewis and Spanier 1979, p. 269)—a concept virtually identical to that of marital adjustment. There have been numerous definitions of marital adjustment or quality (Spanier and Cole 1976), and it may not be fruitful to attempt to define the concept in a sentence or two. Rather, the following description of the factors that constitute marital adjustment or quality may prove more meaningful.

Since Burgess and Cottrell's formulation, scientists have examined extensively the factors constituting marital adjustment. Although there has been no consensus among researchers, factors constituting marital adjustment include *agreement, cohesion, satisfaction, affection,* and *tension.* Agreement between spouses on important matters is critical to a well-adjusted marriage. Though minor differences may broaden their perspectives, major differences between the spouses in matters such as philosophy of life, political orientations, and attitudes toward gender roles are detrimental to marital adjustment. In addition, agreement on specific decisions about family matters must be reached in good accord. Marital cohesion refers to both spouses' commitment to the marriage and the companionship experienced in it. In a well-adjusted marriage, both spouses try to make sure that their marriage will be successful. They also share common interests and joint activities. In a well-adjusted marriage, both spouses must be satisfied and happy with the marriage. Unhappy but long-lasting marriages are not well-adjusted ones. Spouses in well-adjusted marriages share affection, and it is demonstrated as affectionate behavior. Finally, the degree of tension in a well-adjusted marriage is minimal, and when it arises it is resolved amicably, probably in discussion, and the level of tension and anxiety is usually low.

On the basis of a psychological theory of well-being, it has been suggested that marital adjustment or quality has two conceptually distinct factors, marital happiness (or interaction) and marital problems (or instability), and that we should treat these dimensions separately rather than combine them in the concept of marital adjustment or quality (Orden and Bradburn 1968). This position was later supported by a refined statistical analysis (Johnson et al. 1986).

The core component of marital adjustment is marital satisfaction, and it has been extensively studied as a stand-alone concept. As such, it deserves separate consideration. Marital satisfaction has been defined as "the subjective feelings of happiness, satisfaction, and pleasure experienced by a spouse when considering all current aspects of his marriage. This variable is conceived as a continuum running from much satisfaction to much dissatisfaction. Marital satisfaction is clearly an attitudinal variable and, thus, is a property of individual spouses" (Hawkins 1968, p. 648). Again, scientists disagree about the definition. Some scholars conceptualize satisfaction rather as "the amount of congruence between the expectations a person has and the rewards the person actually receives" (Burr et al. 1979, p. 67). Because marital satisfaction is influenced not only by the congruence between expectations and rewards but also by other factors, the former definition is broader than the latter and thus is adopted here.

Although many scientists treat marital satisfaction as a factor of marital adjustment, there exists a possibly major difference between these two concepts about the unit of analysis. Because satisfaction is a subjective property of an actor, there are two kinds of marital satisfaction in a marriage, the husband's and the wife's, and they are conceptually distinct. As Jessie Bernard (1972) stated, there are always two marriages in a family: the husband's marriage and the wife's marriage. Then, do these two marital satisfactions go hand in hand, or are they independent of each other? Research has produced mixed findings. In general, the more satisfied one spouse is with the marriage, the more satisfied is the other, but the correlation between the husband's and the wife's marital satisfactions is far from perfect (Spanier and Cole 1976). Marital adjustment or quality, on the other hand, can be either an individual or dyadic property. When we say "a well-adjusted marriage," we refer to the dyad, while when we say, "She is well adjusted to her marriage," we refer to the individual. No one has proposed valid measurement techniques for examining marital adjustment as a dyadic property, although some observational methods might be considered.

Another difference between marital satisfaction and marital adjustment is that while the former is a static product, the latter can be a dynamic process. In fact, marital adjustment is sometimes defined as a dynamic process, and marital satisfaction is listed as one of the outcomes of the adjustment process (Spanier and Cole 1976, pp. 127–28). It also has been proposed that marital adjustment be defined as a dynamic process and yet be measured as a state at a given point in time, a "snapshot" conception (Spanier and Cole 1976). Nevertheless, this connotation of dynamic process in the term *adjustment* has been criticized (Trost 1985) as a confusion of its meaning because no measure of "adjustment" involves dynamic change, such as negotiation between the spouses.

Without agreeing on which term to use nor on its definition, researchers have tried for decades to measure marital adjustment, quality, or satisfaction. Burgess and Cottrell (1939) created one of the first measures of marital adjustment from twenty-seven questions pertaining to five subareas (agreement, common interests and joint activities, affection and mutual confidences, complaints, and feelings of being lonely, miserable, and irritable). Along with numerous attempts at measuring marital adjustment, Locke and Wallace (1959) modified Burgess and Cottrell's measure and called it the Marital Adjustment Test. Based on factor analysis, the test consists of fifteen questions ranging from the respondent's overall happiness in the marriage, the degree of agreement between the spouses in various matters, how they resolved conflicts, and the number of shared activities, to the fulfillment of their expectations about the marriage. This measure was widely used until a new measure, the Dyadic Adjustment Scale, was proposed (Spanier 1976). It is composed of thirty-two questions and four subscales:

dyadic satisfaction, dyadic cohesion, dyadic consensus, and affectional expression. This scale has been used most widely in the last decade.

All of the above measures have been criticized as lacking a criterion against which the individual items are validated (Norton 1983; Fincham and Bradbury 1987). It has been argued that only global and evaluative items, rather than content-specific and descriptive ones, should be included in marital adjustment or quality measures because the conceptual domain of the latter is not clear. What constitutes a well-adjusted marriage may differ from one couple to another as well as cross-culturally and historically. Whether spouses kiss each other or not every day, for example, may be an indicator of a well-adjusted marriage in the contemporary United States but not in some other countries. Thus, marital adjustment or quality should be measured by the spouses' evaluation of the marriage as a whole rather than by its specific components. Instead of "How often do you and your husband (wife) agree on religious matters?" (a content-specific description), it is argued that such questions as, "All things considered, how satisfied are you with your marriage?" or, "How satisfied are you with your husband (wife) as a spouse?" (a global evaluation) should be used. By the same reasoning, the Kansas Marital Satisfaction Scale (KMS) has been proposed. This test includes only three questions: "How satisfied are you with your (a) marriage; (b) husband (wife) as a spouse; and (c) relationship with your husband (wife)?" (Schumm et al. 1986).

Traditional indices also have been criticized for their lack of theoretical basis and the imposition of what constitutes a "successful marriage." On the basis of exchange theory, Ronald Sabatelli (1984) developed the Marital Comparison Level Index (MCLI), which measures marital satisfaction by the degree to which respondents feel that the outcomes derived from their marriages compare with their expectations. Thirty-six items pertaining to such aspects of marriage as affection, commitment, fairness, and agreement were originally included, and thirty-two items were retained in the final measure. Because this measure is embedded in the tradition of exchange theory, it has strength in its validity.

PREDICTING MARITAL ADJUSTMENT

How is the marital adjustment of a given couple predicted? According to Lewis and Spanier's (1979) comprehensive work, three major factors predict marital quality: social and personal resources, satisfaction with life-style, and rewards from spousal interaction.

In general, the more social and personal resources a husband and wife have, the better adjusted their marriage is. Findings that spouses coming from similar racial, religious, or socioeconomic backgrounds are better adjusted to their marriages are synthesized by this general proposition. Material and nonmaterial properties of the spouses enhance their marital adjustment. Examples include emotional and physical health, socioeconomic resources such as education and social class, personal resources such as interpersonal skills and positive self-concepts, and knowledge they had of each other before getting married. It was also found that good relationships with and support from parents, friends, and significant others contribute to a better adjusted marriage.

The second major factor in predicting marital adjustment is satisfaction with life-style. It has been found that material resources such as family income positively affect both spouses' marital adjustment. Both the husband's and the wife's satisfaction with their jobs enhances better adjusted marriages. Furthermore, the husband's satisfaction with his wife's work status also affects marital adjustment. The wife's employment itself has been found both instrumental and detrimental to the husbands' marital satisfaction (Fendrich 1984). This is because the effect of the wife's employment is mediated by both spouses' attitudes about her employment. When the wife is in the labor force, and her husband supports it, marital adjustment could be enhanced. On the other hand, if the wife is unwilling to be employed, or is employed against her husband's wishes, this can negatively affect their marital adjustment. Marital adjustment is also affected by the spouses' satisfaction with their household composition and by how well the couple is embedded in the community.

Parents' marital satisfaction was found to be a function of the presence, density, and ages of children (Rollins and Galligan 1978). Spouses (particularly wives) who had children were less satisfied with their marriages, particularly when many children were born soon after marriage at short intervals (high density). The generally negative effects of children on marital satisfaction and marital adjustment could be synthesized under this more general proposition about satisfaction with life-style.

It has been consistently found that marital satisfaction plotted against the couple's family life-cycle stages forms a U-shaped curve (Rollins and Cannon 1974). Both spouses' marital satisfaction is highest right after they marry, hits the lowest point when the oldest child is a teenager, and gradually bounces back after all children leave home. This pattern has been interpreted to be a result of role strain or role conflict between the spousal, parental, and work roles of the spouses. Unlike the honeymoon and empty-nest stages, having children at home imposes the demand of being a parent in addition to being a husband or wife and a worker. When limited time and energy cause these roles to conflict with each other, the spouses feel strain, which results in poor marital adjustment. Along this line of reasoning, Wesley Burr et al. (1979) proposed that marital satisfaction is influenced by the qualities of the individual's role enactment as a spouse and of the spouse's role enactment. They argue further, from the symbolic-interactionist perspective, that the relationship between marital role enactment and marital satisfaction is mediated by the importance placed on spousal role expectations.

As seen above, the concept of family life cycle seems to have some explanatory power for marital satisfaction. Researchers and theorists have found, however, that family life cycle is multidimensional and conceptually unclear. Once a relationship between a particular stage in the family life cycle and marital satisfaction is identified, further variables must be added to explain that relationship, variables such as the wife's employment status, disposable income, and role strain between spousal and parental roles (Schumm and Bugaighis 1986). Furthermore, the proportion of variance in marital satisfaction "explained" by the family's position in its life cycle is small, typically less than 10 percent (Rollins and Cannon 1974). Thus, some scholars conclude that family life cycle has no more explanatory value than does marriage or age cohorts (Spanier and Lewis 1980).

The last major factor in predicting marital adjustment is the reward obtained from spousal interaction. On the basis of exchange theory, Lewis and Spanier summarize past findings that "the greater the rewards from spousal interaction, the greater the marital quality" (Lewis and Spanier 1979, p. 282). Rewards from spousal interaction include value consensus, a positive evaluation of oneself by the spouse, and one's positive regard for things such as the physical, mental, and sexual attractiveness of the spouse. Other rewards from spousal interaction include such aspects of emotional gratification as the expression of affection, respect and encouragement between the spouses, love and sexual gratification, and egalitarian relationships. Married couples with more effective communication, expressed in more self-disclosure, frequent successful communication, and understanding and empathy, are better adjusted to their marriages. Complementarity in the spouses' roles and needs, similarity in personality traits, and sexual compatibility all enhance marital adjustment. Finally, frequent interaction between the spouses leads to a better adjusted marriage. The lack of spousal conflict or tensions should be added to the list of rewards from spousal interactions.

Symbolic interactionists also argue that relative deprivation of the spouses affects their marital satisfaction: If, after considering all aspects of the marriage, spouses believe themselves to be as well off as their reference group, they will be satisfied with their marriages. If they think they are better off or worse off than others who are married, they will be more or less satisfied with their marriages, respectively (Burr et al. 1979).

CONSEQUENCES OF MARITAL ADJUSTMENT: MARITAL STABILITY

Does marital adjustment affect the stability of the marriage? Does a better adjusted marriage last longer than a poorly adjusted one? The answer is generally yes, but this is not always the case. Some well-adjusted marriages end in divorce, and many poorly adjusted marriages endure. As for the latter, John Cuber and Peggy Harroff (1968) conducted research on people whose marriages "lasted ten years or more and who said that they have never seriously considered divorce or separation" (p. 43). They claim that not all the spouses in these marriages are happy and that there are five types of long-lasting marriages. In a "conflict-habituated marriage," the husband and the wife always quarrel. In a "passive-congenial marriage," the husband and the wife take each other for granted without zest, while "devitalized marriages" started as loving but have degenerated to passive-congenial marriages. In a "vital marriage," spouses together enjoy such things as hobbies, careers, or community services, while in a "total marriage," spouses do almost everything together. It should be noted that even conflict-habituated or devitalized marriages can last as long as vital or total marriages. For people in passive-congenial marriages, the conception and the reality of marriage are devoid of romance and are different from other people's.

What then determines the stability of marriage and how the marital adjustment affects it? It is proposed that although marital adjustment leads to marital stability, two factors intervene: alternative attractions and external pressures to remain married (Lewis and Spanier 1979). People who have both real and perceived alternatives to poorly adjusted marriages—another romantic relationship or a successful career—may choose divorce. A person in a poorly adjusted marriage may remain in it if there is no viable alternative, if a divorce is unaffordable or would bring an intolerable stigma, or if the person is exceptionally tolerant of conflict and disharmony in the marriage. Nevertheless, it should be emphasized that even though marital stability is affected by alternative attractions and external pressures, marital adjustment is the single most important factor in predicting marital stability.

(SEE ALSO: *Divorce; Family Roles; Interpersonal Attraction; Marriage*)

REFERENCES

Bernard, Jessie 1972 *The Future of Marriage.* New York: World Publishing.

Burgess, Ernest W., and Leonard Cottrell, Jr. 1939 *Predicting Success or Failure in Marriage.* New York: Prentice-Hall.

Burr, Wesley R., Geoffrey K. Leigh, Randall D. Day, and John Constantine 1979 "Symbolic Interaction and the Family." In W. Burr, R. Hill, F. I. Nye, and I. Reiss, eds., *Contemporary Theories about the Family.* New York: Free Press.

Cuber, John F., and Peggy B. Harroff 1968 *The Significant Americans: A Study of Sexual Behavior Among the Affluent.* Baltimore: Penguin Books.

Donohue, Kevin C., and Robert G. Ryder 1982 "A Methodological Note on Marital Satisfaction and Social Variables." *Journal of Marriage and the Family* 44:743–747.

Fendrich, Michael 1984 "Wives' Employment and Husbands' Distress: A Meta-analysis and a Replication." *Journal of Marriage and the Family* 46:871–879.

Fincham, Frank D., and Thomas N. Bradbury 1987 "The Assessment of Marital Quality: A Reevaluation." *Journal of Marriage and the Family* 49:797–809.

Hamilton, Gilbert V. 1929 *A Research in Marriage.* New York: A. and C. Boni.

Hawkins, James L. 1968 "Associations Between Companionship, Hostility, and Marital Satisfaction." *Journal of Marriage and the Family* 30:647–650.

Johnson, David R., Lynn K. White, John N. Edwards, and Alan Booth 1986 "Dimensions of Marital Quality: Toward Methodological and Conceptual Refinement." *Journal of Family Issues* 7:31–49.

Lewis, Robert A., and Graham B. Spanier 1979 "Theorizing about the Quality and Stability of Marriage." In W. Burr, R. Hill, F. I. Nye, and I. Reiss, eds., *Contemporary Theories about the Family.* New York: Free Press.

Lively, E. L. 1969 "Toward Concept Clarification: The Case of Marital Interaction." *Journal of Marriage and the Family* 31:108–114.

Locke, Harvey J., and Karl M. Wallace 1959 "Short Marital-Adjustment and Prediction Tests: Their Reliability and Validity." *Marriage and Family Living* 21:251–255.

Norton, Robert 1983 "Measuring Marital Quality: A Critical Look at the Dependent Variable." *Journal of Marriage and the Family* 45:141–151.

Orden, Susan R., and Norman M. Bradburn 1968 "Dimensions of Marriage Happiness." *American Journal of Sociology* 73:715–731.

Rollins, Boyd C., and Kenneth L. Cannon 1974 "Marital Satisfaction over the Family Life Cycle: A Reevaluation." *Journal of Marriage and the Family* 36:271–282.

Rollins, Boyd C., and Richard Galligan 1978 "The Developing Child and Marital Satisfaction of Parents." In R. M. Lerner and G. B. Spanier, eds., *Child Influences on Marital and Family Interaction.* New York: Academic Press.

Sabatelli, Ronald M. 1984 "The Marital Comparison Level Index: A Measure for Assessing Outcomes Relative to Expectations." *Journal of Marriage and the Family* 46:651–662.

Schumm, Walter R., and Margaret A. Bugaighis 1986 "Marital Quality over the Marital Career: Alternative Explanations." *Journal of Marriage and the Family* 48:165–168.

Schumm, Walter R., Lois A. Paff-Bergen, Ruth C. Hatch, Felix C. Obiorah, Janette M. Copeland, Lori D. Meens, and Margaret A. Bugaighis 1986 "Concurrent and Discriminant Validity of the Kansas Marital Satisfaction Scale." *Journal of Marriage and the Family* 48:381–387.

Spanier, Graham B. 1976 "Measuring Dyadic Adjustment: New Scales for Assessing the Quality of Marriage and Similar Dyads." *Journal of Marriage and the Family* 38:15–28.

———, and Charles L. Cole 1976 "Toward Clarification and Investigation of Marital Adjustment." *International Journal of Sociology of the Family* 6:121–146.

———, and Robert A. Lewis 1980 "Marital Quality: A Review of the Seventies." *Journal of Marriage and the Family* 42:825–839.

Trost, Jan E. 1985 "Abandon Adjustment!" *Journal of Marriage and the Family* 47:1,072–1,073.

YOSHINORI KAMO

MARRIAGE The current low rates of marriage and remarriage and the high incidence of divorce in the United States are the bases of deep concern about the future of marriage and the family. Some have used these data to argue the demise of the family in the Western world (Popenoe 1988). Others see such changes as normal shifts and adjustments to societal changes (Bane 1976). Whatever the forecast, there is no question that the institution of marriage is currently less stable than it has been in previous generations. This chapter explores the nature of modern marriage and considers some of the reasons for its vulnerability.

Marriage can be conceptualized in three ways: as an institution (a set of patterned, repeated, expected behaviors and relationships that are organized and endure over time); a rite/ritual (whereby the married status is achieved); and a process (a phenomenon marked by gradual changes that lead to ultimate dissolution through separation, divorce, or death). In the discussion that follows we examine each of these conceptualizations of marriage, with the greatest attention given to marriage as a process.

MARRIAGE AS INSTITUTION

From a societal level of analysis the institution of marriage represents all the behaviors, norms, roles, expectations, and values that are associated with the legal union of a man and woman. It is the institution in society in which a man and woman are joined in a special kind of social and legal dependence to found and maintain a family. For most people becoming married and having children are the principal life events that pass an individual into mature adulthood. Marriage is considered to represent a lifelong commitment by two people to each other and is signified by a contract sanctioned by the state (and for many people, by God). It thus involves legal rights, responsibilities, and duties that are enforced by both secular and sacred laws. As a legal contract ratified by the state, marriage can be dissolved only with state permission.

Marriage is at the center of the kinship system.

New spouses are tied inextricably to members of the kin network. The nature of these ties or obligations differs in different cultures. In many societies almost all social relationships are based on or mediated by kin, who also may serve as allies in times of danger, be responsible for the transference of property, or are turned to in times of economic hardship (Lee 1982). In the United States, kin responsibilities rarely extend beyond the nuclear family (parents and children). With the possible exception of caring for elderly parents, and even here norms have not yet been developed (Lang and Brody 1983), there are no normative obligations an individual is expected to fulfill for sisters or brothers, not to mention uncles, aunts, and cousins. Associated with few obligations and responsibilities is greater autonomy and independence of one's kin.

In most societies the distribution of power in marriage is given through tradition and law to the male—that is, patriarchy is the rule as well as the practice. For many contemporary Americans the ideal is to develop an egalitarian power structure, but a number of underlying conditions discourage attaining this goal. These deterrents include the tendency for males to have greater income; higher status jobs; and, until recently, higher educational levels than women. In addition, the tradition that women have primary responsibility for child rearing tends to increase their dependency on males.

Historically, the institution of marriage has fulfilled several unique functions for the larger society. It has served as an economic alliance between two families, as the means for legitimizing sexual relations, and as the basis for legitimizing parenthood and offspring. In present-day America the primary functions of marriage appear to be limited to the legitimization of parenthood (Davis 1949; Reiss and Lee 1988) and the nurturance of family members (Lasch 1977). Recently, standards have changed and sexual relations outside of marriage have become increasingly accepted for unmarried people. Most services that were once performed by members of a family for other members can now be purchased in the marketplace, and other social institutions have taken over roles that once were assigned primarily to the family. Even illegitimacy is not as negatively sanctioned as in the past. The fact that marriage no longer serves all the unique functions it once did is one reason that some scholars have questioned the vitality of the institution.

MARRIAGE AS RITE/RITUAL

Not a great deal of sociological attention has been given to the study of marriage as a rite/ritual that transfers status. Philip Slater, in a seminal piece written in 1963, discussed the significance of the marriage ceremony as a social mechanism that underscores the dependency of the married couple and links the new spouses to the larger social group. Slater claims that various elements associated with the wedding (e.g., bridal shower, bachelor party) help create the impression that the couple is indebted to their peers and family members who organize these events. He writes,

> *. . . family and friends [are] vying with one another in claiming responsibility for having "brought them together" in the first place. This impression of societal initiative is augmented by the fact that the bride's father "gives the bride away." The retention of this ancient custom in modern times serves explicitly to deny the possibility that the couple might unite quite on their own. In other words, the marriage ritual is designed to make it appear as if somehow the idea of the dyadic union sprang from the community, and not from the dyad itself* (Slater 1963, p. 355).

Slater describes the ways in which rite and ceremony focus attention on loyalties and obligations owed others: "The ceremony has the effect of concentrating the attention of both individuals on every OTHER affectional tie either one has ever contracted" (Slater 1963, p. 354). The intrusion of the community into the couple's relationship at the moment of unity serves to inhibit husband and wife from withdrawing completely into an intimate unit isolated from (and hence not contributing to) the larger social group.

Martin Whyte (1990) ascertained the lack of information on marriage rituals and conducted a study to help fill this gap. He found that since

1925, wedding rituals (bridal shower, bachelor party, honeymoon, wedding reception, church wedding) have not only persisted but also have increased in terms of the number of people who incorporate them into their marriage plans. Weddings also are larger in scale in terms of cost, number of guests, whether a reception is held, etc. Like Slater, Martin links marriage rituals to the larger social fabric and argues that an elaborate wedding serves several functions. It

> *serves notice that the couple is entering into a new set of roles and obligations associated with marriage, it mobilizes community support behind their new status, it enables the families involved to display their status to the surrounding community, and it makes it easier for newly marrying couples to establish an independent household* (p. 63).

MARRIAGE AS PROCESS

Of the three ways in which marriage is conceptualized—institution, rite/ritual, and process—most scholarly attention has focused on process. Here the emphasis is on the interpersonal relationship. Changes in this relationship over the course of the marriage have attracted the interest of most investigators. Key issues studied by researchers include the establishment of communication, affection, power, and decision-making patterns; development of a marital division of labor; and learning spousal roles. The conditions under which these develop and change (e.g., social class level, age at marriage, presence of children) and the outcomes of being married that derive from them (e.g., degree of satisfaction with the relationship) are also studied. For illustrative purposes, the remainder of this article will highlight one of these components, marital communication, and one outcome variable, marital quality. We also address different experiences of marriage based on sex of spouse: "his" and "her" marriage.

The Process of Communication. The perception of "a failure to communicate" is a problem that prompts many spouses to seek marital counseling. The ability to share feelings, thoughts, and information is a measure of the degree of intimacy between two people, and frustration follows from an inability or an unwillingness to talk and listen (Klagsbrun 1986). However, when the quality of communication is high, marital satisfaction and happiness also are high (Holman and Brock 1986; Gottman and Porterfield 1981; Lewis and Spanier 1979).

The role of communication in fostering a satisfactory marital relationship is more important now than in earlier times because the expectations and demands of marriage have changed. As noted above, marriage in America is less dependent on and affected by an extended kin network than on the spousal relationship. One of the principal functions of contemporary marriage is the nurturance of family members. Perhaps because this function and the therapeutic and leisure roles that help fulfill it in marriage are preeminent, "greater demands are placed on each spouse's ability to communicate (Fitzpatrick 1988, p. 2). The communication of positive affect, and its converse, emotional withdrawal, may well be the essence/antithesis of nurturance. Bloom, Niles, and Tatcher (1985) suggest that one important characteristic of marital dissatisfaction is the expectation that marriage is a "source of interpersonal nurturance and individual gratification and growth" (p. 371), an expectation that is very hard to fulfill.

In the 1990s many studies focused on the role of communication in differentiating distressed from nondistressed marriages (Noller and Fitzpatrick 1990). The findings from this body of research suggest that there are clear communication differences between spouses in happy and in unhappy marriages. Patricia Noller and Mary Anne Fitzpatrick (1990) reviewed this literature, and their findings can be summarized as follows: couples in distressed marriages report less satisfaction with the social-emotional aspects of marriage, develop more destructive communication patterns (i.e., a greater expression of negative feelings, including anger, contempt, sadness, fear, and disgust), and seek to avoid conflict more often than nondistressed couples. Nevertheless, couples in distressed marriages report more frequent conflict and spend more time in conflict. In addition, gender differences in communication are intensified in distressed marriages. For example, husbands have a more difficult time interpreting wives' messages. Wives in general express both negative and positive feelings more directly and are more critical. Spouses in unhappy marriages appear to be unaware that they misunderstand one another. Generally, happily married couples are more likely to engage in positive communication behaviors (agreement, approval, assent, and the use of humor and laughter), while unhappy couples command, disagree, criticize, put down, and excuse more.

Communication patterns may be class-linked. Working-class wives in particular complain that their husbands are emotionally withdrawn and inexpressive (Komarovsky 1962; Rubin 1976). Olsen and his colleagues (1979) assign communication a strategic role in marital/family adaptability. In their conceptualization of marital/family functioning, communication is the process that moves couples along the dimensions of cohesion and adaptability. In another study the absence of good communication skills was associated with conjugal violence (Walker 1979).

Differences between the sexes have been reported in most studies that examine marital communication. The general emphasis of these findings is that males appear less able to communicate verbally and to discuss emotional issues. However, communication is not the only aspect of marriage where sex differences have been reported. Other components of marriage also are experienced differently, depending on the sex of spouse. The following paragraphs report some of these.

Sex Differences. In *The Future of Marriage* (1972), Jessie Bernard pointed out that marriage does not hold the same meanings for wives as for husbands, nor do wives hold the same expectations for marriage as do husbands. These sex differences (originally noted but not fully developed by Emile Durkheim in 1897 in *Le Suicide*) have been observed and examined by many others since Bernard's publication (Larson 1988; Stinnett 1971; Feldman 1982). For example, researchers report differences between husbands and wives in responses to perceptions of marital problems, reasons for divorce (Levinger 1966; Fulton 1979), and differences in perceived marital quality; wives consistently experience/perceive lower quality than husbands. Wives are viewed as the partner who undergoes the most change (adjustment) in marriage (Luckey 1960). They are more susceptible to influence within the marriage (Bernard 1982), and they undergo greater value change than husbands (Barry 1970; Burgess and Wallin 1953; Sanders and Suls 1982).

Sex differences in marriage are socially defined and prescribed (Lee 1982). One consequence of these social definitions is that sex differences get built into marital roles and the division of labor within marriage. For example, it has been observed that wives do more housework (Atkinson and Huston 1984) and child care (McHale and Huston 1984) than husbands. Even wives who work in the paid labor force spend twice as many hours per week in family work as husbands (Benin and Agostinelli 1988). Wives are assigned or tend to assume the role of family kinkeeper (Adams 1968; Rosenthal 1985). To the extent that husbands and wives experience different marriages, wives are thought to be disadvantaged by their greater dependence, secondary status, and the uneven distribution of family responsibilities associated with marriage (Baca Zinn and Eitzen 1990).

All of these factors are assumed to affect the quality of marriage—one of the most studied aspects of marriage (Adams 1988; Berardo 1990). It will be the subject of our final discussion.

Marital Quality. Marital quality may be the "weather vane" by which spouses gauge the success of their relationship. (The reader should be sure to differentiate the concept of marital quality from two other closely related concepts: family quality, and the quality of life in general, called global life satisfaction in the literature. Studies show that people clearly differentiate among these three dimensions of well-being [Ishii-Kuntz and Ihinger-Tallman 1991].)

Marriage begins with a commitment, a promise to maintain an intimate relationship over a lifetime. Few couples clearly understand the difficulties involved in adhering to this commitment or the problems they may encounter over the course of their lives together. More people seek psychological help for marital difficulties than for any other type of problem (Fincham and Bradbury 1987; Veroff, Kulka, and Douvan 1981). For a large number of spouses, the problems become so severe that they renege on their commitment and dissolve the marriage.

A recent review of the determinants of divorce lists the following problems as major factors that lead to the dissolution of marriage: "alcoholism and drug abuse, infidelity, incompatibility, physical and emotional abuse, disagreements about gender roles, sexual incompatibility, and financial problems" (White 1990, p. 908). Underlying these behaviors appears to be the general problem of communication. In their study of divorce, Gay Kitson and Marvin Sussman (1982) reported lack of communication/understanding to be the most common reason given by both husbands and wives concerning why their marriage broke up. The types of problems responsible for divorce have not changed much over time. Older studies list nonsupport, financial problems, adultery, cruelty, drinking, physical and verbal abuse, neglect, lack of love, in-laws, and sexual incompatibility as reasons for divorce (Goode 1956; Harmsworth and Minnis 1955; Levinger 1966).

Not all unhappy marriages end in divorce. Many factors bar couples from dissolving their marriage, even under conditions of extreme dissatisfaction. Some factors that act as barriers to marital dissolution are strong religious beliefs, pressure from family or friends to remain together, and the lack of perceived attractive alternatives to the marriage (Levinger 1965; Lewis and Spanier 1979).

One empirical finding that continues to be reaffirmed in studies of marital quality is that the quality of marriage declines over time, beginning with the birth of the first child (Pineo 1961). Consequently, the transition to parenthood and its effect on the marital relationship has generated a great deal of research attention (Cowen and Cowen 1989; LaRossa and LaRossa 1981; Ruble, Fleming, Hackel, and Stangor 1988; Ryder 1973). The general finding is that marital quality decreases after the birth of a child, and this change is more pronounced for mothers than for fathers. Two reasons generally proposed to account for this decline are that the amount of time couples have to spend together decreases after the birth of a child, and sex role patterns become more traditional (McHale and Huston 1985).

In an attempt to disentangle the duration of marriage and parenthood dimensions, White and Booth (1985) compared couples who became new parents with nonparent couples over a period of several years and found a decline in marital quality regardless of whether the couple had a child. A longitudinal study conducted by Belsky and Rovine (1990) confirmed the significant declines in marital quality over time reported in so many other studies. They also found the reported gender differences. However, their analysis also focused on change scores for individual couples. They reported that while some couples' marital quality declined, this was not true for all couples —it improved or remained unchanged for others. Thus, rather than assume that quality decline is an inevitable consequence of marriage, there is a need to examine why and how some couples successfully avoid this deterioration process. The authors called for the investigation of individual differences among couples rather than continuing to examine the generally well-established finding that marital quality declines after children enter the family and remains low during the child-rearing stages of the family life cycle.

Many students of the family have found it useful to consider marital development over the years as analogous to a career that progresses through stages of the family life cycle (Duvall and Hill 1948; Aldous 1978). This allows for considering changes in the marital relationship that occur because of spouses' aging, duration of marriage, and the aging of children. In addition to changes in marital quality, other factors have been examined, such as differences in the course of a marriage when age at first marriage varies (e.g., marriage entered into at age nineteen as opposed to midthirties), varied duration of child-bearing (few vs. many years), varied number of children (small family vs. large), and the ways in which consumer decisions change over the course of marriage (Aldous 1990).

CONCLUSION

If the vitality of marriage is measured by the extent to which men and women enter marriage, then some pessimism about its future is warranted. Marriage rates are currently lower than during the early Depression years of 1930–1932—which were the lowest in our nation's recent history (Sweet and Bumpass 1987). One conclusion that might be drawn from reading the accumulated literature on marriage, especially the writings that discuss the inequities of men and women within marriage, increasing incidence of marital dissolution, cohabitation as a substitute for marriage, and the postponement of marriage, is that the institution is in serious trouble. These changes have been interpreted as occurring as part of a larger societal shift in values and orientations (Glick 1989) that leans toward valuing adults over children and toward individualism over familism (Glenn 1987; White 1987; see the entire December 1987 issue of *Journal of Family Issues,* devoted to the state of the American family). Supporting this perspective are the data on increased marital happiness among childless couples and lower birth rates among married couples.

Yet every era has had those who write of the vulnerability of marriage and family. For example, in 1920 Edward Alsworth Ross wrote, ". . . we find the family now less stable than it has been at any time since the beginning of the Christian era" (1920, p. 586). Is every era judged to be worse than previous ones when social institutions are scrutinized? More optimistic scholars look at the declining first-marriage rate and interpret it as a "deferral syndrome" rather than as an outright rejection of the institution (Glick 1989; Teachman, Polonko, and Scanzoni 1987). This is because, in spite of declines in the overall rate, the historical 8 percent to 10 percent of never-married in the population has remained constant; almost 90 percent of all women in the United States eventually marry at least once in their lifetime (Norton and Moorman 1987). Also, projections that about two-thirds of all first marriages in the United States will end in divorce (Martin and Bumpass 1989) do not deter people from marrying. In spite of the high divorce rate, an increased tolerance for singleness as a way of life, and a growing acceptance of cohabitation, the majority of Americans continue to marry. Unhappy couples divorce, but most remarry. Marriage is still seen as a source of personal happiness (Campbell, Converse, and Rogers 1976; Kilbourne, Howell, and England 1990).

More fundamentally, marriage rates and the dynamics of marital relationships tend to reflect conditions in the larger society. What appears clear, at least for Americans, is that they turn to marriage as a source of sustenance and support in a society where, collectively, citizens seem to have abrogated responsibility for the care and nurturance of each other. Perhaps it is not surprising that divorce rates are high, given the demands and expectations placed on modern marriages.

(SEE ALSO: *Alternate Life-Styles; Courtship; Family Roles; Heterosexual Behavior Patterns; Intermarriage; Marital Adjustment; Remarriage; Sexual Behavior and Marriage*)

REFERENCES

Adams, Bert N. 1968 *Kinship in an Urban Setting.* Chicago: Markham.

———1988 "Fifty Years of Family Research: What Does it Mean?" *Journal of Marriage and the Family* 50:5–17.

Aldous, Joan 1978 *Family Careers: Developmental Changes in Families.* New York: Wiley.

———1990 Family Development and the Life Course: Two Perspectives on Family Change." *Journal of Marriage and the Family* 52:571–583.

Atkinson, Jean, and Ted L. Huston 1984 "Sex Role Orientation and Division of Labor Early in Marriage." *Journal of Personality and Social Psychology* 41:330–345.

Baca Zinn, Maxine, and D. Stanley Eitzen 1990 *Diversity in Families,* 2nd ed. New York: Harper & Row.

Bane, Mary Jo 1976 *Here to Stay: American Families in the Twentieth Century.* New York: Basic Books.

Barry, W. A. 1970 "Marriage Research and Conflict: An Integrative Review." *Psychological Bulletin* 73:41–54.

Belsky, Jay, and Michael Rovine 1990 "Patterns of

Marital Change Across the Transition to Parenthood: Pregnancy to Three Years Postpartum." *Journal of Marriage and the Family* 52:5–19.

Benin, Mary H., and Joan Agostinelli 1988 "Husbands' and Wives' Satisfaction with the Division of Labor." *Journal of Marriage and the Family* 50:349–361.

Berardo, Felix M. 1990 "Trends and Directions in Family Research in the 1980s." *Journal of Marriage and the Family* 52:809–817.

Bernard, Jessie 1972 *The Future of Marriage.* New York: Bantam Books.

———1982 *The Future of Marriage,* 1982 ed. New Haven, Conn.: Yale University Press.

Bloom, Bernard L., Robert L. Niles, and Anna M. Tatcher 1985 "Sources of Marital Dissatisfaction Among Newly Separated Persons." *Journal of Family Issues* 6:359–373.

Burgess, Ernest, and Paul Wallin 1953 *Engagement and Marriage.* Philadelphia: Lippincott.

Campbell, Angus, Philip E. Converse, and Willard Rogers 1976 *The Quality of American Life.* New York: Russell Sage Foundation.

Cowen, Phillip, and C. Cowen 1989 "Changes in Marriage During the Transition to Parenthood: Must We Blame the Baby?" In G. Michaels and W. Goldberg, eds., *The Transition to Parenthood: Current Theory and Research.* New York: Cambridge University Press.

Davis, Kingsley 1949 *Human Society.* New York: Macmillan.

Durkheim, Emile 1897 *Le Suicide.* Paris: F. Alcan.

Duvall, Evelyn M., and Reuben Hill 1948 "Report of the Committee on the Dynamics of Family Interaction." Paper delivered at the National Conference on Family Life, Washington, DC.

Feldman, L. B. 1982 "Sex Roles and Family Dynamics." In F. Walsh, ed., *Normal Family Processes.* New York: Guilford.

Fincham, Frank D., and Thomas N. Bradbury 1987 "The Assessment of Marital Quality: A Reevaluation." *Journal of Marriage and the Family* 49:797–809.

Fitzpatrick, Mary Anne 1988 "Approaches to Marital Interaction." In P. Noller and M. A. Fitzpatrick, eds., *Perspectives on Marital Interaction.* Clevedon, Eng.: Multilingual Matters, Ltd.

Fulton, Julie 1979 "Parental Reports of Children's Post-Divorce Adjustment." *Journal of Social Issues* 35:126–139.

Glenn, Norval D. 1987 "Tentatively Concerned View of American Marriage." *Journal of Family Issues* 8:350–354.

Glick, Paul C. 1989 "The Family Life Cycle and Social Change." *Family Relations* 38:123–129.

Goode, William J. 1956 *After Divorce.* New York: Free Press.

Gottman, John M., and Albert L. Porterfield 1981 "Communicative Competence in the Nonverbal Behavior of Married Couples." *Journal of Marriage and the Family* 43:817–824.

Harmsworth, Harry C., and Mhyra S. Minnis 1955 "Nonstatutory Causes of Divorce: The Lawyer's Point of View." *Marriage and Family Living* 17:316–321.

Holman, Thomas B., and Gregory W. Brock 1986 "Implications for Therapy in the Study of Communication and Marital Quality." *Family Perspectives* 20:85–94.

Ishii-Kuntz, Masako, and Marilyn Ihinger-Tallman 1991 "The Subjective Well-Being of Parents." *Journal of Family Issues* 12:58–68.

Kilbourne, Barbara S., Frank Howell, and Paul England 1990 "Measurement Model for Subjective Marital Solidarity: Invariance Across Time, Gender and Life Cycle Stage." *Social Science Research* 19:62–81.

Kitson, Gay C., and Marvin B. Sussman 1982 "Marital Complaints, Demographic Characteristics and Symptoms of Mental Distress in Divorce." *Journal of Marriage and the Family* 44:87–102.

Klagsbrun, Francine 1986 *Married People.* New York: Bantam Books.

Komarovsky, Mirra 1962 *Blue-Collar Marriage.* New York: Vintage Books.

LaRossa, Ralph, and M. LaRossa 1981 *Transition to Parenthood.* Beverly Hills, Calif.: Sage Publications.

Lang, Abigail M., and Elaine M. Brody 1983 "Characteristics of Middle-aged Daughters and Help to Their Elderly Mothers." *Journal of Marriage and the Family* 45:193–202.

Larson, Jeffery H. 1988 "The Marriage Quiz: College Students' Beliefs in Selected Myths About Marriage." *Family Relations* 37:3–11.

Lasch, Christopher 1977 *Haven in a Heartless World.* New York: Basic Books.

Lee, Gary 1982 *Family Structure and Interaction: Comparative Analysis.* Minneapolis: University of Minnesota Press.

Levinger, George 1965 "Marital Cohesiveness and Dissolution: an Integrative Review." *Journal of Marriage and the Family* 27:19–28.

———1966 "Sources of Marital Dissatisfaction Among Applicants for Divorce." *American Journal of Orthopsychiatry* 36:803–807.

Lewis, Robert A., and Graham B. Spanier 1979 "Theorizing About the Quality and Stability of Marriage." In W. R. Burr, R. Hill, R. I. Nye, and I. L. Reiss, eds., *Contemporary Theories About the Family,* vol 1. New York: Free Press.

Luckey, Eleanore B. 1960 "Marital Satisfaction and Congruent Self-Spouse Concepts." *Social Forces* 39:153–157.

McHale, Susan M., and Ted L. Huston 1984 "Men and Women as Parents: Sex Role Orientations, Employment, and Parental Roles." *Child Development* 55:1349–1361.

———1985 "The Effect of the Transition to Parenthood on the Marriage Relationship." *Journal of Family Issues* 6:409–433.

Martin, Teresa C., and Larry L. Bumpass 1989 "Recent Trends in Marital Disruption." *Demography* 26: 37–51.

Noller, Patricia, and Mary Anne Fitzpatrick 1990 "Marital Communication in the Eighties." *Journal of Marriage and the Family* 52:832–843.

Norton, A. J., and J. E. Moorman 1987 "Current Trends in Marriage and Divorce Among American Women." *Journal of Marriage and the Family* 49:3–14.

Olsen, David H., D. Sprenkle, and C. Russell 1979 "Circumplex Model of Marital and Family Systems I: Cohesion and Adaptability Dimensions, Family Types and Clinical Applications." *Family Process* 18: 3–28.

Pineo, Peter C. 1961. "Disenchantment in the Later Years of Marriage." *Marriage and Family Living* 23:3–11.

Popenoe, David 1988 *Disturbing the Nest: Family Change and Decline in Modern Societies.* New York: Aldine de Gruyter.

Reiss, Ira L., and Gary R. Lee 1988 *Family Systems in America.* New York: Holt, Rinehart, and Winston.

Rosenthal, Carolyn 1985 "Kinkeeping in the Familial Division of Labor." *Journal of Marriage and the Family* 47:965–974.

Ross, Edward Alsworth 1920 *The Principles of Sociology.* New York: Century Co.

Rubin, Lillian 1976 *Worlds of Pain: Life in the Working Class Family.* New York: Basic Books.

Ruble, Diane, A. Fleming, L. Hackel, and C. Stangor 1988 "Changes in the Marital Relationship During the Transition to First-Time Motherhood: Effects of Violated Expectations Concerning Division of Labor." *Journal of Personality and Social Psychology* 55:78–87.

Ryder, Robert 1973 "Longitudinal Data Relating Marital Satisfaction and Having a Child." *Journal of Marriage and the Family* 35:604–607.

Sanders, Glenn S., and Jerry Suls 1982 "Social Comparison, Competition and Marriage." *Journal of Marriage and the Family* 44:721–730.

Slater, Philip 1963 "On Social Regression." *American Sociological Review* 28:339–364.

Stinnett, Nick 1971 "An Investigation of Selected Attitudes of College Students Toward Marriage." *Journal of Home Economics* 63:33–37.

Sweet, James A., and Larry L. Bumpass 1987 *American Families and Households.* New York: Russell Sage Foundation.

Teachman, Jay D., D. Polonko, and John Scanzoni 1987 "Demography of the Family." In Marvin B. Sussman and Suzanne K. Steinmetz, eds., *Handbook of Marriage and the Family.* New York: Plenum Press.

Veroff, Joseph, Richard Kulka, and Elizabeth Douvan 1981 *Mental Health in America: Patterns of Help-Seeking from 1957 to 1976.* New York: Basic Books.

Walker, Lenore E. 1979 *The Battered Woman.* New York: Harper and Row.

White, Lynn K. 1987 "Freedom Versus Constraint: The New Synthesis." *Journal of Family Issues* 8:468–470.

———1990 "Determinants of Divorce: Review of Research in the Eighties." *Journal of Marriage and the Family* 52:904–912.

———, and Alan Booth 1985 "The Transition to Parenthood and Marital Quality." *Journal of Family Issues* 6:435–449.

Whyte, Martin K. 1990 *Dating, Mating, and Marriage.* New York: Aldine de Gruyter.

MARILYN IHINGER-TALLMAN

MARRIAGE AND DIVORCE RATES

Marriage and divorce rates are measures of the propensity for the population of a given area to become married or divorced during a given year. Some of the rates are quite simple, and others are progressively more refined. The simple ones are called *crude rates* and are expressed in terms of the number of marriages or divorces per 1,000 persons of all ages in the area at the middle of the year. These are the only marriage and divorce rates available for every state in the United States. They have the weakness of including in the base not only young children but also elderly persons, who are unlikely to marry or become divorced. But the wide fluctuations in crude rates over time are obviously associated with changes in the economic, political, and social climate.

More refined rates will be discussed below, but the following illustrative crude rates of marriage for the United States will demonstrate the readily identifiable consequences of recent historical turning points or periods (National Center for Health Statistics 1990a, 1990b).

Between 1940 and 1946 the crude marriage rate for the United States went up sharply, from 12.1 per 1,000 to 16.4 per 1,000, or by 36 percent, showing the effects of depressed economic conditions before, and disarmament after, World War II.

Between 1946 and 1956 the rate went down rapidly to 9.5 per 1,000, or by 42 percent, as the baby boom peaked. The unprecedented increase in the number of young children was included in the base of the rate, and this helped to lower the rate.

Between 1956 and 1964 the rate declined farther to 9.0 per 1,000, or by 5 percent, as the baby boom ended and the Vietnam War had begun. Between 1964 and 1972 the rate went up moderately to a peak of 10.9 per 1,000, or by 21 percent, as the Vietnam War ended and many returning war veterans married.

Between 1972 and 1989 the rate declined irregularly to 9.7 per 1,000, or by 11 percent, because of developments that will be discussed below.

Refined marriage rates show the propensity to marry for adults who are eligible to marry. They exclude from the base all persons who are too young to marry and may also limit the base to an age range within which most marriages occur. Thus, vital statistics annual reports regularly present crude marriage rates for the entire United States, for regions, and for individual states; and historical series on marriage rates for unmarried women under forty-five years of age are presented only for the United States as a whole (National Center for Health Statistics 1990b). More detailed characteristics of brides and grooms are published only for the entire United States. The conventional practice of basing these rates on the number of women rather than all adults has the advantage of making the level of the rates correspond approximately to the number of couples who are marrying. Moreover, the patterns of changes in rates over time are generally the same for men and women.

Changes over time in the tendency for adults to marry are more meaningful and may fluctuate more widely if they are reported in refined rather than crude rates. To illustrate, the crude marriage rate declined between 1972 and 1980 from 10.9 per 1,000 population to 10.6, or by only 3 percent, while the refined rate (marriages per 1,000 women fifteen to forty-four years old) declined from 141.3 to 102.6, or by 27 percent. A change that appeared to be small when measured crudely turned out to be large when based on a more relevant segment of the population. Persons who want to have others believe that the change was small may cite the crude rates, and persons who want to demonstrate that the marital situation was deteriorating rapidly may cite the refined rates. But persons interested in making a balanced presentation may choose to cite both types of results and explain the differences between them.

Still greater refinement can be achieved by computing marriage rates according to such key variables as age groups and previous marital status. Examples appear in table 1 and figures 1 and 3 for the United States from 1971 to 1987. Table 1 and figure 1 show first marriage rates by age for the only marital status category of eligible persons, namely, never-married adults (women) fifteen years old and over. Figure 2 shows divorce rates by age for married women, and figure 3 shows remarriage rates by age for divorced women. The low remarriage rates for widows are not shown here but are treated briefly elsewhere in the article. Rates of separation because of marital discord are also not presented here: Separated adults are still legally married and are therefore included in the base of divorce rates.

The marriage and divorce rates in table 1 were based on data from annual reports published by the National Center for Health Statistics (NCHS). These reports contain information, obtained from

TABLE 1
First Marriage Rates per 1,000 Never-Married Women, Divorced Rates per 1,000 Married Women, and Remarriage Rates per 1,000 Divorced Women by Age: United States, 1970 to 1987

Age (years)	*1970*[a]	*1975*	*1980*[b]	*1983*	*1985*	*1987*
			First Marriage Rate			
15 or over	93	76	68	64	62	59
15 to 17	36	29	22	16	13	12
18 to 19	150	115	92	73	67	58
20 to 24	198	144	122	107	102	98
25 to 29	131	115	104	105	104	105
30 to 34	75	62	60	61	66	69
35 to 39	48	36	33	38	37	42
40 to 44	27	26	22	22	24	22
45 to 64	10	9	8	8	11	10
65 or over	1	1	1	1	1	1
			Divorce Rate			
15 or over	14	NA	20	19	19	19
15 to 19	27	NA	42	48	48	50
20 to 24	33	NA	47	43	47	46
25 to 29	26	NA	38	36	36	34
30 to 34	19	NA	29	28	29	27
35 to 44	11	NA	24	25	22	22
45 to 54	5	NA	10	11	11	11
55 to 64	3	NA	4	4	4	4
			Remarriage Rate			
15 or over	133	117	104	92	82	81
20 to 24	420	301	301	240	264	248
25 to 29	277	235	209	204	184	183
30 to 34	196	173	146	145	128	137
35 to 39	147	117	108	99	97	92
40 to 44	98	91	69	67	63	69
45 to 64	47	40	35	31	36	37
65 or over	9	9	7	5	5	5

[a]First marriage and remarriage rates for 1971.
[b]First marriage and remarriage rates for 1979.

SOURCE: National Center for Health Statistics, 1990b and 1990c.

central offices, of vital statistics in the states that are in the Marriage Registration Area (MRA) and the Divorce Registration Area (DRA). In 1990 the District of Columbia and all but eight states were in the MRA, while the District of Columbia and only thirty-one states were in the DRA. Funding for the central offices is determined by each state's legislature. But for states not in the MRA or DRA the NCHS requests the numbers of marriages and divorces from local offices where marriage and divorce certificates are issued. The reports on divorce include the small number of annulments and dissolutions of marriage. Bases for the marriage and divorce rates in table 1 were obtained from special tabulations made by the U.S. Bureau of the Census from Current Population Survey data. These are tabulations of adults in MRA and DRA states and classified by marital status, age, and sex. Because not all the population of the United States is included in the MRA and DRA, the detailed marriage and divorce statistics published by the NCHS constitute approximations of the marital situation in the country as a whole. This article contains much numerical information that was published in one or more of the three NCHS reports listed among the references.

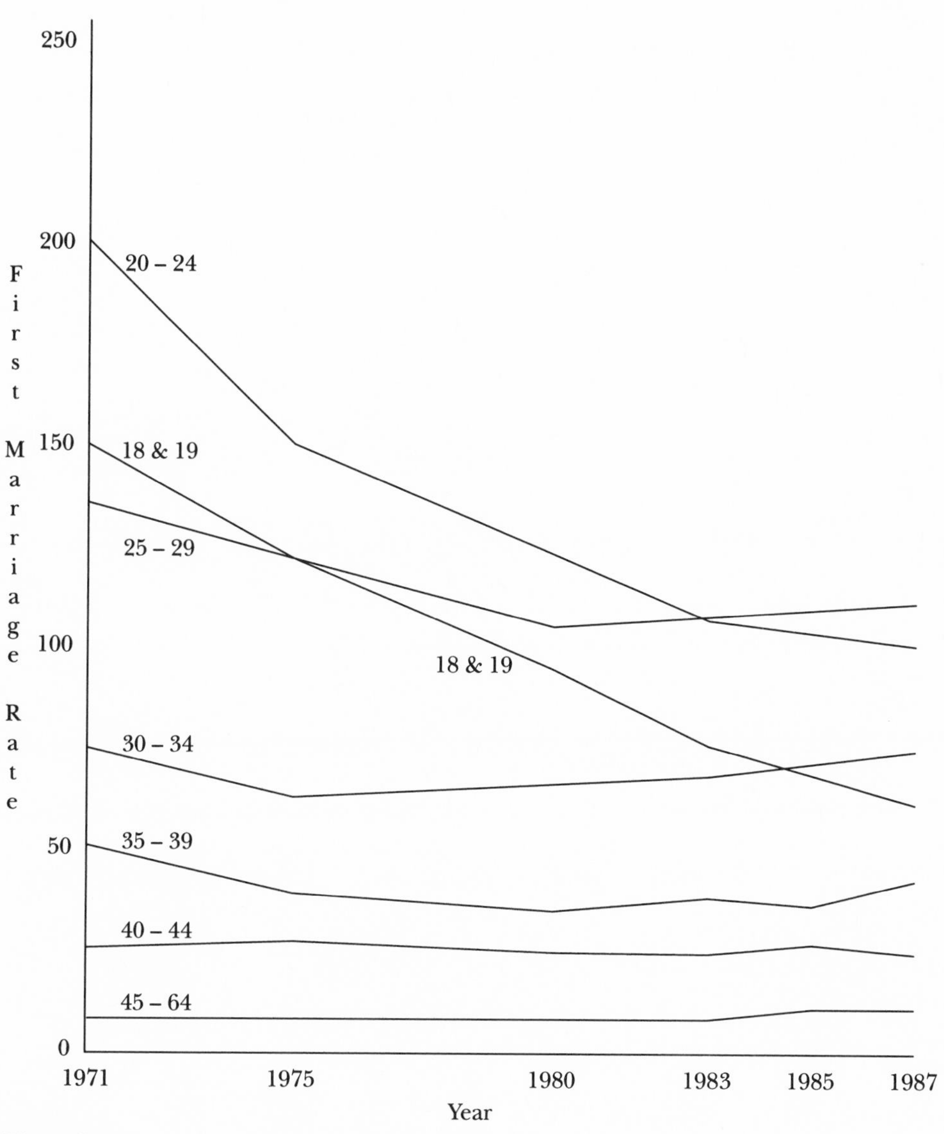

Figure 1
First marriage rate per 1,000 never-married women, by age: United States, 1971–1987

FIRST MARRIAGE RATES BY AGE

Illustrations of first marriage rates appear in table 1. For the United States, the first marriage rates per 1,000 never-married women fifteen years old and over were 93 in 1971 and 59 in 1987. (When this article was prepared, the most recent years for which detailed marriage and divorce rates had been published was 1987. In effect, 9.3 percent of the never-married women in 1971, and 5.9 percent in 1987, became married for the first time.) For men, the corresponding rates were 68 in 1971 and 49 in 1987.

First marriage rates tend to decline with age, and the rates for most of the age groups shown in table 1 were declining over time. The rates for the age groups under twenty years of age were the highest, but they dropped so sharply that they were only about one-third as high in 1987 as they had been in 1971. At the oldest ages, the change appears to have been slight. Obviously, the pro-

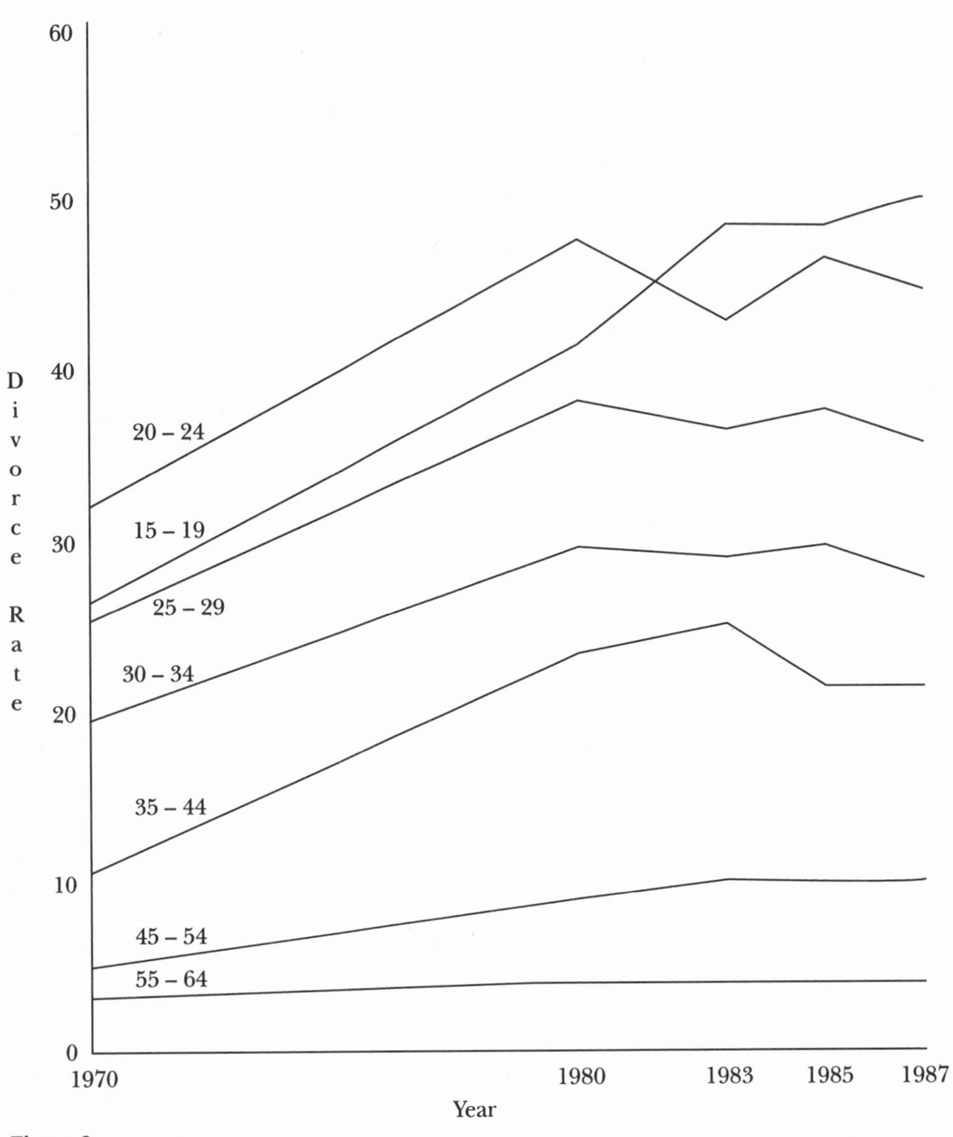

Figure 2
Divorce rate per 1,000 married women, by age: United States, 1970–1987

pensity to marry was falling far more abruptly among the young than among the older singles, probably in reaction to the suddenly changing cultural climate.

The generally downward trend in the marriage rate for each young age group was especially rapid during the early 1970s. By 1975, the veterans of the Vietnam War had already entered delayed marriages, and the upsurge in cohabitation outside marriage was only beginning to depress the first marriage rate. During the 1980s the slight upturn in the first marriage rate for women over thirty years of age probably reflected an increase in marriages among women who had delayed marrying for the purposes of obtaining a higher education and becoming established in the workplace. Research has produced evidence that women who marry for the first time after they reach their thirties are more likely to have stable marriages than those who marry in their twenties

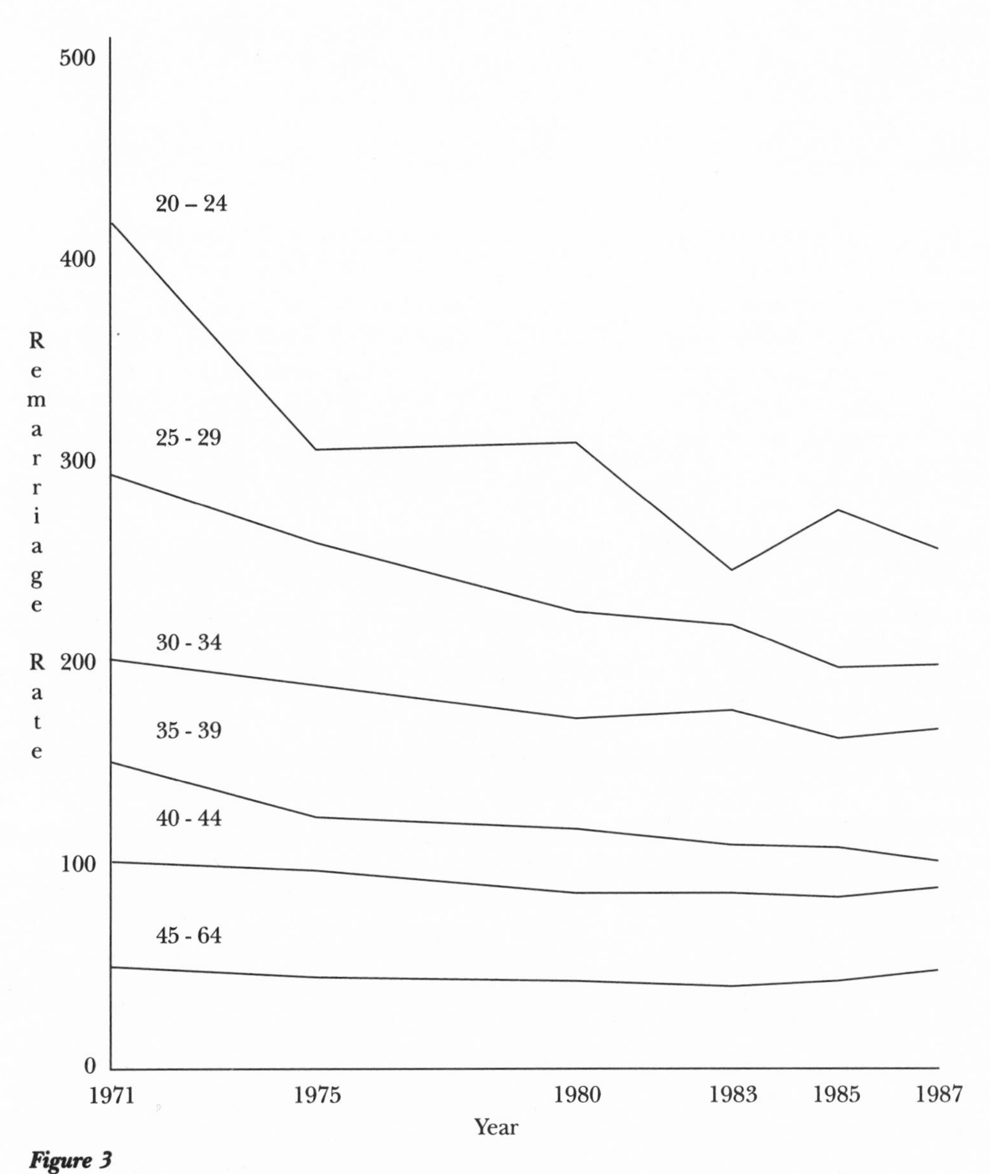

Figure 3
Remarriage rate per 1,000 divorced women, by age: United States, 1971–1987

(Norton and Moorman 1987). Although first marriage rates among adults in their forties are relatively low, they are by no means negligible.

As first marriage rates declined between the mid-1960s and the late 1980s, the median age at first marriage rose at an unprecedented pace over this short period of time. According to vital statistics, the median age at first marriage for women went up from 20.3 years in 1963 to 23.6 in 1987; for men it went up from 22.5 years to 25.3 years. As age at first marriage increased, the distribution of ages at first marriage also increased (Wilson and London 1987).

One of the consequences of the great delay of first marriage has been a very sharp rise in premarital pregnancy. Only 5 percent of births in 1960 occurred to unmarried mothers, but this increased to 24 percent in 1987. Research by Bumpass and McLanahan (1989) showed that one-half of nonmarital births during the late

1980s were first births, and about one-third occurred to teenagers. Moreover, about one-tenth of brides were pregnant at first marriage. Thus, about one-third of the births during the late 1980s were conceived before marriage.

As the first marriage rate declined, the proportion of all marriages that were primary marriages (first for bride and groom) also declined. In 1970, two-thirds (68 percent) were primary marriages, but by 1987 the proportion was barely over one-half (54 percent). Meantime, marriages of divorced brides to divorced grooms nearly doubled, from 11 percent to 19 percent, while marriages of widows to widowers went down from 2 percent to 1 percent.

Men and women, regardless of previous marital status, tend to marry someone whose age is similar to their own. But men who enter first marriage when they are older than the average age of men at marriage have a reasonable likelihood of marrying a woman who has been divorced.

Procedures have been developed for projecting the proportion of adults of a certain age who are likely to enter first marriage sometime during their lives. This measure is, in effect, "a lifetime first marriage rate." One of these procedures was used by Schoen et al. (1985) to find that about 94 percent of men born in the years 1948 to 1950 and who survived to age fifteen were expected to marry eventually; for women, it was 95 percent. Their projections for those born in 1980 were significantly lower, 89 percent for men and 91 percent for women. Despite the implied decline, a level of nine-tenths of the young adults deciding to marry at least once is still high by world standards.

DIVORCE RATES BY AGE

The NCHS publishes annual reports that show the number of divorces occurring among persons in their first marriage, their second marriage, and their third or subsequent marriage (National Center for Health Statistics 1990c). But the required bases for computing first divorce rates and redivorce rates are not available. During the 1980s, about three-fourths of the divorces were obtained by adults in their first marriage, about one-fifth by those in their second marriage, and one-twentieth by those who had been married at least three times.

The divorce rates in table 1 provide illustrations of the magnitude of the rates for the period 1970 to 1987. The divorce rate per 1,000 married women was 14 in 1970 and 19 in 1987. Corresponding rates for men were the same. The rate reached a peak of 20 in 1980, nearly half again as high as in 1970, and declined slightly to 19 in 1987, a level still well above that in 1970.

The divorce rate for married women rose dramatically in every age group during the 1970s and changed relatively little from then through the 1980s. In January 1973 the Vietnam War ended, and at that time the norms regarding the sanctity of marriage were being revised. The advantages of a permanent marriage were being weighed against the alternatives, including freedom from a seriously unsatisfactory marital bond and the prospect of experimenting with cohabitation outside marriage or living alone without any marital entanglements.

Married women under twenty-five years of age have consistently high divorce rates resulting largely from adjustment difficulties associated with early first marriage. Noteworthy in this context is the finding that 30 percent of the women entering a first marriage in 1980 were in their teens, while 40 percent of those obtaining a divorce had entered their marriage while teenagers.

More divorces during the 1980s were occurring to married adults twenty-five to thirty-four years of age than to those in any other ten-year age group. A related study by Norton and Moorman (1987) concluded that women in their late thirties in 1985 were likely to have higher lifetime divorce rates (55 percent) than those either ten years older or ten years younger. This cohort was born during the vanguard of the baby boom and became the trend setter for higher divorce rates. The lower rate for those ten years younger may reflect their concern caused by the adjustment problems of their older divorced siblings or friends.

Married women over forty-five years of age have

quite low divorce rates. Most of their marriages must still be reasonably satisfactory, or not sufficiently unsatisfactory to persuade them to face the disadvantages that are often associated with becoming divorced. Yet, the forces that raised the divorce rate for younger women greatly after 1970 also made the small rate for the older women increase by one-fourth during the 1970s and remain at about the same level through the 1980s.

The median duration of marriage before divorce has been seven years for several decades. This finding is not proof of a seven-year itch. In fact, the median varies widely according to previous marital status from eight years for first marriages to six years for second marriages and four years for third and subsequent marriages. The number of divorces reaches a peak during the third year of marriage and declines during each succeeding year of marriage.

Among separating couples, the wife usually files the petition for divorce. However, between 1975 and 1987, the proportion of husband petitioners increased from 29.4 percent to 32.7 percent, and the small proportion of divorces in which both the husband and the wife were petitioners more than doubled, from 2.8 percent to 6.5 percent. These changes occurred while the feminist movement was becoming increasingly diffused and the birth rate was declining, with the consequence that only about one-half (52 percent) of the divorces in 1987 involved children under eighteen years of age and one-fourth (29 percent) involved only one child. It is not surprising that nine-tenths of children under eighteen living with a divorced parent live with their mother, far more often in families with smaller average incomes than those living with divorced fathers.

Although only about one-tenth of the adults in the United States in 1988 were divorced (7.4 percent) or separated (2.4 percent), the lifetime experience of married persons with these types of marital disruption is far greater. Based on adjustments for underreporting of divorce data from the Current Population Survey and for underrepresentation of divorce from vital statistics in the MRA, Martin and Bumpass (1989) have concluded that two-thirds of current marriages are likely to end in separation or divorce.

REMARRIAGE RATES BY AGE

Annual remarriage rates published by NCHS include separate rates for remarriages after divorce and after widowhood as well as for all remarriages. In this article attention is concentrated on remarriages after divorce, which constitute about nine-tenths of all remarriages. As mentioned above, the remarriage rate after divorce is a measure of the number of divorced women who marry in a given year per 1,000 divorced women at the middle of the year. For example, table 1 shows that the remarriage rate after divorce for the United States was 133 in 1970 and 81 in 1987. Therefore, about 13 percent of the divorced women in 1970 became remarried in that year, as compared with 8 percent in 1987, only three-fifths as much as in 1970.

Divorced men have far higher remarriage rates than divorced women (in 1987, 116 versus 81). This situation and women's greater longevity largely account for the number of divorced women fifty-five years old and over in 1988 being one and one-half times the number of divorced men of that age (U.S. Bureau of the Census 1989).

Like first marriage rates, remarriage rates tend to decline with age, and the rate for each age group declined after 1970. The especially sharp drop during the first half of the 1970s for women under forty years of age resulted from the compounding effect of a rapid increase in divorce and a rapid decline in remarriage during that period.

A large majority of divorced persons eventually remarry. In 1980, among persons sixty-five to seventy-four years old, 84 percent of the men and 77 percent of the women who had been divorced had remarried (U.S. Bureau of the Census 1989). But because of the declining remarriage rates, a projection based on information from the National Survey of Families and Households conducted in 1987 and 1988 shows that 72 percent of the recently separated persons are likely eventually to remarry (Bumpass, Sweet, and Martin 1989).

About 6 percent of those who become separated never become divorced and therefore are not eligible for remarriage. Two-thirds of the remarriages in recent years occurred to women who entered first marriages as teenagers, according to the same study. Moreover, the rate of remarriage declines as the number of young children increases. Among married parents of young children with one or both parents remarried, about one-third of the children were born after the remarriage, and the others are stepchildren with the usually accompanying adjustment problems (Glick and Lin 1987).

In a given year about two of every three adults who marry are marrying for the first time, but this includes those marrying after widowhood as well as divorce. Among those who remarry after divorce, about three-fourths have been married only once, one-fifth have been married twice, and one-twentieth three or more times. Some couples who remarry had been married to each other previously. According to unpublished data from the National Survey of Families and Households, this occurred in about 3.3 percent of all marriages and closer to 5 percent for those in the age range when most remarriages after divorce occur.

Men are older than women, on the average, when they marry for the first time or when they remarry. Moreover, the gap is considerably wider at remarriage than at first marriage, but it narrowed somewhat between 1970 and 1987. Thus, successive marriages have been happening at older ages but with shorter intervals between them. In this context, the wider gap at remarriage than at first marriage may be less socially significant than an identical gap would have been at first marriage.

A woman in her second marriage is likely to be married to a man who is about ten years older than her first husband when she married him. Therefore, her second husband was probably more advanced in his occupation than her first husband was when she married him. But research has established that her first husband was probably about as far advanced ten years after her first marriage as her second husband was when she married him (Jacobs and Furstenberger 1986).

OTHER MARRIAGE AND DIVORCE RATES

Another rate that differs from the rates shown in table 1 is the *total marriage rate.* This rate is intended to show the number of marriages that a group of 1,000 men and women would have if they experienced in their lives the age-sex marriage rates observed in a given year (National Center for Health Statistics 1990b). It is therefore a hypothetical rate analogous to a total fertility rate. The NCHS publishes both total first marriage rates and total remarriage rates annually. Each of the two rates uses as the base the total population in each age group without regard to previous marital status.

The total first marriage rate for the United States in 1987 implied that only 69 percent of men and 70 percent of women would eventually marry. The corresponding remarriage rates were 45 percent for men and 41 percent for women. Because both rates are based on the population regardless of marital status, they are additive. Therefore, the (combined) total marriage rate for 1987 implied that men are likely to have 1.14 marriages during their lifetime and women 1.11. These results may seem low because of the assumptions involved. For instance, if currently about 90 percent of every 100 adults marry, if one-half of the first marriages end in divorce, and if 70 percent of the divorced persons remarry, this would mean that 100 young adults in the 1990s are likely to have 90 first marriages and 32 second marriages after divorce (.90 + .90 × .50 × .70). In addition, many will redivorce and remarry again, and others will become widowed and remarry. Thus, realistically, the average young adult in the 1990s who marries is likely to have more than 1.1 marriages.

Remarriage among widowed adults is not featured in this article. However, the remarriage rate per 1,000 widows declined from 6 in 1982 to 5 in 1987, while the rate for widowers declined from 32 to 26. The remarriage rate for widowers is much higher than the rate for widows because about one-half of them marry widows, who outnumber them five to one (U.S. Bureau of the

Census 1989). Of all men and women who married in 1987, 68 percent had never previously married, 29 percent were divorced, and only 3 percent were widowed.

Divorce rates per 1,000 involved children under eighteen are published annually by NCHS. In 1987, the rate was 17, implying that 1.7 percent of the children under eighteen years of age in the United States were involved in parental divorces in that year. This finding implies further that, if the same rate continued for eighteen years, 30.6 percent of the children would likely experience parental divorce before they reached eighteen years of age. Data from the U.S. Bureau of Census used by Norton and Glick (1986) put the estimate at 40 percent. They also estimated that about an additional 20 percent of children become members of one-parent families because of premarital birth, parental separation that does not end in divorce, or death of a parent. Therefore, about 60 percent of the children born in the 1980s may expect to spend a significant amount of time in a one-parent family before they become eighteen years of age.

Marriage rates vary among countries as a reflection of dissimilar social, demographic, and economic conditions. An analysis of marriage rates in fifteen developed countries revealed that between 1965 and 1980 the rate per 1,000 unmarried women declined in all but two of the countries (Glick 1989). The marriage rates in English-speaking countries and Israel were above the average for the entire group, but the rates were below the average in the Germanic, French, and Scandinavian countries. A special reason for the differences was the extent to which cohabitation had been accepted as at least a temporary alternative to marriage. The generally downward trend among the marriage rates shows that the changing social conditions related to the propensity toward marriage have become widely diffused.

Divorce rates per 1,000 married women in almost all of the fifteen countries went up between 1965 and 1980 and doubled in the majority of them. Most of the countries with divorce rates above the overall average were English speaking. High divorce rates tended to be associated with high marriage rates because remarriages after divorce make an important contribution to the level of the marriage rates per 1,000 unmarried women.

Remarriage rates have been falling in most of the fifteen countries. In Canada a part of the decline between 1965 and 1980 was attributed to a change in the divorce laws and an increase in the delay of remarriage. The remarriage rate in New Zealand actually rose slightly in the context of a baby boom and an increase in immigration of young adults with subsequent high divorce rates. Countries with the highest remarriage rates were English speaking, and those with the lowest were Scandinavian, French, and certain other European countries where cohabitation outside marriage had risen sharply.

Variation in the level of marriage and divorce rates among the American regions and states can be documented only by the use of crude rates. The Northeast and Midwest had consistently lower marriage rates than the South and West. The general pattern is similar for divorce rates. Some of the variations in the rates by states result from differences in the strictness of residence requirements for obtaining a marriage or divorce license. About seven of every eight marriages occur in the state where both the bride and the groom have their usual residence.

SELECTED VARIABLES RELATED TO MARRIAGE AND DIVORCE

Annual marriage and divorce rates are not presented in the NCHS reports by education and race of those involved. However, the reports do show distributions of first marriages and remarriages by several categories of education and race. The 1987 report documents that those marrying for the first time had more education, on the average, than those who were remarrying. Information from the 1980 census showed that women twenty-five to thirty-four years of age who had exactly four years of college training had distinctly the largest proportion with intact first marriages;

those with graduate school training had a somewhat smaller proportion; and those with an incomplete college education had a smaller proportion than those in any other education category (U.S. Bureau of Census 1985).

The 1987 report on marriage provided evidence that white adults tend to marry at a younger age than black adults. The difference was two years for both brides and grooms at first marriage and two years at remarriage after divorce. Information for 1988 from the U.S. Bureau of the Census (1989) indicated that 18 percent of black adults had not married by the time they were forty years old, as compared with 8 percent for white adults of the same age. The pressure to marry and to remain married evidently tends to be less for black adults than white adults.

Interracial marriage occurs between a small but socially significant proportion of those who marry. In 1987, 2 percent of black brides married white grooms, and 6 percent of black grooms married white brides. Also, nearly 2 percent of black women obtaining divorces were married to white men, and more than 4 percent of black men obtaining divorces were married to white women. Thus, among those who intermarried, the marriages of black men to white women tend to be more stable than marriages of white men to black women.

Cohabitation outside marriage increased dramatically from only one-half million heterosexual couples in 1970 to 2.6 million in 1988, with about one million of their households maintained by the woman. This numerical growth occurred primarily among adults below middle age and has contributed importantly to the decline in marriage rates as well as to the increase in the number of separated persons. According to the 1987–1988 National Survey of Families and Households, "almost half of the persons in their early thirties and half of the recently married have cohabited" (Bumpass and Sweet 1989, p. 615). In order to provide some balance on the issue, Thornton (1985, p. 497) has concluded that "even though cohabitation will be experienced by many, most people will continue to spend substantially more time in marital unions than in cohabiting unions."

The health of adults is related to marital selection and marital stability, but NCHS does not provide marriage and divorce rates by the health status of those involved. The center does, however, publish current information on several indicators of the health condition of adults by marital status. Nearly all of the indicators confirm that people with more signs of good health are likely to marry and remain married or to remarry after marital dissolution (Wilson and Schoenborn 1989). Parental divorce tends to be related to health problems of children but largely through the custodial parents' loss of income and time to spend with the children after divorce (Mauldon 1988). And stress prior to an event such as divorce or premarital breakup may actually reduce the impact of the life transition (Wheaton 1990).

Current trends in marriage and divorce rates do not necessarily indicate whether the rates will tend to stabilize at or near their 1990 levels, to resume their movement in historical directions, or to continue fluctuating in response to future social developments. A few more decades of observing the impact of past changes in marriage and divorce rates on the persons involved may be necessary before a definitive evaluation can be made concerning the longtime effect of these changes on family and child welfare.

(SEE ALSO: *Divorce; Marriage; Remarriage*)

REFERENCES

Bumpass, Larry, and Sara McLanahan 1989 "Unmarried Motherhood: Recent Trends, Composition, and Black-White Differences." *Demography* 26:279–286.

Bumpass, Larry, and James A. Sweet 1989 "National Estimates of Cohabitation." *Demography* 26:615–625.

Bumpass, Larry, James A. Sweet, and Teresa Castro Martin 1989 "Changing Patterns of Remarriage." Working Paper 89–02. Madison: Center for Demography and Ecology, University of Wisconsin.

Glick, Paul C. 1989 "The Family of Today and Tomorrow." In K. Ishwaran, ed., *Family and Marriage: Cross-Cultural Perspectives.* Toronto: Wall and Thompson.

Glick, Paul C., and Sung-Ling Lin 1987 "Remarriage after Divorce: Recent Changes and Demographic Variations." *Sociological Perspectives* 30:162–179.

Jacobs, Jerry A., and Frank F. Furstenberg, Jr. 1986 "Changing Place: Conjugal Careers and Women's Marital Stability." *Social Forces* 63:714–732.

Lin, Sung-Ling 1987 "Marital Selection and Child-Bearing and Companionship Functions of Marriage and Remarriage." Ph.D. diss., Arizona State University, Tempe.

Martin, Teresa Castro, and Larry L. Bumpass 1989 "Recent Trends in Marital Disruption." *Demography* 26:37–51.

Mauldon, Jane 1988 "The Effect of Marital Disruption on Children's Health." Paper presented at the Population Association of America meeting, New Orleans.

National Center for Health Statistics 1990a "Births, Marriages, Divorces, and Deaths for 1989." *Monthly Vital Statistics Report* 38, no. 12.

———1990b "Advance Report of Final Marriage Statistics, 1987." *Monthly Vital Statistics Report* 38, no. 12, Supplement.

———1990c "Advance Report of Final Divorce Statistics, 1987." *Monthly Vital Statistics Report* 38, no. 12, Supplement 2.

Norton, Arthur J., and Paul C. Glick 1986 "One-Parent Families: A Social and Economic Profile." *Family Relations* 35:9–17.

Norton, Arthur J., and Jeanne E. Moorman 1987 "Current Trends in Marriage and Divorce among American Women." *Journal of Marriage and the Family* 49:3–14.

Schoen, Robert, William Urton, Karen Woodrow, and John Baj 1985 "Marriage and Divorce in Twentieth-Century American Cohorts." *Demography* 22:101–114.

Thornton, Arland 1988 "Cohabitation and Marriage in the 1980s." *Demography* 25:492–508.

U.S. Bureau of the Census 1985 *1980 Census of Population: Marital Characteristics.* Washington, D.C.: U.S. Government Printing Office.

———1989 "Marital Status and Living Arrangements: March 1988." *Current Population Reports* P-20, no. 433. Washington, D.C.: U.S. Government Printing Office.

Wheaton, Blair 1990 "Life Transitions, Role Histories, and Mental Health." *American Sociological Review* 55:209–223.

Wilson, Barbara F., and Kathryn A. London 1987 "Going to the Chapel." *American Demographics* 9: 26–31.

Wilson, Barbara F, and Charlotte Schoenborn 1989 "A Healthy Marriage." *American Demographics* 11:40–43.

PAUL C. GLICK

MARXIST SOCIOLOGY The concept of a Marxist sociology does not refer to a clearly defined approach to social research; indeed, it is "now employed so widely that it has begun to lose all meaning" (Abercrombie, Hill, and Turner 1988, p. 148). The ambiguity of the term stems from the multiplicity of interpretations of the work of Karl Marx and Friedrich Engels, whose approach to social theory is usually termed *historical materialism.* The most well-known version is that of Soviet communism (Marxism-Leninism) and is identified with the worldview of *dialectical materialism* (a term never used by Marx and Engels), which has served largely the interests of Soviet ideology. The influence of historical materialism in modern sociology, however, stems primarily from the lesser-known independent tradition of European "Western Marxism" and the resulting forms of Marxist sociology (Agger 1979).

Contemporary usage of the term *Marxist sociology* varies considerably. In the United States, for example, the term *Marxist* is often used rather loosely, to designate virtually any type of radical or critical approach influenced by Marxian concepts (e.g., Ollman and Vernoff 1982; Flacks 1982). In societies with more strongly developed social democratic labor movements, as in Europe, the term is more closely identified with Communist parties. Given the inherent ambiguity of the term, it is therefore useful to define Marxist sociology rather narrowly and concretely as a specific form of conflict theory associated with Western Marxism's objective of developing a positive (empirical) science of capitalist society as part of the mobilization of a revolutionary working class.

It is also useful to distinguish three basic types of relations between sociologists and Marxist sociology: those who work directly within the Marxist tradition (Marxist sociology proper) but "incorporate sociological insights, findings, and methodologies"; those who are Marxist-influenced in the sense of being stimulated by its historical approach and the "big questions" Marxists have posed but remain indifferent to "whether the best explanatory answers turn out to be Marxist" (Burawoy and Skocpol 1982, p. vii); and those identifying with highly revisionist critical theories (sometimes still in the name of Marxism) that seek to preserve the emancipatory vision of the Marxist tradition despite abandonment of the conventional notion of working-class revolution (Held 1980; Kellner 1989). It should also be stressed that Marxist sociology in this first sense refers to a historically identifiable—but widely contested—interpretation of the sociological implications of Marx's approach. As the most well-known British Marxist sociologist has concluded with particular reference to the German Frankfurt tradition of critical theory: "The tasks of a Marxist sociology, as I conceive it, are therefore very different from those of a neo-critical theory of society" (Bottomore 1984, p. 81). Marxist sociology in this strict sense thus tends in its most rigid form to resist any eclectic appropriation of sociological concepts: "Marxism has been courted by virtually every conceivable non-Marxist ideology: by existentialism, phenomenology, critical academic sociology, and by several variants of theology. To raise the question of a Marxism of Marxism is to take a resolute stand against all attempts to capture and exploit Marx for non-Marxist purposes; and to adopt as a guiding principle . . . the claim that Marx himself made for his work: that Marxism is a specific science, related to the working class as a guide to socialist revolution" (Therborn 1976, p. 40).

The distinction between Marxism as "science" and as "critique" provides another way of describing the aspirations of Marxist sociology, which most commonly seeks to develop an objective, political economic science of society rather than a critical philosophy of praxis (Bottomore 1975; Gouldner 1980). Such a project is inherently interdisciplinary and often referred to under the heading of *political economy,* a term designating Marxist-oriented research that may be carried out in various disciplines: economics, political science, and history, as well as sociology (Attewell 1984). Though those identifying with neo-Weberian conflict or critical theories accept many of the empirical findings of neo-Marxist sociology and political economy, they tend to disagree about their broader interpretation and relation to political practice and social change.

ORIGINS

All forms of Marxist sociology trace themselves to the general theoretical approach of historical materialism as developed by Marx and Engels (Marx and Engels 1978; Bottomore and Goode 1983; Bottomore et al. 1983). Standard accounts of Marx's theoretical program stress that it does not constitute a unified system so much as diverse, though interrelated, modes of theorizing.

- early writings that outline a theory of philosophical critique, an analysis of alienated labor, and a normative vision of human emancipation;
- a general sociology in the form of historical materialism (i.e., a theory of modes of production) as an approach to historical evolution;
- a specific account of capitalism and its economic contradictions deriving from this general theory; and
- a political philosophy and theory of praxis concerned with translating objective crisis tendencies in capitalism into a revolutionary transformation that would bring about a new form of "socialist" and eventually "communist" society (Giddens 1971, pp. 1–64; Bottomore 1975).

The precise relationship among these areas remains controversial. Though each level of theorizing has sociological implications, Marxist sociology has drawn primarily from the general sociology suggested by historical materialism and the more historically specific analysis of capitalist development that is the empirical focus of Marx's social theory and historical sociology. The key concept of a mode of production serves as the comparative framework for analyzing different social formations in terms of the contradictory relationship between their forces of production (primarily technology) and relations of production (forms of work organization and exploitation). The resulting mode of production directly shapes the specific structures of the class system and the manner in which the economic base determines the cultural superstructure composed of the state and various ideological institutions such as the mass media, education, law, religion, political ideologies, and so forth. In capitalist societies the contradiction deriving from the unresolvable polarization between labor and capital becomes the basis for revolutionary change under conditions of economic crisis.

As a positive science of society, Marxist sociology emerged in the period following Marx's death in 1883 through World War I. Strongly influenced by Engels's conception of "scientific socialism" as elaborated by Karl Kautsky in Germany, it was institutionalized in German Social Democracy and the Second International. Particular stress was placed upon how this approach provided an account of the historical "laws" that explained the causes of changes in modes of production and class formation and struggle. According to these laws a transition to socialism could be deduced from the "necessary" breakdown of capitalism. Extensive further development of such a scientific socialism was carried out by the Austro-Marxists, who deepened the logical analysis of Marxism as a form of causal explanation by drawing upon contemporary debates in the philosophy of science; as well, they extended Marx's theory to new phenomena such as the analysis of nationalism and the ethical foundations of Marxist sociology (Bottomore 1975; 1978; Bottomore and Goode 1978).

These two traditions of scientific socialism, however, did not develop much beyond the level codified in Bukharin's textbook of 1921 (*Historical Materialism: A System of Sociology,* translated in 1925). The primary reason was that there was considerable resistance to Marxism in the academy (related in part to identification of Marxism with the Soviet Union), ignorance of the richness of the suppressed tradition of Western Marxism, and a broad post-World War II institutionalization of sociology that virtually excluded Marxist sociology, despite some marginal influences of research in social stratification and change (e.g., Ralf Dahrhendorf in West Germany and C. Wright Mills in the United States). For all practical purposes the resurgence of Marxist sociology (often identified as "political economy" as opposed to "critical theory") coincides with the parallel emergence of radical and critical theories in the late 1960s, along with the recovery of the deeper foundations of Marxian theory with the proliferation of translations of Western Marxist texts in the 1970s.

It is customary to distinguish two basic starting points of a Marxist sociology based on different interpretations of the base–superstructure metaphor that underlies the concept of a mode of production: economistic or instrumental approaches as opposed to structuralist reproduction models. Economistic interpretations—sometimes associated with the idea of orthodox or "vulgar" Marxism—are based on a more or less reductionistic, causal account of the effects of the economic base or infrastructure upon the cultural superstructure, especially as causally derived from the assumed objective consequences of class interests.

Structuralist theories of social and cultural reproduction, in contrast, argue that the base–superstructure relation is more complex, involving functional relations that ensure the relative (if variable) autonomy of cultural factors, even if the economic is determinant in the last instance. Such structuralist interpretations derive primarily from the concept of the social reproduction of labor power developed in Marx's later works, the theory of cultural hegemony developed by the Italian Marxist leader and theorist Antonio Gramsci (1971) in the 1930s, and the reinterpretation of both Marx and Gramsci by the French philosopher Louis Althusser in the 1960s (Althusser 1971; Althusser and Balibar [1968] 1979).

CONTEMPORARY THEMES IN MARXIST SOCIOLOGY

The most convenient way to speak of contemporary themes in Marxist sociology—thus differentiating it from conflict or critical theory generally—is to restrict the concept to research that continues to adhere to the basic principles of neo-Marxist theory. Such a Marxist sociology would sometimes include adherence to the labor theory of value (which holds that labor is the only source of profit) but more essentially the primacy of economic and class factors, the priority of objective structures over subjectivity and consciousness, and the privileged role of the working class in a transition to socialism as defined by direct state ownership of the means of production (Anderson 1984; Wood 1986; Archibald 1978).

With respect to more recent developments in Marxist sociology, the immense literature and wide national variations make it appropriate to focus primarily—if not exclusively—on the remarkable resurgence of Marxism in American sociology. This phenomenon stems from the 1970s and has been traced to four key influences: the broadened audience of the journal *Monthly Review,* which was founded in 1949 and pioneered the application of Marxist economic theory for an analysis of the United States and its "imperial" role in world politics; Marxist historians who developed a critique of American liberalism and proposed a class-based reinterpretation of American history; the Hegelian Marxism and Critical Theory of the Frankfurt School tradition; and, finally, structuralist Marxism of largely French inspiration that sought to reestablish the credentials of Marx's theory as a science of society (Burawoy 1982, pp. 4–6). To illustrate the concerns of recent Marxist sociology, it is instructive to review some of the most representative examples of research in four key areas: work and the division of labor, class structure, the state and crisis theory, and culture and ideology. Research on the political economy of the world system and dependency theory have also been important but will not be discussed here (see, however, So 1990).

The Labor Process and the New International Division of Labor. Until the late 1960s, Marxist theory was associated primarily with either communist ideologies or economic theory (Sweezy [1942] 1968). Not surprisingly, the pioneering, technically sophisticated Marxist research in the United States was concerned with an economic analysis of the new form of "monopoly capitalism" (Baran and Sweezy 1966). Drawing out the sociological implications of such, political economy is most closely associated with subsequent pathbreaking work involving the rediscovery of the labor process (i.e., Braverman 1974; Burawoy 1979) that gave work the central place that had been lost with the sense of consensus in postwar labor relations (Thompson 1983; Attewell 1984, pp. 93–141). Particular attention was given to the logic of capital's need to cheapen labor costs in ways that degrade and divide workers. More recent work has attempted to emphasize the incorporation of a subjective dimension to the labor process; further, it has developed a comparative perspective through the analysis of factory regimes in different types of economic systems and in relation to the new international division of labor (e.g., Burawoy 1985).

Class. Class analysis of course remains the key aspect of any Marxist sociology, but the focus contrasts sharply with conventional sociological approaches, even those (e.g., Max Weber) that acknowledge the importance of class conflict. Marxist sociology strongly insists on the primacy of the relations of production over the market processes stressed by neo-Weberians (Grabb 1990). The most influential empirical research in this area has stressed the importance of contradictory class locations and of reconnecting the objective and subjective dimensions of class with a theory of exploitation (Grabb 1990, pp. 152–163; Wright 1978; 1985).

Recent Marxist class analysis has been confronted by a number of challenges that pose serious problems for orthodox approaches; for example, the problem of the urban question, the role of ethnicity or race and especially gender as independent sources of domination (Shaw 1985), the emergence of the middle strata and the decline of the traditional "working class" (Walker 1978), the failure of class consciousness and actions to develop in the ways required for revolutionary transition, and other issues. The relation between Marxist and feminist theory has proven most controversial. More orthodox Marxist sociologists have attempted to incorporate gender into the theory of class and modes of production through the concept of unpaid "domestic labor" that contributes to the overall process of social reproduction (Fox 1980). But many feminists have abandoned Marxist sociology precisely because of its insistence on the primacy of class at the expense of gender (and other sources of domination).

The State and Crisis Theory. The contributions of Marxist sociology to the theory of the state have been wide-ranging and influential (Carnoy 1984; Jessop 1982; Holloway and Picciotto 1978). As well, they illustrate most clearly the issues involved in the debate between instrumental and structuralist interpretations of the base–superstructure model. In the context of theories of the state, this issue takes the form of whether the dominant class controls the state directly through its elite connections or indirectly through the functional economic and political imperatives that constrain public policy, regardless of who happens to hold power in a democratic regime. For example, the so-called Miliband-Poulantzas debate sharply defined the different empirical consequences of these two approaches. Miliband ([1969] 1973) stressed the actual empirical link between economic elites and political power of the dominant class, hence the role of the state as an instrument of class rule. Poulantzas ([1968] 1978), on the other hand, analyzed the state as a factor of cohesion that requires relative autonomy in order indirectly to serve the process of social reproduction in the long run.

Another central theme of Marxist sociology has been the relationship between economic crisis tendencies and the state in advanced capitalism (Attewell 1984, pp. 142–206). Research has focused especially on the concept of the "fiscal crisis of the state" (O'Connor 1973). It has been argued that the state is caught between the contradictory pressures of ensuring capital accumulation and legitimating the negative effects of the economy with the safety nets of the welfare state and that these conflicts become the potential basis for the emergence of new class-based oppositional movements.

Culture and Ideology. The most recent flourishing area of research has been in Marxist-influenced analyses of cultural phenomena as manifestations of ideology. The central focus has been on how cultural hegemony (or domination) is formed and the types of resistance that oppressed groups may develop against it. The stress of economistic Marxism has been upon the way in which the cultural superstructure of society "reflects" or "mirrors" economic processes and class relations. This approach often resulted in crude, reductionistic political and class analyses that were often unsatisfactory to those intimately acquainted with both high and popular culture. With the emergence of more sophisticated structuralist models of cultural reproduction, however, the relative autonomy of cultural forms could be acknowledged without obscuring their origins in "material" social relations. In the more extreme form represented by structuralist Marxism, it has been more generally held that all of the cultural institutions of society (e.g., the media, family, law, arts, etc.) functioned in the last instance as "ideological state apparatuses" that served the long-term interests of capital (Althusser 1971). Research based on both instrumentalist and structuralist approaches has been applied to the range of cultural activities (e.g., art, literature, law, sport, etc.), but education and the mass media figure most prominently, and they can serve as illustrations.

In the case of the Marxist sociology of education the result was a shift from an instrumentalist perspective (i.e., the role of capitalist ideology in directly using the educational system to shape consciousness in its interests) to one based on the idea of social reproduction as an indirect form of social control. Initially, structuralist approaches put particular stress upon the formal "correspondence" between the economic base and the hegemonic superstructure, despite the autonomy of the latter. Hence, structuralist research on education attempted to demonstrate the way in which the hidden curriculum of the school "corresponded" to the type of labor required by capital (Bowles and Gintis 1977; Cole 1988). Research on the political economy of the media was more strongly represented by instrumentalist perspectives that stressed the role of the media as instruments of "mind control" on the part of the dominant class and the broader dominance of the American media globally (Schiller 1971; 1973); others argued from a more structuralist perspective that the primary function of the media is the "selling of audiences," irrespective of the specific ideological content of programming (Smythe 1981).

THE CRISIS OF MARXIST SOCIOLOGY

As a specific theoretical approach that seeks to discover the role of economic and class factors in social change, Western Marxist sociology will certainly endure, though its significance will vary with the type of social formation and topic examined. As a philosophy of history or general theory of modes of production, and more especially as part of a particular theory of working-class revolution, orthodox Marxist sociology has been seriously called into question, especially in advanced capitalism. And it has already collapsed in East bloc countries where a completely new tradition of social science is in the process of formation. This is not to say that economic and class factors or Marx become irrelevant, though the broader crisis of historical materialism suggests their significance and relation to social, political, and cultural processes will have to be interpreted in more self-critical, flexible, and historically specific ways (Aronowitz 1981). The complex outcome of the crisis of Marxist sociology in advanced capitalism is suggestively anticipated in the response of three contemporary countertendencies.

So-called analytical Marxism is defined more by its methodological stance than its substantive content. It thus differentiates itself from traditional Marxism in its commitment to abstract theorizing (as opposed to more concrete historical analysis), a search for rethinking the foundations by asking heretical questions, and "using state-of-the-art methods of analytical philosophy and 'positivist' social science" (Roemer 1986, pp. 1–2). Though these developments will undoubtedly have some impact on social theory, they are clearly too heterogeneous and revisionist to fall under the heading of Marxist sociology in the sense used here.

A second, opposing "poststructuralist" strategy is evident in the work of some former Marxists who have retreated from orthodox class concepts, arguing that a "post-Marxism" is required that involves eliminating the notion of the working class as a "universal class" and resurrecting a new conception of socialist democracy (Laclau and Mouffe 1985). Not surprisingly, this (partial) "retreat from class" has been treated with hostility by many neo-Marxists (Wood 1986), but it has provoked important debates about the role of new social movements and democratic processes in any defendable conception of socialist transformation.

A third tendency has been loosely referred to as "cultural Marxism." Such critics of the functionalist tendencies of structuralist Marxism put particular stress upon the contested and uneven character of cultural reproduction in capitalist societies. In particular, various researchers have pointed to how dominated groups resist cultural domination in ways that often become the basis of counterhegemonic social movements. Further, it is argued that a crucial feature of contemporary "postmodern" societies is the distinctive role of the "cultural." The result has been a flowering of cultural research often identified, especially in the British context, with the notion of "cultural studies" (e.g., the work of Raymond Williams, Richard Johnson, Stuart Hall, etc.; see Brantlinger 1990). A related tendency has been the cultural Marxist historiography of E. P. Thompson (Kaye and McClelland 1990) that has influenced a major reinterpretation of Marx as a historical sociologist (Sayer 1983; Corrigan and Sayer 1985). A distinctive aspect of the cultural Marxist tradition, an aspect that has led it away from Marxist sociology in its more restrictive sense, has been its ability actively to engage in debate with and appropriate concepts from a wide variety of non-Marxist approaches. Much of the recent work carried out in the name of cultural Marxism thus increasingly blends with poststructuralist and critical theories of culture, reflecting the circumstance that

"Marxism is no longer a single coherent discursive and political practice" (Nelson and Grossberg 1988, p. 11). One consequence is that it is no longer "possible to talk unproblematically of a 'Marxist' sociology, since Marxism has become a major contributor to sociology in general, while Marxist-influenced sociologists increasingly identify with their discipline (Shaw 1985, p. 16).

(SEE ALSO: *Critical Theory; Macrosociology; Materialism; Socialism*)

REFERENCES

Abercrombie, Nicholas, Stephen Hill, and Bryan S. Turner 1988 *The Penguin Dictionary of Sociology.* 2nd ed. Harmondsworth, England: Penguin Books.

Agger, Ben 1979 *Western Marxism: An Introduction—Classical and Contemporary Sources.* Santa Monica, Calif.: Goodyear.

Althusser, Louis 1974 "Ideology and Ideological State Apparatuses." In *Lenin and Philosophy and Other Essays,* Ben Brewster, trans. New York and London: Monthly Review Press.

———and Etienne Balibar (1968) 1979 *Reading Capital.* Ben Brewster, trans. London: Verso.

Anderson, Perry 1984 *In the Tracks of Historical Materialism.* London: Verso.

Archibald, W. Peter 1978 *Social Psychology as Political Economy.* Toronto: McGraw-Hill.

Aronowitz, Stanley 1981 *The Crisis of Historical Materialism: Class, Politics, and Culture in Marxist Theory.* New York: Praeger and J. F. Bergin.

Attewell, Paul A. 1984 *Radical Political Economy since the Sixties: A Sociology of Knowledge Analysis.* New Brunswick, N.J.: Rutgers University Press.

Baran, Paul A., and Paul M. Sweezy 1966 *Monopoly Capital: An Essay on the American Economic Order.* New York and London: Monthly Review Press.

Bottomore, Tom 1975 *Marxist Sociology.* London: Macmillan.

———1978 "Marxism and Sociology." In Tom Bottomore and Robert Nisbet, eds., *A History of Sociological Analysis.* New York: Basic Books.

———1984 *The Frankfurt School.* London and New York: Ellis Horwood/Tavistock.

———and Patrick Goode (eds.) 1978 *Austro-Marxism* T. Bottomore and P. Goode, trans. Oxford: Clarendon Press.

———1983 *Readings in Marxist Sociology.* Oxford: Oxford University Press.

Bottomore, Tom, et al. (eds.) 1983 *A Dictionary of Marxist Thought.* Cambridge, Mass. and Oxford: Harvard University Press and Basil Blackwell.

Bowles, Samuel, and Herbert Gintis 1977 *Schooling in Capitalist America: Educational Reform and the Contradictions of Economic Life.* New York: Basic Books.

Brantlinger, Patrick 1990 *Crusoe's Footprints: Cultural Studies in Britain and America.* New York and London: Routledge.

Braverman, Harry 1974 *Labor and Monopoly Capital: The Degradation of Work in the Twentieth Century.* New York and London: Monthly Review Press.

Burawoy, Michael 1979 *Manufacturing Consent: Changes in the Labor Process under Monopoly Capitalism.* Chicago and London: University of Chicago Press.

———1982 "Introduction: The Resurgence of Marxism in American Sociology." In Michael Burawoy and Theda Skocpol, eds., *Marxist Inquiries: Studies of Labor, Class, and States.* Chicago and London: University of Chicago Press.

———1985 *The Politics of Production.* London: Verso.

———and Theda Skocpol (eds.) 1982 *Marxist Inquiries: Studies of Labor, Class, and States.* Chicago and London: University of Chicago Press.

Cole, Mike (ed.) 1988 *Bowles and Gintis Revisited: Correspondence and Contradiction in Educational Theory.* London, New York, Philadelphia: Falmer Press.

Corrigan, Philip, and Derek Sayer 1985 *The Great Arch: English State Formation as Cultural Revolution.* Oxford: Basil Blackwell.

Flacks, Richard 1982 "Marxism and Sociology." In Bertell Ollman and Edward Vernoff, eds., *The Left Academy: Marxist Scholarship on American Campuses.* New York: McGraw-Hill.

Fox, Bonnie (ed.) 1980 *Hidden in the Household: Women's Domestic Labour under Capitalism.* Toronto: Women's Press.

Giddens, Anthony 1971 *Capitalism and Modern Social Theory.* Cambridge: Cambridge University Press.

Gouldner, Alvin W. 1980 *The Two Marxisms: Contradictions and Anomalies in the Development of Theory.* New York: Seabury Press.

Grabb, Edward G. 1990 *Theories of Social Inequality: Classical and Contemporary Perspectives.* 2nd ed. Toronto: Holt, Rinehart and Winston.

Gramsci, Antonio 1971 *Selections from the Prison Notebooks,* Quintin Hoare and Geoffrey Nowell Smith, eds. and trans. New York: International Publishers.

Held, David 1980 *Introduction to Critical Theory: Horkheimer to Habermas.* Berkeley and Los Angeles: University of California Press.

Holloway, John, and Sol Picciotto (eds.) 1978 *State and Capital: A Marxist Debate.* London: Edward Arnold.

Jessop, Bob 1982 *The Capitalist State: Marxist Theories and Methods.* Oxford: Martin Robertson.

Kaye, Harvey J., and Keith McClelland (eds.) 1990 *E. P. Thompson: Critical Perspectives.* Philadelphia: Temple University Press.

Kellner, Douglas 1989 *Critical Theory, Marxism, and Modernity.* Baltimore: Johns Hopkins University Press.

Laclau, Ernest, and Chantal Mouffe 1985 *Hegemony and Socialist Strategy: Towards a Radical Democratic Politics,* Winston Moore and Paul Cammack, trans. London: Verso.

Marx, Karl, and Friedrich Engels 1978 *The Marx-Engels Reader,* 2nd ed. Robert C. Tucker, ed. New York: Norton.

Miliband, Ralph (1969) 1973 *The State in Capitalist Society: The Analysis of the Western System of Power.* London: Quartet Books.

Nelson, Cary, and Lawrence Grossberg (eds.) 1988 *Marxism and the Interpretation of Culture.* Urbana and Chicago: University of Illinois Press.

O'Connor, James 1973 *The Fiscal Crisis of the State.* New York: St. Martin's.

Ollman, Bertell, and Edward Vernoff (eds.) 1982 *The Left Academy: Marxist Scholarship on American Campuses.* New York: McGraw-Hill.

Poulantzas, Nicos (1968) 1978 *Political Power and Social Classes,* Timothy O'Hagan, trans. London: Verso.

Roemer, John (ed.) 1986 *Analytical Marxism.* Cambridge: Cambridge University Press.

Sayer, Derek 1983 *Marx's Method: Ideology, Science, and Critique in 'Capital'.* Sussex and Atlantic Highlands, N.J.: Harvester Press and Humanities Press.

Schiller, Herbert I. 1971 *Mass Communications and the American Empire.* Boston: Beacon Press.

———1973 *The Mind Managers.* Boston: Beacon Press.

Shaw, Martin (ed.) 1985 *Marxist Sociology Revisited: Critical Assessments.* London: Macmillan.

Smythe, Dallas W. 1981 *Dependency Road: Communications, Capitalism, Consciousness, and Canada.* Norwood, N.J.: Ablex.

So, Alvin Y. 1990 *Social Change and Development: Modernization, Dependency, and World-System Theories.* Newbury Park and London: Sage.

Sweezy, Paul M. (1942) 1968 *The Theory of Capitalist Development: Principles of Marxian Political Economy.* New York and London: Monthly Review Press.

Therborn, Göran 1976 *Science, Class, and Society: On the Formation of Sociology and Historical Materialism.* London: New Left Books.

Thompson, Paul 1983 *The Nature of Work: An Introduction to Debates on the Labour Process.* London: Macmillan.

Walker, Pat (ed.) 1978 *Between Labor and Capital.* Montreal: Black Rose Books.

Wood, Ellen Meiksins 1986 *The Retreat from Class: A New "True" Socialism.* London: Verso.

Wright, Erik Ohlin 1978 *Class, Crisis, and the State.* London: Verso.

———1985 *Classes.* London: Verso.

RAYMOND A. MORROW

MASS MEDIA RESEARCH The interest of sociologists in mass communication was stimulated by developments in technology allowing the reproduction and speedy transmission of messages. It began with the rise of the popular press, followed by the invention of film, sound broadcasting, and the audiovisual. As a result, all of us live in a world of media-constructed images that, presumably, significantly influence what we think and how we partition our attention, time, and other scarce resources. So pervasive has been the media presence that issues relating to these influences have also drawn the attention of researchers from disciplines other than sociology.

It is to Harold Lasswell (1947), an empirically oriented political scientist, that the social science community owes a succinct formula that lays out the major elements within the field of communication research: *Who* says *what* to *whom* and with what *effect?* The term *how* has since been added to identify the particular channel (face-to-face, print, electronic, etc.) through which communication takes place. Only some channels lend themselves to *mass* communication, which can be defined, in the terms of the above formula, as the transmission by professional communicators (who) of a continuous flow of a uniform content (what) by means of a complex apparatus (how) to a large, heterogeneous, and geographically dispersed audience (to whom).

Not included in this definition of mass communication are its effects or, more broadly speaking, its consequences, toward which most of the sociological research effort has been directed. The physical or electronic transmission of message content does not in itself suffice for communication, which is indisputably social in that it consists of a meeting of minds in the sense of mutual accommodation. Yet the nature and extent of effects have been, over the years, the central problem of sociological interest in media research.

Media effects have been studied on three levels: the atomistic, the aggregate, and the societal. Effects on the atomistic level involve the cognitive processes and behavioral responses of *individuals* who make up the various mass audiences. By contrast, aggregate measures take into account only *distributions* that produce changes in averages usually expressed as net effects. Consequences for society have more to do with the political, cultural, and other *institutional* changes that represent cumulative adaptations over time to the dominance of a particular mass medium. Inferences based on the observation of effects on one level when ascribed to effects on a different level have often turned out to be invalid.

THE ATOMISTIC LEVEL

Much of the research effort has been a response to the operational needs of communicators and propogandists, or of those who wished to defend the public against what was perceived as the pernicious influence of the media. The basic problem has been that of precisely pinpointing effects: What were the characteristics of the potential audience? Who among them was susceptible? What were the determinants of their reactions?

To answer these and similar questions, audience research has typically focused on the situations in which mass communications are received and on the habits and cognitive processes that underlie the responses of individuals either to specific media messages or some significant part of the media fare. The responses under scrutiny have ranged from the arousal of interest, gains in knowledge, the recognition of dangers, changes of opinion, and other attitudinal measures to such behavioral indicators as consumer purchases, electoral decisions, and the "elevation" of cultural taste.

Precisely because of its focus on the individual, this line of research tends to stress the diversity of ways in which individuals relate to media content. First of all, audiences are found to be stratified by education, interest, taste, leisure habits, and so forth, with people at different levels paying attention to different media offerings. The observation that some content had only minimal audience penetration helped explain why some information campaigns failed. Consistent patterns of exposure to different kinds of content further suggested that members of the mass audience, by and large, found what suited their needs and interests.

Second, even common exposure turns out to be a less strong predictor of response than expected. Not everyone understands or understands fully, and reactions are affected by the preconceptions with which people approach the content, by preconceptions rooted in past socialization experience but also reflecting the perspective of groups with which they are associated or identify themselves. Audiences are obstinate and people have options in how they orient themselves to any particular set of messages. They can ignore, misunderstand, accept, find fault with, or be entertained by the same content. In other words, there is no assurance that anyone other than those, for whatever reason, already so disposed will accept the facts, adopt the opinion, or carry out the actions suggested by the mass communicator (Schramm 1973).

This downplaying of the importance of content elements by a methodical partitioning of the mass audience received systematic formulation in the "minimal effects" theorem, derived from Joseph Klapper's review (1960) of certain empirical research findings of studies conducted mostly during the 1940s and 1950s. He generalized that certain factors, such as audience characteristics and a pluralistic media structure, which mediated between content and response, worked primarily in the service of reinforcement of prior attitudes. Changes triggered by exposure were pretty much limited to people whose situations already impelled them to move in that direction. Klapper did, however, acknowledge the power of mass communication to move people on matters with which they were unfamiliar and concerning which they had no distinct views of ingrained habits.

Strong evidence in favor of not-so-minimal effects has come from observations made in the laboratory, especially through the series of experimental studies on children, reported in *Television and Social Behavior,* conducted under the auspices of the U.S. Surgeon General (Murray and Rubinstein 1972). After exposure to programs that included "violent" behavior, subjects often engaged in similar behavior during their play and they were more likely than subjects not so exposed to commit other violent acts.

Still, experiments are generally set up to maximize the possibility of demonstrating direct effects. Thus, in this instance, children, especially young children, would be inclined to model their own behavior on what they see. Moreover, such findings of short-term effects observed in a play situation have to be considered within the context of the whole socialization experience over many years. Longitudinal studies and experimental studies of older children in a more natural setting have yielded results that are more ambiguous (Milavsky et al. 1982). Laboratories do not fully replicate communication situations of real life (Milgram 1973).

But the challenges posed by experimental studies have to be faced. Casual but repeated exposure to televsed messages results in incidental learning. Content gradually intrudes into our consciousness until we associate a product with a particular brand name; issues dominating the news become the criteria by which we measure the effectiveness of a political leadership. Insofar as the various mass media sources transmit similar content and play on similar themes, such limited effects, if they are cumulative, can produce shifts of landslide proportions.

AGGREGATE EFFECTS

Because the responses of persons are so diverse, the effect of communication en masse has to be conveyed in some kind of summary measure—as an average, a trend, a general movement. From this perspective, the magnitude of the shift in the responses of individuals, or whether this represents reinforcement or a reversal, matters less than the overall picture.

How differently effect can appear when viewed from different perspectives may be illustrated by reference to studies of innovations (Rogers 1971). Detailed documentation of the process by which they are adopted and spread suggests that early adopters (also called influentials or opinion leaders, depending on context) are more cosmopolitan in their orientation and hence more attuned to certain media messages. They select from the total stream the ones that best meet their needs and interests. Others will adopt an innovation only after its success has been demonstrated or, if that is precluded—as it would be in most political decisions—out of trust in the expertise of the pacesetters. One can account for the different behavior of leaders and followers in such situations—that is, why one moves ahead and the other is content to wait—in terms of personal characteristics and social relationships. Aggregate effects, on the other hand, have to do with whether or not there has been a general movement toward acceptance or rejection of the innovation.

The most direct measures of aggregate effects are to be found in two-variable relationships, with one variable functioning as an indicator of media presence and the other representing the response. Many such combinations are possible. One can use media penetration (e.g., newspaper circulation or the proportion of homes with a television set) or content characteristics (e.g., the number of violent acts in children's programs, editorial endorsements, or issues emphasized in the news). This rules out media behavior, which is voluntary, and may reflect the influence of still other, often unmeasured, variables that also account for the presumed effect.

As the age of television dawned, opportunities for "controlled" observation—comparing two matched areas, one receiving television and the other not yet within reach of the broadcast signal—were never fully exploited. Rarely did findings about the advent of television go beyond documenting the rather obvious fact that television viewing cut into the use of some other media, especially radio and to a lesser degree movie attendance and children's comic book reading. Nor were the consequences of this reallocation of time at all clear. A study of children in "Teletown" and "Radiotown," the latter community still without television but comparable in other respects, concluded that "before television, many children [had gone] through the same type of change as today from fantasy-seeking media behavior toward reality-seeking media behavior" (Schramm, Lyle, and Parker 1961).

Evidence of this kind is similarly lacking on matters relating to citizen participation among adults. Systematic comparisons between the turnout and overall responsiveness to "party" issues during the 1952 presidential election in counties with high TV-penetration and low TV-penetration revealed no consistent differences, probably because other media were already saturated enough with campaign material to have produced a high level of interest. Situations subject to such "ceiling" effects prevent further movement in response to the presence of a new medium.

Variations in content, when they occur, have offered far more opportunities for controlled observations, many of which have challenged the conventional wisdom. That voters on the west coast of the United States would be dissuaded from voting in the presidential election once television, based on early returns, had declared a winner seemed only logical. Yet studies showed that westerners continued to cast ballots in roughly the same proportions as their compatriots in states where polls had already closed. In voting, they were evidently moved by considerations other than practical utility and by other competing media messages. Whatever the effects of such broadcast returns on the decision to vote or not to vote, they have been too small to measure with any precision. As regards editorial endorsements, where the range of variations is greater, research has shown that such support gives candidates for minor offices, many of whom are only names on a ballot, an incremental but nevertheless distinct advantage over other minor candidates on the same slate.

Correlations that pair a media variable with some measure of response always imply change over time. The alternative is to study change in response to events as they are being communicated via the mass media: a televised speech by a political leader, the announcement of an unexpected reversal of government policy, news of foreign crisis, or simply the flow of information about economic conditions and problems facing the country.

Polls before and after an appropriately timed speech have documented the power of a head of state to move opinion through appeals directed to the public. Speeches can create greater awareness. They are designed to focus attention on those issues and actions from which the politician stands to benefit. The effectiveness of such media events is apt to be greatest when an issue is just surfacing. Leaders also have the ability to make news. Even without an undisputed success, their public appearances, diligently reported by the news media, are used to dramatize their own role in promoting solutions to matters believed to be of general concern.

Careful analysis of the impact of many such events over the years again challenges the conventional wisdom. Neither speeches nor foreign travel by American presidents over nine administrations have, by themselves or in combination, *uniformly* shored up public support. Public response to these events have been highly dependent on the political context—that is, whether they coincided with other events that tended to enhance the president's standing or whether his administration was plagued by intractable problems, such as public concern about a declining economy, an indignation over American hostages whose release it could not effect, or revelations of governmental wrongdoing such as those that surfaced during Watergate and led to the resignation of Richard Nixon (Lang and Lang 1984).

What stands out in a long line of studies is the general correspondence over time between the overall amount of attention a topic, issue, or personality enjoys in the media and the awareness, interest in, and concern about these. Mass communication influences not so much *what* people think (opinion) but what they think *about* (recognition). Insofar as there is enough common emphasis, the media perform an "agenda-setting" function (Iyengar and Kinder 1987). Collectively, they define the terms of public debate. Media attention also confers status on some of the many voices clamoring to be recognized.

This simple formulation, which has been a central focus of effects research in political communication for some years, attributes to the media at one and the same time too much and too little influence. On the one hand, the media do not, all on their own, dictate or control the political agenda. Neither public awareness nor recognition of a problem is sufficient to stir a controversy on which people take sides. On the other hand, access to the media is a major resource for the advocates of particular policies. Concerns become issues through discussion in which political leaders, government officials, news and commentary in the press, and the voices of citizens reciprocally influence one another in a process more aptly characterized as "agenda building" (Lang and Lang 1984).

THE SYSTEMIC PERSPECTIVE

The dissemination of content via the mass communication system occurs in a highly selective fashion. Some information is privileged; other information is available only to those with the interest and resources to pay for it. The upshot of all the efforts to direct communication flow is a repertoire of images of events and ongoing social activities. Media organizations are themselves producers of content. The mass communications through which the world is brought into focus are, in the broadest sense, cultural creations that incorporate the perspectives of the producers and of others whose views have to be taken into account. This influence of the communication system on the content, intended or not, is a source of bias often unrecognized by those responsible for it.

One has to differentiate between two sources of bias: technological and social. Technological bias stems from the physical characteristics of the medium. Harold Innis (1951), the Canadian institutional economist, distinguished between bias toward space and bias toward time. Paper, he averred, because of its light weight, was easily transported but also perishable, and so supported the development of centralized administration. The uniformity thus imposed over a given area (space) was usually at the expense of continuity (time). A more flexible medium could adapt to an oral tradition that favored spontaneous cooperation among autonomous units. There are indeed signs that cheaper and smaller electronic devices may be radically increasing the control individuals have over the information available to them and what to do with it (Beniger 1986).

Applied mechanistically, without regard to who is in control, these categories lead to a simple-minded media determinism. Social bias has to do with how the capabilities intrinsic to the dominant medium are exploited. Television may not have had any demonstrable effect on voter turnout. But a nonpartisan political coverage, designed not to offend, was not only implicit in the economic logic of aiming for the largest possible audience but was reinforced by the regulatory system. The fact that a well-financed candidate could buy nearly unlimited time to air well-targeted political messages may not, in and of itself, have caused the decline of party machines but it certainly contributed to it. Television has helped to make the nominating process far more open to "outsiders" without a firm following among party regulars. And nominating conventions in which political bosses once traded votes were transformed into showpieces, played for a national audience as the curtain raiser for the campaign.

More generally, its penetration into the spheres of other institutions—political, cultural, educational, and so on—is what makes mass communication a potentially powerful influence on the societal level. It hardly matters whether the media are viewed as a resource or as a threat. The publicity generated through mass communication brings the norms of the larger society to bear on actions that once might have been considered privileged or at least shielded from public scrutiny. Conversely, the competition for visibility is an inducement for elite institutions to adopt at least some of the conventions of the media culture.

There remains the question of who sets these norms and standards. Some scholars have argued that repeated exposure to a sanitized media culture results in "mainstreaming." Accordingly, all but a few of the diverse currents that feed into the kaleidoscope of minority cultures receive little or no recognition. Lacking an effective institutional representation, they are more readily marginalized. Content analyses of character portrayal and the values espoused by heroes in the popular entertainment fare have lent some support to the charge of "mainstreaming." Despite the premium on novelty, most media organizations are inclined not to stray too far from what is popularly accepted but will, on the other hand, eagerly imitate any demonstrated success.

The representation of political views is similarly constrained. Despite the independence of the press and a few celebrated instances where a few persistent journalists initiated an inquiry, the more typical pattern is to wait until political actors have highlighted a problem. Usually, it is they, rather than the press, who define the terms of controversies over policy. And, to paraphrase W. Lance Bennett (1988), when the institutional voices speaking in protest are stilled, all but the more radical media are inclined to drop the issue as well. Discussion and diversity exist but usually within self-imposed limits.

It should be clear that major media organizations, though important players, are less than fully separate from other establishments. Their influence on events is greatest when they act in conjunction with other agencies.

(SEE ALSO: *Information Society; Public Opinion*)

REFERENCES

Beniger, James R. 1986 *The Control Revolution. Technological and Economic Origins of the Information Society.* Cambridge, Mass.: Harvard University Press.

Bennett, W. Lance 1988 *News: The Politics of Illusion.* New York: Longman.

Innis, Harold A. 1951 *The Bias of Communication.* Toronto: University of Toronto Press.

Iyengar, Shanto, and Donald R. Kinder 1987 *News That Matters: Television and Public Opinion.* Chicago: University of Chicago Press.

Klapper, Joseph T. 1960 *The Effects of Mass Communication.* New York: Free Press.

Lang, Gladys Engel, and Kurt Lang 1984 *Politics and Television Re-Viewed.* Beverly Hills, Calif.: Sage.

Lasswell, Harold D. 1947 "The Structure and Function of Communication in Society." In L. Bryson, ed., *The Communication of Ideas.* New York: Harper.

Milavsky, J. Ronald, Horst Stipp, Ronald C. Kessler, and William S. Rubens 1982 *Television and Aggression: A Panel Study.* New York: Academic.

Milgram, Stanley 1973 *Television and Anti-Social Behavior: A Field Experiment.* New York: Academic.

Murray, John P., and Eli A. Rubinstein 1972 *Television and Social Behavior: Reports and Papers,* 5 vols. Washington, D.C.: National Institute for Mental Health.

Rogers, Everett M. 1971 *Communication of Innovations. A Cross-Cultural Approach.* New York: Free Press.

Schramm, Wilbur 1973 *Men, Women, Messages and Media.* New York: Harper and Row.

———, Jack Lyle, and Edwin B. Parker 1961 *Television in the Lives of Our Children.* Stanford, Calif.: Stanford University Press.

GLADYS ENGEL LANG
KURT LANG

MATE SELECTION THEORIES Social scientists who study the family have long been interested in the question, "Who marries whom?" On one level, the study of mate selection is conducted from the perspective of family as a social institution. Emphasis is placed on the customs that regulate choice of mates. A counterperspective views the family as an association. This perspective centers instead on the couple and attempts to understand the process of marital dyad formation. Both of these perspectives generate an abundance of knowledge concerning mate selection. Beginning primarily in the 1920s, theoretical and empirical work in the area of mate selection has made great advances in answering the fundamental question, "Who marries whom?"

INSTITUTIONAL PERSPECTIVES ON MATE SELECTION

Anthropologists have studied kinship structures as they relate to mate selection in arranged marriage systems. Sociological inquiry that sees the family as a social institution in the context of the larger society focuses instead on the evolution of courtship systems as societies modernize. In this respect, it is important to note the contributions of scholars such as Bernard Murstein (1974, 1976) who have pointed out the importance of cultural and historical effects on courtship systems that lead to marriage.

Historical evidence suggests that as a society modernizes, changes in the courtship system reflect a movement toward autonomous courtship systems. Thus, parentally arranged marriages diminish in industrialized cultures because arranged marriages are found in societies in which strong extended kinship ties exist or where the marriage has great significance for the family and community in terms of resources or status allocation. As societies modernize, arranged marriages are supplanted by an autonomous courtship system in which free choice of mate is the preferred form. These autonomous courtship systems are also referred to as "love" marriages, since the prerequisite for selection of a mate has shifted from the need to consolidate economic resources to that of individual choice based on love. Of course, family sociologists are quick to point out that the term *love marriage* is somewhat of a misnomer because many other factors operate in the mate selection process.

CORRELATES OF MATE SELECTION

Family social scientists have tried to understand the human mate selection process by using a variety of data sources and theoretical perspectives. The most global or macro-level approaches have made use of vital statistics such as census data or marriage license applications to study the factors that predict mate selection. Attention has been placed on social and cultural background characteristics such as age, social class, race, religion, and educational level.

Norms of endogamy require that people marry those belonging to the same group. While some of these norms have been formalized, such as in U.S. laws that prohibited blacks and whites from marrying, most of the norms operate informally. Thus, analysis of vital statistics on marriage patterns in the United States shows that much similarity exists between marital partners in age, race, social class, religion, and educational level. Although there seems to be more tolerance for exogamous marriages, those marriages occurring between dissimilar partners, the data show that age between partners is similar, with men being about two years older than their wives. Interracial marriage is still rare, with less than 2 percent of all marriages occurring between persons of different races (U.S. Bureau of the Census 1986). Mate selection in the social classes also follows the norm of endogamy, with the upper class being the most restrictive in terms of marriage patterns. Thus, the Cinderella story is more of a fantasy than a reality, and self-help books entitled *How to Marry a Rich Man (Woman)* have little basis in fact.

Census data indicate that the most educationally homogamous marriages occur between individuals with a high school education. In other words, similarity in level of educational attainment was the most pronounced for couples who had not completed college degrees. But as men's educational levels increase, the tendency is for these men to marry women who have less education (Rawlings 1978). The norms have consistently reinforced the notion that women should not have educational levels much more advanced than their husbands'. The general belief that educationally hypergamous marriages (wife has less education than her husband) are more stable and compatible unions than educationally hypogamous (wife has more education than her husband) has empirical support (Houseknech and Macke 1981; Jaco and Shepard 1975).

Again, the effects of industrialization can be

seen in mate selection patterns as they relate to endogamy. The likelihood of marrying across social class, ethnic, and religious boundaries is strongly affected by how homogeneous (similar) the population is (Blau, Blum, and Schwartz 1982). In large cities where the opportunity structures are more heterogeneous (diverse), rates of intermarriage are higher, while in the small rural communities that contain homogeneous populations, the norm of endogamy is even more pronounced.

The factors that operate in the selection process of a mate also function in conjunction with opportunity structures that affect the potential for social interaction. The evidence suggests that propinquity is an important factor in determining who marries whom. Thus, those who live geographically proximate to each other are more likely to meet and marry. Early work by Bossard (1932) shows that at the time of the marriage license application, about 25 percent of all couples live within two city blocks of each other. Bossard's Law, derived from his empirical findings, states, "the proportion of marriages decreases steadily and markedly as the distance between the consenting parties increases." Or, put more simply, "Cupid's wings are best suited for short flights." Of course, current American society has changed since the time Bossard studied mate selection patterns in Philadelphia, and there is a tendency to think that as society becomes more mobile propinquity plays less of a role in the choice of a mate. Propinquitous mate selection does not mean nonmobility, however. It is simply the case that the influence of propinquity shifts as the individual geographically shifts. Thus, one is more likely to marry someone who is currently near than someone previously propinquitous. The overriding effect of propinquity is that people of similar backgrounds will meet and marry because residential homogamy remains a dominant feature of American society.

One interesting area of research that often goes overlooked in discussions of the correlates of mate selection concerns homogamy of physical attractiveness. Based on the equity theory of physical attractiveness, one would expect that persons who are similar in physical attractiveness levels would marry. Many experimental designs have been conducted to test the effects of physical attractiveness on attraction to a potential dating partner. In general, the experimental conditions have yielded the findings that the more highly attractive individuals are the most desired as a dating partner. But studies of couples actually involved in selecting a mate or who are already married support the notion that individuals who are similar in attractiveness level marry. Thus, while attractiveness is a socially valued characteristic in choice of a mate, the norms of social exchange dictate that we select a partner who is similar in attractiveness and is thus attainable. It is only when other highly valued factors such as wealth, wit, or intelligence compensate for deficits in attractiveness that inequity of physical attractiveness in mate selection might occur.

In conclusion, the correlates of mate selection have been widely studied, beginning in the 1920s. But within the past decade emphases have shifted in the studies of mate selection to the examination of the dyadic processes involved. Researchers generally concur that the factors of endogamy, propinquity, and equity of physical attractiveness continue to operate in very important ways, but attention has been expanded to examination of courtship cohabitation and the process of mate selection.

NEED COMPLEMENTARITY

While earlier work on the correlates of mate selection focused on homogamy of background characteristics, the work of Winch (1958) set the stage for further investigation into the hypothesis that "opposites attract," that is, that persons of dissimilar values or personality traits would marry. While value theorists speculated that similarity of values and personality would lead to great affiliation and propensity to marry, Winch posited that persons select mates whose personality traits are complementary (opposite) to their own. Inherent in Winch's theoretical work is the notion that certain specific trait combinations will be gratifying to the individuals involved. For example, a submissive person would find it gratifying or reciprocal to interact with a mate who had a dominant personality. Winch developed twelve such paired complementary personality traits, such as dominant–submissive and nurturant–receptive, for empirical testing using a very small sample of recently married couples. In Winch's work, as well as the work of others, the notion that complementarity of traits was the basis for marriage was not supported by the data.

Although empirical support for need complementarity is lacking, the concept remains viable in the study of mate selection. The appeal of the concept rests in its psychological origins, as work prior to Winch's focused primarily on structural and normative influences in mate selection. The work of Winch set the stage for research commencing in the 1960s that began to examine the processes of mate selection on the dyadic level.

PROCESS THEORIES OF MATE SELECTION

The process of selecting a mate received considerable attention beginning in the 1970s. The basic form these theories take follows the "filter theory" of Kerckoff and Davis (1962). Kerckoff and Davis found empirical support that individuals, having met through the channels of propinquity and endogamy, proceed through a series of stages or steps in the development of the relationship. According to their theory, social status variables such as social class and race operate early on in the relationship to bring people together. The next stage involved the consensus of values, during which time the couple determines the degree of similarity in their value orientations. Couples who share similar values are likely to continue to the third stage, need complementarity. However, the data collected by Kerckoff and Davis offered only weak support for need complementarity as part of the process of mate selection.

Development of process theories of mate selection continued into the 1970s and is exemplified in the work of Reiss (1960), Murstein (1974, 1976), Lewis (1973), and Centers (1975). While these theoretical perspectives differ in terms of the order and nature of the stages, they have much in common. Melding these theories of mate selection, the following assumptions can be made concerning the stages of dyad formation that lead to marriage:

1. There are predictable trajectories or stages of dyadic interaction that lead to marriage.
2. The social and cultural background of the couple provides the context for the interpersonal processes.
3. Value similarity leads to rapport in communication, self-disclosure, and the development of trust.
4. Attraction and interaction depend on the exchange value of the assets and liabilities that the individuals bring to the relationship.
5. There may be conditional factors such as age, gender, or marital history that influence the order, duration of the stages, or probability of the relationship ending in marriage.

All the studies of the mate selection process have struggled with methodological difficulties. Most studies have relied on small, volunteer samples of couples. Most have used college-age, never-married couples. And, finally, most studies have made extensive use of retrospection in assessing the process of dyad formation rather than collecting longitudinal data. These methodological difficulties may, in part, account for the recent decline in the number of studies examining the process of mate selection.

Furthermore, these stages in the mate selection process may or may not result in marriage, but the primary focus of the research is on relationships that endure or terminate in marriage. Therefore, relatively little is known about the mate selection process as it pertains to rejection of a potential mate or how such terminations of relationships affect subsequent mate selection processes.

Many of the theories have also overlooked the influence of peer groups and family members in the mate selection process. The theoretical and empirical inquiry that has paid attention to peer and kin influences is restricted to studies of dating. Unfortunately, studies of dating and studies of mate selection have not been sufficiently integrated to provide the field with adequate data concerning the interrelationships between dating and mate selection processes.

Yet another area of research that has the potential for contributing to further understanding of the mate selection process is the study of romantic love. Process theories of mate selection seldom examine love as the basis, or even as a stage, in the development of a heterosexual relationship. While there is a large body of empirical and theoretical work on romantic love, the studies of love have been treated as conceptually quite distinct from the research on mate selection. Contrary to popular opinion, the relationship between love and marriage is not well understood.

FUTURE DIRECTIONS

As the family system changes in American society, the direction of research on mate selection also shifts. As more couples delay first marriage, examination of courtship cohabitation becomes more salient. Future studies of courtship cohabitation will most likely examine the association between increasing rates of cohabitation and decreasing rates of marriage. On the individual level, the effects of the cohabitation experience on the decision to marry also warrant attention.

Research is just beginning on the mate selection process of remarriage (Bulcroft et al. 1989; Rodgers and Conrad 1986; Spanier and Glick 1980). While some factors that predict first marriage (such as endogamy and propinquity) may remain constant in remarriage, other factors may come into play in remarriage. For example, age homogeneity may be less of a factor in remarriage because the pool of eligible mates is affected by sex ratio imbalance. The exchange relationship in the mate selection process also differs in remarriage because the presence of children, prior marital history, and the economic liabilities of child support or alimony bring new dimensions when considering remarriage. Of particular interest are barriers to remarriage in the middle and later years of the life cycle: Cohabitation or serious dating might offer more long-term rewards to the couple than legal marriage might provide. Thus, the strong profamilial norms that encourage the younger members of society to marry dissipate at mid- and later life. Low rates of remarriage for those individuals over the age of fifty indicate, in part, that societal pressure to marry is greatly reduced.

Lastly, it has generally been assumed that homogeneity of background characteristics leads to similarity of values, shared marital role expectations, rapport, and intimacy in the process of mate selection. But due to changing gender-role expectations, this assumption may no longer be valid. As a result, more attention needs to be given to the process of role negotiation as part of the mate selection process.

In summary, studies of mate selection began with understanding the correlates of mate selection. Social scientists began by studying demographic data on homogamy in religion, social class, age, and other factors as these variables related to who married whom. For a brief period from the 1960s through the early 1980s, attention was turned to theories and data that examined the process of mate selection. Current research has not abandoned the study of the correlates and theories of mate selection, but as the nature of the family system changes, researchers have begun to consider that the generalizability of theories and findings may be limited when trying to explain mate selection at a point later than young adulthood.

(SEE ALSO: *Courtship; Interpersonal Attraction; Love*)

REFERENCES

Blau, Peter, Terry Blum, and Joseph Schwartz 1982 "Heterogeneity and Intermarriage." *American Sociological Review* 47:45–62.

Bossard, James 1932 "Residential Propinquity as a Factor in Marriage Selection." *American Journal of Sociology* 38:219–224.

Bulcroft, Kris, Richard Bulcroft, Laurie Hatch, and Edgar F. Borgatta 1989 "Antecedents and Consequences of Remarriage in Later Life." *Research on Aging* 11:82–106.

Centers, Richard 1975 *Sexual Attraction and Love: An Instrumental Theory.* Springfield, Ill.: C. C. Thomas.

Houseknech, Sharon, and Ann Macke 1981 "Combining Marriage and Career: The Marital Adjustment of Professional Women." *Journal of Marriage and the Family* 43:651–661.

Jaco, Daniel, and Jon Shepard 1975 "Demographic Homogeneity and Spousal Consensus: A Methodological Perspective." *Journal of Marriage and the Family* 37:161–169.

Kerckoff, Alan, and Keith Davis 1962 "Value Consensus and Need Complementarity in Mate Selection." *American Sociological Review* 27:295–303.

Lewis, Robert 1973 "A Longitudinal Test of a Developmental Framework for Premarital Dyadic Formation." *Journal of Marriage and the Family* 35:16–27.

——— 1974 *Love, Sex, and Marriage through the Ages.* New York: Springer.

——— 1976 *Who Will Marry Whom? Theories and Research in Marital Choice.* New York: Springer.

Rawlings, Stephen 1978 *Perspectives on American Husbands and Wives.* Current Population Reports, Ser. P-23, No. 77. Washington, D.C.: U.S. Bureau of the Census.

Reiss, Ira 1960 "Toward a Sociology of the Heterosexual Love Relationship." *Marriage and Family Living* 22:139–145.

Rodgers, Roy, and Linda Conrad 1986 "Courtship for Remarriage: Influences on Family Reorganization after Divorce." *Journal of Marriage and the Family* 48:767–775.

Spanier, Graham, and Paul Glick 1980 "Paths to Remarriage." *Journal of Divorce* 3:283–298.

U.S. Bureau of the Census 1986 *Statistical Abstract of the United States.* Washington, D.C.: U.S. Government Printing Office.

Winch, Robert 1958 *Mate Selection: A Study of Complementary Needs.* New York: Harper and Row.

KRIS BULCROFT

MATERIALISM *Materialism* posits the epistemological primacy of "matter" over "ideas," "mind," "values," "spirit," and other incorporeal phenomena. Philosophical perspectives stressing the central importance of material conditions and physical needs have grown proportionally more elaborate and significant with the increasing differentiation and autonomy of secular systems of knowledge from religion. Materialists pose alternatives to magical, theological, and metaphysical meaning systems and sometimes directly challenge the legitimations of economic and political order. The long-standing debate over materialism and "idealism" (which gives primacy to ideas) has centered on their relative effectiveness as guides to empirical, theoretical, normative, and political practices. In the social sciences, materialists generally view their approach as a metatheory that points to the most fruitful research problems, hypotheses, data, concepts, and theories.

Two contrasting materialist traditions have divergent consequences for the practice of sociology. Epiphenomenalism or reductionism posits that all phenomena are determined strictly by physical causes, and reduces existential knowledge to corporeal explanations. Since it treats psychological and social factors as pure epiphenomena of material conditions lacking independent causal force, this monolithic physicalism denies the behavioral and social sciences their own distinctive content and laws. Nonreductionist materialists, by contrast, recognize emergent or relatively autonomous spiritual, aesthetic, psychological, cultural, and/or social realities that have their own distinct properties, processes, and laws and that exert reciprocal causal influence on the conditions from which they spring. Still, nonreductionists treat material factors as concrete antecedents generating decisive constraints and opportunities for the development of mind, culture, and society that "determine" them "in the last instance." To avert "idealist" fallacies, behavioral and social scientists must take account of the causal linkages with physical realities and accord primacy to materially based inclinations, motives, representations, values, and interests.

Modern materialism is rooted in ancient Greek conceptions of elementary bodies. "Atomist" philosophers contended that nothing exists except empty space and indivisible objects, or atoms, composed of the same stuff and in perpetual motion. Individual things arise from atoms of various sizes and shapes colliding, getting entangled, and forming different combinations. Sensation occurs when atoms pass through the sense organs and collide with the soul (also composed of atoms). Accordingly, all knowledge (sensory, abstract, or whimsical) is a "subjective" manifestation of "objective" reality, deriving from the soul's contacts with imperceptible, individual atoms. From the start, materialists privileged physical reality over experiences and representations of the "subject" (Copleston 1962, pp. 89–92, 145–147).

Atomistic materialism reemerged as a major cultural force during the Renaissance science revolution. Galileo and Newton again portrayed physical reality as ultimate particles moving in empty space. However, their distinction between precisely measurable or primary sensory qualities (i.e., length, width, weight, figure) and nonmathematizable secondary qualities (e.g., color, smell, taste, texture) provided a sharp boundary between objective and subjective experience and a decisive methodological starting point for differentiating scientific knowledge from religion and speculative philosophy. The capacity of different observers, using identical experimental techniques, to arrive at similar findings appeared to support the central materialist assumption about the dependence of mind on an external, object world (Gillispie 1960, pp. 3–150).

The prominence of natural science stimulated materialist explanations of human affairs. For example, Hobbes argued that social actions are also effects of matter in motion. Material primacy is manifested in the dominant drive for self-preservation, pervasive power struggles, and subsequent need for absolute monarchy. And Locke's Newtonian theory of mind argued that primary sense qualities reflect external objects and that complex ideas are built up out of simple ones received directly from sense experience. The extraordinary success of Newtonianism promoted an extensive secularization of knowledge favoring materialism. Yet Descartes's dualistic vision of a thoroughly materialistic, physical world and an autonomous mind blessed with innate ideas of divine origin exemplifies, in the extreme, the tendency of seventeenth-century thinkers to provide separate grounds for science without attacking religion. However, even the more monistic materialists (e.g., Hobbes) of this era left space for God and spiritual realities.

Enlightenment thinkers turned science against religion and paved the way for modern materialism. La Mettrie, D'Holbach, and Diderot argued that all aspects of experience had material causes. Idealizing Newtonian mechanics, the *philosophes* believed that naturalistic explanation of all phenomenal domains would destroy religious and metaphysical superstitions and facilitate rational social reconstruction. Revolutionary advances in eighteenth-century medicine, chemistry, and biology appeared to support this materialist faith in disenchantment and in a bright future of unlimited social progress (Gillispie 1960, pp. 83–116, 164–351; Gay 1977).

Karl Marx set the agenda for modern materialism. Even today's continuing debates about the topic center around different interpretations of his work. Young Marx ([1844] 1964, p. 172) lauded Ludwig Feuerbach's "great achievement" of establishing a "true materialism" and "real science" of humanity focusing on "the social relationship 'of man to man.'" Following Feuerbach, Marx saw religion and its secular idealist substitutes (e.g., Hegelian philosophy) as "inversions" or alienated projections of human capacities and potentialities. He treated humans as purely "natural beings" who must satisfy their fundamental "needs" by appropriating and shaping external objects. Marx shared Hegel's view that people create themselves and their societies entirely through their own historically mediated, social labor. But he opposed Hegel's speculative history of the "spirit." By contrast, Marx called for a recovery of the "real history" of "finite," "particular," "sensuous," "corporeal" human beings (Marx [1844] 1964, pp. 172–182).

Understanding of Marx's materialism is clouded by two terms, "dialectical materialism" and "historical materialism," which were coined, respectively, by Plekhanov and Engels after Marx's death and later codified into a variety of schematic orthodoxies. Dialectical materialism is a philosophy of nature developed first by Engels, later elaborated by Plekhanov and Lenin, and finally fashioned by Marxist-Leninists into an eschatology of the communist movement. The approach has not had much impact on social science outside the communist regimes. Dialectical materialism has served primarily as a political ideology and metalanguage of political action that justifies state socialist bureaucracy as well as communist insurgencies (providing assurance that "revolutionary" ideals can prevail over greater material force). Thus the focus here is on Marx's historical materialism or his metatheory of societal development, which has significant implications for sociology. However, this topic was addressed in different ways by Marx and Engels and has given rise to conflicting interpretations.

The elder Engels ([1891–1894] 1959, pp. 395–400) himself berated younger Marxists for using materialism "as an excuse for not studying history" or as a dogmatic Hegelian "lever for construction" instead of as "a guide to study." Opposing the notion of all-encompassing, mechanistic determination by narrowly conceived economic factors, Engels claimed that he and Marx meant nothing more than "the production and reproduction of real life" (as "the ultimately determining element in history"). Still Engels accepted partial responsibility for the vulgar interpretations, admitting that in their effort to counter idealist opponents, he and Marx presented their point of view too deterministically without proper qualification. Here Engels points to a problematical divide in Marxian materialism. On one hand, Marx and Engels sometimes spoke of progressively unfolding "historical" stages (i.e., primitive communist, ancient, feudal, capitalist, communist) animated by rational, class subjects who propel history toward its "inevitable," emancipatory conclusion (e.g., Marx [1859] 1970, pp. 21–22). Yet they also expressed a multicausal and nonlinear historical materialism that, in Darwinian fashion, breaks with speculative conceptions of progressive evolution, calls for evidential inquiry about concrete historical practices of particular individuals and groups, and demands a constant rethinking of theory and politics in light of the findings.

Like Adam Smith, Marx argued that workers organized collectively in a specialized division of labor attain qualitatively enhanced productive powers far exceeding the efficiency of individual producers. However, Marx specified that the secret of capitalism's extraordinary productivity is its highly developed modes of "social" cooperation, which end the relative "isolation" of premodern production (Marx [1852] 1963, pp. 122–135; [1857–1858] 1973, pp. 471–533). He attacked political economists for obscuring the role of cooperation and for treating capitalist economic exchange and value as a "fantastic . . . relation between things" rather than as a "social relation" (Marx [1887] 1967, pp. 71–83, 322–335). The point here is that by treating the social factor as the most important "material" force, Marx escaped the reductionist physicalism of the early atomists, the awkward dualism of Renaissance thinkers, and the crude technological determinism attributed to him by critics. The social organization of production and the structures of exploitation and domination are decisive for historical materialism.

Marx and Engels ([1845–1846] 1964, pp. 31–32) considered the "first premise of all human history" to be production of "the means of subsistence" and a characteristic "mode of life." As soon as the simplest forms of production are transcended, the accumulation of surplus product allows some individuals or strata to be freed from subsistence activities and makes possible cultural and social differentiation. For Marx, material determination in the "last instance" means that the degree and pattern of societal development depend, ultimately, on the amount, type, and disposition of surplus. But he still stressed the relative autonomy of emergent cultural and social spheres. For example, modern capitalist societies share distinct structural attributes (e.g., complex, specialized, rationalized institutions) that depend on the highly developed productive system. Yet since they are not determined entirely by production, the shape and arrangement of these structures vary widely between and even within capitalist societies. Moreover, they exert reciprocal causal effects that can either facilitate or fetter production and further differentiate individual capitalist societies.

The central hypothesis of historical materialism is that the "mode of production" determines the social, political, and intellectual "forms of intercourse" (Marx and Engels [1845–1846] 1964, pp. 32–33). "Productive forces," or all factors contributing directly to material production (i.e., natural resources, tools, technical knowledge, modes of cooperation, and labor power), and "forms of ownership" providing certain "classes" effective control over the productive process and its products constitute the mode of production and, together, exert a relatively strong determining force on "superstructure" or the modes of social organization (e.g., legal administration) and thought (e.g., ruling ideas) necessary for maintaining the conditions of production and overall reproduction of the social formation. The rest of social life is more loosely determined. Marx conceived of society as a totality of interrelated, interactive, and interdependent social structures and forms of culture. Each part is relatively autonomous (exerting its own distinct influence on the whole), but the mode of production, in the end, is the decisive force shaping the social formation's overall structure and logic of internal relations.

Although Marx implied that productive forces have ultimate analytic primacy, his theoretical and historical writings focus on property relations and consequent class dynamics. He viewed the relationship between owners of productive property and the various strata of producers (who live off their labor) to be the fundamental social condition having the most systematic and fateful consequences for individuals, institutions, and society as a whole. He believed that "class struggles" over productive property are the primary force propelling big social conflicts and transitions. His most disputed contention was that a "final" class struggle, arising from the capitalistic compression of classes into a tiny ownership strata and huge mass of producers, would usher in an emancipated communist epoch of uncoerced cooperation, science, and rational planning and a much milder, pacified, and socially mediated form of material determinism (truly "in the last instance"). Since he spoke prophetically about this hypothesis, its hopeful political scenario is beyond the borders of Marx's "scientific" method.

Marx built on the tradition of eighteenth-century materialism, which sought a nonspeculative foundation for scientific, social, and political practices. Newtonian conceptions of ultimate bodies and absolute space and time underlied this Enlightenment current of thought. However, by the early twentieth century, pathbreaking theories of electromagnetic fields, relativity, and quantum mechanics relativized space and time, eroded the borders between energy and mass, and generally shattered the old mechanistic worldview. The implicit cosmology of the new physics was far more complex, relational, and counterintuitive. In the same period, philosophers such as James, Dewey, Nietzsche, and Heidegger rejected the subject–object dichotomy, dismissed all "foundations" for knowledge, and broke with the conventional epistemological problematic of modern Western thought.

However, dramatic social changes also demanded that class dynamics be rethought. Especially noteworthy was the shift away from early capitalism's emergent, bipolar class structure (i.e., of factory owners and operatives) to a much more complex network of classes with many opposing strata, new types of workplaces, new forms of indirect ownership and control, and an interventionist state that blurred the line between the mode of production and superstructure. Furthermore, capitalism did not melt away, as Marx and Engels had expected, the racial, ethnic, gender, religious, national, regional, and other traditional modes of association, opposition, and identification. But despite these complexities, crude versions of historical materialism abounded. As cited above, Engels critically addressed vulgar materialism in the early 1890s, and about a decade later, Max Weber pitched his heralded "Protestant ethic" thesis, at least, in part, against the same thinkers.

Dialectical materialism became the official ideology of Stalinism and world communism in the late 1920s and 1930s at the same time that sociology was being rapidly transformed into a professionally specialized, empirical discipline in the United States. Talcott Parsons's first translation of Weber and his own *Structure of Social Action* ([1937] 1968) appeared during this period. The strong primacy that Parsons attributed to values and ideas contradicted Marxian materialism. Emphasizing the same idealist theme, his highly influential reading of Weber's corpus pitted Weber directly against Marx. Parsons's leading role in sociological theory (until the late 1960s) solidified opposition to materialism. However, most Cold War social scientists dismissed materialism as ideology whether or not they were acquainted with Parsonian thought. Marx's influence in mainstream sociology was largely reflected in numerous research and theoretical efforts aimed directly or indirectly at refuting materialism by demonstrating the delimited impact of class variables.

Following the multitude of attacks on functionalism and positivism of the middle and later 1960s, Marxian approaches appeared much more prominently in theoretical and empirical sociology. In the same era, Lewis Althusser's ([1965] 1970; Althusser and Balibar [1968] 1970) landmark, anti-Hegelian reading of Marx initiated an intense international debate over materialism, conducted mostly by nonsociologists in interdisciplinary, social theory circles. Later, G. A. Cohen's widely read *Karl Marx's Theory of History* (1978) gave impetus to a growing "analytic" branch of Marxism emphasizing the systematic reconstruction of materialism. Many challenging new works analyzed, criticized, reinterpreted, and applied historical materialism (e.g., Anderson 1974a, 1974b; Hindess and Hirst 1975; Shaw 1978; McMurtry 1978; Rader 1979; Giddens 1981; de Ste. Croix 1981, 1984; McLennan 1981; Bailey and Llobera 1981; Roemer 1982; Elster 1985; Wright 1985; Larrain 1986; Bhaskar 1989; Bertram 1990). Although the studies dwelled mostly on Marx's own materialist point of view, ambiguities in the original texts left plenty of room for developing fresh approaches. The new interpretations generally dispensed with Marxism's Hegelian elements, explicit political features, and nineteenth-century capitalist trappings and delineated clearer, more systematic versions of materialist metatheory. However, some of the new works were stated so abstractly and executed such substantial revisions that the connections to Marx's own materialism seemed obscure (e.g., Habermas 1979, pp. 95–177; see Antonio 1990).

The interdisciplinary debates over historical materialism had a receptive audience among growing numbers of Marxian and other heterodox sociologists. However, poststructuralist and postmodernist approaches, also originating outside sociology, launched linguistic, antirationalist, and antiholist broadsides against the epistemological and normative underpinnings of the materialist tradition (e.g., Baudrillard 1983; Lyotard 1984; see Anderson 1983). Still Marxists and "post-Marxists" alike claimed that neopositivism, middle-range theory, and other mainstream approaches were incapable of coming to terms with emergent changes of momentous proportions (e.g., the collapse of the Eastern Bloc, new democratic movements, worldwide environmental despoliation, internationalization of the economy, and growing class divisions). Although the exact course of future discussion is unpredictable, the sense of impending crisis has stirred renewed interest in metatheory, global social theory, and normative theory, which is likely to carry on and favor continued discussion of materialism. The decline of stereotyped "dialectical materialism," the success of Marxian brands of specialized social science, and growing public concern about material constraints to growth and abundance are also likely to contribute to keeping materialist approaches on the scene.

(SEE ALSO: *Economic Determinism; Marxist Sociology*)

REFERENCES

Althusser, Louis (1965) 1970 *For Marx.* New York: Vintage Books.

———, and Étienne Balibar (1968) 1970 *Reading Capital.* London: New Left Books.

Anderson, Perry 1974a *Passages from Antiquity to Feudalism.* London: New Left Books.

———1974b *Lineages of the Absolutist State.* London: New Left Books.

———1983 *In the Tracks of Historical Materialism.* London: New Left Books.

Antonio, Robert 1990 "The Decline of the Grand Narrative of Emancipatory Modernity: Crisis or Renewal in Neo-Marxian Theory?" In George Ritzer, ed., *Frontiers of Social Theory*. New York: Columbia University Press.

Bailey, Anne M., and Josep R. Llobera 1981 *The Asiatic Mode of Production*. London: Routledge and Kegan Paul.

Baudrillard, Jean 1983 *Simulations*. New York: Semiotext(e).

Bertram, Christopher 1990 "International Competition in Historical Materialism." *New Left Review* 183:116–128.

Bhaskar, Roy 1989 *Reclaiming Reality*. London: New Left Books.

Cohen, G. A. 1978 *Karl Marx's Theory of History*. Princeton, N.J.: Princeton University Press.

Copleston, Frederick, S.J. 1962 *A History of Philosophy: Greece and Rome*, Vol. 1. Garden City, N.Y.: Image Books.

Elster, Jon 1985 *Making Sense of Marx*. New York: Cambridge University Press.

Engels, Friedrich (1891–1894) 1959 "Letters on Historical Materialism." In Lewis S. Feuer, ed., *Basic Writings on Politics and Philosophy: Karl Marx and Friedrich Engels*. Garden City, N.Y.: Anchor Books.

Gay, Peter 1977 *The Enlightenment*, Vol. 2. New York: W. W. Norton.

Giddens, Anthony 1981 *A Contemporary Critique of Historical Materialism*. Berkeley: University of California Press.

Gillispie, Charles Coulston 1960 *The Edge of Objectivity*. Princeton, N.J.: Princeton University Press.

Habermas, Jürgen 1979 *Communication and the Evolution of Society*. Boston: Beacon Press.

Hindess, Barry, and Paul Q. Hirst 1975 *Precapitalist Modes of Production*. London: Routledge and Kegan Paul.

Larrain, Jorge 1986 *A Reconstruction of Historical Materialism*. London: Allen and Unwin.

Lyotard, Jean-François 1984 *The Postmodern Condition*. Minneapolis: University of Minnesota Press.

McLennan, Gregor 1981 *Marxism and the Methodologies of History*. London: New Left Books.

McMurtry, John 1978 *The Structure of Marx's World-View*. Princeton, N.J.: Princeton University Press.

Marx, Karl (1844) 1964 *The Philosophical and Economic Manuscripts of 1844*. New York: International Publishers.

———(1852) 1963 *The Eighteenth Brumaire of Louis Bonaparte*. New York: International Publishers.

———(1857–1858) 1973 *Grundrisse*. New York: Vintage Books.

———(1859) 1970 *A Contribution to the Critique of Political Economy*. Moscow: Progress Publishers.

———(1887) 1967 *Capital*, vol. 1. New York: International Publishers.

———, and Frederick Engels (1845–1846) 1964 *The German Ideology*. Moscow: Progress Publishers.

Parsons, Talcott (1937) 1968 *The Structure of Social Action*, Vols. 1, 2. New York: Free Press.

Rader, Melvin 1979 *Marx's Interpretation of History*. New York: Oxford University Press.

Roemer, John E. 1982 *A General Theory of Exploitation and Class*. Cambridge, Mass.: Harvard University Press.

de Ste. Croix, G.E.M. 1981 *The Class Struggle in the Ancient World*. Ithaca, N.Y.: Cornell University Press.

———1984 "Class in Marx's Conception of History, Ancient and Modern. *New Left Review* 146:94–111.

Shaw, William H. 1978 *Marx's Theory of History*. Stanford, Calif.: Stanford University Press.

Wright, Erik Olin 1985 *Classes*. London: New Left Books.

ROBERT J. ANTONIO

MATHEMATICAL SOCIOLOGY The notion of mathematical sociology has intrigued some scholars for many years, been denounced by others, and been ignored by a sizable portion of the profession. To some extent, the term *mathematical sociology* is misleading because it is neither a subdiscipline nor a methodology per se. This discussion, therefore, is not so much a report on the state of the art as it is a commentary on what mathematical sociology can be and where it is flourishing in the discipline.

In principle, mathematical sociology simply implies the use of mathematics for formulating sociological theory more precisely than can be done by less formal methods. Theory involves abstraction from and codification of reality, formulation of general principles describing what has been abstracted, and deduction of consequences of those formulations for the sake of understanding, predicting, and possibly controlling that reality. When social phenomena can be described in mathematical terms, the deductive power of mathematics enables more precise and detailed derivations and predictions based on original premises.

Mathematical expression also enables sociologists to discover that the same abstract forms and processes sometimes describe what seem to be diverse social phenomena. If the same type of formulation describes both the spread of a disease and the adoption of an innovation, then a common type of process is involved and the theorist can search further for what generates that commonality. Ideally, therefore, mathematics provides the basis for very general and powerful integrative theory.

The vigor of mathematical sociology varies widely over the various subfields of the discipline. Precise formulation requires precise observations and careful induction of general patterns from those observations. Some sociologists have rejected any attempts to quantify human behavior, either on the grounds that what is important is in principle not subject to precise measurement or from a philosophical unwillingness to consider human behavior to be in any way deterministic. That issue will not be addressed here, but clearly it is much easier to obtain precise information in some areas of inquiry than in others. For example, census data provide reasonably precise counts of many sociologically interesting facts, with the consequence that mathematical demography has long flourished.

Mathematics can be thought of as an elegant logic machine. Application of mathematics to any substantive discipline involves careful translation of the substantive ideas into mathematical form, deriving the mathematical consequences, and translating the results back into a substantive interpretation. There are two key aspects to the process: (1) finding a completely satisfactory way of expressing the substantive ideas in mathematical terms and (2) being able to solve the mathematical puzzle.

The mathematical expression of a substantive theory is called a *model.* Often, models are created with primary emphasis on being tractable, or readily solved. Some types of models appear frequently in substantive literature because they are widely known, relatively simple mathematically, and have easy solutions. Basic models and applications can be found in Coleman (1964), Bartholomew (1973); Fararo (1973), and Leik and Meeker (1975). Mathematics and sociological theory are discussed in Fararo (1984). A wealth of more complex models can be found in specialized volumes and in periodicals such as the *Journal of Mathematical Sociology.* When models become too complex to be tractable, they may be incorporated into computer simulations.

Simple models have the advantage of presenting an uncluttered view of the world, although derivations from such models often do not fit observed data very well. When the goal is heuristic, a simple model might be preferable to one that matches more closely the reality being modeled. However, when the goal is accurate prediction and possible control, then more complex models are typically needed.

There are two general questions to be raised in deciding whether developing a mathematical model has been useful. One is whether the mathematics of the model lead to new ideas about how the system being modeled operates. This is purely a theoretical question, concerned with understanding reality better by creating an abstraction of it that enables us to think more clearly about it. The second question concerns how well the model fits that reality. A heuristically useful model may fit poorly, while a model that fits well may provide little in the way of new ideas or understandings. This second question is statistical.

Statistical models are concerned solely with fitting an underlying mathematical model to data from a sample of real-world cases. The underlying model may be complex or simple, but the statistical concerns are whether the sample can be assumed to represent adequately the population from which it was selected and whether the parameter (equation constant) estimates based on that sample can be considered accurate reflections of how the variables of the underlying model are related in that population.

A HISTORY OF RECENT APPROACHES TO THEORY

During much of this century, there has been concern in sociology over the relationship between theory and research. Whereas theory was abstract and typically discursive, research increasingly employed statistical methods. The gulf between verbal statements about theoretical relationships and statistical tests of empirical patterns was great. Zetterberg's (1965) concept of axiomatic theory seemed to offer a bridge over this chasm. The popularized result was *axioms* in the form of monotonic propositions ("The greater the *X*, the greater the *Y*") and hypotheses derived solely from concatenating (multiplying) the signs of the relationships.

For example, axioms of "As *A* increases, *B* increases" and "As *B* increases, *C* decreases" lead to the hypothesis that "As *A* increases, *C* decreases." Standard statistical tests of the deduced hypotheses were presumed to be proper tests of the theory that generated the axioms. The approach was quick, convenient, readily understood, and did not require expertise in mathematics or statistics. Consequently, it quickly became popular.

Numerous inadequacies with such theories soon became apparent, however, and interest turned to *path models,* based on earlier work by Wright (1934). Path models assume that empirical measurements coincide exactly with theoretical concepts, all variables are continuous (or reasonably close to continuous), all relationships (paths) are bivariate, linear, and causal, there is no feedback in the system under analysis (the recursive system assumption), and all relevant variables have been included in the model (the "closed system" assumption). The underlying theoretical model is therefore very simplistic.

If the assumptions are reasonable, then the causal effects, or path coefficients, are equal to ordinary multiple regression coefficients. That is, the underlying mathematical model feeds directly into a well-known statistical model, and the tie between theory and research seems well established. Are the assumptions reasonable?

The closed system assumption, for example, implies that there is no correlation between the prediction errors across the various equations. If error correlations appear, then path coefficient estimates based on the statistical model will be in error, or biased, so the theory will not be tested properly by the statistics. Only two solutions are possible: (1) add more variables or paths to the model or (2) develop a statistical model that can accommodate correlated errors.

The assumption that measurement equals concept poses a different problem whenever various scales or multiple indicators are used to represent a theoretical concept not readily assessed in a single measure. Traditionally, the statistical model called *factor analysis* has been used to handle this measurement–concept problem, but factor analysis was not traditionally linked to the analysis of theoretical systems.

Recent years have seen very extensive development and elaboration of statistical models for linear systems, and these models address both the correlated error and the measurement–concept problems while allowing departure from recursiveness. Called *linear structural models* (Joreskog 1970; Goldberger and Duncan 1973; Long 1983; Hayduk 1987), the underlying mathematical model still says that all variables are continuous and all relationships bivariate, linear, and causal. This development has focused entirely on technical statistical questions about bias in parameter estimates. From a general theory point of view, the underlying linear model's assumptions, which have been imposed for tractability, are highly restrictive. Unfortunately, linear structural models have come to dominate much of sociological theory, even though the models are primarily statistical, and scant attention has been paid to the constraints of the underlying theoretical assumptions.

MOVING BEYOND LINEAR MODELS

Consider the assumption of linearity. If a dynamic process is being modeled, linear relationships will almost always prove faulty. How change in some causal factor induces change in some consequent system property is typically constrained by system limits and is likely to be altered over time through feedback from other system factors.

As a disease like AIDS spreads, for example, the rate at which it spreads depends on how many people are already infected, how many have yet to be infected, and what conditions allow interaction between the not-yet-infecteds and the infecteds. With very few infected, the rate of spread is very small because so few cannot quickly infect a very large number of others. As the number of infecteds grows, so does the rate of spread of the disease, because there are more to spread it. On the other hand, if nearly everyone had already been infected, the rate of spread would be small because there would be few left to spread it to. To complicate theoretical matters further, as the disease has generated widespread concern, norms governing sexual contact have begun to change, influencing the probabilities of transmission of the virus. In mathematical terms, the implication is that the rate of change of the proportion infected (i.e., the rate of spread of the disease) is not constant over time, nor is it a constant proportion of change in any variable in the system. In short, the process is inherently nonlinear.

Nonlinear models take many forms. If the variables are conceived as continuous over time, and the primary theoretical focus is on how variables change as a consequence of changes in other variables, then the most likely mathematical form is differential equations. The substantive theory is translated into statements about rates of change. Most diffusion and epidemiology models, like the AIDS problem just noted, use differential equations. So do a number of demography models. More peripheral to the sociology literature, but just as relevant, are numerous differential equations models dealing with topics such as conflict and arms control.

For relatively simple differential equations models, once the model is developed it is possible to determine the trajectory over time of any of the properties of the system, to ascertain under what conditions the covariation of system properties will shift or remain stable, and to ask whether that system will tend toward equilibrium or some other theoretical limit, oscillate in regular patterns, or even "explode."

None of these questions could be asked of a linear model because the mathematics of the linear model leave nothing about the model itself to be deduced. Only statistical questions can be asked: estimates of the regression coefficients that fit the model to the data and the closeness of that fit. To the extent that sociology addresses questions of process, appropriate theory requires nonlinear models.

What about the assumption of continuous variables? If time or time-related variables were to be treated in discrete units, there are at least three different approaches available. For handling dynamic systems without the calculus of differential equations, difference equations are the appropriate form. Huckfeldt, Kohfeld, and Likens (1982) provide a convenient overview of this approach.

For extensive time series with relatively few variables, there are Box-Jenkins and related types of models, although these have seen relatively little use in sociology. Because they are closer to statistical models than general theoretical models, they are only mentioned here in passing.

Many theories treat systems as represented by discrete states. For example, over a lifetime, an individual is likely to move into and out of several different occupational statuses. Are certain status transitions more likely than others? In simplest form, the implied theoretical model involves a matrix algebra formulation that specifies the probability of moving from each of the states (occupational statuses for this example) to each of the other states. Then the mathematics of matrix algebra allow deduction of a number of system consequences from this "transition matrix." Such a treatment is called a *Markov chain.* Blumen, Kogan, and McCarthy (1955) demonstrated that certain modifications of a Markov chain were needed for the theory to fit the data they had available on occupational transitions. Their work was the initial inspiration for a distinguished string of mathematical social mobility models.

Another type of substantive problem that deals with discrete data is the analysis of social networks such as friendship structures. One of the most vigorous modeling areas in sociology, network analysis has produced a rich and elaborate literature addressing a wealth of substantive issues. Typically, network data consists of whether or not any two cases (nodes in the network) are linked in one or more ways. The resulting data set, then, usually consists of presence or absence of a link of a given type over all pairs of nodes.

Early network analyses concerned friendships, cliques, and rudimentary concepts of structurally based social power. With the introduction of directed graph theory (Harary, Norman, and Cartwright 1965), random or probabilistic net theory, and blockmodeling (Boorman and White 1976), powerful tools have been developed to approach social structure and its consequences from a network point of view. As those tools emerged, the range of questions addressed via network analysis has greatly expanded. Over the past ten years, more articles in the *Journal of Mathematical Sociology* have dealt with networks than with any other single topic. Overviews and examples can be found in Knoke and Kuklinski (1982), Berkowitz (1982), Burt and Minor (1983), and Wellman and Berkowitz (1988).

Small group processes have also generated a variety of mathematical formulations. Because laboratory observations typically generate counts of various types of acts or categorizations of the system in various discrete states over time, micro systems, which are studied in the laboratory, have intrigued model builders since the early 1950s. Recent work on power as a function of the linkages that define the exchange system is an example of such work (cf. Markovsky, Willer, and Patton 1988; Gould and Fernandez 1989).

At the most micro level of sociology, the analysis of individual behavior in social context has a long tradition of mathematical models of individual decision making. Recent developments include the satisfaction-balance decision-making model of Gray and Tallman (1984), which demonstrates improved agreement with experimental data compared to prior models.

The most exciting aspect of these different levels of development is that, increasingly, social-exchange-theory-based inquiries into micro dynamics are working toward formulations compatible with the more general network structural analyses. These joint developments, therefore, promise a much more powerful linking of micro-system dynamics with macro-system structural modeling (cf. Cook 1987; Willer 1987).

One other area of vigorous development deserves attention: the treatment of strings of events that constitute the history of a particular case, process, or situation (Allison 1984; Tuma and Hannan 1984; Heise 1989). Event history analysis has some of its origins in traditional demographers' life tables, but methods and models have experienced a great deal of attention and growth in recent years. If one had lifetime data on job placements, advancements, demotions, and firings (i.e., employment event histories) for a sample of individuals, then event history methods could be used for examining what contributes to differential risks of one of those events occurring, how long someone is likely to be in a given situation ("waiting time" between events), and so forth.

Not all developments in mathematical sociology can be neatly lumped into categories like network analysis or event history analysis. For example, Jasso's (1980) innovative work on models of distributive justice, though linked at a substantive level to a long tradition of inquiry, stands alone as a mathematical formulation of a sociologically important topic. Similarly, affect control theory (Heise 1979; Smith-Lovin and Heise 1988) represents mathematical formulation in an area typically considered not subject to such treatment.

There are many other mathematical formulations appearing in recent years, too many to attempt enumerating or cataloging. There are also a few general texts treating subdisciplines such as criminology or the family in mathematical terms. On the less sanguine side, such works are often ignored by mainstream sociologists.

Mathematical work in sociology is alive and vigorous. It truly does promise a higher level of theoretical precision and integration across the discipline. Unfortunately, too many sociologists are still unaware of what mathematical sociology has to offer.

(SEE ALSO: *Paradigms and Models; Scientific Explanation*)

REFERENCES

Allison, Paul D. 1984 *Event History Analysis: Regression for Longitudinal Event Data.* Beverly Hills, Calif.: Sage.

Bartholomew, D. J. 1973 *Stochastic Models for Social Processes,* 2nd ed. New York: Wiley.

Berkowitz, S. D. 1982 *An Introduction to Structural Analysis.* Toronto: Butterworths.

Blumen, Isadore, Marvin Kogan, and Philip H. McCarthy 1955 *The Industrial Mobility of Labor as a Probability Process.* Ithaca, N.Y.: Cornell University Press.

Boorman, S. A., and H. C. White 1976 "Social Structure from Multiple Networks. II Role Structures." *American Journal of Sociology* 81:1384–1446.

Burt, Ronald S., and Michael J. Minor 1983 *Applied Network Analysis.* Beverly Hills, Calif.: Sage.

Coleman, James S. 1964 *Introduction to Mathematical Sociology.* New York: Free Press.

Cook, Karen S. 1987 *Social Exchange Theory.* Newbury Park, Calif.: Sage.

Fararo, Thomas J. 1973 *Mathematical Sociology.* New York: Wiley.

———(ed.) 1984 *Mathematical Ideas and Sociological Theory.* New York: Gordon and Breach (special issue of the *Journal of Mathematical Sociology).*

Goldberger, A. S., and O. D. Duncan 1973 *Structural Equation Models in the Social Sciences.* New York: Seminar Press.

Gould, Roger V., and Roberto M. Fernandez 1989 "Structures of Mediation: A Formal Approach to Brokerage in Transition Networks." In Clifford C. Clogg, ed., *Sociological Methodology.* Washington, D.C.: American Sociological Association.

Gray, Louis N., and I. Tallman 1984 "A Satisfaction Balance Model of Decision Making and Choice Behavior." *Social Psychology Quarterly* 47:146–159.

Harary, Frank, Robert Z. Norman, and Dorwin Cartwright 1965 *Structural Models.* New York: Wiley.

Hayduk, Leslie A. 1987 *Structural Equation Modeling with LISREL.* Baltimore: Johns Hopkins University Press.

Heise, D. R. 1979 *Understanding Events: Affect and the Construction of Social Action.* New York: Cambridge University Press.

———1989 "Modeling Event Structures." *Journal of Mathematical Sociology* 14:139–169.

Huckfeldt, Robert R., C. W. Kohfeld, and Thomas W. Likens 1982 *Dynamic Modeling: An Introduction.* Beverly Hills, Calif.: Sage.

Jasso, Guillermina 1980 "A New Theory of Distributive Justice." *American Sociological Review* 45:3–32.

Joreskog, Karl G. 1970 "A General Method for Analysis of Covariance Structures." *Biometrika* 57:239–251.

Knoke, David, and James Kuklinski 1982 *Network Analysis.* Beverly Hills, Calif.: Sage.

Leik, Robert K., and Barbara F. Meeker 1975 *Mathematical Sociology.* Englewood Cliffs, N.J.: Prentice-Hall.

Long, J. Scott 1983 *Covariance Structure Models: An Introduction to LISREL.* Beverly Hills, Calif.: Sage.

Markovsky, Barry, David Willer, and Travis Patton 1988 "Power Relations in Exchange Networks." *American Sociological Review* 53:220–236.

Smith-Lovin, L., and D. R. Heise 1988 *Affect Control Theory: Research Advances.* New York: Gordon and Breach.

Tuma, Nancy B., and Michael T. Hannan 1984 *Social Dynamics: Models and Methods.* New York: Academic Press.

Wellman, Barry, and S. D. Berkowitz, eds. 1988 *Social Structures: A Network Approach.* Cambridge: Cambridge University Press.

Willer, David 1987 *Theory and the Experimental Investigation of Social Structures.* New York: Gordon and Breach.

Wright, Sewell 1934 "The Method of Path Coefficient." *Annals of Mathematical Statistics* 5:161–215.

Zetterberg, Hans 1965 *On Theory and Verification in Sociology.* Totowa, N.J.: Bedminster Press.

ROBERT K. LEIK

MEASUREMENT There are many standards that can be used to evaluate the status of a science, and one of the most important is how well variables are measured. The idea of measurement is relatively simple. It is associating numbers with aspects of objects, events, or other entities according to rules, and so measurement has existed for as long as there have been numbers, counting, and concepts of magnitude. In daily living, measurement is encountered in myriad ways. For example, measurement is used in considering time, temperature, distance, and weight. It happens that these concepts and quite a few others are basic to many sciences. The notion of measurement as expressing magnitudes is fundamental, and the observation that *if something exists, it must exist in some quantity* is probably too old to attribute to the proper authority. This notion of quantification is associated with the common dictionary definition of measurement: "The extent, capacity, or amount ascertained by measuring."

A concept such as distance may be considered to explore the meaning of measurement. To measure distance, one may turn to a simple example of a straight line drawn between two points on a sheet of paper. There is an origin or beginning point and an end point, and an infinite number of points between the beginning and the end. To measure in a standard way, a unit of distance has to be arbitrarily defined, such as an inch. Then the distance of any straight line can be observed in inches or fractions of inches. For convenience, arbitrary rules can be established for designating number of inches, such as feet, yards, and miles. If another standard is used—say, meters—the relationship between inches and meters is one in which no information is lost in going from one to the other. So, in summary, in the concept of measurement as considered thus far, there are several properties, two of which should be noted particularly: the use of arbitrary standardized units and the assumption of continuous possible points between any two given points. The case would be similar if time, temperature, or weight were used as an example.

There is another property mentioned above, a beginning point, and the notion of the beginning point has to be examined more carefully. In distance, if one measures one inch from a beginning point on a straight line, and then measures to a second point at two inches, one may say that the distance from the beginning point of the second point is twice that of the first point. With temperature, however, there is a problem. If one measures temperature from the point of freezing using the Celsius scale, which sets 0 degrees at the freezing point of water under specified conditions, then one can observe temperatures of 10 degrees and of 20 degrees. It is now proper to say that the second measurement is twice as many degrees from the origin as the first measure, but one cannot say that it is twice the temperature. The reason for this is that the origin that has been chosen is not the origin that is required to make that kind of mathematical statement. For temperature, the origin is a value known as absolute zero, the absence of any heat, a value that is known only theoretically but has been approximated.

This problem is usually understood easily, but it can be made more simple to understand by illustrating how it operates in measuring distance. Suppose a surveyor is measuring distance along a road from A to B to C to D. A is a long distance from B. Arriving at B, the surveyor measures the distance from B to C and finds it is ten miles, and then the distance from B to D is found to be twenty miles. The surveyor can say that the distance is twice as many miles from B to D as from B to C, but he cannot say that the distance from A to D is twice the distance from A to C, which is the error one would make if one used the Celsius temperature scale improperly. Measuring from the absolute origin for the purpose of carrying out mathematical operations has become known as *ratio level measurement.*

The idea of "levels of measurement" has been popularized following the formulation by the psychologist S. S. Stevens (1966). Stevens first identifies scales of measurement much as measurement is defined above, and then notes that the type of scale achieved depends upon the basic empirical operations performed. The operations performed are limited by the concrete procedures and by the "peculiarities of the thing being scaled." This leads to the types of scales—nominal, ordinal, interval, and ratio—which are characterized "by the kinds of transformations that leave the 'structure' of the scale undistorted." This "sets limits to the kinds of statistical manipulation that can legitimately be applied to the scaled data."

Nominal scales can be of a type like numbering individuals for identification, which creates a class for each individual. Or there can be classes for placement on the basis of equality within each class with regard to some characteristic of the object. *Ordinal* scales arise from the operation of rank ordering. Stevens expressed the opinion that most of the scales used by psychologists are ordinal, which means that there is a determination of whether objects are greater than or less than each other on characteristics of the object, and thus there is an ordering from smallest to largest. This is a crucial point that is examined below. *Interval* scales (equal-interval scales) are of the type discussed above, like temperature or weight, and these are subject to linear transformation with invariance. There are some limitations on the mathematical operations that can be carried out, but in general these limitations do not impede use of most statistical and other operations carried out in science. As noted, when the equal-interval scales have an absolute zero, they are called *ratio* scales. A lucid presentation of the issue of invariance of transformations and the limitations of use of mathematical operations (such as addition, subtraction, multiplication, and division) on interval scales is readily available in Nunnally (1978).

What is important to emphasize is that how the scales are constructed, as well as how the scales are used, determines the level of measurement. With regard to ordinal scales, Nunnally makes a concise and precise statement that should be read carefully: "With ordinal scales, none of the fundamental operations of algebra may be applied. In the use of descriptive statistics, it makes no sense to add, subtract, divide, or multiply ranks. Since an ordinal scale is defined entirely in terms of inequalities, only the algebra of inequalities can be used to analyze measures made on such scales" (1978, p. 22). What this means is that if one carries out a set of operations that are described as making an ordinal scale, the moment one adds, subtracts, divides, or multiplies the ranks, one has treated the scale as an interval scale.

ISSUES ON LEVEL OF MEASUREMENT

A number of issues are associated with the notion of levels of measurement. For example, are all types of measurement included in the concepts of nominal, ordinal, interval, and ratio? What is the impact of using particular statistical procedures when data are not in the form of well-measured interval scales? What kind of measurement appears (epistemologically) appropriate for the social and behavioral sciences?

The last question should probably be examined first. For example, are measures made about attributes of persons nominal, ordinal, or interval? In general, we cannot think of meaningful variables unless they *at least* imply order, but is order all that one thinks of when one thinks about characteristics of persons? For example, if one thinks of heights, say of all males of a given age, such as twenty-five, does measurement imply ordering them on an interval scale? We know that height is a measure of distance, so we assume the way one should measure this is by using a standard. For purposes of the example here, an interval scale is proposed, and the construction is as follows. The smallest twenty-five-year-old male (the category defined as 25 years and 0 days to 25 years and 365 days of age) and the largest are identified. The two persons are placed back to back, front to front, and every other possible way, and the distance between the height of the shortest and the tallest is estimated on a stick. Many estimates are made on the stick, until the spots where agreement begins to show discretely are evident; and so, with whatever error occurs in the process, the locations of beginning and end are indicated on the stick. Now the distance between the beginning and the end is divided into equal intervals, and thus an interval scale has been created. On this scale it is possible to measure every other male who is twenty-five years old, and the measure can be stated in terms of the number of intervals taller than the shortest person. Note that all possible values can be anticipated, and this is a continuous distribution.

Now if a million persons were so measured, how would they be distributed? Here the answer is on the basis of naive experience, as follows. First, there would be very few people who would be nearly as short as the shortest or as tall as the tallest. Where would one expect to find most persons? In the middle of the distance, or at some place not too far from it. Where would the next greatest amount of persons be found? Close to the biggest. With questions of this sort one ends up describing a well-distributed curve, possibly a normal curve or something near it.

It is proper now to make a small diversion before going on with answering the questions about the issues associated with level of measurement. In particular, it should be noted that there are many sources of error in the measurement that has just been described. First, of course, the age variable is specified with limited accuracy. At the limits, it may be difficult to determine exact age because of the way data are recorded. There are differences implied by the fact that where one is born makes a difference in time, and so on. This may seem facetious, but it illustrates how easily sources of error are bypassed without examination. Then it was noted that there were different estimates of the right location for the point of the shortest and the tallest person as marked on the stick. This is an error of observation and recording, and clearly the points selected are taken as mean values. Who are the persons doing the measuring? Does it make a difference if the person measuring is short or tall? These kinds of errors will exist for all persons measured. Further, it was not specified under what conditions the measurement was taken or to be taken. Are the persons barefoot? How are they asked to stand? Are they asked to relax to a normal position or to try to stretch upward? What time of day is used, since the amount of time after getting up from sleep may have an influence? Is the measurement before or after a meal? And so forth.

The point is that there are many sources of error in taking measures, even direct measures of this sort, and one must be alert to the consequences of these errors on what one does with the data collected. Errors of observation are common, and one aspect of this is the limit of the discriminations an observer can make. One type of error that is usually built into the measurement is rounding error, which is based on the estimated need for accuracy. So, for example, heights are rarely measured more accurately than to the half inch or centimeter, depending on the standard used. There is still the error of classification up or down, by whatever rule is used for rounding, at the decision point between the intervals used for rounding. Rounding usually follows a consistent arbitrary rule, such as "half adjusting," which means keeping the digit value if the next value in the number is 0 to 4 (e.g., 24.456 = 24) or increasing the value of a digit by 1 if the next value is 5 to 9 (e.g., 24.789 = 25). Another common rounding rule is simply to drop numbers (e.g., 24.456 = 24 and 24.789 = 24). It is important to be aware of which rounding rule is being used and what impact it may have on conclusions drawn when the data collected are used.

The use of distribution-free statistics (often called nonparametric statistics) was popularized beginning in the mid-1950s, and quickly came to be erroneously associated with the notion that most of the measurement in the social and behavioral sciences is of an ordinal nature. Actually, the use of the distribution-free statistics was given impetus because some tests, such as the sign test, did not require use of all the information available to do a statistical test of significance of differences. Thus, instead of using a test of differences of means, one could quickly convert the data to plus and minus scores, using some arbitrary rule, and do a quick and dirty sign test. Then, if one found significant differences, the more refined test could be carried out at one's leisure. Some of the orientation was related to computing time available, which meant time at a mechanical calculator. Similarly, it was well known that if one used a Spearman rank correlation with larger samples, and if one were interested in measuring statistical significance, one would have to make the same assumptions as for the Pearson product moment correlation, but with less efficiency.

However, this early observation about distribution-free statistics suggests that measures can be thought of in another way. Namely, one can think of measures in terms of how much they are degraded (or imperfect) interval measures. This leads to two questions that are proper to consider. First, what kind of measure is implied as appropriate by the concept? And second, how much error is there in how the measure is constructed if one wants to use procedures that imply interval measurement, including addition, subtraction, multiplication, and division?

What kind of measure is implied by the concept? One way of answering this is to go through the following procedure. As an example, consider a personal attribute, such as aggressiveness. Is it possible to conceive of the existence of a least aggressive person and a most aggressive person? Obviously, whether or not such persons can be located, they can be conceived of. Then, is there any reason to think that persons cannot have any and all possible quantities of aggressiveness between the least and the most aggressive persons? Of course not. Thus, what has been described is a continuous distribution, and with the application of a standard unit, it is appropriately an interval scale. It is improper to think of this variable as intrinsically one that is ordinal because it is continuous. In fact, it is difficult to think of even plausible examples of variables that are intrinsically ordinal. As Kendall puts it, "the essence of ranking is that the objects shall be orderable, and the totality of values of a continuous variate cannot be ordered in this sense. They can be regarded as constituting a range of values, but between any two different values there is always another value, so that we cannot number them as would be required for ranking purposes" (1948, p. 105). While a few comments were published that attempted to clarify these issues of measurement in the 1960s (Borgatta 1968), most methodologists accepted the mystique of ordinal measurement uncritically.

Often measures of a concept tend to be simple questions with ordered response categories. These do not correspond to ordinal measures in the sense of ordering persons or objects into ranks, but the responses to such questions have been asserted to be ordinal level measurement because of the lack of information about the intervals. So, for example, suppose one is attempting to measure aggressiveness using a question such as When you are in a group, how much of the time do you try to get your way about what kinds of activities the group should do next? Answer categories are Never, Rarely, Sometimes, Often, Very Often, and Always. Why don't these categories form an interval scale? The incorrect answer usually given is "because if one assumes an interval scale, one doesn't know where the answer categories intersect the interval scale." However, this *does not* create an ordinal scale. It creates an interval scale with unknown error with regard to the spacing of the intervals created by the categories.

Thus, attention is now focused on the second question of how much error is involved in creating interval scales, and this question can be answered in several ways. A positive way of answering is by asking how much difference it makes to distort an interval scale. For example, if normally distributed variables (which are assumed as the basis for statistical inference) are transformed to flat distributions, such as percentiles, how much impact does this have on statistical operations that are carried out? The answer is "very little." This property of not affecting results of statistical operations has been called robustness. Suppose a more gross set of transformations is carried out, such as deciles. How much impact does this have on statistical operations? The answer is "not much." However, when the transformations are to even grosser categories, such as quintiles, quartiles, thirds, or halves, the answer is that because one is throwing away even more information by grouping into fewer categories, the impact is progressively greater. What has been suggested in this example has involved two aspects: the transformation of the shape of the distribution, and the loss of discrimination (or information) by use of progressively fewer categories.

CONSEQUENCES OF USING LESS THAN NORMALLY DISTRIBUTED VARIABLES

If one has normally distributed variables, the distribution can be divided into categories. The interval units usually of interest with normally distributed variables are technically identified as standard deviation units, but other units can be used. When normally distributed variables are reduced to a small number of (gross) categories,

TABLE 1
Correlation of Scores with Criterion Variable, Average of Five Random Samples (N = 200) of Normal Deviates, Additive Scores Based on Four Items with Correlations of .9, .8, .7, and .6 with the Criterion Variable in the Population

	Correlation Coefficients			*Squared Correlation Coefficients*		
	X	*C*	*ER*	*X**	*C**	*ER**
Scores						
SumX	.921	.896	.532	.848	.802	.294
SumA	.895	.750	.516	.801	.562	.266
SumB	.861	.658	.536	.741	.433	.287
SumC	.819	.762	.428	.671	.581	.183
SumDL	.709	.570	.214	.503	.325	.046
SumDR	.712	.550	.684	.506	.303	.468
SumEL	.635	.438	.169	.403	.192	.029
SumER	.649	.460	.695	.420	.212	.483
SumFL	.534	.334	.122	.285	.112	.015
SumFR	.555	.350	.642	.308	.123	.412

substantial loss of discrimination or information occurs. This can be illustrated by doing a systematic exercise, the results of which are reported below and in Table 1.

The example is for a sample of two hundred cases, beginning with all variables as normally distributed in the population from which the sample is chosen. The exercise is carried out five times (that is, repeated independently five times), and the results are the averages for the five repetitions. There are four predictor variables (items) that are correlated with a criterion variable (X): .6, .7, .8, and .9. These are relatively high correlations corresponding to the types of measures usually available to social and behavioral scientists. With these four items a score (SumX) is created for each of the two hundred cases by adding them together. They are then correlated (product moment correlation) with the criterion variable. The average result of doing this five times is presented in Table 1 as .921. This correlation coefficient is larger than the highest correlation between an item and the criterion variable in the population (.9 above), and this illustrates why it is important to build scores to represent concepts rather than to use single items. Scores, if properly constructed, generally account for more of the variance of the concept than do single items. This example so far represents an ideal situation, since the items usually available are not so well defined as these normally distributed variables.

To continue the example, suppose the items are made less discriminating by grouping the information available into categories. Suppose for a first reduction of discrimination that we create four categories (three dividing points), symmetrically dividing the normal distributions of the items in the middle and at plus and minus one standard deviation unit. Effectively, this divides the distribution roughly as the extreme left 16 percent, the middle left 34 percent, the middle right 34 percent, and the extreme left 16 percent. If we retain the criterion X as the normally distributed variable, and now create scores for the four items (SumA), the average correlation coefficient between these scores and the criterion variable is .895. Obviously, some loss of information is reflected in this lower value. Other examples may be observed as follows: SumB is based on three categories (two dividing points), the same as SumA but omitting the central dividing point, thus extreme left 16 percent, center 68 percent, extreme right 16 percent. For this example the average correlation coefficient between the scores and the criterion variable is .861. SumC is based on only two categories (dichotomies, one dividing point) split in the middle, with 50 percent on the left and 50 percent on the right. For this example the average correlation coefficient is .819.

The next set of examples are all dichotomies, but unlike the above examples they are not symmetric. Each example will have four items on the left (L) or on the right (R). Thus, for SumDL the items are divided 16 percent on the left and 84 percent on the right. For SumDR the division is 84 percent and 16 percent. For SumEL and SumER the division is 10 and 90 percent, and for SumFL and SumFR the division is 5 and 95 percent. In other words, the scores are now being constructed of items that have progressively more extreme dividing points, all the items for each score being biased in the same direction. The average correlation coefficients may be observed in the X column of Table 1, and the progressive reduction is apparent.

In the next set of examples, under column C in Table 1, the same scores are used as in the prior examples, but the criterion variable is altered. Instead of using the normal variable, the criterion variable is transformed into a dichotomy with the dividing point in the middle. The apparent effect of having degraded the criterion variable to a dichotomy may be seen as a reduction in the magnitudes of the correlation coefficients of the scores to the criterion variable. An inconsistency in the pattern is the correlation coefficient between the score SumC and the criterion variable C, where it is seen that if the cutting points of the items and the criterion variable occur in the same location of the distribution (in this case in the middle), the value of the correlation coefficient is higher than might have been anticipated because the amount of information discarded is more than with SumA.

The next set of examples is in column ER of Table 1, and here again the criterion variable is altered to be a dichotomy, but in this case it is with an extreme cutting point, 90 percent on the left and 10 percent on the right. In column ER the values of the correlation coefficients are substantially smaller, but the effect of having items with dividing points near the dividing points of the criterion variables is much more visible. In the comparison of the correlation coefficients of SumEL and SumER with the criterion variable ER, the values are .169 (mismatched) and .695 (matched). The values of SumDL and SumRL, and of Sum FL and FR should also be compared.

While not presented in the table, for the unsymmetric examples scores were also created balancing two items each from the left and the right. The correlation coefficients, as might be expected, fell between the values of the scores based only on left or right items (SumDLR = .483, SumELR = .480, and SumFLR = .422).

Finally, the amount of variance explained by a correlation coefficient is the square of the value, and so the values in columns X, C, and ER have been squared in columns X*, C*, and ER*. These values are more correct to use in estimating the real differences that the transformations on the normal variables create. For example, the comparison of the mismatched SumEL score with that of the matched SumER in correlation with the criterion variable ER, using the squared correlation coefficients, is .029 versus .483 in column ER*, a difference accounting for about fifteen times more variance when the cutting points are matched than when mismatched. The comparison for SumFL and SumFR is even more dramatic in column ER*.

This set of examples illustrates a number of important things about measurement. First, having well-distributed variables is important, and having only a few categories for an item is effectively to have less usable information. Still, if the divisions intersect the population symmetrically and the cutting points are roughly matched, the loss of amount of variance explained may not be excessive. Planning data collection should take this into account. Thus, having items that divide the population symmetrically is important, and by contrast, items that are extreme can create problems of excessive loss of information under particular circumstances. These points can be made extreme by noting that under ideal conditions of having normally distributed items and criterion variable (SumX and X), the amount of variance accounted for in this example is .848, while in the poorest condition of extreme items mismatched to an extreme criterion variable (SumFL and SumFR), the amount of variance accounted for is only .015. How one measures must be considered a most important issue in attempting to build a science.

OTHER MEASURES

The consideration of measurement thus far has concentrated on interval measurement, with some emphasis on how it can be degraded. There are many other issues that are appropriately considered, including the fact that the concepts advanced by Stevens do not include all types of measures. As the discussion proceeds to some of these, attention should also be given to the notion of nominal scales. Nominal scales can be constructed in many ways, and only a few will be noted here. By way of example, it is possible to create a classification of something being present for objects that is then given a label A. Sometimes a second category is not defined, and then the second category is the default, the thing not being present. Or two categories can be defined, such as male and female. Note that the latter example can also be defined as male and not male, or as female and not female. More complex classifications are illustrated by geographical regions, such as North, West, East, and South, which are arbitrary and follow the pattern of compass directions. Such classifications, to be more meaningful, are quickly refined to reflect more homogeneity in the categories, and sets of categories develop such as Northeast, Middle Atlantic, South, North Central, Southwest, Mountain, Northwest, and Pacific, presumably with the intention of being inclusive (exhaustive) of the total area. These are complex categories that differ with regard to many variables, and so they are not easily ordered.

However, each such set of categories for a nominal scale can be reduced to dichotomies, such as South versus Not South; these variables are commonly called "dummy variables." This permits analysis of the dummy variable as though it represented a well-distributed variable. In this case, for example, one could think of the arbitrary underlying variable as being "southernness," or whatever underlies the conceptualization of the "South" as being different from the rest of the regions. Similarly, returning to the male versus female variable, the researcher has to consider interpretatively what the variable is supposed to represent. Is it distinctly supposed to be a measure of the two biological categories, or is it supposed to represent the social and cultural distinction that underlies them?

Many, if not most, of the variables that are of interest to social and behavioral science are drawn from the common language, and when these are used analytically, many problems or ambiguities become evident. For example, the use of counts is common in demography, and many of the measures that are familiar are accepted with ease. However, as common a concept as city size is not without problems. A city is a legal definition, and so what is a city in one case may be quite different from a city in another case. For example, some cities are only central locations surrounded by many satellite urban centers and suburbs that are also defined as cities, while other cities may be made up of a major central location and many other satellite urban centers and suburbs. To clarify such circumstances, the demographers may develop other concepts, like Standard Metropolitan Areas (SMAs), but this does not solve the problem completely; some SMAs may be isolated, and others may be contiguous. And when is a city a city? Is the definition one that begins with the smallest city with a population of 2,500 (not even a geographical characteristic), or 10,000 population, or 25,000 population? Is city size really a concept that is to be measured by population numbers or area, or by some concept of degree of urban centralization? Is New York City really one city or several? Or is New York City only part of one city that includes the urban complexes around it? The point that is critical is that definitions have to be fixed in arbitrary ways when concepts are drawn practically from the common language, and social concepts are not necessarily parsimoniously defined by some ideal rules of formulating scientific theory. Pragmatic considerations frequently intervene in how data are collected and what data become available for use.

An additional point is appropriate here: that in demography and in other substantive areas, important measures include *counts* of discrete entities, and these types of measures do not easily fit the Stevens classification of levels of measurement. A discussion of several technical proposals for more exhaustive classifications of types of measures is considered by Duncan (1984).

CONSTRUCTING MEASURES

There are obviously many ways that measures can be constructed. Some have been formalized and diffused, such as Louis Guttman's cumulative scale analysis, so popular that it has come to be known universally as Guttman scaling, a methodological contribution that was associated with a sociologist and had an appeal for many. An early comprehensive coverage of Guttman scaling can be found in Riley et al. (1954). The essence of Guttman scaling is that if a series of dichotomous items is assumed to be drawn from the same universe of content, and if they differ in difficulty, then they can be ordered so that they define scale types. For example, if one examines height, questions could be the following: 1. Are you at least five feet tall? 2. Are you at least five and a half feet tall? 3. Are you at least six feet tall? 4. Are you at least six and a half feet tall? Responses to these would logically fall into the following types: a "+" to indicate "yes" and a "−" to indicate a "no":

1.	2.	3.	4.
+	+	+	+
+	+	+	−
+	+	−	−
+	−	−	−
−	−	−	−

The types represent "perfect" types, that is, responses made without a logical error. The assumption is that within types, people are equivalent. In the actual application of the procedure, some problems are evident, possibly the most obvious being that there are errors because in applying the procedure in studies, content is not as well specified as being in a "universe" as is the example of height; thus there are errors, and therefore error types. The error types were considered of two kinds: unambiguous, such as − + + +, which in the example above would simply be illogical, a mistake, and could logically be classed as + + + + with "minimum error." The second kind is ambiguous, such as + + − +, which with one (minimum) error could be placed in either type + + − − or type + + + +.

Experience with Guttman scaling revealed a number of problems. First, few scales that appeared "good" could be constructed with more than four or five items because the amount of error with more items would be large. Second, the error would tend to be concentrated in the ambiguous error types. Third, scales constructed on a particular study, especially with common sample sizes of about one hundred cases, would not be as "good" in other studies. There was "shrinkage," or more error, particularly for the more extreme items. The issue of what to do with the placement of ambiguous items was suggested by an alternative analysis (Borgatta and Hays 1952): that the type + + − + was not best placed by minimum error, but should be included with the type + + + −, between the two minimum error locations. The reason for this may be grasped intuitively by noting that when two items are close to each other in proportion of positive responses, they are effectively interchangeable, and they are involved in the creation of the ambiguous error type. The common error is for respondents who are at the threshold of decision as to whether to answer positively or negatively, and they are most likely to make errors that create the ambiguous error types.

These observations about Guttman scaling lead to some obvious conclusions. First, the scaling model is actually contrary to common experience, as people are not classed in ordered types in general but presumably are infinitely differentiated even within a type. Second, the model is not productive of highly discriminating classes. Third, and this is possibly the pragmatic reason for doubting the utility of Guttman scaling, if the most appropriate place for locating nonscale or error types of the common ambiguous type is not by minimum error but between the two minimum error types, this is effectively the same as adding the number of positive responses, essentially reducing the procedure to a simple additive score. The remaining virtue of Guttman scaling in the logical placement of unambiguous errors must be balanced against other limitations, such as the requirement that items must be dichotomous, when much more information can be gotten with more detailed categories of response, usually with trivial additional cost in data collection time.

In contrast with Guttman scaling, simple addition of items into sum scores, carried out with an understanding of what is required for good measurement, is probably the most defensible and useful tool. For example, if something is to be measured, and there appear to be a number of relatively independent questions that can be used to ascertain the content, then those questions should be used to develop reliable measures. *Reliability* is measured in many ways, but consistency is the meaning usually intended, particularly internal consistency of the component items, that is, high intercorrelation among the items in a measure. Items can ask for dichotomous answers, but people can make more refined discriminations than simple yeses and nos, so use of multiple (ordered) categories of response increases the efficiency of items.

The question of whether the language as used has sufficient consistency to make refined quantitative discriminations does not appear to have been studied extensively, so a small data collection was carried out to provide the following example. Suppose people are asked to evaluate a set of categories with the question "How often does this happen?" The instructions state: "Put a vertical intersection where you think each category fits on the continuum, and then place the number under it. Categories 1 and 11 are fixed at the extremes for this example. If two categories have the same place, put the numbers one on top of the other. If the categories are out of order, put them in the order you think correct." A continuum was then provided with sixty-six spaces and the external positions of the first and the last indicated as the positions of 1. Always and 11. Never. The respondents were asked to locate the following remaining nine categories: 2. Almost always; 3. Very often; 4. Often; 5. Somewhat often; 6. Sometimes; 7. Seldom; 8. Very seldom; 9. Hardly ever; and 10. Almost never. It is not surprising that average responses on the continuum are well distributed, with percent locations respectively as 9, 15, 27, 36, 48, 65, 75, 86, and 93; the largest standard deviation for placement location is about 11 percent. Exercises with alternative quantitatively oriented questions and use of a series of six categories from Definitely Agree to Definitely Disagree provide similar evidence of consistency of meaning. In research, fewer than the eleven categories illustrated here are usually used, making the task of discrimination easier and faster for respondents. The point of emphasis is that questions can be designed to efficiently provide more information than simple dichotomous answers and thus facilitate construction of reliable scores.

MEASUREMENT IN THE REAL WORLD

Many variations exist on how to collect information in order to build effective measurement instruments. Similarly, there are alternatives on how to build the measuring instruments. Often practical considerations must be taken into account, such as the amount of time available for interviews, restraints placed on what kinds of content can be requested, lack of privacy when collecting the information, and other circumstances.

With the progressive technology of computers and word processors, the reduced dependence of researchers on assistants, clerks, and secretaries has greatly facilitated research data handling and analysis. Some changes, like Computer Assisted Telephone Interviewing (CATI) may be seen as assisting data collection, but in general the data collection aspects of research are still those that require most careful attention and supervision. The design of research, however, still is often an ad hoc procedure with regard to the definition of variables. Variables are often created under the primitive assumption that all one needs to do is say: "The way I am going to measure XXX is by responses to the following question." This is a procedure of dubious worth, since building knowledge about the measurement characteristics of the variables to be used should be in advance of the research and is essential to the interpretation of findings. It is even more delusory to not measure at all and assume that one may do an analysis intuitively, without measuring variables, on the assumption that such a procedure somehow better corresponds to reality.

The development of well-measured variables in sociology and the social sciences is essential to the advancement of knowledge. Knowledge about how good measurement can be carried out has advanced, particularly in the post–World War II period, but it has not diffused and become sufficiently commonplace in the social science disciplines. In fact, some still believe that it is possible to dismiss the need for systematic empirical research using good measures by stating that attempts to do such research have not been productive, thus more intuitive or qualitative procedures are more appropriate. Much sociological research does not make a sufficient investment to produce the level of knowledge that is possible. However, it is difficult to comprehend how substituting no measurement or poor measurement for the best measurement that sociologists can devise can produce more accurate knowledge. Examples of the untenable position have possibly decreased over time, but they still occur. Note for example: "Focus on quantitative methods rewards *reliable* (i.e. repeatable) methods. Reliability is a valuable asset, but it is only one facet of the value of the study. In most studies, reliability is purchased at the price of lessened attention to theory, validity, relevance, etc." (Scheff 1991). Quite the contrary, concern with measurement and quantification is concern with theory, validity, and relevance!

(SEE ALSO: *Levels of Analysis; Measurement Instruments; Nonparametric Statistics; Reliability, Validity*)

REFERENCES

Borgatta, Edgar F. 1968 "My Student, the Purist: A Lament." *Sociological Quarterly* 9:29–34.

Borgatta, Edgar F., and David G. Hays 1952 "Some Limitations on the Arbitrary Classifications of Non-Scale Response Patterns in a Guttman Scale." *Public Opinion Quarterly* 16:273–291.

Duncan, Otis Dudley 1984 *Notes on Social Measurement.* New York: Russell Sage Foundation.

Kendall, Maurice G. 1948 *Rank Correlation Methods.* London: Griffin and Company.

Nunnally, Jum C. 1978 *Psychometric Theory.* New York: McGraw-Hill.

Riley, Matilda White, John W. Riley, Jr., and Jackson Toby 1954 *Sociological Studies in Scale Analysis.* New Brunswick, N.J.: Rutgers University Press.

Scheff, Thomas J. 1991 "Is There a Bias in *ASR* Article Selection." *Footnotes* 19, no. 2 (February):5.

Stevens, S. S., ed. 1966 *Handbook of Experimental Psychology.* New York: John Wiley.

EDGAR F. BORGATTA

MEASUREMENT INSTRUMENTS

Standardized instruments for measuring key concepts are vital tools for sociological research. As in other branches of science, new instruments tend to produce a flowering of research focused on the newly measurable concept. The Social Distance Scale, first published in 1928 by Bogardus, illustrates that process. Since then a number of excellent instruments have appeared. Many of them are abstracted or reproduced in compendia such as *Sociological Measurement* (Bonjean, Hill, and McLemore 1967), *Handbook of Research Design and Social Measurement* (Miller 1991), *Measures of Occupational Attitudes and Occupational Characteristics* (Robinson, Athanasiou, and Head 1969), *Women and Women's Issues* (Beere 1979), *Handbook of Scales for Research in Crime and Delinquency* (Brodsky and Smitherman 1983), and *Handbook of Family Measurement Techniques* (Touliatos, Perlmutter, and Straus 1990). The current state of instrumentation in sociology, however, is not as robust as these titles might suggest. The data presented below indicate that the development of new measurement instruments has not kept pace with the growth in sociological research. Moreover, the reliability and validity of most of the instruments have not been established. Explanations for these problems will be suggested.

DEFINITION

Measurement instrument as used in this article is synonymous with terms such as *scale* (including Likert, Thurstone, Guttman, and Semantic Differential scales), *index, test, factor score, scoring system* (when used as the indicators for indexes measuring social interaction variables; see Bales 1950), and *latent variables* constructed by use of a structural equation modeling program. The defining feature of each of these types of instruments is that each is "a measure which combines the values of several variables or items [also called indicators, observations, events, questions] into a composite measure . . . used to predict or gauge some underlying continuum which can only be partially measured by any single item or variable" (Nie et al. 1978, p. 529).

ADVANTAGES OF MULTIPLE-INDICATOR INSTRUMENTS

Multiple-indicator measures are emphasized because they are more likely to be valid than single-indicator measures. It is true that a single good item may be enough and thirty bad ones are useless. However, there are reasons why multiple-indicator measures are more likely to be valid. One reason is that most phenomena of interest to sociology have multiple facets that can be adequately represented only by use of multiple indicators. A single question, for example, is unlikely to adequately represent the multiple facets of "community allegiance." At the macrosociological level, a single demographic characteristic, such as the rate of geographic mobility, is not likely to adequately represent the several aspects involved in "community integration."

A second reason for greater confidence in multiple-indicator measurement instruments occurs because of the inevitable risk of error in selecting indicators. If a single indicator is used and there is a conceptual error in formulating the indicator or in scoring it, hypotheses that are tested by using that measure will not be supported even if they are true. However, when a multiple-indicator instrument is used, Straus and Baron (1990) found the adverse effect is limited to a relatively small reduction in validity. In a fifteen-item scale, for example, a defective indicator is only 6.6 percent of the total and therefore will yield findings that are similar to those which would be obtained if all fifteen items were correct. For these and other reasons, a suggested rule of thumb is that three indicators are the minimum needed to reduce the risk involved in staking everything on a single indicator.

Multiple indicators are also desirable because the internal consistency reliability of an instrument as measured by the alpha coefficient (Cronbach 1970) is a function of the number of indicators in the measure and the correlation between them. The more indicators and the higher their correlation with each other, the higher the alpha. If fewer than three items are used, it is almost impossible to achieve a high level of reliability. Reliability needs to be as high as possible because it sets an upper limit on validity. A validity coefficient cannot be greater than the square root of the reliability (Cronbach 1970).

CURRENT STATUS AND TRENDS IN SOCIOLOGICAL MEASUREMENT

There is a rich literature by sociologists on the theory and the procedures needed to construct measures, yet relatively few standardized instruments have been constructed using these methods and subsequently made available for general use. As a result, looking for a standardized, reliable, and valid instrument to measure a sociological concept is usually frustrating.

To investigate the extent of this problem, all the empirical studies published in two major U.S. sociological journals (*American Sociological Review* and *American Journal of Sociology*) and in a methodological journal (*Sociological Methods and Re-*

search) were examined for 1979 and 1989. The relative neglect of measurement instruments can be inferred from the finding that none of the 185 articles (which included articles in a journal devoted to methodology) had as one of its main purposes the presentation of a new measurement instrument. Second, despite the value of multiple indicators, two-thirds of the 185 studies failed to use measures with at least three indicators. Third, even among the third that used multiple-indicator instruments, 89 percent failed to report reliability (77 percent if one adds the 9 percent that reported factor analyses and the 4 percent who used a structural equation model program). Ninety-six percent reported no information on validity. Fourth, there was no significant improvement in respect to these three issues between 1979 and 1989. Finally, the findings from an earlier study of measures of family characteristics (Straus 1964) are very similar, which suggests that there has been no increase in the proportion of multiple-indicator instruments for about twenty-five years.

The inadequate attention in sociology to developing standardized and validated measures contrasts strongly with other sciences. Nobel Prizes have been awarded for new measures in economics and in the physical and biological sciences (Pool 1989). In psychology, the development of new instruments is a recognized and esteemed specialization. Journals such as *Educational and Psychological Measurement* and *Journal of Consulting and Clinical Psychology* publish many articles describing new or improved instruments. A major committee of the American Psychological Association is charged with developing and updating the *Standards for Educational and Psychological Tests.* Courses on psychological measurement are found in many psychology departments. In sociology, as indicated above, there are no journals that encourage articles describing new instruments and such articles are rare in any sociological journal (including journals devoted to methods), the American Sociological Association has never had a committee concerned with standards of measurement, and courses in sociological measurement are rare.

REASONS FOR UNDERDEVELOPMENT OF SOCIOLOGICAL MEASURES

The limited production of standard and validated measures of social characteristics may be attributed to a number of causes. One of these is probably a lack of time and other resources for instrument development, validation studies, and replications to cross-validate. Other likely impediments are in the reward structures, opportunities, and constraints of the discipline. These can be illustrated by a comparison with psychology. First, in psychology, there is an institutionalized reward structure for measure development. Journals devoted to psychological measures and the lack of such journals in sociology were noted above. Moreover, there is a large market for psychological tests, and several firms specialize in publishing such tests. It is a multimillion-dollar industry, and authors of tests can earn substantial royalties. Thus, sociology lacks the symbolic and economic reward system that underlies the institutionalization of test development as a major specialization in psychology.

A second reason for the underdevelopment of sociological measures is a situational constraint inherent in much sociological research, especially survey research. Sociologists often must squeeze the measurement of a dozen or so variables into a single hour or half-hour interview. Practitioners, on the other hand, often can use longer, and therefore more reliable, instruments because their clients have a greater stake in providing adequate data and will tolerate undergoing two or more hours of testing. The constraint on the number of survey questions that can be devoted to measuring each variable also may help explain why so few sociologists report reliability coefficients: when the scale is based on only two to four items, the coefficients are likely to be low.

THE FUTURE OF SOCIOLOGICAL MEASURES

There are grounds for optimism and grounds for concern about the future of sociological measurement instruments. The grounds for concern are, first, that most sociological concepts are measured by a single interview question. Second, even when a multiple-indicator instrument is used, it is rarely on the basis of empirical evidence of reliability and validity. Third, both Bonjean, Hill, and McLemore (1967) and Miller (1991) found that the typical measure developed by a sociologist is never used in another study. One can speculate that this hiatus in the cumulative nature of research occurs because of the lack of evidence of reliability or validity, and because authors rarely provide sufficient information to facilitate use of the instrument by others.

The grounds for optimism are to be found in the sizable and slowly growing number of standardized instruments, such as those to measure socioeconomic status (Nam and Powers 1983), juvenile delinquency (Nye and Short 1957), small group interaction (Bales 1950), personality (Borgatta 1964), family interaction (Straus 1990), and alienation (Seeman 1959). The growth of applied and clinical sociology is also a ground for optimism, but one with a certain irony because basic researchers usually believe that they are the guardians of quality in science. In respect to measurement, however, sociological practitioners tend to demand higher-quality instruments than do basic researchers because the consequences of using an inadequate measure are more serious. When a basic researcher uses an instrument with low reliability or validity, it can lead to a Type II error, that is, failing to accept a true hypothesis. This may result in theoretical confusion or a paper not being published (Spanier 1976); but when a practitioner uses an invalid or unreliable instrument, the worst case scenario can involve injury to a client organization or person. Consequently, practitioners tend to demand more evidence of reliability and validity than do basic researchers. As a result, sociologists in applied fields such as family therapy and evaluation research tend to produce and make available a wider choice of more adequate measures. Finally, it can be hoped that an increasing number of sociologists will heed the advice of Blalock (1979, 1982), who has emphasized that inconsistent findings and failure to find empirical support for sound theories in sociological research may be due to lack of reliable and valid means of operationalizing key concepts in the theories being tested.

(SEE ALSO: *Measurement; Reliability; Validity*)

REFERENCES

Bales, Robert F. 1950 *Interaction Process Analysis: A Method for the Study of Small Groups.* Cambridge, Mass.: Addison-Wesley.

Beere, Carole A. 1979 *Women and Women's Issues: A Handbook of Tests and Measures.* San Francisco: Jossey-Bass.

Blalock, Hubert M. 1979 "Measurement and Conceptualization Problems: The Major Obstacle to Integrating Theory and Research." *American Sociological Review* 44:881–894.

——— 1982 *Conceptualization and Measurement in the Social Sciences.* Newbury Park, Calif.: Sage.

Bogardus, Emory S. 1928 *Immigration and Race Attitudes.* Boston: Heath.

Bonjean, Charles M., Richard J. Hill, and S. Dale McLemore 1967 *Sociological Measurement: An Inventory of Scales and Indices.* San Francisco: Chandler.

Borgatta, Edgar F. 1964 "A Very Short Test of Personality: The Behavioral Self-Rating (BSR) Form." *Psychological Reports* 14:275–284.

Brodsky, Stanley L., and H. O'Neal Smitherman 1983 *Handbook of Scales for Research in Crime and Delinquency.* New York: Plenum.

Cronbach, Lee J. 1970 *Essentials of Psychological Testing.* New York: Harper and Row.

Hodge, Robert W., Paul M. Siegel, and Peter H. Rossi 1964 "Occupational Prestige in the United States, 1925–1963." *American Journal of Sociology* 70:286–302.

Miller, Delbert C. 1991 *Handbook of Research Design and Social Measurement.* Newbury Park, Calif.: Sage.

Nam, Charles B., and Mary G. Powers 1983 *The Socioeconomic Approach to Status Measurement.* Houston, Tex.: Cap and Gown Press.

Nie, Norman H., C. Hadlai Hull, Jean G. Jenkins, Karin Steinbrenner, and Dale H. Bent 1978 *SPSS: Statistical Package for the Social Sciences.* New York: McGraw-Hill.

Nye, F. Ivan, and James F. Short 1957 "Scaling Delinquent Behavior." *American Sociological Review* 22:326–331.

Pool, Robert 1989 "Basic Measurements Lead to Physics Nobel." *Science* 246:327–328.

Robinson, John P., Robert Athanasiou, and Kendra B. Head 1969 *Measures of Occupational Attitudes and Occupational Characteristics.* Ann Arbor, Mich.: Institute for Social Research.

Seeman, Melvin 1959 "On the Meaning of Alienation." *American Sociological Review* 24:783–791.

Spanier, Graham B. 1976 "Measuring Dyadic Adjustment: New Scales for Assessing the Quality of Marriage and Similar Dyads." *Journal of Marriage and Family* 38:15–28.

Straus, Murray A. 1964 "Measuring Families." In Harold T. Christenson, ed., *Handbook of Marriage and the Family.* Chicago: Rand McNally.

——— 1990 "The Conflict Tactics Scale and Its Critics: An Evaluation and New Data on Validity and Reliability." In Murray A. Straus and Richard J. Gelles, eds., *Physical Violence in American Families: Risk Factors and Adaptations to Violence in 8,145 Families.* New Brunswick, N.J.: Transaction Press.

———, and Larry Baron 1990 "The Strength of Weak Indicators: A Response to Gilles, Brown, Geletta, and Dalecki." *Sociological Quarterly* 31:619–624.

———, and Bruce W. Brown 1978 *Family Measurement Techniques,* 2nd ed. Minneapolis: University of Minnesota Press.

Touliatos, John, David Perlmutter, and Murray A. Straus 1990 *Handbook of Family Measurement Techniques,* 3rd ed. Newbury Park, Calif.: Sage.

MURRAY A. STRAUS
BARBARA WAUCHOPE

MEASURES OF ASSOCIATION When each of a set of cases is classified into the categories of two variables simultaneously, the result is known as a *cross-classification table.* For example, when each of a set of manufacturing plants (the cases) is simultaneously classified by product and plant size (the variables), the result is a cross-classification table in which products (e.g., textiles, electronics, automobiles) might be represented in rows, and size (e.g., less than 1,000 employees, 1,000 to 1,999 employees, 2,000 to 2,999 employees) in columns. The usual purpose of such a cross-classification table is to examine the association, or lack of association, between the two variables in the cross-classification. In this instance, the purpose might be to see if plants manufacturing certain types of products are generally larger (have more employees) than plants manufacturing other types of products.

Two variables in a cross-classification table are said to be *statistically independent* if the percentage distribution over the rows is the same for each column, or, alternatively and equivalently, if the percentage distribution over the columns is the same for each row. For example, in the cross classification of manufacturing plants by size and product, these two variables would be statistically independent for the cases in hand if the percent of manufacturing plants in each size category is the same for all product categories. When two variables are statistically independent, there is no *association* between them. Otherwise stated, the row variable provides no clue to the distribution of cases on the column variable, and the column variable provides no clue to the distribution on the row variable. In contrast, when one variable does provide a clue of some kind to the distribution on the other variable, that would imply some degree of association. But it should be clear that finer distinctions can be made than simply no association versus some association, and measures of association have been designed to represent the *degree* of association between variables. While all such measures have this common purpose, and they are typically normed so they vary in absolute value from 0 (no association) to 1 (perfect association), they differ in the way they measure how well a variable provides a clue to the distribution of another. If statistical independence holds for a cross-classification table, all measures of association will indicate 0 association. And if all cases in each row fall into one and only one column unique to that row, all measures of association will indicate perfect association. But for a given cross-classification table in which statistical independence does not hold and in which the cases in each row are not concentrated in one and only one column, different measures of association will indicate different degrees of association because each measures the degree of association in a slightly different way.

While the fundamental concept of association between variables was probably intuitively understood long before there were statisticians, the idea of measuring the degree of association between variables was not developed until late in the nineteenth century, following the development of the coefficient of correlation. A number of such measures have now been developed; indeed, so many different measures of association are available for use that the choice among them is sometimes confusing. A comprehensive review of the measures of association available by the middle of the twentieth century has been provided by Goodman and Kruskal (1954, 1959, 1963, 1972). Some published papers and statistical textbooks also provide a summary of many measures of association (see, e.g., Blalock 1979; Carroll 1961; Costner 1965; Freeman 1965; Loether and McTavish 1974; Mueller, Schuessler, and Costner 1977).

Almost all of the existing measures of association follow one of two master formulas for measuring association. One of these master formulas is based on a statistic known as chi-square, which depends on the discrepancies between the observed joint frequency distribution of two variables, and the joint frequency distribution that would obtain if the variables were statistically independent. When the observed joint frequency distribution is exactly the same as the distribution that would represent perfect statistical independence, chi-square is 0. As the observed joint frequency distribution departs more and more from the distribution that represents statistical independence, chi-square moves farther and farther away from 0. But the chi-square statistic was not developed as a measure of association between variables, and the statistic itself does not serve well as such a measure because (a) it has not been normed to vary in absolute value between 0 and 1 and (b) the magnitude of chi-square for a cross-classification table depends not simply on the degree of association but also on other features, including the number of cases. But when the chi-square statistic is normed to minimize the influence of features other than the degree of association and so it will range from 0 to 1, it can serve as a numerical index of the degree of association exhibited in a cross-classification table. Since there are several possible ways of norming the chi-square statistic for this purpose, there are several measures that are based on this "master formula." An example of a measure of association based on this master formula is Tschuprow's T^2:

$$T^2 = \frac{X^2}{N\,(r-1)\,(c-1)} \tag{1}$$

$$\text{where } X^2 = \text{chi-square} = \sum \frac{(O_{ij} - E_{ij})^2}{E_{ij}}$$

where O_{ij} = the observed frequency in the cell at the intersection of the ith row and the jth column

E_{ij} = the frequency in the cell at the intersection of the ith row and the jth column that would be expected if the two variables were statistically independent

N = sample size, or the number of cases cross-classified in the table

r = the number of rows in the table

c = the number of columns in the table.

Other measures based on this master formula typically use a slightly different norming device. For example, Cramer's V^2 differs from Tschuprow's T^2 in that the former uses the minimum of $(r - 1)$ or $(c - 1)$ rather than the square root of their product (see Loether and McTavish 1974).

In a departure from the traditional chi-square–based measures of association, Jae-on Kim (1984) has devised a measure of association that reflects the proportional reduction in "uncertainty." Very briefly, the measure is parallel to those based on the second master formula, discussed below, and it reflects the reduction in uncertainty in an observed table as compared to a table in which statistical independence holds. Kim's measure provides a normed measure of association closely linked to log-linear models designed to explore contingency structures among several variables simultaneously (see Goodman 1970, 1971, 1972).

The second master formula describes the proportion of the possible reduction in prediction error that can be achieved by a specified prediction rule—that is, a rule for predicting one variable from knowledge of the other (Costner 1965). Such measures are sometimes referred to as "PRE measures"—that is, proportional reduction in error measures. Expressed in general form, this master formula is

$$PRE = \frac{E_1 - E_2}{E_1} \qquad (2)$$

where PRE = the association between variables measured by the proportional reduction in prediction error

E_1 = prediction error using a prediction rule that uses only knowledge of the distribution of the predicted variable—that is, *without* knowledge of the associated or predictor variable

E_2 = prediction error using a prediction rule that does use knowledge of the predictor variable.

The several measures of association that conform to this master formula are defined by a specification of (a) how prediction error is measured and (b) the two prediction rules (with and without knowledge of the predictor variable). Such measures of association, of which the square of the correlation coefficient (r^2) is the most widely cited, also include measures of association specifically for categorical variables (e.g., Goodman and Kruskal's lambda measures and Goodman and Kruskal's tau measures) and specifically for ordinal variables (e.g., Goodman and Kruskal's gamma [Goodman and Kruskal 1954]). Such measures are also discussed in Loether and McTavish (1974) and in Mueller, Schuessler, and Costner (1977).

The proportional reduction in error interpretation for some measures of association is based on a prediction rule that might not seem to be intuitively "natural." For example, the PRE interpretation of gamma requires that one consider the prediction of order for all *pairs* of cases that involve no ties rather than the prediction of a value for each case. The PRE interpretation of the Goodman and Kruskal tau measures is based not on the prediction of a specific outcome for each case but on the prediction of a distribution of outcomes for a set of cases. In some circumstances the reason for desiring a measure of association between variables may suggest the kind of prediction rule that is most appropriate. More commonly, a prediction rule of a particular form is not implied by the reasoning that leads one to explore the degree of association between variables.

Measures of association between variables are commonly used to summarize how closely two variables are linked or the degree to which they vary together. The degree of association in itself is not useful for determining the *reason* two variables are linked or the processes underlying their covariation. Contrary to common belief, a high degree of association between variables does not imply that one has an effect on another. A high degree of association between variables may also occur because each is influenced by the same cause, or because both reflect the same underlying phenomenon. Understanding the reasons for the covariation between variables can be enhanced by including several measures in the analysis, and measures of association are especially useful in describing what happens to an association when other variables are held constant.

(SEE ALSO: *Correlation and Regression Analysis; Nonparametric Statistics; Tabular Analysis*)

REFERENCES

Blalock, Hubert M., Jr. 1979 *Social Statistics,* 2nd ed. New York: McGraw-Hill.

Carroll, John B. 1961 "The Nature of the Data, or How to Choose a Correlation Coefficient." *Psychometrica* 26:347–372.

Costner, Herbert L. 1965 "Criteria for Measures of Association." *American Sociological Review* 30:341–353.

Freeman, Linton C. 1965 *Elementary Applied Statistics: For Students in Behavioral Science.* New York: Wiley.

Goodman, Leo A. 1970 "The Multivariate Analysis of Qualitative Data: Interactions Among Multiple Classifications." *Journal of the American Statistical Association* 65:226–257.

———1971 "Partitioning of Chi-square, Analysis of Marginal Contingency Tables and Estimation of Expected Frequencies in Multidimensional Contingency Tables." *Journal of the American Statistical Association* 66:339–344.

———1972 "A General Model for the Analysis of

Surveys." *American Journal of Sociology* 77:1035–1086.

Goodman, Leo A., and William H. Kruskal 1954 "Measures of Association for Cross Classifications." *Journal of the American Statistical Association* 49:732–764.

———1959 "Measures of Association for Cross Classifications: II. Further Discussion and References." *Journal of the American Statistical Association* 54:123–163.

———1963 "Measures of Association for Cross Classifications: III. Approximate Sampling Theory." *Journal of the American Statistical Association* 58:310–364.

———1972 "Measures of Association for Cross Classifications: IV. Simplification of Asymptotic Variances." *Journal of the American Statistical Association* 67:415–421.

Kim, Jae-on 1984 "PRU Measures of Association for Contingency Table Analysis." *Sociological Methods & Research* 13:3–44.

Loether, Herman J., and Donald G. McTavish 1974 *Descriptive Statistics for Sociologists: An Introduction.* Boston: Allyn and Bacon.

Mueller, John H., Karl F. Schuessler, and Herbert L. Costner 1977 *Statistical Reasoning in Sociology.* Boston: Houghton Mifflin.

HERBERT L. COSTNER

MEDICAL–INDUSTRIAL COMPLEX

The concept of the medical–industrial complex was first introduced in the 1971 book, *The American Health Empire* (Ehrenreich and Ehrenreich 1971) by Health-PAC. The medical–industrial complex (MIC) refers to the health industry, which is comprised of the multibillion dollar congeries of enterprises including doctors, hospitals, nursing homes, insurance companies, drug manufacturers, hospital supply and equipment companies, real estate and construction businesses, health systems consulting and accounting firms, and banks. As employed by the Ehrenreichs, the concept conveys the idea that an important (if not the primary) function of the health care system in the United States is business, that is, to make profits, with two other secondary functions of research and education.

Since that time, a number of authors have examined the medical–industrial complex: Navarro (1976, p. 76, 80), Relman (1980), Waitzkin (1983), Estes et al. (1984), Wohl (1984), McKinlay and Stoeckle (1988), and Salmon (1990). Himmelstein and Woolhandler (1990) argue that health care facilitates profit making by (1) improving the productivity (health) of workers; (2) ideologically ensuring the social stability needed to support production and profit; and (3) providing major opportunities for investment and profit (p. 16). The last function, profit, is now "the driving force," as health care has fully "come into the age of capitalist production" (p. 17).

Arnold Relman (1980), Harvard medical professor and editor of the *New England Journal of Medicine,* was the first physician to employ the concept, observing that recent developments in health care, particularly the corporatization of medicine, are a challenge to physician authority, autonomy, and even legitimacy for the doctors who become health care industry owners. Ginzberg (1988), Gray (1983; Gray and McNerney 1986), and others (Starr 1982; Estes et al. 1984; Light 1986; Himmelstein and Woolhandler 1990; Bodenheimer 1990; Bergthold 1990) have written about the monetarization, corporatization, and proprietarization of "health" care. By the mid-1980s, the author of a book appearing with the title *The Medical Industrial Complex* (Wohl 1984) did not see the need to define it but, rather, began with "the story of the explosive growth of . . . corporate medicine" and focused on "medical moguls" and monopoly and prescription for profit.

The health-care industry has not only contributed to improvements in the health status of the population and protected a plurality of vested interests but also strengthened and preserved the private sector. In U.S. society, the medical–industrial complex functions economically as a source of growth, accumulation of profit, investment opportunity, and employment (Estes et al. 1984, pp. 56–70). It also contributes to the human capital needed for productivity and profit, an able-bodied work force whose work is not sapped by illness (Rodberg and Stevenson 1977).

STRUCTURE OF THE HEALTH-CARE INDUSTRY

Industry Components. Today's medical–industrial complex consists of more than a dozen major components: hospitals; nursing homes; physicians (salaried and fee-for-service); home health agencies; supply and equipment manufacturers; drug companies; insurance companies; new managed-care organizations (HMOs, PPOs, IPAs); specialized centers (urgi, surgi, dialysis); hospices; nurses and all other health-care workers; administrators, marketers, lawyers, planners; and research organizations. In addition to these entities, thousands of other organizations are springing up in long-term care (e.g., case management, respite care, homemaker/chore, independent living centers) and other services for the disabled and aging including social services that have incorporated health-care components such as senior centers (Estes and Wood 1986; Wood and Estes 1988).

Changes in the Structure of the Industry. There were a number of significant changes in the structure of the health-care industry during the 1970s and 1980s, including (1) rapid growth and consolidation of the industry into larger organizations; (2) horizontal integration; (3) vertical integration; (4) change in ownership from government to private, nonprofit and for-profit organizations; and (5) diversification and corporate restructuring (Starr 1982; McKinlay and Stoeckle 1988; White 1990). These changes occurred across the different sectors, which are dominated by large hospital and insurance/managed care organizations.

Rapid Growth and Consolidation. Health care has long been moved from its cottage industry stage with small individual hospitals and solo physician practitioners to large corporate enterprises. The types of health-care corporations are diverse and growing in terms of size and complexity. Hospitals are the largest sector of the health-care industry, accounting for 43 percent of total personal health expenditures (U.S. Department of Commerce [U.S. DOC] 1990). While the growth rate in hospital expenditures was increasing rapidly, the number of community hospitals actually declined from 5,746 in 1972 to 5,533 in 1988 (−3.6%) (American Hospital Association [AHA] 1989) (see Table 1). In 1986 alone, 71 hospitals closed, nearly twice the average annual rate for the previous five-year period. These reductions were primarily in small rural hospitals (AHA 1987). The number of hospital beds also began to decline to 947,000 in 1988 (AHA 1989).

As hospitals are reducing in numbers, they are increasing in size, from an average of 167 to 171 beds between 1978 and 1988 (AHA 1989). The decline in growth in the hospital sector has been accompanied by a decline in average occupancy

TABLE 1
Community Hospitals and Beds by Ownership, 1970, 1980, and 1987

	1972		*1978*		*1988*	
Type of Ownership	*Hospitals*	*Beds*	*Hospitals*	*Beds*	*Hospitals*	*Beds*
Non-Profit	3,301 (57%)	617,000 (70%)	3,339 (57%)	683,000 (70%)	3,242 (59%)	668,000 (71%)
Proprietary	738 (13%)	57,000 (7%)	732 (13%)	81,000 (8%)	790 (14%)	104,000 (11%)
Government	1,707 (30%)	205,000 (23%)	1,778 (30%)	211,000 (22%)	1,501 (27%)	175,000 (18%)
Total	5,746	879,000	5,851	975,000	5,533	947,000

SOURCE: Adapted from American Hospital Association. *Hospital Statistics, 1989–90 Edition.* Chicago: AHA, 1989.
NOTE: Excludes federal psychiatric tuberculosis and other hospitals.

rates from 74 percent in 1978 to 66 percent, a 9 percent decline in admissions, and a 13 percent decrease in inpatient days during the 1978–1988 period (AHA 1989). Although the community hospitals are declining, the number of specialty hospitals, especially psychiatric facilities, has been growing rapidly. Between 1987 and 1988 alone, 47 new investor-owned psychiatric hospitals opened, for a total of 545, and 13 new rehabilitation hospitals with over 1,600 beds were under construction (U.S. DOC 1990).

Nursing homes represent 9 percent of total U.S. health-care expenditures. Nursing homes grew rapidly in numbers of facilities and beds after the passage of Medicaid and Medicare legislation. In 1985, there were approximately 19,000 facilities in the United States providing care for 1.5 million residents (U.S. National Center for Health Statistics 1989). More recently, their overall growth has leveled off, so that growth is not keeping pace with the aging of the population (Harrington, Swan, and Grant 1988).

Home health-care agencies have also grown rapidly since the introduction of Medicare and Medicaid in 1965. In 1980 there were an estimated 16 million home health-care visits provided to 726,000 individuals (U.S. DOC 1990). By 1988, an estimated 37 million visits were provided to 1.3 million individuals by about 11,000 home health-care agencies (U.S. DOC 1990). Expenditures for these services were climbing about 20 percent per year in the latter 1980s (U.S. DOC 1990).

Relatively new and influential corporate forces in the health industry are the managed-care organizations such as health maintenance organizations (HMOs), preferred provider organizations (PPOs), and independent practice associations (IPAs). There has been a large growth in HMOs, which provide health-care services on the basis of fixed monthly charges per enrollee. In 1984 there were only 337 HMOs with 17 million enrollees. By 1988 there were 31 million members enrolled in 643 HMOs (Interstudy 1989). By 1989 there were somewhat fewer HMOs, but enrollment was expected to reach 33 million (U.S. DOC 1990). There have been a number of mergers and acquisitions among HMOs, and some nonprofit HMO corporations have established profit-making operations (Salmon 1990, p. 70). HMOs have rapidly become national firms, so that, by 1988, 49 percent of all HMOs were national firms, with 59 percent of the total HMO enrollment in the United States (Shadle and Hunter 1988).

PPOs are modified HMOs that provide health care for lower costs when the enrollee uses participating providers who are paid on the basis of negotiated or discount rates (U.S. DOC 1990). In 1988 there were about 620 PPOs with about 36 million members. The total number of enrollees in HMOs and PPOs (managed-care programs) was estimated to be 25 percent of the population in the late 1980s, compared with only 3 percent in 1970 (U.S. DOC 1990).

Private health insurance companies are also one of the largest sectors of the health industry. The United States has over 1,000 for-profit, commercial, health insurers and 85 Blue Cross and Blue Shield plans (Feldstein 1988). These private insurance organizations, along with HMOs, PPOs, and other third-party payers, paid for 32 percent ($175 billion out of $540 billion) of the total expenditures in 1988 (U.S. Office of National Cost Estimates [U.S. ONCE] 1990).

Physician practice patterns changed rapidly in the 1970s and 1980s, moving toward larger partnerships and group practices. In 1969 18 percent of physicians were in group practices (with three or more physicians), compared with 28 percent in 1984 (Andersen and Mullner 1989). It is estimated that about 75 percent of all practicing physicians are part of at least one qualified health management organization (U.S. DOC 1990). Thus, physicians are moving toward larger and more complex forms of group practice. In addition, physicians are actively involved in the ownership and operation of many of the newer forms of HMOs, PPOs, IPAs, and other types of corporate health care activities (Relman 1980; Iglehart 1989).

Horizontal Integration. The major changes in corporate arrangements have been the development of multiorganizational systems through horizontal integration. The formation of multihospital systems has grown tremendously within the industry. Ermann and Gable (1984) estimated there were 202 multihospital systems controlling 1,405 hospitals and 293,000 beds in 1975 (or 24 percent of the hospitals and 31 percent of all beds). In 1988, there were 303 multihospital systems controlling 438,433 beds (Table 2). Thus, in 1988 such multihospital systems controlled 38 percent of all hospitals and 35 percent of all hospital beds. This represents a 50 percent increase in the number of multihospital systems between 1975 and 1988.

Multihospital corporations are becoming consolidated, with large companies controlling the largest share of the overall hospital market. In 1986 the five largest nonprofit hospital systems controlled about 13 percent of the hospitals and 17 percent of the nonprofit beds, while the five largest for-profit systems controlled 57 percent of the for-profit hospitals and 71 percent of the for-profit beds (White 1990). Most of the recent increase in these systems has been the result of purchasing or leasing existing facilities and mergers of organizations, rather than of construction of new facilities.

Vertical Integration. Vertical integration involves the development of organizations with different levels and types of organizations and services. One such type of integration has involved the linkage of hospitals and health maintenance organizations and/or insurance companies. For example, National Medical Enterprises owns hospitals, nursing homes, psychiatric hospitals, recovery centers, and rehabilitation hospitals (Federation of American Health Systems [FAHS] 1990). Academic medical center hospitals have relationships with proprietary hospital firms (seventeen in 1985), according to Berliner and Burlage (1990, p. 97). Many of the major investor-owned health care corporations are diversified, with many different types of health care operations.

Changes in Ownership. During the 1970s and 1980s the organizational side of health care witnessed a surge in the growth of for-profit health-care delivery corporations, initially hospitals and later extending to other types of health organizations. The ownership of hospitals shifted from public to nonprofit and for-profit organizations (see Table 1). The percentage of government-owned community hospitals dropped from 30 percent of the total community hospitals in 1972 to 27 percent in 1988, but the percentage of total beds declined from 23 percent to 18 percent between 1972 and 1988 (AHA 1989). In contrast, the percentage of proprietary facilities increased from 13 percent to 14 percent, and the percentage of beds increased from 7 percent to 11 percent, of the total during the 1972–1988 period. The percentage of total U.S. hospitals owned by nonprofit corporations increased from 57 percent to 59 percent during the period, while the percentage of beds was 70 percent in 1972 and 71 percent in 1988 (AHA 1989). While these changes reflected only modest overall shifts, recent growth within multihospital systems was largely proprie-

TABLE 2
Hospitals and Beds in Multihospital Health-Care Systems, by Type of Ownership and Control

	Total Not-for-Profit		*Investor-Owned*		*All Systems*	
Type of Ownership	*Hospitals*	*Beds*	*Hospitals*	*Beds*	*Hospitals*	*Beds*
Owned, leased or Sponsored	1,135 (44%)	266,906 (61%)	865 (34%)	114,090 (26%)	2,000 (78%)	380,996 (87%)
Contracted-managed	254 (10%)	25,724 (6%)	318 (12%)	31,713 (7%)	571 (22%)	57,437 (13%)
Total	1,389 (54%)	292,630 (67%)	1,183 (46%)	145,803 (33%)	2,572 (100%)	438,433 (100%)

SOURCE: Adapted from American Hospital Association. *Hospital Statistics, 1989–90 Edition.* Chicago: AHA, 1989 Table 3, B3.

tary (White 1990). Of the total 303 multihospital systems in 1988, investor-owned systems controlled 46 percent of the hospitals and 33 percent of the beds, compared with nonprofit facilities (AHA 1987).

Multinational health enterprises are an increasingly important part of the medical–industrial complex, with investor-owned and investor-operated companies active not only in the United States but also in many foreign countries. In 1990 a report showed 97 companies reporting ownership or operation of 1,492 hospitals with 182,644 beds in the United States and 100 hospitals with 11,974 beds in foreign countries (FAHS 1990, pp. 16–17). The four largest for-profit chains owned two-thirds of the foreign hospitals (Berliner and Regan 1990). The effects of these developments in foreign countries and the profit-potential of these operations are not clearly understood (Berliner and Regan 1990).

Nursing homes have the largest share of proprietary ownership in the health field (except for the drug and supply industries). In 1985 some 75 percent of all nursing homes were profit-making, 20 percent were nonprofit, and 5 percent were government-run (NCHS 1989). By 1985 chains owned 41 percent of the total nursing home facilities and 49 percent of the nursing home beds (NCHS 1989).

While the largest HMO in the United States is a nonprofit corporation (Kaiser Permanente), the largest growth has been in large investor-owned HMO corporations. By 1988 a total of 84 percent of the national HMOs were for-profit, and they had 54 percent of the total national HMO enrollment, compared with the nonprofit firms (InterStudy 1989).

Investor-owned corporations have also established themselves in many other areas of health care, ranging from primary-care clinics to specialized referral centers and home health care. The number of proprietary home health corporations is increasing rapidly, while the number of traditional visiting nurse associations is declining. In 1982 it was estimated that 14 percent of the Medicare home health charges were by proprietary agencies, 26 percent by nonprofit organizations, 32 percent by visiting nurse associations, 15 percent by facility-based agencies, and 14 percent by other agencies (U.S. Department of Health and Human Services [U.S. DHHS] 1989). By 1988 proprietary agencies accounted for 34 percent of total Medicare charges, nonprofit care for 15 percent, visiting nurses for 20 percent, facility-based agencies for 25 percent, and others for 7 percent (U.S. DHHS 1989). This represents a dramatic shift in ownership structure within a six-year period. The changes brought about by the for-profit chains are more extensive than their proportionate representation among health-care providers might suggest. By force of example and direct competition, for-profit chains have encouraged many nonprofit hospitals and other health entities to combine into chains.

Diversification and Restructuring. Diversification of health-care corporations is continuing to occur. Some large hospital corporations have developed ambulatory care centers (such as Humana, which later sold its centers), while others have developed their own HMOs or insurance (Bell 1987).

By the mid-1980s, many experts expected America's health-care system to be dominated by the four largest for-profit hospital chains: Hospital Corporations of America, Humana, National Medical Enterprises, and American Medical International. Economic problems in the late 1980s resulted in some industry restructuring, by scaling down operations and spinning off substantial segments (Ginzberg 1988). For example, in 1987 the largest multiunit system, Hospital Corporation of America, sold about 25 percent of its hospitals, restructuring to stay competitive (Greene 1988, p. 103). Beverly Enterprises, the nation's largest nursing home corporation, which had been profitable during the early 1980s, experienced financial difficulties in 1987 through 1989 and is in the process of restructuring its corporation (Fritz 1990; Wagner 1988).

As the restructuring of health organizations has been occurring, multihospital systems have continued to grow. In the two years between 1987 and 1989 alone, multihospital systems grew by 9 percent, although the number of total hospitals and beds increased by only 2 percent (AHA 1987; 1989). In spite of the problems of some corporations, the predictions are that corporate growth will continue, although at perhaps a slower pace than in the early 1980s (White 1990).

Financial Status and Profits. The private health sector continues to be extremely healthy financially. *Forbes*'s annual report on investor-owned health corporations shows that the overall median return-on-equity for health corporations during the previous twelve months to its publication was 18.7 percent, well above the 14.3 percent for all U.S. industries (Fritz 1990) (see Table 3). The ten-year average return-on-equity was 18.7

TABLE 3
Selected U.S. Health-Care Investor Corporations, 1990

	Profitability Growth						*Net income*
	Return on equity		*Sales*		*Earnings per share*		
Company	*10-year average %*	*Latest 12 mos. %*	*10-year average %*	*Latest 12 mos. %*	*10-year average %*	*Latest 12 mos. %*	*Latest 12 mos. $ mil*
Health-care services							
Humana	24.4	21.7	16.3	19.0	18.9	11.3	256
Manor Care	22.2	11.8	34.9	16.9	NA	D-P	23
National Medical	15.3	14.5	31.7	15.5	13.1	0.0	152
Universal Health	11.8	5.2	30.7[a]	5.5	NM	Z-P	8
Beverly Enterprises	7.1	def	34.0	3.8	NM	D-D	−118
FHP International	NA	34.9	NA	37.9	NA	31.5	25
PacifiCare Health	NA	24.6	76.2[b]	45.9	NA	83.0	9
United Health Care	NA	61.9	NA	−18.1	NA	D-P	10
US Healthcare	NA	13.7	61.4	29.8	NA	133.3	20
Medians	15.3	14.5	34.0	16.9	NM	83.0	
Drugs							
American Home Prods	35.0	33.7	5.1	5.8	10.9	10.0	1,005
Syntex	31.2	47.9	11.3	5.7	19.8	4.1	312
Merck	30.8	50.3	9.8	9.0	13.5	26.4	1,435
Abbott Laboratories	30.4	33.8	12.3	7.5	18.1	16.4	829
Marion Laboratories	30.0	15.1	21.7	22.0	33.6	−54.3	79
Medians	20.1	19.3	10.1	8.6	10.5	18.2	
Medical Supplies							
CR Bard	20.8	22.6	14.3	6.4	20.7	1.9	74
Medtronic	20.2	21.1	10.9	8.9	14.2	7.3	100
Hillenbrand Inds	19.2	20.5	12.8	15.7	13.0	4.3	72
Bausch & Lomb	16.8	17.1	6.4	27.4	10.2	15.3	109
Medians	14.5	17.1	10.9	8.8	10.2	3.1	
Industry Medians	18.7	18.4	12.5	8.8	10.2	15.2	
All-Industry Medians	14.3	14.4	9.3	8.5	6.4	8.0	

SOURCE: Adapted from M. Fritz, 1990, "Health," *Forbes* January 8: 180–182.
NOTE: D-D: Deficit to deficit D-P: Deficit to profit P-D: Profit to deficit def: Deficit NA: Not available NM: Not meaningful a: Nine-year average b: Eight-year average.

percent for investor-owned health corporations, compared with 14.3 percent for all U.S. industries (Fritz 1990). Median health industry sales for investor-owned companies grew 8.8 percent for 1989 and at a 12.5 percent rate for the ten-year average. Earnings-per-share were 15.2 percent in the most recent twelve months, compared with 12.2 percent for the ten-year average. The earnings per share were much higher than those of 8.0 percent for all U.S. industries in the most recent twelve months in 1989 (Fritz 1990).

The *Forbes* financial reports for the largest health corporations are shown in Table 3 for three different sectors of the industry: health-care services, drugs, and medical supply companies (Fritz 1990). The most profitable health-care service corporation in 1989 was Humana, which owns both hospitals and insurance companies. In 1989 its group health insurance division had almost one million members and a $4 million operating profit (Fritz 1990).

Nursing homes have traditionally been very profitable. Manor Care and National Medical Enterprises own large numbers of nursing homes. These corporations showed 11.8 percent and 14.5 percent returns on equity in 1989, and many have had a 22.2 percent return-on-equity for the previous ten-year period (Fritz 1990, p. 180).

FHP International, PacifiCare Health, United HealthCare, and US Healthcare are large investor-owned HMOs showing high returns on equity and high sales (Fritz 1990). Many of the companies are now offering diversified products and showing high profit levels (Sussman 1990). Life and health insurance had a 32.7 percent earning per share in 1989 over the previous year, compared with a ten-year average of 7.1 percent per share (Clements 1990, p. 185).

Because of the pluralistically financed health-care system in the United States, administrative costs are much higher than those of the national and publicly financed health-care systems of virtually all other Western industrialized nations, with the exception of South Africa (Evans et al. 1989; Himmelstein and Woolhandler 1986). According to one report, 5 percent of total U.S. expenditures ($26 billion in 1988) was spent on program administrative costs and profits for private health insurance (U.S. ONCE 1990). Evans et al. (1989) estimates these costs to be even higher, at approximately one percent of GNP ($40 billion in 1987), excluding many unquantified costs of negotiations, time, and organization. Administrative costs and profits in the United States for private insurance companies range from about 35 percent on individual policies to 7 to 14 percent on group plans and vary by type of plan (Feldstein 1988). The overall administrative costs for the multiple, private, third-party organizations have been estimated to be about 8 percent, whereas both the Medicare program and the Canadian national health program have overhead costs of only 2 to 3 percent (Evans et al. 1989). Thus, these private-sector financing proposals continue to support the private insurance industry and all of the overhead and profits associated with private third-party payers.

Earnings-per-share of drug companies rose by 18.2 percent between 1988 and 1989, which was up from the ten-year average of 10.5 percent (Fritz 1990). Returns-on-equity reported for drug companies increased to 19.3 percent in 1989 and were 20.1 percent on average over the previous ten years (Fritz 1990). While earnings-per-share of medical supply companies were down in 1989 to 3.1 percent over the previous year, their ten-year median earning was 10.2 percent, and their return-on-equity for the previous ten years was 14.5 percent (Fritz 1990). In 1989 a number of large drug company mergers occurred, particularly between U.S. firms and foreign corporations such as Genentech, Inc. and Roche Holding, Ltd. of Switzerland (Southwick 1990). Although the biotechnology industry did not show overall profits in 1989, the sales growth rates were strong, and some companies had high profit rates, such as Diagnostic Products, with a 22.3 percent earnings-per-share and a 23.6 percent return-on-equity in 1989 over the previous year (Clements 1990, p. 182).

It is difficult to determine the overall revenues and profits of the medical–industrial complex. In 1965, according to the Ehrenreichs (1971), the medical–industrial complex reaped an estimated

$2.5 plus billion in after-tax profits. For 1979 Arnold Relman estimated $35 to $40 billion in gross income (about 25 percent of total personal health care costs) for what he defined as the "new medical-industrial complex," or "the vast array of investor owned businesses supplying health services for a profit" (1980, p. 965). However, this estimate excludes profits of the "old medical-industrial complex . . . the businesses concerned with the manufacture and sale of drugs, medical supplies and equipment" (p. 965). As noted, the insurance industry, HMOs, PPOs, and other third-party payers had 32 percent ($175 billion) of the gross revenues for health and another 5 percent ($26 billion) for program administration and profits in the United States in 1988 (U.S. ONCE 1990).

In summary, the 1980s were a decade of rationalization for health care, with the formation of large, complex, bureaucratically interconnected units and arrangements that reached well beyond the hospital and permeated virtually all sectors of the health industry. This vertical and horizontal integration, combined with the revival of market ideologies and government policies promoting competition and deregulation, profoundly altered the shape of U.S. health-care delivery. These changes signal a fundamental transformation of American medicine and a rationalization of the system under private control (Starr 1982).

Reasons for Growth in the For-Profit Sector. In the fifty-five-year period prior to 1965, for-profit medical enterprises were largely confined to the manufacture and sale of drugs, medical equipment, and appliances and to selling health insurance policies (Ginzberg 1988; Relman 1980). A number of factors encouraged the penetration and rapid growth of the for-profit sector in all areas of health care subsequent to 1965.

The federal government was crucial in the development of the medical–industrial complex. After World War II, the federal role expanded as Congress enacted legislation and authorized money for research, education, training, and financing of health services. The passage of Medicare and Medicaid in 1965 was pivotal in expanding the medical–industrial complex, as government became the third-party payer for health-care services (Estes et al. 1984). Public demand for health care among the aged, blind, disabled, and poor (all previously limited in access) was secure. Medicare and Medicaid provided the major sources of long-term capital financing for hospitals and contributed to the marked increase in service volume and technology, as well as to the current oversupply of physicians.

Largely with the help of Medicare's cost-based reimbursement policy (from 1965 to 1983), national expenditures for hospital care catapulted. For nursing home expenditures, Medicaid became a primary payer, with 48 percent of total payments (U.S. DOC 1990). Medicare changes that added coverage of dialysis centers (1972) and coverage for the mentally impaired (1974) also expanded the private sector. Government's share of health spending increased from 25 percent in 1965 to 42 percent in 1988 (U.S. ONCE 1990). In summary, federal financing of health care has performed the very important functions of sustaining aggregate demand through health insurance programs, protecting against financial risks, subsidizing research and guaranteeing substantial financial returns, supporting the system's infrastructure through training subsidies and capital expansion, and regulating competition through licensure and accreditation (LeRoy 1979).

In addition to government spending, third-party insurance offered by Blue Cross/Blue Shield and private commercial companies covered most of the remaining inpatient hospital expenditures and a significant proportion of physician costs. The cost-based service reimbursement by private insurers, Blue Cross, and Medicare created and sustained strong cash flows in the hospital industry (Ginzberg 1988). With public- and private-sector third-party payments covering 90 percent of all inpatient hospital expenditures, the hospital business became virtually risk-free.

Ginzberg (1988) contends the growth in for-profits after the mid-1960s was also related to the overall shortage of hospital beds and the increased demand for health services, particularly in areas of rapid population growth. The growth of for-profit health-care organizations was also further extended by Medicare payments for a return-on-equity for care provided to Medicare beneficiaries (Ginzberg 1988). Medicare also paid for interest payments and depreciation rates on properties purchased by for-profit organizations (Ginzberg 1988).

The for-profit health sector was dramatically expanded by entry into the equity market. The receptivity of Wall Street boosted the medical–industrial complex, as investors willingly raised substantial funds for new corporations and for the purchase of existing facilities and organizations during the 1980s (Ginzberg 1988). The results of these investments paid well, as shown earlier in the high profits of the major corporations.

In the 1980s, two other forces were responsible for the dramatic changes in the medical–industrial complex: a change in the ideological climate with the election of President Reagan and changes in state policies to promote privatization, rationalization, and competition in health care (Estes 1990). These changes contributed to increases in the proportion of services provided by proprietary institutions (Schlesinger, Marmor, and Smithey 1987).

While policies of the 1960s and 1970s encouraged a form of privatization built on the voluntary sector (Estes and Bergthold 1988), President Reagan shifted the direction and accelerated privatization. In the 1980s, the form of privatization was government subsidy of for-profit (rather than nonprofit) enterprise (Bergthold, Estes, and Villanueva 1990) and privatization in the form of a transfer of work from the hospital to the informal sector of home and family (Binney, Estes, and Humphers 1989). Regulatory and legislative devices were important in the health and social services. The Omnibus Reconciliation Act of 1980 and the Omnibus Budget Reconciliation Act of 1981 contributed to competition and deregulation, private contracting, and growth of for-profits in service areas that were traditionally dominated by nonprofit or public providers (e.g., home health care).

Given the long-term historical role of the private, nonprofit sector in U.S. health and social services since the earliest days of the Republic and the rapid organizational changes of the 1980s, vertical and horizontal integration have blurred boundaries between the heretofore distinct nonprofit and for-profit health-care sectors. For-profit entities have nonprofit subsidiaries, and vice versa, and conceptual and structural complexities have multiplied, rendering impossible the simple differentiation of *public* from *private.* It is noteworthy that government-initiated privatization strategies did not reduce public-sector costs (see section on Health-Care Financing).

Issues Raised by the Medical–Industrial Complex. *Commodification, commercialization, proprietarization,* and *monetarization* are all terms used to describe an increasingly salient dynamic in the medical–industrial complex: the potentially distorting effects of money, profit, and market rationality as a (if not the) central determining force in health care. After a decade devoted to market rhetoric, cost containment effort, and stunning organizational rationalization, the bottom line is the complete failure of any of these to stem the swelling tide of problems of access and cost. Meanwhile, public opinion clearly favors change and a national solution that assures access regardless of ability to pay (Bodenheimer 1990), while a nascent movement for national health insurance stirs.

The rapidly growing health-care industry is creating strains on the economic system while it also is creating a financial burden on government, business, and individuals through their payments for health services. These strains are occurring simultaneously with a huge federal debt, increasing fiscal problems at all levels of government, and a sluggish and uncompetitive general economy. Responses to these strains have included cutbacks in services and reimbursements, cost shifts onto consumers, and alterations in the structure of the health-care system itself to accord better with a competitive, for-profit model.

The competition model as a prescription for the nation's health-care woes has restricted access to health care and raised questions of quality of care (Estes et al. 1984, p. 70). Cost shifting to consumers is increasingly limiting access to needed services for those with less ability to pay.

The juxtaposition of the commercial ethos familiar in fast-food chains with health care collides with traditional images of medicine as the embodiment of humane service. Investor-owned health-care enterprises have elicited a number of specific criticisms. It has been argued that commercial considerations can undermine the responsibility of doctors toward their patients and lead to unnecessary tests and procedures and, given other financial incentives, to inadequate treatment (Relman 1980). The interrelationships among physicians and the private health-care sector, particularly for-profit corporations, raises many issues about the effects on quality of care and health-care utilization and expenditures. Many have argued that the potential for abuse, exploitation, unethical practices, and disregard of fiduciary responsibilities to patients is pervasive (Iglehart 1989). Legislation has even been introduced in Congress that would prohibit physicians from referring patients to entities in which they hold a financial interest and from receiving compensation from entities to which they refer patients (Iglehart 1989).

Critics of for-profits argue that such ownership drives up the cost of health care, reduces quality, neglects teaching and research, and excludes those who cannot pay for treatment. Opponents of the market model for health care reflect diverse interests, including members of the medical profession seeking to preserve their professional autonomy, advocates for access to health care for the poor and uninsured, those concerned about the impact of profit seeking on quality of care, and many others. As government and business attempt to restrain health-care spending, cutting into profits and forcing cost reductions, these concerns intensify (Light 1986).

Issues for sociological investigation include the systematic identification of the ways in which the new commercial practices and organization of health care affect health-care delivery. Organizational studies are needed to disentangle the effects of organizational characteristics (e.g., tax status and system affiliation) on the outcomes of equity, access, utilization, cost, and quality of care. Further, the effects on provider–patient interactions of these structural and normative changes in health care require investigation. A general sociological theory of the professions will emerge from understanding the ways in which the dominant medical profession responds to present restructuring of health care and accompanying challenges to its ability to control the substance of its own work, erosions in its monopoly over medical knowledge, diminishing authority over patients resulting from health policy changes, major technological and economic developments, and changes in the medical–industrial complex.

(SEE ALSO: *Health-Care Financing; Health Policy Analysis; Health Services Utilization; Medical Sociology*)

REFERENCES

American Hospital Association 1987 *Hospital Statistics, 1987.* Chicago: AHA.

——— 1989 *Hospital Statistics, 1989–90.* Chicago: AHA.

Andersen, Ronald M., and Ross M. Mullner 1989 "Trends in the Organization of Health Services." In H. E. Freeman and S. Levine, eds., *Handbook of Medical Sociology,* 4th ed., 144–165. Englewood Cliffs, N.J.: Prentice Hall.

Bell, Colin 1987 Multi-Unit Providers. *Modern Healthcare* 17(12):37–58.

Bergthold, Linda A. 1990 "Business and the Pushcart Vendors in an Age of Supermarkets." In J. W. Salmon, ed., *The Corporate Transformation of Health Care: Issues and Directions.* Amityville, N.Y.: Baywood.

———, Carroll L. Estes, and A. Villanueva 1990 "Public Light and Private Dark: The Privatization of Home Health Services for the Elderly in the United States." *Home Health Services Quarterly* 11:7–33.

Berliner, Howard S., and R. K. Burlage 1990 "Proprietary Hospital Chains and Academic Medical Centers." In J. W. Salmon, ed., *The Corporate Transformation of Health Care: Issues and Directions.* Amityville, N.Y.: Baywood.

Berliner, Howard W., and C. Regan 1990 "Multi-National Operations of U.S. For Profit Hospital Chains: Trends and Implications." In J. W. Salmon, ed., *The Corporate Transformation of Health Care: Issues and Directions.* Amityville, N.Y.: Baywood.

Binney, Elizabeth A., Carroll L. Estes, and Susan E. Humphers 1989 Informalization and Community Care for the Elderly. Unpublished manuscript, University of California, San Francisco.

Bodenheimer, Thomas 1990 "Should We Abolish the Private Health Insurance Industry?" *International Journal of Health Services* 20:199–220.

Clements, J. 1990 "Insurance." *Forbes* January 8:184–186.

Ehrenreich, Barbara, and John Ehrenreich 1971 *The American Health Empire: Power, Profits and Politics.* New York: Vintage.

Ermann, Dan, and Jon Gabel 1984 "Multihospital Systems: Issues and Empirical Findings." *Health Affairs* 3:50–64.

Estes, Carroll L. 1990 "The Reagan Legacy: Privatization, the Welfare State and Aging." In J. Quadagno and J. Myles, eds., *Aging and the Welfare State.* Philadelphia: Temple University Press.

———, and Linda A. Bergthold 1988 "The Unravelling of the Nonprofit Service Sector in the U.S." In J. I. Nelson, ed., *The Service Economy.* (special issue of *International Journal of Sociology and Social Policy*) 9:18–33.

———, Lenore E. Gerard, Jane Sprague Zones, and James H. Swan 1984 *Political Economy, Health, and Aging.* Boston: Little, Brown.

———, and Juanita B. Wood 1986 "The Nonprofit Sector and Community-based Care for the Elderly in the U.S.: A Disappearing Resource?" *Social Science and Medicine* 23:1261–1266.

Evans, Robert G., J. Lomas, M. L. Barer, R. J. Labelle, C. Fooks, G. L. Stoddart, G. M. Anderson, D. Feeny, A. Gafni, and G. W. Torrance 1989 "Controlling Health Expenditures: The Canadian Reality." *New England Journal of Medicine* 320:571–577.

Federation of American Health Systems 1990 *1990 Directory.* Little Rock, Ark.: FAHS Review.

Feldstein, Paul J. 1988 *Health Care Economics.* New York: Wiley.

Fritz, M. 1990 "Health." *Forbes* (January 8):180–182.

Ginzberg, Eli 1988 "For Profit Medicine: A Reassessment." *New England Journal of Medicine* 319:757–761.

Gray, Bradford H., ed. 1983 *The New Health Care For Profit.* Washington, D.C.: National Academy Press.

———, and Walter J. McNerney 1986 "For Profit Enterprise in Health Care: The Institute of Medicine Study." *New England Journal of Medicine* 314:1523–1528.

Greene, J. 1988 "Multihospital Systems: Systems Went Back to Basics in 1987, Restructuring to Stay Competitive." *Modern Healthcare* 18:45–117.

Harrington, Charlene, James H. Swan, and Leslie A. Grant 1988 "Nursing Home Bed Capacity in the States, 1978–86." *Health Care Financing Review* 9:81–111.

Himmelstein, David U., and Steffie Woolhandler 1986 "Cost without Benefit: Administrative Waste in the U.S. *New England Journal of Medicine* 314:440–441.

———1990 "The Corporate Compromise: A Marxist View of Health Policy." *Monthly Review* (May):14–29.

Iglehart, John K. 1989 "The Debate over Physician Ownership of Health Care Facilities." *New England Journal of Medicine* 321:198–204.

InterStudy. 1989 "Findings on Open-Ended HMOs Reports by InterStudy." *InterStudy Press Release* March 7. Excelsior, Md.: InterStudy.

LeRoy, Lauren 1979 The Political Economy of U.S. Federal Health Policy: A Closer Look at Medicare. Unpublished Manuscript, University of California, San Francisco.

Light, Donald W. 1986 "Corporate Medicine for Profit." *Scientific American* 255:38–45.

McKinlay, John B., and John D. Stoeckle 1988 "Corporatization and the Social Transformation of Doctoring." In J. W. Salmon, ed., *The Corporate Transformation of Health Care: Issues and Directions.* Amityville, N.Y.: Baywood.

Navarro, Vincente 1976 *Medicine under Capitalism.* New York: Prodist.

Relman, Arnold S. 1980 "The New Medical-Industrial Complex." *New England Journal of Medicine* 303: 963–970.

Rodberg, L., and G. Stevenson 1977 "The Health Care Industry in Advanced Capitalism." *Review of Radical Political Economics* 9:104–115.

Salmon, J. Warren 1990 "Profit and Health Care: Trends in Corporatization and Proprietarization." In J. W. Salmon, ed., *The Corporate Transformation of Health Care: Issues and Directions.* Amityville, N.Y.: Baywood.

Schlesinger, Mark, Theodore R. Marmor, and Richard Smithey 1987 "Nonprofit and For-Profit Medical Care: Shifting Roles and Implications for Health Policy." *Journal of Health Politics and Law* 12(3):427–457.

Shadle, M., and M. M. Hunter 1988 *National HMO Firms 1988.* Excelsior, MN: InterStudy.

Southwick, Karen 1990 "More Merger Mania among Drugmakers." *Healthweek* 4:1, 51.

Starr, Paul 1982 *The Social Transformation of American Medicine.* New York, N.Y.: Basic Books.

Sussman, David 1990 "HMOs Are Still Riding a Wave of Profitability." *Healthweek* 4:12.

U.S. Department of Commerce, International Trade Administration (1990) "Health and Medical Services." *U.S. Industrial Outlook 1990.* Washington, D.C.: U.S. DOC.

U.S. Department of Health and Human Services 1989 *Health United States, 1989.* DHHS 90-1232. Hyattsville, Md.: U.S. DHHS.

U.S. Office of National Cost Estimates (U.S. ONCE) 1990 "National Health Expenditures, 1988." *Health Care Financing Review* 11:1–41.

U.S. National Center for Health Statistics [U.S. NCHS], Hing, E., Sekscenski, E. and Strahan, G. 1989 National Nursing Home Survey: 1985 Summary for the United States. *Vital and Health Statistics* Series 13 Hyattsville, Md.: Public Health Service.

Wagner, L. 1988 "Nursing Homes Buffeted by Troubles." *Modern Healthcare* 33–42.

Waitzkin, Howard 1983 *The Second Sickness: Contradictions of Capitalist Health Care.* New York: Free Press.

White, William D. 1990 "The 'Corporatization' of U.S. Hospitals: What Can We Learn from the Nineteenth Century Industrial Experience?" *International Journal of Health Services* 20:85–113.

Wohl, Stanley 1984 *The Medical Industrial Complex.* New York: Harmony.

Wood, Juanita B., and Carroll L. Estes 1988 The Medicalization of Community Services for the Elderly. *Health and Social Work* 13(1):35–43.

CARROLL L. ESTES
CHARLENE HARRINGTON
SOLOMON DAVIS

MEDICAL SOCIOLOGY

MEDICAL SOCIOLOGY Medical sociology has experienced enormous growth since World War II; indeed, it constitutes the largest of the sections in the American Sociological Association. In Great Britain and Germany, as well as in some other highly industrialized societies, medical sociology is thriving (Bloom 1986; Claus 1983; Wardwell 1982); its burgeoning since World War II was made possible by considerable funding from the respective governments and, in the United States, by private foundations as well. In the United States the National Institutes of Health were a main source of funds, and an appreciable proportion of these funds was devoted to work in mental health.

The term *medical sociology* is in many respects a misnomer. A more proper designation would be the *sociology of health,* because sociological interest in health goes far beyond narrow medical concerns and includes such diverse topics as indigenous health cultures, the structure of health organizations, and the effects of the national economy on health. Because much of the early acceptance of sociologists in the health field required medical acceptance and sponsorship, in addition to the benefits associated with the designation as "medical" sociologists, the use of the title has persisted among many who work in the field. However, a number of medical sociologists in the American Sociological Association have urged that the title of the Medical Sociology Section be changed.

Within the larger discipline of sociology, scholars who identified themselves as medical sociologists were initially charged with ignoring concerns central to the discipline and with merely applying the concepts, skills, and knowledge of the discipline to the needs of the medical profession. Moreover, medical sociology, in contrast to other subfields, such as criminology and sociology of occupations, bordered on domains that were medical or biological and apparently more foreign to established sociological interests and presumably less amenable to the sociological armamentarium.

In 1957 Straus introduced what became a popular distinction to describe two diverging camps of medical sociologists: "sociology in medicine" and "sociology of medicine." The former was intended to describe the efforts of those medical sociologists, usually based in medical schools, nursing schools, public health schools, and other health-professional schools, who addressed the problems defined by health professions, such as the reasons people failed to use health services and to comply with medical regimens. Characteristically, "sociologists in medicine" would seek joint appointments in established sociology departments in an effort to retain their identity, avoid intellectual isolation, and stay abreast of their discipline.

On the other hand, "sociologists of medicine," customarily based in departments of sociology, disavowed any interest in the concerns of health professionals but viewed the health world as any other subject matter that could be used to build sociological knowledge, mainly by studying health occupations, organizations, and institutions. Thus, they would study physicians and nurses as they would lawyers or ministers, or hospitals and health departments as they would other complex organizations. Their work was regarded as more appropriate and respectable by their sociological peers. However, they usually had less familiarity with health phenomena and less access to health settings. Medical sociologists who had worked in public health schools and other organizational environments not only enriched such fields as epidemiology, environmental health, and health policy, for example, but also broadened their own scientific competence by virtue of their exposure to these disciplines.

Since the early influx of sociologists into the health world in the 1950s and 1960s, the status of medical sociology has changed appreciably. Applied sociology has achieved greater respectability, and there is growing appreciation that it is not a mere recipient of the general discipline but a contributor as well (Cockerham 1988; Freeman and Levine 1989). Applied work involves more than mechanically using and applying the theories and bodies of knowledge of the established discipline. As practical problems are tackled, theories are tested, refined, and modified and new formulations are developed. Medical sociologists, for their part, have produced theoretically oriented work that has won the respect of many of their more traditional colleagues. By now, too, the distinction between sociology in medicine and of medicine has become blurred and almost irrelevant. In addition, it is no longer evident that the work in medical sociology being done in the traditional sociology departments is superior to that emerging from the health-professional schools and health organizations.

In the early days, medical sociologists had to overcome the skepticism of health professionals about the legitimacy of sociology's knowledge base and methodology. The work of medical sociologists was mainly confined to enabling medicine and the other health professions to make their services available to people in need of them. As teachers and researchers, medical sociologists sensitized health professionals to the social, cultural, organizational, financial, and communication barriers to the use of services by poor people or members of minority groups.

Medical sociologists introduced sociological variables such as social class, social stress, social cohesion, relative deprivation, and social supports in an effort to explain mortality and diverse forms of morbidity such as alcoholism, heart disease, and mental illness (Syme and Berkman 1976; Dutton 1986). One conspicuous and pervasive finding is that those at the bottom of the stratification system have the highest rates of mortality and morbidity. Sociologists have also provided health professionals with new methodological approaches, methods of data collection, and even new ways of examining quantitative and qualitative data. They alerted physicians to the differential perceptions of symptoms and ways of expressing them and to the different use of health services by men, women, and people of different cultural backgrounds (Zola 1966). Medical sociologists documented the various actions people take when they experience symptoms and rely less on the medical system and more on the lay health culture, self-treatment, and advice from kin, friends, and neighbors (Mechanic 1983); and they reported on the variations in treatment of people of different social classes who present the same mental condition or physical symptoms (Hollingshead and Redlich 1958).

Sociologists also considered the professional education of medical students from the vantage point of adult socialization and considered the influences of their professors as well as their peers (Merton, Reeder, and Kendall 1957; Becker et al. 1961). Freidson (1970) studied medicine as the quintessential profession, which succeeded in having society confer upon it the right to autonomy, the subservience of other health occupations to it, and the privilege of having medical work judged only by medical peers. Medical sociologists have also been interested in the dramatic changes that are going on within medicine and the challenges to medical authority that have arisen recently (Starr 1982). In addition, medical sociologists have been interested in the movement of physicians from solo practice into health organizations, where medical autonomy has been partially curtailed, and in the effects of these developments on physician behavior, satisfaction, and on the quality of care provided to patients (Hafferty 1988; Haug 1988; Light and Levine 1988; McKinlay and Arches 1985; Navarro 1988; Wolinsky 1988).

Health organizations, such as hospitals, clinics, outpatient departments, health centers, as well as the relationships among personnel and patients within them, have commanded the interests of medical sociologists. Others have been interested in the growing public dissatisfaction with the delivery of health care in the United States and the search for more efficient financial and organizational arrangements. Finally, some medical sociologists have addressed the growing ethical and legal issues that have arisen as new, expensive, and sophisticated technologies have been introduced into the medical armamentarium (Fox 1976; Bell 1989).

While not all the work produced by medical sociologists has been greeted enthusiastically by health professionals, many of the concepts and findings have found their way into the health domain. For example, epidemiologists have incorporated various social variables such as social stress, social supports, and networks when designing their studies of the etiology of disease and in planning their courses of instruction (House, Landis, Umberson 1988; Kessler and Wortman 1989). Similarly, teachers of health-services administration make use of sociological findings on social, cultural, and organizational barriers to the use of services.

But it is in the role of social and cultural critic of medicine that medical sociology may have encountered the greatest resistance. Sociologists have encouraged medicine to look critically at its view of the world and to modify some of its fundamental conceptions. Talcott Parsons (1951) led the way in his classic analysis of the "sick role" in which sickness was wrested from the exclusively biological sphere and raised to the social level as a special case of social deviance. Freidson (1970) went further and challenged Parsons's notion of the physician as the possessor of exclusive scientific knowledge to be dispensed in a neutral, impersonal manner. Instead, Freidson pointed to the existence of conflict in the doctor–patient relationship and portrayed the patient as active, negotiating, and contesting.

Medical sociologists helped to dispel the image of the physician as one who is guided by a purely rational calculus. They showed that such medical decisions as which treatments to use, whether to hospitalize or not, or whether to prolong life by heroic measures should best be viewed as decisions made by people with particular values who are performing social roles and are influenced by the specific social contexts in which they are located (Levine 1987). Sociologists have criticized other assumptions of the biomedical perspective such as the notion that disease is caused by a single factor or that disease is to be defined only as a departure from normal biological functioning (Mishler et al. 1981). Sociologists have emphasized the importance of social and cultural factors in the ways in which diseases are defined and classified. In addition, they have directed attention to the role of multiple factors in the etiology of disease, including the biological, social, and physical environment (Hingson et al. 1981). Sociologists have also criticized the growing tendency to "medicalize" many forms of deviant behavior: to treat them as diseases or illnesses that require medical intervention (Conrad and Schneider 1980).

Physicians have been urged to learn more about the social, cultural, and life circumstances of their patients; to pay attention to what patients are saying; to consider that health problems may be related to work, family, and community influences; and to realize the fallacy of viewing patients and their problems solely from the perspective of the biomedical model. On a broader policy level, medical sociologists have criticized health-policy leaders for characteristically seeking the solution of health problems in the greater provision of health services, particularly medical services, and for ignoring the greater influence of social conditions, public health measures, and personal behavior (Levine and Lilienfeld 1986).

It should be added that a small number of physician leaders historically and in recent years have been acutely aware of the social dimensions of health, have advocated greater attention to social factors, and, indeed, have directly and indirectly facilitated the development of medical sociology (Cassel 1976; Susser, Watson, and Hopper 1985; White 1988; and many others).

A review of the medical sociology literature reveals an unusually broad range of interests, from social epidemiology and social psychology to occupational sociology, political sociology, and social movements. Similarly, a wide range of intellectual perspectives is evident, including functionalism, symbolic interactionism, grounded theory, social constructionism, phenonemology, and Marxism. Medical sociologists have been provided with a plethora of opportunities for study of topics that may enrich sociology and contribute to the needs of the health professions and the larger society.

(SEE ALSO: *Comparative Health-Care Systems; Health and Illness Behavior; Health and the Life Course; Health-Care Financing; Health Policy Analysis; Health Promotion; Health Services Utilization; Health Status Measurement; Medical-Industrial Complex; Mental Health; Mental Illness and Mental Disorders*)

REFERENCES

Becker, H. S., B. Geer, E. C. Hughes, and A. Strauss 1961 *Boys in White: Student Culture in Medical School.* Chicago: University of Chicago Press.

Berkman, L. F., and L. S. Syme 1979 "Social Network, Host Resistance and Mortality: A Nine Year Follow-up Study of Alameda County Residents." *American Journal of Epidemiology* 190:186–204.

Bloom, S. W. 1986 "Institutional Trends in Medical Sociology." *Journal of Health and Social Behavior* 27:265–276.

Cassel, J. C. 1976 "The Contribution of the Social Environment to Host Resistance." *American Journal of Epidemiology* 104:107–123.

Claus, L. M. 1983 "The Development of Medical Sociology in Europe." *Social Science and Medicine* 17:1591–1597.

Cockerham, W. C. 1988 "Medical Sociology." In N. J. Smelser, ed., *Handbook of Sociology.* Newbury Park, Calif.: Sage.

Conrad, P., and J. Schneider 1980 *Deviance and Medicalization.* St. Louis, Mo.: C. V. Mosby.

Fox, R. C. 1976 "Advanced Medical Technology—Social and Ethical Implications." *Annual Review of Sociology* 2:231–268.

Freeman, H. E., and S. Levine 1989 "The Present Status of Medical Sociology." In H. E. Freeman and S. Levine, eds., *Handbook of Medical Sociology.* Englewood Cliffs, N.J.: Prentice-Hall.

Freidson, E. 1970 *Profession of Medicine.* New York: Dodd and Mead.

Hafferty, F. W. 1988 "Theories at the Crossroads: A Discussion of Evolving Views of Medicine as a Profession." *The Milbank Quarterly* 66:202–225.

Haug, M. R. 1988 "A Re-examination of the Hypothesis of Physician Deprofessionalization." *The Milbank Quarterly* 66:48–56.

Hingson, R., N. A. Scotch, J. Sorenson, and J. P. Swazey 1981 *In Sickness and in Health: Social Dimensions of Medical Care.* St. Louis, Mo.: C. V. Mosby.

Hollingshead, A. B., and F. C. Redlich 1958 *Social Class and Mental Illness: A Community Study.* New York: Wiley.

House, J. S., K. R. Landis, and D. Umberson 1988 "Social Relationships and Health." *Science* 241:540–545.

Kessler, R. C., and C. B. Wortman 1989 "Social and Psychological Factors in Health and Illness." In H. E. Freeman and S. Levine, eds., *Handbook of Medical Sociology.* Englewood Cliffs, N. J.: Prentice-Hall.

Levine, S., and A. Lilienfeld (eds.) 1986 *Epidemiology and Health Policy.* New York: Tavistock.

Light, D., and S. Levine 1988 "The Changing Character of the Medical Profession." *The Milbank Quarterly* 66:10–32.

McKinlay, J. B., and J. Arches 1985 "Toward the Proletarianization of Physicians." *International Journal of Health Services* 15:161–195.

Mechanic, D. 1983 "The Experience and Expression of Distress: The Study of Illness Behavior and Medical Utilization." In D. Mechanic, ed., *Handbook of*

Health, Health Care, and the Health Professions. New York: Free Press.

Merton, R. K., G. G. Reeder, and P. Kendall 1957 *The Student Physician.* Cambridge, Mass.: Harvard University Press.

Mishler, E. G. 1984 *The Discourse of Medicine: Dialectics of Medical Interviews.* Norwood: Aldex.

Navarro, V. 1988 "Professional Dominance or Proletarianization? Neither." *The Milbank Quarterly* 66: 57–75.

Parsons, T. 1951 *The Social System.* New York: Free Press.

Starr, P. 1982 *The Social Transformation of American Medicine.* New York: Basic Books.

Straus, R. 1957 "The Nature and Status of Medical Sociology." *American Sociological Review* 2:200–204.

Susser, M. W., W. Watson, and K. Hopper 1985 *Sociology in Medicine.* New York: Oxford University Press.

Wardwell, W. 1982 "The State of Medical Sociology—A Review Essay." *Sociological Quarterly* 23:563–576.

White, K. L. 1988 *The Task of Medicine: Dialogue at Wickenburg.* Menlo Park, Calif.: Henry J. Kaiser Family Foundation.

Wolinsky, F. D. 1988 "The Professional Dominance Perspective, Revisited." *The Milbank Quarterly* 66: 33–47.

Zola, I. 1966 "Culture and Symptoms—An Analysis of Patients' Presenting Complaints." *American Sociological Review* 31:615–630.

SOL LEVINE

MENTAL HEALTH The concept of positive mental health was developed by Jahoda (1958), who argues that the notion of mental health can be viewed as an enduring personality characteristic or as a less permanent function of personality and the social situation (Jahoda 1958). This article summarizes Jahoda's approach to mental health, reviews other discussions of the concept, describes a challenge to the assumption that mental health requires the accurate perception of reality, and concludes with a discussion of the value assumptions inherent in the concept.

In her classic book *Current Concepts of Positive Mental Health,* Jahoda (1958) identified the following six approaches to the definition of mental health, which are described in detail below: (1) attitude toward own self; (2) growth, development, and self-actualization; (3) integration; (4) autonomy; (5) perception of reality; and (6) environmental mastery.

1. Acceptance of self, self-confidence, and self-reliance characterize the mentally healthy person. An important attribute of mental health includes the understanding of one's strengths and weaknesses, coupled with the conviction that one's positive characteristics outweigh the negative traits. Independence, initiative, and self-esteem are other indicators of mental health.

2. The realization of one's potential is the underlying assumption of this dimension of mental health. Maslow (1954) explains that self-actualization is a motive that encourages the person to maximize capabilities and talents. It is hypothesized that growth motivation is positively related to mental health. Rather than meeting basic human needs, self-actualization implies movement toward higher goals. This dimension of mental health also implies an investment in living, a concern with other people and one's environment rather than a primary focus on satisfying one's own needs (Jahoda 1958).

3. The mentally healthy person has a balance of psychic forces, a unifying outlook on life, and resistance to stress (Jahoda 1958). Psychoanalysts view integration as the balance of the id, the ego, and the superego. This balance is viewed as changeable, with flexibility as the desired end result. It is also suggested that mental health implies integration at the cognitive level, which implies a unifying philosophy of life that shapes feelings and behaviors. Finally, resistance to stress characterizes the integrated person. The mentally healthy person can adapt to stress without deteriorating. Everyone, it is argued, experiences anxiety when encountering a stressful situation. A mentally healthy response to anxiety and stress implies some tolerance of tension, ambiguity, and frustration.

4. Autonomy implies self-determination and

independence in the decision-making process. The concept suggests that the mentally healthy person is self-directed and self-controlled. The individual acts independently of the outside world; behavior is not dictated by environmental circumstances.

Jahoda points out that some authors interpret autonomy quite differently. Autonomy may be defined as having freedom of choice. An autonomous person freely chooses whether to conform to society's norms. This perspective implies that the person is not independent of the environment but has free choice to decide how to respond to demands made by society.

5. "As a rule, the perception of reality is called mentally healthy when what the individual sees corresponds to what is actually there" (Jahoda 1958, p. 49). Mentally healthy reality perception includes perception free from need distortion. A mentally healthy person views the world without distortions, fitting the perception to objective cues that are present, and does not reject evidence because it does not fit his or her wishes or needs.

Jahoda also argues that this dimension of mental health implies the ability to perceive others in an empathetic manner. This social sensitivity enables a healthy person to put himself or herself in another person's place and anticipate that person's behavior in a given social situation.

6. Mastery of the environment implies achieving success in some social roles as well as appropriate function in those roles. Mental health also includes the ability to have positive affective relationships and adequate interpersonal relations. The social roles involved in environmental mastery may include sexual partner, parent, and worker. Environmental mastery suggests the ability to adapt, adjust, and solve problems in an efficient manner.

OTHER DEFINITIONS OF MENTAL HEALTH

Jourard and Landsman (1980, p. 131) propose similar criteria for mental health: positive self-regard, ability to care about others, ability to care about the natural world, openness to new ideas and to people, creativity, ability to work productively, ability to love, and realistic perception of self.

Jensen and Bergin (1988) conducted a nationwide survey of 425 professional therapists (clinical psychologists, marriage and family therapists, social workers, and psychiatrists) to determine values associated with mental health. Eight themes were identified as important for a positive, mentally healthy life-style: (1) competent perception and expression of feelings (sensitivity, honesty, openness with others); (2) freedom/autonomy/responsibility (self-control, appropriate feelings of guilt, responsibility for one's actions, increasing one's alternatives at a choice point); (3) integration, coping, and work (effective coping strategies, work satisfaction, striving to achieve); (4) self-awareness/growth (awareness of potential, self-discipline); (5) human relatedness/interpersonal and family commitment (ability to give and receive affection, faithfulness in marriage, commitment [to family needs, self-sacrifice); (6) self-maintenance/physical fitness (healthful habits, self-discipline in use of alcohol, drugs, tobacco); (7) mature values (purpose for living, having principles and ideals); and (8) forgiveness (making restitution, forgiving others) (Jensen and Bergin 1988, p. 293). They found a high level of consensus among the practitioners. Many of these values are consistent with the six approaches identified by Jahoda in 1958.

ILLUSIONS AND MENTAL HEALTH

One of these approaches to mental health has been questioned (Snyder 1989). Is accurate reality perception the hallmark of mental health? For most people, reality negotiation is a mentally healthy process. Taylor and Brown (1988, p. 193) explain that "certain illusions may be adaptive for mental health and well being."

According to Taylor and Brown (1988), mentally healthy persons have an unrealistic positive self-evaluation. Normal individuals are more aware of their strengths and less aware of their weaknesses. Mentally healthy persons perceive themselves as better than the average person and view themselves in a more positive light than others see them (Taylor and Brown 1988).

Another illusion of the mentally healthy person is an exaggerated sense of self-control. Taylor and Brown (1988) cite evidence that depressed individuals are more likely to have realistic perceptions of personal control than are nondepressed persons. Positive illusions of personal control over the environment, self-worth, and hopefulness about the future imply mental health and enable people to function in an adaptive manner.

Taylor and Brown (1988) suggest that illusions can promote several criteria of mental health, including happiness or contentment, the ability to care for others, and the capacity for intellectually creative and productive work. While mentally healthy people learn from negative experiences, their illusions help them to cope with stresses and strains (Taylor et al. 1989).

Taylor and Brown (1988, p. 204) conclude that "the mentally healthy person appears to have the enviable capacity to distort reality in a direction that enhances self-esteem, maintains beliefs in personal efficacy, and promotes an optimistic view of the future."

THE ROLE OF UNDERLYING VALUE ASSUMPTIONS

Jahoda (1980) argues that the definition of mental health depends upon underlying value assumptions. The definition of what is mentally healthy varies across societies. In addition, there may be variance across social groups within one society (e.g., social class, gender, race, ethnicity).

For example, there is evidence that there are different standards of mental health for men and women. Broverman et al. (1981) report sex role stereotypes in the clinical judgments of mental health among seventy-nine psychotherapists. The respondents were asked to identify the characteristics that portrayed healthy, mature, and socially competent adults. Broverman et al. (1981, p. 92) found "that healthy women differ from healthy men by being more submissive; less independent; less adventurous; more easily influenced; less aggressive; less competitive."

Finally, according to Jahoda (1988), the definition of mental health is also influenced by the following four assumptions: (1) the criteria for judging health and illness are debatable; (2) mental illness and mental health cannot be defined by the absence of the other; (3) there are degrees of mental health; and (4) a low level of mental health is not synonymous with mental illness. While there is continued debate on how to characterize the mentally healthy person, researchers agree that mental health is more than the absence of mental illness; it represents the enhancement of human potential.

(SEE ALSO: *Health Promotion; Mental Illness and Mental Disorder*)

REFERENCES

Broverman, Inge K., et al. 1981 "Sex-Role Stereotypes and Clinical Judgments of Mental Health." In Elizabeth Howell and Majorie Bayes, eds., *Women and Mental Health.* New York: Basic Books.

Jahoda, Marie 1958 *Current Concepts of Positive Mental Health.* New York: Basic Books.

——— 1980 *Current Concepts of Positive Mental Health,* rev. ed. New York: Arno Press.

——— 1988 "Economic Recession and Mental Health: Some Conceptual Issues." *Journal of Social Issues* 44:13–23.

Jensen, Jay P., and Allen E. Bergin 1988 "Mental Health Values of Professional Therapists: A National Interdisciplinary Survey." *Professional Psychology: Research and Practice* 19:290–297.

Jourard, S. M., and T. Landsman 1980 *Healthy Personality: An Approach from the Viewpoint of Humanistic Psychology,* 4th ed. New York: Macmillan.

Maslow, Abraham H. 1954 *Motivation and Personality.* New York: Harper and Row.

Snyder, C. R. 1989 "Reality Negotiation: From Excuses to Hope and Beyond." *Journal of Social and Clinical Psychology* 8:130–157.

Taylor, Shelley, and Jonathan Brown 1988 "Illusion and Well Being: A Social Psychological Perspective on Mental Health." *Psychological Bulletin* 103:193–210.

Taylor, Shelley, et al. 1989 "Maintaining Positive Illusions in the Face of Negative Information: Getting the Facts Without Letting Them Get to You." *Journal of Social and Clinical Psychology* 8:114–129.

JANET HANKIN

MENTAL ILLNESS AND MENTAL DISORDERS After years of empirical research and theoretical activity, social scientists still do not agree about what mental illness actually is, let alone about what its primary causes are or about the efficacy of various treatments. Sociologists disagree about whether or not mental disorder is truly a disease that fits a medical model of health and illness. They disagree about the relative importance of genetics, personality characteristics, and stress in the onset and course of psychiatric impairment. Nevertheless, sociologists do agree that definitions of mental illness are shaped by the historical, cultural, and interpersonal contexts within which they occur. The significance of any particular set of psychological or behavioral symptoms to a diagnosis of mental disorder lies as much with the audience as with the actor. Given this understanding of mental illness, sociologists are as interested in understanding the consequences of being labeled mentally ill as they are in understanding the causes. Sociologists do, indeed, study the social distribution and determinants of mental disorder. However, they also study social reactions to mental illness and the mentally ill and investigate the ways in which mental-health professionals and institutions can come to serve as agents of social control.

CLASSIFICATION AND DIAGNOSIS

Although psychiatrists themselves have difficulty defining mental illness, the official system for classifying and diagnosing mental disorder in the United States is produced by the American Psychiatric Association (APA). It is known as the *Diagnostic and Statistical Manual of Mental Disorders* (DSM) and was first published in 1952. In its earliest form, DSM-I included a list of sixty separate mental illnesses. By the second edition in 1968, psychiatric definitions of mental illness had changed so markedly that 145 different types of mental disorder were included. Despite the attempt in DSM-II to define more precisely the parameters of mental illness, critics from both within and without psychiatry pointed out that psychiatric diagnoses were extremely unreliable. When different psychiatrists independently used DSM-II to diagnose the same patients, they did so with substantially different results. Studies conducted during the 1960s and 1970s indicated that there was poor agreement about what disease classification was appropriate for any given patient; studies also found that clinicians had difficulty discriminating normal persons from mental patients and that they frequently disagreed about prognosis and the clinical significance of particular symptom patterns (Loring and Powell 1988; Townsend 1980).

After years of debate, some of which was quite heated, the APA published a third edition of DSM in 1980. Mental disorder was defined in DSM-III as "a clinically significant behavioral or psychological syndrome or pattern that occurs in an individual that is typically associated with either a painful symptom (distress) or impairment in one or more areas of functioning (disability)" (American Psychiatric Association 1980, p. 6). DSM-III took a purely descriptive approach to diagnosis; diagnostic criteria, including a list of essential and associated features, were outlined for each disorder, but virtually no attempt was made to explain the etiology of either symptoms or illnesses. Revised again in 1987, the current edition—DSM-IIIR—contains over 200 mental diagnoses, including such disorders as nicotine dependence, caffeine intoxication, and hypoactive sexual desire disorder.

The use of DSM-III and DSM-IIIR criteria has vastly improved the overall reliability of psychiatric diagnoses, thereby enabling psychiatry to meet one of the major criticisms of the medical model of mental disorder. The inclusion of more and more categories of illness in each succeeding version of DSM has led to more precise and consequently more reliable diagnoses. However, some scholars have argued that this expansion of mental diagnoses has less to do with problems of disease classification than it does with "problems" in third-party reimbursement (Mirowsky and Ross 1989). Each increase in the number of disorders listed in DSM has increased the scope of psychiatric practice. As the number of patients with recognized illnesses increases, so too does the amount of compensation that psychiatrists receive from insurance companies.

Even the firmest supporters of DSM-III recognize that the classification of mental disorder is influenced by nonmedical considerations. In order to reduce their payment liabilities, insurance companies have lobbied the APA to reduce the number of diagnoses; changes in public attitudes toward sexual preference issues led, in 1974, to dropping homosexuality from the list of mental disorders; veterans' groups successfully pressed for the inclusion of posttraumatic stress syndrome (Scott 1990); feminists have successfully protested against the male bias implicit in such diagnoses as "gender-identity disorder," a label often attached to girls who liked to play boys' games and with boys' toys. In sum, there is a less than perfect correspondence between some disease-producing entity or syndrome and the diagnosis of a psychiatric disorder; psychiatric diagnosis is based partly in the reality of disordered behavior and emotional pain and partly in the evaluations that society makes of that behavior and pain. Thus, the questions about the validity of psychiatric diagnosis are as troubling for DSM-III and DSM-IIIR as they were for DSM-I. As one observer has noted, "We have learned how to make reliable diagnoses, but we still have no adequate criterion of their validity" (Kendell 1988, p. 374). Given the problems that scholars have in defining mental disorder, and given the validity problems that ensue, it is not surprising that epidemiologists have used a number of different strategies to estimate rates of psychiatric impairment. These different research methodologies often have led to quite different interpretations of the role of social factors in the etiology of mental illness.

MEASUREMENT

The earliest sociological research on mental disorder relied on data from individuals receiving psychiatric care. In a classic epidemiological study, Faris and Dunham (1939) reviewed the records of all patients admitted to Chicago's public and private mental hospitals between 1922 and 1934. They found that admission rates for psychosis were highest among individuals living in the inner city. Several years later, researchers used a similar design to study the social class distribution of mental disorder in New Haven. In contrast to the Chicago study, which focused only on individuals who had been hospitalized, Hollingshead and Redlich (1958) included individuals receiving outpatient care from private psychiatrists in their study. Results from the New Haven study confirmed the earlier findings; the lower the social class, the higher the rate of mental disorder. More recent studies have also used information on treated populations. Studies of patient populations provide useful information, to be sure; findings shed light on the social factors that influence the course of mental-health treatment. Individuals receiving treatment for mental disorder, however, are not a random subset of the population of individuals experiencing psychological distress. Everybody who has potentially diagnosable mental disorder does not receive treatment. Furthermore, pathways to mental-health care may be systematically different for individuals with different social characteristics. Consequently, research based on treated rates of mental disorder seriously underestimates the true rate of mental illness in a population; it also may confuse the effects on psychiatric treatment of variables such as social class, gender, place of residence, or age with the impact of those same variables on the development of psychiatric impairment.

An alternative strategy for studying the epidemiology of mental disorder is the community survey. Early studies, such as the midtown Manhattan study (Srole et al. 1962), used symptom checklists with large random samples to estimate the amount of psychiatric impairment in the general population. Although such studies provided less biased estimates of the prevalence of psychological distress than did research on patient populations, they were subject to a different set of criticisms. The most serious limitation of the early community studies was that they used impairment scales that measured global mental health. Not only did the scales fail to distinguish different types of disorders, they confounded symptoms of physical and psychological disorder (Crandall and Dohrenwend 1967), measured relatively minor forms of psychiatric impairment, and frequently failed to identify the most serious forms of mental illness (Dohrenwend and Crandall 1970). Since it was not clear what relationship psychological symptom scales bore to cases of actual psychiatric disorder, it was also not clear how results from these studies contributed to an understanding of the social causes of mental illness.

Recent advances have solved some of the problems of the early global impairment scales; the development of symptom scales that measure specific forms of psychiatric impairment has done much to improve the reliability and validity of community survey research. The CES-D, for instance, is a twenty-item scale designed to measure depression. Weissman et al. (1977) report that the CES-D accurately distinguishes clinical from normal populations and depression from other psychiatric diagnoses. In addition, methods have now been developed to provide reliable psychiatric diagnoses of community respondents. Probably the most widely used diagnostic instrument of this sort was developed by a team of researchers at Washington University as part of the National Institute of Mental Health (NIMH) Division of Biometry and Epidemiology's Catchment Area Program. Called the Diagnostic Interview Schedule (DIS), the instrument can be administered by nonpsychiatrists doing interviews with the general population. Using DSM-III criteria, it provides both current and lifetime diagnoses for thirty-six adult psychiatric disorders. Enormous amounts of time and money have been devoted to the development of the DIS, and research that makes use of it promises to provide a vital link between studies of clinical and community populations. (See Weissman, Myers, and Ross 1986 for an excellent review and critique of the DIS and other measures used in community mental health research.) Nevertheless, even instruments like the DIS have shortcomings.

Mirowsky and Ross (1989) have challenged the DIS and DSM-III on the grounds that psychiatric diagnosis is a weak form of measurement and that it is of questionable validity. These authors claim that psychiatric disorders are dimensional, not categoric. By collapsing a pattern of symptoms into a single diagnostic case, valuable information is lost about the nature of the disorder. As a result, the causes of mental, emotional, and behavioral problems are obscured. Mirowsky and Ross go on to suggest that the reliance on diagnosis does not give a true, that is, a valid picture of psychiatric distress. Instead, psychiatrists use diagnoses because it allows them to receive payment from insurance companies who will pay only for cases and because it establishes mental distress as a problem that can be treated only by a physician. Although their criticisms are harsh, these authors reestablish the important distinction between the social construction of psychiatric diagnoses and the social causes of psychological pain. It is the latter issue, however, that most sociological research has addressed.

THE EPIDEMIOLOGY OF MENTAL DISORDER

Socioeconomic Status. The inverse relationship between socioeconomic status and mental disorder is now so well established that it has almost acquired the status of a sociological law. The relationship is surprisingly robust; it holds for most forms of mental disorder, no matter how socioeconomic status is measured, and for both patient populations and community samples. The inverse relationship is strongest and most consistent for schizophrenia, personality disorders, and organic syndromes. Findings for the major affective disorders are somewhat less consistent. Studies based on hospital populations (Goodman et al. 1983; Ortega and Rushing 1983) tend to report weak to moderate inverse relationships between social class and the incidence of major affective disorders such as manic depression; lifetime prevalence studies, however, often indicate a positive class gradient (Weissman and Myers 1978). Evidence on the class distribution of minor depression is more clear-cut, with studies almost universally showing higher levels of depressive symptomatology among the lower strata. Similarly, research consistently shows that the highest general levels of distress are also found among those with the lowest income, education, or occupational status.

There are two general qualifications to the pattern outlined above. First, even though socioeconomic status is negatively associated with most types of mental disorder, the relationship is probably not linear. Extremely high rates of disorder are typically found in the lowest stratum. Higher strata do have progressively lower rates, but variation is considerably less between them than between the lowest and the next-to-lowest tier. Some scholars have claimed, therefore, that serious mental illness is primarily an underclass phenomenon. Second, the inverse relationship between social class and mental disorder is probably stronger in urban than in rural areas and in the United States than in other societies. (For a comprehensive review of this literature, see Ortega and Corzine 1990.)

Most, if not all, of the major sociological theories of mental illness begin with the empirical observation that psychological disorder is most prevalent among those individuals with the fewest resources and the least social power. Until recently, researchers focused almost exclusively on one dimension of inequality—social class. Indeed, the dominant paradigms in the sociology of mental health have derived primarily from the attempt to explain this relationship; hypotheses regarding the effects of gender, age, or marital status on psychological distress are often simple elaborations of models derived from the study of social class and mental disorder. Three general models of the relationship between social resources and mental illness have been suggested. These are (1) the "social causation" hypothesis; (2) the "social selection" or "drift" hypothesis; and (3) the "labeling" or "societal reaction" approach.

Social Causation. *Social causation* is a general term, used to encompass a number of specific theories about the class-linked causes of mental disorder. Perhaps the most common version of social causation explains the higher rates of mental disorder among the lowest socioeconomic strata in terms of greater exposure to stress. According to this perspective, members of the lower class experience more stressful life events and more chronic strains. In addition, they are more likely to experience physical hazards in the environment, blocked aspirations, and status frustration (Kleiner and Parker 1963). Taken together, these stresses produce elevated rates of psychiatric impairment. In another version of social causation, scholars have argued that class differences in coping resources and coping styles are at least as important in the etiology of mental disorder as are class differences in exposure to stress (Pearlin and Schooler 1978). In this view, poverty increases the likelihood of mental illness because it (1) disrupts precisely those social networks that might effectively buffer the effects of stressful events and (2) inhibits the development of an active, flexible approach to dealing with problems. For both social and psychological reasons, then, the lower classes make use of less effective coping strategies. Finally, part of the class difference in mental disorder, especially in rates of treated disorder, may stem from class differences in attitudes toward mental illness and psychiatric care. Because of more negative attitudes toward mental illness and because of inadequate access to appropriate psychiatric care, the lower classes may be more seriously ill when they first come in contact with the mental-health-care system, and thus they may be more likely to be hospitalized (Gove and Howell 1974; Rushing and Ortega 1979).

Social Selection and Drift. This perspective implies that, rather than causing mental disorder, low socioeconomic status is a *result* of psychological impairment. Two mobility processes can be involved. According to the drift hypothesis, the onset of mental disorder adversely affects an individual's ability to hold a job and generate income. As a result of psychological disorder, then, individuals experience downward intragenerational mobility and physical relocation to less socially desirable neighborhoods. Social selection, on the other hand, occurs when premorbid characteristics of the mentally disordered individual prevent him or her from attaining as high a social status as would be expected of similar individuals in the general population. Here, the focus is on intergenerational mobility (Eaton 1980; Ortega and Corzine 1991).

Labeling or Societal Reaction. Based on the work of Thomas Scheff (1966), this approach holds that much of the class difference in mental disorder stems not from any real difference in mental illness but rather from a tendency to diagnose or label a disproportionate number of lower class individuals as psychologically impaired. According to Scheff, the process works as follows. Psychiatric symptoms have many different causes, and many people experience them. Only a few individuals, however, are ever labeled as mentally ill. Those who are are drawn from the ranks of those least able to resist the imputation of deviance. Once an individual is identified as mentally ill, a number of forces work to reinforce and solidify a mentally ill self-identity. Once labeled, individuals are encouraged by family and mental-health professionals to acknowledge their illness. They are rewarded for behaving as "good" patients should, a task made easier by virtue of the fact that individuals learn the stereotypes of mental illness in early childhood. When individuals are discharged from the mental hospital, or otherwise terminate treatment, they may be rejected by others. This rejection has psychological consequences that simply reinforce a mentally ill identity. The process is self-fulfilling, leading Scheff to conclude that attachment of the mentally ill label is the single most important factor in the development of chronic mental disorder.

An Assessment. After years of often acrimonious debate, the search for unitary explanations of the mental-disorder-to-social-class relationship has largely been abandoned. Sociologists seldom claim that mental illness derives only from medical factors, is caused only by features of the social environment, or stems purely from societal reaction. Most scholars now believe that different types of disorders require different types of explanations. Genetic and other biomedical factors are clearly involved in the etiology of organic brain syndromes, schizophrenia, and some forms of depression. However, genetics, brain chemistry, and other medical factors do not provide the entire answer since, even among identical twins, concordance rates for mental illness fall only in the range of 30 to 50 percent. Thus, the causes of mental disorder must also be sought in the social environment. Research does suggest a modest relationship between the social stressors attendant to lower class status and the onset of some forms of mental disorder. The evidence is clearest, however, for relatively minor forms of depression or psychological distress. For the more severe forms of mental illness, the drift and selection hypothesis appears to have the most empirical support. Although labeling is not the only cause of chronic mental illness, it is clear that the mental illness label does have negative consequences; the actual status of ex-mental patient, coupled with the ex-patient's expectation of rejection by others, adversely affects earnings and work status (Link 1987). Thus, labeling may be one of the processes through which drift occurs. As researchers refine the measurement of mental illness and more clearly delineate the processes of social causation, drift, and labeling, it is likely that further theoretical convergences will be identified.

Gender. It is not yet clear whether there are significant gender differences in overall rates of mental illness. There is little doubt, however, that certain types of disorders occur more frequently among women than among men. Most research reports that women are more likely to suffer from major and minor depression and anxiety than are men (Fox 1980; Weissman and Klerman 1977). Men, however, are usually found to have higher rates of antisocial personality disorders (Dohrenwend and Dohrenwend 1976). The sex ratio for some forms of mental disorder may be age-dependent; males have higher rates of schizophrenia prior to adolescence, and females have higher rates in later adulthood (Loring and Powell 1988). Studies also find that male–female differences in levels of depression are most pronounced among young adults (Dean and Ensel 1983). Furthermore, gender effects appear to interact with those of marital, occupational, and parental roles.

Scholars continue to disagree about the precise form of the interaction effects of gender and marital status on mental illness. Virtually all studies report that gender differences are most pronounced among married persons; married women consistently show higher levels of depression and anxiety than married men. Evidence on the unmarried, however, is mixed. Research based on treated populations often finds higher rates of disorder among single men. Studies based on community samples more frequently report higher distress levels among unmarried women. The interaction between gender and marital status is further complicated by the presence of children, work outside the home, or both.

Some research on married persons finds that gender differences are reduced when both husbands and wives are employed. Studies comparing groups of women often find that employment has modest, positive effects on mental health. However, other studies report no difference between employed women and housewives, and a few report that married, full-time homemakers with children have fewer worries and more life satisfaction (Veroff, Douvan, and Kulka 1981). These apparently contradictory findings stem, in part, from the different measures of mental health and illness used. It is possible, for instance, that small children can simultaneously increase their mothers' life satisfaction and their overall levels of distress. However, two substantive factors also appear to be involved. First, it is the demands created by children and employment, rather than parental or employment status per se, that cause elevated levels of distress among married women (Rosenfield 1989). The level of demands varies, of course, depending upon the level of male responsibility for child care and housework. Second, employment decreases gender differences in distress only when it is consistent with both the husband's and the wife's desires. Married men's distress levels may, in fact, surpass married women's when wives work but their husbands prefer them not to (Ross, Mirowsky, and Huber 1983).

As is true for social class, explanations for gender differences of mental disorder fall into three broad classes: social causation, social selection, and labeling. Because of the consistency of gender effects (at least for depression and anxiety) and improvements in the reliability of psychiatric diagnoses, most recent work has focused on the ways in which the social and psychological correlates of male and female roles cause variation in rates of mental disorder. Some have argued that differences in sex-role socialization make females more likely to direct frustration inward, toward themselves, rather than toward others, as males might. Thus, women are more likely to develop intropunitive disorders, whereas men are more likely to behave in antisocial ways (Loring and Powell 1988). Others have argued that women are more attached to others and are more sensitive to their needs than are men. As a result, women's mental health is influenced by their own experiences, and, in contrast to men, women are also more psychologically vulnerable to the stresses or losses of loved ones (Kessler and McLeod 1984). According to this perspective, women experience more stressful events and are more psychologically reactive to them than are men. Other explanations—for both direct and interactive effects—of gender on mental illness have focused on male–female differences in power, resources, demands, and personal control. Insofar as employment increases women's power and resources, it is likely to have positive effects on mental health. Well-educated employed women have fewer mental symptoms than nonworking women; among working- and lower class women, however, employment may actually increase anxiety and depression because it elevates demands at the same time that it produces only marginal increases in resources (Sales and Hanson Frieze 1984). Since employed women generally retain full responsibility for children, the demands of caring for children, particularly those under the age of six, exacerbate work-related stress. Thus, male–female differences in power and resources produce differences in the ability to control demands. Gender differences in control, in turn, shape perceptions of personal mastery; personal mastery is the psychological mechanism that connects gender differences in resources and demands to gender differences in mental illness (Rosenfield 1989).

The social selection perspective is valid only for explaining male–female differences in the relationship between marital status and mental disorder. The argument is that mental illness is more likely to select men out of marriage than women. (See Rushing 1979 for a related discussion.) According to this perspective, male forms of mental disorder—psychosis and antisocial personality, for example—prevent impaired men from satisfactorily discharging the traditional male obligation to be a good economic provider, making them ineligible as marriage partners. In contrast, female forms of psychiatric impairment may go undetected for long periods of time and may not seriously interfere with a woman's ability to fulfill the traditional housekeeping role. Thus, the higher rates of female disorder among the married are simply an artifact of the differing probabilities of marriage for mentally disordered men and women.

The labeling explanation for male–female differences in psychiatric impairment begins by challenging the notion that women actually experience more mental symptoms and disorders than men do. Labeling theorists argue that women are overdiagnosed and overmedicated because of biases on the part of predominantly male psychiatrists and because of the male biases inherent in psychiatric nomenclature. Coupled with the greater willingness of females to admit their problems and to seek help for them, these biases simply produce the illusion that women are more likely to be disordered than men. Scholars using the labeling-societal reaction-critical perspective argue that the effects of gender biases are not benign and that they have consequences at two levels. First, individual women are unlikely to receive appropriate services for their real mental-health problems. Second, and at a societal level, critics argue that psychiatry simply legitimates traditional gender roles, thereby buttressing the status quo (Chesler 1973).

A Theoretical Assessment. With the development of DSM-IIIR and with increases in the number of female mental-health professionals, concern over the issues raised by labeling theorists has died down. Trusting that the most blatant instances of sexism have been eliminated, researchers have turned their attention toward specifying the social psychological dynamics of the gender–mental-health equation; considerable progress has been made in elucidating the circumstances under which women are most likely to experience symptoms of mental disorder. Nevertheless, it may be premature to close the question of gender bias in psychiatric diagnosis. In one study, male clinicians appeared to overestimate the prevalence of depressive disorders among women, a tendency that is certainly consistent with gender stereotypes. In the same study, black males were most likely to be diagnosed as paranoid schizophrenics, a view consistent with both gender and racial stereotypes. The advances of DSM-III notwithstanding, the authors of this study concluded that sex and race of client and psychiatrist continue to influence diagnosis even when psychiatric criteria appear to be clear-cut (Loring and Powell 1988).

Age. Among adults, and with the exception of some types of organic brain syndromes, rates of mental illness decrease with age. Rates of schizophrenia, manic disorder, drug addiction, and antisocial personality all peak between the ages of twenty-five and forty-four (Robins et al. 1984). Furthermore, older persons with serious mental disorders are likely to have had their first psychiatric episode in young or middle adulthood. At least 90 percent of older schizophrenics experienced the onset of the disorder in earlier life. Similarly, about two-thirds of older alcholics have a long history of alcohol abuse or dependence (Hinrichsen 1990). Depression is the disorder most likely to occur among the elderly, and a substantial proportion of older community residents do report some of its symptoms. Nevertheless, relatively few of these individuals meet criteria for clinical depression (Blazer, Hughes, and George 1987), and rates of major depression are lower among older adults than in younger age groups. Some older persons, however, are more vulnerable to depression than others. As is true throughout the life cycle, women, individuals with health problems, the unmarried, and those with lower socioeconomic status are at greater risk of depression in late life than their peers. Estimating the true prevalence of depression among the elderly is especially problematic because its symptoms are frequently confused with those of dementia or other forms of organic brain disorder.

According to some estimates, two to four million older Americans suffer some form of chronic organic brain disorder. Of these, roughly half are diagnosed with Alzheimer's, a disease that involves an irreversible, progressive deterioration of the brain. Approximately half of all nursing home residents are estimated to suffer from some form of dementia. Because there is no known treatment for most of these disorders, older mental patients receive little psychiatric care. Critics suggest, however, that many older persons are improperly diagnosed with chronic brain syndromes. A sizable minority may actually be depressed; others may have treatable forms of dementia caused by medications, infection, metabolic disturbances, alcohol, or brain tumors. In many instances, then, the stereotype that senility is a concomitant of the aging process prevents appropriate diagnosis, intervention, and treatment.

Most explanations of the age–mental-health relationship have focused on specific age groups. Clinicians suggest, for instance, that anxiety and depression in middle age are a consequence of hormonal change or of changes in family and occupational roles. The personality disorders of young adulthood are often explained in terms of the stresses produced by the transition from adolescence to full adult roles. Among the elderly, explanations have focused on either organic or environmental factors. The chronic brain syndromes have recognized organic causes. Although neither is a normal part of the aging process, the two major causes of these disorders are the deterioration of the brain tissue, associated with Alzheimer's disease, and cerebral arteriosclerosis. However, environmental factors also contribute to the onset of the brain syndromes. They do so, in part, by increasing the likelihood of stroke or heart attack. In contrast, functional disorders, such as depression, personality disorders, and anxiety, depend more directly upon environmental factors. Some types of depression appear to have a genetic component, but the genetic link appears to be stronger in early- than in late-onset cases. Individuals who have their first episode of clinical depression prior to the age of fifty, for instance, are more likely to have relatives with depression than those who became depressed in later years (Hinrichsen 1990). Consequently, losses typical of late life, losses of health, occupation, income, and loved ones, appear to be the primary causes of mental-health problems among older adults.

Clearly, no single theory can adequately explain the etiology of mental disorder; at each stage of the life cycle, variables that are relevant to the onset of one type of disorder may be insignificant in the onset of other illnesses. Similarly, no single variable or set of variables is likely to explain age differences in overall rates of mental disorder. Nevertheless, efforts are under way to systematically explain the inverse relationship between age and functional psychiatric impairment. Gove and his associates have suggested that psychological distress decreases with age because individuals are able, over time, to find and settle into an appropriate social niche; as individuals move through life, they become less emotional and self-absorbed, function more effectively in their selected roles, and generally become more content with themselves and with others. As a result, rates of mental disorder decrease from late adolescence through late life (Gove 1985; Gove, Ortega, and Style 1989).

Place of Residence. Sociologists have commonly assumed that rates of mental disorder are higher in urban than in rural areas. However, this assumption is based more on the antiurban bias of much sociological theory than it is on empirical research. In a thoughtful and systematic review, Wagenfeld (1982) has argued that there is little evidence in the mental-health literature to suggest the superiority of rural life. In several of the rural community studies Wagenfield cites, researchers report a "probable" case rate for depression and anxiety of 12 to 20 percent. Studies that explicitly compare rural and urban communities generally find that rates of psychosis are higher in rural communities and that rates of depression are somewhat higher in urban areas. Differences in case definition and diagnosis, differences in how rural place of residence is defined and measured, and differences in the time period during which studies were conducted make it difficult to assess whether rural communities have significantly higher overall rates of pathology than urban areas. Results are sufficient, however, to suggest that rural life is not as blissful as it is often claimed to be. Recent declines in the rural economy, the out-migration of the young and upwardly mobile, and the relative paucity of mental-health services are likely to be major contributing factors in the etiology of rural mental-health problems.

Other Factors. Epidemiologists have also explored the relationships between the incidence or prevalence of mental disorder and such variables as race and ethnicity, migration, social mobility, and marital status. In each case, results generally support the view that individuals with the fewest resources—both social and economic—are most likely to experience psychiatric impairment. However, most research has adopted a rather static view; few studies have assessed the extent to which relationships between each of these variables and mental disorder have changed over time. Given the significant change in the mental-health professions over the last decades, this is a striking omission.

AN AGENDA FOR FUTURE RESEARCH

Since the early 1960s, psychiatric sociology has undergone enormous change. During the 1960s and 1970s, much of the literature was sharply critical of psychiatry and of medical models of madness. Although sociologists were divided about the relative importance of labeling processes in the etiology of mental illness, most agreed that psychiatric diagnoses were unreliable and were influenced by social status and social resources, that long-term institutionalization had detrimental effects, and that at least some patients were hospitalized inappropriately. Such criticisms provided one impetus for the substantial change that took place in psychiatric care during this same period. Laws were changed to make involuntary commitment more difficult; steps were taken to deinstitutionalize many mental patients; and a major effort was made to improve the reliability of mental diagnoses. By the time DSM-III was published in 1980, the most flagrant abuses and the sharpest criticisms of psychiatry seemed to have disappeared. Throughout the 1980s, sociologists returned to a medical model of impairment, and research focused on delineating the linkage between social variables, such as gender, age, race, social class, or place of residence, and specific diagnoses. Indeed, the psychiatric view of mental disorder is so well established in sociology that the growing literature on homelessness has generally accepted the assertion of mental-health professionals that most of the homeless are simply individuals who have fallen through the cracks of the mental-health-care system. (For one notable exception, see Snow, Baker, and Anderson 1986.) It is surprising that sociologists have been so uncritical in their acceptance of this position; it is also surprising that they have been so ready to accept the view that mental illness is primarily a problem of brain chemistry, genetics, and so forth and that it can be treated just like any other disease. It is certainly true that enormous strides have been made in the diagnosis and treatment of mental disorder. It is also true that biomedical factors are certainly involved in the etiology of some types of mental illness. Sociologists must, therefore, continue their efforts to develop a model of mental disorder that integrates medical, psychological, and social factors.

As some critics point out, however, the current emphasis on diagnoses and cases of mental disorder has limitations. Acceptance of the psychiatric view of mental disorder and acceptance of the policy implications of that view are not yet firmly grounded in empirical research. Independent of the field trials used in their formulation, few studies to date have assessed the reliability of DSM-III and DSM-IIIR (Mirowsky and Ross 1989); even fewer have assessed the extent to which changes in psychiatric diagnosis or changes in the civil rights guarantees of mental patients have affected the delivery and quality of mental health services. It is far from clear, for instance, that lower class women are any more likely to receive appropriate care in 1990 than they were in 1950 or 1960. It is unclear whether urban–rural differences in rates of mental disorder have changed over time and, if so, to what extent changes in diagnostic systems or service availability are implicated. It is also far from clear that deinstitutionalization of the mentally ill is the primary cause of homelessness in America; it is empirically no less plausible that the economic dislocations of the 1980s are the root causes of homelessness, in both rural and urban communities. Research in the 1990s must adopt a more dynamic or process view of mental-health issues. The consequences of changes in psychiatric diagnosis, of the increased reliance on drug therapies, of changes in mental-health law and policy, and in the availability of mental-health services must be assessed. Changes in the practice of mental-health care must be linked to changes in the composition of the pool of "potential clients" and to issues regarding the development of gender, age, class, and culturally appropriate care.

(SEE ALSO: *Mental Health; Stress*)

REFERENCES

American Psychiatric Association 1980 *Diagnostic and Statistical Manual of Mental Disorders III.* Washington, D.C.: American Psychiatric Association.

Blazer, Dan, Dana C. Hughes, and Linda K. George 1987 "The Epidemiology of Depression in an Elderly Community Population." *Gerontologist* 27: 281–287.

Chesler, Phyllis 1973 *Women and Madness.* New York: Avon Books.

Crandall, D. L., and B. P. Dohrenwend 1967 "Some Relations among Psychiatric Symptoms, Organic Illness, and Social Class." *American Journal of Psychiatry* 123:1,527–1,538.

Dean, Alfred, and Walter M. Ensel 1983 "Socially Structured Depression in Men and Women." In James Greenley, ed., *Research in Community Mental Health,* Vol. 3. Greenwich, Conn.: JAI.

Dohrenwend, Bruce P., and D. L. Crandall 1970 "Psychiatric Symptoms in Community, Clinic, and Mental Hospital Groups." *American Journal of Psychiatry* 126:1,611–1,621.

———, and Barbara Snell Dohrenwend 1976 "Sex Differences in Psychiatric Disorder." *American Journal of Sociology* 81:1,447–1,459.

Eaton, William W. 1980 *The Sociology of Mental Disorders.* New York: Praeger.

Faris, Robert E., and H. Warren Dunham 1939 *Mental Disorders in Urban Areas.* Chicago: University of Chicago Press.

Fox, John W. 1980 "Gove's Specific Sex-Role Theory of Mental Illness: A Research Note." *Journal of Health and Social Behavior* 21:260–267.

Goodman, A. B., C. Siegel, T. J. Craig, and S. P. Lin 1983 "The Relationship between Socioeconomic Class and Prevalence of Schizophrenia." *American Journal of Psychiatry* 140:166–170.

Gove, Walter R. 1985 "The Effect of Age and Gender on Deviant Behavior: A Biopsychosocial Perspective." In Alice S. Rossi, ed., *Gender and the Life Course.* New York: Aldine.

———, and Patrick Howell 1974 "Individual Resources and Mental Hospitalization: A Comparison and Evaluation of the Societal Reaction and Psychiatric Perspectives." *American Sociological Review* 39:86–100.

———, Suzanne T. Ortega, and Carolyn Briggs Style 1989 "The Maturational and Role Perspectives on Aging and Self through the Adult Years: An Empirical Evaluation." *American Journal of Sociology* 94:1,117–1,145.

Hinrichsen, Gregory A. 1990 *Mental Health Problems and Older Adults.* Santa Barbara: ABC–CLIO.

Hollingshead, A. B., and F. C. Redlich 1958 *Social Class and Mental Illness.* New York: Wiley.

Kendell, R. E. 1988 "What Is a Case? Food for Thought for Epidemiologists." *Archives of General Psychiatry* 45:374–376.

Kessler, Ronald C., and Jane D. McLeod 1984 "Sex Differences in Vulnerability to Undesirable Life Events." *American Sociological Review* 49:620–631.

Kleiner, R. J., and S. Parker 1963 "Goal-Striving, Social

Status, and Mental Disorder." *American Sociological Review* 28:129–203.

Link, Bruce 1987 "Understanding Labeling Effects in the Area of Mental Disorders: An Assessment of Expectations of Rejection." *American Sociological Review* 52:96–112.

Loring, Marti, and Brian Powell 1988 "Gender, Race, and DSM-III: A Study of the Objectivity of Psychiatric Behavior." *Journal of Health and Social Behavior* 29:1–22.

Mirowsky, John, and Catherine E. Ross 1989 "Psychiatric Diagnosis as Reified Measurement." *Journal of Health and Social Behavior* 30:11–25.

Ortega, Suzanne T., and Jay Corzine 1990 "Socioeconomic Status and Mental Disorders." In James Greenley, ed., *Research in Community and Mental Health,* Vol. 6. Greenwich, Conn.: JAI.

———, and William A. Rushing 1983 "Interpretation of the Relationship between Socioeconomic Status and Mental Disorder: A Question of the Measure of SES." In James Greenley, ed., *Research in Community and Mental Health,* Vol. 3. Greenwich, Conn.: JAI.

Pearlin, Leonard, and Carmi Schooler 1978 "The Structure of Coping." *Journal of Health and Social Behavior* 19:2–21.

Robins, L. N., J. E. Helzer, M. M. Weissman, H. Orvaschel, E. Gruenberg, J. D. Burke, Jr., and D. A. Regier 1984 "Lifetime Prevalence of Specific Psychiatric Disorders in Three Sites." *Archives of General Psychiatry* 41:949–958.

Rosenfield, Sarah 1989 "The Effects of Women's Employment: Personal Control and Sex Differences in Mental Health." *Journal of Health and Social Behavior* 30:77–91.

Ross, Catherine E., John Mirowsky, and Joan Huber 1983 "Dividing Work, Sharing Work, and In-Between: Marriage Patterns and Depression." *American Sociological Review* 48:809–823.

Rushing, William A. 1979 "The Functional Importance of Sex Roles and Sex-Related Behavior in Societal Reactions to Residual Deviants." *Journal of Health and Social Behavior* 20:208–217.

———, and Suzanne T. Ortega 1979 "Socioeconomic Status and Mental Disorder: New Evidence and a Sociomedical Formulation." *American Journal of Sociology* 84:1,175–1,200.

Sales, Esther, and Irene Hanson Frieze 1984 "Women and Work: Implications for Mental Health." In L. E. Walker, ed., *Women and Mental Health Policy.* Beverly Hills, Calif.: Sage.

Scheff, Thomas J. 1966 *Being Mentally Ill: A Sociological Theory.* Chicago: Aldine.

Scott, Wilbur J. 1990 "PTSD in DSM-III: A Case in the Politics of Diagnosis and Disease." *Social Problems* 37:294–310.

Snow, David, Susan Baker, and Leon Anderson 1986 "The Myth of Pervasive Mental Illness among the Homeless." *Social Problems* 33:407–423.

Srole, L., T. S. Langner, S. T. Michel, M. D. Opler, and T. C. Rennie 1962 *Mental Health in the Metropolis: The Midtown Manhattan Study.* New York: McGraw-Hill.

Townsend, John M. 1980 "Psychiatry versus Societal Reaction: A Critical Analysis." *Journal of Health and Social Behavior* 21:268–278.

Veroff, Joseph, Elizabeth Douvan, and Richard A. Kulka 1981 *The Inner American.* New York: Basic Books.

Wagenfeld, Morton O. 1982 "Psychopathology in Rural Areas: Issues and Evidence." In P. A. Keller and J. D. Murray, eds., *Handbook of Rural Community Mental Health.* New York: Human Sciences Press.

Weissman, Myrna M., and Gerald L. Klerman 1977 "Sex Differences and the Epidemiology of Depression." *Archives of General Psychiatry* 34:98–111.

———, and Jerome K. Myers 1978 "Affective Disorders in a U.S. Urban Community." *Archives of General Psychiatry* 35:1,304–1,311.

———, Jerome K. Myers, and Catherine E. Ross 1986 "Community Studies in Psychiatric Epidemiology: An Introduction." In M. M. Weissman, J. K. Myers, and C. E. Ross, eds., *Community Surveys of Psychiatric Disorders.* New Brunswick, N.J.:Rutgers University Press.

———, D. Scholomskas, M. Pottenger, B. Prusoff, and B. Locke 1977 "Assessing Depressive Symptoms in Five Psychiatric Populations: A Validation Study." *American Journal of Epidemiology* 106:203–214.

SUZANNE T. ORTEGA

MERITOCRACY *See* Equality of Opportunity.

METATHEORY Metatheory in sociology is a relatively new specialty that aims to describe existing sociological theory systematically, and also, to some degree, prescribe what future sociological theories ought to be like. It leaves to other specialties—most notably the sociology and history of sociology and the logic of theory construction—the problems of explaining and predicting how such theories have been, and can be, formulated.

There are two broad varieties of metatheory. One variety, *synthetic,* classifies whole theories according to some overarching typology; the other variety, *analytic,* first dissects theories into their underlying constituents and then classifies these constituents into types.

Some typologies encountered in synthetic metatheory refer to the time-periods when the theories were originated, for example, forerunner, classical, and contemporary (Timasheff and Theodorson 1976 and Eisenstadt 1976 provide examples). Some refer to the places where the theories were originated, for example, French, German, Italian, and American (Bottomore and Nisbet 1978 and Gurvitch and Moore 1945 provide examples). Some refer to the substantive themes of the theories, for example, structural-functional, evolutionist, conflict, and symbolic interactionist (Turner 1986 and Collins 1988 provide examples). Some refer to the ideologies supported by the theories, for example, pro-establishment and anti-establishment (Martindale provides an example). Some refer to various combinations of all the above differences (Wiley 1979 and Ritzer 1983 provide examples).

Analytic metatheory is divisible into two broad classes: one in which the constituents of theories are required to have empirical referents, either directly or indirectly, and another in which these constituents are required or permitted to have nonempirical referents. Thus, one sociologist claims our theory should be brought "closer to nonempirical standards of objectivity" (Alexander 1982), while another claims "sense-based intersubjective verification is indispensable [to sociology]" (Wallace 1983). (This difference in kind of analytic metatheory reflects an applicability of the synthetic-analytic distinction to meta-*method* in sociology: In the synthetic variety of metamethod, whole methods are characterized as *empirical* or *nonempirical, positivistic* or *hermeneutical, experimental* or *participant-observational,* and so on. In the analytic variety, such methods are dissected into their underlying constituents, which are then classified as *measurement, interpretation, speculation, comparison, test, generalization, specification, deduction, induction,* and so on.)

Some types of underlying constituents encountered in empirical analytic metatheory are "control" (Gibbs 1989); "individual actors," "corporate actors," "interests," and "rights" (Coleman 1990); "rational action," "nonrational action," "individualist order," and "collectivist order" (Alexander 1982); "social and cultural structures," "spatial and temporal regularities," "instinct," "enculture," "physiology," "nurture," "demography," "psychical contagion," "ecology," and "artifacts" (Wallace 1983, 1988); and general causal images like "convergence," "amplification," "fusion," "fission," "tension," "cross-pressure," "dialectic," and "cybernetic" (Wallace 1983, 1988). Some types of underlying constituents encountered in nonempirical analytic metatheory have been called (so far, without further explication or specification), "moral implication," "moral commitments," and "moral preferences" (Alexander 1982).

Metatheory in general has been sweepingly condemned as a dead end leading only to the study of "the grounds of other people's arguments rather than substantive problems" (Skocpol 1987), and as holding "little prospect for further developments and new insights" (Collins 1986). Against such characterizations, however, certain unique and indispensable contributions of both synthetic and analytic metatheory to sociology should not be overlooked.

Synthetic metatheory plays obviously central roles in descriptive classifications of sociological theory (e.g., textbooks and course outlines), but they are no less central to the sociology and history of sociology, where efforts to account for the rise and fall of schools, or perspectives, in sociological analysis require systematic conceptualization of such groupings. The contributions of nonempirical analytic metatheory remain unclear (as mentioned, the kinds of ideological commitment and moral foundation to which it refers, and their consequences for sociological theory, have yet to be specified) and, therefore, will not be examined here. The contributions of empirical analytic metatheory will occupy the rest of this article.

THREE CONTRIBUTIONS OF EMPIRICAL ANALYTIC METATHEORY

Empirical analytic metatheory can aid (1) systematic cumulation of the *end product* of sociological investigation (namely, collectively validated empirical knowledge about social phenomena); (2) systematic construction of new versions of the principal *means* employed in generating that end product (namely, collectively shared theory and method); and (3) a sense of discipline-wide *solidarity* among sociologists of all theoretical traditions, all specializations and, eventually one hopes, among all social scientists.

Cumulation of Sociological Knowledge. Knowledge can only cumulate when new knowledge of a given phenomenon is added to old knowledge of that same phenomenon (or, rather, insofar as no phenomenon is ever repeated exactly, that same type of phenomenon). The key to holding such objects of investigation constant is, of course, communication. That is to say, only the communication to investigator B of the identity of the exact phenomenon investigator A has examined, together with the exact results of that examination, can enable investigator B systematically to add new knowledge to A's knowledge.

Disciplinary communication. Now it may be imagined that we already possess such communication in sociology, but we do not. Consider the terms *social structure* and *culture.* One can hardly doubt that, by denoting the substantive heart of our discipline, they indicate what the entire sociological enterprise is about. By virtually all accounts, however, each term signifies very different kinds of phenomena to different sociologists.

Thus, *social structure* has been authoritatively said, at various times for over two decades, to be "so fundamental to social science as to render its uncontested definition virtually impossible" (Udy 1968); to attract "little agreement on its empirical referents" (Warriner 1981); and to possess a meaning that "remains unclear" (Turner 1986). "Few words," it has been said, "do sociologists use more often than 'structure,' especially in the phrase 'social structure.' Yet we seldom ask what we mean by the word" (Homans 1975). In a more detailed statement, one analyst asserts that

> *The concept of social structure is used widely in sociology, often broadly, and with a variety of meanings. It may refer to social differentiation, relations of production, forms of association, value integration, functional interdependence, statuses and roles, institutions, or combinations of these and other factors* (Blau 1975).

Indeed, we can still read that "sociologists use the term ["social structure"] in diverse ways, each of which is either so vague as to preclude empirical application or so broad as to include virtually all collective features of human behavior" (Gibbs 1989). As recent evidence of this diversity, it is noteworthy that, where one sociologist claims that "for sociologists, the units of social structure are conceived of . . . as *relational* characteristics" (Smelser 1988), another refers, without explanation, to a type of "social structure" in which the participants "have *no relations*" (Coleman 1990).

The situation is no different with the term *culture.* Some years ago it was said that "by now just about everything has been thrown into 'culture' but the kitchen sink," and the author of this remark then reflected that "The kitchen sink has been thrown in too" as part of "material culture" (Schneider 1973). Years later, it has again been pointed out that "Theorists of culture remain sorely divided on how best to define culture" (Wuthnow et al. 1984) and, more recently still, "values, orientations, customs, language, norms, [and religion]" have been referred to as though they were all somehow different from "culture" (Coleman 1990). No wonder at least one sociologist has simply given up: *"[A]ny* definition" of culture, he claims, "will be (1) inclusive to the point of being meaningless, (2) arbitrary in the extreme, or (3) so vague as to promise only negligible empirical applicability" (Gibbs 1990).

Sitting squarely in the middle of this disciplinary uncertainty about the empirical referents of social structure and culture, of course, is our persistently unexamined indecision about the empirical referents of the core sociological subject matter, that is, *social phenomena* per se in the generic sense that includes both social structure and culture. Definitions of this subject matter found in introductory textbooks seem to fall into two classes. Either they focus on the individual person as dependent variable and cast social phenomena as independent variables (Tumin 1973 and Orenstein 1985 provide examples) or they focus on social phenomena themselves, as both dependent and independent variables (Broom, Selznick, and Darroch 1981 and Brinkerhoff and White 1985 provide examples). More important than its status as dependent or independent variable, however, is the fact that a social phenomenon is never unequivocally defined in this or any other part of the sociological literature (Durkheim, who might come to mind in this context, gives [1982] two quite different definitions of "social facts" and does not reconcile them).

It therefore seems fair to conclude that modern sociology so far lacks the most indispensable feature of any science, namely, a language for identifying and holding constant the objects of its inquiry. It is this lack that empirical analytic metatheory is specifically aimed at remedying.

Disciplinary direction and priorities. Achieving such a language, it may be noted, should enhance not only our cumulation of knowledge already gained but also our planned pursuit of knowledge yet to be gained. As one sociologist says, "Precisely because of [its cumulation] science has hunches about what problems can now be tackled and what sorts of solutions are likely to emerge. Such continuity gives energy to research and enthusiasm to our intellectual work" (Collins 1986). It hardly seems necessary to add that, without a disciplinary language that can (1) stabilize the objects of our investigations so that knowledge about these objects can be cumulated and (2) provide the terms in which our hunches about possible new knowledge can be collectively debated, there can be no such continuity and no such enthusiasm.

Innovative Theory Construction. The first contribution of empirical analytic metatheory, then, is to the cumulation and projection of sociological knowledge along *existing* theoretical lines. Its second contribution is to the creation of *new* theory.

By reducing existing sociological theories to sets of common elements and common ways of combining these elements, empirical analytic metatheory immediately demonstrates that even the totality of all theories that have ever been proposed by no means exhausts the vast number of ways in which the elements in question *can* be combined. Still less do these theories exhaust the possible explanations of any given social phenomenon. To the extent that empirical analytic metatheory permits us logically to enumerate all these ways and all these explanations, it opens the way to constructing a very large number of testable new theories. It does this much as the periodic table of chemical elements and the theory of chemical bonds facilitate synthesizing new compounds and understanding old ones, and much as dictionaries and grammatical rules facilitate constructing new, as well as understanding old, sentences.

Conceptual Integration and Solidarity of the Discipline. The third contribution of analytic metatheory is to the conceptual integration of sociology and the consequent solidarity of sociologists. That such integration and solidarity are not now present is reflected in comments like "Sociology's fragmentation has accelerated since the 1950s . . . because of a proliferation of seemingly irreconcilable perspectives. . . . Never before has sociology been so fragmented, not just in North America but also in Europe" (Gibbs 1989); "American sociology is 'falling apart' and losing . . . intellectual coherence" (Turner 1989); "the current status [of sociology is] all periphery, no core" (Smelser 1989); "[W]e have become congeries of outsiders to each other, unable to see what the rivalries actually are in . . . fields [other than our own in sociology]" (Collins 1986).

In response to such expressions of disciplinary decline (and acknowledging their strong evidential basis), empirical analytic metatheory falls back on Durkheim's (1982) argument that insofar as "Every scientific investigation concerns a specific group of phenomena which are subsumed under the same definition," it follows that "[the] sociologist's first step must . . . be to define the things he treats so that we may know—he as well—exactly what his subject matter is. This is the prime and absolutely indispensable condition of any proof or verification."

Empirical analytic metatheory, then, seeks a common disciplinary language for sociologists everywhere, regardless of their specializations. Its proponents believe that only with the adoption of some such language can our discipline begin solving its central problems, namely, systematic knowledge cumulation, theory innovation, and solidarity enhancement.

(SEE ALSO: *Epistemology; Scientific Explanation*)

REFERENCES

Alexander, Jeffrey C. 1982 *Positivism, Presuppositions, and Current Controversies.* Berkeley, Calif.: University of California Press.

Blau, Peter M. 1975 "Parameters of Social Structure." In Peter M. Blau, ed., *Approaches to the Study of Social Structure,* pp. 220–253. New York: Free Press.

Bottomore, Tom, and Robert Nisbet 1978 *A History of Sociological Analysis.* New York: Basic Books.

Brinkerhoff, David B., and Lynn K. White 1985 *Sociology.* St. Paul: West.

Broom, Leonard, Philip Selznick, and Dorothy Broom Darroch 1981 *Sociology.* New York: Harper & Row.

Coleman, James S. 1990 *Foundations of Social Theory.* Cambridge, Mass.: Harvard University Press.

Collins, Randall 1986 "Is 1980s Sociology in the Doldrums?" *American Jounral of Sociology,* 91:1336–1355.

———1988 *Theoretical Sociology.* San Diego: Harcourt Brace Jovanovich.

Durkheim, Emile 1982 *The Rules of Sociological Method.* New York: Free Press.

Eisenstadt, S. N., with M. Curelaru 1976 *The Form of Sociology: Paradigms and Crises.* New York: Wiley.

Gibbs, Jack P. 1989 *Control, Sociology's Central Notion.* Urbana, IL: University of Illinois Press.

Gurvitch, Georges, and Wilbert E. Moore 1945 *Twentieth Century Sociology.* New York: Philosophical Library.

Homans, George C. 1975 "What Do We Mean by 'Social Structure'?" In Peter M. Blau, ed., *Approaches to the Study of Social Structure.* New York: Free Press.

Martindale, Don 1979 "Ideologies, Paradigms, and Theories." In William E. Snizek, Ellsworth R. Fuhrman, and Michael K. Miller, eds., *Contemporary Issues in Theory and Research.* Westport, Conn.: Greenwood.

Orenstein, David Michael 1985 *The Sociological Quest: Principles of Sociology.* St. Paul: West.

Ritzer, George 1983 *Contemporary Sociological Theory.* New York: Knopf.

Schneider, Louis 1973 "The Idea of Culture in the Social Sciences: Critical and Supplementary Observations." In Louis Schneider and Charles M. Bonjean, eds., *The Idea of Culture in the Social Sciences.* Cambridge: Cambridge University Press.

Skocpol, Theda 1987 "The Dead End of Metatheory." *Contemporary Sociology* 16:10–12.

Smelser, Neil H. 1988 "Social Structure." In Neil H. Smelser, ed., *Handbook of Sociology.* Newbury Park, Calif.: SAGE.

———1989 "Reviewing the Field of Sociology: A Response." *Contemporary Sociology* 18:851–855.

Timasheff, Nicholas S., and George A. Theodorson 1976 *Sociological Theory,* 4th ed. New York: Random House.

Tumin, Melvin M. 1973 *Patterns of Society.* Boston: Little, Brown.

Turner, Jonathan 1986 *The Structure of Sociological Theory.* Chicago: Dorsey.

———1989 "The Disintegration of American Sociology." *Sociological Perspectives* 32:419–433.

Udy, Stanley H. Jr. 1968 "Social Structure: Social Structural Analysis." In David L. Sills, ed., *International Encyclopedia of the Social Sciences,* Vol. 14. New York: Free Press.

Wallace, Walter L. 1983 *Principles of Scientific Sociology.* Hawthorne, N.Y.: Aldine.

———1988 "Toward a Disciplinary Matrix in Sociology." In Neil J. Smelser, ed., *Handbook of Sociology.* Newbury Park, Calif.: Sage.

Warriner, Charles K. 1981 "Levels in the Study of

Social Structure." In Peter M. Blau and Robert K. Merton, eds., *Continuities in Structural Inquiry*. Beverly Hills, Calif.: Sage.

Wiley, Norbert 1979 "The Rise and Fall of Dominating Theories in American Sociology." In William E. Snizek, Ellsworth R. Fuhrman, and Michael K. Miller, eds., *Contemporary Issues in Theory and Research*, pp. 42–79. Westport, Conn.: Greenwood.

Wuthnow, Robert, James Davison Hunter, Albert Bergesen, and Edith Kurzweil 1984 "Introduction." In Robert Wuthnow et al., eds., *Cultural Analysis*. Boston: Routledge & Kegan Paul.

WALTER L. WALLACE

MEXICAN STUDIES In the eighty-some years since the Mexican Revolution of 1910, Mexico has changed from a society in which three-quarters of the population is agricultural and lived in small villages, to one in which less than a quarter of the population works in agriculture, and most people live in large cities. Contemporary Mexico resembles the contemporary United States much more than the Mexico of 1910 resembled the United States of that year—in the design, technology, and environmental problems of its large cities; in the range and types of employment; in patterns of consumption; and increasingly in certain key demographic indicators, such as the birth rate. The unevenness of Mexico's economic development has resulted, however, in patterns of social inequality, population mobility, and political organization that are markedly different from those of the United States.

U.S.-Mexican relations are different, in a significant respect, from relations between other neighboring countries. The U.S.-Mexican border is the only international frontier that divides a developing and a highly developed country. The contradictory trends of Mexico's development shape U.S.-Mexican relations (Weintraub 1990). The two populations are brought closer to each other in terms of trade, tourism, labor migration, and consumer aspirations. This increasing proximity also creates social distance as each population develops opposing images of the other. These are often based on the misunderstandings that result from wide disparities in income, standards of living, and political and family culture (Pastor and Castañeda 1988).

Despite the propeasant rhetoric of the Mexican Revolution and of its successor governments, the lot of the small, subsistence-oriented farmer—the peasant farmer—has not significantly improved (Warman 1980). Agrarian reform has had only limited success in creating employment opportunities in agriculture, in diversifying the rural economy, and in stimulating development of rural market and service centers. Agricultural modernization in Mexico has meant the displacement of the peasant farmer, and the increasing importance of commercial farming, often linked to agro-industry (Arroyo 1989; Hewitt de Alcantara 1976; Sanderson 1986).

The cornerstone of agrarian reform is the *ejidal* system, based on family farming but with public ownership of and community rights to the land. It has been handicapped by the slowness of land redistribution and the small proportion of *ejidal* land that is irrigated. The expense of producing efficiently for the market deters many members of the *ejido* from continuing in agriculture. The deterrence has increased with the advent of new technological packages that offer substantially improved yields, which indebt the small producer and create dependence on state bureaucracy or on private-sector agro-industries.

The situation of the small-scale farmer is little different, whether *mestizo* or Indian in culture. The Indian population is likely to be materially poorer and to live in villages that are less well connected to market centers than are *mestizo* villages. The Indian population, defined in terms of those who speak an Indian language, has declined from being just over 14 percent of the population in 1940 to about 8 percent currently. Despite the decline in the proportion of Indian-speakers, their numbers have doubled since 1940.

The political structure of the rural areas allows for little local participation. The Mexican peasant is vertically incorporated into national politics through the local organization of the official party, the Partido Revolucionario Institucional (PRI). Rural social movements demanding land

and more government aid, and the increasing numbers of local peasant organizations that are independent of the PRI, indicate that this vertical control has been weakening in recent years. One of the major factors changing the pattern of political incorporation is the extension of government bureaucracy from the 1960s onward (Grindle 1977). In agriculture, this results in a considerable increase in government personnel administering various programs of rural development, of credit, and of technical advice. Direct contacts with government officials enable peasants to bypass local power brokers, thus weakening the broker's position; but it appears to have created a new issue, that of the interface between bureaucracy and the peasant. Bureaucratic officials implement central government policy but pursue their own career goals, and both objectives come into conflict with the strategies of peasant farmers.

The Mexican population has had high rates of growth as a result of significant declines in mortality without offsetting declines in fertility (Alba and Potter 1982). High rates of population growth combined with the lack of economic opportunities in the countryside result in substantial rural-urban and international migration (Massey 1988; Arroyo 1986). One result is the accelerated growth of Mexico's cities.

The urban growth rate of Mexico between 1940 and 1980 averaged 4.7 percent a year, with approximately a third of urban growth due to migration from rural areas. Nearly half of Mexico's population currently live in cities of over 100,000 people. The urban system is characterized by high primacy in which the capital, Mexico City, with a population of over seventeen million, is six times larger than the next largest city, Guadalajara. The high population concentration in Mexico City is based on economic concentration. Mexico City, with less than 20 percent of the national population, accounts for some 48 percent of national production and employment in manufacturing. Mexico City's dominance is similar in other sectors of the economy. This concentration is partly explained by the advantages of agglomeration. Mexico City possesses the major market for consumer goods in Mexico and the most developed economic infrastructure. Mexico City's growth is also promoted by the government's urban bias—substantial subsidies for food consumption, for transportation, and for economic infrastructure are provided by government; without these the profitability of Mexico City enterprises would have been less than that of enterprises in smaller cities (Garza 1985).

The primacy of the system has declined in recent years, and the fastest-growing cities are now intermediate in size, between 100,000 and 2 million. The 1980s saw a spatial restructuring of the urban system in which growth has been fastest in newly important economic regions such as the border with the United States, but also areas in the north-central and southern regions of the country, such as Aguascalientes, Mérida, San Luis Postosí, Guanajuato, and Querétaro.

This restructuring is partly based on Mexico's adoption of an export-oriented model of development based on manufacturing and liberalizing trade. Job creation in Mexican manufacturing is now mainly on the U.S.-Mexico border. The industrial transformation of the northern cities is a complex one. There are assembly-line operations that use cheap, mainly female labor (Fernández-Kelly 1983). There are also plants with high levels of technology that require workers with high levels of qualification and that are prepared to offer attractive conditions of work. The Mexican car industry is shifting to northern Mexico as part of an integrated North American production system, with Mexico shipping cars as well as parts to the United States market (Carillo 1989). These processes are creating a distinct border region straddling the frontier, neither fully Mexican nor fully American (Bustamante 1981; Tamayo and Fernandez 1983).

The consolidation of a border region does not appear to have affected the flow of illegal immigration to the United States. The border cities serve as staging posts for immigration into the United States, but as income opportunities increase in these cities and they develop an extensive infrastructure, they are likely to retain some of the flow of United States-bound population. This flow increased in the 1980s due to the continuing inability of the Mexican rural structure to provide jobs and to the downturn in the urban economies. Migration to the United States becomes the major means by which poor households, whether rural or urban, complement inadequate incomes, attracting even the skilled and better-educated (Massey, Alarcón, Durand, and González 1988).

The existence of large Mexican-origin communities in cities throughout the United States, but particularly in Los Angeles and other cities of the Southwest, provides bridgeheads facilitating immigration.

No matter the Mexican city—whether an established center or a new one—it has been built, to a considerable extent, by its inhabitants with their own hands. Over half the population of Mexico City live in irregular settlements in which the household takes the major responsibility for building the shelter (Ward 1990). Even amenities such as drinking water, sewage, and electricity are mainly secured through the efforts of local inhabitants. They lobby government and international aid agencies for aid, and often provide labor to help install the utilities. The counterpart to this pattern of irregular settlement is the importance of the urban informal sector (Roberts 1989). The informal sector is the set of economic activities, usually small-scale, that avoid state regulation over such matters as Social Security payments, fiscal obligations, and health and safety regulations. Facing difficult access to jobs, and in the absence of state welfare, both migrants and indigenous residents use the informal sector to cheapen the goods or services they offer. They also form an army of domestic outworkers and inexpensive workshop labor with close links to formal enterprises (Benaria and Roldan 1987). The urban informal sector accounts for at least a quarter of urban employment in Mexico.

Despite the significance of the informal sector, Mexico's urban economies have been remarkably successful in absorbing the rapid increase in the urban labor supply (Escobar 1986). Until the mid-1970s, the expansion of wage-earning opportunities, mainly in the formal sector, outpaced the growth of the economically active population. The proportion of the self-employed and unpaid family labor among the economically active urban population declined from 37.9 percent in 1940 to 18.6 percent in 1980. Even migrants from villages and small towns have been successfully integrated into the urban occupational structure. Much of Mexico City's manufacturing labor force is made up of migrants. Migrant-indigenous resident differences in occupational attainment are not substantial, as studies in both Mexico City and Monterrey have shown (Balan, Browning, and Jelin 1973; Muñoz, Oliveira, and Stern 1977).

Service employment, particularly in social and producer services, is the fastest-expanding sector of urban employment, while traditional services and manufacturing are in relative decline (García 1988). Manual workers in manufacturing—the classic industrial proletariat—are only about 14 percent of urban employment. Nonmanual employment, both in the professional, managerial, and technical grades, and in the clerical grades, is expanding faster than manual employment. These nonmanual occupations account for 30 percent of the urban economically active population.

There are three major distinguishing features to Mexico's pattern of social stratification. First is the considerable inequality of income distribution, which worsened between 1950 and 1990. In 1977, the top 10 percent of households absorbed about 36 percent of total national income, whereas the bottom 40 percent of households absorbed about 11 percent of total income. Given the low levels of per capita income, this income distribution produces considerable poverty for perhaps half the working population. Second, there is the presence of the informal sector, mentioned earlier, whose employers and employees have crosscutting interests that are different from those of their counterparts in the formal sector. The existence of these groups creates the potential for additional class identities and new bases for political alliance (Portes 1985). Third is the importance of the state as an employer. The state is a major employer, accounting for 17 percent of total employment, with most state employment concentrated in nonmanual occupations in public administration, health, and educational services.

In the 1980s, the employment categories associated with the informal economy—self-employed, unpaid family workers, owners and employees of enterprises with less than five workers—increased rapidly, while the proportion of employment in formal enterprises declined. The decline in real urban wages that is one of the major consequences of the current recession affects all strata of households. The wage squeeze on such middle-class occupations as teacher, nurse, or bank clerk is particularly severe, making it difficult to maintain or aspire to a middle class life-style. The urban poor are the most drastically affected, since their already low incomes give little leeway for savings other than cutting into basic levels of nutrition or health care. Existing evidence suggests that poor households manage to cope with declining wages through a variety of strategies, but mainly through more members working in the labor market. Surveys show that the number of household members in paid work has increased over the period of the recession, as has the size of the household, since adult children stay longer in the parental home, and other kin or nonkin join existing households (De la Peña, Durán, Escobar, and García de Alba 1990; Selby, Murphy, and Lorenzen 1990).

The household and the neighborhood have become major means of coping with adverse urban conditions (Lomnitz 1977). Though family and community bonds are strengthened, there are also signs of internal discord. Women are particularly heavily burdened. They increasingly have to work the double day of housework and paid work (González de la Rocha 1986). The desire of young adult members of a household to use their earnings individually, rather than contributing to the family pot, also creates tensions.

The struggle to survive in the cities contributes to important changes in politics. Urban politics in Mexico has been dominated by clientelism, with neighborhood leaders seeking to achieve local improvements through favors from the PRI (Cornelius 1975; Eckstein 1977). However, the contemporary size and complexity of cities such as Mexico City, Monterrey, and Guadalajara make clientelism increasingly ineffective. Urban social movements that challenge the official party have been important, particularly in Monterrey and Mexico City (Alonso 1980, Montaño 1976). The declining standard of living of middle classes and working classes is adding to this generalized discontent.

A dramatic manifestation of the extent of change was the 1988 general election, in which the presidential candidate of the PRI, by official figures, won only a bare majority, and lost the election in Mexico City. Though there is no strongly organized opposition party that is sure to wrest political control from the PRI in the near future, Mexican politics are likely to be increasingly open, democratic, and involve more genuine popular participation than in any period since the Revolution.

Mexican and U.S. sociologists are increasingly working together to interpret the above changes and their significance for U.S.-Mexico relations. The concerns of Mexican sociology are closer to those of U.S. sociology than they were twenty years ago—more pragmatic, more attentive to regional issues, more empirical, and less theoretical. In the earlier period, the main debates in Mexico centered around such issues as dependency theory and class analysis (Instituto de Investigaciónes Sociales 1977). This tradition is still reflected to a certain extent in *Revista Mexicana de Sociologia.* More recent journals such as *Estudios Sociologicos* of *El Colegio de Mexico, Frontera Nortes* of *El Colegio de la Frontera Norte,* and *Relaciónes* of *El Colegio de Michoacán,* are more likely to include empirical analyses of labor markets, regional development, migration, and other demographic changes.

(SEE ALSO: *Hispanic-American Studies; Latin American Studies*)

REFERENCES

Alba, Francisco, and Joseph Potter 1982 "Population and Development in Mexico Since the 1940s: An Interpretation." *Population and Development Review* 12:47–73.

Alonso, Jorge 1980 *Lucha Urbana y Acumulación de Capital.* Mexico, D.F.: Ediciónes de la Casa Chata, CISINAH.

Arroyo, Jesus 1986 *Migración a Centros Urbanos.* Guadalajara: Universidad de Guadalajara.

———1989 *El Abandono Rural.* Guadalajara: Universidad de Guadalajara.

Balan, Jorge, Harley Browning, and Elizabeth Jelin 1973 *The Lives of Men.* Austin: University of Texas Press.

Benaria, Lourdes, and Marta Roldan 1987 *The Crossroads of Class and Gender.* Chicago: University of Chicago Press.

Bustamante, Jorge A. 1981 "La Interacción Social en la Frontera Mexico-Estados Unidos: Un Marco Conceptual por la investigación." In Roque González, ed., *La Frontera del Norte.* Mexico, D.F.: El Colegio de Mexico.

Carillo, Jorge V. (ed.) 1989 *La Nueva Era de la Industria Automotriz en Mexico.* Tijuana, B.C.: El Colegio de la Frontera Norte.

Cornelius, Wayne 1975 *Politics and the Migrant Poor in Mexico City.* Stanford, Calif.: Stanford University Press.

De la Peña, Guillermo, Jorge Durán, Agustin Escobar, and Jesus García de Alba, eds. 1990 *Crisis, Conflicto y Sobrevivencia: Estudios Sobre la Sociedad Urbana en Mexico.* Guadalajara: Universidad de Guadalajara/CIESAS.

Eckstein, Susan 1977 *The Poverty of Revolution: The State and the Urban Poor in Mexico.* Princeton, N.J.: Princeton University Press.

Escobar, Agustin 1986 *Con el Sudor de tu Frente: Mercado de Trabajo y Clase Obrera en Guadalajara.* Guadalajara: El Colegio de Jalisco.

Fernández-Kelly, Maria Patricia 1983 *For We Are Sold. I and My People.* Albany: State University of New York Press.

García, Brígida 1988 *Dearrollo Económico y Absorción de Fuerza de Trabajo en Mexico: 1950–1980.* Mexico, D.F.: El Colegio de Mexico.

Garza, Gustavo 1985 *El Proceso de Industrialización en la Ciudad de Mexico, 1821–1970* Mexico, D.F.: El Colegio de Mexico.

González de la Rocha, M. 1986 *Los Recursos de la Pobreza: Familias de Bajos Ingresos de Guadalajara.* Guadalajara: El Colegio de Jalisco/CIESAS.

Grindle, Merilee S. 1977 *Bureaucrats, Politicians and Peasants in Mexico: A Case Study of Public Policy.* Berkeley, CA: University of California Press.

Hewitt de Alcantara, Cynthia 1976 *Modernizing Mexican Agriculture.* Geneva: UNRISD.

Instituto de Investigaciónes Sociales 1977 *Clases Sociales y Crisis Político en América Latina.* Mexico, D.F.: Siglo Veintiuno.

Lomnitz, Larissa 1977 *Networks and Marginality: Life in a Mexican Shantytown.* New York: Academic Press.

Massey, Douglas S. 1988 "Economic Development and International Migration in Comparative Perspective." *Population and Development Review* 14:383–413.

———, Rafael Alarcón, Jorge Durand, and Humberto González 1987 *Return to Aztlán.* Berkeley: University of California Press.

Montaño, Jorge 1976 *Los Pobres de la Ciudad en las Asentamientos Espontáneos.* Mexico, D.F.: Siglo Veintiuno.

Muñoz, Humberto, Orlandina de Oliveira, and Claudio Stern, eds., 1977 *Migración, Desigualdad Social en la Ciudad de Mexico,* Mexico, D.F.: Instituto de Investigaciones Sociales/El Colegio de Mexico.

Pastor, Robert A., and Jorge G. Castañeda 1988 *Limits to Friendship: The United States and Mexico.* New York: Alfred A. Knopf.

Portes, Alejandro 1985 "Latin American Class Structures." *Latin American Research Review* 20:7–39.

Roberts, Bryan 1989 "Employment Structure, Life Cycle, and Life Chances: Formal and Informal Sectors in Guadalajara." In A. Portes, M. Castells, and L. Benton, eds., *The Informal Economy: Comparative Studies in Advanced and Third World Countries.* Baltimore: The Johns Hopkins University Press.

Sanderson, Steven E. 1986 *The Transformation of Mexican Agriculture: International Structure and the Politics of Rural Change.* Princeton, N.J.: Princeton University Press.

Selby, Henry A., Arthur D. Murphy, and S. A. Lorenzen 1990 *Urban Life in Mexico: Coping Strategies of the Poor Majority.* Austin: University of Texas Press.

Tamayo, Jésus, and José Luis Fernandez 1983 *Zonas Fronterizas.* Mexico, D.F.: CIDE.

Ward, Peter M. 1990 *Mexico City: The Production and Reproduction of an Urban Environment.* London: Belhaven Press.

Warman, Arturo 1980 *"We Come to Object." The Peasants of Morelos and the National State.* Baltimore: The Johns Hopkins University Press.

Weintraub, Sidney 1990 *A Marriage of Convenience: Relations Between Mexico and the United States.* New York: Oxford University Press.

BRYAN R. ROBERTS

MIDDLE EASTERN STUDIES Since television, newspapers, and other mass media in the United States have focused on the Persian Gulf crisis, and since there has been an increasing public debate on the military involvement of the United Nations and the United States in that region, it seems appropriate to assess the role of Middle Eastern studies in American sociology. Thanks to the mass media, the general public has "discovered" the importance of such sociocultural phenomena as Ramadan, the *hajj* (pilgrimage to Mecca), and the veiling of women. American troops sent to Saudi Arabia were briefed about the customs of that country and were asked to restrain their celebration of Christmas and Hanukkah in 1990. This sensitivity is a marked change from the focus of the mass media on Middle East terrorism and the taking of hostages. These varying images of the Middle East in the U.S. media clearly call for some critical sociological analysis. There is also a need for a sociological analysis of the prejudice experienced by Middle Eastern immigrants in the United States as a result of events such as the hostage crisis in Iran, hostage taking in Lebanon, and the Arab–Israeli and Gulf wars. Finally, an understanding of the structure of Middle Eastern societies should enrich comparative sociological analysis.

In a paper titled "Sociology" (Sabagh 1976), I examined the development in the United States of the sociology of the Middle East. After a review of articles in four journals, I concluded that "with the possible exception of demographers, the scholarly output of American sociologists on the Middle East is still very modest" (Sabagh 1976, p. 523). If articles on Israel were excluded, this output was even smaller. For the period 1963–1973, of the twelve articles on the Middle East published in the *American Sociological Review* and the *American Journal of Sociology,* eight were on Israel, three on Egypt, and one on Turkey. For the same period *Sociology and Social Research* had even fewer articles on the Middle East, but they were more evenly distributed (two on Israel, two on Turkey, two on Iraq, and one on Israel and Jordan).

One interpretation of this situation, which is still valid today, is that "as long as the research findings tend to be area-oriented rather than hypothesis-oriented they are not likely to be published in American sociological journals" (Sabagh 1976, p. 523). Was the state of Middle Eastern studies in sociology in the 1980s any better than in the early 1970s? The objective of this review is to assess the changes that have occurred since the mid 1970s, more particularly in the 1980s. Three aspects will be considered: (1) trends and distributions in the number of sociologists in the United States specializing in the Middle East, (2) a brief review of the main substantive or methodological concerns of these sociologists, and (3) an indication of some of the theoretical contributions of Middle Eastern studies to American sociology. As background to the discussion, there will first be an overview of the salient socioeconomic characteristics of Middle Eastern countries.

SOCIOECONOMIC AND DEMOGRAPHIC CHARACTERISTICS OF THE MIDDLE EAST

The Middle East includes Iran, Israel, Turkey, and the Arab countries of North Africa and southwest Asia. As shown in Table 1, countries in this vast region vary greatly, not only in population but also in levels of income, education, urbanization, and stages of demographic transition. The most telling differences are those between rich and poor countries, unmatched by the experience of any other Third World region. The range in Gross National Product (GNP) per capita in 1988 was from $170 for Somalia to $13,400 for Kuwait and $15,770 for the United Arab Emirates (UAE). This gap was even greater before the decline in oil prices in the mid 1980s; in 1982 the GNP per capita was around $20,000 in Kuwait, Qatar, and the UAE. The highest incomes are in the least populated countries (Kuwait, UAE, Saudi Arabia); some of the most populous countries (Sudan, Egypt, Morocco) have the lowest incomes.

This income differential is in part responsible

TABLE 1
Selected Demographic, Economic, and Social Characteristics of Middle Eastern Countries and the United States, 1988.

Country, by Level of Income (U.S. dollars)	*GNP per Capita (U.S. dollars) 1988*	*Population (Millions) mid 1988*	*Total Fertility Rate 1988*	*Life Expectancy at Birth 1988*	*Annual Rate of Population Growth 1980–1989*		*Percent of Age Group in Secondary Schools 1987*		*Workers' Remittances as percent of GNP 1988*
					Total	*Urban*	*Total*	*Female*	
Somalia	$ 170	7.1	6.8	47	3.1	5.6	9%	6%	NA
Yemen PDR	$ 430	2.4	6.6	51	3.0	4.7	NA	NA	24.5%
Sudan	$ 480	23.8	6.4	46	3.0	4.1	20	17	2.6
Mauritania	$ 480	1.9	6.5	46	2.6	7.8	16	9	−2.8
Yemen AR	$ 640	8.5	8.0	47	3.4	8.8	26	6	3.5
Egypt AR	$ 660	51.9	4.5	63	2.6	3.5	69	58	9.9
Morocco	$ 830	23.9	4.7	61	2.7	4.4	37	30	6.5
Tunisia	$ 1,230	7.8	4.1	66	2.5	2.9	40	34	5.6
Turkey	$ 1,280	52.4	3.7	64	2.3	3.4	46	34	2.5
Jordan	$ 1,500	3.9	6.4	66	3.7	5.1	NA	NA	13.9
Syrian AR	$ 1,680	11.4	6.7	65	3.6	4.5	59	48	1.1
Algeria	$ 2,360	23.8	5.4	64	3.1	3.9	55	46	0.5
Oman	$ 5,000	1.4	7.1	64	4.7	8.7	38	29	−9.7
Libya	$ 5,420	4.2	6.8	61	4.3	6.7	NA	NA	−2.2
Saudi Arabia	$ 6,200	14.0	7.1	64	4.2	5.8	44	35	−5.7
Bahrain	$ 6,340	0.5	NA	NA	NA	NA	NA	NA	NA
Israel	$ 8,650	4.4	3.0	76	3.0	4.1	83	87	NA
Qatar	$ 9,930	0.4	NA	NA	NA	NA	NA	NA	NA
Kuwait	$13,400	2.0	3.7	73	4.4	5.1	82	79	−4.4
UAE	$15,770	1.5	4.7	71	4.8	4.2	60	66	NA
Iran IR	NA	52.5	5.6	63	3.0	4.1	48	39	NA
Iraq	NA	17.7	6.3	64	3.6	4.8	49	38	NA
Lebanon	NA	2.8	NA	NA	NA	NA	NA	NA	NA
United States	$19,840	246.3	1.9	76	1.0	1.0	98%	99%	− 0.2%

NA = Not available. AR = Arab Republic. IR = Islamic Republic. PDR = People's Democratic Republic. UAE = United Arab Emirates.

SOURCE: World Bank, *World Development Reports 1990* (New York: Oxford University Press, 1990); United Nations, *1988 Demographic Yearbook* (New York: United Nations, 1990).

for a massive labor migration from the poor Arab countries, particularly Egypt and Yemen, to the rich Arab countries (Amin and Awny 1985; Owen 1989). One measure of the importance of this migration is provided by the figures on the share of workers' remittances in the GNP of labor-exporting countries. Workers' remittances constituted 24.5, 13.9, and 9.9 percent of the GNP of Yemen PDR, Jordan, and Egypt, respectively (Table 1). Estimates of the size of the Arab labor-migration streams vary widely (Amin and Awny 1985; Ibrahim 1982), but it increased rapidly in the 1970s and was substantial in 1980. For Egypt alone, one estimate places the number of workers abroad at over one million in 1980, compared with around four hundred thousand in 1975 (Amin and Awny 1985; Fergany 1987). There was also a considerable migration from the poor countries of South and East Asia to Gulf countries, with an estimated seven hundred thousand contract workers in 1987 (Stahl and Asam 1990). After the military occupation of Kuwait by Iraq, there was a massive exodus of many labor migrants from Kuwait and Iraq, creating new economic problems for Arab labor-exporting countries such as Egypt and Jordan. This exodus has continued as a result of the Gulf war.

While a few North Africans and Turks emigrated to the Gulf, most were attracted by expanding economic opportunities in Western Europe; an estimated foreign-stock population of 1.5 million North Africans were in France in 1985, with 1.5 million Turks in Germany in 1988 (Organization for Economic Cooperation and Development 1990, p. 113). As a result of political upheavals such as the Iranian revolution, the Arab-Israeli wars of 1967 and 1973, and the Lebanese civil war, and facilitated by changes in American immigration legislation in the 1960s, there has been a sizable migration of Middle Easterners to the United States; in 1980, of 480,000 persons born in the Middle East, 122,000 were born in Iran (U.S. Bureau of the Census 1984).

The characteristics and implications of the massive labor migration of Middle Easterners and Asians to the rich Arab oil-producing countries have been analyzed by a few American demographers and sociologists (Arnold and Shah 1984; Sabagh 1988; Sell 1988). These and other studies (Amin and Awny 1985; Fergany 1987) have contributed to the analysis of (1) the process of migrant settlement in countries with stringent legislation against settlement, (2) the impact of this migration on social mobility, and (3) the consequences of labor migration on countries of origin.

In almost all Middle Eastern countries, rates of population growth of urban areas are higher, and in some cases much higher, than total population growth. This means that rural–urban migration constitutes an important feature of both rich and poor Middle Eastern societies. This rural exodus is most marked in some of the poorest countries but tends to be lower in poor countries with substantial international labor migration.

While one expects the richest countries to have the highest educational level, the data in Table 1 suggest that this is only partly true. The percentage of persons in secondary school was higher in some of the poorer countries, such as Egypt (69 percent) and Turkey (46 percent), than in some of the richest ones, such as Saudi Arabia (44 percent). Wealth was no guarantee of women's access to education. It is true that in Israel, Kuwait, and the UAE women's educational achievement was as high as or even higher than that of the total population, but the relative gap between the schooling of women and that of the total population was lower in Egypt than in Saudi Arabia.

The demographic indicators of mortality and fertility vary widely among Middle Eastern countries. Expectations of life at birth range from a low of forty-seven years in Somalia to a high of seventy-three in Kuwait and seventy-six in Israel. If we exclude Israel with a total fertility rate (TFR) of 3.0 live births per woman, Middle Eastern countries tend to have high TFRs of around 6, somewhat unrelated to their levels of mortality or income. For instance, Saudi Arabia, with an expectation of life at birth of sixty-four years had an estimated TFR of 7.1, somewhat higher than that of Somalia and Yemen AR, which have the lowest income and highest mortality. Turkey has the same low mortality level as Saudi Arabia, but its TFR (3.7) is nearly half that of Saudi Arabia. Egypt, Morocco, Tunisia, and Kuwait have TFRs of 4.5, 4.7, 4.1, and 3.7, respectively, suggesting that they have experienced some fertility decline.

Clearly, the Middle East is a region worthy of consideration in any analysis of the social and demographic impact of economic modernization and rising levels of income. Its experience poses a real challenge to the theory of demographic transition, in that fertility rates have remained high in spite of rapid modernization and declining mortality. The sudden increase in the wealth of some Arab countries is part of what Ibrahim (1982) has called the "New Arab Social Order," which involves the appearance of new social forces and new values and behavior patterns. This has resulted in a great deal of social chaos and the emergence of new social problems. Partly as a result of this social chaos, there have been significant political and social movements and revolutions that need to be analyzed from a comparative sociological perspective.

The 1973 Arab-Israeli war and the subsequent oil crisis, the civil war in Lebanon, the Iranian revolution of 1978–1979, the Iraq–Iran war of 1980–1988, the Intifadah in the West Bank and Gaza, and now the Gulf war are dramatic events that have increased Americans' awareness of the Middle East. During the Gulf crisis, journalists, military analysts, and political commentators have been the main sources of information for an increasingly puzzled American public. By systematic and comparative analyses of various features of Middle Eastern societies, American sociologists could provide a foundation for a better understanding of these events. This assumes, however, that these sociologists have incorporated the history and experience of Middle Eastern countries into their substantive concerns and theoretical models. The next sections will review the trends in the number of sociologists of the Middle East in the United States and the substantive focus of their work.

NUMBER OF SOCIOLOGISTS OF THE MIDDLE EAST IN THE UNITED STATES

It is significant that an American sociologist, Monroe Berger of Princeton University, was active in the formation of the Middle East Studies Association of North America (MESA) in 1964 and was elected its first president. Nevertheless, in the mid 1970s there were only nine sociologists teaching courses on the sociology of the Middle East in American departments of sociology (Sabagh 1976, p. 524). While growth was slow, the 1980s were marked by a noticeable increase in sociologists teaching or doing research on the Middle East. Sociologist members of MESA increased from twelve in 1968 to twenty-five in 1972, thirty-seven in 1984, fifty-two in 1986, and ninety in 1990 (Sabagh 1976; Bonine 1986; Middle East Studies Association 1990). Not all of these sociologists, however, resided in the United States. In 1986 only 3 percent of MESA members were sociologists, compared with 32 percent who were historians and 21 percent who were political scientists (Bonine 1986, p. 159). In the mid 1980s Bonine (1986, p. 160) could still state that "compared to Latin America, for instance, there are few sociologists and demographers specializing on the Middle East."

While an increasing number of Middle Easterners have come to the United States to obtain a Ph.D. in sociology, most of them have gone back home. But, as a result of the Iranian revolution and its negative effect on the teaching of Western-type sociology in Iran, many Iranians who obtained a Ph.D. in sociology remained in the United States as intellectual exiles. Also, the Iranian revolution provided a real impetus for Iranian students to major in sociology to gain a better understanding of the revolution. According to a special tabulation (MESA members residing in the United States in 1990) provided by Dr. Anne Betteridge, executive secretary of MESA, of the twenty-one members of MESA who received a Ph.D. in sociology prior to 1980, none were Iranians, whereas nearly 60 percent of the nineteen MESA members who received a Ph.D. in sociology in 1980–1989 were born in Iran. By contrast, about 29 percent of the pre-1980 Ph.D. cohort were born in an Arab country, compared with only 10 percent of the 1980–1989 cohort. The creation of the Association of Arab-American University Graduates in 1967 may be partly responsible for this decline. There was also a sharp decline in U.S.-born sociologist members of MESA, from 57 percent of the pre-1980 Ph.D. cohort to 16 percent of the 1980–1990 cohort.

There is some evidence to suggest that the share of U.S.-born sociologist members of MESA will increase in the future. In 1990, about 39 percent of the eighteen sociology student MESA members (for whom information was available) were born in the United States, one was born in an Arab country, four were born in Iran, and six were born in Turkey.

Not all sociologists with a research or teaching interest in the Middle East are members of MESA. One rough estimate of the number of these sociologists is provided by the American Sociological Association's (ASA) *Guide to Graduate Departments of Sociology.* A search of this guide for 1990 showed that thirty-one members of these departments indicated an interest in the Middle East or a Middle Eastern country. Of these, fifteen were members of MESA. Membership in MESA was somewhat higher at universities that had a Middle East/Near East center than those which did not. Fifty percent of sociology student members of MESA were at universities with a Middle East/ Near East center, including Harvard, Michigan, UCLA, SUNY Binghamton, and Texas. With the exception of Texas, sociology faculty members specializing in the Middle East were members of MESA.

SUBSTANTIVE FOCUS OF SOCIOLOGISTS OF THE MIDDLE EAST

It is safe to assume that sociologists who belong to MESA will focus some of their research and theoretical interest on the Middle East. The directory of ASA members (American Sociological Association 1990) provides information on fields of specialization. Unfortunately, there are no tabulations available that would allow comparisons with all sociologists or sociologists who have an interest in other world areas. There were twenty-six nonstudent and nine student members of ASA in 1989 who were also members of MESA. Of the twenty-six nonstudent members, fifteen were in graduate departments of sociology. Members were asked to check four substantive or methodological areas of sociology in order of priority, of which the first and second are analyzed here. The three most important areas of specialization are (1) development and social change, (2) comparative sociology/macro, and (3) political sociology. Next areas in importance are (1) demography, (2) race/ethnic/minority, (3) sociology of sex roles, and (4) social movements.

Unfortunately, no questions were asked about the extent to which sociologists focused on a given region, country, society, or community. For this, it would be necessary to analyze the publications and papers of the thirty-five scholars who were members of both the ASA and MESA. A survey was made of publications and papers by these scholars that were cited in *Sociological Abstracts* for the period 1985–1990. The three most frequent substantive or theoretical topics were (1) the Iranian revolution, (2) historical-sociological analyses of Turkey and Iran, with an emphasis on dependency or world system approaches, and (3) Iranian immigrants in the United States. Other topics included (1) Egyptian international migration, (2) social distance in Egypt, (3) child nutrition, (4) a review of Arab sociology, and (5) the Intifadah. It is likely, however, that there are many more contributions to Middle Eastern studies by sociologists who are not members of MESA. The task of assessing this literature is clearly beyond the scope of this essay. One way to obtain this information is through a survey of these sociologists. In 1983–1984 such a survey was carried out for Arab sociologists or sociologists studying the Arab world (Sabagh and Ghazalla 1986). Ten of the sociologists residing in the United States considered social change and development and the role of Islam to have the highest priority for research on the Arab world.

One issue that needs to be considered is the extent to which sociological research on the Middle East is cited in major American sociological journals. An analysis was made of articles on the Middle East cited in *Sociological Abstracts* for the years 1985–1990 and published in the general and more specialized sociological journals. Since the number of papers on Israel was substantial, they were left out of the analysis. The results of this analysis showed that the situation was even worse now than it was in the period 1963–1973 (Sabagh 1976). There was only one article in the *American Sociological Review* and none in the *American Journal of Sociology* and *Social Forces.* On the other hand, in the 1980s a substantial number of articles on the Middle East were published in the newer or more specialized sociological journals.

An analysis of *Sociological Abstracts* for the period 1985–1990 showed that thirty-one specialized journals had published 104 articles pertaining to the Middle East or to Middle Easterners. The distribution of articles by country or region (exclusive of Israel) was as follows: Iran, thirty-one; Turkey/Ottoman Empire, fourteen; Arab world/Middle East/fifteen; Egypt, fourteen; other Middle Eastern countries, nineteen; Palestinians, five; Arab and Iranian immigrants in the United States, six. The large number of articles on Iran may be explained by the analyses of the Iranian revolution and by the increasing number of Iranian sociologists in the United States. One issue of *State, Culture, and Society* (1985) included eight articles devoted to "The Sociological and Ideological Dimensions of the Iranian Revolution." There were four articles on the Iranian revolution (or comparing the Iranian revolution with other revolutions) in *Theory and Society.* Five specialized journals published ten articles on marriage and the family and the status of women, five of which were on Iran. The period 1985–1990 was also characterized by a substantial number of articles on the Ottoman Empire and Turkey published in the Fernand Braudel Center's *Review.* The Winter 1985 issue of the *Review* included three articles on "From Ottoman Empire to Modern State," and the Spring 1988 issue was devoted to the "Ottoman Empire: Nineteenth-Century Transformations." These articles present critical analyses of the process of incorporation of the Ottoman Empire/Turkey into the world economy. Clearly, sociologists whose research focuses on the Middle East or Middle Easterners have a better chance of getting their articles accepted in specialized sociological journals than in the major and mainstream sociological journals.

THEORETICAL AND METHODOLOGICAL CONTRIBUTIONS OF MIDDLE EASTERN STUDIES TO SOCIOLOGY

There are two major ways in which Middle Eastern Studies can contribute to sociology: (1) dramatic events in the Middle East, such as wars and revolutions present a puzzle to sociologists studying such events, and (2) sociologists specializing in Middle Eastern studies focus on substantive issues that have consequences for sociological theory and methodology. Examples of both types of contributions will be given and discussed.

The Iranian Islamic revolution is clearly one of the most dramatic events of the last decades of the twentieth century. For Arjomand (1988, p. 3) it is a "cataclysm as significant and as unprecedented in world history as the French revolution of 1789 and the Russian revolution of 1917." As could be expected, American sociologists of Iranian origin have contributed many important insights into the causes and consequences of this revolution, and these insights have been and will be incorporated into sociological theories about revolutions (see, e.g., Arjomand 1988; Ashraf and Banuazizi 1985; Ashraf 1988; Dabashi 1984; Moghadam 1989; Parsa 1989). For other sociologists who have studied the nature and sources of revolution, the Iranian revolution presents a real challenge.

This is expressed as follows by Theda Skocpol:

> *The recent overthrow of the Shah, the launching of the Iranian revolution between 1977 and 1979, came as a sudden surprise to outside observers. . . . All of us have watched the unfolding of current events with fascination and, perhaps, consternation. A few of us have also been inspired to probe the Iranian sociopolitical realities behind those events. . . . Its unfolding . . . challenged expectations about revolutionary causation that I developed through comparative-historical research on the French, Russian and Chinese revolutions.* (1982, p. 265)

Skocpol applied her earlier structural analysis of the causes of revolutions to the Iranian case, pointing to the involvement of urban masses in this revolution, the role of the rentier state, and the structural consequences of Shia Islam. When challenged by Nichols (1986, p. 182) that she is "ready to concede the potentially revolutionary content of traditional religious teachings," Skocpol (1986, p. 193) replied that "far from offering a 'subjectivist' or 'ideational' analysis, I point out that Shi'a religion had the cultural potential to facilitate *either* a rebellion against *or* passive acquiescence to secular authority." Arjomand (1988, p. 191) criticizes Skocpol for not recognizing the "normative factor of legitimacy."

Arjomand, Ashraf, and other sociologists indicate the importance of analyzing the 1977–1979 revolution by considering its historical roots, particularly the structural, ideological, and leadership factors in previous uprisings and rebellions. Thus, for Ashraf (1988, p. 550), "The urban uprising of 1963 combined the leadership of a militant charismatic leader, the political resources of the bazaar-mosque alliance, and the sympathy of activist university students . . . a prelude to the Islamic revolution of 1977–79." Arjomand (1988) points to the involvement of "high-ranking members" of the Shiite "clergy" or hierocracy in the constitutional revolution of 1905–1906. Arjomand (1984a, 1984b, 1988) not only traces the history of the relationship between the Shiite hierocracy, the state, and other social groups but also places his analysis of the Iranian revolution in a comparative perspective. Clearly, the Iranian revolution has stimulated an interesting and important sociological theoretical dialogue about the causes of the revolution, but more empirical research is needed to test the various hypotheses and theories that have been advanced.

Somewhat less visible than the Iranian revolution to American sociologists are the various Islamic fundamentalist social movements that have sprung up in many Sunni Muslim countries, partly in response to the impact of the Iranian revolution (Sabagh and Ghazalla 1986). While there have been a number of studies of these movements by sociologists in Egypt and Tunisia, as well as by historians and political scientists in the United States (Arjomand 1984a; Sabagh and Ghazalla 1986; Stowasser 1987), American sociologists specializing in the study of social movements have generally ignored Islamic movements. Not even such dramatic events as the assassination of President Sadat of Egypt by members of an Islamic fundamentalist group have challenged these sociologists. Yet, as Snow and Marshall have stated (1984, p. 145), a sociological analysis of the "resurgence of Islamic militancy" provides an opportunity to inform "our understanding of social movements and changes in the Third World."

One interesting development of the period since 1975 has been the application of the world-system theoretical model to the Ottoman Empire and Turkey. An early issue of the Fernand Braudel Center's *Review* (Winter 1979) included three articles on "The Ottoman Empire and the World-Economy," one of which provides a program of research delineated by Immanuel Wallerstein (1979). The objective of this program was to analyze the process of incorporation of the Ottoman Empire into the world economy, the consequences of this incorporation, and the degree and nature of the peripheralization of the Ottoman Empire and Turkey. This program was carried out by the Research Working Group on the Ottoman Empire and was coordinated by Çağlar Keyder and Immanuel Wallerstein (Kasaba, Keyder, and Tabak 1986). The work of Kasaba (1987, 1988), Kasaba, Keyder, and Tabak (1986), Keyder (1988), Pamuk (1988), and other sociologists, economists, or historians with a world-system perspective has documented the timing and the process of incorporation of the Ottoman Empire into the world economy, the role of the Ottoman bureaucracy, and the emergence of a minority non-Muslim bourgeoisie. Kasaba (1987, p. 842) argues that "between ca. 1750 and ca. 1820 the Ottoman Empire as a whole was incorporated into the capitalist world-economy . . . [and] the history of the Ottoman Empire after the 1820's was that of its peripheralization." Pamuk's (1988) analysis of various indices of foreign trade and investment shows, however, that until 1914 the degree of integration of the Ottoman Empire into the world economy was noticeably lower than that of Latin America or that of Algeria and Egypt. Also, within the Ottoman Empire different sectors of the economy were incorporated in different periods (Çizakça 1985).

One consequence of the process of incorporation into the world economy was the emergence of a new bourgeois class of non-Muslim merchants (Kasaba 1987; Keyder 1988). While there was a social class conflict between these merchants and the Ottoman bureaucracy, this conflict "appeared on the Ottoman agenda to be acted out as Moslem-Christian ethnic-religious conflict" (Keyder 1988, p. 162). The periphery-core status of Safavid Iran and the Ottoman Empire in the seventeenth century is analyzed by Foran (1989, p. 113), who concludes that these states "were far too strong to be colonized and dominated by the core, *and yet* too weak to compete with Europe in the new peripheries of Asia, Southeast Asia, and Africa, not to mention Latin America." Thus, these states were neither core nor periphery.

Janet Abu-Lughod (1989) provides a challenging theoretical emendation of the world-system perspective through a bold analysis of the world system in the period 1250–1350. On the basis of her analysis of linkages and contacts between the cities of western Europe, the Middle East, central Asia and China, and the Indian subcontinent, Abu-Lughod (1990, pp. 276–277) concludes that "what is noteworthy in the world-system of the thirteenth century is that no single cultural, economic, or imperial system was hegemonic" and that the "rise" of this "world-system to its peak in the second half of the thirteenth century and the opening decades of the fourteenth was due primarily to developments in the East, not in the West." While these interpretations and conclusions may be challenged by other sociologists and further historical research, they demonstrate the theoretical relevance of considering the historical experience of Middle Eastern countries.

The sizable migration of Iranians to the United States was another consequence of the Iranian revolution, and the study of this new group of exiles and immigrants has led to some new theoretical insights about immigrant adaptation in this country (Bozorgmehr 1991; Sabagh and Bozorgmehr 1987). According to Bozorgmehr and Sabagh (1988, p. 32), "from a small beginning of perhaps no more than 15,000 individuals in 1965, the Iranian population grew rapidly to at least 121,000 in 1980 and may well have reached 250,000 in 1986." Iranians are the latest wave in migration streams from the Middle East that go back to the 1890s. Cataclysmic events such as the 1948 and 1967 Arab-Israeli wars and the Lebanese civil war also have led to substantial and more recent migration to the United States from the Middle East (Sawaie 1985). Sociological studies of Arab immigrants in the United States provide important insights into the process of ethnicity maintenance among immigrants, showing, for example, the importance of minority status in the country of origin, religion, and entrepreneurship in the United States (Abu-Laban 1989; Abraham, Abraham, and Aswad 1983; Hagopian and Paden 1969; Sawaie 1985; Sengstock 1982; Suleiman and Abu-Laban 1989; Swan and Saba 1974).

The high socioeconomic status of Iranian immigrants in the United States and their ethnoreligious diversity provide a theoretical challenge for the study of the process of immigrant adaptation. Iranian immigrants include Christian Armenians and Assyrians, Baha'is, Jews, Muslims, and Zoroastrians. A challenge for the sociological analysis of immigrant adaptation is the fact that some of these groups have their non-Iranian religious counterparts in the United States. This diversity was the focus of the first extensive study of the adaptation of Iranian immigrants in Los Angeles, which has the largest concentration of Iranians in the United States (Bozorgmehr and Sabagh 1989). Bozorgmehr (1991) has developed the concept of "internal ethnicity" for the analysis of the process of adaptation of ethnically diverse immigrant groups. This concept is applicable not only to Iranians but also to many other early and recent immigrants groups. He shows that the neglect of internal ethnicity in the literature has led to the simplification of a complex process of immigrant adaptation. Some ethnic groups from the Middle East, such as Armenians, have different nationality origins and are characterized by what has been called "subethnicity" (Der Martirosian, Sabagh, and Bozorgmehr [forthcoming]). Thus, some Armenians are born in the United States, whereas others are immigrants from Iran, Iraq, Egypt, Lebanon, Syria, Turkey, or the Soviet Union. Kurds and Assyrians are other Middle Eastern immigrant groups characterized by subethnicity. The basic question for research is the extent to which these groups maintain their subethnicity or become unified as one ethnic minority.

CONCLUSION

Since the 1970s assessment of the state of U.S. sociology of the Middle East, there has been a growth in the number of sociologists involved in the study of the region and in their contributions to sociological theory and methodology. Still, there is much progress to be made. While events in the Middle East, such as the Iranian revolution and the Gulf war capture the headlines in the United States and attract the interest of sociologists, a continuing need exists for incorporating the experiences of this region into sociological models—of wars and revolutions, of social and demographic change, of social movements, and of the role of religion in society. These cataclysmic events have also contributed to the rapid growth of the population of Middle Easterners in the United States and Europe, providing sociologists with a unique opportunity to assess the effects of internal ethnicity, high socioeconomic status, entrepreneurship, and religion on immigrant adaptation.

REFERENCES

Abraham, Sameer Y., Nabeel Abraham, and Barbara C. Aswad 1983 "The Southend: An Arab Muslim Working-Class Community." In Sameer Y. Abraham and Nabeel Abraham, eds., *Arabs in the New World: Studies on Arab-American Communities.* Detroit: Wayne State University Press.

Abu-Laban, Sharon M. 1989 "The Coexistence of Cohorts: Identity and Adaptation Among Arab-American Muslims." *Arab Studies Quarterly* 11:45–83.

Abu-Lughod, Janet 1989 *Before European Hegemony: The World-System A.D. 1250–1350.* New York: Oxford University Press.

———1990 "Restructuring the Premodern World-System." *Fernand Braudel Center Review* 13:273–286.

American Sociological Association 1990a *Guide to Graduate Departments of Sociology.* Washington, D.C.

———1990b *Biographical Directory of Members.* Washington, D.C.

Amin, Galal A., and Elizabeth Awny 1985 *The International Migration of Egyptian Labour: A Review of the State of the Arts.* Ottawa: International Development Research Centre.

Arjomand, Said A. (ed.) 1984a *From Nationalism to Revolutionary Islam.* Albany: SUNY Press.

———1984b *The Shadow of God and the Hidden Imam.* Chicago: University of Chicago Press.

———1988 *The Turban and the Crown: The Islamic Revolution in Iran.* New York: Oxford University Press.

Arnold, Fred, and Nasra M. Shah 1984 *Asian Labor Migration: Pipeline to the Middle East.* Honolulu: East-West Center.

Ashraf, Ahmad 1988 "Bazaar-Mosque Alliance: The Social Basis of Revolts and Revolutions." *Politics, Culture, and Society* 1:538–567.

———, and Ali Banuazizi 1985 "The State, Classes and Modes of Mobilization in the Iranian Revolution." *State and Society* 1:3–40.

Bonine, Michael E. 1986 "MESA and Middle East Studies." *Middle East Studies Association Bulletin* 20:155–170.

Bozorgmehr, Mehdi 1991 "Internal Ethnicity: Armenian, Bahai, Jewish, and Muslim Iranians in Los Angeles." Ph.D. dissertation, University of California, Los Angeles.

———, and Georges Sabagh 1988 "High Status Immigrants: A Statistical Profile of Iranians in the United States." *Iranian Studies* 21:5–36.

———1989 "Survey Research Among Middle Eastern Immigrant Groups: Iranians in Los Angeles." *Middle East Studies Association Bulletin* 23:23–34.

Çizakça, Murat 1985 "Incorporation of the Middle East

into the European World-Economy." *Review* 8:353–377.

Dabashi, H. 1984 "The Revolutions of Our Time: Religious Politics in Modernity." *Contemporary Sociology* 13:673–676.

Der Martirosian, Claudia, Georges Sabagh, and Mehdi Bozorgmehr (Forthcoming) "Subethnicity: Armenians in Los Angeles." In Ivan Light and Parminder Bachu, eds., *Comparative Immigration and Entrepreneurship: Culture, Capital, and Ethnic Networks.*

Dickens, David 1989 "The Relevance of Domestic Traditions in the Development Process: Iran 1963–1979." *International Journal of Contemporary Sociology* 26:55–70.

Fergany, Nader 1987 *Differential Labour Migration: Egypt (1974–1984).* Cairo: Cairo Demographic Centre.

Foran, John 1989 "The Making of an External Arena: Iran's Place in the World-System, 1500–1722." *Review* 12:71–120.

Hagopian, Elaine C., and Ann Paden (eds.) 1969 *The Arab-Americans: Studies in Assimilation.* Wilmette, Ill.: Median University Press International.

Ibrahim, Saad E. 1982 *The New Arab Social Order: A Study of the Social Impact of Oil Wealth.* Boulder, Colo.: Westview Press.

Kasaba, Reşat 1987 "Incorporation of the Ottoman Empire. 1750–1820." *Review* 10:805–847.

———1988 "Was There a Compradore Bourgeoisie in Mid-Nineteenth Century Western Anatolia?" *Review* 11:215–228.

———Çağlar Keyder, and Faruk Tabak 1986 "Eastern Mediterranean Port Cities and Their Bourgeoisie: Merchants, Political Projects, and Nation-States." *Fernand Braudel Center Review* 10:131–135.

Keyder, Çağlar 1988 "Bureaucracy and Bourgeoisie: Reform and Revolution in the Age of Imperialism." *Fernand Braudel Center Review* 11:151–165.

Middle East Studies Association 1990 *Roster of Members 1990.* Tucson, Ariz.

Moghadam, Val 1989 "Populist Revolt and the Islamic State in Iran." In Terry Boswell, ed., *Revolution in the World System.* New York: Greenwood Press.

Nichols, Elizabeth 1986 "Skocpol on Revolution: Comparative Analysis vs Historical Conjecture." *Comparative Social Research* 9:163–186.

Organization for Economic Cooperation and Development 1990 *Continuous Reporting System on Migration. SOPEMI 1989.* Paris: OECD.

Owen, R. 1989 "The Movement of Labor in and out of the Middle East over the Last Two Centuries: Peasants, Patterns, and Policies." In Georges Sabagh, ed., *The Modern Economic and Social History of the Middle East in World Context.* Cambridge: Cambridge University Press.

Pamuk, Şevket 1988 "The Ottoman Empire in Contemporary Perspective." *Fernand Braudel Center Review* 11:127–151.

Parsa, Misagh 1989 *Social Origins of the Iranian Revolution.* New Brunswick, N.J.: Rutgers University Press.

Sabagh, Georges 1976 "Sociology." In Leonard Binder, ed., *The Study of the Middle East.* New York: Wiley.

———1988 "Immigrants in the Arab Gulf Countries: 'Sojourners' or 'Settlers?'" In Giacomo Luciani and Ghassan Salame, eds., *The Politics of Arab Integration.* London: Croom Helm.

———and Mehdi Bozorgmehr 1987 "Are the Characteristics of Exiles Different from Immigrants? The Case of Iranians in Los Angeles." *Sociology and Social Research* 71:77–84.

———and Iman Ghazalla 1986 "Arab Sociology Today: A View from Within." *Annual Review of Sociology* 12:373–399.

Sawaie, Mohammed (ed.) 1985 *Arabic-Speaking Immigrants in the United States and Canada.* Lexington, Ky.: Mazda.

Sell, Ralph R. 1988 "Egyptian International Labor Migration and Social Processes: Toward Regional Integration." *International Migration Review* 22: 87–108.

Sengstock, Mary C. 1982 *Chaldean-Americans: Changing Conceptions of Ethnic Identity.* New York: Center for Migration Studies.

Skocpol, Theda 1982 "Rentier State and Shi'a Islam in the Iranian Revolution." *Theory and Society* 11: 265–283.

———1986 "Analyzing Causal Configurations in History: A Rejoinder to Nichols." *Comparative Social Research* 9:187–194.

Snow, D. A., and S. Marshall 1984 "Cultural Imperialism, Social Movements, and the Islamic Revival." *Research in Social Movements, Conflict and Change* 7: 131–152.

Stahl, Charles W., and Farooq-i-Asam 1990 "Counting Pakistanis in the Middle East: Problems and Policy Implications." *Asian and Pacific Population Forum* 4:1–10, 24–28.

Stowasser, Barbara F. (ed.) 1987 *The Islamic Impulse.* Washington, D.C.: Georgetown University Press.

Suleiman, Michael W., and Baha Abu-Laban 1989 "The Arab Tradition in North America." *Arab Studies Quarterly* 11:1–13.

Swan, Charles L., and Leila B. Saba 1974 "The Migration of a Minority." In Barbara C. Aswad, ed., *Arabic-Speaking Communities in American Cities.* New York: Center for Migration Studies.

U.S. Bureau of the Census 1984 *Socioeconomic Characteristics of U.S. Foreign-Born Population Detailed in Census Bureau Tabulations.* Washington, D.C.: U.S. Government Printing Office.

Wallerstein, Immanuel 1979 "The Ottoman Empire and the Capitalist World-Economy: Some Questions for Research." *Review* 2:389–408.

GEORGES SABAGH

MIGRATION *See* Internal Migration; International Migration.

MILITARY SOCIOLOGY Military sociology has been a relatively obscure field in American sociology. Few sociologists conduct research and write on military topics, and few university departments offer courses of study in this field. To the layperson this circumstance may seem rather myopic, given the sheer size and complexity of the military enterprise and the impact that its products—war and peace—have on individual societies and on the world order as a whole. Some might wonder how sociologists can comprehend the structure and processes of human society without full attention to this major institution. The Persian Gulf War of 1991 is a vivid reminder that military institutions and operations are of importance to most societies.

There is no single reason for this lack of emphasis. One reason, of course, is ideological aversion to military matters. Most sociologists fall on the liberal-left side of the political spectrum, but the same might be said of other social and behavioral scientists who do the bulk of the research on defense-related social issues. Another reason may be that the access and support necessary for most military research requires policy relevance, which defines it as "applied" and therefore of less interest to many sociologists. Unlike other social sciences, sociology has not developed a sizeable cadre of practitioners who conduct research or policy studies in those nonacademic settings where most military research takes place.

There are notable exceptions. One is the classic work by Samuel Stouffer and colleagues during World War II, *The American Soldier* (Stouffer et al. 1949). Its studies of cohesion, morale, and race relations among combat units made critical contributions to both sociological theory and military personnel policies. The work of Morris Janowitz on organizational and occupational changes in the military is also a significant exception to the rule (Janowitz 1960). Charles Moskos at Northwestern University and David and Mady Segal at the University of Maryland are upholding this tradition today, and their universities are among the few that offer courses on military sociology.

In recent years most of the studies that could be classified as military sociology have been carried out in private research institutes and companies or in military agencies, such as the Rand Corporation, the Brookings Institute, the Human Resources Research Organization (HumRRO), the Army Research Institute, and the Office of the Secretary of Defense. Study teams are generally interdisciplinary, with the fields of psychology, economics, political science, and management frequently represented. While these studies have a sociological complexion, they are not limited to sociological concepts or theory, and they usually have a military policy focus.

Much of the published work in this field consists of reports from these various organizations and agencies. No journal is devoted specifically to military sociology, although there is an American Sociological Association Section on Peace and War. *Armed Forces and Society* is an interdisciplinary journal that focuses on social-science topics in the military, and *Military Psychology,* published by the Division on Military Psychology of the American Psychological Association, also covers topics of sociological interest.

This review will emphasize contemporary issues and studies in military sociology, most of which focus on the American military. For reviews that include historical perspectives the reader is referred elsewhere (David R. Segal 1989; Segal and Segal 1991).

THE BASIS OF SERVICE

Without question the most significant issue in American military sociology since World War II is the shift from conscription to voluntary service in 1973. Indeed, many contemporary issues in military sociology—social representation, national service, race, and gender—flow directly or indirectly from this change in the basis of service.

The notion of voluntary service is not new; indeed, compulsory military service has been the exception rather than the rule in the history of most Western societies, although the meaning of "involuntary" and the nature of service has changed over time. Until the Civil War, U.S. military manpower was raised through state militias, which technically encompassed all "able-bodied men" and hence might be thought of as involuntary. But the raising and maintenance of militia was left to the discretion and policies of individual states, and they varied greatly in their representation and effectiveness. Although the desirability and feasibility of national conscription has been debated since the beginning of American history, until 1948 it was employed only during the Civil War and during World Wars I and II. At all other times enlistment was voluntary (Lee and Parker 1977).

The peacetime conscription adopted in 1948 was a significant and historic departure for U.S. military policy. It was prompted by a combination of factors, including Cold War tensions with the Soviet Union, the critical role being played by the United States in defense alliances, and a perception that America had been inadequately prepared for World War II. These conditions led to proposals for a large standing or "active duty" military force that most believed could not be maintained by voluntary methods. The policy was supported by the American public at that time, and it was consistent with the long-standing value that all "able-bodied men" should serve their country.

The end of the peacetime draft occurred in 1973 at the end of the Vietnam War. The debate over draft policies had been intensifying during the 1960s, particularly over the issue of equity. Given the growth in the American youth population (from the post–World War II babyboom), not all men were needed for the military, and a succession of draft-exemption policies—college, occupational, marriage—fueled the debate over the fairness and equity of the draft. Not only were all able-bodied men not serving, those exempted from service tended to be from more affluent classes. In an attempt to solve the equity problem, nearly all exemptions were eliminated during the late 1960s, and a national lottery system was eventually adopted in 1969. These changes did not quell the debate, however; indeed, they probably doomed the draft, since they coincided with one of the most unpopular and unsuccessful of undeclared wars in America's history. Ending exemptions for college students at a time when college students were leading the Vietnam antiwar movement simply fanned the flames of opposition.

On the other side, most defense and military leaders, including many in Congress, initially opposed ending the draft. The conditions leading to a large peacetime military force (over two million active-duty personnel) were unchanged and were not under debate. If such a large force was maintained by voluntary means, it was argued, it would be (1) a mercenary force lacking patriotic motivation and might be either adventuresome or ineffective in large-scale combat; (2) socially unrepresentative, thereby placing the burden of combat on minorities, the poor, and the uneducated; and (3) costly and unaffordable (Segal 1989).

The shift to voluntary service followed definitive recommendations from a presidential commission, known as the Gates Commission, which concluded that a large peacetime force could be adequately maintained with an all-voluntary force (AVF), provided that basic pay was increased to be competitive with comparable civilian jobs. The commission argued that paying enlisted personnel below-market wages was not only unfair but entailed "opportunity" costs in the form of lost productivity of persons who are compelled to work at jobs they would not voluntarily perform. If military pay and benefits were competitive, the commission's studies concluded, a volunteer force would be socially representative and would be as effective as a drafted force. Although some attention was given the social costs of the draft, there is little question that economic analysis and arguments formed the central basis of the commission's report (President's Commission 1970).

THE ALL-VOLUNTEER FORCE

The AVF seemed to work well for the first several years, and the dire predictions of those who opposed ending the draft did not materialize. Enlistment requirements were met, and neither quality nor representation differed much from draft-era enlistments. It appeared that the predictions of the Gates Commission would be validated (Cooper 1977).

During the late 1970s, however, this positive picture changed. Military pay and benefits did not keep up with the civilian sector, and Vietnam antiwar attitudes among youth contributed to a generally negative image of the military. Enlistments began to decline, and increasing numbers were recruited from lower education and aptitude categories. To make matters worse, a misnorming error was discovered in the military aptitude test, and the quality of personnel was even lower than had been thought. By 1980 the Army was particularly affected, with enlistments falling significantly below requirements and with the proportion of lowest-aptitude recruits—those reading at fourth- and fifth-grade levels—reaching 50 percent (Eitelberg 1988).

Some claimed that the Gates Commission had been wrong after all and called for a return to the draft. Others, including a Secretary of the Army, proposed eliminating the aptitude and education standards that had been used since the draft era, arguing that they were not important for military job performance and were potentially discriminatory. Yet others argued that both the AVF and quality standards could be maintained but only by increasing pay and benefits to enable competition with the civilian sector. Critical to this third argument were policy studies led by the Rand Corporation showing a relationship between aptitudes and military job performance and the feasibility of economic incentives for enlistment (Armor et al. 1982; Polich, Dertouzos, and Press 1986)

Substantial increases in pay and other benefits in the early 1980s, as well as changes in recruiting techniques including advertising, had a dramatic impact on recruiting success. By 1986 all military services, including the Army, were not only meeting requirement quotas but were setting new records in the quality of personnel, surpassing even the draft years in the proportion of recruits with high school diplomas and with higher aptitudes. Most military leaders, many of whom had been skeptical about ending the draft, became strong supporters of the AVF and claimed that morale and skills were at all-time highs and discipline problems were at all-time lows. Although this success did require significant increases in the military personnel budget, both the Congress and the public seemed prepared to pay this cost (Bowman, Little, and Sicilia 1986).

The one argument against voluntary service that had never been tested empirically was the combat effectiveness of a market-motivated military. The dramatic success of American forces in the 1991 Persian Gulf war put an end to any doubt about the ability of a volunteer military to operate successfully. Although high-technology weapons systems received much of the publicity during the war, most military leaders gave equal credit to the skill and motivation of their troops.

NATIONAL SERVICE

The increasing success and acceptance of a voluntary military did not end the debate over alternative bases of service. The reasons are numerous, including concern over a shrinking youth population, doubts that a voluntary force can recruit sufficient quality and remain socially representative, and beliefs that it will ultimately be too costly. But the larger issue in this debate involves a clash of fundamental values: whether defense of country should be motivated by monetary incentives or the obligation of citizenry. A major figure in this ideological discussion is Charles Moskos, who describes the change from the draft to the AVF as a transition from "citizen soldier" to "economic man" (Moskos 1988a).

Although few policy leaders call for a return to a draft, there have been serious proposals for a national service policy. Most current national service proposals envisage a program whereby young people devote one or two years to either civilian or military service; they would receive only subsistence wages during their service but at the end would receive a voucher that could be used for college, job training, or home purchase. Most proponents of national service make an argument similar to the "able-bodied men" thesis of the classic militia model. That is, all citizens in a democracy should be willing to serve their country in some fashion, unmotivated primarily by economic gain. Although early proposals for national service envisaged universal military duty, more recent proposals for national service include voluntarism, civilian settings, and monetary incentives—although some see their potential for becoming universal (see Moskos in Evers 1990).

Most military and defense policy leaders who oppose national service argue that the voluntary military is working well and that national service is unnecessary for the purpose of the armed forces. The common refrain would be, "If it isn't broken, don't fix it!" Indeed, some argue that a program for short-term enlistments with subsistence pay plus benefit vouchers would be more costly than current policies because of training costs and the loss of high-quality recruits who would be willing to serve longer terms (Bandow 1988).

Interestingly, while the roots of national service stem from ideologies holding the obligations of citizenship above economic self-interest, all serious national service proposals embrace the key market and economic concepts of the AVF—voluntarism and financial incentives. As long as the voluntary military remains representative, effective, and popular, the debate on national service will generally boil down to costs and affordability as opposed to differences over more fundamental values.

SOCIAL REPRESENTATION AND RACE

The social representation of the American military has been a long-standing issue, predating the debate over the draft and the AVF. It was an issue in the Vietnam War, when some alleged that blacks were overrepresented in combat forces; it was an issue during the draft and AVF debate; and it has remained an issue during the AVF years and in the debates over national service. It was raised once again during the Persian Gulf War, when some black leaders including Jesse Jackson criticized the Department of Defense for the overrepresentation of minorities and the poor in the troops serving in the Gulf.

There are three basic policy questions at stake in the issue of representation. The first and most fundamental question concerns the equity of a military force, or the extent to which the burden of service and risk is borne by all segments of the citizenry. Since a military force has the job of defending the national interests of an entire country, with potential exposure to high risk of death or injury, many national value systems hold that this obligation should be shared uniformly by all citizens, or at least all "able-bodied men." Placing this burden unequally upon certain socioeconomic or racial groups not only violates the canons of fairness in democratic societies but also potentially undermines troop morale and motivation if they perceive the disproportion as unfair (Congressional Budget Office 1989).

A second question involves the impact of social representation on the effectiveness of the armed forces. Since most military leaders believe that the quality of a military force (in other words, its educational and aptitude levels) affects its combat effectiveness, an unrepresentative force might be less effective than a representative force. Although the AVF attained its quality goals during the 1980s, it has not always done so. There has also been continuing concern that the AVF does not include the same proportion of highest-aptitude recruits (above the 35th percentile) as during the draft era. Although the proportion of high-aptitude enlistees has never been large, as in most work forces they occupy a disproportionate share of critical technical and supervisory jobs.

Finally, social representation is sometimes raised as a requirement for a military force's responsiveness to civilian control as well as for its respect for American democratic values and institutions. A military force that overrepresents particular social strata or groups (not necessarily lower strata) might place parochial interests or values over the interests and values of the society as a whole. A force drawn proportionately from all major sectors of a society—regions, races, social classes—is viewed as one most likely to respect and advance the shared values and goals of the total society.

While the issue of representation is not unique to a voluntary military, it has been especially prominent during the AVF era and remains a major argument for proponents of a draft or national service. The most frequent concern has been the overrepresentation of blacks and lower socioeconomic groups. Given the early experience with the AVF, this concern is not without some justification, although the situation improved considerably during the 1980s.

Table 1 shows the percentage of black recruits for several fiscal years: 1973, the last year of the draft; 1979, the highest level of black representation during the AVF era; 1983, the lowest level of black representation during the 1980s; and 1989. Even during the draft years, black representation exceeded the black proportion of the youth population, due in part to higher voluntary enlistment and—prior to the Vietnam War—college exemption policies that applied disproportionately to white youth. But the proportion of black recruits increased dramatically during the 1970s, declined during the 1980s, and increased to 22 percent by 1989.

Socioeconomic representation generally parallels the trends for race, which is not surprising, given the correlation between race and socioeconomic variables. Recruits as a whole come from families with somewhat less education and lower economic levels than the total youth population. In 1989, 19 percent of recruits came from college graduate families and 79 percent from families that owned their homes, compared to 26 percent and 84 percent, respectively, for the general youth population.

Nonetheless, recruits have higher educational and aptitude levels than the youth population because of enlistment eligibility requirements. In 1989, military recruits had reading scores at the 11.2 grade level and 96 percent were high school graduates, compared to reading scores at the 9.4 grade level and 82 percent graduates, respectively, for the youth population. Thus, while the American enlisted forces somewhat underrepresent whites and higher socioeconomic levels, they overrepresent youth with higher personal education and aptitude levels. This means that the current social representation may raise an equity question but not necessarily an effectiveness issue.

It should not be inferred from these data that blacks and the poor are at greater risk of death or injury from combat. In fact, blacks and whites in the enlisted active-duty force are about equally represented in combat jobs such as infantry, gun crews, and combat ships. On the other hand, a

TABLE 1
Percentage of Black Recruits, Active Forces

Fiscal Year	*Army*	*Navy*	*Marine Corps*	*Air Force*	*Total Active Forces*	*Total U.S. population, ages 18–24*
1973	19	11	22	14	17	12
1979	37	16	28	17	26	13
1983	22	14	17	14	18	14
1989	26	22	18	12	22	14

SOURCE: Office of the Assistant Secretary of Defense (1990, p. 19).

higher proportion of blacks occupy administrative, clerical, and supply jobs, while a higher proportion of whites occupy electronic and mechanical repair jobs.

Some argue that these differences in representation present a policy problem, although there is no consensus on what, if anything, should be done about it. Given the AVF experience, it is unclear how a voluntary national service would alter these outcomes, and there are no serious proposals at this time to return to a peacetime draft or compulsory national service. There has been at least one concrete proposal that the Department of Defense adopt limitations or quotas for minority enlistments, but such a practice could be viewed as discriminatory (Walters 1991). The higher black representation reflects a more positive view of the military and a higher demand for military careers among the black population, and any attempt to restrict black enlistments could be legitimately viewed as a denial of equal opportunity to the black community.

WOMEN IN THE MILITARY

Another topic that has received considerable attention from military sociologists since the advent of the AVF is the role of women in the military. Until 1967 women's participation in the military was limited to 2 percent by law, and most military jobs were closed to women. Even after this restriction was lifted by Congress, the representation of women did not change until the AVF policy and the opening of more noncombat jobs to women. From 1973 to 1980 the percentage of women enlistees increased from about 5 percent to about 14 percent and then stabilized. By 1989 women composed about 11 percent of the active enlisted force and 12 percent of the active officer force. This representation is highest among all NATO countries (Office of the Assistant Secretary of Defense 1990; Stanley and Segal 1988).

The growing participation of women in the military reflects both the need for manpower in the AVF era as well as the increased concern for equity in the treatment of men and women in the workplace. Although all military services recruited more women to help alleviate shortfalls during the 1970s, the Department of Defense has also been pressured by Congress and various interest and advisory groups to enlarge the opportunities for women (Segal 1982).

The changing role of women in the military has been accompanied by controversy and debates over a number of issues that remain unresolved. They include the role of women in combat, the provisions for career development within the military job structure, and the problem of sexual harassment. All of these issues were reviewed in a recent Task Force on Women in the Military (Department of Defense 1988).

The most controversial of these issues is the ongoing dialogue on women in combat. While the arguments against women in combat include physical and emotional differences and the potential negative impact on unit cohesion and morale, the overriding reason is one of basic values: Most military leaders and Congress reflect the general public's view that women should be protected from the high risk of death, injury, or capture in combat jobs. Proponents of women in combat counter that (1) women should be judged individually and not as a group for their physical and emotional suitability for combat; (2) the experience of women in noncombatant units has shown no serious adverse impacts on cohesion or morale; and (3) women currently serve in jobs and units that are exposed to increased risks of death, injury, or capture, thereby rendering the moral argument moot and in conflict with current policies (Segal 1982).

Although combatant jobs generally entail the highest risks, it is true that women now serve in many jobs close to or actually in the combat theater, particularly in the Army and Air Force, where risks are substantial due to the technological and doctrinal changes of modern warfare. The experience of the Persian Gulf War, where women were killed, injured, and captured while on duty, confirms the risks of noncombat jobs.

The problem of career development is closely related to the issue of combat job restrictions, particularly for women officers. In many military career fields, career progression and promotion to senior officer status require leadership experience in various kinds of units and positions. Since many types of units are closed to women because of combat restrictions, these requirements are frequently hard to meet, given the number of women competing for promotion. The problem has been especially acute in the surface ship portion of the Navy, where career progression requires a ship command position but where few ships are open to women. As a result of the 1988 Task Force on Women in the Military a number of "combat logistics" ships—which were not actual combatants—were opened to women, thereby enhancing the career progression of women officers in the surface ship Navy.

The concern about sexual harassment is not unique to the military; it has been and continues to be an issue in all mixed-gender work forces. It may be more acute in settings like the military, a traditional male institution, where women compose a relatively small minority of personnel. Very little was known about the extent of sexual harassment in the military until 1988, when the 1988 Task Force on Women in the Military recommended a comprehensive survey of all active-duty personnel. The results indicated rather serious levels of sexual harassment: 5 percent of women reported actual or attempted rape or sexual assault from someone at work during the previous year, 15 percent experienced pressure for sexual favors, 38 percent experienced unwanted touching or cornering, and even higher rates were reported for a variety of other less serious actions (looks, gestures, teasing, jokes). All together, 64 percent of women experienced some form of sexual harassment during a one-year period. About 20 percent of the perpetrators were immediate supervisors, 20 percent were from other higher-ranking persons, and about 50 percent were coworkers (Martindale 1990).

These rates are considerably higher than rates found in a similar survey of federal civilian employees in 1987. The causes of these high rates of harassment are unknown at the present time, but it may be associated in part with the relatively recent increases of women in a traditional male workplace. Another factor may be the attitudes and actions of military leaders and supervisors. Only about half of the women responding believe that the senior leadership of their service and their installation make "honest and reasonable" attempts to prevent sexual harassment, and only 60 percent say their immediate supervisor does so. Whether or not these rates reflect the actual prevention activities of military leaders, there is a perception among many women that not much is being done to stop sexual harassment.

OTHER ISSUES

There are a number of other topics that are studied by military sociologists or that raise important sociological issues. While they have not received the same degree of attention as the topics reviewed above, they deserve mention.

Sociology of Combat. A major focus of *The American Soldier* studies during World War II, the sociology of combat deals with the social processes involved in combat units, such as unit cohesion and morale, leader–troop relations, and the motivation for combat. Recent works include studies of the "fragging" incidents in the Vietnam War and the role of ideology in combat motivation (Moskos 1988b) and unit rotation policies in the Army (Segal 1989).

Family Issues. The proportion of military personnel who are married increased from 38 percent in 1953 to 61 percent by 1980. The active force also has a higher proportion of career personnel than the draft-era forces (50 percent compared to 25 percent), which means more families and family concerns. Much of the increase in military benefits are related to families —housing improvements, medical insurance, overseas schools, child care. Family policy issues include the role and rights of spouses (especially officer spouses) and the issue of child care when single-parent members are deployed in a conflict (Segal 1986; Stanley, Segal, and Laughton 1990).

The Military as Welfare. Somewhat at odds with the social representation issue, some argue that the military should provide opportunity for educational and occupational advancement to the less advantaged in society. The most dramatic example was Project 100,000 begun in 1966 as part of President Johnson's War on Poverty, whereby 300,000 men (mostly black) who did not meet education and aptitude requirements were offered enlistments. According to recent follow-up studies of this group as well as a group of low-aptitude recruits who entered the AVF during the misnorming era, military training and experience do not appear to offer advantages when compared to civilian experiences (Segal 1989; Laurence and Ramsberger 1991)

Military Social Organization. Given changes in military organization at several levels—from draft to AVF, from combat-intensive jobs to technical and support jobs, and from leadership to rational management—some have argued that the military is changing from an institution or "calling" legitimized by normative values to an occupation legitimized by a market orientation (Moskos and Wood 1988). While some of these changes apply to the military as well as to many other American institutions, others suggest that the role of institutional values and traditions is still a dominant characteristic of the American military (Segal 1989).

War and Peace. The most profound impacts of national security policies and their associated military forces are on the relations between whole societies. There is very little serious sociological work at this level, although some of the issues would seem to be fairly critical for sociological theory (e.g., the effectiveness of deterrence policies during the cold war; the role and effects of military alliances; the consequences of war for societal changes). One of the few sociological discussions of these broader issues is found in Segal (1989).

Comparative Perspectives. As in many other fields of sociology, comparative studies of socio-military issues across nations are relatively scarce. Exceptions are some comparative studies of whether the military is an institution or an occupation (Moskos and Wood 1988) and of women in military forces (Stanley and Segal 1988)

CONCLUSION

Although military sociology may have few practitioners, it is not a small field. It should be clear from this review that the types of military issues that are or can be addressed by social scientists have important ramifications for military policy as well as for the development of sociology as a discipline. On the one hand, sociological concepts and perspectives have contributed to rationalizing the basis of service, studying the problems of social representation, and improving the role of women in the military. On the other hand, studies of the structure and processes of military institutions and conflicts can enhance sociological understanding and insights about important forms of social behavior, thereby contributing ultimately to advances in social theory.

(SEE ALSO: *Gender; Peace; War*)

REFERENCES

Armor, D. J., R. L. Fernandez, Kathy Bers, and Donna Schwarzbach 1982 *Recruit Aptitudes and Army Job Performance.* R-2874-MRAL. Santa Monica, Calif.: Rand Corporation.

Bandow, D. 1988 "An Involuntary Military: Paying More for Less." In Lee Austin, ed., *The Anthropo Factor in Warfare: Conscripts, Volunteers, and Reserves.* Washington, D. C.: National Defense University.

Bowman, W., R. Little, and G. T. Sicilia 1986 *The All-Volunteer Force after a Decade.* Washington, D.C.: Pergamon-Brassey's.

Congressional Budget Office 1989 *Social Representation in the U.S. Military.* Washington, D.C.: Congress of the United States.

Cooper, Richard V. L. 1977 *Military Manpower and the All-Volunteer Force.* R-1450-ARPA. Santa Monica, Calif.: Rand Corporation.

Department of Defense 1988 *Report of the Task Force on Women in the Military.* Washington, D.C.: Office of the Assistant Secretary of Defense.

Eitelberg, Mark J. 1988 *Manpower for Military Occupations.* Alexandria, Va.: HumRRO.

Evers, Williamson M. 1990 *National Service, Pro and Con.* Stanford, Calif.: Hoover Institution Press.

Janowitz, Morris 1960 *The Professional Soldier.* Glencoe, Ill.: Free Press.

Laurence, J. H., and P. F. Ramsberger 1991 *Low-Aptitude Men in the Military: Who Profits, Who Pays?* Alexandria, Va.: HumRRO.

Lee, G. C. and G. Y. Parker 1977 *Ending the Draft: The Story of the All-Volunteer Force.* FR-PO-77-1. Alexandria, Va.: HumRRO.

Martindale, Melanie 1990 *Sexual Harassment in the Military: 1988.* Arlington, Va.: Defense Manpower Data Center.

Moskos, Charles C. 1988a *A Call to Civic Service.* New York: Free Press.

———1988b *Soldiers and Sociology.* Alexandria, Va.: U.S. Army Research Institute for the Behavioral and Social Sciences.

———, and F. R. Wood 1988 *The Military: More Than Just a Job?* Washington, D.C.: Pergamon-Brassey's.

Office of the Assistant Secretary of Defense 1990 *Population Representation in the Military Services.* Washington, D.C.: U.S. Government Printing Office.

Polich, J. M., J. N. Dertouzos, and S. J. Press 1986 *The Enlistment Bonus Experiment.* R-3353-FMP. Santa Monica, Calif.: The Rand Corporation.

President's Commission 1970 *Report of the President's Commission on an All Volunteer Force.* Washington, D.C.: U.S. Government Printing Office.

Segal, David R. 1989 *Recruiting for Uncle Sam.* Lawrence: University Press of Kansas.

———, and M. W. Segal 1991 "Sociology, Military." *International Military and Defense Encyclopedia.* New York: Macmillan.

Segal, Mady Wechsler 1982 "The Argument for Female Combatants." In Nancy Loring Goldman, ed., *Female Soldiers: Combatants or Noncombatants?* Westport, Conn.: Greenwood Press.

———1983 "Women's Roles in the U.S. Armed Forces." In Robert K. Fullinwinder, ed., *Conscripts and Volunteers.* Totowa, N.J.: Rowman and Allanheld.

———1986 "The Military and the Family as Greedy Institutions." *Armed Forces and Society* 13:9–38.

Stanley, J., M. W. Segal, and C. J. Laughton 1990 "Grass Roots Family Action and Military Policy Responses." In R. S. Hanks and M. B. Sussman, eds., *Corporations, Businesses, and Families.* New York: The Haworth Press.

Stanley, S. C., and M. W. Segal 1988 "Military Women in NATO: An Update." *Armed Forces and Society* 14:559–585.

Stouffer, S. A., et al. 1949 *The American Soldier.* Princeton: Princeton University Press.

Walters, Ronald 1991 *African-American Participation in the All Volunteer Force.* Testimony before the Committee on Armed Services, U.S. House of Representatives, March 4, 1991.

DAVID J. ARMOR

MINORITY GROUPS *See* Ethnicity; Gender; Race; Segregation and Desegregation.

MODERNIZATION THEORY Modernization theory is a description and explanation of the processes of transformation from traditional or underdeveloped societies to modern societies. In the words of one of the major proponents, "Historically, modernization is the process of change towards those types of social, economic, and political systems that have developed in Western Europe and North America from the seventeenth century to the nineteenth and have then spread to other European countries and in the nineteenth and twentieth centuries to the South American, Asian, and African continents" (Eisenstadt 1966, p. 1). Modernization theory has been one of the major perspectives in the sociology of national development and underdevelopment since the 1950s. Primary attention has focused on ways in which past and present premodern societies become modern (i.e., Westernized) through processes of economic growth and change in social, political, and cultural structures.

In general, modernization theorists are concerned with economic growth within societies as indicated, for example, by measures of gross national product. Mechanization or industrialization are ingredients in the process of economic growth. Modernization theorists study the social, political, and cultural consequences of economic growth and the conditions that are important for industrialization and economic growth to occur. Indeed, a degree of circularity often characterizes discussions of social and economic change involved in modernization processes because of the notion, embedded in most modernization theories, of the functional compatibility of component parts. The theoretical assumptions of modernization theories will be elaborated later.

It should be noted at the outset that the sociological concept of modernization does not refer simply to becoming current or "up to date" but rather specifies particular contents and processes of societal changes in the course of national development. Also, modernization theories of development do not necessarily bear any relationship to more recent philosophical concepts of "modernity" and "postmodernity." Modernity in philosophical and epistemological discussions refers to the perspective that there is one true descriptive and explanatory model that reflects the actual world. Postmodernity is the stance that no single true description and explanation of reality exists but rather that knowledge, ideology, and science itself are based on subjective understandings of an entirely relational nature. While their philosophical underpinnings place most modernization theories of development into the "modern" rather than the "postmodern" context, these separate uses of the term *modernity* should not be confused.

Also, modernization, industrialization, and development are often used interchangeably but in fact refer to distinguishable phenomena. Industrialization is a narrower term than modernization, while development is more general. Industrialization involves the use of inanimate sources of power to mechanize production, and it involves increases in manufacturing, wage labor, income levels, and occupational diversification. It may or may not be present where there is political, social, or cultural modernization, and, conversely, it may exist in the absence of other aspects of modernization. Development (like industrialization) implies economic growth, but not necessarily through transformation from the predominance of primary production to manufacturing, and not necessarily as characterized by modernization theory. For example, while modernization theorists may define development mainly in terms of economic output per capita, other theorists may be more concerned about development of autonomous productive capacity, equitable distribution of wealth, or meeting basic human needs. Also, while modernization theories generally envision democratic and capitalist institutions or secularization of belief systems as components of modern society, other development perspectives may not. Indeed, dependency theorists even talk about the "development of underdevelopment" (Frank 1966).

Each of the social science disciplines pays particular attention to the determinants of modern structures within its realm (social, political, economic) and gives greater importance to structures or institutions within its realm for explaining other developments in society. Emphasis here is given to sociological modernization theory.

Although there are many versions of modernization theory, major implicit or explicit tenets are that (1) societies develop through a series of evolutionary stages; (2) these stages are based on different degrees and patterns of social differentiation and reintegration of structural and cultural components that are functionally compatible for the maintenance of society; (3) contemporary developing societies are at a premodern stage of evolution and they eventually will achieve economic growth and will take on the social, political, and economic features of Western European and North American societies which have progressed to the highest stage of social evolutionary development; (4) this modernization will result as complex Western technology is imported and traditional structural and cultural features incompatible with such development are overcome.

At its core modernization theory suggests that advanced industrial technology produces not only economic growth in developing societies but also other structural and cultural changes. The common characteristics that societies tend to develop as they become modern may differ from one version of modernization theory to another, but, in general, all assume that institutional structures and individual activities become more highly specialized, differentiated, and integrated into social, political, and economic forms characteristic of advanced Western societies.

For example, in the social realm, modern societies are characterized by high levels of urbanization, literacy, research, health care, secularization, bureaucracy, mass media, and transportation facilities. Kinship ties are weaker, and nuclear conjugal family systems prevail. Birth rates and death rates are lower, and life expectancy is relatively longer. In the political realm, the society becomes more participatory in decision-making processes, and typical institutions include universal suffrage, political parties, a civil service bureaucracy, and parliaments. Traditional sources of authority are weaker as bureaucratic institutions assume responsibility and power. In the economic realm, there is more industrialization, technical upgrading of production, replacement of exchange economies with extensive money markets, increased division of labor, growth of infrastructure and commercial facilities, and the development of large-scale markets. Associated with these structural changes are cultural changes in role relations and personality variables. Social relations are more bureaucratic, social mobility increases, and status relations are based less on such ascriptive criteria as age, gender, or ethnicity and more on meritocratic criteria. There is a shift from relations based on tradition and loyalty to those based on rational exchange, competence, and other universally applied criteria. People are more receptive to change, interested in the future, achievement-oriented, concerned with the rights of individuals, and less fatalistic.

Underlying the description of social features and changes that are thought to characterize modern urban industrial societies are theoretical assumptions and mechanisms to explain the shift from traditional to modern societal types. These explanatory systems draw upon the dominant theoretical perspectives in the 1950s and 1960s growing out of classical evolutionary, diffusion, and structural-functionalist theories.

The evolutionary perspective, stemming from Spencer, Durkheim, and other nineteenth-century theorists, contributed the notion that societies evolve from lower to higher forms and progress from simple and undifferentiated to more complex types. Western industrial society is seen as superior to preindustrial society to the extent that it has progressed through specialization to more effective ways of performing societal functions. Diffusionists added the ideas that cultural patterns associated with modern society could be transferred via social interaction (trade, war, travelers, media, etc.) and that there may be several paths to development rather than linear evolution. Structural functionalists (Parsons 1951; Hoselitz 1960; Levy 1966) emphasized the idea that societies are integrated wholes comprised of functionally compatible institutions and roles and that societies progress from one increasingly complex and efficient social system to another. This contributed to the notion that internal social and cultural factors are important determinants or obstacles of economic change.

Research by Smelser (1969) draws on all three traditions in describing modernization of society through processes of social differentiation, disturbances, and reintegration. In a manner similar to other conceptions of modernization, Smelser emphasizes four major changes: from simple to complex technology, from subsistence farming to commercial agriculture, from rural to urban populations, and, most important, from animal and human power to inanimate power and industrialization.

Parsons's (1964) later theoretical work also combines these perspectives in a neo-evolutionist modernization theory that treats societies as self-regulated structural functional wholes in which the main processes of change are social differentiation and the discovery (or acquisition through diffusion) of certain "evolutionary universals" such as bureaucratic organizations and money markets. These, in turn, increase the adaptive capacity of the society by providing more efficient social arrangements and often lead to a system of universalistic norms, "which, more than the industrial revolution itself, ushered in the *modern* era of social evolution" (Parsons 1964, p. 361). A similar neo-evolutionist social differentiation theory of modernization is provided by Eisenstadt (1970).

Another early influence on modernization theory was Weber's work on the Protestant ethic. This work stressed the influence of cultural values on the entrepreneurial behavior of individuals and the rise of capitalism. Contemporary theorists in the Weberian tradition include Lerner, McClelland, Inkeles, and Rostow. Lerner's (1958) empirical studies in several Middle Eastern societies identified empathy, the capacity to take the perspective of others, as a product of media, literacy, and urbanization and as a vital ingredient in producing rational individual behavior conducive to societal development. McClelland (1961) felt that prevalence of individuals with the psychological trait of high "need for achievement" was the key to entrepreneurial activity and modernization of society. In a similar vein, Inkeles and Smith (1974) used interview data from six societies to generate a set of personality traits by which they defined "modern man." They felt that the prevalence of individual modernity in society was determined by such factors as education and factory experience and that individual modernity contributed to the modernization of society. Finally, Rostow's (1960) well-known theory of the stages of economic growth, which he derived from studying Western economic development, emphasized the importance of new values and ideas favoring economic progress along with education, entrepreneurship, and certain other institutions as conditions for societies to "take off" into self-sustained economic growth.

All of these versions of modernization theory depict a gradual and more or less natural transition from "traditional" social structures to "modern" social structures characteristic of Western European and North American societies. More specifically, these theories tend to share to one degree or another the views that (1) modern people, values, institutions, and societies are similar to those found in the industrialized West, that is, the direction of change tends to replicate that which had already occurred in Western industrial societies; (2) tradition is opposite to and incompatible with modernity; (3) the causes of delayed economic and social development (i.e., underdevelopment) are to be found within the traditional society; (4) the mechanisms of economic development also come primarily from within societies rather than from factors outside of the society; and (5) these internal factors (in addition to industrial development) tend to involve social structures, cultural institutions, or personality types.

In keeping with this orientation, empirical studies of sociological modernization tend to deal with the internal effects of industrialization or other economic developments on traditional social institutions or with the social, political, and cultural conditions that facilitate or impede economic growth within traditional or less-developed societies. Examples might include research on the impact of factory production and employment on traditional family relations or the effects of an indigenous land tenure system on the introduction of cash crop farming in society.

Even though modernization theory since the 1960s has been dominated by and sometimes equated with Parsons's neo-evolutionary theory, it is clear that there is no single modernization theory but rather an assortment of related theories and perspectives. In addition to those mentioned, other important contributors of theoretical variants include Hagan (1962), Berger, Berger, and Kellner (1973), Bendix (1964), Moore (1967), Tiryakian (1985), and Lenski and Lenski (1987). Useful reviews include Harrison (1988) and Harper (1989).

Since the 1960s, many critiques of modernization theory and the emergence of competing theories of development have eroded support for modernization theory. Foremost among these are dependency, world systems, and neo-Marxist theories, all of which criticize the ethnocentricity of the modernization concept and the bias in favor of dominant capitalist interests. The focus of these theories is on explaining the contemporary underdevelopment of third world countries or regions of the world in terms of colonization, imperialist interference, and neocolonial exploitation of developing countries since their gaining of independence. In these counter perspectives, both development and underdevelopment are viewed as part of the same process by which certain "center" countries or regions become economically advanced and powerful at the expense of other "periphery" areas. Rather than explaining development and underdevelopment by the presence or absence of certain internal institutions or personalities, these alternative theories argue that both result from unequal exchange relations and coalitions of interests associated with the structural position of societies in the global economy. Rather than interpreting underdeveloped societies as traditional or archaic, both underdeveloped and developed societies are contemporary but asymmetrically linked parts of capitalist expansion. Both are relatively "modern" phenomena.

Attention to modernization theory in sociology has declined as a result of the theoretical and empirical weaknesses raised especially during the 1970s. Nevertheless, it is still the dominant perspective among government officials and international agencies concerned with third world development. Hoogvelt has noted its influence on development policies as follows:

> *Because modernisation theories have viewed the total transformation, that is westernisation, of developing countries to be an inescapable outcome of successful diffusion of the Western economic/technological complex, by methodological* reversal *it is argued that a reorganization of existing social and cultural as well as political patterns in anticipation of their compatibility with the diffused Western economic/technological complex may in fact* facilitate *the very process of this diffusion itself.*
>
> *This monumental theoretical error—which to be fair was not always committed by the theorists themselves—has in fact been made and continues to be made by modernisation policy-makers such as those employed by Western governments, U.N. organizations, the World Bank, and so forth.* (1978, pp. 60–61)

Thus, various *indicators* of social, political, and cultural development (such as degree of urbanization, high literacy rates, political democracy, free enterprise, secularization, birth control, etc.) have frequently been promoted as "conditions" for development.

Interestingly, as modern structures and institutions have spread around the world and created economic, political, social, and cultural linkages, an awareness of global interdependence and of the ecological consequences of industrial development and modern life-styles has grown. It is now clear that finite natural resources and the nature of the global ecosystem could not sustain worldwide modern conditions and practices of European and North American societies even if modernization theory assumptions of evolutionary national development were correct. Thus, new visions and interpretations of national and global development have already begun to replace classical modernization theory.

(SEE ALSO: *Global Systems Analysis; Industrialization in Less Developed Countries*)

REFERENCES

Bendix, Reinhold 1964 *Nation-Building and Citizenship: Studies of Our Changing Social Order.* New York: Wiley.

Berger, Peter L., Brigitte Berger, and Hansfried Kellner 1973 *The Homeless Mind: Modernization and Consciousness.* New York: Vintage Books.

Eisenstadt, S. N. 1966 *Modernization: Protest and Change.* Englewood Cliffs, N.J.: Prentice-Hall.

——— 1970 "Social Change and Development." In S. N. Eisenstadt, ed., *Readings in Social Evolution and Development.* Oxford: Pergamon.

Frank, Andre Gunder 1966 "The Development of Underdevelopment." *Monthly Review* 18 (no.4):17–31.

Hagen, Everett E. 1962 *On the Theory of Social Change.* Homewood, Ill.: Dorsey.

Harper, Charles L. 1989 *Exploring Social Change.* Englewood Cliffs, N.J.: Prentice-Hall.

Harrison, David 1988 *The Sociology of Modernization and Development.* London: Unwin Hyman.

Hoogvelt, Ankie M. M. 1978 *The Sociology of Developing Societies,* 2nd ed. London: Macmillan.

Hoselitz, Berthold F. 1960 *Sociological Aspects of Economic Growth.* New York: Free Press.

Inkeles, Alex, and David H. Smith 1974 *Becoming Modern.* Cambridge, Mass.: Harvard University Press.

Lenski, Gerhard E., and Jean Lenski 1987 *Human Societies: An Introduction to Macrosociology,* 5th ed. New York: McGraw-Hill.

Lerner, Daniel 1958 *The Passing of Traditional Society: Modernizing the Middle East.* New York: Free Press.

Levy, Marion, Jr. 1966 *Modernization and the Structures of Societies,* Vol. 1. Princeton: Princeton University Press.

McClelland, David C. 1961 *The Achieving Society*. New York: Free Press.

Moore, Barrington 1967 *Social Origins of Dictatorship and Democracy: Lord and Peasant in the Making of the Modern World.* Boston: Beacon Press.

Parsons, Talcott 1951 *The Social System*. New York: Free Press.

——— 1964 "Evolutionary Universals in Society." *American Sociological Review* 29:339–357.

Rostow, Walt W. 1960 *The Stages of Economic Growth: A Non-Communist Manifesto.* London: Cambridge University Press.

Smelser, Neil 1966 "The Modernization of Social Relations." In Myron Weiner, ed., *Modernization: The Dynamics of Growth.* New York: Basic Books.

Tiryakian, Edward A. 1985 "The Changing Centers of Modernity." In Erik Cohen, Moshe Lissak, and Uri Almagor, eds., *Comparative Social Dynamics: Essays in Honor of S.N. Eisenstadt.* Boulder, Colo.: Westview Press.

J. MICHAEL ARMER
JOHN KATSILLIS

MONEY Sociologists treat money paradoxically: On the one hand, money is considered a central element of modern society, and yet it remains an unanalyzed sociological category. In classic interpretations of the development of the modern world, money occupies a pivotal place. As "the most abstract and 'impersonal' element that exists in human life" (Weber [1946] 1971, p. 331), it was assumed that money spearheaded the process of rationalization. For Georg Simmel and Karl Marx, money revolutionized more than economic exchange: It fundamentally transformed the basis of all social relations by turning personal bonds into calculative instrumental ties.

But by defining money as a purely objective and uniform medium of exchange, classical social theory eclipsed money's sociological significance. If indeed money was unconstrained by subjective meanings and independent from social relations, there was little left of sociological interest. As a result, economists took over the study of money: There is no systematic sociology of money. Significantly, the *International Encyclopedia of the Social Sciences* devotes over thirty pages to money but not one to its social characteristics. There are essays on the economic effect of money, on quantity theory, on velocity of circulation, and on monetary reform, but nothing on money as a "réalité sociale," using Simiand's apt term (1934).

The sociological invisibility of money is hard to pierce. For instance, the current resurgence of interest in economic sociology has led to a serious revamping of the neoclassical economic model of the market (see, e.g., Granovetter 1985; White 1988; Swedberg 1990). Yet the sociology of markets has not extended into a sociology of money. Or consider the recent literature on the culture of consumption, which boldly reverses our understanding of modern commodities. The new revisionist approach uncovers the symbolic meanings of what money buys, but, curiously, the cultural "freedom" of money itself is never directly challenged (see, e.g., Appadurai 1986; Bronner 1989).

A sociology of money must thus dismantle a powerful and stubborn utilitarian paradigm of a single, neutral, and rationalizing market money. It must show that money is a meaningful, socially constructed currency, continually shaped and redefined by different networks of social relations and varying systems of meanings. There is some evidence that the sociological conversion of money has begun (Turner 1986; Zelizer 1989). And in anthropology, psychology, political science, and history there are also scattered indications that the economic model of money is starting to lose its hold. The following two sections will first discuss the classic approach to money and then propose the basis for a sociology of money.

MARKET MONEY: A UTILITARIAN APPROACH TO MONEY

Many eighteenth-century thinkers saw the monetization of the economy as compatible with or even complementary to the maintenance of a morally coherent social life (see Hirschman 1977; Silver 1990). But the transformative powers of money captured the imagination of nineteenth- and early twentieth-century social theorists. Money turned the world, observed Simmel ([1908]

1950, p. 412), into an "arithmetic problem." On purely technical grounds, the possibility of money accounting was essential for the development of impersonal rational economic markets. But traditional social thinkers argued that the effects of money transcended the market: More significantly, money became the catalyst for the generalized instrumentalism of modern social life. As Simmel ([1900] 1978, p. 346) observed: "The complete heartlessness of money is reflected in our social culture, which is itself determined by money."

The task of social theory was thus to explain the uncontested revolutionary power of money. Presumably, it came from money's complete indifference to values. Money was perceived as the prototype of an instrumental, calculating approach; in Simmel's ([1900] 1978, p. 211) words, money was "the purest reification of means." Unlike any other known product, money was the absolute negation of quality. With money, only quantity mattered. That "uncompromising objectivity" allowed it to function as a "technically perfect" medium of modern economic exchange. Free from subjective restrictions, indifferent to "particular interests, origins, or relations," money's liquidity and divisibility were infinite, making it "absolutely interchangeable" (Simmel [1900] 1978, pp. 373, 128, 441). Noneconomic restrictions in the use of money were unequivocally dismissed as residual atavisms. As money became nothing but "mere money," its freedom was apparently unassailable and its uses unlimited. With money, all qualitative distinctions between goods were equally convertible into an arithmetically calculable "system of numbers" (Simmel [1900] 1978, p. 444).

This objectification of modern life had a dual effect. On the one hand, Simmel argued that a money economy broke the personal bondage of traditional arrangements by allowing every individual the freedom of selecting the terms and partners of economic exchange. But the quantifying alchemy of money had a more ominous chemistry. In an early essay, Marx ([1844] 1964, p. 169) had warned that the transformational powers of money subverted reality: "Confounding and compounding . . . all natural and human qualities . . . [money] serves to exchange every property for every other, even contradictory, property and object: it is the fraternization of impossibilities." As the ultimate objectifier, money not only obliterated all subjective connections between objects and individuals but also reduced personal relations to the "cash nexus." Half a century later, Simmel ([1908] 1950, p. 414) confirmed Marx's diagnosis, dubbing money a "frightful leveler" that perverted the uniqueness of personal and social values. And Max Weber ([1946] 1971, p. 331) pointed to the fundamental antagonism between a rational money economy and a "religious ethic of brotherliness."

The prevailing classic interpretation of money thus absolutized a model of market money, shaped by the following five assumptions:

1. The functions and characteristics of money are defined strictly in economic terms. As a qualityless, absolutely homogeneous, infinitely divisible, liquid object, money is a matchless tool for market exchange.
2. All monies are the same in modern society. Differences can exist in the quantity of money but not in its meaning. Thus, there is only one kind of money—market money.
3. A sharp dichotomy is established between money and nonpecuniary values. Money in modern society is defined as essentially profane and utilitarian in contrast to noninstrumental values. Money is qualitatively neutral; personal, social, and sacred values are qualitatively distinct, unexchangeable, and indivisible.
4. Monetary concerns are seen as constantly enlarging, quantifying, and often corrupting all areas of life. As an abstract medium of exchange, money has not only the freedom but also the power to draw an increasing number of goods and services into the web of the market. Money is thus the vehicle for an inevitable commodification of society.
5. The power of money to transform nonpecuniary values is unquestioned, while the reciprocal transformation of money by values or social relations is seldom conceptualized or else is explicitly rejected.

As the classic view reasons, the monetization of the economy made a significant difference to the organization of social life. For example, it facilitated the multiplication of economic partners and promoted a rational division of labor. But a link is missing from the traditional approach to money. Impressed by the fungible, impersonal characteristics of money, classic theorists emphasized its instrumental rationality and apparently unlimited capacity to transform products, relationships, and sometimes even emotions into an abstract and objective numerical equivalent. But money is neither culturally neutral nor socially anonymous. It may well "corrupt" values and social ties into numbers, but values and social relations reciprocally corrupt money by investing it with meaning and social patterns.

TOWARD A SOCIOLOGY OF MONEY

The utilitarian model has had a remarkable grip on theorizing about money. Coleman (1990, pp. 119–131), for example, builds an extremely sophisticated analysis of social exchange yet continues to treat money as the ultimate impersonal common denominator. Even when analysts recognize the symbolic dimension of modern money, they stop short of fully transcending the utilitarian framework. Parsons (1971a, p. 241; 1971b, pp. 26–27), for instance, explicitly and forcefully called for a "sociology of money" that would treat money as one of the various generalized symbolic media of social interchange, along with political power, influence, and value commitments. In contrast to Marx's ([1858–1859] 1973, p. 222) definition of money as the "material representative of wealth," in Parsons's media theory, money was a shared symbolic language; not a commodity, but a signifier, devoid of use-value. Yet Parsons restricts the symbolism of money to the economic sphere. Money, Parsons (1967, p. 358) contends, is the "symbolic 'embodiment' of economic value, of what economists in a technical sense call 'utility'." Consequently, Parsons's media theory left uncharted the symbolic meaning of money outside the market: money's cultural and social significance beyond utility. Giddens (1990) complains that Parsons incorrectly equates power, language, and money, whereas for Giddens money has a distinctly different relationship to social life. As a "symbolic token," money, in Giddens's analysis, serves as a key example of the "disembedding mechanisms associated with modernity," by which he means the " 'lifting out' of social relations from local contexts of interaction and their restructuring across indefinite spans of time-space" (1990, pp. 22, 25, 21). Giddens's interpretation still ignores the fact that despite the transferability of money, people make every effort to embed it in particular times, places, meanings, and social relations.

Anthropologists provide some intriguing insights into the extraeconomic, symbolic meaning of money, but only with regards to primitive money. For instance, ethnographic studies show that in certain primitive communities, money attains special qualities and distinct values independent of quantity. How much money is less important than *which* money. Multiple currencies, or "special-purpose" money, using Polanyi's (1957, pp. 264–266) term, have sometimes coexisted in one and the same village, each currency having a specified, restricted use (for purchasing only certain goods or services), special modes of allocation and forms of exchange (see, e.g., Bohannan 1959), and, sometimes, designated users.

These special moneys, which Douglas (1967) has perceptively identified as a sort of primitive coupon system, control exchange by rationing and restricting the use and allocation of currency. In the process, money sometimes performs economic functions serving as media of exchange, but it also functions as a social and sacred "marker," used to acquire or amend status, or to celebrate ritual events. The point is that primitive money is transformable, from fungible to nonfungible, from profane to sacred.

But what about modern money? Has modernization indeed stripped money of its cultural meaning? Influenced by economic models, most interpretations establish a sharp dichotomy between primitive, restricted "special-purpose" money and modern "all-purpose" money, which, as a single currency, unburdened by ritual or social controls, can function effectively as a universal medium of exchange. Curiously, when it comes to modern money, even anthropologists seem to surrender their formidable analytical tools. For instance, twenty years ago, Douglas (1967), in an important essay, suggested that modern money may not be unrestricted and "free" after all. Her evidence, however, is puzzlingly limited. Modern money, argues Douglas (1967, p. 139), is controlled and rationed in two situations: in international exchange and at the purely individual personal level, where "many of us try to primitivize our money . . . by placing restrictions at source, by earmarking monetary instruments of certain kinds for certain purposes."

Modern money, however, is marked by more than individual whim or by the different material form of currencies. As François Simiand, one of Durkheim's students, argued (1934), the extra-economic, social basis of money remains as powerful in modern economic systems as it was in primitive and ancient societies. Indeed, Simiand (1934) warned against an orthodox rationalist approach that mistakenly ignores the persistent symbolic, sacred, and even magical significance of modern money. In recent work sociologists, as well as anthropologists, psychologists, historians, and political scientists have finally heeded the warning, proposing long overdue alternatives to the standard utilitarian model of money.

Impatient with their former theoretical blinders, some anthropologists are now claiming modern money for their disciplinary terrain, casting off the fallacy of a single, culturally neutral currency. An important recent collection of essays demonstrates the heterogeneity of money, showing how the multiple symbolic meanings of modern money are shaped by the cultural matrix (Parry and Bloch 1989; see also Lederer 1988). And in psychology, new studies reject the notion that money is psychologically general, maintaining that instead money involves "multiple symbolizations" (Lea, Tarpey, and Webley 1987, p. 335). An exciting literature on "mental accounting" challenges the economists' assumption of fungibility by showing the ways individuals distinguish between kinds of money. For instance, they treat a windfall income much differently from a bonus or an inheritance, even when the sums involved are identical (see, e.g., Thaler 1990; Kahneman and Tversky 1982; for a historian's critique of the economic model of money, see Reddy 1987, and for a political scientist's perspective, Lane 1990).

A sociological accounting of money goes even further. Anthropologists reveal the multiple symbolic representations of modern money in societies outside the centers of capitalism, and psychologists explore individually or household-based differentiations between monies. A sociological model, on the other hand, must show how, even in the most advanced capitalist societies, different networks of social relations and meaning systems mark modern money, introducing controls, restrictions, and distinctions that are as influential as the rationing of primitive money. Special money in the modern world may not be as visibly identifiable as the shells, coins, brass rods, or stones of primitive communities, but its invisible boundaries emerge from sets of historically varying formal and informal rules that regulate its uses, allocation, sources, and quantity. How else, for instance, do we distinguish a bribe from a tribute or a donation, a wage from an honorarium, or an allowance from a salary? How do we identify ransom, bonuses, tips, damages, or premiums? True, there are quantitative differences between these various payments. But surely, the special vocabulary conveys much more than diverse amounts. Detached from its qualitative differences, the world of money becomes undecipherable.

The sociological model of money thus challenges the traditional utilitarian model of market money by introducing different fundamental assumptions in the understanding of money:

1. While money does serve as a key rational tool of the modern economic market, it also exists outside the sphere of the market and is profoundly shaped by different networks of social relations and varying systems of meaning.
2. Money is not a single phenomenon. There are a plurality of different kinds of monies; each special money is shaped by a particular set of

cultural and social factors and is thus qualitatively distinct. Market money does not escape extraeconomic influences but is in fact one type of special money, subject to particular social and cultural influences.

3. The classic economic inventory of money's functions and attributes, based on the assumption of a single general-purpose type of money, is thus unsuitably narrow. By focusing exclusively on money as a market phenomenon, it fails to capture the very complex range of characteristics of money as a social medium. A different, more inclusive coding is necessary, for certain monies can be indivisible (or divisible but not in mathematically predictable portions), nonfungible, nonportable, deeply subjective, and therefore qualitatively heterogeneous.
4. The assumed dichotomy between a utilitarian money and nonpecuniary values is false, for money under certain circumstances may be as singular and unexchangeable as the most personal or unique object.
5. Given the assumptions above, the alleged freedom and unchecked power of money become untenable assumptions. Culture and social structure set inevitable limits to the monetization process by introducing profound controls and restrictions on the flow and liquidity of money. Extraeconomic factors systematically constrain and shape (a) the uses of money, earmarking, for instance, certain monies for specified uses; (b) the users of money, designating different people to handle specified monies; (c) the allocation system of each particular money; (d) the control of different monies; and (e) the sources of money, linking different sources to specified uses.

Exploring the quality of multiple monies does not deny money's quantifiable and instrumental characteristics but moves beyond them; it suggests very different theoretical and empirical questions from those derived from a purely economic model of market money. In fact, a utilitarian theory of money had a straightforward task: explaining how money homogenized and commoditized modern social life. Its critics have a much more complex empirical agenda. The illusion of a fully commoditized world must be rectified by showing how different social relations and systems of meanings actively create and shape a plurality of qualitatively distinct kinds of money. Specifically, a sociological theory of money must come to grips with the remarkably different ways in which people identify, classify, interpret, organize, and use money.

Consider for instance the family economy. Domestic money—which includes wife's money, husband's money, and children's money—is a special category of money. Its meanings, uses, allocation, and even quantity are partly determined by considerations of economic efficiency, but domestic money is equally shaped by ideas about family life, by power relationships, age, gender, and social class (Zelizer 1989; Pahl 1989). For instance, a wife's pin money—regardless of the amount involved—was traditionally reserved for special purchases such as clothing or vacations and kept apart from the "real" money earned by her husband. Or consider the case of gift money. When money circulates among friends or kin as a personal gift for ritual events such as weddings, christenings, bar mitzvahs, or Christmas, it is reshaped into a sentimental currency expressing care and affection. It matters who gives it, when it is given, how it is presented, and how spent. Within formal institutions, money is again redefined this time partly by bureaucratic legislation (Goffman 1961).

These cases are not anomalies or exceptions to value-free market money but typical examples of money's heterogeneity in modern society. In fact, money used for rational instrumental exchanges is simply another socially created currency, not free from social constraints, but subject to particular networks of social relations and its own set of values and norms. A sociological theory of money must explain the sources and patterns of variation between multiple monies. How, for instance, do personal monies, such as domestic and gift monies, which emerge from the social interaction of intimates, differ from the imposed institutional money of inmates? How does the social status of transactors affect the circulation of monies? What determines the relative rigidity or permeability of boundaries between monies? And what are the patterns of conversions between them?

Developing a sociological model of multiple monies forms part of a broader challenge to neoclassical economic theory. It offers an alternative approach not only to the study of money but to all other aspects of economic life, including the market. In the long run, a proper sociological understanding of multiple monies should challenge and renew explanation of large-scale economic change and variation. It should illuminate such phenomena as aggregate expenditures on consumer durables, rates of saving, response to inflation, income redistribution, and a wide range of other phenomena in which individual consumer actions make a large macroeconomic difference. In the sociological model, economic processes of exchange and consumption are defined as one special category of social relations, much like kinship or religion. Thus, economic phenomena such as money, although partly autonomous, intertwine with historically variable systems of meanings and structures of social relations.

(SEE ALSO: *Economic Sociology*)

REFERENCES

Appadurai, Arjun (ed.) 1986 *The Social Life of Things.* Cambridge: Cambridge University Press.

Bohannan, Paul 1959 "The Impact of Money on an African Subsistence Economy." *Journal of Economic History* 19:491–503.

Bronner, Simon J. (ed.) 1989 *Consuming Visions.* New York: Norton.

Coleman, James 1990 *Foundations of Social Theory.* Cambridge, Mass.: Harvard University Press.

Douglas, Mary 1967 "Primitive Rationing." In Raymond Firth, ed., *Themes in Economic Anthropology.* London: Tavistock.

Giddens, Anthony 1990 *The Consequences of Modernity.* Stanford, Calif.: Stanford University Press.

Goffman, Erving 1961 *Asylums.* New York: Anchor.

Granovetter, Mark 1985 "Economic Action and Social Structure: The Problem of Embeddedness." *American Journal of Sociology* 91:481–510.

Hirschman, Albert O. 1977 *The Passions and the Interests.* Princeton, N.J.: Princeton University Press.

Kahneman, Daniel, and Amos Tversky 1982 "The Psychology of Preferences." *Scientific American* 246 (January): 160–173.

Lane, Robert E. 1990 "Money Symbolism and Economic Rationality." Paper presented at the Second Annual Meeting of the Society for the Advancement of Socio-Economics, Washington, D.C., March.

Lea, Stephen E. G., Roger Tarpy, and Paul Webley 1987 *The Individual in the Economy.* New York: Cambridge University Press.

Lederer, Rena 1988 "Pearlshells *In* and *As* Mendi History." Paper presented at the 1988 meetings of the American Anthropological Association, Phoenix, Ariz., November.

Marx, Karl (1844) 1964 "The Power of Money in Bourgeois Society." *The Economic and Philosophic Manuscripts of 1844.* New York: International Publishers.

———(1858–1859) 1973 *Grundrisse.* New York: Vintage.

Pahl, Jan 1989 *Money and Marriage.* New York: St. Martin's Press.

Parry, J., and M. Bloch (eds.) 1989 *Money and the Morality of Exchange.* Cambridge: Cambridge University Press.

Parsons, Talcott 1967 "On the Concept of Influence." In *Sociological Theory and Modern Society.* New York: Free Press.

———1971a "Higher Education as a Theoretical Focus." In Herman Turk and Richard L. Simpson, eds., *Institutions and Social Exchange.* New York: Bobbs-Merrill.

———1971b "Levels of Organization and the Mediation of Social Interaction." In Herman Turk and Richard L. Simpson, eds., *Institutions and Social Exchange.* New York: Bobbs-Merrill.

Polanyi, Karl 1957 "The Economy as an Instituted Process." In Karl Polanyi, Conrad M. Arensberg, and Harry W. Pearson, eds., *Trade and Market in the Early Empires.* New York: Free Press.

Reddy, William 1987 *Money and Liberty in Modern Europe.* New York: Cambridge University Press.

Silver, Allan 1990 "Friendship in Commercial Society: Eighteenth-Century Social Theory and Modern Sociology." *American Journal of Sociology* 95:1,474–1,504.

Simiand, François 1934 "La monnaie, réalité sociale." *Annales sociologiques,* ser. D, pp. 1–86.

Simmel, Georg (1900) 1978 *The Philosophy of Money,* trans. Tom Bottomore and David Frisby. London: Routledge and Kegan Paul.

———(1908) 1950 *The Sociology of Georg Simmel,* ed. Kurt H. Wolf. New York: Free Press.

Swedberg, Richard 1990 *Economics and Sociology.* Princeton, N.J.: Princeton University Press.

Thaler, Richard H. 1990 "Anomalies: Saving, Fungibility, and Mental Accounts." *Journal of Economic Perspectives* 4:193–205.

Turner, Bryan S. 1986 "Simmel, Rationalisation, and the Sociology of Money." *The Sociological Review* 34:93–114.

Weber, Max (1946) 1971 "Religious Rejections of the World and Their Directions." In H. H. Gerth and C. Wright Mills, eds., *From Max Weber: Essays in Sociology.* New York: Oxford University Press.

White, Harrison C. 1988 "Varieties of Markets." In Barry Wellman and S. D. Berkowitz, eds., *Social Structure: A Network Approach.* Cambridge, Mass.: Harvard University Press.

Zelizer, Viviana 1989 "The Social Meaning of Money: 'Special Monies'." *American Journal of Sociology* 95:342–377.

VIVIANA ZELIZER

MORAL DEVELOPMENT *Morality* refers to a set of values that have to do with "how humans cooperate and coordinate their activities in the service of furthering human welfare, and how they adjudicate conflict among individual interests" (Rest 1986, p. 3). Moral behavior is any course of action that serves these functions in a given situation, and moral judgment is the cognitive process by which one determines which particular behavior is morally appropriate.

Moral judgment is but one component of the process that leads to the actual performance of moral behavior. Rest (1986) identifies three other components, specifically (1) a sensitivity to what kinds of behavior are possible in a given situation and how they would affect the interested parties, (2) giving priority to behaving morally as opposed to responding to other personal values (e.g., professional success) that may conflict, and (3) the ability to follow through with the course of action that has been identified as moral.

However, research on moral development over the past thirty-five years has focused primarily on the development of moral judgment. This is due in large part to the influence of psychologists Lawrence Kohlberg (1969, 1971, 1976) and Jean Piaget ([1932] 1948). Both theorists maintained that moral behavior largely depends upon how one perceives the social world and oneself in relation to it. They therefore emphasized the cognitive component as critical to understanding moral development. Furthermore, they viewed moral decision making as a rational process and thus linked the development of moral judgment to the development of rational functioning.

THEORETICAL FOUNDATION

Kohlberg built on Piaget's theory of cognitive development to hypothesize a sequence of six specific stages of moral judgment in individual development. This theory of moral development is based on a fundamental idea from Piaget that the way people think about the physical and social world is the result of an "interactional" process between the human organism's innate tendencies and influences from the environment.

This "cognitive-developmental" approach is thus distinguished from both maturational and environmental theories of development. Maturational theories (Gesell 1956) maintain that patterns of behavior express the organism's inherent tendencies. Development is seen as the natural unfolding of a process determined by hereditary factors. In contrast, environmental theories argue that behavior is determined primarily by external influences. From this point of view, behavior is not innately patterned but is essentially learned, whether as a result of conditioning processes that associate the behavior with particular stimuli, rewards, and punishment, or as a result of observing (and subsequently modeling) the behavior of others.

Social learning theory (Bandura 1977) has produced considerable research on how observational learning explains a variety of behaviors relevant to morality, including prosocial behavior (e.g., sharing, cooperation), aggression, resistance to temptation, and delayed gratification. More recent developments have pursued the question of how individuals exert control over their behavior, thus providing some balance to the theory's focus on environmental influences. Bandura's (1982) self-efficacy theory, for example, emphasizes the individual's expectations as important to the successful performance of a behavior. However, social learning theory has not addressed moral action and moral character in terms of a broad developmental course (Musser and Leone 1986).

Cognitive-developmental theory, on the other hand, focuses on the developmental process by which people come to understand and organize, or "cognitively structure," their experience. It attempts to resolve the "nature–nurture" controversy by emphasizing the development of these cognitive structures as the result of the interaction between organismic tendencies and influences from the outside world. While particular ways of understanding experience may reflect innate tendencies, they develop in response to the individual's specific experiences with the environment.

Thus, development is not seen as primarily maturational, because experience is necessary for cognitive structure to take shape. Also, the rate at which development occurs can be influenced by the individual's experience. However, neither is development thought to be primarily determined by the environment. Rather, cognitive-developmentalists argue that, because the underlying thought organization at each stage is qualitatively different, cognitive development is more than the progressively greater acquisition of information. Furthermore, at any given stage, the current cognitive structure can influence how the world is perceived. Thus, cognitive structure is seen to be "the result of an interaction between certain organismic structuring tendencies and the structure of the outside world, rather than reflecting either one directly" (Kohlberg 1969, p. 352).

THE DOCTRINE OF COGNITIVE STAGES

Piaget's theory of cognitive development maintains that cognitive structures are periodically transformed or restructured as they become unable to account for (or assimilate) new information from the external world adequately. These periods of restructuring result in new ways of understanding that are different from the earlier mental structures as well as from those to be developed later. This allows for the differentiation of distinct cognitive stages, each identifiable by a characteristic approach to processing and organizing one's experience of external reality.

Piaget (1960) identified four main characteristics of cognitive stages. Kohlberg (1969) maintains that these characteristics accurately describe his stages of moral development.

1. Stages refer to distinct *qualitative differences* in the way a person thinks about an experience or solves a problem. Although the focus of attention may be the same, the mode of thinking about it is very different.

2. The progression of stages follows an *invariant sequence* in the development of individuals. That is, the order in which the stages occur is universal for all human organisms. It is possible that the speed or timing at which one progresses through the stages may vary with individual or cultural environments—or even that development may stop at one point or another. However, a given stage cannot be followed by any other stage than the one that is next in the sequence. Conversely, the earlier stage must first be achieved before its inadequacies become apparent and the subsequent transformation to the next stage can occur.

3. The characteristic mode of thinking represents a *structured whole.* Specific cognitive responses to specific tasks depend upon the overall organizational framework within which one processes information. It is this underlying cognitive structure that produces a logical consistency to one's responses. Thus, the stage is not identified by specific responses to specific stimuli but by the pattern in one's responses that indicate a particular underlying cognitive structure.

4. The sequence of stages is *hierarchical.* At each stage, the underlying structure represents a more integrated and complex organizational system that adequately accounts for information that created discrepancies within the previous structure. For example, children in the preoperational period of cognitive development cannot understand that equally sized balls of clay formed into two different shapes still have an equal amount of clay. However, children who have achieved concrete operational thinking understand the principle of conservation and thus recognize that the amount of clay remains the same (is conserved) for both pieces, even though they have changed in shape (Piaget and Inhelder 1969). Thus, the underlying cognitive structure of concrete operational thinking differentiates between amount and shape and integrates the information to achieve a more complex understanding of the phenomenon. It is thus logically superior to preoperational thinking. That the later stages in cognitive development are also more comprehensive and advanced in this way produces a hierarchical element to the sequence. Thus the stages of cognitive development are not just different but also hierarchical in the sense that they provide a progressively more differentiated and integrated—and hence more adaptive—understanding of one's interaction with the environment.

KOHLBERG'S STAGES OF MORAL DEVELOPMENT

Kohlberg's six stages of moral reasoning are divided into three levels, each consisting of two stages. The three levels are differentiated according to what serves as the basis for the person's moral judgment, particularly with regard to the significance given the prevailing, or "conventional," social expectations and authority. Briefly, the "preconventional" level, which is the level of most children under nine years old, is prior to the individual's achieving a full understanding of what is expected or required socially. The "conventional" level, which characterizes most adolescents and adults, refers to an understanding of the social conventions and a belief in conforming to and maintaining the established social order. The "postconventional" level is reached only by a minority of adults who understand and generally accept the social rules and expectations but who recognize that these have been established for the larger purpose of serving universal moral principles. Should the social conventions conflict with these principles, then moral judgment at this level will support the principles at the expense of the conventions.

Within each level, the second stage is a more advanced form than the first. More specifically, the preconventional level refers to judgment based not so much on a sense of what is right and wrong but on the physical consequences that any given act will have for the self. Accordingly, at the first stage within this level, characterized by the *punishment and obedience* orientation, the child will make judgments on the basis of avoiding trouble. This includes obeying authorities to avoid punishment.

At Stage 2, in what is still the preconventional level, the individual has a sense of the needs of others but still makes judgments to serve the self's practical interests. This is called the *instrumental* orientation. Although the person is beginning to understand that social interaction involves reciprocity and exchange among participants, moral judgment is still determined by the significance that the action has for oneself. Thus a child may share candy to get some ice cream.

Next is the conventional level, wherein moral judgment is determined by what is considered "good" according to conventional standards. At this level, the individual has an understanding of what kind of behavior is expected. The first stage at this level (Stage 3) is characterized by the *good boy/nice girl* orientation. Judgment as to what is right is based on living up to the expectations of others. It involves a trust in established authority and conformity for the sake of approval.

At Stage 4, the orientation is toward doing one's duty. This is called the *law and order* orientation. The individual personally subscribes to the existing social order and thus believes that obeying authority and maintaining the social order are good values in their own right. Whereas behaving according to the typical moral conventions is desirable at Stage 3 because it produces approval from others, at Stage 4 the individual has successfully "internalized" these conventions, so that proper behavior is rewarding because it reinforces one's sense of doing one's duty and therefore produces self-approval.

At the postconventional level, one's understanding of what is right and wrong is based on one's personal values and a sense of shared rights and responsibilities. Morality is no longer determined simply by social definition, but rather by rational considerations. Stage 5 is characterized by the *social contract* orientation, which recognizes that conventions are determined by social consensus and serve a social function. There is an emphasis on utilitarian agreements as to what will serve the most good for the most people. Here the person recognizes that rules or expectations are essentially arbitrary. The focus on agreement or contract produces an emphasis on what is legal and on operating "within the system" to achieve one's goals.

Stage 6, however, places the responsibility of a given moral decision firmly on the shoulders of the individual. The basis for moral judgment is found in *universal ethical principles* rather than socially established rules or expectations. One is guided by one's own conscience and recognizes the logical superiority of principles such as respect for human dignity. At Stage 6, it is thus possible to adopt a position that is in conflict with the prevailing social order and maintain this position as morally correct.

MEASURING MORAL JUDGMENT

Kohlberg's procedure for assessing moral judgment involves presenting the subject with a hypothetical "dilemma" that requires the subject to make a moral choice. The most famous example refers to "Heinz," a man whose wife is dying of cancer. The woman could possibly be saved by a new drug, but the druggist who discovered it is charging an exorbitant amount of money for it, ten times what it costs him to make it. Heinz tried but could not raise enough money. Should he steal the drug?

Because Kohlberg's scheme emphasizes cognitive structure, an individual's stage of moral development is indicated not by the actual behavior that is advocated but rather by the pattern of reasoning behind the decision. Thus, two people may arrive at the same decision (e.g., that Heinz should steal the drug to save the life of his dying wife) but for two entirely different reasons. An individual at the preconventional Stage 2, operating within the instrumental orientation, might recommend stealing the drug because any jail term would be short and worth saving his wife. An individual at the postconventional Stage 6 might also recommend stealing the drug but with a different understanding of the dilemma: Although stealing would violate the law, it would uphold the higher principle of valuing human life and allow Heinz to maintain his self-respect.

The difference between the actual behavioral content of a decision and the underlying cognitive structure responsible for making the decision is also illustrated when two people arrive at different decisions but for similar reasons. Thus, the decision not to steal the drug because Heinz would go to jail and probably not be released until after his wife died is also Stage 2 thinking. Even though the ultimate decision advocates the opposite behavior of what was indicated above, it is similarly based on the consideration of what would be most instrumental to Heinz's own self-interest. On the other hand, an individual at Stage 6 might recommend not stealing the drug because, although other people would not blame Heinz if he stole it, he would nonetheless violate his own standard of honesty and lose his self-respect.

Because the stage of moral development is demonstrated not by the behavioral content but by the form of the moral judgment, subjects are allowed to respond freely to these moral dilemmas and asked to explain and justify their answers. The interviewer can probe with specific questions to elicit more information on the basis for the subject's decision. Interviewers are trained to collect relevant information without directing the subject's response.

Subjects' answers are then transcribed and coded for stage of moral development. Kohlberg identified twenty-five aspects of moral judgment, basic moral concepts that refer to such matters as rules, conscience, one's own welfare, the welfare of others, duty, punishment, reciprocity, and motives. Each of the twenty-five aspects was defined differently for each of the six stages of moral development. Originally, Kohlberg used an aspect-scoring system, whereby every statement made by the subject was coded for aspect and rated as to stage ("sentence scoring"). The subject's usage of any given stage of moral reasoning was indicated by the percentage of his or her statements that was attributed to that stage. Aspect scoring also included an overall "story rating," whereby a single stage was assigned to the subject's total response.

Coding difficulties led to the abandonment of the aspect-scoring system. Because the unit of analysis for sentence scoring was so small, coding often became dependent upon the specific content and choice of words and did not lend itself to identifying the general cognitive structure underlying the statement. Conversely, whereas story rating referred to the total response as the unit of analysis, it created some uncertainty when the subject's answer included conflicting themes.

Kohlberg and his colleagues recognized these scoring difficulties and devoted considerable attention to developing a more reliable and valid scoring system. This led to "standardized issue scoring," which relies on the use of a standardized interview format. The subject is presented with three standard dilemmas, and the interviewer probes for only two issues that are specified for each dilemma (e.g., life and punishment in the Heinz dilemma). Scoring of the subject's responses refers to a manual that describes the patterns of reasoning for Stages 1–5 on each issue (Colby et al. 1987). Stage 6 was dropped from the coding procedure, due to its empirically low incidence, but retained as a theoretical construct. Because the focus of the new scoring system is directed more toward the abstract mode of reasoning, the unit of analysis is thus considered larger and less concrete than the single sentence. However, because this approach focuses on specifically identified issues, norms, and elements, it is considered more precise than the global story rating. Despite the qualitative nature of this approach and its potential vulnerability to rater bias, its developers report that long-term study of its inter-rater reliability, test–retest reliability, internal consistency, and validity has produced favorable results (Colby and Kohlberg 1987).

Validity has been a major concern regarding the Moral Judgment Interview. Kurtines and Grief (1974) criticized the low utility of moral judgment scores for predicting moral action. Other questions have been raised about the validity of the data collected, even for purposes of assessing moral judgment. For one, the representativeness of the "classical" dilemmas used in this research has been criticized, in terms of both their addressing hypothetical—as opposed to real-life—circumstances and their reference to a limited domain of moral issues (e.g., property, punishment). A related matter is whether responses are affected by characteristics (e.g., gender) of the story's protagonist. Also, the effect of differences in interviewing style, as interviewers interact with subjects and probe for further information, needs to be considered. Of particular importance is this method's dependence on the subject's verbal expression and articulation skills for the information that is collected. To the extent that the rating might be affected by either the amount of information that is provided or the manner in which it is expressed, the validity of the scoring system is called into question. (See Modgil and Modgil 1986 for discussion of these issues.)

An alternative to Kohlberg's Moral Judgment Interview is the Defining Issues Test (DIT; Rest 1986). This is a standardized questionnaire that presents a set of six moral dilemmas and, for each dilemma, specifically identifies twelve issues that could be considered in deciding upon a course of action. The subject's task is to indicate, on a five-point scale, how important each issue is to deciding what ought to be done in the given situation. The subject also ranks the four most important issues.

Here, the term *issue* is used differently than it is in Kohlberg's new scoring procedure. The items are prototypical statements designed to represent considerations (e.g., "whether a community's laws are going to be upheld") that are characteristic of specific stages of moral reasoning as they are described in Kohlberg's theory. The importance assigned by the subject to items that represent a particular stage is taken to indicate the extent to which the subject's moral judgment is characterized by that stage's mode of thinking.

There are advantages and disadvantages to the DIT compared with the open-ended interview. Whereas the interview is helpful for originally identifying the considerations that may be relevant to resolving a moral dilemma, the DIT provides a more systematic assessment of the relative importance of such considerations. In the open-ended interview, it is never clear whether a specific concern is not identified because it is not important or because the subject failed to articulate it. Similarly, interviews are less comparable to the extent that subjects do not all address the same issues. These problems are avoided by the more structured DIT because the task requires the subject only to recognize what is important rather than to identify and articulate it spontaneously. However, because recognition is an easier task than spontaneous production, it tends to allow higher-level responses. Another important difference is that the DIT measures the maturity of moral judgment as a continuous variable rather than in terms of the step-by-step sequence of cognitive-developmental stages. Researchers must be aware of such differences when interpreting results.

THEORETICAL CRITICISMS

Besides the methodological problems discussed above, Kohlberg's theory of moral development has been criticized on a number of points. The major criticisms include the following:

1. The sequence of stages is more representative of Western culture and thus not universal or invariant across all cultures. Moreover, it is culturally biased in that it maintains the ideals of Western liberalism as the highest form of moral reasoning.

2. Like many theories of personality development, Kohlberg's theory fails to describe accurately the development of women but provides a much better understanding of male development. This is a specific variation of the first criticism, suggesting that the theory itself reflects the sexism of Western culture.

3. Kohlberg's theory fails to describe adult development adequately. In particular, its emphasis on abstract principles fails to recognize how adult moral judgment is more responsive to the specific practical matters of everyday, real-life contexts. Also, its emphasis on cognitive structure fails to recognize that changes in the content of moral reflection may be the most important aspect of adult moral development.

Cultural Bias. A cornerstone of cognitive-developmental theory is that of invariant sequence, the notion that the given developmental progression is universal for all human beings within all cultures. Because the conceptual organization of any given stage is considered logically necessary before the cognitive structure of the next stage can develop, each stage is said to have logical priority to subsequent stages. Shweder and LeVine (1975) take issue with both the notion of logical priority and the doctrine of invariant sequence, although they do not address the development of moral judgment per se. Specifically, they analyze dream concepts among children from the Hausa culture in Nigeria and conclude that there are multiple sequences by which such concepts develop.

Shweder (1982) follows up this initial skepticism with a fuller critique of what he sees as Kohlberg's failure to recognize cultural conceptions of morality as relative to one another. He disagrees with the assertion that there is a rational basis upon which morality can be constructed objectively. Rather, he argues that the postconventional morality that Kohlberg maintains as rationally superior is simply an example of American ideology.

Similarly, others (Broughton 1986; Simpson 1974; Sullivan 1977) argue that Kohlberg's theory is necessarily culture-bound, reflective of the

Western society from which it originates. Simpson suggests that the specific moral dilemmas used in the testing situation may not have the same meaning for people of different cultures and thus the scoring system may not adequately detect legitimate cultural variations in moral structures. Thus, he maintains that the claims to universality are not valid. Sullivan goes even further to suggest that Stage 6 reasoning is so rooted in the philosophical rationale for current Western society that it serves to defend the status quo. In so doing, it distracts attention from the injustices of such societies.

In a response to the charge of cultural bias, Kohlberg, Levine, and Hewer (1983) acknowledge the influence of Western liberal ideology on the theory. They agree there is a need to be more sensitive to cultural differences in the meaning attributed not only to the various elements of the research protocol but, consequently, also to the responses of the subjects themselves. However, they defend the claim to universality for the six-stage sequence of moral development and maintain that empirical research using the scientific method will help to determine to what extent this position is tenable.

They also maintain that, while it is appropriate to remain impartial in the study of moral judgment, this does not make it necessary to deny the relative value of certain moral positions. They assert that some positions are rationally superior to others. They thus continue to subscribe to the ideal that any given moral conflict can be brought to resolution through rational discourse.

Kohlberg's position on invariant sequence has been supported by a number of cross-cultural studies, although postconventional reasoning (Stages 5 and 6) may occur less frequently in nonurbanized cultures (Snarey 1985). However, in a sample of subjects from India, Vasudev and Hummel (1987) not only found the stage of moral development to be significantly related to age, but also found postconventional thinking to occur among a substantial proportion of adults. Concluding that commonalities exist across cultures, Vasudev and Hummel also suggest there is cultural diversity in the way moral principles are expressed, interpreted, and adapted to real life.

Gender Bias. Carol Gilligan (1982) argues that the major theories of personality development describe males more accurately than females. She includes Kohlberg's theory in this assessment and points to the prevalence of all-male samples in his early research as a partial explanation. Gilligan contrasts two moral orientations. The first is the morality of justice, which focuses on fairness, rights, and rules for the resolution of disputes. The second is the morality of care, which focuses on relationships, a sensitivity to the needs of others, and a responsibility for others. Gilligan asserts that the orientation towards morality as justice is more characteristic of males and, conversely, the morality of care and responsibility is especially relevant to females. To the extent that Piaget, Freud, and Kohlberg each address morality as justice, they more accurately represent male moral development but inadequately represent female moral development.

Gilligan argues that women are more likely to rely on the orientation of care to frame personal moral dilemmas. Furthermore, whereas the morality of care focuses on interpersonal relationship, it resembles the Stage 3 emphasis on satisfying the expectations of others. Gilligan believes this resemblance results in a high number of female responses being misrepresented with Stage 3 ratings.

Gilligan thus argues that Kohlberg's theory and scoring system are biased to favor men. However, Walker (1984), after systematically reviewing empirical studies that used Kohlberg's method, concludes that men do not score higher than women, when samples are controlled for education, socioeconomic status, and occupation. Similarly, Thoma (1986) reports that sex differences on the Defining Issues Test actually favor women but that the differences are trivial.

Kohlberg, Levine, and Hewer (1983) address Gilligan's criticisms and agree that the care orientation is not fully assessed by their measurement but disagree that this leads to a biased downscoring of females. They suggest that care and justice may develop together and that Stage 6 nonetheless represents a mature integration of the care and justice moralities. (See also Vasudev 1988.)

Adult Development. A third major issue concerning Kohlberg's theory is whether or not it accurately addresses continued adult development. This issue reflects a more general concern in lifespan developmental psychology regarding the applicability (or inapplicability) of Piaget's model for cognitive development beyond adolescence (Commons, Richards, and Armon 1984). Murphy and Gilligan (1980) provide evidence that college and postcollege subjects not only indicated a greater tendency to appreciate the importance of specific contexts in real-life dilemmas but also indicated a slight tendency to regress from Stage 5 moral reasoning on the classical dilemmas. They suggest that a more mature recognition of the significance of contextual particulars leads one to question the validity of abstract moral principles (hence the regressed score). This argument is consistent with other work suggesting that adult development is marked by a greater appreciation of the practical realities of day-to-day living (Denney and Palmer 1981; Labouvie-Vief 1984; Perry 1970).

Finally, Gibbs (1979) argues that adult development is characterized more by increased reflection on such existential matters as meaning, identity, and commitment than by any structural change in the way one thinks. He suggests that Kohlberg's postconventional stages are not structural advances over the earlier stages but would be more appropriately described in terms of existential development. In response, Kohlberg, Levine, and Hewer (1983) maintain that Stage 5 represents a legitimate cognitive structure. However, they acknowledge the possibility of further nonstructural development in the adult years with regard to both specific contextual relativity and existential reflection. They suggest that such development could be described in terms of "soft" stages that do not strictly satisfy Piaget's formal criteria for cognitive stages.

In spite of the formidable criticisms that have been levied against it, Kohlberg's theory of moral development remains the centerpiece to which all other work in this area is addressed, whether as an elaboration or as a refutation. At the very least, Kohlberg has formulated a particular sequence of moral reasoning that adequately represents the prevalent sequence of development in traditional Western society. To that extent, it serves as a model, not only for building educational devices (see Modgil and Modgil 1986; Nucci 1989; Power, Higgins, and Kohlberg 1989), but also for comparing possible alternatives. Whether or not this sequence is in fact universal or relative to the particular culture—or a particular socialization process within one's culture—is a debate that continues. Nonetheless, the scheme remains the prototype upon which further work in this area is likely to be based.

(SEE ALSO: *Equity Theory; Socialization*)

REFERENCES

Bandura, Albert 1977 *Social Learning Theory.* Englewood Cliffs, N.J.: Prentice-Hall.

———1982 "Self-Efficacy Mechanism in Human Agency." *American Psychologist* 37:122–147.

Broughton, John M. 1986 "The Genesis of Moral Domination." In S. Modgil and C. Modgil, eds., *Lawrence Kohlberg: Consensus and Controversy.* Philadelphia: Falmer Press.

Colby, Anne, and Lawrence Kohlberg 1987 *The Measurement of Moral Judgment,* vol. 1, *Theoretical Foundations and Research Validation.* New York: Cambridge University Press.

———, Lawrence Kohlberg, Alexandra Hewer, Daniel Candee, John C. Gibbs, and Clark Power 1987 *The Measurement of Moral Judgment,* vol. 2, *Standard Issue Scoring Manual.* New York: Cambridge University Press.

Commons, Michael L., Francis A. Richards, and Cheryl Armon (eds.) 1984 *Beyond Formal Operations: Late Adolescent and Adult Cognitive Development.* New York: Praeger.

Denney, Nancy W., and Ann M. Palmer 1981 "Adult Age Differences on Traditional and Practical Problem-Solving Measures." *Journal of Gerontology* 36:323–328.

Gesell, Arnold 1956 *Youth: The Years from Ten to Sixteen.* New York: Harper and Row.

Gibbs, John C. 1979 "Kohlberg's Moral Stage Theory: A Piagetian Revision." *Human Development* 22: 89–112.

Gilligan, Carol 1982 *In a Different Voice: Psychological Theory and Women's Development.* Cambridge, Mass.: Harvard University Press.

Kohlberg, Lawrence 1969 "Stage and Sequence: The Cognitive-Developmental Approach to Socialization." In D. Goslin, ed., *Handbook of Socialization Theory and Research.* Chicago: Rand McNally.

———1971 "From *Is* to *Ought:* How to Commit the Naturalistic Fallacy and Get Away with It in the Study of Moral Development." In T. Mischel, ed., *Cognitive Development and Epistemology.* New York: Academic Press.

———1976 "Moral Stages and Moralization: The Cognitive Developmental Approach." In T. Lickona, ed., *Moral Development and Behavior: Theory, Research, and Social Issues.* New York: Holt, Rinehart, and Winston.

———, Charles Levine, and Alexandra Hewer 1983 *Moral Stages: A Current Formulation and a Response to Critics.* Basel, Switzerland: Karger.

Kurtines, William, and Esther B. Grief 1974 "The Development of Moral Thought: Review and Evaluation of Kohlberg's Approach." *Psychological Bulletin* 81:453–470.

Labouvie-Vief, Gisela 1984 "Culture, Language, and Mature Rationality." In K. McCluskey and H. W. Reese, eds., *Life-Span Developmental Psychology: Historical and Generational Effects.* New York: Academic Press.

Modgil, Sohan, and Celia Modgil 1986 *Lawrence Kohlberg: Consensus and Controversy.* Philadelphia: Falmer Press.

Murphy, John M., and Carol Gilligan 1980 "Moral Development in Late Adolescence and Adulthood: A Critique and Reconstruction of Kohlberg's Theory." *Human Development* 23:77–104.

Musser, Lynn M., and Christopher Leone 1986 "Moral Character: A Social Learning Perspective." In R. T. Knowles and G. F. McLean, eds., *Psychological Foundations of Moral Education and Character Development: An Integrated Theory of Moral Development.* Lanham, Md.: University Press of America.

Nucci, Larry P. (ed.) 1989 *Moral Development and Character Education: A Dialogue.* Berkeley, Calif.: McCutchan.

Perry, William G., Jr. 1970 *Forms of Intellectual and Ethical Development in the College Years.* New York: Holt, Rinehart, and Winston.

Piaget, Jean [1932] 1948 *The Moral Judgment of the Child.* Glencoe, Ill.: Free Press.

———1960 "The General Problems of the Psychobiological Development of the Child." In J. M. Tanner and B. Inhelder, eds., *Discussions on Child Development: Proceedings of the World Health Organization Study Group on the Psychobiological Development of the Child.* New York: International Universities Press.

———, and Barbara Inhelder 1969 *The Psychology of the Child.* New York: Basic Books.

Power, Clark F., Ann Higgins, and Lawrence Kohlberg 1989 *Lawrence Kohlberg's Approach to Moral Education.* New York: Columbia University Press.

Rest, James R. 1986 *Moral Development: Advances in Research and Theory.* New York: Praeger.

Shweder, Richard 1982 "Review of Lawrence Kohlberg's Essays in Moral Development, Vol. 1, The Philosophy of Moral Development: Liberalism as Destiny." *Contemporary Psychology* 27:421–424.

———, and Robert A. LeVine 1975 "Dream Concepts of Hausa Children: A Critique of the 'Doctrine of Invariant Sequence' in Cognitive Development." *Ethos* 3:209–230.

Simpson, Elizabeth L. 1974 "Moral Development Research: A Case Study of Scientific Cultural Bias." *Human Development* 17:81–106.

Snarey, John R. 1985 "Cross-Cultural Universality of Social-Moral Development: A Critical Review of Kohlbergian Research." *Psychological Bulletin* 97:202–232.

Sullivan, Edmund V. 1977 "A Study of Kohlberg's Structural Theory of Moral Development: A Critique of Liberal Social Science Ideology." *Human Development* 20:352–376.

Thoma, Stephen J. 1986 "Estimating Gender Differences in the Comprehension and Preference of Moral Issues." *Developmental Review* 6:165–180.

Vasudev, Jyotsna 1988 "Sex Differences in Morality and Moral Orientation: A Discussion of the Gilligan and Attanucci Study." *Merrill-Palmer Quarterly* 34: 239–244.

———, and Hummel, Raymond C. 1987 "Moral Stage Sequence and Principled Reasoning in an Indian Sample." *Human Development* 30:105–118.

Walker, Lawrence J. 1984 "Sex Differences in the Development of Moral Reasoning: A Critical Review of the Literature." *Child Development* 55:677–691.

THOMAS J. FIGURSKI

MORTALITY *See* Birth and Death Rates; Infant and Child Mortality; Life Expectancy.

MULTINATIONAL CORPORATIONS *See* Transnational Corporations.

MULTIPLE INDICATOR MODELS A primary goal of sociology (and science in general) is to provide accurate estimates of the causal relationship between concepts of central interest to the discipline. Thus, for example, sociologists might examine the causal link between the amount of money people make and how satisfied they are with their life in general. But in assessing the relationship between concepts—such as income and life satisfaction—researchers are subject to making "measurement errors." Such errors will produce biased estimates of the true causal relationship between concepts.

Multiple indicator models are a method of correcting for errors made in measuring a concept or "latent construct." Before examining multiple indicator models, however, the reader should become familiar with the terms and logic underlying such models. Latent constructs are unobservable phenomena (e.g., internal states such as the amount of "satisfaction" a person experiences) or more concrete concepts (e.g., income). It is the "true score" of these latent constructs that social scientists wish to measure (as accurately as possible) for each individual or "case" in a given study. Additionally, an "indicator" is simply another name for the actual measure of a given construct. For example, researchers might measure income through an indicator on a questionnaire that asks people "How much money do you earn per year?"—with the response options being, say, five possible income levels ranging from "income greater than $200,000 per year" (coded as 5) to "income less than $10,000 per year" (coded as 1). Similarly, researchers might provide an indicator for life satisfaction by asking people to respond to the statement, "I am satisfied with my life." The response options here might be "strongly agree" (coded as 5), "agree" (coded as 4), "neither agree nor disagree" (coded as 3), "disagree" (coded as 2), and "strongly disagree" (coded as 1).

Social scientists might expect to find a positive association between the above measures of income and life satisfaction. In fact, a review of empirical studies suggests a correlation coefficient ranging from 0.1 to 0.3 (Larson 1978). Correlation coefficients can have values between 1.0 and −1.0, with 0 indicating no association, and 1.0 or −1.0 indicating a perfect relationship. Therefore, for example, a correlation of 1.0 for income and life satisfaction would imply that we can perfectly predict a person's life-satisfaction score by knowing that person's income. In other words, individuals with the highest income (i.e., scored as a 5) consistently have the highest life satisfaction (i.e., scored as a 5); those with the next highest income (i.e., 4) consistently have the next highest life satisfaction (i.e., 4), and so on. Conversely, a −1.0 suggests the opposite relationship. That is, people with the highest income consistently have the lowest life satisfaction; those with the second-highest income consistently have the second lowest life satisfaction, and so on.

Furthermore, a correlation coefficient of 0.2, as possibly found, say, between income and life satisfaction, suggests a relatively weak association. A coefficient of this size would indicate that individuals with higher incomes only *tend* to have higher life satisfaction. Hence, we should expect to find many exceptions to this "average" pattern. That is, we can predict life satisfaction better by knowing someone's income than if we did not have this information. But we will still make a lot of errors in our predictions.

These errors stem in part from less-than-perfect measures of income or life satisfaction (a topic covered in the next section). However, they also occur because there are many other causes of life satisfaction (e.g., physical health) in addition to income. The more of these additional causes there are, and the stronger their effects (i.e., the stronger their correlation with life satisfaction), the weaker the ability of a single construct such as income to predict life satisfaction. The same principles apply, of course, to any construct used to predict other constructs (e.g., using people's level of stress to predict the amount of aggression they will display).

Correlation coefficients and "path coefficients" are part of the language of causal modeling, including multiple indicator models. Like a correlation coefficient, a path coefficient describes the strength of the relationship between two variables. One can interpret a (standardized) path coefficient in a manner roughly similar to a correlation coefficient. Readers will increase their understanding of the material to follow if they familiarize themselves with these measures of strength of association. (For more information on interpreting correlation and path coefficients, see Blalock 1979.)

SINGLE INDICATOR MODELS

Figure 1 depicts the causal link (solid arrow labeled *x*) between the latent constructs of income and life satisfaction (represented with circles), and the causal link (solid arrows labeled *a* and *b*) between each latent construct (circle) and its respective indicator (box). (The *Z* in Figure 1 represents all causes of life satisfaction that the researcher has not measured and thus not explicitly included in the causal model. The various *E*'s in Figure 1 represent factors that contribute to measurement error.) Because each latent construct (circled I and LS) in Figure 1 has only one indicator (boxed I_1 or LS_1) to measure the respec-

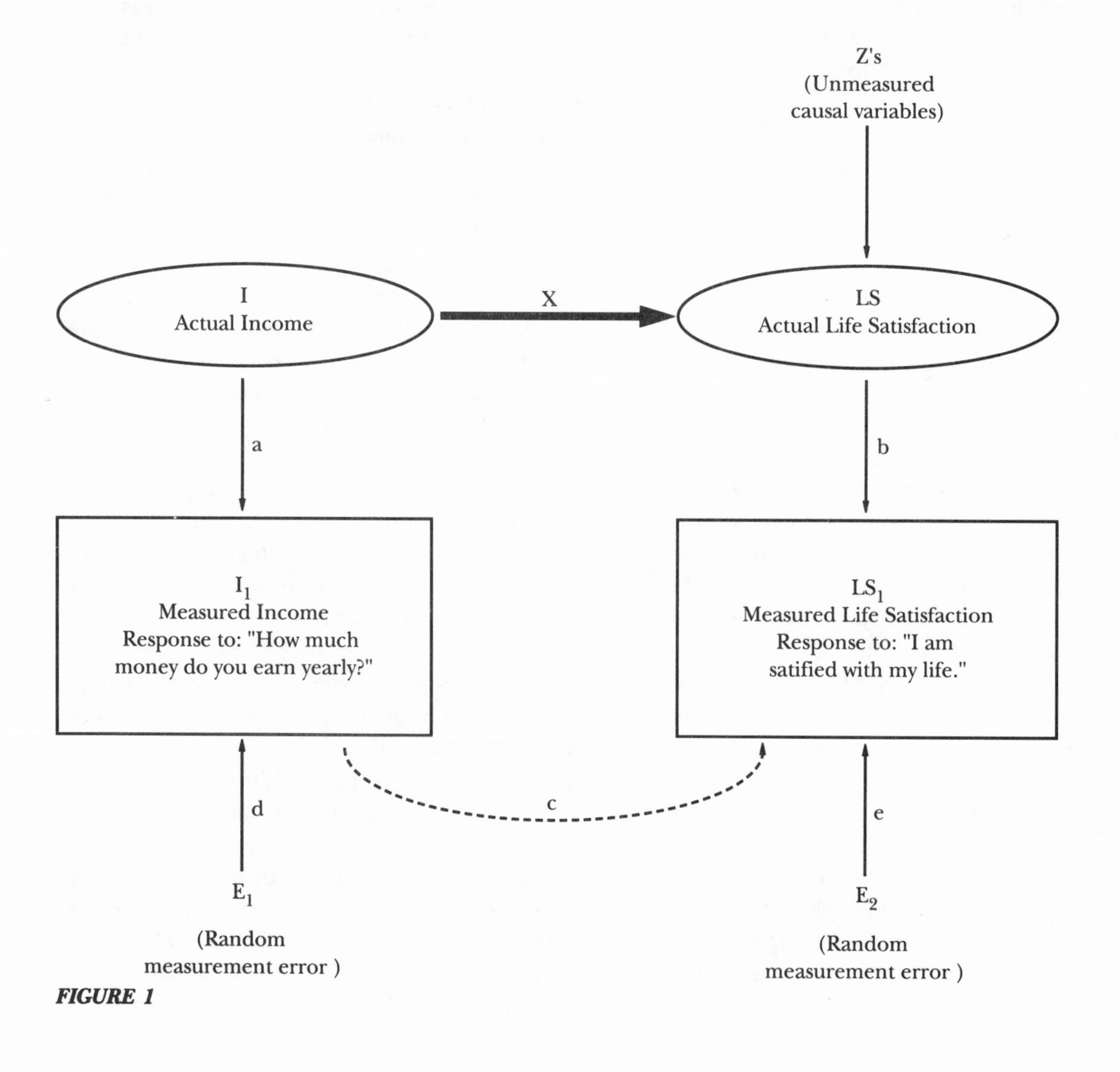

FIGURE 1

tive concept, researchers describe the diagram as a causal model with *single* (as opposed to multiple) indicators. Additionally, Figure 1 displays a dashed arrow (labeled *c*) between the box for income and the box for life satisfaction. This path represents the empirical or *observed* relationship between the indicators of income and life satisfaction. It has a dashed arrow to designate that it is a noncausal relationship, that is, a *spurious* correlation.

What makes the relationship between the indicators for income and life satisfaction noncausal or spurious? Follow the logic diagrammed in Figure 1 for the answer. According to this diagram, an increase in actual income (I) should produce an increase in measured income (I_1). Furthermore, an increase in actual income should also produce an increase in actual life satisfaction (LS), which in turn should produce an increase in measured life satisfaction (LS_1). Note that under these conditions, it will appear that an increase in measured income (I_1) has caused an increase in measured life satisfaction (LS_1). But in fact this positive relationship (i.e., path *c*) is noncausal. In other words, it is a spurious by-product of the causal chain initiated by an increase in actual income.

Note, too, that researchers can never directly observe the *true* causal relationship (i.e., path *x*) between the latent constructs of income (I) and life satisfaction (LS). Researchers can only *infer* such a relationship based on the *observed* (noncausal) relationship (i.e., path *c*) between the empirical indicators—I_1 and LS_1. In other words, social scientists use an observed noncausal relation—path *c*—to estimate an unobserved causal relation—path *x*. Notice that in the presence of random measurement error, path *c* will always be an underestimate of path *x*. Of course, researchers hope that path *c* is the same as the true causal relationship between income (I) and life satisfaction (LS), as represented by path *x*. Put another way, they hope that $c = x$. But *c* will only equal *x* if our measures of income and life satisfaction (I_1 and LS_1) are *perfect*.

To have perfect measures implies that the indicators for income and life satisfaction reflect exactly each person's actual or "true" score on income and life satisfaction. If the indicators for income and life satisfaction are indeed perfect measures, then researchers can attach a (standardized) path coefficient of 1.0 to each path (i.e., *a* and *b*) between the latent constructs and their indicator. Likewise, researchers can attach a path coefficient of 0 to each path (i.e., *d* and *e*) representing the effects of random measurement errors (E_1 and E_2) on the respective indicators for income and life satisfaction.

The path coefficient of 1.0 for *a* and *b* signifies a perfect relationship between the latent construct (i.e., true score) and the measure or indicator for the latent construct (i.e., recorded score). In other words, there is no "slippage" between the actual amount of income or life satisfaction people have and the amount of income or life satisfaction that a researcher records for each person (i.e., there is no measurement error). Therefore, individuals who truly have the highest income will report the most income, those who truly have the lowest income will report the lowest income, and so on. Likewise, people who in fact have the most life satisfaction will always record a life satisfaction score (e.g., 5) higher than those a little less satisfied (e.g., 4) individuals a little less satisfied will always record a life satisfaction score higher than those a little less satisfied yet (e.g., 3), and so forth.

Under the assumption of perfect measurement, social scientists can use the (noncausal) observed correlation (path *c*) between the indicators I_1 and LS_1 to estimate the true causal correlation (path *x*) between income (I) and life satisfaction (LS). Specifically, $c = (a)(x)(b)$; hence, $c = (1.0)(x)(1.0)$ or $c = x$. Thus, if the observed correlation between income and life satisfaction (i.e., path *c*) is, say, 0.2, then the true (unobserved) causal correlation between income and life satisfaction (i.e., path *x*) would also be 0.2. (For more detailed explanations of how to interpret and calculate path coefficients, see Sullivan and Feldman 1979; Loehlin 1987.)

Of course, even if researchers were to measure income and life satisfaction perfectly (i.e., paths *a* and *b* each equal 1.0), there are other possible errors ("misspecifications") in the model shown in Figure 1 that could bias researchers' estimates of how strong an effect income truly has on life satisfaction. That is, Figure 1 does not depict other possible misspecifications in the model, such as "reverse causal order" (e.g., amount of life satisfaction determines a person's income) or "spuriousness" (e.g., education determines both income and life satisfaction and hence only makes it appear that income causes life satisfaction). (For more details on these additional sources of potential misspecification, see also Blalock 1979.)

How realistic is the assumption of perfect measurement? The answer is, "It depends." For example, to assume a path coefficient of 1.0 for path *a* in Figure 1 would not be too unrealistic (the actual coefficient is likely a little less than 1.0—say, 0.90 or 0.95). That is, we would not expect many errors in measuring a person's true income. Likewise, we would expect few measurement errors in recording, say, a person's age, sex, or race. But the measurement of internal states such as "attitudes" or "affective states" (including satisfaction with life) is likely to occur with considerable error. Therefore, researchers would likely misestimate the true causal link between income and life satisfaction if they assumed no measurement error in life satisfaction, that is, a coefficient of 1.0 for path *b* in Figure 1.

How badly researchers misestimate the true causal effect (i.e., path *x*) would depend of course on how much less than 1.0 was the value for path *b*. For the sake of illustration, assume that path *b* equals 0.5. Assume also that income is perfectly measured (i.e., path *a* equals 1.0) and the observed path (*c*) between the indicators for income and life satisfaction is 0.2. Under these conditions, $(1.0)(x)(0.5) = 0.2$, and $x = 0.4$. In other words, researchers who report the observed relationship between income and life satisfaction ($c = 0.2$) would substantially underestimate the strength of the effect ($x = 0.4$) that income actually has on life satisfaction.

But how do researchers know what values to assign to the paths (such as *a* and *b* in Fig. 1) between the latent constructs and their indicators? Unless logic suggests that the concepts in a given model are measured with little error, researchers must turn from *single* indicator models to *multiple* indicator models. As noted earlier, multiple indicator models allow one to make corrections for measurement errors that would otherwise bias estimates of the causal relationships between concepts. (For early developments of multiple indicator models, see Blalock 1968; Costner 1969. For more recent developments in these modeling procedures, see Bentler 1989; Bollen 1989; Hayduk 1987; Jöreskog and Sörbom 1989.)

MULTIPLE INDICATOR MODELS

For researchers to claim that they are using multiple indicator models, at least one of the concepts in a causal model must have more than one indicator. "Multiple indicators" means simply that a causal model contains alternative measures of the same thing (same concept). Figure 2 depicts a multiple indicator model in which income still has a single indicator but life satisfaction now has three indicators (i.e., three alternative measures of the same life satisfaction latent construct). In addition to the original indicator for life satisfaction—"I am satisfied with my life"—there are two new indicators, namely, "In most ways my life is close to my ideal" and "The conditions of my life are excellent." (Recall that the possible response categories range from "strongly agree" to "strongly disagree." See also Diener et al. 1985 for a fuller description of this measurement scale.)

As in Figure 1, the dashed arrows represent the noncausal, observed correlations between each pair of indicators. Recall that these observed correlations are the spurious by-products of the assumed operation of the latent constructs inferred in the causal model. Specifically, an increase in actual income (I) should produce an increase in measured income (I_1) through (causal) path *a*. Moreover, an increase in actual income should also produce an increase in actual life satisfaction (LS) through (causal) path *x*, which in turn should produce an increase in each of the measures of life satisfaction (LS_1, LS_2, and LS_3) through (causal) paths *b, c,* and *d*.

The use of a single indicator for income means

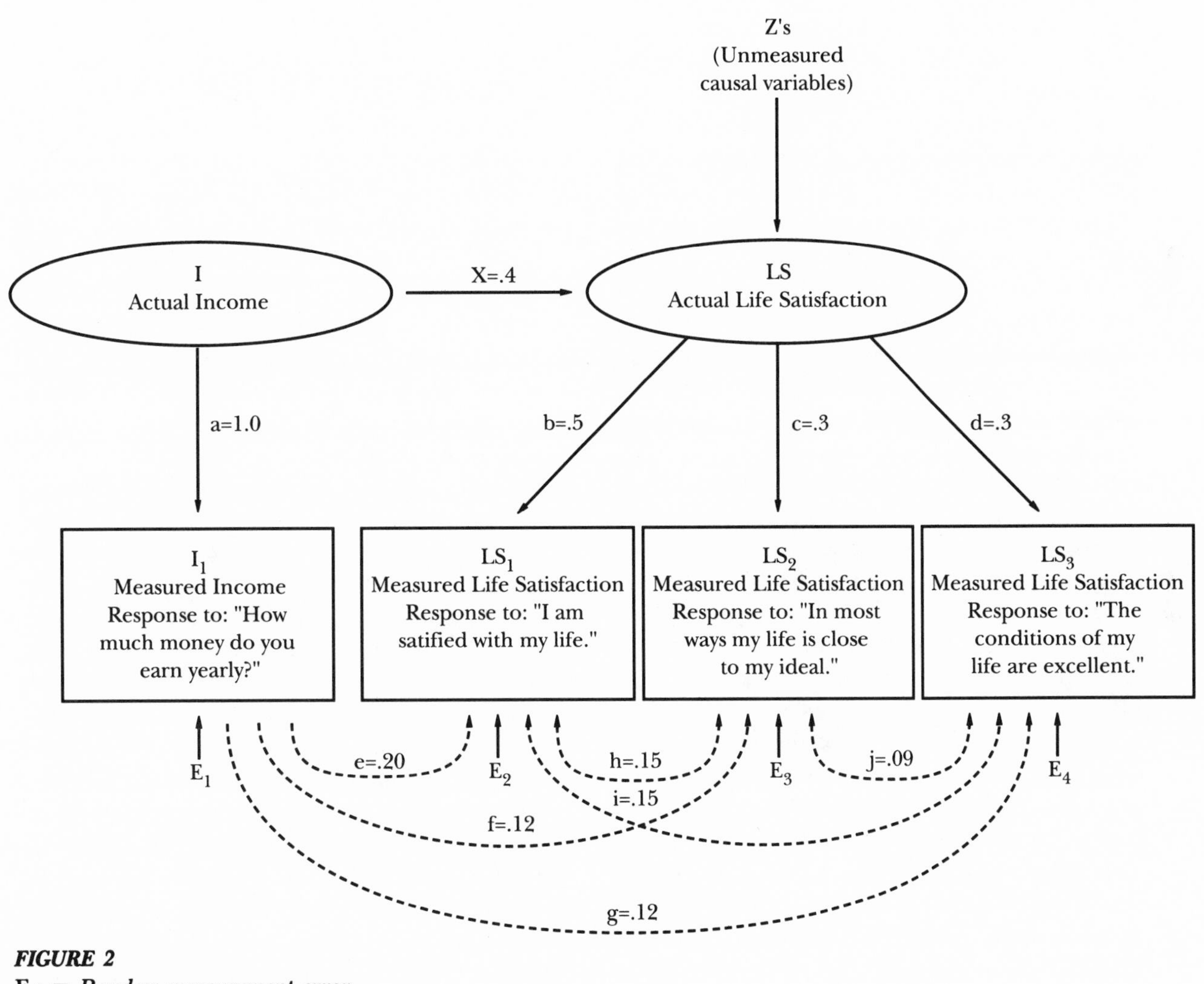

FIGURE 2
E*s* = *Random measurement error*

that researchers must use pure logic to assign a path coefficient to represent "slippage" between the true score (I) and the measured score (I_1). For income, path $a = 1.0$ (i.e., no measurement error) seems like a reasonable estimate. As noted earlier, however, indicators of life satisfaction are not as easily assigned path coefficients of 1.0. That is, there is likely to be considerable error in measuring an internal state such as life satisfaction. Pure *logic* is not very helpful in this situation. Fortunately, however, the use of multiple indicators for the life satisfaction construct permits researchers to provide reasonable estimates of measurement error based on *empirical* results.

More specifically, if the multiple indicator model in Figure 2 is correct, then the observed correlations among the several pairs of indicators should provide researchers with estimates for the unobserved (causal) paths *b, c,* and *d,* that is, estimates of how much "slippage" there is between actual life satisfaction and each measure of life satisfaction. Researchers can use hand calculations involving simple algebra to estimate the paths for such simple multiple indicator models as depicted in Figure 2 (for examples, see Sullivan and Feldman 1979; and Loehlin 1987). But more complicated models are best left to "structural equation" computer programs such as LISREL (Jöreskog and Sörbom 1989) or EQS (Bentler 1989).

In essence, these computer programs go through a series of "iterations" in which different values are substituted for the unobserved paths—in Figure 2: *b, c, d,* and *x.* (Recall that we assigned a value of 1.0 for *a,* so the computer program does not have to estimate a value for this unobserved path.) Ultimately, the program reaches a solution. This solution will reproduce as closely as possible the observed paths—in Figure 2: *e, f, g, h, i,* and *j*—between each of the indicators in the proposed causal model.

For example, to reproduce the observed correlation (path $h = 0.15$) between LS_1 and LS_2, the computer program would have to start with values for paths *b* and *c* considerably lower than 1.0 (i.e., would need to allow for some measurement error). Multiplying the path $b = 1.0$ by the path $c = 1.0$ would not give the correlation of $h = 0.15$; that is, (1.0) (1.0) does not equal 0.15. Conversely, substituting equal values for *b* and *c* of just under 0.4 each would reproduce the observed correlation of $h = 0.15$. But a value of 0.4 for *b* and *c* would *not* reproduce the observed correlations (paths *e* and *f*) between I_1 (the indicator for income) and either LS_1 or LS_2. Given that *e* (0.2) must equal $(a)(x)(b)$—that is, $(1.0)(x)(0.4) = 0.2$—and *f* (0.12) must equal $(a)(x)(c)$—that is, $(1.0)(x)(0.4) = 0.12$—we cannot find a solution for the two equations that uses the *same value* for *x*. That is, for the first equation $x = 0.5$; but for the second equation $x = 0.3$.

Alternatively, if the computer program estimates values of 0.5 and 0.3 for causal paths *b* and *c,* respectively, then it is possible to use the same value of *x* (0.4) for each equation, and still reproduce the appropriate observed correlations for *e* (0.2) and *f* (0.12), as well as *h* (0.15). Furthermore, by also estimating the value of 0.3 for causal path *d,* the computer program would be able to exactly reproduce *all* the observable correlations—*e, f, g, h, i,* and *j*—in Figure 2.

Reproducing the observable correlations among indicators does not, however, establish that the proposed model is correct. One can only disconfirm models, not prove them. Indeed, there are generally a large number of alternative models, often with entirely different causal structures, that would reproduce the observable correlations just as well as the original model specified (see Kim and Mueller 1978 for examples). It should be apparent, therefore, that social scientists must provide rigorous logic and theory in building multiple indicator models, that is, in providing support for one model among a wide variety of possible models. In other words, multiple indicator procedures require that researchers think very carefully about how measures are linked to constructs, and how constructs are linked to other constructs.

Additionally, it is highly desirable that a model contain more observable correlations among indicators than unobservable causal paths to be estimated—that is, is "overidentified." For example, Figure 2 has *six* observable correlations (*e, f, g, h, i,* and *j*) but only *four* unobservable causal paths (*x, b, c,* and *d*) to estimate. Thus, Figure 2 is overidentified. By having an excess of observable correlations versus unobservable causal paths, a researcher can provide tests of the probability that there exist alternative causal paths not specified in the original model.

Conversely, "just-identified" models will contain exactly as many observable correlations as unobservable causal paths to be estimated. Such models will *always* produce estimates (solutions) for the unobservable causal paths that *exactly* reproduce the observable correlations. Unfortunately, however, unlike an overidentified model, a just-identified model does not allow one to detect alternative causal pathways to those specified in the original model.

Finally, the worst possible model is one that is "underidentified," that is, has fewer observable correlations than unobservable causal paths to be estimated. Such models can provide no single (unique) solutions for the unobservable paths. In other words, an infinite variety of alternative estimates for the causal paths are possible.

The number of indicators per latent construct helps determine whether a model will be overidentified or not. In general, one should have at least two and preferably three indicators per latent construct—unless one can assume a single indicator, such as income in Figure 2, has little measurement error. Adding even more indicators for a latent construct rapidly increases the "overidentifying" pieces of information. That is to say, observable correlations (between indicators) grow faster than the unobservable causal paths (between a given latent construct and indicator) to be estimated.

Some additional points regarding multiple indicator models require clarification. For example, in "real life" a researcher would never encounter such a perfect reproduction of the (noncausal) observable paths from the unobservable (causal) paths as Figure 2 depicts. (We are assuming here that the causal model tested in "real life," like that model tested in Fig. 2, is "overidentified." Recall that a just-identified model always exactly reproduces the observed correlations.) Indeed, even if the researcher's model is correctly specified, the researcher should expect *some* discrepancies when comparing the observed correlations among indicators with the correlations among indicators predicted by the (unobserved) causal paths.

Researchers can dismiss as sampling error (i.e., chance) any discrepancies that are not too large (given a specific sample size). At some point, however, the discrepancies do become too large to dismiss as chance. At that point, researchers must reevaluate and respecify their causal models.

Respecification of models generally involves adding new (unobservable) causal paths to improve the fit between the observed versus predicted correlations among indicators. For example, Figure 2, like Figure 1, assumes that measurement error is *random*. That is, Figure 2 depicts the error terms (*E*'s) for each indicator to be *unconnected*. Such random measurement error can occur for any number of reasons: coding errors, ambiguous questions, respondent fatigue, and so forth. But none of these sources of measurement error should produce *correlations among the indicators*.

Where measurement error does produce such correlations, social scientists describe it as *nonrandom*. Under these conditions, the measurement errors of two or more indicators have a common source (a latent construct) other than or in addition to the concept that the indicators were suppose to measure. The focus now becomes one of the *validity* of measures. Are you measuring what you claim to measure or something else?

Failure to include nonrandom—linked—errors in a multiple indicator model will bias the estimates of the causal paths in the model. Figure 3 depicts such a linkage of error terms through the personality variable "optimism" (O). Based on this proposed model, the observed (noncausal) path coefficient (*j*) between the indicators LS_2 and LS_3 would not be entirely due to the effects of life satisfaction (LS) through the causal paths *c* and *d*. In fact, part of the path coefficient *j* would be the

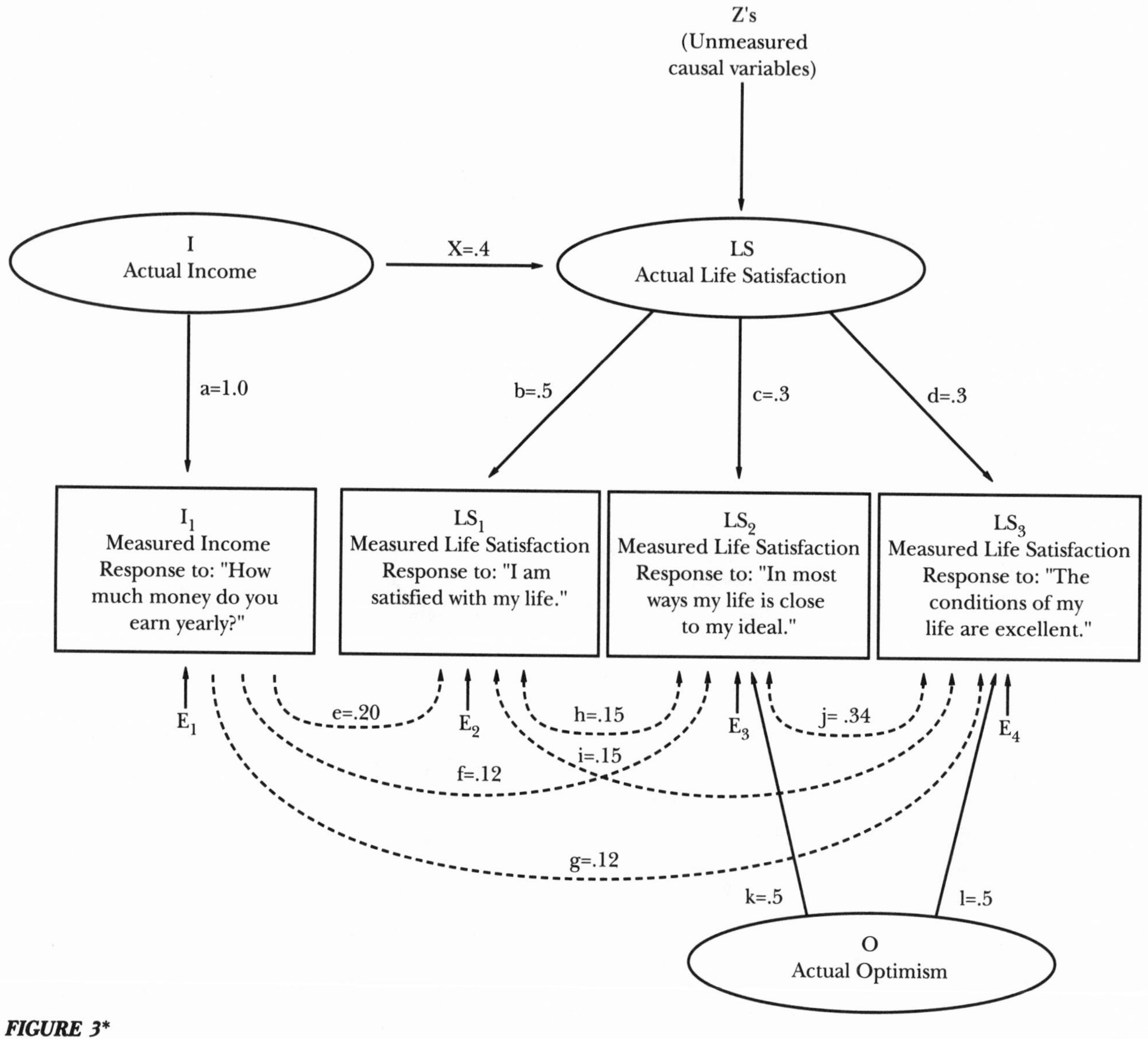

FIGURE 3*
E*s* = *Random measurement error.*
**A "constraint" in this model is that paths* k *and* l *must be equal.*

spurious by-product of the (unobserved) causal paths k and l (which in this model we have constrained to be equal). In other words, the indicators LS_2 and LS_3 measure some of life satisfaction but also optimism. That is, they measure something in addition to what they were intended to measure.

Note that path j is the only observed correlation that differs in strength when comparing Figures 2 and 3. For Figure 2, this path equals 0.09; for Figure 3, this path equals 0.34. The higher observed correlation for j in Figure 3 stems from the additional spurious correlation produced by the effects of optimism through paths k (0.5) and l (0.5). Note that (0.5) (0.5) equals 0.25. If we add 0.25 to the original observed correlation for path j (i.e., 0.09) in Figure 2, we obtain the observed correlation of 0.34 in Figure 3.

Note, too, that we could not obtain a "good fit" with the observed correlations in Figure 3 if we had not added the (unobserved) causal paths (k and l) created by the latent construct of optimism. Indeed, without these additional paths, the computer program would have to increase the path coefficients for c and d (say, to almost 0.6 each), to reproduce the observed correlation of 0.34 for path j. Then, however, the program would fail to reproduce the observed correlations involving LS_2 and LS_3 with other indicators. For example, the observed correlation between I_1 and LS_2 (path f = 0.12) would now be *overestimated,* based on the product of the causal paths that the model suggests determines path f. That is, $f = (a)(x)(c)$; hence, $(1.0)(0.4)(0.6) = 0.24$, which is too high an estimate for the correlation actually observed (i.e., $f = 0.12$).

As the preceding discussion implies, using multiple indicator models requires more thought and complicated procedures than does using more common data analytic procedures such as multiple regression. However, given the serious distortions that measurement errors can produce in estimating the true causal links among concepts, the extra effort in using multiple indicator models can pay large dividends.

(SEE ALSO: *Causal Inference Models; Factor Analysis*)

REFERENCES

Bentler, P. M. 1989 *EQS: Structural Equations Program Manual.* Los Angeles: BMDP Statistical Software, Inc.

Blalock, H. M. 1968 "The Measurement Gap: A Gap between the Languages of Theory and Research." In H. M. Blalock and Ann Blalock, eds., *Methodology in Social Research.* New York: McGraw-Hill.

——— 1979 *Social Statistics,* 2nd ed. New York: McGraw-Hill.

Bollen, K. A. 1989 *Structural Equations with Latent Variables.* New York: Wiley.

Costner, H. L. 1969 "Theory, Deduction, and Rules of Correspondence." *American Journal of Sociology* 75:245–263.

Diener, E., R. A. Emmons, R. J. Larsen, and S. Griffin 1985 "The Satisfaction with Life Scale." *Journal of Personality Assessment* 49:71–75.

Hayduk, L. A. 1987 *Structural Equation Modeling with LISREL.* Baltimore, Md.: John Hopkins University Press.

Jöreskog, K. G. and D. Sörbom 1989 *LISREL 7: A Guide to the Program and Applications,* 2nd ed. Chicago: SPSS Inc.

Kim, J., and C. W. Mueller 1978 *Introduction to Factor Analysis: What It Is and How to Do It.* Beverly Hills, Calif.: Sage.

Larson, R. 1978 "Thirty Years of Research on the Subjective Well-Being of Older Americans." *Journal of Gerontology* 33:109–125.

Loehlin, J. C. 1987 *Latent Variable Models: An Introduction to Factor, Path, and Structural Analysis.* Hillsdale, N.J.: Erlbaum.

Sullivan, J. L. and S. Feldman 1979 *Multiple Indicators: An Introduction.* Beverly Hills, Calif.: Sage.

KYLE KERCHER

MUSIC Music is a significant aspect of social life in every contemporary society. Yet the way music has been manifested historically varies considerably, both among and within different societies. The description and analysis of the diversity of social dimensions of music in social life have been commanding objectives of sociologists since Georg Simmel (Simmel 1882), William I. Thomas (Thomas 1909), and Max Weber (Weber 1912, 1917). For Simmel music as medium of intersubjective communication, for Thomas music as focus of collective action, and for Weber the reflexivity between musical and institutional structures became central themes of inquiry. It is to these scholars that the inception of the field is commonly attributed. The sociology of music aims at generating theoretical propositions that explain this human universal and its particular representations as an aspect of social structure. Yet for most contemporary sociologists, the ever-increasing epidemic of music makes it impossible to do full justice to the value and meaning of every individual musical piece (Silbermann 1963, pp. 4–5).

Sociology defines music empirically. It does not proceed by a priori imputations of what music is and is not, but rather by identifying how specific musical requirements (such as acoustic and architectural conditions, the number of distinct musical parts, the utilization and technological sophistication of musical instruments, or the degree of difficulty of musical execution) stipulate requisite relationships among social actors, and conversely, how social structural dimensions affect the musical situations and structures they support. As a consequence, themes in the literature of related fields of study, such as whether music is divinely inspired, good or bad, beautiful, or elevating or debasing cultural values, are marginal to sociology. Sociology inquires, instead, how music (and meaningful sound) is socially constructed, performed, perceived, and responded to by whom, when, and where. In its study of humans in their collective involvement with music, the sociology of music is concerned with group activities—economic, social, political, and religious—as these impact on the creation, production, dissemination, reception, preservation, and reproduction of music. For scholarly analyses to be classified as part of the sociology of music (rather than of other sociological traditions such as communication, collective behavior, organization, or community relations), it is critical that the phenomena of music are taken to be central both as the starting point of social relationships and objective of sociological explication (Etzkorn 1982).

A selection of recent books with *sociology of music* in the titles offers ready access to the empirical approaches taken in this field. Typically they continue and extend the lines of inquiry set by Simmel and Weber and incorporate other empirical studies in their respective syntheses and bibliographies (Karbusicky 1975; Kneif 1975; Rummenhöller 1978; Haselauer 1980; Blaukopf 1982; DaSilva et al. 1984; Kaden 1985; Supicic 1987; Del Grosso 1989; Etzkorn 1989). This list may be supplemented with other recent volumes with coverage of the sociology of music (Bontinck 1974; Levy 1979; Layton 1981; Mark 1981; Becker 1982; Martorella 1982; Kamerman 1983; Menger 1983; Durga 1984; Ostleitner 1987; Wilson 1986; Silbermann 1973, 1977, 1979, 1986; and Kaplan 1990). In addition, many studies done by ethnomusicologists address identical substantive issues and are distinguishable from the sociology of music principally in their employment of different terminology (Keller 1986; Becker 1989).

Recent work frequently emulates the empirical approach taken by John H. Mueller in his analyses of the social history of musical taste in which he infers from statistical series on the repertories of American symphony orchestras the relative popularity of composers and conductors. European writers include him among the pioneers of the sociology of music (Mueller 1951; Mark 1976). Other studies throw light on the interaction networks between occupants of social roles (composers, publishers, concert managers, publicists), social positions, and the status of musical life (Gilmore 1987), research on the social control of music and cultural productions (Peterson and Berger 1975), or on the relationships between the content of popular music, music videos, and specific factors in the changing social environment (Denisoff 1986, 1987), or on the search for explanations of taste and consumption patterns in popular music (Shepherd 1986), or on degree of social integration and the role of elite music in metropolitan communities (Blau 1988).

European sociologists addressed themselves also to the topic of the impact of mass media policies on the role of music in the cultural lives of their own and of small countries. Careful empirical analyses of changes in symphonic concerts, or of the penetration of official broadcast programs by music from foreign sources, the share of regional music in the sale of recordings, and the percentage of live musical programming versus loudspeaker music reproductions and similar data are combined into indexes of music availability for different nationality and musical taste groups (Heister 1974; Del Grosso 1976; Kneif 1977; Blaukopf et al. 1983; Wallis and Malm 1984; Smudits 1987; Ostleitner 1987; Ling 1988).

The continued indebtedness of both European and North American sociology of music to Max Weber is generally acknowledged (Blomster 1976; Blaukopf 1980; Del Grosso 1982; Feher 1987). Nevertheless, at least one distinguishing characteristic between the continents concerns the respective treatment of the many contributions of Theodor W. Adorno on music as sociology or critical theory (Adorno 1978, 1986). The extensive literary output on musical subjects of Adorno has consistently been more typically considered to represent "sociology" by Europeans than by North Americans. American sociologists found it difficult to reconcile Adorno's axiomatic propagation of musicological principles with the methods of empirical social science, for Adorno's sociological writings are based on the notion that musical developments follow historic laws that are intrinsic to music, independent of the social reality of musical performance (Steinert 1989). American sociologists assumed, instead, that sociological analyses needed to go beyond the analysis of notated scores in two directions, namely the analysis of their social creation and their realization in musical life. In this regard they were consistent with Paul Honigsheim's proposition according to which "an artfully constructed composition that remained in a desk drawer and has never been performed is not of any sociological relevance" (Etzkorn 1989, p. 43). Although some American sociologists may have embraced Adorno's value judgments and aesthetic pronouncements concerning the future of music in mass society, they would not mistake these as representing contributions to sociology. This cannot be said with equal confidence for many of Adorno's European followers (Kolleritsch 1979).

Simultaneous with the ever-increasing reliance on electronic media (the mediatization of musical life) in contemporary society, recent developments in sociological research begin to accompany this growing dependence of musicians on electronic technology for reaching audiences with increasing methodological sophistication. Since the composition and playback of musical sound through electronic equipment (via synthesizers and computers) can eliminate the involvement of other musicians and listeners, traditional notions concerning the entire structure of the composer-performer-audience are being reexamined. The mediamorphosis from live to loudspeaker music and its sociological consequences are the subjects of studies by Silbermann (1987) and Blaukopf (1989). Music that is produced for and reproduced through loudspeakers phenomenologically, and in terms of social relationships, refers to a different social reality than live musicmaking. The former

> *is* objectified *sound, brought into being through the medium of compact disk, tape, or long-playing record, a pair of loudspeakers, or earphones. Moreover it can be manufactured, packaged, commercialized, merchandized, marketed, distributed, sold, bought, used, and stored. Even though there are only a few notions on which sociologists will agree readily, all would subscribe to the premise that they need to differentiate between the study of interpersonal relations and that of relations between persons and material objects* (Etzkorn 1989).

The sociology of music recognizes that there are major differences between the social aesthetics of live and mediated music. In situations in which musical sounds are reproduced from a storage medium, there is as exact a mapping of the once-sounded example as recording technology permits. This musical recording can be reproduced *ad infinitum;* it becomes a commodity for shaping the soundscape (Mowitt 1987). On the other hand, in live musical situations in which musical sounds are the direct result of immediate musicmaking by musicians, each rendition represents a unique realization of the musical script or score. The performers' actions give added significance to the signs in the musical score (Hosokawa 1987); and the skilled performer can modify each realization according to the social context of each moment.

Building on these distinctions between mediated music and live music, sociologists of music discriminate between the definition of the musical situations they study by noting the basic difference in the social action systems that produce the musical sounds. For example, with the exception of live musicmaking, the majority of listening to music takes place through mediated music, by hearing distributed sound commodities, and not by visually and aurally taking in the complex social interplay (among performers and audience) that typically makes each and every live performance a new experience.

Future sociological research on live music will benefit from the study of music as musically defined social activity. On the other hand, the study of the production, distribution, and reception of musical commodities—in short, the many topics of the sociology of mediated music—will clearly gain in importance as media technologies take on ever-increasing significance in our electronic age.

The results of research by the sociology of music can help alert educators and makers of public policy to the double impact of electronic media for the future of musical life. There will be evidence to demonstrate the potential for increased access that the media offer to the wealth of sounds of global music from remote corners. (Media music can, indeed, stimulate involvement in live musical culture.) And there will be evidence that points to the dangers of leveling and dulling musical sensitivities via the commercial mass marketing of commodified sound products.

REFERENCES

Adorno, Theodore Wiesengrund 1978 *Gesammelte Schriften,* vol. 16 (Musikalische Schriften I-III). Frankfurt am Main: Suhrkamp.

———1986 *Die musikalischen Monographien.* Frankfurt am Main: Suhrkamp.

Becker, Howard S. 1982 *Art Worlds.* Berkeley: University of California Press.

———1989 "Ethnomusicology and Sociology: A Letter to Charles Seeger." *Ethnomusicology* 33:275–285.

Blau, Judith R. 1988 "Music as Social Circumstance." *Social Forces* 66:883–902.

Blaukopf, Kurt 1980 "Max Weber und die Musik Soziologie." In Werner Schulze, ed., *Rudolf Haase Festschrift.* Eisenstadt, Germany: Elfriede Rötzer Verlag.

———1982 *Musik im Wandel der Gesellschaft: Grundzüge der Musiksoziologie.* Munich: R. Piper & Co.

———1989 *Beethovens Erben in der Mediamorphose: Kultur- und Medienpolitik für die elektronische Ära.* Heiden, Germany: Verlag Arthur Niggli.

———Irmgard Bontinck, Harald Gardos, and Desmond Mark 1983 *Kultur von Unten: Innovationen und Barrieren in Österreich.* Vienna: Löcker Verlag.

Blomster, Wes V. 1976 "Sociology of Music: Adorno and Beyond." *Telos* 28 (Summer):81–112.

Bontinck, Irmgard (ed.) 1974 *New Patterns of Musical Behaviour of the Young Generation in Industrial Societies.* Vienna: Universal Edition.

Cerulo, Karen 1989 "Sociopolitical Control and the Structure of National Symbols: An Empirical Analysis of National Anthems." *Social Forces* 68 (1):76–99.

DaSilva, Fabio B., Anthony Blasi, and David R. Dees 1984 *The Sociology of Music.* Notre Dame, Ind.: University of Notre Dame Press.

Del Grosso, Luigi Destreri 1976 *Televisione e Stratificazione Sociale. Materiali di Studio.* Trento: Cooperative Libraria Univ.

———1982 "Max Weber e la Sociologia della Musica." *Studi di Sociologie* (Italy) 20 (1):55–62.

———1989 *La Sociologia, La Musica e Le Musiche.* Testi e Studi 80. Milan: Edizioni Unicopoli.

Denisoff, R. Serge. 1986 *Tarnished Gold: The Record Industry Revisited.* New Brunswick, N.J.: Transaction Books.

———1987 *Inside MTV.* New Brunswick, N.J.: Transaction Books.

Durga, S.A.K. 1984 "A New Approach to Indian Musicological Methodology: An Ethnomusicological Perspective." Ph.D. diss., Wesleyan University.

Etzkorn, K. Peter 1982 "On the Sociology of Musical Practice and Social Groups." *International Social Science Journal* 34:555–569.

———(ed. and rev). 1989 *Sociologists and Music: An Introduction to the Study of Music and Society Through the Later Writings of Paul Honigsheim,* 2nd ed. New Brunswick, N.J.: Transaction Books.

Feher, Ferenc 1987 "Weber and the Rationalization of

Music." *International Journal of Politics, Culture and Society* 1:337–352.

Gilmore, Samuel 1987 "Coordination and Convention: The Organization of the Concert World." *Symbolic Interaction* 10:209–227.

Haselauer, Elisabeth 1980 *Handbuch der Musiksoziologie*. Vienna: Herman Böhlaus.

Heister, Hanns-Werner 1983 *Das Konzert: Theorie einer Kulturform*, 2 vols. Wilhelmshaven, Germany: Heinrichshofen.

———, et al. 1974 *Segmente der Unterhaltungsindustrie*. Frankfurt am Main: Suhrkamp.

Hennion, Antoine 1984 "La Sociologie de la musique: Structures et analyses locales." *L'Année sociologique* 34:379–390.

Hosokawa, Shushei 1987 "Technique/Technology and Reproduction in Music." In Thomas A. Sebeok and Jean Umiker-Sebeok, eds., *The Semiotic Web '85: An International Yearbook*. Berlin: Mouton de Gruyter.

Kaden, Christian 1985 *Musiksoziologie*. Wilhelmshaven, Germany: Heinrichshofen.

Kamerman, Jack B., and Rosanne Martorella (eds.) 1983 *Performers and Performances: The Social Organization of Artistic Work*. New York: Praeger.

Kaplan, Max 1990 *The Arts: A Social Perspective*. Rutherford, N.J.: Fairleigh Dickinson University Press.

Karbusicky, Vladimir 1975 *Empirische Musiksoziologie*. Wiesbaden: Breitkopf and Härtel.

Keller, Marcello Sorce 1986 "Sociology of Music and Ethnomusicology: Two Disciplines in Competition." *JGE: The Journal of General Education* 38:167–181.

Kolleritsch, Otto (ed.) 1979 *Adorno und die Musik*. Vienna and Graz: Universal Edition.

Kneif, Tibor 1977 *Politische Musik*. Vienna: Doblinger Verlag.

———(ed.) 1975 *Texte zur Musiksoziologie*. Cologne: Volk-Gerig.

Layton, Robert 1981 *The Anthropology of Art*. New York: Columbia University Press.

Levy, Ernst 1979 *Des Rapports entre la Musique et la Société*. Neuchâtel: La Bacconière.

Ling, Jan 1984 "The Sociology of Music." *Canadian University Music Review* 5:3–16.

———1986 "Music in the World Around Us." In Jack Dobbs, ed., *New Perspectives in Music—New Tasks for Music Education: Papers from the 17th International ISME Conference, Innsbruck, Austria*. London: International Society for Music Education. ISME Yearbook 13:20–30.

———1988 *Musiksociologiskkonferens 1988*. Göteborg: Musikvetenskapliga Avdelningen Musikhögskolan.

Mark, Desmond 1976 "John H. Mueller und sein Beitrag zur Musiksoziologie." *International Review of the Aesthetics and Sociology of Music* 7 (2):312–317.

———(ed.) 1981 *Stock-taking of Musical Life: Music Sociography and Its Relevance to Music Education*. ISME Edition, no 1. Vienna: Doblinger.

———1983 "Pop and Folk as a Going Concern for Sociological Research." *International Review of the Aesthetics and Sociology of Music* 14 (1):93–98.

———1988 "Anmerkungen zum Verhältnis von Musiksoziologie und Musik-Politik in Österreich." In Jan Ling, ed, *Musiksociologisk Konferens 1988*. Göteborg: Musikvetenskapliga Advdelningen Musikhögskolan.

Martorella, Rosanne 1982 *The Sociology of Opera*. South Hadley, Mass.: J. F. Bergin.

Menger, Pierre-Michel 1983 *Le Paradoxe du Musicien: Le Compositeur, le Mélomane et l'État dans la Société Contemporaraine*. Paris: Harmoniques Flammarion.

———1986 "L'Oreille Speculative: Consommation et Perception de la Musique Contemporaine." *Revue Française de Sociologie* 27 (3):445–479.

Middleton, Richard 1990 *Studying Popular Music*. Bristol, Pa.: Open University Press.

Mowitt, John 1987 "The Sound of Music in the Era of Its Electronic Reproducibility." In Richard Leppert and Susan McClary, ed., *Music and Society: The Politics of Composition, Performance and Reception*. Cambridge: Cambridge University Press.

Mueller, John Henry 1951 *The American Symphony Orchestra: A Social History of Musical Taste*. Bloomington: Indiana University Press.

Ostleitner, Elena (ed.) 1987 *Massenmedien, Musikpolitik und Musikerziehung*. Musik und Gesellschaft H. 20. Vienna: Verband der Wissenschaftlichen Gesellschaften Österreichs.

Peterson, Richard A., and David G. Berger 1975 "Cycles in Symbol Production: The Case of Popular Music. "*American Sociological Review* 40 (2):158–173.

Rummenhöller, Peter 1978 *Einführung in die Musiksoziologie*. Wilhelmshaven, Germany: Heinrichshofen.

Sheperd, John C. 1979 "Music and Social Control: An Essay on the Sociology of Musical Knowledge." *Catalyst* (Canada) 13(Spring): 1–54.

———1986 "Music Consumption and Cultural Self-Identities: Some Theoretical and Methodological Reflections." *Media, Culture and Society* 8:305–330.

———, Phil Virden, Graham Vulliamy, and Trevor Wishart 1980 *Whose Music? A Sociology of Musical Languages.* New Brunswick, N.J. Transaction Books.

Silbermann, Alphons 1963 *The Sociology of Music.* In The International Library of Sociology and Social Reconstruction. New York: Humanities Press.

———1973 *Empirische Kunstsoziologie. Eine Einführung mit kommentierter Bibliographie.* Stuttgart: Ferdinand Enke Verlag.

———1977 "Massenkommunikation." In René König, ed., *Handbuch der empirischen Sozialforschung,* vol. dtv Wissenschaftliche Reihe. Stuttgart: Ferdinand Enke Verlag.

———1982 "What Questions Does the Empirical Sociology of Music Attempt to Answer?" *International Social Science Journal* 34 (4):571–581.

——— (ed.) 1987 *Die Rolle der elektronischen Medien in der Entwicklung der Künste.* Frankfurt: Verlag Peter Lang.

———, and Paul Röhrig (eds.) 1987 *Kultur, Volksbildung und Gesellschaft: Paul Honigsheim zum Gedenken seines 100. Geburtstages. Beiträge zum Werk, ausgewählte Texte und ein Verzeichnis der Schriften.* Frankfurt, Bern, New York: Verlag Peter Lang.

Simmel, Georg (1882) 1986 "Psychologische und ethnologische Studien über Musik." *Zeitschrift für Völkerpsychologie und Sprachwissenschaft* 13:261-305. (Translated as "Psychological and Ethnological Studies on Music.") In K. Peter Etzkorn, trans., *Georg Simmel: The Conflict in Modern Culture and Other Essays.* New York: Teachers College Press.

Smudits, Alfred 1987 *New Media: A Challenge to Cultural Policies: Report on a Research Project Undertaken by MEDICACULT.* Vienna: Verband der Wissenschaftlichen Gesellschaften Österreichs.

Stebbins, Robert A. 1976 "Music among Friends: The Social Networks of Amateur Musicians." *Revue Internationale de Sociologie* (Italy) 12 (1–2):52–73.

———1978 "Creating High Culture: The American Amateur Classical Musician." *Journal of American Culture* 1 (3):616–631.

———1979 *Amateurs: On the Margin Between Work and Leisure.* Beverly Hill, Calif: Sage.

Steinert, Heinz 1989 *Adorno in Wien: Über die (Un-) Möglichkeit von Kunst, Kultur und Befreiung.* Vienna: Verlag für Gesellschaftskritik.

Supicic, Ivo 1987 *Music in Society: A Guide to the Sociology of Music.* Stuyvesant, N.Y.: Pendragon Press.

Thomas, William I. 1909 *Sourcebook for Social Origins: Ethnological Materials, Psychological Standpoint, Classified and Annotated Bibliographies for the Interpretation of Savage Societies.* Chicago, Ill: University of Chicago Press.

Wallis, Roger, and Krister Malm 1984 *Big Sounds from Small Peoples: The Music Industry in Small Countries.* London: Constable.

Weber, Max 1917 "Der Sinn der Wertfreiheit der soziologischen und ökonomischen Wissenschaften." *Logos, Internationale Zeitschrift für Philosophie der Kultur* 7:40–88.

———1912 "Vortrag über Soziologie der Musik." Cited on p. 483, in Eduard Baumgarten, 1964 *Max Weber: Werk und Person.* Tübingen: J.C.B. Mohr.

Wilson, Robert N. 1986 *Experiencing Creativity: On the Social Psychology of Art.* New Brunswick, N.J.: Transaction Books.

Zolberg, Vera 1990 *Constructing A Sociology of the Arts.* Cambridge: Cambridge University Press.

K. PETER ETZKORN

N

NATIONALISM Nationalism has been defined in a variety of ways at different levels of analysis (e.g., Kohn 1955, 1968; Symmons-Symonolewicz 1970; Kamenka 1973; Plamenatz 1973; Snyder 1984; Smith, 1976, 1981). The concept combines a sense of identification with a people, an ideology of common history and destiny, and a social movement addressed to shared objectives. This definition raises questions about what differentiates a people or a nation from others, the nature of identification, the conditions under which nationalist ideologies develop, and the course and aims of nationalist movements.

Historically the term *nationalism* was applied to attempts to follow early European models "to make the boundaries of the state and those of the nation coincide" (Minogue 1967), that is, to create loyalty to a nation-state (Kohn 1968). It was also applied to struggles, proliferating after World War II, to gain independence from colonial domination and join the community of sovereign states. More recently, however, analysts have found the confusion between the concepts of state and nation to be a hindrance to understanding contemporary nationalism. Only rarely, if at all, do the boundaries of a state coincide with those of a nation. By *nation* we mean an ethnic group that (1) shares one or more identifying characteristics, such as language, religion, racial background, culture, and/or territory; and (2) is politically mobilized and/or amenable to such mobilization. Thus, *nationalism* should be distinguished from *patriotism,* in that the identification and loyalty in the former is to an ethnic group or nation, and in the latter to the state.

IDENTIFICATION

Debates centering on the intrinsic nature of collective ethnic identification feature variations on two general themes—primordial and structural. Implied in the primordial perspective is a deemphasis on an instrumental view of ethnic ties. Rather, these ties are seen as ends in themselves shaped by forces other than material self-interest; they are persistent and resist the homogenization predicted by convergence and modernization theorists. The essence of these ties "is a psychological bond that joins a people and differentiates it in the subconscious conviction of its members from all other people in the most vital way" (Connor 1978, quoted in Stack 1986, pp. 3, 4). These bonds stem from "immediate contiguity and kin connection mainly, but beyond them . . . from being born into a particular religious community, speaking a particular language, or even a dialect of a language, and following particular social practice" (Geertz 1963, pp. 14, 15). To structuralists, "ethnic identity results instead from objective intergroup differences in the distribution of economic resources and authority" (Hechter 1986, p. 109). Implied here is rational choice and self-interest, that ethnic ties are means to certain ends, and that the boundaries of ethnic groups are changeable.

Neither primordialists nor structuralists would deny the obvious variations in the intensity of identification and in the potential for nationalist movements cross-culturally and over time. Several factors are expected to contribute to these variations. Among the more important of these factors is coterminality of characteristics. In most instances multiple characteristics are involved in distinguishing among ethnic groups—in an overlapping manner at times and coterminously at others. The United States offers an example of overlapping identities where people from different racial backgrounds share the same religious orientations, people with different religious orientation share a common language, and there is no territorial exclusiveness. This overlap in ethnic identification is credited in part with lowering intergroup tensions (Williams 1947). At the other extreme are peoples in southern Sudan, Eritrea, Tibet, and other places for whom all or a combination of racial, religious, linguistic, cultural, and territorial maps largely coincide. The greater the number of factors that coincide, the greater the gulf or "social fault" among ethnic groups along which nationalist sentiments and tensions are likely to intensify.

In addition to differentiating attributes and geographic distributions, a number of features of the social structure contribute heavily to variance in intensity and patterns of nationalism. Hechter (1986) suggests two types of such factors. One is the institutionalization of ethnic differences in legal and normative rules, especially those which govern property and civil rights, as in the case of South Africa. The other is differentiation in positions in the division of labor that shape "specialization experiences as well as material interests." Deutsch (1966) offers another factor in nationalism, attributing membership in a people essentially to a "wide complementarity of social communication" that "consists in the ability to communicate more effectively, and over a wide range of subjects, with members of one large group than with outsiders." Communication is subject not only to commonality of language and cultural background but also to available means. These include networks of social relations as well as the ever-advancing technological means of mass communications.

NATIONALISM

In addition to identification and "consciousness of kind," nationalism involves ideology and mobilization for social movement and political action. The ideology stems from identification, the sense of uniqueness of group origin, history, culture, collective authority, and destiny (Smith 1981). Political mobilization and the course of nationalist movements are greatly influenced by a host of internal and external factors. Important among the internal factors are uneven economic conditions and disparities along cultural lines in control of resources, access to goods, and distribution of positions in the occupational structure. The collective perception of an ethnic group of its deprivation or exploitation may challenge not only the legitimacy of the regime but also of the state itself. The theme of "relative deprivation" has been central to explanations of political violence (e.g., Gurr 1970).

The political system allocates power and authority. An uneven distribution among ethnic groups can be the direct result of exclusionary rules and practices or the indirect result of socioeconomic disparities. Whatever the reason, a cultural distribution of power is as evocative of a nationalist sense of deprivation as a cultural distribution of resources. The close relationship between power and resources led Lasswell (1936) to observe that politics is "Who gets What, When, and How."

Applying a developmental perspective, Huntington (1968) connects political stability/instability to the balance between "institutionalization" and "participation." This line of reasoning suggests to some analysts (e.g., Sanders 1981) a linear relationship between political development and political instability—in this case arising from nationalism, which is credited with having been the most prevalent reason for state-level violence (Said and Simmons 1976). Support for such a pattern of relationships derives also from the expectation that the national integration and political assimilation characteristic of developed societies contribute to a shift from culturally based to functionally based cleavages. The net result is a reduction in the prevalence and intensity of ethnic mobilization in the more politically developed countries. However, clearly implied in Huntington's discussion of relations between demand for participation and institutional capacity is a balance at low levels in the least developed countries and at high levels in the developed ones. Imbalances can be expected at early and middle stages of development, which suggests a curvilinear pattern.

There is no unanimity on the relationships between development and nationalism. This is understandable in view of the complexity of both phenomena and the current state of research. An important voice on these relationships is that of Walker Connor (e.g., 1972), who contends that modernization, the spread of education, and improved means of mass communication are responsible for a resurgence in ethnic nationalism. Juan Linz observes that "in the modern world the aim seems to be to build nations rather than states, a task that is probably beyond the capacity of any state that has not achieved the characteristics of a nation-state before the era of nationalism" (1978, p. 62). The distinction between "level" and "process" of modernization and development is useful in understanding the rise in nationalist sentiments. As Smith has noted, "Perhaps, then, it is not the fact of economic progress or decline that is relevant to ethnic revival, but simply economic change per se. Most change today is painful and uprooting" (1981, p. 34). Tensions, strains, and dislocations associated with change in the structure and distribution of power—political change—are no less painful or uprooting. Attempts by central governments to secularize and to shift loyalties from ethnic groups to the state underlie much of contemporary nationalism.

The rise of nationalism and the forms and directions it takes are significantly influenced by forces external to the respective states—regional and global socioeconomic and political conditions, and the spread of ideologies. The power vacuum created by the liquidation of colonialism after World War II tended to be filled by the newly created states. Regional power struggles, territorial disputes, economic competition, and ideological differences have left many regions of the world fraught with turmoil. Since cultural pluralism is characteristic of most, if not all, of the new states, ethnic nationalism often figures prominently in regional conflicts—as a cause at times, and as a consequence at others. The regional dynamics of ethnonationalism can take many forms.

The phenomenal advancements in means of communication and transportation have enormously increased the intensity and scope of global relations. Four features of these relations are particularly relevant to nationalism. First is the spread of ideologies related to human rights and the right to self-determination. Reports of abuses of these rights are communicated in a rapid, if not an instant, manner. They galvanize global public opinion and prod governments to intercede. Rapid communication also brings to ethnic communities the successes of others who are engaged in struggles or have succeeded in attaining varying measures of autonomy. Second is the presence of world forums to address these issues and bring to bear the weight of the global community, such as the United Nations General Assembly, the Security Council, the International Court of Justice, and other governmental and nongovernmental organizations. Third is the increasing globalization of the economy, which makes it possible for small sociopolitical units to find multilateral niches, thereby reducing dependency on bilateral economic relations with either former colonial powers or states from which they have seceded. Fourth is the geopolitical relations among the superpowers. They have frequently supported different sides of conflicts within pluralistic societies, either directly or through proxies. It is interesting to note that, in the past, both the United States and the Soviet Union have taken positions in support of the doctrine of "self determination." (President Wilson was a staunch spokesman for the principle during and after World War I. Around the same time, "at the Seventh All Russian Democratic Labor Party Conference of May 12, 1917 . . . in a resolution drafted by Lenin, the conference unequivocally endorsed the right of all of the nations forming part of Russia freely to secede and form independent states" [Connor 1984].) In contemporary global relations both nations show less commitment to the principle. Their approaches to nationalism are shaped by strategic and economic interests, tempered by the balance of force that can be brought to the situation. The ebb and flow of relations among superpowers exert considerable influence on ethnonationalism.

NATIONALIST MOVEMENTS

The literature offers two perspectives in explaining the formation of social movements—collective behavior and resource mobilization. In the former, social movements are viewed as responses to a rise in grievances and the actors are seen as "arational" if not "irrational"; in the latter they are considered as goal-oriented, rational responses dependent on organization and mobilization of resources (Jenkins 1983). Debates concerning the strengths and limitations of these two perspectives are yet to be settled. Important to a discussion of nationalism, however, is that literature on social movements, especially on resource mobilization, is primarily Western in conceptualization and empirical foundations. Significant in this respect are differences in aims that guide social movements. More common to Western societies is "changing some elements of the social structure and/or reward distribution of a society" (McCarthy and Zald 1977, pp. 1217, 1218), compared with nationalist movements that press for autonomy, if not for secession. The first type of movement seeks change through influencing political institutions, the legitimacy of which is not in question. Nationalist movements, on the other hand, often challenge, if not outright reject, the legitimacy of the state. This is not to cast doubt on the applicability of theories of social movements to ethnic nationalism but, rather, to point out that the influence of differences among societies in levels of development, political institutions, types of regimes, and movements' aims has not been adequately explored (see McCarthy and Zald 1977; Tilly 1978; Jenkins 1983).

In the following paragraphs we shall outline some of the important features of nationalist movements and the processes of mobilization. More specifically, we shall consider the role of grievance, resources, repertoires of expression, and aims.

The role of grievances remains unresolved. While traditional analysis places grievances stemming from structural strains associated with social change at the root of movements (e.g., Smelser 1962; Gurr 1970; Gusfield 1970), resource mobilization proponents favor structural "causal" explanations (e.g., Tilly 1978). Some feel discontent is ubiquitous and therefore, by itself, cannot explain the emergence of social movements. McCarthy and Zald go even further: "For some purposes, grievances and discontent may be defined, created and manipulated by issue entrepreneurs and organizations" (1977, p. 1215). In line with this perspective is Smith's (1981) account of "ethnic revival." He maintains that the unique and distinguishing rationale of an ethnic group is the emphasis on group belonging and group uniqueness that links successive generations of the group with specific origins and history. Driving the engines of "historicism" and "nationalism" are discontented intellectuals, educators, and professional intelligentsia. Blocked mobility, opposition and repression by traditional authorities, and frustrated expectations concerning recognition, especially on the part of Third World intellectuals, are factors in the radicalization of these groups, which then turn to historicism and inward to their ethnic communities (Smith 1981).

In explaining the spread of "value-oriented movements," Smelser (1962) refers to "structural conduciveness." Two elements of conduciveness are highly applicable to ethnonationalist movements. One is "the availability of means to express grievances" during troubled or uncertain times in order to redress problems. The other relates to the importance of communication in "disseminating a generalized belief"—a position consistent with that of Deutsch and Connor cited earlier.

Attempts to explain nationalist movements must account for the mobilization of resources. McCarthy and Zald outline five central considerations: (1) "aggregation of resources (money and labor)"; (2) the form of organization these resources entail; (3) involvement of individuals and organizations outside the movement; (4) the flow of resources to and from the movement; and (5) "the importance of costs and rewards in explaining individual and organizational involvement" (1977, p. 1216).

The prevailing patterns of social relations are expected to influence the potential for, and forms of, organizations and mobilization. Tilly (1978) maintains that combined strength in identification and interpersonal bonds lead to high levels of organization and to greater possibilities for mobilization. In a similar vein Oberschall (1973) offers a classification for patterns of organization. Along one dimension—relations within collectivities—he identifies three types: "communal," "associational," and "weakly [organized] or unorganized." Mobilization, which is facilitated by communal and associational forms, is rendered difficult by the weakly organized and unorganized structures. Along another dimension Oberschall distinguishes between "vertical" and "horizontal" relations to other collectives and segments of society. Social and political bonds across classes and collectivities can influence mobilization; however, the direction of influence can be expected to vary depending on the type of movement. For example, Oberschall observes: "If in a stratified society there exist [*sic*] strong vertical social and political bonds between upper and lower classes, mobilization into protest movements among lower classes is not likely to take place" (1973, p. 120). While this may be the case in regard to class conflicts, vertical bonds within an ethnic group can significantly facilitate mobilization.

Strength in family and kinship relations underlies Tilly's networks of interpersonal bonds and Oberschall's communal organization. Houseknecht sees strength here as referring "to the extent to which family/kinship obligations and rights take precedence over their nonkinship counterparts" (1990, p. 1). She outlines important ways in which kinship relates to ethnic identification, nationalism, and the organization of movements. Early socialization builds identification with an ethnic culture and commitment to its values and norms, which continue to be strengthened and enforced through kinship ties. Commonality in cultural background facilitates social communication, and the networks of kinship ties are readily available channels for the mobilization of human and material resources. Furthermore, the traditional authority structure afforded by strong family and kinship systems provides protection in resisting pressures applied by the state's central authorities.

While informal networks of kinship and interpersonal relations are important to nationalist movements, the role of formal organizations cannot be overstated. As pointed out by McCarthy and Zald (1977), a social movement may include more than one organization; and all organizations in a movement compose a "social movement industry." Competition over resources can arise between a movement industry and other commitments, as well as among organizations within the same movement industry. The latter form of competition is common to nationalist movements. This frequently encourages the involvement of neighboring states or major powers, and often leads to internal conflicts within movements.

These lines of reasoning concerning the role of kinship and interpersonal relations bring up the unresolved debate over the relative effectiveness of bureaucratic centralized movement organizations compared with those of an informal decentralized nature. While some argue that "a formalized structure with a clear division of labor maximizes mobilization by transforming diffuse commitments into clearly defined roles and . . . centralized decision making," others maintain that "decentralized movements with a minimum division of labor and integrated by informal networks and an overarching ideology are more effective" (Jenkins 1983, p. 539).

Why would individuals and organizations contribute their labor and resources to ethnonationalist movements? To primordialists, the answer is that they do so in order to preserve cultural integrity and a way of life, to maintain group solidarity and social bonds, and to advance the cause of a community from which a sense of security and pride is derived. These are valued ends in themselves. To collective behavior theorists, the answer is in the collective mood, social contagion, and the state of mind that are engendered in response to the perception of grievances. To structuralists and resource mobilization proponents, the answer lies in rational collective action and the pursuit of interests.

The vested interests of other states are usually rooted in resources, trade, security, geopolitical advantage, and/or ideology. While the large states "are likely to intervene for instrumental reasons," the small ones "are more likely to intervene for affective reasons" (Heraclides 1990, p. 377). Regional and global influences may strengthen the state's means of control and repression, contribute to the movement's resources and sanctuary, and/or raise awareness and help mobilize regional and global public opinion. These interests and their expression, directly or through international organizations, expand or inhibit opportunities for nationalist movements.

Opportunities for mobilization are also enhanced by the quality of leadership and its effectiveness in articulating the interests of the group. Smelser explains that the significance of charismatic leadership to value-oriented movements, in such forms as "the dreamer prophet of the cult, the nationalist crusader, and the totalitarian demagogue," is compatible with the character of these movements in certain phases of their development. He goes on to point out, however, that "Insofar as a value-oriented movement receives material from outside sources, and insofar as it inherits an organizational structure, the need for charismatic leadership lessens" (1962, pp. 355, 356). Useful here are categories identified by Hermann (1986) to analyze political leaders. Particularly important are such contextual factors as to whom the leaders are accountable, forms of interaction with followers, the constraints defined by constituents' beliefs and norms, the strength and nature of opposition, and available resources.

Repertoires of expression of ethnic nationalist movements vary along a wide spectrum that includes interest articulation, passive resistance, demonstrations and riots, sabotage, terrorist acts, and internal wars. Patterns of expression are shaped by the style of leadership, the level of organization, and resources. They are also influenced by the reactions of the state as well as by external forces. These expressions represent events in the life history of movements. The points at which these movements begin and end are generally difficult, if not impossible, to ascertain. Thus, what might be referred to as beginnings or outcomes may well represent only arbitrarily defined points in a process.

Ethnic movements differ in aims and strategies. Smith identifies six types:

> *1. Isolation. . . . was the most common strategy for smaller ethnic communities in the past. The ethnic community chooses to stay aloof from society as a whole.*
>
> *2. Accommodation. Here the ethnic community aims to adjust to its host society by encouraging its members to participate in the social and political life of the society and its state. Often, individual members try to assimilate to the host society, or at least become acculturated, for individual advancement.*
>
> *3. Communalism. . . . is simply a more dynamic and active form of accommodation. . . . The aim is communal control over communal affairs in those geographical areas where the ethnic community forms a demographic majority.*
>
> *4. Autonomism. There are . . . various forms and degrees of autonomy. . . . Cultural autonomy implies full control by representatives of the ethnic community over every aspect of its cultural life, notably education, the press and mass media, and the courts. Political autonomy or "home rule" extends this to cover every aspect of social, political, and economic life, except for foreign affairs and defense. Ideally, autonomists demand a federal state structure, and this strategy is really only open to communities with a secure regional base.*
>
> *5. Separatism. This is the classic political goal of ethnonational self-determination. . . . In each*

case, the aim is to secede and form one's own sovereign state, with little or no connection with former rulers.

6. Irredentism. Here an ethnic community, whose members are divided and fragmented in separate states, seeks reunification and recovery of the "lost" or "unredeemed" territories occupied by its members. In general, this is only possible where the ethnic community has its membership living in adjoining states or areas. (1981, pp. 15–17)

Seeking independent rule, as in secessionist or separatist movements, poses the most serious threat to the state. Such movements challenge not only the legitimacy of the government or regime but also the integrity of the state itself.

It is reasonable to expect that factors shaping the intensity of nationalist movements will, in turn, influence the formation of secessionist goals. Territorial coterminality with lines of ethnic identification is a strong contributor, with distance from the ruling center adding to the potential for secessionist claims (Young 1975; Islam 1985; Pankhurst 1988). Timing seems to be important to the rise of such claims as well as to their success. Based on the experiences of several African countries, Young (1975) points out that time is conducive when polity in the parent state falls into disrepute, calling its legitimacy into question because of mismanagement, corruption, and discrimination. He also concludes that times of cataclysmic events in the lives of states offer opportunities for secessionist claims because of the fluidity these events engender, the options they open, and the push for choices to be made. Young cites other antecedents that provide a basis for solidarity and mobilization, such as regional differentials in concentration of wealth and representation in power positions, and at least the minimum political resources to make independent status possible even when economic sacrifice is required. To this list of contributing factors, Islam (1985) adds the magnitude of suffering, the impact of the secession of a region on the rest of the country, whether the seceding region represents a majority or a minority of the population, and the involvement of outside powers.

International relations—regional and global—also influence secessionist movements. The spread of the ideology of minority rights and self-determination plays a special role. In a comparative analysis Sigler (1983) concludes: "There is historical weight to the charge that minority rights is a guise for separatist sentiment" (p. 188). He maintains that the "concept of minority rights briefly blossomed under the minorities treaties system" that followed from the Treaty of Versailles. The system was to protect the rights of minorities in many countries, mostly in Europe, after World War I. It gave jurisdiction to the Permanent Court of International Justice, but litigations became protracted and difficult to adjudicate, thus severely limiting the court's role. It gave power to the Council of the League of Nations to intervene but did not guarantee that disciplinary actions could be carried out against states for infractions. Mutual reinforcement of the system of states as a basis for international relations restrained the various states from interfering in each other's internal affairs. "The collapse of the minorities treaties system . . . has encouraged minority separatist movements. . . . In the absence of a strong international system for the protection of minority rights, resort to separatist politics may have become more prevalent" (Sigler 1983, p. 190). This reinforces Smelser's ideas about structural conduciveness mentioned earlier.

If the odds facing secessionists are great, those facing irredentists are much greater. By definition, irredentism involves multiple secessions, which means contending with the forces of more than one state. An exception is when an ethnic group in one state seeks to attach itself to a neighboring state that includes parts of the same group. This tactic is used by some secessionists to obtain external support (Young 1975).

REACTIONS OF THE STATE

Actions by the authorities and the means of control they employ are largely shaped by the objectives of nationalist movements and greatly affect their course. When perceived as threats to the stability of state and government, they are usually met with repression. However, nationalist movements that remain clandestine and limited under conditions of severe repression tend to gather momentum and erupt into open expression when a new regime reduces coercion. Recent events in the Soviet Union and other countries illustrate the point.

Repression is not the only means used by states in responding to threats of ethnonationalism. Some states, such as the Soviet Union and the People's Republic of China, adopt population redistribution policies aimed at diluting the coterminality of ethnicity with territory. Language policies in education are also used to increase homogenization. Central governments in some pluralist states adopt redistributive policies in regard to resources to assist economic development in lagging regions. Yugoslavia offers good examples of redistributive policies and their effects.

Other means in the state's arsenal are arrangements for power sharing in governance and mechanisms for conflict regulation. Nordlinger (1972) outlines six such mechanisms: (1) a stable governing coalition of political parties involving all major conflict groups; (2) proportional distribution of elective and appointive positions; (3) mutual veto by which government decisions must be acceptable to major conflict organizations; (4) purposive depoliticization in which leaders of conflict groups agree to keep government out of policy areas that impinge upon the various segments' values and interests; (5) regulation by compromise over conflictual issues; and (6) one group granting concessions to another as a way of managing conflicts. He also sees four motives for leaders to engage in conflict regulation: (1) external threats or pressure; (2) negative effects on the economic well-being of the groups involved; (3) aversion to risking violence and human suffering that might result from unregulated conflicts; and (4) the protection of leaders' own power positions.

Lijphart (1977) places equal emphasis on leaders "whose cooperative attitudes and behavior are needed to counteract the centrifugal tendencies inherent in plural societies" (p. 1). The forms he outlines for "consociational" democracies overlap in many ways with Nordlinger's mechanisms for conflict regulation. One important difference, however, is Lijphart's inclusion of "segmental autonomy," that is, federalism. Nordlinger specifically excluded federalism as a mechanism for regulating conflicts because he saw in it a recipe for a breakup of the state.

In conclusion, it can be said that the pervasiveness of nationalism should be self-evident. The socioeconomic, political, and other human costs are frequently staggering. As a major feature of social structure, ethnicity is of central theoretical importance. However, many (and often large) gaps in the state of knowledge exist, both in theory and in accumulated data. There are basically three shortcomings in the literature that account for this. First are conceptual and theoretical limitations, especially at the intermediate levels of abstraction that connect abstract explanatory schemes—of which a notable few exist—with concrete events. Second is that the preponderance of empirical work in this area is in the form of case studies that are mostly historical. They offer uniformity neither in concepts nor in evidence. The third problem with literature on ethnic nationalism is its fragmentation. A coherent picture must draw upon concepts and propositions from a number of traditions. And there are many overriding concepts with which to assemble frameworks to advance theory and to guide the collection of evidence. While they are difficult to plan and execute, there is compelling need for comparative studies to advance understanding of the underlying principles. Clear understanding of nationalism, and of the processes involved, is essential to evolving appropriate educational, policy, constitutional, and other legal means for accommodating cultural diversity.

(SEE ALSO: *Ethnicity; Social Movements*)

REFERENCES

Connor, Walker 1972 "Nation-Building or Nation-Destroying?" *World Politics* 24:319–355.

——— 1978 "A Nation Is a Nation, Is a State, Is an

Ethnic Group, Is a. . . ." *Ethnic and Racial Studies* 1, no. 4:377–400.

——— 1984 *The National Question in Marxist-Leninist Theory and Strategy.* Princeton, N.J.: Princeton University Press.

Deutsch, Karl W. 1984 *Nationalism and Social Communication.* Cambridge, Mass.: MIT Press.

Geertz, Clifford 1963 "The Integrative Revolution: Primordial Sentiments and Civil Politics in the New States." In Clifford Geertz, ed. *Old Societies and New States: The Quest for Modernity in Asia and Africa.* New York: The Free Press.

Gurr, Ted Robert 1970 *Why Men Rebel.* Princeton, N.J.: Princeton University Press.

Gusfield, Joseph R. 1970 "Introduction: A Definition of the Subject." In Joseph R. Gusfield, ed., *Protest, Reform, and Revolt: A Reader in Social Movements.* New York: Wiley.

Hechter, Michael 1986 "Theories of Ethnic Relations." In John F. Stack, Jr., ed., *The Primordial Challenge: Ethnicity in the Contemporary World.* New York: Greenwood Press.

Heraclides, Alexis 1990 "Secessionist Minorities and External Involvement." *International Organization* 44, no. 3 (Summer): 341–378.

Hermann, Margaret G. 1986 "Ingredients of Leadership." In Margaret G. Hermann, ed., *Political Psychology: Contemporary Problems and Issues.* San Francisco: Jossey-Bass.

Houseknecht, Sharon K. 1990 "The Role of Family and Kinship in Ethnic Nationalist Movements." Columbus: Mershon Center, Ohio State University. Mimeograph.

Huntington, Samual P. 1968 *Political Order in Changing Societies.* New Haven: Yale University Press.

Islam, Rafiqul 1985 "Secessionist Self-Determination: Some Lessons from Katanga, Biafra and Bangladesh." *Journal of Peace Research* 22, no. 3:211–221.

Jenkins, J. Craig 1983 "Resource Mobilization Theory and the Study of Social Movements." *Annual Review of Sociology* 9:527–553.

Kamenka, Eugene (ed.) 1973 *Nationalism, the Nature and Evolution of an Idea.* London: Edward Arnold.

Kohn, Hans 1955 *Nationalism.* Princeton, N.J.: D. Van Nostrand.

——— 1968 "Nationalism." In David L. Sills, ed., *International Encyclopedia of the Social Sciences,* vol. 11, Macmillan and Free Press.

Lasswell, Harold D. 1936 *Politics: Who Gets What, When, How.* New York: McGraw-Hill.

Lijphart, Arend 1977 *Democracy in Plural Societies: A Comparative Exploration.* New Haven: Yale University Press.

Linz, Juan J. 1978 "The Breakdown of Democratic Regimes: Crisis Breakdown and Reequilibrium." In Juan J. Linz and Alfred Stepan, eds., *The Breakdown of Democratic Regimes.* Baltimore: Johns Hopkins University Press.

McCarthy, John D., and Mayer N. Zald 1977 "Resource Mobilization and Social Movements: A Partial Theory." *American Journal of Sociology* 82:1212–1241.

Minogue, K. R. 1967 *Nationalism.* New York: Basic Books.

Nordlinger, Eric 1972 *Conflict Regulation in Divided Societies.* Cambridge, Mass.: Center for International Affairs, Harvard University.

Oberschall, A. 1973 *Social Conflict and Social Movements.* Englewood Cliffs, N.J.: Prentice-Hall.

Pankhurst, Jerry G. 1988 "Muslims in Communist Nations: The Cases of Albania, Bulgaria, Yugoslavia, and the Soviet Union." In Anson Shupe and Jeffery Hadden, eds., *The Politics of Religion and Social Change: Religion and Political Order,* vol. 2. New York: Paragon House.

Plamenatz, John P. 1973 "Two Types of Nationalism." In Eugene Kamenka, ed., *Nationalism, the Nature and Evolution of an Idea.* London: Edward Arnold.

Said, Abdul, and Luis Simmons 1976 *Ethnicity in the International Context.* New Brunswick, N.J.: Transaction Books.

Sanders, David 1981 *Patterns of Political Instability.* London: Macmillan.

Sigler, Jay A. 1983 *Minority Rights: A Comparative Analysis.* Westport, Conn.: Greenwood Press.

Smelser, Neal 1962 *Theory of Collective Behavior.* New York: Free Press.

Smith, Anthony D. 1976 "Introduction: The Formation of Nationalist Movements." In Anthony D. Smith, ed., *Nationalist Movements.* London: Macmillan.

——— 1981 *The Ethnic Revival.* Cambridge: Cambridge University Press.

Snyder, Louis L. 1984 *Macro-Nationalism: A History of the Pan-Movements.* Westport, Conn.: Greenwood Press.

Stack, John F., Jr. 1986 "Ethnic Mobilization in World Politics: The Primordial Perspective." In John F. Stack, Jr., ed., *The Primordial Challenge.* New York: Greenwood Press.

Symmons-Symonolewicz, Konstantin 1970 *Nationalist Movements: A Comparative View.* Meadville, Pa.: Maplewood Press.

Tilly, Charles 1978 *From Mobilization to Revolution.* Reading, Mass.: Addison-Wesley.

Williams, Robin M., Jr. 1947 *The Reduction of Intergroup Tensions.* New York: Social Science Research Council.

Young, M. Crawford 1975 "Nationalism and Separatism in Africa." In Martin Kilson, ed., *New States in the Modern World.* Cambridge, Mass.: Harvard University Press.

SAAD Z. NAGI

NATURE VS. NURTURE *See* Gender: Intelligence; Socialization.

NETWORK ANALYSIS *See* Social Network Analysis.

NEW STRUCTURALISM Researchers examining the wage determination process who have focused their attention on structural or contextual factors have been labeled "new structuralists" or "neo-structuralists" (Baron and Bielby 1980). Structural factors define the context within which workers compete for jobs and wages and are compensated for work. In addition to the individual's social background characteristics, new structuralists consider variables relating to the structure of the earnings determination process disagreeing with the position that rewards are uniform across occupational settings. Factors related to the economy, industry, organization, or job, rather than to the characteristics of the individual, are the primary variables of interest. New structuralists argue that rewards vary by structural context, borrowing terms from labor market economists such as *dual economy, industrial sector,* and *internal labor markets* to expand the existing model and explain persistent economic inequalities, poverty, and discrimination.

This article will examine the development of the new-structuralist perspective stemming from individualistic models of wage attainment of both sociologists and economists. A variety of structural components are considered, including contextual effects at a number of economic job levels as well as structural features of the jobs themselves.

A variety of theories, models, and explanations of the wage determination process have been offered by sociologists and economists alike. In the 1960s, Blau and Duncan (1967) introduced the use of path analysis in order to better understand the process by which a father's social standing, education, and occupation affected his son's social standing. The model developed was one of process over the life course from the respondent's social background to his educational achievement, his first occupation, and subsequently, his occupation at the time of interview.

Among the economists, it was Adam Smith ([1776] 1970) who formulated the basic ideas about the forces that determine remuneration for work in competitive labor markets. In this "orthodox" perspective, the market is assumed to be perfectly competitive. Both workers and employers are assumed to have perfect information and attempt to maximize their utility for earnings and profit. Becker (1975) lent explanatory power to the model, arguing that individuals will invest in education and skills (their "human capital") in order to better their potential for success in the labor market, thus explaining the relationship between education and earnings.

In reaction to these individual or atomistic models, neo-institutionalists of economics, like the new structuralists of sociology, introduced structural components to the model that violated the assumptions of perfect information and mobility. They focused their attention on the contexts within which workers are matched to jobs, examining the structural factors related to pricing in labor markets—factors that are not related to the value of an individual's characteristics.

While initiated by economists, structural models in both disciplines have developed along two levels of inquiry; dual economy theory is a macro-level theory that examines the segmentation of industries, firms, and occupations. It concentrates on the linkages between the organization of firms at the macro level and the experiences of individuals who compete for jobs and wages. Segmented labor market theory is a micro-level theory that focuses on the labor market in which individuals compete for jobs. Much confusion has developed concerning the two levels and the degree to which they overlap.

The first level of inquiry, the dual economy theory, suggests that there has been an historical trend toward the development of a dichotomous industrial structure and points to various features of the economic and social organization of production as primarily responsible for this development. A proposed consequence of this trend has been the segmentation of the labor force and labor market along various dimensions ranging from occupational markets to class positions to racial and sexual divisions (Wallace and Kalleberg 1981).

Several theorists have proposed differing concepts to describe the divisions among economic sectors. Averitt (1968) speaks of "center" and "periphery" firms; O'Conner (1973) of "monopoly" and "competitive" sectors; and Bluestone (1970) identifies "core," "periphery," and "irregular" economies which produce segmentation of the structure of industries and are assumed to affect labor market structures.

The center or core firms are primarily characterized as large in size, enabling them to take advantage of an economy of scale. They are thought to be independent or autonomous in relation to market factors and have the ability to adapt to the changing economic environment successfully. In addition, core firms have typically achieved a level of diversification. Periphery firms, on the other hand, generally have no autonomous influence over market prices, have a single product line, and are concerned with short-term profit motives.

The second level of inquiry, segmented labor market theory, has also been described as consisting of two levels—the primary labor market and the secondary labor market—hence, the confusion between the macro and micro theories. "The analysis of labor markets is an important concern for sociological inquiry; it permits an understanding of the way macro forces associated with the economy of a society and elements of social structure impinge on the microrelations between employers and workers in determining various forms of inequality" (Kalleberg and Sorensen 1979, p. 351).

Piore (1975) divides the primary labor market into upper and lower tiers. Upper-tier positions tend not to be dependent on industry type; that is, the upper tier could exist in both primary and secondary markets (positions such as chief executive officer, company president, and higher-level and management). They have a high degree of autonomy, largely as a result of the type of occupational activities. Lower-tier positions consist of mainly white-collar clerical and blue-collar operatives. In the primary market, these positions enjoy the benefits of an internal labor market that is not present in the secondary labor market.

Employees in the secondary labor market are characterized as having inadequate training, erratic work histories, and a lack of applicable on-the-job experience. Segmented labor market theory argues that the secondary (periphery) labor market sectors operate differently than neoclassical economics has postulated and that workers are barred from leaving this sector primarily because of institutional constraints (Kalleberg and Sorensen 1979). Although unions have been responsible for adding an element of stability to and improving benefits in some secondary labor market occupations, they have traditionally discriminated against blacks and have, at times, worked against the interests of women (Milkman 1988). On the other hand, it has also been asserted that racial and sexual discrimination are functional substitutes for the capitalist, each generating a reserve army of cheap, underemployed labor (Bonacich 1972).

An important structural component of segmented labor markets is the existence of internal labor markets. Internal labor markets are the career ladders or promotion systems that exist within a single economic organization. Dunlop describes the internal labor market as "the complex of rules which determines the movement of workers among job classifications within administrative units, such as enterprises, companies, or hiring halls" (1966, p. 32). These markets are in contrast to "external labor markets" where wages and training are controlled by market forces rather than individual firms. For workers, the existence of an internal labor market is a vehicle to both higher wages and greater stability of employment; firms without one (secondary labor market firms) tend to pay less, offer little opportunity for advancement, have poor working conditions, and are associated with unstable employment. There are two main types of internal labor markets. The first refers to a labor market internal to a particular firm with promotional policies, specific career tracks, seniority rights, and few entry ports. The second refers to occupational groups in which certification or membership, such as professional degrees and/or craft guild or union membership, is required (Doeringer and Piore 1971; see also Althauser and Kalleberg 1981).

Confusion concerning the degree of overlap between the two levels of inquiry (macro and micro) has stemmed from the operationalization of dual economy theory, which has often confounded features of the economic organization of firms with characteristics of the labor force and labor market. In addition, the same terminology has been used to describe both macro and micro levels (Sullivan 1981). This is especially confusing, since primary and secondary labor markets are often thought to lie exclusively in core and periphery industries or firms.

> *There is reasoning and evidence enough to justify a framework in which labor markets represent a level of analysis distinct from economic sectors based on firm characteristics. We conclude that the structure, associated characteristics, and origins of internal labor markets (ILM), as well as their consequences for movement between jobs, individual careers, wage levels, or wage functions, cannot be reduced to characteristics of center and peripheral firms or their consequences.* (Althauser and Kalleberg 1981, p. 140)

While features of the economic organization of firms are reflected in labor market outcomes, the correspondence is not as strong as early theorists had assumed.

Dual economy theory has gained some support (Wallace and Kalleberg 1981; Dickens and Lang 1988) but has also attracted strong criticism (Cain 1976; Hodson and Kaufman 1982). Dualistic theories, Cain (1976) argues, have too often been sketchy, vague, and weakened by internal conflict. Many feel the theory is poorly specified, with the dichotomous measure being too simplistic, causing it to underestimate the diversity of macroeconomic factors that may impinge on individual outcomes. In addition, the existence of discrete economic sectors has often been treated as an a priori assumption rather than an empirical question.

Modest support for dual economy and/or segmented labor market theories has primarily focused on specific aspects or pieces of the theories, and a general test of the theory is still wanting. In spite of previous findings reporting a positive relationship between the size of an organization and wages paid to employees (Beck, Horan, and Tolbert 1978), the effect of size varied by gender, occupation (blue- and white-collar), and even industrial sector. Beck, Horan, and Tolbert note that the process by which individual workers are rewarded appears to vary systematically across economic sectors. Taking into account variations among individuals in terms of father's education, father's occupation, age, education, sex, and race, these authors were able to demonstrate evidence of substantial advantages/disadvantages associated with employment in the respective core and peripheral sectors that apparently could not be explained by differences in the skills and/or qualifications of the labor force. While acknowledging a certain oversimplification and lack of refinement in their delineation of core and periphery sectors, the analysis nevertheless points to the existence of certain influences implicit within the economic structure that operate somewhat independently of the impact of individual-level attributes (e.g., education, sex, race).

Looking at regional, as opposed to national labor markets, Parcel (1979) examined earnings as a function of individual social background variables, investment variables, and regional labor market characteristics. She demonstrated that export sector productivity, residential segregation, and racial job competition had notable as well as differential effects on the earnings of blacks and whites even after controlling for individual background characteristics. In another regional study, Semyonov (1988) focused on the impact of labor market segregation on socioeconomic inequality between Jews and Arabs in Israel. His findings support the notion that the regional labor market has strong effects on the success of the worker. Where Arabs working in mono-ethnic labor markets were advantages, those working in bi-ethnic labor markets suffered the effects of occupational and income discrimination more than any other group.

Additional research points to the need to address the existence of internal labor markets, the degree of unionization, and the differential effects of employment in "firms" (Stolzenberg 1978; Baron and Bielby 1980) or "establishments." Villemez and Bridges (1988) found that for white-collar workers, firm size is important, whereas for blue-collar workers, establishment size is more significant. This finding appears to be consistent with Stolzenberg (1978) and Baron and Bielby (1984), who show that large firms are more likely to be in the core sector, offering an internal labor market that promotes stability of employment and career ladders for workers.

Baron and Bielby (1980, 1984) argue that the basic unit of social inequality—the unit that generates inequality through the organization of jobs and that regulates social mobility—is the firm. It is at this level that individuals are hired and assigned tasks that may or may not lead to better jobs. Much prior research on sex segregation used occupational categories that lumped many job titles together. (See also Strang and Baron 1990.) In order to explore lower levels of occupational sex segregation, Baron and Bielby use a data set that allows them to look at individuals with the same job titles at the same establishment. They found that even when the labor pool consists of men and women with similar skills and qualifications, employers continued to segregate workers by sex.

Besides organizational effects, other aspects of the labor market, such as environmental effects, also seem to be important. Kalleberg and Lincoln (1988) discuss five distinctive work structures that define the locations where individuals are employed and rewarded. They include organizations, industries, jobs and occupations, authority positions (class positions), and unions. Each of these has been shown in research to generate inequalities. When comparing male workers in the United States and Japan, Kalleberg and Lincoln find that Americans' earnings are largely determined by job or occupational characteristics and the individual's authority position in the firm. In Japan, seniority and life-cycle variables such as age account for most of the variance in earnings. These findings lend support to the notion that rewards are not uniformly allocated across occupations and that structural characteristics are important in understanding economic inequality in the United States, where structural characteristics of the job accounted for a significant portion of the variation in earnings.

Sorensen and Kalleberg (1981) suggest an alternative model, "vacancy competition," that focuses on tactics used by employees, such as collective bargaining (i.e., unions), to gain control over access to jobs and their wages. In the vacancy model, closed employment relationships are the key to the employees' power. These employment relationships are obtained by the degree of interdependency among jobs, the measurability of productivity, and collective bargaining. Closed relationships are assumed to benefit the employee, since he/she cannot be dismissed or replaced easily. Inequality in earnings is due to differences in job characteristics and the hierarchical organization of jobs in internal labor markets. The job position is seen as separate from the worker, and rewards are distributed on the basis of the position rather than on the basis of individual characteristics. Therefore, for these positions in particular, the typical individual model does not explain earnings well.

A review of the literature indicates multiple dimensions at both the level of organization (i.e., firm or establishment) and the level of the labor market (i.e., consequences of context or regional differences in labor markets). First, at the organizational level, one needs to consider market concentration, economic scale, profits, economic growth, and the expansion of markets. Second, at the labor market level, there are at least four dimensions of segmentation that have crosscutting ramifications: segmentation by primary and secondary markets (including a division of upper and lower tiers within the primary market); segmentation by class or authority positions; segmentation by sex; and segmentation by race.

The consensus in the literature lies in the importance that needs to be given to structural effects. Renewed interest reflects the concern over a wage attainment model that treats jobs, occupations, and employment status as similar in structure. Baron and Bielby (1980) suggest that the macro/micro forces affecting work are played out within the organizational arena of the firm. Additional structural features such as labor market regulations deserve investigation as a source of segmentation that affects both demand and supply. These include legal protection of groups of workers, such as by immigration/guest-worker regulations, affirmative action, and protection codes for women and youth, which may ultimately create more intense competition for the protected parties (Sullivan 1981). It may also be useful to investigate nonmonetary characteristics of both the macro and micro levels (Jencks, Perman, and Rainwater 1988).

Studies of work motivation or satisfaction, occupational sex segregation, and compensating wage differentials point to the need for a better understanding of the components or characteristics of work. Compensating wage differential theory posits that jobs with undesirable work components will be assigned higher wages in order to attract workers who are assumed to maximize their utility for income. While the findings from these studies are mixed, some work components have been found to be tied to wages (e.g., risk of injury/death, risk of unemployment, hours worked). Yet much of the prior research by economists has ignored individual characteristics that may have biased their findings (Brown 1980).

More important, both researchers and policymakers are taking seriously the need to better address issues of comparable worth or equal pay for jobs with comparable characteristics (Baron and Newman 1990). However, as Treiman and Hartmann argue (1981), studies of earnings differences that use job characteristics as explanatory variables do not constitute a definitive body of literature. The few studies that exist typically incorporate, at most, three or four components of work—those most often thought to necessitate compensation. Many of these studies have been examined through the use of job-evaluation systems. Skill, effort, responsibility, and working conditions are the components of work most often measured in job-evaluation systems, primarily because they are widely regarded as compensable. Yet many argue that four compensable factors do not allow for the variety of job tasks found in today's work environment and that currently used job-evaluation systems are biased in their assessment of the important features of jobs.

Overall, new structuralists agree that in order to better understand the process by which workers are matched to jobs, structural or contextual variables need to be examined along with individual characteristics. Both sociologists and economists have much to offer in the way of an explanation of the earnings determination process. To optimize the utility of structural and/or contextual factors, researchers in both disciplines should view the ongoing economic/sociological debate as an agenda for future research (see Smith 1990 and Sorensen 1990 for examples.)

(SEE ALSO: *Economic Sociology; Functionalism; Labor Force*)

REFERENCES

Althauser, Robert P., and Arne L. Kalleberg 1981 "Firms, Occupations, and the Structure of Labor Markets: A Conceptual Analysis." In Ivar Berg, ed., *Sociological Perspectives on Labor Markets*. New York: Academic Press.

Averitt, Robert T. 1968 *The Dual Economy: The Dynamics of American Industry Structure*. New York: Norton.

Baron, James N., and William T. Bielby 1980 "Bringing the Firms Back In: Stratification, Segmentation and the Organization of Work." *American Sociological Review* 45:737–765.

——— 1984 "The Organization of Work in a Segmented Economy." *American Sociological Review* 49: 454–473.

———, and Andrew E. Newman 1990 "For What It's Worth: Organizations, Occupations, and the Value of Work Done by Women and Nonwhites." *American Sociological Review* 55:155–175.

Beck, E. M., Patrick M. Horan, and Charles M. Tolbert II 1978 "Stratification in a Dual Economy: A Sectoral Model of Earnings Determination." *American Sociological Review* 43:704–720.

Becker, Gary S. 1975 *Human Capital,* 2nd ed. Chicago: University of Chicago Press.

Blau, Peter M., and Otis D. Duncan 1967 *The American Occupational Structure.* New York: Wiley.

Bluestone, B. 1970 "The Tripartite Economy: Labor Markets and the Working Poor." *Poverty and Human Resources* 5:15–35.

Bonacich, Edna 1972 "A Theory of Ethnic Antagonism: The Split Labor Market." *American Sociological Review* 37:547–559.

Brown, Charles 1980 "Equalizing Differences in the Labor Market." *The Quarterly Journal of Economics* (Feb.):113–134.

Cain, Glen G. 1976 "The Challenge of Segmented Labor Market Theories to Orthodox Theory." *Journal of Economic Literature* 14:1215–1257.

Dickens, William T., and Kevin Lang 1988 "The Reemergence of Segmented Labor Market Theory." *American Economic Association Papers and Proceedings* (May):129–132.

Doeringer, Peter B., and Michael J. Piore 1971 *Internal Labor Markets and Manpower Analysis.* Lexington, Mass.: D. C. Heath.

Dunlop, John 1966 *The Measurement and Interpretation of Job Vacancies.* Prepared for the National Bureau of Economic Research. New York: Columbia University Press.

Hodson, Randy, and Robert L. Kaufman 1982 "Economic Dualism: A Critical Review." *American Sociological Review* 47:727–739.

Jencks, Christopher, Lauri Perman, and Lee Rainwater 1988 "What Is a Good Job? A New Measure of Labor Market Success." *American Journal of Sociology* 93:1322–1355.

Kalleberg, Arne L., and James R. Lincoln 1988 "The Structure of Earnings Inequality in the United States and Japan." *American Journal of Sociology* 94: S121–S153.

Kalleberg, Arne L., and Aage Sorensen 1979 "The Sociology of Labor Markets." *Annual Review of Sociology* 5:351–379.

Milkman, Ruth 1988 *Gender At Work: The Dynamics of Job Segregation by Sex During World War II.* Urbana: University of Illinois Press.

O'Conner, J. 1973 *The Fiscal Crisis of the State.* New York: St. Martin's Press.

Parcel, Toby L. 1979 "Race, Regional Labor Markets and Earnings." *American Sociological Review* 44: 262–279.

Piore, Michael J. 1975 "Notes for a Theory of Labor Market Stratification." In Richard D. Edwards, Michael Reich, and David M. Gordon, eds., *Labor Market Segmentation.* Lexington, Mass.: Health.

Semyonov, Moshe 1988 "Bi-Ethnic Labor Markets, Mono-Ethnic Labor Markets, and Socioeconomic Inequality." *American Sociological Review* 53: 256–266.

Smith, Adam (1776) 1970 *An Inquiry into the Nature and Causes of The Wealth of Nation.* Harmondsworth, England: Penguin.

Smith, Michael R. 1990 "What is New in 'New Structuralist' Analyses of Earnings?" *American Sociological Review* 55:827–841.

Sorensen, Aage B. 1990 "Throwing the Sociologists Out? A Reply to Smith." *American Sociological Review* 55:842–845.

———, and Arne L. Kalleberg 1981 "An Outline of a Theory of the Matching of Persons to Jobs." In Ivar Berg, ed., *Sociological Perspectives on Labor Markets.* New York: Academic Press.

Stolzenberg, Ross M. 1978 "Bringing the Boss Back In: Employer Size, Employee Schooling, and Socioeconomic Achievement." *American Sociological Review* 43:813–828.

Strang David, and James N. Baron 1990 "Categorical Imperatives: The Structure of Job Titles." *American Sociological Review* 55:479–495.

Sullivan, Teresa A. 1981 "Sociological Views of Labor Markets: Some Missed Opportunities and Neglected Directions." In Ivar Berg, ed., *Sociological Perspectives on Labor Markets.* New York: Academic Press.

Treiman, Donald J., and Heidi I. Hartmann (eds.) 1981 *Women, Work and Wages: Equal Pay for Jobs of Equal Value.* Washington, D.C.: National Academy Press.

Villemez, Wayne J., and William P. Bridges 1988 "When Bigger Is Better: Differences in the Individual-level Effect of Firm and Establishment Size." *American Sociological Review* 53:237–255.

Wallace, Michael, and Arne Kalleberg 1981 "Economic Organization of Firms and Labor Market Consequences: Toward a Specification of Dual Economic

Theory." In Ivar Berg, ed., *Sociological Perspectives on Labor Markets.* New York: Academic.

LYNN M. RIES

NONPARAMETRIC STATISTICS Statistical inference is one of the most important branches of statistics. The field of inference consists of making generalizations, drawing conclusions, and making decisions about population parametrics that are usually unknown, based on sample data and statistics.

Parameters are characteristics of the population being studied, such as mean (μ), standard deviation (σ), or median (Md). Statistics are characteristics of a sample, such as sample mean ($\bar{X}$), and sample median (m). Making inferences from sample(s) to the population(s) necessitates assumptions about the nature of the population distribution, such as a normal population distribution and interval or ratio scales.

There is no general agreement in the literature regarding the meaning of the term *nonparametric statistics.* This term and the term *distribution-free* methods are commonly used interchangeably in the literature, although they have different implications. These statistics require few, or less-stringent, ("weak") assumptions about the nature of the population distribution being studied. They are more flexible in their use and are generally quite robust. Thus, when some types of nonparametric statistics are used, it can be stated that regardless of the nature of the population distribution or the type of measurement involved, conclusions can be drawn about that study.

Both the terms nonparametric and distribution-free statistics are, in a sense, misnomers. The terms do not connote that these tests are not concerned with parameters and they do not signify distribution-free statistics. It is important to note that nonparametric statistics are not assumption-free either, since they must be based on some assumptions applicable to specific tests, such as lack of ties or the independence of two random samples included in the study. Nonparametric statistics may be divided into three major categories: (1) noninferential statistical measures; (2) inferential estimation techniques for point and interval estimation of parametric values of the population; and (3) hypothesis testing, which is considered the primary purpose of nonparametric statistics. (Estimation techniques included in the category above are often used as a first step in hypothesis testing.) These three categories include different types of problems dealing with location, dispersion, goodness-of-fit, association, runs, linear regression, trends, and proportions, which are presented in Table 1.

The major advantages of nonparametric statistics compared to parametric statistics are that they: (1) can be applied to a large number of situations; (2) can be easily understood intuitively; (3) can be used with smaller sample sizes; (4) can be used with more types of data; (5) need fewer or weaker assumptions about the nature of the population distribution; (6) are generally more robust and often not seriously affected by extreme values in data such as outliers; and (7) provide a number of supplemental or alternative tests and techniques to parametric test.

Many critics of nonparametric tests have sometimes erroneously pointed out some of the tests' major drawbacks: (1) they are usually neither as powerful nor as efficient as the parametric tests; (2) they are not as precise or accurate as parametric tests in many cases (e.g., ranking tests with a large number of ties); (3) they might lead to erroneous decisions about rejecting or not rejecting the null hypothesis because of lack of precision in the test; (4) many of such tests utilize data inadequately in the analysis because they transform observed values into ranks and groups; and (5) the sampling distribution and distribution tables for nonparametric statistics are too numerous, often cumbersome, and limited to small sample sizes. Given these advantages and disadvantages, how does one choose between parametric and nonparametric tests?

Many criteria are available for this purpose. Statistical results are expected to be unbiased, consistent, robust, or have a combination of these characteristics. If both tests under consideration are applicable and appropriate, what other criteria may be used in the choice of a preferred test? The power and efficiency of a test are very widely used in comparing parametric and nonparametric tests.

The power of a test is the probability of rejecting the null hypothesis H_0 when it is false. It is defined as 1-β, where β is the probability of a type-II error or accepting a false null hypothesis. If test A and test B both have the same alpha level of significance, same sample sizes, and test B has a higher power, then test B would be considered a preferred choice.

Calculations of the power of a test are often cumbersome. So, two other measures are commonly used. Power efficiency measures the increase in sample size needed to make test B as powerful as test A, given the same significance level and same hypotheses, H_0 and H_1. Power efficiency of test B to test A = 100 (n_A/n_B). Asymptotic relative efficiency (sometimes called Pitman efficiency) is measured without a limit on the increase in sample size of A.

Based on these criteria, it can be generalized that nonparametric tests and techniques tend to be preferred when: (1) nominal or ordinal data scales are involved; (2) robust tests are needed because of outliers in the data; (3) probability distribution or density function of the data is unknown, or cannot be assumed, as in the case of small sample sizes; (4) the effects of violations of specific test assumptions are unknown or only weak assumptions can be made; (5) analogoue parametric tests are not available, as in the case of runs tests and goodness-of-fit tests; and (6) preliminary trials, or supplemental or alternative techniques for parametric techniques are needed.

NONPARAMETRIC STATISTICAL LITERATURE

The historical roots of nonparametric statistics are supposed to go as far back as 1710, when John Arbuthnot(t) did a study that included the proportion of male births in London (Daniel 1990; Hettmansperger 1984) using a sign test, which is a nonparametric procedure. Spearman rank correlation coefficient, which is widely used even today, dates back to 1904, and the forerunner of the chi-square test was introduced in 1900.

Initial major developments in the field that introduced and popularized the study of nonparametric methods appeared in the late 1940s and early 1950s, although a few nonparametric tests were published in the late 1920s and 1930s, such as the Fisher-Pitman test and Kendall's coefficient of concordance respectively. Contributions by Wilcoxon and Mann-Whitney were introduced during the 1940s. The term nonparametric reportedly appeared for the first time in 1942 in a paper by Wolfowitz (Daniel 1990). In the field of sociology, the techniques were probably first introduced by Hare, Borgatta, and Bales (1955). The 1956 publication of Siegel's text on nonparametric statistics popularized the subject to such an extent that the text was the second most-widely cited textbook in the field of statistics for a few years.

The major emphasis in the 1960s and 1970s was on the extension of the field into regression and analysis of variance to develop tests analogous to parametric tests. It was also discovered during this period that nonparametric tests were more robust and efficient than expected previously. The basis for the asymptotic distribution theory was developed during this time period. Computer software for nonparametric tests was developed in the 1970s and 1980s.

A number of elementary texts have been published recently (see Daniel 1990; Krauth 1988; Neave and Worthington 1988; Siegel and Castellan 1988; and Sprent 1989). These texts can be used by those without an extensive statistical background; they have excellent bibliographies and provide adequate examples of applications and scope of the field of nonparametric statistics. In addition, the *Encyclopedia of Statistical Sciences* should serve as an excellent source of material pertaining to nonparametric or distribution-free statistics (Gibbons 1986).

The literature on nonparametric statistics is

TABLE 1
Selected Nonparametric Tests and Techniques

Type of Problem	Type of Data: *One Sample*	*Two Independent Samples*	*Two Related, Paired, or Matched Samples*	k *Independent Samples*	k *Related Samples*
Location	Sign test Wilcoxon signed rank test	Mann-Whitney-Wilcoxon rank-sum test Permutation test Fisher tests Fisher-Pitman test Brown-Mood median test Terry Hoeffding and van der Waerden/normal scores tests Tukey's confidence interval	Sign test Wilcoxon matched-pairs signed-rank test Confidence interval based on sign test Confidence interval based on the Wilcoxon matched-pairs signed-ranks test	Extension of Brown-Mood median test Kruskal-Wallis one-way analysis of variance test Jonckheer test for ordered alternatives Multiple comparisons	Extension of Brown-Mood median test Kruskal-Wallis one-way analysis of variance test Jonckheer test for ordered alternatives Multiple comparisons
Dispersion (Scale Problems)		Siegel-Tukey test Moses' ranklike tests Normal scores tests Tests of the Freunds, Ansari-Bradley, David, or Barton type			
Goodness-of-fit	Chi-square goodness-of-fit Kolmogorov-Smirnov test Lilliefors test	Chi-square test Kolmogorov-Smirnov test		Chi-square test Kolmogorov-Smirnov test	

(continued)

TABLE 1 (con't)

Type of Problem	Type of Data: *One Sample*	*Two Independent Samples*	*Two Related, Paired, or Matched Samples*	k *Independent Samples*	k *Related Samples*
Association	Spearman's rank correlation Kendall's tau_a, tau_b, tau_c Olmstead-Tukey test Phi coefficient λ Yule coefficient Goodman-Kruskal coefficients Cramer's statistic Point biserial coefficient	Chi-square test of independence	Spearman rank correlation H Kendall's tau_a, tau_b, tau_c Olmstead-Tukey corner test	Chi-square test of independence Partial rank correlations Kendall's coefficient of agreement Kendall's coefficient of concordance	Kendall's coefficient of concordance—complete rankings—balanced incomplete rankings
Runs and Randomness	Runs test Runs above and below the median Runs up-and-down test	Wald-Wolfowitz runs test			
Linear Regression		Hollander and Wolfe test for parallelism Confidence interval for difference between two slopes	Theil test Brown-Mood test		
Trends and Changes	Cox-Stuart test Kendall's tau McNemar change test Runs up-and-down test		McNemar change test		
Proportion	Binomial test	Fisher's exact test Chi-square test		Chi-square test	Cochran's *Q* test

extensive. The bibliography published in 1962 by Savage had approximately 3,000 entries. More recent bibliographies have made substantial additions to that list.

The treatment of nonparametric statistics is represented very unevenly in the statistics texts written for sociologists and sociology students. For example, Blalock (1979) deals with more than a dozen tests and has given detailed attention to the subject matter; however, a more recent text by Bohrnstedt and Knoke (1988) has much less coverage of the field.

TESTS AND TECHNIQUES

Table 1 presents a selected list of the more commonly used nonparametric statistical methods and techniques, but it is not intended to be an exhaustive list. It is made up of five columns and eight categories of rows. The five columns describe the nature of the sample and the eight categories of rows identify the major types of problems. Levels of measurement of data are not used in the table as a third dimension; however, references to data scales are made in the narrative part.

The first column in the table consists of tests involving a single sample. The statistics in this category include both inferential and descriptive measurements. They would be used to decide whether a particular sample could have been drawn from a presumed population, or to calculate estimates or to test the null hypothesis. The next column is for two independent samples. The independent samples may be randomly drawn from two populations or randomly assigned to two treatments. In the case of two related samples, the statistical tests are intended to test whether both the samples are drawn from the same population (or identical) populations. The case of k (three or more) independent samples and k-related samples are extensions of the two sample cases.

The eight categories of rows in the table identify the main focus of problems in nonparametric statistics and are described briefly later. Only selected tests and techniques are listed in the table.

Log-linear analyses are not included in this table, though they deal with proportions and meet other criteria for nonparametric tests. The arguments against their inclusion are that they are rather highly developed specialized techniques with some very specific properties of their own.

It may be noted that: (1) many tests cross over into different types of problems (e.g., the chi-square test is included in three types of problems); (2) the same probability distribution may be used for a variety of tests (e.g., in addition to association, proportion, and goodness-of-fit, the chi-square approximation may also be used in Friedman's two-way analysis of variance and Kruskal-Wallis test; (3) many of the tests listed in the table are extensions or modifications of other tests (e.g., the original median test was later extended to three or more independent samples; similarly, the Kruskal-Wallis test spawned the Jonckheere test; (4) the general assumptions and procedures that underlie some of these tests have been extended beyond their original scope (e.g., Hájek's extension of the Kolmogorov-Smirnov test to regression analysis and extension of the two-sample Wilcoxon test for testing the parallelism between two linear regression slopes); (5) many of these tests have corresponding techniques of confidence interval estimates, only a few of which are listed in Table 1; (6) many tests have other equivalent or alternative tests (e.g., when only two samples are used, the Kruskal-Wallis test is equivalent to the Mann-Whitney test); (7) sometimes similar tests are lumped together in spite of differences, as in the case of Mann-Whitney-Wilcoxon test, the Ansari-Bradley type tests or multiple comparison tests; (8) some tests can be used with one or more samples, in which case the tests are listed in one or more categories, depending on common usage; (9) most of these tests have analogous parametric tests; and (10) a very large majority of nonparametric tests and techniques are not included in the table.

Only a few of the commonly used tests and

techniques are selected from Table 1 for illustrative purposes in the sections below. The assumptions listed for the tests are not meant to be exhaustive, and hypothetical data are used in order to simplify the computational examples. Most of the illustrations are two-tailed or two-sided hypotheses at the 0.05 level. Tables of critical values for the tests illustrated here are included in most statistical texts. Modified formulas for ties are not emphasized, nor are measures of estimates illustrated. A description of the eight major categories of rows follows.

Location. Making inferences about location of parameters has been a major concern in the field of statistics. In addition to the mean, which is a parameter of great importance in the field of inferential statistics, the median is a parameter of great importance in nonparametric statistics because of its robustness. The robust quality of the median can be easily ascertained. If the values in a sample of five observations are 5, 7, 9, 11, 13, both the mean and median are 9. If two observations are added to the sample, 1 and 94 (an outlier), the median is still 9, but the mean is changed to 20. Typical location problems include estimating the median, determining confidence intervals for the median, and testing whether two samples have equal medians.

Sign Tests. This is the earliest known nonparametric test used. It is also one of the easiest to understand intuitively because the test statistic is based on the number of positive or negative differences or signs from the hypothesized median. A binomial probability test can be applied to a sign test because of the dichotomous nature of outcomes that are specified by a plus (+) which indicates a difference in one direction or a minus (−) sign which indicates a difference in another direction. Observations with no change or no difference are eliminated from the analysis. The sign test may be a one-tailed or a two-tailed test. A sign test may be used whenever a t-test is inappropriate because the actual values may be missing, or not known, but the direction of change can be determined, as in the case of a therapist who believes that her client is improving. A sign test only uses the direction and not the magnitude of differences in the data.

Wilcoxon Matched-Pairs Signed-Rank Test. The sign test analysis includes only the positive or negative direction of difference between two measures; the Wilcoxon matched-pairs signed-rank test will take into account the magnitude of differences in ordering the data.

Example: A matched sample of students in a school were enrolled in diving classes with different training techniques. Is there a difference? The scores are listed in Table 2.

Illustrative Assumptions: (1) The random sample data consist of pairs; (2) the differences in pair values have an ordered metric or interval scale, are continuous, and independent of one another; and (3) the distribution of differences is symmetric.

TABLE 2
Total Scores for Five Dive Trials

Pairs	*Team A*	*Team B*	*Differences*	*Signed Rank of Differences*	*Negative Ranks*
1	37	35	−2	−1	1
2	39	46	7	+4	
3	32	24	−8	−5.5	5.5
4	21	34	13	+7	
5	20	28	8	+5.5	
6	9	12	3	+2	
7	14	9	−5	−3	3
				$T^{+}=18.5$ $T^{-}=9.5$	9.5

Hypotheses: Two-sided test is used in this example.

H_0: Sum of positive ranks = sum of negative ranks in population

H_1: Sum of positive ranks ≠ sum of negative ranks in population

Test statistic or procedures: The differences between the pairs of observations are obtained and ranked by magnitude. T is the smaller of the sum of ranks with positive or negative signs. Ties may be either eliminated or the average value of the ranks assigned to them. Z can be used as an approximation even with a small n except in cases with a relatively large number of ties. The formula for Z may be substituted when $n>20$.

$$Z = \frac{T - N(N+1)/4}{\sqrt{N(N+1)\,(2N+1)/24}}$$

Efficiency: The power efficiency of the test varies around 95 percent, based on the sample sizes.

Decision: We fail to reject the null hypothesis (or do not reject the null hypothesis) of no difference between the two groups, with an N of 7 at the 0.05 level.

Related nonparametric test: t-test for matched pairs.

Analogous nonparametric test(s): Sign test; randomization test for matched pairs; Walsh test for pairs.

Kruskal-Wallis One-Way Analysis of Variance Test. This is a location measure with three or more independent samples. It is a one-way analysis of variance that utilizes ranking procedures.

Example: The weight loss in kilograms for thirteen randomly assigned patients to one of the three diet programs is listed in Table 3 along with the rankings. Is there a significant difference in the sample medians?

Illustrative Assumptions: (1) Ordinal data scales; (2) three or more random samples, and (3) independent observations.

Hypothesis: A two-sided test without ties is used in this example.

H_0: Md_1 = Mdl2 = Md_2. The populations have the same median value.

H_1: All the populations do not have the same median value.

Test statistic or procedures: The procedure is to rank the values and compute the sums of those ranks for each group and calculate the H statistic. The formula for H is

$$H = \left(\frac{12}{N(N+1)} \sum_{i=1}^{k} \frac{R_i^2}{N_i} \right) - 3\,(N+1)$$

where N_i = the case in the ith category of rank sums

R_i = the sum of ranks in the ith sample.

$$H = \frac{12}{13\,(13+1)} \left[\frac{(46)^2}{5} + \frac{(16)^2}{4} + \frac{(29)^2}{4} \right]$$

$$- 3\,(13+1) = 45,9857 - 42$$

$$H = 3.99$$

Decision: Do not reject null hypothesis, as the critical value for 2 df at the 0.05 level is 5.99 and the H value of 3.99 is less than the critical value.

Efficiency: Asymptotic relative efficiency of Kruskal-Wallis test to F test is 0.955 if each population is normally distributed.

TABLE 3
Diet Programs and Weight-Loss Rankings

Group 1	*Rank*	*Group 2*	*Rank*	*Group 3*	*Rank*
2.8	3	2.2	1	2.9	4
3.5	7	2.7	2	3.1	6
4.0	11	3.0	5	3.7	9
4.1	12	3.6	8	3.8	10
4.9	13				
	$R_1=46$		$R_2=16$		$R_3=29$

Related parametric test: F test.

Analogous nonparametric test(s): Jonckheere test for ordered alternatives.

Friedman Two-Way Analysis of Variance. This is a nonparametric two-way analysis of variance based on ranks and is a good substitute for the parametric F test when it cannot be used.

Example: Three groups of telephone employees from each of the work shifts were tested for their ability to recall fifteen-digit random numbers, under four conditions or treatments of sleep deprivation. The observations are listed in Table 4. Is there a difference in the population medians?

$$F_r = \left[\frac{12}{Nk\,(k+1)} \sum_{j=1}^{k} R_j^2\right] - 3\,N(k+1)$$

N = number of rows (groups of subjects)

k = number of columns

(variables or conditions or treatments)

R_j = sum of ranks in the jth column.

$$F_r = \left[\frac{12}{3\,(4)\,(4+1)}\right] [(11)^2 + (6)^2 + (3)^2 + (10)^2] - 3$$

$$(3)\,(4+1)$$

$$F_f = (0.20)\,(266) - 45 = 8.2$$

Illustrative Assumptions: There is no interaction between blocks and treatment. Ordinal data with observable magnitude or interval data.

Hypotheses:

H_0: $Md_1 = Md_2 = Md_3 = Md_4$. The different levels of sleep deprivation do not have differential effects.

H_1: One or more equality is violated. The different levels of sleep deprivation have differential effects.

Test statistic or procedures: The formula and computations are listed above.

Decision: The critical value at the 0.05 level of significance in this case for N=3 and K=4 is 7.4. Reject the null hypothesis because the F_r value is higher than the critical value. Conclude that the ability to recall is affected.

Efficiency: The power efficiency of Friedman's test is affected by the number of columns or conditions in the test. Compared with the F test, the power efficiency of this test is 0.64 when k=2 (k being number of columns or categories), and goes up to 0.91 when k=20. Similarly, the asymptotic relative efficiency of this test depends on the nature of the underlying population distribution.

Analogous parametric test: F test.

Analogous related nonparametric test(s): Page test for ordered alternatives.

Mann-Whitney-Wilcoxon Test. A combination of different procedures are used to calculate the probability of two independent samples being drawn from the same population or two populations with equal means. This group of tests is analogous to the t-test, and can be used with fewer assumptions, and uses rank sums.

Example: Table 6 lists the verbal ability scores for a group of boys and a group of girls who are

TABLE 4
Scores of Three Groups by Four Levels of Sleep Deprivation

Conditions	I	II	III	IV
Group 1	7	4	2	6
Group 2	6	4	2	9
Group 3	10	3	2	7

TABLE 5
Rank of Three Groups by Four Levels of Sleep Deprivation

Ranks	I	II	III	IV
	4	2	1	3
	3	2	1	4
	4	2	1	3
	R_j=11	6	3	10

TABLE 6
Verbal Scores for Boys and Girls < 1 Year Old

Boys N_1 (sample A): 10, 15, 18, 28
Girls N_2 (sample B): 12, 14, 20, 22, 25, 30, 30, 31, 32

less than one year old. (The scores are arranged in ascending order for each of the groups.) Do the data provide evidence for significant differences in verbal ability of boys and girls?

Mann-Whitney-Wilcoxon U Test

The following formulas may be used to calculate U.

$$U_1 = N_1N_2 + \frac{N_1(N_1 + 1)}{2} - R_1$$

$$U_2 = N_1N_2 + \frac{N_2(N_2 + 1)}{2} - R_2$$

$$R_1 = 1 + 4 + 5 + 9 = 19$$

$$R_2 = 2 + 3 + 6 + 7 + 8 + 10.5 + 10.5 + 12 + 13 = 72$$

R_1 and R_2 refer to the sum of ranks for group 1 and group 2, respectively.
$U_2 = (4)(9) + [9(9 + 1)/2] - 72 = 9$ and $U_1 = 27$, for $U_1 + U_2 = (N_1N_2) = 36$.

Illustrative Assumptions: Samples are independent. Ordinal data.

Hypotheses: Two-sided test is used in this example.

H_0: $Md_1 = Md_2$. There are no significant differences in the verbal ability of boys and girls.

H_1: Md_1 j Md_2. There is a significant difference in the verbal ability of boys and girls.

Test statistic or procedures: Rearrange all the scores in an ascending or descending order (see Table 7). The test statistic is U_1 or U_2 and the calculations are illustrated above.

Decision: Retain null hypothesis. At the 0.05 level, we fail to reject the null hypothesis of no difference in verbal ability. The rejection region for U in this case is 4 or smaller for samples of 4 and 9.

Efficiency: For large samples, the power efficiency approaches 95 percent.

Analogous parametric test: F test.

Related nonparametric test(s): Behrens-Fisher problem test, robust rank order test.

Z can be used as a normal approximation if $N>12$, or N_1 or $N_2 > 10$

$$Z=\frac{R_1-R_2-(N_1-N_2)(N+1)/2}{\sqrt{N_i\,N_2(N+1)/3}}$$

Dispersion. Dispersion refers to spread or variability. Dispersion measures are intended to test for equality of dispersion in two populations.

The two-tailed null hypothesis in the Ansari-Bradley-type tests and Moses-type tests assumes that there is no difference in the dispersion of the populations. The Ansari-Bradley test assumes equal medians in the population. The Moses test has wider applicability because it does not make that assumption.

Dispersion tests are not widely used because of the limitations on the tests imposed by the assumptions, the low power efficiency of the tests, or both.

Goodness-of-Fit. This test is a one-sample design that allows for nominal data scales. Because chi-square techniques are used to test the goodness-of-fit, these measures are also

TABLE 7
Ranked Verbal Scores for Boys and Girls < 1 Year Old

Scores:	10	12	14	15	18	20	22	25	28	30	30	31	32
Rank:	1	2	3	4	5	6	7	8	9	10.5	10.5	12	13
Comp:	A	B	B	A	A	B	B	B	A	B	B	B	B

called chi-square goodness-of-fit tests. A specific distribution is postulated for the presumed population in the null hypothesis. The observed frequencies in the sample are compared against the expected distribution in the population to assess the probability that the observed frequencies could have been sampled from that population.

Goodness-of-fit tests would be used in making decisions based on the prior knowledge of the population; for example, sentence length in a new manuscript compared with that in other works by an author to decide whether the manuscript is by that author; or a manager's observation of a greater number of accidents in the factory on some days of the week as compared to the average figures could be tested for significant differences. Test procedures used in X^2 are applicable to goodness-of-fit measures. The expected frequency of accidents is based on the assumption of no differences in the number of accidents by days of the week.

The Kolmogorov-Smirnov test is another major goodness-of-fit test. It has two versions, the one-sample and the two-sample tests. It is different from the chi-square goodness-of-fit in that the Kolmogorov-Smirnov test is based on observed and expected differences in cumulative distribution functions and can be used with individual values instead of having to group them.

Association. There are two major approaches to measures of association. The consist of: (1) measurements of the degree of association among the variables, and (2) measures to test the existence (relationship) or nonexistence (independence) of association among the variables. Different measures of association are utilized in the analysis of nominal and nominal data, nominal and ordinal data, nominal and interval data, ordinal and ordinal data, and ordinal and interval data.

Measures belonging to the first category include Spearman's rank correlation coefficient (one of the oldest nonparametric techniques) and Kendall's tau coefficients. A number of other measures, such as gamma statistic, Somer's index of asymmetric association, phi coefficient, biserial coefficient, and point and interval estimates of the population, also fall into this category.

Kendall's tau is a measure of correlation and also tests for independence of the two variables observed. It assumes at least ordinal data. The values of tau range from -1 to $=1$. The asymptotic relative efficiency of tau is in the 0.9 range.

Tau_a may be used when there are no ties
Tau_b is a modified corrected formula for ties
Tau_c is used in the case of grouped data

X^2 test is an example of the second approach to measures of association. It is a test of independence between two or more variables. X^2 is one of the most useful and widely used nonparametric tests. The test can be used either with nominal or other types of data and may consist of one or more samples.

Runs and Randomness. A run is a gambling term that in statistics refers to a sequence or order of occurrence of events; for example, if a coin were tossed ten times, it could result in the following sequence of heads and tails: H T H H H T T H H T. The purpose of runs test is to test and determine whether the run or sequence of events occurs in a random order.

Another type of runs test would be to test whether the run scores are higher or lower than the median scores. A runs up-and-down test compares each observation with the one immediately preceding it in the sequence. Runs tests are not very robust, as they are very sensitive to variations in the data.

As there are no direct parallel parametric tests for testing the random order or sequence of a series of events, the concept of power or efficiency is not really relevant in the case of runs tests.

Linear Regression. The purpose of regression tests and techniques is to predict one variable based on its relationship with one or more other variables. The procedure most often used is to try to fit a regression line based on observed data. Only a few simple linear regression techniques are included in Table 1. This is one of the more active areas in the field of nonparametric statistics.

Trends and Changes. Comparisons between before and after experiment scores are among the most commonly used procedures of research designs. The obvious question in such cases is whether there is a pattern of change and, if so, whether the trends can be detected. Demographers, economists, executives in business and industry, and the departments of commerce are always interested in trends—whether downward, upward, or existing at all. The Cox-Stuart change test or test for trend is a procedure intended to answer these kinds of questions. It is a modification of the sign test. The procedures are very similar to the sign test.

Example: We want to test a statement in the newspaper that there is no changing trend in snowfall in Kalamazoo between the last twenty years and twenty years before that. The assumptions, procedures, and test procedures are similar to the sign test. These data constitute twenty sets of paired observations. If the data are not chronological, then values below the median and above the median would be matched in order. The value in the second observation in the set is compared to the first and would be coded as positive or plus, negative or minus, and no change. A large number of positive or negative signs would indicate a trend and the same number of positive and negative signs would indicate no trend. The distribution here is dichotomous, and hence a binomial test would be used. If there are seven positive signs and thirteen negative signs, it can be concluded that there is no statistically significant upward or downward trend in snowfall at the 0.05 level as $p(k=7/20/0.50)$ is greater, k being the number of positive signs. The asymptotic relative efficiency of the test compared to rank correlation is 0.79. Spearman's coefficient of rank correlation and Kendall's tau may also be used to test for trends.

Proportion. The terms *portion* or *share* are also used to convey the same idea in day-to-day usage. A sociologist might be interested in the proportion of working and nonworking mothers in the labor force, or in comparing the differences in the proportion of people who voted in a local election and the voter turnout in a national election. In case of a dichotomous situation, a binomial test can be used as a test of proportion. But there are many other situations where more than two categories and two or more independent samples are involved. In such cases, the chi-square distribution may also be viewed as a test of differences in proportion between two or more samples.

Cochran's Q test is another test of proportions that is applicable to situations with dichotomous choices or outcomes for three or more related samples. For example, in the context of an experimental situation, the null hypothesis would be that there is no difference in the effectiveness of treatments. Restated, it is a statement of equal proportions of success or failures in the treatments.

NEW DEVELOPMENTS

There are many new developments taking place in the field of nonparametric statistics to be included here. Only two major trends are referenced here. The scope of application of nonparametric tests is gradually expanding. Often, more than one nonparametric test may be available to test the same or similar hypotheses. Again, many new appropriate and powerful nonparametric tests are being developed to replace or supplement the original parametric tests.

Many topics and subtopics in nonparametric statistics have developed into full-fledged specialties or subspecialties, such as extreme value statistics, which is used in studying floods, air pollution, and other types of extreme values. Similarly, a large number of new techniques and concepts—such as (1) the influence curve for comparing different robust estimators, (2)*M*-estimators for generalizations that extend the scope of traditional location tests, and (3) adaptive estimation procedures for dealing with unknown distribution—are being developed in the field of inferential statistics. Attention is also being directed to the development of measures and tests with nonlinear data. These trends are expected to contribute to the development of nonparametric statistics and a more precise assessment of its utility. In addition, some tentative attempts are being made by nonparametric statisticians to incorporate other branches of statistics, such as Bayesian statistics.

Parallel Trends in Development. There are two parallel developments in nonparametric and parametric statistics. first, the field of nonpatametric statistics is being extended to develop more tests analogous to parametric tests. Recent developments in computer software include many of the new nonparametric tests and alternatives to parametric tests. Second, the field of parametric statistics is being extended to develop and incorporate more robust tests to increase the stability of parametric tests. The study of outliers, for example, is now gaining significant attention in the field of parametric statistics.

Recent advancements have accelerated parallel developments in nonparametric and parametric statistics, narrowing many distinctions and bridging some of the differences between the two types, and bringing the two fields conceptually closer.

(SEE ALSO: *Measurement; Measures of Association; Statistical Inference)*

REFERENCES

Blalock, Hubert M., Jr. 1979 *Social Statistics,* rev. 2nd ed. New York: McGraw-Hill.

Bohrnstedt, George W., and David Knoke 1988 *Statistics for Social Data Analyses,* 2nd ed. Ithaca, N.Y.: Peacock.

Daniel, Wayne W. 1990 *Applied Nonparametric Statistics,* 2nd ed. Boston: PWS-KENT.

Gibbons, Jean Dixon 1986 "Distribution-Free Methods." In S. Kotz and N. L. Johnson, eds., *Encyclopedia of Statistical Sciences,* Vol. 2. New York: Wiley.

Hare, A. Paul, Edgar F. Borgatta, and Robert F. Bales 1955 *Small Groups: Studies in Social Interaction.* New York: Knopf.

Hettmansperger, Thomas P. 1984 *Statistical Inference Based on Ranks.* New York: Wiley.

Krauth, Joachim 1988 *Distribution-Free Statistics: An Application-Oriented Approach.* Amsterdam: Elsevier.

Neave, H. R., and P. L. Worthington 1988 *Distribution-Free Tests.* London: Unwin Hyman.

Savage, I. R. 1962 *Bibliography of Nonparametric Statistics.* Cambridge: Harvard University Press.

Siegel, Sidney 1956 *Nonparametric Statistics for the Behavioral Sciences.* New York: McGraw-Hill.

——— and N. John Castellan, Jr. 1988 *Nonparametric Statistics for the Behavioral Sciences,* 2nd ed. New York: McGraw-Hill.

Sprent, P. 1989 *Applied Nonparametric Statistical Methods.* London: Chapman and Hall.

SUBHASH R. SONNAD

NURSING HOMES Long-term care of the elderly in the United States has generally been provided in the context of institutional settings that are broadly classified as nursing homes. Nursing homes are primarily oriented toward treating chronic, long-term patients and provide less technically sophisticated forms of treatment than general hospitals. Medicare and Medicaid certify nursing homes as eligible for reimbursement based on the level and quality of care provided. Until recently the levels of such facilities ranged from certified skilled nursing facilities (SNFs), which provided twenty-four-hour nursing services under registered nurse (RN) supervision, to intermediate care facilities (ICFs), which provided less extensive nursing service and more custodial-oriented care to older persons capable of more independent living (Sirrocco 1989). However, since the Nursing Home Reform Act was passed in 1987, ICFs have been required to provide the same range of services as the SNFs, thus eliminating the need for a distinction in terms. All nursing homes are now classified as nursing facilities (NFs) (Richardson 1990).

Nursing homes are of interest to sociologists on both the macro and the micro level. On the macro level they reflect society's orientation to financing, regulating, and delivering long-term care services to its older and/or frail citizens who are no longer capable of fully autonomous community living. Sociologists have been particularly interested in those factors affecting long-term care delivery which reflect social construction of the reality of the lives of marginal individuals such as the aged.

On a micro level nursing homes represent

formal organizations that regulate and control the daily lives of frail elders while providing them with medical and social care. The tension between expectations for rehabilitative or prosthetic services and actual delivery of palliative care or dependency-inducing treatment with iatrogenic consequences has been a particular source of fascination and concern to sociologists (Goffmann 1961; Kahana, Kahana, and Riley 1989). Complementing this interest has been the search for understanding person-environment interactions, interpersonal and intergroup relationships involving residents, staff, and families within the institutional context (Gubrium 1975; Johnson and Grant 1985).

Even as we aim to review sociological contributions to the understanding of nursing homes, it is important to note that information about this subject has been obtained through the research efforts of diverse disciplines, with epidemiologists, political scientists, social workers, psychologists, nurses, and physicians all contributing to the literature. In fact, medical sociologists have focused their investigation primarily on acute health care delivery in general hospitals, and many of the theoretical constructs they have developed are more applicable to acute illness than to chronic disability (Wolinsky 1988). Consequently, this discussion of the nursing home draws upon multidisciplinary sources.

The following discussion about nursing homes will be divided into an introductory section providing background demographic and statistical information followed by a discussion of macrolevel issues focused on the nursing home as an institution. There is also a section dealing with microlevel, resident-focused issues. The article will conclude with a discussion of emerging trends in nursing home care and the future of nursing homes in the United States.

MODELS OF CARE IN NURSING HOMES

Nursing homes have developed from two traditions reflecting different orientations to care. The medical model of care considers nursing homes as health care institutions designed to deliver high-quality chronic care to patients. As such, nursing homes are expected to provide competent and well-trained personnel to meet health care needs of patients. In principle, the criterion for successful care is improved health of the patient. In practice, quality of care is generally approached by the organization through adherence to certain standards of care delivery, such as adequate staff recruitment and training, and high staff-patient ratios (Nyman and Geyer 1989).

The social model (Kane and Kane 1978) considers the nursing home to be a sheltered housing arrangement for older adults who can no longer function independently in the community. The goal of a successful nursing home is ensuring good quality of life for residents through encouragement of maximum autonomy in a homelike setting. The criterion for successful care is defined in terms of sustained psychosocial well-being, self-esteem, and life satisfaction of residents. While medical definitions of care dictate provision of diagnostic and treatment activities, social definitions suggest emphasis on comfort, choice, and adaptation. Advocates of quality-of-life approaches have often argued for major redirection in the way of handling long-term care. They seek greater support for the home-based rather than the institutional-based model of care (Brody 1985).

The very term *nursing home* embodies the dual aspects of care provided in such settings or, alternatively, the ambivalence of society about the needs that are to be met and the services that are to be delivered. Accordingly, the literature refers to nursing home occupants as either patients or residents. While the former implies a medical orientation and the latter reflects social definitions, it has become accepted practice to use these terms interchangeably. Nor is research on the effects of institutional living governed exclusively by principles of social or medical definitions of care. Focus on the medical model may be most useful for understanding prevailing efforts by society to ensure high-quality care through regulation. Focus on the social model is particularly salient for governing research on the effects of institutionalization on the individual.

UTILIZATION OF NURSING HOMES

In 1986, 4.3 percent of American elderly over the age of sixty-five were residing in nursing homes (Sirrocco 1988). However, rates of institutionalization over time for any given individual over age sixty-five are considerably higher (9 to 12 percent), and the risk of residing in a nursing home just prior to death increases to over 26 percent (Wingard et al. 1987). Furthermore, old-old persons aged eighty-five and older have a much higher likelihood of living in a nursing home (23.7 percent) than those aged sixty-five to seventy-four (1.2 percent) (Sirrocco 1989). Although the vast majority of nursing home residents are elderly, about 10 percent are younger than sixty-five (Burns et al. 1988).

The majority of nursing home placements are due to a combination of functional impairments, mental infirmity, and unavailability of caregivers (Rovner et al. 1986; Wingard et al. 1987; Sirrocco 1989). It has been noted that for every frail elder living in a nursing home, there are at least two elderly with comparable impairments living in the community (General Accounting Office 1977). Older women are twice as likely as older men to reside in nursing homes, both because of their longevity and because they are more likely to be widowed and without caregivers (Densen 1987). Accordingly, 71 percent of nursing home residents are women. Blacks are underrepresented in nursing homes compared with whites (Sirrocco 1989). Both greater willingness of black families to care for elders and barriers to utilization of nursing homes by minorities have been cited as possible reasons for these differences.

The majority of elderly enter a nursing home immediately after discharge from an acute care hospital. Most of these elderly need ongoing medical care and often require rehospitalization (Densen 1987). Others enter a nursing home directly from the community due to multiple risk factors including physical and cognitive frailty and nonavailability of caregivers. In addition, some elderly were transferred to nursing homes from mental hospitals during the era of deinstitutionalization of the mentally ill.

Nursing homes generally provide custodial or palliative rather than rehabilitative care. Although there has been recent emphasis on the role of nursing homes as short-term rehabilitative facilities, few in fact offer intensive rehabilitative programs. There is evidence that patients who stay for ninety days or more in nursing facilities are likely to remain there for the rest of their lives (Brody 1985). Nevertheless, about one-third of nursing home patients eventually return to the community (Lewis et al. 1985). Another noteworthy recent trend is the increasing use of nursing homes for short-term respite care that provides caregivers with a break from providing assistance to frail elders (Burdz et al. 1988).

DISTRIBUTION AND ORGANIZATION

As of 1986 there were about 16,400 nursing homes in the United States with approximately 1.5 million beds, reflecting an average nursing home size of 92 beds (Sirrocco 1989). Over 75 percent of nursing homes are proprietary, about 20 percent are nonprofit, and 5 percent are government-sponsored facilities (Richardson 1990). As of 1985, 41 percent of all nursing homes were run by large, commercial organizations operating a group or chain of facilities (Richardson 1990).

There is a discrepancy in the rate of utilization and number of homes according to geographical locale. The Northeast has the highest occupancy rates and highest utilization rates for nursing homes. However, they have some of the lowest bed rates (number of beds available). The aged in the Midwest have the greatest number of nursing home beds available to them. The lowest utilization percentages and lowest bed rates are in Hawaii, Arizona, Florida, and Nevada (Sirrocco 1989).

These rates of occupancy may be influenced by migration patterns. Many retirees may move to warmer "Sunbelt" regions when they are in good health, in order to seek a better life-style and improved quality of life. However, failing health and the desire to be close to family during times of illness may influence these migrants to return to their states of origin (Longino 1990). Such moves and countermoves may affect the utilization rates of nursing homes in certain regions.

FINANCING

It has been argued that in the United States funding mechanisms have been largely responsible for shaping the delivery of health care in general and the delivery of long-term care in particular (Kane and Kane 1990). Acute and rehabilitative health care of the aged has generally been financed by Medicare, a universal age-based entitlement program. Most nursing home costs, however, are not covered by Medicare.The majority of nursing home care, an estimated 70 percent, is paid for by the need-based, state-administered, third-party payment program of Medicaid. Most elderly start their nursing home stays as privately paying patients. Nursing home care, in fact, represents the major portion (82.5 percent) of out-of-pocket health care expenses of the elderly (Rice 1989). After personal resources are depleted (usually in less than a year), patients become eligible for Medicaid financing. Private nursing home insurance has been advocated as an important protection for older adults, but only very limited coverage is available (Rivlin and Weiner 1988).

Escalating health care costs, along with increased utilization of nursing homes by growing segments of the old-old, have resulted in increased federal and state expenditures for long-term care services. In 1985 costs of nursing home care accounted for 36 billion dollars nationally, with 14.7 billion dollars covered by Medicaid. There is growing pressure for cost containment to reduce those burdens, and in response there have been suggestions ranging from rationing of health care to the old to shifting the burden of financing health care to families (Callahan 1987). Efforts directed at cost containment through reduced payments for care pose a serious threat to provision of high-quality services. In addition, the profit motive inherent in proprietary health care may be seen as posing a conflict of interest with provision of high-quality care. This link among sponsorship, financing, and quality of care is evidenced by successful lobbying efforts of the nursing home industry to cut back on funds for nursing home inspections (Williams 1986).

ENSURING STANDARDS OF NURSING HOME CARE

Ensuring high quality of care and standards for services has posed a major challenge to the nursing home field (Vladeck 1980). Problems have been encountered in terms of poor staff training, high staff turnover rates, and limited physician involvement (Johnson and Grant 1985). Social workers, psychologists, and occupational and physical therapists are typically involved in patient care only as consultants rather than as full time staff (Kane and Kane 1978). Nurses' aides, staff members with the most limited training and education and at the lowest end of the pay scale, provide a majority of the patient care in nursing homes (Stannard 1973). Evidence of poor quality of care has been noted by Vladeck (1980), who states that the most common diagnoses among nursing home residents admitted to general hospitals include infections and bedsores. There is also evidence of inappropriate use and overuse of drugs, in particular psychotropic medications, in nursing homes (Beers et al. 1988). In an observational study of a large variety of nursing homes, Gottesman and Bourestom (1974) documented that inactivity among residents and neglect by staff were common. Instances of patient abuse have been cited, although there is no clear evidence that abuse is a widespread problem (Stannard 1973).

Alternative approaches to ensuring standards for services have been advanced through regulation or free market economy (Nyman and Geyer 1989). Regulation seeks to enforce high quality of care through staffing standards, care plans, and result audits. In general, it aims to ensure the most basic aspects of quality of care, such as appropriate medication use, sanitary living conditions, sufficient exercise, adequate diet, and at least limited privacy for residents. Regulatory efforts are widely employed and have had at least limited success in defining and monitoring quality of health care. However, regulation is seen by some as a costly and often ineffective approach that is dependent on enforcement of a limited set of universally agreed-upon standards (Nyman and Geyer 1989).

In free market competition, consumers do the work of raising quality by making informed choices and purchasing high-quality services. Ensuring standards through the use of the free market economy rests on the assumption that the consumer has researched the market and will choose to reside in a facility that provides the best care. Third-party payment systems limit the effectiveness of consumers in exercising market choices. Severely impaired nursing home patients (who lack family or advocates) are also limited in their ability to exercise sufficient rational market choice for ensuring nursing home quality.

Alternative approaches to improving quality of care have been noted in addition to those of regulation or competition. For example, increased community involvement may enhance care by increasing public awareness and accountability. Community advocacy programs that involve local citizens to press for patient rights and improved care delivery have been found to be useful (Williams 1986).

The Omnibus Reconciliation Act (OBRA) of 1987 represents a major step in the direction of federal legislation for improving and bringing nursing home care in the United States up to a uniform standard. This legislative act set federal standards for care in homes funded by Medicare and Medicaid. Based on a study conducted by the Institute of Medicine (1986), the Health Care Financing Administration set forth guidelines for ensuring uniform standards for nursing home care. OBRA uses a two-pronged approach that addresses both quality of care and quality of life. Quality of care is addressed by increasing nursing and social work staff in nursing homes and improving training for nurses' aides. OBRA also enforces a regulation that sets standards of care by increasing financial sanctions for noncompliance. Accordingly, noncompliant homes could be subject to fines and have Medicaid and Medicare payments withheld.

In an effort to enhance quality of life, OBRA mandates a national system for resident assessments and institutes activity programs to meet individual needs (Morris et al. 1990). It guarantees patients' rights to privacy and to freedom from chemical and physical restraints, and supports patient autonomy by encouraging resident participation in treatment decisions. It also provides patients with the freedom to choose their own physicians.

Regulations and policies mandated by OBRA came into effect in 1990. Thus, it is too early to assess the actual impact of this legislation on quality of nursing home care in the United States. It is also important to recognize that even if they are successful, regulatory efforts cannot transform nursing homes into sophisticated rehabilitation facilities. Nor can the basic character of the nursing home as an institution be restructured to provide a truly homelike environment that approximates community living (Kahana 1973).

FOCUS ON THE NURSING HOME RESIDENT: EFFECTS OF INSTITUTIONALIZATION

We will now consider those aspects of institutionalization that impact on the experiences, lifestyles, and well-being of the individuals who enter even the best of nursing homes. To do so we will shift our focus from the macro or societal level to the micro or individual or small group level of analysis. It is primarily this area of inquiry, relating social processes to the life experiences of the individual patient, to which sociologists have addressed their research on nursing homes. Considering the individual resident in the context of the physical and social milieu of a given institution, we can appreciate both the factors which induce negative reactions and those resources which facilitate positive responses to institutionalization. On this level of analysis, the sociologist moves away from considering the patient as a mere object of care and notes the interactive nature of the encounter between the institutionalized person and elements within the nursing home environment.

The problems brought about by institutionalization go beyond problems of quality health care and in fact may inhere in the very nature of congregate care. Accordingly, sociologists have recognized that the nursing home, by its very nature, represents a unique social context with homogenizing qualities, and that even in the best facility providing high-quality care, there are alterations in normal patterns of interaction and social exchange.

Goffmann's (1961) classical depiction of the total institution still serves as a standard for understanding the problems of institutional living. The total institution is described as a place where inmates are brought together under a common authority, are stripped of their normal identities, and are expected to engage in activities of daily living according to formal rules and a rational plan that regiments them. Activities of work, play, and sleep overlap and are typically conducted in the presence of others. The institution (which is often located at a distance from friends and the previous community of the resident) also effectively cuts residents off from social ties in the outside world. It has been suggested that among nursing home residents, isolation from society and loss of control over one's life lead to learned helplessness (Avorn and Langer 1982; Baltes 1982).

Frail older persons who typically enter nursing homes are particularly vulnerable because of physical and mental infirmities and loss of social supports that have created the need for such placement (Johnson and Grant 1985; Kahana, Kahana, and Kinney 1990). Such vulnerable individuals are particularly sensitive to environmental change, adverse environmental conditions, and stress (Lawton 1980). Elderly living in the community generally fear institutional placement and seldom plan for a move to an institution (Kahana, Kahana, and Young 1985). Anticipation of entering an institution has been found to be particularly stressful; it is associated with diminished morale and self-esteem, and even cognitive disorganization (Tobin and Lieberman 1976).

The transition to living in a nursing home is typically involuntary, with patients seldom playing major roles in the decision. Physicians and hospital social workers have been found to be most influential in decision making (York and Calsyn 1977). Furthermore, the new setting is unfamiliar in terms of both physical features and social expectations. Less than half of family members visit facilities prior to placement of an elder. Schultz and Brenner (1977) reviewed research on relocation stress as it pertains to institutional placements and concluded that unpredictability and uncontrollability are major risk factors accounting for the negative outcomes of institutional relocation.

It is difficult to establish conclusively which elements of institutionalization are responsible for negative outcomes among residents because the effects of morbidity, relocation, and institutionalization occur concurrently and are difficult to separate. Yet the negative personal consequences of life in total institutions have been documented in terms of loss of self-esteem and future orientation, withdrawal, apathy, and depression (Gubrium 1975; Vladeck 1980; Isaacs et al. 1972). Collectively these ill effects have been referred to as depersonalization (Townsend 1962). Ill effects of institutionalization have also been demonstrated in terms of both physical and psychological decline, particularly during the first year of institutional living (Lieberman and Tobin 1983).

In spite of evidence of adverse effects of institutionalization, there is a growing body of research and clinical observations that documents positive features and potential benefits of residential life in nursing homes. The term *nursing home* implies residence in a social unit, akin to a family, where members are connected by expressive functions (Johnson and Grant 1985). For isolated older persons who can no longer care for themselves, the nursing home can offer protection and improved living conditions. Advantages of living in a nursing home can also include behavioral expectations that are well matched with the competencies of the frail resident (Lawton 1980).

Nutritious meals, regular medical care, and supervised administration of medications may maximize health for frail elders living in nursing homes. Proximity to other residents allows for social needs to be met, and organized activities can lead to meaningful social participation. Indeed, there is some evidence that resident satisfaction subsequent to institutionalization exceeds expectations (Kahana, Kahana, and Young 1985). Some studies have noted improved morale (Spasoff et al. 1978) and enhanced family relationships subsequent to institutionalization of elders (Smith and Bengtson 1979).

Residents of nursing homes have been found to perceive less stress attributed to recent life events than do community-living elderly (Stein et al. 1983). The nursing home may thus be viewed as a supportive setting that shelters elderly from responsibilities of decision making and helps them cope with stress. Well-being among residents subsequent to institutionalization may reflect not only positive influences of institutional life but also the resilience and survival skills of residents. Accordingly, Lieberman and Tobin (1983) demonstrated that even in the face of major involuntary environmental changes such as institutionalization, many elderly continue to preserve a coherent and consistent self-image.

THE RESIDENT AS AN ACTIVE RESPONDER: ADAPTATION IN INSTITUTIONS

The major focus of research on institutional living has been on older persons as objects, victims at worst and beneficiaries at best, of institutional influences. Yet there is growing evidence supporting the view that residents are active agents who attach meaning to and actively impact their environment (Kahana, Kahana, and Young 1985).

Goffmann (1961) describes a range of adaptive responses among inmates of total institutions. *Withdrawal* refers to the resident's efforts to curtail interaction with others and to withhold emotional investment in his/her surroundings. *Intransigence* is a response that challenges institutional authority through noncooperation. These two modes of responding are likely to result in further alienation and to invite negative responses from staff and other residents. *Colonization* represents a strategy of maximizing satisfactions within the confines of the institution through accepting the rules and norms of institutional life. *Conversion* represents an identification with both outward characteristics and values of staff. Patients who opt for conversion submerge their identities into their patient roles. Although Goffmann's conceptualization and description provide the earliest and possibly richest sociological efforts to understand resident adaptation in nursing homes, there has been little follow-up research to confirm the typologies he proposed.

Research has documented that there are active efforts even among institutionalized elderly to adapt to demands and stresses of institutional living (Tobin and Lieberman 1976). Instrumental coping strategies have been associated with maintenance of psychological well-being subsequent to institutionalization, whereas affective modes of coping have been related to decline in morale (Kahana, Kahana, and Young 1987).

Appraisals of life in a nursing home may contribute greatly to perceptions of stress, coping responses, and ultimately to adaptive outcomes. In fact, an understanding of the interpretive meaning of institutional life may help integrate conflicting findings about effects of selection, relocation, and institutionalization on psychosocial well-being of elders residing in nursing homes.

Aspects of physical frailty that create a need for institutional placement, along with perceived or real abandonment by family, require major reappraisals of both one's worldview and one's self-concept. Given a vulnerable self and loss of intimacy with significant others, the safety of one's physical and social milieu becomes a critical concern. To the extent that new residents of nursing homes can appraise their physical and social environment as safe, and other residents who comprise their new reference group as intact, satisfied, and helpful, instrumental adaptations may be possible and depersonalization may be avoided. Accordingly, research by Kahana, Kahana, Sterin, Fedirko, and Brittis (1990) reveals that perceptions of even minor acts of helpfulness by other residents help institutionalized elderly reinterpret their surroundings as benign. Formation of social ties with other patients or social integration represents an important mode of positive adaptation for nursing home residents. About half of institutionalized elderly form friendships with fellow residents (Miller 1986).

Personal backgrounds of residents as well as environmental influences affect adaptations that residents make in institutions. Lack of mental impairment and few mobility limitations and sensory deficits are associated with maintenance of close social ties within the nursing home (Bitzan and Kruzich 1990). Personality and cognitive traits such as impulse control have been found to be associated with psychosocial well-being subsequent to institutionalization (Kahana and Kahana 1976). The potential interactions of the institutional setting with personal orientations are illustrated in findings that external rather than internal locus of control predicts high morale in institutional settings (Felton and Kahana 1974). It is likely that in environments where there is little opportunity for personal control, residents who realistically appraise their situations make the best adjustment.

PERSON-ENVIRONMENT INTERACTION IN NURSING HOMES

In order to better understand and operationalize person-environment transactions in nursing homes, several conceptual models have been articulated that take into account both personal and environmental features. Lawton's (1980) ecological model focuses on the importance of matching environmental elements to personal competencies of frail elders. Kahana's (1982) person-environment congruence model emphasizes the role of individual differences in needs and environmental preferences, and specifies alternative formulations for expected outcomes based on oversupply, undersupply, or congruence of environmental characteristics, such as stimulation or homogeneity, in relation to personal preferences.

Interactionist perspectives lead to a better understanding of social influences in nursing homes by calling attention to the importance of both personal reactions and environmental presses. Environmental design and intervention approaches in nursing homes have focused on changing personal competencies of residents by providing environments that benefit residents in general, or interventions that improve fit between the environment and personal needs of residents. Furthermore, specification of salient dimensions of the institutional milieu has been one important area of progress toward designing better nursing home environments. Moos (1978) has conducted pioneering work in providing reliable and valid indicators of social dimensions of the institutional environment.

Specific components of the institutional environment that determine the demands, constraints, and benefits of institutional life include the administrative structure, the physical environment, and the social environment. The social environment may be further subdivided into staff environment, patient environment, and environmental input from community representatives such as volunteers, or friends and family, who visit the resident in the institution. Research on administrative structure has focused primarily on size, financing, and type of ownership. Although it has been argued that proprietary ownership may result in poorer quality of care, the link between type of ownership and level of care has not been conclusively established. Similarly suggested links between size of home or proportion of Medicaid patients and quality of care have not been fully documented (Johnson and Grant 1985).

Staffing patterns have also been associated with the quality of care provided. Specifically, a major study of one thousand male patients transferred from general medical hospitals to nursing homes (Linn et al. 1977) found that a higher professional staff to patient ratio predicted patients' survival, improvement, or discharge six months after entering the home. Negative staff attitudes, poor staff training, and high turnover rates have adverse effects on patient care (Johnson and Grant 1985; Wright 1988). There is evidence that intrusive and excessive assistance in self-care activities can result in learned helplessness among nursing home residents (Avorn and Langer 1982). Conversely, positive staff interventions with residents may enhance autonomy (Kahana and Kiyak 1984).

Similarities in ethnic, cultural, and social backgrounds of staff and residents appear to facilitate positive interactions, whereas discrepancies in cultural values have been found to hamper communication and mutual understanding (Kahana, Kahana, Sterin, Fedirko, and Taylor 1991; Harel 1987). Institutional norms as well as formal policies have been found to shape the impact of institutions on residents (Kiyak et al. 1978).

The patient environment in the nursing home presents an important influence in terms of homogeneity or heterogeneity of resident composition. Widespread practices of functional integration in nursing homes surround "well" residents with those who manifest disruptive behavior due to mental health problems or mental impairment. While such combined living arrangements may be beneficial to the more impaired residents, they can have adverse consequences for the better-functioning ones (Kahana, Kahana, and Riley 1989).

Interactions with family also play an important role in social integration of residents. Research has underscored that the majority of institutionalized elderly continue to maintain meaningful ties and interactions with family members (York and Calsyn 1977; Smith and Bengtson 1979). Ties appear closest to children who visit most frequently (Bitzan and Kruzich 1990), followed by other family members and friends (Kahana, Kahana, and Young 1985). Proximity of family members and previous history of extensive social interactions facilitate continued contact (York and Calsyn 1977). In turn, visitation by families and friends has been associated with enhanced residential functioning and well-being (Greene and Monahan 1982).

While sociologists have generally focused on the specification of broad social features of nursing homes that impact on the life and welfare of the resident, psychologists, nurses, and social workers have been more involved in implementing specific and usually limited intervention efforts in nursing homes. Direct interventions to improve functioning and/or quality of life in nursing homes have been limited by absence of systematic theories, on the one hand, and lack of commitment of needed resources, on the other. Diverse efforts to improve care have generally yielded some success, suggesting that almost any type of intervention can improve the quality of life or functioning of residents. Interventions may be broadly classified as those aiming to improve the physical or social environment of the setting, and those aiming to improve coping strategies, psychosocial well-being, or cognitive functioning of residents.

Intergenerational programs that promote interaction between nursing home residents and children or young adults have been found to be successful in enhancing quality of life for nursing home patients as well as young children (Newman 1985). Such programs have generally been found to improve activities and social interactions of the elderly. Reality orientation has been a therapeutic strategy aimed at reinforcing orientation to time, place, and person among cognitively impaired elderly (Whanger 1980). Fantasy validation therapy takes a divergent view, providing acceptance to nursing home patients through expressing empathy in response to unrealistic beliefs or behaviors (Feil 1982).

Behavioristic approaches to treatment of psychiatric problems in nursing homes include reinforcement of appropriate behaviors through token economies or habit training (Whanger 1980). Educational opportunities to enhance competent coping strategies have also been advocated (Kahana and Kahana 1983). Focusing on the physical environment, prosthetically designed environments in nursing homes have been found to retard decline among mentally impaired elderly (Lawton et al. 1984). Milieu therapy is a systematic approach to enhancing all aspects of the social and physical environment in order to encourage social interactions among residents (Coons 1978).

As illustrated in the above discussion of environmental influences and interventions in nursing homes, much of the empirical work relevant to person-environment transactions focuses on only one of the two related influences: the patient or the milieu. Thus, while conceptual frameworks recognize the dynamic nature of person-institution transactions, operationalization of these complex interactions has not yet been widely implemented.

CONCLUSIONS

The foregoing discussion highlighted a series of counterpoints in consideration of nursing home care on the macro and micro levels. On the macro level distinctions between medical and social models of care, quality of care, and quality of life issues have been discussed. Societal needs for cost containment have been juxtaposed with the need to invest greater resources in long-term care to ensure provision of high-quality care. Regulation and free market competition have been presented as alternative strategies to improve standards of care.

On a micro level we have noted evidence for depersonalizing aspects of institutional living along with data about protective features and benefits of long-term care environments. Furthermore, residents of nursing homes have been described as frail and vulnerable, on the one hand, and as adaptable and resilient, on the other. Ultimate well-being of nursing home residents is seen as a function of the environment, of the person, or of transactions between the two. These dualities are useful to propel dialogue and permit a thorough examination of nursing home care. At the same time they hold the danger of oversimplification of issues that may be approached from a unidimensional framework as proponents advocate one pole of the duality or the other. In fact, a sociological understanding of nursing homes underscores the complexity and multidimensionality of the social context and social world of the nursing home. Thus, there is great benefit in attempting to integrate insights gained from both poles of the dualities discussed.

The nursing home resident of the future is likely to be ever more frail, especially if we succeed in developing more home-based alternatives to care. Hence, we cannot reject the medical model in favor of a social model of care or focus on quality of life rather than on quality of care exclusively. Instead, we need to complement concerns of high-quality health care with those of high standards for social care. Similarly, just as proprietary care is likely to remain a part of health care, so regulation is here to stay. Financing mechanisms that enhance the ability of the consumers of such care to exercise control can complement regulatory efforts to upgrade quality of care in nursing home settings. On the broadest societal level, both decisions about commitment of resources and development of creative alternatives to institution-based, long-term care are likely to shape the parameters and qualities of nursing homes of the future.

The experience of any given individual being cared for in a nursing home must ultimately be understood in the context of the complex matrix of influences posed by institutional living. Accordingly, it is not fruitful to focus on either the ill effects or the benefits of institutionalization. Review of nursing home care (Johnson and Grant 1985) continues to focus on normative understandings, generally highlighting poor quality of care in such facilities. Empirical support for such negative conclusions generally derives from qualitative research (Stannard 1973; Gubrium 1975).

Quantitative studies generally provide little support for expectations of decline and adverse patient reactions. In an effort to understand conflicting conclusions of different genres of research in this area, it is useful to focus on personal as well as environmental and situational influences that moderate the effects of institutional living. More carefully designed nursing home-based research is needed to specify conditions of both person and environment that maximize well-being of the individual requiring institutional care (Lawton et al. 1984).

Even advocates of alternative forms of long-term care acknowledge that nursing home care is here to stay and will continue to be needed by the increasing segment of old-old citizens. Sanctions, incentives, and interventional programs have all been shown to be beneficial, at least to a limited extent, in improving the quality of care and the quality of life in nursing homes.

Enhancing the quality of nursing home care places a challenge on society to commit greater resources generated by currently productive citizens to the care of those who have made previous contributions. The resources society devotes to long-term care ultimately mirror the value placed by society on its frail or dependent citizens. Thus, a devaluing of older people is likely to result in a devaluing of institutions that care for them, along with a devaluing of the providers of their care (Arnold 1989). Conversely, more positive societal attitudes toward frail elders are likely to be translated into increasing involvement by high-caliber, trained professionals in the care of the institutionalized elderly. In addition, positive societal attitudes should bring community representatives into closer contact with institutions and help break down barriers between the nursing home and community living.

(SEE ALSO: *Death and Dying; Long-Term Care; Social Gerontology*)

REFERENCES

Arnold, M. D. 1989 "The Politics of Assuring Quality of Care for Elders." *Generations* (Winter):34–37.

Avorn, J., and E. Langer 1982 "Induced Disability in Nursing Home Patients: A Controlled Trial." *Journal of the American Geriatrics Society* 31:387–400.

Baltes, M. M. 1982 "Environmental Factors in Dependency Among Nursing Home Residents: A Social Ecology Analysis." In T. W. Wills, ed., *Basic Processes in Helping Relationships.* New York: Academic Press.

Beers, M., et al. 1988 "Psychoactive Medication Use of Intermediate Care Facility Residents." *Journal of the American Medical Association* 260, no. 20:3016–3020.

Bitzan, J. E., and J. M. Kruzich 1990 "Interpersonal Relationships of Nursing Home Residents." *The Gerontologist* 30, no. 3:385–390.

Brody, E. M. 1985 "Parent Care as Normative Family Stress." *The Gerontologist* 25, no. 1:19–29.

Burns, B., et al. 1988 "Mental Disorders Among Nursing Home Patients: Preliminary Findings from the National Nursing Home Survey Pretest." *International Journal of Geriatric Psychiatry* 3:27–35.

Burdz, M. P., W. O. Eaton, and J. B. Bond 1988 "Effect of Respite Care on Dementia and Nondementia Patients and Their Caregivers." *Psychology and Aging* 3, no. 1:38–42.

Callahan, D. D. 1987 *Setting Limits: Medical Goals in an Aging Society.* New York: Simon and Schuster.

Coons, D. 1978 "Milieu Therapy." In W. Reichel, ed., *Clinical Aspects of Aging.* Baltimore: Williams & Wilkins.

Densen, P. M. 1987 "The Elderly and the Health Care System: Another Perspective." *Milbank Memorial Fund Quarterly* 65:614–638.

Feil, N. 1982 *Validation: The Feil Method.* Cleveland: Edward Feil Productions.

Felton, B., and E. Kahana 1974 "Adjustment and Situationally Bound Locus of Control Among Institutionalized Aged." *Journal of Gerontology* 29, no. 3:295–301.

General Accounting Office 1977 *The Wellbeing of Older People in Cleveland, Ohio.* Washington, D.C.:

Goffman, Erving 1961 *Asylums.* New York: Anchor Books.

Gottesman, L. E., and N. C. Bourestom 1974 "Why Nursing Homes Do What They Do." *The Gerontologist* 14, no. 6:501–506.

Greene, V. L., and D. Monahan 1982 "The Impact of Visitation on Patient Well-being in Nursing Homes." *The Gerontologist* 22, no. 4:418–423.

Gubrium, J. F. 1975 *Living and Dying in Murray Manor.* New York: St. Martin's.

Harel, Z. 1987 "Ethnicity and Aging: Implications for Service Organizations." In C. H. Hayes, R. A. Kalish, and D. Guttman, eds., *European-American Elderly.* New York: Springer.

Institute of Medicine 1986 *Improving the Quality of Care in Nursing Homes.* Washington, D.C.: National Academy Press.

Isaacs, B., M. Livingston, and Y. Neville 1972 *Survival of the Unfittest.* London: Routledge and Kegan Paul.

Johnson, C. L., and L. A. Grant 1985 *The Nursing Home in American Society.* Baltimore: Johns Hopkins University Press.

Kahana, B., and E. Kahana 1976 "The Relationship of Impulse Control to Cognition and Adjustment Among Institutionalized Aged Women." *Journal of Gerontology* 30, no. 6:679–687.

Kahana, E. 1973 "The Humane Treatment of Old People in Institutions." *The Gerontologist* 3, no. 3:282–289.

——— 1982 "A Congruence Model of Person–Environment Interactions." In M. P. Lawton, P. G. Windley, and T. O. Byerts, eds., *Aging and the Environment: Theoretical Approaches.* New York: Springer.

———, and B. Kahana 1983 "Environmental Continuity, Discontinuity, Futurity and Adaptation of the

Aged." In G. Rowles and R. Ohta, eds., *Aging and Milieu: Environmental Perspectives on Growing Old.* New York: Academic Press.

———, B. Kahana, and J. M. Kinney 1990 "Coping Among Vulnerable Elders." In Z. Harel, P. Ehrlich, and R. Hubbard, eds., *Understanding and Servicing Vulnerable Aged.* New York: Springer.

———, B. Kahana, and K. P. Riley 1989 "Contextual Issues in Quantitative Studies of Institutional Settings for the Aged." In S. Reinharz and G. D. Rowles, eds., *Qualitative Gerontology.* New York: Springer.

———, B. Kahana, G. Sterin, T. Fedirko, and R. Taylor 1991 "Adaptation to Institutional Life Among Polish, Jewish, and Western-European Elderly." In C. Barresi and D. Stull, eds., *Ethnicity and Long-Term Care.* New York: Springer.

———, B. Kahana, G. Sterin, T. Fedirko, and S. Brittis 1990 "Patterns of Mutual Assistance and Well-being Among Ethnic Nursing Home Residents." Paper presented at the meeting of the Society for Traumatic Stress, New Orleans.

———, B. Kahana, and R. Young 1985 "Social Factors in Institutional Living." In W. Peterson and J. Quadagno, eds., *Social Bonds in Later Life: Aging and Interdependence.* Beverly Hills, Calif.: Sage.

——— 1987 "Strategies of Coping and Post-Institutional Outcomes." *Research on Aging* 9, no. 2:182–199.

Kahana, E., and A. Kiyak 1984 "Attitudes and Behavior of Staff in Facilities for the Aged." *Research on Aging* 6, no. 3:395–416.

Kane, R. L., and R. A. Kane 1978 "Care of the Aged: Old Problems in Need of New Solutions." *Science* 200, no. 26:913–919.

——— 1990 "Health Care for Older People: Organizational and Policy Issues." In R. H. Binstock and L. K. George, eds., *Handbook of Aging and Social Science,* 3rd ed. New York: Academic Press.

Kiyak, A., E. Kahana, and N. Lev 1978 "The Role of Informal Norms in Determining Institutional Totality in Homes for the Aged." *Long Term Care and Health Administration Quarterly* 2, no. 4:102–110.

Larson, D. B., et al. 1989 "A Systematic Review of Nursing Home Research in Three Psychiatric Journals: 1966–1985." *International Journal of Geriatric Psychiatry* 4:129–134.

Lawton, M. P. 1980 *Environment and Aging.* Monterey, Calif.: Brooks/Cole.

———, M. Fulcomer, and M. H. Kleban 1984 "Architecture for the Mentally Impaired Elderly." *Environment and Behavior* 16, no. 6:730–757.

Lewis, M. A., S. Cretin, and R. L. Cane 1985 "The Natural History of Nursing Home Patients." *The Gerontologist* 25, no. 4:382–388.

Lieberman, M. A., and S. S. Tobin 1983 *The Experience of Old Age: Stress, Coping and Survival.* New York: Basic Books.

Linn, M. W., L. Gurel, and B. S. Linn 1977 "Patient Outcome as a Measure of Quality Nursing Home Care." *American Journal of Public Health* 67:337–344.

Longino, C. F. 1990 "Geographic Distributions and Migration." In R. H. Binstock and L. K. George, eds., *Handbook of Aging and the Social Sciences,* 3rd ed. San Diego: Academic Press.

Miller, S. J. 1986 "Relationships in Long-Term Care Facilities." *Generations* 10, no. 4:65–68.

Moos, R. H. 1978 "Specialized Living Environments for Older People: A Conceptual Framework for Evaluation." *Journal of Social Issues* 36, no. 2:75–94.

Morris, J. N., C. Hawes, B. E. Fries, C. D. Phillips, V. Mor, S. Katz, K. Murphy, M. L. Drugovich, and A. S. Friedlob 1990 "Designing the National Resident Assessment Instrument for Nursing Homes." *The Gerontologist* 30, no. 3:293–302.

Newman, S. J. 1985 "Housing and Long-Term Care: The Suitability of the Elderly's Housing to the Provision of In-Home Services." *The Gerontologist* 25, no. 1:35–40.

Nyman, J. A. 1988 "Excess Demand, the Percentage of Medicaid Patients, and the Quality of Nursing Home Care." *Journal of Human Resources* 13, no. 1:76–92.

Nyman, J. A., and C. R. Geyer 1989 "Promoting the Quality of Life in Nursing Homes: Can Regulations Succeed?" *Journal of Health Politics, Policy and Law* 14, no. 4:797–816.

Rice, Thomas 1989 "The Use, Cost, and Economic Burden of Nursing-Home Care in 1985." *Medical Care* 27, no. 12:1133–1147.

Richardson, H. 1990 "Long-Term Care." in A. R. Kovner, ed., *Health Care Delivery in the United States.* New York: Springer.

Rivlin, A. M., and J. M. Weiner 1988 *Caring for the Disabled Elderly: Who Will Pay?* Washington, D.C.: The Brookings Institution.

Rovner, B. W., S. Kafonek, L. Filipp, M. J. Lucas, and M. F. Folstein 1986 "Prevalence of Mental Illness in a Community Nursing Home." *American Journal of Psychiatry* 143:1446–1449.

Schultz, R., and G. Brenner 1977 "Relocation of the Aged: A Review and Theoretical Analysis." *Journal of Gerontology* 32:323–333.

Sirrocco, A. 1988 "Nursing and Related Care Homes as Reported from the 1986 Inventory of Long-Term Care Places. *Advance Data from Vital and Health Statistics* no. 147, DHHS Pub. no. (PHS) 88–1250. Hyattsville, Md.: National Center for Health Statistics, Public Health Service.

——— 1989 "Nursing Home Characteristics: 1986 Inventory of Long-Term Care Places." *Vital and Health Statistics* ser. 14, no. 33, DHHS Pub. no. (PHS) 89–1828. Washington, D.C.: U.S. Government Printing Office.

Smith, K., and V. Bengtson 1979 "Positive Consequences of Institutionalizations: Solidarity Between Elderly Parents and Their Middle-Aged Children." *The Gerontologist* 19, no. 5:438–447.

Spasoff, R. A., et al. 1978 "A Longitudinal Study of Elderly Residents of Long-Stay Institutions." *The Gerontologist* 18, no. 3:281–292.

Stannard, C. 1973 "Old Folks and Dirty Work: The Social Conditions for Patient Abuse in a Nursing Home." *Social Problems* 20, no. 3:329–342.

Stein, S., et al. 1983 "The Impact of Environment on Perception of Stress and Symptoms of the Elderly." *Adaptation and Aging* 3, no. 4:39–48.

Tobin, S. S., and M. A. Lieberman 1976 *Last Home for the Aged.* San Francisco: Jossey-Bass.

Townsend, P. 1962 *The Last Refuge: A Survey of Residential Institutions and Homes for the Aged in England and Wales.* London: Routledge and Kegan Paul.

Vladeck, B. C. 1980 *Unloving Care: The Nursing Home Tragedy.* New York: Basic Books.

Whanger, A. D. 1980 "Treatment Within the Institutions." In *Handbook of Geriatric Psychiatry.* New York: Van Nostrand Reinhold.

Williams, C. 1986 "Improving Care in Nursing Homes Using Community Advocacy." *Social Science and Medicine* 23, no. 12:1297–1303.

Wingard, D. L., D. W. Jones, and R. M. Kaplan 1987 "Institutional Care Utilization by the Elderly: A Critical Review." *The Gerontologist* 27, no. 2:156–163.

Wolinsky, F. D. 1988 *The Sociology of Health: Principles, Practioners, and Issues, 2nd ed.* Belmont, Calif.: Wadsworth.

Wright, L. K. 1988 "A Reconceptualization of the 'Negative Staff Attitudes and Poor Care in Nursing Homes' Assumption." *The Gerontologist* 28, no. 6:813–820.

York, J., and R. Caslyn 1977 "Family Involvement in Nursing Homes." *The Gerontologist* 17, no. 6:500–505.

EVA KAHANA
SARAJANE BRITTIS

O

OBJECTIVITY *See* Scientific Explanation.

OBSERVATION SYSTEMS The most sensitive, sophisticated, and flexible instrument of observation available today is the human being. Systematic methods of observation may vary the unit of analysis, shift the boundaries of categories, and adjust the level of judgment allowed, but sociologists are ultimately left with the basic reality of human beings watching other human beings. The role of the methodologist is to make this process systematic.

Most sociological data are filtered through the perceptions of informants in an idiosyncratic manner. Retrospective accounts of events, opinion polls, and surveys measure the output of the social perception process. Only systematic observation, with valid and reliable instruments, provides a record of the events themselves rather than the retrospective reconstruction of the events. The more rigorously defined the categories, the more confident the researcher can be that the data reflect the events and not just the biases and preconceptions of the informants.

While some of the systems that are described below were developed for specific purposes such as the observation of business case-study groups or the diagnosis of psychiatric patients, most attempt to capture the full range of social behavior and may thus be applied to a wide range of settings. Not included here are the specialized systems that have been developed for single contexts such as the classroom behavior of small children, the responses of subjects in a tightly controlled laboratory experiment, or the evaluation of employees. One fast-food restaurant, for example, has developed a thirty-one category checklist—including items such as "There is a smile," "The bag is double folded," and "Change is counted efficiently"—that managers can use to observe and evaluate counter staff.

Observation systems have been used for a wide variety of purposes over the years. Early uses included psychiatric diagnosis, job placement, and basic research into group development. As corporate assessment centers came into widespread use for the selection of executives, early observation systems reappeared for the analysis of leaderless group exercises. More recent applications have included research and consulting on team building, training and evaluation of social workers, prediction of success or failure of military cadets, the study of leadership networks in large corporations, the evaluation and treatment of problem children in the classroom, the evaluation of psychiatric interventions, the analysis of delinquent behavior and resocialization, and consultation on mergers and consolidations (Polley, Hare, and Stone 1988).

SINGLE CATEGORY SYSTEMS

Elliot D. Chapple introduced the "interaction chronograph" in 1940. It was a simple device that consisted of two telegraph keys. Observers were instructed to press key "A" when person "A" spoke and key "B" when person "B" spoke. A record of the conversation was kept on a moving paper tape. Not surprisingly, inter-rater reliabilities were nearly perfect. Twenty-five years later, the human observers were replaced by voice-activated microphones attached to analog-digital converters (Wiens, Matarrazo, and Saslow 1965). That such a simple device could replace the human observer suggests that the systems were not taking full advantage of the observers' capabilities. In reality, the decision to record such objective and basic information simply shifted the burden of interpretation from the observer to the researcher. Chapple and his successors developed elaborate schemes for interpreting the patterns of lines and blanks that appeared on their paper tapes. At the peak of its popularity, the interaction chronograph was used for everything from psychiatric diagnosis to employee placement.

MULTIPLE CATEGORY SYSTEMS

Chapple's work serves as an important bench mark. The near-perfect reliability is achieved at the cost of validity. The observation systems that followed it generally traded off a measure of reliability for greater validity. More meaningful sets of categories will almost certainly be harder to employ with any degree of inter-rater reliability.

Interaction process analysis (IPA) was one of the earliest attempts to devise more meaningful categories. Bales (1950) began with an encyclopedic list of behaviors and gradually consolidated them into an elegant set of twelve basic categories. Forty years later, his original system is still actively employed in research.

The IPA category list was evolving at the same time that Parsons and Bales (1955) were developing a model of family socialization. They saw family leadership in the 1940s and 1950s as divided between the father and the mother. IPA reflects this division through its primary dimension; six categories are provided for coding task-oriented behaviors and six categories are for coding social-emotional behaviors (Table 1). When Slater (1955) suggested that this role differentiation could be extended to a general model of effective leadership in groups, he sparked a continuing controversy.

Additional symmetries are built into IPA. Three

TABLE 1
Interaction Process Analysis (IPA)

Category	*Emotion*	*Task*	*Problem*
1. Shows Solidarity	Positive		Reintegration
2. Shows Tension Release	Positive		Tension Reduction
3. Agrees	Positive		Decision
4. Gives Suggestion		Answer	Control
5. Gives Opinion		Answer	Evaluation
6. Gives Orientation		Answer	Communication
7. Asks for Orientation		Question	Communication
8. Asks for Opinion		Question	Evaluation
9. Asks for Suggestion		Question	Control
10. Disagress	Negative		Decision
11. Shows Tension	Negative		Tension Reduction
12. Shows Antagonism	Negative		Reintegration

SOURCE: Adapted from Bales (1950).

of the six social-emotional categories carry positive affect and each has a direct counterpart on the negative side. Task-oriented behavior is seen as the process of asking questions and offering answers, though the answers—in the form of suggestions, opinions, and orientation (or information) —may be in response to questions asked or unasked. Finally, the functionalist orientation of Parsons and Bales (1955) appears in the identification of six problems faced by groups: communication, evaluation, control, decision, tension reduction, and reintegration.

Like Chapple, Bales developed and marketed a moving-paper tape recording device. The interaction recorder allowed for observation of groups rather than just dyads; the tape was divided into twelve rows and moved past a window at a constant speed so that the observer could write a code, indicating who was speaking to whom, within a category-by-time sector on the tape. This added complexity but enlarged the unit of analysis. The interaction recorder provided a continuous on–off record' while IPA recorded discrete acts. The coding unit was, however, kept small. IPA coders often record two or three acts for a single sentence and are expected to record *all* acts.

The first serious challenge to Bales's IPA system was Borgatta's (1963) interaction process scores (IPS) system. Borgatta argued that the twelve categories failed to make some crucial distinctions. His redefinition of the boundaries resulted in an eighteen-category system that had the advantage of greater precision and the disadvantages of greater complexity and lack of symmetry. The former problem was largely solved by the availability of a self-training workbook (Borgatta and Crowther 1965).

The next logical step after categorization is the organization of categories. IPA had an implicit internal organization that was lacking in IPS. This, and the fact that IPA had twelve rather than eighteen categories, made IPA the easier system to learn and use. As Weick (1985) points out, however, there is the problem of "requisite variety." A system for understanding a phenomenon must be at least as complex as the phenomenon itself. Weick uses the metaphor of a camera with variable focal length. In order to photograph objects at twenty different distances, the camera must have at least twenty focal settings or the pictures will not all be of equal clarity. This creates real problems for the interaction chronograph. Clearly social behavior is more complex than Chapple's "on–off" category system. Unfortunately, it is also more complex than IPA's twelve-category system or IPS's eighteen-category system. This creates a dilemma. The mind can hold only so many categories at once; even with only twelve categories, most observers tend to forget the rare ones in an attempt to simplify their job.

MULTIDIMENSIONAL SYSTEMS

Leary (1957) proposed one of the first observation systems based primarily on dimensions rather than categories. His interpersonal diagnosis system placed sixteen categories at the compass points of a two-dimensional circumplex. The dimensions, Dominance–Submission and Love–Hate, would prove to be the two most common dimensions among the systems that followed. While intended primarily for the diagnosis of psychiatric disorders, the system also identified the "normal," or less intense, variant of each behavior as well as the likely response that each behavior would generate in other people. For example, the general behavior in the direction of dominance is "manage, direct, lead"; this behavior "provokes obedience" in others, and the extreme version of the category is "dominate, boss, order." This falls into a larger category of behavior that is described as "managerial" when in the normal range and "autocratic" when in the abnormal range. More than a method of observation, the interpersonal diagnosis system was a remarkably well-articulated theory of interpersonal relations. Were it not for Leary's well-publicized advocacy of LSD, the system might very well be in common use today. While the research was briefly resurrected by McLemore and Benjamin (1979), it never had a major impact either on social psychology or psychiatry.

Leary's two dimensions were theoretically derived. In a 1960 doctoral dissertation, Arthur

Couch pioneered the application of factor analysis to interpersonal behavior, thus offering an empirical alternative for the derivation of dimensions. Couch's six dimensions of interpersonal behavior were derived from the factor analysis of a vast amount of data on twelve groups of five undergraduates each. The individuals were given a large battery of personality tests, and the twelve groups were observed participating in a wide variety of tasks across five meetings each. While factor analysis is not independent of the original categories of measurement and observation, Couch's data set was so exhaustive as to deserve credence.

MULTILEVEL SYSTEMS

The three dimensions of Bales, Cohen, and Williamson's (1979) SYMLOG (System for the Multiple Level Observation of Groups) owe much to both IPA and Couch's empirical work. Dominant–Submissive (U-D) was the first factor from Couch's analysis; in IPA it corresponds to total amount of talking rather than to interaction in any set of categories. Friendly–Unfriendly (P-N) was Couch's second factor and corresponds to the positive and negative affect from the six social-emotional categories of IPA. Task-Oriented–Emotional (F-B), the controversial distinction from IPA, was a compromise that created one bipolar dimension out of two of Couch's remaining factors. These three dimensions, generally referred to by the code letters shown above, define a three-dimensional conceptual space. Like Leary, Bales and his colleagues then defined the compass points of the space. In this case, definitions were produced for all twenty-six of the vectors in the three dimensional space. Thus, a dominant, unfriendly, task-oriented act (UNF) is defined as "authoritarian and controlling," and a submissive, unfriendly, emotional act (DNB) is described as "withdrawn and alienated." This is a creative solution to the dilemma of providing requisite variety while keeping the number of categories at a manageble size. While there are twenty-six categories, they are organized into three-dimensions, so coders can hold the three-dimensional space, rather than the twenty-six categories, in mind.

In addition to the basic level of behavior described above, SYMLOG provides definitions for the twenty-six vectors on the level of nonverbal behavior. This level is coded when unintentional messages are sent through nonverbal behavior or when the nonverbal—or paralinguistic—cues are at variance with the overt verbal cues. In developing his descriptions of facial expression and nonverbal cues, Bales drew on the work of the eighteenth-century French Encyclopedists. He found that Diderot and his colleagues had developed a more sophisticated understanding of facial expressions and nonverbal nuance than have modern social scientists.

SYMLOG also allows for the coding of verbal content. Theoretically, the two levels of behavior —overt and nonverbal—could be coded without reference to the content of the message. Conversely, the content of messages could be coded from written transcripts without reference to the behaviors of the speakers. The content coding level attends only to evaluative statements. Each statement is first coded PRO (for statements in favor of something) or CON (for statements against something). The content of the value statement is then coded in the same three-dimensional space that was used for behavior. Finally, the level of the value statement is recorded. Levels begin with the self and move out: Self, Other, Group, Situation, Society, and Fantasy.

When the full SYMLOG system is used for coding a conversation, the result is a set of simple sentences written in code. For example, Figure 1

123	JOE	BIL	A	UNF	Stop contradicting me!	C	N	BIL
123	BIL	JOE	A	UNB	Don't give me orders.	C	UNF	JOE
124	RON	GRP	A	UPF	I think we should all calm down.	P	DP	GRP

FIGURE 1
Sample SYMLOG Coding

records a brief exchange that took place from 1:23 to 1:24. Joe ordered Bill to stop contradicting him. The behavior was authoritarian and the value statement was against negativity in Bill (C N BIL). Bill responded in a rebellious manner (UNB) and made a value statement against Joe's authoritarianism (C UNF JOE). Ron intervened in a "purposeful and considerate" manner (UPF) and made a value statement in favor of reducing the level of conflict (P DP GRP). If we see contradictions between the overt and nonverbal behavior, we could add lines such as: 123 JOE GRP N DN. This would indicate that underneath Joe's authoritarianism is a note of insecurity and nervousness. (The first "N" in the message stands for "nonverbal;" the "A" in each of the messages in Figure 1 stands for "act.") Clearly, the system requires fairly extensive training of coders. Most SYMLOG coders have been through a fifteen-week course that is run as a self-analytic group. During this time, they alternate between serving as group participants and retreating behind a mirror to serve as observers and SYMLOG coders.

SYMLOG adds depth and sophistication to the coding of social interaction but again enlarges the unit of measurement. While IPA is an act-by-act coding system, SYMLOG is a "salient act" coding scheme. Since it takes much longer to record a SYMLOG observation, the coder must select the most important acts for recording. Clearly, this results in a loss of reliability as disagreements may result not only from two observers interpreting the same act differently but from two observers recording different acts. Because of this, two observers are generally sufficient for IPA, but five or more are recommended for SYMLOG. One measure lacking in the SYMLOG coding scheme is intensity. However, when multiple coders are used, more intense acts are likely to be selected as salient by more coders and will thus be weighted more heavily than the less intense acts that may be picked up by only one or two coders.

The issue of reduced reliability is directly related to the problem of subjectivity. Moreno (1953) was an early critic of IPA; he argued that the observations of nonparticipants were meaningless because they could not possibly comprehend the life of a group to which they did not belong. While his position was extreme, it raised a difficult problem for any system that relies on the observations of outsiders. By standing outside of the group, the observer gains distance and "objectivity." Unfortunately, it is not clear that objectivity has any real meaning when speaking of interpersonal interaction. IPA sidestepped the problem by providing very clear specifications of categories. SYMLOG confronts the problem directly since observers are required to make fairly strong inferences as to the meaning of a behavior. The coder is instructed to take the perspective of the "generalized other," or the "average" group member. When a group is polarized, this may be impossible. Half of the group is likely to interpret an act in one way and the other half in a different way. This is another reason for having multiple observers. It is hoped that the various biases of observers will cancel one another out if five or more people observe. Polley (1979) goes a step further by providing "descriptive reliabilities." Instead of simply reporting a reliability figure, descriptive reliabilities allow for a systematic analysis of observer bias. It is argued that observations tell as much about the observer as about the observed. This is particularly valuable information when group members are trained to serve as observers, as is the case in the self-analytic groups led by Bales and his colleagues.

Both IPA and SYMLOG have been repeatedly criticized for their use of a bipolar model of the relationship between "task-oriented" and "emotional" behavior. Two of these critiques have proposed adding a fourth dimension. Hare (1976) went back to Parsons's original AGIL system and concluded that the task-emotion dimension should be divided into two dimensions: Serious versus Expressive and Conforming versus Nonconforming. Wish, Deutsch, and Kaplan (1976) proposed leaving the Task–Emotion dimension intact, even though it did not seem to be quite bipolar, and adding a fourth dimension: Intensity. Polley (1987) has argued that emotionality is already captured in the Friendly–Unfriendly dimension and that the third dimension should be reserved for recording Conventional versus Unconventional behavior. This solution contends that the polarization of Task and Emotion is an artifact from the 1950s and has largely lost its meaning since then. If work is defined as devoid of emotional satisfaction, then Task and Emotion are bipolar. As soon as we recognize the possibility of having an emotional reaction—positive or negative—to work, the two dimensions become orthogonal. As Stone (1988, p. 18) points out, the Task–Emotion polarity "implies that most work involves the sublimation of the libido, and demands impulse control. Moreover, it becomes difficult to imagine management's task orientation . . . fostering individual creativity as some so-called excellent companies have been able to do." It is becoming increasingly apparent that no "universal" scheme for coding interpersonal interaction exists totally independent of cultural and temporal context.

SPECIALIZED SYSTEMS

While Leary's system was intended primarily for psychiatric diagnosis, and IPA was originally designed for the coding of case discussion groups at Harvard Business School, the methods discussed above represent attempts to develop comprehensive and general coding schemes. In addition to these all-purpose methods, observation systems have been devised for somewhat more specific relationships or channels of communication.

Richard Mann's (1967) sixteen-category system codes only the one-way relationships from members to leader. By narrowly defining the relationships to be observed, Mann is able to provide a much more detailed picture. Coding categories are provided for four types of impulse, four different expressions of affection, three variations of dependency, and five ego states. The additional sophistication is achieved by drastically reducing the number of observed relationships. If we observe a ten-person group using Mann's leader–member relationship scheme, we are looking at nine one-way relationships. If we use one of the all-purpose methods, we are coding forty-five two-way relationships.

The most thoroughly studied channel of communication is probably the nonverbal. While this is a small part of the SYMLOG system, proxemic behavior has been exhaustively categorized by Hall (1963) in terms of posture, orientation of bodies, kinesthetic factors, touch code, visual code, thermal code, olfaction code, and voice loudness. The potential complexity of this mode of communication is further illustrated by the fact that Birdwhistell (1970) has developed an equally elaborate system for the coding of movement. While Hall's system codes states, Birdwhistell's codes state-to-state transitions. While each of these coding schemes concentrates on the physical nature of nonverbal behavior, Mehrabian's (1970) system attempts to record directly the meaning of the behavior via a three-dimensional model that closely parallels SYMLOG. Again, the difference is in whether meaning is inferred by the observer or deferred to the researcher.

The other channel of communication that has been studied in depth is content. Again, this channel is a small piece of SYMLOG; all content that does not carry a positive or negative evaluation is ignored. In 1966, Philip Stone and his colleagues published *The General Inquirer,* a computerized content analysis system. While many of the applications involve the coding of written text, it has also been used for the coding of transcribed conversations. In one of the first applications of the method, Dexter Dunphy used *The General Inquirer* to code descriptions that group members had written of recent sessions. The great advantage of the method is that it allows the user to define the dictionary. Three of the earliest dictionaries were the Harvard III Psychosocial Dictionary, the Stanford Political Dictionary, and the Need-Achievement Dictionary. It would also be possible to develop a SYMLOG value-level dictionary. In the case of a computerized content analysis system, the dictionary designer infers meaning *before* the behavior is coded.

THE FUTURE OF OBSERVATION SYSTEMS

Observation systems have been used less and less in recent years for a mundane reason: cost. Training observers is time consuming, as is the actual process of observing and coding behavior. At this point, serious research using direct SYMLOG observation is being done at only two or three institutions. In contrast, the much less time-consuming method of retrospective rating (using either the Bales items or the Polley revisions) is currently in use in at least fifty institutions around the world. While there are some indications of a resurgence of interest in direct observation, it is clear that the method requires a substantial commitment of time and money on the part of the researcher.

While the costs of direct observation are high, it is clear that there are a great many aspects of social behavior that simply cannot be understood without it. Basic research still needs to be done on group development, particularly as it relates to team building in organizations. The effects of various leadership styles and decision-making processes on group functioning are still not thoroughly understood. A wide range of styles is currently used by group therapists, but these styles are more often backed by rival schools of thought than by empirical evidence.

As with content analysis, the future of observation systems may well lie in computerization. Johansen (1989) recently coined the term *groupware* to refer to computer systems for the support of groups or teams. To date, most of the systems have provided little more than an "electronic flipchart" for nominal group technique sessions. With advances in artificial intelligence, more sophisticated examples of groupware are likely to emerge. Speech recognition programs for the automatic transcription of meetings would greatly reduce the cost of using content analysis. Programs have also been developed for recognizing emotional content in speech. If these could be combined with voice-activated microphones, some automatic scoring of behavior—at least at the paralinguistic level—may be possible. Until technology substantially reduces the costs, a return to the widespread use of observation systems seems unlikely.

(SEE ALSO: *Small Groups; Social Psychology*)

REFERENCES

Bales, Robert F. 1950 *Interaction Process Analysis.* Chicago: University of Chicago Press.

———, Stephen P. Cohen, and Stephen A. Williamson 1979 *SYMLOG: A System for the Multiple Level Observation of Groups.* New York: Free Press.

Birdwhistell, Ray 1970 *Kinesics and Context.* Philadelphia: University of Pennsylvania Press.

Borgatta, Edgar 1963 "A New Systematic Interaction Observation System." *Journal of Psychological Studies* 14:24–44.

———, and Betty Crowther 1965 *A Workbook for the Study of Social Interaction Processes.* Chicago: Rand McNally.

Chapple, Elliot D. 1940 "Measuring Human Relations: An Introduction to the Study of the Interaction of Individuals." *Genetic Psychology Monographs* 27:3–147.

Couch, Arthur S. 1960 "Personality Determinants of Interpersonal Behavior." Ph.D. diss., Harvard University, Cambridge, Mass.

Hall, Edward T. 1963 "A System for the Notation of Proxemic Behavior." *American Anthropologist* 65:1003–1026.

Hare, A. Paul 1976 *Handbook of Small Group Research,* 2nd ed. New York: Free Press.

Johansen, Robert 1989 *Groupware.* New York: Free Press.

Leary, Timothy 1957 *Interpersonal Diagnosis of Personality.* New York: Ronald Press.

McLemore, Clinton, and Lorna Benjamin 1979 "Whatever Happened to Interpersonal Diagnosis?" *American Psychologist.* 34:17–34.

Mann, Richard D. 1967 *Interpersonal Styles and Group Development.* New York: Wiley.

Mehrabian, Albert 1970 "A Semantic Space for Nonverbal Behavior." *Journal of Consulting and Clinical Psychology* 35:248–257.

Moreno, Jacob 1953 *Who Shall Survive?* Beacon, N.Y.: Beacon House.

Parsons, Talcott, and Robert F. Bales 1955 *Family,*

Socialization, and Interaction Process. New York: Free Press.

Polley, Richard B. 1979 "Investigating Individual Perceptual Biases of Group Members in Rating and of Observers in SYMLOG Interaction Scoring." In R. F. Bales, S. P. Cohen, and S. A. Williamson, *SYMLOG: A System for the Multiple Level Observation of Groups.* New York: Free Press.

——— 1987 "The Dimensions of Interpersonal Behavior: A Method for Improving Rating Scales." *Social Psychology Quarterly* 50:72–82.

———, A. Paul Hare, and Philip J. Stone, eds. 1988 *The SYMLOG Practitioner: Applications of Small Group Research.* New York: Praeger.

Slater, Philip E. 1955 "Role Differentiation in Small Groups." *American Sociological Review* 20:300–310.

Stone, Philip J. 1988 "SYMLOG for Skeptics." In R.B. Polley, A. P. Hare, and P.J. Stone, eds., *The SYMLOG Practitioner: Applications of Small Group Research.* New York: Praeger.

———, Dexter C. Dunphy, Marshall S. Smith, and Daniel M. Ogilvie 1966 *The General Inquirer: A Computer Approach to Content Analysis.* Cambridge, Mass.: MIT Press.

Weick, Karl E. 1985 "Systematic Observational Methods." In G. Lindzey and E. Aronson, eds., *The Handbook of Social Psychology,* 3rd ed. New York: Random House.

Wiens, A. N., J. D. Matarazzo, and G. Saslow 1965 "The Interaction Recorder: An Electronic Punched Paper Tape Unit for Recording Speech Behavior During Interviews." *Journal of Clinical Psychology* 21:142–145.

Wish, Myron, Morton Deutsch, and S. Kaplan 1976 "Perceived Dimensions of Interpersonal Relations." *Journal of Personality and Social Psychology* 33:409–420.

RICHARD BRIAN POLLEY

OCCUPATIONAL AND CAREER MOBILITY Occupational and career mobility in adulthood is often referred to as intragenerational social mobility. It involves change in an individual's position in the labor market over the adult life course. Change is studied with respect to both type of work and the rewards derived from work. The term *career* refers to an individual's job history. Empirical *regularity* in the careers of individuals in the labor force defines what we call a "career line" or "job trajectory," since a work history common to a portion of the labor force reflects the existence of structurally determined linkages among jobs in the economy. Jobs are located in particular firms, whereas occupations and industries encompass jobs in many firms. An individual may remain in the same occupation or industry but change firms and jobs within the same firm any number of times. Since the process of job change does not necessarily involve a change of occupation or industry, but a change of occupation or industry always involves a job change, the process of job change provides a more detailed account of career movement. Changes in the rewards derived from work usually accompany job changes but can also occur during the course of tenure in a job.

Research on intragenerational mobility has focused on the labor force as a whole and on employees in particular occupations and firms. Research on the labor force as a whole has usually considered change in occupation and industry, as measured for detailed categories or more aggregated groupings that define broad occupational and industrial groups. It has also considered change in the rewards derived from work, focusing primarily on occupational prestige and earnings. Research on particular occupations and firms has usually focused on job status and authority changes within organizational hierarchies and on changes in work rewards.

Early work on intragenerational mobility involved the mathematical modeling of transition probabilities, usually among a few, highly aggregated categories (see Mayer 1972 for a review). This work used Markov models and semi-Markov models to analyze transition probabilities in a sequence under the assumption that the job category an individual will occupy in the future depends only on the job category occupied in the present and not on job categories occupied previously. Although there is empirical support for this assumption in some studies (see, e.g., White 1970; March and March 1977), it has not been found to be broadly applicable. In semi-Markov models transition probabilities are permitted to vary with time and for subgroups of the population. These models capture declines in mobility with age or duration of stay and allow for the fact that some individuals are more likely to move than others. There is evidence to indicate that mobility is an exponentially declining function of time (Mayer 1972) and that some individuals become "movers" while others become "stayers" (Blumen, Kogan, and McCarthy 1955).

Later analyses have considered more refined models of job change, focusing on job shifts as elementary acts in the mobility process. Job shifts also occur at a decreasing rate with time, and the rate of mobility varies with characteristics of the individual, the job, and the environment (Sørensen 1975b; Felmlee 1982; Rosenbaum 1984). Change in the rewards derived from work usually accompanies a job shift (Sørensen 1974, 1975a; Rosenbaum 1984) but may also occur during the course of a job. For the labor force as a whole, occupational prestige and earnings increase over the adult working life. The shape of these trajectories tends to be concave downward —with a rise early in the career, a plateau during the middle years, and a slight decline as the end of the work career approaches. Status and earnings trajectories have the same form, but the former is flatter (Mincer 1974; Rosenfeld 1980). There is also variation in the shape of these trajectories for those in different career lines (Spilerman 1986).

Given the heterogeneity of career lines and the important role that age, or duration since career entry, plays in shaping career lines, there have been attempts to study the path of careers in recent years. For example, mobility not only declines sharply with age, but job changes that occur later in an individual's work life tend to involve jobs requiring skills that are more similar than those that occur earlier in the work life (Spenner, Otto, and Call 1982). There is also evidence that early career experiences have an important affect on later career outcomes. This evidence indicates not only that those entering *different* career lines, who receive different rewards at career entry, can expect different career outcomes (Sewell and Hauser 1975; Marini 1980; Spenner, Otto, and Call 1982), but also that early experiences *within* a career line can condition subsequent progression and the level of reward attained relative to others who enter the same career line (Rosenbaum 1984). The career lines most often studied have been trajectories within institutional structures, but there have also been attempts to describe career lines that cross institutional boundaries (Spilerman 1977; Spenner, Otto, and Call 1982).

LABOR MARKET STRUCTURE

The concept of "career line" or "job trajectory" derives from the view that the labor market is structured in a way that makes some types of job changes more likely than others. Early work on career mobility ignored this structural differentiation, estimating the overall (linear) relationship between the status and earnings of an individual's first job and the status and earnings of a job held later in the career (Blau and Duncan 1967; Coleman et al. 1972; Jencks et al. 1972; Sewell and Hauser 1975; Marini 1980). Jobs resembling each other in status, pay, and working conditions, however, are sometimes part of a career line and sometimes not, and even if part of a career line can be attached to *different* career lines. Jobs providing similar current rewards may therefore not offer the same prospects for future mobility.

Since career lines are rooted in labor market structure, their existence demonstrates that intragenerational mobility is influenced by the structure of the labor market, as well as the demography of the labor force and individual characteristics that affect movement within segments of the labor market. If jobs have entry requirements and confer rewards, the structure of jobs plays a critical role in establishing the link between the attributes of individuals and work rewards. Recognition that the labor market is structured in a way that produces segmentation among career lines has led to attempts not only to describe career lines but to identify the forces shaping them.

During the 1940s and 1950s, institutional economists called for an understanding of well-defined systems of jobs and firms, drawing a distinction between internal and external labor markets. For example, Dunlop (1957) argued that within a firm there are groups of jobs, or "job clusters," each of which is linked together by technology, the administrative organization of the production process, and the social customs of the work community. A job cluster usually contains one or more key jobs and a group of associated jobs, and the wage rates for the key jobs mediate the effects of labor market influences, including union and government wage policies, and forces in the market for products on the wage structure of the firm. The distinction between internal and external labor markets was later reintroduced by Doeringer and Piore (1971), who discussed what they called a "mobility cluster." The central idea was that administrative rules and procedures tend to set up separate markets for those already hired (an internal labor market) and those seeking employment (an external labor market). A firm hires workers from the outside labor market into "entry jobs," and other jobs are filled internally as workers progress on well-defined career ladders by acquiring job-related skills, many of which are firm-specific. Thus, firms make investments in individuals, and these investments segment the work force with respect to advancement opportunity.

The concept of the internal labor market was developed further in what was first called *dual* and then *segmented* labor market theory (Gordon 1972; Kalleberg and Sørensen 1979). This theory draws a distinction between primary and secondary jobs, arguing that the internal labor market is only one kind of work setting. *Primary* jobs emphasize long-term attachment between workers and firms and offer built-in career ladders and promotion opportunities, whereas *secondary* jobs do not offer these advantages. The distinction between primary and secondary jobs may occur within the same firm or between firms, since primary jobs are considered more likely to be found in oligopolistic, unionized industries, and secondary jobs in competitive industries.

Dual and other segmented labor market theories came under attack as being too crude to meaningfully characterize the multiple dimensions on which labor markets vary. Attempts to measure labor market segmentation by crude topologies, including industrial and occupational categories, were also criticized (Baron and Bielby 1980; Hodson and Kaufman 1982). Because there is extensive heterogeneity within industrial and occupational categories, and there is no way to link them to the kinds of job clusters hypothesized to exist, more disaggregated analyses of jobs and firms were argued to be needed. Many subsequent analyses have focused on particular bureaucracies or firms.

Attempting to develop a systematic conceptual scheme for studying labor market segmentation, Althauser and Kalleberg (1981 p. 130) argued that "the concept of an internal labor market should include any cluster of jobs, regardless of occupational titles, or employing organizations, that have three basic structural features: (a) a job ladder, with (b) entry only at the bottom, and (c) movement up this ladder, which is associated with a progressive development of knowledge and skill." Based on four possible pairings of type of control and prospects for advancement, they differentiated four types of labor market structures: (1) firm internal labor markets, which are internal labor markets controlled by firms; (2) occupational internal labor markets, which are internal labor markets controlled by occupational incumbents; (3) firm labor markets, which provide firm-specific security without advancement prospects; and (4) occupational labor markets, which provide occupational security without advancement prospects. Within an occupation or firm, there may be multiple job ladders that vary in length. Advancement prospects depend on the length of job ladders and the interconnections between them (Rosenbaum 1984; Baron, Davis-Blake, and Biebly 1986; DiPrete 1989). In an analysis of the U.S. federal civil service, for instance, DiPrete (1989) found a two-tiered job ladder system for clerical and administrative work.

Although there is general agreement that the technical character of work influences organizational development, existing variation in personnel structures, especially cross-nationally, indicates that the technical character of work alone does not determine job ladders and career lines.

These are affected by the historical circumstances surrounding an organization's founding, including the gender, racial, and ethnic composition of the work force, market conditions that affect the rate of employment growth, and the negotiating strength of various bargaining units. A number of specific explanations have been advanced for the emergence of distinct labor market segments. Becker (1964) noted that when workers receive firm-specific training, it is in the interest of employers to bind them to the firm with promises of promotion, salary increases, and employment security. A related explanation that has received substantial empirical support is that internal labor markets result from employers' needs for renewable supplies of otherwise scarce, highly skilled workers. This explanation is linked to explanations emphasizing firm-specific skills and on-the-job training, since firm-specific skills are, by definition, not available on the external market and on-the-job training often produces firm-specific skills or skills that are scarce on the external market. Another explanation, offered by Bulow and Summers (1986), is that job hierarchies offering promotion prospects and wage increases are an important means of motivating workers when individual performance is not easily monitored.

The emergence and spread of internal labor markets has also been seen as related to the development of personnel departments, formalized rules, and the rise of bureaucratic control. There is some empirical support for this view, but at least some internal labor markets preceded the emergence of these bureaucratic control systems and rules (Althauser 1989). Spilerman (1986) has noted that workers have an interest in barring lateral entry and in having high-level positions filled through promotion. Workers may also wish to limit employer discretion by having decisions about promotion and layoff tied to seniority. These worker interests cause labor unions to work to create more widespread job hierarchies and promotion. Because firms characterized by high profit levels, oligopolistic pricing, and large organizational size can better afford to create internal labor markets, these firms have been argued to be more likely to do so; however, there is evidence that internal labor markets are not merely a derivative feature of core-economy organization (Althauser 1989).

Because mobility depends on the availability of positions, the shape of organizational hierarchies constrains the probability of career advancement. Most organizational hierarchies are pyramidal, with many more low-level than high-level positions. The average employee's advancement therefore must slow down over time. Aggregate age-promotion curves appear to be described by an exponential-decline function where the highest promotion changes occur at the outset, declines are a fixed proportion of an individual's current chances, and promotion chances become increasingly rare but not impossible. In short, promotion favors youth, declines gradually, but does not disappear for older workers. In keeping with human capital theory, there may also be chances for an increase in promotion during the initial career years, when most of the on-the-job training occurs.

Career lines not only involve substantial movement between job ladders within firms but often cross firm and industry boundaries rather than remaining within them. For example, it has been estimated that only somewhat over a quarter of U.S. workers are continuously employed by the same employer for twenty years or more (Hall 1982). In some careers, such as the salaried professions, crafts, and "secondary" labor market positions, firm and industry are not a locus of career line structure. Nevertheless, moves between firms and industries often occur between related positions so that labor market segmentation emerges even without institutional barriers.

Because the availability of vacancies in organizational hierarchies affects career advancement, promotion is affected by demographic factors such as cohort size and the rate of exit from positions (Stewman and Konda 1983). It is also affected by organizational growth and contraction that result in the creation and termination of jobs. This change in the actual structure of jobs occurs in response to social and economic influences, including technological development.

WORKER CHARACTERISTICS

Given the structure of the labor market, particularly the local labor market where most job search occurs, entry into a career line is affected by worker characteristics, such as job-related credentials (e.g., education, intelligence, physical attributes), job preferences, and access to resources (e.g., information, material support, sponsorship by influential others). In some career lines worker characteristics at entry may also influence career progression, whereas in others such characteristics may have little effect after access to a career line is obtained. If worker characteristics at entry continue to have an effect, they may do so in part because they influence subsequent on-the-job training and performance.

Human capital theory has been advanced by economists to explain change in work rewards. In human capital theory, workers are seen as rational actors who make investments in their productive capacities to maximize lifetime income (Becker 1964; Mincer 1974). The investments usually studied are education and on-the-job training, although the theory applies to other investments, such as effort, job search, geographic mobility, and health. It is assumed that labor markets offer open opportunity and that earnings growth is a function of how hard individuals work and the ability, education, and training they possess. Individuals can increase their productivity not only through formal education but by learning on the job. On-the-job training occurs in formal training programs provided by employers or as a result of informal instruction by supervisors and coworkers and simply by doing the job. Time away from the job, in contrast, can lead to skill depreciation. Because investments in education and training are costly, workers concentrate their investments in the early part of their careers, sacrificing immediate earnings for better long-term career prospects.

Although worker qualifications that may affect productivity are associated with advancement, these associations are consistent with explanations other than that afforded by human capital theory. As many critics have pointed out, the assumption that worker characteristics such as formal education, labor market experience, and interruptions in employment reflect differences in productivity has not been adequately tested. These variables are assumed to reflect productivity, but they may reflect other influences. For instance, formal education may be used by employers as a credential for screening workers and may affect wages because it affects access to jobs (Spence 1974). Labor market experience may affect wages because it is a proxy for seniority so that wages rise with seniority and job tenure regardless of productivity. For women, labor market experience may be an outcome rather than a determinant of career mobility if entry into career lines offering little opportunity for advancement affects labor force participation.

Although information on the actual productivity of workers is difficult to obtain, evidence on the relationships of worker characteristics such as formal education and labor market experience to productivity within occupations suggests that although these variables have some bearing on productivity, their effects on career advancement are largely independent of productivity (Horowitz and Sherman 1980; Medoff and Abraham 1980, 1981; Maranto and Rodgers 1984). Moreover, much variability is seen across occupations and work contexts in the extent to which education and work experience affect either productivity or earnings (Horowitz and Sherman 1980; Spilerman 1986). Evidence also contradicts the "tradeoff hypothesis"—that individuals sacrifice earnings at the beginning of their careers for better long-term career prospects. Individuals with lower earnings early in their careers actually have lower rather than higher job status and earnings later.

Recently, new explanations of the relationships of education and experience to career advancement have been surfacing. Some economists now attribute the relationship between experience and earnings to the desire of employers, especially those who make large investments in screening and training employees, to retain workers and motivate high performance over time (Lazear 1981; Lazear and Rosen 1981; Bulow and Summers 1986). Promotions and wage increases are seen as a means of eliciting effort from workers when the monitoring of their efforts and outputs is prohibitively expensive. These new explanations deviate from the view that labor is paid its marginal product in each short period, assuming that workers are paid their marginal product over the life cycle or in some cases in excess of their marginal product. So far, none of these explanations has an empirical basis, and, as single-factor explanations, they are unlikely to account for the diverse compensation schemes observed across occupations and work settings (Talbert and Bose 1977; Spilerman 1986).

Sociologists view the relationships of education and experience to career advancement as influenced primarily by the organizational, and even the broader societal, context in which the administrative arrangements that govern salary advancement and promotions arise. Spilerman (1986) has suggested that education and experience bear weaker relationships to earnings and promotion when organizational rules rigidly prescribe the temporal paths of earnings and occupational advancement. These rigid schedules are usually found in workplaces where the majority of workers are engaged in a very few career lines, or where multiple career lines exist, but there is little opportunity for transferring among them. Such schedules often result from unionization, since labor unions seek to standardize work arrangements. Even the effects of education and experience that exist under this type of personnel system vary across cities in ways suggesting an influence of general societal beliefs that educated and experienced workers should be paid more. Because such beliefs do not specify how much more, compensation schedules vary widely. Education and experience appear to bear stronger relationships to earnings in large nonunionized organizations that encompass many occupational specialties. However, even in these organizations, societal notions of equity and custom may affect wage structures. In Japan, for example, both seniority and family size are major determinants of salary in large companies (Dore 1973).

Sociological accounts differ from economic explanations in recognizing that the rewards of work derive from job occupancy and that a relatively enduring structure of jobs determines the relationships of individual effort, ability, and performance to work rewards. In the sociological view, jobs are assigned wage rates via processes operating at the societal and organizational levels, and the mechanisms that match individuals to jobs produce associations between individual effort, ability, and training, on the one hand, and work rewards, on the other. Jobs differ in the routes by which they are entered and in the extent to which performance can affect work rewards.

Within the organizational hierarchies of firms and occupations, patterned relationships among jobs produce job ladders and career lines composed of multiple job ladders. To the extent that upward mobility is possible and the shape of the hierarchy is pyramidal, workers entering a career line are in competition with others at the same level for advancement to the next highest level. Because jobs at the next level are filled from those occupying positions in the level below, entry to a job ladder and performance at each step on the ladder affect ultimate career attainments. Rosenbaum (1984) describes the process by which a cohort of employees is progressively differentiated throughout their careers in a series of implicit competitions as being like a tournament. Selections among the members of a cohort occur continually as careers unfold, and each selection affects the opportunity to advance further. Over time, career histories come to differ in the timing and occurrence of advancement, and factors affecting performance and selection early in the career have more important effects because more of the future remains to be determined.

What influences advancement is not the attributes of individuals per se, but their attributes in relation to organizational positions. Organizations define the criteria by which ability is identified and to the extent that ability is not tied to those criteria, it will not be recognized and rewarded. If individuals of limited ability are able by chance or other more calculated means to meet the criteria by which ability is identified, they will be assumed to have ability by an inference process in which the direction of causality is reversed. An important consequence of this system is that factors affecting access to positions, of which ability is only one, and factors affecting performance in accordance with organizationally recognized criteria, including the willingness to conform to organizational goals and practices, have an important influence on long-term career outcomes.

Given the importance of the structure of jobs in mediating the relationship between individual attributes such as education and experience and job rewards, it is not surprising that these attributes have little direct effect on rewards within job status categories. However, they have an important effect on careers via their influence on access to positions in the structure of jobs. Education is a major determinant of access to job ladders and career lines, and movement within these produces relationships between education and experience and work rewards. The organizational hierarchies to which college graduates, especially those from preferred colleges, have access increase the effects of college on career attainments over time. These hierarchies are moved through via experience. The job structure also mediates the relationship of ascriptive characteristics such as gender, race, and ethnicity to job rewards, where these characteristics become a basis for the differentiation of job ladders and career lines, as well as a basis for access to the jobs within them (Spilerman 1977; DiPrete 1989; Marini 1989).

SELECTION BY EMPLOYERS

Movement within a career line is affected not only by the characteristics of workers but by the characteristics and actions of those empowered by employers to make hiring and promotion decisions. Evaluation of performance and ability is usually based on incomplete information. In many jobs performance is difficult to assess, and ability is even harder to assess because it is inferred from performance. In addition, human perceptive capabilities are limited and variable. As a result, employers tend to rely on readily available information, or "signals," such as the amount of education attained, where it is attained, the amount and types of prior job experience, observable personal attributes, and evidence of past performance such as the rate of career advancement and prior job status and earnings. The criteria on which individuals are evaluated are therefore often superficial, and having the resources (i.e., money, knowledge, and skill) to identify the way the evaluation process works and acquire an appropriate set of signals plays an important role in career advancement. Because of the difficulty of obtaining information, employers are also susceptible to employee attempts to supply and manipulate information about themselves as well as others.

Another influence on the evaluation of ability and performance is attitudes and beliefs previously acquired by those with decision-making authority. Information is unconsciously filtered and interpreted through that cognitive lens. The effect of prior attitudes and beliefs is evident in the prejudice and stereotyping triggered by ascriptive characteristics such as gender, race, and ethnicity (Hamilton 1981; Marini 1989), which have been a focus of theories of discrimination in the labor market (see, e.g., Blau 1984).

In addition to the difficulties that arise in assessing performance and ability, personal relationships and political coalitions influence mobility. There is growing evidence that personal contacts and relationships constitute important sources of information and influence in gaining access to jobs (Granovetter 1984). An employee's position in workplace political coalitions can also affect career advancement.

(SEE ALSO: *Labor Force; Professions; Work and Occupations; Work Orientation*)

REFERENCES

Althauser, Robert P. 1989 "Internal Labor Markets." *Annual Review of Sociology* 15:143–161.

———, and Arne L. Kalleberg 1981 "Firms, Occupations and the Structure of Labor Markets: A Conceptual Analysis." In I. Berg, ed., *Sociological Perspectives on Labor Markets.* New York: Academic.

Baron, James N., and William T. Bielby 1980 "Bringing the Firms Back In: Stratification, Segmentation, and the Organization of Work." *American Sociological Review* 45:737–765.

Baron, James N., Alison Davis-Blake, and William T. Biebly 1986 "The Structure of Opportunity: How Promotion Ladders Vary within and among Organizations." *Administrative Science Quarterly* 31:248–273.

Becker, Gary S. 1964 *Human Capital.* New York: National Bureau of Economic Research.

Blau, Francine D. 1984 "Discrimination against Women: Theory and Evidence." In W. Darity, Jr., ed., *Labor Economics: Modern Views.* Boston: Kluwer-Nijhoff.

Blau, Peter M., and Otis Dudly Duncan 1967 *The American Occupational Structure.* New York: Wiley.

Blumen, Isadore, M. Kogan, and P. J. McCarthy 1955 *The Industrial Mobility of Labor as a Probability Process. Cornell Studies in Industrial and Labor Relations,* vol. 6. Ithaca: New York State School of Industrial and Labor Relations, Cornell University.

Bulow, J. I., and Larry H. Summers 1986 "A Theory of Dual Labor Markets with Application to Industrial Policy, Discrimination, and Keynesian Unemployment." *Journal of Labor Economics* 4:376–414.

Coleman, James S., Zahava D. Blum, Aage B. Sørensen, and Peter H. Rossi 1972 "White and Black Careers during the First Decade of Labor Force Experience. I. Occupational Status." *Social Science Research* 1:243–270.

DiPrete, Thomas A. 1989 *The Bureaucratic Labor Market.* New York: Plenum.

Doeringer, Peter B., and M. J. Piore 1971 *Internal Labor Markets and Manpower Analysis.* Lexington, Mass.: Heath.

Dore, Ronald P. 1973 *British Factory—Japanese Factory.* Berkeley: University of California Press.

Dunlop, John 1957 "The Task of Contemporary Wage Theory." In G. W. Taylor and F. C. Pierson, eds., *New Concepts in Wage Determination.* New York: McGraw-Hill.

Felmlee, Diane H. 1982 "Women's Job Mobility Processes within and between Employers." *American Journal of Sociology* 80:44–57.

Gordon, David M. 1972 *Theories of Poverty and Underemployment.* Lexington, Mass.: Heath.

Granovetter, Mark 1984 *Getting a Job: A Study of Contacts and Careers.* Cambridge, Mass.: Harvard University Press.

Hall, Robert E. 1982 "The Importance of Lifetime Jobs in the U.S. Economy." *American Economic Review* 72:716–724.

Hamilton, David L. 1981 *Cognitive Processes in Stereotyping and Intergroup Behavior.* Hillsdale, N.J.: Erlbaum.

Hodson, Randy, and Robert Kaufman 1982 "Economic Dualism: A Critical Review." *American Sociological Review* 47:727–739.

Horowitz, Stanley A., and Allan Sherman 1980 "A Direct Measure of the Relationship between Human Capital and Productivity." *Journal of Human Resources* 15:67–76.

Jencks, Christopher, M. Smith, H. Ackland, M. Bane, D. Cohen, H. Gintis, B. Heyns, and S. Michelson 1972 *Inequality: A Reassessment of the Effect of Family and Schooling in America.* New York: Basic Books.

Kalleberg, Arne, and Aage B. Sørensen 1979 "The Sociology of Labor Markets." *Annual Review of Sociology* 5:351–379.

Lazear, Edward P. 1981 "Agency, Earnings Profiles, Productivity, and Hours Restrictions." *American Economic Review* 71:606–620.

———, and S. Rosen 1981 "Rank-order Tournaments as Optimum Labor Contracts." *Journal of Political Economy* 89:841–864.

Maranto, Cheryl L., and Robert C. Rodgers 1984 "Does Work Experience Increase Productivity? A Test of the On-the-job Training Hypothesis." *Journal of Human Resources* 19:341–357.

March, James C., and James G. March 1977 "Almost Random Careers: The Wisconsin School of Superintendency, 1940–1972." *Administrative Science Quarterly* 22:377–409.

Marini, Margaret Mooney 1980 "Sex Differences in the Process of Occupational Attainment: A Closer Look." *Social Science Research* 9:307–361.

——— 1989 "Sex Differences in Earnings in the United States." *Annual Review of Sociology* 15:343–380.

Mayer, Thomas 1972 "Models in Intragenerational Mobility." In J. Berger, M. Zelditch, Jr., and B. Anderson, eds., *Sociological Theories in Progress,* vol. 2. Boston: Houghton Mifflin.

Medoff, James L., and Katherine G. Abraham 1980 "Experience, Performance, and Earnings." *Quarterly Journal of Economy* 95:703–736.

——— 1981 "Are Those Paid More Really More Productive? The Case of Experience." *Journal of Human Resources* 16:186–216.

Mincer, Jacob 1974 *Schooling, Experience, and Earnings.* New York: National Bureau of Economic Research.

Rosenbaum, James E. 1984 *Career Mobility in a Corporate Hierarchy.* New York: Academic.

Rosenfeld, Rachel A. 1980 "Race and Sex Differences

in Career Dynamics." *American Sociological Review* 45:583–609.

Sewell, William H. and Robert M. Hauser 1975 *Education, Occupation, and Earnings.* New York: Academic.

Sørensen, Aage B. 1974 "A Model for Occupational Careers." *American Journal of Sociology* 80:44–57.

——— 1975a "Growth in Occupational Achievement: Social Mobility or Investment in Human Capital." In K. L. Land and S. Spilerman, eds., *Social Indicator Models.* New York: Russell Sage Foundation.

——— 1975b "The Structure of Intragenerational Mobility." *American Sociological Review* 40:456–471.

Spence, Michael A. 1974 *Market Signaling.* Cambridge: Harvard University Press.

Spenner, Kenneth I., Luther B. Otto, and Vaughn R. A. Call 1982 *Career Lines and Careers.* Lexington, Mass.: Lexington Books.

Spilerman, Seymour 1977 "Careers, Labor Market Structure, and Socioeconomic Achievement." *American Journal of Sociology* 83:551–593.

——— 1986 "Organizational Rules and the Features of Work Careers." *Research in Social Stratification and Mobility* 5:41–102.

Stewman, Shelby, and S. L. Konda 1983 "Careers and Organizational Labor Markets: Demographic Models of Organizational Behavior." *American Journal of Sociology* 88:637–685.

Stiglitz, Joseph E. 1973 "Approaches to the Economics of Discrimination." *American Economic Review* 63:287–295.

Talbert, Joan, and Christine E. Bose 1977 "Wage Attainment Processes: The Retail Clerk Case." *American Journal of Sociology* 83:403–424.

White, Harrison C. 1970 *Chains of Opportunity.* Cambridge: Harvard University Press.

MARGARET MOONEY MARINI

OCCUPATIONAL PRESTIGE Individuals have repeatedly demonstrated an ability to rank occupations according to their relative social standing or prestige, a concept embodying elements of socioeconomic status and social honor. The modern study of occupational prestige dates to a landmark survey fielded in 1947 by the National Opinion Research Center (NORC) under the direction of Cecil C. North and Paul K. Hatt (Reiss et al. 1961), in which prestige scores for ninety occupational titles were constructed. Although others had conducted earlier investigations in the United States, NORC's national sample and broad coverage of the occupational hierarchy became the model for later inquiries. Perhaps the best-known product of the North-Hatt study was Duncan's (1961) Socioeconomic Index, which assigned to each detailed occupational category a predicted prestige score based on the age-standardized education and income characteristics of occupational incumbents reported by the census of 1950. This index exploited the limited occupational titles evaluated by the North-Hatt study to construct the first metric scale of socioeconomic status for all occupations.

In the 1960s, a second generation of studies was carried out by NORC (Hodge, Siegel, and Rossi 1964). Piecing together surveys from 1963, 1964, and 1965, Siegel (1971) generated the first prestige scale for all census occupations. This scale served for twenty years as the foundation of socioeconomic status scores, and it became the backbone of Treiman's (1977) International Prestige Scale. In 1980, however, a major change in the occupational classification system employed by the Bureau of the Census called into question scores based on earlier classifications of occupational titles. In 1989, the NORC General Social Survey undertook another periodic sounding of Americans' evaluations of the general social standing of occupations (Nakao and Treas 1990). The 1989 survey, the first to collect evaluations for all occupational categories at one time, yielded new prestige and socioeconomic scores.

Five generalizations may be drawn from the research about occupational prestige.

First, very different methods for soliciting occupational evaluations yield very similar prestige hierarchies. Presenting respondents with an occupational title (e.g., electrician), the North-Hatt study asked them to "pick out the statement that best gives your personal opinion of the general standing that such a job has." Five response categories, ranging from "excellent standing" to "poor standing," were presented along with a "don't know" option. One might readily fault the ambiguous instructions calling for both a "personal" opinion and a reading of "general" standing. Nonetheless, the resulting hierarchical order proved virtually identical to those of the 1964 and 1989 surveys, which asked respondents to sort cards bearing occupational titles onto a "ladder of social standing." The 1964 study went on to ask respondents to sort occupations onto a horizontal ruler according to another specific dimension (e.g., freedom and independence, perceived income, how interesting the work). However different the tasks, the correlation with social standing evaluations was over 0.90 for eight of nine dimensions.

Even when respondents are instructed to cluster occupations according to their similarity (rather than rank them by social standing), multidimensional scaling methods reveal that the organizing principle behind judged similarity is a prestige hierarchy. Burton (1972) first demonstrated this with a nonrandom sample of volunteers solicited from an advertisement in the Harvard student newspaper. Kraus, Schild, and Hodge (1978) achieved similar results with a representative sample of 463 urban Israelis. To confirm that people view occupations in terms of an up–down classification scheme, Schwartz (1981) showed that ranking occupations according to "vertical" paired adjectives (e.g., top/bottom) yields results highly correlated with prestige scores, while rankings based on evaluative (e.g., kind/cruel), potency (e.g., big/little), and activity (e.g., slow/fast) dimensions fail to replicate prestige orderings. In short, the prestige hierarchy is so central to how we evaluate occupations that it emerges from virtually any reasonable effort to elicit it.

Second, overall prestige rankings are very stable over time. Hodge, Siegel, and Rossi (1964) reported a correlation of 0.99 between the 1947 North-Hatt study and their own in the mid-1960s. Nakao and Treas (1990) find a correlation of 0.96 between the mid-1960s and 1989. This stability is not surprising. First, the relative income and education levels associated with various occupations are quite stable over time (Treiman and Terrell 1975). Second, to the extent that prestige is fixed by the division of labor and workplace authority, we do not expect the prestige of flight attendants to soar above that of pilots.

This is not to say that prestige never changes. Hodge, Siegel, and Rossi (1964) noted modest gains for blue-collar occupations, an upswing in scientific occupations and the "free" professions (e.g., "physician"), and a downturn in artistic, cultural, and communication occupations. Nakao and Treas (1990) point out that the bottom of the American occupational prestige distribution shifted upward between 1964 and 1989. Low-status service and farming occupations came to be more favorably evaluated. The case of farmers suggests that change occurs not because of the succession of new generations who hold different views, but rather because all age groups change their thinking about the relative standing of occupations. Changes in the general public's familiarity with an occupation can also affect its rating, as demonstrated for "nuclear physicist" between 1947 and 1963 (Hodge, Siegel, and Rossi 1964). Thus, individual occupations change even though the overall ranking of occupations remains quite stable over time.

Third, prestige evaluations are surprisingly comparable from one society to another. Arguing that industrialization everywhere demands a similar organization and reward of work, Treiman (1977) assembled 85 prestige studies for 60 nations, tribal societies, and territories. Comparing the United States with fifty-nine other societies yielded an average intercorrelation of 0.837; in other words, about 70 percent of the variation in U.S. prestige evaluations is shared in common with the "average" society available to Treiman. To be sure, the correlations ranged from 0.98 for Canada to 0.54 for Zaire. Prestige hierarchies are similar, but not identical. Notable differences relate to level of economic development (Treiman 1977) and the greater appreciation of manual labor in socialist societies (Penn 1975; for a Chinese exception, see Lin and Xie 1988).

Fourth, subgroups within a society also tend to agree about the relative ranking of occupations. Efforts to discern differences between blacks and whites, between those employed in more versus less prestigious jobs, have typically found little effect of the respondent's social location on his/her view of the occupational hierarchy (e.g., Goldthorpe and Hope 1972; Kraus, Schild, and Hodge 1978). To be sure, higher-status groups assign somewhat higher absolute rankings to high-status jobs than do lower-status groups, who tend to boost lower-status jobs somewhat (Hodge and Rossi 1978). Apparently, this phenomenon does not arise because groups hold self-serving views of the social order. Instead, high-status individuals agree more among themselves and, therefore, avoid random ranking errors that move both high- and low-status occupations toward the middle of the distribution. Since one's location in the social structure has been shown to influence so many other attitudes, it is surprising that groups agree so closely on the order of occupations. The mechanisms leading to this consensus are not well understood. By early adolescence, however, children can agree how jobs rank (Gunn 1964).

Fifth, the main factors associated with an occupation's prestige are its education and income levels. Socioeconomic scores based on these two factors account for about 80 percent of the variation in prestige attributed to different occupations (Hodge 1981). Since socioeconomic status scores beat prestige scores when it comes to accounting for fathers' occupational influences on sons' occupational achievements (Treas and Tyree 1979), it is tempting to dismiss occupational prestige. This would be a mistake. Subgroups of raters agree not only on the prestige of an occupation, but also how prestige differs from the occupation's socioeconomic location (Hodge 1981).

However important the educational requirements and economic rewards of occupations, they are not alone in determining the prestige accorded occupations. The racial, age, and sex composition of jobs also figure in their public evaluation. Even controlling for education and occupation, a higher proportion of nonwhites in an occupation is associated with lower prestige ratings (Siegel 1971). Occupations dominated by the very young or very old are similarly disadvantaged (Siegel 1971).

There is no conclusive evidence that American respondents consistently downgrade the status of female-gendered occupational titles (e.g., policewoman) as compared with male titles (e.g., policeman). Male (but not female) respondents do downgrade the standing of occupations in which women find employment—a relation that holds after the income and education levels of workers are taken into account (Meyer 1978).

(SEE ALSO: *Social Stratification; Status Attainment*)

REFERENCES

Burton, Michael 1972 "Semantic Dimensions of Occupational Names." In A. Kimball Romney, Roger N. Shepard, and Sara Nerlove, eds., *Multidimensional Scaling: Theory and Applications in the Behavioral Sciences.* Vol. 2, *Applications.* New York: Seminar.

Duncan, Otis Dudley 1961 "A Socioeconomic Index for All Occupations." In Albert J. Reiss, Jr., et al., eds., *Occupations and Social Status.* New York: Free Press.

Goldthorpe, John H., and Keith Hope 1972 "Occupational Grading and Occupational Prestige." In Keith Hope, ed., *The Analysis of Social Mobility: Methods and Approaches.* Oxford: Clarendon Press.

Gunn, Barbara 1964 "Children's Conceptions of Occupational Prestige." *Personnel and Guidance Journal* 42:558–563.

Hodge, Robert W. 1981 "The Measurement of Occupational Prestige." *Social Science Research* 10:396–415.

———, and Peter M. Rossi 1978 "Intergroup Consensus in Occupational Prestige Ratings: A Case of Serendipity Lost and Regained." *Sozialwissenschaftliche Annalen* 2:B59–73.

———, Paul M. Siegel, and Peter Rossi 1964 "Occupational Prestige in the United States, 1925–1963." *American Journal of Sociology* 70:286–302.

Kraus, Vered, E. O. Schild, and Robert W. Hodge 1978 "Occupational Prestige in the Collective Conscience." *Social Forces* 56:900–918.

Lin, Nan, and Wen Xie 1988 "Occupational Prestige in Urban China." *American Journal of Sociology* 93:793–832.

Meyer, Garry S. 1978 "Sex and Marriage of Raters in the Evaluation of Occupations." *Social Science Research* 7:366–388.

Nakao, Keiko, and Judith Treas 1990 "Occupational Prestige in the United States Revisited: Twenty-five Years of Stability and Change." Paper presented at the Annual Meeting of the American Sociological Association, Washington, D.C.

Penn, R. 1975 "Occupational Prestige Hierarchies: A Great Empirical Invariant?" *Social Forces* 54:352–364.

Reiss, Albert J., Jr., with Otis D. Duncan, Paul K. Hatt, and Cecil C. North 1961 *Occupations and Social Status.* New York: Free Press.

Schwartz, Barry 1981 *Vertical Classification: A Study in Structuralism and the Sociology of Knowledge.* Chicago: University of Chicago Press.

Siegel, Paul M. 1971 "Prestige in the American Occupational Structure." Ph.D. diss., Department of Sociology, University of Chicago.

Treas, Judith, and Andrea Tyree 1979 "Prestige Versus Socioeconomic Status in the Attainment Processes of American Men and Women." *Social Science Research* 8:201–221.

Treiman, Donald J. 1977 *Occupational Prestige in Comparative Perspective.* New York: Academic Press.

———, and Kermit Terrell 1975 "Women, Work and Wages—Trends in the Female Occupation Structure." In Kenneth C. Land and Seymour Spilerman, eds., *Social Indicator Models.* New York: Russell Sage Foundation.

KEIKO NAKAO

OCCUPATIONS *See* Professions; Work and Occupations.

ORGANIZATIONAL EFFECTIVENESS

Organizational effectiveness is the ability of an organization, formal or informal, to achieve its goals. While defining effectiveness as the ability to achieve goals seems straightforward, assessing organizational effectiveness is a complex task. Crucial elements in evaluating organizational effectiveness include both determining the desired goal or goals of an organization and assessing how and why the organization is succeeding or failing in attaining goals.

Early models of organizational effectiveness assumed a clear organizational goal—usually a production goal—and focused on the organization's ability to achieve this goal by best utilizing the resources available to the organization. Researchers such as Frederick Winslow Taylor (1911) and Frank and Lillian Gilberth (1917) promoted what they labeled "scientific management," which involved the scientific analysis of work tasks, to determine the most efficient means of production. One of Taylor's applications of scientific management was in the handling of pig iron at Bethlehem Steel. Taylor argued that although the work process was by nature crude, the average of 12½ long tons handled per man per day could be nearly quadrupled by the application of scientific principles and the use of economic incentives. In this case a 60 percent increase in wages owing to a bonus system increased production by almost 400 percent. Although the principle that workers are economically motivated was widely accepted, the overall scientific management model met considerable resistance. First, workers resisted attempts to control their performance and did not universally respond to incentive systems. Second, managers resented the usurpation of their judgment and prerogatives by the standardization of work practices. The study of how best to design work to increase human efficiency continues by researchers in the areas of human factors and industrial engineering.

Some of the early efforts by researchers to measure factors that promoted worker productivity and organizational effectiveness were successful in unanticipated ways. For example, several organizational researchers in the 1930s began a series of experiments designed to examine the role that workplace conditions played in the productivity of workers. These studies, known as the Hawthorne experiments, were conducted over a period of years in separate relay assembly and bank wiring rooms in a General Electric manufacturing plant outside of Chicago. Researchers, including F. J. Roethlisberger and W. J. Dickson (1939) as well as Elton Mayo (1945), sought to investigate productivity by varying general work conditions rather than specific characteristics of tasks. These researchers changed things such as the timing and length of coffee and lunch breaks, the kind of meals served to workers (including whether the meals were hot or cold), and the lighting conditions under which the workers were assembling the product. Worker productivity continued to improve over the course of the studies, regardless of the type of change instituted by the researchers. Lighting levels were raised, and worker productivity increased. Lighting levels were lowered, and worker productivity increased. The number of coffee breaks was expanded, and so did productivity; coffee breaks were eliminated, and productivity increased. In an effort to examine the sources of this phenomenon, working conditions were returned to exactly those at the beginning of the study, and productivity still continued at a higher level. It became apparent that something more fundamental than changing working conditions was going on—the very presence of the investigators in the work rooms was acting to promote worker productivity. The workers were enjoying the attention that they were receiving, and may also have been mindful that they held valuable jobs in a time of a declining economy. This unintended effect became known as the "Hawthorne effect." The Hawthorne studies spawned an entire school of research, known as the "human relations" school, which examines the effects of personal interaction on organizational effectiveness. Current research in this area is largely conducted in the disciplines of organizational behavior and industrial psychology.

While researchers in the United States initially focused on factors affecting worker productivity, others were examining the relationship between overall organizational structure and effectiveness. Max Weber (1968), the most prominent of the European scholars, drew attention to the rationalization of organizations. He argued that "modern," "rational," bureaucratic organizations that are characterized by routines and regulations are more efficient than traditional forms of social organization. Bureaucracy makes organizations effective, because it makes activities routine—if you wish to process an order for a product, for instance, you simply follow the rules laid out for that task. There is no need to treat each case individually; rules and regulations replace innovation in finding solutions to organizational problems. This means that while bureaucracies provide an effective means of dealing with routine activities, the solution of unique problems is made more difficult. Hence, bureaucracies solve some problems of organizational effectiveness while creating others. For example, Kanter, in *When Giants Learn to Dance,* focuses on efforts to implement innovation in large, rule-bound, heavily bureaucratic organizations.

Fundamental to determining the source of organizational effectiveness is understanding an organization's goals. As research progressed, it became clear that organizational goals are complex. For instance, organizational goals may change over time; organizations, once created, have inertial properties that seek to maintain the organization's existence regardless of its effectiveness in achieving external goals. Robert Michels noted in *Political Parties* that leaders of organizations often have a strong stake in the survival of the organization and may change its goals to ensure survival. He felt that this tendency had strong implications for the ability of organizations to remain democratically controlled over time. Mayer Zald and Patricia Denton (1963), in a classic study of the YMCA, demonstrate the presence of maintenance goals. The organization, originally designed to provide housing for single Christians in urban areas, became a general-purpose, nondenominational recreational center as its initial goal was achieved or became obsolete.

In addition to having a goal that may change over time, organizations typically have multiple goals. The existence of multiple goals suggests that effective organizations may *satisfice,* that is, be less than fully optimal or efficient in working toward any one goal—but instead may be seeking to pursue a set of goals simultaneously.

Another way to view the presence of multiple goals in an organization, from the point of view of a leader or manager with a single goal, is that a series of means–ends chains need to be constructed and maintained (Simon 1957). This should be done in such a way that while individuals and interest groups within the organization can pursue their own subgoals, that pursuit of subgoals acts as a set of means for pursuing some larger goal. In this way, organizations remain goal-oriented at the highest level, even though individuals may not have any direct connection with the goals of the whole organization. For example, a bricklayer can pursue the construction of a particular wall, with little stake in the overall completion of a building. In the extreme, organizations can be viewed not as monolithic entities with a single interest, but as coalitions of interest groups. Different individuals and interest groups within the organization may have different goals, which may or may not be synonymous with stated organizationwide goals (Weick 1976). Therefore, in order to study organizational effectiveness, researchers often find they are examining a set of goals rather than a single goal.

Evaluation of organizational effectiveness, either in achieving a single goal or a set of goals, requires measuring goal attainment. The choice of measure(s) may have substantial consequences for the organization. First, different measures may provide a very different picture of the organization's effectiveness. For instance, an increase in gross sales might reflect successful growth but could be accompanied by either an increase or a decrease in net profits. Second, the measure(s) chosen—and the overall evaluation process—may alter the effectiveness of the organization. The placement of sensors to measure outputs can distort the work of the organization; the practice of "storming" in an effort to meet monthly quotas is one consequence of a system of evaluating organizational effectiveness (Berliner 1956). In a similar way, the use of errors as an indicator of a baseball player's defensive ability may in fact yield counterproductive behavior, since the players who contribute most to a team's effectiveness may be those who consistently cover more territory, and thus have more opportunities to fail. Hence, the person who does the most may also make the most mistakes.

Even when measures are readily available, evaluation of the effectiveness of the organization is still not straightforward. The assessment of organizational effectiveness may differ when evaluated in different time frames. For example, an organization may be successful in achieving a goal at a single point in time, but may be unable to maintain that success over longer time periods. The effectiveness of a software manufacturer may look particularly good in the months before its competitors ship equivalent products, and decrease steadily as competition increases.

This raises a further point, which is the complexity of evaluating the source of organizational effectiveness. For example, an organization may be effective at achieving a goal for some period of time, and then, with identical structures and behavior, may find itself to be ineffective owing to a change in its environment. Reconsidering the previous example, the source of a software company's effectiveness may come more from being the first to market with a particular product. As the environment changes, especially as underlying operating systems change, a company's product, while being successfully maintained and upgraded, nevertheless may be bypassed by products oriented toward different operating systems.

Efforts to evaluate organizational effectiveness can serve to clarify the meaning of goals, how goal achievement might be measured, the time frame in which they are to be evaluated, and the sources of effectiveness in meeting a particular goal at a particular point in time. Further, simple goals, such as product produced, profit achieved, and members gained, can give members and leaders of organizations the power and ability to guide the organization toward accomplishing complex, interrelated tasks.

Great strides have been made in the subtlety and thoroughness with which researchers and practitioners understand and evaluate effectiveness.

(SEE ALSO: *Complex Organizations; Organizational Structure*)

REFERENCES

Berliner, J. S. 1956 "A Problem in Soviet Business Administration." *Administrative Science Quarterly* 1:86–100.

Gilbreth, F. B., and L. M. Gilbreth 1917 *Applied Motion Study*. New York.

Gouldner, Alvin W. 1959 "Organizational Analysis." In Robert Merton, Leonard Broom, and Leonard S. Lothell, Jr., eds., *Sociology Today*. New York: Basic Books.

Kanter, Rosabeth M. 1989 *When Giants Learn to Dance*. New York: Simon and Schuster.

Mayo, Elton 1945 *The Social Problems of an Industrial Civilization.* Boston: Graduate School of Business Administration, Harvard University.

Michels, Robert 1915 (1949 trans.) *Political Parties.* Glencoe, Ill.: Free Press.

Roethlisberger, F. J., and William J. Dickson 1939 *Management and the Worker.* Cambridge: Harvard University Press.

Selznick, Philip 1949 *TVA and the Grass Roots.* Berkeley: University of California Press.

Simon, H. A. 1957 *Administrative Behavior,* 2nd ed. New York: Macmillan.

Taylor, F. W. 1911 *The Principles of Scientific Management.* New York: Harper.

Weber, Max 1968 *Economy & Society.* New York: Bedminster Press.

Weick, K. 1976 "Educational Organizations as Loosely Coupled Systems." *Administrative Science Quarterly* 21:1–19.

Zald, Mayer N., and Patricia Denton 1963 "From Evangelism to General Service: The Transformation of the YMCA." *Administrative Science Quarterly* 8:214–234.

NANCY E. DURBIN
ANDREW L. CREIGHTON

ORGANIZATIONAL STRUCTURE Organizations are composed of a variety of elements. Perhaps the fundamental component is *organizational structure,* the set of interrelationships (social bonds) between positions. Even organizations of globe-encircling proportions, such as multinational corporations, have their origin in the most elemental social bond, "the consciously coordinated activities of two or more people" (Barnard 1938, p. 73). Similarly, it may be argued that relationships between and among *sets* of such organizations form the social structure of whole societies.

Within an organizational structure, groups or sets of social relationships can be differentiated by task specialization, known as the *division of labor.* People are assigned to specific positions within an organizational structure in order to increase the specificity of tasks and the reliability with which they are performed. Organizational structure is both (1) an outcome resulting from interactive processes between elements within the organization as well as between the environment and the organization; and (2) a determinant of those interactive processes. Organizational structure constitutes a grant of authority calling for or inhibiting particular behaviors by organizational participants.

Interaction among parties to a relationship gives rise to particular shared understandings that become part of an organization's culture. Focusing as it does on relationships constituting organizational structure, the social systems perspective for organizational analysis has been criticized as having a static cast. By contrast, study of social processes among constituent parties is said to give organizational analysis a dynamic focus because it examines how social change occurs as participants grant or withhold their consent for collective actions. When the volitional and cognitive exigencies among constituents change, their behavior toward each is altered. For a specific set of participants, negotiations on emergent interests lead to the creation of new relationships, fluidity in existing relationships, and the potential for breaking off long-standing relationships. The processes influencing expectation and negotiation are complicated by the structural advantages enjoyed by dominant constituent parties. Whether change in agreed-upon relations is viewed as desirable often depends on whether a given constituent party perceives change to be disproportionately beneficial to itself when compared with the benefits to specific constituent groups or the overall organization. Moreover, more powerful constituents can, to their own benefit, cloud less powerful constituents' perceptions of what is actually in the latter's self-interest.

Much traditional theory and research on organizations implicitly (occasionally explicitly) assumes that decisions by upper participants benefit the entire collectivity. Most analyses do not differentiate benefit to the collectivity from benefit to upper-, middle-, or lower-level participants. Most researchers simply proceed on the assumption that owners and managers are prime, if not sole, legitimate beneficiaries of organizational structure. If measured by their contributions to organizational survival, actual and potential beneficiaries of organizational structure compose a much broader array of constituents. Researchers need explicitly to identify and differentiate *all* participants and constituents that contribute directly or indirectly to an organization. Allocation of resources to an organization's tasks, defined through the division of labor, critically affects the power balance between participants, thus raising important and politically disturbing questions. Organizational structure, composed of collectively endorsed resource allocation agreements, can be usefully understood from a "distributive justice" theoretical perspective. A key feature is differential distribution of types of people to types of tasks.

Distributive justice research seeks to understand how resources are allocated in ways believed to be "fair" by various interactants. Meindl (1989) notes two perspectives on distributive justice: (1) where the allocator uses a set of "distributive rules" to allocate resources, and (2) where recipients exhibit levels of satisfaction according to their perception of the just distribution of allocations. The invention and implementation of distribution rules by allocators focuses on *attributes* and *contributions* of recipients (Cook and Yamagishi 1983). Attributes can be personal characteristics such as gender, age, and ethnicity, which are used to determine social status. Contributions refer to valued inputs made by participants in an exchange relationship; among these valued inputs are performance, ability, and effort.

Organizational theorists frequently focus on workers' contributions in creating distribution rules and ignore workers' attributes. Given the level of ethnic and gender segregation within the work force, particular tasks appear to be associated with certain attributes as workers are distributed into organizational positions. Additionally, institutional factors, such as state legislation, and cultural values may affect allocators' distribution rules. In some cases distribution rules for constituents related to a given organization through its impact on their culture, economy, or community may differ from distribution rules for those participating directly in an organization. Recipients of allocated resources compare their contributions and rewards for tasks with other individuals' or groups' contributions and rewards. While most theorists perceive people to make comparisons solely on the basis of income, Martin (1981) notes that people broadly compare themselves to others simultaneously on such bases as income, age, education, seniority, and productivity. Further, not all workers believe their attributes such as organizational loyalty, ethnicity, or gender are justly rewarded, so they may discount the market (monetary) value of their labor as an indicator of its true worth.

In order better to assess the distributive implications of organizational structure, researchers should devote more attention to Blau and Scott's (1962) *cui bono* criterion, which explicitly raises the question of who benefits from particular policies and characteristics of organizational structure. Blau and Scott suggest a fourfold topology of organizations: (1) mutual benefit organizations, such as clubs, where presumably egalitarian *members* are prime beneficiaries; (2) business or industrial organizations, where *owners* are prime beneficiaries; (3) service organizations, such as hospitals, where *clients* are prime beneficiaries; (4) commonweal organizations, such as the State Department, in which the *public-at-large* is prime beneficiary. For each type of organization, researchers should systematically examine patterns of benefit by virtue of a constituency's location either (1) externally in an input–output exchange relationship to the organization, or (2) internally as upper-, middle-, or lower-level participants in its organizational structure (Etzioni 1961). A fully developed distributive justice perspective would evaluate the benefit a constituency derives from the organization relative to its contribution to the organization's sustained existence (Alvarez 1979).

This review is categorized into four functional requirements for social system survival posited by Parsons (1960): (1) adaptation to the environment; (2) goal attainment; (3) integration of its members into a "whole"; and (4) creation of cultural understandings among members by which the meaning of collective action can be judged. We do not suggest Parsons's AGIL scheme is the only or definitive way to classify organizational structures or attendant activities. Rather, the scheme implies a focus on the totality of a particular organization and subsequently raises questions of how its organizational structures come into being, change, and persist; within each category we question "who benefits" from consensual, consciously coordinated activities.

ADAPTATION TO THE ENVIRONMENT

"Environment" refers to a broad array of elements that are "outside" organizational boundaries but are relevant to organizational functioning. Organizational boundaries are the set of agreed-upon relationships that constitute organizational structure. Dill (1958, p. 410) defines the task, or technical, environment as all features of the environment "potentially relevant to goal setting and goal attainment." Established beliefs and practices embedded within the organization may systematically affect the shape and operation of the focal organization's structure. Scott (1986) terms these influences the *institutional environment* of organizations; others refer to it as organizational culture. An organization may seek to control or reshape all or some elements in its environment as a means to lessen uncertainty about its capacity to endure. An organization might reshape its own organizational structures if it is unable to reshape the environment (e.g., Aldrich 1979). Dess and Beard (1984) suggest that Aldrich's (1979) topology of environmental characteristics may be classified into three categories: (1) munificence, or the environmental availability of resources needed by organizations; (2) complexity, or the similarity or dissimilarity of environmental entities and their distribution across the environment; and (3) dynamism, or the degree of change in the environment.

Organizations exist within larger societies. Societal culture (relatively integrated sets of values and value-based orientations) of a given society affects directly the kinds of organizational structures that can be sustained by organizations. Nevertheless, organizational structures and their internal organizational culture might be a stronger determinative force than the outer societal culture. Hence, some organizations are often viewed as determinative importers of social change into some societies (e.g., technology transfers by multinational corporations). Organizational culture and the external societal culture inevitably affect one another. Findings vary as to how societal culture affects multinational firms. Birnbaum and Wong (1985) for example, found that organizational structure was "culture free." Researchers still have to find ways to identify and measure cultural effects as differentiated from global characteristics of societies such as their economy, legal systems, and demographic composition.

The state (the system of governance in a society) is another global element with pervasive repercussions for organizational functioning. The state may regulate the organizations directly by instituting programs within them or indirectly by state regulation of what an organization may produce or how it may transact with other organizations such as suppliers or consumers. Organizations may attempt to influence governmental actions so that public policy does not constrain them or so that it will actively benefit them. Organizations frequently influence legislation directly, as by activities of lobbyists on retainer. Organizations often mount campaigns either to achieve or prevent the enactment of specific legislation by directly influencing general public opinion and particular voters. Even if legislation is passed over their opposition, organizations can achieve their purposes by subsequently influencing the allocation of resources for its enforcement.

Communities are attentive to organizations located in their midst since changes in organizational structure can have considerable repercussions for the community at large. As Scott (1986) points out, not all organizations are strongly tied to the communities in which they are located. Locally based firms have a greater vested interest in community prosperity than do geographically dispersed firms, and they may act to assure continued community prosperity. Organizations may strongly affect the allocation of public goods and services as well as specifications in local policies, such as zoning and tax laws. The number, size, and type of organizations located in a community also have widespread consequences for individual local residents. South and Xu (1990) compared industries that dominate their local metropolitan economy with those that do not, finding that employees in dominant industries earn higher wages. Thus, organizations have important political, economic, and normative effects on individuals with or without organizational membership and on their community's organized power structures.

We now explore how organizations respond to and create their own environments. "Gate-keepers" are organizational participants at various levels who "selectively" permit information and people to traverse boundaries into and out of an organization. They "legitimate" particular environmental constituencies, with whom the organization then establishes institutional relations. Relations with constituencies not so "selected" become invisible, neutralized, or illegitimate. The breadth of the environmental domain that an organization claims in this manner has consequences for its stability. Narrow domains are associated with greater stability, while broad, inconsistently defined domains are associated with loss of function (Meyer 1975).

"Loose coupling," the seemingly weak relationship between parts of an organization to one another (Pfeffer and Salancik 1978), is one of many ways in which organizations learn to deal with a broad environmental domain. This weak relationship allows change in one part of an organization to precipitate minimal or no change in other parts. Relationships between subunits or individuals in organizations, and relationships between the organization and other environmental entities, may be loosely coupled. Organizations may respond to potentially coercive environmental pressures, such as state regulation, by very limited conformity in a specific sector, and yet this limited conformity projects an aura of complete organizational compliance. In reality, affected components of organizational structure may be effectively uncoupled from many other components and processes, resulting merely in the appearance of compliance (DiMaggio and Powell 1983). Loose coupling can also lead to structural "inertia" in an organization's response to environmental changes, causing "lags" between environmental changes and adaptations to them on the part of various organizational structures.

Who benefits in the adaptation of organizations to the environment? Elites (fiduciaries, executives, and high level managers) are only one kind of constituency vying for potential benefits derived from organizational structure. Middle and lower level organizational participants are often neglected in the research literature on organizational structure. Often, when research findings indicate that either an "organization" or a "community" benefits from a particular activity, what is really meant is that *upper* level participants benefit. Certain populations (women and ethnic minorities, for example) participate differentially at upper, middle, and lower levels of organizational structure; thus, a focus on upper participants is insufficient to fully describe patterns of benefit.

GOAL ATTAINMENT

"Goal" refers to a desirable future state of affairs. *Official* goals are the formal statements put forth by organizations to state their general purposes (Perrow 1961). *Operative* goals, on the other hand, refer to "what the organization is actually trying to do" (Perrow 1961, p. 855). The degree of congruency between official and operative goals is variable. It is important to distinguish organizational goals from the motives of individual organizational participants (Simon 1964). However, researchers need to clarify how particular goal activity differentially benefits specific internal or external constituencies. Goals serve to limit and direct organizational decision making and to suggest criteria by which organizational performance can be measured.

Over time, organizations tend to establish multiple, often disparate, and sometimes conflicting goals. Kochan, Cummings, and Huber (1976) argue that goal multiplicity and conflict are associated with both horizontal (number of tasks at the same level of structure) and vertical (number of levels between the "highest" and "lowest" units) differentiation of organizational structure. In the pursuit of multiple goals, coordination of effort is necessary, leading to vertical differentiation of organizational structure. Organizations change their goals over time, both for external and internal reasons. Thompson and McEwen (1958) contend that goals vary because interaction with elements *external* to the organization can be of two kinds: competitive or cooperative. The only competitive option in their discussion we call *bounded competition,* referring to the fact that the interaction takes place within the bounds of the normative structure (institutional environment) of the larger social system. *Raw* or *unbounded competition* takes place outside of any normative order common to the contending parties and is not accounted for by Thompson and McEwen's discussion. Accordingly, Thompson and McEwen define competition as rivalry between two or more organizations mediated by a third party. Organizations compete for resources viewed as desirable for organizational functioning. Thompson and McEwen discuss three cooperative styles of interaction between organizations and external elements, each underscored by a decreasing level of hostility: co-optation, bargaining, and coalition. Co-optation is the absorption of an external element into the organization, neutralizing its potential hostility by incorporating it within the organization's structure. Bargaining is direct interaction with environmental entities in which some kind of exchange takes place so that the organization can get what it desires. Coalition is an agreement, usually of specific duration for specific collective purposes, combining the efforts of two or more organizations, and restricting the right of each to set goals unilaterally. Notice that coalition requires very low levels of hostility between an organization and its partners; indeed, a potential outcome may be loss of separate identity and structural unification. These strategies can increase or decrease the size and complexity of organizational structure and the allocation of resources within it.

Organizational goals also change for *internal* reasons. Constituencies within the organization frequently form *coalitions,* initially for self-protection against real or imagined threats to the pursuit of their own interests. Each, unable to impose its will on others, but fearing imposition, makes alliances with other constituencies perceived to be friendly. Some such alliances capture key positions of the organizational structure, thus giving greater access to the allocation of organizational resources. This dominance can be maintained over time by securing the cooperation of other elements and coalitions within the organization through the selective distribution of resources. How central a given goal is to an organization may depend on the composition of the dominant coalition and the relative balance of power within it.

This discussion has emphasized the complexity of goals and goal setting given a variety of internal and external factors. The processes by which groups or members of organizations gain power, and the loose coupling between goals and motivations, have a large impact on goal setting. It is useful to discuss the processes of power in organizations in more depth. Many theorists have proposed definitions of power, but one of the most useful is Emerson's (1962); power resides in the dependency of one on the resources of another. Resource control theorists believe that individuals or organizational subunits exercise power because they allocate resources needed by others to reduce uncertainty or because their resources are specialized or are central to the work flow of the organization (Lachman 1989). Researchers have paid much attention to structural conditions associated with power in organizations. Spaeth (1985) found that resource allocation is central to task performance since lower level employees are assigned to produce given outputs and are provided with the necessary resources to do so. The higher the level of the worker, the more discretionary resources she or he will have to allocate. Recently, researchers have explored the relationship between technological innovation and shifts of power among organizational members. Burkhardt and Brass (1990) found that early adopters of a computerized information system in a federal agency increased their centrality and power in organizational networks. These shifts did not completely alter the power structure since those in power were not completely displaced by early technology adopters. Barley (1986) makes clear that technology provides organizational members an occasion for "structuring." The same technological system may have different implications and cause different social changes in different organizational structures. Thus, Barley disputes the claims by some researchers that technology has objective material consequences regardless of the social contexts within which it exists.

Scott (1986) writes that organizations attempt to build structures, not only to accomplish a division of labor but to create a structure of authority. As organizations become more formalized, that is, as procedures and rules are explicitly formulated, power differentials are built into the system and institutionalized. The distributive advantage of upper participants is not obvious since hierarchy is presumably built on specific task competence and power is vested for specific task achievement. Those with institutionalized power need not mobilize to have their interests served, since they control the flow of resources and information. The institutionalization of power contradicts resource control theory, which asserts that those who control the contingencies for change in organizations gain power. Lachman (1989) emphasizes that when the relative power of subunits changes, the new power structure is significantly affected by the previous one. He found that the greatest predictor of subunit power after organizational change was its degree of power before the change, regardless of its control over organizational contingencies or changes.

Setting and attainment of goals are complex processes affected by factors internal and external to organizations and by processes for power distribution. The *cui bono* criterion alerts the researcher not to take formal goals at face value but to identify how key actors and groups in coalitions differentially benefit from goal activity. In spite of its tendency to persist, organizational structure can be and is altered to reflect the power of new alliances among internal and external constituencies who benefit from new institutional arrangements. Organizations survive because powerful constituent alliances continue to derive benefit from them.

THE INTERNAL INTEGRATION OF ORGANIZATIONAL STRUCTURE

Organizations cohere in part because some elements of organizational structure are designated to coordinate other organizational elements into a collective "whole" in the pursuit of goals. The discussion of integration will examine: (1) how some organizational variables affect composition of organizational structural; (2) structure's differential outcomes for stratified groups; and (3) who benefits from integration.

One factor important to integrating organizational members is technology, knowledge about how to get things done. Organizations often must increase coordinative activity to achieve technically complicated tasks. Galbraith (1977) notes mechanisms to increase task coordination: (1) rules standardize both acceptable actions and agreed-upon ends; (2) schedules coordinate interdependent activities or multiple activities occurring at the same time; (3) departmentalization routinizes the division of labor by grouping homogeneous tasks together; (4) organizational hierarchy helps to coordinate tasks that are interrelated among departments. Organizational size can be an important factor affecting internal structure. Several measures have been used for size, including the physical plant, number of clients, or number of employees (Kimberly 1976). Most researchers have treated size as a determinant of organizational structure. It can be an indicator of demand for organizational services or products, providing constraints or opportunities for structural change.

These two variables are related to a number of structural outcomes, the most important of which are complexity or differentiation, formalization, and centralization. Complexity is the diversity of factors that must be simultaneously coordinated to get a task done. Horizontal differentiation is the specification of component elements of tasks performed at the same level of organizational structure. Vertical differentiation is the number of levels of importance, power, and control among units. Multiple and complex technologies are associated with increased structural differentiation (Dewar and Hage 1978). Increased size (number of participants) is necessary to achieve high degrees of structural differentiation, although a large organization may be minimally differentiated and simply coordinated. Nevertheless, larger organizations are generally more structurally differentiated and more complexly coordinated (cf. Blau and Schoenherr 1971).

Formalization is the extent that rules for behaviors and relations in organizations are explicitly specified for participants directly or indirectly associated with particular tasks. This means that formalized positions have standardized powers and duties, regardless of the particular individual incumbent. Organizations with routine technology have a greater degree of formalization (Dornbusch and Scott 1975) at a more minute level of detail. Glisson (1978) contends that routinized technology may produce greater formalization. Formalization, however, is only moderately associated with organizational size (e.g., Blau and Schoenherr 1971).

Centralization refers to the extent to which decision making in an organization is concentrated or dispersed. Dornbusch and Scott (1975) point out that organizations may engage multiple technologies that vary in terms of clarity, predictability, and efficacy. Tasks high on these dimensions are more likely to be centralized, but tasks low on the dimensions are likely to be allocated to specialists, decentralizing organizational authority. Centralization through rules is associated with use of routine technology (Hage and Aiken 1967). There is an inverse relationship between size and centralization: Larger organizations tend to decentralize decision making.

Consistent with generalized values in the host society, organizational structure has differential outcomes for people of diverse identities. Labor theorists offer various explanations for occupational segregation, the organizational practice of reserving specific kinds of jobs for people of given ethnicity or gender. Occupational segregation results in lower earnings in jobs traditionally held by relatively powerless groups—minority men and white and minority women. Kaufman (1986) found that black men were more likely than white men to be employed in highly routinized, less skilled jobs and were less likely to be in job ladders involving increasing levels of status dominance over other workers. Tienda, Smith, and Ortiz (1987) found that, although women's earnings increase as they move into jobs traditionally held by males, male incumbents experience a greater increase in earnings than their female counterparts. Some researchers contend that market forces have created an occupationally segregated labor force, while others believe that organizational practices are responsible. Bridges and Nelson (1989) argue that although market forces produce gender-related inequalities (as expected), these are exacerbated by intraorganizational decisions resulting in preservation of occupational segregation.

Although hierarchy appears to be determined rationally by high-level managers and by owners, labor theorists reveal that organizational structure has differential outcomes for people based on ethnicity and gender. Further, the structural inequalities between wages and perquisites for workers at various levels of the organization may be quite large and not necessary to maintain a task-oriented division of labor on which an organization's survival might depend. Marxists, work redesign theorists, and researchers exploring organizational "structuring" explicitly address how organizations benefit, or fail to benefit, worker categories. These perspectives challenge the presumption of rationality for organizational structures imbalanced in favor of a given constituency. Problems in assessing benefit are due to the assumption that managers or the environment determine what middle and lower participants do without exploring resistance to more generally beneficial institutional policies by upper participants. Researchers examining the impact of variables such as size on formalization frequently exclude human agents, and thereby reify organizational structure. Such research fails to give due consideration to how organizational structuring might account for these phenomena. To the extent that workers subvert, modify, or resist organizational structuring of their activities, researchers cannot justify the assumption that structure is the sole result of owner, managerial, or environmental influences.

LATENT FACTORS IN STRATEGIC PLANNING

Values guide and give meaning to activities. A set of activities, however, may be variously interpreted from alternative value perspectives. Activities that are rational and meaningfully appropriate for an organizational task (in a bank, for example) may, unbeknownst to organizational participants, also be in substantial congruity with prescriptions and proscriptions of, say, an ostensibly unrelated religious organization serving the same client population. This hidden or *latent* positive affinity might make a bank clerk appear particularly productive as new customers are attracted to the bank and give favorable reactions for service received from the bank in spite of, rather than because of, role performance as bank clerk. The latent import could be negative, in which case the bank clerk might look particularly unproductive.

Although there is no assurance an organizational structure staffed with a demographically diverse population has a higher probability of survival, rational theorists believe its chances are increased. As an organization takes in participants with demographic characteristics different from those of previous participants, modalities of personal values at different participant levels will change. This creates a latent potential for future pressure to change goals and procedures. For effective long-term strategic planning, decision makers are well advised to consider implications of alternative demographic concentrations among actual or potential external constituencies and among each internal participant level. Cultivation of new markets to absorb organizational output may require recruitment from populations with new attributes as much as recruitment from new populations to reduce labor costs may require acceptance of new types of participant contributions. Such changes inherently precipitate structural change. An organization setting narrow limits to organizational culture may as a latent consequence inadvertently limit its capacity to adapt to altered environmental conditions and thus decrease its capacity to survive.

While organizational culture is an important result of organizational structure, it appears to have been given both narrow and exaggerated importance by writers whose focus is on profit-making organizations. Most such corporate culture theorists erroneously posit upper participants as its sole determinants and beneficiaries. They view corporate culture to be a normative framework created and manipulated as a tool by upper participants to effectively set their own corporate goals and efficiently manage lower participants. Managers are assumed capable of spreading it unidirectionally downward within an organization by coordinating both material and symbolic rewards that give meaning to organizational behavior. How well lower participants are indoctrinated into the corporate culture is thought to set limits to their coordination and control; degree of convergence between participant values and corporate norms enhances commitment to organizational goals and procedures. Some researchers assert that "strong" (tight coordination and control over workers) corporate cultures lead to organizational success (e.g., Deal and Kennedy 1982). Deal and Kennedy also view corporate culture as existing in a delicate balance to be protected by managers at all costs. Participants attacking a corporation's unique culture would presumably undermine the rationale for virtually all actions in the firm. Such assertions fly in the face of "loose coupling" research findings. Moreover, maintaining control over corporate culture may be used as an excuse for preventing entry into the organization by new demographically diverse participants.

In sharp contrast to the determinism of corporate culture theorists, others argue that culture is how *all* constituencies give meaning to their own existence. Smircich (1983a, p. 339) comments that "those of a skeptical nature may . . . question the extent to which the term corporate culture refers to anything more than an ideology cultivated by management for the purpose of control and the legitimation of activity." The issue here is how much of values essential to its own well-being will each constituency surrender in return for the benefit of continued organizational participation? Upper participants are evidently only one constituency potentially benefiting from organizational culture, since other groups may use it as a vehicle to express resistance to, or interest in, a wide array of organizational conditions. If upper participants seek effectiveness in goal achievement and efficient productivity for increased profits, lower participants might seek security of employment and quality of working conditions. Organizational culture may be seen as a forum within which each group of organizational participants expresses its own self-interests in the context of collective concern for organizational survival by all participants. Depending on their relative power within the organizational structure, constituents may enact and establish understandings about the distribution of rewards given their structural position and contribution relative to organizational survival.

To increase their power, participant groups may enter into coalitions with each other. Organizational theorists are increasingly interested in groups of overlapping or "nested" cultures that may support, merely coexist, or conflict with each other (Louis 1983). Which nested cultural views become dominant may depend on the relative structural power and resources of participants, giving upper managers a better chance of formalizing their views into policy. Formalization of structural diversity requirements in the policy-making process may allow workers an opportunity to inject their views. Another factor influencing membership is the competence that people exhibit as members of the local culture. Members must show that they grasp the meaning of key symbols, values, ideals, and relationships within the culture to function within it. Meaning may also be imported into organizations from the environment, which can help to structure meanings for ambiguous events. Metaphors, used as the basis of vocabularies with which to describe organizational change, provide meaning to new and relatively ambiguous sets of relationships by grounding those relationships in culturally recognizable contexts (Pondy 1983). External populations with specific cultural identities, on whose good will the organization depends, may tilt the balance of power in favor of specific internal constituencies.

If participants decide the distribution of rewards is unsatisfactory or inequitable relative to some other group or individual, relative deprivation theorists argue that they will attempt systemic or individual remedies. Indeed, lower participants may choose to treat "official" cultural accounts with disbelief or to subvert them (Smircich 1983b). Martin (1981) differentiates between pessimistic and optimistic deprivation. People who expect injustice are likely to take violent or destructive actions against individuals or systems. People not expecting injustice are more likely to take "constructive" action, engaging in system-wide reform or self-improvement efforts. However, researchers have failed to demonstrate how unfavorable comparisons cause behavioral outcomes. Historically, groups of workers have understood existence of ethnicity and gender inequality in the work place, but not all groups have taken steps to remedy the problems. The distributive justice perspective may allow exploration of organizational structuring as a process in which agency exists on the parts of participants and constituents of organizations at both aggregate and individual levels in accord with their cultural orientation.

CONCLUDING REMARKS

Current theory and research on organizational structure has been characterized by both managerial determinism and by a vague environmental determinism used to exonerate owners and managers from detrimental consequences of their structural designs upon middle and lower participants within the organization. Owners and higher level managers often overemphasize short-term gains achieved by production and managerial techniques undermining relative empowerment of lower participants. On their behalf, organizational theorists and researchers are said to contribute unwittingly to intensification of unnecessary control over workers, consumers, community residents, and other types of participants (Clegg 1981). Research guided by a distributive justice perspective may reduce an overemphasis on the competitive advantage of upper participants (disguised as advantage by the *organization* against external adversaries) and open new vistas on cooperative actions beneficial to all participants and related to the perceived value of their contributions to organizational survival. In the final analysis, perhaps the only justification for rewards received by a category of organizational participants is the criticality of the contribution it makes to the essential task of organizational survival (Alvarez 1979).

(SEE ALSO: *Complex Organizations*)

REFERENCES

Aldrich, Howard E. 1979 *Organizations and Environments.* Englewood Cliffs, N.J.: Prentice-Hall.

Alvarez, Rodolfo 1979 "Institutional Discrimination in Organizations and Their Environments." In R. Alvarez and K. Lutterman, eds., *Discrimination in Organizations: Using Social Indicators to Manage Social Change.* San Francisco: Jossey-Bass.

Barnard, Chester I. 1938 *The Functions of the Executive.* Cambridge, Mass.: Harvard University Press.

Barley, Stephen R. 1986 "Technology as an Occasion for Structuring: Evidence from Observations of CT Scanners and the Social Order of Radiology Departments." *Administrative Science Quarterly* 31:78–108.

Birnbaum, Phillip H., and Gilbert Y. Wong 1985 "Organizational Structure of Multinational Banks from a Culture-Free Perspective." *Administrative Science Quarterly* 30:262–277.

Blau, Peter M., and Richard Schoenherr 1971 *The Structure of Organizations.* New York: Basic Books.

Blau, Peter, and W. Richard Scott 1962 *Formal Organizations.* New York: Wiley.

Bridges, William P., and Robert L. Nelson 1989 "Markets in Hierarchies: Organizational and Market Influences on Gender Inequality in a State Pay System." *American Journal of Sociology* 95:616–658.

Burkhardt, Malene E., and Daniel J. Brass 1990 "Changing Patterns or Patterns of Change: The Effects of a Change in Technology of Social Network Structure and Power." *Administrative Science Quarterly* 35:104–127.

Clegg, Stewart 1981 "Organization and Control." *Administrative Science Quarterly* 33:24–60.

Cook, Karen S., and Toshio Yamagishi 1983 "Social Determinants of Equity Judgments." In David M. Messick and Karen Cook, eds., *Equity Theory.* New York: Praeger.

Deal, Terrence, and Allan Kennedy 1982 *Corporate Cultures.* Reading, Mass.: Addison-Wesley.

Dess, Gregory G., and Donald W. Beard 1984 "Dimensions of Organizational Task Environment." *Administrative Science Quarterly* 29:52–73.

Dewar, Robert D., and Jerald Hage 1978 "Size, Technology, Complexity and Structural Differentiation: Toward a Theoretical Synthesis." *Administrative Science Quarterly* 23:111–136.

Dill, William R. 1958 "Environment as an Influence on Managerial Autonomy." *Administrative Science Quarterly* 25:120–128.

DiMaggio, Paul J., and Walter W. Powell 1983 "The Iron Cage Revisited: Institutional Isomorphism and Collective Rationality in Organizational Fields." *American Sociological Review:* 147–160.

Dornbusch, Sanford M., and W. Richard Scott 1975 *Evaluation and the Exercise of Authority.* San Francisco: Jossey-Bass.

Emerson, Richard M. 1962 "Power–Dependence Relations." *American Sociological Review:*31–40.

Etzioni, Amitai 1961 *A Comparative Analysis of Complex Organization.* New York: Free Press.

Galbraith, Jay 1977 *Organization Design.* Reading, Mass.: Addison-Wesley.

Glisson, Charles 1978 "Dependence of Technological Routinizations of Structural Variables in Human Service Organizations." *Administrative Science Quarterly* 23:383–395.

Hage, Jerald and Michael Aiken 1967 "Relationship of Centralization to Other Structural Properties." *Administrative Science Quarterly* 12:72–91.

Kaufman, Robert L. 1986 "The Impact of Industrial and Occupational Structure on Black–White Employment Allocation." *American Sociological Review:*310–323.

Kimberly, John 1976 "Organizational Size and the Structuralist Perspective." *Administrative Science Quarterly* 29:571–597.

Kochan, Thomas, George Cummings, and Larry Huber 1976 "Operationalizing the Concepts of Goals and

Goal Incompatibility in Organizational Behavior Research." *Human Relations* 29:544–577.

Lachman, Alan 1989 "Power from What?" *Administrative Science Quarterly* 34:231–251.

Louis, Meryl Reis 1983 "Organizations as Cultural-Bearing Milieux." In Louis Pondy, ed., *Organizational Symbolism.* Greenwich, Conn: JAI.

Martin, Joanne 1981 "Relative Deprivation: A Theory of Distributive Injustice for an Era of Shrinking Resources." In L.L. Cummings and Barry Staw, eds. *Research in Organizational Behavior.* Greenwich, Conn.: JAI.

Meindl, James R. 1989 "Managing to Be Fair: An Exploration of Values, Motives, and Leadership." *Administrative Science Quarterly* 34:252–276.

Meyer, Marshall W. 1975 "Leadership and Organizational Structure." *American Journal of Sociology* 81:514–542.

Parsons, Talcott 1960 *Structure and Process in Modern Society.* New York: Free Press.

Perrow, Charles 1961 "The Analysis of Goals in Complex Organizations." *American Sociological Review* 26:854–866.

Pfeffer, Jeffrey, and Gerald R. Salancik 1978 *The External Control of Organizations.* New York: Harper and Row.

Pondy, Louis 1983 "The Role of Metaphors and Myths in Organization and in the Facilitation of Change." In Louis Pondy, ed., *Organizational Symbolism.* Greenwich, Conn.: JAI.

Scott, W. Richard 1986 *Organizations.* Englewood Cliffs, N.J.: Prentice-Hall.

Simon, Herbert A. 1964 "On the Concept of Organizational Goals." *Administrative Science Quarterly* 9:1–22.

Smircich, Linda 1983a "Concepts of Culture and Organizational Analysis." *Administrative Science Quarterly* 28:339–358.

——— 1983b "Organizations as Shared Meanings." In Louis Pondy, ed., *Organizational Symbolism.* Greenwich, Conn.: JAI.

South, Scott J., and Weiman Xu 1990 "Local Industrial Dominance and Earnings Attainment." *American Sociological Review* 55:591–599.

Spaeth, Joe L. 1985 "Job Power and Earnings." *American Sociological Review* 50:603–617.

Thompson, James D., and William McEwen 1958 "Organizational Goals and Environments: Goal Setting as an Interaction Process." *American Sociological Review* 23:23–31.

Tienda, Marta, Shelley A. Smith, and Vilma Ortiz 1987 "Industrial Restructuring, Gender Segregation, and Sex Differences in Earnings." *American Sociological Review* 52:195–210.

RODOLFO ALVAREZ
LEAH ROBIN

ORGANIZED CRIME Organized crime is considered one of the most serious forms of crime for two reasons: (1) It is so often lucrative and successful; and (2) it is so difficult to counteract. In the broadest terms, organized crime can be viewed as any form of group conduct designed to take advantage of criminal opportunities, whether on a one-time or a recurring basis. More commonly, the label *organized crime* has more restricted usage.

It should not be a surprise to find criminals associating for the purpose of committing crime. The achievement of goals through cooperative efforts is a common element of contemporary life. Association with other criminals creates an interesting dilemma for the individual criminal. Having coconspirators increases the visibility of criminal conduct, the risks of apprehension, and, upon apprehension, the risk of betrayal. On the other hand, some types of criminal opportunities can be exploited only through group behavior. Offenders who fail to join with others may thereby limit their rewards from criminal conduct. For organized crime to persist, it must function both to overcome the risks of associating with others and result in positive benefits and increased rewards for those who participate.

No one knows how much organized crime is committed every year. Rather than being measured in numbers of events, the significance of organized crime is generally recorded in the dollar volume of activities. Some have argued that revenue estimates for organized crime are advanced more in the interest of drama than of accuracy, but the estimates are nonetheless staggering. For example, annual revenue from the sale of drugs is placed in the $40 to $60 billion range, and annual revenue from illicit gambling operations, at $20 to $40 billion.

Organized crime is unlikely to be reflected in

official crime statistics for three reasons: first, crime statistics record information about individual criminal events rather than about the individuals or groups committing them; second, many of the activities of organized crime groups involve so-called victimless crimes where no report of a crime is made; and third, persons who are victimized by organized crime groups may be unlikely or unwilling to come forward and report their victimization.

Organized crime is best understood by examining the nature of ongoing criminal organizations, their activities, and societal response to the behavior of these organizations. A secondary use of the term, referring to criminal support systems that aid all offenders, is also briefly noted.

ONGOING CRIMINAL ORGANIZATIONS

Organized crime usually refers to the activities of stable groups or gangs that commit crimes on an ongoing basis. While not all group crime is properly labeled "organized crime," there exists no standard definition of the term. Instead, the phenomenon has been variously described as "a cancerous growth on American society" (Andreoli 1976, p. 21); "one of the queer ladders of social mobility" (Bell 1970, p. 166); "a society that seeks to operate outside the control of the American people and its governments" (President's Commission 1967, p. 1); and "the product of a self-perpetuating criminal conspiracy to wring exorbitant profits from our society by any means" (Salerno and Tompkins 1969, p. 303).

Scholars have identified the following as elements that characterize all groups labeled as organized crime: a hierarchical organizational structure, dominated by a strong leader; a territorial imperative, exhibited in attempts to monopolize all lucrative criminal opportunities within a geographic area; a predilection to violence both to enforce internal norms and to advance economic objectives; and a desire to influence the social response to criminal conduct, as demonstrated in significant investments in public corruption. Cressey (1969) identified these latter two characteristics—the "element of enforcement" and the "element of corruption"—as the essential features of organized crime.

In the United States, organized crime has been personified in ethnically based criminal organizations and, in particular, the twenty-four fictive "families" believed to make up the American Mafia. Joseph Valachi, in testimony before the United States Senate in 1963, revealed a sordid and secret world in which he claimed these criminal organizations operated and prospered.

While some scholars pointed to inconsistencies in Valachi's statements, and other criminals would later question the depth of his experience and knowledge, his testimony spawned a series of books and movies that placed Italian criminal organizations in the forefront of the public's consciousness with respect to organized crime.

The term *mafia* (with either upper- or lowercase letters) is used variously to apply to a secret criminal organization or to a life-style and philosophy that developed in sixteenth- and seventeenth-century southern Italy and Sicily in opposition to a series of foreign rulers who dominated the area. The life-style combines the idea of manliness in the face of adversity with an antagonism to authority and a closeness and reliance on family and clan.

Smith (1975) argues that applying the "mafia" label to Italian criminal organizations in the United States was both fateful and calculated. It was fateful because it imbued these organizations with international connections that there was little evidence they had. This may in turn have helped these organizations consolidate and solidify their power, in competition with other ethnic (primarily Irish) criminal organizations that were actually more prevalent in the early decades of the twentieth century. Use of the label was calculated in that it gave Italian criminal organizations a subversive and sinister character designed to ensure public support for extraordinary law enforcement efforts to eradicate these groups.

Overlooked in much of the attention paid to Mafia "families" was the fact that bands of brigands and smugglers, displaying many of the same organizational attributes as "mafia," were well established in Elizabethan England; that criminal organizations linked to a life-style based on the primacy of male-dominated families and the concept of dignity and manliness are common in Central and Latin America; and that criminal societies and associations have been successful vehicles for social mobility in many cultures, for example, the Chinese Triads or the Japanese Yakuza.

Also overlooked were some significant changes occurring during the late 1960s and early 1970s in the major cities in which the Mafia "families" were believed to operate. These changes signaled what Ianni (1974) called "ethnic succession" in organized crime: That is, as the populations of inner cities came to be dominated by racial minorities, so too were the ranks of those running criminal organizations. This gave rise to law enforcement characterizations of such groups as the "Mexican Mafia" or the "Black Mafia," not because of their associations with Mafia "families" but as a shorthand way of communicating their organizational style and methods of operating.

By the 1980s, the term *organized crime* had lost its ethnic distinction. Instead, the label started being applied to many more criminal associations, from motorcycle and prison gangs to terrorist groups to some juvenile gangs. Observed in all these groups were the organizational characteristics that had first been identified as distinctive of Mafia "families."

ACTIVITIES OF ORGANIZED CRIME GROUPS

The activities in which organized crime groups are involved constitute another distinctive hallmark. Broadly defined, the term *organized crime* can be used to describe the activities of a band of pickpockets, a gang of train robbers, or a cartel of drug smugglers. Practically speaking, however, use of the term is somewhat more restrictive.

Commentators, scholars, and lawmakers generally use the term when referring to criminal conspiracies of an entrepreneurial nature—in particular, enterprises focused in black-market goods and services. Black markets are those in which contraband or illegal goods and services are exchanged. In this more restrictive use of the term, the activities of drug smugglers would be included while the conduct of pickpockets or train robbers would not.

These latter groups, and others involved in various forms of theft and extortion, commit what are best termed *predatory crimes.* As such, they are generally regarded as social pariahs. Society and the forces of social control will actively seek to root out such groups and bring them to justice. This is despite the fact that such groups may display a highly evolved organizational structure, a strong sense of territory, and a tendency toward violence.

Contrast this with groups engaged in entrepreneurial conduct. These groups supply the society with goods and services that are illegal but in demand. While some in society may still view these criminals as social pariahs, many in society will not. Instead, the criminal group establishes patron–business relationships with criminal and noncriminal clients alike. The forces of social control are not so bent on eradicating these groups because of the widespread social support they garner. This support, when added to the profits reaped as criminal entrepreneurs, creates both the means and the conditions for corruption.

If any one activity can be considered the incubator for organized crime in the United States, it would be the distribution and sale of illegal alcohol during Prohibition. The period of Prohibition (1920–1933) took a widely used and highly desired commodity and made it illegal; it also created the opportunity for a number of predatory criminal gangs to evolve as entrepreneurs. These entrepreneurs then developed important client and business relationships and emerged from Prohibition as wealthy and somewhat more respectable members of their communities.

Gambling and other vices have similar social support profiles. Purveyors of these services are widely perceived as engaged in victimless crimes, that is, black-market transactions involving willing buyers and sellers. Their activities, while morally unacceptable to many, arouse little social concern.

Societal ambivalence becomes even more pronounced where gray-market goods and services are involved. These are situations where legal goods or services are being provided in an illicit manner or to persons ineligible to receive them. Abuses of wartime rations is a good example of a gray-market situation, as is the negotiation of so-called sweetheart labor contracts or the illegal disposal of hazardous waste.

Criminal groups involved in gray-market activities are very tightly meshed in the economic and social fabric of the legitimate community. The persona of such groups is more likely to be legal than illegal, and the capacity of their members to become closely affiliated with persons of power and authority is likely to be great. Public corruption becomes not only likely but inevitable.

Combined with the characteristics that groups of criminals exhibit, the activities in which they engage are also likely to define such groups as organized crime. Some commentators feel it is impossible to separate a group's character from the nature of the crimes it commits. To this way of thinking, selling drugs requires a certain level of organization, but it is impossible to tell whether a group has evolved an organizational style in order to sell drugs or began to sell drugs as a consequence of its organizational capacity.

What is clear is that the capacity to exploit one type of criminal opportunity can be parlayed into other legal and illegal endeavors. Similarly, profits from organized crime activities can permit individual criminals to climb that "queer ladder of social mobility" that wealth creates.

SOCIETY AND ORGANIZED CRIME GROUPS

The final aspect of organized crime that distinguishes it from other forms of crime is its relationship with the society in which it operates. Organized crime is the one form of crime that assesses criminal opportunities in light of the probable social response as well as the possible economic and social rewards.

Cressey (1969) identified this capacity of organized crime as a "strategic planning" capability. Using this capability, organized crime groups choose "safe crime": where there is high social tolerance or at least ambivalence toward the conduct; where the chances of apprehension are therefore not great; where, even if apprehended, the chances of conviction are small; and where, even if convicted, the likelihood of serious consequences is also small.

In this assessment, society's attitudes toward various criminal activities become a key determinant in the nature of organized crime activities that will be displayed. Society's attitudes, as embodied in the criminal law, become even more significant.

Packer (1969) argued that in black- and gray-market situations, the criminal law may actually serve as a protective tariff. As such, the law limits the entry of entrepreneurs into the proscribed marketplace while guaranteeing, for those who do enter the market, exorbitant profits. The theory of deterrence does not work in such markets because as the sanction increases so do the likely rewards.

A similar analysis by Smith (1978) suggests that the law operates in many marketplaces to segment generic demand, labeling some legal and some illegal. By so doing, the law does not reduce demand; what it does is change the dynamics of the market, creating the "domain" or market share of organized crime. In this sense, it is society—through its legislative enactments—that generates and structures the dynamics of organized crime opportunities.

Social institutions also play a role in structuring the nature and success of organized crime. The nature of government and the underpinnings of justice systems loom large in determining how organized crime groups will operate and succeed. Anglo-American legal systems, founded on the principle of individual responsibility for criminal acts, deal at best ineptly with group crime. When faced with more sophisticated criminal conspiracies, they appear to falter.

Where criminal organizations are armed with investments in public corruption, justice systems will not operate properly. Where government operates ineffectively or unfairly, the black market will flourish. Where there is the tendency to proscribe what cannot be controlled, criminal organizations will reap social support and financial rewards.

CRIMINAL SUPPORT SYSTEMS

A secondary use of the term *organized crime* refers to support systems that aid the criminal activities of all offenders. The typical list of support systems includes the tipster, the fix, the fence, and the corrupt public official. Each of these mechanisms serves to reduce the risks of criminal conduct or to lessen its consequences.

For example, tipsters function to provide criminals with information critical to committing a crime, such as the internal security schedule for a building or the timing of valuable cargo shipments. By doing so, they reduce the uncertainties the offenders face and enhance the chances for success. As a reward, tipsters receive a percentage of the "take," or proceeds of the crime.

The fix arranges for special disposition of a criminal's case, once it is in the justice system. This might mean seeing that paperwork is lost, or that a light sentence is imposed. Usually, the fix operates with the aid of corrupt public officials who are in a position to accomplish the required improper acts.

The fence serves as the market for stolen property, transforming it into cash or drugs for thieves. In the role of middleman, the fence determines what thieves steal, how much they are paid to do so, and, consequently, how often they steal. Fences provide structure and stability to a wide range of offenders. Like other criminal support systems, they impose organization on the activities of criminal groups and individual criminals.

Not all criminals can access the services of criminal support systems. These mechanisms will not act to serve the notorious or the psychotic. In this way, criminal elites are established and preserved. For those who use these support systems, crime is organized, the justice system is predictable, and success is likely.

There was a time when the "criminal underworld" was a physical place, a true sanctuary to hide and protect criminals. Now the underworld exists as a communication system, an important dimension of which involves support systems that can aid and protect offenders. The manner in which these systems function provides stability and organization to the underworld.

SUMMARY

Organized crime refers primarily to the broad range of activities undertaken by permanent criminal organizations having the following characteristics: a hierarchical organizational structure; a territorial imperative; a predilection for violence; and the capacity and funds to corrupt public officials.

These groups tend to locate in gray or black markets where they establish patron–client relationships with much of society. The funds they earn as entrepreneurs, combined with social support for their activities, permit them to influence the social response to their acts. They may become upwardly mobile as a result of investing their profits in both legal and illegal endeavors.

Organized crime also refers to criminal support systems such as the tipster, the fix, the fence, and the corrupt official, who impose organization and stability in the underworld.

(SEE ALSO: *Criminology*)

REFERENCES

Abadinsky, Howard 1981 *Organized Crime.* Boston: Allyn and Bacon.

Anderson, Annelise Graebner 1979 *The Business of Organized Crime.* Stanford, Calif.: Hoover Institution Press.

Andreoli, P. D. 1976 "Organized Crime Enterprises—Legal." In S. A. Yefsky, ed., *Law Enforcement Science and Technology: Proceedings of the First National Conference on Law Enforcement Science and Technology.* Chicago: IITRI.

Bell, Daniel 1970 "Crime as an American Way of Life." In M. E. Wolfgang, L. Savitz, and N. Johnson, eds., *The Sociology of Crime and Delinquency.* New York: Wiley.

Chambliss, William J. 1978 *On the Take: From Petty Crooks to Presidents.* Bloomington: Indiana University Press.

Cressey, Donald R 1969 *Theft of the Nation: The Structure and Operations of Organized Crime in America.* New York: Harper and Row.

Homer, Frederic D. 1974 *Guns and Garlic: Myths and Realities of Organized Crime.* West Lafayette, Ind.: Purdue University Press.

Ianni, Francis A. J. 1974 *Black Mafia: Ethnic Succession in Organized Crime.* New York: Simon and Schuster.

Kwitny, Jonathan 1979 *Vicious Circles: The Mafia in the Marketplace.* New York: Morton.

Maas, Peter 1968 *The Valachi Papers.* New York: Putnam.

Packer, Herbert L. 1969 *The Limits of the Criminal Sanction.* Stanford, Calif.: Stanford University Press.

President's Commission on Law Enforcement and the Administration of Justice 1967 *Task Force Report: Organized Crime.* Washington, D.C.: U.S. Government Printing Office.

Robertson, Frank 1977 *Triangle of Death: The Inside Story of the Triads—The Chinese Mafia.* London: Routledge and Kegan Paul.

Salerno, Ralph, and John S. Tompkins 1969 *The Crime Confederation: Cosa Nostra and Allied Operations in Organized Crime.* Garden City, N.Y.: Doubleday.

Smith, Dwight C., Jr. 1975 *The Mafia Mystique.* New York: Basic Books.

———1978 "Organized Crime and Entrepreneurship." *International Journal of Criminology and Penology* 6:161–177.

Walsh, Marilyn E. 1977 *The Fence: A New Look at the World of Property Theft.* Westport, Conn.: Greenwood Press.

MARILYN E. WALSH

OVERPOPULATION *See* Human Ecology and the Environment; Population.

P

PARADIGMS AND MODELS The terms *paradigm* and *model* have enjoyed considerable popularity in sociology, in part because they have a range of meanings. In everyday language, "model" has two senses: (1) a replica of the object being modeled, for example, a model of a building; and (2) an exemplar to be emulated, as in "role model." "Paradigm" is somewhat more esoteric in everyday usage, but has become quite important in academic disciplines, including sociology, largely due to Thomas S. Kuhn's 1962 book, *The Structure of Scientific Revolutions.*

The original meaning of "paradigm" overlaps "model" in the sense of exemplar. The term comes from the study of grammar, where a paradigm provides a model of, for instance, the way to conjugate all the regular verbs of a particular type (I love, you love, he/she loves, etc.). Its appearance in sociology predates Kuhn, but since Kuhn, it is a much grander idea. Merton (1949, p. 13) used the device of analytical paradigms for presenting codified materials, by which he means a technique for exposing the "complete array of assumptions, concepts and basic propositions employed in a sociological analysis." Parsons treated "paradigm" in a similar way when he presented paradigms for social interaction and social change and emphasized that these are distinct from theories (1951, p. 485).

It is quite clear, however, that Kuhn's work has brought "paradigm" from relative obscurity to a central place in the discourses of the humanities, the social sciences, and the history and philosophy of science. Kuhn's paradigm and his model of change in science are highly controversial; yet they have had considerable influence in these academic fields. Some of the effects Kuhn intended; many effects, however, were unintended, causing Kuhn to disavow explicitly some of the interpretations of his work (Kuhn 1970; 1974). Crews (1986) comments that a loose reading of Kuhn's book—which he calls the most frequently cited academic book of modern times—even justifies the rejection of science as empirical.

WORKING DEFINITIONS

A useful definition of "model" draws on Kaplan (1964, p. 263): "Any system A is a model of a system B if the elements and relationships of A aid in the understanding of B without regard to any direct or indirect causal connection between A and B." For example, one could use ideas about political change (system A)—stable government, crisis, revolution, new government attains stability—to model change in science (system B). Models range from informal analogies or metaphors (e.g., society as an organism) to highly formal equation systems.

A model contains elements that have (or are given) properties, that is, are characterized by descriptive terms, and connections among some or all of these elements. One could construct a physical model of a social network using balls with holes in them and rods that fit into the holes. The rods would connect some but not all of the balls; the balls (elements of the model) would represent individuals in the network and the rods (connections) would link those individuals who communicate with one another.

The critical property of a model is an isomorphism with its object, the thing being modeled. Strictly speaking, isomorphism is a one-to-one correspondence between the elements and relationships in the model and the elements and relationships in its object. Needless to say, strict isomorphism is not satisfied by many metaphors and analogies even though these can aid understanding; the lack of strict isomorphism, however, should serve as a caution in taking analogies too literally. Similar caution applies to models in general, since it is all too easy to reify the model, that is, confuse the model with its object. Models do not capture all the properties of their objects, so that even with strict isomorphism, a model inevitably omits significant aspects of the object. As long as those concerned with a model recognize this limitation, they can employ the model fruitfully and unproblematically.

A loose usage of "model" treats it as synonymous with "theory" or as theory expressed in mathematical symbols. While it is possible to have a model of a theory, the working definition given above rules out synonymous usage because a model of "x" must resemble "x" in terms of pattern or structure, whereas a theory about "x," that predicts or explains "x," need not, and generally does not, resemble "x." In short, theories of "x" do not have to be isomorphic with "x"; models do.

In formulating a working definition of "paradigm," it would seem reasonable to follow Kuhn, since he is largely responsible for the contemporary significance of the idea. This presents serious difficulties, however, for as Laudan observes, "Kuhn's notion of paradigm has been shown to be systematically ambiguous . . . and thus difficult to characterize accurately" (1977, p. 73). While constructing a definition of "paradigm" is a formidable task, it is an essential one because the term is critical to an understanding of Kuhn, and Kuhn's work plays an important role in many of the current controversies in sociology. Some of the ambiguity disappears if one distinguishes between what a paradigm *is* and what a paradigm *does;* still, it would be presumptuous to believe that one could fully capture Kuhn's concept with all its nuances. The following working definition has the more modest goal of representing many of his key ideas: A paradigm is a significant scientific achievement recognized by a particular community of scientists that provides a model from which springs a coherent tradition of scientific research and also a general way of looking at the world.

The principal functions of a paradigm include: (1) determining what kinds of problems are appropriate objects of study; (2) specifying appropriate ways to study these problems; and (3) delimiting the types of theories and explanations that are acceptable. For instance, one could consider Durkheim's *Suicide* ([1897] 1951) as a paradigm for many sociologists that provides a model for research and a way to look at phenomena. For Durkheimians, *Suicide* is an exemplar that specifies ways to look for, and at, social facts and limits explanations of given social facts to other social facts, rather than, for example, explaining social facts with psychological ideas such as motives.

It is important to distinguish "paradigm" from "theory." While a well-developed paradigm may contain a number of specific theories, a paradigm is "metatheoretical." A "theory" makes statements about the world, whereas a paradigm involves statements about the nature of acceptable theory, the appropriate entities to investigate, and the correct approaches to these investigations. As an exemplar, a paradigm serves as a normative standard; hence, it is a special type of model, a model of what the given scientific community considers to be exemplary work.

KUHN'S MODEL OF SCIENTIFIC CHANGE

Kuhn developed a model of change in science built around his concept of paradigm. The model employs several concepts related to "paradigm" that extend its meaning: normal science, anomaly, crisis, revolution, paradigm shift, and incommensurability. Brief explications of these ideas follow (page references are to Kuhn 1970):

Normal Science: When a paradigm gains acceptance in a scientific community, it is largely in terms of a promise of success if researchers in the community follow the exemplar. "Normal science consists in the actualization of that promise, an actualization achieved by extending the knowledge of those facts that the paradigm displays as particularly revealing, by increasing the extent of the match between those facts and the paradigm's predictions, and by further articulation of the paradigm itself" (p. 24). To Kuhn, normal science involves "mopping-up operations (that) engage most scientists throughout their careers" (p. 24) and is primarily devoted to puzzle solving: "Perhaps, the most striking feature of the normal research problems . . . is how little they aim to produce major novelties, conceptual or phenomenal" (p. 35).

Anomaly: This refers to "the recognition that nature has somehow violated the paradigm-induced expectations that govern normal science" (p. 52).

Crisis: A crisis, a period of "pronounced professional insecurity" (pp. 68–69), occurs when enough anomalies accumulate so that scientists question the appropriateness of the paradigm.

Revolution: Kuhn takes scientific revolutions to be "those non-cumulative developmental episodes in which an older paradigm is replaced in whole or in part by an incompatible new one" (p. 92).

Paradigm Shift: Kuhn argues that scientists with a new paradigm do not merely have new interpretations for what they observe, but rather "see" things differently. The difference in perception is in a sense similar to the gestalt switch studied by psychologists, where the same figure can yield a right-hand face or a left-hand face depending on how it is viewed.

Incommensurability: During crisis periods, rival paradigms coexist and advocates of rival paradigms cannot understand one another because they have different ways of seeing the world, different standards for appraisal, and different objectives for their scientific community. Consequently, paradigm conflicts are not resolvable by appeal to a set of shared criteria.

These concepts allow a sketch of Kuhn's model:

Paradigm I→ Normal Science →Anomalies→Crisis→

Revolution→Paradigm II

When the members of a scientific community accept a paradigm, that acceptance generates a set of shared commitments to objectives, methods for achieving those objectives, and criteria for appraising theories and research. These commitments are the foundation for a period of normal science, since what to study, how to study it, and what constitutes adequate explanations are not problematic. During normal science, the community regards the paradigm itself as unalterable and immune to challenge. Scientists work to solve the puzzles that the paradigm presents and for which the paradigm guarantees solutions; in this process of puzzle solving, refutations for theories contained in the paradigm arise and empirical studies come up with unexpected findings. The more serious refutations and the more surprising findings come to be regarded as anomalies, and as these anomalies accumulate, scientists are at a loss as to how to deal with them. In the crisis period, rival paradigms arise, but because paradigms are incommensurable, scientists adhering to rivals have no common basis for choosing among the competitors. Paradigm II wins out because some scientists undergo the conversion experience of a paradigm shift where they see the world in a new way or the adherents of Paradigm II are especially persuasive or the adherents of Paradigm I die off.

Kuhn's model questions ideas of cumulation and progress in science. While normal science is cumulative, revolutions do not preserve all, or even the most important, achievements of previous paradigms. "There are losses as well as gains in scientific revolutions" (Kuhn 1970, p. 167). Furthermore, the incommensurability thesis argues that Paradigm II does not win out because it is better or more progressive; the lack of shared standards preclude definitive judgments.

CRITIQUE

Kuhn's work has raised important questions for scholars in the history, philosophy, and sociology of science and has generated a large literature in these areas. Interestingly enough, it has also had broad appeal to intellectuals outside these specialized fields. Although Kuhn presented his basic model in 1962, his ideas continue to command attention and engender controversy, both within relevant technical fields and in broader academic circles. His work seems to have had less impact in the natural sciences, although it attacks the conventional views of many natural scientists.

Kuhn's emphasis on scientific communities and on noncognitive factors in the development of science clearly appeals to sociologists, especially sociologists of science, for example, those who study social networks among scientists or the effects of reward systems. His model provides an antidote to the mythology of cumulative, linear growth of knowledge, the view that characterizes science as building one discovery on another, and with each increment, coming closer to total truth about nature. Nearly thirty years after his initial publication, it is difficult to appreciate how dominant such mythology was when Kuhn challenged it.

But if prior views overemphasized cognitive and rational factors and held to a naive and simplistic view of progress in science, many post-Kuhnians underemphasize the cognitive and the rational or overemphasize the social and political; moreover, some totally deny the possibility of scientific progress. For many, Kuhn provides the license to remove science from its pedestal, to deny that science has any distinctive character or special claim on society's attention or support, and to demand that social sciences cease their attempts to be scientific. Close examination of a few of his key ideas indicates how Kuhn came to be used in ways he, himself, disavowed.

The first problem is the ambiguity of the term "paradigm." Masterman (1970), a sympathetic critic, has pointed to twenty-one different senses of paradigm in the 1962 book, and Kuhn has added to the problem with later modifications of his ideas (1970, 1974). Laudan notes, "Since 1962 most of Kuhn's philosophical writings have been devoted to clearing up some of the ambiguities and confusions generated (by the 1962 book) . . . to such an extent that . . . [m]ore than one commentator has accused the later Kuhn of taking back much of what made his message interesting and provocative in the first place" (1984, pp. 67–68).

The metaphorical language in Kuhn's model poses a second serious problem. As Laudan puts it:

> *Notoriously, he speaks of the acceptance of a new paradigm as a "conversion experience," conjuring up a picture of the scientific revolutionary as a born-again Christian, long on zeal and short on argument. At other times he likens paradigm change to an "irreversible Gestalt-shift." . . . Such language does not encourage one to imagine that paradigm change is exactly the result of a careful and deliberate weighing-up of the respective strengths of rival contenders* (1984, p. 70).

Although Laudan believes that problems of misinterpretation can be "rectified by cleaning up some of the vocabulary," and Kuhn has assumed some responsibility for the misunderstandings due to his own rhetoric (1970, pp. 259–260), it should be noted that Kuhn's ambiguity and his vivid metaphors are important reasons behind much of the enthusiastic embracing of his model. The possibility of reading into the meaning of paradigm and paradigm shift enables the model to serve a variety of agendas.

Kuhn's incommensurability thesis is both the most frequently criticized and the most commonly misused element of his model. It has provided ammunition for a radical subjectivism that denies all standards (Scheffler 1967). In attacking those who use Kuhn to justify any sweeping paradigm of their own, Crews writes, "By incommensurability Kuhn never meant that competing theories are incomparable but only that the choice between them cannot be *entirely* consigned to the verdict of theory-neutral rules and data" (1986, p. 39, emphasis added). Since Kuhn never clearly specified how rules and evidence entered into paradigm change and because he understated the degree to which different scientific communities can share rules and objectives, it is not surprising that this thesis became a rallying point for attacks on scientific rationality.

Another major criticism—and one that goes to the heart of Kuhn's model—involves the indivisible character of paradigms. Paradigm shift is an all-or-nothing process; a paradigm is accepted or rejected as a whole. Treating the parts of a paradigm as inseparable almost requires the transition from one paradigm to another to be a conversion experience; moreover, such a holistic view does not provide an accurate picture of how large-scale changes of scientific allegiance occur (Laudan 1984, pp. 71–72).

Many of these criticisms are widely held. Nevertheless, Kuhn's model remains important to many disciplines, including sociology. Some scholars remain adherents to the basic features of the model; others believe they must respond to the model's challenges to contemporary philosophy and methodology of science.

USE OF "PARADIGM" IN SOCIOLOGY

While several leading British sociologists of science who focus on the sociology of knowledge reflect the intellectual mood of Kuhnian analysis (Collins 1983), the main applications of "paradigm" have occurred in either descriptive or normative efforts in the sociology of sociology.

Analysts have employed versions of Kuhn's concept to classify sociological activities as belonging to one or another paradigm; for example, Ritzer (1975) distinguishes three paradigms for the field at large—social facts, social definition, and social behavior—while Bottomore (1975) identifies four paradigms of macrosociology—structural-functionalist, evolutionist, phenomenologist, and structuralist. Other sociologists discriminate varying numbers of paradigms from as few as two to as many as eight for a single subfield. Some writers classify theories into different paradigms; others categorize research strategies; still others codify more general philosophical orientations. In addition to disputing the number of paradigms, sociologists also disagree about whether paradigm applies to the field in general or only to subfields and whether there are any paradigms at all in sociology, that is, whether the field is preparadigmatic.

A few studies have applied Kuhn to examine historical development of a paradigm. Colclough and Horan (1983), for instance, use content analysis of status attainment studies to illustrate Kuhn's model. Their analysis finds evidence for a stage of normal science and a stage in which anomalies arise and they suggest the onset of a crisis for status attainment research.

Sociologists who use Kuhn focus on different properties of paradigms and debate the utility of their approaches or their faithfulness to Kuhn (cf. Ritzer 1975, 1981a, 1981b; Eckberg and Hill 1979; Hill and Eckberg 1981; Harvey 1982). Compounding the confusion are the many interpreters who read their own meanings into Kuhn. One critic argues:

> *for the most part the use of the term paradigm in sociology fails to reflect the analytic elements of Kuhn's concept . . . Arbitrary pigeon-holing schemes of varying degrees of sophistication, are constructed and theories of, ideas about, and approaches to, sociology are dropped in. The result is a personalized schematic device that . . . plays little part in providing . . . any explanation or understanding of the growth of knowledge. The labelling of such pigeon-holes as paradigms legitimizes the scheme and implies an authority it does not possess* (Harvey 1982, p. 86).

The disarray led Bell to ask: "Does the term 'paradigm' carry too many possible meanings for rigorous thinking? Has it become quasi-mystical? Is it time to review its many usages and to consider discarding it in favor of more precise terms that convey to others more accurately what we mean to say?" (1990, p. 17) Bell went on to answer "yes" to all three questions.

MODELS IN SOCIOLOGY

The first basic distinction necessary to characterize the use of models in sociology is among substantive, measurement, and statistical models. The substantive modeler's objective is to model a specific theory, phenomenon, or process in order to learn (or teach) something about the specific object of the model. For example, Pfeffer and Salancik (1978) use a theory of interpersonal power and dependence (Emerson 1962) to model interorganizational relations, and Gamson (1969) creates an elaborate game that simulates the operation of key features of a society. In both instances, the model focuses on a particular problem—to learn about organizational relations in the first, or to teach students about major aspects of society in the second.

The objective of a measurement model is to create and justify a measuring instrument that has a wide range of applicability. One measurement area to which sociologists have devoted considerable attention is attitude measurement, developing models for scaling attitudes. These scaling models provide the rationale for assigning numbers to represent different expressions of the attitude. For example, Bogardus (1925), in a classic work, created a measure of social distance on the analogy of physical distance, in which allowing a member of some ethnic group into your family represented less social distance than only allowing that person to live in your neighborhood. Guttman (1950) developed one of the most frequently used attitude scaling models that defines and justifies procedures for ordering a set of attitude questions.

Statistical models are the basis for the systematic quantitative analysis of sociological data, and most empirical research in the field employs one or more statistical models. These models are general tools, broadly applicable to diverse problems; the nature of the subject matter that the data reflect is largely irrelevant to the model as long as the data have certain properties, for example, are drawn randomly from some population. A large number of different statistical models appears in the sociological literature. Some are simple, for instance, using the analogy of coin tossing to evaluate the likelihood that a given event occurred by chance. Others are highly complex, using systems of equations to represent the structure of relationships in a set of variables. Models for multivariate analysis have become extremely important to sociology, including, for example, structural equation models, also known as path or causal models (Bielby and Hauser 1977), and log-linear models (Goodman 1984).

FUNCTIONS OF MODELS

A model, first of all, is an abstract representation of what the modeler regards as important aspects of the object being modeled. It involves assumptions, explicit or tacit, about that object, elements of the object, and the relationships among these elements. The definition given above requires that modeling leads to increased understanding; examining the relationships assumed in the model—ascertaining those that fit the object well, those that fit it somewhat, and those that do not fit at all—serves this most important function. In other words, scrutinizing ways the model resembles the object and ways it does not can uncover previously unrecognized features of the object. In more formalized models, one can employ logical or mathematical tools to derive conclusions from the model's assumptions and then test whether these conclusions represent hitherto unknown properties of the object. A model, in general, provides the means to ask new questions about the phenomenon it represents and thus functions to generate new ideas.

A model provides a vehicle for communication. Since a model is more abstract than its object and since it omits many properties of the object, it is easier for writer and audience to share understanding of the model. Caution, however, is necessary, particularly when the model is a vague analogy (e.g., society as a living organism); the possibility of reading into analogies and metaphors can defeat shared understanding when the audience focuses on aspects that are unintended.

A model may display the complexities of the object. Attempting to represent the ties among members of a social group, for example, may require the elaboration of a simple model that represents only the presence or absence of a relationship to one that distinguishes types of relationships—attraction, task interdependence, relative status, and so on. Even if a model inadequately represents its object, it can enhance the understanding of that object by exposing issues that need to be addressed. One important class of models—those known as "baseline models"—is developed in order to study how the object deviates from the model's minimal representation. Investigating discrepancies between a baseline representation and the object can direct the construction of a more complex model (Cohen 1963).

The last general function to be noted is that a model can serve to relate what appear to be different phenomena. An abstract model can apply to a variety of different objects, therefore calling attention to their common aspects; sometimes, especially with metaphors and analogies, the features of one phenomenon serve as the model for another. Using drama as a model for everyday interaction calls attention to some common elements, for instance, what it means to play a role.

Berger et al. (1980) present a typology of models based on more specific functions. Although their concern is mathematical models, their typology has more general application. They distinguish: (1) explicational; (2) representational; and (3) theoretical construct models. Explicational models are those for which the primary goal is to explicate or render precise one or more concepts. Many social network models are explicational models in that they provide an explication of the concept of social structure (Marsden and Lin 1982). While all models are representational, in this typology, the term refers to those models that attempt to represent a particular observed social phenomenon. The majority of models developed in sociology are representational in this sense as long as one has some latitude in interpreting "observed"; in many cases, the object of the model is a generalization from observed phenomena. Coleman (1964, 1973) has formulated a number of representational models dealing with social change and with collective action.

Theoretical construct models are those that formalize an explanatory theory. In sociology, these models have focused on a variety of substantive topics, as the following examples illustrate: Fararo and Skvoretz (1989) have devised a model that draws on social structural theories of Blau (1977) and Granovetter (1973); Hannan and Freeman (1989) have constructed models of organizational birth and death processes based on bioecological theories; Berger, Fisek, and Norman (1977) have formulated a model of status characteristic theory (Berger, Cohen, and Zelditch 1966, 1972).

Sociological models are models in a sense that is close to the everyday meaning of model as a replica or representation. It is even reasonable to think of many of them in the other everyday sense as exemplars, since we can point to sociological research traditions devoted to their development and test. Only with the benefit of more hindsight than is presently available, however, will it be possible to judge whether any of these models are paradigmatic.

(SEE ALSO: *Mathematical Sociology; Scientific Explanation)*

REFERENCES

Bell, Wendell 1990 "What Do We Mean by 'Paradigm.'" *Footnotes* 18:17.

Berger, Joseph, Bernard P. Cohen, and Morris Zelditch, Jr. 1966 "Status Characteristics and Expectation States." In Joseph Berger, Morris Zelditch, Jr., and Bo Anderson, eds., *Sociological Theories in Progress,* Vol. 1. Newbury Park, Calif.: Sage.

——— 1972 "Status Characteristics and Social Interaction." *American Sociological Review* 37:241–255.

Berger, Joseph, Bernard P. Cohen, Morris Zelditch, Jr., and J. Laurie Snell 1980 *Types of Formalization in Small-Group Research.* Westport, Conn.: Greenwood Press.

Berger, Joseph, M. Hamit Fisek, and Robert Z. Norman 1977 "Status Characteristics and Expectation States: A Graph-Theoretic Formulation." In Joseph Berger, M. Hamit Fisek, Robert Z. Norman, and Morris Zelditch, *Status Characteristics and Social Interaction: An Expectation States Approach.* New York: Elsevier.

Bielby, William T., and Robert M. Hauser 1977 "Structural Equation Models." *Annual Review of Sociology* 3:137–161.

Blau, Peter 1977 *Inequality and Heterogeneity.* New York: Free Press.

Bogardus, Emery S. 1925 "Measuring Social Distance." *Journal of Applied Sociology* 9:299–308.

Bottomore, Tom 1975 "Competing Paradigms in Macrosociology." *Annual Review of Sociology* 1:191–202.

Cohen, Bernard P. 1963 *Conflict and Conformity: A Probability Model and Its Application.* Cambridge: MIT Press.

Colclough, Glenna, and Patrick M. Horan 1983 "The Status Attainment Paradigm: An Application of the Kuhnian Perspective." *The Sociological Quarterly* 24:25–42.

Coleman, James 1964 *Models of Change and Response Uncertainty.* Englewood Cliffs, N.J.: Prentice-Hall.

——— 1973 *The Mathematics of Collective Action.* Chicago: Aldine.

Collins, H. M. 1983 "The Sociology of Scientific Knowledge: Studies of Contemporary Science." *Annual Review of Sociology* 9:265–285.

Crews, Frederick 1986 "In the Big House of Theory." *N.Y. Review of Books,* May 29.

Durkheim, Emile (1897) 1951 *Suicide.* New York: Free Press.

Eckberg, Douglas L., and Lester Hill, Jr. 1979 "The Paradigm Concept and Sociology: A Critical Review." *American Sociological Review* 44:925–937.

Emerson, Richard 1962 "Power-Dependence Relations." *American Sociological Review* 27:31–41.

Fararo, Thomas J., and John Skvoretz 1989 "The Biased Net Theory of Social Structures and the Problem of Integration." In Joseph Berger, Morris Zelditch, Jr., and Bo Anderson, eds., *Sociological Theories in Progress: New Formulations.* Newbury Park, Calif.: Sage.

Gamson, William A. 1969 *SIMSOC: Simulated Society.* New York: Free Press.

Goodman, Leo A. 1984 *The Analysis of Cross-Classified Data Having Ordered Categories.* Cambridge, Mass.: Harvard University Press.

Granovetter, Mark S. 1973 "The Strength of Weak Ties." *American Journal of Sociology* 78:1360–1380.

Guttman, Louis 1950 "The Basis for Scalogram Analysis." In Samuel A. Stouffer et al., eds., *Measurement and Prediction.* Princeton, N.J.: Princeton University Press.

Hannan, Michael T., and John Freeman 1989 *Organizational Ecology.* Cambridge, Mass.: Harvard University Press.

Harvey, Lee 1982 "The Use and Abuse of Kuhnian Paradigms in the Sociology of Knowledge." *Sociology* 16:85–101.

Hill, Lester, Jr., and Douglas L. Eckberg 1981 "Clarifying Confusions about Paradigms: A Reply to Ritzer." *American Sociological Review* 46:248–252.

Kaplan, Abraham 1964 *The Conduct of Inquiry.* San Francisco: Chandler.

Kuhn, Thomas S. 1962 *The Structure of Scientific Revolutions.* Chicago: University of Chicago Press.

——— 1970 "Postscript." *The Structure of Scientific Revolutions,* 2nd ed., Chicago: University of Chicago.

——— 1974 "Second Thoughts on Paradigms." In Frederick Suppe, ed., *The Structure of Scientific Theories,* Urbana: University of Illinois Press.

Laudan, Larry 1977 *Progress and Its Problems: Towards a Theory of Scientific Growth.* Berkeley: University of California.

——— 1984 *Science and Values: The Aims of Science and Their Role in Scientific Debate.* Berkeley: University of California Press.

Marsden, Peter V., and Nan Lin, eds. 1982 *Social Structure and Network Analysis.* Beverly Hills, Calif.: Sage.

Masterman, Margaret 1970 "The Nature of a Paradigm." In Imre Lakatos and Alan Musgrave, eds., *Criticism and the Growth of Knowledge.* Cambridge: Cambridge University Press.

Merton, Robert K. 1949 *Social Theory and Social Structure.* New York: Free Press.

Parsons, Talcott 1951 *The Social System.* New York: Free Press.

Pfeffer, Jeffrey, and Gerald R. Salancik 1978 *The External Control of Organizations.* New York: Harper and Row.

Ritzer, George 1975 *Sociology: A Multiple Paradigm Science.* Boston: Allyn and Bacon.

——— 1981a "Paradigm Analysis in Sociology: Clarifying the Issues." *American Sociological Review* 46:245–248.

——— 1981b *Toward an Integrated Sociological Para-*

digm: The Search for an Exemplar and an Image of the Subject Matter. Boston: Allyn and Bacon.
Scheffler, Israel 1967 *Science and Subjectivity.* Indianapolis: Bobbs-Merrill.

BERNARD P. COHEN

PARENTAL ROLES In the closing years of the twentieth century, most adults still become parents. The ages at which they start having children, as well as the number of children they have, differ significantly from earlier generations, as do the social and economic conditions of parenthood.

In this article, several major aspects of parenthood in the contemporary United States are discussed. First, several demographic patterns associated with parenting are reviewed. Second, the rewards and costs associated with parenting are examined. Third, changes in the responsibilities of parents, as defined by social perceptions of the nature of childhood, are discussed. In this section, special attention is given to gender and social class differences in parenting styles. The fourth section examines the impact of the first child's birth on the parents. The paper closes with a discussion of parent–child relations in later life.

DEMOGRAPHIC TRENDS IN PARENTING

One of the most dramatic changes in the nature of parenthood has been the decline in the average number of births to each woman. Over the past 200 years, this number has decreased from seven births per woman, on the average, to less than two. This downward trend has not been steady or consistent. During some periods, such as the Great Depression of the 1930s, the rate of decline was much more pronounced, while at other times, most notably during the post–World War II babyboom, the number of births per woman actually increased. In 1936, the middle of the depression, American women were giving birth to two children, on the average, while in 1957, the number reached 3.6 births per woman. Today, the average number of births each woman has is slightly under two. There are, however, racial and socioeconomic differences in fertility. In the United States, white women have the fewest number of births, followed by black and Hispanic women (Zinn and Eitzen 1990, p. 290).

Race and ethnicity differences in fertility can be explained largely in terms of socioeconomic factors. Blacks and Hispanics in the United States tend to be disproportionately poor, uneducated, and underemployed. Such persons are likely to place a high value on childbearing and to believe in traditional gender roles. For people with limited occupational options, childbearing and child rearing may offer rewards that are lacking in employment. Moreover, high fertility may be viewed by people of lower socioeconomic status as one way of lifting the family out of poverty insofar as it may increase the family's likelihood of having at least one child of superior talent or ability in some area. In addition, people of lower socioeconomic status tend to marry earlier than those of higher status and thus have a longer marital childbearing period. Finally, affiliation with the Roman Catholic church, which has a restrictive policy toward fertility control, may be responsible for the higher fertility rate among Hispanic women (Zinn and Eitzen 1990, p. 295).

Why has the average number of births per woman decreased over the past 200 years? One major reason for the current low fertility rates is that women are marrying at a later age than during the babyboom years. As a result, the number of marital childbearing years is lower and the number of children that can be born is also lower. The relatively high divorce rate has had a similar effect on fertility. Another major reason for the low fertility rate is the high female labor force participation rate. Child-rearing duties decrease the amount of time and energy mothers can devote to their jobs; therefore, women who are career oriented often choose to forgo childbearing altogether or to limit the number of children they have. A final factor that has reduced the average number of births per woman is the legalization of abortion. Currently, 30 percent of all pregnancies that do not end in stillbirth or miscarriage are aborted (Zinn and Eitzen 1990, pp. 290–291).

These social changes have been reflected not only in a reduction in the average number of children born per woman but also in the age at which women begin to have children. In the past twenty years, more and more couples are postponing parenting. In 1970, women under age twenty-five accounted for four out of every five first births that were occurring. By the late 1980s, women of this age accounted for only one out of every two first births. More women were waiting to have their first babies until their late twenties, thirties, and even forties (U.S. Bureau of the Census 1988, p. 3).

Another significant change in fertility is the increase in births to unmarried women. Over 20 percent of all births in the United States today are to unwed mothers. The rate is higher among blacks than it is among whites. Nearly 60 percent of all black babies are born to unmarried mothers (U.S. Bureau of the Census 1989).

As a consequence of the high out-of-wedlock birth rate and the high divorce rate, an increasing number of women are engaging in solo parenting. About one-fourth of all American families with children have only one parent (U.S. Bureau of the Census 1988). Some experts predict that two out of every three white children and nine out of ten black children born in 1980 will be living in a single-parent household by age eighteen (Brophy 1986). Children spend between six and eight years, on the average, living in a single-parent home (Hofferth 1985). Most tend to have little contact with their nonresidential parent. In fact, one study revealed that about two out of every five children of divorce had no contact with their fathers in over five years. Some did not even know whether their fathers were still living (Furstenberg and Nord 1982).

Single-parent families headed by women have many special problems, not the least of which is limited economic resources. The average income of such families is only one-third that of families with two parents (Johnson 1980). Nearly one-half of female-headed families live below the poverty level (Payton 1982). A major contributing factor to this "feminization of poverty" is the fact that not all noncustodial fathers are ordered by the courts to pay child support after divorce, and, of those who are, less than half actually pay the full amount (Weitzman 1985).

Economic need has led to a dramatic increase in the employment of mothers, married as well as divorced. In 1960, fewer than one in every five mothers of preschool children was employed. Today, well over 60 percent are employed (U.S. Bureau of the Census 1989). The increased demand for substitute child care has become one of the most pressing social problems in the 1990s.

THE CHILDBEARING DECISION: THE REWARDS AND COSTS OF PARENTING

Since individuals are now better able to control their reproductive functions due to advances in contraceptive technology and access to legal abortion, it is important to examine why the majority of adults still choose to become parents. For most people, becoming a parent involves a decision-making process in which the anticipated rewards and costs of parenting are weighed. One major influence on this choice is societal pressure. The United States is often referred to as "pronatalist," which means that dominant values and attitudes promote and encourage childbearing.

Studies of the value of children to their parents have identified many major rewards that child rearing provides (Hoffman and Hoffman 1973; Hoffman and Manis 1979). In one national study (Hoffman and Manis 1979), respondents were asked to identify the advantages and disadvantages of having children. One major type of reward provided by children is self-preservation and family continuity. The birth of children ensures that the father's family name will continue into the future, at least for one more generation, and it may give the parents a sense of immortality, a feeling that part of them will survive after death. Moreover, in earlier historical periods, children were valued in large part because their labor could greatly enhance a family's economic survival. Today, children continue to have economic value for some parents who view them as a type of old age insurance. A small minority of parents, typically those from rural areas, also see children's ability to participate in household labor as a valuable asset. Children may also enable a family to maintain control over property or a family-owned or operated farm or business. For most families, though, children may be more of an economic liability than a benefit. Their primary value to their parents is emotional and symbolic. Understanding the nonmaterial benefits of child rearing helps in understanding why most people choose to become parents when they are no longer forced to do so by biological necessity.

One major type of nonmaterial reward provided by children is self-enhancement. Becoming a parent leads to a change in social identity. It bestows adult status, which carries with it implications of maturity and stability. In fact, for many people, parenthood is *the* event that gives a sense of feeling like an adult (Hoffman and Manis 1979). Having children may also produce a sense of achievement, not only for the physical fact of conception but also for the challenges of raising a child. Moreover, many parents also feel a sense of accomplishment through their children's achievements. Finally, during the child-rearing years, the legitimate authority that is attached to the parent role, as well as the resulting power and influence parents have over their children's lives, may be self-enhancing, especially to parents who lack such influence and control in other aspects of their lives.

The most frequently mentioned reward of child rearing is the provision of primary group ties and affection. Children are expected to help prevent loneliness and to provide love and companionship. These rewards may be particularly important to blue-collar couples, insofar as their marriages may not provide adequate companionship and affection (Rainwater 1960).

The stimulation and fun that child rearing provides are also identified as rewards of the parent role. The presence of a new baby in the home is an immediate source of novelty. As they grow and mature, children continue to provide new experiences for their parents.

Finally, many people regard childbearing as a sacred duty and may feel that by becoming parents they are fulfilling a divine commandment (Scanzoni and Scanzoni 1988). Moreover, the physical and symbolic sacrifices involved in child rearing are perceived by some as a sign that parents are more virtuous and altruistic than childless adults.

There are also costs, financial and socio-emotional, associated with parenting. Over the years, economists have estimated the direct (e.g., food, clothing, shelter, medical and dental care, toys, recreation, leisure, and education) and indirect costs (e.g., foregone savings and investments, lower standards of living, loss of potential income for parents who leave the labor market to care for the child) of child rearing. In 1985, raising a child, including sending her or him to a state university for four years, cost parents $232,000 (Belkin 1985). While couples may be aware of the magnitude of financial costs associated with child rearing, most are not deterred by their awareness (Hoffman and Manis 1979). Economic considerations play only a small role in the decision to become a parent (Blake 1979).

The presence of children may also be costly to adults through the restriction of their activities and the resulting loss of freedom. Parents are responsible for the mental, emotional, physical, spiritual, and social development of their offspring. Obviously, such responsibility may consume much of the parents' time and attention and may require a readjustment of lifestyle to take the children's needs and activities into account. Consequently, parenting may have negative effects on marriage. Studies have shown that the birth of children may hurt a couple's affectional and sexual relationship, due largely to frequent interruptions, a loss of privacy, and increased demands on time and energy (Glenn and McLanahan 1982; Hoffman and Levant 1985; Miller and Sollie 1980). The birth of children often results in role segregation, which means that spouses engage in fewer joint activities as they attempt to fulfill their parental responsibilities.

Our society, however, is very effective in overemphasizing the positive outcomes of parenting while downplaying the negative. Some scholars have concluded that it is necessary for every society to do this in order to ensure that adults do not try to avoid taking on these difficult but essential societal functions (LeMasters and DeFrain 1983; LeMasters 1970). The set of folk beliefs that depict children as fun, cute, clean, healthy, and intelligent, and child rearing as easy and enjoyable are not always supported by facts. Indeed, most studies reveal that adults believe these overly positive depictions of children and child rearing only until they become parents and reality sets in (LaRossa and LaRossa 1981).

Largely as a result of powerful pronatalist forces, then, most adults choose to have children. Throughout this century, the proportion of childless marriages ranged from 5 to 10 percent. The rates have doubled in the past twenty years, however, and some experts are predicting that between 25 and 30 percent of American women now in their late twenties and early thirties will remain childless throughout their lives (Bloom and Bennett 1986).

For the small minority of persons who are voluntarily child-free, the anticipated costs of having children outweigh the anticipated rewards. Adults who choose to remain childless may believe that having children would interfere with their ability to achieve in their careers or in other types of public service. They may feel that caring for children would drain away the time and energy that could be devoted to other highly valued pursuits. Another important consideration for such adults is the expectation that the commitment to parenthood would reduce the time available to commit to the marital relationship. To voluntarily childless couples, marriage is the primary source of affection and sense of belonging. Children are not needed to provide such rewards. Finally, voluntarily childless couples may believe that children would create a monotonous routine and reduce the time and money available for valuable adult activities (Veevers 1979; 1980).

THE RESPONSIBILITIES OF PARENTS

For most of human history, simple physical survival of children was the dominant issue in child rearing (Skolnick 1987). Prior to the seventeenth century, parental love was rarely identified by child-rearing experts as a critical factor in the development of a child. Parents provided physical care, consistent discipline, and a model for proper behavior (Kagan 1977). Today, parents are responsible not only for the child's physical well-being but also for his or her psychological adjustment. Often, flaws in a person's adjustment are traced to a lack of parental love or some other parental shortcoming (Skolnick 1987).

Ideas about ideal parental behavior have varied in conjunction with conceptions of children's needs. Today, Americans assume that children have a distinct nature that distinguishes them from adults. While adults work, assume responsibility, act in a controlled and rational manner, think abstractly, and seek and maintain sexual relationships, children play and forgo assumption of responsibility, act in an irrational and emotional manner, think in concrete terms, and are asexual creatures (Benedict 1938). As a result of children's undeveloped state, parents are assigned responsibility for protecting, providing, and psychologically shaping them.

The concept of childhood as a separate developmental stage of life is a relatively modern invention. In premodern societies a different concept of childhood dominated. Children were seen as "miniature" adults (Aries 1962). As such, they participated fully in the adult world. For instance, in preindustrial Europe, children were involved in various occupations such as farming, baking, shoemaking, the law, business, pharmacy, administration, and the clergy. School was part of the adult world, as well, and was not age-graded. Students made their own rules and were unsupervised by adults. They could enter college at the age of nine or ten, completing their studies at age thirteen. In fact, children could be found in all places where adults regularly spent their time—at work, in the army, and in taverns and houses of ill repute.

A similar process occurred in the emergence of adolescence as a distinct stage of development in Western societies. Although Americans think of the period between puberty and the assumption of adult roles, which lasts anywhere from ten to fifteen years, as a biologically determined stage, it is, in reality, a social invention. In some societies, contrary to our own, puberty leads directly from childhood to adulthood. Adolescence was not established as a distinct stage of social development in our society until the early 1900s, after industrialization had reduced the significance of the family as the unit of economic production, compulsory education was institutionalized, and child labor laws removed children from the work force (Skolnick 1987, p. 350). The teenage years became a time of occupational choice and preparation rather than a period of apprenticeship in the occupation of one's parents. Thus, the period of children's dependence on their parents increased further.

There is some reason to believe that this period of preadulthood is being lengthened even further. Keniston (1971) proclaimed the existence of a "youth" stage between adolescence and adulthood and that this stage was emerging because rapid social change was making it increasingly difficult for young people to establish their own independent identity. Indeed, during the 1980s, more and more young people past the conventional age of independence were still living in their parents' home (Glick and Lin 1986). Nearly two-thirds of the young men and about half of the young women between the ages of eighteen and twenty-four were living with their parents in the mid-1980s. This suggests that parents may continue to feel responsibility for their children into the third decade of their children's lives.

The Mother Role. To many people, parenting is synonymous with mothering, and mothering is believed by many to be an instinct found in all women. While scientists have yet to find an instinctual motive for motherhood among humans, they have demonstrated a strong learned need among women to have children. Most women, given the choice to become a mother, would choose to do so and most women who are already mothers would choose the role again (Genevie and Margolies 1987).

The belief that motherhood is necessary for women's fulfillment and for the normal healthy development of children has waxed and waned throughout our history, largely in response to economic conditions. When women's labor is not needed outside the home, the mother role is glorified and exalted; when women's labor is essential to the economy, the importance of the mother child bond is downplayed (Margolis 1984). Earlier in our history, when our economy was agrarian, parenting was more of a joint venture. Child rearing was shared among a larger number of adults and the mother-child bond was not regarded as primary. Only after industrialization and urbanization changed the nature of work and family life did the role of mother in child development become preeminent. As will be discussed below, similar changes are under way in regard to the father role.

The Father Role. While the verb *to mother* is used to refer to the nurturance and care given to children, usually by women, the verb *to father* has a much more restricted meaning. To many, this simply refers to the male role in procreation. The responsibilities attached to the father role have traditionally been economic. To be a good father, a man had to be a good provider. Participation in the daily custodial care of the child was not expected, nor was companionship or nurturance. In recent decades, with the entrance of large numbers of mothers into the labor force, the expectations attached to the father role are beginning to change. Men can no longer be good fathers simply by being good providers. They must also participate more fully in the daily care of their children and in the socialization process (Pleck 1979).

It appears that these expectations are being reflected in changed behavior (Pruett 1987). More men are attending child birth education classes with their wives and are present at the births of their children (Bigner 1979). Additionally, reports of the average amount of time men spend with their children has increased since the early 1970s, from thirty-eight seconds per day with infants in the early 1970s (Rebelsky and Hanks 1971) to eight minutes per weekday in the mid-1980s (Fischman 1986). These changes provide support to studies that have shown that men are psychologically capable of participating in all parenting behaviors (except for gestation and lactation, which they are biologically incapable of performing; Fein 1980). Perhaps the most telling evidence of the extent to which Americans' ideas about the father role have changed since the 1940s can be found in the expert advice on parenting. In the first edition of his classic book, *Baby and Child Care,* published in 1945, Dr. Benjamin Spock reminded fathers that they need not be as involved in child care as mothers, at most "preparing a formula on Sundays." By the 1980s, Dr. Spock admonished fathers to take on half of all child care and housework tasks (Spock and Rothenberg 1985).

Social Class Variations in Parental Values. As noted above, ideas about the proper role of parents have varied historically. Sociologists have also identified significant variation in child-rearing attitudes by social class (Kohn 1969). The values parents attempt to convey to their children are learned through personal experience in the occupational world. Because jobs differ significantly in many ways, workers learn different ways of coping on the job to ensure success in the work world. When these behaviors bring occupational success to workers, they attempt to apply similar traits to other areas of their lives. Higher status jobs permit, even require, self-direction. They encourage flexibility, creativity, and decision making. People who hold these jobs come to value these traits and attempt to instill them in their children with the hope that they will bring them success. Lower status jobs, on the other hand, rarely provide opportunities for self-direction and require conformity to authority. Thus, lower class and working-class parents believe that the most important trait they can teach their children is obedience and conformity.

Parental disciplinary tactics reflect these values. While both middle class and working-class parents emphasize behavior control in their approach to child rearing, they look for the source of this control in different places. Middle class parents expect their children to be self-directed, to have inner control, whereas lower and working-class parents expect their children to be obedient to external sources of control. As a result, working-class parents will punish any disobedient acts, whereas middle class parents will punish only those disobedient acts that they view as having violent intent. These findings apply to mothers as well as to fathers and to black parents as well as to white parents (Scanzoni 1977). At one point, scholars believed that lower class parents were simply more likely than middle class parents to use physical punishment (Kerckhoff 1972, p. 42). A closer reexamination of the evidence has called this conclusion into question (Pearlin 1972; Straus 1971). The major difference seems to be the conditions under which parents will use physical punishment, not how likely they are to use it (Kohn 1969).

TRANSITION TO PARENTHOOD

Some sociological studies have found that many couples experience the birth of their first child as a crisis (LeMasters 1957; Dyer 1964). The changes brought about by the addition of a baby to a household are indeed extensive. Occupational commitments, particularly of the mother, may be reduced, and family economics must be reorganized as spending increases and earnings are reduced. Household space must be reallocated to accommodate the infant's lifestyle. The parents' time and attention must be redirected toward the infant. Relationships with kin, neighbors, and friends must be redefined to include the baby's schedule. The marital relationship itself may be disrupted due to the enormous demands for time, energy, and attention made by the baby. As a result, new mothers frequently report unexpected fatigue, confinement to the home and a sharp reduction in social contacts, and loss of satisfaction that accompanied outside employment. New fathers feel added economic pressure and a general disenchantment with the parent role (LaRossa and LaRossa 1981).

The severity of the crisis experienced by new

parents does not seem to be related to the quality of the marital relationship before the birth of the child or to the degree to which the child was planned and wanted. Instead, it may be the degree to which the parents had romanticized parenthood in conjunction with their lack of preparation for the role that leads to a feeling of crisis. As a result of the tremendous changes brought about by the presence of children and the burdens associated with child rearing, marital satisfaction appears to decline sharply around the time of the first child's birth and to remain low until children leave the home (Rollins and Cannon 1974).

There is some indication that the transition to parenthood is more difficult for middle class couples than it is for blue-collar couples. The reasons for this are many. Working-class women may place a greater intrinsic value in child rearing, may have fewer alternative sources of gratification outside the family, may have more experience in caring for children, may have fewer conflicting demands from occupational aspirations, and may have had less companionate, less satisfying marital relationships prior to the arrival of children. Thus, for these couples, the birth of the first child may offer more rewards than it produces costs.

PARENTING IN THE LATER YEARS OF LIFE

Research has demonstrated that the rewards of parenting persist through life (Long and Mancini 1989). Feelings of continued attachment to their children help to minimize elderly parents' sense of isolation and loneliness. Believing that their children would take care of their needs, regardless of the time, energy, or money involved, helps to build a sense of security in old age and is important in day-to-day survival. However, opportunities to continue to provide nurturance to their children are also highly valued by elderly parents. Their contributions to their adult children occur in many forms, from financial assistance to help with housework and care of grandchildren. Adults derive a great sense of pride and satisfaction from their parental role, even when their sons and daughters are middle-aged adults with children of their own. Being recognized by their children for their value and competence in the role of parent helps them to maintain high levels of self-esteem (Long and Mancini 1989).

(SEE ALSO: *American Families; Family Roles; Socialization)*

REFERENCES

Aries, Phillipe 1962 *Centuries of Childhood: A Social History of Family Life.* New York: Alfred A. Knopf.

Belkin, Lisa 1985 "Parents Weigh the Costs of Children." *New York Times* May 23.

Benedict, Ruth 1938 "Continuities and Discontinuities in Cultural Conditioning." *Psychiatry* 1:161–167.

Bigner, Jerry 1979 *Parent–Child Relations: An Introduction to Parenting.* New York: Macmillan.

Blake, Judith 1979 "Is Zero Preferred? American Attitudes Toward Childlessness in the 1970s." *Journal of Marriage and the Family* 41:245–257.

Bloom, David, and Neil Bennett 1986 "Childless Couples." *American Demographics* 8:23–25, 54–55.

Brophy, Beth 1986 "Children Under Stress." *U.S. News and World Report* October 27, pp. 58–63.

Clemens, Audra, and Leland Axelson 1985 "The Not-So-Empty Nest: The Return of the Fledgling Adult." *Family Relations* 34:259–264.

Dyer, Everett 1964 "Parenthood as Crisis." *Marriage and Family Living* 25:196–201.

Fein, Robert 1980 "Research on Fathering." In Arlene Skolnick and Jerome Skolnick, eds., *The Family in Transition.* Boston: Little, Brown.

Fischman, Joshua 1986 "The Children's Hours." *Psychology Today,* October 10.

Furstenburg, Frank, and Christine Nord 1982 "Parenting Apart: Patterns of Childrearing After Marital Disruption." *Journal of Marriage and the Family* 47:893–904.

Genevie, Lou, and Eva Margolies 1987 *The Motherhood Report: How Women Feel About Being Mothers.* New York: Macmillan.

Glenn, Norvall, and Sara McLanahan 1982 "Children and Marital Happiness: A Further Specification of the Relationship." *Journal of Marriage and the Family* 44:64–72.

Glick, Paul, and Sung-Ling Lin 1986 "More Young Adults Are Living with Their Parents: Who Are They?" *Journal of Marriage and the Family* 48:107–112.

Hofferth, Sandra 1985 "Updating Children's Life Course." *Journal of Marriage and the Family* 47:93–115.

Hoffman, Lois, and Martin Hoffman 1973 "The Value of Children to Parents." In James T. Fawcett, ed., *Psychological Perspectives on Population.* New York: Basic Books.

Hoffman, Lois, and Jean Manis 1979 "The Value of Children in the United States: A New Approach to the Study of Fertility." *Journal of Marriage and the Family* 41:583–596.

Hoffman, Susan, and R. F. Levant 1985 "A Comparison of Child-Free and Child-Anticipated Married Couples." *Family Relations* 34:197–203.

Johnson, Beverly 1980 "Single Parent Families." *Family Economics Review* (Summer-Fall):22–27.

Kagan, Jerome 1977 "The Child in the Family." *Daedalus* 106:33–56.

Keniston, Kenneth 1971 "Psychosocial Development and Historical Change." *Journal of Interdisciplinary History* 2:329–345.

Kerckhoff, Alan 1972 *Socialization and Social Class.* Englewood Cliffs, N.J.: Prentice-Hall.

Kohn, Melvin 1969 *Class and Conformity: A Study in Values.* Homewood, Ill.: Dorsey.

LaRossa, Ralph, and Maureen LaRossa 1981 *Transition to Parenthood: How Infants Change Families.* Beverly Hills, Calif.: Sage.

LeMasters, E. E. 1957 "Parenthood as Crisis." *Marriage and Family Living* 19:352–355.

——— 1970 *Parents in Modern America: A Sociological Analysis.* Homewood, Ill.: Dorsey.

———, and John DeFrain 1983 *Parents in Contemporary America.* Homewood, Ill.: Dorsey.

Long, Janie, and Jay Mancini 1989 "The Parental Role and Parent–Child Relationship Provisions." In Jay Mancini, ed., *Adult Parents and Adult Children.* Lexington, Mass.: Lexington Books.

Margolis, Maxine 1984 *Mothers and Such: Views of American Women and Why They Changed.* Berkeley: University of California Press.

Miller, Brent, and D. Sollie 1980 "Normal Stresses during the Transition to Parenthood." *Family Relations* 29:459–465.

Payton, Isabelle 1982 "Single-Parent Households: An Alternative Approach." *Family Economics Review* (Winter):11–16.

Pearlin, Leonard 1972 *Class Context and Family Relations: A Cross-National Study.* Boston: Little, Brown.

Pleck, Joseph 1979 "Men's Family Work: Three Perspectives and Some New Data." *Family Coordinator* 28:481–489.

Pruett, Kyle 1987 *The Nurturing Father: Journey Toward the Complete Man.* New York: Warner Books.

Rainwater, Lee 1960 *And the Poor Get Children.* Chicago: Quadrangle.

Rebelsky, F., and C. Hanks 1971 "Fathers' Verbal Interactions with Infants in the First Three Months of Life." *Child Development* 42:63–68.

Rollins, Boyd, and Kenneth Cannon 1974 "Marital Satisfaction over the Family Life Cycle: A Reevaluation." *Journal of Marriage and the Family* 36:271–282.

Rossi, Alice 1984 "Gender and Parenthood." *American Sociological Review* 49:1–19.

Scanzoni, John 1977 *The Black Family in Modern Society: Patterns of Stability and Security.* Chicago: University of Chicago Press.

Scanzoni, Letha, and John Scanzoni 1988 *Men, Women, and Change: A Sociology of Marriage and Family.* New York: McGraw-Hill.

Skolnick, Arlene 1987 *The Intimate Environment: Exploring Marriage and the Family.* Boston: Little, Brown.

Spock, Benjamin 1945 *Baby and Child Care.* New York: Pocket Books.

———, and Michael Rothenberg 1985 *Dr. Spock's Baby and Child Care.* New York: Pocket Books.

Straus, Murray 1971 "Some Social Antecedents of Physical Punishment: A Linkage Theory Interpretation." *Journal of Marriage and the Family* 33:658–663.

U.S. Bureau of the Census 1988 "Households, Families, Marital Status and Living Arrangements: March 1988." *Current Population Reports,* Series P-20, no. 432. Washington, D.C.: U.S. Government Printing Office.

———1989 "Fertility of American Women: June 1988." *Current Population Reports,* Series P-20, No. 436. Washington, D.C.: U.S. Government Printing Office.

———1989 *Statistical Abstract of the United States, 1989.* Washington, D.C.: U.S. Government Printing Office.

Veevers, Jean 1979 "Voluntary Childlessness: A Review of Issues and Evidence." *Marriage and Family Review* 2:1–26.

———1980 *Childless by Choice.* Toronto: Butterworths.

Weitzman, Lenore 1985 *The Divorce Revolution.* New York: Free Press.

Zinn, Maxine Baca, and D. Stanley Eitzen 1990 *Diversity in Families,* 2nd ed. New York: Harper and Row.

CONSTANCE L. SHEHAN

PARTICIPANT OBSERVATION *See* Field Methods.

PARTICIPATORY RESEARCH Participatory research integrates scientific investigation with education and political action. Researchers work with members of a community to understand and resolve community problems, to empower community members, and to democratize research. The methods of participatory research include group discussions of personal experience, interviews, surveys, and analysis of public documents. Topics that have been investigated with this approach include community issues such as polluted water supplies and the school curriculum, employment issues such as working conditions and unionization, and theoretical issues about consent and resistance to domination. For social scientists who question the traditional values of being detached and value-free and who seek an approach that is less hierarchical and that serves the interests of those with little power, participatory research is a valuable alternative.

Participatory research can be identified by five characteristics: (1) participation by the people being studied; (2) inclusion of popular knowledge; (3) a focus on power and empowerment; (4) consciousness-raising and education of the participants; and (5) political action. A precise definition should be avoided so that each group that does participatory research can be free to develop some of its own methods.

Participation in the research process by the people being studied is best viewed as a continuum that includes low levels of participation, such as asking people who are interviewed to read and comment on the transcripts of their interviews, as well as high levels of participation. Ideally, community members have a significant degree of participation *and control,* and help determine the major questions and overall design of the study.

Second, participatory research validates popular knowledge, personal experience and feelings, and artistic and spiritual expressions as useful ways of knowing. If researchers are to work with community members as coinvestigators, they must respect people's knowledge. Moreover, one of the rationales for community participation in research is the assumption that people understand many aspects of their situation better than outsiders do. Practitioners have used group discussions, photography, theater, and traditional tales to draw on popular knowledge (Barndt 1980; Luttrell 1988).

A focus on power and empowerment also distinguishes most participatory research. "The core issue in participatory research is power . . . the transformation of power structures and relationships as well as the empowerment of oppressed people," states Patricia Maguire in her excellent analysis of the field (1987, p. 37). Participatory researchers differ widely in their positions on empowerment, and include radicals who try to transform the power structure by mobilizing peasants to wrest land from the ruling class, as well as conservatives who ignore power relations and focus on limited improvements such as building a clinic or a collective irrigation system.

The fourth characteristic of participatory research—consciousness-raising and education—is closely related to power. Group discussions and projects typically attempt to reduce participants' feelings of self-blame and incompetence and try to relate personal problems to unequal distributions of power in the community and the society. Participants often become visibly more confident and effective as they speak out in discussions, learn that others share some of their experiences, and learn research skills and relevant technical information.

Finally, participatory research includes political action, especially action that cultivates "critical consciousness" and is oriented toward structural change, not toward adjusting people to oppressive environments (Brown and Tandon 1983). Some scholars argue that "real" participatory research must include actions that radically reduce inequality and produce "social transformation." Research and action, from this perspective, should be guided by a general theory like Marxism to help identify the underlying causes of inequality and the best strategies for changing society. Others caution against expecting to achieve radical changes because "social transformation requires . . . organizing, mobilizing, struggle" as well as knowledge (Tandon 1988, p. 12). These researchers point to the value of small collective actions in educating people about the local power structure, creating greater solidarity and feelings of power, and providing new knowledge about how power is maintained and challenged. Many projects include little or no collective action and are limited to changing the behavior of individual participants, strengthening or "creating a community network" and "fostering critical knowledge" (Park 1978, p. 20).

In some cases, participatory research produces major changes, as exemplified by a project with residents of a small town in the state of Washington. The town was going to be destroyed by the expansion of a dam, and the U.S. Army Corps of Engineers was planning to disperse the community. But with the assistance of Professor Russell Fox and numerous undergraduates from Evergreen State College, residents clarified their own goals for a new community, learned about the planning process, and produced a town-sponsored plan for a new town. Their plan was accepted by the Corps of Engineers after prolonged struggle involving the courts and the U.S. Congress. The new town thrived and continued to involve the entire community in planning decisions (Comstock and Fox 1982).

A study of the working conditions of bus drivers in Leeds, England, illustrates the mixed results that are more typical of participatory research. As a result of greater pressure at work accompanying Prime Minister Margaret Thatcher's program of deregulation, bus drivers were experiencing increasing stress, accidents, and conflicts at home (Forrester and Ward 1989). With the help of professors from the University of Leeds who were running an adult education program for workers, a group of eight bus drivers, selected by their local union, decided to do research that would investigate stress at work and motivate the drivers' union to take action. They designed and carried out a survey of a sample of drivers and their families, studied accident records, and measured physical signs of stress. Although the report presenting their findings failed to produce the desired action by the union, the project was successful in many other ways—workers' stress became part of the agenda for the union and the national government, and the report was used by workers in other countries to document the need for improved working conditions. The participants in the research gained research skills and knowledge about work stress, and the professors produced academic papers on work stress and participatory research. The professors had a dual accountability (as they put it) to both the bus workers and to the university; their projects produced results that were valuable to both groups.

THE HISTORY OF THE FIELD AND RELATIONS TO OTHER FIELDS

Participatory research was developed primarily by Third World researchers, and most projects have been in Third World communities. In the 1970s it became clear that mainstream economic development projects were failing to reduce poverty and inequality. In response, researchers began to develop alternative approaches that increased the participation of the poor in development programs and aimed at empowering poor rural and urban communities as well as improving their standard of living (Huizer 1979; Tandon 1981, 1988). For example, in the Jipemoyo Project in Tanzania, researchers and villagers investigated traditional music and dance practices and developed cooperative, small-scale industries based on these traditions, such as the production of "selo drums" for sale in urban areas (Kassam and Mustafa 1982). In other projects, peasants and farmers participated with agricultural and social scientists to determine the most appropriate and productive farming methods. Several projects in Latin America, led by Orlando Fals Borda and labeled "participatory action research," integrated the knowledge of peasant activists and academics to build rural organizations and social movements.

Participatory researchers in the Third World are closely associated with Paulo Freire, an exiled Brazilian educator with roots in Marxism and critical theory. His book *Pedagogy of the Oppressed* is the most influential work in participatory research. Freire argues that teaching and research should not be dominated by experts but should be based on dialogue with a community of oppressed people. Through dialogue and collective action, people can develop critical consciousness, learn the skills they need to improve their situation, and liberate themselves. A similar approach has been developed by the influential Highlander Research and Education Center in the southern United States. Organized by Myles Horton and others in the 1930s, Highlander has inspired many participatory researchers with its success in educating and empowering poor rural people (Gaventa and Horton 1981; Gaventa, Smith, and Willingham 1990). Another important center of participatory research has been the Participatory Research Network in Toronto, focusing on adult education (Hall 1975, 1981).

The development of participatory research in the 1970s was also fostered by challenges to positivist social science by feminists, Marxists, critical theorists, and others (Bernstein 1983; Harding 1986). The critics emphasized the links between knowledge and power. They argued that the positivists' emphasis on objectivity, detachment, and value-free inquiry often masked a hidden conservative political agenda, and encouraged research that justified domination by experts and elites and devalued oppressed people. The critics proposed alternative paradigms that integrated research and theory with political action, and gave the people being studied more power over the research (Carr and Kemmis 1986; Lather 1986; Rose 1983).

The development of alternative paradigms, together with the emergence of participatory research in the Third World and the politicial activism accompanying social movements of the 1960s and 1970s, sparked a variety of participatory research projects by North American social scientists. John Gaventa investigated political and economic oppression in Appalachian communities, and grass-roots efforts to challenge the status quo, and Peter Park criticized mainstream sociology from the perspective of participatory research and critical theory. Health-related issues such as wife-battering, health collectives, and toxic wastes were studied by Patricia Maguire and others, while researchers in education examined community efforts to improve public schools and participatory methods of teaching (Luttrell 1988). Issues at the workplace such as struggles for unionization have been investigated by many participatory researchers; they have documented the impact of factors such as ethnic divisions and women's work culture on the success of unionization (Bookman and Morgen 1988).

Participatory research is closely related to several other fields. Feminist approaches to research and teaching often closely resemble participatory research and emphasize nonhierarchical relations between researcher and researched, raising consciousness, taking action against sexism and other forms of domination, and valuing expressive forms of knowledge (see Smith 1987; Stanley and Wise 1983). Feminists have done the majority of the participatory research projects in North America, but they do not use the label, and feminists and participatory researchers rarely consult each other's work.

A similar approach has been developed by William F. Whyte, who works with representatives of managment and workers to study organizational problems such as reducing production costs, or redesigning training programs. His approach differs from participatory research in that it gives little attention to power and empowerment, or consciousness-raising and education, and the action component of the projects is coordinated with management and does not directly challenge the existing power structure. Whyte labels his approach "participatory action research," which will cause confusion since the same term is used to describe Orlando Fals Borda's very different, more radical approach.

Participatory research also overlaps with several traditional social science methods, especially participant observation, ethnography, and intensive interviews, all of which rely on empathic interpretation of popular knowledge and everyday experience and that lead researchers to be engaged with the people being studied, not detached from them. Applied research also focuses on social action, but usually for the privileged—those with the money and sophistication to employ researchers or consultants.

ISSUES IN PARTICIPATORY RESEARCH

Two issues underlie many of the problems confronted by academic participatory researchers: the relations between researchers and the researched; and the tensions between being politically active and producing objective, academic studies.

Relations between researchers and researched are problematic at each stage of a participatory research project (on stages, see Maguire 1987; Vio Grossi 1981; Hall 1981). At the beginning of the project the researchers must consider what segments of the community will participate. Although some participatory researchers talk about "the oppressed" people in a community or "the poor" as if they were a homogeneous group, most communities are complex and internally stratified, and the more powerless people usually are more difficult to include.

The power of the researcher versus the researched also is problematic in the next stage of a project, when participants identify and discuss community problems. Researchers have specific skills in facilitating the group and obtaining information, and typically have more time, money, and other resources. Therefore, they can take more responsibility (and power) in the project, and community members often want a researcher to take charge in some areas. There are also conflicts during group discussions between validating participants' knowledge and power versus educating for critical consciousness and validating the researchers' power (Vio Grossi 1981).

When the project moves to the stage of designing research on community problems, researchers are especially likely to have a power advantage, since community members typically lack the skills and the interest to carry out this task. If community members are to be equal participants in designing a complex research project, they first need an extended educational program like the adult education classes for the Leeds bus drivers. Otherwise, the research probably will have to be fairly limited, or the researchers will control the research design, while community members participate as consultants and trained research assistants. In this case it becomes especially important that community members have substantial power in setting the research agenda (e.g., Merrifield 1989).

Conflicts between activism and involvement versus academic objectivity and detachment are another source of problems. However, many of the problems can be resolved by questioning the assumed incompatibility between being involved with the people one is studying and producing objective or valid evidence. On the one hand, involved researchers often produce valid knowledge. Sociology and anthropology include many examples of systematic, highly regarded ethnographies and interview studies by researchers who were very involved with the community. Moreover, participating as an activist probably yields just as valid an account as being a traditional participant observer. On the other hand, research methods associated with being detached, such as surveys and quantitative analysis, often contribute to effective political action. For example, a research group in Bombay organized a participatory census of pavement-dwellers in a large slum. Their results documented that slum-dwellers had been underenumerated by the official census and had been unjustly denied census-dependent services. Participants also created strong community organizations and learned how to use existing services

(Patel 1988). In this project, community involvement and academic standards were compatible. In other projects, participatory researchers have experienced many conflicts between serving the interests of the community being researched, and producing knowledge that is valuable to the academic community.

(SEE ALSO: *Field Research Methods; Qualitative Methods; Social Movements*)

REFERENCES

Acker, Joan, Kate Berry, and Joke Esseveld 1983 "Objectivity and Truth: Problems in Doing Feminist Research." *Women's Studies International Forum* 6:423–435.

Barndt, Deborah 1980 *Education and Social Change: A Photographic Study of Peru.* Dubuque, Iowa: Kendal/Hunt.

Bernstein, Richard 1983 *Beyond Objectivism and Relativism.* Philadelphia: University of Pennsylvania Press.

Bookman, Ann, and Sandra Morgen, eds. 1988 *Women and the Politics of Empowerment.* Philadelphia: Temple University Press.

Bredo, Eric, and Walter Feinberg (eds.) 1982 *Knowledge and Values in Social and Educational Research.* Philadelphia: Temple University Press.

Brown, L. David, and Rajesh Tandon 1983 "The Ideology and Political Economy of Inquiry: Action Research and Participatory Research." *Journal of Applied Behavioral Science and Technology: An International Perspective* 19:277–294.

Carr, Wilfred, and Stephen Kemmis 1986 *Becoming Critical: Education, Knowledge and Action Research.* London: Falmer Press.

Comstock, Donald, and Russell Fox 1982 "Participatory Research as Critical Theory: North Bonneville U.S.A. Experience." Paper presented at 10th World Congress of Sociology, Mexico City. (Available from Russell Fox, Evergreen State College, Olympia, Wash. 98505.)

Fals Borda, Orlando 1988 *Knowledge and People's Power: Lessons with Peasants: Nicaragua, Mexico and Colombia.* New York: New Horizons Press.

Forrester, Keith, and Kevin Ward 1989 "The Potential and Limitations: Participatory Research in a University Context." Participatory Research Conference Case Study, Division of International Development, International Centre, Calgary, Alberta.

Freire, Paulo 1970 *Pedagogy of the Oppressed.* New York: Continuum.

Gaventa, John 1980 *Power and Powerlessness: Quiescence and Rebellion in an Appalachian Valley.* Urbana: University of Illinois Press.

——— 1988 "Participatory Research in North America." *Convergence* 21:19–29.

———, and Billy Horton 1981 "A Citizen's Research Project in Appalachia, U.S.A." *Convergence* 14:30–40.

———, Barbara Smith, and Alex Willingham (eds.) 1990 *Communities in Economic Crisis.* Philadelphia: Temple University Press.

Hall, Bud 1975 "Participatory Research: An Approach for Change." *Prospects* 8:24–31.

——— 1981 "The Democratization of Research in Adult and Non-Formal Education." In P. Reason and J. Rowan, eds., *Human Inquiry.* New York: Wiley.

Harding, Sandra 1986 *The Science Question in Feminism.* Ithaca, N.Y.: Cornell University Press.

Huizer, Gerrit, and Bruce Mannheim (eds.) 1979 *The Politics of Anthropology: From Colonialism and Sexism Toward a View from Below.* Paris: Mouton Publishers.

Kassam, Yusuf, and Mustafa Kemal (eds.) 1982 *Participatory Research: An Emerging Alternative Methodology in Social Science Research.* New Delhi: Society for Participatory Research in Asia.

Lather, Patti 1986 "Research as Praxis." *Harvard Educational Review* 56:257–277.

Luttrell, Wendy 1988 *Claiming What Is Ours: An Economics Experience Workbook.* New Market, Tenn.: Highlander Research and Education Center.

Maguire, Patricia 1987 *Doing Participatory Research: A Feminist Approach.* Amherst: Center for International Education, School of Education, University of Massachusetts.

Merrifield, Juliet 1989 "Putting the Scientists in Their Place: Participatory Research in Environmental and Occupational Health." *Highlander Center Working Paper,* Highlander Research and Education Center.

Mies, Maria 1983 "Towards a Methodology for Feminist Research." In G. Bowles and R. Klein, eds., *Theories of Women's Studies.* London: Routledge and Kegan Paul.

Park, Peter 1978 "Social Research and Radical Change." Presentation at 9th World Congress of Sociology, Uppsala, Sweden.

———, Budd Hall, and Ted Jackson (eds.) Forthcoming *Knowledge, Action and Power: An Introduction to Participatory Research.* South Hadley, Mass.: Bergin and Garvey.

Participatory Research Network 1982 *Participatory Research: An Introduction.* New Delhi: Society for Participatory Research in Asia.

Patel, Sheela 1988 "Enumeration as a Tool for Mass Mobilization: Dharavi Census." *Convergence* 21:120–135.

Rose, Hilary 1983 "Hand, Brain and Heart: A Feminist Epistemology for the Natural Sciences." *Signs: Journal of Women in Culture and Society* 9:73–94.

Shor, Ira (ed.) 1987 *Freire for the Classroom: A Sourcebook.* Portsmouth, N.H.: Heinemann.

Smith, Dorothy 1987 *The Everyday World as Problematic: A Feminist Sociology.* Boston: Northeastern University Press.

Stanley, Liz, and Sue Wise 1983 *Breaking Out: Feminist Consciousness and Feminist Research.* London: Routledge and Kegan Paul.

Tandon, Rajesh 1981 "Participatory Research in the Empowerment of People." *Convergence* 14:20–29.

——— 1988 "Social Transformation and Participatory Research." *Convergence* 21:5–18.

Vio Grossi, Francisco 1981 "Socio-Political Implications of Participatory Research." *Convergence* 14:43–51.

Whyte, William F. 1989 "Advancing Scientific Knowledge Through Participatory Action Research." *Sociological Forum* 4:367–386.

FRANCESCA M. CANCIAN
CATHLEEN ARMSTEAD

PEACE The study of peace is not a tidy, well-ordered field, but it is flourishing. In recent decades, work in peace research, peace studies, peace science, conflict resolution, and nonviolent action has expanded greatly in the United States, Western Europe, and many other parts of the world. The work has been truly global and interdisciplinary, but this article emphasizes recent writing by U.S. sociologists and other social scientists drawing from sociological theory and research.

The concept of peace is a matter of controversy. Some writers use the term in distinction to war; this is *negative peace,* defined as the absence of direct physical violence. Other writers stress *positive peace;* this may entail integrative and cooperative relations, or the absence of great inequalities in the life chances of different populations. Some writers' conception of peace includes relations among all kinds of groups and between individuals, as well as between countries; others define peace in terms of global actors in a world system.

This article is about international peace, but it also considers peace processes among various social units and levels. Reflecting considerable consensus in the field, we examine the social conditions fostering integration, equity, and mutual security, not merely the absence of war. Not focusing on the causes of war, reviewed elsewhere in this volume, we discuss sociological work regarding: (1) *peacebuilding,* creating conditions that prevent the emergence of violent conflicts; (2) *peacemaking,* developing processes that contribute to the deescalation and settlement of conflicts; and (3) *peacekeeping,* creating conditions for maintaining and expanding nonviolent relations and equitable outcomes.

As for any conflict, important factors shaping developments at each of those stages of international struggles arise from three major sources: (1) within one of the primary adversaries; (2) in the relationship between them; and (3) in the social system of which they are a part (Kriesberg 1982). Analysts tend to stress one or another of these sources, and each will be discussed as it relates to peacebuilding, peacemaking, and peacekeeping.

A final introductory observation: Much of the sociological work concerning peace follows traditional directions, analyzing empirical data about when and how actions contributing to peace have occurred. Some of it takes a critical stance, examining the social conditions and processes that produce wars and other forms of violent international struggle and stressing factors that are not conventionally used to account for and justify the struggles. Finally, still other writing is more policy- and futurist-oriented, emphasizing possibilities for fostering peace.

PEACEBUILDING

Considerable research and theorizing have been done about the conditions within societies that generate international conflicts and wars.

Unmasking those conditions is sometimes expected to lead to changing them and thus building peace. Following in the tradition of C. Wright Mills, one subject of such work is the military-industrial complex. The assumption of much of this work is that preparing to fight a war, even if justified in terms of defense or to deter war, has a dynamic of its own. Consequently, it becomes disproportionate to the goals sought, generates mutual mistrust, and hence increases the likelihood of war. The dynamic is driven by military, industrial, and political elites with a vested interest in maintaining high military expenditures. Popular support for this military preparedness is mobilized, and people in mass societies are particularly vulnerable to appeals for national solidarity against a terrible external threat.

Illustrative works include Sanders's (1983) study of the Committee on the Present Danger, which effectively pressured the U.S. government in the mid-1970s to increase weapons development and procurement; and Wolfe's (1979) analysis of the domestic coalitions, which explained the changing perceptions of a Soviet threat. The end of the Cold War is providing additional kinds of evidence about the significance of internal factors within both the American and Soviet societies for sustaining the cold war between them.

Influenced by the feminist tradition, attention is now being given to the importance of gender socialization as a domestic factor affecting peacebuilding. Men tend to view social relations in a more adversarial and competitive way than do women, who tend to emphasize integrative relations. This is manifested, too, in different conceptions of war, peace, and security and in gender differences in supporting reliance on military versus noncoercive means of conducting international relations (Boulding 1977; Northrup 1990). Societal differences in the socialization of men and women then would help explain differing national predispositions toward fighting and the use of violence.

The way in which language is used to frame conflict and means of waging struggles is also a matter of considerable recent attention. Discourses of the mass media and of films have been analyzed as sources for overreliance on violence and the threat of violence in conducting conflicts (Gibson 1989). Such work also illuminates the processes of dehumanization in social conflicts that supports the disproportional character of much conflict escalation and intractability.

The role of social structure and culture in setting the style of conducting conflicts is a matter of great significance. Attention has been given to the repertoire of methods to conduct conflicts. Information about effective nonviolent ways of settling conflicts may become peacebuilding methods added to a society's repertoire.

In addition to internal conditions, we note two of the several aspects of relations between global actors that affect the likelihood that those actors will conduct their relations peacefully. One longstanding area of work has been the effects of integration between societies, including the exchange of peoples, goods, and ideas. On the whole, research supports the generalization that such integration enhances mutual security and reduces the chances of waging wars or threatening each other's security. Increased integration not only creates greater bonds of mutual identity and interest but also improves communication and exchanges that parties will regard as equitable.

Recent work has given particular attention to alternatives to traditional reliance on military threat as a means of sustaining security. Sharp's (1973, 1990) studies of nonviolent action as a means of achieving social change and of defending a society against aggression are increasingly significant as the Cold War ends. The development of nonviolent or civilian-based defense clearly is less threatening and therefore less provocative in intersocietal relations.

Finally, the global system within which adversaries interact also affects the likelihood that their relations will be peaceful. In this context, the concepts of positive peace and structural violence are particularly significant. Unlike personal violence, structural violence is indirect. It refers to the "avoidable denial of what is needed to satisfy fundamental needs" (Galtung 1980, p. 67). Thus, structural conditions may damage and cut short people's lives by restrictions of human rights or by malnutrition and illness while other people using conventionally available knowledge do not suffer the same deprivations. Such inequities are built into many social systems and into the global order and constitute negative peace. This has been an influential idea and has stimulated a variety of studies, particularly regarding conditions in the Third World.

Another area of considerable sociological work pertains to the expansion in number, size, and scope of international nongovernmental organizations (NGOs). Many kinds of transnational organizations perform activities and are arenas for interactions that supplement or even compete with states and international governmental organizations. NGOs include multinational corporations, religious and ideological organizations, professional and trade associations, trade union federations, and ethnically based associations. These groupings provide important bases of identity and action that cross-cut country borders (Angell 1969; Evan 1981; Boulding 1988).

International and supranational governmental organizations have also been examined by sociologists. They have sought to understand the conditions in which such institutions emerge and survive and serve as agencies to prevent conflicts from arising and escalating to violence (Etzioni 1965).

PEACEMAKING

Recent work has focused particularly on the ways in which the escalation of conflicts is limited, how transitions occur toward deescalation, and how negotiations end conflicts. Domestic, relational, and contextual factors all contribute to such peacemaking, as discussed next.

Among domestic conditions, sociological work gives attention to popular forces that pressure governments to move toward an accommodation with adversaries. This interest combines with the recent growth in theory and research about social movements to generate considerable work on peace movements (Lofland and Marullo 1990). For example, McCrea and Markle (1989) analyzed the nuclear freeze campaign of the early 1980s as well as earlier campaigns against nuclear weapons. There is a variety of evidence that at least within the United States and Western Europe, public opinion and organized public pressure have influenced governments on foreign policy issues, often in the direction of peacemaking.

Most work on peacemaking focuses on the relations between adversaries, and for U.S. analysts this has meant the U.S.-Soviet conflict. Contributions have been made about the extent to which that conflict and the proxy wars associated with it have been based on misunderstandings and on processes of dehumanization that foster conflict escalation (e.g., Gamson and Modigliani 1971).

Other writing has drawn from and contributes to studies of conflict resolution and negotiation. This work focuses on unilateral, conciliatory gestures and other initiatives in deescalating conflicts, on managing crises and transforming intractable conflicts into negotiable problems, and on strategies and techniques for negotiating mutually acceptable agreements (Patchen 1988; Kriesberg 1988).

Finally, sociological attention is given to the role of nonofficial groups that serve as links and channels of communication between adversaries (Schwartz 1989). Sometimes based in one camp, they provide some mediating services in deescalating a protracted conflict, acting as quasi-mediators.

This is closely related to aspects of the global context that may advance peacemaking. Sociologists have contributed to understanding, for example, the possible roles of mediation in conflict deescalation and resolution. Practice and analysis pertain to getting parties to the negotiating table, facilitating meetings, creating new options, and building support for agreements (Burton 1990; Laue, Burde, Potapchuk, and Salkoff 1988).

Although much of this attention has been focused on nonofficial and informal mediation, the roles of governmental actors, often with great resources, and of international governmental organizations are also being examined (e.g., Rubin 1981).

PEACEKEEPING

Sustaining cease-fires, settlements about disputes, and peace agreements, as well as general accommodations between former adversaries are all part of peacekeeping. The development of vested interests within each society for the maintenance of peace is similar to the domestic processes and conditions related to peacebuilding discussed earlier and will not be further elaborated on here.

Peacekeeping between adversaries is being changed by new conceptions of security. Led by work done in Western Europe, many analysts stress the reality that seeking security by threatening the security of others is inadequate, and this perspective has fostered examining new ways of achieving mutual security. In addition, the very concept of security has been broadened to include more than state security by military means. For example, threats to life and well-being arising from environmental developments and global inequities, as well as changes in the means by which security is attained, are receiving new attention (Stephenson 1988).

The international system includes international governmental organizations that have played important roles in peacekeeping, as have individual governments and ad hoc multinational groups. Sociologists have studied the working of such peacekeeping forces and the impact of that experience on the soldiers so involved (Moskos 1976).

CONCLUSIONS

Sociological students of peace have generally sought to be relevant for policy as well as theory. For U.S. analysts this has generally meant focusing on the U.S.-Soviet conflict and the threat of nuclear war (Gamson 1990). One important task now is to assess different explanations for the end of the Cold War. To what extent do the analysts who emphasized the unrealistic nature of the Cold War and the positive contributions of official and popular peacemaking efforts convincingly explain the transformation, or to what extent are those who stressed the primacy of coercion and military threat vindicated?

The Cold War served as the paradigm-setting conflict in recent peace research. Its end gives new significance to other enduring conflicts and issues as well as to emerging challenges to peace. The United States is now the single military and economic superpower; its role as a guarantor of peace and as a threat to peace will need to be examined intensively. This examination, in the new global context, will provide new tests for old ideas.

Long-standing sociological interest in community, tradition, and collective identity will be helpful in understanding the impact of the new prominence of ethnic and nationalist conflicts, and the reduced prominence of unversalistic ideological struggles. These newly significant conflicts will also seem to be more realistically grounded struggles over territory and authority than was the U.S.-Soviet rivalry.

Other conflicts evoke global identifications and perspectives. They entail common interests as well as conflicting ones. The conflicts pertain to environmental challenges, economic development, and human rights. In these struggles, nonstate actors are increasingly important, and the sociological attention to such movements and NGOs is therefore especially relevant.

Finally, the rapidly changing nature of world conflicts means that new perspectives for analysis and for policy will be pitted against each other. The ideas of conflict resolution, of framing and reframing conflicts, and of participation by nongovernmental forces and actors across the world in the construction of peace will take on increased importance.

(SEE ALSO: *Global Systems Analysis; Military Sociology; Religion, Politics, and War; War*)

REFERENCES

Angell, Robert C. 1969 *Peace on the March: Transnational Participation.* New York: Van Nostrand Reinhold.

Boulding, Elise 1977 *Women in the Twentieth Century World.* New York: Sage.

——— 1988 *Building a Global Civic Culture.* New York: Teachers College Press.

Burton, John 1990 *Conflict: Resolution and Provention.* New York: St. Martin's Press.

Etzioni, Amitai 1965 *Political Unification.* New York: Holt, Rinehart and Winston.

Evan, William M. (ed.) 1981 *Knowledge and Power in a Global Society.* Beverly Hills, Calif.: Sage.

Galtung, Johan 1980 *The True Worlds: A Transnational Perspective.* New York: Free Press.

Gamson, William A. 1990 "Sociology and Nuclear War." In H. Gans, ed., *Sociology in America.* Beverly Hills, Calif.: Sage.

———, and André Modigliani 1971 *Untangling the Cold War: A Strategy for Testing Rival Theories.* Boston: Little, Brown.

Gibson, James William 1989 "American Paramilitary Culture and the Reconstitution of the Vietnam War." In J. Walsh and J. Aulich, eds., *Vietnam Images: War and Representation.* New York: St. Martin's Press.

Kriesberg, Louis 1982 *Social Conflicts,* 2nd ed. Englewood Cliffs, N.J.: Prentice-Hall.

——— 1988 "Strategies of Negotiating Agreements: U.S.-Soviet and Arab-Israeli Cases." *Negotiation Journal* 4:19–29.

Laue, James H., Sharon Burde, William Potapchuk, and Miranda Salkoff 1988 "Getting to the Table: Three Paths." *Mediation Quarterly* 20:7–21.

Lofland, John, and Sam Marullo (eds.) 1990 *Peace Movement Dynamics.* New Brunswick, N.J.: Rutgers University Press.

McCrea, Frances B., and Gerald E. Markle 1989 *Minutes to Midnight.* Newbury Park, Calif.: Sage.

Moskos, Charles C., Jr. 1976 *Peace Soldiers: The Sociology of a United Nations Military Force.* Chicago: University of Chicago Press.

Northrup, Terrell A. 1990 "Personal Security, Political Security: The Relationship Between Conceptions of Gender, War, and Peace." In L. Kriesberg, ed., *Research in Social Movements, Conflicts and Change,* vol. 12. Greenwich, Conn.: JAI Publications.

Patchen, Martin 1988 *Resolving Disputes Between Nations: Coercion or Conciliation?* Durham, N.C.: Duke University Press.

Rubin, Jeffrey Z. 1981 *Dynamics of Third Party Intervention: Kissinger in the Middle East.* New York: Praeger.

Sanders, Jerry W. 1983 *Peddlers of Crisis.* Boston: South End Press.

Schwartz, Richard D. 1989 "Arab-Jewish Dialogue in the United States: Toward Track II Tractability." In L. Kriesberg, T. A. Northrup, and S. J. Thorson, eds., *Intractable Conflicts and Their Transformation.* Syracuse, N.Y.: Syracuse University Press.

Sharp, Gene 1973 *The Politics of Nonviolent Action.* Boston: Porter Sargent.

——— 1990 *Civilian-Based Defense.* Princeton, N.J.: Princeton University Press.

Stephenson, Carolyn M. 1988 "The Need for Alternative Forms of Security: Crises and Opportunities." *Alternatives: Social Transformation and Humane Governance* 13:55–76.

Wolfe, Alan 1979 *The Rise and Fall of the "Soviet Threat": Domestic Sources of the Cold War Consensus.* Washington, D.C.: Institute for Policy Studies.

LOUIS KRIESBERG

PENSION SYSTEMS *See* Retirement; Social Security.

PERSONAL RELATIONSHIPS Personal relationships permeate the social environment. People have relatives, friends, parents, siblings, spouses, and/or children to whom they are more or less obligated, more or less committed, and more or less close. These relationships involve sentiments, values, shared activities, public declarations of commitment, and exchanges of information, thoughts, feelings, and services. Paradoxically, these relationships also involve issues of conflict and power.

Much attention has been directed toward the study of personal relationships in recent years. The argument has even been made that personal relationships should be a separate discipline (Kelley 1986). However, this argument overlooks the fact that some aspects of personal relationships, such as marriage and courtship, have a long history of sociological research and study (see, e.g., Waller 1938; Simmel 1950). The following essay argues that personal relationships are sociologically relevant because they create social structure and are affected by that structure. After contrasting primary relationships with secondary relationships, key theories and examples of research findings are presented. Throughout the essay a special emphasis is placed on friendship and its characteristics as an important type of personal relationship. Finally, the essay considers the absence of personal relationships by looking at research on loneliness and concludes by examining possibilities for future research.

Relationships exist along a continuum, moving from the most impersonal (secondary relationships) to the most intimate (primary relationships). Secondary relationships are formal and, often, instrumental in nature. People at this end of the continuum respond to each other on the basis of their statuses or roles rather than considering the unique and personal characteristics of the individual. Secondary relationships may be of short duration with little or no intimacy. Examples of secondary relationships include coworkers or sales clerk and customer. Primary relationships, however, are informal, enduring, and expressive, involving intimate interactions over a period of time. Primary relationships need not be sexually intimate. As Simmel suggests, "it is by no means only erotic relations which attain a special, significant timbre, beyond their describable content and value, through the notion that an experience like theirs never existed before" (1950, p. 125). Examples of primary relationships include spouses and friends. Of course, secondary relationships can move toward primary relationships by becoming closer and more intimate; and primary relationships can move toward secondary relationships by becoming less close and less intimate (as in the case of a divorced couple, for example). Personal relationships are, therefore, primary relationships. As McCall (1970) suggests, however, personal relationships are probably best conceived as a combination of both secondary and primary relationships.

It has been observed that strong, intimate bonds tend to confine people to limited social circles, limiting relationships to in-group associations and fragmenting society. Nevertheless, weak social bonds between people integrate society by establishing intergroup relationships (Blau 1977; Granovetter 1973). Couple and kinship relationships are strong bonds constraining individual behavior through their obligatory nature. In addition, kinship bonds are also strong due to their ascribed status. A marriage, by its very nature (e.g., exclusivity, commitment, social sanctions), is a strong bond that hinders the individual's participation in other relationships. Friendship can have varying degrees of closeness and intimacy, but it is neither obligatory nor ascribed (at least in Western society). Therefore, friendship (except perhaps for best-friendship) is a weaker bond than marriage and, as such, encourages intergroup relationships, thus creating community.

The most intimate type of primary relationship is marriage. It is characterized by ceremony, legal recognition, and normative expectations of mutual loyalty and obligation. Cohabitation, which since the late 1970s has become increasingly common (Bumpass 1990), is a personal relationship of importance and interest equal to marriage. Since some have argued that cohabitation is a stage leading to marriage (Blumstein and Schwartz 1983; Bumpass 1990), the study of cohabitation can answer questions about the process by which some relationships move from less committed to more committed and why some relationships do not make that transition. In addition, Blumstein and Kollock (1988) argue that it is useful to compare cohabiting couples with married couples because they are comparable on all structural variables, except for the institutionalized nature of marriage.

Some researchers have considered the distinction between secondary and primary friendships. Friendship, like marriage and cohabitation, is expressive, focusing on the unique characteristics of the individuals involved. Of course, friends may use friends in an instrumental way. This is permissible as long as it is understood that the friend is not a friend solely because of his/her usefulness (Allan 1979). For example, Kurth (1970) examined the difference between friendships and friendly relations. According to Kurth, friendly relations lack a sense of uniqueness about the individuals involved, there is little intimacy, and there are few obligations. As friendly relations take on these characteristics of personal uniqueness, intimacy, and obligations, they move toward primary relationships, either of friendship or courtship. Using a structural approach, Kurth further argues that some relationships are constrained from forming due to three important variables: age, gender, and marital status. Friendships form between those of the same age, same gender, and same marital status. Research supports the idea that same-sex friendship is the norm (Rose 1985; Bell 1981; Allan 1979; Booth and Hess 1974). Researchers have also found evidence for general equality between friends due to similarities in age, social class, and marital status (Bell 1981; Allan 1979). However, important empirical questions follow. For example, to what extent is friendship inhibited on the basis of these factors? To what degree are friendships exploitative when they cross the barriers of age, gender, and marital status?

Waller's (1938) principle of least interest may explain why some relationships continue and others do not. According to this principle, the individual with the least interest in continuing the relationship has the most power. Personal relationships, therefore, may become exploitative to the extent that those with more interest in the relationship, and therefore less power, are unable to negotiate fair exchanges (Kurth 1970). Ironically, power issues operate alongside the notion of reciprocity. Gouldner (1960) reasons that reciprocity is a norm with two aspects. First, a friend should repay a favor received; and second, a friend should not do harm to a person who has given a favor.

Two important theories are exchange theory and equity theory. Exchange theory, as developed by Thibaut and Kelley (1959), attempts to account for much of the variability in personal relationships by a cost/reward analysis. All social relationships incur both costs and rewards for the individuals. Often a person must decide between one relationship and another on the basis of an analysis of cost and reward (Kelley 1979). This analysis occurs at two levels. At the comparison level the individual evaluates costs and rewards within the relationship based on his/her own standards. At the comparison level for alternatives, the individual evaluates the costs and rewards based on the possibility of alternative relationships. Consequently, whether the relationship continues depends on the cost/reward analysis. Equity or fairness within the relationship is theoretically important (Walster et al. 1978; Kelley 1986). Researchers have found that personal relationships that are equitable are more satisfying to the individuals involved. In a study of lesbian couples by Caldwell and Peplau (1984), satisfaction with the relationship was related to equity.

A zero-sum view of social involvements holds that increased involvement in one relationship demands decreased involvement in other relationships (Johnson and Leslie 1982). When the individual assumes a new role—that of a spouse, for example—all other role identities must be reprioritized because of the costs incurred with the new role. Therefore, the dyadic withdrawal hypothesis proposes that as a couple move closer together, their social network decreases (Burgess and Huston 1979). For example, Johnson and Leslie (1982), in a study of 419 college students, found that the number of friends reported by couples decreased, according to the stage of the couple relationship, from occasional dating to marriage. The reasons given by the authors for this finding is the exclusive nature of the couple relationship, the requirement of long-term commitment, and the increasing time requirement of the relationship.

Two models of personal relationships have been developed to capture the diversity of relationships. The first is Backman's (1981) four-stage theory of relationship development. The first stage describes the movement from no contact to unilateral awareness. In this stage physical proximity is essential. The second stage focuses on the processes of first impressions and sorting on the basis of similarities, physical attractiveness, and self-presentation. Obviously, most of the important work regarding interpersonal attraction occurs in this stage. The third stage involves the development of interdependence and role negotiation in which self-disclosure, exchanges, and attribution are central. The last stage concerns those processes that lead either to maintenance or to dissolution of the relationship. The last two stages are important to both exchange and equity theorists. The advantage of this model is that the focus remains on the dyad. It is also a process model, as opposed to a structural model.

The second model is by Blumstein and Kollock

(1988), who identified five key characteristics or dimensions of personal relationships: (1) whether the relationship is kinship based, (2) whether the relationship has a sexual-romantic aspect, (3) whether the individuals live together, (4) whether the relationship is hierarchical or egalitarian, and (5) whether it is a cross-sex or same-sex relationship. Using this model, personal relationships can then be classified on each dimension. For example, individuals in a marriage are nonkin, sexual-romantic, cohabiting, and cross-sex. Since the authors argue that researchers need to take a comparative approach in analyzing relationships, one could compare marriages as described above with commuter marriages (in which individuals do not cohabit) to determine the differences between the two types of marriage. Such a study would be complicated, however, by the fact that in any marriage relationships are more or less egalitarian, more or less hierarchical.

The absence of personal relationships often creates a condition identified as loneliness. Loneliness can be conceived as the absence of a relationship with another and, therefore, "represents a very specific relation to society" (Simmel 1950, p. 120). This area has experienced much recent attention, primarily from psychologists (see, e.g., Hojat and Crandall 1989), coinciding with growth of interest in personal relationships (Perlman 1989). What is the societal significance of loneliness? How is it experienced differently by gender? by class? by race? Research has shown that loneliness is experienced disproportionately by the elderly, suggesting that the study of personal relationships in relation to the life course is important. Theoretically the sociologist needs to be concerned with loneliness because it fragments society and weakens controls on behavior (see Hirschi 1969 for a discussion on control theory).

Several studies on friendship have indicated that the life cycle is an important factor in predicting the friendship patterns of couples. Reisman (1981) found that friends dominate the lives of single, young adults and the elderly but decrease in importance during the childbearing and career-building years, a finding also observed by Rubin (1985) and Fischer and Oliker (1983). It is unlikely that life stage is important only in friendships.

The following excerpt captures the importance of personal relationships in a commonsense yet elegant manner:

> *Man is gifted with reason; he is life being aware of itself; he has awareness of himself, of his fellow man, of his past, and of the possibilities of his future. This awareness of himself as a separate entity, the awareness of his own short life span, of the fact that without his will he is born and against his will he dies, that he will die before those whom he loves, or they before him, the awareness of his aloneness and separateness, of his helplessness before the forces of nature and of society, all this makes his separate, disunited existence an unbearable prison. He would become insane could he not liberate himself from this prison and reach out, unite himself in some form or other with men, with the world outside.* (Erich Fromm, *The Art of Loving*, pp. 6–7.)

One way in which knowledge regarding personal relationships can be advanced is by studying other societies in order to understand the ways in which personal relationships vary depending on societal norms. As Brain (1976) found, friendships vary cross-culturally, with other cultures having more norms regarding appropriate friendship behavior. He concludes that in Western societies friendship is often disposable. This, however, may be more often the case for friendly relations (secondary relationships) than for friendships (primary relationships).

This essay has briefly reviewed the general area of personal relationships, distinguishing between primary and secondary relationships. A special emphasis was placed on friendship as a type of primary relationship. In addition, key theories and models were presented. One question remains, however: Should personal relationships be a separate discipline? The answer here is no. Sociologists need to reclaim the study of relationships precisely because they are central to people's lives and form the basis for society. The study of the dyad in sociology has a long history, from Cooley (1902) to Waller (1938) to Simmel (1950). Sociologists need to be concerned with the subject matter because it focuses on the most fundamental of all social groups, the dyad, rather than on the individual.

(SEE ALSO: *Interpersonal Power; Symbolic Interaction Theory*)

REFERENCES

Allan, G. A. 1979 *A Sociology of Friendship and Kinship.* London: George Allen and Unwin.

Backman, C. W. 1981 "Attraction in Interpersonal Relationships." In M. Rosenberg and R. H. Turner, eds., *Social Psychology: Sociological Perspectives.* New York: Basic Books.

Bell, R. R. 1981 *Worlds of Friendship.* Beverly Hills, Calif.: Sage.

Blau, P. 1977 *Inequality and Heterogeneity.* New York: Free Press.

Blumstein, P., and P. Kollock 1988 "Personal Relationships." *Annual Review of Sociology* 14:467–490.

Blumstein, P., and P. Schwartz 1983 *American Couples.* New York: Morrow.

Booth, A., and E. Hess 1974 "Cross-Sex Friendships." *Journal of Marriage and the Family* 36:38–47.

Brain, R. 1976 *Friends and Lovers.* New York: Basic Books.

Brown, R. 1965 *Social Psychology.* New York: Free Press.

Bumpass, L. L. 1990 "What's Happening to Family? Interactions Between Demographic and Institutional Change." *Demography* 27, no. 4: 483–496.

Burgess, R. L., and T. L. Huston 1979 *Social Exchange in Developing Relationships.* New York: Academic Press.

Caldwell, M. A., and L. A. Peplau 1984. "The Balance of Power in Lesbian Relationships." *Sex Roles* 10, no. 7/8:587–599.

Cooley, C. H. 1902 *Human Nature and the Social Order.* New York: Scribners.

Fischer, C. S., and S. J. Oliker 1983 "A Research Note on Friendship, Gender, and the Life Cycle." *Social Forces* 62, no. 1:124–133.

Gouldner, A. W. 1960 "The Norm of Reciprocity: A Preliminary Statement." *American Sociological Review* 25, no. 2:161–178.

Granovetter, M. S. 1973 "The Strength of Weak Ties." *American Journal of Sociology* 78, no. 6:1360–1380.

Hirschi, T. 1969 *Causes of Delinquency.* Berkeley: University of California Press.

Hojat, M., and R. Crandall (eds.) 1989 *Loneliness: Theory, Research and Applications.* Newbury Park, Calif.: Sage.

Johnson, M. P., and L. Leslie 1982 "Couple Involvement and Network Structure: A Test of the Dyadic Withdrawal Hypothesis." *Social Psychology Quarterly* 45, no. 1:34–43.

Kelley, H. H. 1979 *Personal Relationships: Their Structures and Processes.* Hillsdale, N.J.: Erlbaum.

——— 1986 "Personal Relationships: Their Nature and Significance." In R. Gilmour and S. Duck, eds., *The Emerging Field of Personal Relationships.* Hillsdale, N.J.: Erlbaum.

Kurth, S. B. 1970 "Friendship and Friendly Relations." In G. McCall, ed., *Social Relationships.* Chicago: Aldine.

McCall, G. 1970 "The Social Organization of Relationships." In G. McCall, ed., *Social Relationships.* Chicago: Aldine.

Perlman, D. 1989 "Further Reflections on the Present State of Loneliness Research." In M. Hojat and R. Crandall, eds., *Loneliness: Theory, Research and Applications.* Newbury Park, Calif.: Sage.

Reisman, J. M. 1981 "Adult Friendships." In S. Duck and R. Gilmour, eds., *Personal Relationships,* vol. 2. New York: Academic Press.

Rose, S. M. 1985 "Same- and Cross-Sex Friendships and the Psychology of Homosociality." *Sex Roles* 12:73–74.

Rubin, L. 1985 *Just Friends: The Role of Friendship in Our Lives.* New York: Harper and Row.

Simmel, G. 1950 *The Sociology of Georg Simmel,* K. H. Wolff, ed. and trans. New York: Free Press.

Thibaut, J., and H. H. Kelley 1959 *The Social Psychology of Groups.* New York: Wiley.

Waller, W. 1938 *The Family: A Dynamic Interpretation.* New York: Dryden.

Walster, E., G. W. Walster, and E. Berscheid 1978 *Equity: Theory and Research.* Boston: Allyn and Bacon.

KATHLEEN A. WARNER

PERSONALITY AND SOCIAL STRUCTURE Three questions underlie the study of social structure and personality: What is social structure? What is personality? And, what is the relationship between the two? The history of this area and the current state of knowledge contain tremendous variability in the answers to the questions.

For example, social structure includes whole cultural configurations, social institutions such as family and the state, social stratification and class, the nature of roles, organizational structures, group dynamics, and microfeatures of day-to-day interactions. Social structure also includes process and change at the group level such as economic depression or recession, modernization, revolution, war, organizational growth and decline, human development and aging, and life course transitions (e.g., school to work, retirement).

Concepts and approaches to personality also have a rich history and many variations. These concepts include attitudes, abilities, affective and attributional styles, values, beliefs, cognitive schema, identities, aspirations, views of the self and others, and individual behaviors. The concept of personality, too, connotes both structure and process or change. Most contemporary observers would agree with a definition of personality as "regularities and consistencies in the behavior of individuals in their lives" (Snyder and Ickes 1985, p. 883). In some approaches, attitude and the self precede and determine behavior; in other approaches, people observe behavior and infer their own mental states and features of self.

Neither a simple answer nor close consensus exists among scholars on the question of the nature of the relationship between social structure and personality, although most would agree that the relationship is reciprocal rather than asymmetric, and modest rather than extremely strong or extremely weak (House and Mortimer 1990). That is, multiple areas of research provide clear evidence that variations in social structures shape components of personality, and variations in personality have effects on social structure. Humans are neither completely pawns in the face of social forces, nor are they entirely independent, autonomous agents, unfettered by social influences. The study of human lives shows clear evidence of both forms.

The study of social structure and personality has its roots in the disciplines of sociology, psychology, and anthropology. The scholars whose ideas and research offered inspiration include Marx (1963), Freud (1928), Mead (1934), Lewin (1951), Gerth and Mills (1953), Inkeles and Levinson (1954), Smelser and Smelser (1963), and Turner (1956).

Although an oversimplification, in the 1930s, 1940s, and early 1950s the focus of scholarship was to define the basic concepts and processes for personality, for social structure, and for the relationship between the two. This era produced and elaborated developments such as field theory, role theory, interactionist perspectives on the self, along with concepts such as self, significant other, role-taking, socialization, the authoritarian personality, modal personality, and national character.

In the 1950s, sociological research on social structure and personality focused on macroscopic empirical studies of national character: What was national character? How did it vary? Could it be defined in terms of modal personality types? A long tradition of comparative anthropological studies of culture and personality informed these studies. For example, some of these studies considered the relationship between social class and personality: With social class defined as white collar or blue collar, personality referred to some underlying continuum of "adjustment," and the link between the two occurred in socialization, in particular child-rearing practices.

The 1960s produced major changes in the study of personality and social structure. First, the quantity of research increased significantly, concurrent with the massive growth of sociology and psychology as disciplines and the growth of higher education. Second, research in the area became more diffuse and differentiated. What was a fairly identifiable area of research divided into subareas of scientific disciplines such as the sociology of medicine, social stratification, small group dynamics, or attitude–behavior research. The research problems multiplied; research methods and strategies multiplied; theories and explanations multiplied; and, the journal outlets and books multiplied. At the same time, communication, integration, and cross-fertilization across research areas declined, although in the 1980s this seemed to change. In short, since the 1960s social structure and personality became an umbrella description for many different lines of investigation that were only loosely connected.

The third major change in the 1960s was a refocusing of research on social structure and personality, one that continued into the 1990s. The empirical macroscopic studies of national character and the emphasis on holistic conceptions of culture and national character declined. On the sociological side the emphasis shifted to studying "aspects of societies in relation to aspects of individuals" (House 1981, p. 526). On the psychological side a looser, multidimensional approach to personality replaced the earlier Freudian approach that was based on a coherent dynamic system and personality types and structures (DiRenzo 1977).

House (1981) described this major refocusing of research in terms of three principles that also define ideals for the investigation of personality and social structure. First, the components principle suggests that social structures such as roles, positions, and systems are multidimensional, and theory should specify which dimensions are important for which personality phenomena (such as stress, self-esteem, locus of control, and so on). Second, the proximity principle suggests focusing first on understanding the more proximate stimuli that affect people and then mapping the causal patterns across broader levels of social structure in time and space. Third, the psychological principle identifies the importance of specifying the psychological processes involved when social structures and processes affect the self, personality, and attitudes. House's three principles nicely summarize many advances in the study of social structure and personality. They also define the nature of limitations in current knowledge and identify research frontiers.

In the 1990s sociological research on social structure and personality is a patchwork of problems and areas. These include social stratification, work and personality (Kohn et al. 1983; Kohn and Slomczynski 1990), social structure and health, both physical and psychological (Mirowsky and Ross 1986), disjunctive social changes (war, economic depression) and individual adjustment (Elder 1974), role transitions and psychological changes (O'Brien 1986), variations in self-concept by structural position (Gecas 1989), human development, aging, and social change (Featherman and Lerner 1985), and political and disciminatory attitudes, social institutions, and change (Kiecolt 1988), to mention just a few.

One of the most substantial and important areas of research involves the study of social stratification, work and personality, and the program of research of Kohn et al. (1983). The Kohn–Schooler model reflects the dominant approach in this particular area and illustrates the major sociological approach to the study of social structure and personality. Spenner (1988a; 1988b) provides detailed review of their research. In comparison, approaches in psychology are more microscopic—in focusing on shorter intervals of time and smaller arenas of social space—and more likely to rely on experiments and lab studies or on field research rather than on large-scale survey research of people's work lives and personality histories.

The Kohn–Schooler model begins with dimensions of jobs that are defined and measured as objectively as possible (versus subjective dimensions and measures of individuals' jobs). These structural imperatives of jobs include: occupational self-direction (substantive complexity of work, closeness of supervision, and routinization); job pressures (time pressure, heaviness, dirtiness, and hours worked per week); extrinsic risks and rewards (the probability of being held responsible for things outside of one's control, the risk of losing one's job or business, job protections, and job income); and organizational location (ownership, bureaucratization, and hierarchical position). The three basic dimensions of personality in this research include intellectual flexibility, self-directedness of orientation, and sense of well-being or distress. Among the subdimensions of these organizing dimensions are: authoritarian conservatism, personally responsible standards of morality, trustfulness, self-confidence, self-deprecation, fatalism, anxiety, and idea-conformity.

The type of analysis used in the Kohn–Schooler research estimates the lagged and contemporaneous reciprocal relationships between conditions of work and dimensions of personality in nonexperimental, panel, survey data. The major data come from a national sample of over 3,000 persons, representative of the male, full-time labor force, ages sixteen and over in 1974. About one-third of these men were reinterviewed about ten years later, with measures being taken of work conditions and personality at both points in time. Most of the studies of women in this tradition refer to wives of men in the sample.

In a series of structural equation-model analyses that adjust for measurement error in dimensions of jobs and personality, the authors document an intricate pattern of lagged (over time) and contemporaneous selection and socialization effects. Selection effects refer to the effects of personality on work and social structure; socialization effects refer to the effects of work (social structure) on self and personality. Most of the effects of personality on work are lagged, as workers appear to select jobs of given types depending on measured aspects of their personality, or workers slowly mold jobs to match their personalities. Conversely, the effects of jobs on personalities appear to be somewhat larger and involve both contemporaneous and lagged effects. The largest relationships center on components of occupational self-direction, in particular, substantive complexity of work. For example, substantive complexity of work environments increases intellectual flexibility for men by an amount that is one-fourth as great as the effect of earlier intellectual flexibility a decade earlier, net of controls for other variables and confounding influences.

Kohn et al. interpret their findings with a "learning-generalization" explanation. According to this explanation, people learn from their jobs and generalize the lessons directly to spheres of their lives away from their jobs rather than using alternate psychological mechanisms such as displacement or compensation. The structural imperatives of jobs affect workers' values, orientations to selves, their children, and society, and cognitive functioning. The collected research shows that these generalizations appear to hold under a broad range of controls for spuriousness, alternate explanations, and extensions. The extensions include men's and women's worklives, self-direction in leisure activities, housework, and educational domains, and a number of replications of the basic model including careful comparisons with samples from Poland and Japan.

Similar summaries exist for many other areas of research in social structure and personality, but this line of research has been one of the most important. The limitations of the Kohn–Schooler program of research illustrate some of the frontiers facing research on work and personality. First, are these conditions of work the most important dimensions of social structure? Do they combine and exert their effects in a more complicated manner? Are there other features of context that should be considered? Second, are these the appropriate dimensions and combinations of personality? Are there left-out dimensions or other larger meta- or organizing dimensions of personality such as flexibility, rigidity, or general affectivity (Spenner 1988a) or processual dimensions of personality that might be more important?

Third, there are many alternate explanations that replace or extend the learning-generalization explanation for how jobs and personality reciprocally relate (for review, see O'Brien 1986). They include: (1) fit hypotheses, in which the quality of the match between dimensions of personality and dimensions of social structure determines the effects of person on job and vice versa; (2) needs and expectancy explanations, in which additional layers of cognitive weighting, interpretation, and processing mediate the relationships among job attributes, personality dimensions, and work attitude outcomes; (3) buffering and mediational hypotheses, in which the effects of social structure on personality (or vice versa) are accentuated or damped for certain extreme combinations of work conditions, or outside influences such as social support buffer the effects of social structure on personality; and (4) social information processing and attributional explanations, which posit additional perceptual/judgmental, evaluational/choice or attributional processes that affect job–attitude and attitude–behavior linkages.

At more microscopic levels (shorter time intervals such as seconds or minutes and smaller domains of social space such as intrapsychic or face-to-face interactions) the challenge for research on social structure and personality is to discover the meanings and processes that underlie longer-term, larger-scale correlations between the two. This challenge applies not only to how job or social structure affects personality but also to how a domain of personality selects a worker into an occupational or another role or serves as a catalyst for human agency and leads to attempts by people to modify their roles and circumstances. The field understands many of the ingredients but not the specific recipe.

At a mezzoscopic level, one of careers, the human life span, organizations, and other institutional settings and mechanisms, the challenge to research on social structure and personality is to put the snapshots of relationships in motion and understand the dynamics over longer periods of time. For example, in the Kohn–Schooler model, how are its findings nested in adult development, and how is adult development affected by the dynamics implied in this model?

Finally, at the macroscopic level of decades and centuries and whole institutional spheres and societies, the challenges confronting research in social structure and personality include discovering the larger sociohistorical, psychological, and biological contexts and processes in which social structure–personality relationships are embedded and then to map and trace the lines of influence across levels. This challenge also includes discovering how long-term variations in human personality feed back to long-term variations in social structures, shaping history and defining what is possible for the evolution of social forms and processes.

(SEE ALSO: *Personality Theories; Social Psychology*)

REFERENCES

DiRenzo, Gordon J. 1977 "Socialization, Personality, and Social Systems." In A. Inkeles, J. Coleman, and N. Smelser, eds., *Annual Review of Sociology*. Vol. 3. Palo Alto, Calif.: Annual Reviews.

Elder, Glen H., Jr. 1974 *Children of the Great Depression*. Chicago: University of Chicago Press.

Featherman, David L., and Richard M. Lerner 1985 "Ontogeneses and Sociogenesis: Problematics for Theory and Research about Development and Socialization across the Life-Span." *American Sociological Review* 50:659–676.

Freud, Sigmund 1928 *The Basic Writings of Sigmund Freud*, ed. and trans. A. A. Brill. New York: Random House.

Gecas, Victor 1989 "The Social Psychology of Self-Efficacy." In W. R. Scott and J. Blake, eds., *Annual Review of Sociology*. Vol. 15. Palo Alto, Calif.: Annual Reviews.

Gerth, Hans, and C. Wright Mills 1953 *Character and Social Structure*. New York: Harcourt.

House, James S. 1981 "Social Structure and Personality." In M. Rosenberg and R. H. Turner, eds., *Social Psychology: Sociological Perspectives*. New York: Basic Books.

———, and Jeylan T. Mortimer 1990 "Social Structure and the Individual: Emerging Themes and New Directions." *Social Psychology Quarterly* 53:71–80.

Inkeles, Alex, and Daniel Levinson 1954 "National Character: The Study of Modal Personality and Social Systems." In G. Lindzey, ed., *Handbook of Social Psychology*. Cambridge, Mass.: Addison-Wesley.

Kiecolt, K. Jill 1988 "Recent Developments in Attitudes and Social Structure." In W. R. Scott and J. Blake, eds., *Annual Review of Sociology*. Vol. 14. Palo Alto, Calif.: Annual Reviews.

Kohn, Melvin L., Carmie Schooler with the collaboration of J. Miller, K. Miller, C. Schoenbach, and R. Schoenberg 1983 *Work and Personality: An Inquiry into the Impact of Social Stratification*. Norwood, N.J.: Ablex.

Kohn, Melvin L., and Kazimierz M. Slomczynski 1990 *Social Structure and Self-Direction*. Cambridge, Mass.: Blackwell.

Lewin, Kurt 1951 *Field Theory in Social Science*. New York: Harper.

Marx, Karl 1963 *Karl Marx: Early Writings*, ed. and trans. T. B. Bottomore. New York: McGraw-Hill.

Mead, George H. 1934 *Mind, Self, and Society*. Chicago: University of Chicago Press.

Mirowsky, John, and Catherine E. Ross 1986 "Social Patterns of Distress." In R. Turner and J. Short, eds.,

Annual Review of Sociology, Vol. 12. Palo Alto, Calif.: Annual Reviews.

O'Brien, Gordon E. 1986 *Psychology of Work and Unemployment.* New York: Wiley.

Smelser, Neil J., and William T. Smelser 1963 *Personality and Social Systems.* New York: Wiley.

Snyder, Mark, and William Ickes 1985 "Personality and Social Behavior." In G. Lindzey and E. Aronson, eds., *Handbook of Social Psychology.* Vol. 2, *Special Fields and Applications.* New York: Random House.

Spenner, Kenneth I. 1988a "Social Stratification, Work, and Personality." In W. R. Scott and J. Blake, eds., *Annual Review of Sociology,* Vol. 14. Palo Alto, Calif.: Annual Reviews.

———1988b "Occupations, Work Settings, and the Course of Adult Development: Tracing the Implications of Select Historical Changes." In P. B. Baltes, D. L. Featherman, and R. M. Lerner, eds., *Life-Span Development and Behavior,* Vol. 9. Hillsdale, N.J.: Erlbaum.

Turner, Ralph H. 1956 "Role-Taking, Role Standpoint, and Reference Group Behavior." *American Journal of Sociology* 61:316–328.

KENNETH I. SPENNER

PERSONALITY THEORIES Problems of definition arise with the terms *personality* and *personality theories.* Personality is understood by some people to mean self-concept; by others, the consensus of other people's opinions about one's character, and by others, one's true character. Some personality theories have elaborate coordinated concepts discussing how personality originates and develops from conception to senescence, taking up cognitive, conative, and affective aspects of the mind as well as free will, holism, philosophy, and other issues. On the other hand, there are relatively simple, one-dimensional theories of personality that pay little attention to what seems important to other theorists.

This topic is complicated not only by its complexity and variations but also by intellectual belligerence among those who favor one theory over another and those who differ about the same theory. The analogy to religions is inescapable.

In view of this situation, personality theories will be handled in an unusual way. Sentences in italics are reprinted from *Personality Theories, Research, and Assessment* (Corsini and Marsella 1983). They contain quotes of selected assertions about the various theories written by authorities of nine major systems.

Table 1 is a list of a number of other important personality theories.

PSYCHOANALYSIS (SIGMUND FREUD, 1856–1939)

Psychoanalysis is both a theory of personality and a form of psychotherapy (see Freud 1952–1974). Highly controversial throughout Freud's lifetime, it continues to be so.

Freud saw personality as a dynamic conflict within the mind between opposing instinctual and social forces. *The topographical hypothesis views the mind in terms of three systems.* They are: the unconscious, the preconscious, and the conscious. *The mind is composed of the id, ego, and superego.* The id consists of primitive instinctual demands, the superego represents society's influence restricting the id's demands, and the ego is dynamically in between the two. *Fundamental motives are instinctual.* Instincts are the basic forces (drives) of the psyche. The aim of drives is their satisfaction. *All instincts are basically sexual.* Freud's concept of sexuality was equivalent to physical pleasures. *There is a series of built-in stages of sexual development.* Freud postulated that people went through three sexual stages: An oral stage following the primary infantile narcissistic stage, then an anal phase, and finally a phallic phase. *Children develop libidinal attitudes towards parents.* This notion of the Oedipus and Electra complex of children having sexual attractions to parents of the opposite sex has especially generated controversy.

The psyche develops a number of defenses. To survive, the human being's ego develops a number of processes intended to repress awareness of conflicts. Repression is the main mental mechanism, but others defenses are related to it, including rationalization, displacement, identification and conversion. *Dreams have meaning and purpose.*

TABLE 1
Some Personality Theories and Their Originators

Abelson, R. P.	Least effort
Allport, Gordon W.	Personalism
Angyll, Andreas	Organismic theory
Assiogoli, Roberto	Psychosynthesis
Berne, Eric	Transactional analysis
Binwangers, Ludwig	Daseinanalysis
Branden, Nathaniel	Biocentrism
Burrow, Trigant	Phyloanalysis
Bühler, Charlotte	Humanistic psychology
Bühler, Karl	Funktionlust
Boss, Medard	Daseinanalysis
Cattell, Raymond	Multivariate theory
Combs, Arthur	Phenomenology
Ellis, Albert	Rational-emotive theory
Erikson, Erik	Developmental theory
Eysenck, Hans	Developmental theory
Frankl, Victor	Logotherapy
Fromm, Erich	Humanistic psychoanalysis
Heider, Fritz	Balance theory
Horney, Karen	Sociopsychological theory
Jackson, Don	Systems theory
Kelly, Charles	Neo-Reichian theory
Korsybski, Alfred	General semantics
Lecky, Philip	Self-consistency
Lewin, Kurt	Topological psychology
Lowen, Alexander	Bio-energetics
Maltz, Albert	Psychocybernetics
Maslow, Abraham	Self-actualizations
May, Rollo	Existentialism
Mead, G. H.	Social interaction
Miller, Neal	Learning theory
Meyer, Adolf	Psychobiological theory
Moreno, J. L.	Sociometry
Mowrer, O.H.	Two-factor theory
Murphy, Gardner	Biosocial theory
Murray, H. A.	Need-press theory
Osgood, Charles	Congruity theory
Perls, Frederick	Gestalt theory
Piaget, Jean	Developmental theory
Rank, Otto	Will theory
Reich, Wilhelm	Character analysis
Rolf, Ida	Structural integration
Rotter, Julian	Social learning
Sarbin, Theodore	Role theory
Sheldon, William	Morphological theory
Sullivan, H.S.	Interpersonal theory
Van Kaam, Adrian	Transpersonal psychology
Werner, Heinz	Developmental theory
Wolpe, Joseph	Behavior theory

According to Freud, dreams are disguised desires permitting people to sleep by permitting expressions of illicit desires disguised by various symbolisms.

INDIVIDUAL PSYCHOLOGY (ALFRED ADLER, 1870–1937)

Alfred Adler's personality theory is distinguished by its common sense and simple language (see Adler 1956). In contrast to Freud and Jung, Adler's views demonstrate social concern.

Man, like all forms of life, is a unified organism. This basic holistic notion contradicts Freud's classifications and opposing theses and antitheses. Adler viewed the individual as an indivisible totality that could not be analyzed or considered in sections. *Life is movement, directed towards growth and expansion.* Adler took a dynamic and teleological attitude toward life, that people were always striving toward goals of personal self-improvement and enhancement. *Man is endowed with creativity and within limits is self-determined.* Instead of taking the usual position that only biology and society were to be considered in the formation of personality, Adler posited a third element: personal creativity or individual responsibility, akin to the concept of free will. Adler accepted that we all have certain biological and social givens and what is made of them is the responsibility of individuals.

Man lives inextricably in a social world. Adler had a social personality theory. *Individuale* in German does not have the same denotation as *individual* in English but rather denotes indivisibility or unity. Adler did not see humans apart from society. *The important life problems—human relations, sex, occupation—are social problems.* Adler believed that to be successful in life all humans had to complete the life tasks of socialization, family, and work.

Social interest is an aptitude that must be consciously developed. Social interest is the criterion of mental health. Social interest is operationally defined as social usefulness. This trio of related statements is an explicit philosophy unique for personality theories. Adler believed that psychological normality depended on *Gemeinschaftsgefühl*—social interest. He saw all human failures, such as criminals, the insane, and neurotics, as lacking this element.

ANALYTICAL PSYCHOLOGY (CARL G. JUNG, 1875–1961)

Jung's analytical psychology stresses unconscious mental processes and features elements in personality that derive from mankind's past (Jung 1953–1972).

Personality is influenced by potential activation of a collective transpersonal unconscious. Jung believed that individuals upon conception came with something from the past that directed their personalities, a concept somewhat like Lamarckism relative to physical heredity. *Complexes are structured and energized around an archetypical image.* This is an extension of the first assertion. Complexes refer to important bipolar aspects of personality, such as introversion–extraversion. Complexes, directed by archetypes, are seen as innate and universal capacities of the mind to organize human experiences. Archetypes are considered innate potentials of the mind derived from the experiences of ancestors, a kind of directing blueprint of one's character.

The ego mediates between the unconscious and the outside world. According to Jung, a strong, well-integrated ego is the ideal state for a person. *Unconscious psychic reality is as important as the outside world.* Jung stressed the importance of phenomenology in contrast to overt behavior. He explored people's inner realms with great diligence. He even exceeded Freud in concentrating on the importance of the unconscious. *Personality growth occurs throughout the life cycle.* Jung saw individuals in constant growth and development with imperceptible stages that sometimes, as in the case of adolescence and midlife crises, became evident. *The psyche spontaneously strives towards wholeness, integration, and self-realization.* This last statement is echoed in many different ways by a number of other theorists, including the two just considered, and is made a central point by some theorists such as Carl Rogers and Kurt Goldstein.

PERSON-CENTERED THEORY (CARL ROGERS 1902–1987)

Carl Rogers developed his theory as part of his system of client-centered or nondirective therapy (see Rogers 1951). He had a lifelong abiding faith in the potentials of people to correct the errors of their past if a therapeutic environment could be created in which the client felt understood and accepted by a neutral nonevaluative therapist. His system emerges from one central theme, the first assertion below.

Each person has an inherent tendency to actualize unique potential. Rogers viewed each person as having a built-in tendency to develop all his or her capacities in ways that serve to maintain or enhance the organism. *Each person has an inherent bodily wisdom which enables differentiation between experiences that actualize and those that do not actualize potential.* Rogers's trust in people is indicated here: There is a wisdom of the body in that everyone knows what is best for one's self in terms of the ultimate goal of self-realization.

It is crucially important to be fully open to all experiences. Experiencing becomes more than bodily sensing as one grows older. Through complex interactions with our body and with other persons we develop a concept of self. These three assertions belong together, and in them Rogers is taking up the nature–nurture, heredity–environment controversy. Essentially, his position is that personality is a function of bodily wisdom and the effect of others (primarily parents).

One can sacrifice the wisdom of one's own experiences to gain another's love. Rogers as a therapist came to the conclusion that a great deal of human suffering is due to the tendency of people to sacrifice their own body wisdom to gain positive regard from others. Children, in order to gain acceptance by their parents, will too often agree with them, accept their premises, and maintain them throughout life, generating problems thereby if the premises are incorrect. His therapeutic system was intended to get people to understand their historical processes and to be able to revise the history of their life. *A rift can develop between what is actually experienced and the concept of self.* The same theme is here elaborated. A person may deny reality to gain approval from others, and this bifurcation can generate a host of problems. *When the rift between experiencing and self is too great, anxiety or disorganized behavior can result.* Once again, the same theme is emphasized. We all want to be loved and accepted, but the continued pursuit of acceptance may separate us from reality. *Validating experiencing in terms of others can never be completed. All maladjustments come about through denial of experiences discrepant with the self-concept.* And so, one must depend on one's self for reality and not on others. Adler believed that maladjusted people lacked social interest, while Rogers stated that maladjustment essentially came from people listening to others rather than to their own bodily wisdom.

PERSONAL CONSTRUCTS THEORY (GEORGE A. KELLY, 1905–1967)

Kelly was a highly original thinker. He developed a unique cognitive system that called for the use of idiosyncratic language (see Kelly 1955). While his personal constructs theory covers all of psychology from the ideographic point of view, he bypassed usual terms and concepts such as *learning* and *emotions* and paid no attention to the environment or heredity.

All our interpretations of the universe are subject to revision. Kelly starts with a skepticism about beliefs and takes the position that there is no absolute reality. He took the position of constructive alternativism to indicate that people with differences of opinions could not necessarily be divided in terms of right and wrong. Two people can view the same situation in quite different ways and both can be right, both can be wrong, or one or the other may be right. *No person needs to be a victim of his own biography.* Here we have a statement of the free-will concept in a different form.

A person's processes are psychologically channelized by the ways in which he anticipates events. This is Kelly's fundamental postulate. Essentially, this viewpoint states that what is important is how events are interpreted rather than the events themselves. This assertion leads naturally to

Kelly's major contribution to personality theory, a series of other personal constructs, relative to how people view reality. We need not attempt to cover all of his constructs, but a few of them will give the reader a sense of Kelly's thinking: *A person anticipates events by construing their replication.* (The construction corollary.) *Persons differ from one another in their construction of events.* (The individuality corollary.) *A person may successively employ a variety of construction subsystems which are inferentially incompatible with each other.* (The fragmentation corollary.) This last corollary relates directly to Carl Rogers's theme that maladjustment comes from divergent forces: from within and from without.

Many of the important processes of personality and behavior arise as a person attempts to change or is threatened with forced change in his construct system. Kelly's point here is echoed by many other theorists, that one establishes some sort of life pattern or life-style, but changes in thinking about one's self and others will disrupt the individual.

Kelly's system is the purest cognitive system of any discussed here, solely dependent on perceptions and interpretations.

OPERANT REINFORCEMENT THEORY (B.F. SKINNER, 1904–1990)

Skinner has denied that his operant reinforcement is a personality theory, but rather that it covers all aspects of overt human behavior (Skinner 1938). In contrast to those theorists who view personality as essentially phenomenological, Skinner decries the term mind and concerns himself solely with overt behavior. As a radical behaviorist, Skinner does not deny internal processes but considers them not relevant to psychology as an objective science of behavior.

Personality is acquired and maintained through the use of positive and negative reinforcers. Skinner applies operant reinforcement to all aspects of human behavior. We tend to repeat what works and to give up what does not work, to continue behavior that leads to pleasant consequences and to discontinue behavior that leads to unpleasant consequences. *Behavior may be altered or weakened by the withholding of reinforcers.* If other people change their ways of operating towards an individual, this in turn will affect that person's behavior and consequently his personality.

Personality develops through a process of discrimination. In life, we experience all kinds of consequences, and we have to make decisions about our future behavior to these consequences. *Personality becomes shaped or differentiated.* Over time, our personalities are shaped by generalizations about ways that lead to the achievement of goals.

SOCIAL LEARNING THEORY (ALBERT BANDURA, 1925–)

Bandura, like Skinner, came to his opinions about personality mostly through research (Bandura and Walters 1963). His system is of the cognitive-learning type stressing the capacity of individuals to generalize in terms of symbols.

The causes of human behavior are the reciprocal interaction of behavioral, cognitive, and environmental influences. Bandura believes personality is a function of how we think and act and our responses of the environment's reactions to our behavior. In terms of the three elements of biology, society, and creativity, Bandura stresses the latter two. Heredity is discounted as a major determiner in personality development: How a person thinks and acts and how the environment responds to a person's behavior determines one's personality. *Behavior can be self-governed by means of self-produced consequences (self-reinforcement).* This assertion also emphasizes the importance of reciprocity: life is interaction: the individual versus the world, with the individual changing the world and the world changing the individual.

Individuals may be influenced by symbols which act as models. Reality to people need not only be direct stimuli, such as a smile or a slap, but reality can also be via symbols, such as pictures or words. Bandura's major research studies called for children to watch the behavior of others. He found that if a person considered to be a model acted in an aggressive manner and got what he wanted, that observers were likely to imitate the model. Consequently, not only direct stimuli and responses (as per Skinner) but symbolic experiences also determine personality. *Reinforcements (and punishment) can operate in a vicarious manner.* This is more of the above. Various kinds of behavior can be changed by seeing what happens to others. We learn not only by doing and getting responses but also by observing.

EXISTENTIAL PERSONALITY THEORY

Existential psychology is a loosely organized and ill-defined set of concepts mostly based on the work of philosophers and theologians (see Blackham 1959; Grimsley 1955). Essentially, existentialists see individuals as being in search of meaning. People are also seen as striving to achieve authenticity.

Personality is primarily constructed through attribution of meaning. Essentially, this point of view is similar to Kelly's concept of constructs. *Persons are characterized by symbolization, imagination, and judgment.* These are seen as attempts to find meaning. The human being is always trying to make sense out of existence, others, and self and uses mental processes in interaction with self and the world.

Life is best understood as a series of decisions. The human individual not only has to make evident decisions such as what to eat, but more subtle and important ones, such as who he or she really is. One has to decide what the world is like, what is real, what is important, and how to participate in the world. *Personality is a synthesis of facticity and possibility.* Facticity means the givens of heredity and environment and possibility becomes the creative aspect of personality. The facts of reality limit behavior variations.

A person is always faced with the choice of the future, which provokes anxiety, and the choice of the past, which provokes guilt. The human condition is such that people looking backwards in time can find reasons to be guilty and looking forward can find reasons to be afraid. Existentialists see anxiety and guilt as essential elements of the human being.

Ideal development is facilitated by encouraging individuality. Here we find traces of Carl Rogers's concept of the importance of listening to one's own body or Adler's and Kelly's requirement for personal courage. A human problem is to escape the effects of one's early environment, especially the effects of one's family.

CONSTITUTIONAL THEORIES

The oldest theories of personality formation are the constitutional that state that personality is a function of the nature of one's corporeal body. Aristotle (1910) in his *Physiognomica,* for example, stated that the "ancients" had a variety of theories to explain differences in human character. The Greek physician Galen took Hippocrates's physiological explanation of bodily health as a function of the balance between certain bodily fluids and stated that various personality types were a function of excesses of these fluids. Gall and Spurzheim (1809) extolled phrenology (the shape of the human head) in establishing personality. Kretschmer (1922) declared that people with certain kinds of body types tended to have particular types of mental conditions. Lombroso (1911) declared that criminal types were distinguished by a number of physiological anomalies. The list goes on and on. At present there are a variety of constitutional personality theories, some of which will be discussed below.

Structural Approach. William Sheldon (see Sheldon and Stevens 1942) classified individuals in terms of body shapes claiming that there was a positive correlation between various structural variations and personality types. He spent many years in doing basic research to find evidence for his theory. He found strong evidence to support the validity of his views. Other investigators also found supporting evidence but not to any useful degree.

The somatotype provides a universal frame of reference for growth and development that is independent of culture. This statement by implication discounts society and creativity. Born with a particular body type and you will have a specific personality type. *Three polar extremes called endomorphy, mesomorphy, and ectomorphy identify the essential components of the somatotype.* Sheldon had a somewhat complex classificatory system with three main body types: mesomorphs had an excess of muscle, endomorphs an excess of fat, and ectomorphs were relatively thin. For example, mesomorphs were considered to be bold, endomorphs to be extraverted and ectomorphs to be introverted.

Experiential Approach. This particular constitutional position is championed by Schilder (1950) and Fisher (1970) among others. It is a combined learning/physiological approach, referring to the nature of the experiences that a person has via contact during life, between the inner viscera, the skin, and the environment's effect on the body.

Body sensations provide the primary basis for initial differentiation of self from environment. The basic notion is that an unborn infant is only aware of internal sensations, but following birth, now becomes aware of stimuli from the outside world. Thus, the body surface becomes the locus of separation of self from the environment and the child now becomes able to identify the self and the outer world. *The development of the body image proceeds through stages, each of which has a lasting effect upon the body image as a whole.* This assertion has elements of the Freudian sexual stages and of Skinner's behaviorism in that contact with the outside world not only establishes the world but also the individual's personality.

Holistic Approach. Kurt Goldstein, who worked primarily with brain-injured patients, is primarily identified with this viewpoint (see Goldstein 1939). In working with various cases of physical pathology, such as stroke victims, he came to the realization of the importance of a human's attempt to maximize and organize potentials to survive and to enhance one's situation.

The normal human organism is equipped to maximize self-actualization, provided environmental forces do not interfere. This statement is accepted in a variety of ways by a number of other personality theorists, but Goldstein made this his central point. Of those theorists already discussed, Adler, Jung, and Rogers would have agreed completely. *Self-actualization is manifested by maximum differentiation and by the highest possible level of complexity of an integrated system.* This statement follows from the prior one and gives emphasis to the concept of the wisdom of the body. *The key to effective behavior is adequate functioning of part-whole relations.* Goldstein used Gestalt concepts of figure and ground to give evidence of the importance of understanding behavior as a totality, and consequently he can be considered an holistic theorist.

SUMMARY

At present there are a considerable number of personality theories, each working as it were completely independently of one another. There is lack of a common vocabulary that in turn leads to different people saying the same thing in different words. A complete eclectic theory would consider all elements mentioned, taking up the issue of personality in terms of the issues of heredity, environment and creativity, self and the environment.

(SEE ALSO: *Personality and Social Structure; Social Psychology*)

REFERENCES

Adler, A. 1956 *The Individual Psychology of Alfred Adler.* H. L. Ansbacher and R. Ansbacher, eds., New York: Basic Books.

Aristotle 1910 *Physiognomica.* Oxford: Oxford University Press.

Bandura, A., and R. Walters 1963 *Social Learning Theory and Personality Development.* Englewood Cliffs, N.J.: Prentice-Hall.

Blackham, G. W. 1959 *Six Existential Thinkers.* New York: Harper and Row.

Corsini, R. J., and A. J. Marsella 1983 *Personality Theories, Research, and Assessment.* Itasca, Ill.: Peacock.

Fisher, S. 1970 *Body Experience in Fantasy and Behavior.* New York: Appleton-Century-Crofts.

Freud, S. 1952–1974 *The Complete Psychological Works of Sigmund Freud.* London: Hogarth Press (24 volumes).

Gall, F. J., and J. C. Spurzheim 1809 *Recherches sur la système nerveux.* Paris: Schoell.

Goldstein, K. 1939 *The Organism.* New York: American Book Co.

Grimsley, R. 1955 *Existentialist Thought*. Cardiff: University of Wales Press.

Jung, C. G. 1953–1972 *The Collected Works of C. G. Jung*. Princeton, N.J.: Princeton University Press.

Kelly, G. A. 1955 *The Psychology of Personal Constructs*. New York: W. W. Norton.

Kretschmer, E. 1922 *Physique and Character*. London: Paul, Trench Trubner.

Lombroso, C. 1911 *The Criminal Man*. Boston: Little, Brown.

Rogers, C. R. 1951 *Client-Centered Therapy*. Boston: Houghton Mifflin.

Schilder, P. 1950 *The Image and Appearance of the Human Body*. New York: International Universities Press.

Sheldon, W. H., and S. S. Stevens 1942 *Varieties of Human Temperament*. New York: Harper and Row.

Skinner, B. F. 1938 *The Behavior of Organisms*. New York: Appleton-Century-Crofts.

RAYMOND J. CORSINI

PERSUASION From 1963 to 1976 the average number of hours the television set was on in American households increased from 5.6 to 6.8 hours a day. The trend since that time is less clear, but television viewing time continues to increase, if at a slower rate (Peterson 1981). When not watching their 6.8 hours of television, most people spend the bulk of their leisure time in talk with others. Much of this talk is geared, if only implicitly, not just to making oneself understood but to convincing someone else of the value and correctness of one's viewpoint. The average adult spends the majority of his or her waking hours at work, where, depending on the job, much activity involves efforts to get others to do one's bidding or being the object of such efforts. All this television watching, conversation, and work takes place in a social and political climate that, in theory if not in practice, encourages the exchange and dissemination of ideas among large numbers of people.

These facts have led some to conclude that this is an era of persuasion in which understanding who says what to whom in what way and with what effect is of critical importance (Lasswell 1948). In fact, some argue that the current era of persuasion is one of the few periods in the four millennia of Western history characterized by such a degree of openness to argument (McGuire 1985).

Whether the present era is unique in this manner, more and more people are becoming conscious of the persuasive contexts in which they spend most of their time. Indeed, if the increasingly ingenious efforts of advertisers to pique and retain interest are any indication, people are becoming increasingly savvy about others' efforts to persuade them in one way or another. This means that people facing attempts to persuade them have a very practical interest in understanding just how persuasion works. It also means that those sinking millions of dollars into the business of persuasion have at least a financial interest in whether they succeed. Finally, it means that social scientists, and social psychologists in particular, have an interest in understanding and explaining a pervasive social phenomenon.

In fact, social psychologists' preoccupation with attitudes and attitude change led some to argue that social psychology is the study of attitudes (Thomas and Zaniecki 1918). However, research on attitudes has waxed and waned since its beginnings in the early 1900s. During the 1920s and 1930s psychologists focused on describing the attitudes people hold. This led to the development of techniques for measuring attitudes, primarily scales such as the Likert scale, which continue to be used today by persuasion researchers. The second period of interest in research occurred during the 1950s and 1960s, with the main focus moving from description to the study of attitude change and the effects of attitudes on behavior. (For a review of the research on attitude-behavior consistency, see Ajzen and Fishbein 1977.) This interest waned considerably during the next two decades as social psychologists became increasingly interested in social perception, or how people selectively perceive, interpret, and respond to their social environment. The resurgence of interest in attitudes, and particularly in persuasion, that followed, and that continues today, is thus largely informed by social psychology's more general emphasis on how people process the information they take in from their environment.

One might speculate that the greater interest in persuasion or attitude change, rather than the simple description of attitudes, reflects the increasing influence of mass media. However, this coincidence of research interest and social change is belied by the lack of communication between those studying the effects of mass media on attitudes and those studying persuasion in more immediately interpersonal contexts (Roberts and Maccoby 1985). This essay reflects the split in research foci, concentrating solely on persuasion research in face-to-face, interpersonal contexts and dealing only peripherally with research on the effects of mass media on attitudes. (See Roberts and Maccoby 1985 for a review of this literature.) The issue of brainwashing, an extreme form and method of persuasion, is considered only when it has direct relevance to less extreme persuasion contexts.

Of relevance to research on persuasion is the study of normative compliance occurring in settings where no active attempt is made to influence, but people change their opinions or judgments nonetheless. Asch's (1951) research on conformity demonstrated that subjects involved in a simple task of judging the length of a line were highly influenced by the judgments of others present, even when no overt influence attempts were made. In these studies some people working with the experimenter gave incorrect assessments of the relative lengths of lines viewed. Even in cases of obviously incorrect judgments, most subjects conformed to the majority's assessment. Normative compliance is found to be greater the closer to unanimity the majority view, the larger the number holding it, and the more the conforming subject is attracted to and invested in group membership.

The persistence of findings of normative compliance, even in the absence of overt attempts at influence, raises an obvious question: What happens when such overt attempts are made? This and related questions are the focus of persuasion research. The focus in persuasion research is on attitude change "occurring in people exposed to relatively complex messages consisting of a position advocated by a communicator and usually one or more arguments designed to support that position" (Eagly and Chaiken 1984, p. 256). More simply defined, persuasion is an effort to change people's attitudes, these being the emotional and cognitive responses they have to objects, people, experiences, and so on.

FACTORS AFFECTING THE LIKELIHOOD OF PERSUASION

The guiding question of who says what to whom in what way with what effect has largely determined what factors researchers look to in explaining and predicting persuasion. These factors fall into four general classes: source or communicator variables, message variables, channel variables, and receiver variables. Reflecting two decades of research on social cognition, studies of the effects of these variables on persuasion investigate how these factors affect persuasion by shaping the way in which people process information in the persuasion context. Indeed, the term *process* reflects the computer analogy often used to capture the manner in which people perceive, interpret, and respond to their environment.

For example, in studying the effects of source characteristics (the characteristics of the person communicating the persuasive message) researchers might examine how the likability of the source leads the receiver (the object of persuasion) either to attend to or to ignore the quality of the arguments accompanying the message. Similarly, researchers examine other aspects of cognition (e.g., attention, comprehension, receptivity, retention) for the manner in which they mediate the effects of source, message, channel, and receiver variables on persuasion. However, since research has focused primarily on argument scrutiny, this discussion will do so as well.

Source Variables. The source variable of greatest interest is the credibility of the person communicating the persuasive message, including the communicator's apparent knowledge, social class, attractiveness, and likability. Consistent with common sense, the more credible the source, the more persuasive the source and the more likely that the receiver will change his or her attitude in the direction of the persuasive message. More interesting, however, is the combination of source credibility with other factors, and their combined effect on persuasion. For example, if the target person is not personally involved with the issue at hand, source credibility is more likely to enhance persuasion than if the person is highly involved in the issue. This is because personal involvement is likely to be associated with greater argument scrutiny, leading the target person to be less immediately accepting of a credible source's position (Chaiken 1980).

The effects of source credibility on persuasion are thus mediated by the extent to which the target is motivated to thoughtfully scrutinize the supporting arguments presented by the source. Personal involvement in the issue is one such motivation, but specific knowledge of the topic (without any particularly emotionally charged investment in it) and being educated in general are also factors that mediate the effect of source credibility because of their impact on the manner in which the target processes information at his or her disposal. Level of involvement, knowledge, and education are all characteristics of the receiver. The above example thus reveals the complex relationships between the factors that affect persuasion and their joint effects on information processing.

Message Variables. Many aspects of the persuasive message itself have been examined by research on persuasion. These include message style, ordering of arguments presented, speed of delivery, and message repetition. The effects of message repetition on persuasion are particularly interesting because they reveal the often unexpected combined effects of variables. For example, a study by Cacioppo and Petty (1979) revealed that only if supporting arguments are strong does repetition enhance persuasion, since repetition leads to greater argument scrutiny by the receiver, which enhances persuasion only to the extent that arguments are convincing.

Common sense might tell us that the use of humor in a message will enhance its persuasiveness by increasing the attractiveness of the source or, in the case of weak supporting arguments, distracting target's attention from the content. Researchers have hypothesized that humor should enhance persuasion with a highly credible source, but not with a less credible source, since humor is likely to further reduce credibility in the latter case. However, there is little evidence to support the expected effects of humor on persuasion. The observed effects are rarely significant, and are as often negative as positive. Furthermore, the combined effects of humor with source credibility, or its impact on interest, retention, or source evaluation are not found (McGuire 1985).

Channel Variables. Channel variables refer to the medium in which the message is communicated. For example, message persuasiveness varies depending on whether the message is given in person or in verbal, written, audio, or video form. In addition, channel variables include factors such as distraction, either created by the behavior of the source or indirect distraction such as repeated external noise during message communication.

Petty and Cacioppo (1981) studied the effects of distraction on persuasion, and found that its effects are mediated by cognitive factors such as the target's ability or motivation to scrutinize the arguments. If the message is accompanied by a distracting noise, for example, this will enhance persuasion if accompanying arguments are weak, since it decreases receiver's ability or motivation to pay close attention to the supporting arguments. Conversely, if the supporting arguments are strong, distraction decreases the likelihood of persuasion, especially with knowledgeable targets, since it makes it unlikely they will pay attention to the strong arguments designed to persuade them.

Similarly, other channel variables, such as the use of catchy music in television ads, affect persuasion to the extent that they motivate the receiver to generate positive rather than negative thoughts in response to the message. Generating thoughts is distinguished from argument scrutiny because it refers to the additional arguments or ideas the receiver brings to bear in evaluating the message, not to the supporting arguments provided by the communicator. Channel or other variables enhance persuasion to the extent that they generate positive thoughts or supporting arguments in the target (Greenwald 1968). Like the other factors affecting persuasion, then, the impact of channel variables on persuasion is mediated by the resulting cognitive processes engaged in by the target of the persuasive message.

Receiver Variables. Since persuasion is oriented toward convincing some person to adopt a particular viewpoint or endorse an opinion, it makes sense that the person himself or herself has some impact on the persuasion process. Interest in the personality correlates of persuasion was high during the 1950s, but waned in the following decades as individual-level explanations of social phenomena became less popular among social psychologists. However, more recent work has revived interest in the effect of receiver variables on persuasion.

One aspect of individual difference that has not lost popularity among social scientists is gender, and persuasion researchers have continued to examine the effects of gender on influenceability. A summary of 148 such studies (Eagly and Carli 1981) confirms earlier findings that women are more easily influenced than men. However, as consistent as these findings are, the magnitude of gender differences in influenceability is small enough to raise doubts about its practical significance for people's everyday lives (McGuire 1985).

However trivial these differences may be, they have inspired persuasion researchers to search for an explanation. One plausible account provided by Eagly and Carli (1981) is that "greater female susceptibility and greater male predictability might derive from socialization differences such that conforming pressures are exerted more strongly and uniformly on women, compressing them into a narrow band of high influenceability . . ." (McGuire 1985, p. 288). Thus, the receiver variable *gender* does not affect influenceability because of some biologically determined difference, but is the result of the different social experiences of men and women (for example, the greater likelihood that women will hold jobs in which they will receive more persuasion attempts than they themselves perform).

An additional receiver variable, self-esteem, has generated less uniform results. Researchers predict that greater self-esteem will decrease the likelihood of persuasion to the extent that it increases the likelihood that the receiver will carefully scrutinize arguments, and decreases the likelihood of the receiver's being swayed by a credible source in the absence of strong supporting arguments. Therefore, like the other factors affecting persuasion, self-esteem exerts its effects on persuasion through the variables related to the manner in which the receiver processes the information available in the persuasion context.

Results of studies of self-esteem and persuasion offer mixed results. For example, the effects of self-esteem on suggestibility are negligible (Barber 1964). However, a study of conformity among children (Endler et al. 1972) found self-esteem to be negatively related to conformity. That is, the lower the self-esteem, the greater the tendency to conform, especially when the aspect of self-esteem involved is closely related to the issue at hand.

In some cases the effects of self-esteem are far more complicated than they are hypothesized to be, especially when combined with other variables. For example, greater influenceability is associated with higher, not lower, self-esteem as the complexity of the persuasive message increases. Clearly, as with all the other variables considered, the receiver variable *self-esteem* requires further research before its relationships to other factors affecting persuasion can be fully understood.

APPROACHES TO THE STUDY OF PERSUASION

While all studies of persuasion tend to focus on some combination of the variables discussed above, more general research orientations are not uniform. One way of dividing research approaches to persuasion is to distinguish between the descriptive and the mathematical models. The former may focus on any combination of variables affecting persuasion, but their predictions tend to be stated in the form of a verbal argument or a set of hypotheses. Mathematical or probabilistic models, on the other hand, cast their predictions about persuasion in the form of equations, with variables and their relationships represented in algebraic terms. While the choice of research approach does not dictate which variables the researcher focuses on, some argue that the greater precision of probabilistic models makes for a more exact understanding of the conditions likely to produce persuasion (McGuire 1985). On the other hand, others (e.g., Eagly and Chaiken 1984) refer to these models as "normative," meaning that they describe how persuasion ought to work, not necessarily how it works in reality.

CONCLUSIONS

Whatever the relative merits of descriptive and probabilistic approaches, there is some consensus among persuasion researchers that a more general theory of persuasion is necessary if the vast research findings in the area are to be integrated in a meaningful manner (Eagly and Chaiken 1984). As this discussion shows, the research on persuasion is blessed with a large number of well-conceptualized variables, most of which are easy to operationalize, that is, to create in a laboratory setting. This discussion also shows, however, that even when a small portion of all the possible combinations of these variables are matched with one or two of the potential mediating cognitive processes, the resulting insights into persuasion are far from some of the commonsense notions alluded to throughout this discussion. This fact lends support to the call for a more unifying theory of persuasion to integrate the somewhat fragmented picture that emerges from a combining-of-variables approach.

A final word concerning the ethical issues relating to persuasion is warranted. Two questions may be raised to address this: When is being easily persuaded good? When is resistance good, and how can it be taught? If Americans are spending 6.8 hours a day in front of their television sets, and the rest of their waking hours in persuasive communications with others on the job or at leisure, teaching resistance to all this persuasion might become a top priority. For example, when research reveals that motivating people to generate reasons for their attitudes toward a product ultimately causes them to change their initial attitude, and even to purchase a product on the basis of their changed attitude (only to regret it later), attention is called to the conditions under which enhancing persuasion might be better avoided (Wilson et al. 1989). On the other hand, when research shows that two years of viewing "Sesame Street" caused both black and white children to manifest more positive attitudes toward blacks and Hispanics, something is learned about the conditions under which enhancing attitude change and persuasion is desirable (Bogatz and Ball 1971).

Strong resistance to the potential losses of autonomy involved in persuasion is probably not surprising in a culture that places a premium on individuality and freedom. Indeed, resistance or reactance to persuasion is common enough to have become an object of study in its own right. This research shows that when people perceive persuasive messages as threats to their freedom, they resist persuasion and maintain their original views or, in some cases, adopt a position opposite to the one advocated in the message (Brehm 1966).

However, many of the attempts at persuasion that people face in natural settings are specifically designed to minimize the threatening aspect of such attempts and thus to reduce resistance (hence the use of the word *seductive* to refer to arguments, advertisements, etc.). Are people continually at risk, then, of potentially harmful persuasion?

One could argue that in people's ability to be persuaded lies the possibility of autonomy. If people are easily persuaded, then they are in similar measure unlikely to be overwhelmingly persuaded by a particular viewpoint over all others. They may be likely to resist total indoctrination, if only because they are susceptible to some other credible source sending a convincing message in a captivating medium.

(SEE ALSO: *Coercive Persuasion and Attitude Change; Compliance and Conformity; Social Psychology*)

REFERENCES

Ajzen, I., and M. Fishbein 1977 "Attitude-Behavior Relations: A Theoretical Analysis and Review of Empirical Research." *Psychological Bulletin* 84: 888–918.

Asch, S. E. 1951 "The Effects of Group Pressure upon the Modification and Distortion of Judgments." In H. Guetzkow, ed., *Groups, Leadership, and Men.* Pittsburgh, Pa.: Carnegie Press.

Barber, T. X. 1964 "Hypnotizability, Suggestibility and Personality: V. A Critical Review of Research Findings." *Psychological Reports* 14:299–320.

Bogatz, G. A., and S. J. Ball 1971 *The Second Year of Sesame Street: A Continuing Evaluation.* 2 vols. Princeton, N.J.: Educational Testing Service.

Brehm, J. W. 1966 *A Theory of Psychological Reactance.* New York: Academic Press.

Cacioppo, J., and R. Petty 1979 "Effects of Message Repetition and Position on Cognitive Response, Recall, and Persuasion." *Journal of Personality and Social Psychology* 37:97–109.

Chaiken, S. 1980 "Heuristic Versus Systematic Information Processing and the Use of Source Versus Message Cues in Persuasion." *Journal of Personality and Social Psychology* 39:752–766.

Eagly, A. H., and L. Carli 1981 "Sex of Researchers and Sex-typed Communication as Determinants of Sex Differences in Influenceability: A Meta-analysis of Social Influence Studies." *Psychological Bulletin.* 90:1–20.

Eagly, A. H., and S. Chaiken 1984 "Cognitive Theories of Persuasion." In L. Berkowitz, ed., *Advances in Experimental Social Psychology,* Vol. 17. New York: Academic Press.

Endler, N. S., D. L. Wiesenthal, and S. H. Geller 1972 "The Generalization Effects of Agreement and Correctness on Relative Competence Mediating Conformity." *Canadian Journal of the Behavioral Sciences* 4:322–329.

Greenwald, A. G. 1968 "Cognitive Learning, Cognitive Response to Persuasion, and Attitude Change." In A. G. Greenwald, T. S. Brock, and T. M. Ostrom, eds., *Psychological Foundations of Attitudes.* New York: Academic Press.

Lasswell, H. D. 1948 "The Structure and Function of Communication in Society." In L. Bryson, ed., *Communication of Ideas.* New York: Harper.

McGuire, W. J. 1985 "Attitudes and Attitude Change." In G. Lindzey and E. Aronson, eds., *The Handbook of Social Psychology,* Vol. 2. New York: Random House.

Peterson, R. A. 1981 "Measuring Culture, Leisure, and Time Use." *Annals of the American Academy of Political and Social Science* 453:1969–1979.

Petty, R. E., and J. T. Cacioppo 1981 *Attitudes and Persuasion: Classic and Contemporary Approaches.* Dubuque, Iowa: W. C. Brown.

Roberts, D. F., and N. Maccoby 1985 "Effects of Mass Communication." In G. Lindzey and E. Aronson, eds., *The Handbook of Social Psychology,* Vol. 2. New York: Random House.

Thomas, W. I., and F. Znaniecki 1918 *The Polish Peasant in Europe and America.* Chicago: University of Chicago Press.

Wilson, T. D., D. S. Dunn, D. Kraft, and D. J. Lisle 1989 "Introspection, Attitude Change, and Attitude-Behavior Consistency: The Disruptive Effects of Explaining Why We Feel the Way We Do." In L. Berkowitz, ed., *Advances in Experimental Social Psychology,* Vol. 22. New York: Academic Press.

SUSAN MCWILLIAMS

PHENOMENOLOGY Phenomenology is a movement in philosophy that has been adapted by certain sociologists to promote an understanding of the relationship between states of individual consciousness and social life. As an approach within sociology, phenomenology seeks to reveal how social action, social situations, and society are products of human awareness (Natanson 1970).

Phenomenology was initially developed by Edmund Husserl (1859–1938), a German mathematician who felt that the objectivism of science precluded an adequate apprehension of the world (Husserl 1931, 1970). He presented various philosophical conceptualizations and techniques designed to locate the sources or essences of reality in the human mind. It was not until Alfred Schutz (1899–1959) came upon some problems in Max Weber's theory of action that phenomenology entered the domain of sociology (Schutz 1967). Schutz distilled from Husserl's rather dense writings a sociologically relevant approach. Schutz set about describing how subjective meanings produce an apparently objective social world (Schutz

1962, 1964, 1966, 1970; Schutz and Luckmann 1973; Wagner 1983).

Schutz's migration to the United States prior to World War II, along with that of other phenomenologically inclined scholars, resulted in the transmission of this approach to American academic circles and to its ultimate transformation into interpretive sociology. Two expressions of this approach have been called *reality constructionism* and *ethnomethodology.* Reality constructionism synthesizes Schutz's distillation of phenomenology and the corpus of classical sociological thought to account for the possibility of social reality (Berger 1963, 1967; Berger and Berger 1972; Berger and Kellner 1981; Berger and Luckmann 1966). Ethnomethodology integrates Parsonian concerns into phenomenology and examines the means people use to make ordinary life possible (Garfinkel 1967; Garfinkel and Sacks 1970). Reality constructionism and ethnomethodology are recognized to be among the most fertile orientations in the field of sociology (Ritzer 1988).

Phenomenology is used in two basic ways in sociology: (1) to theorize about substantive sociological problems and (2) to enhance the adequacy of sociological research methods. Since phenomenology insists that society is a human construction, sociology itself and its theories and methods are also constructions (Cicourel 1964; 1973). Thus, phenomenology seeks to offer a corrective to the field's emphasis on positivist conceptualizations and research methods that may take for granted the very issues that phenomenologists find of interest. Phenomenology presents theoretical techniques and qualitative methods that illuminate the human meanings of social life.

Phenomenology has until recently been viewed as at most a challenger of the more conventional styles of sociological work and at the least an irritant. Increasingly, phenomenology is coming to be viewed as an adjunctive or even integral part of the discipline, contributing useful analytic tools to balance objectivist approaches (Levesque-Lopman 1988; Luckmann 1978; Psathas 1973; Rogers 1983).

TECHNIQUES

Phenomenology operates rather differently from conventional social science (Darroch and Silvers 1982). Phenomenology is a theoretical orientation, but it does not generate deductions from propositions that can be empirically tested. It operates more on a metasociological level, demonstrating its premises through descriptive analyses of the procedures of self-, situational, and social construction. Through its demonstrations, audiences apprehend the means by which phenomena, originating in human consciousness, come to be experienced as facts of the world.

Current phenomenological techniques in sociology include the method of "bracketing" (Ihde 1977). This approach lifts an item under investigation from its meaning context in the commonsense world, with all judgments suspended. For example, the item "alcoholism as a disease" (Peele 1985) is not evaluated within phenomenological brackets as being either true or false. Rather, a "reduction" is performed in which the item is assessed in terms of how it operates in consciousness: What does the disease concept do for those within its domain? A phenomenological reduction both plummets to the essentials of the notion and ascertains its meanings independent of all particular occasions of its use. The reduction of a bracketed phenomenon is thus a technique to gain theoretical insight into the meaning of elements of consciousness.

Phenomenological tools include the use of introspective and *Verstehen* methods to offer a detailed description of how consciousness itself operates (Hitzler and Keller 1989). Introspection requires the phenomenologist to use his or her own subjective process as a resource for study, while *Verstehen* requires an empathic effort to move into the mind of the other (Truzzi 1974). Not only are introspection and *Verstehen* tools of phenomenological analysis, but they are procedures used by ordinary individuals to carry out their projects. Thus, the phenomenologist as analyst might study himself or herself as an ordinary subject dissecting his or her own self-consciousness and action schemes (Bleicher 1982). In this technique, an analytic attitude toward the role of consciousness in designing everyday life is developed.

Since cognition is a crucial element of phenomenology, some theorists focus on social knowledge as the cornerstone of their technique (Berger and Luckmann 1966). They are concerned with how common-sense knowledge is produced, disseminated, and internalized. The technique relies on theoretical discourse and historical excavation to the foundations of knowledge that is taken for granted. Frequently, religious thought is given primacy in the study of the sources and legitimations of mundane knowledge (Berger 1967).

Phenomenological concerns are frequently researched using qualitative methods (Bogdan and Taylor 1975). Analyses of small groups, social situations, and organizations using face-to-face techniques of participant observation are frequently undertaken by phenomenological researchers (Bruyn 1966; Turner 1974). Ethnographic research frequently utilizes phenomenological tools (Fielding 1988). Intensive interviewing to uncover the subject's orientations or his or her "life world" is also widely practiced. Qualitative tools are used in phenomenological research either to yield insight into the microdynamics of particular spheres of human life for its own sake or to exhibit the constitutive activity of human consciousness.

Techniques particular to the ethnomethodological branch of phenomenology have been developed to unveil the practices used by people to accomplish everyday life (Leiter 1980; Mehan and Wood 1975). At one time, "breaching demonstrations" were conducted to reveal the essentiality of taken-for-granted routines and the means by which threats to these routines were handled. Since breaching these routines sometimes resulted in serious disruptions of relationships, this technique has been virtually abandoned. Social situations are video- and audiotaped to permit the painstaking demonstration of the means by which participants produce themselves, their interpretations of the meanings of acts, and their sense of the structure of the situation. Conversational analysis is a technique that is frequently used to describe how people make sense of each other through talk and how they make sense of their talk through their common background knowledge (Schegloff and Sacks 1974). The interrelations between mundane reasoning and abstract reasoning are also examined in great depth as researchers expose, for example, the bases of scientific and mathematical practice in common-sense thinking (Knorr-Cetina and Mulkay 1983).

THEORY

The central task in social phenomenology is to demonstrate the circularity of interrelations among the processes of human action, situational structuring, and reality construction. Rather than contending that any aspect is a causal factor, phenomenology views all dimensions as constitutive of all others. Phenomenologists use the term *reflexivity* to characterize the way in which all dimensions serve as both foundation and consequence of all human projects. The task of phenomenology, then, is to make manifest the incessant tangle or reflexivity of action, situation, and reality in the various contexts of being in the world.

Phenomenology commences with an analysis of the "natural attitude." This is understood as the way ordinary individuals are in the world, taking its existence for granted, assuming its objectivity, and undertaking action projects as if these fit in with given patterns. Language, culture, and common sense are experienced as features of an external world that are internalized by actors in the course of their lives.

The openness of humans to patterned social experience, their striving toward meaningful involvement in a knowable world, and their tendency to classify sense data characterize a typifying mode of consciousness. Humans experience the world in terms of *typifications;* that is, humans categorize what is presented to them: Children are exposed to the common sounds and sights of particular animals, people, vehicles, and so on and come to apprehend the categorical identity and typified meanings of each in terms of conventional linguistic forms. In a similar manner, individuals learn the formulas for doing common activities. These practical means of doing are called *recipes for action.* Typifications and recipes, once internalized, tend to settle beneath the level of full awareness, that is, become sedimented as do layers of rock. Thus, in the natural attitude, the foundations of actors' knowledge of meaning and action are obscured to the actors themselves.

Actors assume that knowledge is objective and all people reason in a like manner. Each assumes that every other knows what he or she knows of this world: They believe they share common sense. However, each person's biography is unique, and each develops a relatively distinct stock of typifications and recipes. Therefore, interpretations may diverge. Everyday social interaction is replete with ways in which actors create feelings that common sense is shared, that mutual understanding is occuring, and that everything is all right. Phenomenology emphasizes that humans live within an intersubjective world, yet they at best approximate shared realities. While a "paramount reality" is commonly experienced in this manner, particular realities or "finite provinces of meaning" are also constructed and experienced by diverse cultural, social, or occupational groupings.

For phenomenology, all human consciousness is practical—it is always of something. Actors intend projects into the world; they act in order to implement goals based on their typifications and recipes, their stock of knowledge at hand. Consciousness as an "intentional process" is composed of thinking, perceiving, feeling, remembering, imagining, and anticipating directed toward the world. The objects of consciousness, these intentional acts, are the sources of all social realities.

Thus, typifications derived from common sense are internalized, becoming the tools that individual consciousness uses to constitute a social world that is experienced as factual. Common sense serves as an ever-present resource to assure actors that the reality that is projected from human subjectivity is an objective reality. Since all actors are implicated in this intentional work, they sustain the collaborative effort to reify their projections and thereby reinforce the very frameworks that provide the construction tools.

Social interaction is viewed phenomenologically as a process of reciprocal interpretive constructions of actors applying their stock of knowledge at hand to the occasion. Interactors orient themselves to others by taking into account typified meanings of actors in typified situations known to them through common sense. Action schemes are geared by each to the presumed projects of others. The conduct resulting from the intersection of intentional acts indicates to members of the collectivity that communication or coordination or something of the like is occurring among them. For these members, conduct and utterances serve as "indexical" expressions of the properties of the situation enabling each to proceed with the interaction while interpreting others, context, and self. Through the use of certain interpretive practices, members order the situation for themselves in sensical and coherent terms: In their talk they gloss over apparent irrelevancies, fill in innumerable gaps, ignore inconsistencies, and assume a continuity of meaning, thereby formulating the occasion itself.

Ongoing social situations manifest patterned, routine conduct that appears to positivist investigators to be normative or rule-guided. Phenomenologically, rules are "indexical expressions" of the interpretive processes applied by members in the course of their interactions. Rules are enacted in and through their applications. In order to play by the book, the interpreter endeavors to use the rule as an apparent guide. However, he or she must use all sorts of background expectancies to manage the fit somehow between the particular and the general under the contexted conditions of the interaction, and in so doing is acting creatively. Rules, policies, hierarchy, and organization are accomplished through the interpretive acts or negotiations of members in their concerted efforts to formulate a sense of operating in accord with a rational, accountable system. This work of doing structure to the situation further sustains its common-sensical foundations as well as its facticity.

Phenomenologists analyze the ordering of social reality and how the usage of certain forms of knowledge contributes to that ordering. It is posited that typified action and interaction become "habitualized." Through sedimentation in layered consciousness, human authorship of habitualized conduct is obscured and the product is externalized. As meaning-striving beings, humans create theoretical explanations and moral justifications in order to legitimate the habitualized conduct. Located in higher contexts of meaning, the conduct becomes objectivated. When internalized by succeeding generations, the conduct is fully institutionalized and exerts compelling constraints over individual volition. Periodically, the institutions might be repaired in response to threats, or individuals might be realigned if they cognitively or affectively migrate.

The reality that ordinary people inhabit is constituted by these legitimations of habitualized conduct. Ranging from common sense typifications of ordinary language to theological constructions to sophisticated philosophical, cosmological, and scientific conceptualizations, these legitimations compose the paramount reality of everyday life. Moreover, segmented modern life, with its proliferation of meaning-generating sectors, produces multiple realities, some in competition with each other for adherents. In the current marketplace of realities, consumers, to varying degrees, may select their legitimations, as they select their occupation and, increasingly, their religion.

IMPLICATIONS

For phenomenology, society, social reality, social order, institutions, organizations, situations, interactions, and individual actions are constructions that appear as suprahuman entities. What does this suggest regarding humanity and sociology? Phenomenology advances the notion that humans are creative agents in the construction of social worlds (Ainlay 1986). It is from their consciousness that all being emerges. The alternative to their creative work is meaninglessness, solipsism, and chaos: a world of dumb puppets, in which each is disconnected from the other, and where life is formless (Abercrombie 1980). This is the nightmare of phenomenology. Its practitioners fear that positivist sociologists actually theorize about such a world (Phillipson 1972).

Phenomenologists ask sociologists to note the misleading substantiality of social products and to avoid the pitfalls of reification. For the sociologist to view social phenomena within the natural attitude as objects is to participate in legitimation rather than to offer analysis. A phenomenological sociology would investigate social products as humanly meaningful acts, whether these products are termed attitudes, behaviors, families, aging, ethnic groups, classes, societies, or otherwise (Armstrong 1979; Gubrium and Holstein 1987; Herek 1986; Petersen 1987; Starr 1982). The sociological production of these fictive entities would be understood within the context of their accomplishment, that is, the interview setting, the observational location, the data collection situation, the field, the research instrument, and so forth (Schwartz and Jacobs 1979). The meaning contexts applied by the analyst would correlate with those of the subjects under investigation and would explicate the points of view of the actors as well as do justice to the expression of their life world. A phenomenological sociology would strive to reveal how actors construe themselves, all the while recognizing that they themselves are actors construing their subjects and themselves.

Phenomenologically understood, society is a fragile human construction, thinly veneered by abstract ideas. Phenomenology itself is evaluatively and politically neutral. Inherently, it promotes neither transformative projects nor stabilization. In the work of a conservatively inclined practitioner, the legitimation process might be supported, while the liberative practitioner might seek to puncture or debunk the legitimations (Morris 1975). Phenomenology can be used to reveal and endorse the great constructions of humankind or to uncover the theoretical grounds of oppression and repression (Smart 1976). Phenomenologists insist upon the human requirements for meaning, subjective connectedess, and a sense of order. These requirements may be fulfilled within existent or emancipative realities (Murphy 1986).

The phenomenological influence upon contemporary sociology can be seen in the increased humanization of theoretical works, research methods, testing procedures, and instructional modes (Darroch and Silvers 1982; O'Neill 1985). The future impact of phenomenology will depend on its resonance with the needs and aspirations of the rising generations of sociologists.

(SEE ALSO: *Ethnomethodology; Qualitative Methods*)

REFERENCES

Abercrombie, Nicholas 1980 *Class, Structure and Knowledge.* New York: New York University Press.

Ainlay, Stephen C. 1986 "The Encounter with Phenomenology." In James Davison Hunter and Stephen C. Ainlay, eds., *Making Sense of Modern Times: Peter L. Berger and the Vision of Interpretive Sociology.* London: Routledge and Kegan Paul.

Armstrong, Edward G. 1979 "Black Sociology and Phenomenological Sociology." *Sociological Quarterly* 20:387–397.

Berger, Peter L. 1963 *Invitation to Sociology: A Humanistic Perspective.* New York: Anchor.

——— 1967 *The Sacred Canopy: Elements of a Sociological Theory of Religion.* New York: Doubleday.

———, and Brigitte Berger 1972 *Sociology: A Biographical Approach.* New York: Basic Books.

———, and Hansfred Kellner 1981 *Sociology Reinterpreted.* New York: Doubleday.

———, and Thomas Luckmann 1966 *The Social Construction of Reality: A Treatise in the Sociology of Knowledge.* New York: Doubleday.

Bleicher, Josef 1982 *The Hermeneutic Imagination: Outline of a Positive Critique of Scientism and Sociology.* London: Routledge and Kegan Paul.

Bogdan, Robert, and Steven J. Taylor 1975 *Introduction to Qualitative Research Methods: A Phenomenological Approach to the Social Sciences.* New York: Wiley.

Bruyn, Severn T. 1966 *The Human Perspective in Sociology: The Methodology of Participant Observation.* Englewood Cliffs, N.J.: Prentice-Hall.

Cicourel, Aaron V. 1964 *Method and Measurement in Sociology.* New York: Free Press.

——— 1973 *Theory and Method in a Study of Argentine Fertility.* New York: Wiley.

Darroch, Vivian, and Ronald J. Silvers (eds.) 1982 *Interpretive Human Studies: An Introduction to Phenomenological Research.* Washington, D.C.: University Press.

Fielding, Nigel G. (ed.) 1988 *Actions and Structure: Research Methods and Social Theory.* London: Sage Publications.

Garfinkel, Harold 1967 *Studies in Ethnomethodology.* Englewood Cliffs, N.J.: Prentice-Hall.

———, and Harvey Sacks 1970 "The Formal Properties of Practical Actions." In John C. McKinney and Edward A. Tiryakian, eds., *Theoretical Sociology.* New York: Appleton-Century-Crofts.

Gubrium, Jaber F., and James A. Holstein 1987 "The Private Image: Experiential Location and Method in Family Studies." *Journal of Marriage and the Family* 49:773–786.

Herek, Gregory M. 1986 "The Instrumentality of Attitudes: Toward a Neofunctional Theory." *Journal of Social Issues* 42:99–114.

Hitzler, Ronald, and Reiner Keller 1989 "On Sociological and Common-Sense *Verstehen.*" *Current Sociology* 37:91–101.

Husserl, Edmund 1931 *Ideas: General Introduction to Pure Phenomenology.* W. R. Boyce Gibson, trans. New York: Humanities Press.

——— 1970 *The Crisis of European Sciences and Transcendental Phenomenology.* David Carr, trans. Evanston, Ill.: Northwestern University Press.

Ihde, Don 1977 *Experimental Phenomenology: An Introduction.* New York: Putnam.

Knorr-Cetina, Karin, and Michael J. Mulkay (eds.) 1983 *Science Observed.* London: Sage Publications.

Leiter, Kenneth 1980 *A Primer on Ethnomethodology.* New York: Oxford University Press.

Levesque-Lopman, Louise 1988 *Claiming Reality: Phenomenology and Women's Experience.* Totowa, N.J.: Rowman and Littlefield.

Luckmann, Thomas (ed.) 1978 *Phenomenology and Sociology: Selected Readings.* New York: Penguin.

Mehan, Hugh, and Houston Wood 1975 *The Reality of Ethnomethodology.* New York: Wiley.

Morris, Monica B. 1975 "Creative Sociology: Conservative or Revolutionary?" *American Sociologist* 10: 168–178.

Murphy, John W. 1986 "Phenomenological Social Science: Research in the Public Interest." *Social Science Journal* 23:327–343.

Natanson, Maurice 1970 "Alfred Schutz on Social

Reality and Social Science." In Maurice Natanson, ed., *Phenomenology and Social Reality*. The Hague: Nijhoff.

O'Neill, John 1985 "Phenomenological Sociology." *Canadian Review of Sociology and Anthropology* 22:748–770.

Peele, Stanton 1985 *The Meaning of Addiction: Compulsive Experience and Its Interpretation*. Lexington, Mass.: Lexington Books.

Petersen, Eric E. 1987 "The Stories of Pregnancy: On Interpretation of Small-Group Cultures." *Communication Quarterly* 35:39–47.

Phillipson, Michael 1972 "Phenomenological Philosophy and Sociology." In Paul Filmer, Michael Phillipson, David Silverman, and David Walsh, eds., *New Directions in Sociological Theory*. Cambridge, Mass.: MIT Press.

Psathas, George (ed.) 1973 *Phenomenological Sociology: Issues and Applications*. New York: Wiley.

Ritzer, George 1988 *Contemporary Sociological Theory*. New York: Knopf.

Rogers, Mary F. 1983 *Sociology, Ethnomethodology, and Experience: A Phenomenological Critique*. New York: Cambridge University Press.

Schegloff, Emmanuel, and Harvey Sacks 1974 "Opening Up Closings." In Roy Turner, ed., *Ethnomethodology*. Baltimore: Penguin.

Schutz, Alfred 1962 *Collected Papers I: The Problem of Social Reality*. Maurice Natanson, ed. The Hague: Nijhoff.

——— 1964 *Collected Papers II: Studies in Social Theory*. Arvid Brodersen, ed. The Hague: Nijhoff.

——— 1966 *Collected Papers III: Studies in Phenomenological Philosophy*. The Hague: Nijhoff.

——— 1967 *The Phenomenology of the Social World*. George Walsh and Frederick Lehnert, trans. Evanston, Ill.: Northwestern University Press.

——— 1970 *Reflections on the Problem of Relevance*. Richard Zaner, ed. New Haven: Yale University Press.

———, and Thomas Luckmann 1973 *The Structure of the Life World*. Evanston, Ill.: Northwestern University Press.

Schwartz, Howard, and Jerry Jacobs 1979 *Qualitative Sociology: A Method to the Madness*. New York: Free Press.

Smart, Barry 1976 *Sociology, Phenomenology, and Marxian Analysis: A Critical Discussion of the Theory and Practice of a Science of Society*. London: Routledge and Kegan Paul.

Starr, Jerold M. 1982 "Toward a Social Phenomenology of Aging: Studying the Self Process in Biographical Work." *International Journal of Aging and Human Development* 16:255–270.

Truzzi, Marcello 1974 *Verstehen: Subjective Understanding in the Social Sciences*. Reading, Mass.: Addison-Wesley.

Turner, Roy (ed.) 1974 *Ethnomethodology: Selected Readings*. Baltimore: Penguin.

Wagner, Helmut R. 1983 *Alfred Schutz: An Intellectual Biography*. Chicago: University of Chicago Press.

MYRON ORLEANS

POLICE For modern sociology the core problem of police has been, and continues to be, the extrication of the concept *police* from the forms and institutions in which it has been realized and the symbols and concealments in which it has been wrapped. Doing so is essential to the interpretive understanding of the idea of police and is prerequisite to mature answers to the question of what policing means, has meant, and can mean. In one form or another it is the project that has occupied sociologists of police since the early 1960s, and although there is occasional overlap and interchange, attention to it is primarily what distinguishes contributions to the sociology of police from scholarly efforts in the study of police administration, jurisprudence, criminalistics, and police science.

THE POLICE: A SOCIOLOGICAL DEFINITION

By the end of the 1960s a small number of now-classic empirical studies of police had made it apparent that conventional understandings of the idea of police were fundamentally and irreparably flawed. In the face of large-scale studies by Reiss (1971) and Black (1971) which showed that the model tour of duty of a patrol officer in the high-crime areas of the nation's largest cities did not involve the arrest of a single person, it became impossible for sociologists to continue to speak of police as "law enforcers" or of their work as "law enforcement." Likewise, both Skolnick's *Justice Without Trial* (1966) and Wilson's *Varieties of Police Behavior* (1968) illustrated dramatic differences in the way police were organized and the relationships they elected to enjoy with courts and law. Similarly, early studies of both the exercise of patrol officer discretion (Bittner 1967a, 1967b) and requests for police service (Cumming et al. 1965; Bercal 1970) cast substantial doubt on the notion that a substantial, much less a defining, activity of police was "fighting crime."

Police Role and Functions. The task of extricating the concept of police from these common misconceptions was assumed by Egon Bittner in his *The Functions of Police in Modern Society* (1970). A fundamental theme of Bittner's work was that to define police as "law enforcers," "peacekeepers," "agents of social control," "officers of the court," or, indeed, in any terms that suppose what police should do, confuses police role and function. Throughout history, in this country and in others, police have performed all sorts of functions. In fact, the functions, both manifest and latent, which police have performed are so numerous and so contradictory that any attempt to define police in terms of the functions they are supposed to perform or the ends they are supposed to achieve is doomed to failure.

Force as the Core of the Police Role. Sociologically, policing cannot be defined in terms of its ends; it must be defined in terms of its means. In *Functions* Bittner advanced an approach to understanding the role of the police that was based on the single means which was common to all police, irrespective of the ends to which they aspired or were employed. The means Bittner found to define police was a right to use coercive force. Police, said Bittner, are "a mechanism for the distribution of non-negotiably coercive force" (1971). No police had ever existed, nor is it possible to conceive of an entity that could be called police ever existing, that did not claim the right to use coercive force.

Sociologically, Bittner's formulation had three major virtues. First, it was universal. It was applicable to police everywhere and at all times, police as diverse as the sheriff's posse of the old West, the London bobby, the FBI, or the police of Hitler's Third Reich or Castro's Cuba. Second, it was politically and morally neutral. It could be used to refer to police whose behavior was exemplary as readily as it could be applied to police whose behavior was appalling. And, third, it made it possible to make explicit and to probe in systematic ways a host of questions about the role of police that could not previously be explored because they had been concealed in the confusion between role and function: Why do all modern societies, from the most totalitarian and most tyrannical to the most open and democratic, have police? What does having police make available to society that no other institution can supply? What functions are appropriate to assign to police and what are best left to other institutions?

These questions are of such enormous consequence and so fundamental to an understanding of the role of the police that it is difficult to conceive of a sociology of police existing prior to their recognition.

Why Police? If police are a "mechanism for the distribution of non-negotiably coercive force," why should all modern societies find it necessary to create and sustain such a mechanism? What does having such a mechanism make available to modern societies that no other institution can provide?

Bittner's answer is that no other institution has the special competence required to attend to "situations which ought not to be happening and about which something ought to be done NOW!" (1974; p. 30). The critical word in Bittner's careful formulation of the role of the police is "now." What the right to distribute coercive force gives to police is the ability to resolve situations that cannot await a later resolution. The crucial element is time. Turning off a fire hydrant against the wishes of inner-city street bathers, preventing the escape of a serial murderer, halting the escalation of a domestic dispute, or moving back the curious at the scene of a fire so that emergency equipment can pass—these and hundreds of other tasks fall to police because their capacity to use force may be required to achieve them "now."

This view of police radically inverts some conventional conceptions. While popular opinion holds that police acquire their right to use coercive force from their duty to enforce the law, the sociology of police holds that police acquire the duty to enforce the law because doing so may require them to invoke their right to use coercive force. Similarly, focus by police on the crimes and misdemeanors of the poor and humble, and their relative lack of attention to white-collar and corporate offenders, is often promoted as reflecting a class or race bias in institutions of social control. While not denying that such biases can exist and do sometimes influence the direction of police attention, if such biases were eliminated entirely, the distribution of police effort and attention would undoubtedly remain unchanged. It would remain unchanged because the special competence of police, their right to use coercive force, is essential in enforcement efforts in which offenders are likely to physically resist or to flee. In white-collar and corporate crime investigations, the special competence of lawyers and accountants is essential, while the special competence of police is largely unnecessary.

INSTITUTIONAL FORMS

Although all modern societies have found it necessary to create and maintain some form of police, it is obvious that any institution which bears the right to use coercive force is extraordinarily dangerous and highly subject to abuse and corruption. The danger of the institution of police would appear to be magnified when it gains a monopoly or a near monopoly on the right to use coercive force and those who exercise that monopoly are almost exclusively direct and full-time employees of the state. Appearances and dangers notwithstanding, these are nevertheless the major terms of the institutional arrangement of police in every modern democracy. Some comment on the sociology of this institutional uniformity may be helpful.

Avocational Policing. For most of human history most policing has been done by individuals, groups, associations, and organizations in the private sector. This type of private-sector policing, done by citizens not as a job but as an avocation, may be classified into at least three types, each of which offered a somewhat different kind of motivation to private citizens for doing it (Klockars 1985). Historically, the most common type is *obligatory avocational policing.* Under its terms private citizens are compelled to police by the threat of some kind of punishment if they fail to do so. In American police history the sheriff's posse is perhaps the most familiar variety of this type of policing. The English systems of frankpledge (Morris 1910) and parish constable (Webb and Webb 1906) were also of this type.

A second type of private-sector policing, *voluntary avocational policing,* is done by private citizens not because they are obliged by a threat of punishment but because they, for their own reasons, want to do it. The most familiar American example of this type of policing is vigilante groups, over three hundred of which are known to have operated throughout the United States up to the end of the nineteenth century (Brown 1975).

A third type, *entrepreneurial avocational policing,* includes private citizens who as English thief takers, American bounty hunters, French agents provocateurs, and miscellaneous paid informants police on a per-head, per-crime basis for money.

The institutional history of these avocational forms of policing is thoroughly disappointing, and modern societies have largely abandoned these ways of getting police work done. The central flaw in all systems of obligatory avocational policing is that as the work of policing becomes more difficult or demanding, obligatory avocational policing takes on the character of forced labor. Motivated only by the threat of punishment, those who do it become unwilling and resistant, a situation offering no one any reason to learn or cultivate the skill to do it well. All forms of voluntary avocational policing suffer from the exact opposite problem. Voluntary avocational police, vigilantes and the like, typically approach their work with passion. The problem is that because the passionate motives of voluntary avocational police are their own, it is almost impossible to control who and where and what form of police work they do and on whom they do it. Finally, the experience with entrepreneurial forms of avocational policing—thief takers, bounty hunters, and paid informants—has been the most disappointing of all. The abuse and corruption of entrepreneurial avocational police has demonstrated unequivocally that greed is too narrow a basis on which to build a police system.

Sociologically, the shortcoming of all forms of avocational policing is that none of them offers adequate means of controlling the police. This observation leads directly to the question of why one might have reason to suspect that a full-time, paid police should be easier to control than its avocational precedents. What new means of control is created by establishing a full-time, paid, police vocation?

The answer to this problem is that only when policing becomes a full-time, paid occupation is it possible to dismiss, to *fire,* any particular person who makes his or her living doing it. The state can only hire entrepreneurial avocational police, bounty hunters, paid informants, and thief takers; it cannot fire them. Vigilantes are driven by their own motives and cannot be discharged from them. Obligatory avocational police are threatened with punishment if they don't work; most would love to be sacked. Because the option to fire, to take police officers' jobs away from them, is the only essential means of controlling police work that separates the police vocation from all avocational arrangements for policing, how that option is used will, more than anything else, determine the shape and substance of the police vocation.

The Police Vocation. The English, who in 1829 created the first modern police, were intimately familiar with the shortcomings of all forms of avocational policing. They had, in fact, resisted the creation of a paid, full-time police for more than a century, out of fear that such an institution would be used as a weapon of political oppression by the administrative branch of government. To allay the fears that the "New Police" would become such a weapon, the architects of the first modern police, Home Secretary Robert Peel and the first commissioners of the New Police, Richard Mayne and Charles Rowan, imposed three major political controls on them. Peel, Mayne, and Rowan insisted that the New Police of London would be unarmed, uniformed, and confined to preventive patrol. Each of these features shaped in profound ways the institution of the New Police and, in turn, the police of the United States and other Western democracies that explicitly copied the English model.

Unarmed. Politically, the virtue of an unarmed police is that its strength can be gauged as a rough equivalent of its numbers. Weapons serve as multipliers of the strength of individuals and can increase the coercive capacity of individuals to levels that are incalculable. One person with a rifle can dominate a dozen citizens; with a machine gun, hundreds; with a nuclear missile, thousands. One person with a police truncheon is only slightly stronger than another, and that advantage can be quickly eliminated by the other's picking up a stick or a stone. In 1829 the individual strength of the three thousand-constable, unarmed New Police offered little to fear to London's 1.3 million citizens.

While this political virtue of an unarmed police helped overcome resistance to the establishment of the institution, the long-run sociological virtue of an unarmed police proved far more important. Policing is, by definition, a coercive enterprise. Police must, on occasion, compel compliance from persons who would do otherwise. Force is, however, not the only means to compel compliance. Sociologically, at least three other bases for control are possible: authority, power, and persuasion.

Unarmed and outnumbered, the New Police "bobby" could not hope to police effectively on the basis of force. Peel, Mayne, and Rowan knew that if the New Police were to coerce successfully, they would have to do so on the basis of popular respect for the authority and power of the institution of which they were a part. The respect owed each constable was not owed to an individual but to a single, uniform temperament, code of conduct, style of work, and standard of behavior that every constable was expected to embody.

In order to achieve this uniformity of temperament, style, conduct, and behavior, the architects of the New Police employed the option to dismiss with a passion. "Between 1830 and 1838, to hold the ranks of the New Police of London at a level of 3300 men required nearly 5000 dismissals and

6000 resignations, most of the latter not being altogether voluntary" (Lee 1971; p. 240). During the first eight years of its organization, every position on the entire force was fired or forced to resign more than three times over!

Unlike their earlier London counterparts, the new American police were undisciplined by the firing option. What prevented the effective use of the firing option by early American police administrators was that police positions were, by and large, patronage appointments of municipal politicians. In New York, for example, the first chief of police did not have the right to fire any officer under his command. So while London bobbies were being dismissed for showing up late to work or behaving discourteously toward citizens, American police were assaulting superior officers, taking bribes, refusing to go on patrol, extorting money from prisoners, and releasing prisoners from the custody of other officers.

In New York, Boston, Chicago, and other American cities the modern police began, in imitation of London's bobbies, as unarmed forces; but, being corrupt, undisciplined, and disobedient, they could not inspire respect for either their power or their authority. In controlling citizens they had no option but to rely on their capacity to use force. The difficulty with doing so unarmed is that someone armed with a multiplier of strength can always prove to be stronger. Gradually, against orders, American police armed themselves, at first with the quiet complicity of superior officers and later, as the practice became widespread, in open defiance of departmental regulations. Eventually, in an effort to control the types of weapons their officers carried, the first municipal police agencies began issuing standard service revolvers.

The long-run sociological consequence of arming the American police can be understood only by appreciating how it shaped American police officers' sense of the source of their capacity to control the citizens with whom they dealt. While the London bobbies drew their capacity for control from the profoundly social power and authority of the institution of which they were a part, American police officers understood their capacities for control to spring largely from their own personal, individual strength, multiplied if necessary by the weapon they carried on their hips. This understanding of the source of their capacity for control led American police officers to see the work they did and the choices they made in everyday policing to be largely matters of their individual discretion. Thus, the truly long-run sociological effect of the arming of the American police has been to drive discretionary decision making to the lowest and least public levels of American police agencies. Today how an American police officer handles a drunk, a domestic disturbance, an unruly juvenile, a marijuana smoker, or a belligerent motorist is largely a reflection not of law or agency policy but of that particular officer's personal style. This is not to say that law or agency policy cannot have influence over how officers handle these types of incidents. However, one of the major lessons of recent attempts by sociologists to measure the impact of changes in law or police policy in both domestic violence and drunken driving enforcement is that officers can resist those changes vigorously when the new law or policy goes against their views of proper police response (see Dunford et al. 1990; Mastrofski et al. 1988).

Uniformed. Politically, the requirement that police be uniformed is a guarantee that they will not be used as spies; that they will be given information only when their identity as police is known; that those who give them information, at least when they do so in public, are likely to be noticed doing so; and that they can be held accountable, as agents of the state, for their behavior. The English, who had long experience with uniformed employees of many types, understood these political virtues of the uniform completely. In fact, an incident in 1833 in which a police sergeant assumed an ununiformed undercover role resulted in such a scandal that it nearly forced the abolition of the New Police.

By contrast, the early American understanding of the uniform was totally different. Initially it was seen to be a sign of undemocratic superiority. Later it was criticized by officers themselves as a demeaning costume and resisted on those grounds. For twelve years, despite regulations that required them to do so, early New York policemen successfully refused to wear uniforms. In 1856 a compromise was reached by allowing officers in each political ward to decide on the color and style they liked best.

Despite the early resistance to the uniform and the lack of appreciation for its political virtues, American police eventually became a uniformed force. But while the London bobby's uniform was explicitly designed to have a certain "homey" quality and reflect restraint, the modern American police officer's uniform is festooned with the forceful tools of the police trade. The gun, ammunition, nightstick, blackjack, handcuffs, and Mace, all tightly holstered in shiny black leather and set off with chromium buckles, snaps, badges, stars, flags, ribbons, patches, and insignia, suggest a decidely military bearing. The impression intended is clearly one not of restraint but of the capacity to overcome the most fearsome of enemies by force.

The Military Analogy and the War on Crime. To understand the sociology of the American police uniform, it is necessary to see in it a reflection of a major reform movement in the history of the American police. Around 1890 American police administrators began to speak about the agencies they administered as if they were domestic armies engaged in a war on crime (Fogelson 1977).

The analogy was powerful and simple. It drew upon three compelling sources. First, it sought to connect police with the victories and heroes of the military and to dissociate them from the corruption and incompetence of municipal politics. Second, it evoked a sense of urgency and emergency in calls for additional resources. From the turn of the century to the present day, the war on crime has proved a useful device for getting municipal governments and taxpayers to part with money for police salaries and equipment. And, third and most important, the war on crime and the military analogy sought to create a relationship between police administrators and politicians at the municipal level that was similar to the relationship enjoyed by military generals and politicians at the national level. At the national level Americans have always conceded that the decision on whether to fight a war was a politicians' decision, but how that war was to be fought and the day-to-day discipline of the troops was best left to the generals. By getting the public and the politicians to accept these terms of the police-politics relationship, the early police administrators found a way to wrest from the hands of politicians the tool they needed to discipline their troops: the option to fire disobedient officers.

The uniform of the war-ready American police officer is testimony to the fact that since the 1940s, American police administrators have won the battle to conceive of police as engaged in a war on crime. And in doing so they have gained control of the option to fire for administrative purposes. However, the cost of that victory has been enormous.

A major problem is the idea of a war on crime and the expectation police have promoted that they can, in some sense, fight or win it. In point of fact, a war on crime is something police can neither fight nor win for some fundamental sociological reasons. It is simply not within the capacity of police to change those things—unemployment, the age distribution of the population, moral education, civil liberties, ambition and the social and economic opportunities to realize it—that influence the amount and type of crime in any society. These are the major social correlates of crime, and despite presentments to the contrary, police are but a small tail on a gigantic social kite. Moreover, any kind of real "war on crime" is something that no democratic society would be prepared to let its police fight. No democratic society would be able to tolerate the kinds of abuses to the civil liberties of innocent citizens that fighting any real "war" on crime would necessarily involve. It is a major contribution of the sociology of police since the 1960s to demonstrate that almost nothing police do can be shown to have any substantial effect on reducing crime.

The problems of policing in the name of crime when one cannot do much of anything about it are enormous. It is not uncommon for patrol officers to see their employers as hypocritical promoters of a crime-fighting image that is far removed from what they know to be the reality of everyday police work. They may seek to explain what they know to be their failure to do much about crime in terms of the lack of courage of their chief, the incompetence of police administration, or sinister political forces seeking to "handcuff" the police. They often close off what they regard as the disappointing reality of what they do in cynicism, secrecy, and silence—the "blue curtain," the occupational culture of policing.

Equally problematic as a spoil of the early chiefs' victory in their war on crime is the quasi-military police administrative structure. Although once heralded as a model of efficiency, it is now regarded as an organizationally primitive mode of management. It works, to the extent that it works, by creating hundreds and sometimes even thousands of rules and by punishing departures from those rules severely. The central failing of such an administrative model is that it rests on the unwarranted assumption that employees will not discover that the best way to avoid punishment for doing something wrong is to do as little as possible. The administration can, in turn, respond by setting quotas for the minimum amount of work it will tolerate from employees before it moves to punish them, but if it does so, that minimal amount of work is, by and large, all it will get.

Preventive Patrol. The third major mechanism with which architects of the New Police sought to neutralize their political uses was to confine police to preventive patrol. This restriction was understood to have the effect of limiting the uniformed, patrolling constable to two relatively apolitical types of interventions: situations in which constables would be called upon for help by persons who approached them on the street and situations that, from the street, constables could see required their attention. These political virtues of patrol impressed the architects of the New Police, particularly Sir Richard Mayne. Mayne postponed the formation of any detective unit in the New Police until 1842, and for his 40 years as commissioner held its ranks to fewer than 15 detectives in a force of more than 3,500.

In the early American experience uniformed patrol served the principal purpose of imposing some semblance of order on unruly officers. Patrol offered some semblance of assurance that officers could be found at least somewhere near the area to which they were assigned. And while American police created detective forces almost immediately after they were organized, patrol has become in the United States, as in Britain and other modern democracies, the major means of getting police work done.

Sociologically, patrol has had tremendous consequences for the form and substance of policing. It has, for example, been extraordinarily amenable to the three most profound technological developments of the past century: the automobile, the telephone, and the wireless radio. And while there is no evidence that increasing or decreasing the amount of patrol has any influence whatsoever on the crime rate, each of these technological developments has made police patrol more convenient and attractive to citizens who wish to call for police service. It is not an exaggeration to say that the vast majority of the activity of most modern police agencies is driven by a need to manage citizen demand for patrol service.

In recent years, attempts to manage this demand have taken many forms. Among the most common are the creation of computer-aided dispatch systems that prioritize the order in which patrol officers are assigned to complaints and increasingly stringent policies governing the types of problems for which police will provide assistance. Also increasingly common are attempts to handle complaints that merely require a written report, by taking that report over the telephone or having the complainant complete a mail-in form. In no small part, such efforts at eliminating unnecessary police response and making necessary police response efficient have produced some of the increasing cost for police labor.

REORIENTING POLICING

Despite efforts at prioritization, limitation of direct police response, and development of alternative ways of registering citizen complaints, demand for police service continues to grow. And despite the fact that individual citizens appear to want this form of police service more than any other, some contemporary approaches suggest that the entire idea of "dial-a-cop," "incident-driven" policing requires reconsideration. Two such approaches, "community-oriented policing" (Skolnick and Bayley 1986) and "problem-oriented policing" (Goldstein 1979, 1990), have been advanced as the next generation of "reform" movements in American policing (Greene and Mastrofski 1988).

As theories of police reform, both "problem-oriented" and "community-oriented" policing are grounded in the suspicion that the traditional police response of dispatching patrol officers in quick response to citizen complaints does little to correct the underlying problem that produced the complaint. To some degree at least, this suspicion is confirmed by studies which tend to show that a fairly small number of addresses tend to generate disproportionate numbers of calls for police service, and that patrol officers commonly return to such "hot spots" again and again to attend to similar problems (Sherman et al. 1989).

Both problem-oriented and community-oriented policing offer strategies to deal with such problems that go beyond merely dispatching an officer to the scene. Problem-oriented policing offers a generic, four-step, problem-solving strategy—scanning, analysis, response, and assessment—that police can use to identify problems and experiment with solutions. Community-oriented policing, by contrast, does not offer a mechanism for problem analysis and solution. It is, however, committed to a general strategy that calls for cooperative, police-community efforts in problem solving. In such efforts it encourages the employment of a variety of police tactics—foot patrol, storefront police stations, neighborhood watch programs—that tend to involve citizens directly in the police mission.

While both approaches to reorienting policing have been heralded as revolutionary in their implications for the future of policing, both confront some major obstacles to their realization. The first is that neither problem-oriented nor community-oriented police efforts have been able to reduce the demand for traditional patrol response. Unless that demand is reduced or police resources are increased to allow it to be satisfied along with nontraditional approaches, the community- and problem-oriented policing approaches will most likely be relegated, at best, to a secondary, peripheral role.

The second problem confronting both community- and problem-oriented policing stems from the definition of police and the role appropriate to it in a modern democratic society. The special competence of police is their capacity to use force, and for that reason all modern societies find it necessary and appropriate to have them attend to situations that cannot await a later resolution. Reactive, incident-driven, dial-a-cop patrol is a highly popular, extremely efficient, and, as near as possible, politically neutral means of delivering that special competence. To expand the police role to include responsibility for solving the root problems of neighborhoods and communities is an admirable aspiration. But it is a responsibility that seems to go beyond the special competence of police and to require, more appropriately, the special competence of other institutions.

(SEE ALSO: *Criminal Sanctions; Criminology; Social Control*)

REFERENCES

Bercal, T. E. 1970 "Calls for Police Assistance: Consumer Demand for Governmental Service." *American Behavioral Scientist* 13, no. 2 (May–August):221–238.

Bittner, E. 1967a "Police Discretion in Apprehension of Mentally Ill Persons." *Social Problems* 14 (Winter):278–292.

——— 1967b "The Police on Skid Row: A Study of Peace Keeping." *American Sociological Review* 32 (October):699–715.

——— 1970 *The Functions of Police in Modern Society.* Washington, D.C.: U.S. Government Printing Office.

——— 1974 "Florence Nightingale in Pursuit of Willie Sutton: A Theory of Police." In H. Jacob, ed., *The Potential for Reform of Criminal Justice.* Beverly Hills, Calif.: Sage.

Black, D. 1971 "The Social Organization of Arrest." *Stanford Law Review* 23 (June): 1087–1111.

Brown, R. M. 1975 *Strain of Violence: Historical Studies of American Violence and Vigilantism.* Oxford: Oxford University Press.

Cumming, E., I. Cumming, and L. Edell 1965 "Policeman as Philosopher, Guide, and Friend." *Social Forces* 12, no. 3:276–286.

Dunford, F. W., D. Huizinga, and D. S. Elliott 1990 "The Role of Arrest in Domestic Assault: The Omaha Police Experiment." *Criminology* 28, no. 2:183–206.

Fogelson, R. 1977 *Big City Police.* Cambridge, Mass.: Harvard University Press.

Goldstein, H. 1979 "Improving Policing: A Problem-Oriented Approach." *Crime and Delinquency* 25 (April): 236–258.

——— 1990 *Problem-Oriented Policing.* New York: McGraw-Hill.

Greene, J., and S. Mastrofski 1988 *Community Policing: Rhetoric or Reality.* New York: Praeger.

Klockars, C. B. 1985 *The Idea of Police.* Beverly Hills, Calif.: Sage.

Lee, M. 1971 *A History of Police in England.* Montclair, N.J.: Patterson Smith.

Mastrofski, S., R. R. Ritti, and D. Hoffmaster 1988 "Organizational Determinants of Police Discretion: The Case of Drunk Driving." *Journal of Criminal Justice* 15:387–402.

Morris, W. A. 1910 *The Frankpledge System.* New York: Longmans, Green and Co.

Reiss, A. J., Jr. 1971 *Police and the Public.* New Haven, Conn.: Yale University Press.

Sherman, L. W., P. Gartin, and M. E. Buerger 1989 "Hot Spots of Predatory Crime: Routine Activities and the Criminology of Place." *Criminology* 27:27–55.

Skolnick, J. K. 1966 *Justice Without Trial.* New York: John Wiley.

———, and D. Bayley 1986 *The New Blue Line.* New York: Free Press.

Webb, S., and B. Webb 1906 *English Local Government from the Revolution to the Municipal Corporations Act: The Parish and the County.* New York: Longmans, Green and Co.

Wilson, J. Q. 1968 *Varieties of Police Behavior: The Management of Law and Order in Eight Communities.* Cambridge, Mass.: Harvard University Press.

CARL B. KLOCKARS

POLISH SOCIOLOGY To understand the past and present status of Polish sociology, one should take into account its peculiarity, namely, its particularly tight, intrinsic link with the course of Polish national history, overabundant with uprisings, wars, revivals, and transformations. The nineteenth century and the period up to World War II were characterized by the reception of the dominant European trends of social thought. The organicism of Herbert Spencer is reflected in the works of Jozef Supinski (1804–1893), called the founder of Polish sociology. He formulated, for the first time, the problem of the interplay between the nation and the state, which became persistent later in Polish sociology. Ludwik Gumplowicz (1838–1909) was one of the classic exponents of the conflict tradition and probably the only Polish sociologist of that period who entered the standard textbooks of the history of sociology. He published several works, mainly in German: *Der Rassenkampf* (1883), *Grundriss der Soziologie* (1885), *Die soziologische Staatsidee* (1892), and *Soziologie und Politik* (1892). Gumplowicz's peculiarity consisted in being an advocate of sociologism before Durkheim. The psychologism of Gabriel Tarde and Gustave Le Bon influenced the ideas of Leon Petrazycki (1867–1931), whose three fundamental works were originally published in Russian: *The Introduction to the Study of Politics and Law* (1892), *An Introduction to the Study of Law and Morality* (1905), and *The Theory of Law and State* (1907). Also his *Die Lehre vom Einkommen* (two volumes, 1893–1895) was published in Berlin. For Petrazycki observation is a basic method of investigating and studying objects and phenomena. As regards psychical phenomena, the observation consists in self-observation, or introspection. The task of sociology was to detect objective tendencies of social phenomena. Unconscious adaptation processes might be replaced by deliberate steering of man's destiny with the help of law. The ideal pursued by Petrazycki consisted in the human psyche being so fitted to the requirements of social life that law, state, and other normative systems (e.g., morality) would prove unnecessary. Another advocate of psychologism was Edward Abramowski (1868–1918). His main writings include *Individual Elements in Sociology* (1899) and *Theory of Psychical Units* (1899), where he sketched his theory of sociological phenomenalism. Its main thesis was that the development of societies is based on the constant interaction between objective phenomena and human consciousness, which are causes and effects alternately. In three works—*Problems of Socialism, Ethics and Revolution,* and *Socialism and the State,* written before 1899 and published in *Social Philosophy: Selected Writings* (1965)—he applied sociological phenomenalism to the analysis of the strategy of class struggle and to the realization of the socialist system. Social revolution should be preceded by "moral revolution"—a deep transformation of conscience. A cooperative is a germ of a socialist society, while the state is its enemy. Cooperatives can get transformed into a real republic—a cooperative *res publica.* Ludwik Krzywicki (1859–1941) was the foremost representative of the first Polish Marxists' generation. Among his works are *Modern Social Issue* (1888), *Political Economy* (1899), *Sociological Studies* (1923), and *Idea and Life* (1957). Krzywicki was under the substantial influences of Darwin and Comte, which led him to the idea of society as a section of natural phenomena and social evolution as a part of universal evolution. The merging of historical materialism with positivistic scientific criteria produced a natural-evolutionistic branch of Marxism comprising the canon of "iron historical laws," of which Krzywicki himself was the representative. His conception of "historical background" allowed him to invent the original typology of social systems. Also, he was the author of original conception of "industrial feudalism," being the precursor of the "welfare state" theory. Another follower of Marx's ideas, Kazimierz Kelles-Krauz (1872–1906), published among other works *The Law of Revolutionary Retrospection* (1895), *Sociological Law of Retrospection* (1898), *Economic Basis of Primitive Forms of the Family* (1900), *A Glimpse on XIX Century Sociology* (1901), and *Economic Materialism* (1908). He defined the sociological theory of Marxism as monoeconomism, according to which the whole of social life is determined by the mode of production. However, the central point of his sociological conception was the law of revolutionary retrospection. It referred exclusively to the sphere of social consciousness and was supposed to explain the origins of the revolutionary ideal in a way parallel to monoeconomics: The ideals by which the whole reformatory movement wishes to substitute the existing social norms are always similar to norms from the more or less distant past. Stefan Czarnowski (1879–1937), in his works *Leading Ideas of Humanity* (1928), *Culture* (1938), and *Works* (2 volumes, 1956), continued Durkheim's ideas. *Culture* is Czarnowski's top achievement, in which he claims the culture is the whole of objective elements of social heritage, common for several groups and because of its generality able to expand in space. Czarnowski overcame the dualism of Durkheim's conception granting both society and culture the character of reality *sui generis.* Characteristic of all these conceptions was the overt impact of the actual sociopolitical conditions on the content of social theory.

Florian Znaniecki's (1882–1958) sociology and Bronislaw Malinowski's (1884–1942) social (or cultural) anthropology were different from those mentioned above in at least two respects. First, both gained worldwide recognition; second, both produced general conceptions not restricted in scope by particular conditions of time, place, and culture. Znaniecki, a coauthor (with W. I. Thomas) of *The Polish Peasant in Europe and America* (1918–1920) and author of numerous books, such as *Cultural Reality* (1919), *Introduction to Sociology* (1922), *The Laws of Social Psychology* (1925), *Sociology of Education* (two volumes, 1928–1930), *The Method of Sociology* (1934), *Social Actions* (1936), *The Social Role of the Man of Knowledge* (1940), *Cultural Sciences* (1952), and the posthumous *Social Relations and Social Roles,* is well known as the author of the concept of "humanistic coefficient," and of a theoretical system unfolding the postulate of universal cultural order and axionormatively ordered social actions. Bronislaw Malinowski, the author of *Argonauts of Western Pacific* (1922), *The Sexual Life of Savages in North-Western Melanesia* (1929), *Coral Gardens and Their Magic* (1935), *A Scientific Theory of Culture and Other Essays* (1944), and *Freedom and Civilization* (1947), among other works, found world esteem as one of the most influential scholars in establishing the functional approach in cultural anthropology.

POSTWAR YEARS TO MARTIAL LAW, 1949–1981

The history of Polish sociology in this period remains to be written. It was a time that sociology underwent severe criticism (including the condemnation in the period 1949–1956), a time of the great shift toward Marxist orientation, but also a time of continuation of traditional lines of theorizing and of implementing in Polish sociology several novelties emerging in Western sociology (especially after 1956, when it was brought back to life). It was certainly the time of a strong group of Marxist sociologists, including, among others, Zygmunt Bauman, Julian Hochfeld, Wladyslaw Markiewicz, and Jerzy Wiatr. On the other hand, in this period the following were especially active: Jozef Chalasinski (1904–1979), who wrote *Young Generation of Peasants* (1938), *Society and Education* (1948), *Young Generation of the Villagers in People's Poland* (a series of volumes, 1964–1969), and *Culture and Nation* (1968); he was a prominent student of Polish intelligentsia, peasantry, and youth; Stanislaw Ossowski (1897–1963), who wrote *On the Peculiarities of Social Sciences* (1962) and *Class Structure in the Social Consciousness* (1963, English ed.), the latter containing fresh, stimulating, and critical overviews of theories of both class and social stratification; Andrzej Malewski (1929–1963); and Stefan Nowak (1925–1990), whose work will be mentioned in the next section. While Ossowski studied class structure and stratification theoretically, Jan Szczepanski initiated empirical research around the problems of the emergence of a socialist-grown working class and an intelligentsia. His book *Polish Society* (Szczepanski 1970) summarizes about thirty monographs that emerged from this research project between 1956 and 1965.

MAJOR CONTEMPORARY CONTRIBUTIONS

In the realm of theory, most characteristic of current Polish sociology is a rather large number of works that are in some sense secondary, however novel, interpretations of contemporary sociological theories. Functionalistic orientation was extensively studied by several sociologists, among others by Piotr Sztompka (*System and Function: Toward a Theory of Society,* 1974), or social anthropologists such as Andrzej Paluch (*Conflict, Modernization, and Social Change: An Analysis and Critique of the Functional Theory,* 1976). Another extensively studied orientation is interactionist theory by theoreticians such as Marek Czyzewski (*The Sociologist and Everyday Life: A Study in Ethnomethodology and Modern Sociology of Interaction,* 1984), Elzbieta Chalas (*The Social Context of Meanings in the Theory of Symbolic Interactionism,* 1987), Zdzislaw Krasnodebski (*Understanding Human Behavior: On Philosophical Foundations of Humanistic and Social Sciences,* 1986), Ireneusz Krzeminski (*Symbolic Interactionism and Sociology,* 1986), and Marek Ziolkowski (*Meaning, Interaction, Understanding: A Study of Symbolic Interactionism and Phenomenological Sociology as a Current of Humanistic Sociology,* 1981). There are also good examples of innovative works within the domain of conflict theory by Janusz Mucha (*Conflict and Society,* 1978), Marxist theory by Andrzej Flis (*The Great Vision Fractured: A Reassessment of Marxist Understanding of History,* 1990), social exchange theory by Marian Kempny (*Exchange and Society: An Image of Social Reality in Sociological and Anthropological Theories of Exchange,* 1988), and "sociological theory of an individual's identity" by Zbigniew Bokszanski (*Identity—Interaction— Group: Individual's Identity in Perspective of Sociological Theory,* 1989). Since social anthropology is used to be treated in Poland as closely related to sociology, I should mention Piotr Chmielewski's work *Culture and Evolution,* 1988, in which he gives penetrating theoretic insight of evolutionistic theory since Darwin till contemporaries, and Zdzislaw Mach's book *The Culture and Personality Approach in American Anthropology,* which presents critical evaluation of this influential theoretical paradigm.

Original, creative efforts at the level of history of social thought, metatheory, and sociological theory have been quite substantial in the postwar period. In the domain of history of sociology an important achievement is the monumental, two-volume *History of Sociological Thought* by Jerzy Szacki (Szacki 1979). The work is not just a simple presentation of theories of significant social thinkers from social philosophy of antiquity to contemporary sociological controversies of the 1970s. Critical analysis of each conception is accompanied by a penetrating account of its place in intellectual history, its relation to other orientations, and its role in the development of the social sciences. It can be said that this work presents "the true history of social thought." That work does not have its equivalent in world literature. One should also mention two another original, creative works in the history of sociology. The first, a book edited by Piotr Sztompka, *Masters of Polish Sociology* (Sztompka 1984), presents a comprehensive account of Polish sociology since its beginnings up to martial law in 1981 and after—the closing date is being called the period of the search for the new perspective for Polish sociology. The same kind of work is a book written by Andrzej Paluch, *The Masters of Social Anthropology* (Paluch 1990), in which the author evaluates ten theories of the most consequential figures in the history of social anthropology, from Edward Tylor to Claude Lévi-Strauss. Still another work by Piotr Sztompka should be included to substantial achievements in the field of history of sociology, namely the book *Robert K. Merton: An Intellectual Profile* (Sztompka 1986), the aim of which is to give the fullest possible description of its hero as a "classic" of modern sociology. The greatest achievements in the fields of metatheory and/or philosophy of social sciences include two books by Stefan Nowak and Edmund Mokrzycki. Nowak's book, *Understanding and Prediction: Essays in Methodology of Social and Behavioral Sciences* (Nowak 1976), can be treated as the vehicle by which Polish sociology entered metatheoretical debates of contemporary social sciences as a fully mature partner. Nowak discusses several issues crucial for sociological metatheory, such as usefulness of the "humanistic coefficient," laws of science vs. historical generalizations, inductionism vs. deductionism, the time dimension, causal explanations, reduction of one theory to another, and axiomatizized theories. Solutions he proposes are novel and enlightening. The same can be said about Edmund Mokrzycki's book, *Philosophy and Sociology: From the Methodological Doctrine to Research Practice* (Mokrzycki 1983). He argues that since early positivism started in the 1950s circulating as the methodological foundation of sociology, as a result empirical sociology lost the character of a humanistic discipline without acquiring the status of a true scientific discipline. As a way out, Mokrzycki proposes to put sociology within the framework of a broadly understood theory of culture. In the field of sociological theory the following achievements should be pointed out. First, one should mention the theoretical group dealing with class, social structure, and stratification headed by Wlodzimierz Wesolowski, whose work *Classes, Strata, and Power* (Wesolowski 1979) serves as their leading theoretical achievement. The crux of the argument is that while theoretically relationship to the means of production determines attributes of social position such as income, work, prestige, uniformity of that relationship created under socialism makes that the means of production lose their determining properties. In this circumstance status becomes disengaged from class and tends to "decompose" so that we encounter the phenomenon of "leapfrogging" by groups along certain dimensions. This statement was the point of departure for further studies on meritocratic justice, educational meritocracy, stratification, and structure in comparative perspective (Slomczynski, Miller, and Kohn 1981; Slomczynski 1989), social mobility (Wesolowski and Mach 1986), and other studies. A second group of works deals with problems in the field of sociology but bordering on microsociology and social philosophy. Pawel Rybicki's *The Structure of* the Social World (Rybicki 1979) introduces to sociological debates in Poland for the first time in a very comprehensive way problems of micro-macro link, the problematics of a small group, and ontological dilemmas especially related to the individualism vs. holism controversy. On the other hand, Andrzej Malewski's work (Malewski 1975), aimed primarily at modification and experimental testing of social-psychological theories of L. Festinger, M. Rokeach, and N. E. Miller, also undertakes fundamental methodological and theoretical problems of the integration of social sciences, which he tries to solve through theoretical reduction. Jacek Szmatka's work (Szmatka 1989) tries to reach virtually all the same goals that his predecessors mentioned above tried to reach. The final result of these endeavors is his structural microsociology, based on assumptions of emergent sociological structuralism, the structural conception of the small group, and specific conception of short- and long-range social structures. Still another type of theorizing is present in the next two important theoretical works, Piotr Sztompka's theory of social becoming (Sztompka 1991) and Jadwiga Staniszkis' ontology of socialism (Staniszkis 1989). Both works are very different in style of theorizing and the level of abstraction but have one goal in common: to produce theoretical conceptions that would account for tensions, problems, and processes in Polish society. Sztompka, who develops his conception around such categories as human agency and social movements, is highly abstract and stays within the Marxian tradition. Staniszkis engages in her analysis categories such as power, politics, legitimization, and ideology; is less abstract (she refers frequently to concrete societies); but she also stays within the Marxian tradition. *Sociology of Culture* by Antonina Kloskowska (Kloskowska 1983) is a work that continues vital traditions of this field in Polish sociology and that also provides several theoretical innovations. Sociology of culture is understood here as a branch of sociological theory, being culture-oriented, and operating with various types of cultural data. Basic subject matter for this theory is symbolic culture, while basic explananda are conditions and functions of symbolic culture in the domain of societal culture. Kloskowska develops, among other theories, communication theory of symbolic culture and theory of symbolic culture development; one of her statements is that symbolic culture can play its functions only when it preserves its original character, and its values remain intrinsic, autotelic, sought for their own sake.

The most vital and extensively cultivated, however, is empirical sociology of Polish society. Especially extensive are studies on several aspects of social consciousness of Polish society (continuing Ossowski's 1963 work); its changes in time perspective (Koralewicz 1987); value system, attitudes, and aspirations (Nowak 1980, 1982, 1989); class consciousness and political participation (Ziolkowski 1988); and collective subconsciousness and the concept of collective sense (Marody 1987, 1988). Other important and vital fields of research are studies on the political and legal system of Polish society (Staniszkis 1987), legitimation of the social order (Rychard 1987), repressive tolerance of the political system (Gorlach 1989), local power elite (Wasilewski 1989), and deviance and social control (Kwasniewski 1987). The third domain of research consists of different aspects of social and economic organization of Polish society, namely self-management and current economical crisis (Morawski 1987), determinants of economic interests (Kolarska-Bobinska 1988), and conditions of social dimorphism (Wnuk-Lipinski 1987). There are also interesting studies on life values of youth in Poland (Sulek 1985), the role of the army in the Polish political and social scene (Wiatr 1988), and appraisals of the birth and the role of the Solidarity movement (Staniszkis 1984).

HOW WILL SOCIOLOGY DEVELOP IN POLAND?

Studies mentioned above were characterized by an overt link between empirical investigation of "society in transition" and sociological theorizing. If it is true that sociological theory undergoes essential changes that lead it from overarching frameworks for all sociology, to theory-oriented to empirical knowledge of specific domains, to theory that is abstract and general but has empirical import, then the same will happen to Polish sociology in the near future. A particular focus of Polish sociology will be on more "middle range" theory, as a system of interrelated concepts and propositions that are abstract, general, and have empirical import. From this bulk of empirical studies should emerge a number of such theories of legitimation, inequality, power elite recruitment, functions of social mobility, etcetera.

REFERENCES

Gorlach, Krzysztof 1989 "On Repressive Tolerance: State and Peasant Farm in Poland." *Sociologia Ruralis* 28:23–33.

Kloskowska, Antonina 1983 *Sociology of Culture.* Warsaw: Polish Scientific Publishers.

Kolarska-Bobinska, Lena 1988 "Social Interests, Egalitarian Attitudes, and the Change of Economic Order." *Social Research* 55:111–138.

Koralewicz, Jadwiga 1987 "Changes in Polish Social Consciousness During the 1970s and 1980s: Opportunism and Identity." In J. Koralewicz, I. Bialecki, and M. Watson, eds., *Crisis and Transition: Polish Society in the 1980s.* Oxford: Berg.

Kwasniewski, Jerzy 1987 *Society and Deviance in Communist Poland: Attitudes to Social Control.* Oxford: Berg.

Malewski, Andrzej 1975 *For a New Shape of the Social Sciences—Collected Papers.* Warsaw: Polish Scientific Publishers.

Marody, Miroslawa 1987 "Social Stability and the Concept of Collective Sense." In J. Koralewicz, I. Bialecki, and M. Watson, eds., *Crisis and Tradition: Polish Society in the 1980s.* Oxford: Berg.

——— 1988 "Antinomies of Collective Subconsciousness." *Social Research* 55:97–110.

Mokrzycki, Edmund 1983 *Philosophy and Sociology: From the Methodological Doctrine to Research Practice.* London: Routledge and Kegan Paul.

Morawski, Witold 1987 "Self-Management and Economic Reform." In J. Koralewicz, I. Bialecki, and M. Watson, eds., *Crisis and Tradition: Polish Society in the 1980s.* Oxford: Berg.

Nowak, Stefan 1976 *Understanding and Prediction: Essays in Methodology of Social and Behavioral Sciences.* Dordrecht, Netherlands: Reidel.

——— 1980 "Value System of the Polish Society." *Polish Sociological Bulletin* 2:5–20.

——— 1982 "Value System and Social Change in Contemporary Poland." *Polish Sociological Bulletin* 1–4:119–132.

——— 1989 "The Attitudes, Values and Aspirations of Polish Society." *Sisyphus. Sociological Studies* 5:133–163.

Paluch, Andrzej K. 1990 *The Masters of Social Anthropology: On the Development of Anthropological Theory.* Warsaw: PWN.

Rybicki, Pawel 1979 *The Structure of the Social World.* Warsaw: Polish Scientific Publishers.

Rychard, Andrzej 1987 "The Legitimation and Stability of the Social Order in Poland." In J. Koralewicz, I. Bialecki, and M. Watson, eds., *Crisis and Tradition: Polish Society in the 1980s.* Oxford: Berg.

Slomczynski, Kazimierz M. 1989 *Social Structure and Mobility: Poland, Japan, and the United States.* Warsaw: Polish Academy of Sciences, Institute of Philosophy and Sociology.

——— Joanne Miller, and Melvin L. Kohn 1981 "Stratification, Work, and Values: A Polish-United States Comparison." *American Sociological Review* 46:720–744.

Staniszkis, Jadwiga 1984 *Poland: Self-Limiting Revolution.* Princeton, N.J.: Princeton University Press.

——— 1987 "The Political Articulation of Property Rights: Some Reflections on the 'Inert Structure.'" In J. Koralewicz, I. Bialecki, and M. Watson, eds., *Crisis and Tradition: Polish Society in the 1980s.* Oxford: Berg.

——— 1989 *The Ontology of Socialism.* Warsaw: In Plus.

Sulek, Antoni 1985 "Life Values of Two Generations: From a Study of the Generational Gap in Poland." *Polish Sociological Bulletin* 1–4:31–42.

Szacki, Jerzy 1979 *History of Sociological Thought.* Westport, Conn.: Greenwood Press.

Szczepanski, Jan 1970 *Polish Society.* New York: Random House.

Szmatka, Jacek 1989 *Small Social Structures: Introduction to Structural Microsociology.* Warsaw: Polish Scientific Publishers.

Sztompka, Piotr 1986 *Robert K. Merton: An Intellectual Profile.* London: Macmillan.

——— (ed.) 1984 *Masters of Polish Sociology.* Krakow: Ossolineum.

——— 1991 *Society in Action: Theory of Social Becoming.* Cambridge: Polity Press/Chicago: The University of Chicago Press.

Wasilewski, Jacek 1989 "Social Processes of Power Elite Recruitment." *Sisyphus. Sociological Studies* 5:205–224.

Wesolowski, Wlodzimierz 1979 *Classes, Strata, and Power*. London: Routledge and Kegan Paul.

———, and Bogdan W. Mach 1986 "Unfulfilled Systemic Functions of Social Mobility I: A Theoretical Scheme." *International Sociology* 1:19–35.

Wiatr, Jerzy 1988 *The Soldier and the Nation*. Boulder, Colo.: Westview Press.

Wnuk-Lipinski, Edmund 1987 "Social Dimorphism and Its Implications." In J. Koralewicz, I. Bialecki, and M. Watson, eds., *Crisis and Tradition: Polish Society in the 1980s*. Oxford, England: Berg.

Ziolkowski, Marek 1988 "Individuals and the Social System: Values, Perceptions, and Behavioral Strategies." *Social Research* 55:139–177.

JACEK SZMATKA

POLITICAL CRIME Political crime has been more often an object of partisan assertion than of independent research. Passions are easily aroused, facts are difficult to establish. Nevertheless, a growing number of studies have contributed to (1) articulating the issues in defining political criminality; (2) describing instances and patterns of resistance to political-legal authority; (3) cataloging and analyzing governmental efforts to prevent and counter such challenges; and (4) proposing research agendas.

THE PROBLEM OF DEFINITION

Political criminality may be narrowly or broadly defined, with greater or lesser regard for definitions offered by laws and interpretations by authorities. Moreover, the values and politics of observers frequently influence their conceptions of what and who is politically criminal. The resulting mélange of definitions has led Kittrie and Wedlock (1986, p. xlii) to conclude pessimistically, "It may be that an objective and neutral definition of political crime is impossible, because the term seems to involve relativistic relationships between the motives and acts of individuals and the perspectives of government toward their conduct and allegiances." However, an alternative view is implicit in their understanding of political criminality as perceptual and relational, defined in interaction between opposing parties.

Whose perceptions decide what is to be called political crime? Apart from partisan and subjective answers, the empirical reality of political criminality is that it is defined by those with enough power to impose their perceptions. Insofar as a political authority structure has been established, one may argue that the dominant parties within it by definition have the power to define criminality (Turk 1982a, pp. 11–68, 1984, pp. 119–121; see also Ingraham 1979, pp. 13, 19). However, this view leaves unsettled the question of how authorities themselves may be defined as political criminals.

The most common resolution is to expand the definition to include anyone who commits extralegal acts defending or attacking an authority structure. For example, Roebuck and Weeber (1978, pp. 16–17) consider political crime to be any illegal or disapproved act committed by "government or capitalistic agents" or by "the people against the government." This very subjective definition (disapproved by whom?) leaves one unable to distinguish either between acts against and on behalf of authority or between legal and nonlegal behavior. A more promising approach is to recognize that criminality may be defined at different levels of political organization—international as well as national. To the extent that sanctions are likely to be applied to offenders, the Universal Declaration of Human Rights, formally accepted by nearly all members of the United Nations (Henkin 1989, p. 13), may eventually serve to define political crime by national and international elites as well as their challengers. Within nations, acts by local authorities may be effectively treated as political crimes (subversive of the authority structure) by national elites, as in the U.S. federal government's historic crackdown on southern state and local violations of constitutionally guaranteed civil rights.

Another question is whether political criminality is to be defined only as behavior. While one may agree that only specified harmful acts *should* be punishable, the historical fact is that in addition to offending behavior, nonbehavioral attributes such as ethnicity and class background have frequently been used by antagonists as criteria of intolerable political deviance. Moreover, imputed as well as observed deviations or threats have been used. Anticipation as well as reaction are involved in the identification of political criminality. In sum, political criminality is most realistically defined as whatever is treated as such by specified actors (usually governments, dominant groups, or their agents) in particular historical situations.

RESISTING AUTHORITY

Resistance to political authority may be more or less deliberate, organized, or planned. The appearance or potential of resistance may be sufficient for authorities to act against perceived challengers. Resisters may be engaged in activities ranging from merely disrespectful comments to the most violent assaults, from spontaneous eruptions to carefully orchestrated attacks, from individually motivated acts to organized strategies of rebellion. Acts of resistance may be categorized as evasion, dissent, disobedience, or violence.

Resisters may simply evade the orders and demands of the powerful. Avoiding masters, bosses, tax collectors, and military conscription has generally been safer than explicit defiance—because open defiance tends to force authorities to respond, while tacit evasion is more easily ignored or minimized.

The right to speak out against authority is enshrined in many legal traditions but in practice is limited by the varying tolerance of authorities and people—decidedly lower in wartime and economic hard times. After centuries of attempting to deter such offenses as seditious libel and treasonous utterances, more democratic governments have de facto concluded that the effort is incompatible with the concept of free speech (Law Commission 1977; Stone 1983; Hurst 1983; cf. Franks 1989). However, other labels may be invoked to authorize punishing those whose dissent is especially galling, especially when authorities feel particularly threatened. U.S. Senator Joseph McCarthy, for instance, achieved the lasting notoriety of "McCarthyism" by freewheeling accusations of "subversion" against a wide spectrum of targets—from known communists to President Eisenhower.

Dissenting is one thing, actually disobeying rules and commands is another. Lower class people have historically suffered many demonstrations of their vulnerability, so have characteristically been less likely than higher class people either to dissent or to disobey overtly (Turk 1982a, pp. 69–114). On the other hand, dissenting or disobedient higher class, especially youthful, resisters have typically been subjected to less punitive treatment. For instance, sentences of Vietnam draft resisters decreased in response to the political repercussions of imprisoning growing numbers of higher class young men (Hagan and Bernstein 1979). Not surprisingly, civil disobedience has been more likely to be a higher class than a lower class mode of resistance—that is, a tactic of those whose backgrounds encourage them to believe, perhaps erroneously, in their own significance and efficacy and in legal rights and protections.

Violent resistance by individuals and small organizations seldom threatens authority structures directly, but does indirectly weaken them in that authorities facing or fearing violence typically adopt extralegal and repressive control measures —which contradict beliefs in legal restraints on governmental power. The more actually and ideologically democratic the political order, the greater the contradiction—which is associated with the greater vulnerability of democratic than despotic regimes to terrorism (Turk 1982b, p. 127).

Political offenders have commonly been viewed as morally or mentally defective. However, even the most violent assassins and terrorists appear unlikely to exhibit psychopathology (Turk 1983, 1984, p. 123; cf. Schafer 1974). The effort to understand political resisters begins in recognizing that they may vary enormously in political consciousness and motivation, organizational involvement, and readiness to commit violent acts, in addition to other characteristics, such as class origins. Distinctions must be made among deliberate political actors, emotional reactors to climates of political instability and violence, and apolitical opportunists such as ordinary criminals who merely seek to profit from their contacts with resistance figures and movements.

ASSERTING AUTHORITY

Political dominance is defended legally and often extralegally at all institutional levels. The highest and broadest level is typified by national (and increasingly international) policies of insulation, sanctioning, and persuasion designed to ensure that potential resisters lack the opportunities, resources, and will to challenge authority (Gamson 1968). More specifically focused on controlling resistance is political policing—the organized effort to gather relevant intelligence, manipulate channels of communication, neutralize opposition, and deter challenges.

Because the value of information can never be fully anticipated, intelligence-gathering is inherently limitless. Advancing technologies of surveillance and analysis enable ever more extensive and intensive monitoring of human behavior and relationships. The distinction between public and private is increasingly dubious in both law and practice. Recurring legislative and judicial efforts to impose legal restraints have occasionally slowed but never stopped the trend (Marx 1988).

Authorities have never been entirely comfortable with the ideal of free and open communications. Even where that ideal has been most firmly asserted in law, in practice the right to disseminate critical information and ideas has been limited (Kittrie and Wedlock 1986, passim). Openly or subtly, communications favoring the status quo have been facilitated, while dissent has been inhibited to a greater or lesser degree.

When resistance is encountered, some blend of enclosure and terror tactics is used—that is, methods designed not only to suppress resistance but also to convince offenders that apprehension is inevitable and punishment unbearably severe. Psychological as well as physical coercion is accomplished by subjecting targets to sanctions varying from character assassination to torture and extermination. International covenants notwithstanding, torture and other violations of human rights continue throughout the world (Amnesty International 1984). Clearly, authorities facing serious challenges are unlikely to be restrained by legal or other norms.

The ultimate goal of political policing is general deterrence. Insofar as the subject population does not knowingly and willingly accept the political order, fear and ignorance may still ensure acquiescence. Surveillance, censorship, and neutralization are designed not only to repress political deviance but also to discourage any inclination to question the social order. But intimidation must be supplemented by persuasion if superior power is to be legitimated—transformed into authority. A classic technique is the political trial, in which legal formalities are used to portray the accused as a threat to society, to convey the impression that political policing is legally restrained, and to reinforce the sense that political dominance is both right and irresistible (Kirchheimer 1961; Christenson 1986).

RESEARCH AGENDAS

Studies of political criminality have raised far more questions than they have answered. In the future, not isolated, small-scale investigations but ongoing research programs are essential if the quest for systematic explanations of political criminality is to be successful. Such programs will necessarily be multilevel, integrating research on the political socialization of individuals, the radicalization of defenders as well as challengers of authority, the interaction of resistance and policing strategies, and the conditions under which the political organization of social life is relatively viable (low rates of both resistance and repression).

The viability of a political authority structure can in principle be objectively defined: The probability of its survival increases or decreases. Accordingly, research can identify progressive actions (increase viability) and destructive actions (decrease viability) by anyone involved in political conflict. Turk (1982a, pp. 181–191) hypothesizes that random violence, economic exploitation, and weakening social bonds are destructive, while nonviolent actions increasing the life chances of everyone instead of only some people are likely to be progressive.

(SEE ALSO: *Criminology; Social Control; White-Collar Crime)*

REFERENCES

Amnesty International 1984 *Torture in the Eighties.* London: Amnesty International Publications.

Christenson, Ron 1986 *Political Trials: Gordian Knots in the Law.* New Brunswick, N.J.: Transaction Books.

Franks, C. E. S., ed. 1989 *Dissent and the State.* Toronto: Oxford University Press.

Gamson, William A. 1968 *Power and Discontent.* Homewood, Ill.: Dorsey Press.

Hagan, John, and Ilene Bernstein 1979 "Conflict in Context: The Sanctioning of Draft Resisters, 1963–76." *Social Problems* 27:109–122.

Henkin, Louis 1989 "The Universality of the Concept of Human Rights." *Annals of the American Academy of Political and Social Science* 506:10–16.

Hurst, James Willard 1983 "Treason." In Sanford H. Kadish, ed., *Encyclopedia of Crime and Justice,* vol. 4. New York: Free Press.

Ingraham, Barton L. 1979 *Political Crime in Europe: A Comparative Study of France, Germany and England.* Berkeley: University of California Press.

Kirchheimer, Otto 1961 *Political Justice: The Use of Legal Procedure for Political Ends.* Princeton, N.J.: Princeton University Press.

Kittrie, Nicholas N., and Eldon D. Wedlock, Jr. (eds.) 1986 *The Tree of Liberty: A Documentary History of Rebellion and Political Crime in America.* Baltimore: Johns Hopkins University Press.

Law Commission 1977 *Codification of the Criminal Law: Treason, Sedition, and Allied Offences.* Working Paper 72. London: Her Majesty's Stationery Office.

Marx, Gary T. 1988 *Undercover: Police Surveillance in America.* Berkeley: University of California Press.

Roebuck, Julian, and Stanley C. Weeber 1978 *Political Crime in the United States: Analyzing Crime by and against Government.* New York: Praeger.

Schafer, Stephen 1974 *The Political Criminal: The Problem of Morality and Crime.* New York: Macmillan.

Stone, Geoffrey R. 1983 "Sedition." In Sanford H. Kadish, ed., *Encyclopedia of Crime and Justice,* vol. 4. New York: Free Press.

Turk, Austin T. 1982a *Political Criminality: The Defiance and Defense of Authority.* Newbury Park, Calif.: Sage.

——— 1982b "Social Dynamics of Terrorism." *Annals of the American Academy of Political and Social Science* 463:119–128.

——— 1983 "Assassination." In Sanford H. Kadish, ed., *Encyclopedia of Crime and Justice,* vol. 1. New York: Free Press.

——— 1984 "Political Crime." In Robert F. Meier, ed., *Major Forms of Crime.* Newbury Park, Calif.: Sage.

AUSTIN T. TURK

POLITICAL ORGANIZATIONS Political organizations are formally organized, named groups that seek to influence the public policy decisions of governmental policy makers (Wilson 1973, p. 9; Berry 1984, p. 4). They are distinct from political parties, whose primary purpose is to elect candidates to public office and only incidentally to press for specific policy agendas. This definition of political organizations also excludes public agencies, which may act at times to promote their own policy preferences, and private profit-making corporations, which may include a government affairs office to lobby for preferential treatment by legislators and regulators. It also leaves aside social movement organizations whose primary tactics involve rallies, demonstrations, and violent forms of protest (including revolutionary actions intended to overthrow the government) rather than working within routine channels of the political system. Most political organizations take the form of a voluntary association of persons or organizations that pools financial and other resources from its members and constituents and attempts through routine political tactics to influence the policy decisions of public officials. The most common synonyms for this type of organization are "interest groups," "pressure groups," and "collective action organizations."

Political organizations include voluntary associations holding a wide range of formal goals, associations such as labor unions, professional societies, business and trade associations, churches, neighborhood and community organizations, fraternities and sororities, nationality and racial-ethnic federations, civic service, philanthropic, and cooperative groups, medical and legal societies, conservation leagues, and even recreational and hobby clubs. Political goals need not be their primary objective nor compose the majority of their activities, but the critical requirement is that they go beyond merely providing direct services to their members by seeking to change or preserve the social, economic, cultural, or legal conditions faced by their members or those on whose behalf they operate. One interesting type of political organization is the so-called citizens' group or public interest group (PIG), which purports not to benefit narrow sectarian or economic self-interests but to promote the broader collective values of the society (Berry 1977; McFarland 1976). For example, civil rights, civil liberties, environmental protection, feminist, and consumer advocacy associations frequently proclaim a disinterested agenda. A close examination of their supporters and activities suggests they do not differ fundamentally from other political organizations in methods of operation (Schlozman and Tierney 1986, pp. 30–35). Based on listings compiled by various American directories, perhaps as many as 15,000 voluntary associations operate at the national level (many with dozens or hundreds of chapters and branches in state and local communities). Of these, perhaps half qualify as political organizations based on their efforts to communicate their positions on national policy issues to the federal government (Knoke 1990, p. 208). They range in size from the American Association of Retired Persons with more than 31 million members to small staff organizations with fewer than a dozen operatives bankrolled by foundations or public donations.

Recent theorizing and research on political organizations have concentrated on four themes: How and why such organizations are created; how participation and support of members are maintained; the internal governance of associations; and their roles in public policy making. Only brief summaries of key findings are possible here.

The founding and expansion of political organizations seem to occur in cycles corresponding to national political and economic dynamics (Berry 1977, p. 13; Schlozman and Tierney 1986, pp. 74–82). American labor unions established a national policy presence during the New Deal, and public interest groups blossomed during the civil rights, antiwar, and feminist social movements of the 1960s. Business advocacy associations flocked to Washington in the 1970s and 1980s in reaction to restrictions imposed by newly established federal regulatory agencies for environment, occupational safety and health, consumer protection, and equal employment opportunity (Vogel 1989, pp. 148–192). Increasingly, mass membership organizations have yielded ground to institutionally based political organizations such as corporations and confederations of state and local governments (Salisbury 1984). Interest groups rarely form spontaneously but require leadership and resources. Salisbury (1969) argued that interest group origins and growth are best understood as an exchange between entrepreneurial organizers, who invest capital in a set of benefits offered to potential members as the price of membership and members who pay dues in order to receive these benefits. Intergroup subsidies may occur; for example, the United Auto Workers supported Cesar Chavez's United Farm Workers union. While citizen activists such as Ralph Nader or John Gardner occasionally provide an energizing impetus for launching new organizations, many public interest groups rely on wealthy individuals or foundation sponsors as well as favorable mass media treatment (Walker 1983).

Once an organization is created, its survival and expansion depends on its ability to attract and hold members or other sponsoring organizations. Labor unions and business associations can acquire substantial war chests through dues and assessments on their members, while PIGs have more limited capacities to take potential constituents' money. For almost three decades, a central paradigm to explain member contributions has been Mancur Olson Jr.'s *Logic of Collective Action* (1965). He proposed a rational choice explanation of conditions under which people would voluntarily contribute resources to an organized group that seeks a public good such as a governmental policy from which no eligible persons can be excluded. He argued that utility-maximizing actors will refuse to pay for public goods that will be produced regardless of their contributions and thus will take a "free ride" on the efforts of other members. As a result, most political organizations would fail to mobilize their potential supporters if they were to rely solely on public goods to attract support. Olson concluded that such entities would become viable only if they offered "selective incentives" to prospective members in exchange for their contributions toward the lobbying effort. These inducements included magazine subscriptions, group insurance, social gatherings, certification and training programs, and similar benefits from which noncontributors can be effectively excluded by the organization unless they pay dues and assessments. In Olson's formulation, a political organization's policy-influencing objectives are reduced to a secondary "by-product" of its members' and supporters' interests in obtaining personal material benefits.

Despite his appealing analytical arguments, Olson's propositions were repeatedly challenged by empirical investigations of the incentive systems of real voluntary organizations. Members often respond to diverse inducements apart from personal material gains, including normative and purposive appeals and organizational lobbying for public goods (Moe 1980, pp. 201–231; Knoke 1988; 1990, pp. 123–140). For example, the decision by members to remain in Common Cause, a citizen lobby for good government, is extensively influenced by their valuation of the collective benefits produced by the organization (Rothenberg 1988; McFarland 1984, pp. 57–58). The internal economies of political organizations turn out to be more complex than originally believed. Organizational leaders have an important impact in defining the conditions and prospects for their members and persuading them to contribute toward collective efforts that may run counter to the members' short-term personal interests.

The internal governance of political organizations is often posed as a question of oligarchy versus democracy. Persistent leadership and staff cliques in labor unions, trade associations, fraternal organizations, professional societies, and other types of associations are frequently interpreted as evidence of an inevitable "iron law of oligarchy." But, apart from labor unions (with their legal monopolies on occupational representation within certain industries), most voluntary groups are too dependent on their members for critical resources to enable officials to flout the memberships' interests in the long run. Consequently, most political organizations' constitutions provide for an array of democratic institutions including competitive elections, membership meetings, referenda, and committee systems (Berry 1984, pp. 92–113; Knoke 1990, pp. 143–161). But, actual practices of consulting members to formulate collective actions vary widely, and researchers are just beginning to investigate how the democratic control of political organizations shapes their capacity to engage in collective actions. The task is complicated by the interaction of governance processes with executive and leadership actions, bureaucratic administration, environmental conditions, and the internal economy of member incentives.

Political organizations serve a dual function for a political system. On the one hand, as combatants in policy arenas, they aggregate the interests of citizens holding similar preferences, enabling them effectively to press these demands on government officials. By articulating societal demands and pooling the scarce resources of weak individuals, they fashion a loud voice that cannot be ignored by those in positions charged with public policy decision making. In turn, organizations provide public authorities with channels to communicate policy information and provide benefits to their constituencies. The fragmentation of power among numerous policy arenas in the American federal system offers many aggrieved groups several access points—legislatures, executive agencies, regulatory bodies, and courts at the local, state, and national levels—through which to raise their demands and promote their preferred solutions onto the public policy agenda for debate and resolution. This dualism of political organizations at the interface between the state and its citizenry assures that the interest-group system exerts a critical, if constitutionally ambiguous, impact on shaping the outcomes of collective political action.

Substantial research has gone into uncovering the techniques that political organizations use in attempting to influence national policy makers (Schlozman and Tierney 1986, pp. 261–385; Berry 1984, pp. 114–211; Knoke 1990, pp. 187–213). Campaign contributions and litigation are relatively rare methods, while contacting governmental officials (legislative, executive, regulatory), testifying at hearings, presenting research findings, and mobilizing their mass memberships are the most prevalent tactics. The relative effectiveness of these approaches in producing the policy outcomes desired by political organizations is unclear. One comparative study of multiple policy decisions in the American national energy and health domains revealed that complex strategic resource exchanges occur between public authorities and interest groups in reaching the collective outcomes of legislative proposals (Laumann and Knoke 1987, pp. 343–373). In agricultural policy, interest groups carved out specialized identities and occupied narrow issue niches, rarely allying themselves with or becoming adversaries of other interests (Browne 1990). The filing of amicus curiae (friend of the court) briefs by interest groups substantially increases the probability the Supreme Court will grant the petition for case review, as the justices apparently make inferences about the significance and impact of their decisions from the demands of outside parties (Caldeira and Wright 1988). Although case study and anecdotal evidence can be marshaled on all sides, only systematic comparisons across numerous attempts at influencing policy events will ascertain the impact of power resources mobilized by the various participants. More extensive research is necessary to determine the conditions under which policy-making influence occurs, especially across national polities. For example, are business organizations more effective when negotiating with public officials as individual corporations or through collective representation by a trade association? Do alliances between labor unions and status-group organizations (race, gender, ethnic group) advance their common goals at the cost of specific objectives?

In recent years, debates outside the United States over the organized representation of societal interests have concentrated on corporatism as a distinctive form of interest intermediation (Berger 1981). Although many definitions of corporatism and neocorporatism abound (Cox and O'Sullivan 1988), the dominant theme concerns how interest groups become incorporated into public policymaking processes through institutionalized access to the levers of state power rather than as seekers of intermittent influence and access that characterize pluralist systems such as the United States. A corporatist arrangement involves policy negotiations between state agencies and interest groups; subsequently, policy agreements are implemented through these political organizations, who use their ability to enforce compliance by their members. The corporatist state takes a highly interventionist role by forming private-sector "peak" (encompassing, nonvoluntary, monopolistic) interest groups; delegating to them quasi-public authority to determine binding public policy decisions; and brokering solutions to conflicts. In return for a stable share of power, privileged corporatist organizations are expected to discipline their members to accept the imposed policy decisions. Within national labor and other policy domains a closed tripartite network of state agencies, business, and labor organizations collaborates on solutions to such problems as workplace regulation and income distribution and imposes these compromises on the society. Although much corporatist bargaining occurs primarily within the executive sector of government, the social partnership aspect of regulated class conflicts should carry over into the parliamentary arena. The corporatist organizations representing capital, labor, and state interests jointly sponsor legislative proposals originated by agreement with the executive branch. Other competitive interest groups are effectively excluded from participating in these corporatist agreements, resulting in a pattern of cumulative cleavages between them and the corporatist core. These disgruntled, excluded status groups are sources of new social movements against the corporatist monopolies; ecological, antinuclear, feminist, homeless, and immigrant groups are examples of these deprived segments.

The study of political organizations is thriving at several levels of analysis, from the individual members to organizational political economies to the integration of societal interests into the national polity. Renewed attention must be paid to linking these diverse foci into a comprehensive explanation of interest organization behaviors situated in their environments. Especially promising avenues include developing formal models of rational social choice at the micro and macro levels; developing intra- and interorganizational networks of exchange relations; accounting for historical and institutional differences in interest representation processes across diverse national settings; and the functions of intergovernmental agencies (such as the World Health Organization) and nongovernmental pressure groups (e.g., Amnesty International) in the world system. Given the vastly expanded sociopolitical functions of modern states in all their varieties, a better understanding of the roles that political organizations play as developers, mediators, expressers, and manipulators of societal interests is indispensable.

(SEE ALSO: *Political Party Systems; Voluntary Associations*)

REFERENCES

Berger, Suzanne D. (ed.) 1981 *Organizing Interests in Western Europe: Pluralism, Corporatism, and the Transformation of Politics.* Cambridge: Cambridge University Press.

Berry, Jeffrey M. 1977 *Lobbying for the People.* Princeton: Princeton University Press.

——— 1984 *The Interest Group Society.* Glenview, Ill.: Scott, Foresman.

Browne, William P. 1990 "Organized Interests and Their Issue Niches: A Search for Pluralism in a Policy Domain." *Journal of Politics* 52:477–509.

Caldeira, Gregory A., and John R. Wright 1988 "Organized Interests and Agenda Setting in the U.S. Supreme Court." *American Political Science Review* 82:1,109–1,127.

Cox, Andrew, and Noel O'Sullivan (eds.) 1988 *The Corporate State: Corporatism and the State Tradition in Western Europe.* Hants, England: Edward Elgar.

Knoke, David 1988 "Incentives in Collective Action Organizations." *American Sociological Review* 53: 311–329.

——— 1990 *Organizing for Collective Action: The Political Economies of Associations.* Hawthorn, N.Y.: Aldine de Gruyter.

Laumann, Edward O., and David Knoke 1987 *The Organizational State: A Perspective on National Energy and Health Domains.* Madison: University of Wisconsin Press.

McFarland, Andrew S. 1976 *Public Interest Lobbies.* Washington, D.C.: American Enterprise Institute.

——— 1984. *Common Cause.* Chatham, N.J.: Chatham Press.

Moe, Terry 1980 *The Organization of Interests: Incentives and the Internal Dynamics of Political Interest Groups.* Chicago: University of Chicago Press.

Olson, Mancur, Jr. 1965 *The Logic of Collective Action.* Cambridge, Mass.: Harvard University Press.

Rothenberg, Lawrence S. 1988 "Organizational Maintenance and the Retention Decision in Groups." *American Political Science Review* 82:1,129–1,152.

Salisbury, Robert H. 1969 "An Exchange Theory of Interest Groups." *Midwest Journal of Political Science* 13:1–32.

——— 1984 "Interest Representation: The Dominance of Institutions." *American Political Science Review* 78:64–76.

Schlozman, Kay L., and John T. Tierney 1986 *Organized Interests and American Democracy.* New York: Harper and Row.

Vogel, David 1989 *Fluctuating Fortunes: The Political Power of Business in America.* New York: Basic Books.

Walker, Jack L. 1983 "The Origins and Maintenance of Interest Groups in America." *American Political Science Review* 77:390–406.

Wilson, James Q. 1973 *Political Organizations.* New York: Basic Books.

DAVID KNOKE

POLITICAL PARTY SYSTEMS Political parties have been defined both normatively, with respect to the preferences of the analyst, and descriptively, with respect to the activities in which parties actually engage. Normative definitions tend to focus on the representative or educational functions of parties. Parties translate citizens' preferences into policy and also shape citizens' preferences. Parties are characterized as "policy seeking." Thus, Lawson (1980) defines parties in terms of their role in linking levels of government to levels of society. She states that "parties are seen, both by their members and by others, as agencies for forging links between citizens and policy-makers." And von Beyme (1985, p. 13) lists four "functions" that political parties generally fulfill: (1) the identification of goals (ideology and the program); (2) the articulation and aggregation of social interests; (3) the mobilization and socialization of the general public within the system, particularly at elections; and (4) elite recruitment and government formation.

Descriptive definitions usually stay closer to Max Weber's observation that parties are organizations that attempt to gain power for their members, regardless of constituent wishes or policy considerations. Parties are characterized as "office seeking." "Parties reside in the sphere of power. Their action is oriented toward the acquisition of social power . . . no matter what its content may be" (Weber 1968, p. 938). Schumpeter ([1950] 1975) applied this type of definition to a democratic setting. He argues that parties are organizations of elites who compete in elections for the right to rule for a period. Or as Sartori (1976, p. 63) puts it, "a party is any political group identified by an official label that presents at elections, and is capable of placing through elections (free or nonfree), candidates for public office."

The present article employs a descriptive definition but also investigates how well parties perform functions described in the normative definitions. Thus, a party system may be characterized as the array or configuration of parties competing for power in a given polity. The focus here will be almost exclusively on Western-style democracies.

ORIGINS

Beyme (1985) suggests three main theoretical approaches to explain the emergence of political parties: institutional theories, historical crisis situation theories, and modernization theories (see also La Palombara and Weiner 1966).

Institutional Theories. Institutional theories explain the emergence of parties as largely due to the way representative institutions function. Parties first emerge from opposing factions in parliaments. Continuity, according to such theories, gives rise to stable party constellations based on structured cleavages. These theories seem most relevant to countries with continuously functioning representative bodies, like the United States, Great Britain, the Scandinavia countries, Belgium, and the Netherlands. However, institutional theories do not explain developments well in some countries like France, because continuity of parliament has been absent, and its strength and independence has come repeatedly into question. The timing of the franchise is also relevant, but its effect is indeterminate because a party system was often partly established before the franchise was fully extended. Moreover, liberal bourgeois parties that helped establish parliamentary government were often opposed to extending the franchise to the lower classes, while leaders like Bismarck or Napoleon III sometimes extended the franchise in nonparliamentary systems for tactical political reasons (von Beyme 1985, p. 16). Likewise, Lipset (1983, chap. 6) argues that a late and sudden extension of the franchise sometimes contributed to working class radicalism because the lower classes were not slowly integrated into an existing party system. Voting laws can also affect the structure of the party system. Single-member districts, with a first-past-the-post plurality winner, as in the United States and Great Britain, are said to encourage a small number of parties and ideological moderation (competition for the center). National lists, with proportional representation (PR), are said to encourage multipartism (fractionalization) and ideological polarization. However, PR may have this effect only if it is implemented concurrently with the extension of the franchise, because already-established parties may otherwise be well entrenched and leave little room for the generation of new parties. Lijphart (1985) notes that voting laws may also affect other features of political life, like voter turnout and efficacy or system legitimation, but that these have not been extensively investigated.

Crisis Theories. Critical junctures in a polity's history may generate new political tendencies or parties. Crisis theories are especially associated with the Social Science Research Council's (SSRC) project on Political Development (e.g., La Palombara and Weiner 1966; Grew 1978). According to SSRC scholars, five such crises can be identified in political development: the crises of national identity, state legitimacy, political participation, distribution of resources, and state penetration of society. The sequence in which these crises are resolved (if only temporarily) and the extent to which they may coincide can affect the emerging party system. Thus, Great Britain's well-spaced sequence contributed to the moderation of its party system. The recurrent piling up of crises in Germany from the mid-nineteenth century to the mid-twentieth century, and the attempt to solve problems with penetration (strong-state measures) contributed to the fragmentation, polarization, and instability of its party system. And the piling up of all five crises in mid-nineteenth century America contributed to the emergence of the Republican party—and the second party system. From a slightly different perspective, von Beyme (1985) noted three historical crisis points that generated parties. First, the forces of nationalism and of integration during the nation-building process often took on roles as political parties. Second, party systems have been affected by breaks in legitimacy as a result of dynastic rivalries, as between Legitimists, Orleanists, and Bonapartists in mid-nineteenth-century France. Third, the collapse of parliamentary democracy to fascism produced characteristic features in the party systems of postauthoritarian democracies: "a deep distrust of the traditional right; an attempt to unify the centre right; [and] a split on the left between the socialists and the Communists" (Beyme 1985, p. 19).

Modernization Theories Some theories, following the tenets of structural functionalism, argue that "parties will not in fact materialize unless a measure of modernization has occurred" (La Palombara and Weiner 1966, p. 21). Modernization includes such factors as a market economy and an entrepreneurial class, acceleration of communications and transportation, increases in social and geographic mobility, increased education and urbanization, an increase in societal trust, and secularization. La Palombara and Weiner argue that the emergence of parties requires one or both of two circumstances: a change in citizen attitudes whereby they come to perceive a "right to influence the exercise of power," or some group of elites or potential elites may aspire to gain or maintain power through public support. Clearly, not all elements of modernization are necessary, since the first party systems (in the United States and Great Britain) emerged in premodern, agrarian, and religious societies. Also, not all modernization theories are functionalist. Thus, Moore (1966) and others have suggested the emergence of a bourgeoisie increases the probability of the emergence of democracy.

Probably the most influential theory of the origins of party systems is by Lipset and Rokkan (1967) and Lipset (1983). While ostensibly anchored in Parsonian functionalism, theirs is a comparative-historical approach that borrows from each of the categories listed here. According to Lipset and Rokkan, the contours of the party systems for western European states can be understood in the context of the specific outcomes of three historical episodes. The three crucial junctures are (1) the Reformation, "the struggle for the control of the ecclesiastical organizations within the national territory" (p. 37); (2) the "Democratic Revolution," related to a conflict over clerical or secular control of education beginning with the French Revolution; and (3) the opposition between landed and the rising commercial interests in the towns early in the Industrial Revolution. A significant fourth struggle between owners and workers emerges in the later stages of the Industrial Revolution. Lipset and Rokkan suggest that the shape of current party systems was determined largely during the stages of mass mobilization in the pre–World War I West.

Following Lipset and Rokkan, von Beyme (1985, pp. 23–24) lists ten types of parties that have emerged from this historical development: (1) liberals in conflict with the old regime, that is, with: (2) conservatives; (3) workers parties against the bourgeois system (after ca. 1848) and left-wing socialist parties (after 1916); (4) agrarian parties against the industrial system; (5) regional parties against the centralist system; (6) Christian parties against the secular system; (7) communist parties against the Social Democrats (after 1916–17) and antirevisionist parties against "real Socialism"; (8) fascist parties against democratic systems; (9) protest parties in the petty bourgeoisie against the bureaucratic welfare state system (e.g., Poujadisme in France); (10) ecological parties against a growth-oriented society. No one country contains all ten sorts of parties, unless one includes splinter groups and small movements.

PARTY SYSTEMS AND SOCIETY

Even under a purely office-seeking definition, parties in a democracy must have some connection to society since they have to appeal to voters' material or ideal interests. Yet the connection between the party system and social structure or social values is rather weak in most countries—and much weaker than would be expected under a theory that sees parties as mediating between society and the state. In many cases, organizational or institutional factors may be much more important than social factors in determining party strength.

Social Cleavages. The party types listed above clearly have some connection to divisions or cleavages in society. Parties may seek to represent social classes, religious denominations, linguistic communities, or other particular interests. Three types of politically relevant social cleavages may be identified.

Positional cleavages correspond to a party supporter's place in the social structure. This may be an ascriptive position into which one is born, like race, ethnic group, or gender, or it may be a social structural position like social class or religious denomination, which one might be able to change in the course of a lifetime. Of course, the distinction between ascriptive and social structural position is not absolute but may itself be determined partly by social norms. Also, against Marxist expectations, class determinants of party support are generally overshadowed by racial, ethnic, religious, regional, or linguistic determinants, when these are also present. One explanation for this finding is that, while one can split differences on class (especially monetary) policies, similar compromises are much more difficult where social "identity" is concerned.

"Behavioral" cleavages, especially membership, generally have a greater impact on party support than positional cleavages. Studies have shown that while working class status is mildly correlated to support for leftist parties, union membership is quite strongly correlated. And while religious denomination is correlated to support for religious parties (e.g., Catholics and Christian Democrats in Germany), strength of belief or church attendance is much more strongly correlated.

Ideological cleavages are preferences—values, worldviews, and the like—that may not correspond entirely with one's position in society. Indeed, ideological orientations may overshadow positional cleavages as a determinant of partisan preferences. For instance, several of the ostensibly working class communist parties of Western Europe have traditionally drawn large percentages of their support from middle class leftists.

Not all cleavages or issues that exist in a society are politically relevant at any given time, or if they are they may not correspond to party support. One can distinguish between latent and actual cleavages around which politics are mobilized. Some cleavages may remain latent for a very long time before becoming politicized. For instance, women's issues had been relevant for decades before the "gender gap" emerged in the elections of the 1980s. One can also consider the process of politicization as a continuum that begins when a new social division or issue emerges, develops into a (protest) movement, then a politicized movement, and ends—at an extreme—with the creation of a new political party or the capture of an existing party. Of course, this process may be halted or redirected at any stage.

Party Loyalty and Party System Change: Alignment, Realignment, Dealignment. Parties may persist over time, and the party system alignment may be stable. There are several possible reasons for this. First, the social cleavages around which a party was built may persist. Second, voters may grow up in a stable party system and be socialized to support one or another party. Studies show that when a new cleavage line emerges in party alignment, it begins with the youngest generations. These generations then carry their new party loyalties with them throughout their lives, though perhaps to a decreasing extent if the events that originally motivated them fade over time. Likewise, older generations tend to resist alignments along newly emerging cleavage lines because they remain loyal to the parties they began to support in their own youth. Third, parties may become organizationally entrenched and difficult to dislodge. Even if cleavages or issues emerge that cause voter dissatisfaction with existing parties, these parties may have the organizational resources to outmaneuver new movements or parties. They may be able to "steal" the new parties' issues and absorb or co-opt their constituencies, or they may be able to stress other issues that distract voters from the new issues.

However, newly emerging cleavage structures may overwhelm these inertial tendencies. The party system may respond in three ways to new social cleavages. The first two are processes of party "realignment." First, new parties may be formed to appeal to the new constituencies. A classical example is the emergence of the British Labour Party in the late nineteenth and early twentieth centuries when the Liberals and Conservatives did not pay sufficient attention to the concerns of the growing working classes. The more recent emergence of Green parties in some European countries is another example. The creation of the American Republican Party in the 1850s shows the explosive impact a new party can have: Lincoln's election precipitated Southern secession. Second, existing parties may change their policies to appeal to new constituencies. For instance, existing parties seem now to be in the process of killing the European Greens by adopting their issues. Perhaps the best example of this process is found in American history. Bryan's Democrats moved to absorb the Populist Party, and Al Smith's and Franklin Roosevelt's Democrats moved to absorb the growing urban ethnic constituencies (Burnham 1970; Chambers and Burnham 1975). Third, if neither of these changes occurs, there may be a period of "dealignment" in which much of the population—especially new constituencies—is alienated from all parties and turnout or political participation declines. New constituencies may organize themselves into pressure groups or social movements that fail either to form new parties or capture existing parties. Existing parties may become internally more heterogeneous and polarized, single-issue actions may proliferate, referenda may increase, and citizen action groups may simply bypass parties. Scholars since the mid-1960s have debated whether Western polities are going through a period of realignment or dealignment (Dalton, Flanagan, and Beck 1984). Of course, both processes may be occurring: Dealignment may be a way station on the road to party realignment.

STRUCTURAL FEATURES

Certain structural features of the party system may be important independently of parties' connections to society.

Representativeness. The electoral system determines how votes are translated into seats in the legislature. The results can vary widely. At one extreme, a system of proportional representation (PR) with a single-national list enables even tiny parties to get representatives into the legislature. Thus, if one hundred parties each received 1 percent of the vote, each would receive one seat in a one-hundred seat legislature. Such systems put no obstacles in the way of party system fragmentation. At the other extreme, first-past-the-post plurality voting with single-member constituencies tends to overrepresent larger parties and underrepresent smaller parties. Thus, if party A wins 40 percent of the vote in every district, and parties B and C each win 30 percent of the vote in every district, party A would get all the seats in the legislature, and parties B and C would get none at all. Such systems discourage party system fragmentation. Still, regionally concentrated minority parties tend to be less underrepresented than minority parties whose support is spread across all districts. If each of 100 parties were completely concentrated in each of one hundred districts, the electoral system could not prevent fragmentation. Some election systems combine features. German voters have two votes, one for a district candidate and one for a party list. If any candidates receive a majority in their district, they get a seat. The remaining seats are allocated proportionately according to the list votes. Furthermore, a party must receive at least 5 percent of the national vote to get any seats from the list portion. This system attempts to reduce party system fragmentation and at the same time to reduce over- or underrepresentation. It was once thought that PR reduces government stability and endangers democracy. However, recent research gives little support for this proposition: "Electoral systems are not of overriding importance in times of crisis and even less in ordinary times" (Taagepera and Shugart 1989, p. 236).

Volatility. Party system volatility, or fluctuations in electoral strength, encompasses several different processes (Dalton, Flanagan, and Beck 1984; Crewe and Denver 1985). It includes the gross and net flow of voters between parties as well as into and out of the electorate because of maturity, migration, death, and abstention. And it includes realignment and dealignment: changes in the electoral alignment of various constituencies and the overall weakening of party attachments. Scholars have long debated whether electoral volatility contributed to the collapse of democracies in the 1930s, especially the mobilization of first-time or previously alienated voters. Recently, Zimmermann and Saalfeld (1988) concluded that volatility encouraged democratic collapse in some, but not all, countries. Studies also show that most postwar antidemocratic "surge" parties draw support disproportionately from voters who are weakly attached to parties or weakly integrated in politically mobilized subcultures like labor, religious, or ethnic organizations. Yet volatility and protest do not always flow in an antidemocratic direction. On the contrary, they are also normal components of democratic politics. Few would argue that the New Deal realignment harmed American democracy or that most New Left or ecology movements are antidemocratic. In order for volatility to cause trouble for democracy, it must be accompanied by antidemocratic sentiments. Indeed, massive vote-switching among *democratic* parties may be the best hope for *saving* democracy during a crisis. Everything depends on the propensity of voters to support antidemocratic parties.

Fragmentation. In the wake of World War II, some scholars argued that the fragmentation of party systems, partly caused by proportional representation, contributed to the collapse of European democracies. In a fragmented party system, they argued, there are too many small parties for democratic representation and effective government. Citizens are confused and alienated by the large array of choices. And because parties have to form coalitions to govern, voters' influence over policy is limited, and they become further disenchanted with democracy. With so many small parties, governing coalitions can be held hostage to the wishes of very minor parties. Empirical studies show some support for these theses. Fragmentation is associated with reduced confidence in government and satisfaction with democracy. And governments in fragmented party systems tend to be unstable, weak, and ineffective in addressing major problems. However, other scholars argue that party system fragmentation is not the main culprit. Fragmentation contributes to problems, but other factors are more important. Since fragmented party systems are often composed of blocs of parties (e.g., the Netherlands, Italy), voters have less difficulty reading the terrain than alleged. Besides, party system polarization may contribute to governmental instability and ineffectiveness more than fragmentation.

Scholars have looked at this possibility in both the interwar period and in the postwar period. While the evidence is not overwhelming, it tends to support the thesis.

Polarization. Sartori's (1966; 1976) model of "polarized pluralism" is the most influential account of party system polarization. In a polarized party system, according to Sartori, a large (but not majority) party governs more or less permanently in unstable coalitions with various other parties. And at least one extremist (antisystem) party is in quasi-permanent opposition. Extremist parties are sufficiently unacceptable to others that they cannot form alternative coalitions, but they are strong enough to block alternative coalitions that do not include themselves. Sartori argues that this leads to stagnation and corruption at the center, frustration and radicalization at the periphery, and instability of governing coalitions. He cites Weimar Germany, Fourth Republic France, and contemporary Italy as examples. Much empirical evidence supports Sartori's model. Polarization is associated with illiberal values in postauthoritarian democracies like West Germany, Austria, Italy, and Spain. And the dynamic may also work in reverse. When intolerant and distrustful relations among political actors were institutionalized by constitutional guarantees in some postauthoritarian countries, they became crystallized in a polarized party system. Cross-national research shows that polarization harms other aspects of democracy, as well. Polarization is negatively related to democratic legitimation and trust in government, and it is positively associated with cabinet instability. However, other elements of Sartori's model have been disputed. In particular, studies in the early 1980s of Italy—the model's current exemplar—called into question Sartori's claim that polarized pluralism generates extremism and thus harms democracy. These studies claimed that the Italian communists had moderated and that the centrist Christian Democrats had become less intolerant of them. However, the studies' own evidence were not entirely persuasive, and subsequent developments—while not reversing course—do not present a decisive break with earlier patterns.

COALITIONS

Single-party government in Western democracies is relatively rare (Laver and Schofield 1990). The multiparty systems of most countries necessitate coalition government. Even in two-party America, a president and Congress of different parties produce a kind of coalition government. (Indeed, internal party discipline is so weak in America—as well as in some parties in Italy, Japan, and other countries—that one can characterize parties themselves as coalitions of political actors.) Most work on coalition government attempts to predict which parties get into office. One of the most influential theories predicts that "minimum connected winning" (MCW) coalitions will form most often. This theory combines office-seeking and policy-seeking approaches, predicting that parties will form bare-majority coalitions (so that the spoils can be divided among the smallest number of winners) among contiguous parties on the ideological dimension (so that there is not too much disagreement about policy). MCW theory succeeds fairly well in predicting coalitions in unidimensional party systems but less well in multidimensional systems—which are often fragmented, polarized, or based on rather heterogeneous societies. Likewise, research suggests that in unidimensional systems, offices are most often allocated among the winning parties proportionately to their electoral strength. But in multidimensional systems, offices are allocated less according to parties' electoral strength than according to their "bargaining" strength, that is, how much they are needed to complete the majority. Thus, if three parties won 45 percent, 10 percent, and 45 percent of the vote, the small party would have just as much bargaining strength as either of the larger parties.

Research also shows that party system fragmentation and polarization, and the presence of antisystem parties, all contribute to cabinet instability. Theorists have sometimes posited that cabinet instability leads to instability of democracy—that it may reduce governments' capacity to solve problems effectively, and that this may reduce the regime's legitimacy. Yet research gives only mixed support for this conjecture. Investigators have found that cabinet instability tends to depress the electorate's evaluation of "the way democracy works." But its effects on other measures of democratic legitimation and confidence in government are inconsistent. Research on contemporary democracies shows that cabinet instability is related to civil disorder and governmental ineffectiveness. But research on the period between the world wars indicates that cabinet instability cannot be definitely tied to the collapse of democracy. Cabinets in France and Belgium were as unstable as those in Germany and Austria, but only the latter democracies collapsed (British and Dutch cabinets were more stable). Why is cabinet instability not more clearly tied to problems for democracy? One possibility is that cabinet instability simply reflects the severity of problems. Just as electoral volatility may reflect citizens' desire for change, cabinet instability may reflect elites' flexible response to the problems. Neither of these need reflect a desire for a regime change, simply for a policy change. Indeed, cabinet *immobilism* might be more damaging to effectiveness and democratic legitimation if problems are severe enough. In this respect, cabinet instability, like electoral volatility, probably has an indeterminate effect on democratic survival.

Oversized grand-coalition governments also have ambiguous effects on liberal democracy. The most important theory is Lijphart's (1977, 1984) model of "consociational democracies," plural societies with high levels of intercommunal conflict. In such polities, parties are unwilling to go into opposition because they risk losing too much and because party strength—closely tied to the size of the ascriptive communities—changes too slowly to make their return to office likely. Thus, formal opposition could lead to more extreme conflict. The alternative is a grand coalition government of all major parties, combined with a degree of federalism and proportional allocation of state services according to party or communal size. Since potential conflict is too dangerous, open opposition is delegitimated and suppressed. In this respect, consociational procedures are intended to be a method for *reducing* extreme underlying intercommunal conflict through contact among opponents (at the elite level), which promotes trust. If these measures succeed, the "game among players" can move to one in which moderate conflict and tolerance of opponents becomes legitimated. This appears to have succeeded in the Netherlands and Austria and failed most miserably in Lebanon. On the other hand, if grand coalitions are formed in societies *without* extreme underlying conflict, they may *initiate* a vicious circle of intolerance and delegitimation. To form a grand coalition, prosystem parties generally move closer to the center of the policy spectrum than they would otherwise do. This move may leave their more militant (but still prosystem) constituents politically homeless, and they may seek harder positions in a more extremist party or movement. These constituents do not so much abandon their party as the party abandons them. Thus, if a grand coalition submerges a moderate competitive structure, it can generate polarization. The grand coalition government of 1966–1969 in West Germany—a country with little intercommunal conflict—was probably largely responsible for the rise of antisystem voting at the time. If the grand coalition government had not ended fairly quickly, it might have caused serious problems for West German democracy.

(SEE ALSO: *Coalitions; Democracy; Political Organizations; Voting Behavior*)

REFERENCES

Beyme, Klaus von 1985 *Political Parties in Western Democracies.* Gower, England: Aldershot.

Burnham, Walter Dean 1970 *Critical Elections and the Mainsprings of American Politics.* New York: W.W. Norton.

Chambers, William Nisbet, and Walter Dean Burnham (eds.) 1975 *The American Party Systems,* 2nd ed. New York: W.W. Norton.

Crewe, Ivor, and David Denver (eds.) 1985 *Electoral Change in Western Democracies: Patterns and Sources of Electoral Volatility.* New York: St. Martin's Press.

Dalton, Russell J., Stephen C. Flanagan, and Paul A. Beck 1984 *Electoral Change in Advanced Industrial*

Democracies. Princeton, N.J.: Princeton University Press.
Grew, Raymond (ed.) 1978 *Crises of Political Development in Europe and the United States.* Princeton, N.J.: Princeton University Press.
La Palombara, Joseph, and Myron Weiner (eds.) 1966 *Political Parties and Political Development.* Princeton, N.J.: Princeton University Press.
Laver, Michael, and Norman Schofield 1990 *Multiparty Government. The Politics of Coalition in Europe.* New York: Oxford University Press.
Lawson, Kay (ed.) 1980 *Political Parties and Linkage.* New Haven, Conn.: Yale University Press.
Lijphart, Arend 1977 *Democracy in Plural Societies.* New Haven, Conn.: Yale University Press.
——— 1984 *Democracies: Patterns of Majoritarian and Consensus Government in Twenty-One Countries.* New Haven, Conn.: Yale University Press.
——— 1985 "The Field of Electoral Systems Research: A Critical Survey." *Electoral Studies* 4:3–14.
Lipset, Seymour Martin 1983 "Radicalism or Reformism: The Sources of Working-Class Politics." *American Political Science Review* 77:1–18.
———, and Stein Rokkan 1967 "Cleavage Structures, Party Systems, and Voter Alignments." In Seymour Martin Lipset and Stein Rokkan, eds., *Party Systems and Voter Alignments.* New York: Free Press.
Moore, Barrington, Jr. 1966 *Social Origins of Dictatorship and Democracy.* Boston: Beacon Press.
Sartori, Giovanni 1966 "European Political Parties: The Case of Polarized Pluralism." In Joseph La Palombara and Myron Weiner, eds., *Political Parties and Political Development.* Princeton, N.J.: Princeton University Press.
———1976 *Parties and Party Systems: A Framework for Analysis.* Cambridge: Cambridge University Press.
Schumpeter, Joseph (1950) 1975 *Capitalism, Socialism, and Democracy.* New York: Harper Colophon.
Taagepera, Rein, and Matthew Soberg Shugart 1989 *Seats and Votes: The Effects and Determinants of Electoral Systems.* New Haven, Conn.: Yale University Press.
Weber, Max 1968 *Economy and Society.* Berkeley and Los Angeles: University of California Press.
Zimmermann, Ekkart, and Thomas Saalfeld 1988 "Economic and Political Reactions to the World Economic Crisis of the 1930s in Six European Countries." *International Studies Quarterly* 32:305–334.

FREDERICK D. WEIL

POPULAR CULTURE Since the 1960s, studies of popular culture in the United States have proliferated and a range of novel arguments have been proposed, linking patterns of popular culture production and consumption to systems of stratification and power. Before the 1960s in Europe, Roland Barthes ([1957] 1972) and Fernand Braudel ([1949] 1966) championed (for quite different reasons) increased attention to everyday culture and its social significance, and members of the Frankfurt school emigrating to the United States brought new theories of mass culture to American academics (Rosenberg and White 1957; Lowenthal 1961), but American scholars still did not generally see any value in studying popular culture.

Beginning in the mid-1960s, as the American middle class began to be targeted by the mass media as the desired audience, more American educators started to show more interest in media-based popular culture, even though in much of academia, studying popular culture was either declassé or taboo (Ross 1989). A few hardy souls from sociology and literary criticism looked at popular culture as a realm of interesting fads and fashions, ephemeral cultural forms that plummeted through modern urban life with regularity, gave rise to much cultural entrepreneurship, and left ordinary citizens running to keep up with what was "happening." Sociologists found it a bit easier to justify ongoing attention to these social ephemera because of the established tradition in sociology of examining urban and suburban communities and their cultures (Park 1955; Lynd and Lynd 1929). By the mid-1960s a quite active community of scholars around Bowling Green University proliferated empirical and descriptive accounts of everything from fast-food restaurants to rock and roll (Keil 1966; Nye 1972; Cawelti 1972; Browne 1982). At roughly the same time, a small group of literary scholars drew on long-standing literary interest in the voices of the people in literature (Shiach 1989, chaps. 2 and 4), and argued that to understand contemporary uses of language, one had to study commercial language in popular culture (McQuade and Atwan 1974). This work did not have much success in changing either sociology or literature. In sociology, it was eclipsed conceptually by sociological work that linked patterns of popular culture to systems of institutional control (Cantor 1971; Denisoff 1974; Hirsh 1972). This work had greater legitimacy because it addressed the organizations' literature, but it also reinforced the sense that the study of popular culture was not really important enough to stand on its own.

By the end of the 1960s, as the political climate shifted, radical scholars began to champion studies of popular culture either to understand the world of "the people" (disregarded by elites) or to account for the political passivity of the working class and poor. They tried to resuscitate questions about elite distaste for popular culture itself and its relation to systems of social control. These questions gave popular culture new importance, not as an aesthetic or commercial system but as a political actor in systems of stratification and power (Schiller 1969; Guback 1969; Aronowitz 1973; Gans 1974).

This legacy has been carried into present-day popular culture research as it has spread through sociology, literature, anthropology, history, and cultural studies. Ongoing fascination with "politics from below" has made this subfield a conceptually complex and politically "left" branch of cultural studies, not concerned so much with the moral fabric of society or the ideational sources of its integration (subjects derived from the Weberian tradition of cultural studies), but rather with the use of culture to exert or avoid systematic domination from above.

Many contemporary attempts to explain patterns of cultural domination through popular culture are indebted to (and in different ways critical of) the work on mass culture and consciousness begun by the Frankfurt school. Members of the Frankfurt Institute of Social Research originally organized themselves to examine the philosophical underpinnings of Marxism, but when Hitler came to power, since most of the leading members of the group were Jewish, this project was disrupted and many figures came to the United States. The work on mass culture that developed from this group was (not surprisingly) devoted to understanding the success of Nazism by dissecting and analyzing the psychological and political effects of mass society (Jay 1973). Members of the Frankfurt school perceived mass culture as aesthetically and politically debilitating, reducing the capacities of audiences to think critically and functioning as an ideological tool to manipulate the political sentiments of the mass public. They argued that in modern industrial societies, the pursuit of economic and scientific rationality provided an impoverished environment for human life. The realm of culture, which might have provided respite from the drudgery of everyday life, was itself being industrialized, yielding a commercial mass culture that atomized audiences and lulled them with emotionally unsatisfactory conventionality. This world of commodities only added to the dissatisfactions that deflected people from their desires. The dulling of their senses made them politically passive and their emotional discontent made them easy targets for propaganda that addressed their powerful inner feelings. This combination, according to theory, was what made the propaganda in Nazi Germany so effective (Horkheimer and Adorno 1972).

During the 1960s, critical theory, as the work of the Frankfurt school came to be known, continued in U.S. intellectual circles to be used to explain the political conservatism of the working class, but it was also taken up in the student movement as a critique of commercial mass culture that justified the efforts by flower children to create radical social change through cultural experimentation. The problem was that, for the latter purpose, critical theory was too deterministic to have much room for human agency, including cultural strategies for change. Constructivist models from the sociology of culture could be and were used to explain how ordinary people could break the hold of political institutions over their imaginations (Blumer 1969; Goffman 1959; Berger and Luckmann 1966; Schutz 1967; Becker 1963), but they did not explain how ideological control of populations by elites could work. The insights of the Italian communist political writer Antonio Gramsci (1971) about hegemony seemed a better scheme for explaining both the role of ideology in systems of power and the constructed nature of social reality. According to Gramsci, elites maintained their power and legitimacy by creating hegemonic definitions of reality that were accepted as common sense by the population. By subscribing to these views, nonelites collaborated in their own oppression. Gramsci's work, available in English translations and popularized in the academic community in the 1970s, gave the study of culture and power in the English-speaking world new direction.

By the 1970s, much innovative work on popular culture was coming out of Great Britain. The British school of cultural studies drew attention to the role of nonelites in systems of power, but it focused more on working-class culture—particularly its role as a crucible for cultural resistance, innovation, and change. This school had its roots in the work of E. P. Thompson (1963) and Raymond Williams (1961; 1977; 1980). These authors began from the premise that the working class is not just defined by relations of production, but a self-consciousness bred in a class-based way of life. The working class has its own history and traditions that give its members distinct values and a complex relation to societal level systems of power. In their own cultural enclaves, class members are active producers of their own political institutions and popular entertainments (and through them defined social realities). So while the public culture of Western industrialized societies may be dominated by elites who control the mass media and who try to use cultural systems for exerting power, their hegemonic control is circumscribed by the cultures of subordinated groups. The realm of popular culture, in this tradition, is an arena of conflict in which cultural identity, authority, and autonomy are contested. Social rifts are made manifest in the multiplicity of points of view that enter into the public sphere along with the hegemonic messages of much mass culture (Curran, Gurevitch, and Woolacott 1979; Hall and Whannel 1965).

While early British cultural studies paid greatest attention to working-class culture, the ideas about cultural resistance were easily transferred to the analysis of other subordinated groups such as women, youth, and minorities. This broader approach to cultures of resistance gave birth to the kind of subcultural analysis conducted, for example, by Dick Hebdige (1979). He argues that innovations in youth culture come from marginalized working-class youths rebelling against both their parents and hegemonic culture. New developments in music and dress are culled from the cultural possibilities made available in mass society, both in commercial commodities and local cultures. These cultural resources are mixed and reassembled to create new subcultural styles. Much innovation of this sort comes from minority communities and is picked up by middle-class kids in part because it is so offensive to their parents. The irony, of course, is that if they make these styles popular, they end up making them part of the world of mass culture, economic mainstays of the entertainment industry.

One of the most interesting literatures spawned in America by this British school comes from historians looking to the realm of popular culture to try to understand class, gender, and ethnic relations in the United States. Roy Rosenzweig (1983), Kathy Peiss (1985), and George Lipsitz (1990) look at how class, gender, and ethnic culture are sustained and dissolved over time in patterns of resistance, co-optation, mutual influence, and change. They identify ways that residues of older cultural traditions both resist and are incorporated into the cultural mainstream, and how different groups have absorbed and used elements of both traditional and mass culture to fashion distinct identities and ways of life.

Rosenzweig (1983), studying the white working class in nineteenth-century America, treats popular culture as a site of resistance to work discipline in the factory. The division of life into periods of work and leisure for workers in this period was not, to Rosenzweig, the articulation of two spheres of activity, but a political division that was part of a struggle over control of time by workers.

Peiss (1985) looks at women workers in nineteenth-century cities. She demonstrates that young working women used their new economic independence to resist the constraints of the family as well as of the factory. They were able to develop new styles of dress, dancing, and play, but could not free themselves from their highly structured gender relations.

Lipsitz (1990) looks at how ethnic and class cultures have been sustained and dissolved in the late twentieth century in the United States. He sees popular culture forming a kind of popular memory, obscuring and yet reviving the U.S. working class's immigrant past and ethnic complexity. Centralized mass media such as television have helped to create and record the decline of immigrant identity under the force of consumerism. In contrast, more participatory cultural forms like street dancing and parading during Mardi Gras and some popular music forms have allowed ethnic groups to play their identities and create an urban mixed culture that simultaneously embraces and rejects traditional ethnic identity.

Another direction in the analysis of class and culture has been developed by Pierre Bourdieu (1984) and his colleagues in France. They have been looking for the mechanisms by which domination has been sustained across generations. If social constructivists are right and social life must necessarily be "created" by each new generation, then social *stability* over time needs theoretical explanation. To Bourdieu, culture is a main source of class stability. He argues that each rank has its own kind of cultural tastes, some systems of taste constituting cultural capital that can be exchanged for economic capital. People at the top of the hierarchy have a class culture with a high amount of cultural capital. They teach this culture to their children and thereby give them an economic edge. This kind of elite culture is also taught in school, but kids from less affluent backgrounds often resist learning it. This cultural resistance by the working class is not a victory for Bourdieu; rather, it is a trap for reproducing the class system.

Bourdieu's theory of cultural and social stratification is interestingly unlike most models found in the United States and Britain because it has no special place for a homogenizing mass culture. Bourdieu argues that members of different social ranks may see the same films (or other forms of mass culture), but they see them in different ways and they like or dislike them for different reasons. Elite culture is more abstract and formal than working-class culture, so elite filmgoers pay more attention to film language while nonelites care more about plots and stars. These differences in cultural consumption are more significant to Bourdieu than differences of cultural production (mass versus handmade culture) because elites identify with formal approaches to culture and prefer to associate with (and hire) those who share their views.

Scholars in both Britain and the United States have been profoundly influenced by Bourdieu. Paul DiMaggio (1982), in a study of the Boston Symphony and its development in the nineteenth century, paid attention to the differentiation of tastes and social ranks at issue when concerts for elite audiences were purged of popular songs and were used to define a special repertoire of classical music. This happened when the symphony was established as an elite musical institution and drove out competing musical organizations that had more "democratic" tastes. DiMaggio argues that this cultural differentiation took place when immigrant groups grew dramatically in Boston and took over local politics there. The superiority of traditional elites was no longer visible in the public sphere, but it remained central to the economy. The creation of cultural institutions identifying this elite with elevated tastes helped to make class power visible and to sustain it over time by giving upper-class Bostonians a distinctive culture.

In Britain, Paul Willis (1977) has confirmed Bourdieu's perceptions about class reproduction through his study of the education of working-class youths. He argues that distaste for the "elevated" values of the school among working-class youths is expressed in school by resistance to lessons. This resistance does not have the optimistic possibilities found in the theories of Williams (1977) or Hebdige (1979), but results in class reproduction. Working-class youths, in eschewing elite cultural values, end up reproducing their own domination within the class system. MacLeod (1987) in the United States finds much the same thing, although he focuses on differences between blacks and whites. Members of gangs from both ethnic communities who lived in the same housing project found difficulty escaping their social rank because of difficulties at school. The blacks believed that by going to school they could achieve mobility, while the white kids did not. Still, both groups were kept in their "places" by a lack of cultural capital.

Since the end of the 1970s, there has been a growing literature, stimulated by the women's movement, on gender stratification and popular culture. The bulk of it addresses two media—novels and film—because of the centrality of women to the economic development of these two areas of popular entertainment. As Ann Douglas (1977) pointed out in her seminal and controversial book, *Feminization of American Culture,* women readers and women writers helped to establish this form of popular novel writing in the United States during the nineteenth century. Sentimental novels were tailored to the domesticated women in the period, who had to stay home and devote their attention to familial relations and child rearing. The novels focused on interpersonal relations and problems of individuals' morals (as opposed to large issues of morality)—just the kind of thing that both fit and justified middle class women's highly circumscribed lives. Douglas decries the role of women writers in shaping this disempowering literature for women and praises in contrast more "masculine" and male writings from the period (hence generating much controversy about her easy acceptance of the literary canon). Most important for students of popular culture, she argues that the sentimental novels were models of mass culture that have been used ever since in romance novels and soap operas.

Janice Radway (1984) questioned this easy dismissal of romance novels, and went out to study in a quasi-ethnographic fashion the readers of contemporary romance novels to see how they were affected by their reading. She found that the novels had more mixed effects than Douglas supposed. While they taught traditional gender relations (including male violence toward women), they also celebrated the gentler side of men and (more important) were used by women readers as a reason to deflect demands on their time by husbands and children. Women claimed their reading time as their own, and used it to withdraw temporarily from the uninterrupted flow of demands on their attention.

Gaye Tuchman's (1989) book provides some interesting history that serves as a vantage point from which to view the controversy between Douglas and Radway. She shows how around the turn of the century, publishing houses began to reject the women novelists and their sentimental novels and to favor male novelists. Publishers were central to the switch to the canons of modernism, and the "expulsion" of women from the profession of novel writing. Women readers still constituted the major market for novels, but their market had become so lucrative that high status male poets, who had eschewed the novel before, began to be interested in it. Once this occurred, their tastes were taken as authoritative and the novel was quickly placed in their hands. Tuchman makes clear that changes in taste like this were neither arbitrary nor grounded purely in aesthetics; they were the result of economic changes in the literary market, institutional decisions about how to address them, and institutional trivialization of women and their culture.

The attention to gender and film has been inspired not by the importance of the female audience or the centrality of women to the film industry (the opposite is the case), but rather the importance of actresses, of the faces and bodies of film stars, to the commercial and cultural success of the industry. When feminist studies of film began in the 1970s, most of the work was on the exploitation of the female body in films by male filmmakers and for a male audience. This kind of analysis stressed how commercial films used male-centered notions of sexuality and power, presenting women in films as objects of desire and/or violence (Weibel 1977; Tuchman, Daniels, and Benet 1978). In the 1980s, researchers turned away from the study of film production and toward analyses of film language and film consumption to construct a psychology of film watching (Modleski 1982; Mulvey 1989). Much of this literature focuses on the voyeuristic pleasure film watching provides men by allowing them to gaze at women's bodies while sitting in a dark theater where the female objects of the gaze cannot look back. Scholars in this tradition examine in shot-by-shot detail how men and women are differentially presented on film: men are generally in medium shots, carrying the action of films, while women stand in the background (or are dissected in close-ups to appear as faces or other body parts, available to the male gaze). Because this type of analysis seems to prove so decisively that films are constructed for a male audience, recent feminists have wondered why women seem to find so much pleasure going to the movies. How could women look at other women through the male gaze without feeling alienated or demeaned? One answer is that some films contain strong and interesting female characters who address issues of concern to female audiences. Another is that interpretations of films are not overwhelmingly determined by the filmmaker's point of view (or a male gaze). Drawing on reader response theory, Nancy Chodorow's (1978) ideas about female psychology, Carol Gilligan's (1982) ideas about female reasoning, Lacanian psychology, and poststructuralist views of the politics of interpretation (Eagleton 1983), a new psychology of film reading is looking at how audiences (particularly women) construct meaningful messages from film texts (Mulvey 1985, 1989; Erens 1979).

In the 1980s, two opposite developments in culture theory have emerged from renewed attention (in poststructuralism in general and in the film theory described above) to the multivocality of texts and the proliferation of meanings through multiple readings. The upbeat one emphasizes the liberatory nature of culture, and is related to: (1) the poststructuralist argument that asserting alternative interpretations undermines the authority of canonical readings; (2) feminist versions of reader response theory that contend that how you use culture is central to what it is; and (3) the idea from the British school of cultural studies that competing social voices enter into the public sphere and are available for readers/audiences to find. Advocates of this position claim that efforts at social control through culture do not work very well because, in their own life worlds, people use the cultural resources around them in their own ways. These new constructivists—for example, Robert Bellah (Bellah et al. 1985) Ann Swidler (1986), Joseph Gusfield (1989), and Michael Schudson (1989)—are much like Goffman (1959) and earlier symbolic interactionists who presented everyday life as a cultural achievement, but they see the construction of meaning in everyday life (in an optimistic reversal of Foucault and other poststructuralists) as a healthy exercise of power as well as symbolic manipulation (Foucault 1970, 1975, 1979; Jameson 1984; Zukin 1988).

This optimistic view of the proliferation of meanings in everyday life is countered by students of postmodernism who derive from structuralism and poststructuralism an interest in the languages of culture and see in modern urban society a loss of meaning resulting from the multiplication of signs and their decontextualization/reappropriation. They argue that commercial culture has such a need to assign meaning to objects (in order to make sense of their consumption and use) that signs are proliferated, reappropriated, mixed, and reused until they lose their meaning. For example, as famous paintings are used to sell cosmetics, images of the Old West are used to signify the solidity of banks, and bits and pieces of past architecture are mixed to construct a new built environment, history is made meaningless. The play with signs goes on without serious thought to what this does to human life. The result is (to postmodernists) an overwhelming alienation. Cultural production and counterproduction, the argument goes, may reduce hegemony by undermining attempts to define "common sense," and may give people pleasure through the free play of signs, but they provide only an illusion of freedom, and breed alienation. This view of modern urban life contains some of the unremitting pessimism of the Frankfurt school, but it is tied to a view of cultural decentralization that is at odds with traditional critical theory.

The diverse approaches to popular culture that have developed since the 1960s seem to have produced a proliferation of meanings for popular culture itself, but the result has not been alienation. Popular culture research has gained an analytic richness that it lacked when few scholars dared or cared to approach it. Conflicting theoretical views about what makes popular culture significant may make it more difficult to define and characterize (much less understand) popular culture. The theories often begin from quite different assumptions about the sources of structure and agency in human life. But they share a common origin in the critique of culture as a source of social control, and they remain committed to the view that through the study of popular culture one can learn something about the worlds of nonelites and their relations to systems of power. All the debates consider how groups come to understand the world they live in, and how those understandings subordinate or alienate them (on the one hand) or liberate them to make meaningful lives, in spite of efforts by others to control them. This heritage is clear, and gives both meaning and direction to popular culture studies.

(SEE ALSO: *Mass Media Research; Postmodernism; Social Movements*)

REFERENCES

Aronowitz, Stanley 1973 *False Promises.* New York: McGraw-Hill.

Barthes, Roland (1957) 1972 *Mythologies.* New York: Hill and Wang.

Becker, Howard 1963 *Outsiders: Studies in the Sociology of Deviance.* New York: Free Press.

Bellah, Robert N., et al. 1985 *Habits of the Heart.* Berkeley: University of California Press.

Berger, Peter, and T. Luckmann 1966 *Social Construction of Reality.* Garden City, N.Y.: Doubleday.

Blumer, Herbert 1969 *Symbolic Interactionism: Perspective and Method.* Berkeley: University of California Press.

Bourdieu, Pierre 1984 *Distinction: A Social Critique of the Judgment of Taste.* Cambridge, Mass.: Harvard University Press.

Braudel, Fernand (1949) 1966 *The Mediterranean and the Mediterranean World in the Age of Phillip II.* New York: Harper.

Browne, Ray 1982 *Objects of Special Devotion.* Bowling Green, Ohio: Popular Press.

Cantor, Muriel 1971 *The Hollywood Producer.* New York: Basic Books.

Cawelti, J. G. 1972 *The Six-Gun Mystique.* Bowling Green, Ohio: Popular Press.

Chodorow, Nancy 1978 *Reproduction of Mothering.* Berkeley: University of California Press.

Curran, James, Michael Gurevitch, and Janet Woolacott 1979 *Mass Communication and Society.* New York: Russell Sage Foundation.

Denisoff, Serge 1974 *Solid Gold: The Popular Record Industry.* New Brunswick, N.J.: Transaction Books.

DiMaggio, Paul 1982 "Cultural Entrepreneurship in Nineteenth-Century Boston: The Creation of an Organizational Base for High Culture in America." *Media, Culture and Society* 4:33–50.

Douglas, Ann 1977 *Feminization of American Culture.* New York: Knopf.

Eagleton, Terry 1983 *Literary Theory.* Minneapolis: University of Minnesota Press.

Erens, P. 1979 *Sexual Stratagems.* New York: Horizon.

Foucault, Michel 1970 *The Order of Things.* New York: Random House.

——— 1975 "What is an Author?" *Partisan Review* 4:603–614.

——— 1979 *Discipline and Punish.* New York: Vintage.

Gans, Herbert 1974 *Popular Culture and High Culture.* New York: Basic Books.

Gilligan, Carol 1982 *In a Different Voice.* Cambridge, Mass.: Harvard University Press.

Goffman, Erving 1959 *Presentation of Self in Everyday Life.* Garden City, N.Y.: Anchor.

Gramsci, Antonio 1971 *Selections from the Prison Notebooks.* New York: International Publishers.

Guback, Thomas 1969 *The International Film Industry: Western Europe and America Since 1945.* Bloomington: Indiana University Press.

Gusfield, Joseph 1989 *On Symbols and Society.* Chicago: University of Chicago Press.

Hall, Stuart, and Paddy Whannel 1965 *The Popular Arts.* New York: Pantheon.

Hebdige, Dick 1979 *Subculture: The Meaning of Style.* New York: Methuen.

Hirsh, Paul 1972 "Processing Fads and Fashions: An Organization-Set Analysis of Cultural Industry Systems." *American Journal of Sociology* 77:639–659.

Horkheimer, Max, and Theodor Adorno (1944) 1972 *Dialectic of Enlightenment,* New York: Seabury.

Jameson, Frederic 1984 "Postmodernism, of the Cultural Logic of Late Capitalism." *New Left Review* 146:53–93.

Jay, Martin 1973 *The Dialectical Imagination: A History of the Frankfurt School and the Institute of Social Research 1923–50.* Boston: Little, Brown.

Keil, C. 1966 *Urban Blues.* Chicago: University of Chicago Press.

Lipsitz, George 1990 *Time Passages.* Minneapolis: University of Minnesota Press.

Lowenthal, Leo 1961 *Literature, Popular Culture and Society.* Englewood Cliffs, N.J.: Prentice-Hall.

Lynd, Robert and H. Lynd 1929 *Middletown.* New York: Harcourt, Brace, and World.

MacLeod, Jay 1987 *Ain't No Making It.* Boulder, Colo.: Westview Press.

McQuade, Donald, and Robert Atwan 1974 *Popular Writing in America.* New York: Oxford University Press.

Modleski, Tania 1982 *Loving with a Vengeance.* Hamden, Conn.: Archon Books.

Mulvey, Laura 1985 "Film and Visual Pleasure." In G. Mast and M. Cohen, eds., *Film Theory and Criticism.* New York: Oxford University Press.

———1989 *Visual and Other Pleasures.* Bloomington: Indiana University Press.

Nye, R. B. 1972 *New Dimensions in Popular Culture.* Bowling Green, Ohio: Popular Press.

Park, Robert 1955 *Society.* New York: Free Press.

Peiss, Kathy 1985 *Cheap Amusements: Working Women and Leisure in New York City, 1880 to 1920.* Philadelphia: Temple University Press.

Radway, Janice 1984 *Reading the Romance.* Chapel Hill: University of North Carolina Press.

Rosenberg, Bernard, and David Manning White 1957 *Mass Culture.* New York: Free Press.

Rosenzweig, Roy 1983 *Eight Hours for What We Will: Workers and Leisure in an Industrial City, 1870–1920.* Cambridge and New York: Cambridge University Press.

Ross, Andrew 1989 *No Respect: Intellectuals and Popular Culture.* New York: Routledge and Kegan Paul.

Schiller, Herbert 1969 *Mass Communication and American Empire.* New York: Kelly.

Schudson, Michael 1989 "How Culture Works." *Theory and Society.* 18:153–180.

Schutz, Alfred 1967 *Collected Papers.* Vol. 3, *The Problem of Social Reality.* The Hague: Martinus Nijhoff.

Shiach, Morag 1989 *Discourse on Popular Culture.* Stanford, Stanford University Press.

Swidler, Ann 1986 "Culture in Action: Symbols and Strategies." *American Sociological Review* 51:273–286.

Thompson, E. P. 1963 *The Making of the English Working Class.* New York: Vintage.

Tuchman, Gaye 1989 *Edging Women Out.* New Haven, Conn.: Yale University Press.

———, Arlene Daniels, and James Benet 1978 *Hearth and Home.* New York: Oxford University Press.

Weibel, Kathryn 1977 *Mirror, Mirror.* Garden City, N.Y.: Anchor.

Williams, Raymond 1961 *The Long Revolution.* New York: Columbia University Press.

——— 1977 *Marxism and Literature.* Oxford: Oxford University Press.

——— 1980 *Problems in Materialism and Culture.* London: Verso.

Willis, Paul 1977 *Learning to Labor.* New York: Columbia University Press.

Zukin, Sharon 1988 "The Post-Modern Debate over Urban Form." *Theory, Culture and Society* 5:431–446.

CHANDRA MUKERJI

POPULATION Because "population" is such a comprehensive term, the study of human populations might seem to include all the activities of the social sciences and many of the life sciences. In practice, however, the topic more modestly refers to the number and composition of various social groupings and to the dynamics of change in these characteristics. It extends to the determinants and consequences of levels, differentials, and changes in fertility, mortality, and spatial distribution. Within the social sciences, population study has a broad concern with the cultural, social, economic, and psychological causes and consequences of these characteristics (see Hauser and Duncan 1959; Coleman and Schofield 1986; Stycos 1987; Namboodiri 1988). Within sociology, the main concern is with linkages between social institutions and the dynamics of population change and equilibrium (see Taeuber, Bumpass, and Sweet 1978). Demography, an important component of population study, focuses on data collection, measurement, and description (for an inventory of demographic methods, see Shryock and Siegel 1971).

OVERVIEW OF POPULATION HISTORY

In the course of providing an overview of major changes in population characteristics, it is possible to indicate some of the linkages between social life and these characteristics. (For a more detailed discussion see, for example, Wrigley 1969 and Petersen 1975.)

During Neolithic times, hunting and gathering groups probably consisted of only a few dozen individuals. Based on the carrying capacity of that technology and the area believed to have been populated, it is estimated that in about 8000 to 6000 B.C. the population of the world was only five million to ten million (Yaukey 1985, p. 38). Probably about half of all children died before age five. Mainly because of the high mortality of infants and children, life expectancy was probably only about twenty years, although some adults would have survived to advanced ages. Maternal mortality was also high, probably resulting in considerably shorter life expectancy for females than for males (United Nations 1973, p. 115). In such a setting, which until recently has been observable in certain remote locations, the social consequences of these fundamental demographic facts would have been enormous. Many of our current social values and institutions have their roots in this kind of harsh environment.

Death was sudden, random, and frequent—about five times as common, in a population of a given size, as it would be in a developed country today. A major function of religion was to enable people to interpret death as a part of the life course and to surround it with rituals. New births to offset these deaths were essential for the survival of a group. There can be no doubt that many groups, of various sizes, failed in this effort, but the survivors were our ancestors. Children were important to the micro economy of the household and community from an early age; young adults were crucial for the survival of older adults. Practices and institutions to encourage fertility—of humans, as well as of the environment of plants and animals—were essential. Marital unions of some type would have been virtually universal and would have begun at an early age. It is likely that unions would have been arranged by the parents, partly because they occurred at such early ages, as well as because of the social advantages of arranged marriages for strengthening an intergenerational network of social obligations. Thus a case can be made that the social institutions of religion, marriage, and the extended family, among others, had some of their original impetus in the extremely high mortality of human prehistory and the consequent imperative for high fertility and child survivorship.

One of the most remarkable functions of social institutions is that they provide valves or mechanisms by which population size can be regulated to be compatible with the prevailing environmental circumstances and level of technology (Davis 1963). As just mentioned, high mortality must be accompanied by comparably high fertility if a population is to sustain itself. For the most part, it is the level of mortality that drives the level of fertility, through various intervening mechanisms, although mortality (e.g., infanticide) has sometimes served as a means of population control. Therefore social regulation of population size usually takes the form of increasing or decreasing the average number of births per woman.

Humans have a much greater capacity to reproduce than is often recognized, and even in situations of very high mortality and fertility there is usually an untapped potential for even higher fertility. There are well-documented populations in which the average woman who survives the childbearing ages has ten to eleven children after age twenty, and it is estimated that the average after age fifteen could be as high as sixteen children under some circumstances. (Of course, if maternal mortality is high, many women will not survive the childbearing years.) The potential supply of births is adequate to balance even the most severe conditions; if it were not, the species would not have survived.

Over the long run, there has been a general pattern of increased life expectancy with two major transitions. The transition from hunting and gathering to settled agriculture and larger human settlements produced a net increase in life expectancy, although with some shifts in causes of death. Larger settlements have a higher incidence of infectious diseases because of inadequate sanitation and sources of clean drinking water. The second major transition began in the seventeenth century with industrialization and the progressive reduction of deaths from infectious diseases and will be discussed in the next section.

Fluctuations in mortality due to transitory influences have been superimposed on these two main transitions (Tilly 1978; Wrigley and Schofield 1981). Some of the short-term increases in mortality, due to wars, famines, and epidemics, have been devastating; for example, the Black Death in fourteenth-century Europe eliminated more than one third of the population in several areas.

Trends and fluctuations in mortality have direct consequences for population size and indirect consequences for reproduction, through socially sanctioned regulatory mechanisms. Consider, for example, the transition to agriculture and larger settlements. Mortality fell and population size increased, so that at the beginning of the Christian era, the world population is estimated to have been about three hundred million. However, at some point a new equilibrium was achieved, with relative stability at the higher size. The increase in carrying capacity with a new technology and social organization probably had its principal effect on reproduction at the household level (Laslett and Wall 1972; Goody 1976, 1983). If territory for new settlements is absent or inaccessible, too many children will result in too much division of land and property. Some kind of limitation on reproduction will result.

The most important social mechanism or lever for regulating fertility has probably been limitation of exposure to the risk of conception—in short, regulation of sexual activity. Thus, in preindustrial Europe, the age at marriage was high—on average, in the mid-twenties. The motivation for delaying marriage and the formation of new households probably arose at the micro level, because the parental generation had limited land to pass to their children. Marriage and childbearing were deferred until a viable household could be established. These micro-level motives led to a general consensus that marriage at later ages was preferable. Associated with late age at marriage were voluntary rather than arranged marriages, and apprenticeships or domestic service for many young people. Alternatives to married life developed—for example, in celibate religious communities. These behaviors can be viewed as mechanisms for fertility limitation, even though they certainly had other functions as well. Within marriage there was probably very little use, or even knowledge, of contraception.

Similarly, the response to short-term increases in mortality, when they occurred, was to increase the prevalence of marriage and to reduce the mean age at marriage. Again, these motivations operated primarily at the micro level, in the sense that when mortality rose, there were increased opportunities for land division and settlement, and new households could be formed more quickly.

This has been an effort to characterize population growth and homeostasis in the broadest terms, up to the beginning of the industrial era in the West. Because of limited space, this description has glossed over enormous differences worldwide in the patterns of reproduction and social structure and their linkages. There have been several ethnographic and historical analyses of these variations (see, e.g., Hanley and Wolf 1985).

MORTALITY DECLINE

The declines in mortality and fertility, and the rapid increase in population over the past three centuries, are described as the demographic transition. This topic is discussed elsewhere and will treated here only briefly.

The transformation of mortality from a common event, occurring most often to children, to a relatively rare event, occurring most often to the elderly, arose from a confluence of technological and social developments. Most important among these was the control of infectious diseases spread by microorganisms in the air and water. An improved understanding of the etiology of these diseases, together with technical capacity and political support for public health measures, led to childhood vaccinations, clean drinking water, and improved sanitation (McKeown 1976). Standards of personal hygiene and cleanliness of clothing improved. There is little evidence that improvements in diet were important, and curative (as contrasted with preventive) medicine played a relatively small role in the main part of the transformation.

In developed countries, the infant mortality rate has steadily fallen from about 250 deaths (in the first year of life) per 1,000 births to a present level of less than 10 per 1,000 (Mosley and Chen 1984). One consequence of a decline in the risk of infant and child deaths is to increase the sense of parental control over reproduction. It is more rational to develop notions of desired numbers of children when the survivorship of children is less random. Similarly, as survivorship improves, it is more rational to invest in children's future by providing them with formal education. The value of children—to their parents and to the larger society—increases as child mortality falls and life expectancy improves (see, e.g., Easterlin 1976).

The increase in life expectancy, currently about seventy-three years in the developed countries, has also resulted in a rise in the mean age of the population, in a substantial increase in the proportion who are elderly or retired, and in a shift to causes of death associated with old age. These trends have broad social implications—for example for the employment of and advancement opportunities for young people, the resilience of political structures, and the support of retirement programs and medical care for the elderly.

Fewer births per woman, together with the now negligible rates of maternal mortality in developed countries, have resulted in a substantially greater life expectancy for women than for men. The differential, now about seven years, works against the typically earlier age at marriage for women than for men. Although at birth there are about 104 males for every 100 females, there are progressively more females, per male, for every age after about age thirty in the United States. Thus the elderly population consists disproportionately of women, and women typically experience much longer periods of widowhood and living alone than men do.

In today's developing countries, the pace of mortality decline has been much more rapid than it was in the developed countries, because an accumulation of Western public health measures could be introduced nearly simultaneously. Most of the decline has occurred since World War II and the ensuing independence of most of these countries from colonial powers, but some of it can be traced back to earlier decades of the twentieth century. The rapidity of the mortality decline and its largely exogenous nature have been factors in the delay of a subsequent fertility decline in many cases (see Preston 1978).

FERTILITY DECLINE

The lag between the decline in mortality and the decline in fertility resulted in substantial population growth in the West. In Europe, the onset of substantial reductions in fertility occurred first in France early in the nineteenth century, and last in Ireland early in the twentieth century. In the earliest cases, it can be argued that the onset of fertility control coincided with mortality decline rather than following it. In the United States as in Britain, 1880 is regarded as a watershed year for widespread initiation of contraception.

With no exceptions, from the cases of France through Ireland, the initiation and the bulk of the modern fertility declines occurred as a result of contraception rather than delayed marriage, and in contexts in which contraception was publicly regarded as immoral, supplies and information were illegal, and methods were primitive by today's standards. Substantial proportions of married couples actually had no children or only one child, but the main reduction came about through the truncation or termination of family formation after some point. As a generalization, births were not intentionally spaced or postponed; rather, attempts were made to terminate childbearing at some earlier parity than would have been the case without intervention. The main contraceptive method was withdrawal (coitus interruptus). Abstinence was probably not infrequently used as a last resort. Rhythm may have been used, but probably incorrectly; douching was common but is now known to be ineffective. Sterilization was not available, although it is likely that a high proportion of hysterectomies served the same function. Condoms were not widely available until the twentieth century.

It is clear that the motivation to control fertility was both powerful and personal. It is unfortunate that it is so difficult at this distance to reconstruct the specific strategies that were employed, patterns of communication between couples, and sources of information. However, at least two generalizations can be made. One is that the practice of contraception required an ideational justification, to the effect that individual couples have a personal right to control their family size. From a modern perspective it is easy to overlook the fundamental role of this concept. It is not just a coincidence that France was the first country to experience contraception on a wide scale and was also the home of the Enlightenment and was the first European country to experience a fundamental political revolution. Intervention to prevent a birth rests on the premise that it is legitimate for an individual—or a couple—to make critical choices affecting personal welfare. Contraception can be viewed as the ultimate micro-level manifestation of a macro-level value for personal freedom, even in the face of strong pronatalist positions by both church and state.

A secondary condition for contraceptive use in the West appears to have been some degree of local development, as evidenced by higher literacy and a higher standard of living. Historical research continues into the importance of specific factors such as the relative status of women, the transition to a wage-earning class, local industrialization, improvements in Social Security and public welfare, and so on. (For more details on specific countries see, e.g., Ryder 1969; Livi Bacci 1977; Teitelbaum 1984. For a general discussion of these factors in Europe, see van de Walle and Knodel 1980. For theoretical discussions see Caldwell 1976 and 1978.)

In the economically less developed countries, one to two generations of reduced mortality combined with a traditional high level of fertility have resulted in annual growth rates often over 3 percent. However, beginning in the late 1960s, some Asian countries, particularly Taiwan and South Korea, began to experience rapid declines in fertility. At present these countries have reached approximate equilibrium between fertility and mortality rates, although they continue to grow because of their youthful age distributions. About a decade later, Thailand and Indonesia and several Latin American countries such as Colombia and Mexico showed rapid reductions in their fertility rates. At present, dramatic fertility declines are under way in most countries outside of Africa, South Asia (excluding Sri Lanka and the Indian state of Tamil Nadu, which have experienced significant declines), and the Islamic Middle East. The declines are due in small part to delayed marriage, but for the most part to use of contraception—primarily sterilization, and secondarily reversible methods such as intrauterine devices (see Bulatao and Lee 1983; Cleland and Hobcraft 1985).

The conditions for these fertility declines show both similarities and differences from the Western declines. It appears critical to have the concept that it is appropriate to intervene in the procreative process. In Pakistan, for example, it is commonly held that the number of births, as well as their gender and survivorship, is in the hands of Allah, and there is virtually no effective use of contraception. Contraception tends to be found where the concepts of political and economic self-determination are better established, particularly among women.

In contrast with the Western experience, however, it also appears critical to have institutional support for contraception. The countries that have shown the clearest declines in fertility have had national family planning programs and visible support for these programs at the highest levels of the government. The most effective programs have integrated family planning services into a general program of maternal and child health (see Lapham and Mauldin 1987).

The consequences of population growth for economic development have been much debated

(Simon 1977; Birdsall 1980). There are many cases, such as Japan and South Korea, in which rapid economic expansion occurred simultaneously with rapid increases in population. Virtually all such cases, however, were transitional, and the fertility of those countries is currently at the replacement level.

A growing population has a young age distribution, with many new entrants to the labor force and relatively few old people in need of pensions and health care. These factors may stimulate economic growth, but they must be balanced against the costs of supporting and educating large numbers of children. In several countries, such as the Philippines, the economy is unable to employ large cohorts of young people satisfactorily, especially those who are better educated, and they emigrate in large numbers. In addition, household welfare can be adversely affected by large numbers of children, even in situations of economic expansion at the macro level. The consequences of rapid growth extend beyond the economy and into the areas of health, social welfare, political stability, and the environment.

CHANGES IN POPULATION DISTRIBUTION

Superimposed on the major trends in population size described above, there have been enormous changes in geographical distribution. Many of the social problems attributed to rapid population growth are more accurately diagnosed as consequences of increasing concentration. Urban areas, in particular the megalopolises of developing countries such as Mexico City, Buenos Aires, and New Delhi, have been growing during the twentieth century at more than twice the rate of the countries in which they are located. This growth has exacerbated the problems of inadequate housing, sanitation, transportation, schooling, unemployment, and the crime associated with urban life. On the other hand, cities are centers of concentration of economic, intellectual, and political life (see Hawley 1981).

The growth of cities has resulted in part from the excess of births over deaths in rural areas. Individuals have been displaced from these areas, which cannot absorb them, and have moved to cities, which are perceived to have better economic opportunities. Often that perception is incorrect. With a few exceptions, such as Pakistan, fertility is lower in cities than in rural areas.

A second major type of population redistribution in recent centuries has, of course, been across national borders. Movement to the Americas was greatest during the half-century between 1880 and 1930, and continues to the present. There are many streams of both short-term and long-term international migration, for example out of South and Southeast Asia and into the Middle East, Europe, and North America, and from Africa into Europe and North America, and the economies of several sending countries are strengthened by monthly remittances from their emigrants (United Nations 1979).

POPULATION OF THE UNITED STATES

The United States had a population of approximately 250 million at the time of the 1990 census and a growth rate of about 1 percent annually, roughly one-fifth of which is due to immigration and four-fifths to natural increase. Fertility is slightly below replacement level, but there are more births than deaths because of the large size of the babyboom cohort, born from the late 1940s through the early 1960s. Age-specific fertility rates are increasing for women in their thirties, mainly because of postponed first and second births rather than from higher-order births. Rates have been declining for women below age twenty but are still higher than in most other developed countries.

Perhaps the most serious issues related to fertility are the large numbers of unplanned births to young women and the high numbers of abortions —about two for every five births—that could have been averted by contraception. Few developed countries have a range of contraceptive methods as limited as the United States. As mentioned earlier, most of the fertility decline in the West occurred while contraception was considered immoral and was explicitly illegal. Although contraception and even abortion are now legal, deep cultural ambiguities remain in the linkage between sexuality and procreation. A litigious environment has inhibited the development of new contraceptives by American pharmaceutical companies, or the marketing of new contraceptives developed elsewhere, and the U.S. government plays a minimal role in such development.

Life expectancy in 1987 in years was 72.2 for white males, 78.9 for white females, 67.3 for nonwhite males, and 75.2 for nonwhite females (National Center for Health Statistics 1989). Although life expectancy is increasing for both males and females, the female advantage is also increasing. The greatest improvements in mortality are in the highest age groups. Because of increases in the number of elderly and projected changes in the age distribution of the labor force, the age at receipt of full Social Security benefits is scheduled to increase gradually, from sixty-five to sixty-six by the year 2009 and to sixty-seven by the year 2027 (Binstock and George 1990).

Life expectancy for black males is currently falling, due mainly to deaths by homicides to black males in their twenties and a greater prevalence of cardiovascular disease among blacks (Keith and Smith 1988). Infant mortality rates for nonwhite babies are increasing, due to low birth weights and inadequate prenatal care. These reversals of earlier long-term improvements are indicators of worsening conditions among poorer Americans.

For more description of the population of the United States, see Bogue 1985; Lieberson and Waters 1988; Sweet and Bumpass 1988.

FUTURE POPULATION

The overriding concern of world population policy at present is the achievement of a new equilibrium between fertility and mortality so that growth will be slowed or stopped. At the present rate of growth, about 2 percent annually, the world population of about five and a third billion (in 1990) will double in about thirty-five years (see United Nations 1988 for a range of projections). Even if reproduction immediately came into balance with mortality, in the sense that each woman had a little more than two births (and the net reproduction rate were 1.0), the momentum due to the youthful age distribution of the population would produce an excess of births over deaths (i.e., growth) for nearly half a century. Under optimistic projections, it is expected that by the year 2025 the world population will be eight and a half billion. This projected growth will occur almost entirely in the less developed countries (World Bank 1990).

The net reproduction rate is currently less than 1.0 (that is, fertility is below the long-term level needed to balance mortality) in virtually all of the more developed countries. The quarter of the world's population that resides in those countries will increase scarcely at all, and much of that growth will be the result of immigration from developing countries. It is projected that the median age in Europe may rise to the mid-forties. Policies directed at increasing fertility in European countries have met with little success (see Calot and Blayo 1982; van de Kaa 1987).

In urban settings with a high standard of living, children lose much of their earlier value as a source of economic activity, household wealth, and security in old age. They become increasingly expensive in terms of direct costs such as clothing, housing, and education, and in terms of opportunity costs such as forgone labor force activity by the mother.

In brief, there are probably two main reasons why fertility has not declined even further in the developed countries. One is the adherence to a powerful norm for two children that was consolidated around the middle of the twentieth century. Surveys show an overwhelming preference for exactly two children—preferably one boy and one girl—with little flexibility either above or below that number. Actual childbearing often departs from the norm, more commonly by being below two children, so that fertility is below replacement.

Second, children provide parents with a primary social group. There is no longer an expectation that they will provide support in old age, nor an important concern with carrying on the family name, but children do provide psychic and social rewards. To bear children is to emulate the behavior of one's parents and to replicate the family of orientation.

Although the world as a whole is far indeed from experiencing a decline in population, and European demographers have been concerned for decades about the specter of national declines, the low reproductivity of some countries and subpopulations raises questions of more than intellectual interest about the future mechanisms for restraining an indefinite decline in fertility. This is not to argue that some decline in population or changes in the balance of national populations would be undesirable, but simply to speculate on the long-term scenario (see Teitelbaum and Winter 1985; Davis, Bernstam, and Ricardo-Campbell 1986).

Major reductions in fertility in the past have been the result of delayed marriage and contraception and have been motivated at the level of the household. Maintenance of equilibrium in the future will require an increase in desired family size and less use of contraception. The norm for two children is pervasive, but norms are also fragile and largely reflect recent and current behavior. As increasing numbers of women opt for no children or only one, it is possible that the widespread preference for two will weaken. The other influence mentioned above, the desire for a primary group analogous to the family of orientation, could be satisfied with a single child rather than two. Indeed, this has been demonstrated in the surprisingly general acceptance of the one-child policy in urban China. For these reasons, it is easier to project a continued decline in fertility, rather than a significant upturn, in the absence of major changes or interventions in the micro economy of the household.

(SEE ALSO: *Demography; Demographic Transition; Life Expectancy*)

REFERENCES

Binstock, Robert H., and Linda K. George (eds.) 1990 *Handbook of Aging and the Social Sciences.* London: Academic Press.

Birdsall, Nancy 1980 "Population Growth and Poverty in the Developing World." *Population Bulletin* 35 (5).

Bogue, Donald J. 1985 *The Population of the United States: Historical Trends and Future Projections.* New York: Free Press.

Bulatao, Rodolfo, and Ronald D. Lee 1983 *Determinants of Fertility in Developing Countries.* New York: Academic Press.

Caldwell, John G. 1976 "Toward a Restatement of Demographic Transition Theory." *Population and Development Review* 2:321–366.

——— 1978 "A Theory of Fertility: From High Plateau to Destabilization." *Population and Development Review* 4:553–577.

Calot, G., and Chantal Blayo 1982 "The Recent Course of Fertility in Western Europe." *Population Studies* 36:349–372.

Cleland, John, and John Hobcraft, eds. 1985 *Reproductive Change in Developing Countries.* Oxford: Oxford University Press.

Coleman, David, and Roger Schofield, eds. 1986 *The State of Population Theory.* Oxford: Basil Blackwell.

Davis, Kingsley 1963 "The Theory of Change and Response in Modern Demographic History." *Population Index* 29:345–366.

———, Mikhail S. Bernstam, and Rita Ricardo-Campbell, eds. 1986 *Below-Replacement Fertility in Industrial Societies: Causes, Consequences, Policies. Population and Development Review,* a supplement to Vol. 12.

Easterlin, Richard A. 1976 "The Conflict Between Resources and Aspirations." *Population and Development Review* 2:417–425.

Goody, Jack 1976 *Production and Reproduction.* Cambridge: Cambridge University Press.

——— 1983 *The Development of the Family and Marriage in Europe.* Cambridge: Cambridge University Press.

Hanley, Susan B., and Arthur P. Wolf (eds.) 1985 *Family and Population in East Asian History.* Stanford, Calif.: Stanford University Press.

Hauser, Philip M., and Otis Dudley Duncan (eds.) 1959 *The Study of Population.* Chicago: University of Chicago Press.

Hawley, Amos H. 1981 *Urban Society.* New York: Wiley.

Keith, Verna M., and David P. Smith 1988 "The Current Differential in Black and White Life Expectancy." *Demography* 25:625–632.

Lapham, Robert J., and W. Parker Mauldin 1987 "The Effects of Family Planning on Fertility: Research Findings." In R. J. Lapham and G. B. Simmons, eds., *Organizing for Effective Family Planning Programs.* Washington, D.C.: National Academy Press.

Laslett, Peter, and Richard Wall (eds.) 1972 *Household and Family in Past Time.* Cambridge: Cambridge University Press.

Lieberson, Stanley, and Mary C. Waters 1988 *Ethnic and Racial Groups in Contemporary America.* New York: Russell Sage Foundation.

Livi Bacci, M. 1977 *A History of Italian Fertility.* Princeton, N.J.: Princeton University Press.

McKeown, Thomas 1976 *The Modern Rise of Population.* New York: Academic Press.

Mosley, W. Henry, and Lincoln C. Chen (eds.) 1984 *Child Survival: Strategies for Research. Population and Development Review,* a supplement to Vol. 10.

Namboodiri, Krishnan 1988 "Ecological Demography: Its Place in Sociology." *American Sociological Review* 53:619–633.

National Center for Health Statistics 1989 *Monthly Vital Statistics Report* 38 (5).

Petersen, William 1975 *Population.* New York: Macmillan.

Preston, Samuel H. 1978 *Mortality Patterns in National Populations.* New York: Academic Press.

Ryder, Norman B. 1969 "The Emergence of a Modern Fertility Pattern: United States 1917–1966." In S. J. Behrman, ed., *Family Planning: A World View.* Ann Arbor: University of Michigan Press.

Shryock, Henry S., and Jacob S. Siegel 1971 *The Methods and Materials of Demography.* Washington, D.C.: U.S. Bureau of the Census.

Simon, Julian 1977 *The Economics of Population Growth.* Princeton, N.J.: Princeton University Press.

Stycos, J. Mayonne (ed.) 1987 *Demography as an Interdiscipline.* Special issue of *Sociological Forum* 2 (4).

Sweet, James A., and Larry L. Bumpass 1988 *American Families and Households.* New York: Russell Sage Foundation.

Taeuber, Karl E., Larry L. Bumpass, and James A. Sweet (eds.) 1978 *Social Demography.* New York: Academic Press.

Teitelbaum, Michael S. 1984 *The British Fertility Decline: Demographic Transition in the Crucible of the Industrial Revolution.* Princeton, N.J.: Princeton University Press.

———, and Jay M. Winter 1985 *The Fear of Population Decline.* San Diego, Calif.: Academic Press.

Tilly, Charles (ed.) 1978 *Historical Studies of Changing Fertility.* Princeton, N.J.: Princeton University Press.

United Nations 1973 *The Determinants and Consequences of Population Trends: New Summary of Findings on Interaction of Demographic, Economic and Social Factors,* vol. 1. *Population Studies* 50. New York.

——— 1979 *Trends and Characteristics of International Migration Since 1950.* New York.

——— 1988 *World Demographic Estimates and Projections, 1950–2025.* New York.

Van de Kaa, Dirk J. 1987 "Europe's Second Demographic Transition." *Population Bulletin* 42 (1).

Van de Walle, Etienne, and John Knodel 1980 "Europe's Fertility Transition: New Evidence and Lessons for Today's Developing World." *Population Bulletin* 34 (6).

World Bank 1990 *World Development Report 1990.* Washington, D.C.: Oxford University Press.

Wrigley, E. A. 1969 *Population and History.* New York: McGraw-Hill.

———, and R. S. Schofield 1981 *The Population History of England 1541–1871: A Reconstruction.* London: Edward Arnold.

Yaukey, David 1985 *Demography: The Study of Human Population.* New York: St. Martin's.

THOMAS W. PULLUM

PORNOGRAPHY Sexually explicit material—a live show, book, magazine, movie, play, videotape, photograph, sculpture, painting, or song lyric—is popularly termed *pornography,* but the term is usually defined as content that violates the laws against obscenity. Pornographic material is prosecuted in accordance with the laws against obscenity.

The U.S. Supreme Court has ruled that in order to be considered obscene, material must meet three criteria: It is patently offensive, it appeals to the prurient interest of the average adult applying contemporary community standards, and it lacks literary, artistic, political, or scientific value (*Miller v. California* 1973). "Community" refers not to a national but to a local community, which may be a county, state, or several counties, depending on the jurisdiction.

Sociological research on sexually explicit materials, much of it conducted under the auspices of the President's Commission on Obscenity and Pornography (1971), has established that there is no special demographic subgroup that uses such materials; the content appears to have no long-term negative effects; the materials have little effect on the incidence of sex offenses, except perhaps to lead to a decline in some offenses; satiation occurs after intensive exposure to sexually explicit media; and women can be as responsive as men to sexually oriented material. The commission, headed by a law school dean, commissioned a substantial body of research on pornography.

X-rated videotapes, which represent perhaps one-sixth of the stock of videotape stores, account for almost two-fifths of the rentals at the stores. This interest of Americans in sexually explicit materials began to emerge in the early 1970s as the result of a number of factors: the availability of inexpensive super-8 film projectors and ten- to twelve-minute cartridges of explicit "loop" materials; a series of liberal U.S. Supreme Court decisions in the 1960s declaring a number of movies and novels not to be obscene; the promulgation in 1968 of the movie rating system, which gave respectability to X-rated movies, some of which starred mainstream actors (e.g., Marlon Brando in *Last Tango in Paris* in 1973) or won Best Picture Academy Awards (e.g., *Midnight Cowboy* in 1969); and a general loosening of sexual attitudes (Winick 1977).

In the 1980s, a major institutional spur to increasing audiences for explicit materials was the Federal Communications Commission's decision not to regulate cable television. As a result, in dozens of American cities, cable television nightly presents all kinds of sexual representations. As the audiences for such materials increase, it becomes less likely that the adults who compose the audiences, and who also may function as jurors who may try obscenity cases, will convict a film, book, or magazine.

The Attorney General's Committee on Obscenity and Pornography (1985), headed by a prosecutor, conducted public hearings and recommended stricter enforcement of the existing laws against pornography. Federal and state laws against pornography are essentially similar, and the decision on jurisdiction or venue is often made on the relative expectations of the prosecutors about where a conviction is most likely.

Pornography involving children is illegal and is not commercially available. Materials combining sex and violence are also not generally sold in the United States. Even the most hard core materials tend to have relatively conventional content. There appears to be no relationship between pornography and prostitution; consumers of pornography are unlikely to be customers of prostitutes because of differences in the nature of the gratifications provided by the two activities.

The President's Commission on Obscenity and Pornography recommended, in the absence of any data demonstrating negative long-term effects of sexually explicit materials, that such materials should be legally available to adults but not to children. Similar recommendations were subsequently made in every country that has conducted a systematic study, including England, Sweden, Norway, Denmark, Israel, and Germany.

Long-term follow-up studies of the effects of legalization of explicit print (1967) and pictorial (1968) media in Denmark have concluded that there were no negative consequences and that there may have been some positive consequences. One major finding of the Danish experience was the public's loss of interest in the materials, soon after they became available, because the materials' novelty had ceased to be a contributor to their attractiveness (Kutchinsky 1985).

Surveys have generally found community attitudes toward sexually explicit materials to be accepting and positive, even in traditionally conservative areas like the South and Midwest. Some communities have established specific zoning regulations for the concentration of movies, bookstores, and other licit sexually oriented businesses in designated "adult entertainment" areas. Such segregation, as in Boston and Detroit, makes it easier for the motivated consumer to shop for "adult" materials and makes it less likely that a nonconsumer will be offended by an unexpected encounter with a movie marquee or bookstore window.

Beginning in the 1980s, the great increase in videocassette recorder (VCR) use made it easier for an adult to view sexually explicit materials inexpensively and conveniently at home. In response to this huge market, there was an explosion of the number of commercially prepared, sexually explicit, X-rated videotapes—to as many as 4,000 new titles a year by 1990. In recent years, approximately one-third of adult males and one-fifth of adult females have seen an X-rated movie videotape in a given year.

Research has identified a number of functions served by sexually explicit materials: They provide fantasy, information, sexual stimulation, and reassurance about one's body and about specific practices; they ease anxiety; they serve as items for those interested in collecting materials or following the careers of specific performers; they facilitate communication about sex as a result of desensitization; they encourage communication between sexual partners; and they provide a socially acceptable substitute for masturbation and for acting out of socially harmful sexual acts (Winick 1971).

Sociological investigations of pornography include studies of users of pornography and of organizations of the adult entertainment industry, surveys of the general public's attitudes toward the materials, studies of the career lines of performers and personalities, investigations of pornography's relationship to incidence of criminal activity, analyses of the effects of court decisions, and discussions of the content of pornographic material.

(SEE ALSO: *Deviance; Legislation of Morality*)

REFERENCES

Attorney General's Committee on Obscenity and Pornography 1985 *Final Report.* Washington, D.C.: U.S. Government Printing Office.

Kutchinsky, B. 1985 "Pornography and Its Effects in Denmark and the United States." *Comparative Social Research* 8:301–330.

President's Commission on Obscenity and Pornography 1971 *Final Report.* Washington, D.C.: U.S. Government Printing Office.

Winick, C. 1971 "A Study of Consumers of Explicitly Sexual Materials: Some Functions Served by Adult Movies." In *President's Commission on Obscenity and Pornography, Technical Report,* Volume IV. Washington, D.C.: U.S. Government Printing Office.

——— 1977 "From Deviant to Normative." In E. Sagarin, ed., *Deviance and Social Change.* Beverly Hills, Calif.: Sage Publications.

CHARLES WINICK

POSITIVISM

POSITIVISM The term *positivism* is now ambiguous. Indeed, its most explicit connotation is a pejorative smear for certain kinds of intellectual activity in the social sciences, sociology in particular. Most frequently, at least within sociology, positivism is associated with such undesirable states as "raw empiricism," "mindless quantification," "antihumanism," "legitimation of the status quo," and "scientific pretentiousness." With few exceptions (e.g., Turner 1985), sociologists are unwilling to label themselves "positivists." Yet, the titular founder of sociology—Auguste Comte—used this label as a rallying cry for developing formal and abstract theory that could still be used to remake society; so, the current use of the term does not correspond to its original meaning. If anything, the term connotes almost the exact opposite of Comte's vision (1830–42). It is proper, therefore, to review Comte's original conception of positivism and its use in early sociology, and then we can seek to discover how and why the meaning of positivism changed.

In *Cours de philosophie positive,* Comte began by asserting that "the first characteristic of Positive Philosophy is that it regards all phenomena as subject to natural *Laws*" (1830, p. 5); then he emphasized that "research into what are called *causes,* whether first or final," is "in vain" (1830, p. 6); and by the time he was well into *Cours de philosophie positive,* he stressed that a "great hindrance to the use of observation is the empiricism which is introduced into it by those who . . . would interdict the use of any theory whatever" because "no real observation of any kind of phenomena is possible, except in as far as it is first directed, and finally interpreted, by some theory" (1830, p. 242). Rather, the goal of positivistic sociology is to "pursue an accurate discovery of . . . Laws, with a view to reducing them to the smallest possible number," and "our real business is to analyze accurately the circumstance of phenomena, to connote them by natural relations of succession and resemblance" (1830, p. 6). Comte's exemplar for this advocacy was Newton's law of gravitation, an affirmation of his early preference to label sociology as "social physics." Moreover, such laws were to be used to reconstruct society; and while Comte went off the deep end on this point, proclaiming himself late in his career to be the "high priest of humanity" (Comte 1851–1854), it is difficult to see Comte's positivism as antihumanistic, as conservative, or as legitimating the status quo.

How, then, did Comte get turned on his head? The answer to this question cannot be found in nineteenth-century sociology, for the most positivistic sociologists of this period—Herbert Spencer (1874–1896) and Emile Durkheim ([1893] 1947; [1895] 1938)—could hardly be accused of "raw" and "mindless" empiricism, nor could they in the context of their times be considered antihumanistic, conservative, and apologists of the status quo (the label "conservative" for these thinkers is imposed retrospectively, through the refraction of contemporary eyeglasses). Moreover, early American sociologists—Albion Small, Frank Lester Ward, Robert Park, William Graham Sumner, and even the father of statistical methods and empiricism in American sociology, Franklin Giddings—all advocated Comtean and Spencerian positivism before World War I. Thus, the answer to this question is to be found in the natural sciences, particularly in a group of scientist-philosophers who are sometimes grouped under the rubric "the Vienna Circle," despite the fact that several intellectual generations of very different thinkers were part of this circle.

Before the "circle" was evident, the nature of the issues was anticipated by Ernst Mach (1893), who argued that the best theory employs a minimum of variables and does not speculate on unobservable processes and forces. Mach emphasized reliance on immediate sense data, rejecting all speculation about causes and mechanisms to explain observed relations among variables. Indeed, he rejected all conceptions of the universe as being regulated by "natural laws" and insisted that theory represent mathematical descriptions of relations among observable variables. Although Mach was not a member of the Vienna Circle, his ideas framed the issues for those who are more closely identified with this group. Yet, his ideas did not dictate their resolution. Many in the Vienna Circle were concerned primarily with logic and systems of formal thought, almost to the exclusion of observation (or, at least, to the point of subordinating it to their primary concerns). A split thus developed in the Vienna Circle over the relative emphasis on empirical observation and systems of logic; a radical faction emphasized that truth can be "measured solely by logical coherence of statements" (which had been reduced to mathematics), whereas a more moderate group insisted that there is a "material truth of observation" supplementing "formal truths" (Johnston 1983, p. 189). Karl Popper, who was a somewhat marginal figure in the Vienna Circle of the 1930s, is perhaps the best-known mediator of this split, for he clearly tried to keep the two points of emphasis together. But even here the reconciliation is somewhat negative (Popper 1959; 1969): A formal theory can never be proven, only disproven; and so, data are used to mount assaults on abstract theories from which empirical hypotheses and predictions are formally "deduced."

Why did the philosopher-scientists in the Vienna Circle have any impact on sociology, especially American sociology? In Europe, of course, sociology had always been firmly anchored in philosophy, but in American sociology during the 1920s and 1930s, the rise of quantitative sociology was accelerating as the students of Franklin Giddings assumed key positions in academia and as Comtean and Spencerian sociology became a distant memory (it should be noted, however, that Marx, Weber, and Durkheim had yet to have much impact on American sociology in the late 1920s or early 1930s). But American sociology was concerned with its status as science and, hence, was receptive to philosophical arguments that could legitimate its scientific aspirations (Turner and Turner 1990). Mach was appealing because his advocacy legitimated statistical analysis of empirical regularities as variables; and Popper was to win converts with his uneasy reconciliation of observation and abstract theory. Both legitimated variable analyses; and for American sociologists in the 1930s and later from the 1940s through the early 1960s, this meant sampling, scaling, and statistically aggregating and analyzing empirical "observations." Members of the Vienna Circle had even developed an appealing terminology, *logical positivism,* to describe this relation between theory (abstract statements organized by a formal calculus) and research (quantitative data for testing hypotheses logically deduced from abstract statements). The wartime migration of key figures in the late Vienna Circle to the United States no doubt increased their impact on the social sciences in the United States (despite the fact that the "logical" part of this new label for "positivism" was redundant in Comte's original formulation). But logical positivism legitimated American empiricism in this sense: The quantitative data could be used to "test" theories, and so it was important to improve upon gathering data and analyzing methodologies in order to realize this lofty goal. Along the way, the connection of theory and research was mysteriously lost, and positivism became increasingly associated with empiricism and quantification, per se.

There was a brief and highly visible effort, reaching a peak in the late 1960s and early 1970s, to revive the "logical" side of positivism by explaining to sociologists the process of "theory construction." Indeed, numerous texts on theory construction were produced (e.g., Zetterberg 1965; Dubin 1969; Blalock 1969; Reynolds 1971; Gibbs 1972; Hage 1972), but the somewhat mechanical, cookbook quality of these texts won few converts, and so the empiricist connotations of positivism were never successfully reconnected to abstract theory. Even the rather odd academic alliance of functional theory with quantitative sociology—for example, Merton and Lazarsfeld at Columbia and Parsons and Stouffer at Harvard —was unsuccessful in merging theory and research, once again leaving positivism to denote quantitative research divorced from theory.

Other intellectual events, anticipated by various figures of the Vienna Circle, created a new skepticism and cynicism about the capacity to develop "objective" science, especially social science. This skepticism stressed the arbitrary nature of symbols and signs and hence their capacity to represent and denote the universe independently of the context in which such signs are produced and used. Such thinking was supplemented by Kuhn's (1970) landmark work and by the sociology of science's (e.g., Whitley 1984) emphasis on the politico-organizational dynamics distorting the idealized theory–data connection as advocated by Popper (1969). Out of all this ferment, a new label increasingly began to appear: *postpositivism.* This label appears to mean somewhat different things to varying audiences, but it connotes that Comte's original vision and Popper's effort to sustain the connection between empirical observations and theory are a thing of the past—just as "rationalism" and "modernity" are giving away to "postmodernism." Thus, one hears about a "postpositivist" philosophy of science, which, despite the vagueness and diversity of usages for this label, is intended to signal the death of positivism. Curiously, this postpositivism is meant as an obituary for the older Comtean positivism or its resurrection as logical positivism by the Vienna Circle, where abstract logic and observation were more happily joined together.

The result is that the term *positivism* no longer has a clear referent, but it is evident that, for many, being a positivist is not a good thing. It is unlikely, then, that positivism will ever be an unambiguous and neutral term for sociological activity revolving around the formulation and testing of theory and the use of plausible theories for social engineering (or in more muted form, for sociological "practice"). Other labels are likely to be employed in light of the negative connotations of positivism in an intellectual climate dominated by "post-isms."

(SEE ALSO: *Epistemology; Scientific Explanation)*

REFERENCES

Blalock, Hubert M., Jr. 1969 *Theory Construction: From Verbal to Mathematical Formulations.* Englewood Cliffs, N.J.: Prentice-Hall.

Comte, Auguste 1830 *Cours de philosophie positive: Les*

Préliminaires géneraux et la philosophie mathématique. Paris: Bachelier.

——— 1851–1854 *Système de politique: ou, Traite de sociologie, instituant la religion de l'humanite.* Paris: L. Mathias.

Dubin, Robert 1969 *Theory Building.* New York: Free Press.

Durkheim, Emile [1893] 1947 *The Division of Labor in Society.* New York: Free Press.

——— (1938) 1985 *The Rules of the Sociological Method.* New York: Free Press.

Gibbs, Jack 1972 *Sociological Theory Construction.* Hinsdale, Ill.: Dryden Press.

Hage, Jerald 1972 *Techniques and Problems of Theory Construction in Sociology.* New York: Wiley.

Johnston, William M. 1983 *The Austrian Mind: An Intellectual and Social History, 1848–1938.* Berkeley: University of California Press.

Kuhn, Thomas 1970 *The Structure of Scientific Revolutions,* 2nd ed. Chicago: University of Chicago Press.

Mach, Ernst 1893 *The Science of Mechanics,* trans T. J. McCormack. La Salle, Ill.: Open Court.

Popper, Karl 1959 *The Logic of Scientific Discovery.* London: Hutchinson.

——— 1969 *Conjectures and Refutations.* London: Kegan and Paul.

Reynolds, Paul Davidson 1971 *A Primer in Theory Construction.* Indianapolis: Bobbs-Merrill.

Spencer, Herbert 1874–1896 *The Principles of Sociology,* 3 vols. New York: D. Appleton.

Turner, Jonathan H. 1985 "In Defense of Positivism." *Sociological Theory* 3:24–30.

Turner, Stephen Park, and Jonathan H. Turner 1990 *The Impossible Science: An Institutional Analysis of American Sociology.* Newbury Park, Calif.: Sage.

Whitley, Richard 1984 *The Intellectual and Social Organization of the Sciences.* Oxford: Clarendon Press.

Zetterberg, Hans L. 1965 *On Theory and Verification in Sociology,* 3rd ed. New York: Bedminster Press.

JONATHAN H. TURNER

POSTINDUSTRIAL SOCIETY *Postindustrial society* is a concept used to characterize the structure, dynamics, and possible future of advanced industrial societies. As with the more recent concepts *postmodern society* and *radically modern society,* the concept *postindustrial society* attempts to make sense of the substantial changes experienced by advanced industrial societies since the end of World War II. In providing a depiction of the character and future of these societies, analyses usually attempt to shape the futures they describe. Such efforts illustrate an awareness among sociologists of the reflexive character of much social science—an awareness that analyses of society become elements of the social world which have the potential to shape the future.

Social analysts have long been aware of the potential effects of their ideas, at times engaging in work precisely because it may have an effect on the future through such mechanisms as social engineering, social movements, and the application of technology. The nineteenth-century theorists of industrial society, like postindustrial theorists a century later, tried to make sense of the diverse changes surrounding them, often in an effort to help shape the future. In the early nineteenth century Claude-Henri de Saint-Simon attempted to provide an image of what was then a barely emerging industrial society, an image he hoped would enable scientists and industrialists to see the crucial roles they were to play in a society consciously directed by scientific knowledge. Similarly, in the mid nineteenth century Karl Marx and Friedrich Engels were outlining the characteristics of industrial capitalism, including the revolutionary role of the proletariat, at a time when the factory system in England was still in its infancy and the work force "was still heavily concentrated in agriculture and domestic service, with the remainder mostly employed in the old craft industries" (Kumar 1977, p. 133). Although there were areas in which theorists of industrial society may not have been fully correct, their recognition of some major correlates of industrialization provided a surprisingly accurate portrait of a form of society qualitatively different from prior modes of human organization. The emerging industrial society was one that increasingly utilized technology and machinery for work; it was a society with substantial increases in communication, transportation, markets, and income; it was a society within which urbanism became a way of life and the division of labor became increasingly complex; it was a society marked by an increasing role for the state, and bureaucratization in government and the economy; and it was a society marked by increasing secularization and rationalization.

The concept *postindustrial society* indicates significant changes in some of these central characteristics of industrial society. In probably the earliest use of the concept, the guild socialist Arthur Penty (1917) called for development of a postindustrial state that reversed key characteristics of industrial society. He called for development of a mode of organization reflecting the artisan workshop, in which work, leisure, and family would be once again brought together. Although Penty may have been the first to use the concept *postindustrial society,* it was not until the 1960s that the concept took on its present character, focusing on quantitative changes separating postindustrial from industrial society. Interest in the future and in postindustrial society developed at that time as a response to the dramatic changes occurring in advanced industrial societies. These changes included the technological and organizational expansion accompanying economic growth after World War II, the expansion of the welfare state, and an increased concern over the dark side of industrialism. An array of terms emerged to characterize the social milieu of advanced industrial societies, including *technocratic era* (Brzezinski 1970), *service class society* (Dahrendorf 1967), *personal service society* (Halmos 1970), *post-scarcity society* (Bookchin 1971), *post-economic society* (Kahn and Wiener 1967), *knowledge society* (Drucker 1969), *postmodern society* (Etzioni 1968), and *postindustrial society* (Touraine 1971; Richta et al. 1969). Although differing in focus, the analyses overlapped considerably with Daniel Bell's work on postindustrial society (1973, 1989), which has been considered the best and most complete analysis (Kumar 1978). The following effort to characterize postindustrial society uses Bell's analysis as the organizing framework. This is followed by an examination of the related concepts *postmodern society* and *radically modern society.*

CHARACTERISTICS OF POSTINDUSTRIAL SOCIETY

For analytical purposes Bell divides society into three parts: social structure, culture, and polity. The concept *postindustrial society* focuses primarily on changes in social structure, that is, changes in the economy, technology, and occupational structure. Although social structure, polity, and culture may influence one another, it is not assumed that there is a harmonious relation among the three. In fact, changes in any one may pose problems for the others (Bell 1976).

Bell's depiction of postindustrial society (1973, 1989) focuses on two dimensions: the centrality of codified theoretical knowledge and the expansion of the service sector, especially professional and human services. The centrality of theoretical knowledge is viewed as the most important dimension, or axial principle, of postindustrial society. The institutions that most embody this dimension are the university and the research institute. In postindustrial society major innovations are more a product of the application of theoretical knowledge (e.g., Albert Einstein's discussion of the photoelectric effect for the development of lasers, holography, photonics) than the product of persons skilled in the use of equipment (e.g., Alexander Graham Bell and Thomas Edison). The use of theoretical knowledge increases the importance of advanced education, which is reflected in substantial enrollments in colleges and universities, as well as in substantial numbers of scientists, engineers, and persons with advanced degrees. For example, between 1939 and 1964, as the United States moved from an industrial to a postindustrial society, the number of scientists and engineers increased over fivefold, from 263,000 to 1,475,000 (Bell 1973). Relatedly, the percentage of those twenty to twenty-four years old who were studying for a college degree went from 4 percent in 1900 to 15 percent in 1940, 26 percent in 1950, and 34 percent in 1960 (estimated from Bell 1973, Table 3-4). Related estimates show tertiary enrollment rates going from 32 percent in 1960 to 40 percent in 1965 and to 57 percent in 1985 (World Bank 1980, 1988).

Accompanying the importance of science and theoretical knowledge is an occupational structure in which more persons are involved in services, with professional and helping services especially important. This includes increased employment in education, science, and engineering, which is a natural consequence of a society committed to science and education. It also involves expansion of the number of white-collar workers and professionals in government and the helping services, resulting from an expanded welfare state and increased attention to health care. Such trends are illustrated in the following data on the percentage of the work force in white-collar and professional occupations in the United States and in twenty developed countries (fifteen Western European countries, plus Canada, Australia, New Zealand, Japan, and Israel) (U.S. Bureau of the Census 1975, 1990; ILO 1965–1988).

Increased employment in white-collar and professional occupations occurs largely at the expense of agricultural employment and, to a lesser extent, of manufacturing employment. The economic dynamic behind such changes consists of shifts in relative demand toward services as disposable income increases (Clark 1960), and of the greater responsiveness of agriculture and manufacturing to technical innovation (Fuchs 1968). As incomes rise, the percentage of total income used for food and agricultural products declines, and the need for basic manufactured products is more easily met. Thus, relative demand for health, education, and an array of other services may increase. At the same time technical innovations increase productivity in agriculture and manufacturing, thereby lowering the demand for labor in these sectors. However, technical change is less able to displace workers in services, even though technical advances aid productivity. This is most clearly seen in health care, where technical change may increase both the services available and the need for personnel to provide new services. Thus, economic and technical developments shift relative consumer demand and labor toward services. Such economic dynamics indicate that development of an increasingly service-oriented postindustrial economy does not mean agriculture and manufacturing are ignored (Cohen and Zysman 1987). It means that technology takes over much of what people formerly did, and shifts productive efforts and labor toward services.

Accompanying the rising importance of theoretical knowledge and the service sector are several other changes. These include changes in women's roles, especially increased participation in the formal labor force. In addition, the class structure of postindustrial society increasingly comes to center on education and technical expertise, creating possible tensions between expertise and populist sentiments. New political issues and attitudes concerned with the environment and quality of life move onto the political agenda (Ingelhart 1977; Lipset 1976). Technocratic rule may begin to take hold in organizations and to confront the problem of rationalized means becoming ends. Corporations may come under pressure to take into account objectives other than profit maximization. Efforts at social planning increase, and confront the problem of establishing a rational calculus for maximizing benefits throughout the society. The society becomes more politicized and conflictive as citizenship expands and groups seek a place in the polity.

Such conditions provide the basis for changes in consciousness and cosmology, as individuals confront a world of information and expanding

	1900	1940	1960	1970	1980
Percent White-Collar Occupations					
United States	17.6	31.1	40.1	44.8	48.0
Percent Professional Occupations					
United States	4.3	7.5	10.8	13.8	14.1
20 Developed Countries			8.1	11.3	14.7

specialized knowledge. The world becomes less one in which the individual interacts with nature and machines, and more one of persons interacting with persons. The reciprocal consciousness of self and other becomes increasingly important in defining the world. The culture may come to show contradictions between values of self-restraint, discipline, and work as a calling, and emerging postindustrial values of consumption and the negation of traditional bourgeois life (Bell 1976).

The image of postindustrial society provided by Bell and other social analysts is that of a society in which technological advances have made possible the development of a society characterized by the expansion and use of theoretical knowledge, and the concomitant expansion of white-collar and especially professional employment. A commitment to human welfare and social planning facilitates expansion of the welfare state and human services, further increasing white-collar and professional employment. Yet such a society is not without tensions and conflict, both within the social structure and among social structure, polity, and culture. It is by pointing out such tensions and problems that postindustrial theorists attempt not only to describe the present and future but also to shape the future.

In one of the most recent contributions to the postindustrial literature, Fred Block is clear about the role social analysis plays in shaping the future. He points out that "[social theory] has real consequences, because individuals cannot do without some kind of conception of the type of society in which [they] live" (Block 1990, p. 2). Block's book represents a return to the analysis of postindustrial society after a brief hiatus during the 1980s that Block attributes to the breakdown of mainstream and leftist social theory, and the reemergence of a tradition of economic liberalism quiescent since the Great Depression. Block's analysis carries forward the focus of prior postindustrial theory on social structure, yet gives scant attention to the role of codified theoretical knowledge, the university, and professional groups. Instead, Block looks at key aspects of the changing postindustrial economy of the United States in an effort to develop alternative possibilities for the future. He notes that a postindustrial economy utilizing advanced technology, and having a substantial service sector, would be most productive if it kept some distance from the dictates of classical economic theory.

Specifically, productivity is likely enhanced by (1) economic organization some distance from classic competetive markets, allowing for greater predictability and more accurate information; (2) labor relations emphasizing cooperation between labor and management, since skilled labor in technologically sophisticated industries and the professions has substantial knowledge and is expensive to replace; (3) treating capital not merely as a physical asset but also as part of a productive process that includes the organization of persons working with capital; (4) developing measures of economic well-being that incorporate positive and negative utilities currently excluded from measures like gross national product (e.g., child care and pollution as positive and negative utilities, respectively); (5) using various hybrid forms of market, state, and other regulatory mechanisms to enhance quality growth.

Block's work provides a useful extension of postindustrial theory into the more traditional economic domains of labor, capital, and measured economic output. The book may represent a revival of analysis of postindustrial society, perhaps under the alternative concept *postmodern society*. However, before considering postmodern society, some criticisms of the concept *postindustrial society* need to be mentioned. Much of the critical literature focuses on Bell's work, since it is viewed as one of the best expressions of postindustrial theory.

One criticism of postindustrial theory is that it overemphasizes the role of theoretical knowledge in decision making. Although critics acknowledge that formal knowledge is more important than ever before, they contend that technical experts and scientific knowledge have not come to play the central role in decision making in government or corporations that postindustrial theorists said they would. Within government, political dynamics of the industrial era persist, and within the corporation "the expert and his knowledge are, for the most part, embedded in the corporate bureaucracy" (Cohen and Zysman 1987, p. 260). Also, critics point out that while there may be more scientists, more persons with advanced education, and more money spent on research and development, these may be only tenuously related to increases in the amount and effective use of theoretical knowledge (Kumar 1978).

Critics also question the attention given by postindustrial theorists to the service sector and to white-collar and professional work. As with theoretical knowledge, critics agree the service sector has grown, yet question the focus of postindustrial theorists. Critics remind us that the service sector has always been a major segment of preindustrial and industrial society (Hartwell 1973), that most service employment is in low-skilled, low-paid work, and that increases in white-collar and professional employment are a consequence of dynamics embedded in industrial society. Relatedly, most of the increases in white-collar and professional employment are in clerical positions and jobs like teaching and nursing, jobs that carry less autonomy and lower income than traditional professional occupations. Perhaps most important, critics argue that a focus on the service sector fails to adequately acknowledge the key role that manufacturing would play in a postindustrial economy, including the dependence of the service sector on a dynamic manufacturing sector (Cohen and Zysman 1987).

One response to these and other criticisms (e.g., Ritzer 1989; Frankel 1987) would be to point out that postindustrial theory often acknowledges points made by critics, such as the fact that the political order can check trends in the economy, that the bulk of services are in low-skilled, low-paid labor, and that a sophisticated and dynamic manufacturing sector is important for an economy as large as that of the United States. Postindustrial theory merely chooses to focus on other developments that may hold insights into the future of advanced industrial society. A related response to criticisms is to point out that critics have frequently acknowledged the validity of postindustrial claims of an increasing role for formal and theoretical knowledge, the increasing importance of technical developments in information processing, and the rise of a service sector with a good number of white-collar and professional workers. The points of contention between postindustrial theory and its critics appear to center on the general portrait of society provided by postindustrial theorists: Is this society best seen as a new type of society, or as a logical extension of advancing industrialization (Kumar 1978, 1988; Ritzer 1989; Giddens 1990)? Also, what are the implications of this image of society, not only for describing the present and future but also for shaping both?

POSTMODERN SOCIETY

Recent discussions of the character and future of advanced industrial societies have been framed within the concept *postmodern society.* Although the variety of work dealing with postmodern society makes a clear definition difficult (Smart 1990), it seems reasonable to say postmodern society differs from postindustrial society in having the more nebulous reference point of "modern" society. Whereas studies of industrial society understandably give substantial attention to technical and economic factors, studies of modern society broaden the focus to bring political and especially cultural phenomena more to the center of analysis. This shift in focus helps explain why analyses of the cultural dynamics of postindustrial society are frequently considered in terms of the dynamics of postmodern society (e.g., Baudrillard 1988), and why studies of the economic characteristics of postmodern society look very much like studies of postindustrialism (e.g., Clegg 1990).

Analyses of postmodern society may differ from postindustrial analyses not only in substantive focus but also in basic presuppositions regarding the nature of social reality. While studies of postmodern society often reflect a standard social science framework, what has come to be called postmodern theory includes methodological presuppositions some distance from traditional social scientific inquiry. Although the central tenets of postmodern theory are still unclear (Smart 1990), it is possible to note some major themes.

Reflecting the influence of literary criticism, postmodern theory often views "social and cultural reality, and the social sciences themselves [as] linguistic constructions" (Brown 1990, p. 188). Authoritative images of what is real are seen to emerge through rhetorical processes in which "peoples establish repertoires of categories by which certain aspects of what is to be the case are fixed, focused, or forbidden" (Brown 1990, p. 191). Postmodern theory critiques the notion that what is real exists separate from the symbols used to convey it. The reality of the social world described by social scientists is viewed as inseparable from the discourse through which social scientists come to designate some descriptions of the world as more legitimate than others. The traditional hierarchy in which reality occupies a privileged status separate from the symbols used to describe it is broken down, or deconstructed. The deconstruction project of postmodern theory not only critiques the separation of reality from symbols describing it but also critiques other hierarchies, such as those separating expert knowledge from common knowledge, and high culture from low. The project even moves to deconstruct the possibility of a generalizing social science, and the idea of a social world (Foucault 1980; Baudrillard 1983). In such bold forms a postmodern sociology becomes a contradiction in terms, undermining its own basis for existence (Turner 1990; Smart 1990; Bauman 1988). However, although a postmodern sociology may be difficult to establish, a sociology of postmodernism that examines postmodern society, and draws from postmodern theory, is possible.

Attempts to characterize postmodern society reflect the contributions of postmodern theory as well as more conventional sociological approaches. From postmodern theory comes a view of postmodern society as a technologically sophisticated, high-speed society with access to vast amounts of information, and fascinated by consumer goods and media images. Mass consumption of goods and information is seen as facilitating a breakdown of hierarchies of taste and development of an explicit populism. Technology and speed blur lines separating reality from simulation as television, videos, movies, advertising, and computer models provide simulations of reality more real than reality. People may realize this hyperreality is simulation, yet are fascinated by it and come to make it part of their lives, thus transforming much of reality into simulation (Baudrillard 1983). Under such conditions history comes to have little meaning, and the fast-paced present becomes increasingly important. People may attempt to come to grips with such a world, but the world comes to undermine major assumptions, or grand narratives, of rationality and progress, thus generating a sense of exhaustion (Lyotard 1984). An acute sense of self-consciousness and unease may develop, as "the current age stumbles upon the very transvaluation of Western values and vocabularies that Nietzsche urged more than a century ago" (Baker 1990, p. 232).

Views of postmodern society from more conventional social science frameworks echo some of these themes. For example, both Daniel Bell (1976) and Christopher Lasch (1979) point to the development of cultural themes in postindustrial society emphasizing consumption and personal gratification at the expense of themes emphasizing self-restraint, work, commitment, and a sense of historical connection and continuity. In a Marxist analysis Fredric Jameson (1984) points to the loss of a sense of historical connection in the consumer-oriented world of late capitalism.

One productive approach to postmodern society starts from the assumption that a central process defining modern society is differentiation. Thus, the type of society coming after modern society is viewed as reversing this process. The process of dedifferentiation is illustrated in the cultural arena in the conflation of high and popular culture noted above, as well as in the general deconstruction project of postmodernist theory (see also Lash 1988). Within the economic arena dedifferentiation appears in the reversal of the processes of bureaucratization and the division of labor characteristic of the assembly line (Clegg 1990). Such trends have been viewed as part of the changing character of production in the world economy since 1960, and have been examined under such terms as the *second industrial divide* (Piore and Sabel 1984) or the *emergence of disorganized capitalism* (Lash and Urry 1987). The changes frequently include a shift to smaller organizations or subunits of organizations, a less formalized and more flexible division of labor, increased variation in the character of products, more decentralized managerial structures, and the use of computers. Such organizations are engaged in services, information processing, or production using computer-controlled, flexible production techniques (Heydebrand 1989; Clegg 1990). The postbureaucratic character of these organizations is made possible by computers that do routine tasks, as well as by the need to respond flexibly to diverse clientele and markets, and the sophisticated capabilities of employees who operate complex manufacturing equipment and provide professional services.

Although postmodern production techniques and organizations are becoming more prominent and important in advanced industrial societies, they may express themselves in different ways and do not eclipse other forms of production and organization. Workers in low-skill tasks in manufacturing and services will likely comprise a substantial segment of the work force far into the future, creating the possibility of increased variation in skill and income in postmodern society (Burris 1989). Also, postmodern organizations can vary substantially among themselves. For example, Clegg (1990) argues that Japan and Sweden stand as alternative expressions of postmodernist futures. Sweden provides the more optimistic democratic scenario with fairly broad representational rights of workers in organizations. Japan represents a less optimistic view with an enclave of privileged workers formed on exclusive principles of social identity, such as gender, ethnicity, and age.

RADICALLY MODERN SOCIETY

Much as critics of the concept of postindustrial society pointed out that postindustrial trends were best seen as the logical extension of major characteristics of industrial society, so Anthony Giddens (1990) questioned the notion that postmodern trends actually represent a break with modern society. Giddens acknowledges current trends of complexity and widespread change accompanied by a lack of a clear sense of progress, and also would likely admit to trends of dedifferentiation in some organizations. However, Giddens does not see this as constituting postmodernity. Instead, he refers to such trends as characterizing radically modern societies, for these societies represent the logical extension of three essential characteristics of modernity. The first characteristic is an increase in complexity, as the major processes of industrialization, class formation, and rationalization proceed apace and shape one another. The second is the separation of much of what humans experience as social reality from concrete instances of time and space. Thus, money represents an element of social reality that designates a mechanism of exchange not bound to any specific instance of exchange, and experts represent specialized knowledge that may be called upon for a variety of purposes at a number of times and places. Science is one of the clearer expressions of such knowledge, with its esoteric and changing images of the character of the natural and physical universe.

As societies become more modern, humans are viewed as increasingly experiencing the world through such abstract, or "disembedded," categories as money, expertise, and science. Realization of the disembedded nature of social life helps facilitate development of the third characteristic of modernity, its reflexivity. As noted earlier, reflexivity refers to the fact that efforts and information used to understand social reality become part of reality, and thus help shape the present and the future. According to Giddens, awareness of reflexivity is not confined to social scientists but is embedded in the nature of modernity. Modern societies generate theories of what they are, which become important constitutive elements that shape society, including the future character of theories. All three of the characteristics of modernity find expression in each of four interrelated institutional complexes: capitalism, the nation-state, the military, and industrialization. Thus, radically modern societies are those in which major institutions are highly complex, abstract or disembedded, and reflexive. Such societies will be more difficult for individuals to understand concretely; will require substantial amounts of trust in abstract and expert systems; and will generate high levels of self-consciousness as persons seek to use personal resources to more reflexively construct personal identity and meaning. Thus, radically modern societies may produce the unease and sense of powerlessness that some postmodern theorists see in postmodern societies. By avoiding the concept of postmodern society, Giddens is able to illustrate how current trends are part of the logic of modernity, and to provide a more optimistic view of the future than some postmodern theorists by underscoring the reflexive and transformative power of ideas and action.

POSTMODERN SOCIETY AND THE WORLD SYSTEM

Most analyses of postindustrial, postmodern, and radically modern societies carry with them a view of societal change occurring within an increasingly interconnected world system. Giddens is quite explicit in this regard, pointing out how the complexity, abstractness, and reflexive character of modernity move beyond the nation-state to become a world-level phenomenon. This is most clearly expressed in the development of a world capitalist system, a nation-state system, a world military order, and an international division of labor. Although Giddens does not systematically consider the dynamics of these aspects of the world system in discussing radical modernity, his conceptualization is a useful reminder of the possible utility of considering multiple dimensions of the world system in efforts to understand postmodern societies. As the review of postindustrial and postmodern literature suggested, most analyses consider the role of the world system in terms of economic exchanges (Bell 1989), new technologies, and new modes of economic organization (Piore and Sabel 1984; Lash and Urry 1987; Clegg 1990).

Analysts have drawn increasing attention to cultural dimensions of the world system (e.g., Featherstone 1990), pointing out how themes associated with modern, postmodern, and postindustrial society have become elements of an emerging world culture (Meyer 1991; Smith 1990; Robertson 1989, 1990). Giddens touched on these themes when he noted how the abstract and reflexive character of modernity has become a global phenomenon, making theories of modernity part of contemporary culture. Meyer (1980, 1991) also notes the role that ideologies of modernity and postindustrialism may play in the contemporary world, pointing out how rationalized conceptions of modern society, including social scientific discourse, have become part of a contemporary world cultural framework. For example, modern images of society that indicate economic development, national integration, and personal and societal progress are the product of individuals with specialized knowledge, are said to have become a world-level assumption, and have generated expansion of educational enrollments between 1950 and 1970 (Meyer et al. 1977; Boli and Ramirez 1986; Fiala and Gordon Lanford 1987).

Relatedly, postindustrial images of the role of specialized knowledge in society are viewed as an important factor affecting the worldwide expansion of higher education and professional employment in the post–World War II era (Meyer and Hannan 1979). Such images may account for part of the 95 percent increase from 1960 to 1980 in the percentage of the labor force employed in professional occupations among forty-three less-developed countries (LDCs), a significant increase considering the substantial population and labor force growth in LDCs during this period. This increase contrasts with an 81 percent increase for the twenty developed countries (DCs) reported earlier and the 31 percent increase for the United States. When comparing percentage point increases, the 3.5 point increase for LDCs falls behind the 6.6 point increase for twenty DCs, although it is greater than the 3.3 point increase for the United States. While economic growth may account for some of these increases in professional employment, the relatively high growth rates for LDCs, especially compared with the United States, indicates that other variables likely play a role. It seems plausible that postindustrial images regarding the importance of specialized knowledge and personnel may have an effect.

CONCLUSION

Efforts to understand the character and future of advanced industrial societies in the latter half of the twentieth century have occurred under the rubric of at least three major concepts. The concept *postindustrial society* focused attention on social structural or economic dimensions of society, especially the changing character of technology, knowledge, occupations, and the market. The concept *postmodern society* continued to bring attention to structural and economic aspects of society, yet gave increased attention to political, cultural, and psychological dimensions, at times with an explicit critique of standard social science methodology. The concept *radically modern society* underscored the links between contemporary changes and the basic dynamics of modernity, while introducing the useful idea that radically modern societies are characterized by high levels of abstractness and reflexivity. Each of the three concepts acknowledges that changes are occurring within an increasingly interconnected world system.

The current review clearly illustrates the reflexive character of much social science. In postindustrial theory this was largely a recognition that formal scientific knowledge may shape the future. In postmodern theory, and especially in radically modern theory, this reflexivity became part of the culture itself, affecting the consciousness of much of the population. This creates a vastly more complex image of society, with a diverse array of possible futures, and may account for the unease that postmodern theory sees as characterizing postmodern society.

While work on postmodern and radically modern society offers insightful ideas, most empirical research has been done on postindustrial society and on economic aspects of postmodern society. Future studies should attempt to examine some of the major elements of postmodern and radically modern approaches, as well as continue to clarify areas of ambiguity within postindustrial theory. For example, within the postindustrial framework attention should be given to understanding the influence of various segments of a knowledge class on specific institutions in society, and to trying to explain national variation in the expansion of various types of service employment. Within the postmodernist framework, it would be informative to assess whether, and to what extent, persons in advanced industrial societies experience a sense of exhaustion regarding the future, and to try to explain national and temporal variation in this area. Relatedly, it would be productive to have the notions of reality and simulation more clearly specified and, if possible, to assess the degree to which individual biographies become simulations. Drawing from the view of radically modern societies, it would be useful to examine the idea that modern cultures increasingly incorporate reflexive elements. One possible project could examine media coverage of the process of news coverage in the 1991 Persian Gulf war, compared with wars in which the United States was involved earlier in the twentieth century. Last, to assess hypotheses regarding the effects of world cultural themes, research could examine the effects of an ideology of specialized knowledge and expertise on expansion of professional employment. The data presented above suggest the plausibility of such an effect but do not offer firm support.

Issues such as those above are but a few of the avenues of research that may help provide a clearer image of the character and future of advanced industrial societies. In posing the issues and in providing answers, social science will likely help shape the future it describes.

(SEE ALSO: *Global Systems Analysis; Information Society; Macrosociology; Technology and Society*)

REFERENCES

Baker, Scott 1990 "Reflection, Doubt, and the Place of Rhetoric in Postmodern Social Theory." *Sociological Theory* 8:232–245.

Baudrillard, Jean 1983 *In the Shadow of the Silent Majorities . . . or the End of the Social.* New York: Jean Baudrillard and Semiotext.

———1988 *Selected Writings.* Mark Poster, ed. Stanford, Calif.: Stanford University Press.

Bauman, Zygmunt 1988 "Is There a Postmodern Sociology?" *Theory, Culture and Society* 5:217–237.

Bell, Daniel 1973 *The Coming of Post-Industrial Society: A Venture in Social Forecasting.* New York: Basic Books.

———1976 *The Cultural Contradictions of Capitalism.* New York: Basic Books.

———1989 "The Third Technological Revolution." *Dissent* 36:164–176.

Block, Fred 1990 *Postindustrial Possibilities: A Critique of Economic Discourse.* Berkeley: University of California Press.

Bogard, William 1990 "Closing Down the Social: Baudrillard's Challenge to Contemporary Sociology." *Sociological Theory* 8:1–15.

Boli, John, and Francisco Ramirez 1986 "World Culture and the Institutional Development of Mass Education." In John Richardson, ed., *Handbook of Theory and Research for the Sociology of Education.* Westport, Conn.: Greenwood Press.

Bookchin, Murray 1971 *Post-Scarcity Anarchism.* Berkeley, Calif.: Ramparts Press.

Brzezinski, Zbigniew 1970 *Between Two Ages: America's Role in the Technocratic Era.* New York: Viking Press.

Brown, Richard Harvey. 1990. "Rhetoric, Textuality, and the Postmodern Turn in Sociological Theory." *Sociological Theory* 8:188–197.

Burris, Beverly 1989 "Technocratic Organization and Control." *Organization Studies* 10:1–22.

Clark, Colin 1960 *The Conditions of Economic Progress,* 3rd ed. New York: Macmillan.

Clegg, Stewart R. 1990 *Modern Organizations: Organization Studies in the Postmodern World.* Newbury Park, Calif.: Sage.

Cohen, Stephen, and John Zysman 1987 *Manufacturing Matters: The Myth of the Post-Industrial Economy.* New York: Basic Books.

Dahrendorf, Ralf 1967 *Society and Democracy in Germany.* Garden City, N.Y.: Doubleday.

Drucker, Peter 1969 *The Age of Discontinuity: Guidelines to Our Changing Society.* New York: Harper & Row.

Etzioni, Amitai 1968 *The Active Society.* New York: Free Press.

Featherstone, Mike 1990 *Global Culture: Nationalism, Globalization and Modernity.* Newbury Park, Calif.: Sage.

Fiala, Robert, and Audri Gordon Lanford 1987 "Educational Ideology and the World Educational Revolution 1950–1970." *Comparative Education Review* 31:315–332.

Foucault, Michel 1980 *Power/Knowledge: Selected Interviews and Other Writings, 1972–1977.* Colin Gordon, ed. and trans. New York: Pantheon.

Frankel, Boris 1987 *The Post-Industrial Utopians.* Cambridge: Polity Press.

Fuchs, Victor 1968 *The Service Economy.* New York: Columbia University Press.

Giddens, Anthony 1990 *The Consequences of Modernity.* Stanford, Calif.: Stanford University Press.

Halmos, P. 1970 *The Personal Service Society.* London: Constable.

Hartwell, R. M. 1973 "The Service Revolution: The Growth of Services in the Modern Economy." In Carlo Cippola, ed., *The Industrial Revolution, 1700–1914.* Brighton, England: Harvester Press.

Heydebrand, Wolf 1989 "New Organizational Forms." *Work and Occupations* 16:323–357.

Ingelhart, Ronald 1977 *The Silent Revolution: Changing Values and Political Styles Among Western Publics.* Princeton, N.J.: Princeton University Press.

International Labour Organization. 1965–1988. *Yearbook of Labor Statistics.* Geneva: ILO.

Jameson, Fredric 1984 "Postmodernism, or the Cultural Logic of Late Capitalism." *New Left Review* 146:59–92.

Kahn, Herman, and Anthony Wiener 1967 *The Year 2000.* New York: Macmillan.

Kumar, Krishnan *Prophecy and Progress: The Sociology of Industrial and Post-Industrial Society.* London: Allen Lane.

———1988 *The Rise of Modern Society.* New York: Basil Blackwell.

Lasch, Christopher 1979 *The Culture of Narcissism.* New York: Norton.

Lash, Scott 1988 "Postmodernism as a Regime of Signification," *Theory, Culture and Society* 5:311–336.

———, and John Urry 1987 *The End of Organized Capitalism.* Madison: University of Wisconsin Press.

Lipset, Seymour 1976 *Rebellion in the University.* Chicago: University of Chicago Press.

Lyotard, Jean-Francois 1984 *The Postmodern Condition.* Minneapolis: University of Minnesota Press.

Meyer, John 1980 "The World Polity and the Authority of the Nation State." In Albert Bergesen, ed., *Studies of the Modern World System.* New York: Academic Press.

———1991 "Concluding Commentary: The Evolution

of Modern Stratification Systems." In David Grusky, ed., *Social Stratification: Class, Race and Gender in Sociological Perspective.* Boulder, Colo.: Westview Press.

Meyer, John, and Michael Hannan 1979 "National Development in a Changing World System: An Overview. In J. Meyer and M. Hannan, eds., *National Development and the World System: Educational, Economic, and Political Change, 1950–1970.* Chicago: University of Chicago Press.

Meyer, John, Francisco Ramirez, Richard Rubinson, and John Boli-Bennett 1977 "The World Educational Revolution, 1950–1970." *Sociology of Education* 50:242–258.

Penty, Arthur 1917 *Old Worlds for New: A Study of the Post-Industrial State.* London: Allen & Unwin.

Piore, Michael, and Charles Sabel 1984 *The Second Industrial Divide: Possibilities for Prosperity.* New York: Basic Books.

Richta, Radovan, et al. 1969 *Civilization at the Crossroads: Social and Human Implications of the Scientific and Technological Revolution,* 3rd ed. New York: International Arts and Sciences Press.

Ritzer, George 1989 "The Permanently New Economy: The Case for Reviving Economic Sociology." *Work and Occupations* 16:243–272.

Robertson, Roland 1990 "Mapping the Global Condition: Globalization as the Central Concept." In Mike Featherstone, ed., *Global Culture: Nationalism, Globalization and Modernity.* Newbury Park, Calif.: Sage.

——— 1989 "Globalization, Politics and Religion." In J. A. Beckford and T. Luckmann, eds., *The Changing Face of Religion.* Newbury Park, Calif.: Sage.

Smart, Barry 1990 "Modernity, Postmodernity and the Present." In Bryan S. Turner, ed., *Theories of Modernity and Postmodernity.* Newbury Park, Calif.: Sage.

Smith, Anthony 1990 "Towards a Global Culture?" In Mike Featherstone, ed., *Global Culture: Nationalism, Globalization and Modernity.* Newbury Park, Calif.: Sage.

Touraine, Alain 1971 *The Post-Industrial Society.* New York: Random House.

Turner, Bryan 1990 "Periodization and Politics in the Postmodern." In Bryan S. Turner, ed., *Theories of Modernity and Postmodernity.* Newbury Park, Calif.: Sage.

U.S. Bureau of the Census 1975 *Historical Statistics of the United States,* Part I, *Colonial Times to 1970.* Washington D.C.: U.S. Government Printing Office.

———1990 *Statistical Abstract of the United States 1990: The National Data Book.* Washington D.C.: U.S. Government Printing Office.

World Bank 1980 *World Development Report 1980.* New York: Oxford University Press.

———1988 *World Development Report 1988.* New York: Oxford University Press.

ROBERT FIALA

POSTMODERNISM In 1959, C. Wright Mills speculated that "the Modern Age is being succeeded by a post-modern period" in which assumptions about the coherence of the Enlightenment values of scientific rationality and political freedom were being challenged (1959, p. 166). Critical theorists had earlier speculated about how the revolutionary potential of the urban laboring classes of the nineteenth century was co-opted by the shift to a postindustrial twentieth-century society, a society characterized by mass consumerism and war economies. The characteristics of postindustrial societies were explored more recently in Daniel Bell's analysis of contemporary capitalism (1976). In the modern information societies, Bell argues that the class forces that drove nineteenth-century social change have been replaced by new processes. Under welfare capitalist states, scientists, technicians, managers, and bureaucrats formulate social tensions as administrative and technical issues based on political consensus. For Bell, postindustrial societies with their information bases hold the key to social harmony and the end of misery.

Alain Touraine's view (1984) is different. He also stresses how class antagonism has changed under welfare capitalism, but for Touraine the information managers, guided by technological thinking, tend to "steer the entire social order toward the perfectly programmed society, the ultimate technocratic prison" (Baum 1990, p. 5). Touraine also writes that the categories of basic sociological analysis have become out of touch with changes in contemporary societies. In particular, he rejects the modernist supposition of evolutionary progress over time, culminating in what he calls "the impoverishing homogeneity of modern civilization" (Touraine 1984, p. 38), the sociologist's conception of the national states as units of analysis, and the gradual expunging of the cultural diversity of traditional societies. The collapse of modernism arises from a failure of sociology to keep abreast of the developing autonomy of cultural products, the globalization of capital, and the rise of new forms of social control and of public resistance to them. In this analysis, "the crisis of modernity . . . is not all-encompassing . . . the crisis in modernity is not considered to be total or terminal but limited in scope, if deep" (Smart 1990, p. 408). Though Bell and Touraine have been associated with critiques of postindustrial societies, the meaning of "postmodernism" has become far more radical, and draws on earlier sources.

De Saussure's "structural" theory of linguistics (1959) distinguished the "sign" from the "signified" and developed a science based on the discovery that symbolic systems might have formal properties that were unrelated to the meanings of the objects they signified but that might hold across different systems of symbols. The system for describing, for example, the animal kingdom and the protocols for siting teepees might reflect the same logic—without any inherent equivalence to the things they described or organized (Giddens 1987). "Poststructuralism" deepened this disinterest in the signified objects by dismissing any link binding words/symbols to things. Things were only the hypostatizations of language. All analysis was "deconstruction," or unmasking of phenomena in terms of their underlying rhetorical conventions. For poststructuralists, texts only pointed to other texts. The world was viewed as an intertwining of systems of representation without any derivation from or basis within "terra firma." Everything became text—including violent speech and violent symbolic acts such as incest, war, or spousal abuse.

The postmodern twist is the application of the linguistic implications of poststructuralism to the three core principles connecting contemporary civilizations with the project of the Enlightenment: scientific knowledge (Truth), aesthetics (Beauty), and morality (the Good). The Enlightenment project—"modernism"—refers to the rise of the Age of Reason. It was characterized by the gradual shift away from religious sensibilities and to scientific objectivity, the rational exploitation of nature for human needs, the perspectival representation of nature in art and humanistic truth in fiction, and the struggle for a humane society. Modernism was realist in its epistemology and progressive in its politics. Truth could be attained —particularly with scientific advances. Beauty could be distinguished from trash. Humanism could nurture moral conduct and decent conditions of life. And history was purposive and progressive.

Postmodernism is the sensibility that arises when the credibility of these "master narratives" is questioned. The postmodern period, as described by Lyotard (1984) and Baudrillard (1983), is the one we now confront. Though it is often dated as a creature of the post-World War II period, it is thought only to have become generalized with mass consumerism in the age of electronics and to have been initiated by dramatic changes in contemporary capitalism. Capitalism has ushered in global communication and exchange, and has created a self-sustaining cybernetic system that almost completely transcends the ability of individual governments to control their directions and objectives. As a result, postmodernity is sometimes referred to as posthistorical society in the sense that the mission or sense of purpose that guided nation-states in the past through events such as the French Revolution has been overtaken by global consumerism. The view of history as a struggle for the gradual liberation of humanity and progressive evolution of more humane societies is dismissed by Lyotard as mythic. In addition, the transcendence of communities by electronic representations makes the idea of "the social" purely illusory (Bogard 1990). The objectivity of societies, nation-states, communities, and history is viewed only as "narratives" or "simulacra" (Baudrillard 1983). Referents disappear in favor of a world of simulations, models, performatives, and codes—in short, "information" (broadly conceived), which becomes the predominant phenomenon of exchange among the masses through the mass media.

One of the important theoretical aspects of the postmodernist position is its explicit rejection of Marxism in general and Habermas' theorizing about creating a rational society through communicative competence. Where Habermas (1973, p. 105) speculates that a rational community might be able to "arrive at the conviction that in the given circumstances the proposed norms are 'right,' " Lyotard rejects the myth of reason behind the Habermasian project. The project implies that there is a correct moral and scientific standard to which communities ought to aspire. Enforcement of such standards valorize conformity and, as witnessed in the fascist European states in the 1920s and 1930s, promote terrorism to extract it. This introduces a tension within postmodernism that has not been worked through (Frank 1990). On the positive side, the supposition of "multivocality" in scientific and moral discourse promotes the "excavation" of minority voices and minority experiences which have been occluded in "master" modernist ways of thinking. Every point of view can be heard, none can be privileged. On the other side, postmodernism seems ill equipped to distinguish between any particular moral or objective position and any other, including the fascist discourse that is associated with modernism. Choosing between Holocaust history and Holocaust denial would seem in principle to be a matter of rhetorical preference —which is clearly nihilistic.

When we move away from epistemology to postmodernity's impact on art and architecture, the situation is different. Postmodernism celebrates a rejection of hegemonic traditions and styles by mixing elements from competing schools and by bringing the rim of representation into focus as an organic element of the depiction. Novels exploit the discontinuities in perspective and the fragmentations in contemporary society. In architecture, postmodernism represents a repudiation of high-density ("efficient") functionality based on centralized city planning with an emphasis on no-frill construction. Decentralized planning emphasizes collage and eclecticism and the development of spaces to heighten aesthetic possibilities (Harvey 1989). The globalization of experience encourages such exchanges and experimentation. However, the replacement of "efficient" spaces like public housing, with their brutalizing side effects, with more particularistic designs is part of the emancipatory interest of modernity—so that at least here, postmodernity is still part and parcel of the Enlightenment. This raises three questions.

To what extent has the case been made that the changes in capitalism during the past two decades have been so profound as to represent a destruction of modernist society and a disappearance of history and "the social" (i.e., real face-to-face community)? Some critics dispute the claim (Baum 1990); others point out that Baudrillard's evidence is unconvincing since his own postmodern manner of exposition is self-consciously rhetorical, inflationary, and, consistent with the idiom, only one possible reading of recent history (Smart 1990). Secondly, if we have no careful (i.e., modernist) analysis of the factors that have contributed to the demise of our confidence in the "master narratives" of modernism, would it not seem to be impossible to discern which ones have been shaken, and how seriously our confidence in them has been eroded? Skepticism is insufficient. Finally, under these circumstances, is it not predictable that there is no consensus about the meaning of postmodernism? Arguably this dissensus is inherent in the perspective. For Baudrillard (1983), postmodernism spells the end of sociology (and other modernist subjects); for Bauman (1988), it is simply a new topic—a sociology of postmodernism, but not a postmodern sociology. For Brown (1990), it is an opportunity to rethink the continuing relevance of the role of rhetoric in politics and science in order to employ knowledge in guiding human conduct. Under these circumstances, the proclamation of the death of modernism would seem premature.

(SEE ALSO: *Popular Culture; Postindustrial Society; Social Philosophy*)

REFERENCES

Baudrillard, Jean 1983 *In the Shadow of the Silent Majorities*. New York: Semiotext(e).

Baum, Gregory 1990 "The Postmodern Age." *Canadian Forum* (May): 5–7.

Bauman, Z. 1988 "Is There a Postmodern Sociology?" *Postmodernism*, special issue of *Theory, Culture and Society* 5(2–3):217–238.

Bell, Daniel 1976 *The Cultural Contradictions of Capitalism*. New York: Basic Books.

Bogard, William 1990 "Closing Down the Social: Baudrillard's Challenge to Contemporary Sociology." *Sociological Theory* 8(1):1–15.

Brown, Richard H. 1990 "Rhetoric, Textuality, and the Postmodern Turn in Sociological Theory." *Sociological Theory* 8(2):188–197.

Frank, Arthur 1990, "Postmodern Sociology/Postmodern Review." *Symbolic Interactionism* 14(1):93–100.

Giddens, Anthony 1987 "Structuralism, Post-structuralism and the Production of Culture." In A. Giddens and J. Turner, eds., *Social Theory Today*. Stanford, Calif.: Stanford University Press.

Habermas, J. 1973 *Legitimation Crisis*. Boston: Beacon Books.

Harvey, David 1989 *The Condition of Postmodernity*. Oxford: Blackwell.

Lyotard, Jean-Francois 1984 *The Postmodern Condition: A Report on Knowledge*. Minneapolis: University of Minnesota Press.

Mills, C. Wright 1959 *The Sociological Imagination*. New York: Oxford University Press.

Saussure, Ferdinand de 1959 *Course in General Linguistics*. C. Bally and A. Sechehaye, eds.; Wade Baskin, trans. New York: McGraw-Hill.

Smart, Barry 1990 "On the Disorder of Things: Sociology, Postmodernity and 'The End of the Social.'" *Sociology* 24:397–416.

Touraine, Alain 1984 "The Waning Sociological Image of Social Life." *International Journal of Comparative Sociology* 25:33–44.

AUGUSTINE BRANNIGAN

POVERTY Concerning poverty, scholarly as well as ideological debate has long centered on the most elementary questions: What is poverty? How can it be measured? What causes it? Is it a natural phenomenon or a symptom of a poorly ordered society? Although answers exist for all of these questions, no definitive answer exists for any one of them; nor can there ever be, for the questions are not purely demographic but moral, ethical, and political as well. Poverty is a concept, not a fact, and must be understood as such. If no definitive answers are possible, this does not mean that all other answers are thereby equal, since many may be based on ignorant assumptions and ill-formed judgments. Sociologists involved in poverty research seek to be sure that all understand the meaning and consequences of various points of view and that both theoretical and policy research are based soundly, on clear definitions and reliable data.

Even the definition of poverty is problematic. The word derives from the French *pauvre* (meaning "poor"), and means simply the state of lacking material possessions, of having little or no means to support oneself. All would agree that anyone lacking the means necessary to remain alive is in poverty, but beyond that there is little agreement. Some scholars and policy makers would draw the poverty line at the bare subsistence level, as did Rowntree (1902): "the minimum necessaries for the maintenance of merely physical efficiency." Others argue for definitions that include persons whose level of living is above subsistence but who have inadequate means; among those holding to the latter, further arguments concern the definition of adequacy. Social science cannot resolve the most basic arguments. For example, the level of living implied by the poverty threshold in the United States would be seen as desirable and unattainable in many other countries, yet few would suggest that poverty in the United States be defined by such outside standards. Sociologists can evaluate the demographic and economic assumptions underlying standards of poverty, but not the standards themselves.

CONCEPTIONS OF POVERTY

Poverty can be defined in absolute or relative terms. The subsistence line is a good example of an absolute definition. A criterion based on some arbitrary formula, such that poverty equals some fraction of the median income or below, is a good example of a relative definition. In all industrial societies an absolute definition will result in far fewer persons officially in poverty than will a relative definition, creating natural political pressure for absolute definitions (e.g., a study in 1976 revealed that if poverty was defined as 50 percent of the median income, data on income distributions would show that an unchanging 19 percent of the population would have been poor for almost the previous two decades; see U.S. Department of Health, Education, and Welfare 1976). Beyond that, there are valid arguments for both types of definitions. There is evidence that most people see poverty in relative terms rather than as an absolute standard (Rainwater 1974; Kilpatrick 1973). That is, popular conceptions of what level of living constitutes poverty have been found to change as general affluence goes up and down. Advocates of relative measures point out that any absolute measure is arbitrary and thus meaningless. A reasonable definition of the poor, they argue, should be one that demarcates the lower tail of the income distribution as the poor, whatever the absolute metric represented by that tail, for those persons will be poor by the standards of that time and place. As the average level of income rises and falls, what is seen as poverty will, and should, change.

Advocates of absolute measures of poverty do not deny that poverty is intimately tied to distributional inequality, but they argue that relative definitions are too vague for policy purposes. An absolute standard, defined on some concrete level of living, is a goal that can possibly be attained. Once it is attained, a new goal could be set. Eliminating poverty as defined by relative standards is a far more difficult goal, both practically and politically. Marshall (1981, p. 52) noted: "the question of what range of inequality is acceptable above the 'poverty line' can only marginally, if at all, be affected by or affect the decision of where that line should be drawn."

Relative versus absolute poverty is a distributional distinction, but there are other important ones as well. A social distinction, and one with considerable political import, is that usually made between the deserving poor and the undeserving poor. In their brief summary of the historical origins of this distinction, Morris and Williamson (1986, pp. 6–12) maintain that it became significant in the fourteenth century, when, for a variety of reasons (the decline of feudalism, the rise of a market economy with concomitant periodic labor dislocations, bubonic plague-induced regional labor shortages), the poor became geographically mobile for the first time. Before that, the local Catholic parish, with its "blessed are the poor" theology, was the primary caretaker of the indigent. Mobility caused an increase in the number of able-bodied individuals needing temporary assistance, and troubles arising from their presence contributed to a growing antipathy toward the able-bodied poor. Feagin (1975, Chapter 2) locates the origins of negative attitudes toward the poor in the Protestant Reformation. Under Protestantism, he notes, the "work ethic"—the ideology of individualism—became a central tenet of the Western belief system. Poverty, in the extreme Calvinist version of this viewpoint, is largely a consequence of laziness and vice and can even be regarded as just punishment from a righteous God. The rise of Puritan thought contributed to the increasing disfavor with which the unemployed and destitute were regarded. It became a matter of faith that poverty was individually caused and must thereby be individually cured. These ideas became secularized, and programs to aid the poor thereafter focused on curing the individual faults that led to poverty—potential problems in the structure of society that caused unemployment and underemployment were not to be scrutinized in search of a solution. The notion of poverty continues to be in flux. As Marshall (1981) noted, the concept has been with us since antiquity, but its meaning has not been constant through the ages.

THEORY AND POLICY

The epitome of the individual viewpoint in the social sciences was the once-dominant "culture of poverty" explanation for destitution. Oscar Lewis (1961; 1966) is usually credited with this idea, which sees poverty not only as economic deprivation, or the absence of something, but also as a way of life, the presence of specific subcultural values and attitudes passed down from generation to generation. Lewis saw the structure of life among the poor as functional, a set of coping mechanisms without which the poor could not survive their harsh circumstances. But there were negative consequences of the value system as well, he noted. Family life was disorganized, there was an absence of childhood as a prolonged life-cycle stage, a proliferation of consensual marriages, and a very high incidence of spouse and child abandonment—all of which left individuals unprepared and unable to take advantage of opportunities. Exacerbating the problem, the poor were divorced from participation in and integration into the major institutions of society, leading to constant hostility, suspicion, and apathy. Many have maintained that the culture of poverty viewpoint dovetailed perfectly into a politically liberal view of the world. It blamed the poor as a group for their poverty but held no single person individually responsible, nor did it blame the structure of the economy or the society. This view of the poor led to antipoverty policies directed at changing the attitudes and values of those in poverty so that they could "break out" of the dysfunctional cultural traits they had inherited. It led political liberals and radicals to attempt to "organize the poor." Political conservatives transformed the explanation into one that held the poor more culpable individually and the problem into one that was intractable—"benign neglect" being then the only sensible solution (Banfield 1958; 1970; Katz 1989).

There are many problems with the culture of poverty explanation. Most serious was the fact that the cultural scenario simply does not fit. Only a minority of the poor are poor throughout their lives; most move in and out of poverty. Also, a substantial proportion of those in poverty are either women with children who fell into poverty when abandoned by a spouse, or the elderly who became poor when their worklife ended—neither event could be explained by the culture of the class of destination. Many studies falsified specific aspects of the culture of poverty thesis (for a review see Katz 1989, pp. 41 ff.), and Rodman's (1971) influential notion of the "lower-class value stretch" offered an alternative explanation. Rodman argued that the poor actually share mainstream values but must "stretch" them to fit their circumstances. Remove the poverty, and they fit neatly into the dominant culture, Rodman believed. Furthermore, attempts to alter their "culture" are unnecessary and meaningless, since "culture" is not the problem.

Nonetheless, the culture of poverty thesis was (and to some extent still is) a very popular explanation for poverty. This is probably so, in part, because it fits so well the individualistic biases of the majority of Americans. Surveys of attitudes toward poverty have shown that most people prefer "individualistic" explanations of poverty, those that place the responsibility for poverty primarily on the poor themselves. A minority of Americans have subscribed to "structural" explanations that blame external social and economic factors, and in the early 1970s this minority consisted largely of the young, the less educated, lower income groups, nonwhites, and Jews (Feagin 1975, p. 98).

One of the most influential recent works on poverty policy has been that of Murray (1984). Murray argued that the viewpoint that individuals ultimately caused their own poverty changed in the 1960s to the viewpoint that the structure of society was ultimately responsible. This alteration in the intellectual consensus, which freed the poor from responsibility for their poverty, was fatally misguided, he argues, and caused great damage to the poor. Despite enormously increased expenditures on social welfare from 1965 on, he maintains, progress against poverty ceased at that point. In the face of steadily improving economic conditions, the period 1965 to 1980 was marked by increases in poverty, family breakdown, crime, and voluntary unemployment. Murray argues that this occurred precisely because of the increased expenditures on social welfare, not despite them. Work incentive declined during these years because of government policies that rewarded lack of employment and nonintact family structure. It is a standard economic principle that any activity that is subsidized will tend to increase. Murray's arguments have had policy impact but have been subject to extensive criticism by students of the field.

As evidence of the disincentive to work brought about by social welfare payments, Murray cites the Negative Income Tax (NIT) experiments. These were large social experiments designed to assess the effects of a guaranteed income. The first NIT experiment was a four-year study in New Jersey from the late 1960s to the early 1970s. In this study, 1,375 intact "permanently poor" families were selected, and 725 of them were assigned to one of eight NIT plans. It was found that the reduction in labor market activity for males caused by a guaranteed income was not significant but that there were some reductions for females (5 to 10 percent of activity), most of which could be explained by the substitution of labor market activity for increased child care (home employment). In a larger NIT study conducted throughout the 1970s, the Seattle-Denver Income Maintenance Experiment (usually referred to in the literature as the SIME-DIME study), much larger work disincentives were found, about 10 percent for men, 20 percent for their spouses, and up to 30 percent for women heading single-family households (see Haveman 1987, Chapter 9, for an excellent summary of the many NIT experiments). Murray offered these findings as evidence that existing welfare programs contributed to poverty by creating work disincentives. Cain (1985) pointed out that the experiments provided much higher benefits than existing welfare programs and also noted that, given the low pay for women at that level, the 20 percent reduction for wives would have a trivial effect on family income. If it resulted in a proportionate substitution of work at home, the reduction could actually lead to an improvement in the lives of the poor. Commentators have presented arguments against almost every point made by Murray, insisting that either his measures or interpretations are wrong. For example, Murray's measure of economic growth, the GNP, did increase throughout the 1970s, but real wages declined, and inflation and unemployment increased—poverty was not increasing during good times, as he argues. His other assertions have been similarly challenged (see McLanahan et al. 1985 and Katz 1989, Chapter 4, for summaries), but the broad viewpoint his work represents remains important in policy deliberations.

MEASURES OF POVERTY

In the United States, official poverty estimates are based on the Orshansky Index. The index is named for Mollie Orshansky of the Social Security Administration, who first proposed it (Orshansky 1965). It is an absolute poverty measure based on the calculated cost of food sufficient for an adequate nutritional level and on the assumption that people must spend one-third of their after-tax income on food. Thus, the poverty level is theoretically three times the annual cost of a nutritionally adequate "market basket." This cost was refined by stratifying poor families by size, composition, and farm or nonfarm residence and creating different income cutoffs for poverty for families of differing types. Originally there were 124 income cutoff points, but by 1980 the separate thresholds for farm families and female-headed households had been eliminated and the number of thresholds reduced to forty-eight. Since 1969 the poverty line has been updated regularly using the consumer price index to adjust for increased costs. The original index was based on the least costly of four nutritionally adequate food plans developed by the Department of Agriculture. Since a 1955 Department of Agriculture survey of food consumption patterns had determined that families of three or more spent approximately one-third of their income on food, the original poverty index was simply triple the average cost of the economy food plan. This index was altered for smaller families to compensate for their higher fixed costs and for farm families to compensate for their lower costs (the farm threshold began as 70 percent of the nonfarm for an equivalent household and was raised to 85 percent in 1969). Originally, the poverty index was adjusted yearly by taking into account the cost of the food items in the Department of Agriculture economy budget, but this changed in 1969 to a simple consumer price index adjustment (U.S. Bureau of the Census 1982).

Over the years there have been many criticisms of the official poverty measure and its assumptions (for summaries and extended discussion see U.S. Department of Health, Education, and Welfare 1976; Haveman 1987). The first set of problems, some argue, come from the fact that the very basis of the measure is flawed. The economy food budget at the measure's core is derived from an outdated survey that may not reflect changes in tastes and options. Further, the multiplication of food costs by three is only appropriate for some types of families; other types must spend greater or lesser proportions on food. Some estimates indicate that the poor spend one-half or more of their income on food; the more well-to-do spend one-third or less. And, even if the multiplier was correct, the original Department of Agriculture survey discovered it for post-tax income; in the poverty measure it is applied to pre-tax income, though the poor pay little in taxes. Other problems often cited include the fact that the "economy budget" assumes sufficient knowledge for wise shopping—a dubious assumption for the poor—and the fact that the poor are often locked into paying much higher prices than average because of a lack of transportation. An additional problem is that the poverty thresholds are not updated by using changes in the actual price of food but instead by changes in the consumer price index, which includes changes in the price of many other items such as clothing, shelter, transportation, fuel, medical fees, recreation, furniture, appliances, personal services, and many other items probably irrelevant to the expenses of the poor. Findings are mixed, but it is generally agreed that the losses in purchasing power suffered by the poor in inflationary periods is understated by the consumer price index (see Oster, Lake, and Oksman 1978, p. 25). A second set of problems derives from the fact that the definition is based on income only. Both in-kind transfers and assets are excluded. Excluding in-kind transfers means that government-provided food, shelter, or medical care is not counted. Excluding assets means that a wealthy family with little current taxable or reportable income might be counted as poor.

DEMOGRAPHY OF POVERTY

In 1987 the average poverty threshold for a family of four was $11,611 per year (all figures in this paragraph are from U.S. Bureau of the Census 1989; 1990). This means the assumed annual cost of an adequate diet for four persons was $3,870.33, or about 88 cents per meal per person. For a single person the poverty threshold was $5,778 and the food allowance $1.76 per meal. In 1986 the same poverty threshold was $11,203, allowing 85 cents per meal, and in 1988 it had risen to $12,091, or 92 cents per meal. In the United States in 1987 there were 32,341,000 persons below the poverty threshold, or 13.4 percent of the population. In 1988 there were 31,878,000, or 13.1 percent, almost one-half million fewer persons below official poverty than the year before. These figures underestimate official poverty somewhat since they are based on the Current Population Survey, which is primarily a household survey and thus does not count the homeless not in shelters. The decline from 1987 to 1988 in the number in poverty is part of a long-term trend. In 1960 there were eight million more—39,851,000 persons—who by today's guidelines would have been counted as officially in poverty, representing 22.2 percent of the population. By the official, absolute standard, poverty has greatly decreased since the early 1960s, both in terms of the actual number of persons below the threshold and, even more dramatically, in terms of the percentage of the population in poverty (U.S. Bureau of the Census 1989). This decrease was actually over two decades, since the number in poverty in 1970 had declined to only 25,420,000, or 12.6 percent of the population, and the number and percentage has risen since then, but never back as high as the 1960 levels. Poverty is not evenly spread over the population. Of those below the official poverty level in 1988, 57.1 percent were female, 29.6 percent were black, and 16.9 percent were Hispanic. Female-headed families with children were disproportionately poor. In 1988, 38.2 percent of all such white families were in poverty, and 56.3 percent of all such black families were in poverty (this is a gender phenomenon, not a single-parent one, since in 1988 only 18 percent of male-headed single-parent families were below the poverty threshold). The age composition of the poor population has changed. In 1968, 38.6 percent of those in poverty were of working age (eighteen to sixty-four), while twenty years later 49.6 percent of those in poverty were of working age. From 1968 to 1988 the proportion of the poor population over sixty-five declined from 18.2 percent to 10.9 percent, and the proportion that were children under eighteen declined from 43.1 percent to 39.5 percent. A higher percentage of working-age poor is seen by some as a sign of worse times. It almost certainly reflects not only economic downturns but also in part ideological biases toward helping the presumedly able-bodied poor; most antipoverty programs have been specifically aimed at the old or the young.

Despite extensive debate about the policy implications of various definitions of poverty, one can have confidence that the poor are being counted with considerable precision. More than one generation of social scientists has contributed to the refinement of the measures of poverty, and existing statistical series are based on data collected by the U.S. Bureau of the Census—an organization whose technical competence is unparalleled. Nonetheless, there is one group, the extremely poor, whose numbers are in doubt. All current measurement relies on the household unit and assumes some standard type of domicile. As Rossi (1989, p. 73) puts it, "our national unemployment and poverty statistics pertain only to that portion of the domiciled population that lives in conventional housing." An extremely poor person living, perhaps temporarily, in a household where other adults had sufficient income would not be counted in poverty. Even more important, the literally homeless who live on the street, and those whose homes consist of hotels, motels, rooming houses, or shelters are not counted at all in the yearly Current Population Survey (the decennial census does attempt to count those in temporary quarters, but the 1990 census was the first even to attempt to count those housed in unconventional ways or not at all). The studies of Rossi and his colleagues indicate that the number of extremely poor people in the United States (those whose income is less than two-thirds of the poverty level) is somewhere between 4 and 7 million. The number of literally homeless poor people, those who do not figure into the official poverty counts, must be estimated. The best available estimate is that they number between 250,000 and 350,000, about 5 to 8 percent of the extremely poor population (Rossi 1989). The number of extremely poor people has more than doubled since 1970, while the population has increased by only 20 percent (Rossi 1989, p. 78). The extremely poor are at considerable risk of becoming literally homeless. When they do so, they will disappear from official statistics (just as the unemployed cease being officially unemployed soon after they run out of benefits and/or give up the search for work). To see that official statistics remain reliable in the face of increasing extreme poverty is the most recent methodological challenge in the field.

The study of poverty is a difficult field and is not properly a purely sociological endeavor. As even this brief overview shows, a thorough understanding requires the combined talents of sociologists, economists, demographers, political scientists, historians, and philosophers. All of these fields have contributed to our understanding of the phenomenon.

(SEE ALSO: *Homelessness; Income Distribution in the United States; Social Mobility; Social Stratification*)

REFERENCES

Banfield, Edward C. 1958 *The Moral Basis of a Backward Society.* New York: Free Press.

———1970 *The Unheavenly City.* Boston: Little, Brown.

Cain, Glen 1985 "Comments on Murray's Analysis of the Impact of the War on Poverty on the Labor Market Behavior of the Poor." In Sara McLanahan, et al. *Losing Ground: A Critique*. Special Report no. 38. Madison: University of Wisconsin, Institute for Research on Poverty.

Feagin, Joe R. 1975 *Subordinating the Poor: Welfare and American Beliefs*. Englewood Cliffs, N.J.: Prentice-Hall.

Haveman, Robert H. 1987 *Poverty Policy and Poverty Research: The Great Society and the Social Sciences*. Madison: University of Wisconsin Press.

Katz, Michael B. 1989 *The Undeserving Poor: From the War on Poverty to the War on Welfare*. New York: Pantheon Books.

Kilpatrick, R. W. 1973 "The Income Elasticity of the Poverty Line." *Review of Economics and Statistics* 55:327–332.

Lewis, Oscar 1961 *The Children of Sanchez*. New York: Random House.

———1966 *La Vida: A Puerto Rican Family in the Culture of Poverty—San Juan and New York*. New York: Random House.

Marshall, T. H. 1981 *The Right to Welfare and Other Essays*. New York: Free Press.

McLanahan, Sara, et al. 1985 *Losing Ground: A Critique*. Special Report no. 38. Madison: University of Wisconsin, Institute for Research on Poverty.

Morris, Michael, and John B. Williamson 1986 *Poverty and Public Policy: An Analysis of Federal Intervention Efforts*. Westport, Conn.: Greenwood Press.

Murray, Charles 1984 *Losing Ground: American Social Policy, 1950–1980* New York: Basic Books.

Orshansky, Mollie 1965 "Counting the Poor: Another Look at the Poverty Profile." *Social Security Bulletin* 28(1): 3–29.

Oster, Sharon M., Elizabeth E. Lake, and Conchita Gene Oksman 1978 *The Definition and Measurement of Poverty* Boulder, Colo.: Westview Press.

Rainwater, Lee 1974 *What Money Buys: Inequality and the Social Meaning of Income*. New York: Basic Books.

Rodman, Hyman 1971 *Lower-Class Families: The Culture of Poverty in Negro Trinidad*. London: Oxford University Press.

Rossi, Peter H. 1989 *Down and Out in America: The Origins of Homelessness*. Chicago: University of Chicago Press.

Rowntree, B. S. 1902 *Poverty: A Study of Town Life* London: Macmillan.

U.S. Bureau of the Census 1982 "Changes in the Definition of Poverty." *Current Population Reports*. Series P-60, no. 133. Washington, D.C.: U.S. Government Printing Office.

———1989 "Poverty in the United States: 1987." *Current Population Reports*. Series P-60, no. 163. Washington, D.C.: U.S. Government Printing Office.

———1989b "Money Income and Poverty Status in the United States: 1988." *Current Population Reports*. Series P-60, no. 166. Washington, D.C.: U.S. Government Printing Office.

———1990 "Measuring the Effect of Benefits and Taxes on Income and Poverty: 1989." *Current Population Reports*. Series P-60, no. 169-RD. Washington, D.C.: U.S. Government Printing Office.

U.S. Department of Health, Education, and Welfare 1976 *The Measure of Poverty: A Report to Congress as Mandated by the Education Amendments of 1974*. Washington, D.C.: U.S. Government Printing Office.

WAYNE J. VILLEMEZ

POWER *See* Interpersonal Power.

PRAGMATISM Pragmatism, whose Greek root word means action, grew out of a turn-of-the-century reaction in American philosophy to Enlightenment conceptions of science, human nature, and social order. Generally, it has sought to reconcile incompatibilities between philosophical idealism and realism. In the former, reality is conceived as existing only in human experience and subjectivity and is given in the form of perceptions and ideas. In the latter, reality is proposed as existing in the form of essences or absolutes that are independent of human experience. These two traditions have grounded different approaches to empiricism and in their extremes can be found, respectively, in the solipsism of the British philosopher George Berkeley and the positivistic embracement of natural law by the French sociologist Auguste Comte.

As a response and alternative to these traditions, pragmatism has not been developed as a unified philosophical system. Rather, it has existed as a related set of core ideas and precepts that are expressed as versions or applications of pragmatic thought. Variation within that thought ranges across the realism–idealism continuum and is largely a function of different analytical agendas. Despite that variation, however, pragmatism has become quite broad in its application to theoretical and research problems. Acknowledged as the most distinctive and profound contribution of American intellectual thought, its influence can be found in all contemporary disciplines in the humanities and social sciences. Its intellectual roots are described in Rucker (1969), Martindale (1960), and Konvitz and Kennedy (1960), and its core ideas are described in Shalin (1986), Rochberg-Halton (1986), and Rosenthal (1986).

MAIN IDEAS AND VARIATIONS

In summary form, the main ideas embodying the thrust of pragmatism are as follows. First, humans are active, creative organisms, empowered with agency rather than passive responders to stimuli. Second, human life is a dialectical process of continuity and discontinuity and therefore is inherently emergent. Third, humans shape their worlds and thus actively produce the conditions of freedom and constraint. Fourth, subjectivity is not prior to social conduct but instead flows from it. Minds (intelligence) and selves (consciousness) are emergent from action and exist dialectically as social and psychical processes rather than only as psychic states. Fifth, intelligence and consciousness are potential solutions to practical problems of human survival and quality of life. Sixth, science is a form of adjustive intelligibility and action that is useful in guiding society. Seventh, truth and value reside simultaneously in group perspectives and the human consequences of action. Eighth, human nature and society exist in and are sustained by symbolic communication and language. In these core ideas can be seen the neo-Hegelian focus on dialectical processes and the concurrent rejection of Cartesian dualisms, the Darwinian focus on the emergence of forms and variation through adjustive processes, and the behavioristic focus on actual conduct as the locus of reality and understanding. These ideas were embraced and developed by a variety of scholars and thinkers, including Ralph Waldo Emerson, Percy Bridgman, C. I. Lewis, Morris Cohen, Sidney Hook, Charles Morris, Charles Peirce, William James, Charles Horton Cooley, John Dewey, and George Herbert Mead. The latter five will be reviewed here for purposes of assessing the relevance of pragmatism to social science and sociology.

Charles S. Peirce (1839–1914) is generally credited as the originator of the term *pragmatism* and the formulation of some of its basic tenets. One of his earliest statements (1877–1878) pertained to methods for resolving doubt about conclusions, in which he argued in favor of science because of its flexibility and self-correcting processes. This view contrasts sharply with the Cartesian basis of science in subjectivism and individualism proposed by Descartes. Rather than focusing on belief and consciousness as definitive, Peirce focused on probability. Both truth and scientific rationality rest in a community of opinion in the form of perpetual doubt and through a process of revisions are measured in terms of movement toward the clarification of ideas. The emphasis in this process is both evolutionary, since Peirce saw modes of representing knowledge moving from chance (firstness) to brute existence (secondness) to generality or order (thirdness), and pragmatic, since truth is meaningful only in terms of future consequences for human conduct (the "pragmatic rule").

William James (1842–1910) was driven by the problem of determinism and free will. This problem was expressed in his monumental *Principles of Psychology* (1890), in which he established a functional view assimilating biology and psychology and treated intelligence as an instrument of human survival, and in his brilliant analysis of consciousness (1904), in which he characterized human experience as an ongoing flow instead of a series of psychic states. Pragmatist principles were sharply articulated in these works. He accepted Peirce's pragmatic rule that the meaning of anything resides in experimental consequences. Accordingly, the distinction between subject and object as fundamental was denied and was replaced with the idea that relations between the knower and the known are produced by and in ongoing experience. This more dialectical conceptualization informed his theory of emotions, which stressed bodily responses as producers of emotional responses (e.g., we feel afraid because we tremble) and his theory of the self, emphasizing the "I" (self as knower) and the "Me" (self as known) as tied to multiple networks of group affiliation. His focus throughout was on the operations of ongoing experience, and his formulations not only specified and elaborated pragmatist principles but anticipated or contributed to behaviorism, gestalt psychology, and operationalism.

Charles Horton Cooley (1864–1929), building on the work of James, rejected the legitimacy of all dualisms. In his famous statement that "self and society are twin-born," he asserted the inseparability of individuals and society. Individuals, he proposed, are merely the distributive phase and societies the collective phase of the same social processes. The indissoluble connection of self and society, which was the dominant theme of Cooley's writings, is manifested in their necessary interdependence. His theory of the social self held that self-concepts are behaviorally derived through reflected appraisals of the actions of others—the looking-glass self. Especially important in the process of self-acquisition are primary groups (family, friends), which link the person to society. Correspondingly, society significantly exists in the form of personal imaginations or mental constructs; society, Cooley stated, is an interweaving and interworking of mental selves. Cooley's approach was thoroughly holistic and organic, with human consciousness and communication being the most critical processes, and his work added further to the pragmatist's dismantling of the Cartesian split between mind and society.

John Dewey (1859–1952) was perhaps the most influential and prolific of the early pragmatists. Coming philosophically to pragmatism from Hegelianism, he emphasized intelligence, process, and the notion that organisms are constantly reconstructing their environments as they are being determined by them. He contributed forcefully to the critique of dualistic thought in his analysis of stimulus-response theory (1896). Instead of constituting an arc, in which the stimulus leads to a response (a dualistic conception), Dewey argued that they are merely moments in an overall division of labor in a reciprocal, mutually constitutive process (a dialectical conception). Central to those dialetics was communication, which according to Dewey was the foundation and core mechanism of social order. He developed an instrumentalist theory of language (1925)—language as a tool—which was generalized into a broader instrumentalism. One of his central interests was moral and social repair through the application of intelligence and scientific methods. He merged theory and practice in the view that ideas are instruments for reconstructing and reconstituting problematic situations. Those ideas may be moral judgments or scientific findings, but both take the general form of hypotheses, which are proposals for action in response to difficulties. Dewey thus built from Peirce's and James's pragmatic rule by arguing that validity and truth statements, whether theological or scientific, are established by examining the consequences of action derived from hypotheses.

The last pragmatist briefly to be considered is George Herbert Mead (1863–1931). He sought understanding of emergent human properties such as the ability to think in abstractions, self-consciousness, and moral and purposive conduct. His central argument was that these properties are grounded in the development of language and social interaction as humans adjust to the conditions of their environments and group life (Mead 1934). His position is said to be one of social behaviorism, in which the social act is the unit of analysis and out of which minds and selves develop. The act has covert and overt phases. It begins in the form of an attitude (an incipient act), is constructed through role-taking processes (imaginatively placing oneself in the position of others), and is manifested in overt conduct. All social behavior involves a conflation of subjective and objective processes through which persons adjustively contend with the facts of their environments and simultaneously create social situations. Mead's explicit theory of time and sociality places these adjustments squarely in the dialectics of continuity and discontinuity (Maines, Sugrue, and Katovich 1983).

In these five brief summaries can be seen how the early pragmatists wove together strands of scientific method, evolutionary theory, language, and behaviorism into a radically new perspective. Pragmatism provided a clear alternative to perspectives based on Cartesian dualisms and reconstituted science, morality, aesthetics, political theory, and social development in terms of dialectical transactions. Philosophical idealism and realism were brought into a common framework in the proposition that human experience and facts of nature and society (the "world that is there," as Mead called them) are only phases of ongoing social processes that mediate persons and their environments in terms of transacted meanings. The variation within pragmatism hinges largely on individual affinitives for idealism and realism: James and Cooley tended toward idealism, Peirce toward realism, and Dewey and Mead toward a transactional midpoint between the two. Moreover, there is variation in pragmatism's influence in the social sciences and humanities. Dewey has been enormously influential in education and communication, Mead and Cooley in sociology and social psychology, Peirce in semiotics, and James in psychology. That variation, however, only represents modal tendencies, since pragmatism as a whole has had a significant impact across disciplines.

INFLUENCE IN SOCIAL SCIENCE

Since 1980 there has been a major resurgence of interest in pragmatism (Bernstein 1986). Its compatibilities with quantum mechanics and relativity theory have been articulated, as has its relevance for the development of a more social semiotics and discourse analysis (Perinbanayagam 1986). The relation of pragmatism to hermeneutics, from the tradition of German Idealism, is being reexamined (Dallmayr 1987), as is its relation to critical theory in the work of Jürgen Habermas (McCarthy 1984), literary criticism (Rorty 1982), phenomenology (Ricoeur 1985), cultural studies (Carey 1989), and modernization theory (Rochberg-Halton 1986). According to some, such as Richard Bernstein, this resurgence indicates that the early pragmatists were ahead of their time. Certainly the breaking down of traditional disciplinary boundaries through the increasing interdisciplinary nature of social scientific work is compatible with pragmatism's holistic approach. Moreover, the collapse of hegemonic theories and the corresponding import of postpositivistic debate in social scientific theorizing has brought the basic tenets of pragmatism directly into the segmented and decentered interdisciplinary search for new paradigms in social theory.

These recent influences and developments notwithstanding, there has been a long tradition of direct influence of pragmatism on social science research and theory. Sociology's first research classic was Thomas and Znaniecki's (1918–1920) study of Polish immigrant adaptation to American urban life. They were interested in questions of personal adjustment, family relations, neighborhood formation, delinquency, and cultural assimilation, and they used the principles of pragmatism, especially as expressed by G. H. Mead, to answer those questions. Their monumental five-volume work presented their attitude–value scheme as a general theory of the adjustive relations between individuals and society. "Attitudes" referred to the individual's tendencies to act and represented human subjectivity; "values" referred to the constraining facts of a society's social organization and represented the objective social environment. Both are present in any instance of human social conduct, they argued, but the relationships between the two are established in processes of interpretation that they called "definitions of the situation." Thomas and Znaniecki thus placed human agency at the center of their explanations, and they conceptualized society as the organization of dialectical transactions.

That research contained pragmatist ideas pertaining to the social psychological and social organizational aspects of human behavior. These aspects were developed during the 1920s and 1930s at the University of Chicago by Ellsworth Faris and Robert Park. Faris (1928) examined attitudes, especially in terms of the nature of their influence on behavior. He argued that human subjectivity is a natural datum for sociological research and proposed that wishes and desires, not attitudes, have a direct bearing on overt conduct. Park

(1926) was more interested in large-scale historical issues such as urban organization and racial stratification. He directly applied Dewey's focus on society as communication to his research on urban communities. These communities, he argued, have objective spatial patterns, but those patterns are not separable from human consciousness. Urban ecology thus has a moral dimension composed of meanings that collectivities attribute to urban areas.

The pragmatist themes of individual/society inseparability and human behavior as transactions were pursued by other sociologists. In 1937, Herbert Blumer coined the phrase *symbolic interaction* to refer simultaneously to how humans communicate and to a sociological perspective. He applied that perspective to a wide range of research areas such as social psychology, collective behavior, race relations, and social problems (Maines 1989). Blumer's posthumous volume on industrialization and social change (1990) elaborates the Thomas and Znaniecki formulations by presenting a conceptualization of causal influences that hinge on human agency and interpretation. Stone's (1962) research on clothing and fashion similarly focuses on human behavior as transactions. In particular, his analysis of identity establishment identifies dialectical processes of communication through which individuals are located and placed in the social organization of society. His treatment of interpersonal identities is sympathetic to Cooley's emphasis on the importance of primary groups, while his treatment of structural relations corresponds with Thomas and Znaniecki's concept of values and predates contemporary social psychological research on individuals and social structure.

Studies of social organization have been directly influenced by pragmatist principles, as previously mentioned, but that influence has been especially apparent since the early 1970s (see Hall 1987 for a summary). Anselm Strauss's research on occupations and formal organizations has been prominent in this recent work and has led to the development of the "negotiated order" perspective (Strauss 1978). Negotiations, he argues, are processes through which collective actions occur and tasks are accomplished. These processes are influenced by actor characteristics, the immediate situation, and larger structural contexts. However, those larger contexts also are influenced reciprocally by actual negotiations and their situations. Strauss's model of social organization thus is a recursive and dialectical one. Stryker (1980) presents a slightly different version but one that is no less pragmatist. He incorporates traditional role theory to argue that social structural arrangements limit options and opportunities by channeling people into status and role positions. So located, people construct their identities in terms of social meanings that are hierarchically organized. Both Strauss's and Stryker's applications of pragmatism have stimulated considerable research and theoretical development.

One of the distinctive characteristics of social science research and theory that has been grounded in pragmatism is the reluctance to give credence to dualisms such as micro–macro or individual–society. While issues of scale have always been acknowledged and used, as the work of Park, Blumer, Stone, Stryker, and Strauss has demonstrated, the focus has been directed toward the examination of social processes that produce, maintain, and change social orders. Those social processes generally have been conceptualized as communicative in nature, and the central thrust has been on how large- and small-scale phenomena are simultaneously or similarly transacted by individuals and groups. The focus on those processes has maintained the action orientation of pragmatism, and the central precepts of the perspective are finding wide currency and relevance in contemporary work in the social sciences and humanities.

(SEE ALSO: *Social Philosophy; Social Psychology*)

REFERENCES

Bernstein, Richard 1986 *Philosophical Profiles.* Philadelphia: University of Pennsylvania Press.

Blumer, Herbert 1990 *Industrialization as an Agent of Social Change: A Critical Analysis.* Hawthorne, N.Y.: Aldine de Gruyter.

Carey, James 1989 *Communication as Culture.* Boston: Unwin Hyman.

Dallmayr, Fred 1987 *Critical Encounters Between Philosophy and Politics.* Notre Dame, Ind.: University of Notre Dame Press.

Dewey, John 1896 "The Reflex Arc Concept in Psychology." *The Psychological Review* 3:363–370.

——— 1925 *Experience and Nature.* Chicago: Open Court.

Faris, Ellsworth 1928 "Attitudes and Behavior." *American Journal of Sociology* 33:271–281.

Hall, Peter 1987 "Interactionism and the Study of Social Organization." *The Sociological Quarterly* 28: 1–22.

James, William 1890 *Principles of Psychology.* New York: Henry Holt.

——— 1904 "Does Consciousness Exist?" *Journal of Philosophy, Psychology, and Scientific Method* 1:477–491.

Konvitz, Milton, and Gail Kennedy (eds.) 1960 *The American Pragmatists.* Cleveland, Ohio: World Publishing Co.

McCarthy, Thomas 1984 *The Critical Theory of Jürgen Habermas.* Cambridge: Polity Press.

Maines, David 1989 "Repackaging Blumer: The Myth of Herbert Blumer's Astructural Bias." In Norman Denzin, ed., *Studies in Symbolic Interaction.* Greenwich, Conn.: JAI Press.

———, Noreen Sugrue, and Michael Katovich 1983 "The Sociological Import of G. H. Mead's Theory of the Past." *American Sociological Review* 48:151–173.

Martindale, Don 1960 *The Nature and Types of Sociological Theory.* Boston: Houghton Mifflin.

Mead, George Herbert 1934 *Mind, Self, and Society.* Chicago: University of Chicago Press.

Park, Robert 1926 "The Urban Community as a Spatial and Moral Order." In Ernest Burgess, ed., *The Urban Community.* Chicago: University of Chicago Press.

Peirce, Charles 1877–1878 "Illustrations of the Logic of Science." *Popular Science Monthly* 12:1–15, 286–302, 604–615, 705–718; 13:203–217, 470–482.

Perinbanayagam, Robert 1986 "The Meaning of Uncertainty and the Uncertainty of Meaning." *Symbolic Interaction* 9:105–126.

Ricoeur, Paul 1985 *Time and Narrative.* Chicago: University of Chicago Press.

Rochberg-Halton, Eugene 1986 *Meaning and Modernity: Social Theory in the Pragmatic Attitude.* Chicago: University of Chicago Press.

Rorty, Richard 1982 *Consequences of Pragmatism.* Minneapolis: University of Minnesota Press.

Rosenthal, Sandra 1986 *Speculative Pragmatism.* Amherst: University of Massachusetts Press.

Rucker, Darnell 1969 *The Chicago Pragmatists.* Minneapolis: University of Minnesota Press.

Shalin, Dmitri 1986 "Pragmatism and Social Interactionism." *American Sociological Review* 51:9–29.

Stone, Gregory 1962 "Appearance and the Self." In Arnold Rose, ed., *Human Behavior and Social Processes.* Boston: Houghton Mifflin.

Strauss, Anselm 1978 *Negotiations.* San Francisco: Jossey-Bass.

Stryker, Sheldon 1980 *Symbolic Interactionism: A Social Structural Version.* Menlo Park, Calif.: Benjamin/Cummings.

Thomas, William I., and Florian Znaniecki 1918–1920 *The Polish Peasant in Europe and America,* 5 vols. Chicago: University of Chicago Press.

DAVID R. MAINES

PREJUDICE Gordon Allport, in his classic, *The Nature of Prejudice,* defined prejudice as "an antipathy based upon a faulty and inflexible generalization" (1954, p. 9). This phrasing neatly captures the notion that both inaccurate beliefs and negative feelings are implicated in prejudice. To these "cognitive" and "affective" dimensions of prejudice, some analysts add "conative," referring to action orientation (Klineberg 1972) and prescription (Harding et al. 1969). Allport's circumspection on the conative implications of prejudice—he said prejudice "may be felt or expressed" (1954, p. 9)—foreshadowed our growing understanding that the correspondence of behavior with cognitions and feelings is uncertain and a research issue in its own right (Schuman and Johnson 1976).

Racial and ethnic prejudice was Allport's primary interest. Emerging social issues have brought expanded attention to other forms of prejudice—against women, the elderly, handicapped persons, AIDS patients, and others. This discussion will focus on racial prejudice among white Americans, in the expectation that parallels and points of contrast will continue to make race relations research relevant to other forms of prejudice.

TRENDS AND PATTERNS

For many years, derogatory stereotypes, blatant aversion to interracial contact, and opposition in principle to racial equality were seen as the central manifestations of race prejudice, virtually defining the social science view of the problem. Indicators of these beliefs and feelings show a clear positive trend (Jaynes and Williams 1989; Schuman, Steeh, and Bobo 1985). White Americans who believed in the innate intellectual inferiority of blacks declined from 53 percent in 1942 to about 20 percent in the 1960s, when the question was discontinued in major national surveys. The percentage of whites who said it wouldn't make any difference to them if a Negro of equal social status moved into their block rose from 36 percent to 85 percent between 1942 and 1972. White opinion that blacks should have "as good a chance as white people to get any kind of job" climbed from 45 percent in 1944 to 97 percent in 1972. Smith and Sheatsley sum up this picture without equivocation: "Looking over this forty-year span, we are struck by the steady, massive growth in racial tolerance" (1984, p. 14).

Recurrent outbursts of overt racial hostility serve as unfortunate reminders that some white Americans still cling to blatant prejudice. More importantly, even the majority of whites, those on whom Smith and Sheatsley focused, appear unambiguously tolerant only if attention is confined to such traditional survey indicators as those described above. A confluence of developments has broadened the study of race prejudice and transformed our understanding of white racial attitudes. First, evidence of widespread, subtle prejudice has been revealed in research using disguised, "nonreactive" methods. Second, "social cognition" scholarship, prominent in the psychological wing of social psychology, has been powerfully applied to intergroup relations. Third, evolution of the struggle for racial equality in the United States has shifted attention to a new domain of racial policy-related beliefs and feelings. These perspectives provide ample evidence that white racial prejudice is not a thing of the past but exists today in complex forms that have yet to be thoroughly charted.

Evidence from "Nonreactive" Studies. Given the clear dominance of "liberal" racial norms evidenced in public opinion data, it might be expected that needs for social acceptability and self-esteem would lead many whites to withhold evidence of negative racial feelings and cognitions whenever possible. Disguised, "nonreactive" research (Webb et al. 1981) provides substantial evidence that, indeed, traditional survey approaches underestimate negative racial feeling. Field experiments reveal that whites often provide less help to victims who are black (Crosby, Bromley, and Saxe 1980), sometimes redefining the situation so as to justify their lack of response (Gaertner 1976). Such elements of nonverbal behavior as voice tone (Weitz 1972) and seating proximity (Word, Zanna, and Cooper 1974) have been found to reveal negative racial feelings and avoidance. Reaction time studies suggest the existence of a subtle form of stereotyping, not derogating blacks, but reserving positive characteristics for whites (Dovidio, Mann, and Gaertner 1989). Thus, accumulating evidence reveals that "microaggressions" (Pettigrew 1989) often accompany self-portrayals of liberalism.

Social Cognition Perspectives. In recognizing aspects of prejudice as predictable outgrowths of "natural" cognitive processes, Allport (1954) was ahead of his time. The current wave of social cognition research on intergroup relations was set in motion by Tajfel (1969), who demonstrated that mere categorization—of physical objects or of people—encourages exaggerated perception of intragroup homogeneity and intergroup difference. Even in "minimal groups" arbitrarily created in psychology laboratories, these effects of social categorization are often accompanied by outgroup discrimination (Brewer 1979; Hamilton 1979). Accumulating evidence of the negative consequences of ingroup–outgroup categorization has spurred research aimed at identifying conditions of intergroup contact that are likely to decrease category salience and promote "individuation" or "decategorization" (Brewer and Miller 1988; Wilder 1978) or at least to reduce the negativity of outgroup stereotypes (Rothbart and John 1985; Wilder 1984).

The study of attributional processes (Heider 1958; Jones and Davis 1965) also has been usefully applied to intergroup relations, calling attention to such issues as whether whites believe that black economic hardship results from discrimination or lack of effort. Research evidence has linked stereotypic thinking to attributions of outgroup behavior (Hamilton 1979). Specific predictions are developed in Pettigrew's (1979) discussion of the "ultimate attributional error," the tendency to hold outgroups personally responsible for their failures but to "discount" their responsibility for successes, attributing successes to such factors as luck or unfair advantage.

The Expanded Racial Attitude Domain. Over the past twenty-five years, evolution in the struggle for racial equality has brought new complexity to the public debate about racial issues. Notions that barriers to black equality consist solely of white hostility and aversion or formal denial of rights now appear naive. Advocates insist that structural barriers far more complex and pervasive than formal denial of access prevent actual equality of opportunity and desegregation, making questions about acceptance by white individuals a moot point for millions of black Americans.

In the current era of U.S. race relations, traditional manifestations of race prejudice recede in relevance, and different forms of race-related belief and feeling take center stage—reactions to agitation for change, recognition and interpretation of continuing inequality, support for proposed remedies. By all indications, such white "perceptions, explanations, and prescriptions" (Apostle et al. 1983, p. 18) show far less consensus and support for racial change than appeared in traditional race survey data. Asked about specific policies and programs designed to increase racial equality—fair housing guarantees, school desegregation plans, affirmative action in hiring and college admission—white Americans show substantially less support than they voice for racial equality in principle (Schuman, Steeh, and Bobo 1985). In the minds of many white Americans, recent black gains and benefits of affirmative action are exaggerated, and remaining inequality is underestimated (Kluegel and Smith 1982). There is substantial white resentment of black activism and perceived progress (Bobo 1988a; Schuman, Steeh, and Bobo 1985).

The influence of attribution research in social psychology and earlier societal analyses (Ryan 1971; Feagin 1975) is reflected in a remarkable convergence of recent scholarly opinion that explanations are at the heart of the matter. The research evidence tells a clear story: Whites explain the economic plight of black Americans more often as the result of such "individualistic" factors as lack of motivation than as the result of such "structural" factors as discrimination (Apostle et al. 1983; Kluegel and Smith 1986; Sniderman and Hagen 1985). Furthermore, individualistic attributions are linked to a variety of policy-relevant beliefs and opinions including opposition to affirmative action (Kluegel and Smith 1983; 1986).

CHARACTERIZATIONS OF WHITE RACIAL ATTITUDES

Efforts to characterize the complex pattern of racial attitudes held by white Americans emphasize an array of themes:

1. *Natural cognitive processing.* As noted earlier, social cognition analyses claim that a substantial part of the race prejudice once thought to have sociocultural or psychodynamic roots actually stems from ordinary cognitive processing, particularly categorization (Hamilton 1979). Social cognition portrayals have become somewhat more eclectic in recent years, allowing motivational and social influences (Hamilton and Trolier 1986; Fiske 1987), but there remains a tone of contrast between cognitive explanations and what Tajfel called "blood and guts" notions (1969, p. 80).

2. *Strain between individualism and egalitarianism.* Current racial policy issues are said to pull whites between two cherished American values, individualism and egalitarianism (Lipset and Schneider 1978). *Qualified* support for social programs exists, in this view, because egalitarian sentiments prevail only until a proposal challenges individualistic values.

3. *Ambivalence.* Adding psychodynamic flavor to the idea of a strain between individualism and egalitarianism, some analysts describe current white feelings as an ambivalence that produces an unpredictable mix of amplified positive and negative responses (Katz, Wackenhut, and Hass 1986).

4. *Aversive racism.* A desire to avoid interracial contact, muted negative feelings, and egalitarian self-concepts are the mix Kovel (1970) characterized as aversive racism. Aversive racism leads one to avoid positive interracial behavior when the situation can be defined to permit it and to express negative feelings when there are ostensible nonracial justifications (Gaertner 1976; Gaertner and Dovidio 1986).

5. *Self-interest.* Collective self-interest is sometimes identified as the primary basis of whites' interracial beliefs and feelings (Jackman and Muha 1984; Wellman 1977). If zero-sum assumptions prevail, redistribution in favor of blacks will be seen as a losing proposition to whites. Self-interest is at the heart of what Bobo (1988b) calls an "ideology of bounded racial change": white acceptance of racial change ends when the changes are perceived to threaten the well-being of whites.

6. *Symbolic or modern racism.* Anti-black affect instilled by childhood socialization and the sense that racial change threatens fondly held individualistic values, not self-interest, constitute Sears's (1988) "symbolic" racism. "Modern" racism contains the added ingredient of denying continuing racial inequality (McConahay 1986).

7. *Dominant stratification ideology.* A belief that opportunity is plentiful and equally distributed, and thus that effort is economically rewarded and economic failure is deserved, compose the "dominant stratification ideology" (Huber and Form 1973; Kluegel and Smith 1986). Although personal status and strands of American "social liberalism" also play a role, unyielding adherence to this American "dominant ideology" is portrayed as a major impediment to public support for redistributional claims in general and to calls for racial change in particular (Kluegel and Smith 1986). On a foundation of ignorance resulting from social segregation, whites' own experiences of economic success work to prevent recognition of the continuing barriers to full opportunity for black Americans (Kluegel 1985).

PRESCRIPTIONS FOR MODERN PREJUDICE

When the lessons from cognitive social psychology are counterposed with those from other perspectives on modern race prejudice, an apparent dilemma is revealed. Though social cognition findings indicate that category salience can promote stereotype change under some circumstances (Cook 1984; Pettigrew and Martin 1987; Rothbart and John 1985), much of the cognitive literature insists that categorization is a central contributor to race prejudice and negative race relations: Color-consciousness is often portrayed as an evil, color-blindness as the ideal. From other scholars of modern prejudice, the analysis and prescription are nearly a mirror image of this view. Color-blindness is said to impede forthright problem solving in desegregated institutions (Schofield 1986); to represent ignorance of the structural barriers faced by black Americans (Kluegel 1985); and to be used as a weapon by those opposing black claims of collective rights (Jackman and Muha 1984; Omi and Winant 1986). The solution implied or stated by these analysts is for whites to adopt a color-consciousness that fully acknowledges the historical impact of racial subordination and the continuing liabilities of direct and indirect discrimination. The two streams of advice present this challenge: How to promote in the white public a racial understanding that avoids the psychological liabilities of ingroup and outgroup categorization while acknowledging the full sociological implications of the past and continuing color line.

(SEE ALSO: *Attitudes; Discrimination; Race; Segregation and Desegregation; Segregation Indices*)

REFERENCES

Allport, Gordon 1954 *The Nature of Prejudice.* Cambridge, Mass.: Addison-Wesley.

Apostle, Richard A., Charles Y. Glock, Thomas Piazza, and Marijean Suelzle 1983 *The Anatomy of Racial Attitudes.* Berkeley: University of California Press.

Bobo, Lawrence 1988a "Attitudes Toward the Black Political Movement: Trends, Meaning, and Effects on Racial Policy Preferences." *Social Psychology Quarterly* 51:287–302.

——— 1988b "Group Conflict, Prejudice, and the Paradox of Contemporary Racial Attitudes." In Phyllis A. Katz and Dalmas A. Taylor, ed., *Eliminating Racism.* New York: Plenum Press.

Brewer, Marilynn B. 1979 "Ingroup Bias in the Minimal Intergroup Situation: A Cognitive-Motivational Analysis." *Psychological Bulletin* 86:307–324.

Brewer, Marilynn B., and Norman Miller 1988 "Contact and Cooperation: When Do They Work?" In Phyllis A. Katz and Dalmas A. Taylor, eds., *Eliminating Racism.* New York: Plenum Press.

Cook, Stuart W. 1984 "Cooperative Interaction in Multiethnic Contexts." In Norman Miller and Marilynn B. Brewer, eds., *Groups in Contact: The Psychology of Desegregation.* New York: Academic Press.

Crosby, Faye J., Stephanie Bromley, and Leonard Saxe 1980 "Recent Unobtrusive Studies of Black and White Discrimination and Prejudice: A Literature Review." *Psychological Bulletin* 87:546–563.

Dovidio, John F., Jeffrey Mann, and Samuel L. Gaertner 1989 "Resistance to Affirmative Action: The Implications of Aversive Racism." In Faye J. Crosby and Fletcher A. Blanchard, eds., *Affirmative Action in Perspective.* New York: Springer-Verlag.

Feagin, Joe R. 1975 *Subordinating the Poor.* Englewood Cliffs, N.J.: Prentice-Hall.

Fiske, Susan T. 1987 "On the Road: Comment on the Cognitive Stereotyping Literature in Pettigrew and Martin." *Journal of Social Issues* 43:113–118.

Gaertner, Samuel L. 1976 "Nonreactive Measures in Racial Attitude Research: A Focus on 'Liberals.'" In Phyllis A. Katz, ed., *Toward the Elimination of Racism.* New York: Pergamon.

Gaertner, Samuel L., and John F. Dovidio 1986 "The Aversive Form of Racism." In John F. Dovidio and Samuel L. Gaertner, eds., *Prejudice, Discrimination, and Racism.* Orlando, Fla.: Academic Press.

Hamilton, David A., and Tina K. Trolier 1986 "Stereotypes and Stereotyping: An Overview of the Cognitive Approach." In Phyllis A. Katz and Dalmas A. Taylor, eds., *Eliminating Racism.* New York: Plenum Press.

Hamilton, David L. 1979 "A Cognitive-Attributional Analysis of Stereotyping." In Leonard Berkowitz, ed., *Advances in Experimental Social Psychology.* Vol. 12. New York: Academic Press.

Harding, John, Harold Proshansky, Bernard Kutner, and Isador Chein 1969 "Prejudice and Intergroup Relations." In Gardner Lindzey and Elliot Aronson, eds., *Handbook of Social Psychology.* 2d ed. Reading, Mass.: Addison-Wesley.

Heider, Fritz 1958 *The Psychology of Interpersonal Relations.* New York: Wiley.

Huber, Joan, and William H. Form 1973 *Income and Ideology.* New York: Free Press.

Jackman, Mary R., and Michael J. Muha 1984 "Education and Intergroup Attitudes: Moral Enlightenment, Superficial Democratic Commitment, or Ideological Refinement?" *American Sociological Review* 49:751–769.

Jaynes, David Gerald, and Robin M. Williams, Jr. 1989 *A Common Destiny: Blacks and American Society.* Washington, D.C.: National Academy Press.

Jones, Edward E., and Keith E. Davis 1965 "From Acts to Dispositions: The Attribution Process in Perception Perception." In Leonard Berkowitz, ed., *Advances in Experimental Social Psychology.* Vol. 2. New York: Academic Press.

Katz, Irwin, Joyce Wackenhut, and R. Glen Hass 1986 "Racial Ambivalence, Value Duality, and Behavior." In John F. Dovidio and Samuel L. Gaertner, eds., *Prejudice, Discrimination, and Racism.* Orlando, Fla.: Academic Press.

Klineberg, Otto 1972 "Prejudice: The Concept." In David L. Sills, ed., *International Encyclopedia of the Social Sciences.* New York: Macmillan and Free Press.

Kluegel, James R. 1985 "If There Isn't a Problem, You Don't Need a Solution." *American Behavioral Scientist* 28:761–784.

———, and Eliot R. Smith 1982 "Whites' Beliefs about Blacks' Opportunity." *American Sociological Review* 47:518–532.

——— 1983 "Affirmative Action Attitudes: Effects of

Self-Interest, Racial Affect, and Stratification Beliefs on Whites' Views." *Social Forces* 61:797–824.

——— 1986 *Beliefs about Inequality: Americans' Views of What Is and What Ought to Be.* New York: Aldine de Gruyter.

Kovel, Joel 1970 *White Racism: A Psychohistory.* New York: Pantheon.

Lipset, Seymour Martin, and William Schneider 1978 "The Bakke Case: How Would It Be Decided at the Bar of Public Opinion?" *Public Opinion* 1:38–44.

McConahay, John B. 1986 "Modern Racism, Ambivalence, and the Modern Racism Scale." In John F. Dovidio and Samuel L. Gaertner, eds., *Prejudice, Discrimination, and Racism.* Orlando, Fla.: Academic Press.

Omi, Michael, and Howard Winant 1986 *Racial Formation in the United States from the 1960s to the 1980s.* New York: Routledge and Kegan Paul.

Pettigrew, Thomas F. 1979 "The Ultimate Attribution Error: Extending Allport's Cognitive Analysis of Prejudice." *Personality and Social Psychology Bulletin* 5:461–476.

——— 1989 "The Nature of Modern Racism." *Revue internationale de psychologie sociale* 2:291–305.

———, and Joanne Martin 1987 "Shaping the Organizational Context for Black American Inclusion." *Journal of Social Issues* 43:41–78.

Rothbart, Myron, and Oliver P. John 1985 "Social Categorization and Behavioral Episodes: A Cognitive Analysis of the Effects of Intergroup Contact." *Journal of Social Issues* 41:81–104.

Ryan, William 1971 *Blaming the Victim.* New York: Vintage.

Schofield, Janet Ward 1986 "Causes and Consequences of the Colorblind Perspective." In John F. Dovidio and Samuel L. Gaertner, eds., *Prejudice, Discrimination, and Racism.* Orlando, Fla.: Academic Press.

Schuman, Howard, and Michael P. Johnson 1976 "Attitudes and Behavior." *Annual Review of Sociology* 2:161–207.

Schuman, Howard, Charlotte Steeh, and Lawrence Bobo 1985 *Racial Attitudes in America: Trends and Interpretations.* Cambridge: Mass.: Harvard University

Sears, David O. 1988 "Symbolic Racism." In Phyllis A. Katz and Dalmas A. Taylor, eds., *Eliminating Racism.* New York: Plenum Press.

Smith, Thomas W., and Paul B. Sheatsley 1984 "American Attitudes toward Race Relations." *Public Opinion* 6:14–15, 50–53.

Sniderman, Paul M., with Michael Gray Hagen 1985 *Race and Inequality: A Study in American Values.* Chatham, N.J.: Chatham House Publishers.

Tajfel, Henri 1969 "Cognitive Aspects of Prejudice." *Journal of Social Issues.* 4:79–97.

Webb, Eugene J., Donald T. Campbell, Richard D. Schwartz, Lee Sechrest, and J. B. Grove 1981 *Nonreactive Measures in the Social Sciences.* 2nd ed. Boston: Houghton Mifflin.

Weitz, Shirley 1972 "Attitude, Voice, and Behavior: A Repressed Affect Model of Interracial Interaction." *Journal of Personality and Social Psychology* 32: 857–864.

Wellman, David T. 1977 *Portraits of White Racism.* New York: Oxford University Press.

Wilder, David A. 1978 "Reduction of Intergroup Discrimination through Individuation of the Out-Group." *Journal of Personality and Social Psychology* 36:1,361–1,374.

——— 1984 "Intergroup Contact: The Typical Member and the Exception to the Rule." *Journal of Experimental Social Psychology* 20:177–194.

Word, Carl O., Mark P. Zanna, and Joel Cooper 1974 "The Nonverbal Mediation of Self-Fulfilling Prophecies in Interracial Interaction." *Journal of Experimental Social Psychology* 10:109–120.

MARYLEE C. TAYLOR
THOMAS F. PETTIGREW

PROBABILITY THEORY Sociologists, as much as researchers in any field perhaps, use a variety of approaches in the investigation of their subject matter. Quite successful and important are the historical and exegetical approaches and those in the traditions of anthropology and philosophy. Also of great importance are the systematic approaches that use mathematical models. Here the social investigator proposes a model, a mathematical depiction of social phenomena. A successful mathematical model can be very powerful, providing not only confidence in the theory from which the model was derived, giving us an explanation of the phenomena, but producing as well a method for predicting, giving us a practical means for controlling or affecting the social phenomena.

The social mathematical model is first of all a description of the relationship of the properties of social objects—groups, states, institutions, organizations, even people. If the model is derived from a theory, or if it contains features implied by a theory, and if the model fits data (i.e., has been found to satisfy some criterion of performance), the model can in addition be regarded as evidence to support that theory. In this case we can think of a true, underlying model that generated the observations we are studying and a proposed model that will be tested against data. Quantitative analysis begins, then, with some theoretical understanding of the properties of groups of social objects; this understanding leads to the specification of a model of the interaction of these properties, after which observations of these properties on a sample of the objects are collected. The performance of the model is then evaluated to determine to what degree the model truly describes the underlying process.

The measurement of a property of a social object is called a *variable.* Variables can be either fixed or random. Fixed variables are those determined by the investigator; they usually occur in experiments and will not be of concern in this chapter. All other variables are random. The random nature of these variables is the unavoidable consequence of two things; first, the fact that our observations are *samples,* that is, groups of instances of social objects drawn from a population (that is, a very large number of possible instances to be observed); second, the fact that our theories and data collection are often unable to account for all the relevant variables affecting the variables included in the analysis. Probability theory in social models, or, equivalently, random variables in social models, will derive from these two subtopics: sampling and the specification of residual or excluded variables in the models.

A certain philosophical difference of opinion arises among probability theorists about the nature of the true source of the randomness in nature. One group argues that these features are inherent in reality, and another argues they are simply the consequence of ignorance. The primary modeling tool of the former group is the *stochastic process* (Chung 1974), while that of the latter is the *Bayesian statistical model* (de Finetti 1974).

MAIN CONCEPTS

Models that contain random variables automatically invoke the theory of probability. A random variable is actually a *function* that assigns a value or *probability* to the outcome of a measurement. The measurement of a property of a social object is usually called an observation. Thus, the record of a person's response to a question about educational background or income, for example, is an observation. Let X_i be a random variable representing educational background of the ith person in a group of people for which educational background has been measured. Next, let x represent one of the members of the set of all possible outcomes: 1—less than eighth grade; 2—more than eighth grade and less than college; 3—at least some college. Then $PR(X_i = 1)$ is the probability that the measurement of the ith person on educational background will be less than an eighth-grade education, $PR(X_i = 2)$ is the probability that the measurement will be more than eighth grade and less than college, and so on. In this example the *probability distribution function* (or PDF) is a discrete function. The PDF may also be a continuous function. Continuous PDFs are usually called probability *density* functions.

Probability distribution functions may be empirical (i.e., the probabilities are determined from observations) or theoretical. The latter play an important role in social models. An example is the normal density function:

$$Pr(X_i = x) = \frac{1}{\sqrt{2\pi\sigma^2}} e^{\frac{-(x-\mu)^2}{2\sigma^2}} \quad (1)$$

where μ and σ^2 are parameters. The normal density function is the most widely used distribution in social models, first because it has advantageous mathematical properties and second because its specification in many cases can be justified on the basis of the central limit theorem (Hogg and Tanis 1977, p. 155).

Other important concepts in probability theory

are the *cumulative distribution function* (or CDF), *joint distributions* (distributions involving more than one variable), and *conditional distributions.* The CDF is the probability of X being less than or equal to x, that is, $Pr(X < x)$. An accessible introduction to probability may be found in Hogg and Tanis (1977).

SAMPLING

In physics all protons behave similarly. To determine their properties, any given instance of a proton will do. Social objects, on the other hand, tend to be complex, and their properties can vary considerably from instance to instance. It is not possible to draw conclusions about all instances of a social object from a given one in the same manner we might from a single instance of a proton. Given equivalent circumstances we can't expect everyone to respond the same way to a question about their attitudes toward political issues or to behave the same way when presented with a set of options.

For example, suppose we wish to determine the extent to which a person's education affects his or her attitudes towards abortion. Let A_i represent a measurement of the attitude of some person, labeled the *i*th person, scored 0 if they are opposed to abortion or 1 if not. Let B_i be the measurement of the person's education, scored 0 for less than high school, 1 for high school but no college, or 2 for at least some college.

Given measurements on a sample of people, we would find that they would be distributed in some fashion across all of the six possible categories of the two variables. Dividing the number that fall into each category by the total number in the sample would give us estimates of the empirical distribution for the probabilities: $PR(A = 0, B = 1)$, $PR(A = 0, B = 2)$, and so on. We might also model this distribution. For example, an important type of model is the loglinear model (Goodman 1972; Haberman 1979; Agresti 1990), which models the log of the probability:

$$\log PR(A = i, B = j) = \lambda_i^A + \lambda_j^B + \lambda_{ij}^{AB} \qquad (2)$$

where λ_i^A, λ_j^B, and λ_{ij}^{AB} are parameters (actually sets of parameters). In this model the λ_{ij}^{AB} parameters represent the associations between A and B, and an estimate of these quantities might have important implications for a theory.

Given a sample distribution, computing an estimate of λ_{ij}^{AB} is straightforward (Bishop, Fienberg, and Holland 1975). It is important, however, to realize that such an estimate is itself a random variable, that is, we can expect the estimate to vary with every sample of observations we produce. If the sample is properly selected, in particular if it is a simple random sample in which each person has an equal chance of being included in the sample, it can be shown that the estimates of λ_{ij}^{AB} have, in large samples at least, a normal distribution (Haberman 1973). Our estimates, then, are themselves parameters of a distribution, usually the means of a normal distribution. It follows that the fundamental parameters upon which a theory will depend can never be directly observed and that we must infer its true value from sample data.

All research on social objects is unavoidably research on samples of observations. Therefore all such research will necessarily entail at the very least a probabilistic sampling model, and the conclusions drawn will require properly conceived statistical inference.

MODELS WITH EXCLUDED VARIABLES

The Regression Model. The most well-known and widely used statistical model is the regression model. It is a simple linear hypersurface model with an added feature: a disturbance term, which represents the effects on the dependent variable of variables that have not been measured. To the extent that the claims or implications of a theory may be put into linear form, or at least transformed into linear form, the parameters (or regression coefficients) may be estimated and statistical inference drawn by making some reasonably benign assumptions about the behavior of the variables that have been excluded from measurement. The key assumption is that the excluded variables are uncorrelated with included variables. The failure of this assumption gives rise to *spurious* effects; that is, parameters may be under- or overestimated, and this results in faulty conclusions. The statistical inference also requires a homogeneity of variance of the disturbance variables, called *homoscedasticity.* The variation of the excluded variables must be the same across the range of the independent variables. This is not a critical assumption, however, because the consequence of the violation of this assumption is inefficiency rather than bias, as in the case of the spurious effects. Moreover, the underlying process generating the heteroscedasticity may be specified, which would yield efficient estimates, or a modified inference may be computed, based on revised estimates of the variances of the distribution of the parameter estimates (White 1980).

For example, a simple regression of income, say, on years of education may be described, $y_i = b_0 + b_1 x_i + \varepsilon_i$, where y_i and x_i are observations on income and years of education, respectively, of the ith person, b_0 and b_1 are regression coefficients, and ε_i is the disturbance term. Estimates of b_0 and b_1 may be found (without making any assumptions about the functional form of the distribution of ε_i) by using perhaps the most celebrated theorem in statistics, the Gauss-Markov theorem, and they are usually called *ordinary least squares estimates.*

If we gather the observations into matrices, we can rewrite the regression equation as functions of matrices: $Y = XB + E$, where Y is an $N \times 1$ vector of observations on the dependent variable, X an $N \times K$ matrix of observations on K independent variables, B a $K \times 1$ vector of regression coefficients, and E an $N \times 1$ vector of disturbances. With this notation the estimates in B may be described $\hat{B} = (X'X)^{-1}X'Y$, where the "ˆ" over the B emphasizes that they are estimates of the parameters.

Our observations are samples, and since our estimates of B will vary from sample to sample, it follows that these estimates will themselves be random variables. Appealing again to the Gauss-Markov theorem, it is possible to show that the ordinary least squares estimates have a normal distribution with variance–covariance matrix equal to $\text{VarCov}(\hat{B}) = \sigma_\varepsilon^2(X'X)^{-1}X'Y$, where σ_ε^2 is estimated by $\sigma_\varepsilon^2 = (Y - XB)'(Y - XB)/(N - K - 1)$.

Other Models. The regression model in the previous section is a "single equation" model, that is, it contains one dependent variable. A generalization of the regression model incorporates multiple dependent variables. This model may be represented in matrix notation as $BY = \Gamma X + Z$, where Y is an $N \times L$ matrix of L *endogenous* variables (i.e., variables that are dependent in at least one equation), B is an $L \times L$ matrix of coefficients relating endogenous variables among themselves, X is an $N \times K$ matrix of K *exogenous* variables (i.e., variables that are never dependent), Γ is an $L \times K$ matrix of coefficients relating the exogenous variables to the endogenous variables, and Z is an $N \times L$ matrix of disturbances. Techniques have been developed to produce estimates and statistical inference for these kinds of models (Judge et al. 1982; Fox 1984).

Measurement error is another kind of excluded variable, and models have been developed to incorporate them into the regression and simultaneous equation models. One method for handling measurement error is to use multiple measures of an underlying *latent* variable (Bollen 1989; Jöreskog and Sörbom 1988). A model that incorporates both measurement error and excluded variable disturbances may be described in the following way:

$$
\begin{aligned}
Y &= \Lambda_y \eta + \epsilon_y \\
X &= \Lambda_x \xi + \epsilon_x \\
B\eta &= \Gamma \xi + \zeta
\end{aligned}
\qquad (3)
$$

where Y and X are our observations on the endogenous and exogenous variables respectively, Λ_y and Λ_x are coefficient matrices relating the underlying variables to the observed variables, η and ξ are the latent endogenous and exogenous variables respectively, B and Γ are coefficient matrices relating the latent variables among themselves, ε_y and ε_x are the measurement error disturbances, and ζ is the excluded variable disturbance.

This model incorporates three sources of randomness, measurement error disturbance, excluded variable disturbance, and sampling error. Models of the future may contain a fourth source of randomness: a structural disturbance in the coefficients. These latter models are called random coefficient models and are a special case of the most general kind of probabilistic model called the *mixture model* (Judge et al. 1982; Everitt 1984).

The models described to this point have been linear. Linearity can be a useful approximation that renders the problem tractable. Nonlinearity may be an important aspect of a theoretical specification, however, and methods to incorporate nonlinearity in large-scale models have been developed (Amemiya 1985). It also appears to be the fact that most social measures are not continuous, real variables, which is what is assumed by the regression and simultaneous models described above. Thus, much work is now being devoted to the development of models that may be used with measures that are limited in a variety of ways—they are categorical, ordinal, truncated, or censored, for example (Muthén 1984; Maddala 1983). Limited variable methods also include methods for handling variations on the simple random method of sampling.

Probability theory has had a profound effect on the modeling of social processes. It has helped solve the sampling problem, permitted the specification of models with excluded variables, and provided a method for handling measurement error. This article has covered only the most successful applications of probability theory. Less widely applied but not less important are applications of stochastic processes to social processes (Tuma and Hannan 1984). These latter models take explicit account of time in social processes; eventually, perhaps, the most fundamental descriptions of all processes, whether social or not, will be described by stochastic process models.

(SEE ALSO: *Mathematical Sociology; Sampling Procedures; Statistical Inference*)

REFERENCES

Agresti, A. 1990 *Categorical Data Analysis.* New York: Wiley.

Amemiya, T. 1985 *Advanced Econometrics.* Cambridge, Mass.: Harvard University Press.

Bishop, Y. M. M., S. E. Fienberg, and P. W. Holland 1975 *Discrete Multivariate Analysis: Theory and Practice.* Cambridge, Mass.: MIT Press.

Bollen, K. A. 1989 *Structural Equations with Latent Variables.* New York: Wiley.

Chung, K. L. 1974 *Elementary Probability Theory with Stochastic Processes.* Berlin: Springer-Verlag.

de Finetti, B. 1974 *Theory of Probability.* 2 vols. New York: Wiley.

Everitt, B. S. 1984 *An Introduction to Latent Variable Models.* London: Chapman and Hall.

Fox, J. 1984 *Linear Statistical Models and Related Methods.* New York: Wiley.

Goodman, L. A. 1972 "A General Model for the Analysis of Surveys." *American Journal of Sociology* 37:28–46.

Haberman, S. J. 1973 "Loglinear Models for Frequency Data: Sufficient Statistics and Likelihood Equations." *Annals of Mathematical Statistics* 1:617–632.

——— 1979 *Analysis of Qualitative Data.* Vol. 2, *New Developments.* Orlando, Fla.: Academic Press.

Hogg, Robert V., and Elliot A. Tanis 1977 *Probability and Statistical Inference.* New York: Macmillan.

Jöreskog, K. G., and Dag Sörbom 1988 *LISREL VII.* Chicago: SPSS.

Judge, George G., R. Carter Hill, William Griffiths, Helmut Lütkepohl, and Tsoung-Chao Lee 1982 *Introduction to the Theory and Practice of Econometrics.* New York: Wiley.

Maddala, G. 1983 *Limited-Dependent and Qualitative Variables in Econometrics.* Cambridge: Cambridge University Press.

Muthén, B. 1984 "A General Structural Equation Model with Dichotomous, Ordered Categorical, and Continuous Latent Variable Indicators." *Psychometrika* 49:115–132.

Tuma, Nancy Brandon, and Michael T. Hannan 1984 *Social Dynamics: Models and Methods.* Orlando: Academic Press.

White, H. 1980 "A Heteroskedasticity-Consistent Covariance Matrix Estimator and a Direct Test for Heteroskedasticity." *Econometrica* 48:817–838.

RONALD SCHOENBERG

PROBATION AND PAROLE The criminal justice system is the primary institution responsible for the formal social control of criminal deviance. Those who violate the criminal law are subject to a variety of sanctions, ranging from the reprimand of a police officer to execution by hanging. Most offenders are not apprehended, and among those who are arrested many are not prosecuted nor convicted of a crime. For offenders who are found guilty, either by trial or more often by negotiated guilty plea, the sentence handed down by the court typically mandates correctional supervision, usually either some form of probation or incarceration with early release to some form of parole.

Even though probation and parole have been integral components of corrections since the nineteenth century, the differences between them are not always clear. Both are postconviction alternatives to incarceration that include supervision in the community by a probation or parole officer, who, depending on the jurisdiction, may be the same person. They are conditional releases to the community that are contingent on compliance with stipulated conditions, which if violated, may lead to revocation. Many probation and parole programs are similar (e.g., intensive supervision) or they share clientele. Last, as alternatives to incarceration, both are less expensive, less punitive, and probably more effective strategies of crime control.

The major difference between probation and parole is that probationers are sentenced directly to community supervision without being incarcerated, while parolees serve part of their sentence incarcerated before they are released to parole. Parole is a conditional release from confinement, whereas probation is a conditional suspension of a sentence to confinement. In both cases, a new crime or technical violation of conditions may lead to enhanced restrictions or incarceration. A general definition of *probation* is the conditional supervised release of a convicted offender into the community in lieu of incarceration (Allen et al. 1985). *Parole* is the conditional supervised release of an incarcerated offender into the community after serving part of the sentence in confinement (Clear and Cole 1986).

PROBATION

Before informal probation was created in Boston in 1841 by philanthropist John Augustus, and the first statewide probation law was enacted in Massachusetts in 1978, convicted offenders were typically fined or imprisoned, often serving their full sentence. Probation was instituted as an alternative to incarceration at a time when jail and prison overcrowding became a critical management and humanitarian issue. Probation was considered a front-end sentencing solution to overcrowding, intended specifically for less serious, first-time, and juvenile offenders amenable to "rehabilitation."

Over the years, rehabilitation has remained the primary goal of probation, and to this end, probation facilitates behavioral reform in a variety of ways. First, the often negative practical and symbolic consequences of the stigma of being an "ex-con" are neutralized. As less notorious and visible "probationers," the label will have less deleterious effects on the rehabilitative process. Second, the contaminating effects of imprisonment are avoided. This is particularly important for the less experienced offender, who may learn more about crime from more sophisticated, and sometimes predatory, inmates. The "pains of imprisonment" also produce anger, resentment, hostility, cynicism, and many other dysfunctional attitudes and feelings that make it more difficult to reform. Third, probation supports the existing social integration of the offender in the free community of noncriminals, including family, neighbors, employers and co-workers, friends, teachers and classmates, and others who are critical to the informal social control of crime. The offender released from incarceration will have the more difficult task of "reintegration." Fourth, the rehabilitative programs and services available to probationers are generally less coercive and more varied, flexible, and effective than those provided for prisoners. Fifth, the implied trust in leaving an offender in the community to demonstrate the ability to conform reinforces a positive attribution of self and expectations of appropriate behavior. Probation is more likely than incarceration to contribute to a self-fulfilling prophecy of rehabilitation.

Secondary goals of probation are more punitive. Probation is a penal sanction by virtue of the restrictions placed on the freedom of the offender. The conditions range from very lenient (e.g., weekly phone contact with a probation officer) to very punitive (e.g., twenty-four-hour home confinement), depending on the nature of the offense and offender characteristics. The goal of crime control can also be addressed by enhanced monitoring of probationers' compliance with the terms of probation, particularly their whereabouts. This can be accomplished by increasing the number and duration of meaningful (namely, face-to-face) contacts between probationer and probation officer, in the department's office, at home, at work, in a residential or nonresidential program facility, or anywhere else in the community. More comprehensive control is possible with electronic monitoring devices; for example, transmitter anklets can verify the location of a probationer within, or outside of, a stipulated free movement area. The goal of deterrence is served to the extent that rehabilitation and punishment succeed in preventing probationers from committing more crimes and returning to the criminal justice system. Finally, justice is achieved when probation is the appropriate sentence for the offense and offender, and its application is equitable and uniform across race, sex, and socioeconomic status categories (McAnany, Thomson, and Fogel 1984).

The decision to grant probation is the product of a complex organization of legal actors, sentencing procedures, decision criteria, and system capacity. The decision may be initiated by the prosecutor, who negotiates a guilty plea in exchange for a recommendation to the judge that the defendant be sentenced to probation. Or it may await conviction at trial. In either case, a presentence investigation report prepared by a probation officer may support the recommendation by providing background information on the offender and an assessment of the public risks and prospects for probation success.

There are intense organizational pressures to minimize the number of trials and to divert convicted offenders from incarceration: There are huge case backlogs in the courts (Meeker and Pontell 1985) and tremendous overcrowding in jails and prisons, as evidenced by the almost forty states in 1988 that were under court order to reduce inmate populations in order to meet a variety of correctional standards (Petersilia 1987). Incredibly, it has been estimated that more than 90 percent of convictions for felonies are the result of negotiated guilty pleas (McDonald 1985), and a high percentage of those receive probation since, by state, from 25 to 70 percent of convicted felons are sentenced to probation (Petersilia 1985). It is clearly in the personal and organizational interests of the defendant, prosecutor, judge, and even the jailer and prison superintendent to support "copping" a plea for probation.

Whether the conviction is negotiated or decided at trial, the judge sentences the offender, within the constraints imposed by the sentencing model and guidelines used in the jurisdiction. Most states use indeterminate sentencing, where judges have substantial discretion in rendering sentences and parole authorities are responsible for release decisions of incarcerated offenders. The trend is toward determinate sentencing, where judges and parole boards have much less influence on sentence and release decisions. In both models, probation is a widely used sentencing option, especially for less serious offenders but even for many serious offenders: Nationally, as high as 20 percent of violent offenders receive probation, including 13 percent of defendants convicted of rape and 9 percent of those convicted of homicide (Lisefski and Manson 1988).

Despite the confluence of the trend toward determinate sentencing, more pervasive justice model practices in corrections, and increased public pressure to be more punitive with criminals, there are relatively more offenders on probation than incarcerated or on parole than there were two decades ago (Petersilia et al. 1985). More serious offenders are being incarcerated for more fixed sentences, but the concomitant institutional overcrowding has produced a greater utilization of probation, as well as a variety of types of probation designed to meet the needs of both less serious and middle-range offenders, who in the past would have been more likely to be incarcerated. In addition to "standard probation," characterized by assignment to a probation officer with a caseload of as many as two hundred probationers and nominal contact, supervision, and rehabilitative services, a whole range of "intermediate sanctions" has been created that includes programs that are typically more punitive, restrictive, intensive, and effective than standard probation (Petersilia 1987; Morris and Tonry 1990). Judges now have a diversity of probation alternatives at sentencing: intensive supervised probation, home confinement, electronic monitoring, residential centers (halfway houses), and split sentences (jail/probation). These alternatives are often combined and coupled with other probation conditions that require restitution to victims, employment or education, payment of program costs, random urinalysis, specialized treatment or classes (e.g., Alcoholics Anonymous), or community service. Many of the intermediate sanctions are also used in the supervision of parolees.

PAROLE

Like probation, parole in the United States was created to relieve the serious overcrowding problem in prisons at the beginning of the nineteenth century. Years before informal probation began, some prison wardens and correctional administrators were releasing prisoners before their full sentence was served. They were either released outright, much as if they had received a pardon, or were monitored informally by the police. Based on the European correctional innovations of "good time" and "ticket of leave," formal parole emerged toward the end of the nineteenth century, with the first indeterminate sentencing law passed in 1876 in New York (Champion 1990).

Until Maine abolished parole in 1976, all states had indeterminate sentencing and parole authorities. In general, within these systems a prisoner earns good time by productive participation in institutional programs and good conduct. The accumulated good time is subtracted from the sentence to determine the time incarcerated. This decision is typically made by a parole board, which is often a group of political appointees from a variety of occupations and constituencies. The offender is then released (or awarded a leave) to the supervision of a parole officer. If an offender does not commit a new crime or violate the conditions upon which release to parole is contingent, he or she can complete the remainder of the sentence as a parolee, to the time of discharge and freedom.

The goals of parole are anchored in indeterminate sentencing and the tenets of the rehabilitative ideal. It is assumed that offenders are amenable to reformation, through both the rehabilitation provided by the prison's treatment, educational, and vocational programs and the reintegration back into the free world facilitated by the transitional programs and services of parole. These twin primary goals of "rehabilitation" and "reintegration" drive the decisions and actions of the parole system. Parole is granted when the prisoner is considered ready for release, based on behavior during confinement, the extent to which rehabilitation is evident, and the apparent risk to public safety. In practice, many offenders spend a relatively small proportion of their sentence incarcerated; for instance, a convicted murderer with a life sentence may "do hard time" for as few as, say, ten years and serve the rest of the sentence on parole. Parole is revoked, or modified, when there are indications that reintegration is in jeopardy or unlikely, owing to violation of parole conditions. A new crime, in particular, but even a technical violation may be sufficient for the parole board to reincarcerate a parolee. The parole board also has the discretionary authority to set dates for parole hearings, fix minimum terms and release dates, determine good time credits, and specify parole conditions and requirements.

Like probation, the secondary goals of parole

include punishment, crime control, and deterrence. After all, parole is a part of the penal sanction defined by the sentence to imprisonment, and, depending on the type of parole and stipulated conditions, the parole experience can be very restrictive and quasi-custodial. Effective rehabilitation, supervision, and monitoring of parolees should also produce deterrent effects—the combination of reformation and punishment should prevent future criminal conduct among parolees.

Unfortunately, by the mid-1970s, evidence had accumulated that suggested that parole was not an especially effective crime control strategy (Martinson 1974), and the shift away from the rehabilitative ideal to a more punitive justice philosophy (von Hirsch 1976) began in earnest. About one-third of states have returned to some form of determinate sentencing, and more are likely to follow. The discretionary power of judges in rendering sentences and of parole boards in implementing them has been abridged, in order to make decisions more rational and fair by linking them to the severity of the offense rather than the characteristics of the offender. Offenders are now more likely to be serving sentences in confinement —since 1980, the rate of incarceration has increased by 76 percent (Bureau of Justice Statistics 1989). They are also less likely to be placed on parole by a paroling authority—between 1977 and 1987, releases from imprisonment decided by parole boards dropped from about 70 percent to 40 percent of all releases, while mandatory releases increased from roughly 5 percent to 30 percent of the total (Hester 1988). With determinate sentencing, many states simply do not have paroling authorities or parole supervision in the community.

These changes have also affected the types of parole that are still available in a majority of states. Although many parole and probation programs are similar, the usually more serious offenses and criminal histories of parolees and the shift toward more punitive correctional systems have led to a hardening of the conditions of (cf. U.S. Sentencing Commission 1987) and less utilization of "standard parole" and a greater emphasis on protecting public safety by extending custody from the institution to the community. The goals of rehabilitation and reintegration have become less important, while crime control and deterrence have become more important. Consequently, there is greater reliance on transitional programs that maximize monitoring and supervision, while providing opportunities and services (e.g., employment, school, counseling, drug treatment) intended to facilitate reentry into the community and desistance from crime during parole and, ultimately, after discharge from correctional supervision. These programs are more intensive and custodial, often involving residential placement in a halfway house, intensive parole supervision, or home confinement with electronic monitoring. From these community bases, parolees may participate in work or school releases, home furloughs, counseling, religious services, and a variety of other reintegrative activities.

Although parole is not used to the extent that it was before the advent of determinate sentencing, and there are those who believe that it should be abolished in all states, some research suggests that determinate sentencing is no more a panacea than prior correctional reforms. There may be a leveling of sentencing disparities, and more offenders are being incarcerated. But they, on the average, are doing less time and, after release, may be as likely to be reconvicted and reincarcerated (Covey and Mande 1985).

RESEARCH

While the research evidence on the efficacy of determinate sentencing may be sketchy, there are many studies of other issues in probation and parole that have produced more substantive results. Social scientific research on probation and parole has tended to revolve around a set of related issues that are common to both: program effectiveness, recidivism, and classification and prediction. The overriding empirical and policy question is "What works?" Attempts to address the question vary in rigor and quality, and the answers are neither direct nor simple.

There are innumerable studies of program

effectiveness, most of them not producing useful, much less compelling, evidence of program success or failure. For example, many studies conclude that a probation program is successful because 30 percent of participants recidivate or that a parole program is successful because 40 percent of participants recidivate. There are serious problems with those kinds of studies. First, they do not compare the program being evaluated with others, either with other probation or parole programs, or across correctional alternatives (e.g., release, probation, incarceration, and parole).

Second, without comparison groups, one can only evaluate program effectiveness in relation to some standard of success. But preordained acceptable levels of recidivism are determined normatively, not empirically. Normative criteria of success cannot be applied uniformly across the incredible variation in probation and parole programs. For instance, some probation programs, because of the very low risk participants, should probably generate recidivism rates that are closer to 5 percent than 30 percent.

Third, recidivism is often not defined or measured adequately. Generically, recidivism has come to mean "reoffending," particularly by offenders who have had contact with the criminal justice system, as measured typically by rearrest, reconviction, reincarceration, or some variation or combination thereof. But what does a probationer or parolee relapse to, and what is the most appropriate and accurate measure? The answers are complicated by the fact that probation and parole can be revoked if an offender commits a crime that becomes known to criminal justice authorities or by a noncriminal violation of release conditions (a "technical violation"). Paradoxically, practically all studies ignore the substantial amount of successful criminal behavior that remains hidden from officials, but many use both revocation criteria as measures of recidivism. Which measure is used can dramatically affect judgments about program effectiveness. Evaluations of three intensive probation supervision programs show that technical violations, as compared to new crimes, account for the majority of revocations. The revocation rates due to technical violations for these programs were 56 percent, 70 percent, and 85 percent, respectively. However, if the technical violations are not counted in the recidivism rates, the rates drop to 7 percent, 8 percent, and 5 percent, respectively (Petersilia 1987). Depending on program objectives, recidivism, no matter how measured, may not be the only or most appropriate criterion of program effectiveness. It may also be useful to assess relative costs and savings, impacts on jail and prison overcrowding, effects on public perceptions of safety, performance at school or in the workplace, changes in offenders' attitudes and self-concept, and so on.

More rigorous studies utilize comparison groups in order to assess the relative effectiveness of different correctional strategies. A typical study compares the recidivism rates of various combinations of offenders on probation, incarcerated, and on parole, and concludes that probationers are least likely and ex-prisoners are most likely to recidivate. Of course, one would predict those results based on the differences between the groups in their risk to recidivate. The selection biases of the court place the least serious, low-risk offenders on probation and the most serious, high-risk offenders in institutions. The observed differences in recidivism do not reflect the relative effectiveness of the programs, but the original differences in the recidivism risks of the comparison groups.

Some studies attempt to produce more comparable groups by using more objective probation and parole prediction instruments to classify and then compare offenders by level of recidivism risk across programs. That is, they try improve comparability by "matching" offenders within the different program groups. For example, a study of the relative effectiveness of standard probation, intensive supervision probation, and incarceration with parole classified offenders within each group into low-, medium-, high-, and maximum-risk levels. Comparisons of recidivism, measured by rearrest, reconviction, and reincarceration, across the three program alternatives for each of the four categories of offenders (namely, least likely to most likely to recidivate) show that parole is least effective in preventing recidivism at all levels of recidivism risk. But the differences between standard and intensive probation are not as consistent: no matter how recidivism is measured, the rate is higher among intensive supervision probationers who are low- and high-risk offenders; among medium-risk offenders, it varies by the measure of recidivism; and for maximum-risk probationers, there seems to be little difference in the effectiveness of standard or intensive supervision, except for the somewhat higher reincarceration rate among intensive supervision probationers (Erwin 1986).

The equivocal findings of this and many similar studies reflect the difficulty in predicting recidivism risk with any degree of accuracy. The most comprehensive and statistically sophisticated techniques (e.g., cluster analyses, linear models, complex contingency tables) are not much more accurate than bivariate tabular procedures developed seventy years ago by Ernest Burgess. And no technique is able to predict recidivism with higher than 70 percent accuracy, with most slightly better than chance (Blumstein et al. 1986). Therefore, it is virtually impossible to make groups comparable on the basis of recidivism risk, or any other prediction criteria, which compromises the validity of the findings regarding differential program effectiveness.

The mixed results probably also reflect the paradox of intensive supervision programs in general: Increasing supervision and monitoring may increase, rather than decrease, the probability of recidivism. The offender is at greater risk to recidivate, simply because there is a better chance that unacceptable conduct will be observed. However, depending on the declared program goals, this may indicate success rather than failure: If intensive supervision probation and parole are intended to enhance crime control and public safety, rather than to rehabilitate, higher rates of recidivism may demonstrate program effectiveness (Gottfredson and Gottfredson 1988).

Research on probation and parole effectiveness cannot produce compelling findings from studies that depend on comparisons of typically noncomparable groups. What is necessary are "equivalent" groups that are created through random assignment within experiments. Unfortunately, experimental designs are usually more expensive and more difficult to implement and complete in natural settings. Consequently, they are extremely rare in research on probation and parole. For instance, there are more than one hundred studies of the effectiveness of intensive probation supervision, but none have an experimental design with random assignment to program conditions (Petersilia 1987). There are some current efforts to implement studies of probation and parole that have experimental designs, but if the objective is to produce valid and useful knowledge on "what works," there must be a greater commitment on the part of the criminal justice system, funding agencies, and the social science research community.

(SEE ALSO: *Court Systems of the United States; Criminal Sanctions; Criminology; Social Control*)

REFERENCES

Allen, Harry E., Chris Eskridge, Edward Latessa, and Gennaro Vito 1985 *Probation and Parole in America.* New York: Free Press.

Blumstein, Alfred, Jacqueline Cohen, Jeffrey Roth, and Christy Visher, eds. 1986 *Criminal Careers and "Career Criminals."* Washington, D.C.: National Academy Press.

Bureau of Justice Statistics 1989 *Prisoners in 1988* (bulletin). Washington, D.C.: U.S. Department of Justice.

Champion, Dean J. 1990 *Probation and Parole in the United States.* Columbus, Ohio: Merrill.

Clear, Todd, and George F. Cole 1986 *American Corrections.* Belmont, Calif.: Brooks/Cole.

Covey, Herbert C., and Mary Mande 1985 "Determinate Sentencing in Colorado." *Justice Quarterly* 2:259–270.

Erwin, Billie S. 1986 "Turning Up the Heat on Probationers in Georgia." *Federal Probation* 50:17–24.

Gottfredson, Michael, and Don M. Gottfredson 1988 *Decision Making in Criminal Justice.* New York: Plenum.

Hester, Thomas 1988 *Probation and Parole, 1987.* Washington, D.C.: U.S. Department of Justice.

Lisefski, Edward, and Donald Manson 1988 *Tracking*

Offenders. Washington, D.C.: U.S. Department of Justice.

Martinson, Robert 1974 "What Works? Questions and Answers About Prison Reform." *Public Interest* 35: 22–54.

McAnany, Patrick D., Doug Thomson, and David Fogel (eds.) 1984 *Probation and Justice: Reconsideration of a Mission.* Cambridge, Mass.: Oelgeschlager, Gunn and Hain.

McDonald, William F. 1985 *Plea Bargaining: Critical Issues and Common Practices.* Washington, D.C.: U.S. Department of Justice.

Meeker, James, and Henry M. Pontell 1985 "Court Caseloads, Plea Bargains, and Criminal Sanctions: The Effects of Section 17 P.C. in California." *Criminology* 23:119–143.

Morris, Norval, and Michael Tonry 1990 *Between Prison and Probation: Intermediate Punishments in a Rational Sentencing System.* New York: Oxford.

Petersilia, Joan 1985 *Probation and Felony Offenders.* Washington, D.C.: U.S. Department of Justice.

——— 1987 *Expanding Options for Criminal Sentencing.* Santa Monica, Calif.: Rand.

———, Susan Turner, James Kahan, and Joyce Peterson 1985 *Granting Felons Probation: Public Risks and Alternatives.* Santa Monica, Calif.: Rand.

U.S. Sentencing Commission 1987 *United States Sentencing Commission Guidelines Manual.* Washington, D.C.: U.S. Sentencing Commission.

Von Hirsch, Andrew 1976 *Doing Justice.* New York: Hill and Wang.

JOSEPH G. WEIS

PROFESSIONS The idea of a "profession" did not exist in ancient times. Although there were people who did what is currently denoted as professional work, these "professionals" often labored in dependent positions. For example, physicians in the Roman Empire were slaves in wealthy households, and architects worked as salaried public employees. These "professionals" also had little education. Lawyers in ancient Greece were merely friends of the litigants who spoke before a gathering of their peers. Neither lawyers nor physicians received formal training (Carr-Saunders and Wilson 1933).

By medieval times, the three classic professions—medicine, law, and the clergy (which included university teaching)—began to approximate more closely the modern conception of a profession. With the development of universities, then under religious auspices, would-be professionals completed lengthy training in their chosen fields. They also began to constitute a new class of intellectuals. As society increasingly secularized, the professions emerged from under religious control and began to organize professional associations. By the eighteenth century they had achieved independent status.

In the nineteenth century, middle class occupations such as dentistry, architecture, and engineering began to professionalize, aspiring to the gentlemanly status of the classic, learned professions (Dingwall and Lewis 1983). "Gentlemanly" was the appropriate description, since the majority of professionals were men. It was not until the 1970s that women began to make significant inroads into these occupations, and even today men predominate in the status professions.

In the nineteenth and early twentieth centuries, professionalism developed in concert with the increasing division of labor and rationalization characteristic of industrializing Europe and the United States. As competitors in market economies, occupational incumbents sought to professionalize to improve their status. In addition, they wanted to better their economic positions by securing occupational niches for their services (Ritzer and Walczak 1986). In the United States, at least, universities played the key role of transferring both the technical know-how and the culture of professionalism to new generations of professional aspirants (Bledstein 1976).

WHICH OCCUPATIONS ARE PROFESSIONS?

Today the term *profession* includes a range of occupations arrayed along a continuum of high to medium levels of prestige. First, at the high end of the continuum are the classic, or "status," professions of medicine, law, clergy, and university teaching. Incumbents in these occupations usually receive high incomes, exercise job autonomy, and receive deference from the public and those lower in the status hierarchy. They are also typically male—in 1988, women's representation among college and university teachers, physicians, lawyers, and the clergy were 38, 20, 19, and 9 percent, respectively (U.S. Bureau of Labor Statistics 1989).

Second, somewhat lower on the continuum are the "newer" professions such as dentistry, engineering, accounting, and architecture, which also command respect and relatively high salaries. Men also predominate in these occupations—in 1988, 9, 7, and 15 percent of dentists, engineers, and architects were women. Only in accounting have women made significant inroads—by 1988, nearly half of all accountants and auditors were women. This feminization is attributable largely to that occupation's dramatic occupational growth in the 1970s (Reskin and Roos 1990).

Third, still lower on the professional continuum are the marginal professions (e.g., pharmacy, chiropractic) and the semiprofessions (e.g., nursing, public school teaching, librarianship). These occupations exhibit some characteristics of the classic professions but have not acquired full professional status. They have been unable to professionalize fully because of opposition from established professions and an inability to convince the public that they command unique expertise. As a consequence, they are less prestigious and are paid less than incumbents in either the classic or new professions. Moreover, because they concentrate in bureaucratic settings, incumbents in these occupations exercise less job autonomy than higher-status professionals. An important feature of the marginal and semiprofessions is that the former are predominantly male (in 1988, 32 percent of pharmacists were female), the latter predominantly female (women composed 95, 73, and 85 percent of nurses, public school teachers, and librarians, respectively).

Finally, while not professionals per se, paraprofessionals work with, but as subordinates to, members of the other professions. They are generally technicians associated with various professional occupations. Paralegals, for example, work closely with lawyers, and physicians delegate certain tasks and responsibilities to physicians' assistants. As in the semiprofessions, women tend to predominate in paraprofessional occupations.

THE PROCESS OF PROFESSIONALIZATION

Given the stratification of the U.S. occupational structure, it is clear why workers desire to professionalize. Professionalization brings higher income, higher prestige, and greater job autonomy. It also protects incumbents from competition. The "process of professionalization" posits a common sequence of development that occupations undergo. Some scholars accept Harold Wilensky's (1964) depiction of this process. First, people begin to work full time at a specific set of tasks that will form the new occupation's core jurisdiction. Second, those in the occupation establish a university-affiliated training program, and some incumbents undertake the responsibility for training new generations of practitioners. Third, practitioners and teachers combine to form a professional association that identifies the occupation's core tasks and makes claims regarding skill jurisdiction. Fourth, occupational incumbents seek to protect their jurisdictional claims by political means. Professionals lobby for legal protection, in the form of licensing and certification requirements, to generate labor market shelters that ensure their monopoly of skills. Finally, incumbents develop a formal code of ethics that embodies rules to protect clients, eliminate the unqualified, and spell out the occupation's service ideal.

APPROACHES TO THE STUDY OF THE PROFESSIONS

What distinguishes the professions from other occupations? Theoretical approaches in studying this question have changed over time and remain in flux. Scholars have also developed new methods to address these questions.

The Trait Approach. After World War II, the trait approach was the dominant one in scholarship on the professions (Freidson 1986). Scholars —mostly American academics—tried to define the professions by generating an exhaustive list of characteristics. These traits, scholars hoped, would distinguish professions from nonprofessions and higher-status professions from those of lower status. The main method used was the case study. Scholars carefully scrutinized particular occupations to determine how well they approximated an ideal-typical profession.

Theorists posited that four major criteria, or traits, existed in the ideal-typical profession (Hodson and Sullivan 1990). First, professions have esoteric knowledge. Professionals are experts, possessing abstract knowledge and skills that set them apart from ordinary people. Second, because of their unique expertise, professionals are able to exercise autonomy on the job. Codes of ethics help to ensure autonomy from outside control by permitting professionals to police misconduct internally. Third, their esoteric knowledge allows professionals to claim authority over their clients and subordinate occupational groups. Finally, the professions are altruistic, that is, service- rather than profit-oriented. Underlying these four traits is a fifth characteristic—the public must recognize the occupation as a profession. Regardless of an occupation's *claim* of unique expertise, if the public does not view the occupation's knowledge as abstract, it is difficult for those working in it to claim professional status and the perquisites that accompany it.

Scholars used these criteria to differentiate among the professions, most particularly in comparing the female semiprofessions to the typically male status professions. While the semiprofessions have a body of knowledge, they lack a monopoly over that knowledge. They also have a difficult time convincing the public that their skills are professional. The public is less likely to recognize their expertise (e.g., teaching children, servicing library patrons) as particularly esoteric. Semiprofessionals typically work in bureaucratic settings and, as a consequence, are subject to heteronomy, or supervision by organizational superiors and professional colleagues. Thus, semiprofessionals can make only limited claims to autonomy.

The Power Approach. In the 1960s, scholars in the United States and Great Britain began to criticize the trait approach for being static and ideological. Power theorists also shifted to historical methods to understand the sources of professional power. These scholars argued that occupations we view as professions do not necessarily exhibit the requisite traits. Rather, incumbents in these occupations simply have the power to convince the public that they possess these traits. Power thus became the operative word, supplanting expertise as the mechanism whereby professionals achieve market control and prestige. Power theorists viewed the professions as monopolistic organizations intent on gaining and retaining professional control and ensuring their status in the stratification system. Eliot Freidson (1986), for example, described his early work as focusing on the political and cultural influences of the professions and as depicting how professions establish protected labor markets for their services. Magali Sarfatti Larson (1977) argued that the professions are market organizations in the capitalist economy, explicitly seeking to dominate the market for their expertise.

For these theorists, the so-called objective characteristics of the trait approach are ideological attempts to preserve the professions' status and privilege (Freidson 1986). For example, they posited that, rather than being truly altruistic, the professions create the myth of service orientation to gain public goodwill, enhance their status, and minimize external control. In addition, they contended that professionals abuse their autonomy by failing to police themselves—incompetent doctors and lawyers fleece the public with little fear of reprisal from their peers. Finally, the professional's authority over clients has also declined in recent years as the public has become more active in activities seen as the province of professionals (e.g., getting second opinions on medical recommendations and becoming more educated consumers regarding medical and legal issues).

The historical battles between physicians, on the one hand, and pharmacists and chiropractors on the other, illustrate how an established profession exercises power against competing occupations (Starr 1982). When the pharmacist's traditional task of compounding drugs shifted to pharmaceutical companies, they lost their diagnostic expertise (and hence monopoly over their knowledge). With respect to chiropractors, the American Medical Association has lobbied to keep this occupation from threatening their jurisdictional claims by restricting access through licensing laws or blocking reimbursement from private insurance companies. As a consequence, pharmacy and chiropractic remain marginal to the established professions and have not achieved full professional status.

What enables professions to wield power? According to power theorists, the major sources for professional power are indeterminancy and uncertainty (Ritzer and Walczak 1986). Those professions that have achieved and maintained power are those whose tasks cannot be broken down or otherwise routinized (indeterminancy). Similarly, those that deal with areas of uncertainty are also likely to preserve their power. As Wilensky (1964) described it, professional knowledge involves a "tacit" dimension, in Polanyi's (1967) terminology. Their lengthy training and years of practical application ensure that physicians "know" what treatments to use for which symptoms. Similarly, lawyers "know" what legal strategies work best, given the particulars of the cases they take to court. Reading a textbook or consulting computerized data bases is not equivalent to tacit knowledge. This kind of knowledge—expertise refined by years of experience—is not easily routinized. Physicians and lawyers also deal with areas of high uncertainty for their clients, the former with physical health and the latter with legal affairs. Clients need these professionals to translate medical and legal jargon into everyday language they can more readily understand.

The System of Professions. Andrew Abbott's (1988) theory of professions critiques previous approaches, especially the notion that professions undergo a common process of development. Employing historical and comparative methods, Abbott provides a wealth of evidence that the history of the professions is much more complicated than that suggested by a linear process of professionalization. Rather than a history of professions that established systems of control (e.g., schools, professional associations, licensing and certification), Abbott's account is of interprofessional competitions, squabbles over jurisdictions, and professional births and deaths.

Abbott's contention is that professionalization must be seen as part of a larger "system of professions." Professions make up an interdependent system, and understanding modern professions entails articulating their histories of conflict with other professions. Thus, comprehending the realities of modern medicine, for example, depends more on an investigation of its historical conflicts with closely related professions such as psychiatry and chiropractic than on the particulars of medieval or nineteenth-century medicine.

Recognizing the interdependence of professions is important because it clarifies that professions emerge, grow, change, and die within the historical context of competition with other professions. Interprofessional competition means that occupations compete over closely related jurisdictions. Jurisdictional disputes arise out of one of the characteristics peculiar to the professions—abstract knowledge. Professionals can use their abstract knowledge to define a core set of tasks (their jurisdiction), defend that jurisdiction from others, or appropriate the tasks of others. When any of these events occur, or when some outside force such as technology impinges on how professionals perform their jobs, the changes reverberate throughout the system. The professions reequilibrate, with some occupations accepting a subordinate or advisory role, some agreeing to split jurisdictions or clients, and others exiting the professions altogether.

SEX DIFFERENCES IN THE PROFESSIONS

In 1988, women composed 45 percent of the employed labor force but 50 percent of professionals, suggesting that women have equal access to professional occupations (U.S. Bureau of Labor Statistics 1989). However, a closer look at the statistics reveals a different story. As noted, women heavily concentrate in the semiprofessions (as nurses, public school teachers, and librarians) and men in the higher-status professions (as physicians, lawyers, and engineers). Incumbents in the former earn less and exercise less autonomy than workers in the latter. As in the entire labor force, the professions are thus highly segregated by sex.

Even within the higher-prestige professions, women work in different, lower-paying, and less-prestigious jobs than men. Women lawyers, for example, work in government jobs, in research rather than litigation, and in certain specialties such as trust and estates; women physicians are more likely than men to specialize in pediatrics and to work in health maintenance organizations (HMOs); female clergy specialize in music or education (Reskin and Phipps 1988).

Part of the reason for this differential job distribution by sex has to do with a characteristic unique to the professions. The high level of uncertainty inherent in prestigious professional jobs means that employers are careful to choose recruits who "fit in" with those already on the job. Thus, as Rosabeth Moss Kanter (1977) suggested, employers tend to recruit people much like themselves, a process she calls "homosocial reproduction." The predominance of males in the status professions thus ensures the perpetuation of sex segregation.

Other factors reducing women's access to high-status professions are entrance restrictions such as certification and licensing. Physicians, for example, consolidated their control over medical jurisdictions by successfully pressing for legislation to outlaw midwives and prohibit the licensing of those trained at "irregular" schools, activities that disproportionately affected women. In 1872, the Supreme Court restricted women's ability to practice law, arguing that "the natural and proper timidity and delicacy which belongs to the female sex unfits it for many of the occupations of civil life" (Reskin and Phipps 1988). Professionals, most of whom were males, were thus able to establish labor market shelters to protect themselves from competition from women as well as other "undesirables."

But what of the present day? Since 1970, women have made inroads into some of the professions, including occupations such as medicine, law, and pharmacy. Indications are, however, that internal differentiation within the professions perpetuates occupational segregation by sex (Reskin and Roos 1990). For example, Polly Phipps (1990) found that women's representation in pharmacy nearly tripled (from 12 to 32 percent) between 1970 and 1988. Phipps also noted, however, that women pharmacists concentrate in the lower-paying hospital sector, while men predominate in the higher-paying retail sector. Similar ghettoization exists in other professions that are admitting more women.

THE CHANGING PROFESSIONS

Some view the future of the professions as bleak, pointing to ongoing proletarianization or deprofessionalization as eliminating the professions' unique traits. The proletarianization thesis argues that an increasing division of labor and bureaucratization within the professions are routinizing knowledge and transferring authority from professionals to organizational superiors. The deprofessionalization thesis documents declines in the professions' monopolistic control over their knowledge, their exercise of autonomy on the job, their ability to protect their jurisdiction from encroachments, and the public's deference to professional authority (Ritzer and Walczak 1986).

Some occupations, of course, have deprofessionalized. As noted, as pharmaceutical companies increasingly absorbed the compounding of drugs, and as chains replaced independent pharmacies, pharmacists lost some of their autonomy and monopoly of their knowledge to physicians. Taking a broad view of the professions, however, Freidson (1984) provided evidence that the presumed incompatibility between bureaucratization and professionalization is overstated. Working in organizations, he argued, has been the norm for most professions from their inception, with engineers the most obvious example. In addition, organizations that employ professionals tend to diverge enough from the ideal-typical bureaucracy to protect professional privilege. For example, professionals in organizations often exercise a lot of autonomy, working under senior members of their own profession rather than nonprofessional managers. Freidson thus portrays organizations as accommodating professionals.

Freidson (1984) also found no evidence that the prestige of the professions as a whole has declined. Nor did he find that public trust in professionals has deteriorated relative to other American institutions. Thus, when viewed as a set of occupations, he argued that the professions have not deteriorated in status. Moreover, the professions' continuing ability to erect labor market barriers to competition is important evidence of their enduring power. Professionals today continue to remain strong enough to exert their will against others lower in the occupational hierarchy. Professional privilege thus remains intact in the American occupational structure.

(SEE ALSO: *Work and Occupations; Work Orientation*)

REFERENCES

Abbott, Andrew 1988 *The System of Professions: An Essay on the Division of Expert Labor.* Chicago: University of Chicago Press.

Bledstein, Burton J. 1976 *The Culture of Professionalism: The Middle Class and the Development of Higher Education in America.* New York: W. W. Norton.

Carr-Saunders, A. M., and P. A. Wilson 1933 "Professions." In Edwin R. A. Seligman and Alvin Johnson, eds., *Encyclopaedia of the Social Sciences.* New York: Macmillan.

Dingwall, Robert, and Philip Lewis 1983 *The Sociology of the Professions: Lawyers, Doctors and Others.* London: Macmillan.

Freidson, Eliot 1984 "The Changing Nature of Professional Control." *Annual Review of Sociology* 10:1–20.

——— 1986 *Professional Powers: A Study of the Institutionalization of Formal Knowledge.* Chicago: University of Chicago Press.

Hodson, Randy, and Teresa A. Sullivan 1990 *The Social Organization of Work.* Belmont, Calif.: Wadsworth.

Kanter, Rosabeth Moss 1977 *Men and Women of the Corporation.* New York: Harper and Row.

Larson, Magali Sarfatti 1977 *The Rise of Professionalism: A Sociological Analysis.* Berkeley: University of California Press.

Phipps, Polly A. 1990 "Industrial and Occupational Change in Pharmacy: Prescription for Feminization." In Barbara F. Reskin and Patricia A. Roos, *Job Queues, Gender Queues: Explaining Women's Inroads into Male Occupations.* Philadelphia, Pa.: Temple University Press.

Polanyi, Michael 1967 *The Tacit Dimension.* Garden City, N.Y.: Anchor Books.

Reskin, Barbara F., and Polly A. Phipps 1988 "Women in Male-Dominated Professional and Managerial Occupations." In Ann H. Stromberg and Shirley Harkess, eds., *Women Working: Theories and Facts in Perspective.* Mountain View, Calif.: Mayfield.

Reskin, Barbara F., and Patricia A. Roos 1990 *Job Queues, Gender Queues: Explaining Women's Inroads into Male Occupations.* Philadelphia: Temple University Press.

Ritzer, George, and David Walczak 1986 *Working: Conflict and Change.* 3rd ed. Englewood Cliffs, N.J.: Prentice-Hall.

Starr, Paul 1982 *The Social Transformation of American Medicine: The Rise of a Sovereign Profession and the Making of a Vast Industry.* New York: Basic Books.

U.S. Bureau of Labor Statistics 1989 *Employment and Earnings,* Vol. 36 (January). Washington, D.C.: U.S. Government Printing Office.

Wilensky, Harold L. 1964 "The Professionalization of Everyone?" *American Journal of Sociology* 70:137–158.

PATRICIA A. ROOS

PROSTITUTION Prostitution is the granting of nonmarital sexual access for remuneration that provides part or all of the prostitute's livelihood. Most prostitution involves a woman who services male clients; perhaps 5 percent involves males servicing other males in the United States.

There is a prostitution subculture that involves pimps and a range of intermediaries such as convention personnel, bartenders, taxi drivers, and hotel bellhops. The pimp is a confidante, protector, and manager who usually gets all of the woman's earnings. The intermediaries, who steer the client to the woman, typically receive around 40 percent of her charge to the client. If the woman works out of a call house, the madam receives half of the payment. If the woman works in a brothel, the madam also gets half.

A brothel is an apartment or house where there is a manager and a number of prostitutes on duty so that the customer can choose one and go to a room for the sexual activity. The brothel, also called a whorehouse or bawdy house and formerly concentrated in specific areas called red light districts, exists today on a limited basis. It used to be the most frequent American format for prostitution until World War II, when the large number of young men away from home led to concern about the many brothels that opened near the training camps but that were soon closed by new federal laws. The brothels have largely been supplanted by hotels, bars, streetwalking, and quasilegal activities like escort services and massage parlors.

Call girls are at the apex of prestige of prostitution; streetwalkers are at the bottom. Women are relatively unlikely to move from one type or format of prostitution to another. Prostitution is one occupation in which age is negatively correlated with success because of the extent to which youth is prized by customers.

A variety of positive social functions has been cited for prostitution. It has been said to provide a sexual outlet for male immigrants or males who do not marry, to offer a form of sexual initiation for young men, to make available sexual satisfaction for handicapped men and others with exotic tastes that cannot be satisfied conventionally, to encourage marital stability by providing outlets for husbands with unusual sexual requirements that cannot be satisfied in the home, to meet fantasy needs of men and provide an activity that is collateral to gambling and spectator athletics (Winick and Kinsie 1972).

Beginning in the 1960s, some feminist writers began discussing prostitution as an ultimate degradation and symbol of men's exploitation of women. Other feminists saw prostitutes as the only honest women because they charge for their services rather than submit to a marriage contract that forces them to work for life without pay.

Prostitution is a crime in each of the fifty states, although Nevada law permits each county to decide if it wishes to permit legalization. Fifteen of the state's seventeen counties have opted for legalization.

Half the states have a "customer amendment" that considers a patron as guilty of a crime as the prostitute. However, the law against patrons is seldom implemented. Laws against prostitutes are themselves implemented inconsistently and are not assigned a high priority in most communities by prosecutors, police, or citizens. If prostitutes are arrested, they are likely to be given a small fine, serve a short prison term, or both.

The United Nations (1968) treaty on prostitution prohibited government licensing of prostitution and recommended that houses of prostitution be closed. It prohibited exploitation of prostitutes by third persons, recommended a program of rehabilitation of prostitutes, and emphasized the need for each country to follow a flexible course because of cultural traditions. Probably a majority of the countries in the world are following the United Nations treaty recommendations. The United States, which did not ratify the treaty, is unique in that its prohibitionist approach punishes both prostitutes and clients.

In many large cities, at least half the prostitutes are taking drugs such as heroin or cocaine (Goldstein 1979). Some may have become prostitutes in order to get money for illegal drugs, and others began using drugs after entering the occupation, as one way of coping with their work. Prostitutes' drug use has become a social issue because of the extent to which intravenous drug users are implicated in the spread of AIDS as a result of sharing infected needles. Non-drug using prostitutes have not been significant contributors to venereal disease because they generally examine clients' genitalia, take prophylactic doses of drugs like penicillin, and use condoms, even when providing oral sex. In general, prostitutes do not represent a significant contributor to AIDS and other sexually transmitted diseases.

Most countries are ambivalent about prostitution and are unable to resolve the differences between its seeming ubiquity and the norms against it. A few countries, like the Netherlands, have made prostitution a legal occupation; the government requires prostitutes to pay income taxes and makes social services available to them. Most Western countries, like England, permit prostitution so long as it does not represent a public nuisance such as aggressive street soliciting.

When sexual attitudes became more liberal in the 1960s, there was speculation that prostitution would decline. However, it did not decline and actually developed new formats. In recent years, there has been an increase in the number of women working as part-time prostitutes. Unless prostitution assumes the kind of salience as a public issue that it had early in the twentieth century, when it was known as "the master problem" or "the social evil," it is unlikely to attract the kind of legislative and political attention that will lead to significant changes in policy.

Sociologists have studied the subculture and social structure of prostitution, methods of induction into the occupation, prostitution's different formats, trends in customers and services, relations to patterns of sexual behavior in the larger society, and indirect cooperation by structural arrangements within the community (Frey, Reichert, and Russell 1981).

(SEE ALSO: *Deviance; Heterosexual Behavior Patterns; Legislation of Morality*)

REFERENCES

Frey, J. H., L. R. Reichert, and K. V. Russell 1981 "Prostitution, Business, and Police: The Maintenance of an Illegal Economy." *The Police Journal* 54:239–249.

Goldstein, P. 1979 *Prostitution and Drugs.* Lexington, Mass.: Lexington Books.

United Nations 1968 *Study on Traffic in Persons and Prostitution.* New York: United Nations.

Winick, C., and P. M. Kinsie 1972 *The Lively Commerce: Prostitution in the United States.* New York: New American Library.

CHARLES WINICK

PROTEST MOVEMENTS Protest movements have been of high interest to sociological research since the inception of the discipline in the early nineteenth century, during the periods of great industrial and urban development in Europe and North America. During massive changes in the economic structure and mass rural-to-urban and cross-national migration, a variety of protest movements developed, and they caught the attention of Comte, Le Bon, Weber, and other early sociological analysts. In the United States the first widely used introductory sociology textbook, developed by Chicago School sociologists Park and Burgess (1921), was organized around the concept of collective behavior, with protest movements occupying a substantive part of the text.

Such movements have generally been seen as an interim form of collective challenge to some aspect of the social status quo. The protest continuum ranges from localized groups and crowds that organize around specific and short-term delimited grievances to mass protest movements about social conditions and perceived injustices. These mass protests are designed to generate comprehensive and fundamental changes in a society and sometimes across societies (Heberle 1968, p. 439; Turner and Killian 1986, p. 401). More so than localized acting crowds and less so than systemic social movements, protest movements encompass mass behavior that extends beyond a localized situation, and they have the potential of generating social movements when a variety of conducive conditions exist (Gusfield 1968; Smelser 1962; Tilly 1978).

The twentieth century has been characterized by a wide variety of protest movements. In the United States, industrial labor protests were common for the first third of the century, as were anti-immigration protests. The suffragette movement early in the century was a precursor to the women's movement for equal treatment and opportunity in the latter third of the century; the civil rights movement, led by blacks in the 1950s and 1960s, precipitated countermovements (another characteristic of protest movements) including the White Citizens' Council protests and the reemergence of the Ku Klux Klan. Poor people in Chile, El Salvador, Nicaragua, and other Latin American countries have protested the privileges of an elite economic class as vestiges of an unproductive and rigid class colonial structure. Such protest movements have also occurred in Africa, the Middle East, and Asia.

A common thread through the wide variety of protest movements is their political nature. In various ways governmental authority is challenged, changed, supported, or resisted in specific protest movements. To advance their prospects for success, protest movement leaders often engage in coalition politics with more powerful individuals and groups who, for their own interests and values, support the challenge raised by the movement (Piven and Cloward 1977; Rustin 1965). When protest movements succeed in generating sufficient public support to secure all or most of their goals, governments may offer policy legitimization of the movement as a means of adapting to or modifying a movement's challenge to the state of pre-movement affairs.

Such political legitimation has taken a variety of forms. The labor protest movements culminated in the passage of the National Labor Relations Act of 1935, which legitimized labor–management collective bargaining agreements. The suffragette movement resulted in passage of the Nineteenth Amendment to the Constitution, guaranteeing that the right to vote in the United States could not be denied or abridged on account of sex. The civil rights movement attained support with passage of the comprehensive Civil Rights Act of 1964 and the Economic Opportunity Act and Elementary and Secondary Education Act, both in 1965.

Success of these and other movements is often tempered by countermovements, participants of which perceive their relative positions and interests to be threatened. For instance, the women's movement experienced a series of challenges from those, often from fundamentalist religious groups, adhering to patriarchy (a male-dominated hierarchy). As a consequence, women's progress was slowed in winning various forms of equal treatment and opportunity in economic, political, and social areas of life, and the U.S. Congress failed to pass the Equal Rights Amendment.

More generally, after passage of civil rights legislation in the mid-1960s, a series of protest movements within the Democratic and, more extensively, the Republican parties resulted in growing administrative, legislative, and judicial resistance to equality in educational, occupational, and housing opportunities. The countermovement result has been a reentrenchment of a long-established economic structure of racism and low income class rigidity that functions independently of personalized racist feelings and beliefs (Wilson 1987, pp. 11–12). A reflection of such countermovement pressure is the growth in perception among white males that affirmative action educational and occupational policies directed toward racial and ethnic minorities and women constitute a form of reverse or "affirmative discrimination" (Glazer 1975).

Countermovements have generated their own countermovements, known as counter-counter protest movements. This variation of Hegelian dialectic does not result in a return to whatever constituted premovement normalcy; in conventional political terms the results are more conservative, reactionary, liberal, or radical than what existed before the protest movement. These terms may apply to the participants of a specific protest movement as well as to established authorities. Further, while a predominant orientation may exist among protest activists and another among established authorities, in complex, mass modern societies, values and political orientations are usually contending among protestors and their supporters and among established authorities and their supporters, against whom the protest is directed (Mueller and Judd 1981).

The U.S. civil rights movement can be viewed in historical terms, if not in contemporary political terms, as a primarily conservative movement. The predominant aim of activists and organizations was to allow blacks and other minorities to break into the political and economic system rather than to break the established system. In contrast, the late 1980s' and early 1990s' liberal to radical protest movements in Poland, Hungary, Rumania, and other Eastern European countries aimed to break the system of exclusive communist political and economic domination.

In the United States, protest ideologies are largely reminiscent of established, liberal democratic political ideals. This is evidenced in the way protest groups adopt language from the Declaration of Independence to fit their purposes. For example, the Black Panthers, popularly perceived as a radical group, adopted a statement of purpose that held, "We hold these truths to be self-evident, that all black and white [*sic*] men are created equal and endowed by their creator with certain unalienable rights." Similarly, the National Organization for Women inserted into their declaration of purposes the wording that "men and women" were created equal.

Protest movements attain mixed and sometimes changed results. These results occur because of institutional inertia (certain things have been done certain ways over a long period of time) and because of countermovements within institutional centers such as schools, businesses, and local, state, and national government offices. In the United States, reactions to the civil rights movement have resulted in private and public attitudes and behaviors that have combined to disadvantage more severely low income racial and ethnic minorities (Bonacich 1988). It is also the case that despite all the countermovement resistance to educational, economic, and political advances for minority status groups, census bureau reports document a growing number and proportion of blacks, women, and other minority status group members moving into educational institutions, occupational settings, and political positions from which they were formerly excluded *de jure* or *de facto* (e.g., see U.S. Bureau of the Census 1983; 1984).

Examples from history and other cultures demonstrate the mixed potential and results of protest movements. The German Nazi protest movement in the 1920s illustrated that a movement could be radical *and* reactionary, in that case toward further destabilization of the Weimar Republic's democratic government, which was perceived as being decreasingly effective and legitimate by growing sectors of the German public (Shirer 1960). After the Nazis succeeded in countering various democratic and communist protest movements, Germany saw a more comprehensive institutionalization of Nazi ideological and authoritarian control during the 1930s. More recently, in 1989, the Chinese student democratic protest movement in Tiananmen Square resulted in a government-sponsored countermovement that physically shattered the student protest and resulted in a system of political, economic, and educational controls that were more comprehensively rigid than those that existed before the protest movement.

It is evident that there is a wide range of protest participants and of protest methods employed. The characteristics of protest participants and the methods they employ have been central concerns of research on such movements.

PROTEST PARTICIPANTS AND METHODS OF PROTEST

If protest participants could alleviate their grievances or sense of injustice individually, there would be no likely motivation for them to become active in a protest movement. Protest participants thus have two central characteristics: (1) they have insufficient influence to gain a desired change in their circumstances, and (2) they seek active association with relatively like-minded persons to gain relief from their aggrieved state.

These two characteristics can be seen among protest participants over time and in different locales. In the 1960s civil rights movements in the United States, leading activists—including blacks, Hispanics, Native Americans, and women—expressed a strong sense of unequal treatment and opportunity while associating with and supporting activists to achieve equal opportunities in schools, jobs, elected offices, and other social settings. College students, the most active participants in the civil rights movement, could not generally be characterized in these minority status terms. Yet, they were not yet an established part of the economic and political order being challenged and were in a position to be critical of that order

(Lipset 1971). Other participant supporters such as labor unions, selected corporate leaders, and religiously motivated persons often saw protest related change needed in terms of their own long-term interests and worked either to help the civil rights movement succeed or to preempt or co-opt it (Gamson 1975, pp. 28–31). The broad political support base for the comprehensive 1964 Civil Rights Act had all these protest movement participant elements.

The individuals who are most likely to initiate and support a protest movement tend to be those with long-developed grievances within a society. A case in point is Solidarity, the labor group that precipitated the successful 1980s protest movement against communist rule in Poland and that helped precipitate other successful Eastern European protest movements. The initial work stoppage, instrumental in offering a political challenge to Polish and Soviet Marxist authority, occurred at the Lenin Shipyard in Gdansk, a center of Cassubian ethnic residence. For a long time Cassubians have held a minority status in Polish society (Lorentz 1935). As the protest movement proceeded to secure broad-based support among Polish citizens, it was no accident that Cassubians, who have experienced prejudice and discrimination beyond communist rule in Poland, would be at the forefront. It is also not surprising that Solidarity was led by a Cassub, Lech Walesa. It is also noteworthy that the protest movement received strong support from another Cassub, Pope John Paul II, whose original name of Karol Wojtyla ends with a Cassubian "a" rather than the more typical Polish "ski."

In the United States, the civil rights movement was manifestly initiated and led by blacks (Morris 1984). Jews, who have experienced more prejudice and discrimination than most other whites in American society, where they constitute less than 3 percent of the population, composed the largest group of whites in the movement. In the Congress of Racial Equality (CORE), one of the leading mass civil rights protest organizations, almost one-half of the white participants identified themselves as Jewish or as secularists whose parents were Jewish (Bell 1968).

The methods employed by protest participants and leaders tend to reflect a lack of institutionalized power. When such institutionalized power is available, it can be exercised to redress grievances without resorting to mass protests. Within democratic political processes in the United States and in other democratic societies, much organized protest on such issues as trade policies, road construction and placement, and taxation can be viewed in more normative, adaptive terms.

When such normative activities do not result in a resolution of grievances, the potential for a protest movement increases. In such a context, legitimized guarantees of the right to protest, as embedded in the U. S. Constitution's First Amendment guarantee of the right to assemble and petition for redress of grievances, do not preclude protest strategies that go beyond legal or normative boundaries of protest behavior.

Methods of protest are related to prospects of success and levels of frustration. When a protest movement or a countermovement has broad public support and is likely to receive a positive response from targeted authorities, protest activities are likely to be peaceful and accepted by such authorities. Such is the case with pro-choice protests on the abortion issue, protests for clean air, and protests in support of Jewish and other minority religious status groups in the Soviet Union. All these protest activities have relatively broad American support, even when they experience a minority activist opposition.

A variety of nonlegitimate strategies are used when protest movements address issues and involve participants with relatively little public support and active opposition. One such nonlegitimate strategy is Ghandi's nonviolent confrontation. Adapted by Martin Luther King, Jr., and most other black civil rights protest leaders in the 1950s and early 1960s, the strategy of nonviolence was designed to call general public attention in a nonthreatening manner to perceived injustices experienced by blacks. With such techniques as sit-ins at racially segregated lunch counters and boycotts of segregated public buses, this nonviolent method generates conflict by breaking down established social practices. The aim of such nonviolent methods is to advance conflict resolution by negotiating a change in practices that produced the protest. The most famous case is perhaps the 1955 Montgomery, Alabama, bus boycott, which was one of several major precipitants of the national black-led civil rights movement (Mauss 1975, p. 520; Morris 1984).

Other, violent, forms of protest include both planned strategies and unplanned spontaneous crowd action. In either case such activity tends to be perceived by authorities and their supporters as disorderly and lawless mob behavior. Masses of protest participants are likely to be drawn to violent action when the general perception (or emergent norm) (Turner and Killian 1986, pp. 21–25) develops that redress of felt grievances cannot be achieved either in normal conditions before protest or by peaceful means. The history of violent protest is a long one and includes the forcible occupation of farms and fields by landless French peasants in the eighteenth century, American attacks on British possessions and military posts prior to the Declaration of Independence, and bread riots by Russian urban dwellers in World War I (Graham and Gurr 1969).

Violent protests usually concern specific issues such as taxes, conscription into the military, and food shortages, issues that are confined to particular situations and times. Although these types of protests do not evolve into major social movements, they have had severe and immediate consequences, as in 1863, during the Civil War, when Irish Catholics protested what they perceived as the unfair nature of the military draft in New York City. These protests left several hundred dead. Likewise, college students in the late 1960s and early 1970s revolted against the draft during the unpopular Vietnam War, and these revolts included loss of human life.

Unplanned violence may also be a form of protest. As reported by the National Advisory Commission on Civil Disorders and other research on over two dozen urban racial riots in the 1960s in the United States, these riots, which resulted in over a hundred deaths and over $100 million in property damage, were disorganized extensions of the black civil rights movement (National Advisory Commission on Civil Disorders 1968; Fogelson 1971). These violent events closely fit Davies's (1974) J-curve thesis, which argues that rising expectations, produced by legal successes in the mid-1960s by the black civil rights movement, were frustrated by the declining urban ghetto environments and growing Vietnam War tensions, both of which were related to the fact that large numbers of blacks were being drafted while most white college students were exempted.

Overall, protest movements are more frequent in societies that legitimize the right of protest. In such societies, social conflict generated by protest movements is often functional in resolving conflict over issues between challenging and target groups (Coser 1956). Still, urban and campus riots of the 1960s illustrate that formal rights of protest do not preclude democratic authorities and their public supporters from responding with police force or from beginning a countermovement. Authoritarian societies may experience fewer protest movements, but when they do occur, such movements are far more likely to be intense and to have the potential for massive social movements designed to transform the society. This could be seen in widely disparate societies including most Eastern European nations and the Soviet Union, El Salvador, Nicaragua, Namibia, South Africa, Iran, and mainland China.

CONSEQUENCES OF PROTEST MOVEMENTS

Given the long and continuing history of protest movements, there has been growing interest in the long-term consequences of such movements. Some assessments concentrate on historical, comparative analysis such as Snyder and Tilly's (1972) analysis of French collective violence in response to government-sponsored repression between 1830 and 1968, or Bohstedt and Williams' (1988) analysis of the diffusion of riotous protests in Devonshire, England, between 1766 and 1801. Other studies of long-term consequences make empirical assessments of the aftermath of more contemporary protest movements. Examples include Gordon's (1983) community-based assessment of black and white leadership accommodation in the decade following the Detroit race riots of 1967 and Morris's (1980) assessment of the decade-long impact on national public values of the environmental movement of the late 1960s.

The need for more short- and long-term assessment of the consequences of protest movements is evident in reviews of past movements. William Gamson's consideration of fifty-three protest movements in the United States between the 1830s and 1930s illustrates the need. Gamson categorized each movement's own specific goals in one of four ways: co-opted, preempted, full response success, or collapsed failure (Gamson 1975, pp. 145–153). Gamson assessed each protest movement's success in achieving its goals during its own period of organized activity: For instance, Gamson assessed such groups as the German American Bund (1936–1943), the American Proportional Representation League (1893–1932), and the Dairymen's League (1907–1920).

Of the fifty-three identified protest movements, twenty-two, the largest single proportion, were categorized as being collapsed failures, twenty as achieving full response success, six as being preempted, and five as being co-opted. Protest movements categorized as collapsed failures and full response successes demonstrate the need for assessment of protest movements long beyond their activist periods. Listed under collapsed failures were major long-term successful movements including the abolitionist North Carolina Manumission Society (1816–1834) and the American Anti-Slavery Society (1833–1840). In contrast, among full response success movements was the American Committee for the Outlawry of War (1921–1929), a major force in the achievement of the international Kellogg-Briand Pact of 1928, which outlawed war between nations, a short-lived success that for most of the rest of the twentieth century proved a grand failure.

Successful or unsuccessful in the short or long term, protest movements are periodically a part of social change at local, national, and global levels and in situational, institutional, and cross-cultural concerns. In the United States and other modern mass urban societies, protest movements are becoming more professionalized and are mobilizing more resources to more effectively challenge entrenched interests (McCarthy and Zald 1973). Modern communication systems, international economic interdependence, and economical movement of masses of people over great distances assures that protest movements of the future will increasingly be characterized by a combination of ideas, people, and organization across all of these areas of social life.

(SEE ALSO: *Segregation and Desegregation; Social Movements; Student Movements*)

REFERENCES

Bell, Inge Powell 1968 *CORE and the Strategy of Non-Violence.* New York: Random House.

Bohstedt, John, and Dale E. Williams 1988 "The Diffusion of Riots: The Patterns of 1766, 1795, and 1801 in Devonshire." *Journal of Interdisciplinary History* 19 (no. 1):1–24.

Bonacich, Edna 1988 "Sociology of Race Relations in the United States." In E. F. Borgatta and K. S. Cook, eds., *The Future of Sociology.* Beverly Hills, Calif.: Sage.

Coser, Lewis 1956 *The Functions of Social Conflict.* New York: Free Press.

Davies, James C. 1974 "The J-Curve and Power Struggle Theories of Collective Violence." *American Sociological Review* 39:607–612.

Fogelson, Robert 1971 *Violence as Protest: A Study of Riots.* New York: Anchor.

Glazer, Nathan 1975 *Affirmative Discrimination.* Cambridge, Mass.: Harvard University Press.

Gamson, William A. 1975 *The Strategy of Social Protest.* Homewood, Ill.: Dorsey.

Gordon, Leonard 1983 "Aftermath of a Race Riot: The Emergent Norm Process Among Black and White Community Leaders." *Sociological Perspectives* 26:115–135.

Graham, Hugh D., and Ted Gurr, eds. 1969 *The History of Violence in America: Report of the National Commission on the Causes and Prevention of Violence.* New York: Bantam.

Gusfield, Joseph R. 1968 "The Study of Social Movements." In D. L. Sills, ed., *International Encyclopedia of the Social Sciences.* New York: Macmillan and Free Press.

Heberle, Rudolf 1968 "Types and Functions of Social Movements." In D. L. Sills, ed., *International Encyclopedia of the Social Sciences.* New York: Macmillan and Free Press.

Lipset, Seymour M. 1971 *Rebellion in the University.* Boston: Little, Brown.

Lorentz, Frederick 1935 *The Cassubian Civilization.* London: Faber and Faber.

Mauss, Armand L. 1975 *Social Problems as Social Movements.* New York: J. B. Lippincott.

McCarthy, John, and Mayer Zald 1973 *The Trend of Social Movements in America: Professionalization and Resource Mobilization.* Morristown, N.J.: General Learning.

Morris, Aldon D. 1984 *The Origins of the Civil Rights Movement: Black Communities Organizing for Change.* New York: Free Press.

Morris, Denton 1980 "The Soft Cutting Edge of Environmentalism: Why and How the Appropriate Technology Notion Is Changing the Movement." *Natural Resources Journal* 20:275–298.

Mueller, Carol, and Charles Judd 1981 "Belief Consensus and Belief Constraint." *Social Forces* 60:182–187.

National Advisory Commission on Civil Disorder 1968 *Report of the National Advisory Commission on Civil Disorders.* New York: Bantam.

Park, Robert E., and Ernest W. Burgess 1921 *Introduction to the Science of Sociology.* Chicago: University of Chicago Press.

Piven, Frances Fox, and Richard A. Cloward 1977 *Poor People's Movements: Why They Succeed, How They Fail.* New York: Vintage.

Rustin, Bayard 1965 "From Protest to Politics: The Future of the Civil Rights Movement." A *Commentary* Reprint. New York: Institute of Human Relations.

Shirer, William 1960 *The Rise and Fall of the Third Reich.* New York: Simon and Schuster.

Smelser, Neil J. 1962 *Theory of Collective Behavior.* New York: Free Press.

Snyder, David, and Charles Tilly 1972 "Hardship and Collective Violence in France: 1830 to 1960." *American Sociological Review* 37:520–532.

Tilly, Charles 1978 *From Mobilization to Rebellion.* Reading, Mass. Addison-Wesley.

Turner, Ralph, and Lewis M. Killian 1986 *Collective Behavior.* 3rd ed. Englewood Cliffs, N.J.: Prentice-Hall.

U.S. Bureau of the Census 1983 *Handbook of Labor Statistics.* Washington, D.C.: U.S. Government Printing Office.

——— 1984 *Employment and Earnings.* Washington, D.C.: U.S. Government Printing Office.

Wilson, William J. 1987 *The Truly Disadvantaged: The Inner City, the Underclass, and Public Policy.* Chicago: University of Chicago Press.

LEONARD GORDON

PUBLIC OPINION Public opinion is characterized, on the one hand, by its form as elementary collective behavior (Blumer 1972) and, on the other, by its function as a means of social control (Ross 1901). It comes into play in problematical situations characterized by some degree of normative ambiguity in one of several senses: The situation is novel and unprecedented, so that persons cannot cope by falling back on generally accepted codes of conduct; people actively disagree over the appropriate way of coping with the situation; or existing practices have been challenged by a dissident group. In the extreme case, controversy over what should be done can heat up to a point where order gives way to violent intragroup conflict or revolution.

Interest in public opinion is historically linked to the rise of popular government. Although rulers have always had to display some minimum sensitivity to the needs and demands of their subjects, they felt little need, unlike most of today's governments that must face voters in mandated elections, to anticipate their constituents' reactions to events that were yet to occur or to policies still to be implemented. But public opinion operates equally outside the relationship of citizens to the state. Its influence is felt throughout civil society, where on many matters, including personal taste in dress, music, or house furnishings, people remain sensitive to the changing opinions of peers and neighbors. They court approval by showing themselves in step with the times.

Opinions have behind them neither the sanctity of tradition nor the sanctions of law. Their only force is agreement, and people can change their minds. Labeling something as "opinion" implies a certain willingness to acknowledge the validity of contrary views, which opens the issue to discussion. Those involved to the degree that their attention is focused on the issue and they are ready to take sides make up a public. It usually expands in size as an issue heats up, to contract again as the focus shifts to new problems. There are in fact as many publics as there are issues.

In the center of early sociological studies of public opinion was the question of competence. Analysts sought to distinguish conceptually between the reasoned opinions developed in discussion and the nondebatable demands voiced by the greatly feared "mob" acting under the sway of emotion. But two works, one in Germany and one in America, coincidentally published the same year, analyzed the problem in structural terms. Tönnies (1922) pointed to the press and to associations who usurped for themselves the role of articulating public opinion. To Lippmann (1922) the notion that ordinary citizens—even the most well-educated among them—had the time and incentive to acquire the expertise necessary to grasp the complex problems of the day in sufficient detail to direct the course of events was a false ideal. Drawing on a wide range of literature, he showed how the public saw the world in stereotypes fed to them by the press. Whenever the public attempted to intervene in the policy process, he argued, it was inevitably as the dupe or unconscious ally of special interests. The role of the public was necessarily limited to identifying the problems and areas in need of remedial action of some sort and to deciding which party, institution, or agency should be trusted to work out solutions. Mostly he saw the public as a potentially effective "reserve force" to be mobilized in support of the procedural norms of democracy.

The list of social scientists echoing these skeptical views about "rule by public opinion" under modern conditions includes Mannheim (1940), Schumpeter (1942), Schattschneider (1960), Bogart (1972), and most recently Ginsberg (1986). "The paradox of mass politics," writes Neuman (1986, p. 3), "is the gap between the expectation of an informed citizenry put forward by democratic theory and the discomforting reality revealed by systematic survey interviewing." Where pluralists see a public made up of many competing interests, each with its own leadership, Neuman sees only three: a tiny percentage of sophisticated citizens with some input into policy; uninterested and inactive know-nothings, who make up roughly one-fifth; and a large middle mass that votes largely out of a sense of duty but with only a very limited understanding of the issues their vote is meant to decide. The discrepancy from the ideal, which appears over and over again in public opinion polls, cannot be discounted as attributable to flaws in techniques.

Polls do, of course, vary in quality. The reliability and validity of any particular survey as a measure of public opinion hinges on three general factors: who is interviewed, the situation in which the interview takes place, and the questions asked. Insofar as elections are opportunities for the public to go on record with its "opinion," the utility of polling as a research tool can be ascertained by comparing pre-election readings with the actual vote count.

The two fiascoes in polling history have been painstakingly diagnosed. We will never see again the wildly incorrect 1936 forecast by the *Literary Digest* that Roosevelt, who won by a landslide, would lose the presidential election. Poll-takers learned the hard way not to rely solely on sample size, and to shed the common-sense belief that larger automatically means better. The *Digest* poll was based on 2.3 million returns from over ten million straw ballots mailed to persons drawn from automobile registration lists and telephone books. Owners of cars and telephones were somewhat less supportive of Roosevelt than those too poor to own either or both such conveniences. A second, actually more important, source of bias was the large number of Republicans, compared with Democrats, motivated to respond by using the straw ballot to register a protest against the party in power.

When in 1948 the public pollsters, despite more skillfully designed samples and more sophisticated methods, nevertheless wrongly predicted the defeat of incumbent Harry Truman, this became the occasion for one of the most extensive inquiries into polling practices by a committee of the Social Science Research Council (Mosteller et al. 1949). Its report stressed the importance of samples based on random selection that would give every voter the same chance of being contacted, an objective often difficult to implement. Polling techniques have come a long way since, but, as an investigation by Crespi (1988) of the factors associated with accurate prediction in 430 pre-election polls during the 1980s showed, the extra effort invested in callbacks still pays off in greater accuracy. Persons missed because they are hard to get hold of or refuse to answer often differ from the rest in ways difficult to estimate.

As to the interview situation, answering the questions of a poll-taker is hardly the same as casting a vote, all the more so when the election is months away. The large margins by which Truman had been trailing in the early fall of 1948 caused several pollsters to cease polling weeks before voting day. Thus, they never registered the strong Democratic rally that occurred toward the end of the campaign. Crespi's more recent tabulations show that proximity to the election remains a major determinant of the accuracy in pre-election polls. Much depends on how far in advance people first make up their minds, on the firmness of their convictions, and on the influence of such major events as occur during the election campaign. Responses to polls taken too early may be artifacts of the interview situation. These non-attitudes, as they are called, are an especially dangerous contaminant in low-turnout elections with little-known candidates and in referendums on questions beyond the understanding of most voters.

The problems encountered in election research, where the issue boils down to a choice between two leading candidates, are more elusive when there is no outside standard against which to validate the opinions voiced in the interview. Poll-takers have long learned to omit from their tabulations of pre-election surveys anyone identified as a likely nonvoter. Similar "filters" are used to eliminate the responses of people questioned about matters of little concern to them, to which they have given no thought, and of which they may not even have been aware except for the question having been put to them. Respondents who admit to being unfamiliar with or unconcerned about an issue are asked no further questions about it. This still leaves those reluctant to make such an admission. One survey that deliberately inserted a question about a nonexistent act allegedly under consideration in Congress had significant minorities respond that they had heard of it, with some going on to fabricate an opinion about it.

Measures of public opinion based on a single question can be misleading. They take no account of the complexities of the underlying issue. Thus, a poll taken in 1971, when concern over American involvement in Vietnam was higher than over any other issue on the public agenda, put the following direct question to respondents: "Do you favor or oppose the withdrawal of all American troops from Vietnam by the end of the year?" The result: Two out of three respondents replied that they favored withdrawal. On another question in the same survey about whether they favored withdrawing all troops "regardless of how the war was going," they split with a bare plurality of 44 percent against 41 percent in favor. Does the 22-point difference between the 66 percent found in favor on the first question and the 44 percent on the second identify a group ready to take back an off-the-cuff answer because of the reminder of possible consequences? Or were they confident that South Vietnam would not fall, in which event the contingency incorporated into the second question was purely hypothetical and had no practical relevance for them? There is still a third possibility: Were they afraid to admit to the interviewer that they did not care whether or not America was forced to withdraw in defeat?

Polls on the Vietnam war exemplify how responses to differently phrased questions can give contradictory readings of where the public actually stands on a complex policy question. Thus, at the same time majorities declared their support for both immediate withdrawal and stepping up the air war on North Vietnam. Many people who thought Vietnam a mistake nevertheless remained steadfast backers of Johnson's Vietnam policy. Nor were self-styled "doves" necessarily in sympathy with student protesters. One needs a series of probing questions to assess what is on people's mind.

There are alternatives to the survey, but these, too, require caution. Letters, telegrams, and phone calls to political leaders may reflect nothing more than the effort of a well-organized minority. On the other hand, a rise in the number who refuse draft calls or desert from the armed forces, a change in the incidence of certain crimes, or the number of demonstrations, strikes, and other forms of protest can be important clues—not necessarily to general opinion but at least to what the groups most affected by some problem may be unwilling to settle for (Tilly 1978).

Studies of public opinion have to contend with a broad range of beliefs. Located at one extreme are the more stable political allegiances; at the other, the often fluctuating "gut" responses to whatever happens to be current. Specific opinions, as Converse (1964) showed through surveys taken during the early 1960s, do not form clearly defined ideological clusters; the relation of each opinion to others is rather loose.

Other more general ideas that underlie the legitimacy of the political system have greater stability insofar as they build on childhood experience within the family, where children tend to adopt the views of their parents. Early views are then elaborated or modified, as the children grow up, by sustained contact with other major institutions like school or church and, to some extent (especially during major catastrophes affecting the country or its leaders), by the news media (Renshaw 1977). The content of the political culture assimilated differs from milieu to milieu.

Controversy is likely to arise during crises that highlight the endemic cleavages related to position in social structure and in historical time. The activation of old loyalties causes public opinion to divide in predictable ways—by region, race, religion, ethnicity, class background, educational experiences, and so forth. If the cleavage is deep enough, issues stand a good chance of escalating into coercive conflict. The more powerful groups will dominate.

Yet changes in basic attitudes do occur, though slowly, partly through replacement and partly through the diffusion of new experience. Differential birth rates, migration, social mobility, and the metabolic succession of generations are processes that disturb the existing balance without any change on the individual level and despite evidence of political continuity between parents and offspring. Distinct intergenerational differences are believed to develop in response to certain critical experiences, like the encounter, early in adulthood before one's outlook has fully crystallized, with general poverty and war, or participation in social struggles.

Attitudes on race are a good example of how diffusion and replacement operate in conjunction with each other. Surveys taken over time show a distinct movement toward greater racial tolerance (Schuman and Bobo 1985). All groups moved in the same direction, even if at greatly different speeds. The young showed the way, often with tacit support of sympathetic parents not yet themselves prepared to issue a radical challenge to segregation. Rising levels of education and replacement of the more conservative account for part of the shift, while people in regions where segregationist practices were most firmly entrenched changed more rapidly than the rest of the country, once the full force of public opinion had been brought to bear on them.

The day-to-day shifts in public opinion on matters great and small are more subject to influence by the media of mass communication, the great force toward homogenization that helped intransigent Southerners opposed to racial desegregation to see themselves as the rest of the country saw them. More generally, the news of major events gives the public a common focus. By highlighting a problem or giving space and air time to some political figure to do so, the media collectively define the public agenda (agenda setting). Their treatment of the principal actors, of the causes and consequences of the problems, has a distinct influence on the terms on which the issue is debated (agenda building). This role is well documented in case studies of Watergate (Lang and Lang 1983) and of child abuse as an emergent social problem (Nelson 1984).

Media power is nevertheless limited (Paletz and Entman 1981). Some problems, like corruption in high places or a bad turn in foreign relations, about which no one would know unless alerted, depend more on media recognition than do inflation or shortages, which directly impinge on nearly everyone, or grievances anchored in group experience. The latter will not go away for mere lack of mention. Moreover, media managers are less than fully independent. They have to accommodate other actors intent on publicizing only those issues (or aspects of issues) that work in their favor. This is where the highly developed art of news management comes into play. Whoever succeeds in controlling the coverage gains. Public discussion and, indirectly, public opinion have come to be governed by media strategies aimed less at persuading opponents than at neutralizing them.

Shifts in attention cause revaluation. The measures most consistently used for tracking public opinion are the presidential approval ratings. Incoming presidents typically stand high in the polls. On the assumption that the public reacts primarily to policy issues, Mueller (1973) attributes the progressive erosion of popularity to a coalition of minorities: Each decision the president makes will antagonize some constituency. In fact, most of the public is not issue-oriented but reacts to the general image of presidential performance. "Good" news of any kind tends to bolster that image, with one major exception. A national crisis generally sets in motion a rally to the flag. Oppositional voices are stilled, at least temporarily, in a show of patriotic unity.

As to the effects of such opinions, at least two presidents have been driven from office when confronted with clear erosion of public support. Following the all too evident failure of his Vietnam policy, Lyndon B. Johnson declared himself out of the race for reelection, even though as a sitting president he would have been assured renomination as the standard bearer of his party (Schandler 1977). Richard M. Nixon made several concessions and ultimately bowed to public opinion in releasing the tapes with the incriminating evidence that made his impeachment and removal from office, subsequent to a Senate trial, a near certain probability (Lang and Lang 1983).

Popularity is an obvious asset, not only for a president but for anyone aspiring to influence. Social control often works subtly to discourage those who feel out of step from asserting themselves as confidently and forcefully as they might otherwise. They may actually lapse into silence and, however reluctantly, go along with the apparent majority. Noelle-Neumann (1984) refers to the process underlying such bandwagon effects as a "spiral of silence," which further strengthens the already dominant opinion. There is no question about the effectiveness of such silencing. The control of public opinion by totalitarian regimes depends to a large extent on their control over the conversational channels through which ideologically deviant tendencies may spread. In societies governed by the norm of free discussion, all but the most intransigent will recognize when an issue has been settled to a point where further debate becomes superfluous. Likewise, the need to display unity in a crisis or moral fervor, whipped up in crusades against alleged internal enemies, is apt to keep discussion within acceptable bounds. Leaders become cautious and dissidents lie low. Whether such spirals generally operate in ways described by Noelle-Neumann (1984) remains questionable.

Whether elected or not, the leaders of major institutions have proved distinctly sensitive to trends in public opinion that bear on their policies or measures under consideration. Congress, understandably, keeps its finger on the public pulse. Lacking evidence of majority support, members have been inclined to wait, watching to see which way the public tilts. In the controversy over Roosevelt's plan to pack the Supreme Court as well as the one over Nixon's complicity in Watergate, opinion was moved by events, including events generated by the debate. On civil rights, major legislation was passed only after mass demonstration and media attention to discriminatory practices had created public concern and support for the principle had reached or exceeded the two-thirds mark. Laws subsequent to the initial path-breaking legislation could then be enacted without direct pressure from below. But none of these things could have been achieved without effective political leadership.

Legal decisions, at least in principle, are seen as insulated from the direct pressure of public opinion. Yet even the U.S. Supreme Court, the most august of all judicial bodies, so Marshall (1989) concludes, has been an essentially majoritarian institution. Of 142 decisions from the mid-1930s to the mid-1980s for which there were comparable opinion data, over four-fifths turned out to be consistent with expressed public preferences. The linkage, strongest in times of crisis, may be explained by the court's sensitivity to legislative and executive concerns incorporating public opinion rather than as a direct response to public pressure.

It is on questions relating to the constitutional rights of dissident minorities that the court has most consistently set itself against majority opinion. Other countermajoritarian opinions have either articulated a rising trend, strengthened by the voice of the court, or been modified by later decisions that, in an apparent response to public opinion, carved out exceptions and introduced qualifications to the broad rule laid down during the original case. By and large, opinions with majority support are less likely to be reversed by subsequent courts.

Although many measures cast doubt on the public's qualifications, political leaders do experience constraints, even when dealing with the more obscure issues usually cleared through networks known mostly to insiders. The prudent ones are forever listening and managing appearances. Rarely does the public become aroused by some all too apparent failure, a scandal, or some official act involving its own interest. It is on these occasions that the power of the public as a "reserve force," wisely or otherwise, is felt most directly.

(SEE ALSO: *Attitudes; Mass Media Research; Social Indicators; Survey Research*)

REFERENCES

Blumer, Herbert 1972 "Outline of Collective Behavior." In Robert R. Evans, ed., *Readings in Collective Behavior.* Chicago: Rand McNally.

Bogart, Leo 1972 *Polls and the Awareness of Public Opinion.* New York: Wiley.

Converse, Philip E. 1964 "The Nature of Belief Systems in Mass Publics." In David Apter, ed., *Ideology and Discontent.* New York: Free Press.

Crespi, Irving 1988 *Pre-Election Polling; Sources of Accuracy and Error.* New York: Russell Sage.

Ginsberg, Benjamin 1986 *The Captive Public: How Mass Opinion Promotes State Power.* New York: Basic Books.

Lang, Gladys Engel, and Kurt Lang 1983 *The Battle for Public Opinion: The President, the Press, and the Polls during Watergate.* New York: Columbia University Press.

Lippmann, Walter 1922 *Public Opinion.* New York: Macmillan.

Mannheim, Karl 1940 *Man and Society in an Age of Reconstruction.* New York: Harcourt, Brace.

Marshall, Thomas 1989 *Public Opinion and the Supreme Court.* Boston: Unwin Hyman.

Mosteller, Frederick, Herbert Hyman, Philip J. McCarthy, Eli S. Marks, and David B. Truman 1949 *The Preelection Polls of 1948,* Bulletin no. 68. New York: Social Science Research Council.

Mueller, John E. 1973 *War, Presidents, and Public Opinion.* New York: Wiley.

Nelson, Barbara 1984 *Making an Issue of Child Abuse: Agenda Setting for Social Problems.* Chicago: University of Chicago Press.

Neuman, W. Russell 1986 *The Paradox of Mass Politics: Knowledge and Opinion in the American Electorate.* Cambridge, Mass.: Harvard University Press.

Noelle-Neumann, Elisabeth 1984 *The Spiral of Silence.* Chicago: University of Chicago Press.

Paletz, David L., and Robert F. Entman 1981 *Media Power Politics.* New York: Free Press.

Renshaw, Stanley A., ed. 1977 *A Handbook of Political Socialization.* New York: Free Press.

Ross, Edward A. 1901 *Social Control: A Survey of the Social Foundations of Order.* New York: Macmillan.

Schandler, Herbert J. 1977 *The Unmaking of a President: Lyndon B. Johnson and Vietnam.* Princeton: Princeton University Press.

Schattschneider, E. E. 1960 *The Semisovereign People: A Realist's View of Democracy in America.* Hinsdale, Ill.: Dryden Press.

Schuman, Howard and Lawrence Bobo 1985 *Racial Attitudes: Trends and Interpretations.* Cambridge, Mass.: Harvard University Press.

Schumpeter, Joseph A. 1942 *Capitalism, Socialism, and Democracy.* New York: Harper and Row.

Sigel, Roberta S., ed. 1989 *Political Learning in Adulthood: A Sourcebook of Theory and Research.* Chicago: University of Chicago Press.

Tilly, Charles 1978 *From Mobilization to Revolution.* New York: Random House.

Tönnies, Ferdinand 1922 *Kritik der öffentlichen Meinung.* Berlin: Springer.

KURT LANG

PUBLIC POLICY ANALYSIS Public policy analysis is a large, sprawling intellectual enterprise involving numerous academic disciplines, private research organizations, and governmental agencies, each sharing a common concern with the formulation, implementation, or consequences of public policy decisions. There are approximately thirty journals published in the English language alone, and nearly twenty professional associations, that are devoted more or less exclusively to policy analysis. Departments, centers, and institutes dealing in whole or in part with policy analysis can be found at over forty American universities.

As currently practiced, policy analysis involves contributions from the entire gamut of scientific disciplines. Much present-day public policy analysis is undertaken by scholars from the various applied physical and biological sciences (for example, environmental impact studies, technology assessments, seismic risk analyses, and the like). The focus here, however, is on public policy analysis as it is conducted within the social and behavioral sciences, principally economics, political science, and sociology.

The diversity of research work conducted under the rubric of public policy analysis, even when restricted to the social science component, is perhaps the distinguishing characteristic of the subject. In the space available here we can do little more than indicate the range of topics and approaches with which policy analysts are concerned. Rogers (1989) has developed a typology of public policy research that is useful for this purpose; the following is adapted from his discussion.

PROBLEM DEFINITION OR NEEDS ASSESSMENT

Public policy usually addresses real or sensed problems, and a great deal of public policy analysis is therefore devoted to defining or clarifying problems and assessing needs. What are the health-care needs of a particular neighborhood? What are the housing or nutritional needs of the nation's poverty population? What social services do homeless persons require? It is obvious that the development and formulation of public policy will be enhanced when underlying needs have been adequately described and analyzed. There is a large literature on the theory and practice of problem definition and needs assessment (see especially Johnson et al. 1987).

VALUE EXPLORATION OR CLARIFICATION

Given a demonstrated need, any number of policies might be developed to address it. Which policies, goals, or outcomes are most desirable? If an area is found to have unmet health needs, is it better to open freestanding clinics or provide subsidized health insurance? Are the housing needs of the poor best addressed through public housing projects or through housing vouchers that can be used in lieu of rent? Should our policies with respect to the homeless attempt to ameliorate the conditions of a homeless existence or prevent people from becoming homeless in the first place?

Assessing the relative desirability of policy options is only rarely an empirical matter; such decisions are more often ethical or ideological. MacRae (1985) stresses the unavoidable role of values in the process of policy analysis and the ensuing conflicts for the policy analyst. He identifies four principal "end values" widely shared throughout American society and against which policy decisions can be compared: economic benefit, subjective well-being, equity, and social integration. Sadly, policies that maximize equity may not maximize net economic benefit; those that enhance social integration may destroy subjective well-being. Thus, public policy analysis is not an arena for those who wish to pursue "value-neutral" science nor is it one for the morally or ideologically faint of heart.

CONCEPTUAL DEVELOPMENT

Much work in the area of public policy analysis consists of developing conceptual schemes or typologies that help sort out various kinds of policies or analyses of policies (such as the typology used here). Nagel (1984) and Dubnick and Bardes (1983) review numerous conceptual schemes for typifying policies and policy analyses and make useful suggestions for synthesis; the former is an especially good overview of the field as a whole.

POLICY DESCRIPTION

Adequate description of public policy is essential for proper evaluation and understanding, but many public policies prove frustratingly complex, especially as delivered in the field. "Poverty policy" in the United States consists of a vast congeries of federal, state, and local programs, each focused on different aspects of the poverty problem (income, employment, housing, nutrition) or on different segments of the poverty population (women, children, women with children, the disabled, the elderly). The same can obviously be said of housing policy, tax policy, environmental policy, health policy, and on through a very long list. Even a single element of poverty policy such as Aid to Families with Dependent Children (AFDC) has different eligibility requirements, administrative procedures, and payment levels in each of the fifty states. Thus, accurate policy description is by no means a straightforward task. Outstanding examples of policy description, both focused on poverty policy, are Haveman (1977) and Levitan (1985).

METHODOLOGICAL RESEARCH

Unlike much basic disciplinary research in the social and behavioral sciences, whose results are largely inconsequential except to a handful of specialists, the results of policy studies will often influence people's lives and well-being, and the cost of being wrong can run into millions or billions of dollars. Thus, issues of internal and external validity, errors of measurement and specification, proper statistical modeling, and the like are more than methodological niceties to the policy analyst; they are worrisome, ever-present, and potentially consequential threats to the accuracy of one's conclusions and to the policy decisions that ensue. A technical error in a journal article can be corrected in a simple retraction; an equivalent error in a policy analysis might result in wrongheaded or counterproductive policies being pursued.

Much of the literature on public policy analysis, and especially on impact evaluation (see below), is therefore mainly methodological in character; indeed, many recent innovations in research procedure have been developed by scholars working on applied, as opposed to basic, problems. There are many texts available on the methodology of public policy analysis. Rossi and Freeman (1989) provide a comprehensive overview; Judd and Kenny (1981) are highly recommended for the more advanced student.

POLICY EXPLANATION

Much public policy analysis undertaken by political scientists focuses on the processes by which policy is made at federal, state, and local levels. Classic examples are Marmor's (1970) analysis of the passage of Medicare and Moynihan's (1973) study of the ill-fated Family Assistance Plan proposed early in the Nixon administration but never enacted.

Explanations of how public policy is made are invariably replete with the "dirty linen" of the political process: competing and often warring constituencies, equally legitimate but contradictory objectives and values, vote-trading, compromises and deals, political posturing by key actors, intrusions by lobbying, advocacy and special interest groups, manipulation of public sentiment and understanding, in short, the "booming, buzzing confusion" of a fractious, pluralistic political system. For those whose understanding of such matters does not extend much beyond the obligatory high school civics lesson in "how a bill becomes a law," the policy explanation literature is a revelation.

POLITICAL INTELLIGENCE OR PUBLIC OPINION

In a democratic society, public opinion is supposed to "count" in the policy formation process. Sometimes it does, often it does not. Policy analysis thus sometimes involves plumbing the depths and sources of support or opposition to various policy initiatives and, in a larger sense, explicating the process by which policy becomes legitimated.

There is no easy answer to the question whether (or under what conditions) public opinion dictates the direction of public policy. It is evident that policymakers are sensitive to public opinion; many presidents, for example, are morbidly fascinated by their standing in the polls (e.g., Sussman 1988). It is equally evident, however, that many policies with strong majority support are never enacted into law. An interesting study of the effects of public opinion on policy formation is Verba and Nie (1975).

EVALUATION RESEARCH

The ultimate analytic question to be asked about any public policy is whether it produced (or will produce) its intended effects (or any effects, whether intended or not). The search for bottom-line effects—impact assessment—is one of two major activities subsumed under the rubric of evaluation research. (The other is so-called process evaluation, discussed below under "implementation analysis.")

There are many formidable barriers to be overcome in deciding whether a policy or program has produced its intended (or any) effects. First, the notion of "intended effects" presupposes clearly defined and articulated program goals, but many policies are enacted without a clear statement of the goals to be achieved. Thus, many texts in evaluation research recommend an assessment of the "evaluability" of the program prior to initiating the evaluation itself. A second barrier is the often-pronounced difference between the program as designed and the program as delivered. This is the issue of program implementation discussed later.

The most troublesome methodological issue in evaluation research lies in establishing the *ceteris paribus* (or "all else equal") condition or, in other words, in estimating what might have happened in the absence of the program to be evaluated. In an era of declining birth rates, any fertility reduction program will appear to be successful; in an era of declining crime rates, any crime reduction program will appear to be successful. How, then, can one differentiate between program effects and things that would have happened anyway owing to exogenous conditions? (Students of logic will see the problem here as the *post hoc, ergo propter hoc* fallacy.)

Because of this *ceteris paribus* problem, many evaluations are designed as experiments or quasi-experiments. In the former case, subjects are randomly assigned to various treatment and control conditions and outcomes monitored. Randomization in essence "initializes" all the starting conditions to the same values (except for the vagaries of chance). In the recent history of evaluation research, the various Negative Income Tax experiments (see Rossi and Lyall 1976) are the best-known examples of large-scale field experiments of this general sort. "Quasi-experiments" are any of a number of research designs that do not involve randomization but use other methods to establish the *ceteris paribus* condition; the definitive statement on quasi-experiments is Cook and Campbell (1979).

A final problem in doing evaluation research is that most policies or programs are relatively small interventions intended to address rather large, complex social issues. The poverty rate, to illustrate, is a complex function of the rate of employment, trends in the world economy, prevailing wage rates, the provisions of the social welfare system, and a host of additional macrostructural factors. Any given antipoverty program, in contrast, will be a relatively small-scale intervention focused on one or a few components of the larger problem, often restricted to one or a few segments of the population. Often, the overall effects of the various large-scale, macrostructural factors will completely swamp the program effects—not because the program effects were not present or meritorious but because they are very small relative to exogenous effects.

The literature on the theory and practice of evaluation research is expansive; students seeking additional information will find themselves well served by Rossi and Freeman (1989).

OUTCOME ANALYSIS

Assuming that a program has been adequately evaluated and an effect documented, one can then analyze that effect (or outcome) to determine whether it was worth the money and effort necessary to produce it. Outcome analysis thus examines the cost-effectiveness or cost-beneficiality of a given policy, program, or intervention.

Cost-benefit and cost-effectiveness analysis are intrinsically complex, technically demanding subjects. One complication lies in assessing the so-called opportunity costs. A dollar spent in one way is a dollar no longer available to use in some other way. Investing the dollar in any particular intervention thus means that one has lost the "opportunity" to invest that dollar in something that may have been far more beneficial.

A second complication is in the "accounting perspective" one chooses to assess benefits and costs. Consider the Food Stamp program. A recipient receives a benefit (a coupon that can be redeemed for food) at no cost; from the accounting perspective of that recipient, the benefit-to-cost ratio is thus infinite. The Food Stamp program is administered by the U.S. Department of Agriculture. From the USDA perspective, the benefit of the program presumably lies in the contribution it makes to relieving hunger and malnutrition in the population; the cost lies in whatever it takes to administer the program, redeem the coupons once submitted by food outlets, and so forth. Accounted against the USDA perspective, the benefit-to-cost ratio will be very different, and it will be different again when accounted against the perspective of society as a whole. The latter accounting, of course, requires asking what it is worth to us as a nation to provide food to those who might otherwise have to go without, clearly a moral question more than an empirical or analytic one.

This last example illustrates another thorny problem in doing cost-*benefit* analyses, namely, the incommensurability of benefits and costs. The dollar costs of most programs or policies can be reasonably well estimated. (The dollar costs are usually not the only costs. There may also be ethical or political costs that cannot be translated into dollars and cents but that are, nonetheless, real. Let us ignore the nondollar costs, however.) Unfortunately, the benefits of most interventions cannot be readily expressed in dollars; they are expressed, rather, in less tangible (but equally real) terms: lives saved, improvements in the quality of life, reductions of hunger, and the like. If the outcome cannot be converted to a dollar value, then a strict comparison to the dollar costs cannot be made and a true benefit-to-cost ratio cannot be calculated.

Cost-*effectiveness* analysis, in contrast, compares the benefits of one program (expressed in any unit) at one cost to the benefits of another program (expressed in the same unit) at a different cost. Thus, a program that spends $10,000 to save one life is more cost-effective than another program that spends $20,000 to save one life. Whether either program is cost-*beneficial,* however, cannot be determined unless one is willing to assign a dollar value to a human life.

Many texts by economists deal at length with these and related complexities; an accessible overview is Levin (1975).

IMPLEMENTATION ANALYSIS

"Much is the slippage between the spoon and the mouth." A program as it is delivered in the field is rarely identical to the program as designed in the policymaking process; sometimes, there is only a superficial resemblance. Since slippage between design and implementation might provide one explanation for the failure to achieve significant program effects, implementation analysis is an essential component of all capable policy evaluations.

There are many reasons that programs as delivered differ from programs as designed: technical impossibility, bureaucratic inertia, unanticipated conditions, exogenous influences. An elegantly designed policy experiment can fail at the point of randomization if program personnel let their own sentiments about "worthy" and "unworthy" clients override the randomizing process. Many educational policy initiatives are subverted because teachers persist in their same old ways despite the program admonition to do things differently. Welfare reform will mean little if caseworkers continue to apply the same standards and procedures as in the past. More generally, the real world finds ways to impinge in unexpected and often unwanted ways on any policy initiative; failure to anticipate these impingements has caused many a policy experiment to fail.

Loftin and McDowell (1981) provide a classic example of the utility of implementation analysis in their evaluation of the effects of the Detroit mandatory sentencing law. The policy as designed required a mandatory two-year "add on" to the prison sentence of any person convicted of a felony involving a firearm. Contrary to expectation, the rate of firearms crime did *not* decline after the law was enacted. Implementation analysis provided the reason. Judges, well aware of the overcrowded conditions in the state's prisons, were loathe to increase average prison sentences. Yet, state law required that two years be added to the charge. To resolve the dilemma, judges in firearms cases would begin by *reducing* the main sentence by two or so years and then *adding* the mandated two-year add-on, so that the overall sentence remained about the same even as the judges remained in technical compliance with policy.

UTILIZATION

A consistent frustration expressed throughout the literature is that policy analysis seems only rarely to have any impact on actual policy. Many reasons for nonutilization have been identified. One of the most important is timeliness. Good research takes time, whereas policy decisions are often made quickly, well before the results of the analysis are in. The Negative Income Tax experiments mentioned earlier were stimulated in substantial part by a Nixon administration proposal for a modified negative income tax to replace the then-current welfare system. The shortest of the experiments ran for three years; several ran for five years; none were completed by the time the Nixon proposal was killed mainly on political grounds.

A second factor in the nonutilization of policy studies is that research is seldom unequivocal. Even the best-designed and best-executed policy researches will be accompanied by numerous caveats, conditions, and qualifications that strictly limit the safe policy inferences one may draw from them. Policymakers, of course, prefer simple declarative conclusions; policy research rarely allows one to make such statements.

Finally, even under the most favorable conditions, the scientific results of policy analyses are but one among many inputs into the policymaking process. There are, in addition, normative, economic, political, ethical, pragmatic, and ideological inputs that must be accommodated, and in the process of accommodation, the influence of scientific research is often obscured to the point where it can no longer be recognized. It should not be inferred from this that the policy analysis has not been utilized, only that the research results are only one voice in the cacophony of the process. And while policy analysts and evaluation researchers often bemoan this state of affairs, it is as it should be; otherwise, we would have long since concluded that cannibalism is the solution to both world hunger and overpopulation.

(SEE ALSO: *Evaluation Research; Health Policy Analysis; Sociology and Federal Research Support*)

REFERENCES

Cook, Thomas, and Donald Campbell 1979 *Quasi-Experimentation.* Chicago: Rand MacNally.

Dubnick, Melvin, and Barbara Bardes 1983 *Thinking about Public Policy: A Problem Solving Approach.* New York: Wiley.

Haveman, Robert 1977 *A Decade of Federal Antipoverty Programs: Achievements, Failures, and Lessons.* New York: Academic Press.

Johnson, D., L. Meiller, L. Miller, and G. Summers 1987 *Needs Assessment: Theory and Methods.* Ames: Iowa State University Press.

Judd, Charles, and David Kenny 1981 *Estimating the Effects of Social Interventions.* New York: Cambridge University Press.

Levin, Henry 1975 "Cost-Effectiveness Analysis in Evaluation Research." In M. Guttentag and E. Struening, eds., *Handbook of Evaluation Research.* Newbury Park, Calif.: Sage Publications.

Levitan, Sar 1985 *Programs in Aid of the Poor.* Baltimore: Johns Hopkins University Press.

Loftin, Colin, and David McDowell 1981 "One with a Gun Gets You Two: Mandatory Sentencing and Firearms Violence in Detroit." *Annals of the American Academy of Political and Social Science* 455:150–168.

MacRae, Duncan 1985 *Policy Indicators: Links between Social Science and Public Debate.* Chapel Hill: University of North Carolina Press.

Marmor, Theodore 1970 *The Politics of Medicare.* New York: Aldine.

Moynihan, Daniel 1973 *The Politics of a Guaranteed Annual Income: The Nixon Administration and the Family Assistance Plan.* New York: Vintage.

Nagel, Stuart 1984 *Contemporary Public Policy Analysis.* Birmingham: University of Alabama Press.

Rogers, James 1989 "Social Science Disciplines and Policy Research: The Case of Political Science." *Policy Studies Review* 9:13–28.

Rossi, Peter, and Howard Freeman 1989 *Evaluation: A Systematic Approach.* Newbury Park, Calif.: Sage Publications.

Rossi, Peter, and Kathryn Lyall 1976 *Reforming Public Welfare.* New York: Russell Sage Foundation.

Sussman, Barry 1988 *What Americans Really Think and Why Our Politicians Pay No Attention.* New York: Pantheon.

Verba, Sidney, and Norman Nie 1975 *Participation in America: Political Democracy and Social Equality.* New York: Harper and Row.

JAMES D. WRIGHT

Q

QUALITATIVE METHODS Qualitative methods are ways of studying the qualities of everyday life, from life's actions and narratives to its signs, circumstances, and sense of reality. Participant observation involves the qualitative researcher directly in the social setting, observing more or less openly in various membership roles (Adler and Adler 1987). Conversation analysis focuses on talk in interaction and is concerned with the analysis of communicative competencies that underlie ordinary social activity (Heritage 1984). Discourse analysis is more concerned with language use, highlighting practice and contextuality (Gubrium and Holstein 1990). Content analysis explicates documents for general categories of meaning, from personal papers such as letters and psychiatric reports, to human interest stories (Plummer 1983). Ethnographic interviewing is relatively unstructured, is usually focused, and explores with respondents the texture and flow of select experiences (Spradley 1979).

THEORY AS METHOD

Qualitative sociology is distinctive because method and theory are inseparable; methodology pertains not only to the logic of procedure but also to the logic of analysis. In most areas of empirical sociology, method connotes only technique. Survey research methodology comprises sampling processes, questionnaire formatting, interview management, code construction, and statistical analysis. The design of experiments includes diverse structural and temporal controls to enhance subject comparisons. Qualitative sociology is in contrast in that, besides traditional techniques such as participant observation and content analysis, theory itself is treated as a method.

In nonqualitative studies, hypotheses are formed before data collection and are interpreted or tested afterward, although this may not be clear-cut in practice. Formally theorizing about data while they are being collected is considered methodologically problematic. In qualitative research, hypothesis generation, concept formation, and development of typologies, among other forms of theorizing, are part of the data-gathering process. Data take shape and meaning from the concurrent theoretical activity of the researcher. There is a continual movement, back and forth, between conceptualization on the one hand and data collection on the other.

The difference can be explained in terms of the primary object of research interest in qualitative studies: the organization of meaning. Two questions are addressed: What is the meaning of conduct and how is meaning socially organized? The first question pertains to native meaning, that is, meaning as understood and used by participants. While an event or act might appear to the outside observer as, say, an instance of child abuse, the qualitative researcher aims to discover "the subjective meaning attached" by those concerned to the conduct under consideration, reflecting Max Weber's (1947, p. 88) classic definition of action. The second question refers to circumstance or context. Because meaning is conceived of as being attached to conduct, the meaning of conduct varies with the conditions of description. Since qualitative research does not conceive of meaning as settled or fixed, but rather as socially and circumstantially variable, it is not hypothesized about before its investigation. The research task is to build theory in relation to the discovery of meaning and its social organization.

THEORETICAL SHAPING OF METHODS

There are diverse forms of qualitative theorizing, from symbolic interaction (Mead 1934; Blumer 1969) to ethnomethodology (Garfinkel 1967; Heritage 1984) and semiotics (Manning 1987). Because qualitative sociology does not separate theory and methods, theoretical differences serve to distinguish what, ostensibly, are the same methods. Participant observation, for example, is known to be a hallmark method in the area. Yet what is done under the aegis of participant observation is understood differently, depending on whether the method is informed, say, by symbolic interactionism or by ethnomethodology. Symbolic interactionists tend to observe meaningful patterns of behavior, whereas ethnomethodologists are inclined to document the interactional production and management of meaningful events and circumstances.

Symbolic Interactionism. In the American context, the oldest form of sociological theorizing informing qualitative methods is symbolic interactionism, in particular the variety associated with the so-called Chicago school (Bulmer 1984). Centered on the relation between selves, roles, and significant others, symbolic interactionists, notably Herbert Blumer (1969), situate meaning in social interaction, not separate from it. Blumer presents this point of view in three premises. The first premise is that we act in terms of the meanings that objects and events have for us. The second is that meaning arises out of social interaction; those engaged in various domains of everyday life construct its meanings. The third premise is that meanings are transformed in the process of interaction.

Native definitions and understandings are focal; symbolic interactionists grant no special privilege to official or institutionally sanctioned versions of reality. Howard Becker (1963), for example, is concerned with how interpretation and circumstance serve to define marijuana use as deviant and users' experiences as euphoric. Becker argues that it is not the drug itself that produces particular personal and public reactions but the social organization of definitions and rhetoric. The task is to describe how marijuana users define and experience their drug use and how its deviance is socially established and imposed. The assumption is that all domains of everyday life are meaningful in their own right. In a pioneering study, W. I. Thomas and Florian Znaniecki (1917) traced changing attitudes toward self and others among Polish peasant immigrants to the United States by analyzing definitions of daily experience contained in the immigrants' correspondence with relatives in Poland. It is thought that the contents of letters reveals the changing self-definition of the immigrant and, thereby, indicates that meanings grow out of, and are transformed by, relations with others.

Sentiments about the ubiquity of native meaning incline symbolic interactionists to prove their point by documenting the organization of so-called deviant experiences, in which organized meanings are often claimed not to exist. William Foote Whyte's (1943) classic observational study of the young adult street gang is notable in this regard. At the time, Whyte wrote that the common view of gangs and other underworld activity was that the activity was without norms, or amoral; holding sway was the law of the jungle, an alleged Hobbesian world without order where life was nasty, brutish, and short. Whyte's method was to immerse himself in, and observe, the interactions of gang members on their own terms, as close to their natural state as possible. As if following Blumer's premises, Whyte took for granted that meanings arise out of, and in turn affect, social interaction. Whyte discovered a complex array of rules of conduct, in which gang members' definitions of self were affected by the roles they played, which, correspondingly, shaped their continuing social relations.

A naturalistic view of experience underpins studies informed by symbolic interaction (Hammersley and Atkinson 1983). Qualitative researchers associated with the Chicago school are committed to "go out there, to where the action is." There is an implicit prohibition against assuming that the researcher already knows the definition of the meaning of life by subjects. There are native meanings, located in subjects' living environments —held by gangs in their territories, felons in prisons, and others—that cannot be understood separate from their natural contexts. The methods considered most conducive to revealing the empirical products of this view are participant observation, analysis of personal documents, and ethnographic interview. Given the naturalistic bent, the methods are understood to be vehicles for revealing the diverse meanings of life on the meanings' own terms.

Yet this theoretical shaping of method, with its underlying naturalism, remained a relatively informal design for research, more an oral tradition than formal methodology, until Barney Glaser and Anselm Strauss (1967) formulated explicit strategies for qualitative research, calling them the *grounded theory approach.* Naturalistically oriented, their view is that the goal of qualitative sociology is to *discover* theory, not formulate it before one has had a chance to observe what life in its various circumstances means to participants. Accordingly, theory generation proceeds from the ground up, from the careful observation and documentation of native categories of meaning based on sampling strategies sensitive to everyday life, to the design of general theory that reflects subjects' substantive experiences.

Ethnomethodology. When Harold Garfinkel (1967) writes that the task of ethnomethodology is to document the processes by which the organized character of everyday reality is produced and managed by its members, the socially natural itself comes under scrutiny. Unlike symbolic interactionists, who take it for granted that meanings are "out there" to be discovered in the native circumstances of their adherents, ethnomethodologists set aside ("bracket") the assumption, in order to document the processes by which meanings are assigned to experience to *produce* a sense of reality or social order. The qualitative aspect of this approach is to specify members' own methods for articulating understandings of reality within select domains of experience.

Qualitative methods take on a different character in ethnomethodology. Some approaches can be more intrusive than in symbolic interactionist research, aiming to make readily visible the conventions and borders of the socially natural by disrupting them. Garfinkel describes informal experiments that show how members work at producing and sustaining a sense of reality in particular situations. So-called breaching experiments entail the introduction by the researcher of behavior anomalous to a situation, in order to "breach" its taken-for-grantedness. The object is to document the methods used by members to sustain the existing sense of reality, or to define it otherwise.

In one breaching experiment, undergraduates are asked to act as if they are boarders in their own homes and to conduct themselves in a "circumspect and polite fashion. They are to avoid getting personal, to use formal address, to speak only when spoken to" (p. 47). Garfinkel reports that this produces astonishment and bewilderment. But what is important in the responses is that family members try to make sense of the behavior and sustain the existing reality of family life by casting the behavior in *relatedly* sensible terms. Garfinkel writes that "explanations were sought in previous, understandable motives of the student: the student was working too hard in school; the student was ill; there had been another fight with a fiancee" (p. 48). Family members use biographically relevant *accounts* to sustain a familial, not institutional or otherwise nondomestic, reality in the household. There are other forms of response, of course, but they are equally methodical, engaging participants in the work of "doing reality."

Ethnomethodological research extends beyond breaching experiments to include wide-ranging studies of interactional encounters, practical decision making, and rule use as processes of reality construction. Ethnographic adaptations of the ethnomethodological perspective describe the social practices through which the observable, reportable features of everyday life are locally accomplished and managed. For example, analyses have been done of the production and management of social order in a halfway house for narcotics offenders, a traffic court, and a public assistance agency.

Conversation analysis, a research approach deriving from ethnomethodological assumptions, seeks descriptions of the communicative procedures that ordinary speakers use and rely upon to participate in intelligible, socially organized interaction (Heritage 1984). Focal is the structure of conversation itself: principles that underpin its sequential organization, local management of turn taking, and issues related to openings and closings. Conversation analysts' theoretical commitment to the minute details of interaction as the foundation of social order mandates methodological interest in mundane talk, generally gathered by means of audio or video recordings. Once again, theory and method are inseparable.

Recently, generic features of competent, ordinary conversation have been addressed in institutional settings (Drew and Heritage 1991). Conversation analysts have begun to examine the ways in which principles of conversation are relevant to institutional interactions, as well as how interaction is conditioned and constrained by various types of institutional settings.

Practical Ethnography. In studying the social organization of meaning, symbolic interactionism highlights natural, *substantive* differences, while ethnomethodology underscores *processes* of meaning production. The difference has prompted some qualitative sociologists to ask whether the two emphases might be combined. One effort in this direction has been practical ethnography (Gubrium 1988). The production of meaning is treated as a practical matter located within, and influenced by, concrete settings. The image of the actor is that of a practitioner of everyday life. The practitioner's task is to apply locally available, generally recognized categories, ideas, and accounts to meaningfully sort, design, and execute plans of action, investing everyday life with a particular sense of reality. On the one hand, available concepts and categories that are constantly developing in their own right—local culture—provide the resources for assigning meaning to objects and events (Gubrium 1989). Local cultures comprise possible, not actual, meanings of things. This emphasis draws on symbolic interactionism's substantive focus on the study of meaning, but it also accentuates the everyday communicative work of sorting, designing, and enacting meanings through interactional practices that constitute everyday reality. While the possible meanings of objects and events are diversely, locally available and, thus, socially distributed, the practitioner of everyday life applies and manages meaning with considerable discretion. This emphasis borrows from the ethnomethodological tenet that the reality of everyday life is an "artful" accomplishment, linking the socially productive quality of interaction to traditional qualitative concerns with the structure of social worlds, to produce an ethnography of social practice.

Discourse, or what people do with words, not the formal structure of conversation, is the focus of practical ethnography. For example, Jaber Gubrium and David Buckholdt (1982) distinguish two images of recovery in a study of how patient progress is documented and communicated in a physical rehabilitation hospital. An educational image offers a discourse of teaching and learning, while a medical image makes available a discourse of curing. The images provide descriptive resources for conveying progress as a function, respectively, of either patient motivation and achievement or clinical skill. The discourse used to sort pertinent rehabilitation facts and figures depends on whether the audience communicated with is defined as the patient, the family, other staff members, or third-party payers. Third-party payers receive medical accounts describing progress as curing. Families, especially patients, are more likely to receive educational accounts, placing the onus of recovery on the learner (usually the patient).

In studies of involuntary mental hospitalization proceedings, James Holstein (1987) documents how locally viable gender depictions and a delimited number of available understandings of mental health care discursively enter into the construction of biographical particulars for candidate mental patients to constitute pertinent arguments for or against hospitalization. In a practical ethnography of a work incentive program in a welfare agency, Gale Miller (1991) shows how depictions of labor markets and worker motivation provide local ideologies, not just concrete job conditions, for assigning meaning to participants' success in the program. While the ideologies are clear and distinct as interpretive resources, they are used and applied with considerable discretion by program staff.

Each practical ethnography presents aspects of everyday life as they are locally produced by reference to generally recognized collective representations (Durkheim 1961). The analytic orientation of practical ethnography relies upon traditional ethnographic techniques of qualitative methodology but develops an approach to descriptive practice. Participant observation, ethnographic interviews, and the content analysis of both official and personal documents provide means for cataloguing local categories and understandings. The ethnomethodologically informed analysis of ordinary talk and practical reasoning offers a way of making visible the emergent quality of meaning assignment.

THE GROWING EDGE

Theory as method in qualitative sociology is currently veering in several opposing directions, with divergent technical implications. For example, framed in terms of cultural studies and informed by deconstructionist thinking, especially the work of Jacques Derrida and Jean Baudrillard, Norman Denzin's (1990) argument forcefully promotes the indeterminacy of meaning. Drawing on literary deconstruction with direct application to social life, Denzin argues that there are no determinate codes for assigning meaning to objects and events, only a "continuous play of difference." While the position underscores variation and discretion, it ignores meaning's social organization. The study of social organization being irrelevant, traditional methods of qualitative sociology are displaced by the reflexively inventive analysis of texts, akin to what has been called the new, new literary criticism.

Feminist social thinkers argue that talking and listening from women's standpoint has important implications for qualitative methods (Roberts 1981; Smith 1987). Marjorie Devault (1990) notes that qualitative methods are particularly useful in distinguishing and analyzing the gender-related qualities of experience. Yet these methods, she argues, in particular the traditional ethnographic interview, cannot capture categorical and existential diversity. The methods must be reconceived so as to acknowledge their experientially constitutive qualities. She suggests that sociological analysis must acknowledge that participant observation and ethnographic interviewing not only elicit information from settings and subjects but also enable interviewers and interviewees to construct experience differently in the process. Most important, women construct experience differently from men. Devault points out that technique itself is gendered.

Drawing on semiotics, the science of signs, Peter Manning (1987) offers yet another option for qualitative method. From fieldwork on policing and narcotics use and studies of the logic of disease, Manning moves away from rich ethnographic detail to derive formal taxonomies for the related practices of everyday life. Signs and sign systems, he argues, provide the sum and substance of meaning in social life. Taking language as a model for life, the approach does not so much offer understanding as seek "to identify the rules or principles that guide *signification* (the process by which objects in the world communicate meaning)" (p. 9). Objects, not subjects, convey meaning; thus, the approach's rationalist inclination.

(SEE ALSO: *Case Studies; Conversation Analysis; Ethnomethodology; Field Research Methods; Life Histories; Symbolic Interaction Theory)*

REFERENCES

Adler, Patricia A., and Peter Adler 1987 *Membership Roles in Field Research.* Newbury Park, Calif.: Sage.

Becker, Howard 1963 *Outsiders.* New York: Free Press.

Blumer, Herbert 1969 *Symbolic Interactionism.* Englewood Cliffs, N.J.: Prentice-Hall.

Bulmer, Martin 1984 *The Chicago School of Sociology.* Chicago: University of Chicago Press.

Denzin, Norman K. 1990 "Reading Cultural Texts: Comment on Griswold." *American Journal of Sociology* 95:1577–1580.

Devault, Marjorie L. 1990 "Talking and Listening from Women's Standpoint: Feminist Strategies for Interviewing and Analysis." *Social Problems* 37:96–116.

Drew, Paul, and John C. Heritage, eds. 1991 *Talk at Work: Interaction in Institutional Settings.* New York: Cambridge University Press.

Durkheim, Emile 1961 *The Elementary Forms of the Religious Life.* New York: Collier-Macmillan.

Garfinkel, Harold 1967 *Studies in Ethnomethodology.* Englewood Cliffs, N.J.: Prentice-Hall.

Glaser, Barney G., and Anselm L. Strauss 1967 *The Discovery of Grounded Theory.* Chicago: Aldine.

Gubrium, Jaber F. 1988 *Analyzing Field Reality.* Newbury Park, Calif.: Sage.

——— 1989 "Local Cultures and Service Policy." In Jaber F. Gubrium and David Silverman, eds., *The Politics of Field Research: Sociology Beyond Enlightenment.* London: Sage.

———, and David R. Buckholdt 1982 *Describing Care: Image and Practice in Rehabilitation.* Cambridge, Mass.: Oelgeschlager, Gunn & Hain.

———, and James A. Holstein 1990 *What Is Family?* Mountain View, Calif.: Mayfield.

Hammersley, Martyn, and Paul Atkinson 1983 *Ethnography: Principles in Practice.* London: Tavistock.

Heritage, John C. 1984 *Garfinkel and Ethnomethodology.* Cambridge: Polity Press.

Holstein, James A. 1987 "Producing Gender Effects on Involuntary Mental Hospitalization." *Social Problems* 34:301–315.

Manning, Peter 1987 *Semiotics and Fieldwork.* Newbury Park, Calif.: Sage.

Mead, George Herbert 1934 *Mind, Self & Society.* Chicago: University of Chicago Press.

Miller, Gale 1991 *Enforcing the Work Ethnic.* Albany, N.Y.: SUNY Press.

Plummer, Ken 1983 *Documents of Life.* London: Allen & Unwin.

Roberts, Helen (ed.) 1981 *Doing Feminist Research.* London: Routledge.

Smith, Dorothy E. 1987 *The Everyday World as Problematic: A Feminist Sociology.* Boston: Northeastern University Press.

Spradley, James P. 1979 *The Ethnographic Interview.* New York: Holt, Rinehart & Winston.

Thomas, William I., and Florian Znaniecki 1923 *The Polish Peasant in Europe and America.* Chicago: University of Chicago Press.

Weber, Max 1947 *Theory of Social and Economic Organization.* New York: Free Press.

Whyte, William Foote 1943 *Street Corner Society.* Chicago: University of Chicago Press.

JABER F. GUBRIUM
JAMES A. HOLSTEIN

QUALITATIVE MODELS Qualitative models describe structure and metamorphosis among things or events or among discrete properties of things or events. Sociologists have several approaches for creating such models.

Qualitative modeling based on *logic* involves the following ideas. Propositions can be true or false, and negation of a proposition transforms truth into falsity or falsity into truth. Compound statements are formed when two or more propositions are placed in disjunction or conjunction, signified in English by the words *or* (or *nor*) and *and* (or *but*). Compound statements are true if all their component propositions are true, and compound statements are false if all their component propositions are false. Disjunction of true and false propositions yields a compound statement that is true, whereas conjunction of true and false propositions yields a compound statement that is false. These definitions are sufficient for logical analyses, but a supplementary definition is useful: The conditional "P implies Q" or "if P then Q" means that whenever proposition P is true, proposition Q is true also, but when P is false, Q may be either true or false.

Set theory corresponds closely with logic, to the point that logic formulations can be interpreted in terms of sets, and information about the existence of elements in sets and subsets can be interpreted in terms of logic. Logic also can be translated to Boolean algebra (which operates as does ordinary algebra, except that there are only two numbers, 0 and 1, and $1 + 1 = 1$), so any formulation in terms of logic can be transformed to an algebraic problem and processed mathematically.

Logic models have been used to delineate sociological entities. Balzer (1990), for example, employed logic plus some additional mathematical ideas in order to synthesize sociological perspectives regarding social institutions into a comprehensive and precise definition.

Znaniecki (1934) systematized *analytic induction* as a method for deriving logic models from statements known to be true as a result of sociological research. For example (alluding to a study by Becker 1953 that applied the method), field research might have disclosed a set of fourteen males who are marijuana users, all of whom were taught to enjoy the drug; a set of three females who use marijuana, though they never were taught to enjoy it; a set of six males who were taught how to enjoy marijuana, but who do not use it; and implicitly it is understood that other people never were taught to enjoy marijuana and do not use it. From this information one might conclude that for males like the ones who were studied, using marijuana implies being taught to enjoy the drug. Robinson's (1951) critique of analytic induction led to a hiatus in the development of logic models in sociology until modeling difficulties were understood better.

Ragin (1988) developed a method for constructing logic models from cross-sectional data. Empirically valid propositions about all cases in a population are conjoined into a complex compound statement, transformed into Boolean algebra format, and processed by a computer program (Drass 1988). The result is a reduced compound statement that is empirically true for the cases and the propositions studied. The approach differs from statistical analysis of multifold tables in ignoring count information (other than whether a cell in a table has zero cases or more than zero cases) and in describing data patterns in terms of logic statements rather than in terms of the effects of variables and their interactions.

Abell (1987) and Heise (1989) developed a logic model approach for *event sequence analyses,* and Heise and Lewis (1988) developed a computer implementation. Logic models for sequences do not predict what will happen next but instead offer developmental accounts indicating what events must have preceded a focal event. A narrative of events is elicited from a culturally competent consultant who also defines prerequisites of the events in terms of other events within the happening. Since prerequisites define implication relations, such an elicitation yields a logic model that accounts for sequencing of events within the happening and that can be tested as a possible explanation of event sequencing in other happenings. Routines that appear to have little surface similarity may be accountable by abstract events in a logic model; for example, Corsaro and Heise (1990) showed that an abstract model accounted for observed play routines among children in two different cultures. Abell (1987) suggested that abstraction involves homomorphic reduction: That is, abstract events categorize concrete events that have identical logical relations with respect to events outside the category.

Careers are sequences in which the events are status transformations. Heise's (1990) logic model analysis of careers emphasized that individuals' sequences of status transformations are generated in limited patterns from institutional taxonomies of roles. *Guttman scaling* can be employed as a means of analyzing individual experiences in order to infer logic models that are generating career sequences (e.g., see Wanderer 1984). Abbott and Hrycak (1990) applied *optimal matching* techniques to the problem of comparing career sequences, with the similarity of two sequences being measured as the minimum number of transformations required to change one sequence into the other; clusters of similar sequences discovered from the similarity measures are identified as genres of career patterns that actually exist.

A *formal grammar* defines sequences of symbols that are acceptable in a language, being "essentially a deductive system of axioms and rules of inference, which generates the sentences of a language as its theorems" (Partee, ter Meulen, and Wall 1990, p. 437). A grammar, like a logic model, is explanatory rather than predictive, interpreting why a sequence was constructed as it was or why a sequence is deviant in the sense of being unprincipled. Grammars have been applied for modeling episodes of social interaction, viewing sequences of social events as symbolic strings that are, or are not, legitimate within a language of action provided by a social institution (Skvoretz and Fararo 1980; Skvoretz 1984). The grammatical perspective on institutionalized action can be reformulated as a *production system* model in which a hierarchy of if–then rules defines how particular conditions instigate particular actions (Axten and Fararo 1977; Fararo and Skvoretz 1984).

Case frame grammar (Dirven and Radden 1987) deals with how syntactic position within a sequence or group of symbols designates function. For example, syntactic positioning in a sentence can designate an event's agent, action, object, instrument, product, beneficiary, and location (e.g., "the locksmith cut the blank with a grinder into a key for the customer in his shop"). Montague grammar (Dowty, Wall, and Peters 1988) employs logic and higher-order logics to develop sophisticated formal models depicting how the meaning of a grammatical sequence emerges from the meaning of its components and the way they are put together. Related ideas arise in sociology. For example, in network theory "leader," "isolate," "broker," and so forth are roles that can be identified from structural position, and a case-grammar approach could focus on how characteristics of individuals combine with roles to yield unique systems. The case-grammar perspective informed Heise's (1979) symbolic-interactionist modeling of social interaction by providing an agent–action–object–location framework for analyzing social events. Guttman's *facet mapping sentences* (see Shye 1978) implicitly employ a case-grammar framework for analyzing a conceptual domain in terms of sets of concepts that fit into different syntactic slots and thereby generate a large number of propositions related to the domain. For example, Grimshaw (1989) developed a complex mapping sentence that suggested how different kinds of ambiguities arise in conversation and are resolved as a function of a variety of factors.

The mathematics of *abstract groups* provide a means for modeling some deterministic systems. Suppose a few different situations exist, and combining any two situations establishes another one of the situations; the result of a string of combinations can be computed by combining adjacent situations two at a time in any order. Also suppose that any situation can be reproduced by combining it with one particular situation, and this identity situation can be obtained from any other situation through a single combination. Then the set of situations and the scheme for combining them together constitute a group, and the group describes a completely deterministic system of transformations. Kosaka (1989) suggested a possible application of abstract groups by modeling the aesthetic theory of a Japanese philosopher in which there are sixty-four defined transformations; for example, *yabo* ("rusticity") combines with *hade* ("flamboyance") to produce *iki* ("chic urbanity").

A classic sociological application of groups involved kinship. Classificatory kinship systems (which are common in aboriginal cultures) put every pair of people in a society into a kinship relationship that may have little relation to genetic closeness, and each person implicitly is in a society-wide kinship class that determines relationships with others. White (1963) showed through mathematical analysis that classificatory rules regarding marriage and parentage generate clans of people who are in the same kinship situation and that the resulting classificatory kinship system operates as an abstract group; then he demonstrated that existing kinship systems accord with analytic results.

Models of social networks sometimes employ the notion of *semigroup*—a set of situations and a scheme for combining them (i.e., a group without an identity situation). For example, Breiger and Pattison (1986) examined economic and marriage relations among elite families in fifteenth-century Florence and showed that each family's relations to other families constituted a semigroup that was part of the overall semigroup of family relations in the city; they were able to identify the allies and enemies of the famous Medici family from the structure of family relationships. Social network research, the most sophisticated area of qualitative modeling in sociology, employs other algebraic and graph-theoretic notions as well (Marsden and Laumann 1984).

In general, qualitative models describe the systematic nature of social constructions and provide a basis for further empirical investigations. Thus, they serve the same functions that formal models serve in quantitative research.

(SEE ALSO: *Paradigms and Models; Qualitative Methods)*

REFERENCES

Abbott, Andrew, and Alexandra Hrycak 1990 "Measuring Resemblance in Sequence Data: An Optimal Matching Analysis of Musicians' Careers." *American Journal of Sociology* 96:144–185.

Abell, Peter 1987 *The Syntax of Social Life: The Theory and Method of Comparative Narratives.* New York: Oxford University Press.

Axten, N., and Thomas J. Fararo 1977 "The Information Processing Representation of Institutionalized Social Action." In P. Krishnan, ed., *Mathematical Models of Sociology.* Sociological Review Monograph 24. Keele, United Kingdom: University of Keele. Reprinted 1979, Totowa, N.J.: Rowan and Littlefield.

Balzer, Wolfgang 1990 "A Basic Model for Social Institutions. *Journal of Mathematical Sociology.* 16:1-29

Becker, Howard S. 1953 "Becoming a Marijuana User." *American Journal of Sociology* 59:235–243.

Breiger, Ronald L., and Philippa E. Pattison 1986 "Cumulated Social Roles: The Duality of Persons and Their Algebras." *Social Networks* 8:215–256.

Corsaro, William and D. Heise 1990 "Event Structure Models from Ethnographic Data." In C. Clogg, ed., *Sociological Methodology: 1990.* Cambridge, Mass.: Basil Blackwell, 1990.

Dirven, René, and Günter Radden (eds.) 1987 *Fillmore's Case Grammar: A Reader.* Heidelberg, Germany: Julius Groos Verlag.

Dowty, D. R., R. E. Wall, and S. Peters 1988 *Introduction to Montague Semantics.* Boston: D. Reidel.

Drass, Kriss 1988 Qualitative Comparative Analysis Version 2.02 (QCA 2.02). Dallas: Southern Methodist University, Department of Sociology.

Fararo, Thomas J., and John Skvoretz 1984 "Institutions as Production Systems." *Journal of Mathematical Sociology* 10:117–182.

Grimshaw, Allen D. 1989 *Collegial Discourse: Professional Conversation among Peers.* Norwood, N.J.: Ablex.

Heise, D. R. 1979 *Understanding Events: Affect and the Construction of Social Action.* New York: Cambridge University Press.

——— 1989 "Modeling Event Structures." *Journal of Mathematical Sociology* 14:139–169.

——— 1990 "Careers, Career Trajectories, and the Self." In J. Rodin, C. Schooler, and K. W. Schaie, eds., *Self-Directedness: Cause and Effects Throughout the Life Course.* New York: Erlbaum.

———, and Elsa Lewis 1988 ETHNO Version 2.0. Durham, N.C.: Duke University Press, National Collegiate Software.

Kosaka, Kenji 1989 "An Algebraic Reinterpretation of IKI NO KOZO (Structure of IKI)." *Journal of Mathematical Sociology* 14:293–304.

Marsden, Peter V., and Edward O. Laumann 1984 "Mathematical Ideas in Social Structure Analysis." *Journal of Mathematical Sociology* 10:271–294.

Partee, B. H., A. ter Meulen, and R. E. Wall 1990 *Mathematical Methods in Linguistics.* Boston: Kluwer Academic Publishers.

Ragin, Charles C. 1988 *Between Complexity and Generality: The Logic of Qualitative Comparison.* Berkeley: University of California Press.

Robinson, W. S. 1951 "The Logical Structure of Analytic Induction." *American Sociological Review* 16:812–818.

Shye, S. (ed.) 1978 *Theory Construction and Data Analysis in the Behavioral Sciences: A Volume in Honor of Louis Guttman.* San Francisco: Jossey-Bass.

Skvoretz, John 1984 "Languages and Grammars of Action and Interaction: Some Further Results." *Behavioral Science* 29:81–97.

———, and T. J. Fararo 1980 "Languages and Grammars of Action and Interaction: A Contribution to the Formal Theory of Action." *Behavioral Science* 25:9–22.

Wanderer, J. J. 1984 "Scaling Delinquent Careers over Time." *Criminology* 22:83–95.

White, Harrison C. 1963 *An Anatomy of Kinship: Mathematical Models for Structures of Cumulated Roles.* Englewood Cliffs, N.J.: Prentice-Hall.

Znaniecki, Florian 1934 *The Method of Sociology.* New York: Farrar and Rinehart.

DAVID R. HEISE
ALEX DURIG

QUALITY OF LIFE Although the concept of quality of life (QL) is not new, quality of life as an area of research and scholarship dates back only to the 1960s. Schuessler and Fisher (1985) recently noted that President Eisenhower's 1960 Commission on National Goals and Bauer's book on social indicators (1966) are often credited as providing the impetus for the development of QL as an area of research. Campbell (1981) suggested that the 1960s were favorable times for the development of QL research because of the emergence then of a concern that people must examine the quality of their lives and must do so in an environment that goes beyond providing material goods to foster individual happiness. Campbell quotes President Johnson, who stated in 1964:

> *The task of the Great Society is to ensure our people the environment, the capacities, and the social structures which will give them a meaningful chance to pursue their individual happiness. Thus the Great Society is concerned not with how much, but with how good—not with the quantity of goods but with the quality of their lives.* (Campbell 1981, p. 4)

Schuessler and Fisher (1985) note that the Russell Sage Foundation promoted QL and research on social indicators in the 1960s and 1970s and that the Institute for Social Research at the University of Michigan and the National Opinion Research Center at the University of Chicago have conducted QL research since the late 1960s. Despite the high volume of QL research during the 1960s and 1970s, it was not until 1979 that "Quality of Life" became an index entry in *Sociological Abstracts.*

The emerging QL research in the 1970s provided a departure from previous work that focused on objective indicators, primarily economic in nature, of individual well-being. The book *The Quality of American Life: Perceptions, Evaluations, and Satisfactions,* written by Campbell, Converse, and Rodgers in 1976, particularly promoted the use of subjective or psychological indicators of well-being. The work reported was founded on the conviction that the relationship between objective and subjective well-being indicators was weak and poorly understood. Moreover, the rising affluence of the post-World War II era had been accompanied by steady increases in social problems afflicting American society as well as other Western societies.

The year 1976 also saw the publication of another major work focusing on subjective indicators of well-being. *Social Indicators of Well-Being: Americans' Perceptions of Life Quality* by Andrews and Withy (1976) reported findings from interviews with representative samples of more than 5,000 Americans. The interviews focused on satisfaction with the quality of various life domains. A more recent volume, titled *Research on the Quality of Life,* edited by Frank Andrews (1986), brought together a variety of papers originating at a symposium honoring the memory of Angus Campbell, one of the founders of the Institute for Social Research. And, although this volume included important papers on cross-national differences in life satisfaction and papers on blacks and Hispanics, a number of the papers had no direct relationship to QL research. Rockwell (1989) noted that a useful focus of the field was lost in this volume, the focus on subjective indicators of the quality of life. Andrews also noted that support for large-scale, wide-ranging surveys become increasingly difficult in the 1980s in the United States resulting in a lack of replication of the national surveys conducted in the previous decade by the Institute for Social Research.

Parallel to the large national surveys of subjective well-being during the 1970s, there was a proliferation of studies focusing on the subjective well-being of the elderly. In a useful article, Larson (1978) reviewed three decades of research that focused on the psychological well-being of older people. Perhaps no other area of research in the emerging field of gerontology had received as much attention during the 1960s and 1970s as the area of life satisfaction, morale, mental health, and psychological well-being in general. Much of this research was spurred by the lively debate over the merits of disengagement theory (proposed by Cumming and Henry 1961) and activity theory (identified with various authors, including Havighurst, Neugarten, and Tobin 1968; Maddox 1968, 1970) in predicting "successful aging." Gerontological work in the 1980s showed a marked decline in the number of articles predicting life satisfaction and morale and an increase in articles focusing on specific dimensions of psychological well-being, such as depression and psychological distress, as well as articles focusing on the prediction of physical health outcomes (Markides 1989).

The relative decline in research on the subjective quality of life of Americans in general as well as the subjective well-being of the elderly observed in the 1980s was accompanied by a marked increase in QL research in medicine. In 1989, for example, the *Journal of the American Medical Association* published three major articles on quality of life (Stewart et al. 1989; Tarlov et al. 1989; Wells et al. 1989) of various kinds of patients. In contrast, not a single paper focusing on quality of life was published in the *American Sociological Review* in the same year. A careful examination of the 1990 program of the annual meeting of the American Sociological Association revealed no sessions or papers focusing directly on QL research.

Within medicine, there has been particular interest in studying the quality of life of cancer patients. Before 1970, cancer research focused almost exclusively on survival and its extension. With extended survival from cancer becoming the rule, research has given increasing attention to the quality of life of the surviving patients afflicted with cancer or patients treated for cancer. In 1987, for example, a volume entitled *The Quality of Life of Cancer Patients* was published. The volume, edited by Aaronson and Beckman (1987), contains papers from researchers in a number of European countries as well as the United States.

Another parallel to this work has been the recent focus on active life expectancy. The work has gone beyond predicting extension of life in general to investigating the extent to which recent extensions of life expectancy have been accompanied by extensions of "active" life.

DEFINITIONS OF QUALITY OF LIFE

As seen in the previous section, there has been a movement in recent decades away from objective, quantitative research toward subjective, qualitative assessments of QL in sociology and other fields. But even within these broad approaches to QL, there appears to be little agreement about an appropriate definition of QL.

Some writings include under QL research the social indicators movement. Land (1971) noted that in the early years of the movement, the most popular definition of social indicators was given in *Toward a Social Report* (U.S. Department of Health, Education, and Welfare 1969, p. 97):

> *A social indicator . . . may be defined to be a statistic of direct normative interest which facilitates concise, comprehensive and balanced judgments about the condition of a major aspect of a society. It is in all cases a direct measure of welfare and is subject to the interpretation that, if it changes, in the "right" direction, while other things remain equal, things have gotten better, or people are "better off." Thus statistics on the number of doctors or policemen could not be social indicators whereas figures on health or crime rates could be.*

Land criticized the above definition and proposed a broader one that treats social indicators as both "outputs" and "inputs" in "a sociological model of a social system or some segment thereof" (1971; p. 324). Thus, for example, the number of doctors is essential to understanding the health of the population, as are other factors. Land's definition has been largely accepted by the social indicators movement (Mukherjee 1989; p. 53).

This entry will give only limited attention to

social indicators because a separate article is devoted to it. Yet the term is often used interchangeably with QL, at least with respect to what Mukherjee (1989; p. 49) calls "need-based" quality of life research. Moreover, the journal *Social Indicators Research* is subtitled *An International Journal of Quality of Life Measurement.*

In his book *The Quality of Life Valuation in Social Research,* Mukherjee notes that QL researchers employ several dichotomies such as "quantity" and "quality," "behavior" and "perception," and "objective" and "subjective" indicators. He argues:

> *Economists and planners . . . are almost exclusively concerned with behavioural research on the basis of quantitative variables to improve the quality of life of the people. In that context, they ignore qualitative variations in the appraisal of a better quality of life or treat these variations as introducing a classificatory . . . distinction in the field of enquiry. They also equate the individual-wise subjective perception of reality to a group-wise "objective" perception by experts. Their appraisal of social reality in this manner leads them to formulate what the people* need *in order to improve their quality of life.* (Mukherjee 1989, pp. 37–38)

This need-based approach to QL research is not limited to the work of economists and planners. For example, as mentioned above, the social indicators movement is largely need-based research.

Need-based research has been criticized on a variety of grounds. Michalos argues:

> *The existence of a great gap between Maslow-type needs and specific items of actions in the world is one reason why the attempt to develop indicators from needs does not seem worthwhile. . . . Indeed, contrary to those who think we might be able to construct a theory of value based on needs. I am sure that the logic of the situation is just the reverse. Values are* prior *to needs and required for their definition. To see that this is so, consider what one means to say about something when one says that it is needed. At the very least it is assumed that if someone needs something, that person would suffer from some form of* deterioration *in its absence.* (Michalos 1974, p. 125)

This argument favors a "want-based" approach to QL research that focuses on people's perceptions, expectations, aspirations, and achievement orientations (Mukherjee 1989; p. 44). Bharadwaj and Wilkening argue, for example:

> *The recognition that the economic health of a nation is not synonymous with individual satisfaction and well-being had led to the development of social indicators to assess individual quality of life. . . . The new emphasis is on the monitoring of change in goals, values, attitudes and satisfaction that affect individual lives and nations. The overall thrust appears to be "the development of a set of 'dependent variables'."* (Bharadwaj and Wilkening 1980, p. 377)

Similarly, in describing the results of their research, Campbell, Converse, and Rogers argue:

> *The research with which this book is concerned derives from the conviction that the relationship between objective conditions and psychological states is very imperfect and that in order to know the quality of life experience it will be necessary to go directly to the individual himself for his description of how his life feels to him.* (Campbell, Converse, and Rogers 1976, p. 4)

From this kind of perspective, quality of life typically involves "a sense of achievement in one's work, an appreciation of beauty in nature and the arts, a feeling of identification with one's community, a sense of fulfillment of one's potential" (Campbell, Converse, and Rogers 1976, p. 1).

The "dependent variables" of this research tend to be items or scales measuring satisfactions or happiness. Milbrath (1978, p. 36), for example, argues: "I have come to the conclusion that the only defensible definition of quality of life is a general feeling of happiness." And even though such global evaluations have been common, much of the research has focused on describing and explaining satisfactions with various life "domains" such as work, family, housing, and so forth.

In discussing subjective indicators of QL, Land noted the difficulties in relating them to objective indicators. He noted, for example, that while income levels tend to be associated with satisfactions and happiness within given countries and at given times, "higher per capita levels of national income do not produce higher average levels of national satisfaction over time or cross sectionally" (1983, p. 5). He goes on to suggest that from the standpoint of generating theory of social change, it is not clear that satisfaction indexes are the most desirable subjective indicators as opposed to values, aspirations, or expectations, nor is it clear that satisfaction indexes provide an unambiguous criterion for the formulation of public policy. He notes, for example, that research by Andrews and Withy (1976), among others, has found that areas most critical to individual satisfactions do not seem very amenable to public policy interventions.

MEASURING QUALITY OF LIFE

The broadest and most commonly employed distinction in measures of QL is between objective and subjective measures. Among the former are indicators such as per capita income, average calorie consumption, percent of adult illiteracy, quality of air, average daily temperature, crime rates, life expectancy, and a myriad of other indicators that are best seen as causes of quality of life.

Any one of the above has shortcomings. For example, GNP per capita has been acknowledged to suffer from many well-known limitations, including that it may not capture the spending power of the masses but rather that of a small minority (Mukherjee 1989, p. 42). To overcome the limitations of single indicators, researchers have proposed a number of composite indexes such as the Physical Quality of Life Index (PQLI; see Morris 1977) that includes, among other variables, life expectancy at birth, infant mortality, and literacy. The purpose of the PQLI was to rank countries by physical well-being. Yet it has limitations, as its proponent acknowledges, including that "it is based on the assumption that the needs and desires of individuals initially and at the most basic level are for larger life expectancy, reduced illness, and greater opportunity" (Morris 1977, p. 147).

Another composite index of objective indicators of QL is the Index of Social Progress (ISP) proposed originally by Estes (1984) and revised more recently by the same author (Estes 1988). The latest version (ISP83) consists of thirty-six indicators and is divided into ten subindexes covering "education, health status, status of women, defense effort, economic, demographic, political participation, cultural diversity and welfare effort" (Estes 1988, p. 1). A number of equally important indicators are not included because reliable data are not available on the 124 nations studied (e.g., crime rates, suicide rates, maldistribution of wealth). Estes goes on to acknowledge further the index's limitations as a measure of quality of life:

> *[The ISP is not] a tool that attempts to assess personal happiness, satisfaction with life, or the degree of personal "fulfillment" experienced by individuals living in particular nations. Rather, the ISP measures the changing capacity of nations to provide for the basic social and material needs of their populations as a whole. . . . Consequently, the ISP should be regarded as a quantitative measure of national human welfare, and is not to be construed as a tool that can be used to assess directly varying degrees of personal fulfillment.* (Estes 1988, p. 4)

There has also been a lively interest in developing indexes consisting of objective indicators to rank quality of life of American cities. Liu (1976), for example, utilized 1970 U.S. Census data covering five major domains of quality of life: economic, environmental, health and education, political, and social. Weighting was employed to create an overall index as well as domain-specific subindexes. Other similar indexes were offered by J. Wilson (1967), Smith (1972), Boyer and Savageau (1981), Rosen (1979), and Berger, Blomquist, and Waldner (1987). Such rankings of cities typically elicit national attention and often surprise individuals about how high or low their community ranks. Rankings also do not often correlate with each other. For example, Berger, Blomquist, and Waldner (1987) found that their revealed-preference ranking had a correlation of −0.075 with those proposed by Boyer and Savageau (1981) and a correlation of 0.048 with Liu's (1976) rankings.

There have been numerous subjective measures of QL, with most relating to happiness or life satisfaction. Some measures are global in the sense that they aim at capturing happiness or satisfaction with life as a whole, while others pertain to happiness or satisfaction with certain life-domains.

The studies by Andrews and Withy (1976) and Campbell, Converse, and Rogers (1976) included measures of both domain-specific and global life satisfaction and employed the former as predictors of the latter. In general, they found that the best predictors of global satisfaction are marriage and family life, leisure activities, work and finances, housing, the community, and friendships.

Well before these landmark studies, W. Wilson (1967) reviewed prior literature on subjective well-being and concluded that the "happy person emerges as a young, healthy, well-educated, well-paid, extroverted, optimistic, worry-free, religious, married person with high self-esteem, high job morale, modest aspirations, of either sex and of a wide range of intelligence" (1967, p. 294). He also concluded that little progress had been made in understanding happiness since the time of the Greek philosophers.

Diener (1984) noted that between W. Wilson's 1967 article and 1984, over 700 studies on subjective well-being had been published. In general, Wilson's conclusions regarding predictors of well-being appeared supported by the literature, including that little theoretical progress had been made in the field since the ancient Greeks.

This voluminous literature on subjective well-being has employed a variety of single-item and multiple-item measures of happiness and life satisfaction. Among the best-known single-item measures are: Cantril's (1965) "self-anchoring ladder," which asks respondents to place themselves on a nine-rung ladder ranging from "best possible for you" to "worst possible for you"; Gurin, Veroff, and Feld's (1960) item, "Taking all things together, how would you say things are these days?", with possible response choices being "very happy," "pretty happy," and "not too happy"; and Andrews and Withy's (1976) item, "How do you feel about how happy you are?", with seven choices ranging from "delighted" to "terrible."

A problem with single-item measures is that because internal reliability estimates cannot be computed, the only way of assessing their reliability is through temporal correlation, which makes it difficult to separate measurement error from true change. However, convergence with other measures of well-being has suggested that these single-item measures enjoy moderate levels of validity. They do suffer from other limitations, however, such as positive skewness, acquiescence, and inability to capture the various dimensions of well-being (Diener 1984).

There have also been a variety of multi-item scales employed. Some of the best-known general scales include: the Affect Balance Scale (Bradburn 1969), which consists of items capturing positive and negative well-being, the two being relatively independent of each other, and Campbell, Converse, and Rogers's (1976) Index of General Affect, which asks respondents to describe their present lives using semantic differential scales (miserable–enjoyable, hard–easy, boring–interesting, useless–worthwhile, lonely–friendly, discouraging–hopeful, empty–full, disappointing–rewarding, and doesn't give me a chance–brings out the best in me).

Although happiness and satisfaction are often used interchangeably, many writers believe they are distinct measures of well-being. George, for example, suggests that "happiness refers to an affective assessment of quality of life," while "life satisfaction refers to an assessment of the overall conditions of life, as derived from a comparison of one's aspirations to one's actual achievements" (1981, p. 351). Campbell, Converse, and Rogers (1976) prefer satisfaction measures over happiness measures because they are more sensitive to intervention. While happiness tends to be transitory and volatile, life satisfaction changes gradually and systematically in response to changing life conditions (see also Stull 1987). Satisfaction scales have been particularly popular in gerontology.

QUALITY OF LIFE IN THE ELDERLY

An area in which lively interest has been shown in subjective indicators of QL has been the emerging field of gerontology. As mentioned earlier, use of subjective measures of well-being was particularly high during the 1960s and 1970s, when social gerontologists were occupied with assessing the merits of disengagement and activity theories. In the late 1970s, Larson (1978) reviewed three decades of research and concluded that the most consistent predictor of subjective well-being are self-reports of health.

Although gerontological studies have employed general well-being measures (e.g., the Affect Balance Scale), they have also employed scales specifically developed for use with older people. The two best known are the Life Satisfaction Index A (Neugarten, Havighurst, and Tobin 1961) and the Philadelphia Geriatric Morale Scale (Lawton 1975). The Life Satisfaction Index A consists of twenty items, with which respondents agree or disagree. A combined life satisfaction score is obtained by summing scores on all twenty items. Because the index covers a variety of areas, including happiness, satisfaction, and "activation level" (see Cherlin and Reeder 1975), the combined score confounds separate dimensions of well-being (Stull 1987). The Philadelphia Geriatric Center Morale Scale (PGCMS) originally consisted of twenty-two items (Lawton 1972), and the revised version consisted of seventeen items (Lawton 1975). Factor analyses with the latter have produced three dimensions: Agitation, Attitude toward Own Aging, and Lonely Dissatisfaction. The scale has problems similar to those of the Life Satisfaction Index, such as the confounding of satisfaction and happiness. The two scales are in many ways similar (in fact, they share some items) and have been found to be highly intercorrelated ($r = 0.76$; see Lohman 1977).

Liang (1985) attempted to integrate the Life Satisfaction Index A and the Affect Balance Scale by selecting seven items from the former and eight from the latter. His analysis yielded four factors (congruence, happiness, positive affect, and negative affect) that correspond to dimensions of well-being discussed by Lawton (1983). However, Liang acknowledged a gap between the operationalization of well-being and its theoretical operationalization: "Most instruments were developed with only a general conceptual definition, and the sampling of the item domain is usually based on intuition, experience, and empirical experimentation" (Liang 1985, p. 553).

After reviewing the voluminous literature on subjective well-being among the elderly, Gubrium and Lynott (1983) concluded that it was time to "rethink life satisfaction" in old age. One of their key concerns was that the dominant measures employed tended to dwell on the earlier years of people's lives and have less relevance for their current circumstances. In addition, "current measures do not allow for co-equal dialogue between subject and researcher about the content of items and responses" (Gubrium and Lynott 1983, p. 37).

Possibly because of these and other conceptual and methodological problems in subjective well-being measures, we have seen a substantial decline in published studies in major journals aiming at predicting life satisfaction, morale, and related concepts during the 1980s. Social gerontologists have instead concentrated on predicting more narrow dimensions of well-being, such as psychological distress and depression, and are increasingly employing a life course perspective that involves examination of main and interactive effects of stress, social support, and related factors (e.g., George 1989). Measures of depression and psychological distress are being employed more frequently, perhaps because they are perceived as more amenable to intervention than are measures of life satisfaction and morale. Other measures of well-being that are more amenable to intervention are various indicators of physical health that are also increasingly being studied from a life course perspective (Markides and Cooper 1989).

STUDIES OF THE QUALITY OF LIFE OF PATIENTS

Perhaps the most activity in the area of quality of life is currently found in medicine, much of it conducted by behavioral and social scientists. Interest in QL after medical treatments is based on the realization that chronic diseases cannot be cured, and, therefore, the goal of much therapy becomes to limit the effects of illness so that patients may live productive, comfortable, and satisfying lives. Traditionally, success of medical treatment was evaluated in terms of lengthening lives and post-treatment complications. However, there has been a realization that medical and surgical treatments may extend survival but often reduce quality of life (Eisman 1981).

Hollandsworth (1988) reviewed studies evaluating the impact of medical treatment on QL during the period 1980 to 1984 and compared his results with those of studies conducted during 1975 to 1979 (Najman and Levine 1981). Hollandsworth's (1988) comparison revealed a marked increase between the two time periods in both quantity and quality of studies. Although recent studies tended to be more sophisticated, the majority nevertheless relied on convenience samples. One marked improvement in the recent research is the increase in use of subjective measures of quality of life, with 60 percent of the recent studies employing at least one such measure, compared to only around 10 percent in the earlier period.

Another interesting outcome of Hollandsworth's (1988) analysis was the increase over time in the proportion of studies that do not report favorable outcomes. Studies published in the late 1970s were almost unanimous in claiming favorable outcomes of treatment, but this optimism must be tempered by the many methodological limitations of these studies (Najman and Levine 1981). Of the more sophisticated studies published from 1980 to 1984, almost one-half reported either negative outcomes or at least mixed results. In fact, it appeared that the probability of reporting negative outcomes (or lack of positive results) tended to be correlated with the methodological sophistication of the studies (Hollandsworth 1988).

The impact of a variety of medical treatments have been examined, including cardiovascular therapies (e.g., Jenkins et al. 1983; Wenger et al. 1984), end-stage renal disease (e.g., Evans et al. 1985), and chronic obstructive pulmonary disease (e.g., McSweeney et al. 1982). However, by far the most frequently studied area is that relating to outcomes of cancer treatment (see Aaronson 1989; Aaronson and Beckman 1987; Cella and Cherin 1988). Aaronson (1989, p. 69) noted that while "there is no universally accepted definition of the quality of life concept, in oncology it is most often used to describe such aspects of health status as physical symptoms, daily activity level, psychological well-being, and social functioning." This increasing use of subjective QL indicators is becoming an integral part of evaluation in clinical cancer research, but a major challenge facing researchers is the development of measures capturing all dimensions of QL while meeting rigorous standards of reliability and validity (Aaronson 1988).

An overview of the literature on medical treatment outcomes does indeed reveal increasing use of subjective quality of life measures. As in the broader QL field, many studies tend to employ single-item global indicators capturing life satisfaction or happiness. However, an increasing number of studies are employing general multiple-item measures discussed earlier, such as the Affect Balance Scale and the Life Satisfaction Index Z. Other scales capturing more specific and narrow dimensions of QL include measures of mood, anxiety, self-concept, and depression (Hollandsworth 1988) as well as more comprehensive instruments that capture physical, emotional, and social functioning, such as the McMaster Health Index Questionnaire (Chambers et al. 1982).

CONCLUSION

This brief and selective overview of the field of quality of life indicates a variety of perspectives employed within sociology and related fields. In fact, it may be said that there is more interest in QL outside of the mainstream of sociology, as, for example, in the area of medical treatment. While much of the pioneer work and large-scale national studies in the 1970s were conducted by sociologists, research on quality of life remains very much outside the mainstream of sociology. For example, Schuessler and Fisher's (1985) review uncovered only one article (Gerson 1976) explicitly on quality of life published in the *American Sociological Review* way back in 1976.

This overview also reveals some patterns and trends in QL research in the last three decades. First, there have been two broad approaches, one focusing on objective indicators and one focusing on subjective indicators. Related dichotomies noted by Mukherjee (1989) include quantity versus quality and behavior versus perception. It is clear that there has been a trend away from relying simply on objective indicators to relying increasingly on people's subjective reports about the quality of their lives. Objective measures have been the domain primarily of the social indicators movement, with subjective approaches to QL increasingly perceived as the domain of QL research (Mukherjee 1989).

Within the subjective QL approach, we also see a trend away from single-item indicators capturing global happiness and life satisfaction to multiple-item scales such as the Affect Balance Scale and the Life Satisfaction Index Z. At the same time, there have been attempts to measure subjective quality of life in specific life domains. And, there has been continuing interest by sociologists, economists, and others (including popular magazines) to rank urban areas according to a variety of QL indicators.

During the 1960s and 1970s a great deal of subjective QL research was conducted by social and behavioral gerontologists, who used measures of life satisfaction and morale as indicators of successful aging. For a number of reasons, gerontologists began abandoning research on life satisfaction and morale in favor of measures more amenable to intervention, such as measures of psychological distress, depression, and physical health function. Perhaps the most exciting research on QL currently being conducted is in the area of medical treatment outcomes, particularly cancer treatment.

It is becoming increasingly difficult to obtain funding to conduct large-scale national surveys of subjective quality of life such as those conducted during the 1970s. The future of QL research is uncertain, at least as a broad unified field of inquiry. Studies ranking urban areas are likely to continue, if anything because of the immediate and broad appeal they elicit. It is also safe to predict that the concept of quality of life will continue to have some appeal in social gerontology. The most exciting work may well take place in the area of medical intervention outcomes. Sociologists and other behavioral scientists are increasingly conducting research related to medicine, and much of this research relates to quality of life. It is becoming apparent that medical interventions (as well as other factors) are enabling us to live longer, but it is not clear that the added years of life are "quality" years. There will be increasing interest in finding ways to improve the quality of the added years, and sociologists have an opportunity and responsibility to help find ways of accomplishing that.

(SEE ALSO: *Attitudes; Health and Illness Behavior; Health Status Measurement; Mental Health; Social Gerontology; Social Indicators*)

REFERENCES

Aaronson, Neil K. 1989 "Quality of Life: What Is It? How Should It Be Measured?" *Oncology* 2:69–74.

———, and J. H. Beckman (eds.) 1987 *The Quality of Life of Cancer Patients*. New York: Raven.

Andrews, Frank M. (ed.) 1986 *Research on the Quality of Life*. Ann Arbor: University of Michigan, Institute for Social Research.

———, and Stephen B. Withey 1976 *Social Indicators of Well-Being: Americans' Perceptions of Life Quality*. New York: Plenum.

Bauer, Raymond A., ed. 1966 *Social Indicators*. Cambridge, Mass.: MIT Press.

Berger, Mark C., Glenn C. Blomquist, and Werner Waldner 1987 "A Revealed-Preference Ranking of

Quality of Life for Metropolitan Areas." *Social Science Quarterly* 68:761–778.

Bharadwaj, Lakshmi K., and E. A. Wilkening 1980 "Life Domain Satisfactions and Personal Social Integration." *Social Indicators Research* 7:337–351.

Boyer, Rick, and D. Savageau 1981 *Places Rated Almanac.* Chicago: Rand McNally.

Bradburn, Norman 1969 *The Structure of Psychological Well-Being.* Chicago: Aldine.

Campbell, Angus 1981 *The Sense of Well-Being in America: Recent Patterns and Trends.* New York: McGraw-Hill.

———, Phillip Converse, and Willard L. Rogers 1976 *The Quality of American Life: Perceptions, Evaluations, and Satisfactions.* New York: Russell Sage Foundation.

Cantril, Hadley 1965 *The Pattern of Human Concerns.* New Brunsick, N.J.: Rutgers University Press.

Cella, David F., and E. A. Cherin 1988 "Quality of Life during and after Cancer Treatment." *Comprehensive Therapy* 14:69–75.

Chambers, Larry W., Lorry A. MacDonald, Peter Tugwell, W. Watson Buchanan, and Gunnar Kraag 1982 "The McMaster Health Index Questionnaire as a Measure of Quality of Life for Patients with Rheumatoid Disease." *Journal of Rheumatology* 9:780–784.

Cherlin, Andy, and Leo G. Reeder 1975 "The Dimensions of Psychological Well-Being: A Critical Review." *Sociological Methods and Research* 4:189–214.

Cumming, Elaine, and William E. Henry 1961 *Growing Old: The Process of Disengagement.* New York: Basic Books.

Diener, Ed 1984 "Subjective Well-Being." *Psychological Bulletin* 95:542–575.

Eisman, B. 1981 "The Second Dimension." *Archives of Surgery* 116:11–13.

Estes, Richard J. 1984 *The Social Progress of Nations.* New York: Praeger.

——— 1988 *Trends in World Social Development: The Social Progress of Nations. 1970–1987.* New York: Praeger.

Evans, R. W., D. L. Manninen, L. P. Garrison, L. G. Hart, C. R. Blagg, R. A. Gutman, A. R. Hull, and E. G. Lowrie 1985 "The Quality of Life of Patients with End-Stage Renal Disease." *New England Journal of Medicine* 312:553–559.

George, Linda K. 1981 "Subjective Well-Being: Conceptual and Methodological Issues." *Annual Review of Gerontology and Geriatrics* 2:345–382.

——— 1989 "Stress, Social Support, and Depression over the Life Course." In Kyriakos S. Markides and Cary L. Cooper, eds., *Aging, Stress and Health.* Chichester, United Kingdom: Wiley.

Gerson, Elihu M. 1976 "On 'Quality of Life'." *American Sociological Review* 41:793–806.

Gubrium, Jaber F., and Robert J. Lynott 1983 "Rethinking Life Satisfaction." *Human Organization* 42:30–38.

Gurin, Gerald, J. Veroff, and S. Feld 1960 *Americans View Their Mental Health.* New York: Basic Books.

Havighurst, Robert J., Bernice Neugarten, and Sheldon S. Tobin 1968 "Disengagement and Patterns of Aging." In Bernice L. Neugarten, ed., *Middle-Age and Aging.* Chicago: University of Chicago Press.

Hollandsworth, James G. 1988 "Evaluating the Impact of Medical Treatment on the Quality of Life: A Five-Year Update." *Social Science and Medicine* 26:425–434.

Jenkins, C. David, Babette A. Stanton, J. A. Savageau, P. Denlinger, and M. D. Klein 1983 "Coronary Artery Bypass Surgery: Physical, Psychological, Social, and Economic Outcomes of Six Months Later." *Journal of the American Medical Association* 250:782–88.

Land, Kenneth C. 1971 "On the Definition of Social Indicators." *American Sociologist* 6:322–325.

——— 1983 "Social Indicators." *Annual Review of Sociology* 9:1–26.

Larson, Reed 1978 "Thirty Years of Research on Subjective Well-Being of Older Americans." *Journal of Gerontology* 33:109–125.

Lawton, M. Powell 1972 "The Dimensions of Morale." In Donald Kent, Robert Kastenbaum, and Sylvia Sherwood, eds., *Research, Planning, and Action for the Elderly.* New York: Behavioral Publications.

——— 1975 "The Philadelphia Geriatric Center Morale Scale: A Revision." *Journal of Gerontology* 30:85–89.

——— 1983 "The Varieties of Well-Being." *Experimental Aging Research* 9:65–72.

Liang, Jersey 1985 "A Structural Integration of the Affect Balance Scale and the Life Satisfaction Index A." *Journal of Gerontology* 40:552–561.

Liu, Ben-Cheih 1976 *Quality of Life Indicators in U.S. Metropolitan Areas.* New York: Praeger.

Lohman, Nancy 1977 "Correlations of Life Satisfaction, Morale, and Adjustment Measures." *Journal of Gerontology* 32:73–75.

McSweeney, A. J., I. Grant, R. K. Heaton, K. Adams, and R. M. Timms 1982 "Life Quality of Patients with Chronic Obstructive Pulmonary Disease." *Archives of Internal Medicine* 142:473–478.

Maddox, George L. 1968 "Persistence of Life Styles among the Elderly: A Longitudinal Study of Patterns of Social Activity in Relation to Life Satisfaction." In Bernice L. Neugarten, ed., *Middle-Age and Aging.* Chicago: University of Chicago Press.

——— 1970 "Themes and Issues in Sociological Theories of Aging." *Human Development* 13:17–27.

Markides, Kyriakos S. 1989 "Aging, Gender, Race/ Ethnicity, Class, and Health: A Conceptual Overview." In K. S. Markides, ed., *Aging and Health: Perspectives on Gender, Race, Ethnicity, and Class.* Newbury Park, Calif.: Sage.

———, and Cary L. Cooper (eds.) 1989 *Aging, Stress, and Health.* Chichester, United Kingdom: Wiley.

Michalos, Alex C. 1974 "Strategies for Reducing Information Overload in Social Reports." *Social Indicators Research* 8:385–422.

Milbrath, L. W. 1978 "Indicators of Environmental Quality." In UNESCO, ed., *Indicators of Environmental Quality and Quality of Life.* UNESCO Reports and Papers in the Social Sciences, No. 38. Paris: UNESCO.

Morris, David M. 1977 "A Physical Quality of Life Index (PQLI)." In J. W. Sewell, ed., *The United States and the World Development Agenda 1977.* New York: Praeger.

Mukherjee, Ramkrishna 1989 *The Quality of Life Valuation in Social Research.* New Delhi: Sage Publications.

Najman, J. M., and Sol Levine 1981 "Evaluating the Impact of Medical Care and Technologies on the Quality of Life: A Review and Critique." *Social Science and Medicine* 15(F):107–115.

Neugarten, Bernice L., Robert J. Havighurst, and Sheldon S. Tobin 1961 "The Measurement of Life Satisfaction." *Journal of Gerontology* 16:134–143.

Rockwell, R. C. 1989 Review of *Research on Quality of Life,* ed. F. M. Andrews. In *Social Forces* 67:824-826.

Rosen, Sherwin 1979 "Wage-Based Indexes of Urban Quality of Life." In Peter Mieszkowski and Mahlon Straszheim, eds., *Current Issues in Urban Economics.* Baltimore: Johns Hopkins University Press.

Schuessler, Karl F., and G. A. Fisher 1985 "Quality of Life Research in Sociology." *Annual Reviews of Sociology* 11:129–149.

Smith, David M. 1972 "Towards a Geography of Social Well-Being: Inter-State Variations in the United States." *Antipode Monographs in Social Geography* 1:17–46.

Stewart, Anita L., S. Greenfield, R. D. Hays, K. Wells, W. H. Rogers, S. D. Berry, E. A. McGlynn, and J. E. Ware 1989 "Functional Status and Well-Being of Patients with Chronic Conditions: Results from the Medical Outcomes Study." *Journal of the American Medical Association* 262:907–913.

Stull, Donald E. 1987 "Conceptualization and Measurement of Well-Being: Implications for Policy Evaluation." In Edgar F. Borgatta and Rhonda J. V. Montgomery, eds., *Critical Issues in Aging Policy.* Newbury Park, Calif.: Sage.

Tarlov, Alvin R., J. E. Ware, S. Greenfield, E. C. Nelson, E. Perrin, and M. Zubkoff 1989 "The Medical Outcomes Study: An Application for Monitoring the Results of Medical Care." *Journal of the American Medical Association* 262:925–930.

U.S. Department of Health, Education, and Welfare 1969 *Toward a Social Report.* Washington, D.C.: U.S. Government Printing Office.

Wells, Kenneth B., A. Stewart, R. D. Hays, M. A. Burnam, W. Rogers, M. Daniels, S. Greenfield, and J. Ware 1989 "The Functioning and Well-Being of Depressed Patients." *Journal of the American Medical Association* 262:914–919.

Wenger, Nanette K., Margaret E. Mattson, Curt D. Furberg, and Jack Elinson (eds.) 1984 *Assessment of Quality of Life in Clinical Trials of Cardiovascular Therapies.* New York: Le Jacq Publishing.

Wilson, John O. 1967 *Quality of Life in the United States: An Excursion into the New Frontier of Socioeconomic Indicators.* Kansas City, Mo.: Midwest Research Institute.

Wilson, Warner 1967 "Correlates of Avowed Happiness." *Psychological Bulletin* 67:294–306.

KYRIAKOS S. MARKIDES

QUASI-EXPERIMENTAL RESEARCH DESIGNS The goal of most social scientific research is to explain the causes of human behavior in its myriad forms. Researchers generally attempt to do this by uncovering causal associations among variables. For example, researchers may be interested in whether a causal relationship exists between income and happiness. One might expect a positive association between these two variables. That is, an increase in income, the independent variable, produces an increase in happiness, the dependent variable. Unfortunately, observing a positive correlation between these two variables does not prove that income causes happiness. In order to make a valid causal inference, three conditions must be present: (1) there must be an association between the variables (e.g., income and happiness); (2) the variable that is the presumed cause (e.g., income) must precede the effect (e.g., happiness) in time; and (3) the association between the two variables cannot be explained by the influence of some other variable (e.g., education) that may be related to both of them. The purpose of any research design is to construct a circumstance within which a researcher can achieve these three conditions and thus make valid causal inferences.

Experimental designs are one of the most efficient ways to accomplish this goal of making valid causal inferences. Several characteristics are common to all true experimental designs. First, researchers *manipulate* the independent variable. That is, they actively modify people's environment (e.g., provide some people with money they otherwise would not have received)—as contrasted with passively observing the existing, "natural" environment (e.g., simply measuring the amount of income people normally make). Second, researchers have complete control over *when* the independent variable is manipulated (e.g., when people receive supplementary income). Third, researchers have complete control over *what* they manipulate. That is, they can specify the exact content of the different "treatment conditions" (different levels) of the independent variable to which subjects are exposed (e.g., how much supplementary income people receive and the manner in which they receive it). Fourth, researchers have complete control over *who* is assigned to which treatment condition (e.g., who receives the supplementary income and who does not, or who receives higher versus lower amounts of income).

Control over who receives specific treatments is especially important in making valid causal inferences. As a consequence of this control, researchers can use a very powerful technique called *random assignment.* For example, in evaluating the effect of income on happiness, investigators might randomly assign individuals who are below the poverty level to treatment groups receiving varying levels of supplementary income (e.g., none versus $1,000).

Table 1*a* illustrates this example. It depicts an experimental design in which subjects are randomly assigned to one of two groups. At time 1, researchers manipulate the independent variable (*X*): Each subject in group 1 receives $1,000 in supplementary income. Conversely, no subjects in group 2 receive any supplementary income. At time 2, researchers observe (measure) the average level of happiness (*O*) for group 1 versus group 2. The diagram $\uparrow X_{\text{income}} \rightarrow O_{\text{happiness}} \uparrow$ indicates an expected increase in happiness when supplementary income increases. That is, the average happiness score should be higher for group 1 than for group 2.

By assigning each subject to a particular treatment condition based on a coin flip or some other random procedure, experimental designs ensure that each subject has an equal chance of appearing in any one of the treatment conditions (e.g., levels of supplementary income). Therefore, as a result of random assignment, the different treatment groups depicted in Table 1*a* should be approximately equivalent in all characteristics (average education, average physical health, average religiosity, etc.) except their exposure to different levels of the independent variable (i.e., different levels of supplementary income). Consequently, even though there are a large number of other variables (e.g., education, physical health, or religiosity) that might affect happiness, none of these variables can serve as plausible alternative explanations for why the higher-income group has higher average happiness than does the lower-income group.

For example, due to random assignment, physically healthy versus unhealthy persons should be approximately equally distributed between the higher versus lower supplementary income treatment groups. Hence, a critic could not make a plausible argument that the treatment group receiving the higher amount of supplementary income (i.e., group 1) also has better health, and it is the better health and not the greater income that is producing the higher levels of happiness in

TABLE 1
Types of Research Designs

Causal inference for each design: $\uparrow X_{income} \rightarrow O_{happiness} \uparrow$

True Experimental Design:

a. Posttest-Only Control Group

	Time 1	Time 2
Group 1	$X_{\$1000}$	$O_{happiness}$
↑ Random Assignment ↓		
Group 2	$X_{\$0}$	$O_{happiness}$

Pre-Experimental Designs:

b. One-Group Pretest-Posttest

	Time 1	Time 2	Time 3	Time 4
Group 1	$X_{\$0}$	$O_{happiness}$	$X_{\$1000}$	$O_{happiness}$

c. Static-Group Comparison

	Time 1	Time 2
Group 1	$X_{\$1000}$	$O_{happiness}$
Group 2	$X_{\$0}$	$O_{happiness}$

Quasi-Experimental Designs:

d. Time Series

	Time 1	Time 2	Time 3	Time 4	Time 5	Time 6	Time 7	Time 8	Time 9	Time 10
Group 1	$X_{\$0}$	$O_{happiness}$	$X_{\$0}$	$O_{happiness}$	$X_{\$1000}$	$O_{happiness}$	$X_{\$0}$	$O_{happiness}$	$X_{\$0}$	$O_{happiness}$

e. Nonequivalent Control Group

	Time 1	Time 2	Time 3	Time 4
Group 1	$X_{\$0}$	$O_{happiness}$	$X_{\$1000}$	$O_{happiness}$
Group 2	$X_{\$0}$	$O_{happiness}$	$X_{\$0}$	$O_{happiness}$

f. Multiple Time Series

	Time 1	Time 2	Time 3	Time 4	Time 5	Time 6	Time 7	Time 8	Time 9	Time 10
Group 1	$X_{\$0}$	$O_{happiness}$	$X_{\$0}$	$O_{happiness}$	$X_{\$1000}$	$O_{happiness}$	$X_{\$0}$	$O_{happiness}$	$X_{\$0}$	$O_{happiness}$
Group 2	$X_{\$0}$	$O_{happiness}$	$X_{\$0}$	$O_{happiness}$	$X_{\$0}$	$O_{happiness}$	$X_{\$0}$	$O_{happiness}$	$X_{\$0}$	$O_{happiness}$

g. Regression-Discontinuity

[See Figure 1]

Non-Experimental Designs:

h. Passive Static Group Comparison[1]

	Time 1
Group 1	$(X_{high\ income}\ O_{happiness})$
Group 2	$(X_{medium\ income}\ O_{happiness})$
Group 3	$(X_{low\ income}\ O_{happiness})$

i. Panel (Passive Nonequivalent Control Group)[2]

	Time 1	Time 2
Group 1	$(X_{\$0}\ O_{happiness})$	$(X_{high\ income}\ O_{happiness})$
Group 2	$(X_{\$0}\ O_{happiness})$	$(X_{medium\ income}\ O_{happiness})$
Group 3	$(X_{\$0}\ O_{happiness})$	$(X_{low\ income}\ O_{happiness})$

O = Observed effect on the dependent variable
X = Independent variable (the cause)
↑X = Value of the independent variable increases
↑O = Value of the dependent variable increases
→ = Causal effect

[1] Parentheses around independent & dependent variable (XO) indicates measure of X and O (income and happiness) occur at the same time.
[2] The panel design depends on statistical controls to make groups equivalent in income (and happiness) at Time 1.

that treatment group. Indeed, this same logic applies no matter what other causal variables a critic might substitute for physical health as an alternative explanation for why additional income is associated with greater happiness.

In sum, strong causal inferences are possible where social scientists manipulate the independent variable and retain great control over when treatments occur, what treatments occur, and who receives the different treatments. But there are times when investigators, typically in "field" (i.e., nonlaboratory, natural, or real-world) settings, are interested in the effects of an intervention but cannot do true experiments. More specifically, there are times when researchers in naturally occurring settings can manipulate the independent variable and exercise at least some control over when the manipulation occurs and what it includes. But these same field researchers may have less control over who receives the treatment conditions. In other words, there are many real-world settings in which *random assignment is not possible.*

Where random assignment and thus true experiments are not possible, a large number of potential threats to valid causal inference can occur. Under these less-than-optimal field conditions, investigators may resort to a number of alternative research designs that help reduce at least some of the threats to making valid causal inferences. These alternative procedures are collectively referred to as *quasi-experimental designs.* (See also Campbell and Stanley 1963; Cook and Campbell 1979.)

These designs are not as powerful as true experiments in establishing causal relationships. But some of the designs are able to overcome the absence of random assignment such that they approximate the power of true experiments. Conversely, where the designs are particularly weak in establishing causal relationships, Campbell and Stanley (1963) have described them as *pre-experimental designs.* Furthermore, social scientists describe as *non-experimental designs* those studies in which the researcher can only measure (observe) rather than manipulate the independent variable. As we shall see, however, one type of non-experimental design—the "panel"—may surpass pre-experimental designs and approach the power of some quasi-experimental designs in overcoming threats to valid causal inference.

The subsequent sections of this article describe common threats to "internal validity" (i.e., making valid causal inferences) in field settings, the conditions under which such threats are likely to occur, and representative research designs and strategies used to combat the threats. Later sections will briefly examine threats to "external validity," "construct validity," and "statistical conclusion validity," as well as strategies used to reduce these threats.

THREATS TO INTERNAL VALIDITY

Where researchers are unable to assign subjects to treatment conditions randomly, a large number of threats to internal validity (causal inference) can occur. These potential threats include effects due to history, maturation, testing, instrumentation, regression to the mean, selection, mortality, and reverse causal order. (See Cook and Campbell 1979 for a more elaborate list.)

Research designs vary greatly in *how many* and *which* of these potential threats are likely to occur—that is, are likely to serve as plausible alternative explanations for an apparent causal relationship between an independent and dependent variable. As an example of a weak (pre-experimental) research design in which most of the various threats to internal validity are plausible, consider the "one group pretest-posttest design" (Campbell and Stanley 1963). Furthermore, assume that researchers have adapted this design to study the effect of income on happiness. As depicted in Table 1*b*, investigators observe the happiness ($O_{\text{happiness}}$) of persons at time 2 following a period (during time 1) in which subjects (all below the poverty line) receive no supplementary income ($X_{\$0}$). Subsequently, subjects receive a $1,000 "gift" ($X_{\$1,000}$) at time 3, and their happiness is remeasured ($O_{\text{happiness}}$) at time 4.

The investigators find that posttest happiness (i.e., time 4 $O_{\text{happiness}}$) is indeed substantially higher than pretest happiness (i.e., time 2 $O_{happiness}$). Accordingly, an increase in supplementary income is associated with an increase in happiness. But is this association due to supplementary income *causing* an increase in happiness? Or is the association due to some alternative explanation?

Given this weak, pre-experimental research design, there are a number of threats to internal validity that serve as plausible alternative explanations for increases in happiness other than the $1,000 gift. These plausible threats include effects due to history, maturation, testing, instrumentation, and regression to the mean, with less likely or logically impossible threats due to selection, mortality, and reverse causal order.

History effects refer to some specific event that exerts a causal influence on the dependent variable, and that occurs at roughly the same time as the manipulation of the independent variable. For example, during the period between the pretest (time 2) and posttest (time 4) measure of happiness as outlined in Table 1*b*, Congress may have declared a national holiday. This event could have the effect of elevating everyone's happiness. Consequently, even if the $1,000 gift had no effect on happiness, researchers would observe an increase in happiness from the pre- to posttest measure. In other words, the effects of the $1,000 gifts are totally confounded with the effects of the holiday, and both remain reasonable explanations for the change in happiness from time 2 to time 4. That is, a plausible rival explanation for the increase in happiness with an increase in income is that the holiday and not the additional income made people happier.

Maturation effects are changes in subjects that result simply from the passage of time (e.g., growing hungrier, growing older, growing more tired). Simply put, "people change." To continue with our current example using a weak, pre-experimental research design, assume that individuals, as they grow older, increase in happiness owing to their improved styles of coping, increasing acceptance of adverse life events, or the like. If such developmental changes appear tenable, then maturation becomes a plausible rival explanation for why subjects' happiness increased after receiving the $1,000 gift. That is, subjects would have displayed an increase in happiness over time even if they had *not* received the $1,000 gift.

Testing effects are the influences of taking a pretest on subsequent tests. In the current study of income and happiness, pretest measures of happiness allow participants to become familiar with the measures' content in a way that may have "carryover" effects on later measures of happiness. That is, familiarity with the pretest may make salient certain issues that would not be salient had subjects not been exposed to the pretest. Consequently, it is possible that exposure to the pretest could cause participants to ponder these suddenly salient issues and therefore change their opinions of themselves. For example, people may come to see themselves as happier than they otherwise would have perceived themselves. Consequently, posttest happiness scores would be higher than pretest scores, and this difference need not be due to the $1,000 gift.

Instrumentation effects are a validity threat that occurs as the result of changes in the way that a variable is measured. For example, in evaluating the effect of income on happiness, researchers may make pretest assessments with one type of happiness measure. Then, perhaps to take advantage of a newly released measure of happiness, researchers might use a different happiness measure on the posttest. Unless the two measures have exactly parallel forms, however, scores on the pre- and posttests are likely to differ. Accordingly, any observed increase in happiness may be due to the differing tests and not to the $1,000 gift.

Regression to the mean is especially likely to occur whenever two conditions are present in combination: (1) researchers select subjects who have extreme scores on a pretest measure of the dependent variable, and (2) the dependent variable is less than perfectly measured (i.e., is less than totally reliable owing to random measurement error). It is a principle of statistics that individuals who score either especially high or low on an imperfectly measured pretest are most likely to have more moderate scores (i.e., regress toward their respective mean) on the posttest. In the social sciences, almost all variables (e.g., happiness) are less than perfectly reliable. Hence, whenever social scientists assign subjects to treatment conditions based on high or low pretest scores, regression to the mean is likely to occur. For example, researchers may believe that those persons who are most unhappy will benefit most from a $1,000 gift. Therefore, only persons with low pretest scores are allowed into the study. However, low scorers on the pretest are likely to have higher happiness scores on the posttest simply as a result of remeasurement. Under such circumstances, regression to the mean remains a plausible rival explanation for any observed increase in happiness following the $1,000 gift.

Selection effects are processes that result in different kinds of subjects being assigned to one treatment group as compared to another. If these differences (e.g., sex) affect the dependent variable (e.g., happiness), then selection effects serve as a rival explanation for the assumed effect of the hypothesized causal variable (e.g., income). Because there is not a second group in the one-group pretest-posttest design illustrated here, the design is *not* subject to validity threats due to selection. That is, because the same group receives all treatment conditions (e.g., no gift versus $1,000 gift), the characteristics of subjects (e.g., number of females versus males) remain constant across treatment conditions. Thus, even if females tended to be happier than males, this effect could not explain why an increase in happiness occurred after subjects received the $1,000 gift.

Mortality effects refer to the greater loss of participants (e.g., due to death or disinterest) in one treatment group compared to another. For example, in the study of the effects of income on happiness, the most unhappy people are more likely than other subjects to drop out of the study before its completion. Because these dropouts appear in the pre- but not the posttest, the average level of happiness will increase. That is, an increase in happiness would occur even if the supplementary income had no effect whatsoever. Mortality is *not,* however, a plausible alternative explanation in the current example of a study using the one-group pretest-posttest design. Researchers can simply exclude from the study any subjects who appear in the pre- but not posttest measure of happiness.

Reverse causal order effects are validity threats due to ambiguity about the direction of a causal relationship, that is, does *X* cause *O,* or does *O* cause *X?* The one-group pretest-posttest design is *not* subject to this internal validity threat. The manipulation of the independent variable (giving the $1,000 gift) clearly precedes observation of the dependent variable (degree of happiness). In general, where research designs manipulate rather than measure the independent variable, they greatly reduce the threat of reverse causal order.

As an overview, the reader should note that the various threats to internal validity, where plausible, violate the last two of three conditions necessary for establishing a valid causal inference. Recall that the three conditions are: (1) an association between two variables is present; (2) the presumed cause must precede the presumed effect in time; and (3) the association between the two variables cannot be explained by the influence of a third variable that may be related to both of them.

Only the violation of the *first* condition is *not* covered by the list of specific threats to internal validity. (But see a later section on threats to "statistical conclusion validity.") Reverse causal order is a threat to internal validity that violates the *second* condition of causal inference. Furthermore, history, maturation, testing, instrumentation, regression to the mean, selection, and mortality are all threats to internal validity that one can broadly describe as the potential influence of a third variable—threats that violate the *third* condition of causal inference. That is, each of these threats represents a specific type of third variable that affects the dependent variable and coincides with the manipulation of the independent variable. In other words, the third variable is *related* to both the independent and dependent variable. Because the third variable affects the dependent variable at the same time that the independent variable is manipulated, it will *appear* that the independent variable causes a change in the dependent variable. But in fact this apparent causal relation is a *spurious* (i.e., noncausal) by-product of the third variable's influence.

As an illustration, recall how validity threats caused by history can produce a spurious correlation between income and happiness. In the example used earlier, Congress declared a national holiday that increased subjects' happiness and coincided with subjects receiving a $1,000 gift. Hence, the occurrence of a national holiday represents a third variable that is related both to income and happiness, and makes it appear (falsely) that income increases happiness.

Research, in its broadest sense, can be viewed as an investigator's attempt to convince the scientific community that a claimed causal relationship between two variables really exists. Clearly, the presence of one or more threats to internal validity challenges the researcher's claim. That is, the more likely a validity threat seems, the less convincing is the investigator's claim.

When confronted with the specific threats to internal validity in field settings, investigators can attempt to modify their research design to control one or more of these threats. The fact that a specific threat is *possible* for a given research design, however, does not mean it is *plausible*. Implausible threats do little to reduce the persuasiveness of researchers' claims. Therefore, the specific design researchers' use should be determined in large part by the specific threats to validity that are considered most plausible.

Furthermore, as noted earlier, each research design has a given number of possible threats to internal validity. And some designs have more plausible threats than do other designs. But only a certain number of these threats will be plausible for *the specific set of variables under study*. That is, different sets of independent and dependent variables will carry different threats to internal validity. Thus, researchers may select weaker designs where the plausible threats for a given set of variables are relatively few and not among the possible threats for the given design. Campbell and Stanley (1963) note, for example, that the natural sciences can often use the one-group pretest-posttest design despite its long list of *possible* threats to internal validity. Given the carefully controlled laboratory conditions and focus on variables measuring nonhuman phenomena, *plausible* threats to internal validity are low.

The next section examines some common quasi-experimental designs and plausible threats to internal validity created by a given design. The discussion continues to use the concrete example of studying the relationship between income and happiness. Examples using a different set of variables might, of course, either reduce or increase the number of plausible threats for a given design.

QUASI-EXPERIMENTAL DESIGNS

When researchers have the opportunity to make more than a single pretest and posttest, some form of *time series* design becomes possible. Table 1*d* illustrates the structure of this design. The *O*'s designate a series of observations (measures of happiness) on the same individuals (group 1) over time. The table shows that subjects receive no supplementary income ($X_{\$0}$) through the first two (time 2 and 4) observational periods. Then at time 5 subjects receive the $1,000 gift ($X_{\$1,000}$). Their subsequent level of happiness is then observed at three additional points (time 6, 8, and 10).

This quasi-experimental design has a number of advantages over the single-group pretest-posttest (pre-experimental) design. For example, by examining the trend yielded by multiple observations prior to providing the $1,000 gift, it is possible to rule out validity threats due to maturation, testing, and regression to the mean. In contrast, instrumentation could still be a threat to validity, if researchers changed the way they measured happiness—especially for changes occurring just before or after giving the $1,000 gift. Moreover, artifacts due to history remain uncontrolled in the time series design. For example, it is still possible that some positive event in the broader environment could occur at about the same time as providing the $1,000 gift. Such an event would naturally serve as a plausible alternative explanation for why happiness increased after the treatment manipulation.

In addition to eliminating some threats to internal validity found in the one-group pretest-posttest design, the time series design provides measures of how long a treatment effect will occur. That is, the multiple observations (*O*'s) following the $1,000 gift allow researchers to assess for how long happiness will remain elevated after the treatment manipulation.

In some circumstances, the time series design may not be possible owing to constraints of time or money. In such cases, other quasi-experimental designs may be more appropriate. Consequently, as an alternative strategy for dealing with some of the threats to internal validity posed by the single-group pretest-posttest (pre-experimental) design, researchers may add one or more *comparison groups*.

The simplest multigroup design is the *static-group comparison* (Campbell and Stanley 1963). Table 1*c* provides an illustration of this design. Here, observations are taken from two different groups (G_1 and G_2) at the same point in time. The underlying assumption is that the two groups differ only in the treatment condition ($1,000 gift versus no gift) they receive prior to the measure of happiness. In many instances, this is not a safe assumption to make.

The static-group comparison design does reduce some potential threats to internal validity found in the single-group pretest-posttest design; namely, history, testing, instrumentation, and regression to the mean. That is, each of these threats should have *equal* effects on the two experimental groups. Thus, these threats cannot explain why experimental groups differ in posttest happiness.

Conversely, the static-group comparison design adds other potential threats—selection, reverse causal order, and mortality effects—not found in the single-group pretest-posttest design. Indeed, these threats are often so serious that Stanley and Campbell (1963) refer to the static-group comparison, like the single-group pretest-posttest, as a "pre-experimental" design.

Selection effects are generally the most plausible threats to internal validity in the static-group comparison design. That is, in the absence of random assignment, the treatment groups are likely to differ in the type of people they include. For example, researchers might assign poverty-level subjects to the $1,000-gift versus no-gift treatment groups based on physical health criteria. Subjects in poor health would receive the supplementary income; subjects in better health would not. Note, however, that poor health is likely to reduce happiness, and that less healthy—and therefore less happy—people appear in the $1,000 treatment condition. Hence, it is possible that this selection effect based on physical health could *obscure* the increase in happiness due to the supplementary income. In other words, even if the $1,000 gift does have a positive effect on happiness, researchers might make a false causal inference; namely, that supplementary income has *no* effect on happiness.

This result illustrates the point that threats to internal validity are not always ones that refute a claim that a causal effect occurred. Threats to internal validity can also occur that refute a claim that a causal effect did *not* happen. In other words, threats to internal validity concern possible false-negative findings as well as false-positive findings.

The preceding example showed how false-negative findings can result due to selection effects in the static-group comparison. False-*positive* findings can, of course, also occur due to selection effects in this design. Consider, for example, a situation in which researchers assign subjects to treatment conditions based on contacts with a particular governmental agency that serves the poor. Say that the first twenty subjects who contact this agency on a specific day receive the $1,000 gift, and the next twenty contacts serve as the no-gift comparison group. Furthermore, assume that the first twenty subjects that call have extroverted personalities that made them call early in the morning. In contrast, the next twenty subjects are less extroverted and thus call later in the day. If extroverted personality also produces higher levels of happiness, then the group receiving the $1,000 gift would be happier than the no-gift comparison group even before the treatment manipulation. Accordingly, even if supplementary income has no effect on happiness, it will appear that the $1,000 gift increased happiness. In other words, extroverted personality is a third variable that has a positive causal effect on both level of supplementary income and happiness. That is, the more extroversion, the more supplementary income; and the more extroversion, the more happiness. These causal relationships therefore make it appear that there is a positive, causal relationship between supplementary income and happiness. But in fact this latter correlation is *spurious.*

Reverse causal order effects are another potential threat to internal validity when researchers use the static-group comparison design. Indeed, reverse causal order effects are really just a special case of selection effects. More specifically, reverse causal order effects will occur whenever the dependent variable is also the third variable that determines who is assigned to which treatment groups.

By substituting happiness for extroversion as the third variable in the preceding example, one can demonstrate how this reverse causal order effect could occur. Recall that subjects who contacted the government agency first were the most extroverted. Assume now, instead, that the earliest callers were happier people than those who called later (because unhappy people are more likely to delay completing tasks). Under these conditions, then, prior levels of happiness comprise a third variable that has a positive causal effect on both level of supplementary income and subsequent happiness. That is, those subjects who are initially happier are more likely to receive supplementary income; and those subjects who are initially happier are more likely to experience subsequent (posttest) happiness. These causal relationships thus make it appear that there is a positive, causal association between supplementary income and happiness. In fact, however, this correlation is spurious. Indeed, it is not supplementary income that determines happiness; it is happiness that determines supplementary income.

Mortality is another possible threat to internal validity in the static-group comparison design. Even if the treatment groups have essentially identical characteristics before the manipulation of the independent variable (i.e., no selection effects), differences between the groups can occur as a consequence of people dropping out of the study. That is, by the time researchers take posttest measures of the dependent variable, the treatment groups may no longer be the same as when they started.

For example, in the study of income and happiness, perhaps some individuals in the no-gift group hear that others are receiving a $1,000 gift. Assume that among those people, the most likely to drop out are those who have a "sour" disposition, that is, those who are likely to be the most unhappy members of the group in general. Consequently, the no-gift comparison group will display a higher posttest measure of happiness than the group would have if all members had remained in the study. Thus, even if the $1,000 gift increases happiness, the effect may be obscured by the corresponding, "artificial" increase in happiness in the no-gift comparison group. In other words, mortality effects may lead researchers to make a false causal inference; namely, that there isn't a causal relationship between two variables, when in fact there is.

One of the most common quasi-experimental designs is the *nonequivalent control group* design. This design is an elaboration of the static-group comparison design. The former is a stronger design than the latter, however, because researchers administer pretests on all groups prior to manipulating the independent variable. Table 1*e* illustrates this design.

A major advantage of the pretests is that they allow researchers to *detect the presence* of selection effects. Specifically, by comparing pretest scores for the different treatment groups before manipulation of treatment conditions, it is possibly to discern whether the groups are initially different. If the groups differ at the time of the pretest, any observed differences at the posttest may simply be a reflection of these pre-existing differences.

For example, in the income and happiness study, if the group receiving the $1,000 gift is happier than the no-gift comparison group at the time of the pretest, it would not be surprising for this group to be happier at posttest, even if supplementary income had no causal effect. The point is that the nonequivalent control group design, unlike the static-group comparison design, can test whether this difference is present. If there is no difference, then researchers can safely argue that selection effects are not a threat to internal validity in their study.

The inclusion of pretest scores also permits the nonequivalent control group design to detect the presence or absence of other threats to internal validity not possible using the static-group comparison design—namely, mortality and reverse causal order. Recall that threats due to reverse causal order are a special subset of selection effects. Thus, the ability of the nonequivalent control group design to detect selection effects means it should also detect reverse causal order effects. Selection effects occur as a consequence of differences in pretest measures of the dependent variable. Therefore, in the present example, differences between groups in pretest happiness would indicate the possibility of reverse causal order effects. In other words, the amount of pretest happiness determined the amount of supplementary income subjects received ($1,000 gift versus no gift), rather than the converse, that the amount of supplementary income determined the amount of posttest happiness.

Furthermore, the pretest scores of the nonequivalent control group design also allow assessment of mortality effects. Regardless of which subjects drop out of which treatment condition, the researcher can examine the pretest scores for the remaining subjects to ensure that the different treatment groups have equivalent initial scores (e.g., on happiness).

In sum, the nonequivalent control group design is able to reduce all the threats to internal validity noted up to this point. Unfortunately, it is unable to detect one threat to internal validity not previously covered—*selection by maturation interactions.* (For a more complete list of interactions with selection, see Cook and Campbell 1979.) This threat occurs whenever the various treatment groups are maturing—growing more experienced, tired, bored, and so forth—at different rates.

For example, consider a situation in which the pretest happiness of the group receiving no gift is as high as the group receiving the $1,000 gift. Moreover, the pretest measures occur when both groups are in stimulating environments, in contrast to the boring environments for the posttest measures. Assume now that there is a greater proportion of people who become bored easily in the no-gift as compared to the $1,000-gift group. That is, there is a selection effect operating that results in different kinds of people in one group as compared with another. But this difference doesn't manifest itself until a nonstimulating environment triggers the maturational process that generates increasingly higher levels of boredom. The differential rates at which boredom occurs in the two groups result in higher levels of boredom and corresponding unhappiness in the no-gift as compared to the $1,000-gift group. In other words, the group receiving the $1,000 gift will display higher levels of posttest happiness than the no-gift group, even if supplementary income has no effect on happiness.

The *multiple time series* design incorporates aspects of both the nonequivalent control group and time series designs. Table 1*f* illustrates the results of this combination. By extending the number of pretest and posttest observations found in the nonequivalent control group design, the multiple time series design can detect selection-maturation interactions. For instance, if differential reactions to boredom explain why the group receiving the $1,000 gift has higher happiness than the no-gift group, then we should expect to see these differences in at least some of the additional pretest measures (assuming that some of these additional group comparisons occur in nonstimulating environments). We would also expect the differential reaction to boredom to manifest itself in the additional posttest measures of the multiple time series design. That is, whenever researchers take posttest measures in stimulating environments, they should observe no group differences. Conversely, whenever researchers take posttest measures in nonstimulating environments, they should observe higher happiness among the group receiving the $1,000 gift.

Furthermore, by adding a second group to the original, single-group time series, the multiple time series reduces the threat of history that is a major problem with the single-group design. Events (e.g., national holidays) that coincide with the manipulation of the independent variable (e.g., $1,000 gift versus no gift) should have equal impacts on each group in the analysis.

By incorporating multiple groups with pretests and posttests, the multiple time series and nonequivalent control group designs can be effective at reducing a long list of internal validity threats. To actually reduce a number of these threats, however, researchers must demonstrate that the different treatment groups are functionally equivalent prior to manipulating the independent variable. Pretest scores allow researchers to detect, at least in part, whether this condition of equivalence is present. But what if the groups are not initially equivalent? Under these conditions, researchers may attempt to equate the groups through "matching" or other, "statistical," adjustments or controls (e.g., analysis of covariance). Matching, however, is never an acceptable technique for making groups initially equivalent (see Nunnally 1975; Kidder and Judd 1986); and statistical controls are a better but still less-than-desirable procedure for equating groups at the pretest (see Lord 1967; Dwyer 1983; Rogosa 1985).

In sum, an overview of pre- and quasi-experimental designs using multiple groups indicates the importance of establishing the equivalence of the groups through pretest measures. Further, to more firmly establish this equivalence, researchers should try to obtain as many additional observations as possible both before and after manipulating the treatments. When groups are nonequivalent at the outset, however, it is extremely difficult to discern whether treatment manipulations have a causal effect.

In certain field settings, however, ethical considerations may *mandate* that groups be nonequivalent at the outset. That is, researchers must assign subjects to certain treatment conditions based on who is most "needy" or "deserving." And if the dependent variable (e.g., happiness) is associated with the criteria (e.g., physical health) that determines who is most needy or deserving, then the experimental groups will not display pretest equivalence (e.g., the people with the worst health and hence lowest pretest happiness must be assigned to the group receiving the $1,000 gift).

Fortunately, the *regression-discontinuity* design (Thistlethwaite and Campbell 1960; Cook and Campbell 1979) often allows researchers to make relatively unambiguous interpretation of treatment effects, even where groups are not initially equivalent. To continue with the example of income and happiness, researchers may feel compelled to give the $1,000 gift to those individuals with the poorest health. The investigators would therefore begin by developing a scale of need in which participants below a certain level of physical health receive the gift and those above this cutting point do not. This physical-health scale constitutes the "pseudo"-pretest necessary for the regression-discontinuity design. The usual posttest measures of the dependent variable—happiness—would follow the manipulation of the no-gift versus $1,000-gift treatment conditions. Researchers would then regress posttest happiness measures on pretest measures of physical health. This regression analysis would include the calculation of separate regression lines for (1) those subjects receiving the $1,000 gift and (2) those subjects not receiving it.

Figure 1 provides an illustration of the results using the regression-discontinuity design. (The structure of the design does not appear in Table 1 due to its relative complexity.) If the $1,000 gift has a discernible impact on happiness, a "discontinuity" should appear in the regression lines at the cutting point for "good" versus "poor" physical health. An essential requirement for the regression-discontinuity design is a clear cutting point that defines an unambiguous criterion (e.g., degree of physical health) by which researchers can

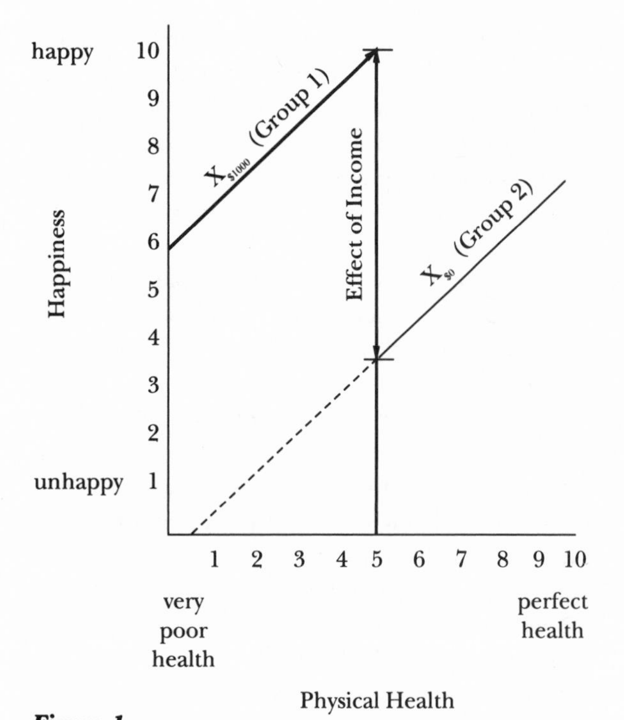

Figure 1

Regression–Discontinuity Design Showing Treatment Effect of Income on Happiness

----- = Projected Happiness scores for Group 1 if the $1,000 treatment had no effect on happiness

assign subjects to the treatment conditions. It is the clarity of the decision criterion, not its content, that is important.

An interesting characteristic of the regression-discontinuity design is that it works even if the decision criterion has no effect on the outcome of interest (e.g., happiness). Indeed, as the variable that forms the decision criterion approaches a condition in which it is totally unrelated to the outcome, the decision criterion becomes the functional equivalent of *assigning subjects randomly* to treatment conditions (Campbell 1975). That is, the study more closely approximates a true experimental design.

There are, however, several threats to internal validity that can occur when using the regression-discontinuity design. One threat emerges when the relationship between the pseudopretest measure (e.g., physical health) and the posttest measure (e.g., happiness) does not form a linear pattern. In fact, a curvilinear relationship near the cutting point may be indistinguishable from the discontinuity between the separate regression lines. Moreover, another threat to internal validity arises if the investigators do not strictly adhere to the decision criterion (e.g., feeling sorry for someone who is close to qualifying for the $1,000 and thus giving them the "benefit of the doubt"). Additionally, if only a few people receive a given treatment condition (e.g., if only a few $1,000 awards can be made for financial reasons), the location of the regression line may be difficult to estimate with any degree of accuracy for that particular treatment condition. Thus, researchers should include relatively large numbers of subjects for all treatment conditions.

In summary, quasi-experimental designs allow researchers to maintain at least some control over what and when they manipulate the independent variable, but researchers lose much control over who receives specific treatment conditions (i.e., the designs do not permit random assignment). Quasi-experimental designs differ in how closely they approximate the power of true experiments to make strong causal inferences. As a general rule, the more observations quasi-experimental designs add (i.e., the more *O*'s as depicted in the diagrams of Table 1), the more the designs are able to reduce threats to internal validity.

NON-EXPERIMENTAL DESIGNS

In contrast to quasi-experimental designs, *non-experimental designs* do *not* manipulate the independent variable. Thus, researchers have no control over who falls into which category of the independent variable, when there is a change from one to another category of the independent variable, or what content the various levels of the independent variable will contain. Rather than serving as an agent that actively changes (manipulates) the independent variable, the researcher must be content to passively observe (measure) the independent variable as it naturally occurs. Hence, some social scientists also refer to nonexperimental designs as *passive-observational* designs (Cook and Campbell 1979).

When researchers can only measure rather than manipulate the independent variable, threats to internal validity increase greatly. That is, reverse causal order effects are much more likely to occur. And there is a much greater probability that some third variable has a causal effect on both the independent and dependent variable, therefore producing a spurious relationship between the latter two variables.

To illustrate these points, consider the most widely used research design among sociologists; namely, the static-group comparison design, with measured rather than manipulated independent variables—or what we will refer to here as the *passive static-group comparison.* Table 1*h* depicts the structure of this non-experimental, cross-sectional design. Researchers generally combine this design with a "survey" format—in which subjects self-report their scores on the independent and dependent variables (e.g., report their current income and happiness).

Note that the structure of this non-experimental design is basically the same as the static-group comparison design found in Table 1*c*. To capture the various levels of naturally occurring income better, however, the diagram in Table 1 expands the number of categories for income from two *manipulated* categories ($1,000 gift versus no gift) to three *measured* categories (high, medium, and low personal income). Furthermore, whereas the original static-group design manipulated income *before* measuring happiness, the passive static-group design measures both personal income and happiness at the *same time* (i.e., when subjects respond to the survey). Consequently, the temporal ordering of the independent and dependent variable is often uncertain.

Indeed, because researchers do not manipulate the independent variable, and because they measure the independent and dependent variable at the same time, the threat of reverse causal order effects is particularly strong in the passive static-group comparison design. In the present example, it is quite possible that the amount of happiness a person displays is a determinant of how much money that person will subsequently make. That is, happiness causes income rather than income causes happiness. Or, even more likely, both causal sequences occur.

Additionally, the passive static-group comparison design is also especially susceptible to the threat of "third" variables producing a spurious relationship between the independent and dependent variable. For example, it is likely that subjects who fall into different income groupings (high, medium, and low) also differ on a large number of other (selection effect) variables. That is, the different income groups are almost certainly non-equivalent with regard to characteristics of subjects in addition to income. One would expect, for example, that the higher-income groups have more education, and that education is associated with greater happiness. In other words, there is a causal link between education and income, and education and happiness. More specifically, higher education should produce greater income, and higher education should also produce greater happiness. Hence, education could produce a spurious association between income and happiness.

As noted earlier, researchers can attempt to equate the various income groups with regard to third variables by making statistical adjustments (i.e., controlling for the effects of the third variables). But this practice is fraught with difficulties (again, see Lord 1967; Dwyer 1983; Rogosa 1985).

It is especially sobering to realize that a design as weak as the passive static-group comparison is so widely used in sociology. Note, too, that this design is a substantially weaker version of the static-group comparison design that Campbell and Stanley (1963) considered so weak that they labeled it pre-experimental. Fortunately, there are other non-experimental, longitudinal designs that have more power to make valid causal inferences. Most popular among these designs is the *panel* design. (For additional examples of passive longitudinal designs, see Rogosa 1988; von Eye 1990).

Table 1*i* depicts the structure of this longitudinal survey design. It is very similar to the non-equivalent control group design in Table 1*e*. It differs from the quasi-experimental design, however, because the independent variable is measured rather than manipulated, and the independent and dependent variable are measured at the same time.

In its simplest, and weaker, two-wave form (shown in Table 1), the panel design can address at least some threats due to reverse causal order and third variables associated with the independent and dependent variable. (This ability to reduce threats to internal validity is strengthened where investigators include three and preferably four or more waves of measures.) The most powerful versions of the panel design include data analysis using simultaneous equations with multiple indicators (see Kessler and Greenberg 1981; Dwyer 1983). Simultaneous equations involve statistical adjustments for reverse causal order and causally linked third variables. Thus, the standard admonishments noted earlier about using statistical control techniques apply here too.

TRUE EXPERIMENTS REVISITED

The great problems that non-experimental designs encounter in making causal inferences help illustrate the increased power researchers obtain when they move from these passive-observational to quasi-experimental designs. But no matter how well a quasi-experimental design controls threats to internal validity, there is no quasi-experimental design that can match the ability of true experiments to make strong causal inferences. Indeed, threats to internal validity are greatly reduced when researchers are able to assign subjects to treatment groups randomly. Therefore, the value of this simple procedure cannot be overstated.

Consider the simplest and most widely used of all true experiments, the *posttest-only control group* design (Campbell and Stanley 1963), as depicted in Table 1*a*. Note that it is similar in structure to the very weak, pre-experimental, static-group comparison design in Table 1*c*. These two designs differ primarily with regard to whether they do or do not use *random assignment*.

The addition of random assignment buys enormous power to make valid causal inferences. With this procedure, and the manipulation of an independent variable that temporally precedes observation of the dependent variable, reverse causal order effects are impossible. Likewise, with the addition of random assignment, other threats to internal validity present in the static-group comparison design dissipate. Specifically, selection effects are no longer a major threat to internal validity. That is, selection factors—different kinds of people—should appear approximately evenly distributed between categories of the independent variable (e.g., $1,000 gift versus no gift). In other words, the different groups forming the treatment conditions should be roughly equivalent prior to the treatment manipulation. Further, given this equivalence, threats due to selection-maturation interactions are also reduced.

Conversely, given that pretest measures of the dependent variable (e.g., happiness) are absent, mortality effects remain a potential threat to internal validity in the posttest-only control group design. Of course, for mortality effects to occur, different kinds of subjects have to drop out of one experimental group as compared to another. For example, in the study of income on happiness, if certain kinds of subjects (say, those who are unhappy types in general) realize that they are not in the group receiving the $1,000 gift, they may refuse to continue. This situation could make it appear (falsely) that people receiving the $1,000 gift are less happy than those not receiving the gift.

Naturally, the probability that *any* subjects drop out is an increasing function of how much time passes between manipulation of treatment conditions and posttest measures of the dependent variable. The elapsed time is generally quite short for many studies using the posttest-only control group design. Consequently, in many cases, mortality effects are not a plausible threat.

In sum, one may conclude that random assignment removes, at least in large part, all the major threats to internal validity. (But see Cook and Campbell 1979 for some additional qualifications.)

Two more points are noteworthy with respect to random assignment. First, it is important to realize that this procedure does *not ensure* that third variables that might influence the outcome will be evenly distributed between groups in any particular experiment. For example, random assignment does not ensure that the average level of education will be the same for the group receiving the $1,000 gift as for the group receiving no gift. Rather, random assignment allows researchers to *calculate the probability* that third variables (such as education) are a plausible alternative explanation for an apparent causal relationship (e.g., between supplementary income and happiness). Researchers are generally willing to accept that a causal relationship between two variables is real if the relationship could have occurred by chance—that is, due to the *coincidental* operation of third variables—less than one time out of twenty.

Some researchers add pretests to the posttest-only control group design to evaluate the "success" of the random assignment procedure and to add "statistical power." According to Nunnally (1975), however, the use of a pretest is generally not worth the attendant risks. That is, the pretest may sensitive subjects to the treatment conditions (i.e., create a treatment-testing interaction). In other words, the effect of the independent variable may not occur in other situations where there are no pretest measures. Thus, any gain from pretest information is likely to be offset by this threat to "construct validity." (For an example of a treatment-testing interaction, see the later section on threats to construct validity.)

Second, random *assignment* of subjects is different from random *selection* of subjects. Random assignment means that a subject has an equal probability of entry into each treatment condition. Random selection refers to the probability of entry into the study as a whole. The former issue bears on internal validity (i.e., whether observed outcomes are unambiguously due to the treatment manipulation); the latter is an issue of external validity (i.e., the extent to which the results of the study are generalizable).

THREATS TO EXTERNAL VALIDITY

Whereas internal validity refers to whether or not a treatment is effective, *external validity* refers to the conditions under which the treatment will be effective. That is, to what extent will the (internally valid) causal results of a given study apply to different people and places?

One type of threat to external validity occurs when certain treatments are likely to be most effective on certain kinds of people. For example, researchers might find that a $1,000 gift has a strong effect on happiness among a sample of young adults. Conversely, a study of extreme elderly persons might find that the $1,000 has no effect on happiness (say, because very old people are in general less stimulated by their environment than are younger age groups). Cook and Campbell (1979) label this external validity threat an *interaction between selection factors and treatment.*

Researchers sometimes mistakenly assume that they can overcome this threat to external validity by *randomly selecting* persons from the population across which they wish to generalize research findings. Random samples do not, however, provide appropriate tests of whether a given cause–effect finding applies to different kinds of people. Obtaining a random sample of, say, the U.S. population would not, for example, reproduce the above (hypothetical) finding that a $1,000 gift increases happiness among younger but not older people. Combining younger and older persons in a representative sample would only lead to an averaging or "blending" of the strong effect for youths with the no-effect for the elderly. In fact, the resulting finding of a "moderate" effect would not be an accurate statement of income's effect on happiness for either the younger or older population.

Including younger and older people in a random sample would only increase external validity if the researchers *knew* to provide separate analyses for young and old—among an infinite variety of *possible* human characteristics that researchers might choose for subsample analyses (e.g., males and females). If researchers suspected that the treatment might interact with age, however, then they could simply make sure that their nonrandomly selected "convenience" sample contained sufficient numbers of both youths and elderly to allow separate analyses on each age group.

Additionally, threats to external validity can

occur because certain treatments work best in certain settings. Giving $1,000 to a person at a shopping mall may increase their happiness substantially compared to the same gift given to someone stranded on a desert island with nowhere to spend the money. Cook and Campbell (1979) label this external validity threat an *interaction between treatment and setting*. Given that quasi-experimental designs are most often located in "real-life" field settings, they are somewhat less susceptible to this threat than are true experiments—which most often occur in "artificial" laboratory settings.

Note that threats to external validity are concerned with restricting cause–effect relationships to particular persons or places. Therefore, the best procedure for reducing these restrictions is to *replicate* the findings on different people and in different settings—either within a single study or across a series of studies (Cook and Campbell 1979).

THREATS TO CONSTRUCT VALIDITY

Construct validity refers to the accuracy with which researchers manipulate or measure the construct intended rather than something else (Cook and Campbell 1979). Thus, for example, investigators might establish that their manipulation of a variable labeled "income" does indeed have a causal effect on their measure of the outcome labeled "happiness." That is, the researchers have avoided plausible threats to internal validity and, consequently, have presented a convincing claim for a cause-and-effect relationship. Critics might question, however, whether the manipulation labeled "income" and the measure labeled "happiness" do in fact represent the concepts that the investigators claim they have manipulated and measured, respectively.

In providing supplementary income to selected subjects, for example, researchers might also have manipulated, say, the perception that the researchers really are concerned about the welfare of the subjects. And it may be subjects' perceptions of this "caring attitude," and not an increase in "economic well-being," that produced the effect the $1,000 gift had on happiness. In other words, investigators were manipulating a dimension in addition to the economic dimension they intended to manipulate.

Likewise, in asking subjects to answer a questionnaire that purportedly measures "happiness," researchers may not be measuring happiness but rather the degree to which subjects will respond in socially desirable ways (e.g., some subjects will respond honestly to questions asking how depressed they are, and other subjects will hide their depression).

Cook and Campbell (1979) provide an extensive list of threats to construct validity. The description of these threats is rather abstract and complicated. Hence, the following discussion includes only a few concrete examples of potential threats. For a more complete list and discussion of these threats, the interested reader should consult the original article by Cook and Campbell, as well as other volumes on the construct validity of measures and manipulations (e.g., Costner 1971; Nunnally 1978).

One type of threat to construct validity occurs in research designs that use pretests (e.g., the nonequivalent control group design). Cook and Campbell (1979) label this threat an *interaction of testing and treatment*. This threat occurs when something about the pretest makes participants more receptive to the treatment manipulation. For example, in the study of income and happiness, the pretest may make salient to participants that "they don't have much to be happy about." This realization may, in turn, make subjects more appreciative and thus especially happy when they later receive a $1,000 gift. In contrast, the $1,000 gift might have had little or no causal impact on happiness if subjects were not so sensitized, that is, were not exposed to a pretest. Accordingly, it is the combination of the pretest and $1,000 gift that produces an increase in happiness. Neither condition alone is sufficient to create the causal effect. Consequently, researchers who use pretests must be cautious in claiming that their findings would apply to situations in which pretests are not present. Because quasi-experimental designs are dependent on pretest observations to overcome threats to internal validity (i.e., to establish the initial equivalence of the experimental groups), researchers cannot safely eliminate these measures. Thus, to enhance the construct validity of the manipulation, researchers should strive to use as unobtrusive measures as possible (e.g., have trained observers or other people familiar with a given subject secretly record the subject's level of happiness).

Another set of potential threats to construct validity concerns what Campbell and Stanley (1963) describe as *reactive arrangements.* Cook and Campbell (1979) have subsequently provided more specific labels for these threats: *hypothesis-guessing within experimental conditions, evaluation apprehension,* and *experimenter expectancies* (see also Rosenthal and Rosnow 1969). Threats due to reactive arrangements occur as a consequence of the participants' knowing they are in a study and thus behaving in a way that they might not in more natural circumstances. Subjects receiving the $1,000 gift, for example, may guess the hypothesis of the study when they are subsequently asked to respond to questions about their state of happiness. Realizing that the study may be an attempt to show that supplementary income increases happiness, participants may try to be "good subjects" and confirm the experimental hypothesis by providing high scores on the happiness questionnaire. In other words, the treatment manipulation did in fact produce an increase in the assumed *measure* of "happiness," but the measure was actually capturing participants' willingness to be good subjects.

To reduce threats to construct validity due to reactive arrangements, researchers may attempt, where feasible, to disguise the experimental hypothesis, to use unobtrusive measures and manipulations, and to keep both the subject and the person administering the treatments "blind" to who is receiving what treatment conditions. These disguises are generally easier to accomplish in the naturally occurring environments of quasi-experimental designs than in the artificial settings of laboratory experiments. Finally, there are additional, sophisticated procedures for discerning where reactive arrangements may be present in a study, and for making "statistical adjustments" to correct for the bias that these threats would otherwise introduce (Costner 1971).

THREATS TO STATISTICAL CONCLUSION VALIDITY

Before researchers can establish whether an independent variable has a causal effect on the dependent variable, they must first establish whether an *association* between the two variables does or does not exist. *Statistical conclusion validity* refers to the accuracy with which one makes inferences about an association between two variables—without concern for whether the association is causal or not (Cook and Campbell 1979). The reader will recall that an association between two variables is the first of three conditions necessary to make a valid causal inference. Thus, statistical conclusion validity is closely linked to internal validity. To put it another way, statistical conclusion validity is a necessary but not sufficient condition for internal validity.

Threats to statistical conclusion validity concern either one of two types of errors: (1) inferring an association where one does not exist (described as a "Type-I error"), or (2) inferring no association where one does exist (described as a "Type-II error"). Researchers' ability to avoid Type-II errors depends on the power of a research design to uncover even weak associations, that is, the power to avoid making the mistake of claiming an association is due to chance (is statistically insignificant) when in fact the association really exists. Type-II errors are more likely to occur the lower the probability level that researchers set for accepting an association as being statistically significant; the smaller the sample size researchers use; the less reliable their measures and manipulations; and the more random error introduced by (1) extraneous factors in the research setting that affect the dependent variable, and (2) variations among subjects on extraneous factors that affect the dependent variable (Cook and Campbell 1979).

Investigators can reduce Type-II errors (false claims of no association) by: (1) setting a higher probability level for accepting an association as being statistically significant (e.g., $p < .05$ instead of $p < .01$); (2) increasing the sample size; (3) correcting for unreliability of measures and manipulations (see Costner 1971); (4) selecting measures that have greater reliability (e.g., using a ten-item composite measure of happiness instead of a single-item measure); (5) making treatment manipulations as consistent as possible across occasions of manipulation (e.g., giving each subject the $1,000 gift in precisely the same manner); (6) isolating subjects from extraneous (outside) influences; and (7) controlling for the influence of extraneous subject characteristics (e.g., gender, race, physical health) suspected to impact the dependent variable (Cook and Campbell 1979).

Type-I errors (inferring an association where one does not exist) are more likely the higher the probability level that researchers set for accepting an association as being statistically significant, and the more associations a researcher examines in a given study. The latter error occurs because the more associations one includes in a study, the more associations one should find that are statistically significant "just by chance alone." For example, given 100 associations and a probability level of .05, one should on the average find 5 associations that are statistically significant due to chance.

Researchers can reduce threats of making Type-I errors by setting a higher probability level for statistical significance, particularly when examining many associations between variables. Of course, decreasing Type-I errors increases the risk of Type-II errors. Hence, one should set higher probability levels in conjunction with obtaining reasonably large samples—the latter strategy to offset the risk of Type-II errors.

Research designs vary greatly in their ability to implement strategies for reducing threats to statistical conclusion validity. For example, very large sample sizes (say, 500 subjects or more) are generally much easier to obtain for nonexperimental designs than for quasi-experimental or experimental designs. Moreover, experimental designs generally occur in laboratory rather than naturally occurring settings. Thus, it is easier for these designs to control for extraneous factors of the setting (i.e., random influences of the environment). Additionally, experimental designs are generally better able than quasi-experimental designs to standardize the conditions under which treatment manipulations occur.

SUMMARY AND CONCLUSIONS

Quasi-experimental designs offer valuable tools to sociologists conducting field research. This article has reviewed various threats that researchers must overcome when using such designs. In addition, to provide a context in which to evaluate the relative power of quasi-experimental designs to make valid causal inferences, this article also reviewed examples of experimental and non-experimental designs.

It is important to note that the quasi-experimental designs described here are merely illustrative; they are representative of the types of research designs that sociologists might use in field settings. These designs are not, however, exhaustive of the wide variety of quasi-experimental designs possible. (See Campbell and Stanley 1963; Cook and Campbell 1979 for more extensive reviews.) In fact, great flexibility is one of the appealing features of quasi-experimental designs. It is possible literally to combine bits and pieces from different standard designs to evaluate validity threats in highly specific or unusual situations. This process highlights the appropriate role of research design as a *tool* in which the specific research topic dictates which design investigators should use. Unfortunately, investigators too often use a less-appropriate design for a specific research topic simply because they are most familiar with that design. When thoughtfully constructed, however, quasi-experimental designs can provide researchers with the tools they need to explore the wide array of important topics in sociological study.

(SEE ALSO: *Causal Inference Models; Experiments; Reliability; Scientific Explanation; Validity*)

REFERENCES

Campbell, D. T. 1975 "Reforms as Experiments." In M. Guttentag and E. Struening, eds., *Handbook of Evaluation Research.* Beverly Hills, Calif.: Sage.

———, and J.C. Stanley 1963 "Experimental and Quasi-experimental Designs for Research on Teaching." In N. L. Gage, ed., *Handbook of Research on Teaching.* Chicago: Rand McNally.

Cook, T. D. and D. T. Campbell 1979 *Quasi-Experimentation: Design and Analysis Issues for Field Settings.* Chicago: Rand McNally.

Costner, H. L. 1971 "Utilizing Causal Models to Discover Flaws in Experiments." *Sociometry* 34:398-410.

Dwyer, J. H. 1983 *Statistical Models for the Social and Behavioral Sciences.* New York: Oxford University Press.

Kessler, R. C., and D. F. Greenberg 1981 *Linear Panel Analysis: Models of Quantitative Change.* New York: Academic.

Kidder, L. H., and C. M. Judd 1986 *Research Methods in Social Relations,* 5th ed. New York: Holt, Rinehart and Winston.

Lord, F. M. 1967 "A Paradox in the Interpretation of Group Comparisons." *Psychological Bulletin* 68:304-305.

Nunnally, J. 1975 "The Study of Change in Evaluation Research: Principles Concerning Measurement, Experimental Design, and Analysis." In M. Guttentag and R. Struening, eds. *Handbook of Evaluation Research.* Beverly Hills, Calif.: Sage.

——— 1978 *Psychometric Theory,* 2nd ed. New York: McGraw-Hill.

Rogosa, D. 1985 "Analysis of Reciprocal Effects." In T. Husen and N. Postlethwaite, eds., *International Encyclopedia of Education.* London: Pergamon.

——— 1988 "Myths about Longitudinal Research." In K. W. Schaie, R. T. Campbell, W. Meredith, and S. C. Rawlings, eds., *Methodological Issues in Aging Research.* New York: Springer.

Rosenthal, R., and R. L. Rosnow 1969 *Artifacts in Behavioral Research.* New York: Academic.

Thistlethwaite, D. L., and D. T. Campbell 1960 "Regression-Discontinuity Analysis: An Alternative to the Ex Post Facto Experiment." *Journal of Educational Psychology* 51:309-317.

von Eye, A. (ed.) 1990 *Statistical Methods in Longitudinal Research,* vols. I and II. New York: Academic.

KYLE KERCHER

R

RACE The study of race and race relations has long been a central concern of sociologists. The assignment of individuals to racial categories profoundly affects the quality and even the length of their lives. These assignments are ostensibly made on the basis of biological criteria, such as skin color, hair texture, and facial features. Yet the biological meaning of race is so unclear that some social scientists argue that *race,* as a biological phenomenon, does not exist. Others take the less extreme position that while different races exist, extensive interbreeding in many societies has produced large numbers of people of mixed ancestry. The assignment of these people to racial categories depends on social, rather than on biological, criteria. Thus the social consequences of biologically inherited traits is the fundamental issue of the sociological study of race.

BIOLOGICAL CONCEPTIONS OF RACE

While the terms *race* and *ethnicity* are often used interchangeably, it is more precise to see race as a special case of ethnicity (van den Berghe 1981). *Ethnic groups* are extended kinship groups; that is, membership in an ethnic group is based on common ancestry. Members of ethnic groups also share a common culture: language, religion, and styles of dress and cooking are cultural markers that identify individuals as members of a given ethnic group. Furthermore, members of ethnic groups generally marry within their group, a practice known as endogamy, which tends to preserve the distinctiveness of the group and prevents its assimilation into other groups. Finally, shared ancestry and cultural heritage produce a sense of solidarity among ethnic group members; they identify themselves as members of the group and are so identified by others.

For most of human history, ethnic groups living in close proximity did not differ significantly in physical appearance. Thus the observable biological differences associated with race were not used as ethnic markers, and interracial antagonisms were unknown. The rapid, long-distance migration required to bring members of different racial groups together is a comparatively recent phenomenon that was accelerated by trade and the large-scale European exploration and colonial expansion of the sixteenth through the nineteenth centuries (van den Berghe 1981). It was also during this period that Western science assumed a central role in the attempt to understand the natural and social worlds. Thus, as Europeans became aware of peoples who differed from them in culture and appearance, the concept of race entered the popular and scientific vocabularies as a means of classifying previously unknown groups.

Not content merely to classify people into racial groups, nineteenth- and early-twentieth-century scientists attempted to uncover differences between groups. Darwin's theory of evolution, which holds that species are engaged in a struggle for existence in which only the fittest will survive, was gaining widespread acceptance during this period. Herbert Spencer, William Graham Sumner, and other early social theorists extended this evolutionary argument, suggesting that different social groups, including races, were at different stages of evolution; the more advanced groups were destined to dominate groups less "fit." This idea, called social Darwinism (which Darwin himself did not support), provided justification for imperialism by the British and others, and for America's treatment of its racial minorities.

Building on the notion that some races were at a more-advanced stage of evolution than others, a number of scientists tried to measure differences between the races, especially in the area of intelligence. The first intelligence test was developed by Alfred Binet and Theodore Simon in 1905. Modified versions of this test were administered to approximately one million American soldiers in World War I, and the results were used to argue that there were large, genetically determined differences in intelligence between blacks and whites. Such a conclusion implied that blacks could not benefit from education to the extent that whites could; these findings were then used as a justification for the inferior education made available to blacks.

Binet himself rejected the notion that intelligence was a fixed quantity determined by heredity, or that intelligence could be measured with the kind of precision claimed by other intelligence testers, especially in the United States. Furthermore, other scholars demonstrated that the tests were heavily biased against members of certain ethnic, class, and cultural groups, including blacks. While the *average* scores of blacks have tended to fall below the average scores of whites, greater variation occurs within each group than between the two groups; that is, many blacks outscore many whites. Since these tests measure academic achievement and middle-class cultural knowledge, rather than potential, the impoverished backgrounds and substandard educations of some blacks offer reasonable explanations for their lower average scores. Research has repeatedly failed to demonstrate that racial groups differ in terms of their innate capacity for learning. Today, therefore, the vast majority of social scientists reject the idea that any one race is superior in intelligence or any other ability, at least to the extent that such abilities are determined by heredity. (For an interesting account of the race–intelligence controversy, see Gould 1981; Montagu 1975.)

Controversy continues however on the subject of race itself. In the nineteenth century the concept was defined quite loosely, and the idea was widely held that people of similar appearance but different nationalities constituted different races. As recently as World War II it was not uncommon to hear people speak of the "British race," the "Jewish race," and so on. Some physical anthropologists narrowed the concept to include three main groups: the Negroid, Caucasoid, and Mongoloid races. Others argue that human populations have always exhibited some degree of interbreeding; that this has greatly increased during the last few centuries, producing large groups of people who defy such racial classification. "Pure races" have probably never existed, and certainly do not exist now. According to this argument, race is a cultural myth, a label that has no biological basis but is attached to groups in order to buttress invidious social distinctions (Lieberman 1975).

SOCIAL CONCEPTIONS OF RACE

Two conclusions may be drawn from the above discussion of biological conceptions of race. First, if one follows common practice and assigns individuals to one of three main "racial" groups, no evidence exists that those groups differ in the distribution of intelligence or other innate abilities. Second, the biological meaning of race, and racial categorization, is unclear. Human beings can be classified in any number of ways, according to shoe size, forearm length, and so on, ad infinitum. While race may be of little or no biological significance, it does have tremendous social significance. Racial distinctions are meaningful because we *attach* meaning to them, and the consequences vary from prejudice and discrimination to slavery and genocide.

Since people believe that racial differences are significant, and behave accordingly, those differences become significant. Hitler, for example, believed that Jews constituted a distinct and inferior race, and the consequences of his belief were very real for millions of Jews. Thus the major questions confronting sociologists who study race relations concern the social consequences of racial categorization. To what degree are different racial and ethnic groups incorporated into the larger society? How can we account for variations in the economic, political, legal, and social statuses of different groups?

American sociologists have found their own society to be a natural laboratory for the study of these issues. The United States has a wide variety of racial and ethnic groups, and some of these have fitted more successfully into American society than have others. Within any group there is substantial variation in economic achievement; still, considered as groups, Jews and Japanese have been more successful in America than have blacks and Mexicans. One explanation for these differences that has found some acceptance both within and outside scientific circles is that the cultures and values of these groups differ. Some groups' values are believed to be more conducive to success than others. Jews, for example, have traditionally valued scholarship and business acumen; as a result they have worked hard in the face of discrimination, educated their children, and pulled themselves up from poverty. African Americans, by contrast, allegedly lacked these values; the result is their continued concentration in the poor and working classes.

Most sociologists reject this argument, which Stephen Steinberg (1981) refers to as the "ethnic myth." Steinberg argues that this line of reasoning is simply a new form of social Darwinism, in which the fittest *cultures* survive. A closer look at the experiences of immigrants in America (including African Americans) reveals that not all immigrant groups start at the bottom; some groups arrive with the skills necessary to compete in the American labor market while others do not. Furthermore, the skills possessed by some groups are in high demand in the United States, while other groups find fewer opportunities. Thus Steinberg argues that the success of an immigrant group depends on the occupational structure of its country of origin, the group's place in that structure, and the occupational structure of the new country.

Steinberg uses the case of American Jews to support his argument. In terms of education, occupation, and income, Jews have been highly successful. In 1971, 36 percent of the adult Jewish population had graduated from college, compared with 11 percent of non-Jews. Seventy percent of Jews were in business or the professions, compared with roughly a third of non-Jews. The median family income of Jews in 1971 was fourteen thousand dollars, approximately 30 percent more than the average American family. It is possible to overstate Jewish success, since many Jews are still poor or working-class; middle-class Jews are concentrated in small business and the professions and are nearly absent from corporate hierarchies. Furthermore, Jews have experienced a great deal of economic and social discrimination. Nevertheless, compared with other ethnic and racial groups in America, they have been quite successful.

This success, Steinberg argues, is attributable in part to the origins of Jewish immigrants, most of whom came from Russia and Eastern Europe, and arrived in the United States in the late nineteenth and early twentieth centuries. Since Jews in Eastern Europe could not own land, they tended to live in cities; even those who lived in rural areas were mostly merchants and traders, rather than farmers. The urban concentration and above-average literacy rates of Jews affected their occupational distribution: in 1897, 70 percent of Russian Jews worked as artisans or in manufacturing or commerce; even unskilled Jews worked in industrial occupations. Of the immigrants who arrived in America between 1899 and 1910, 67 percent of Jews were skilled workers, compared with 49 percent of English immigrants, 15 percent of Italians, and 6 percent of Poles.

Furthermore, Jewish immigrants were disproportionately represented in the garment industry, which was growing at two to three times the rate of other American industries. Jobs in the garment industry were better paid than other industrial jobs, and Jews, with their higher skill level, tended to have the better-paid jobs within the industry. The garment industry also offered unusual opportunities for individual entrepreneurship, since little capital was required to start a small clothing business.

In sum, Jewish immigrants did well in America because they brought industrial skills to an industrializing country. Although the majority of Jewish immigrants arrived with little money and encountered widespread discrimination, American industry could not afford to exclude them completely. Steinberg concludes that while a case can be made that Jews have traditionally valued educational and occupational achievement, and that this contributed to their success, Jews do not hold a monopoly on these values. Furthermore, if they had encountered an occupational structure that offered no hope for the fulfillment of these aspirations, Jews would have scaled their goals down accordingly.

The inability of other racial and ethnic groups to match the success achieved by Jewish Americans has also been attributed to the cultures and values of those groups. Glazer and Moynihan (1970), for example, blame the persistent poverty of blacks on "the home and family and community . . . It is there that the heritage of two hundred years of slavery and a hundred years of discrimination is concentrated; and it is there that we find the serious obstacles to the ability to make use of a free educational system to advance into higher occupations and to eliminate the massive social problems that afflict colored Americans and the city" (pp. 49, 50). Yet, as Gutman (1976) has shown, the black family emerged from slavery relatively strong and began to exhibit signs of instability only when blacks became concentrated in urban ghettos. Furthermore, for generations after emancipation, blacks faced extreme educational and employment discrimination; the notion that a free educational system provided a smooth path to the higher occupations is simply inconsistent with blacks' experience in America.

Most sociologists tend, like Steinberg, to locate the cause of blacks' poverty relative to white immigrant groups in the structure of opportunity that awaited them after slavery. The South was an economically backward region where blacks remained tied to the land and subject to conditions that were in many cases worse than those they had known under slavery. The vast majority of white immigrants settled in the North, where industry provided jobs and taxpaying workers provided schools. The more agricultural South had fewer educational opportunities to offer blacks or whites. Immediately after the Civil War, when they were provided access to education, blacks flocked to southern schools. This opportunity was short-lived, however, since the scarcity of educational resources made it advantageous for whites to appropriate the blacks' share for themselves, a temptation they did not resist.

By the time large numbers of blacks migrated north, the period of industrial expansion that had provided so many jobs for immigrants was drawing to a close. Moreover, the newly freed slaves did not have industrial skills and were barred from industrial occupations. Given the generations of social, economic, political, and legal discrimination that followed, and the fact that blacks did take advantage of the opportunities that presented themselves, it is unnecessary to call on "inferior values" to explain the difference in achievement between American blacks and white immigrants to the United States. (For a historical account of the struggle of blacks in the postbellum South and North, as well as that of nonwhites in South Africa, see Frederickson 1981; for a comparison of the conditions faced by U.S. blacks and white immigrants, and the effects of these differences on each group's success, see Lieberson 1980.)

CONCLUSIONS

Ever since Darwin proposed that the evolutionary process of natural selection ensures that only the fittest species survive, social science has been bedeviled by the notion that some human groups, especially races, are more biologically or culturally fit than others. This extension of Darwin's principle to competition for survival *within* the human species, especially when applied to modern industrial societies, cannot withstand close scrutiny. While differences in pigmentation, the distribution of body fat, height, and so on, may have been important earlier in human history they are hardly relevant in today's school or workplace.

Furthermore, cultural differences between groups can be identified, and these differences may have economic consequences, but they are more likely to reflect a group's historical experiences than the value its members attach to economic success. Thus, the current trend in sociology is to explain differences in the success of racial and ethnic groups in terms of the economic and political resources possessed by those groups, and by the groups with whom they are in competition and conflict.

One reason for the longevity of the biological and cultural forms of social Darwinism may be that for many years most natural and social scientists have been white, and middle-class to upper-class. While the objective search for truth is the goal of the scientific enterprise, race is an emotionally and ideologically loaded concept, and even the most sincere humanitarians have been led to faulty conclusions by their own biases. The greatest prospect for the advancement of the scientific study of race, then, is the recruitment of new scholars with a wide diversity of backgrounds, from both within and outside the United States. This increasing diversity will ensure that the exchange of ideas so necessary to scientific inquiry will be more balanced and less subject to bias than it has been in the past.

(SEE ALSO: *Ethnicity; Intelligence*)

REFERENCES

Frederickson, George M. 1981 *White Supremacy.* New York: Oxford University Press.

Glazer, Nathan, and Daniel Patrick Moynihan 1970 *Beyond the Melting Pot.* Cambridge, Mass: MIT Press.

Gould, Stephen Jay 1981 *The Mismeasure of Man.* New York: Norton.

Gutman, Herbert 1976 *The Black Family in Slavery and Freedom.* New York: Pantheon.

Lieberman, Leonard 1975 "The Debate over Race: A Study in the Sociology of Knowledge." In Ashley Montagu, ed., *Race and IQ.* New York: Oxford University Press.

Lieberson, Stanley 1980 *A Piece of the Pie: Blacks and White Immigrants Since 1880.* Berkeley: University of California Press.

Montagu, Ashley (ed.) 1975 *Race and IQ.* New York: Oxford University Press.

Steinberg, Stephen 1981 *The Ethnic Myth.* New York: Atheneum.

van den Berghe, Pierre L. 1981 *The Ethnic Phenomenon.* New York: Praeger.

SUSAN R PITCHFORD

RACISM *See* Apartheid; Discrimination; Prejudice; Race; Segregation and Desegregation.

RAPE *See* Sexual Violence and Abuse.

RATIONAL CHOICE THEORY A relatively straightforward way of gaining a sense of rational choice theory in sociology is to specify three criteria that many would agree should be met if any theory in sociology is to be wholly satisfactory: (1) The set of phenomena to be explained by the theory is the behavior of social systems (large or small) and not the behavior of individuals. Explanation of the behavior of social systems requires explanation in terms of the behavior of actors in the system, thus implying the other criteria, which consist of (2) a theory of transitions between the level of social system behavior and the level of behavior of individual actors, often expressed as the micro–macro problem; and (3) a psychological theory or model of the springs of individual action.

No wholly satisfactory theory exists in sociology because no theory has been able simultaneously to meet these three criteria. Different theoretical traditions can be characterized by the criterion or criteria that they sacrifice or give short shift to. These sacrifices constitute theoretical wagers that the element sacrificed is less important than those taken as problematic.

The class of theories that maintain the first criterion and sacrifice the second and third can be termed holistic. Such theories remain at the level of the system, never descending, for explanatory purposes, to the level of the actors within it. Functionalist theory is perhaps the most prominent example but is by no means the sole member of this class. The versions of structuralism in which agency plays no role is another specimen of this class of theory.

The class of theories that maintain criteria 1 and 3 but ignore criterion 2 consists of those which explain system behavior as a direct aggregation of behavior or tendencies on the part of individuals. The micro–macro transition is assumed to occur through simple aggregation. This class is exemplified by theories of panic or crowd behavior that posit some emotional "tendency" at the individual level that gives rise to the behavior that, when aggregated, constitutes panic. Another example consists of individualistic theories of the initiation of revolution, such as "rising expectations" theories. These theories see revolution as the result of the simultaneous frustration of large numbers of the population whose expectations have risen rapidly, leading to reactions that, when aggregated, bring about a revolution. In these theories, what is taken as problematic are the properties of individual psychology that lead to the tendencies to behave in the observed ways, as in various forms of collective behavior. What is given short shrift is the combination or organization of individual actions to produce a systemic outcome. The danger in this mode of theorizing is that the assumption of simple aggregation, ignoring social organization, leads to incorrect conclusions about the sources of change at the level of the system.

Rational choice theory in sociology belongs to still another class of theories, those that give short shrift or pay little attention to criterion 3, that is, the criterion that the theory have a psychological theory or model of the springs of individual action.

It may seem a mistake to describe a theoretical approach labeled according to its psychological assumptions as giving short shift to its psychological components. This is accurate, however. What is taken as problematic in rational choice theory is not individual psychology; it is rather criterion 2—the transitions between the micro level of individual action and the macro level of system behavior. This component can otherwise be described as institutional structure. An example will illustrate the point. The free rider phenomenon is a mainstay of rational choice theory in sociology. But the free rider phenomenon does not refer to some aspect of individual psychology. It refers to the structure of incentives, a structure that would lead a "normal" or "reasonable" or "rational" person to act in a way that benefits the self, at a cost to others affected by the action. No matter that experiments with such structures nearly always show that some persons do not free ride. Rational choice theory would argue that the problem is with the experimenter, who has allowed other incentives to creep in: the ties of friendship or merely the desire to be thought well of by others.

This is not to say that rational choice theory is always right in holding to the principle that persons act "rationally," even if the incentives are fully specified. It is, rather, to say that this constitutes one strategy for developing theory about the way institutional structures produce systemic behavior. It is a strategy that blinds itself to deviations from rationality, with the aim of getting on with a different task: the task of moving between micro and macro levels.

The institutional structure through which transitions between micro and macro levels occur in many applications of rational choice theory is the market. In economic systems, markets are complex systems of interactions between independent individuals that translate preferences at the micro level into prices at the macro level, and prices at the macro level into transactions at the micro level.

Markets are not the only form of institutional structure through which the micro–macro transitions occur, though many other institutions, including formal organizations, can be conceptualized as consisting of structured markets of some form.

THE POWER OF RATIONAL CHOICE THEORY

Rational choice theory's power derives from its injunction that persons pursue goals actively. This means that the theorist is not free to conceive of persons as merely passive objects of others' actions. A description of a social system consisting of active oppressors and passive oppressed, active exploiters and passive exploited, is not satisfactory for a rational choice theorist, no matter that power differentials in the system may be great. In rational choice theory, every actor in the system is acting to realize his or her interests within resource constraints. This orientation leads to a different theoretical approach to crime, to the welfare system, to social stratification, and to formal organization than does much other social theory. It puts rational choice theories at odds with that portion of social theory that depends on active–passive or subject–object dichotomies.

In addition, rational choice theory does not permit specifying a person's "reactions" in an ad hoc way. In rational choice theory persons do not accept influence from others without a reason. External "causes" of action are always mediated by purpose. Explanation of a phenomenon is satisfactory only if the actions that bring it about are seen to be motivated.

In its more highly specified form, the secret of rational choice theory's power as a theory lies in one word: optimization. Given various courses of action, the theory postulates that the individual will take that course which is best, or optimal, for him. Optimization finds its most explicit expression in the principle of maximizing utility. When the utility of each course of action for the individual is specified, the individual is postulated to take that action which maximizes utility. This locates the major problem of rational choice theory as that of specifying the utilities that the individual sees each action to hold.

At the system level, this principle of action gives power to the theory through the criterion of efficiency, or equilibrium. Two levels of efficiency are important: If different persons' utilities cannot be compared, the state of "Pareto-efficiency" is one in which no person's utility can be increased without another's being decreased. Under the principle of voluntaristic action, this implies an equilibrium: No change can be made to which all would agree.

A stronger criterion of efficiency exists when there is some single medium, such as money, through which all persons' utilities may be compared. Then, the efficiency or equilibrium criterion at the system level is maximization of the quantity of this medium, that is, wealth maximization (or if all possible states impose a cost, cost minimization). For example, Ellickson (1990) accounts for emergence of norms in terms of wealth maximization.

In the theory of games, which employs rational choice theory, the various solution concepts for a game are based on some form of the equilibrium principle. For example a widely used equilibrium concept for non-zero sum games, Nash equilibrium, is a state in which no player has an incentive to move from the state.

Optimization and efficiency provide for rational choice theory its potential for explanatory power. In this, it differs sharply from most other types of social theory.

RATIONAL CHOICE VERSUS STANDARD SOCIOLOGICAL THEORY

Aspects of rational choice theory lead its adherents in directions that are often diametrically opposed to dominant assumptions in sociology. One such aspect is that rational choice theory assumes all actors to act purposively and, in most versions of rational choice theory, self-interestedly. This leads rational choice theorists to see persons who commit crimes as purposive and self-interested actors, while criminology in sociology has characteristically viewed such persons as passive objects, victims of environmental circumstance. The policy implications are very different: Rational choice theorists see a change in the structure of incentives, that is, increased measures of deterrence, as appropriate policy (see Becker 1976; Ehrlich 1973). Standard sociology sees criminals as objects to be molded, via rehabilitative treatment, into non-crime-oriented persons (see Sutherland and Cressey 1970; Cloward and Ohlin 1960). The question of what policy is most effective in the long or the short run is a test between these two theoretical orientations, but what is especially striking is the direct opposition between the orientations: rational choice theory, regarding the actor to be the subject of action and taking that actor's perspective but evaluating the action from the point of view of the larger social system; and standard sociological theory, assuming the actor to be a passive object of others' actions but evaluating that action from the point of view of the actor, who is often regarded as a victim of environmental circumstances.

This opposition between "purposive action" of rational choice theory and "environmental determinism" of other branches of social theory leads to a general ideological difference, in which rational choice theorists tend to see persons as responsible for their own actions, and for the outcomes of those actions, while many other sociologists tend to see outcomes for persons as due to forces beyond their control. It is likely that neither is entirely correct: Economics, the discipline in which rational choice theory is most fully developed, is well known for having no place for coercion in its conceptual structure, an absence that could not be tolerated outside economics. At the opposite extreme, to see all outcomes as the result of the powerful exploiting the weak is a *reductio ad absurdum* and constitutes in effect a resignation from the task of social theory construction.

Another dimension on which rational choice theory differs from standard sociological theory is that some rational choice theory pays attention to general equilibrium in a market (or stated otherwise, social) system, while standard sociological theory seldom does so. An example is Gary Becker's analysis of the systemic consequences of discrimination—that is, when some employers have a "taste for discrimination," for example, a preference for men as employees over women when all other attributes are equal. Becker (1971) shows that at market equilibrium, nondiscriminating employers will gain, and the favored group of workers (men in this example) will gain, while the discriminating employers and the nonfavored workers will lose, compared to a system without discrimination. These are nonobvious and nontrivial deductions from the theory.

The simple assumption of pure rationality serves rational choice theorists better under certain circumstances than under others. As an example of a circumstance in which the theory is faulty due to its spare model of individual action, psychologists have shown the importance of "framing effects" on action, while the effect of frames of reference on action has no place in rational choice theory (Kahneman, Slovic, and Tversky 1982).

Rational choice theory has trod upon ground that traditional sociologists have carefully protected from individualistic approaches. An example is the question of how and why group solidarity arises. In much social theory, groups and thus group solidarity are taken as given. But rational choice theory, beginning with rational, self-interested individuals, takes group solidarity as problematic (Hechter 1987). Another example concerns social norms. Again, much social theory takes norms as given and studies behavior only within the given framework of norms. Rational choice theory, not content with this, asks how we can account for the emergence of norms that constrain or encourage actions. The answer it gives is in terms of a demand for norms, which arises when a person's action affects others. This leads those who are affected to attempt to control the action, through norms enforced by sanctions. But these sanctions may or may not take place, depending on properties of the social structure (Coleman 1990). This is an example of the general program of rational choice theory: to assume nothing except that individuals begin as self-interested purposive actors. This leads to questions that otherwise remain unasked: Why do solidary groups form? Why and how do norms emerge?

The range of sociological problems to which rational choice theory has been applied is extensive. It includes the question of how groups make collective decisions (Mueller 1989), marriage and divorce (Becker 1991), interactions in small groups and social networks (Homans 1958; Cook 1987), how groups form constitutions (Ostrom 1989), the conditions under which collective action arises or fails to arise (Heckathorn 1989), the conditions under which revolutions occur (Tullock 1974; Lindenberg 1989), the viability of formal organizations (Coleman 1990), and how risk is managed by social institutions (Heimer 1985).

THE PROGRAM OF RATIONAL CHOICE THEORY

Rational choice theory can be described as seeing the functioning of social systems as the outcome of a game, with players and rules as the game's components. The task of social theory in this view is to uncover the rules and to discover how the rules shape and combine the actions of players to bring about the systemic behavior observed in reality. This view also lends itself to the task of constructing rules that will bring about actions resulting in systemic behavior that meets some criterion. It is this that leads rational choice theory to have close connections to normative theory, in which criteria of optimality play a part.

Note that in this view of the tasks of social theory, the players are regarded as interchangeable, with variations in social system behavior due not to variations in players but to variations in the rules under which they act. It is in this sense that rational choice theory gives short shrift to psychological theory.

Another way of expressing the program of rational choice theory is to say that it casts the cold hard light of purposive self-interested individual action on any explanation of a social phenomenon, asking whether the explanation is consistent both with what "reasonable" or "rational" persons would do in those circumstances and with the institutional structures through which individual actions combine to bring about a systemic outcome.

This program may be too restrictive: the cold hard light may be too cold and hard; that is, persons *do* sometimes act in others' interests. It may be incorrect in other ways: Persons may deviate systematically from maximizing expected utility. For example, they may be unable to prevent themselves from acting in ways they would not have wished in advance of the event and will later regret, inexplicably so from the perspective of rational choice theory (Elster 1979). They may change their preferences, values, or tastes, a matter on which rational choice theory is strangely silent. Psychologists (or advertisers) may easily trap them in inconsistencies. These are the casualties of the strategy that rational choice theory has taken: to give short shrift to a theory of the springs of action and to concentrate on the behavior of social systems and on the institutional structures through which actions of purposive individuals give rise to behavior of a social system.

WHY HAS RATIONAL CHOICE BECOME PROMINENT?

Part of the explanation for the growth of rational choice theory in sociology lies in the theoretical vacuum created by the failure of Parsonian functionalism. Part, however, lies elsewhere. Increasingly, we live in a world that we construct, a world from which physical constraints have been removed. Ascriptive statuses, and the institutions in which they are embedded, have given way to achieved statuses, located in institutions or organizations whose design creates criteria for achievement. If we want social theory to be more than description of an inexorable fate, that is, to be useful in institutional design, then one strategy is to develop theories about how different incentive structures will lead the actions of "normal," "standard," or "rational" persons to result in differing systemic behavior. This is the program of rational choice theory. It is a program fitted for an activist theoretical stance, one oriented to having social theory used in the design of social institutions. It is an approach peculiarly fitted for a time in which institutions are increasingly the product of human design.

(SEE ALSO: *Cognitive Consistency Theories; Decision-Making Theory and Research; Exchange Theory*)

REFERENCES

Becker, Gary S. 1971 *The Economics of Discrimination,* 2nd ed. Chicago: University of Chicago Press.

——— 1976 *The Economic Approach to Human Behavior.* Chicago: University of Chicago Press.

——— 1991 *A Treatise on the Family,* 2nd ed. Cambridge, Mass.: Harvard University Press.

Cloward, Richard A., and Lloyd E. Ohlin 1960 *Delinquency and Opportunity.* New York: Free Press.

Coleman, James S. 1990 *Foundations of Social Theory.* Cambridge, Mass.: Harvard University Press.

Cook, Karen S. 1987 *Social Exchange Theory.* Newbury Park, Calif.: Sage Publications.

Ehrlich, I. 1973 "Participation in Illegitimate Activities: A Theoretical and Empirical Investigation." *Journal of Political Economy* 81: 521–564.

Ellickson, R. 1988 "A Critique of Economic and Sociological Theories of Social Control." *Journal of Legal Studies* 16:67–99.

Elster, Jon 1979 *Ulysses and the Sirens.* Cambridge: Cambridge University Press.

Hechter, Michael 1987 *Principles of Group Solidarity.* Berkely: University of California Press.

Heckathorn, Douglas 1989 "Collective Action and the Second-Order Free-Rider Problem." *Rationality and Society* 1:78–100.

Heimer, Carol A. 1985 *Reactive Risk and Rational Action.* Berkeley: University of California Press.

Homans, G. 1958 "Social Behavior As Exchange." *American Journal of Sociology* 65:597–606.

Kahneman, D., P. Slovic, and A. Tversky, 1982. *Judgement Under Uncertainty: Heuristics and Biases.* Cambridge: Cambridge University Press.

Lindenberg, Siegwart 1989 "Social Production Functions, Deficits, and Social Revolutions: Prerevolutionary France and Russia." *Rationality and Society* 1:51–77.

Mueller, Dennis C. 1989 *Public Choice II.* Cambridge: Cambridge University Press.

Ostrom, Elinor 1989 "Microconstitutional Change in Multiconstitutional Political Systems." *Rationality and Society* 1:11–50.

Sutherland, Edwin H., and Donald R. Cressey 1970 *Criminology.* 8th ed. Philadelphia: Lippincott.

Tullock, G. 1974 *The Social Dilemma: The Economics of War and Revolution.* Blacksburg, Va.: University Publications.

JAMES S. COLEMAN

REFERENCE GROUP THEORY In the 1942 monograph *The Psychology of Status,* Herbert Hyman introduces the term *reference group* while examining an individual's conception of his or her own status positions relative to referent others, or members of various groups with which one psychologically identifies (Kuhn 1967; Shibutani 1967; Schmitt 1972). Following Hyman's work, Merton and Kitt (1950) introduced this term to sociologists by noting that Stouffer and his associates had utilized the reference group idea in their work on relative deprivation (Kuhn 1967). Symbolic interactionists, who study the emergence of social structure through daily interaction (Federico and Schwartz 1983), claim that the reference group idea is a "simplification and specification" of their concept of the generalized other, or the composite expectations of society with regard to a particular role (Kuhn 1967; Turner 1956). Other researchers have also utilized the reference group concept, resulting in slightly varied definitions of this concept (for a more detailed discussion, see Schmitt 1972). There are common elements, however, within the various definitions, and these elements have been used to construct a general definition of a reference group. That is, a *reference group* refers to a set of individuals whose standing or perspective is taken into account by an actor when selecting a course of action or when making a judgment about a specific issue (Shibutani 1967; Kemper 1968). Individuals can serve the same functions as reference groups but should be distinguished as reference individuals (Merton 1957).

Reference groups and reference individuals serve two functions: (1) as a normative group and (2) as a comparison group (Gecas 1982). As a normative group, reference groups are a source of norms and values, providing guidelines or having certain expectations with which the individual is able to identify. As a comparison group, reference groups provide standards for self-evaluation with regard to such issues as the legitimacy of one's actions and attitudes or the adequacy of one's performance (Kemper 1968; Gecas 1982). Kemper (1968) further identifies four types of comparison groups: (1) equity groups—reference groups used by an individual to judge whether her or his situation is fair or equitable; (2) legitimator groups—reference groups used by an individual to determine the legitimacy of her or his behavior or opinions; (3) role model—a reference individual (or group) that demonstrates for another individual how things are actually done; and (4) accommodator group—a reference group or individual providing another individual with a cue for a complementary or parallel response (for a more detailed discussion of these types, see Kemper 1968).

The reference group idea gained popularity among social scientists as well as the lay public. According to Kuhn (1967), this popularity was due in part to the prestige of its initial users and the ease with which the concepts could be adapted to survey research. Despite this popularity, however, the reference group idea has not gone without criticism. First, Borgatta (1960) argues that the reference group idea as defined by its normative function can be covered in a discussion of socialization (the interactive process of becoming a member of society), since this particular usage merely describes the way in which an individual is socialized. Schmitt (1972) criticizes the reference group concept as being too inclusive, and researchers for inconsistently using this concept. Beyond these conceptual/definitional problems, research done on reference groups assumes rather than verifies the existence of reference groups (Kuhn 1967). It is not uncommon to find researchers asking subjects about the composition of their particular "reference groups." Much of the research on reference groups is also retrospective in nature. Researchers often require subjects to identify the members of their reference group(s) used to make some past decision. As an example of such work, Walsh, Ferrell, and Tolone (1972) examined the selection of reference groups with regard to sexual permissiveness by asking subjects to identify their most important "reference group" with regard to this issue. Finally, Borgatta (1960) suggests that analyses involving reference groups as defined by their comparative function have primarily been used to explain rather than predict behavior, thus limiting their contribution to a "predictive social science."

The direction for future work in this area should include clarifying the conceptual definition of a reference group, ascertaining whether reference groups do indeed exist, examining the process by which reference groups are selected, and, finally, determining the extent to which an individual's behavior is influenced by his or her reference group(s).

(SEE ALSO: *Role Theory; Self-Concept*)

REFERENCES

Borgatta, Edgar F. 1960 "Role and Reference Group Theory." In Leonard S. Kogan, ed., *Social Science Theory and Social Work Research.* New York: National Association of Social Workers.

Federico, Ronald C., and Janet S. Schwartz 1983 *Sociology.* Menlo Park, Calif.: Addison-Wesley.

Gecas, Viktor 1982 "The Self-Concept." *Annual Review of Sociology* 8:1–33.

Kemper, Theodore D. 1968 "Reference Groups, Socialization, and Achievement." *American Sociological Review* 33:31–45.

Kuhn, Manford H. 1967 "The Reference Group Reconsidered." In J. Manis and B. Meltzer, eds.,

Symbolic Interaction: A Reader in Social Psychology. Boston: Allyn and Bacon.

Merton, Robert K. 1957 *Social Structure.* Glencoe, Ill.: Free Press.

———, and Alice S. Kitt 1950 "Contributions to the Theory of Reference Group Behavior." In R. Merton and P. Lazarsfeld, eds., *Continuities in Social Research: Studies in the Scope and Method of "The American Soldier."* Glencoe, Ill.: Free Press.

Schmitt, Raymond L. 1972 *The Reference Other Orientation: An Extension of the Reference Group Conept.* Carbondale: Southern Illinois University Press.

Shibutani, Tamotsu 1967 "Reference Groups as Perspectives." In J. Manis and B. Meltzer, eds., *Symbolic Interaction: A Reader in Social Psychology.* Boston: Allyn and Bacon.

Turner, Ralph H. 1957 "Role-Taking, Role Standpoint, and Reference-Group Behavior." *American Journal of Sociology* 61:316–328.

Walsh, Robert H., Mary Z. Ferrell, and William L. Tolone 1972 "Selection of Reference Group, Perceived Reference Group Permissiveness, and Personal Permissiveness Attitudes and Behavior: A Study of Two Consecutive Panels (1967–1971; 1970–1974)." *Journal of Marriage and the Family* 34: 495–507.

YVETTE FARMER

REFUGEES *See* International Migration.

REGRESSION EFFECTS *See* Quasi-Experimental Research Designs.

RELIABILITY Everyday we use terms such as *consistent* and *single-minded* to describe the performances of others around us, realizing that these are no more than averages that summarize considerable intra-individual variability in performance. There is also variability in the measurement of performances. The variability we observe in the performances of others, whether mental or physical, is due to a number of factors, including variations in mental and physical efficacy, the conditions under which the performance occurs, the specific tasks associated with the performance, and inconsistencies in the evaluation itself—inconsistencies due to the imperfection of both the instruments used and the humans recording the performance (Feldt and Brennan 1989). Factors that lead to inconsistencies in performance constitute *errors in measurement.*

For all intents and purposes, all human assessment contains errors in measurement. Some errors are systematic, as in the case of an athlete who "clutches" under the pressure of a game or the person whose low self-esteem causes him or her to perform poorly in oral classroom work. Other error is essentially random, due to chance variations. Examples of random variation include one's mood or the failure to understand instructions when responding to an assessment instrument. When the term *measurement error* is used in the context of measurement and assessment, it almost always refers to random errors of measurement; such is the case in this exposition.

In its most general sense, *reliability* refers to the degree of consistency we exhibit in recording human behaviors, whether using technical instruments (e.g., computers), questionnaires, interviews, or structured observations. To the degree that an instrument or technique yields reliable observations, one would expect a set of *N* individuals to be ranked the same from measurement to measurement unless the phenomenon under investigation had itself changed from measurement to remeasurement.

Two methods have been used to estimate the degree of consistency of measurement. One is to band scores with a confidence interval of sorts (called the *standard error of measurement),* the other is to compute a *reliability coefficient* (Feldt and Brennan 1989). Among sociologists the latter method is by far the more popular, and therefore we will restrict our attention to it.

TRUE SCORES

When measuring human behavior, whether of individuals or of groups, most sociologists assume that at the moment of measurement some "true" score on the variable under investigation exists for the person or group being assessed. The scientist's task is to measure individuals' statuses on the true score as accurately as possible. However appealing this Platonic notion of a true score is (Sutcliffe 1965), classical measurement theory takes a much different view of what a true score is. A true score is one's average on a variable, assuming that one could be measured an infinite number of times. More precisely, a true score τ_p is $E_p(x) = \tau_p$ where $E_p(x)$ refers to the expected value for a single person, *p*, measured an infinite number of times. The reader may have problem digesting this, but not to fret. In fact reliability can be assessed with as few as two measurements of the same behavior across time or by use of as few as two separate assessments of the behavior at the same time.

CLASSICAL TEST THEORY

Classical test theory begins with the assumption that observed scores are due to the sum of two components—a true score component and a measurement error component. If we assume we are measuring *N* individuals on a variable *x* with a true score τ and measurement error ϵ, then the relationship among these components is given by

$$x=\tau+\epsilon \tag{1}$$

As indicated earlier, we assume that all measurement error is random—that is, on average, zero, or more formally:

$$E(\epsilon)=0 \tag{2}$$

Furthermore, the classical measurement model assumes that the errors are random with respect to the value of the true scores—that is, the errors in measurement are assumed to be uncorrelated with the true scores:

$$C(\tau, \epsilon) = 0 \tag{3}$$

where $C(.,.)$ stands for the covariance of two variables. The errors of measurement error associated with one variable also are assumed to be uncorrelated with the true score of another variable. Thus, for two variables x_i and x_j we assume:

$$C(\tau_j, \epsilon_i) = 0 \tag{4}$$

From these assumptions the fundamental variance relationship in classical test theory follows:

$$\sigma_x^2 = \sigma_\tau^2 + \sigma_\epsilon^2 \tag{5}$$

That is, the observed variance for a variable *x* is equal to the sum of the true score and the error variance.

A more complete and comprehensive overview can be found in Lord and Novick (1968); a more elementary introduction, in Nunnally (1967).

RELIABILITY DEFINED

The definition of the reliability of a measure *x*, labeled ρ_x, is the ratio of true score variance to observed variance:

$$\rho_x = \sigma_\tau^2/\sigma_x^2 \tag{6}$$

With a little algebra, it follows from (5) and (6) that

$$\rho_x = 1 - (\sigma_\epsilon^2/\sigma_x^2) \tag{7}$$

as well. Hence (7) is an alternative expression that can be, and often is, used for the reliability. Since a variance is a nonnegative quantity, it follows from this last equation that the reliability is between 0 and 1. And the greater the amount of error variance relative to the observed variance, the closer the reliability will be to 0. Conversely, when the error variance is 0, the reliability will equal 1.

THE EFFECT OF UNRELIABILITY ON STATISTICAL ESTIMATES

While one would expect that unreliability would affect statistics such as the mean, standard deviation, and correlation coefficients, to this point we have not been explicit about those effects. It follows directly from the relationship assumed between the true and observed scores as shown in (1), and the assumption that the mean of the measurement errors is 0, that the mean of the observed scores is equal to the mean of the true scores:

$$\mu_x = \mu_\tau \tag{8}$$

When one knows the reliability, it follows immediately from the definition of reliability (see [6]) that

$$\sigma_\tau^2 = \sigma_x^2\rho_x \tag{9}$$

That is, the true score variance of x equals the observed variance multiplied by the reliability of the measure. If a measure is perfectly measured, the true score and observed variances will be equal. At the other extreme, if the reliability of the measure is 0, the true score variance will also equal 0.

Interestingly, the covariance is *un*affected by measurement error. Since the covariance is the backbone of the correlation coefficient, one might assume that correlations would be unaffected by measurement errors in x and y as well. This is not the case. Instead,

$$\rho_{\tau_x\tau_y} = \rho_{xy} \Big/ \sqrt{\rho_x\rho_y} \qquad (10)$$

Notice that if there were no errors in measurement, the observed correlation between x and y would equal the correlation between τ_x and τ_y. Equation (10) is the best known of a class of *attenuation formulas.* It expresses the fact that the true relationship between x and y is attenuated by errors in measurement.

Interestingly, regression coefficients are affected only by errors in measurement related to the independent variables. Thus, in the two-variable case, where $\beta_{\tau_y\tau_x}$ is the population regression coefficient,

$$\beta_{\tau_y\tau_x} = \beta_{xy}/\rho_x \qquad (11)$$

The effects of measurement error in the three-variable case can be found in Bohrnstedt (1983).

RELIABILITY AS A FUNCTION OF THE NUMBER OF INDEPENDENT MEASURES

It makes intuitive sense that one's confidence in an estimate should increase as the number of independent measurements of a phenomenon increase for a given level of reliability of measurement. One would be more confident with a pair of independent measures of political liberalism, each with a reliability of 0.6, than with a single scale measure. And we would be even more confident if we had four such independent measures, and so on. It is this intuitive reasoning that forms the rationale for using multiple items rather than a single one to measure a construct (Curtis and Jackson 1962). The assumption is that errors in measurement are random, that is, will cancel each other out, and the average of all the measurements is a better estimate of the true value than any single measurement.

It is also clear that one needs fewer independent measures to achieve a given level of confidence when the reliability of each individual measurement is high. If one knows a measure has a reliability of 0.9, one might accept a single measurement, whereas one might need eight or nine independent assessments for a measure with a reliability of 0.5 to have the same degree of confidence in what the true value is.

The relationship between the reliability of a composite x_n (where $x_n = \sum_{i=1}^{n} x_i$) and n parallel measures of known reliability was derived independently by Spearman (1910) and Brown (1910). They showed that the reliability of a measure n times longer than the original is

$$\rho_{x_n} = \frac{n\rho_x}{1 + (n - 1)\rho_x} \qquad (12)$$

where ρ_{x_n} is the reliability of the composite. The verbal interpretation of (12) is as follows: The reliability of a measure composed of parallel items is a joint function of (a) the number of items comprising it and (b) the reliability of those individual items. The higher the reliability of the individual items in the composite, the fewer items needed to achieve a given level of reliability.

Figure 1 shows the increase in reliability as a function of the number of independent items for various initial reliabilities. The implication is obvious. When one has good items, relatively few are needed to construct a composite score with a high degree of reliability; the lower the reliability of the items, more are needed. For example, if one demands a reliability of 0.8 for x_n, it can be achieved with two items with reliabilities of 0.7, four with reliabilities of 0.5, or ten with reliabilities of 0.3.

TYPES OF RELIABILITY

To this point, our discussion of reliability has been largely theoretical and historical. We now briefly discuss specific ways to assess reliability.

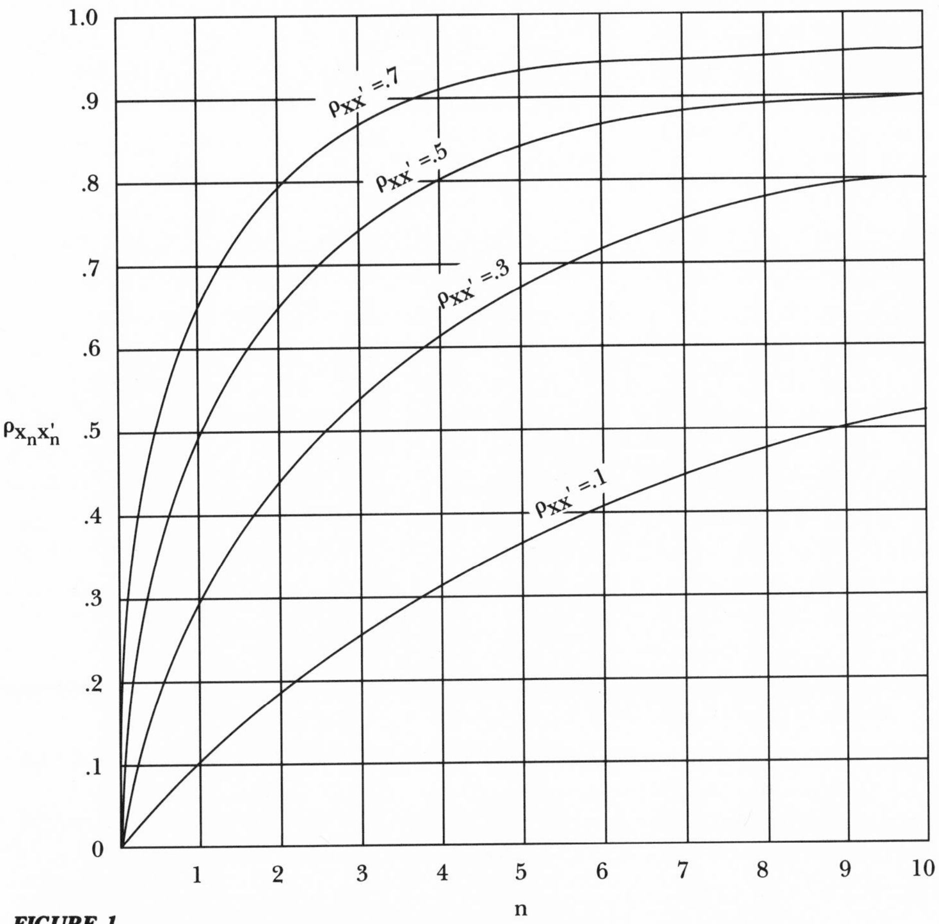

FIGURE 1
Diagram Showing Increase in Reliability as a Function of Increase in the Length of Scale (n) *for Different Initial Reliabilities*

Generally, reliability measures can be divided into two major classes: measures of *stability* and measures of *equivalence*.

Measures of Stability. A person's response to a particular item or set of items may vary from occasion to occasion. The respondents may not be certain how they feel about an issue or a person, may be distracted by other matters, may be tired or ill, and so on. All of these will contribute to errors of measurement and therefore depress the reliability of the items. Given that error exists, the problem is how to assess it in a way that satisfies the definition of reliability given above. Historically, the most popular way to evaluate it has been to correlate respondents' responses at one point in time with their responses at some later point in time. Reliability evaluated by correlating a measure across time is called a *measure of stability* or, more commonly, *test-retest* reliability.

There are problems with test-retest reliability estimates, however. For several reasons one is likely to obtain different estimates, depending on the amount of time between measurement and remeasurement. First there is the problem of memory. If the interval between the measurement and remeasurement is short, the respondents may remember their earlier responses, thus making them appear more consistent with respect to the true content than they in fact are. To handle this problem, some researchers employ a *parallel forms* test-retest procedure. A different but presumably parallel form of the measure is used at the second administration. Truly parallel items have the same error variance, correlate identically with each other, and correlate identically with criterion variables. Obviously these are difficult, if not impossible, conditions to meet, and it should be clear that few "parallel forms" of measures are in fact parallel. However, if one can be satisfied that two forms are reasonably parallel, their employment across time reduces the degree to which respondents' memory can inflate the reliability estimate.

A second problem with the test-retest approach has to do with the assumption that the errors of measurement ϵ_1 and ϵ_2 are uncorrelated. If the errors of measurement are in some sense systematic and not random, one would expect that the same sources of bias might operate each time measurement occurs, thereby making the assumption of uncorrelatedness of errors in measurement highly suspect.

A third problem is that true change cannot be distinguished from unreliability in a simple test-retest reliability design, and obviously the longer the time interval between measurement and remeasurement, the greater the probability that respondents will have in fact changed on the underlying unobserved variable. It should be clear that if individuals have in fact changed, a low test-retest correlation does not necessarily mean that the reliability of one's measure is poor. While the technical details are beyond the scope of this introduction to reliability, several approaches to deal with the problem of disentangling true change from unreliability have appeared in the literature. Building on the innovative work of Heise (1969), papers by Wiley and Wiley (1970), Werts, Jöreskog, and Linn (1971), and Hargens, Reskin, and Allison (1976) have all extended this line of work.

Measures of Equivalence. Whereas historically reliability has more often been assessed using measures of stability, in recent decades an alternative approach has gained in popularity—the use of measures of equivalence. Parallel items administered at the same point in time and correlated to estimate reliability is an example of a measure of equivalence. The assumption is made that the two items have the same underlying true score and as such are equivalent, and hence equally good measures of the true score. In a sense, the two items can be thought of as an instant test-retest. As noted earlier, one need not be limited to a pair of parallel items. Indeed, since reliability is partially a function of the number of items used, it makes good sense to build composites or scores that are sums of items so long as one can assume the items in a given score have the same underlying true score.

One of the earliest equivalence measures to appear was the split-half method. In the split-half approach to reliability the total number of items in a composite is divided into halves and the half-scores are then correlated. Since the actual measure is twice as long as the half-score being correlated, the correlation is usually inserted in the Spearman-Brown prophecy formula with $n = 2$ (see [12]) to get an estimate of the reliability of the total composite. Some researchers used the odd-numbered items for one half-test and the even-numbered for the other. Another approach was to use the first $n/2$ items for one half-test and the last $n/2$ items for the other (where n refers to the total number of items). Yet another version of the split-half approach was to use randomly selected items (without replacement) to build the half-tests. Obviously each of these methods could yield conflicting estimates of the reliability of the half-tests. Indeed, for a composite $2n$ items long, the total number of splits is $(2n!)/2(n!)(n!)$. For example, for a 10-item score there are 126 different possible splits. It is small wonder that split-half techniques began to fall into disuse as more precise methods for estimating reliability were developed.

It should be mentioned in passing that split-half methods have often been used in a test-retest format where one version is used at time 1 and a second version is used at time 2. In this case the splits are assumed to be parallel composites. This procedure is followed as a possible way to deal with memory effects that might confound test-retest reliability estimates using the same composite across time.

The split-half techniques have gradually been replaced by internal consistency methods for the estimate of reliability with cross-sectional data. Internal consistency reliability estimates utilize the covariances among all the items simultaneously rather than concentrating on a single correlation between two arbitrary splits.

Kuder and Richardson (1937) were the first to devise a measure of equivalence that utilized all the covariances among the items. However, their formulas KR20 and KR21 could be used only with dichotomous items. Hoyt (1941) and Guttman (1945) presented generalizations of the KR formulas for polychotomous items. But by far the most popular generalization has been coefficient α developed by Cronbach (1951), where

$$\alpha = \frac{n}{n-1}\left[1 - \frac{\sum_{i=1}^{n} V(y_i)}{\sum_{i=1}^{n} V(y_i) + 2\sum_{i=1}^{n}\sum_{j=1}^{n} C(y_i,y_j)}\right] \quad (13)$$

where $i \neq j$. Then, after some algebra, it follows that

$$\alpha = \frac{n}{n-1}\left[1 - \frac{\sum_{i=1}^{n} V(y_i)}{\sigma_x^2}\right] \quad (14)$$

where $x = \sum_{i=1}^{n} y_i$. Importantly, α exactly equals the reliability if one has parallel measures. In general, however, α is a *lower bound* to the reliability of an unweighted composite of n items (Novick and Lewis 1967). That is, $\rho_x \geq \alpha$. However α equals the reliability of the composite if the n measures under three conditions that are successively less restrictive than parallel measures. τ-equivalent measures are defined as measures with the same true scores but without the necessity of having equal measurement error variances. Essentially, *τ-equivalent measures* allow for differences in error variances and in item means. Finally, *congeneric measures* relax the requirements of parallel measures even further. True scores for items can differ by as much as a linear relationship. Jöreskog (1971) has shown how *confirmatory factor analysis* can be used to determine whether a set of items can be fit by the congeneric assumption. The details can be found in Bohrnstedt (1983) or Alwin and Jackson (1980).

In spite of the fact that the congeneric assumption is much more likely to fit the items used in sociological research than the other, more restrictive items, at best most of our items are what Alwin and Jackson (1980) call "near congeneric."

SUMMARY

All measurement contains error. The amount of error is inversely proportional to the reliability of a measurement tool. In this essay we have provided a brief overview of the major types of reliability and ways in which reliability can be estimated. In addition, we have quickly reviewed the effects of unreliability on statistical estimates. Fuller treatments of the subject can be found in Feldt and Brennan (1989), Zeller and Carmines (1980), or Bohrnstedt (1983).

(SEE ALSO: *Measurement; Measurement Instruments; Replication; Scientific Explanation*)

REFERENCES

Alwin, D. F., and D. J. Jackson 1980 "Measurement Models for Response Errors in Surveys: Issues and Applications. In Karl F. Schuessler, ed., *Sociological Methodology: 1980.* San Francisco: Jossey-Bass.

Bohrnstedt, G. W. 1983 *Handbook of Survey Research.* New York: Academic Press.

Brown, W. 1910 "Some Experimental Results in the Correlation of Mental Abilities." *British Journal of Psychology 3:296–322.*

Cronbach, L. J. 1951 "Coefficient Alpha and the Internal Structure of Tests." *Psychometrika* 16: 297–334.

Curtis, R. F., and E. F. Jackson 1962 "Multiple Indicators in Survey Research." *American Journal of Sociology* 72:1–16.

Feldt, L. S., and R. L. Brennan 1989 "Reliability." In R. L. Linn, ed., *Educational Measurement.* New York: Macmillan.

Guttman, L. 1945 "A Basis for Analyzing Test-Retest Reliability." *Psychometrika* 10:255–282.

Hargens, L. L., B. F. Reskin, and P. D. Allison 1976 "Problems in Estimating Error from Panel Data: An Example Involving the Measurement of Scientific Productivity." *Sociological Methods and Research* 4 (May):439–458.

Heise, D. R. 1969 "Separating Reliability and Stability in Test-Retest Correlation." *American Sociological Review* 34 (February):93–101.

Hoyt, C. 1941 "Test Reliability Estimated by Analysis of Variance." *Psychometrika* 6:153–160.

Jöreskog, K. G. 1971 "Statistical Analysis of Sets of Congeneric Tests." *Psychometrika* 36:109–134.

Kuder, G. F., and M. W. Richardson 1937 "The Theory of the Estimation of Test Reliability." *Psychometrika* 2:135–138.

Lord, F. M., and M. R. Novick 1968 *Statistical Theories of Mental Test Scores*. Reading, Mass.: Addison-Wesley.

Novick, M. R., and C. Lewis 1967 "Coefficient Alpha and the Reliability of Composite Measurements." *Psychometrika* 32:1–13.

Nunnally, J. C. 1967 *Psychometric Theory*. New York: McGraw-Hill.

Spearman, C. 1910. "Correlation Calculated with Faulty Data." *British Journal of Psychology* 3:271–295.

Sutcliffe, J. P. 1965 "A Probability Model for Errors of Classification. I. General Considerations." *Psychometrika* 30: 73–96.

Werts, C. E., K. G. Jöreskog, and R. L. Linn 1971 "Comment on 'The Estimation of Measurement Error in Panel Data." *American Sociological Review* 36 (February):110–112.

Wiley, D. E., and J. A. Wiley 1970 "The Estimation of Measurement Error in Panel Data." *American Sociological Review* 35 (February):112–117.

Zeller, R. A., and E. G. Carmines 1980 *Measurement in the Social Sciences*. Cambridge: Cambridge University Press.

GEORGE W. BOHRNSTEDT

RELIGION, POLITICS, AND WAR

The outcome and settlement of World War II made the independent sovereign nation-state the dominant system of action for managing and governing populations (Nettl and Robertson 1968; Meyer 1980). The most important factors affecting the likelihood that religion has a role in the political affairs of a nation-state are: (1) the religious traditions that are present in a nation-state's population and (2) a nation-state's institutional and social organization.

The symbols, myths, and ideology of a religious tradition are a cultural resource that may affect politics. Whether a religious tradition has the capacity to affect politics depends on the ethical and doctrinal components of its symbols, myths, and ideology. Ethics and doctrines vary in terms of orientation to the affairs of the everyday world, the extent to which adherents are expected to express their beliefs in the practical affairs of a society, and whether claims are made on politically controlled social and economic resources. Differences on those dimensions determine the likelihood that a religious tradition encourages political action. For example, within Protestant Christian traditions in the United States, Pentecostals emphasize individual religious experience and behavior, while many mainline denominations tend to stress social action and reform (Roof and McKinney 1987; Poloma 1989). Pentecostals are less likely to be involved in politics than members of mainline Protestant denominations. Some religious traditions (for example, Theravada Buddhism) value withdrawal from the everyday world as a path to enlightenment and salvation (Gombrich 1988). Others, such as Calvinistic Protestantism, stress the methodical performance of ordinary tasks and jobs (including political roles) as a religious duty and calling (Poggi 1983). Adherents of world-rejecting traditions are less likely to be involved in politics than followers of world-affirming traditions.

Claims on the resources of a society are a major focus of political action. By rejecting in principle the authority of any state and, thereby, the mechanisms of resource distribution that are embedded in governments, some religious traditions exclude themselves from ordinary politics. Jehovah's Witnesses fit into this category (Stroup 1945). On the other hand, subject to constitutional and other constraints that may be imposed by national regimes, the Roman Catholic Church has an interest in obtaining resources that are distributed through state action, thereby implicating itself in politics.

Whether religion becomes a force in the internal factional politics of a nation-state depends in part upon the extent of religious diversity in a population in addition to predisposing ethical or doctrinal factors. Religious diversity alone, however, is seldom a direct cause of political action and conflict. Religion in combination with other properties of a nation-state's population provides a basis for politics that can be affected by religious differences. Those properties include differences in language, race, patterns of settlement, and class. Religiously inspired political tension and conflict can occur where religious differences are correlated with differences in language and other social characteristics (Eversley 1989). If religious differences are only weakly related to other significant divisions in a population, it is unlikely that religion will be implicated in the internal politics of a nation-state (cf. Lipset 1960).

Secular ideological alternatives to religion—communism, for example—can also be a basis for population diversity and political conflict (O'Toole 1977). Major intranational conflicts in the twentieth century that pitted secular and religious forces or their representatives against one another include the Spanish Civil War (1936–1939) and the movement to democratize Poland at the end of the cold war. Controversies over abortion, censorship, and sexual orientation frequently involve clashes between the adherents of secular and religious ideologies (Simpson 1983; Luker 1984).

Variation in the religious characteristics of populations and their relationships with language, race, class, and patterns of settlement provide clues regarding the likelihood that a population's capacity for religiously based politics will be manifested in action. A population's characteristics that enhance or discourage a tie between religion and politics, however, should always be considered in the context of the institutional and social organization of nation-states. Institutional and social organization influence the likelihood that population characteristics that enhance or inhibit religiously based politics will be expressed in action.

Economic, political, and cultural spheres of action including religion constitute the institutional sectors of the nation-state. Nation-states vary according to the extent to which their institutional sectors are intertwined or stand as differentiated and autonomous sources of action (cf. Luhmann 1982). Those differences affect the forms that religiously based conflict and politics may take.

The relationship between the religious and the political institutions of a nation-state can be classified in terms of three models: (1) the theocratic/caesaropapist model; (2) the two-powers model; (3) the strict-separation model. The theocratic/caesaropapist model assumes an identity of interests and an interpretive unity in religious and political fields of action. At the limit no distinction is made between religious and political or military acts. Politics is an explicit expression of the divine will, and war is holy. Supreme authority in both religious and political matters lies in either a lay ruler (caesaropapism) or clergy, priests, or other religious officials (theocracy).

Historically, caesaropapism is identified with the Christian rulers of the Roman Empire (313–395) and the Byzantine Empire (330–1453; Walker 1959). Today, theocracy is best exemplified within Islam, whose founder, Muhammad (570–632), was both the secular and religious leader of his followers. His cultural legacy, normative Islam, makes no distinction, in principle, between the political and religious institutions of a society (Cragg and Speight 1988). The Republic of Iran is a contemporary example of a theocracy where Islamic law and ethics are established and public officials tend to be religiously qualified persons (Akhavi 1986).

While the theocratic/caesaropapist model is usually found where a single religious ideology dominates, the form of the model may also apply in the case of dominant secular ideologies. Thus, under communism as advocated by Lenin, no distinction was made between a political and an ideological ("religious") act. Positions of power were occupied by Communist party members, and, in principle, there were no ideological differences across the institutional sectors of a society or between those in responsible positions. One had to be ideologically qualified in order to occupy an office (Tucker 1975).

Unlike theocracy or caesaropapism, the two-powers model assumes the differentiation of religious and political action and the distinct authority of both secular rulers and religious functionaries in their respective domains of action. The origin of the model can be traced to the exile of the ancient Hebrews in Babylon following the conquest of the Kingdom of Judah in the sixth century B.C. (Zeitlin 1984). There, under foreign domination, religious observance was adapted and elaborated without the support of a Hebrew state and in the absence of worship in the Temple. The idea that religion could be independent of protective state power entered history. Following a strand of its Hebrew roots, early Christianity recognized the authority of the state while asserting the autonomy of its own spiritual sphere of action, a notion summed up in the saying attributed to Jesus: "Render therefore to Caesar the things that are Caesar's and to God the things that are God's." Although Christianity became the official religion of the Roman Empire in the fourth century under Constantine the Great, the Western Christian notion of separate spiritual and temporal realms of power expressed in distinct but complementary organizational milieux persisted and proved to be a basis for accommodation and conflict throughout European history (Walker 1959).

Under the two-powers model the religious and political spheres have separate and, in principle, equal standing in a society. A common arrangement is church establishment where the state recognizes the preeminence of a particular religious tradition and grants a religious monopoly and material support in return for the recognition of its authority and legitimacy by the established religion. In that circumstance jurisdictional conflicts over control of resources and authority can arise. Where the state enforces a religious monopoly, religiously based conflict and politics is likely to involve matters related to dissent from the established religion.

In contrast to both the theocratic/caesaropapist and two-powers models, the model of strict separation eliminates all ties between religious and political institutions. The model can be traced to the Anabaptist movement in sixteenth-century Europe, which viewed the church as a community of the redeemed and the state as an institution with no competence in matters of faith and conscience (Littel 1958). Church and state operate with distinct and different interpretive modes and logics and do not exchange resources. Religious adherence is voluntary, and legal barriers may be erected to prevent one sector from intruding on the other. Where the strict-separation model holds, religious belief and practice may become a private, individual matter without reference to arenas of public action (Luckmann 1967; Neuhaus 1984). In that circumstance religiously inspired politics is likely to involve conflict over church–state boundaries and safeguards that protect religious freedom.

In modernized nation-states elements from the three models may be mixed together. Thus, features of both the two-powers and strict-separation models are found in Western nation-states where an established church exists—Sweden and the United Kingdom, for example—and the voluntary principle of membership is recognized through official toleration of all religions (Martin 1978). No effective limitations are placed on religious freedom. Modern Japan combines elements of a modified theocratic/caesaropapist model with the strict-separation model. Although he is no longer revered as a divine ruler, the emperor of Japan is honored as the symbolically dominant spirit of the nation in a society where eclectic patterns of religious observance are not unusual and no formal or legal constraints are placed on religious practice (Kitagawa 1987).

The institutional arrangements in a nation-state underwrite preferred modes of patterned action. Those arrangements receive empirical specificity in social organization where action is realized. The state–society relationship is the most important social feature affecting the form and expression of religion in the public arena.

While nation-states are formally similar (all are units with sovereign territorial jurisdiction and a governing apparatus), there is considerable variation in the state–society relationship. Civil society—a sector of public action separate from the domains of the state and the church—developed in the West in the eighteenth century (Poggi 1978). The extent to which civil society is a source of authoritative action, however, is not uniform across nation-states (Swanson 1967; 1971).

Where private interests have no public significance or legitimacy or are proscribed as a basis for action, the state does not (or will not) factor those interests into its actions. The one-party states of Eastern Europe that arose in the aftermath of World War II exemplified that pattern. All public actions were, in principle, the actions of agents of the state, and no public legitimacy was accorded actions not explicitly defined by the state as legitimate. In Poland, Czechoslovakia, and Hungary the Roman Catholic church played an important role in democratizing those countries by supporting and promoting the emergence of civil society as a source of action and meaning independent of the state (Michel 1990).

Where civil society is a source of authoritative action, organized private interests can penetrate the state. The party politics of stable Western democracies exemplify that pattern. Religious interests may be expressed in the normal course of politics (Clark 1945). If religious differences are highly correlated with other differences in a population, such as language, patterns of settlement, and so forth, it is likely that religiously based political parties will be among those contesting the right to govern a nation-state, as in the Netherlands and Switzerland (McRae 1974). If religious differences are not highly correlated with many other significant cleavages in a population, then major national political parties will not be organized around religious traditions. The United States is a case in point. There, religious interest groups enter the arena of party politics on an ad hoc basis, but the major parties are not organized around religious or well-defined and articulated ideological traditions as some parties are, for example, in Germany (Martin 1978).

While religion may affect the internal politics of nation-states under the conditions outlined above, it is also the case that religion can be implicated in conflicts between nation-states or between nationalities within states. Such conflicts now occur in a world made into a single place by technological, economic, and social developments (Meyer 1980; Wallerstein 1983; Robertson and Chirico 1985). Increasingly, what is done in one locale can have significant effects on what happens elsewhere in the world within a short time span and despite great geographic distances, national boundaries, and differences in language, culture, local political traditions, and economic development. In that circumstance, communications media construct a global arena of events where the identities of nation-states and nationalities are at stake.

In the global arena religion may be an ingredient in the formation and projection of a national identity. Some nations project an identity that is founded on religion, for example, Iran. In other cases, groups or movements may seek to redefine the image of a nation-state in terms of a religious or ideological tradition (Liebman and Wuthnow 1983; Liebman and Don-Yehiya 1984). Some nation-states project an explicitly secular image (France) or an atheistic image (Albania).

The images that nations or contending groups within nations project into the global arena either coincide or are in conflict with an emergent set of global cultural norms that have a structural base in various transnational cultural, scientific, and educational organizations and in such bodies as the United Nations. Global cultural norms include: (1) respect for the principle of national sovereignty and self-determination; (2) respect for human rights; (3) adherence to the notion that the nation-state should be progressive in its orientation to its citizens and underwrite and promote their economic and social welfare; (4) respect for the environment; (5) the recognition of science as the universal mode of knowledge construction (Thomas and Meyer 1984).

The norms of global culture are invoked in the arena of global events, where they may be reinforced or contradicted and opposed by religious groups following the doctrines and ethics of their traditions. If nation-states or nationalities project and defend an image based on religious absolutes, conflict with the norms of global culture and other religious traditions is inevitable. Whether such conflicts rise to the level of armed aggression between nation-states or groups within nation states depends on many contingencies including the economic, political, and military capacity to wage war in a given circumstance. Whatever the case, the potency of religion as a factor in national identity formation underscores its importance as one enduring source of conflict in the global arena (Swatos 1989).

(SEE ALSO: *Global Systems Analysis; Social Aspects of World Religions; Sociology of Religion; War*)

REFERENCES

Akhavi, Shahrough 1986 "State Formation and Consolidation in Twentieth-Century Iran: The Reza Shah Period and the Islamic Republic." In A. Banuazizi and M. Weiner, eds., *The State, Religion, and Ethnic Politics: Afghanistan, Iran, and Pakistan*. Syracuse, N.Y.: Syracuse University Press.

Clark, S. D. 1945 "The Religious Sect in Canadian Politics." *American Journal of Sociology* 51:207–216.

Cragg, Kenneth, and R. Marston Speight 1988 *The House of Islam*. Belmont, Calif.: Wadsworth.

Eversley, David 1989 *Religion and Employment in Northern Ireland*. London: Sage Publications.

Gombrich, Richard F. 1988 *Theravada Buddhism*. London: Routledge Chapman Hall.

Kitagawa, Joseph M. 1987 *On Understanding Japanese Religion*. Princeton, N.J.: Princeton University Press.

Liebman, Charles S., and Eliezer Don-Yehiya 1984 *Religion and Politics in Israel*. Bloomington: Indiana University Press.

Liebman, Robert C., and Robert Wuthnow 1983 *The New Christian Right*. New York: Aldine.

Lipset, Seymour Martin 1960 *Political Man*. Garden City, N.Y.: Doubleday.

Littel, Franklin H. 1958 *The Anabaptist View of the Church*. Boston: Starr King Press.

Luckmann, Thomas 1967 *The Invisible Religion*. London: Macmillan.

Luhmann, Niklas 1982 *The Differentiation of Society*. New York: Columbia University Press.

Luker, Kristin 1984 *Abortion and the Politics of Motherhood*. Berkeley: University of California Press.

Martin, David 1978 *A General Theory of Secularization*. New York: Harper and Row.

McRae, Kenneth D., ed. 1974 *Consociational Democracy*. Toronto: McClelland and Stewart.

Meyer, John W. 1980 "The World Polity and the Authority of the Nation-State." In A. J. Bergesen, ed., *Studies of the Modern World-System*. New York: Academic Press.

Michel, Patrick 1990 *Politics and Religion in Eastern Europe*. Cambridge, England: Polity Press.

Nettl, J. P., and Roland Robertson 1968 *International Systems and the Modernization of Societies*. New York: Basic Books.

Neuhaus, Richard John 1984 *The Naked Public Square: Religion and Democracy in America*. Grand Rapids, Mich.: Eerdmans.

O'Toole, Roger 1977 *The Precipitous Path*. Toronto: Martin.

Poggi, Gianfranco 1978 *The Development of the Modern State*. Stanford, Calif.: Stanford University Press.

——— 1983 *Calvinism and the Capitalist Spirit*. Amherst: University of Massachusetts Press.

Poloma, Margaret M. 1989 *The Assemblies of God at the Crossroads*. Knoxville: University of Tennessee Press.

Robertson, Roland, and JoAnn Chirico 1985 "Humanity, Globalization, and Worldwide Religious Resurgence." *Sociological Analysis* 46:219–242.

Roof, Wade Clark, and William McKinney 1987 *American Mainline Religion*. New Brunswick, N.J.: Rutgers University Press.

Simpson, John H. 1983 "Moral Issues and Status Politics." In Robert C. Liebman and Robert Wuthnow, eds., *The New Christian Right*. New York: Aldine.

Stroup, Herbert H. 1945 *The Jehovah's Witnesses*. New York: Columbia University Press.

Swanson, Guy E. 1967 *Religion and Regime*. Ann Arbor: University of Michigan Press.

——— 1971 "An Organizational Analysis of Collectivities." *American Sociological Review* 36:607–623.

Swatos, William H., Jr., ed. 1989 *Religious Politics in Global and Comparative Perspective*. Westport, Conn.: Greenwood Press.

Thomas, George M., and John W. Meyer 1984 "The Expansion of the State." In R. H. Turner and J. F. Short, Jr., eds., *Annual Review of Sociology*. Vol. 10. Palo Alto, Calif.: Annual Reviews.

Tucker, Robert, ed. 1975 *The Lenin Anthology*. New York: W. W. Norton.

Walker, Williston 1959 *A History of the Christian Church*. New York: Charles Scribner's Sons.

Wallerstein, Immanuel 1983 *Historical Capitalism*. London: Verso.

Zeitlin, Irving M. 1984 *Ancient Judaism*. Cambridge, England: Polity Press.

JOHN H. SIMPSON

RELIGIOUS FUNDAMENTALISM

Fundamentalism has four distinct meanings. These different meanings are often intermingled in both mass media and scholarly usage, with the result of considerable confusion and misunderstanding of the phenomenon. Significant theological (Barr 1977; Sandeen 1970) and historical (Marsden 1980) literatures are available on fundamentalism, but neither a theoretical nor an empirical sociological literature is well developed. This article identifies the four distinct meanings of fundamentalism, locates each in historical context, and then concludes with a brief discussion of the utility of the concept for comparative sociological research.

First, fundamentalism refers to a Christian *theological* movement that experienced its greatest strength in the first quarter of the twentieth century; it was concerned with defending the faith against an internal movement seeking to make changes to accommodate Protestant Christianity to the modern world. As a theological movement, fundamentalism sought to purge the teachings of "modernism" from churches and theological schools. Modernist teachings emerged during the late nineteenth century as a means of accommodating Christian doctrine to the evidence and teachings of science (Hutchinson 1976).

The most basic teaching of fundamentalism is that the scriptures are inerrant—that is, literally true (Scofield 1945). Closely related is the doctrine of *millenarianism,* which prophesies the imminent return of Christ. In the early days of the fundamentalist movement, these theological battles were waged in the leading theological seminaries of the nation (e.g., Princeton Theological Seminary).

An important development in this struggle was the publication, between 1910 and 1915, of a series of twelve books that sought to defend and reaffirm "fundamental" Christian principles in the face of the teachings of liberal scholars who did not believe that the Bible should be understood as literal truth. Leading scholars from the United States and England contributed articles to the books, titled *The Fundamentals.* Published by two wealthy Christian brothers, Lyman and Milton Steward, *The Fundamentals* were distributed gratis to over a quarter-million clergy, seminary students, and teachers throughout the United States. These tracts provided the inspiration for the name of the movement, but the term *fundamentalism* was not coined until 1920 by a Baptist newspaper editor, Curtis Lee Laws (Marsden 1980, p. 159).

Defense of the faith against the encroachment of modernist theological teachings was at the core of the fundamentalist movement. But fundamentalism was profoundly influenced by the *holiness* movement, which was just as concerned with correct behavior as fundamentalism was with correct belief. The personal piety and renunciation of "worldly" vices of the holiness movement was combined with the combative spirit of theological fundamentalism to produce a *political fundamentalism,* the second distinct kind of fundamentalism.

The first wave of political fundamentalism was a short-lived but vigorous conservative movement with several agendas, including temperance and anticommunism. The critical and ultimately fatal crusade of the fundamentalist movement occurred in the arena of public education policy. Charles Darwin's theory of evolution, which had gained popularity among scientists and teachers, was clearly incompatible with a literal reading of the Bible. Among other incompatible passages, the Genesis story of creation in the Bible states that the earth and all that dwells therein were created in six days. The fundamentalists launched a campaign to prohibit the teaching of Darwinism in public schools, a campaign that initially met with considerable success.

The struggle came to a climax in 1925 in one of the most celebrated trials of the twentieth century. John Scopes, a substitute biology teacher, was charged with violating a Tennessee state law that prohibited the teaching of evolution. Dubbed "the Monkey Trial," this epochal event drew two of America's greatest trial lawyers to the tiny town of Dayton, Tennessee. For the prosecution was William Jennings Bryan, brilliant orator, three times presidential nominee of the Democratic Party, and the unchallenged leader of the fundamentalist political movement. Scopes was defended by Clarence Darrow, a bitter foe of organized religion who was believed by many to be the outstanding trial lawyer in the nation (Stone 1941). Darrow gained prominence as a defender of labor unions and in litigation against monopolistic corporations.

The highlight of the trial came when, in a surprise move, Darrow called Bryan as a witness. While Bryan claimed to have been a scholar of the Bible for fifty years, his ability to defend some of the finer points and implications of fundamentalist theology proved wanting. In the end, his testimony was a debacle for the prosecution. George Marsden, the premier historian of fundamentalism, described the scene thus: "Bryan did not know how Eve could be created from Adam's rib, where Cain got his wife, or where the great fish came from that swallowed Jonah. He said that he had never contemplated what would happen if the earth stopped its rotation so that the sun would 'stand still' "(Marsden 1980, p. 186).

The trial was quintessentially a confrontation between the emerging modern world and the forces of traditionalism. The drama was played out on the turf of traditionalism—a sleepy, small town in Tennessee—but it was communicated to the world by journalists who were sages of the new modern order. The fundamentalists were portrayed as fossilized relics from an era long past. Darrow himself portrayed the trial as a struggle of modern liberal culture against "bigots and ignoramuses" (Marsden 1980, p. 187). John Scopes was convicted, but that fact seemed inconsequential. The forces of modernity and tradition had met face to face, and modernity triumphed. William Jennings Bryan collapsed and died a few days after the trial without ever leaving Dayton, Tennessee. In popular myth, Bryan died of a broken heart. Bryan had planned a national campaign to compel schools across the nation to teach evolution as a theory, not a scientific fact (Stone 1941, p. 464). There was no one else of Bryan's stature to pick up the cause. The first wave of political fundamentalism died when Bryan was unable to defend its theological underpinnings.

The third distinct meaning of fundamentalism emerges from a melding of the two movements to create a popular caricature of small-town Americans as culturally unenlightened religious fanatics. H. L. Mencken (1919–1927) and Sinclair Lewis (1927), writing in the second and third decades of this century, set the tone and style of a genre of lambasting literature that subsequent generations of writers have admired and sought to emulate. Fundamentalists were portrayed as backwater fools preyed on by hypocritical evangelists, but most certainly a withering species destined to disappear from the modern world. They could be meddlesome and annoying, but they were not viewed as politically dangerous. In time they would most certainly die off, even in the rural hinterlands of America.

The Scopes trial clearly marked the demise of the first wave of political fundamentalism. Fundamentalists in the major Protestant denominations did lose ground to the modernists, but biblical fundamentalism did not so much wane as it passed from high public visibility. A number of leaders bolted from mainline Protestant churches and formed new denominations and seminaries. But out of the limelight of the press and mainstream culture, fundamentalism did not wither as had been forecast. Rather, it continued to grow, particularly in the Midwest and South (Carpenter 1984a). Fundamentalists also were schism-prone, so that none of the scores of groups developed into large new denominations, such as occurred with the Baptists and Methodists in the nineteenth century (Finke and Stark forthcoming). This, too, served to diminish the fundamentalists' visibility.

An important development occurred during the 1940s when fundamentalism effectively divided into two camps. The first, which was more insular and combative toward the larger culture, joined with Carl McIntire to create the American Council of Christian Churches (ACCC). McIntire was militantly antimodernist, and he viewed the ACCC as an instrument for doing battle with the liberal Federal Council of Churches (FCC), which in 1950 became the National Council of Churches. There was yet another large contingent of fundamentalists who were neither with the militant McIntire contingent nor the modernist tradition aligned with the FCC. In 1942 this second group of fundamentalists founded the National Association of Evangelicals (NAE). Theologically the NAE might have considered themselves neo-fundamentalists, but they recognized the negative cultural stereotype associated with fundamentalism. The use of the term *evangelical* was a reappropriation of a term that most Protestant groups used to describe themselves before the modernist-fundamentalist schism. It was more respectable and, clearly, the members of the NAE wanted to put some distance between themselves and other fundamentalists who had joined forces with Carl McIntire. But theologically the NEA was not much different from the fundamentalist movement of the early part of the century (Marsden 1987).

Publicly NAE leaders stressed their desire to emphasize the positive aspects of their beliefs in contrast to the highly negative and combative posture of the ACCC toward both theological modernism and political liberalism (Carpenter 1984b, p. 12). Some of the leaders of the NAE later admitted that the reappropriation of the name "evangelical" was a strategy to escape the negative cultural stereotypes against fundamentalism. Whether a self-conscious strategy or not, the label "evangelical" has served to mainstream millions of Christians whose theological beliefs are hardly discernible from those who are identified as fundamentalists. Billy Graham, perhaps the most respected religious leader of the second half of the twentieth century, is considered an evangelical. Theologically speaking, his basic beliefs are virtually indistinguishable from those of fundamentalist Jerry Falwell or the leadership of the Southern Baptist Convention, which staged a takeover of the Southern Baptist denomination during the 1980s.

Notwithstanding an underlying core of basic beliefs, fundamentalism in the United States is highly varied in terms of social organization, nuances of belief, and social class backgrounds. To the general public, however, fundamentalists are known in terms of the caricature that is the legacy of the Scopes trial debacle—people who are narrow-minded, bigoted toward persons different from their own kind, obscurantist, sectarian, and hostile to the modern world. The mass media dredge up enough examples of people exhibiting these traits to keep the stereotype alive (Hadden and Shupe 1990).

From the 1930s forward there have been periodic flurries of right-wing political activity led by preachers and laypersons who have been labeled fundamentalists. During the Depression William Dudley Pelley, Gerald B. Winrod, and Gerald L. K. Smith led movements that blended religion with anti-Semitism (Ribuffo 1983). For many decades from the 1940s forward, Carl McIntire was a strident anti-Catholic propagandist. Frederick C. Schwarz, Billy James Hargis, and Edgar Bundy were among the most visible anticommunist crusaders of the post–World War II era (Forster and Epstein 1964). Liberal political pundits and scholars have always viewed these groups with mixed feelings. Some have unequivocally looked on them with great alarm (e.g. Clabaugh 1974), and that sense of alarm has always been greatest during periods when their movements were highly visible. Outside of periods of high visibility, the general consensus of scholars is that the fundamentalist right embodies doctrines and attracts an element that is on the fringe of the mainstream of American politics. While perhaps repugnant to the liberal ethos, they have not been widely perceived as a serious threat to democratic institutions.

In 1979 Jerry Falwell, a fundamentalist television preacher, founded a political organization named the Moral Majority. Initially the media paid little attention, but when Falwell and his fellow right-wing fundamentalists organized to help elect presidential candidate Ronald Reagan, interest picked up. When Reagan reached out and embraced the fundamentalists, attention escalated (Hadden and Swann 1981, pp. 130–133). Following the Reagan victory, along with the defeat of several ranking senators and congressmen, Falwell claimed responsibility. Pollster Lou Harris agreed that the fundamentalist vote was the margin of victory for Reagan. Postelection analysis did not support this claim (Hadden and Swann 1981), but the high media profile of Falwell and his fellow televangelists give fundamentalism its highest public profile since the 1920s.

This most recent wave of concern about the political power of fundamentalists might have blown over quickly were it not for the timing of this development with the rise of the Islamic imam Ayatollah Khomeini, who led a revolution that deposed the shah of Iran; shortly thereafter, Khomeini's followers held sixty-two Americans hostage for fourteen months. Political analysts concerned with the power of the fundamentalists in America were soon comparing the religious right in America with the followers of Ayatollah Khomeini and other radical Muslim factions in the Middle East. From these comparisons was born the concept "Islamic fundamentalism." This linkage was quickly followed by the labeling of selected politically active religious groups around the world as "fundamentalist."

Thus was born the concept *global fundamentalism,* the fourth distinct meaning of fundamentalism. During the 1980s the idea of global fundamentalism became widely accepted by the mass media and scholars alike. But like previous uses of the term, global fundamentalism has suffered from lack of systematic conceptualization and consistent application. The global application of the concept thus has many of the same underlying presuppositions of the popular caricature of fundamentalism in U.S. Protestantism. It is an uncomplimentary epithet for religious groups that are viewed as out of sync with the modern world. Fundamentalism, whether the American variety or of some other culture and faith, is characterized by blind adherence to a religious dogma or leader and zealous rejection of the modern world. It is also widely assumed that fundamentalists are contemptuous of democratic institutions.

Inconsistencies in the application of the concept were readily available. Perhaps this is nowhere so apparent as with discussions of the Afghan Muslim guerrillas who fought the Soviet army to a standoff during the 1980s. Both theologically and politically the Afghan rebels were unmistakably Islamic fundamentalists, but they were almost never so identified in the Western press. Rather, these Afghans are almost always referred to as the *mujaheddin,* usually with positive references such as courage, bravery, and freedom fighters. But seldom did anyone mention that *mujaheddin* means, literally, one who fights a *jihad* or holy war. This and other instances of inconsistent application suggest that the concept of fundamentalism is reserved for religious zealots who are disapproved.

In sum, both popular and scholarly use of the concept of fundamentalism during the twentieth century has had a strong ideological bias. This bias has carried over to the creation of the notion of global fundamentalism. Given this history, it might be proposed that fundamentalism has not been a concept of great utility for sociological analysis and thus its use should be discouraged. In support of this proposition can be added the observation that social scientists have not developed any instruments that have been widely used to measure fundamentalism. Such a proposal may be premature.

Even though popular use of the concept of global fundamentalism had tended to connote the same stereotypical content as the term has conveyed when applied to Protestant fundamentalists in the United States, the suggestion that the phenomenon might exist across cultures and world religions invites comparative analysis that was lacking when the concept was restricted to American Protestantism. By the late 1980s serious comparative analysis of fundamentalism had begun (e.g., Caplan 1987; Lawrence 1989).

Comparative sociological inquiry suggests that the characterization of fundamentalism as an unenlightened backwater form of resistance to modernization involves a misplaced emphasis. The forces of tradition have always resisted innovation. Bruce Lawrence, along with others, argues that fundamentalism is a product of modernity and thus is a phenomenon that did not exist prior to modernity, and "because modernity is global, so is fundamentalism" (Lawrence 1989, p. 3). In a similar argument, Anson Shupe and Jeffrey K. Hadden contend that "fundamentalism is a truly modern phenomenon—modern in the sense that the movement is always seeking original solutions to new, pressing problems" (Shupe and Hadden 1989, p. 112). Shupe and Hadden note that *secularization,* the cognitive counterpart to modernization, has progressively compartmentalized religion from and defined it as irrelevant to other institutional spheres. Fundamentalism may be viewed as a proclamation of reclaimed authority of a sacred tradition that is to be reinstated as an antidote for a society that has strayed from its cultural moorings. Sociologically speaking, fundamentalism involves (1) a refutation of the radical differentiation of the sacred and the secular that has evolved with modernization, and (2) a plan to dedifferentiate this institutional bifurcation and thus bring religion back to center stage as an important factor of interest in public policy decisions.

So conceived, fundamentalism is not antimodern. Fundamentalists, for example, are typically not against the use of modern technology, but rather certain applications of it. Further, they have proven themselves to be particularly adept at utilizing technology, particular communications technology, to their own ends. From the invention of radio to the development of syndicated television broadcasting, fundamentalists have dominated the use of the airwaves for religious broadcasting in the United States. They have also succeeded in developing a significant global presence. In terms of sheer volume, the four major international religious broadcasting organizations transmit more hours per week in more languages than the BBC, Radio Moscow, and the Voice of America together (Hadden 1990, p. 162).

Fundamentalism is clearly an assault on the cognitive components of modernization. Insofar as the process of modernization is not globally uniform, the development of fundamentalism may be expected to manifest a different character in different cultures. The most ambitious comparative study of fundamentalism to date was launched in 1987 by the American Academy of Arts and Sciences with a substantial grant from the John D. and Catherine T. MacArthur Foundation. Over a period of five years the Fundamentalism Project brought together scholars of religion from around the world to prepare studies of groups that have been identified as fundamentalist. This project has encouraged a large number of scholars to study the phenomenon seriously. In addition, the published papers from the project will provide a rich source of original studies for comparative and synthesizing work (Marty and Appleby 1991).

(SEE ALSO: *Religious Movement; Sociology of Religion*)

REFERENCES

Barr, James 1977 *Fundamentalism.* Philadelphia: Westminster Press.

Caplan, Lionel, ed. 1987 *Studies in Religious Fundamentalism.* Albany: State University of New York Press.

Carpenter, Joel A. 1984a "The Renewal of American Fundamentalism, 1930–1945," Baltimore: Ph.D. diss., The Johns Hopkins University.

——— 1984b "From Fundamentalism to the New Evangelical Coalition." In George Marsden, ed., *Evangelicalism and Modern America.* Grand Rapids, Mich.: Eerdmans.

Clabaugh, Gary K. 1974 *Thunder on the Right: The Protestant Fundamentalists.* Chicago: Nelson-Hall.

Finke, Roger, and Rodney Stark (Forthcoming) *The Churching of America: 1776–1990.* New Brunswick, N.J.: Rutgers University Press.

Forster, Arnold, and Benjamin R. Epstein 1964 *Danger on the Right.* New York: Random House.

Hadden, Jeffrey K. 1990 "Precursors to the Globalization of American Televangelism." *Social Compass* 37:161–167.

———, and Anson Shupe 1990 "Elmer Gantry: Exemplar of American Televangelism." In Robert Abelman and Stewart M. Hoover, eds., *Religious Television: Controversies and Conclusions.* Norwood, N.J.: Ablex.

———, and Charles E. Swann 1981 *Prime Time Preachers.* Reading, Mass.: Addison-Wesley.

Hutchinson, William R. 1976 *The Modernist Impulse in American Protestantism.* Cambridge, Mass.: Harvard University Press.

Lawrence, Bruce B. 1989 *Defenders of God.* San Francisco: Harper and Row.

Lewis, Sinclair 1927 *Elmer Gantry.* New York: Harcourt, Brace.

Marsden, George M. 1980 *Fundamentalism and American Culture.* New York: Oxford University Press.
——— 1987 *Reforming Fundamentalism.* Grand Rapids, Mich.: Eerdmans.
Marty, Martin E., and R. Scott Appleby (eds.) 1991 *Fundamentalism Observed.* The Fundamentalism Project, vol. 1. Chicago: University of Chicago Press.
Mencken, Henry Louis 1919–1927 *Prejudices,* 6 vols. New York: Alfred A. Knopf.
Ribuffo, Leo P. 1983 *The Old Christian Right.* Philadelphia: Temple University Press.
Sandeen, Ernest R. 1970 *The Roots of Fundamentalism: British and American Millenarianism 1800–1930.* Chicago: University of Chicago Press.
Scofield, Cyrus Ingerson 1945 *The Scofield Reference Bible.* New York: Oxford University Press.
Shupe, Anson, and Jeffrey K. Hadden 1989 "Is There Such a Thing as Global Fundamentalism?" In Jeffrey K. Hadden and Anson Shupe, eds., *Secularization and Fundamentalism Reconsidered.* Religion and the Political Order, vol. 3. New York: Paragon House.
Stone, Irving 1941 *Clarence Darrow for the Defense.* Garden City, N.Y.: Doubleday, Doran.

JEFFREY K. HADDEN

RELIGIOUS MOVEMENTS Most people do not perceive of religious beliefs as changing very much over the centuries. Religions, after all, are engaged in the propagation of eternal truths. And whereas religious organizations may change, that process is perceived to occur only very slowly.

Contrary to these popular perceptions, both religious beliefs and religious organizations are dynamic, ever-changing phenomena. Changes in the beliefs and structure of religions reflect adaptations, accommodations, and innovations to continuously changing cultural, political, and economic environments. Without more or less constant change, religions become irrelevant to their environments and simply become defunct.

Some changes in religious organizations occur as the result of decisions by leaders empowered to do so. Some changes in beliefs occur so slowly that adherents and leaders alike hardly notice. But much change occurs as the result of movements. *Religious movements* may be understood as a subcategory of *social movements*—that is, organized efforts to cause or prevent change. There are three discrete types or categories of religious movements. First, *endogenous religious movements* constitute efforts to change the internal character of the religion. Second, *exogenous religious movements* attempt to alter the environment in which the religion resides. Third, *generative religious movements* seek to introduce new religions into the culture or environment.

Religions consist of beliefs, symbols, practices, and organizations. *Endogenous movements* seek to change one or more of these aspects of a religion (Stark and Bainbridge 1985, p. 23). Some endogenous movements have had monumental impact on both history and culture—for example, the great schism that split Christianity into Western Catholicism and Eastern Orthodoxy in the eleventh century; and the Reformation, which developed in the sixteenth century and which split Protestantism from Roman Catholicism. Other movements, while important to the participants, have been of little cultural significance.

Endogenous movements frequently result in a schism—the division of the religious organization into two or more independent parts (Stark and Bainbridge 1987, p. 128). Protestantism has been particularly schism-prone. J. Gordon Melton (1989) has identified more than 750 Protestant groups in North America alone. New religious groups formed through the process of schism are known as *sects.* Sectarian movements tend to be led by laity or lower-echelon clergy. Many religious movements result in reform rather than schism. Reform is a more likely outcome when movements are initiated by the religious leaders, or when the religious hierarchy responds to and co-opts grassroots demands for change.

The Second Vatican Council (1962–1965) was called by Pope John XXIII in response to strong internal pressures to modernize the Roman Catholic Church and improve relations with other faiths. The Council produced many wide-sweeping changes in the Catholic church. In addition, it spawned many other religious movements within the Catholic church (e.g., liberation theology, the women's ordination movement, and movements for greater lay participation). A second important hierarchically initiated movement of the twentieth century was the Protestant ecumenical movement. After several centuries of denominational proliferation, the second half of the twentieth century has witnessed a powerful ecumenical movement that has resulted in the union of diverse Protestant traditions.

Exogenous movements constitute a second general type of religious movement. They are concerned with changing some aspect of the environment in which a religious organization exists. Religious organizations bring to the environments in which they exist the interests of (1) survival; (2) economics; (3) status; and (4) ideology (Hadden 1980). As long as these interests are secure, the religious organization may be said to exist in equilibrium or harmony with its environment. But when any of these interests are threatened, or the leadership of the religious organization seeks to enhance or expand its interests, religious movements may ensue. Often, exogenous religious movements are indistinguishable from social movements and, indeed, are frequently pursued in coalition with secular social movement organizations.

The very essence of religious organizations is that they carry cultural values, ideals, customs, and laws that claim transcendental character. When religious leaders engage in exogenous religious movements, they almost always draw on these transcendental principles to legitimate their cause. The claim that movement objectives are part of a divine plan, or that God is on the side of the movement, may serve as a powerful motivation for adherents of the faith to participate. Witness, for example, the many occasions during the 1980s when Islamic leaders exhorted their followers to engage in *jihad* (holy war).

In addition to legitimating religious movements with transcendental principles, religious leaders are often enlisted by secular social movement leaders to legitimate their movements. As a general proposition, religious leaders are specialists in the legitimation of social movement causes.

The civil-rights movement in the United States was substantially a religious movement. It was led by black ministers, activities were organized in black churches, funds were raised in liberal white churches, white clergy bolstered the troops who marched and picketed, and idealistic black and white youth—motivated by their religious traditions—participated in civil-rights campaigns and projects. The strength of the movement came not only from the broad base of religious participation but also from the ability of the leaders to legitimate the movement constantly in terms of sacred religious principles. For example, civil-rights leaders repeatedly quoted the passage in the Declaration of Independence that acknowledges the role of the Creator in human rights: "We hold these Truths to be self-evident, that all Men are created equal, that they are endowed by their Creator with certain unalienable Rights, that among these are Life, Liberty, and the Pursuit of Happiness . . ."

The Solidarity labor movement in Poland, which was the first major social movement that led to the collapse of communism in Eastern Europe, sought and received legitimacy from the Catholic church. Not only in Poland but also throughout Eastern Europe, religious traditions were deeply involved in the movement for liberation from communism (Echikson 1990).

Not all exogenous religious movements are movements of liberation. Around the globe religious groups call on divine providence to help them in struggles against other religions, ethnic rivals, and unsympathetic governments.

There are literally hundreds of these movements around the globe in various stages of ascendancy or abatement. In predominantly Hindu India, Muslims in the northern province of Kashmir seek independence or union with Pakistan, while Sikhs in the nearby province of Punjab have for many years waged a bloody confrontation with the government for independence. In Sri Lanka, just off India's southern shores, Tamils, members of a Hindu sect, seek an independent state in a nation that is predominantly Buddhist. In Northern Ireland, Protestants and Catholics have experienced periodic conflict since Protestant settlers arrived in the middle of the seventeenth century, but since 1968 the two rivals have been locked in a high level of tension punctuated with intermittent outbursts of violence (Bruce 1986, p. 412).

The third type of religious movement is *generative*—a deliberate effort to produce a new religious movement. New religions are introduced to a culture either externally by missionaries or are products of innovation (invention) by members of the culture. Whereas schismatic movements produce variations on an existing religion within a culture, new religions are novel to the host culture (Stark and Bainbridge 1987, p. 157). Sociological scholars refer to these new religions as *cults.*

New religions are not necessarily newly created. Hare Krishnas, adorned in saffron robes and chanting on street corners, first appeared in the United States during the mid-1960s. The Krishnas brought Hindu beliefs and practices that were clearly novel to North America, but they were first practiced in India in the sixteenth century (Rochford 1985, p. 11). In contrast, the Reverend Sun Myung Moon, a Korean and founder of the Unification Church, created a religion that involved a blending of significantly reconstructed Christian beliefs along with important elements of eastern religions. In still another example, L. Ron Hubbard, a science fiction writer, published a book in 1950 titled *Dianetics,* which outlined psychotherapeutic or mental-health techniques. The book became a best seller, and in 1954 Hubbard founded the Church of Scientology.

In these three groups we have examples of the importation of an old religion based on sacred texts of Hinduism (Hare Krishnaism), a newly created religion based on reported revelation from the God of the monotheistic traditions of Judaism and Christianity (Unificationism), as well as an indigenous religion based on techniques of modern psychotherapy (Scientology). All are new and novel to North American culture.

The late 1960s and early 1970s produced a flurry of new religious movements in the United States. The youth counterculture of the 1960s provided a receptive environment for new religions. Equally important, the repeal of the Oriental Exclusion Acts in 1965 paved the way for many Eastern gurus to come to the United States as missionaries of their faiths (Melton and Moore 1982, p. 9). While not nearly as extensive, this activity can be compared to that of the Christian missionaries who flocked to Africa and Asia during the late nineteenth and early twentieth centuries to seek converts to their faith.

This period of rapid cult formation was not particularly unique. The nineteenth century, for example, produced a large number of cults and sectarian movements in the United States. Christian Science, Mormonism, Seventh-day Adventism, the Jehovah's Witness movement, and Theosophy are but a few examples of groups emerging in that time frame that remain viable in the late twentieth century.

Significant social-science literature exists on all three types of religious movements: endogenous, exogenous, and generative. The focus of inquiry has shifted significantly over time, and the discipline of the investigators has influenced the selection of questions addressed.

During the formative years of sociology much attention was devoted to discerning how new religions arise and evolve (Glock 1973, pp. 207–208). Max Weber (1958) and Ernst Troeltsch (1960) conceptualized what is known as the "sect-church" theory. Sects develop as a result of dissent within churches, which break away and form sects. Over time, sects institutionalize and gradually become more like the churches they earlier broke from, even as new sects are being formed. H. Richard Niebuhr (1929) postulated that sects recruit disproportionately from "the disinherited" or economically deprived classes. Benton Johnson (1961) argued that sectarian groups socialize their members to the dominant middle-class values of society.

Until the mid-1960s, much of the sociological literature focused on what has here been identified as endogenous movements. Much of this literature concerned questions relating to the formation of religious movements. Most explanations could be classified as theories of (1) deprivation (socioeconomic and other); (2) social dislocation; or (3) socioeconomic change (McGuire 1981, p. 121).

Historical work has focused on exogenous and generative movements, although this literature supports much sociological work that concludes that religions groups emerge on the fringe of society. Norman Cohn's monumental work *The Pursuit of the Millennium* concludes that revolutionary millenarian movements during the eleventh and sixteenth centuries drew their strength from groups on the margin of society. By marginal Cohn means persons who are not just poor but who also have no "recognized place in society [or] regular institutionalized methods of voicing their grievances or pressing their claims" (1970, p. 282).

Anthropological literature focuses on generative movements. The question that has dominated their inquiry was inherited from the evolutionary agenda of Social Darwinism in the late nineteenth century: What are the origins of religion? New religions, they conclude, emerge during periods of rapid social change, disorganization, and dislocation (Hine 1974, p. 646). In anthropological literature, this cultural strain is most often identified as the result of the invasion of an indigenous culture by a militarily advanced culture—the typical pattern of conquest and colonization by European cultures from the late fifteenth century forward.

The new religions are variously identified as "cargo cults," "messianic movements," "nativistic movements," and "revitalization movements." Anthropological literature postulates that new religions emerge as a means of dealing with cultural stress. Weston La Barre (1972) generalizes from the scores of ethnographic studies of anthropologists to locate the origins of all religions in cultural crisis. Vittorio Lanternari, surveying anthropological and historical literature on new religions that emerge as a result of intercultural conflict, concludes that these religions "tend to seek salvation by immediate action through militant struggle or through direct and determined opposition to the foreign forces" (1965, p. 247).

Psychological literature has been much less concerned with religious movements. Following the logic of Sigmund Freud's cultural bias against religion, some psychologists have identified the leaders of religious movements as psychopathological and their followers as psychologically defective. This literature has not been particularly productive of insights about religious movements (see Saliba 1987, pp. xvii–xxxix; Anthony 1990).

The ferment of generative religious movements in the wake of the youth counterculture of the late 1960s stimulated a tremendous volume of sociological inquiry (Bromley and Hadden forthcoming). In terms of sheer volume, research and theorizing about "new religious movements" eclipsed all other subtopics of inquiry in the social scientific study of religion during the 1970s and 1980s. In addition to new conceptual perspectives on how religious groups form (Stark and Bainbridge 1987; Stark 1987), studies have examined (1) the organizational development of new religions (Robbins 1988); (2) the structural and social-psychological dynamics of affiliation (Snow and Machalek 1984) and disaffiliation (Bromley 1988); and (3) the persistence of intragroup conflict between new and established religious traditions (Shupe, Bromley, and Oliver 1984).

(SEE ALSO: *Religious Organizations; Sociology of Religion*)

REFERENCES

Anthony, Dick 1990 "Religious Movements and Brainwashing Litigation." In Thomas Robbins and Dick Anthony, eds., *In Gods We Trust,* 2nd ed. New Brunswick, N.J.: Transaction Books.

Bromley, David G. (ed.) 1988 *Falling from Faith: Causes and Consequences of Religious Apostasy.* Newbury Park, Calif.: Sage.

———, and Jeffrey K. Hadden (eds.) Forthcoming *Handbook of Cults and Sects in America,* 2 vols. Greewich, Conn.: JAI Press.

Bruce, Steve 1986 "Protestantism and Politics in Scotland and Ulster." In Jeffrey K. Hadden and Anson Shupe, eds., *Prophetic Religions and Politics.* Religion and the Political Order, vol 1. New York: Paragon House.

Cohn, Norman 1970 *The Pursuit of the Millennium.* New York: Oxford University Press.

Echikson, William 1990 *Lighting The Night: Revolution in Eastern Europe.* New York: William Morrow.

Glock, Charles Y. 1973 "On the Origin and Evolution of Religious Groups." In Charles Y. Glock, ed.,

Religion in Sociological Perspective. Belmont, Calif.: Wadsworth.

Hadden, Jeffrey K. 1980 "Religion and the Construction of Social Problems." *Sociological Analysis* 41: 99–108.

Hine, Virginia H. 1974 "The Deprivation and Disorganization Theories of Social Movements." In Irving I. Zaretsky and Mark P. Leone, eds., *Religious Movements in Contemporary America.* Princeton, N.J.: Princeton University Press.

Johnson, Benton 1961 "Do Holiness Sects Socialize in Dominant Values?" *Social Forces* 39:309–316.

La Barre, Weston 1972 *The Ghost Dance.* New York: Delta.

Lanternari, Vittorio 1965 *The Religions of the Oppressed.* New York: Mentor Books.

McGuire, Meredith B. 1981 *Religion: The Social Context.* Belmont, Calif.: Wadsworth.

Melton, J. Gordon 1989 *The Encyclopedia of American Religions,* 3rd ed. Detroit, Mich.: Gale Research.

Melton, J. Gordon, and Robert L. Moore 1982 *The Cult Experience.* New York: Pilgrim Press.

Niebuhr, H. Richard 1957 *The Social Sources of Denominationalism.* Cleveland, Ohio: Meridian Books.

Robbins, Thomas 1988 *Cults, Converts and Charisma.* Newbury Park, Calif.: Sage.

Rochford, E. Burke, Jr. 1985 *Hare Krishna in America.* New Brunswick, N.J.: Rutgers University Press.

Saliba, John A. 1987 *Psychiatry and the Cults: An Annotated Bibliography.* New York: Garland.

Shupe, Anson D., Jr., David G. Bromley, and Donna L. Oliver 1984 *The Anti-Cult Movement in America.* New York: Garland.

Snow, David A., and Richard Machalek 1984 "The Sociology of Conversion." In Ralph H. Turner and James F. Short, Jr., eds., *Annual Review of Sociology,* vol. 10. Palo Alto, Calif.: Annual Reviews.

Stark, Rodney 1987 "How New Religions Succeed: A Theoretical Model." In David G. Bromley and Phillip E. Hammond, eds., *The Future of New Religious Movements.* Macon, Georgia: Mercer University Press.

———, and William Sims Bainbridge 1985 *The Future of Religion.* Berkeley, Calif.: University of California Press.

———1987 *A Theory of Religion.* New York: Peter Lang.

Troeltsch, Ernst 1960 *The Social Teachings of Christian Churches,* 2 vols. New York: Harper & Row.

Wallace, Anthony F. C. 1966 *Religion: An Anthropological View.* New York: Random House.

Weber, Max 1958 "The Social Psychology of the World's Religions." In H. H. Gerth and C. Wright Mills, eds. and trans., *From Max Weber: Essays in Sociology.* New York: Oxford University Press.

JEFFREY K. HADDEN

RELIGIOUS ORGANIZATIONS The social organization of religion in the United States is diverse and complex. Most religious organizations are local churches (congregations, parishes, synagogues) tied to national religious bodies (usually referred to as denominations). According to the *Yearbook of American and Canadian Churches,* there are almost 350,000 churches in 219 denominations in the United States. The membership reported by these churches equals almost 59 percent of the U.S. population (Jacquet 1989). The largest denominations are the Roman Catholic Church (53,496,862 members in 1988), the Southern Baptist Convention (14,722,617 members), and the United Methodist Church (9,124,575 members). Most denominations are quite small. In all, the twenty-three denominations with membership in excess of one million members account for more than 127,000,000 members—about 90 percent of all church members in the United States. In contrast, the 108 denominations with fewer than 25,000 members account for about 730,000 members, about 0.5 percent of church members (above figures calculated from information in Jacquet 1989).

Local churches typically hold worship services at least once a week and also have educational activities, especially for children and youth. Most churches organize various groups within the church to accomplish particular tasks (for example, missions, evangelism, or community action) or for the association of persons with common interests, for instance, women, youth, or senior citizens. Women's groups are especially active. Moreover, churches often serve as community centers providing space for meetings of all sorts of neighborhood and community organizations.

Local churches usually have a pastor (priest, rabbi) and a lay governing board. There is great variation from denomination to denomination on the authority of lay boards, and, within denominations, there is variation from church to church in informal power. Research has shown that control by inner circles of informal leaders is likely to emerge when formal mechanisms of control and official leaders are not performing effectively (Hougland and Wood 1979).

The degree to which the denomination exercises control over the local church depends in large part upon the polity, or political structure, of the denomination. Students of religious organizations place denominations in three categories according to polity. Congregational polity is the weakest. In this polity the local church owns its own property and hires and fires its own pastor. In contrast, in a hierarchical (often episcopal) polity the national (or regional) body holds title to the property and controls the placement of pastors. An in-between category is often called presbyterial. There are a number of correlates of polity. For example, denominations with strong polities were more active supporters of the civil-rights movement and more aggressively pressed for the integration of their churches (Wood 1981).

Though the organization of Jewish synagogues is similar to that of many Protestant churches, the Jewish perspective on religious organization is somewhat different. In 1987 the officials of the congregational organizations of the Orthodox, Conservative, and Reform branches of Judaism reported 3,750,000 persons associated with their synagogues and temples. However, there are approximately six million Jews in the United States considered an ethnic, social, and religious community (Jacquet 1989, pp. 243–244). Daniel Elazar stresses that Jews see no meaningful line of separation between "churchly" purposes and other communal needs, hence Jewish organizations are not neatly divided into religious and nonreligious ones. "It is *not simply* association with a *synagogue* that enables a Jew to become part of the organized Jewish community. Affiliation with *any of a whole range of organizations,* ranging from clearly philanthropic groups to 'secularist' cultural societies, offers the same option" (Elazar 1980, p. 131). Elazar argues that local Jewish federations for welfare, educational, and cultural activities should be seen as religious organizations (p. 133).

RELIGIOUS ORGANIZATIONS IN SOCIOLOGICAL CONTEXT

Religious organizations provide patterns for the interaction of religious individuals. Social forces change these patterns, but in turn the collective action of religious people influences society. Sociologists looking at religious organizations have been interested especially in their importance as plausibility structures that foster specific beliefs and values (Berger 1967) and as structures of action that mobilize people to seek social change.

Until the 1970s the sociological approach to religious organizations was guided primarily by the church–sect typology. This theoretical framework helped to explain the number and variety of religious bodies and differences in their behaviors by reference to the social class of their adherents. Max Weber distinguished between a church, a continuously operating rational, compulsory association that claims a monopolistic authority, and a sect, "a voluntary association [that] admits only persons with specific religious qualifications" (Weber 1978, p. 56). One becomes a member of the church by birth, but a "sect . . . makes membership conditional upon a contractual entry into some particular congregation" (p. 456). Weber's student, Ernst Troeltsch (1961), developed a typology from these concepts, and some variation of the church–sect typology has been used repeatedly in studying U.S. religious organizations.

In the Weberian tradition, H. Richard Niebuhr stressed the sociological sources of sect formation and the way in which social forces tended to turn sects into churches. He argued that sects originate "in the religious revolts of the poor, of those who were without effective representation in church or state" and who employed a democratic, associational pattern in pursuing their dissent because it was the only way open to them. Niebuhr observed that the pure sectarian character of organization seldom lasts more than one generation. As children are born to the voluntary members of the first generation,

> *the sect must take on the character of an educational and disciplinary institution, with the purpose of bringing the new generation into conformity with ideals and customs which have become traditional. Rarely does a second generation hold the convictions it has inherited with a fervor equal to that of its fathers, who fashioned these convictions in the heat of conflict and at the risk of martyrdom. As generation succeeds generation, the isolation of the community from the world becomes more difficult. Furthermore, wealth frequently increases when the sect subjects itself to the discipline of asceticism in work and expenditure; with the increase of wealth the possibilities for culture also become more numerous and involvement in the economic life of the nation as a whole can less easily be limited.* (Niebuhr 1954, pp. 19–20)

Nancy Ammerman's work continues the research tradition that relates the evolution of churches to social class backgrounds. Ammerman traces the rise of fundamentalism in the Southern Baptist Convention to the erosion of cultural support for traditional beliefs. She found that fundamentalism decreased with increased levels of education and with increased levels of income. But "many at the edges of this transition are likely to respond by embracing fundamentalist beliefs more vigorously than ever (Ammerman 1986, p. 487).

According to James Beckford, "The question of the degree to which any particular organisation was church-like or sect-like was taken seriously for what it implied about that organisation's capacity to survive in the modern world" (Beckford 1984, p. 85). The church–sect theorizing was dominated by considerations of rationalization and compromise. Beckford detected a shift in the focus of sociologists studying religious organizations in the 1970s toward "the capacity of religious organisations to foster a sense of personal authenticity, conviction and self-identity" (p. 85). The 1970s saw a great many studies about recruitment and mobilization by religious organizations. Many of these studies focused on the growth and decline of traditional organizations, but many others dealt with religious movements that were new, or at least new upon the U.S. scene. Beckford refers to a number of authors who have found that cultlike formations are appropriate to an age marked by rationalization, bureaucratization, and privatization. That is, small groups of people cultivating esoteric religion in private are flexible and adaptable to the conditions of highly mobile and rapidly changing societies. Some of these scholars have linked cults' ability to inspire and mobilize their members to their distinctive forms of organization.

In recent years more emphasis is placed on applying general organization theory to religious organizations. Many recent studies of religious organizations are characterized by an open systems approach, which views organizations as adaptive organisms in a threatening environment (Scherer 1980). The questions of adaptability to the modern world and that of inspiration and mobilization of followers come together in studies of the Roman Catholic Church. Seidler and Meyer (1989) examine that denomination's accommodations to the modern world, many of which involve important structural changes, such as priest's councils, and other changes that allowed both priests and lay people to have more say in the operation of the church.

A relatively new theoretical perspective within the sociology of organizations and social movements—resource mobilization—has illuminated much of the current scene of new religious movements. Bromley and Shupe (1979) did a detailed resource mobilization analysis of the Unification Church. They argue that one key element in the church's establishment in the United States was the development of mobile fund-raising teams.

CURRENT ISSUES

A more varied theoretical approach to religious organizations has allowed scholars to focus on different kinds of issues. A major concern has been the decline of the liberal mainline denominations and the significance of that decline (Roof and McKinney 1987; Hoge and Roozen 1979). The liberal mainline churches in the United States share with other churches in a vast mobilization of voluntary time and money in activities caring for individuals such as the poor, the sick, and the elderly. Churches are particularly effective at such mobilization because they instill philanthropic values and present information and opportunities for philanthropic activities in face-to-face settings such as worship services and Sunday School classes. The liberal churches have played the additional role of implementing socially liberal policies, that is, policies designed to change the structure of society so that, for example, income as well as opportunities for individual achievement are more widely distributed throughout society. The liberal social agenda also includes sharp criticism of the U.S. government's role as promoter of U.S. business interests abroad. Mobilizing individuals and groups to press for the acceptance and implementation of a liberal social agenda may be these churches' most significant contribution to U.S. society (Wood 1990).

Religious organizations also play an important role in the process of consensus formation in our society. Amitai Etzioni (1968) argues that a healthy society is one in which the relationship between citizens and national leaders is mediated by a large network of groups and organizations where multiple perspectives are reduced toward consensus. The effect of any direct appeal by national leaders or by mass media campaigns to individual citizens is determined largely by the multiple membership of the citizens in groups and organizations. This mediation protects against mass emotional manipulation. At the national level the many "legislatures" within the major religious bodies in this country are of enormous importance in shaping the working consensus that enables both the formulation and the implementation of national policies. The representative selection procedures for national meetings and the deliberative consensus formation processes typical of the major denominations are an important contribution to informed public opinion in U.S. society.

At the local level, meetings of the congregation or its committees provide a forum in which differing opinions can be expressed in a context of mutual respect. Knoke and Wood (1981) show that a wide variety of nonreligious social influence associations did not attract people with views as diverse as those in the church. They suggest that "the goals of these organizations are fairly clear to members before they join. Members know what they are getting into. And in most of these organizations, policy-dissatisfied members probably do not feel the social pressure to remain in the organization comparable to that felt by dissatisfied church members" (p. 103). Churches' multiple goals and the emotional and value ties provide holding power that keeps members with different views together in the same church. Voluntary associations in which individuals can debate the critical issues face to face encourage individuals to act out their selfless values rather than their selfish interests and provide a bulwark against the manipulation of the public by computer-generated direct mailings and mass media campaigns for a particular group's vested interest in ideology, money, or power.

OTHER RELIGIOUS ORGANIZATIONS

Wuthnow (1988) has described the rise of numerous special purpose organizations that are rooted in religion and draw legitimation and resources from the more traditional religious organizations but with the objective of achieving a quite specific purpose. These organizations provide new options for religious people in addition to participation in local churches. A wide variety of purposes are pursued, including the advancement of nuclear disarmament and meeting the spiritual needs of senior citizens. Wuthnow suggests that "as far as the society as a whole is concerned, these organizations may be the ones that increasingly define the public role of American religion. Rather than religion's weight being felt through the pressure of denominations, it may be exercised through the more focused efforts of the hundreds of special purpose groups now in operation" (1988, p. 121). Though these special purpose groups are in many ways a revitalizing influence on traditional religious organizations (denominations and local churches), they may have important sociological implications for them.

For example, while the traditional organizations have often held together people of diverse social backgrounds, special purpose groups may have a tendency toward homogeneity.

There are also a number of important umbrella organizations, such as the National Council of Churches and the National Association of Evangelicals, that facilitate the cooperation of sets of denominations. The National Council of Churches was particularly important in mobilizing a segment of the church population into the civil rights movement (Wood 1972). There has also been a growth of community councils of churches.

In the news in recent years there have been a number of religious organizations that are unrelated either to the Judeo–Christian heritage or to immigrant groups. They draw their adherents largely from the broad center of the U.S. middle class. Ellwood and Partin (1988) discuss more than forty of these groups. None of them is very large and in the majority most of their members remain affiliated for less than a year. Perhaps their greatest importance from the sociological perspective is that they introduce new organizational models into the U.S. scene.

THE FUTURE

New immigrant people are bringing their religions. Islam in particular is growing rapidly. People in the United States may have to start thinking of themselves as a Protestant, Catholic, Jewish, Islamic nation. According to one source, in 1973 there were fifteen or twenty local centers of Muslim worship in the United States; by 1980 Muslim centers were reported in all of the 300 largest cities in the United States. Two million adherents were reported in 1980; six million were reported in 1989. Most Islamic organizations in the United States are local centers (variously called Islamic Society, Islamic Center, or Muslim Mosque). These organizations provide a place of worship and a center for other religious, social, and educational activities. Islam does not have an organized hierarchy, but several regional and national groups help to coordinate the work of local groups and promote unity among them (Jacquet 1989). If, as Elazar (1980) contends, many Jewish organizations in addition to the synagogue play a religious role, in Islam it appears that the religious centers play many roles in addition to the religious one. Perhaps this is always the case with the churches of recent immigrants.

Stark and Bainbridge (1985) think that traditionally organized religion may decline drastically as more and more people pursue individualistic "careers" of going from one self-enhancement group to another. If they are correct, any societal influence of religious organizations would be felt more through influence on individuals than through collective action of large religious bodies. However, there is much evidence that the traditional structure of religious organization in the United States will persist.

(SEE ALSO: *Organizational Structure; Sociology of Religion*)

REFERENCES

Ammerman, Nancy T. 1986 "The New South and the New Baptists." *The Christian Century* May 14, pp. 486–488.

Beckford, James A. 1984 "Religious Organisation: A Survey of Some Recent Publications." *Archives de Sciences Sociales des Religions* 57:83–102.

Berger, Peter L. 1967 *The Sacred Canopy.* Garden City, N.Y.: Doubleday.

Bromley, David G., and Anson D. Shupe, Jr. 1979 *"Moonies" in America: Cult, Church, and Crusade.* Beverly Hills, Calif.: Sage.

Elazar, Daniel J. 1980 "Patterns of Jewish Organization in the United States." In Ross P. Scherer, ed., *American Denominational Organization.* Pasadena, Calif.: William Carey Library.

Ellwood, Robert S., and Harry B. Partin 1988 *Religious and Spiritual Groups in Modern America.* Englewood Cliffs, N.J.: Prentice-Hall.

Etzioni, Amitai 1968 *The Active Society.* New York: Free Press.

Hoge, Dean R., and David A. Roozen 1979 *Understanding Church Growth and Decline: 1950–1978.* New York: Pilgrim Press.

Hougland, James G., Jr., and James R. Wood 1979

"'Inner Circles' in Local Churches: An Application of Thompson's Theory." *Sociological Analysis* 40:226–239.

Jacquet, Constant H., Jr. (ed.) 1989 *Yearbook of American and Canadian Churches.* Nashville, Tenn.: Abingdon Press.

Knoke, David, and James R. Wood 1981 *Organized for Action: Commitment in Voluntary Associations.* New Brunswick, N.J.: Rutgers University Press.

Niebuhr, H. Richard 1954 *The Social Sources of Denominationalism.* Hamden, Conn.: Shoe String Press.

Roof, Wade Clark, and William McKinney 1987 *American Mainline Religion: Its Changing Shape and Future.* New Brunswick, N.J.: Rutgers University Press.

Scherer, Ross P. 1980 *American Denominational Organization.* Pasadena, Calif.: William Carey Library.

Seidler, John, and Katherine Meyer 1989 *Conflict and Change in the Catholic Church.* New Brunswick, N.J.: Rutgers University Press.

Stark, Rodney, and William S. Bainbridge 1985 *The Future of Religion: Secularization, Revival, and Cult Formation.* Berkeley: University of California Press.

Troeltsch, Ernst 1961 *The Social Teachings of the Christian Churches.* New York: Harper and Row.

Weber, Max 1978 *Economy and Society.* Berkeley: University of California Press.

Wood, James R. 1972 "Unanticipated Consequences of Organizational Coalitions: Ecumenical Cooperation and Civil Rights Policy." *Social Forces* 50:512–521.

——— 1981 *Leadership in Voluntary Organizations: The Controversy over Social Action in Protestant Churches.* New Brunswick, N.J.: Rutgers University Press.

——— 1990 "Liberal Protestant Social Action in a Period of Decline." In Robert Wuthnow and Virginia A. Hodgkinson, eds., *Faith and Philanthropy in America: Exploring the Role of Religion in America's Voluntary Sector.* San Francisco: Jossey-Bass.

Wuthnow, Robert 1988 *The Restructuring of American Religion: Society and Faith since World War II.* Princeton, N.J.: Princeton University Press.

JAMES R. WOOD

RELIGIOUS ORIENTATIONS Sociologists generally conceive of religion as a system of symbols that evokes a sense of holistic or transcendent meaning (Bellah 1970, p. 16; Geertz 1973, pp. 90–125). This definition reflects sociology's claim that symbols are essential to the human capacity to experience and interpret reality (Berger and Luckmann 1966). Symbols are acts, objects, utterances, or events that stand for something—that is, that give meaning to something by connecting it to something else. Symbols give order and meaning to life. Without them, life would be experienced as senseless and chaotic. Indeed, research suggests that individuals are able to experience and understand only those aspects of their worlds for which they have symbols (Farb 1973).

Sociologists' emphasis on holistic or transcendent meaning as the defining feature of religion arises from their view that meaning is always contextual (Langer 1951). The meaning of a particular word depends on the other words that form its immediate context. For example, the word "courts" means one thing if it appears with the word "tennis," but something different when the words "justice" or "dating" are present. Similarly, in their daily lives people give meaning to their activities by associating them with various frames of reference. Hitting a tennis ball has meaning, for example, because it is associated with the rules of the game of tennis. Each frame of reference, moreover, has meaning because it can be placed within a more encompassing symbolic context (tennis, say, within the context of physical exercise and health). But if each symbolic framework requires a broader framework to have meaning, then, some form of holistic or transcendent symbol system that embraces all of life must be present. These are what sociologists call religious orientations or religious systems (Berger 1967; Roberts 1984).

The questions that typically invoke religious symbols involve the quest to make life itself meaningful. Such questions arise at the extremities of human existence: Where did I come from? Why am I here? What happens when I die? These questions, framed at the individual level, may also be asked about the collectivity to which one belongs or about humanity in general: How did our tribe originate? Where is humanity headed? Other questions focus on the absolutes or landmarks that make life recognizable in its most basic sense: What is beauty? What is truth? How can we know truth? What is essential about the human condition? There are also questions that arise because the events they deal with make no sense to us on the surface: Why must I die? Why is there suffering in the world? What is the reason for evil?

Transcendent symbol systems address these questions at a variety of levels. Elaborate philosophical and theological doctrines sometimes supply rational answers that satisfy canons of logic and empirical evidence. In daily life these questions are more likely to be addressed through narratives, proverbs, and maxims, and ikonic representations rich with experiential connotations. Religious orientations are likely to be structured less by abstract deductive reasoning than by parables that raise questions but leave open precise answers, by personal stories that link experience with wider realities, and by creeds and images that have acquired meaning through long histories of interpretation in human communities (Greeley 1982, pp. 53–70).

Like other symbol systems, religious orientations are thought to be the products of social interaction. Although the role of such factors as divine revelation cannot be ruled out, sociologists focus on the ways in which symbols come to have meaning through the interaction of individuals and groups in human communities. Sometimes these communities invent collective symbols to articulate powerful experiences they may have undergone. More commonly, communities borrow symbols available within their cultural traditions, but then adapt these symbols to their own use, giving them new meanings and interpretations. Communities also underwrite the plausibility of religious belief systems (Berger 1967, p. 45). They do so by providing evidence that such beliefs are not the product of individual imaginations alone, by encouraging the public expression of beliefs, and by creating occasions on which beliefs may be enacted and predictions fulfilled. Without the ongoing interaction of people in communities, it is doubtful whether belief systems could long be sustained. Research has also demonstrated that personal religious orientations are more likely to have behavioral consequences if these orientations are supported by communities of like-minded individuals (Roof 1978).

In defining religion as a symbol system that deals with ultimate questions, sociologists assume that humans have the capacity to question their experience and a desire to make sense of their worlds. Whether all people pursue this desire with equal intensity is more doubtful. It is possible, for example, to explain a plane crash by observing that a rivet came loose. It is also possible to let the incident raise questions about the meaning of pain, the frailty of human existence, or the meaning and purpose of one's own life. How much the quest for holistic meaning and transcendence enters into people's lives is, therefore, a matter of variation. Studies indicate that most people say they have thought about the meaning and purpose of life, but individuals vary in the extent to which they have been troubled by this issue. They also vary in the amount of explicit attention they have devoted to it and in their views about the possibility of arriving at definite answers (Stark and Glock 1968, p. 77). Agnosticism, for example, is a religious orientation that grants the importance of ultimate questions about meaning and purpose but denies the possibility of finding answers to these questions.

The kinds of symbols that come into play in relation to such questions are also matters of variation. While all such symbol systems may perform functionally similar roles, it is useful to distinguish them substantively. These substantive distinctions are usually the basis on which religious orientations are delineated in popular discourse. At the broadest level, sociologists distinguish theistic meaning systems, which recognize the existence of a God or divine being, from atheistic systems, which do not acknowledge a divine being (Glock and Stark 1965, pp. 3–17). Christianity is an example of the former; Marxism, of the latter. Insofar as it addresses the same higher-order questions about the meaning of life, Marxism would be considered functionally similar to Christianity. But this does not mean that Marxism necessarily functions this way. Just as one might study Marxism to derive economic principles, so one might study Christianity simply as an example of literature. In neither case would it be appropriate to say that a religious orientation is at work. Only as they function to evoke holistic meaning and transcendence do symbol systems become religious orientations.

The distinction between theistic and atheistic meaning systems is useful when the relevant concept is the presence or absence of a divine entity. But this distinction may be less useful in other contexts. For example, contemporary discussions in theology and in science sometimes distinguish religious orientations on the basis of whether they posit a reality that is humanly knowable or ultimately mysterious, whether reality is empirical or includes a supraempirical dimension, or whether being implies something that is not being itself but the ground of being. In these debates the boundary between varieties of ultimate meaning systems is often ambiguous.

In contemporary societies religious orientations are often distinguished in popular belief according to the dominant force or power that people perceive as governing their lives (Wuthnow 1976). Some people may conceive of this force as God; others, as luck or fate. Natural or human causes may also be considered dominant; for example, the force of heredity, of scientific law, society, or individual willpower. Whether a part of elaborate philosophical systems or simple pieces of folk wisdom, such understandings help people to make sense of their lives by identifying the causal agents that control human events.

Sociologists have insisted that religious orientations become important to the study of human behavior insofar as these orientations are internalized as part of the individual's worldview. A worldview can be defined as a person's guiding outlook on life. The essential aspects of a religious orientation are the person's beliefs and assumptions about the meaning of life and such matters as the existence and nature of God, goodness and evil, life beyond death, truth, and the human condition. These beliefs and assumptions help the individual make sense of life cognitively. They also have an emotional dimension, perhaps including a feeling of awe, reverence, fear, or peace, comfort, and security. In addition, they are regarded as behavioral predispositions that lead to various actions, such as participation in worship, prayer, or ethical decisions (Spilka, Hood, and Gorsuch 1985).

The importance of religious orientations for ethical decisions has been of long-standing interest to sociologists. In the classical work of Max Weber (1963), religious orientations were conceived of as symbolic frameworks that made sense of the world, in part, by providing explanations for the existence of evil (also known as theodicies). Some religious orientations, for example, explained evil as a struggle between God and the devil, others saw evil as part of a cycle of regeneration and renewal, while still others attributed evil to the workings of an all-powerful but inscrutable deity. The implications for ethical action derived from the prescriptions for salvation implied by these different conceptions of evil. In one tradition, for example, people might be expected to pray and meditate in order to escape from the cycle of evil and regeneration; in another tradition, they might be expected to do good deeds as a way of siding with the forces of good against those of evil.

Much of the research by sociologists on religious orientations has dealt with their subjective aspects (Blasi and Cuneo 1986). Assuming that the important feature of symbolism is its meaning, researchers have tried to discover what religious symbols mean to individuals. Efforts have been made to tap the deeper predispositions presumed to underlie such religious expressions as prayer and worship, to say how deeply implanted the religious impulse is, and to classify varieties of religious outlooks and experiences.

Recent developments in sociological theory have resulted in some rethinking of this emphasis on subjective religiosity. Current research is beginning to focus more on the observable manifestations of religious symbolism itself, rather than claiming to know what lies beneath the surface in the subjective consciousness of the individual (Wuthnow 1987). Discourse, language, gesture, and ritual have become more important in their own right (Tipton 1982). The contrast between this and the earlier approach can be illustrated by comparing two statements: "I believe God exists" and "God speaks to us through the Word." A subjective approach would treat both statements as manifestations of some inner conviction of the individual. The more recent approach would pay closer attention to the language itself, noting, for example, the more personalized style of the first statement and the collective reference contained in the second.

The value of the more recent approach is that it recognizes the public or social dimension of religious orientations. Observers may not know what goes on in the dark recesses of the believer's soul. But if that person tells a story, or participates in worship, the researcher can then study the observable manifestations of that person's faith.

To account for variations in religious orientations sociologists usually look at the social conditions to which people are exposed. They assume that most people do not make up their own religions from scratch. Rather, they borrow from the various symbol systems that are available in their environment. The most significant borrowing occurs in early childhood. Family is thus an important factor, and it, in turn, is influenced by broader conditions such as social class, levels of education, race and ethnicity, and exposure to regional subcultures.

A generation ago, sociologists often held the view that scientific generalizations could be made about the relationships between social factors and religious orientations. For example, much work was inspired by the hypothesis that theistic religious orientations were more common among persons with lower levels of education than among persons in better-educated social strata. Another common hypothesis suggested that religious orientations were likely to be associated with various kinds of social deprivation, since the deprived would presumably seek solace in otherworldly beliefs. Empirical studies have found some support for such hypotheses. But the ability to make generalizations has remained limited. Different relationships seem to be present in different communities and in different time periods.

More attention has turned in recent years, therefore, toward describing the rich and complex processes by which religious orientations and social environments intermingle. In one setting people without college educations may turn to religious views that shield them from the uncertainties of science and other modern ideas. In another setting people with high levels of education may also turn to religion, but do so in a way that combines ideas from science and Scripture or that focuses on the therapeutic needs of people working in the professions. In both settings, religious orientations provide answers to ultimate questions. But the composition of these orientations reflects ideas present in the different social settings.

An earlier generation of social theorists also sought to explain the variations in religious orientations in ways that often reduced them to little more than the by-products of social or psychological needs. Sociologists following in the tradition of Karl Marx, for example, regarded religion merely as a reflection of class struggles, while some following Emile Durkheim viewed it as a reflection of the corporate authority of society (Swanson 1960, 1967). The reductionism in these approaches consisted not only of regarding social structure as more basic than religion but also of implying that religion would gradually disappear as people became more aware of its origins (Fenton 1970). Recent work is decidedly less reductionistic in its assumptions about religion. It still assumes that religion fulfills human needs and that it is influenced by social conditions, but regards religion as a more active contributor to human experience and considers its future more viable.

In addition to the more general social conditions that may influence the religious orientations of individuals, sociologists have also been particularly interested in the institutions that devote specific energies to the promulgation of religious orientations. These institutions supply the resources needed for religious orientations to be perpetuated. Leadership, producers of religious knowledge, specialists in the dissemination of such knowledge, organizational skills, physical facilities, and financial resources are all required for religious orientations to be maintained over time. Religious institutions must compete with other institutions, such as governments, businesses, and families, for these resources.

In most modern societies competition is also present among the adherents of various religious orientations (Wuthnow 1988a). When such competition has been recognized either governmentally or culturally, we say that a condition of religious pluralism exists (Silk 1988). Pluralism often becomes a kind of religious orientation itself, imposing norms of civility and tolerance on particularistic religious traditions. When multiple religious orientations are forced to compete with one another, the plausibility of any one such tradition may be diminished as a result of believers' seeing others who hold views different from their own. At the same time, pluralism appears to contribute to the overall vitality of religious orientations in a society by encouraging competition among them for adherents and by giving believers more options from which to choose (Christiano 1987).

It has been common in the past for individuals to choose one particular religious orientation with which to identify. Often these orientations have been defined by religious institutions, such as the Roman Catholic church, or by denominational organizations, such as the Presbyterian or Methodist churches (Greeley 1972). Increasingly, however, it appears that individuals in modern societies are exposed to a variety of religious institutions and orientations. As a result, they may pick and choose particular elements from several different faiths and traditions. Their religious orientation therefore takes on a more personalized character (Bellah et al. 1985, pp. 219–249; Roof and McKinney 1987, pp. 40–71).

Although some individuals work out highly coherent religious orientations that have internal consistency and integrity, it appears that the more common result of living in religiously pluralistic settings is a form of personalized eclecticism. People become heteroglossic—that is, they gain the capacity to speak with many religious voices. Their religious orientations may not provide a guiding philosophy of life that maintains an orderly view of the world. Rather, religious orientations become tool kits (Swidler 1987) assembled from a variety of personal experiences, social contacts, books, sermons, and other cultural repertoires, and from which the individual is able to draw as he or she is confronted with the challenges of life.

At present, research studies indicate that large proportions of the population in societies like the United States hold theistic religious orientations (Wuthnow 1988b). In other societies where religious institutions have had fewer resources in the past, such orientations are less common. In all societies, though, theistic orientations are confronted by the humanistic orientations promulgated by secular institutions. The outcome appears to involve a balance between pressures to adapt, on the one hand, and tendencies by religious adherents to resist these pressures, on the other hand (Hammond 1985; Beckford 1989). Much of the struggle depends on the ability of religious leaders to articulate visions that grow out of particular confessional traditions in ways that appeal to the universalistic norms governing wider social audiences.

Although religious orientations have become more diverse and eclectic as a result of cultural contact and mass communication, evidence also suggests that in some societies a basic polarization has emerged between those whose orientation involves traditionalistic, fundamentalistic, or conservative norms, on one side, and those whose orientation involves progressive, modernistic, or liberal norms, on the other side (Wuthnow 1988b). Conservatives are characterized by adherence to the authority of traditional scriptural texts, while liberals emphasize more the relativity of these texts and the need for reason and experience in interpreting them. Liberal religious orientations have been nurtured by relativistic views in higher education, in the professions, and in the mass media in market-oriented societies, but conservative orientations have grown as well, not only in reaction to liberalism, but also as a result of conservatives gaining educational or political advantages and seizing on opportunities created by the ill effects of rapid societal change (Ammerman 1987; Hunter 1987). Whereas earlier discussions predicted the demise of fundamentalist religious orientations, current studies are more concerned with the ongoing tensions between fundamentalist and more liberal or more humanistic religious orientations.

(SEE ALSO: *Social Philosophy; Sociology of Religion*)

REFERENCES

Ammerman, Nancy Tatom 1987 *Bible Believers: Fundamentalists in the Modern World.* New Brunswick, N.J.: Rutgers University Press.

Beckford, James A. 1989 *Religion and Advanced Industrial Society.* London: Unwin Hyman.

Bellah, Robert N. 1970 *Beyond Belief: Essays on Religion in a Post-Traditional World.* New York: Harper and Row.

———, Richard Madsen, William M. Sullivan, Ann Swidler, and Steven M. Tipton 1985 *Habits of the Heart: Individualism and Commitment in American Life.* Berkeley: University of California Press.

Berger, Peter L. 1967 *The Sacred Canopy: Elements of a Sociological Theory of Religion.* Garden City, N.Y.: Doubleday.

———, and Thomas Luckmann 1966 *The Social Construction of Reality: A Treatise in the Sociology of Knowledge.* Garden City, N.Y.: Doubleday.

Blasi, Anthony J., and Michael W. Cuneo 1986 *Issues in the Sociology of Religion: A Bibliography.* New York: Garland.

Christiano, Kevin J. 1987 *Religious Diversity and Social Change: American Cities, 1890–1906.* Cambridge: Cambridge University Press.

Farb, Peter 1973 *Word Play.* New York: Bantam.

Fenton, John Y. 1970. "Reductionism in the Study of Religion." *Soundings* 53:61–76.

Geertz, Clifford 1973 *The Interpretation of Cultures.* New York: Harper and Row.

Glock, Charles Y., and Rodney Stark 1965 *Religion and Society in Tension.* Chicago: Rand McNally.

Greeley, Andrew M. 1972 *The Denominational Society: A Sociological Approach to Religion in America.* Glenview, Ill.: Scott Foresman.

———1982 *Religion: A Secular Theory.* New York: Free Press.

Hammond, Phillip E. (ed.) 1985 *The Sacred in a Secular Age.* Berkeley: University of California Press.

Hunter, James Davison 1987 *Evangelicalism: The Coming Generation.* Chicago: University of Chicago Press.

Langer, Susanne K. 1951 *Philosophy in a New Key.* New York: Mentor.

Roberts, Keith A. 1984 *Religion in Sociological Perspective.* Belmont, Calif.: Wadsworth.

Roof, Wade Clark 1978 *Community and Commitment: Religious Plausibility in a Liberal Protestant Church.* New York: Elsevier.

———, and William McKinney 1987 *American Mainline Religion: Its Changing Shape and Future.* New Brunswick, N.J.: Rutgers University Press.

Silk, Mark 1988 *Spiritual Politics: Religion and America Since World War II.* New York: Simon and Schuster.

Spilka, Bernard, Ralph W. Hood, Jr., and Richard L. Gorsuch 1985 *The Psychology of Religion: An Empirical Approach.* Englewood Cliffs, N.J.: Prentice-Hall.

Stark, Rodney, and Charles Y. Glock 1968 *American Piety: The Nature of Religious Commitment.* Berkeley: University of California Press.

Swanson, Guy E. 1960 *The Birth of the Gods: The Origin of Primitive Beliefs.* Ann Arbor: University of Michigan Press.

———1967 *Religion and Regime: A Sociological Account of the Reformation.* Ann Arbor: University of Michigan Press.

Swidler, Ann 1987 "Culture in Action: Symbols and Strategies." *American Sociological Review* 51:273–286.

Tipton, Steven M. 1982 *Getting Saved from the Sixties: Moral Meaning in Conversion and Cultural Change.* Berkeley: University of California Press.

Weber, Max 1963 *The Sociology of Religion.* Boston: Beacon.

Wuthnow, Robert 1976 *The Consciousness Reformation.* Berkeley: University of California Press.

———1987 *Meaning and Moral Order: Explorations in Cultural Analysis.* Berkeley: University of California Press.

———1988a "Sociology of Religion." In Neil J. Smelser, ed., *Handbook of Sociology.* Beverly Hills, Calif.: Sage.

———1988b *The Restructuring of American Religion: Society and Faith Since World War II.* Princeton, N.J.: Princeton University Press.

ROBERT WUTHNOW

REMARRIAGE In Colonial America, remarriage frequently followed the death of a spouse. Demos (1970, p. 194) reported that in the Plymouth Colony, approximately 40 percent of men and 26 percent of women over the age of fifty had been married more than once. The interval between the death of the first spouse and remarriage was often less than a year, since remaining single posed both social and economic problems. The organization of the community assumed that most adults would be married, and maintaining a household required the efforts of both a husband and wife, particularly when there were orphaned children.

The tendency toward remarriage has continued into the twentieth century; however, the majority of remarriages now occur following divorce, owing to the combination of the dramatic decrease in the mortality rate in the first few decades of the century and the increase in the divorce rate from the 1960s through the early 1980s. By the early 1980s, almost ten times as many remarriages followed divorce than followed widowhood (Wilson 1989).

TRENDS IN REMARRIAGE

Remarriages in contemporary America have become almost as common as first marriages—in fact, in recent years, almost half of all marriages involved at least one spouse who had been married previously (U.S. Bureau of the Census 1990). Remarriage rates in the United States (the number of people remarrying each year per 1,000 persons divorced or widowed) increased during the 1960s, declined precipitously across the 1970s, and has continued to decline in the 1980s, although at a much slower rate (Sweet and Bumpass 1988; U.S. Bureau of the Census 1990). While the remarriage rates are related to changes in divorce rates, the trends are not always similar. For example, the rise in remarriage rates in the 1960s accompanied the rise in divorce rates, but the decline in remarriage rates in the 1970s occurred at a time when the divorce rates were still growing.

Remarriage happens fairly quickly. For example, in 1983, the mean number of years between divorce and remarriage was 3.0 for divorced men and 3.3 for divorced women (Wilson 1989). Men whose first marriage ended with the death of a spouse also remarried relatively quickly (3.5 years); in contrast, the interval for women who became widowed was 6.1 years.

Who Remarries? Rates of remarriage vary substantially by age, gender, race and ethnicity, and marital status (i.e., divorced or widowed). Among older people, remarriage also varies by health—those in better health are more likely to remarry (Bulcroft et al. 1989).

Age at the time of termination of the first marriage is clearly the best predictor of remarriage, with younger people remarrying at much higher rates. For example, 89 percent of women who were under the age of twenty-five when their first marriage ended eventually remarry, while only 31 percent of women over the age of forty at the termination of the first marriage remarry (Bumpass, Sweet, and Martin 1990, p. 753).

Remarriage rates also differ by race and ethnicity. The importance of this factor is shown by Bumpass, Sweet, and Martin (1990, p. 752) in their report that the remarriage rate among African-Americans is only one-fourth that among white non-Hispanics, while the remarriage rate among Hispanics is only half that of white non-Hispanics.

Gender is a particularly important factor to consider when discussing remarriage, not only because remarriage rates vary by gender but because gender interacts with several other factors that predict remarriage. For example, not only are men more likely to remarry than are women, but the *difference* in men's and women's likelihood of remarriage increases substantially across the life course. For example, among individuals who were under the age of twenty at the time of separation, 78 percent of the women had remarried by the end of ten years, and 83 percent of the men had remarried (Sweet and Bumpass 1988, p. 196). In contrast, among individuals between the ages of thirty and thirty-four at the time of separation, only 40 percent of the women had remarried by the end of ten years, compared to 63 percent of the men. Differences between men's and women's likelihood of remarriage continue to increase across the life course, with the greatest discrepancies occurring between men and women after the age of sixty.

The effect of the presence of children on likelihood of remarriage also varies by gender.

The presence of children has no effect on the likelihood of remarriage for men but affects the likelihood of remarriage for women in most age groups. Among women under twenty-five at the time of separation, having children decreases the likelihood of remarriage, while for women separated at ages twenty-five to thirty-four, the presence of children has no effect on remarriage. In contrast, among women separated when over thirty-five, those who have children are *more* likely to remarry (Koo and Suchindran 1980).

Various explanations for the overall lower remarriage rates for women than for men have been developed. The most commonly cited explanation focuses on the limited "marriage market" or the field of eligibles for women who experience the termination of their marriage through divorce or death. First, there are fewer men than women, and this discrepancy increases with age (U.S. Bureau of the Census 1990), providing fewer men for women in the older age groups. Also, women tend to marry men who are older than themselves, further limiting the pool of eligibles for women who are themselves older.

MATE SELECTION AMONG THOSE REMARRYING

One of the most striking phenomena in first marriages is the tendency for individuals to marry others with similar social characteristics such as age, educational attainment, religion, and socioeconomic background—a pattern known as homogamy. Although there is also a tendency toward homogamy in remarriage, the degree of similarity is less than in first marriages.

The reduced tendency toward status similarity in remarriage can be seen by examining the differences in age homogamy. Individuals who remarry tend to select mates from a wider field of eligibles compared to first marrieds, resulting in a greater age difference between spouses in remarriage (Wilson 1989, p. 2). When both parties are marrying for the first time, the groom is, on average, two years older than the bride; however, when both parties are divorced, the groom is approximately four years older.

Individuals appear to select mates on the basis of more pragmatic criteria for remarriages than for first marriages. While love remains a consideration in selecting a partner for remarriage, the decision to remarry is often also based on fulfilling some instrumental need such as assistance with parenting, household labor, and financial responsibilities.

One of the primary explanations for the instrumental focus in mate selection for remarriage is that the individuals are older and more experienced compared to those entering their first marriage. Remarried men and women are approximately a decade older than individuals marrying for the first time. The median age for those who remarry after a divorce is the mid-thirties compared to the mid-twenties for first marrieds. An even sharper contrast, of course, is the median age of remarriage for widowers, which is sixty for men and fifty-three for women (Wilson 1989).

SUCCESS OF REMARRIAGES

While the popular press has debated the relative happiness of first marriages and remarriages research on this issue has failed to find important differences. The most comprehensive review of research on this topic to date (Vemer et al. 1989) found that first marrieds report only slightly greater marital satisfaction than do remarrieds. Elizabeth Vemer and her colleagues suggest that even this small difference may be accounted for by the fact that most studies combined data from individuals who had married twice with those who had married more than twice, and there is evidence that individuals in the latter group are less happy in general. Vemer and her colleagues also found that remarried men were more satisfied with their relationships than were remarried women—however, the differences were very small and paralleled the differences often found between women's and men's satisfaction with first marriages. Thus, taken together, the findings indicate little difference in satisfaction between first marriages and remarriages for either men or women.

One question that is often raised in both the

popular and scholarly literature is the effect of the presence of children on marital quality. The presence of children has generally been found to have a negative effect on parents' marital quality; however, the effects of children specifically on *remarried* couples is less clear. While White and Booth (1985) found that the presence of stepchildren was associated with somewhat lower marital quality, Martin and Bumpass (1989) found no effect, and both Albrecht, Bahr, and Goodman (1983) and Kurdek (1989) reported that the presence of stepchildren was weakly but *positively* associated with marital quality. The findings regarding mutual children are also inconsistent. Ganong and Coleman (1988) found that mutual children had no effect on marital quality, but Albrecht, Bahr, and Goodman found a weak but positive effect. Thus, it is unclear how the presence of either mutual children or stepchildren affects marital quality among remarrieds.

Clearly, remarriages and first marriages differ in complexity, due to the ties that are developed during the first marriage. The remarried couple must develop ways of interacting with the former spouse, children from the former marriage (regardless of whether the children are minors or adults), and, in some cases, both the extended kin and new partner of the former spouse. In addition, the emotional history of the relationship with the first spouse, positive and negative, may carry over to influence the new relationship, regardless of whether the first marriage was terminated by death or divorce. Further, there are material possessions and financial considerations emanating from the first marriage that often have a significant impact on second marriages.

This complexity, and perhaps the attendant problems, might help explain the slightly higher rate of divorce among remarried couples. Whereas about half of first marriages end in divorce, approximately 60 percent of remarriages do so (Ihinger-Tallman and Pasley 1987).

There are several explanations for the higher rate of divorce of remarriages. Cherlin (1978) has suggested there is an "incomplete institutionalization" of remarriage. Remarriage, according to Cherlin is more difficult than a first marriage due to the lack of guidelines in language, law, and custom for remarried couples.

Another interpretation of the higher rate of divorce among remarrieds is offered by Furstenberg and Spanier (1984b), who identify the predisposition to divorce of remarrieds as the key explanatory factor. According to this perspective, since remarried individuals have already demonstrated their willingness to leave an unsatisfactory marriage, they will be willing to do so again if dissatisfied with the current relationship. Therefore, it may not be the quality of the marital relationship that precipitates divorce but the propensity to leave an unsatisfactory relationship.

Last, Martin and Bumpass (1989) have suggested that the higher rate of divorce among remarrieds can be accounted for by the fact that individuals who remarry have characteristics that increased the likelihood that their first marriage would end in divorce. These characteristics include early age at first marriage, lower socioeconomic status, and parental divorce.

In sum, while the literature on remarriage emphasizes differences between first marriages and remarriages, it is important to reiterate that, overall, there is substantially more similarity than difference between these two types of marriages. The patterns of mate selection, marital quality, and marital stability of individuals who remarry do not differ markedly from the patterns of individuals marrying for the first time.

STEPFAMILIES

Almost two-thirds of remarriages involve children from a former marriage (Cherlin and McCarthy 1985). A substantial body of literature on stepfamilies has developed in recent years. The present discussion will highlight two issues that have received particular attention (see Coleman and Ganong 1990; Ihinger-Tallman 1988; and Spanier and Furstenberg 1987 for comprehensive reviews)—the effects on children and stepparenting.

A major focus of research on stepfamilies has been the effect of remarriage on children. Ganong and Coleman's (1984) review of the research on stepchildren concluded that children in stepfamilies and children in other family forms did not differ in terms of problem behaviors, self-concepts, or school performance. A recent study by Baydar (1988) supports this overall conclusion. Baydar found that mothers' remarriages had an initial detrimental effect on children's emotional well-being but that this effect disappeared within the first few years. Thus, children in stepfamilies are not necessarily at a disadvantage relative to children in other families, at least after a short time.

Many authors have noted that stepmothers often experience difficulty establishing satisfying relationships with their stepchildren. The primary explanation for this phenomenon focuses on the fact that the large majority of stepmothers and stepchildren do not live together, thus limiting the day-to-day interaction that facilitates the development of intimacy (Ambert 1986; Ihinger-Tallman and Pasley 1987). Nevertheless, stepmothers are often expected to assume a major role in parenting during their stepchildren's visits. This situation often leads to conflict between stepmothers and stepchildren as well as between stepmothers and their spouses—particularly regarding discipline (Ahrons and Rodgers 1987).

Although there are special concerns and greater complexity in family relationships in stepfamilies, there are also unique strengths. For example, as Furstenberg and Spanier (1984a) point out, stepfamilies add kin to family networks, extending the potential for warm nurturing relationships with more people. Thus, stepfamilies generally function as effective family units, with the same variation in relationship quality found in more traditional family forms.

CONCLUSION

In conclusion, married life in America today often involves a sequence of marriage, divorce, and remarriage, sometimes followed by a subsequent divorce. Many sociologists suggest that the high rate of remarriage following divorce in American society indicates a strong commitment to married life, albeit of a slightly different form. These scholars argue that contemporary Americans are not rejecting marriage, they are only rejecting specific relationships that became unsatisfying. Taken together, the literature on remarriage and stepfamilies suggests that individuals who choose to follow this pattern have approximately as great a likelihood of finding a satisfying and stable relationship as do those who marry for the first time.

(SEE ALSO: *Divorce; Marriage; Marriage and Divorce Rates; Widowhood*)

REFERENCES

Ahrons, Constance R., and Roy H. Rodgers 1987 *Divorced Families: A Multidisciplinary Developmental View.* New York: Norton.

Albrecht, Stan L., Howard M. Bahr, and Kristen L. Goodman 1983 *Divorce and Remarriage: Problems, Adaptations and Adjustments.* Westport, Conn.: Greenwood Press.

Ambert, Anne-Marie 1986 "Being a Stepparent: Live-in and Visiting Stepchildren." *Journal of Marriage and the Family* 48:795–804.

Baydar, Nazli 1988 "Effects of Parental Separation and Reentry into Union on the Emotional Well-Being of Children." *Journal of Marriage and Family* 50:967–981.

Benson-Von Der Ohe, Elizabeth 1987 *First and Second Marriages.* New York: Praeger.

Bulcroft, Kris, Richard Bulcroft, Laurie Hatch, and Edgar F. Borgatta 1989 "Antecedents and Consequences of Remarriage in Later Life." *Research on Aging* 11:82–106.

Bumpass, Larry, James Sweet, and Teresa Castro Martin 1990 "Changing Patterns of Remarriage." *Journal of Marriage and the Family* 52:747–756.

Cherlin, Andrew 1978 "Remarriage as an Incomplete Institution." *American Journal of Sociology* 84:634–650.

———, and James McCarthy 1985 "Remarried Couple Households: Data from the June 1980 Current Population Survey." *Journal of Marriage and the Family* 47:23–30.

Coleman, Marilyn, and Lawrence H. Ganong 1990 "Remarriage and Stepfamily Research in the 1990s: Increased Interest in an Old Family Form." *Journal of Marriage and the Family* 52:925–940.

Demos, John 1970 *A Little Commonwealth: Family Life in Plymouth Colony.* London: Oxford University Press.

Furstenberg, Frank F., Jr., and Graham B. Spanier 1984a *Recycling the Family: Remarriage after Divorce.* Beverly Hills, Calif.: Sage.

———1984b "The Risk of Dissolution in Remarriage: An Examination of Cherlin's Hypothesis of Incomplete Institutionalization." *Family Relations* 33:433–441.

Ganong, Lawrence H., and Marilyn Coleman 1984 "The Effects of Remarriage on Children: A Review of the Empirical Literature." *Family Relations* 33:389–406.

———1988 "Do Mutual Children Cement Bonds in Stepfamilies?" *Journal of Marriage and the Family* 50:687–698.

Glick, Paul C. 1989 "Remarried Families, Stepfamilies, and Stepchildren: A Brief Demographic Profile." *Family Relations* 38:24–27.

Ihinger-Tallman, Marilyn 1988 "Research on Stepfamilies." In W. R. Scott, ed., *Annual Review of Sociology.* Vol. 14. Palo Alto, Calif.: Annual Reviews.

———, and Kay Pasley 1987 *Remarriage.* Beverly Hills, Calif.: Sage.

Koo, Helen P., and C. M. Suchindran 1980 "Effects of Children on Women's Remarriage Prospects." *Journal of Family Issues* 1:497–515.

Kurdek, Lawrence A. 1989 "Relationship Quality for Newly Married Husbands and Wives: Marital History, Stepchildren, and Individual-Difference Predictors." *Journal of Marriage and the Family* 51:1053–1064.

Martin, Teresa Castro, and Larry Bumpass 1989 "Recent Trends in Marital Disruption." *Demography* 26:37–51.

Spanier, Graham B., and Frank F. Furstenberg, Jr. 1987 "Remarriage and Reconstituted Families." In M. Sussman and S. Steinmetz, eds., *Handbook of Marriage and the Family.* New York: Plenum.

Sweet, James A., and Larry L. Bumpass 1988 *American Families and Households.* New York: Russell Sage Foundation.

U.S. Bureau of the Census 1990 *Statistical Abstract of the United States, 1990.* Washington, D.C.: U.S. Government Printing Office.

Vemer, Elizabeth, Marilyn Coleman, Lawrence H. Ganong, and Harris Cooper 1989 "Marital Satisfaction in Remarriage: A Meta-Analysis." *Journal of Marriage and the Family* 51:713–725.

White, Lynn K., and Alan Booth 1985 "The Quality and Stability of Remarriages: The Role of Stepchildren." *American Sociological Review* 50:689–698.

Wilson, Barbara Foley 1989 "Remarriages and Subsequent Divorces." *National Vital Statistics.* Series 21, no. 45. Hyattsville, Md.: National Center for Health Statistics.

NANCY E. SACKS
J. JILL SUITOR

REPLICATION Philosophers have long identified replicability, also called "intersubjective testability," "reliability," and "verifiability by repetition," as a key element that distinguishes science from other forms of intellectual inquiry. In recent years philosophically oriented sociologists have attacked the claim that replicability logically distinguishes scientific knowledge, arguing that researchers' judgments as to what counts as a replication are historically contingent products of social negotiation (cf. Collins 1985). Practicing scientists nevertheless continue to emphasize replication as an important means of distinguishing truth from error. For this reason, nearly all scientific papers contain a section that describes the methods and materials used in a research project so that, at least hypothetically, others can repeat the work in an attempt to reproduce the reported results. Successful replication gives scientists confidence in each others' work and reassures them about the fruitfulness of their general line of inquiry. The meaning of an unsuccessful attempt to replicate earlier work is ambiguous; it may cast doubt upon the work but may also be due to such factors as inadequate specification of research procedures, the existence of a stochastic element in the production of results, and researchers' incompetence (Aronson and Carlsmith 1968).

One may distinguish a continuum that ranges between *exact replication* and *weakly approximate replication.* The former refers to attempts to repeat exactly the conditions, materials, and procedures of a previous study to determine whether the same results are obtained. Approximate replication refers to attempts to improve upon a new finding or to extend it to other topics. When successful, such work indirectly replicates the original procedure or finding. Most scientists value successful approximate replication more than successful exact replication because it contributes something new to existing knowledge.

Attempts to replicate published work exactly are rare and are mostly confined to cases of suspected self-delusion or fraud. This is partly because exact replications are often difficult and costly to perform; researchers are therefore reluctant to perform them unless the suspect work is theoretically important or has potential practical value. In addition, researchers ordinarily have trouble publishing exact or nearly exact replications. Journal editors are reticent to publish such work because (1) little new knowledge results when an exact replication reproduces a previous study's findings and (2) when an attempt at exact replication fails to reproduce a study's findings, the original researcher can usually counter that the attempt did not really reproduce the original procedures. The difficulty in publishing even nearly exact replications leads to competition for priority in reporting research results and encourages researchers to specialize in order to reduce the chance of being "scooped" (Hagstrom 1965, pp. 69–104). Such specialization reduces the likelihood of exact and nearly exact replications.

Exact replications are almost nonexistent in the social sciences, especially for nonexperimental studies such as sample surveys, because social science research is done in changing social and historical contexts. Consequently, failures to reproduce a finding exactly can nearly always be ascribed to failing to recreate the social and historical context of the previous study. This difficulty makes especially ambiguous the meaning of failures to replicate previous results in the social sciences (Schuman and Presser 1981).

Weakly approximate replications, the overwhelming majority of all replications, can achieve many goals. For example, they may demonstrate that a finding can be generalized beyond the population originally studied or can shed light on the construct validity of an experimental manipulation (Aronson and Carlsmith 1968). However, weakly approximate replications are often not identified as such because, if successful, their main contribution is to improve or extend the original work. When an approximate replication fails to yield the results earlier work suggested, researchers rarely conclude that the earlier work was incorrect because, by attempting to go beyond it, the approximate replication does not constitute a fair test of the validity of the earlier work.

Social scientists have long advocated increased reliance on replication of previous research. This concern is due partly to their dependence on statistical inference. Researchers using statistical inference can only reject or fail to reject a null hypothesis, and each of these two outcomes is subject to error due to the probabilistic nature of statistical hypothesis testing—sometimes researchers reject a null hypothesis when it is actually true (type-one error) and sometimes they fail to reject a null hypothesis when it is actually false (type-two error). Replications can help assess whether previously reported results were the result of one of these two kinds of error.

Concern about the possibility that a substantial proportion of published results is due to type-one error is a second reason for emphasis on the desirability of increased replications (Sterling 1959). Because failure to reject a null hypothesis does not justify accepting it, studies that do not yield rejections are usually judged as contributing little substantively and are published infrequently. To ensure that they will be able to reject a null hypothesis, researchers may use procedures that maximize the chance that statistically significant results will result (cf. Selvin and Stuart 1966). These practices capitalize on chance and are likely to yield findings that are due to type-one error. Concern about the possible prominence of type-one error in the published literature is also prevalent in the medical sciences, in which physicians might adopt expensive and invasive treatments on the basis of results contained in a single research report.

Although the traditional view of replication entails the collection of new data—including data on additional cases or additional measures—statisticians and social scientists have suggested alternative replication strategies. One is to build replication into a study from the start. For example, a researcher can draw a sample large enough to allow its random partition into two subsamples. Data in one subsample can then be used to check conclusions drawn from analysis of data in the other. A more recent approach, requiring the intensive use of computing resources, is to draw multiple random subsamples from already collected data and then use these subsamples to cross-validate results (Finifter 1972). This general strategy, which includes such techniques as "jackknifing" and "bootstrapping," is also used to assess sampling variances for complex sampling designs. Another elaboration of the basic idea of replication is the general approach called *meta-analysis.* Here an analyst treats existing studies on a topic as a sample of approximate replications and analyzes them to determine if they show similar results and if variation in study design accounts for variation in results (Rosenthal 1984).

Despite calls for increased replication, behavioral science journals publish few studies aimed at replicating previously published work. In an early study of this issue, Theodore Sterling (1959) reported that among 362 articles in psychology journals, 97 percent of those reporting a test of significance rejected the null hypothesis but that none was an explicit replication. Ironically, many have replicated Sterling's results (cf. Dickersin 1990; Gaston 1979; Reid, Soley, and Rimmer 1981). These studies may underestimate the prevalence of replication, however, because they do not count papers reporting a set of experiments that comprise both an original result and one or more approximate replications of it. Nevertheless, many argue that scholarly journals in the behavioral sciences should more actively encourage replication studies, perhaps by reserving a certain amount of space for them. By not encouraging replication, behavioral science journals may foster elaborate and vacuous theorizing at the expense of identifying factual puzzles that deserve theoretical analysis (Cook and Campbell 1979, p. 25).

(SEE ALSO: *Reliability; Scientific Explanation*)

REFERENCES

Aronson, Elliot, and J. Merrill Carlsmith 1968 "Experimentation in Social Psychology." In Gardner Lindzey and Elliot Aronson, eds., *Handbook of Social Psychology,* 2nd ed. Reading, Mass.: Addison-Wesley.

Collins, H. M. 1985 *Changing Order: Replication and Induction in Scientific Practice.* London: Sage.

Cook, Thomas D., and Donald T. Campbell 1979 *Quasi-Experimentation: Design and Analysis Issues for Field Studies.* Chicago: Rand McNally.

Dickersin, Kay 1990 "The Existence of Publication Bias and Risk Factors for Its Occurance." *Journal of the American Medical Association* 263:1,385–1,389.

Finifter, Bernard M. 1972 "The Generation of Confidence: Evaluating Research Findings by Random Subsample Replication." In Herbert L. Costner, ed., *Sociological Methodology 1972.* San Francisco: Jossey-Bass.

Gaston, Jerry 1979 "The Big Three and the Status of Sociology." *Contemporary Sociology* 8:789–793.

Hagstrom, Warren O. 1965 *The Scientific Community.* New York: Basic Books.

Reid, L. H., L. C. Soley, and R. D. Rimmer 1981 "Replications in Advertising Research: 1977, 1978, 1979." *Journal of Advertising* 10:3–13.

Rosenthal, Robert 1984 *Meta-Analytic Procedures for Social Research.* Beverly Hills, Calif.: Sage.

Schuman, Howard, and Stanley Presser 1981 "Mysteries of Replication and Non-Replication." In Howard Schuman and Stanley Presser, *Questions and Answers in Attitude Surveys.* New York: Academic Press.

Selvin, Hannan C., and Alan Stuart 1966 "Data-Dredging Procedures in Survey Analysis." *American Statistician* 20:20–23.

Sterling, Theodore D. 1959 "Publication Decisions and Their Possible Effects on Inferences Drawn from Tests of Significance—Or Vice Versa." *Journal of the American Statistical Association* 54:30–34.

LOWELL L. HARGENS

RETIREMENT Retirement is primarily a twentieth-century phenomenon that developed through a convergence of public and private employment policies, a restructuring of the life span relative to work activity, and a redefinition of the terms of monetary compensation for work performed. It may be tempting to view retirement as the "natural" development of a social institution matched to the needs of older people experiencing declines in capacity and competency. But the invention of a distinctive status called *retirement* was not simply a response to the phenomenon of human aging. Rather, in reconciling a transformed economy to an aging population with an increasing amount of surplus labor, an explicit policy of job distribution was produced. Retirement policies incorporated age as a characteristic that served as both a qualifying and an exclusionary principle for work and income. The fact that these policies were age-based can be linked to the social production of age as a valid predictor of individual capacity and potential, a production that had ideological roots in the science and larger culture of the time.

HISTORICAL DEVELOPMENTS

While *retirement contracts* existed in traditional Europe (Gaunt 1987) and colonial America (Fischer 1977), Plakans (1989) argues that this preindustrial retirement was a more gradual transition that allowed the head of a household to transfer legal title to an heir in exchange for some combination of monetary payments, material provisions, and services as stipulated by the aged person or couple. These contracts were typical of agrarian economies in which land was the main factor in production; they represented the final step in a long and sometimes elaborate process of property transfer. These "stepping down" practices were therefore most immediately linked to inheritance patterns; they could be used to ensure that family control of the land was maintained (Sorensen 1989).

Between 1790 and 1820, American legislatures introduced policies of mandatory retirement for certain categories of public officials. By the late 1800s, the majority of businesses still had no formal policies of fixed-age retirement; however, most used informal policies to eliminate older workers from their labor forces (Fischer 1977). This decline in the demand for older workers can be linked to changes in the structure of American capitalism. During the late 1800s the structure of American capitalism began to change from small-producer, competitive capitalism to large-scale corporate capitalism (Sklar 1988). Part of this reconstruction involved attempts to rationalize age relations in the workplace, a process that was embedded in a more general disenchantment with older workers and a devaluation of their skills. Indeed, the employment rates for men aged sixty-five and over showed a steady decline during this period, from 80.6 percent in 1870 to 60.2 percent in 1920 (Graebner 1980). According to Graebner's analysis, retirement became the impersonal and egalitarian method adopted by both public and private employers for dealing with superannuated workers. It allowed employers to routinize the dismisal of older workers, thereby restructuring the age composition of their work forces in a way they believed would enhance efficiency, a belief supported by the principles of scientific management. Pension plans legitimized this process and, at the same time, served as an effective labor control device.

The first pension plan (1875) is credited to the American Express Company, but benefits were restricted to permanently incapacitated workers who were at least sixty-five years old with a minimum of twenty years of service (Schulz 1976). In 1920, the first general piece of retirement legislation, the Civil Service Retirement Act, provided pension coverage for federal civilian employees. One year later, the Revenue Act of 1921 encouraged businesses to implement private plans by exempting both the income of pension and profit-sharing trusts and the employer contributions to these trusts from income-tax liability. Nevertheless, coverage remained concentrated in a few industries, and 85 percent of the work force continued to be without pension coverage (Schulz 1976).

By the 1930s, the question of how to solve the problem of superannuated workers was coupled with the more general problem of managing surplus labor. The changing technology of the workplace, the speeding up and mechanization that were part of the transformation of the labor process, the subsequent increase in worker productivity, and the growing recognition of the cyclical crises inherent in industrial capitalism broadened the concern beyond that of simple superannuation to that of job distribution and consumption capacity.

The Great Depression of the 1930s greatly exacerbated the growing problem of old-age poverty and unemployment. By 1935 unemployment rates among those sixty-five and older were well over 50 percent (Holzman 1963). Even those with pension benefits did not escape poverty; trade union plans were collapsing, and state and local governments were decreasing or discontinuing pension payments (Olsen 1982). Legislative proposals for alleviating some of these problems included the Townsend Plan and the Lundeen Bill. The Townsend Plan proposed a flat $200 monthly pension for older Americans; recipients had to spend the pension within thirty days. The Lundeen Bill proposed benefits at the level of prevailing local wages for all unemployed workers aged eighteen and older (including the elderly) until suitable employment was located (Olsen 1982). Neither of these plans was directly related to a retirement transition. The Townsend Plan would grant equal benefits to all nonemployed persons over age sixty. The Lundeen Bill focused more on job creation for workers of all ages than on limiting labor supply through age exclusions.

In 1934, President Franklin Roosevelt appointed the Committee on Economic Security (CES) to develop legislation to address the problems of old-age poverty and unemployment. The Social Security Act of 1935 offered a solution that based benefits on the level of worker contributions to a general trust fund. Upon their retirement, covered workers (primarily those in manufacturing) could draw retirement benefits, assuming they met the age and work eligibility requirements.

For the CES, retirement referred to complete withdrawal from the labor force. As stated by Barbara Armstrong, an original member of the CES, "Retirement means that you've stopped working for pay." According to Armstrong, the option facing the Roosevelt administration pitted older workers against younger workers (Graebner 1980, p. 186). Retirement would reduce unemployment by moving older workers out of the labor force, allowing industries characterized by surplus labor to transfer jobs from older to younger workers. The federal government could facilitate this process by shifting the focus of older workers' financial dependency from the wage contract to a federal income maintenance program. In that sense, the Social Security Act of 1935 established what was primarily a program of old-age relief; its limited coverage and low benefit levels precluded its serving as an effective instrument of retirement. However, in establishing a measure of income support for retired older workers, the act reinforced the view that in the competition for jobs, age was a legitimate criterion, and youth had the "higher claim" (Graebner 1980). Ironically, the mobilization for World War II created job opportunities for older workers, as it did for women. Even though these opportunities proved temporary, they called into question the connection between retirement and superannuation, a connection that was asserted more emphatically when the supply of labor exceeded the demand.

During the next several decades, considerable growth in private pension plans occurred; coverage increased from 4 million workers in the late 1930s to 10 million workers in 1950 and 20 million workers in 1960. The expansion was spurred by a number of factors including the desire of firms to encourage loyalty and reduce turnover, favorable tax treatment, and the 1949 Supreme Court decision to uphold a National Labor Relations Board ruling that pensions were appropriate issues of negotiation through collective bargaining (Schulz 1976). During this same period, an increasing number of occupations were included under the umbrella of Social Security, and Congress continued to raise benefits in response to changes in the cost of living, although actual benefit levels remained relatively low (Derthick 1979).

RETIREMENT RESEARCH

Early research on retirement was centrally concerned with the question of voluntarism in the retirement transition, as well as with the financial, social, and psychological consequences of leaving the labor force. Even though the expansion of both public and private pensions had improved the economic situation of older people in retirement, poverty rates among the elderly were still high. By 1960, 35.2 percent of persons aged sixty-five and over were below the poverty line, compared with 22.4 percent of the general population. Poverty was the norm for older white women and older blacks, although, among blacks, the risk of poverty was not as greatly exacerbated by age (U.S. Bureau of the Census 1987).

During the 1950s, the Social Security Administration began studying the characteristics of newly entitled beneficiaries. Initial reports stated that early retirement occurred primarily because of poor health and difficulties with finding and keeping jobs; the availability of Social Security retirement benefits played a secondary role (Wentworth 1945; Stecker 1955). Although these studies relied on beneficiary-reported reasons for retirement, a measurement strategy that was criticized because of its susceptibility to social desirability bias, their findings cannot be totally discounted. Retirement in the 1950s was not a financially attractive status for many older workers. Given that retirement income programs offered "fixed" benefits (benefits that remained nominally the same but, with inflation, declined in real terms), the financial security of middle- and working-class retirees was in jeopardy.

During the 1950s, retirement grew as a social phenomenon. Insurance companies led the way in developing "retirement preparation" programs, as researchers attempted to define strategies for "successful aging." In 1961, Cumming and Henry argued that disengagement, the gradual relinquishment of social roles and positions of authority and responsibility, was a natural process of aging that served positive functions for both the individual and society. By extension, retirement from the labor force was a process older workers should not resist. This perspective contrasted sharply with the tenets of activity theory, which held that successful aging resulted from remaining active and involved in social networks.

In an era of postwar prosperity, retirement came to be viewed as a "period of potential enjoyment and creature experience which accrues as a social reward for a life-time of labor" (Donahue, Orbach, and Pollak 1960, p. 361). Researchers investigating the effect of retirement on life satisfaction found that "retirement does not cause a sudden deterioration in psychological health as [had] been asserted by other writers" (Streib and Schneider 1971). Rather than rejecting the idea of retirement, the policy concerns advanced by advocacy groups for the elderly emphasized the conditions of retirement, in particular the adequacy of retirement income. Mandatory retirement had not yet become an issue (Achenbaum 1983). Instead, the trend was in the direction of earlier retirement, that is, before the age of sixty-five. In 1956, women, and in 1962 men, were allowed to retire at age sixty-two by accepting actuarially reduced Social Security benefits.

During the mid-1960s, in the context of Lyndon Johnson's War on Poverty, the issue of poverty of the elderly again captured the attention of elected officials. In the Older Americans Act of 1965, Congress established a "new social contract for the aged" (Achenbaum 1983, p. 95) by specifying a series of objectives that, if met, would significantly improve the quality of life enjoyed by older people. Among these objectives was the entitlement of older people to "equal opportunity to the full and free enjoyment of . . . an adequate income in retirement in accordance with the American standard of living . . . [and] retirement in health, honor, and dignity" (U.S. Department of Health, Education, and Welfare 1976).

It was during Richard Nixon's presidency that the era of modern retirement was inaugurated (Myles 1988). Whereas earlier amendments to the Social Security Act had brought more and more workers into the system, they had not significantly improved the level of retirement benefits (Munnell 1977). The presumption that Social Security benefits should serve as retirement income supplements rather than as the primary source of income had not been challenged. But the persistently high rates of old-age poverty lent credence to the charge that benefits were inadequate. During the decade following passage of the Older

Americans Act, benefits increased five times and, in 1972, were indexed relative to changes in the consumer price index. Both the "real" level of benefits and the replacement rate of benefits to previous earnings were improved. These enhancements in the "retirement wage" allowed workers to maintain their standard of living across the retirement transition and helped redefine retirement as a legitimate nonwork status that average-income workers could afford to enter voluntarily (Myles 1988). During the decade of the 1970s, private pension plans were also being reorganized. In 1974, passage of the Employee Retirement Income Security Act regularized vesting plans and provided workers with some protection against benefit loss (Schulz 1976). Private-sector initiatives aimed at inducing early retirement were also becoming more common (Barfield and Morgan 1969). Until the 1970s, workers choosing early retirement virtually always accepted reduced benefits. During the 1970s, however, private plans began providing early retirement benefits greater than their actuarial equivalent (Schulz 1976).

The parallel changes in labor force participation rates and in poverty rates among the elderly are noteworthy. During the 1970s, labor force participation rates for older men dropped significantly, especially among early-retirement-aged workers. For men aged 55 to 64, rates dropped from 83 percent in 1970 to 75.6 percent in 1975 and 72.1 percent in 1980 (U.S. Department of Labor 1983). In addition, at the beginning of the decade, 24.6 percent of those aged 65 and older were living below the poverty line, twice the 12.1 percent that characterized the general population. By the end of the decade, the poverty rate among the elderly had dropped to 15.2 percent, compared with an overall poverty rate of 11.7.

During the 1970s and 1980s, retirement research produced a fairly consistent picture of the retirement process. Most of this research was being conducted by economists and sociologists. These studies concentrated on workers' circumstances at the time of their retirements rather than on post hoc explanations that retirees offered for their behavior, an analytic design facilitated by federally funded longitudinal surveys such as the Retirement History Surveys and the National Longitudinal Survey of Older Men (NLS), both of which began in the mid to late 1960s.

Economists typically conceptualized retirement as an individual decision based in utility theory and the underlying assumption that equates choice with revealed preference. Individuals attempt to maximize pleasure and minimize discomfort; therefore, they "choose" to retire when the "benefits" of entering retirement exceed the "costs." Clark and Barker (1981) argue that increased wealth may make work less attractive and that variation in retirement behavior can be explained by individual differences in personal characteristics, in preferences for work versus leisure, and in work opportunities. These econometric studies frequently focused on establishing the determinants of early retirement. They consistently documented the importance of retirement income in retirement decision making: eligibility for benefits (both Social Security and private pension benefits), benefit amount, and financial consequences of postponing retirement benefits. Health limitations also continued to reliably predict early retirement (Bowen and Finegan 1969), and several studies (e.g., Quinn 1977) reported that the availability of retirement income, especially Social Security benefits, had a stronger effect on health-impaired workers than on healthy workers.

Sociologists have largely shared an individualistic orientation to retirement decision making, but they have also introduced structural features of older workers' situations into models of retirement behavior. A central argument in this literature derives from traditional theories of stratification and stresses the importance of occupational structure in shaping behavioral contingencies. Workers in different structural locations face different opportunities/constraints on their behaviors (Hardy 1985). Some positions (e.g., unionized manufacturing) are structured in ways that protect older workers through seniority systems; at the same time, they encourage early retirement by providing pension plans that make retirement financially feasible, especially for workers with many years of continuous service, and by socializing workers to the benefits of early retirement. However, older workers are also vulnerable to plant closings and job dislocations that accompany mergers, downsizing, and cutbacks in government spending (Schulz 1976). This perspective does not argue that all workers in similar circumstances behave in the same way. But it does suggest that the likelihood of certain outcomes (as referenced by the incidence of certain behaviors) varies across structural contexts, thereby producing different "normative patterns" of retirement. In this perspective, retirement is embedded in work careers, with late-career behaviors being at least partially contingent on earlier career opportunities. In addition, retirement behavior is embedded in more general macroeconomic conditions. Rates of unemployment, changes in both private and public pension policies, and the age structure of the population are all involved in defining the supply-and-demand relations for labor and, ultimately, in the encouragement or discouragement of retirement.

By the time of the 1978 amendments to the Age Discrimination and Employment Act that raised allowable mandatory retirement from age sixty-five to seventy in most occupations and removed it completely in federal civil service, retirement studies were reporting that mandatory retirement policies play only a minor role in the process of labor force withdrawal among older workers (Burkhauser and Quinn 1983), a factor that may be due, at least in part, to the increasing orientation of larger firms toward retirement incentives rather than compulsory terminations. In a 1966 survey of industrial firms in the United States with fifty or more employees, Slavick (1966) found that mandatory policies were more common in large firms and firms that offered private pensions. Though only a minority of firms enforced mandatory retirement, approximately half of wage-and-salary workers were believed to be subject to these policies. Although the number of potential "forced" retirements was quite large, the actual number of workers whose retirements appeared to be the result of mandatory retirement was quite small: Parnes and Less (1985) reported that fewer than 5 percent of the retired men in the NLS were forced out through mandatory plans.

CHANGING DEFINITIONS OF RETIREMENT

As the incidence and study of retirement increased, so did the ambiguity of the concept. Armstrong's definition of "no longer working for pay" was being replaced by a variety of definitions that revolved around factors other than work activity per se. In general, these definitions differ in the way they frame the transition that is central to retirement. Whereas Armstrong's definition focused on the worker's exit from the labor force, other definitions are oriented toward transitions out of career employment or full-time work or changes in major income sources (the receipt of retirement pension benefits) or in identity structures (e.g., through self-identification as a retiree). As definitions of retirement shifted toward pensions and the inclusion of part-time workers (Atchley 1982), the concerns of government turned toward the escalating cost of retirement and the advisability of delaying it.

A more recent refinement in using labor force participation as the criterion for retirement has been to distinguish among subcategories of nonparticipation, that is, differentiating the retired from the disabled older worker. Studies invoking this distinction document different patterns of withdrawal by occupational category. Professionals, managers, and salesmen tend to delay retirement, whereas skilled and semiskilled blue-collar workers move more rapidly into retirement; clerical workers move more quickly into both retirement and disability statuses, and service workers experience relatively high rates of disability and death out of employment (Hayward, Hardy, and Grady 1989).

Older, discouraged workers have received less attention. The official category of discouraged workers is a relatively recent creation of the Bureau of Labor Statistics denoting former workers who would like to work but are not seeking employment because they believe either that no jobs are available or that their skills or their age make them unhirable. The discouraged worker hypothesis, that older workers leave the labor force after unsuccessful job searches, suggests that labor force exits should be responsive to changes in levels of unemployment. Bowen and Finegan (1969) demonstrate that the responsiveness of labor force participation to changes in unemployment increases with age for both men and married women, and Rosenblum (1975) argues that workers aged fifty-five or older had the highest rates of discouragement.

All of these developments in defining retirement have expanded and refined the status beyond that of a single category of older nonworkers. Studies that distinguish retirees from older disabled workers reflect the change in the social definition of what it means to be retired. Whereas earlier views defined retirement as a status for people who couldn't work because of illness or couldn't find work, retirement gradually became redefined as a distinct life stage devoted to the enjoyment of leisure activities before the onset of disabling health conditions (Atchley 1985). Definitions that allowed retirees to also be workers became more common as the propensity for older workers to maintain marginal attachments to the labor force through temporary or part-time work increased. More recent studies (e.g., Beck 1984) have reported that a significant minority of those who leave the labor force reenter at a later time. For some, retirement is a partial or temporary status rather than a complete and final exit.

ISSUES OF GENDER AND RACE

The development of retirement policy has been predominantly male-centered. The structure of "retirement wages" has been oriented to the work careers of men, predominantly white men. The original Social Security program excluded industries in which women and blacks were concentrated. Although later amendments eventually covered these categories of workers, the benefit structure continued to reward long and continuous attachment to the labor force and penalize workers for extended or frequent absences from the labor force, regardless of the reasons for these absences. The temporal organization of women's lives relative to work and family activities has important ramifications for their retirement. Women whose work careers are interrupted by years of childbearing and child rearing may find it difficult to retire, since they are "off schedule" in the accumulation of retirement income (O'Rand and Henretta 1982a, 1982b).

African-Americans are more likely to exit from the labor force through disability and also more likely to continue to work intermittently after retirement. However, Gibson (1987) argues that disability is simply another pathway to retirement for older African-Americans, one that offers financial advantages. The work patterns of African-Americans also present special challenges to retirement researchers. In youth, as well as in old age, work patterns among them can appear sporadic, a factor that creates ambiguity in determining the exact timing of retirement (Gibson 1987; Jackson and Gibson 1985). In addition, work histories characterized by frequent spells of unemployment, illness, or temporary disability are linked to lower average retirement benefits.

The career disadvantages of women and African-Americans translate into higher poverty rates for these groups. Married women who qualify for Social Security benefits in their own right frequently find it to their advantage to claim dependents' benefits based on their husbands' work histories (Quadagno 1988). Benefit structures in private pension plans are also weighted in favor of long-tenured employees, both in eligibility requirements and benefit amounts. A study by the U.S. Bureau of Labor Statistics reported that 26.7 percent of the sampled plans required thirty years of service for normal retirement benefits (Bell and Marclay 1987).

Dramatic changes in women's work patterns during this century have made the gendered structure of retirement income programs a source of increasing concern. Whereas the labor force participation rates of U.S. men have shown steady decline, the rates for women have held steadier in both the 55–64 and 65 and older age ranges (Treas 1981). The studies addressing the retirement determinants for older women workers suggest that women's plans are strongly influenced by their own eligibility for Social Security and, when applicable, private pensions (Shaw 1984). They also appear more likely to retire early or late, rather than at the conventional age of 65, and more likely to retire for health reasons (Atchley 1982).

The increasing rates of labor force participation among married women have led some researchers to argue that retirement should be viewed as a joint decision. In fact, there is evidence to suggest that couples may prefer to retire at the same time; however, wives who are younger than their husbands tend to continue working after their husbands retire (Henretta and O'Rand 1980).

INTERNATIONAL COMPARISONS

Discussion of the connection between the development of retirement as a labor force policy and the changes in economic and political organization occurring within the last century need not be limited to a case study of the United States. A comparison across nations can provide valuable insight into the retirement process by showing how different societies regulate the relationship between age and labor markets. Cross-national comparisons indicate that the age of retirement has been declining dramatically in many industrialized nations (Guillemard 1985; Meyer and Featherman 1989). Pampel (1985) reports that, among advanced industrial nations, a pattern of low labor force participation among aged males is related to the level of industrialization and population aging. Mirkin (1987) notes that, among countries of Western Europe and North America, the broadening of eligibility for retirement and disability programs is a favored policy for alleviating unemployment. Although the United States has recently modified public retirement policy in an effort to encourage workers to postpone retirement, early retirement policies in Europe have been more pervasive, a difference he attributes to the greater severity of unemployment problems in Western Europe and the difference in the pace of population aging. In apparent contrast with the experiences of Western Europe, Canada, and the United States, labor force participation rates in Japan appear relatively high (Organization for Economic Co-operation and Development [OECD] 1988). However, in making comparisons on the basis of rates of labor force participation, it is important to take into account national differences in census procedures, how the labor forces are defined, and what types of activities constitute work (Holden 1978). In addition, labor force participation rates do not measure partial retirement. However, because countries differ in the paths workers take to retirement, using pension receipt as an indicator is also flawed. In Germany and France, for example, disability benefits and intermediate unemployment benefits also provide access to early retirement.

Though there is little variation among industrialized nations in the legal retirement age, nations appear to be on different trajectories with regard to retirement policy. In 1983 in the United States, amendments to the Social Security Act legislated a gradual increase in the age of full entitlement. In 1982 France lowered its legal retirement age to sixty. Whereas recent debate in the United States has centered on the financial burdens of supporting a growing population of retirees and the desirability of reversing the trend toward early retirement, Guillemard notes that, in France, "old age is seen as a time in life when work is illegitimate" (Guillemard 1983, p. 88). In trying to understand the difference between these two views, it is necessary to consider more than the characteristics of older workers and retirees; it is necessary to consider how the rights and privileges of different age groups are constructed relative to each other.

(SEE ALSO: *Disengagement Theory; Labor Force; Social Gerontology; Social Security Systems*)

REFERENCES

Achenbaum, W. Andrew 1983 *Shades of Gray: Old Age, American Values, and Federal Policies since 1920*. Boston: Little, Brown.

Atchley, Robert 1982 "Retirement: Leaving the World

of Work." *Annals of the Academy of Political and Social Science* 464:120–131.

———1985 *Social Forces and Aging*. Belmont, Calif: Wadsworth.

Barfield, Richard E., and James N. Morgan 1969 *Early Retirement: The Decision and the Experience.* Ann Arbor, Mich.: University of Michigan Press.

Beck, Scott 1985 "Determinants of Labor Force Activity Among Retired Men." *Research on Aging* 7(2): 251–280.

Bell, Donald, and William Marclay 1987 "Retirement Eligibility and Pension Trends." *Monthly Labor Review* April:18–25.

Bowen, William G., and T. Aldrich Finegan 1969 *The Economics of Labor Force Participation.* Princeton, N.J.: Princeton University Press.

Burkhauser, Richard V., and Joseph F. Quinn 1983 "Is Mandatory Retirement Overrated? Evidence from the 1970s." *Journal of Human Resources* 18(3):337–358.

Clark, Robert, and David T. Barker 1981 *Reversing the Trend toward Early Retirement.* Washington, D.C.: American Enterprise Institute.

Cumming, Elaine, and William E. Henry 1961 *Growing Old: The Process of Disengagement.* New York: Basic Books.

Derthick, Martha 1979 *Policymaking for Social Security.* Washington, D.C.: Brookings Institution.

Donahue, Wilma, Harold Orbach, and Otto Pollak 1960 "Retirement: The Emerging Social Pattern." In Clark Tibbitts, ed., *Handbook of Social Gerontology.* Chicago: University of Chicago Press.

Fischer, David H. 1977 *Growing Old in America.* New York: Oxford University Press.

Gaunt, David 1987 "Rural Household Organization and Inheritance in Northern Europe." *Journal of Family History* 2:121–141.

Gibson, Rose 1987 "Reconceptualizing Retirement for Black Americans." *Gerontologist* 27(6):691–698.

Graebner, William 1980 *A History of Retirement: The Meaning and Function of an American Institution, 1885–1978.* New Haven, Conn.: Yale University Press.

Guillemard, Anne-Marie 1983 "The Making of Old Age Policy in France: Points of Debate, Issues at Stake, Underlying Social Relations." In Anne-Marie Guillemard, ed., *Old Age and the Welfare State.* Beverly Hills, Calif.: Sage.

———1985 "The Social Dynamics of Early Withdrawal from the Labor Force in France." *Aging and Society* 5(4):381–412.

Hardy, Melissa A. 1985 "Occupational Structures and Retirement." In Zena Blau, ed., *Current Perspectives on Aging and the Life Cycle.* Greenwich, Conn.: JAI Press.

Hayward, Mark D., Melissa A. Hardy, and William R. Grady 1989 "Labor Force Withdrawal Patterns among Older Men in the United States." *Social Science Quarterly* 70(2):425–448.

Henretta, John, and Angela O'Rand 1980 "Labor Force Participation Patterns of Older Married Women." *Social Security Bulletin* 43:10–16.

Holden, Karen C. 1978 "Comparability of the Measured Labor Force of Older Women in Japan and the United States." *Journal of Gerontology* 33(3):422–426.

Holzman, Abraham 1963 *The Townsend Movement: A Political Study.* New York: Bookman.

Jackson, James, and Rose Gibson 1985 "Work and Retirement Among the Black Elderly." In Zena Blau, ed., *Current Perspectives On Aging and the Life Cycle.* Greenwich, Conn.: JAI Press.

Mayer, Karl Ulrich, and David L. Featherman 1989 "Methodological Problems in Cross-National Research on Retirement." In David Kertzer and K. Warner Schaie, eds., *Age Structuring in Comparative Perspective.* Hillsdale, N.J.: Erlbaum.

Mirkin, Barry 1987 "Early Retirement as a Labor Force Policy: An International Overview." *Monthly Labor Review* March:19–33.

Munnell, Alicia H. 1977 *The Future of Social Security.* Washington, D.C.: Brookings Institution.

Myles, John 1988 "Postwar Capitalism and the Extension of Social Security into a Retirement Wage." In Margaret Weir, Ann Orloff, and Theda Skocpol, eds., *The Politics of Social Policy in the United States.* Princeton, N.J.: Princeton University Press.

Olsen, Laura Katz 1982 *The Political Economy of Aging: The State, Private Power, and Social Welfare.* New York: Columbia University Press.

O'Rand, Angela, and John Henretta. 1982a. "Delayed Career Entry, Industrial Pension Structure and Retirement in a Cohort of Unmarried Women." *American Sociological Review* 47:365–373.

———1982b. "Women at Middle Age: Developmental Transitions." *Annals of the Political and Social Sciences,* 464:57–64.

Organisation for Economic Co-operation and Development 1988 *Aging Populations: The Social Policy Implications.* Paris: OECD.

Pampel, Fred 1985. "Determinants of Labor Force Participation Rates of Aged Males in Developed and

Developing Nations, 1965–1975." In Zena Blau, ed., *Current Perspectives on Aging and the Life Cycle.* Greenwich, Conn.: JAI Press.

Parnes, Herbert S., and Lawrence J. Less 1985 "The Volume and Pattern of Retirements, 1966–1981." In Herbert S. Parnes, et al., eds., *Retirement Among American Men.* Lexington, Mass.: D. C. Heath.

Plakans, Andrejs 1989 "Stepping Down in Former Times: A Comparative Assessment of Retirement in Traditional Europe." In David Kertzer and K. Warner Schaie, eds., *Age Structuring in Comparative Perspective,* Hillsdale, N.J.: Erlbaum.

Quadagno, Jill 1988 "Women's Access to Pensions and the Structure of Eligibility Rules: Systems of Production and Reproduction." *Sociological Quarterly* 29(4):541–558.

Quinn, Joseph 1977 "Microeconomic Determinants of Early Retirement: A Cross Sectional View of White Married Men." *Journal of Human Resources* 12:329–346.

Rosenblum, Marc 1975 "The Last Push: From Discouraged Worker to Involuntary Retirement." *Industrial Gerontology* 2:14–22.

Schulz, James H. 1976 *The Economics of Aging.* Belmont, Calif.: Wadsworth.

Shaw, Lois 1984 "Retirement Plans of Middle-Aged Women." *Gerontologist* 24 (2):154–159.

Sklar, Martin J. 1988 *The Corporate Reconstruction of American Capitalism, 1890–1916.* New York: Cambridge University Press.

Slavick, Fred 1966 *Compulsory and Flexible Retirement in the American Economy.* Binghamton, N.Y.: Hall.

Sorensen, Aage B. 1989 "Old Age, Retirement, and Inheritance." In David Kertzer and K. Warner Schaie, eds., *Age Structuring in Comparative Perspective.* Hillsdale, N.J.: Erlbaum.

Stecker, Margaret 1955 "Why Do Beneficiaries Retire? Who Among Them Return to Work?" *Social Security Bulletin* 18:3.

Streib, Gordon F., and Clement Schneider 1971 *Retirement in American Society.* Ithaca, N.Y.: Cornell University Press.

Treas, Judith 1981 "Women's Employment and Its Implications for the Status of the Elderly in the Future." In Sara B. Keisler, James N. Morgan, and Valerie Oppenheimer, eds., *Aging, Social Change.* New York: Academic Press.

U.S. Bureau of the Census. 1987. *Statistical Abstract of the United States 1986.* Washington, D.C.: U.S. Government Printing Office.

U.S. Department of Health, Education, and Welfare 1976 *Older Americans' Act of 1965, as Amended and Related Acts, Bicentennial Compilation, March 1976.* Washington, D.C.: Office of Human Development, Administration on Aging.

U.S. Department of Labor, Bureau of Labor Statistics 1983 Current Population Reports, Series P-60, No. 148. Washington, D.C.: U.S. Government Printing Office.

Wentworth, Edna C. 1945 "Why Beneficiaries Retire." *Social Security Bulletin* 8:16–20.

MELISSA HARDY

REVOLUTIONS *Revolutions* are rapid, fundamental transformations of a society's socioeconomic and political structures (Huntington 1968). Social revolutions differ from other forms of social transformation, such as rebellions, coups d'état, and political revolutions. *Rebellions* involve the revolt of society's subordinate classes—peasants, artisans, workers—but do not produce enduring structural changes. *Coups d'état* forcibly replace the leadership of states but do not alter state structures. *Political revolutions* transform state structures but leave social structures largely intact. What is distinctive to social revolutions is that basic changes in social structures and political structures occur in a mutually reinforcing fashion (Skocpol 1979).

Recent sociological work on revolutions recognizes their importance to the making of the modern world order and the opportunities revolutions offer for building theories of social and political change. These opportunities were most emphatically embraced by Marx, who placed the study and the project of revolution at the center of his lifework. Virtually all theories of revolution since Marx share his concern with three separate yet interrelated phenomena: (1) the social conditions that lead to revolution or its absence; (2) the character of participation in revolutions; and (3) the outcomes of revolutions (see Tucker 1978). This review compares Marx's analysis with significant contemporary interpretations in order to examine how events after his death have changed theories of revolution and to consider how much Marx's legacy might endure in future work.

First, Marx understood modern revolutions to be by-products of the historical emergence of capitalism. Revolutionary situations emerged when contradictions between the forces of production (how the means of existence are produced) and the relations of production (how labor's product is distributed) within an existing mode of production reached their limits. These contradictions were evident in the crises of overproduction that well up from time to time in capitalist economies. Revolutions brought the resolution of crises by serving as bridges between successive modes of production, enabling the ascent of capitalism over feudalism and, later, the replacement of capitalism by socialism.

Second, Marx held that revolutions were accomplished through class struggle. Revolutionary situations intensified conflict between the existing dominant class and the economically ascendant class. Under feudalism class conflict pitted the aristocracy against the ascendant bourgeoisie. Under capitalism the differing situations of segments of society determined their revolutionary tendency. Some classes, such as the petite bourgeoisie, would become stakeholders in capitalism and allies of the dominant bourgeoisie. Others, such as the peasantry, that did not fully participate in wage labor and lacked internal solidarity, would stay on the sidelines. The industrial proletariat would be the midwife of socialist revolution, for wage labor's concentration in cities would generate collective consciousness of the proletariat's exploitation by the bourgeoisie. Class consciousness was a necessary (though not a sufficient) condition for revolution.

Third, Marx believed that revolutions so thoroughly transformed class relations that they put in place new conditions enabling further economic advance. Revolutions were locomotives of history that brought in train new structures of state administration, property holding, and political ideology. Reinforcing the fundamental changes in class relations, these transformations culminated the transition from one mode of production to another.

In sum, Marx's theory identified the conditions that spawn revolutionary situations, the classes that would make revolutions, and the outcomes of revolutions. How well has Marx's analysis served later generations of scholars and revolutionaries? Many of the sociopolitical transformations since his death were unanticipated by Marx. In light of these events, contemporary sociologists have reconsidered his thinking.

Consider first the social conditions making for revolution or its absence. Social revolutions are rare. Modern capitalist societies have experienced deep economic crises that intensified class conflicts and gave the appearance of revolutionary situations, but they have skirted actual revolution. Capitalist economies have great staying power, and reform rather than revolution is the rule in advanced nations. Indeed, the great revolutions of France, Russia, and China, and those in Third World states such as Cuba, Vietnam, and Nicaragua, have occurred in predominantly agrarian economies where capitalist relations of production were only moderately developed. The 1917 Russian Revolution stands as proof of Lenin's claim that revolution was possible in Russia despite its failure to develop a fully capitalist economy in the manner of Western European states.

Rather than growing from contradictions between the forces and the relations of production, revolutionary situations arise in political crises occasioned by international competitive pressures. States with relatively backward economies are vulnerable to military defeats, as occurred in Russia in 1917, and to financial crises like that of 1789 France after a century of costly struggle with Britain. Countries that are disadvantaged within the international states system are most at risk to externally induced crises and to the possibility of social revolution.

A state's vulnerability to crisis, however, depends fundamentally on its relationship to elites, whether nobles, landlords, or religious authorities. State managers are forever caught in the cross pressures between attempts to meet international competitive challenges by increasing revenues and resistance by angry elites to resource extraction. States that are weakly bureaucratized, where elites control high offices and key military posts, cannot act autonomously. When powerful elites can paralyze the state's resource accumulation, severe conflicts occur, as in the English, French, and Chinese revolutions (Goldstone 1986).

However, externally induced crises may initiate an "elite revolution," as occurred in Japan's 1868 Meiji restoration and Ataturk's 1919 revolution in Turkey. In such regimes a bureaucratic elite of civil and military officials emerged that lacked large landholdings or ties to merchants and landlords. In the face of Western military threats to national sovereignty and, consequently, to their own power and status, these elites seized control of the state apparatus. With the aim of resolving economic and military difficulties, they transformed existing sociopolitical structures through land reform, leveling of status distinctions, and rapid industrialization (Trimberger 1978). These transformative episodes, sometimes called "revolutions from above," are distinguished by the absence of popular revolts "from below."

Neopatrimonial regimes are highly vulnerable to revolutionary overthrow (Eisenstadt 1978). Examples include pre-1911 Mexico, pre-1959 Cuba, pre-1979 Nicaragua, and pre-1979 Iran. Centered on the personal decisions of a dictator, these regimes operate through extensive patronage networks rather than a bureaucratized civil service and professional military. Their exclusionary politics makes reform nearly impossible and, in the event of a withdrawal of support by stronger states, invites challenges that may overwhelm corrupt armed forces.

In contrast, revolution is unlikely in open, participatory regimes typical of modern capitalist democracies. By enfranchising new groups, these systems successfully incorporate challengers. By redistributing wealth and opportunity, they are able to mute class antagonisms.

In sum, contradictions between the state apparatus and the dominant classes have been crucial to the onset of revolutionary situations. State bureaucrats are caught in the cross pressures between meeting the challenges of the international states system and yielding to the competing claims of elites. Consequently state structures differ in their vulnerability to political crises.

Consider next the character of participation in revolutions. Challengers of Marx's voluntarist theory assert that no successful social revolution has been made by a self-consciously revolutionary movement. They allow that revolutionaries do guide the course of revolutions, but assert that they do not create revolutionary situations, which emerge from externally induced political crises. These theorists also offer a different reading of the roles of social classes in revolutions. Urban workers, favored by Marx's theory, played important parts in revolutions. However, their numbers were small and their contribution was less crucial than that of peasants, who comprised the vast bulk of producers. When political crises immobilized armies and weakened supervision, they opened the way for peasant revolts that provided the "dynamite" to bring down old regimes (Moore 1966). Revolts against the landed upper classes made it impossible to continue existing agrarian class relations and thereby reduced the prospects for liberalism or counterrevolution. It was the conjunction of political crisis and peasant insurrection that brought about the fundamental transformations identified with social revolution (Skocpol 1979).

But peasants often do not act alone. A key difference between earlier and twentieth-century revolutions is the greater importance of coalitions in the latter (Tilly 1978). Peasants in France and Russia lived in solitary and relatively autonomous villages that afforded them the solidarity and tactical space for revolt (Wolf 1969). Elsewhere, professional revolutionaries provided leadership and ideologies that cemented disparate local groups into potent national movements. The success of their efforts depended in part on the breadth of the coalition they were able to realize among peasants, landless and migrant laborers, rural artisans, and sometimes landlords (Goodwin and Skocpol 1989).

Urban groups have played crucial parts in Third World revolutions. In Cuba and Nicaragua students, professionals, clerics, and merchants joined workers and peasants in coalitions that toppled dictatorical regimes. The 1979 overthrow of the Shah of Iran resulted from an urban revolution that met little resistance from powerful military forces (Farhi 1990).

Finally, revolutionary leaderships have not come from among those who controlled the means of production nor from the ranks of a risen proletariat. Rather, marginal political elites were most likely to consolidate power, for they were both skilled in the running of state organizations and tied by identity and livelihood to the aggrandizement of national welfare and prestige. Their role is clearest in revolutions from above but is no less prominent in social revolutions.

Consider, last, the outcomes of revolutions. For Marx revolutions were bridges between successive modes of production. Bourgeois revolutions marked the transition from feudalism to capitalism; socialist revolutions, the transition from capitalism to communism, history's final stage. Once completed, socialist revolution would open the way to the end of class struggle and the disappearance of state power.

That revolutions transform social and political institutions is undeniable, but the mechanisms of transformation are open to question. In all historically successful revolutions, the resultant sociopolitical transformations were accomplished by new state structures. The state did *not* wither away.

Moreover, the new states were more centralized and bureaucratized. Liberal parliamentary regimes appeared in the early phases of the French and Russian revolutions. However, these gave way in the face of counterrevolutionary threats and international pressures that were met with rationalized state institutions. Revolutionary events in the twentieth century also make clear that the completion and political consolidation of social revolutions depend on the openings offered by military conflicts and the international balance of power. Liberal parliamentary regimes have met similar fates in successful twentieth-century revolutions.

Through the centralization of political power, what changed most in revolutions was the mode of social control of the lower strata. All revolutions ended in the consolidation of new mass-mobilizing state organizations through which peasants and urban workers were for the first time directly incorporated into national economies and politics. National liberation movements in Asia and Africa combined aspirations for independence and for incorporation in a fashion similar to these newly formed revolutionary states.

Finally, much as revolutionary situations are in part determined by world historical events like wars and depressions, revolutionary outcomes transform the structure of the international states system and of world markets. Revolutions break old alliances and create new ones. They launch new programs of agricultural and industrial production. Past revolutions stand as models for present and future revolutions. In all these ways revolutions shape the possibilities for revolution and reform in the modern world order.

Sociologists who study revolutions have been engaged in a project of revision. Informed by recent sociopolitical transformations and new research on past revolutions, their work questions and qualifies much of Marx's analysis. It considers revolutions in the context of the world economy and the international states system. It places the relations between states and social classes in a new light. And it examines how transformations in the recent or distant past weigh on the course of revolutionary events. But, on balance, it largely confirms and continues the main thrust of Marx's method, notably his focus on actors embedded in concrete organizational settings within historically specific circumstances. This view, rather than a focus on the alternatives of personality, collective mentality, or system dysfunction, distinguishes the sociology of revolution. It owes much to Marx's legacy.

(SEE ALSO: *Marxist Sociology*)

REFERENCES

Eisenstadt, S. N. 1978 *Revolution and the Transformation of Societies.* New York: Free Press.

Farhi, Farideh 1990 *States and Urban-Based Revolutions: Iran and Nicaragua.* Urbana: University of Illinois Press.

Goldstone, Jack A. 1986 "The Comparative and Historical Study of Revolutions." In J. A. Goldstone, ed., *Revolutions*. San Diego: Harcourt Brace Jovanovich.

Goodwin, Jeff, and Theda Skocpol 1989 "Explaining Revolutions in the Contemporary Third World." *Politics & Society* 17:489–509.

Huntington, Samuel P. 1968 *Political Order in Changing Societies*. New Haven: Yale University Press.

Moore, Barrington, Jr. 1966 *Social Origins of Dictatorship and Democracy*. Boston: Beacon Press.

Skocpol, Theda 1979 *States and Social Revolutions*. New York: Cambridge University Press.

Tilly, Charles 1978 *From Mobilization to Revolution*. Reading, Mass.: Addison-Wesley.

Trimberger, Ellen Kay 1978 *Revolution from Above: Military Bureaucrats and Development in Japan, Turkey, Egypt, and Peru*. New Brunswick, N.J.: Transaction Books.

Tucker, Robert (ed.) 1978 *The Marx–Engels Reader*. New York: Norton.

Wolf, Eric R. 1969 *Peasant Wars of the Twentieth Century*. New York: Harper and Row.

ROBERT C. LIEBMAN

ROLE CONFLICT *Role conflict* is a social-psychological concept used to investigate and explain individuals' experiences of competing or conflicting demands. The concept was born of two sociological frameworks: *role theory* and *symbolic interactionism*. Role theory provides the underlying metaphor—that social life is structured and individuals occupy social positions such as employee, spouse, and parent in much the same way as actors occupy roles in a play. To explain individual and social activity, role theory focuses primarily on the influences of objective social structures and external forces (e.g., organizational job descriptions for specific work duties, religious norms for wedding ceremonies, cultural expectations of parental responsibility, etc.). Though similar to role theory, symbolic interactionism emphasizes the importance of individuals' subjective appraisals of their role experiences as well as their ability to redefine their roles (see Stryker and Statham 1985 for a thorough discussion of role theory and its relationship to symbolic interactionism). Role conflict draws on both these theoretical frameworks in that it was developed to describe and interpret individuals' subjective experiences of objective role forces.

According to Robert Kahn and his associates, who presented the first systematic treatise of role conflict in their 1964 book, *Organizational Stress: Studies in Role Conflict and Ambiguity*, individuals have jobs or functions (i.e., roles) that typically depend on a steady exchange of role-relevant information with others. For example, secretaries and supervisors depend on each other, through exchanges of facts, feedback, and directives, to work effectively. Communications are laden with expectations that constitute *role pressure*. For a particular individual (a *focal person*), these role pressures are communicated by one or more *role senders*, who, along with the individual, constitute the members of a *role set*. According to Kahn et al. (1964), role conflict (specifically, *sent role conflict*) occurs in three forms: (1) *intersender conflict* occurs when incompatible expectations or demands are communicated by two or more members of a role set; (2) *intrasender conflict* occurs when incompatible expectations or demands are communicated by a single member of a role set; and (3) *interrole conflict* occurs when incompatible expectations or demands are communicated by members of different role sets.

Whereas each of these three forms involves conflict between multiple expectations or demands, it is also possible for a single demand to conflict with the focal individual's personal beliefs or preferences. In other words, *person–role conflict* occurs when an expectation or demand by a member of a role set is incompatible with the focal person's own belief's.

Additionally, Kahn et al. (1964) described the occurrence of overwhelming, though not necessarily conflicting, role pressures as *role overload*. This occurs when one or more role pressures, conflicting or otherwise, are overwhelming.

Because role conflict has an objective or environmental component (what the role senders expect) as well as a subjective or psychological component (what the focal person experiences), researchers have been interested in discovering why objective role conflict does not always result in the psychological experience of role conflict. Kahn et al. (1964) suggest that three sets of factors influence the relations between role senders and focal persons: (1) *organizational factors,* for example, organizational size and management structure; (2) *interpersonal factors,* for example, degree of interdependence among members within and between role sets; and (3) *personality factors,* for example, particular beliefs and motives of role set members. However, despite many empirical investigations, findings on the effects of these moderating factors have been inconsistent (Fisher and Gitelson 1983; Jackson and Schuler 1985; Van Sell, Brief, and Schuler 1981).

In contrast, empirical findings clearly link the subjective experience of role conflict with important outcome measures like role satisfaction. For example, reviews by Jackson and Schuler (1985) as well as Fisher and Gitelson (1983) have linked high levels of employee reports of role conflict with low levels of satisfaction with such aspects of their jobs as coworkers and job content. Similarly, these researchers found that employees who reported high levels of role conflict were more likely than those reporting low levels to consider leaving their job. On average, these studies found the strength of association between role conflict and employee outcomes was "moderate," with absolute correlations of about 0.3 reported.

What is the current state of role conflict measures in social science research? Most studies of role conflict in places of work have used an eight-item self-report instrument developed by Rizzo and his colleagues (1970) and based on the original research by Kahn et al. (1964). This composite includes statements such as "I receive an assignment without adequate resources and materials to execute it," to which respondents reply. In reviewing the psychometric properties of the Rizzo et al. measure of role conflict (as well as a related measure of "role ambiguity"), King and King (1990) concluded that the role conflict measure had several conceptual shortcomings that need to be addressed to improve theory and research in this area. Specifically, they conclude that (1) the eight-item composite may not measure the full breadth of different types of role conflict (as defined by Kahn et al. 1964), (2) the content validity of individual items is tenuous, and (3) evidence of discriminant validity between the role conflict scale and a scale of role ambiguity (theoretically separate constructs) is weak. Given the significance of the concept of role conflict in organizational research, and the intimate connection between theory and measurement, improving the psychometric properties of role conflict measures is critical.

Finally, although the initial measures and studies of conflict focused primarily on role experiences at places of work, self-report measures for assessing conflict within other roles such as marriage and parenting, as well as between work and other roles, have also been developed (Holahan and Gilbert 1979). Consistent with results from studies of role conflict at work, the evidence to date suggests that role conflict experienced in nonwork roles is also related to important role outcomes such as marital satisfaction (see Suchet and Barling 1986). Thus, as research on role conflict expands and improves, it promises to advance both theory and knowledge of how individuals experience conflicting pressures within and between important life domains.

(SEE ALSO: *Role Theory; Stress*)

REFERENCES

Fisher, C. D., and R. Gitelson 1983 "A Meta-analysis of the Correlates of Role Conflict and Ambiguity." *Journal of Applied Psychology,* 68:320–333.

Holahan, C. K., and L. A. Gilbert 1979 "Conflict between Major Life Roles: Women and Men in Dual Career Couples." *Human Relation* 32:451–467.

Jackson, S. E., and R. S. Schuler 1985 "A Meta-analysis and Conceptual Critique of Research on Role Ambiguity and Role Conflict in Work Settings." *Organizational Behavior and Human Decision Processes* 36:16–78.

Kahn, R. L., D. M. Wolfe, R. P. Quinn, J. D. Snoek, and R. A. Rosenthal 1964 *Organizational Stress: Studies in Role Conflict and Ambiguity.* New York: Wiley.

King, L. A., and D. W. King 1990 "Role Conflict and Role Ambiguity: A Critical Assessment of Construct Validity." *Psychological Bulletin* 107:48–64.

Rizzo, J. R., R. J., House, and S. I. Lirtzman, 1970

"Role Conflict and Ambiguity in Complex Organizations." *Administrative Science Quarterly* 15:150–163.

Stryker, S., and A. Statham 1985 "Symbolic Interactionism and Role Theory." In G. Lindzey and E. Aronson, eds., *The Handbook of Social Psychology,* 3rd ed. Reading, Mass.: Addison-Wesley.

Suchet, M., and J. Barling 1986 "Employed Mothers: Interrole Conflict, Spouse Support and Marital Functioning." *Journal of Occupational Behaviour* 7: 167–178.

Van Sell, M., A. P. Brief, and R. S. Schuler 1981 "Role Conflict and Role Ambiguity: Integration of the Literature and Directions for Future Research." *Human Relations* 34:43–71.

ERIC LANG

ROLE MODELS The acceptance of role models as an important concept is evident by the popularity of the term among social scientists as well as laypersons (Jung 1986; Kemper 1968; and Speizer 1981). Kemper (1968) describes a role model as a person who "possesses skills and displays techniques which the actor lacks (or thinks he lacks), and from whom, by observation and comparison with his own performance, the actor can learn." In other words, a role model demonstrates for the actor how something is done. According to Jung (1986), the role model concept is derived from the concepts of role (based on role theory) and modeling (based on social learning theory).

Role theory is a misnomer in the sense that it is not one grand theory (Thomas and Biddle 1966). Biddle (1986) identifies five perspectives, each with its own version of role theory. They include *functional role theory*—focusing on the roles or characteristic behaviors of persons who occupy social positions within a stable social system; *symbolic interactionist role theory*—focusing on the roles of individual actors, the evolution of those roles through social interaction, and how social actors understand and interpret behavior; *structural role theory*—focusing on social structures or social positions that share the same patterned behaviors that are directed toward other social positions in the structure; *organizational role theory*—focusing on roles associated with identified social positions in preplanned, task-oriented, and hierarchical social systems; and *cognitive role theory*—focusing on relationships between role expectations and behavior (for a detailed discussion of these theories, see Biddle 1986). There are, however, certain ideas and concepts that most of these perspectives accept. These common elements are focused on in the following discussion of role theory.

According to Sarbin (1954), role theory attempts to explain human behavior at a complex level. Role theory is concerned with the notion that human behavior can be both different and predictable, depending on an actor's social identity and the context of the situation (Biddle 1986). The theory began as a theatrical metaphor applying terms such as "parts" and "scripts" to explain human conduct. To elaborate on this metaphor, a triad of concepts appears central to role theory. The three concepts are:

1. *expectations*—there are two types of expectations: rights are role expectations in which an actor anticipates certain behaviors from an actor in a reciprocal role; and obligations are role expectations in which an actor of a role anticipates certain behaviors directed toward an actor of a reciprocal role
2. *role or roles*—patterned sequence of learned actions performed by an individual in an interaction situation
3. *social position or positions*—a cognitive organization of role expectations or expected actions of individuals who enact a certain role.

Basically, expectations or scripts generate roles or characteristic behaviors associated with social positions or parts to be played.

Social learning theory is also a misnomer in the sense that there are many variations of this theory. The type of social learning theory of interest here is that which includes imitation or modeling, represented by the work of Bandura and his colleagues (1962; 1963).

Some social learning theories discuss the acquisition of behavior patterns as a slow, gradual process based on differential reinforcement (e.g., classical and operant conditioning). With exposure to a model, Bandura and Walters (1963) claim that behavior patterns can be acquired in large segments or in their entirety. They distinguish among three possible effects of exposure to a model: (1) a modeling effect, indicating that an observer has acquired new response patterns; (2) an inhibitory or disinhibitory effect, involving an increase or decrease in the frequency, latency, or intensity of response patterns similar to the model's response patterns; and (3) a possible eliciting effect, where the observation of a model's responses encourages similar responses by an observer that are neither new nor inhibited as a result of prior learning.

Blending the concepts of role and modeling is an attractive way to explain how an actor is socialized into new roles. In general, an observer learns a particular role through exposure to a model. Certain types of role modeling described in the literature imply the existence of an affectional bond that Jung (1986) claims must be present for a model to be able to influence an observer. For Jung, having an affectional bond distinguishes role modeling from modeling.

Merton (1957) distinguishes role models from referent individuals by indicating that the latter is an individual for whom behavior and values in several roles are emulated, while the former is an individual for whom behavior and values in one or only a few roles are emulated. This distinction indicates that an affectional bond is more likely to exist between a referent individual and an actor than with a role model and an actor. It may be that there are degrees of affectional bonding with modeling at one end of the continuum, referent individuals at the opposite end, and role models lying somewhere in the middle of that continuum.

Much of the research on role modeling examines the learning that takes place in children after exposure to the behavior of a model. Jung (1986) notes that role models for children may include characters in television cartoons, but Speizer (1981) claims that the most often examined role models for children are their parents. She further notes that even though several studies have examined the effects of parental role models on children's career choice and aspirations, the findings remain ambiguous.

SEX ROLE MODELS

To be consistent, sex roles should refer to behaviors that are characteristic of one sex or the other. A review of the literature in this area, however, reveals that attempts to define sex roles have centered on expectations and positions as well as characteristic behaviors (Angrist 1969; Lipman-Blumen and Tickamyer 1975). For the sake of conceptual clarity, sex roles will refer here to those behaviors characteristic of one sex or the other.

Appropriate sex-typed roles are learned through the process of socialization that occurs in social structures such as families and institutions (Lipman-Blumen and Tickamyer 1975). Within these structures are sex role models or individuals who demonstrate appropriate behaviors given their respective sex. In families, the male role model engages in behaviors that differ from those of the female role model. For example, females are typically more involved with household and child care activities even when both spouses work outside the home (Hochschild 1973). In addition, parents engage in differential treatment of their children depending upon whether the children are identified as male or female. For example, parents talk to and cuddle with girls more than boys, while boys are handled more often and more roughly than girls (Lipman-Blumen and Tickamyer 1975).

With regard to sex role models in institutions, several studies have focused on faculty members at both the high school and college levels. In reviewing the work on mentoring relationships, Farmer et al. (1990) note the importance of having a mentor in higher education who, by definition, assists his or her protégé in gaining access to a given profession. They also note that females are disadvantaged in finding same-sex mentors due to the relatively few female faculty members in most academic departments.

In attempting to address the issue of whether it's advantageous for students to have same-sex mentors, Speizer (1981) reports that the findings are variable and sometimes contradictory. Some examples of the type of findings that are reported in the literature are as follows: Female students tend to major in departments with more female faculty members; undergraduate female students who could identify a female faculty role model had significantly higher degree expectations than females who could not identify a role model; and female students report an absence of collegial relationships with male faculty members as well as fewer opportunities to engage in collaborative work with faculty.

These findings do not substantiate the popular notion that female students need female role models to attain maximum achievement, and it is therefore necessary to evaluate critically what has been reported. With regard to the finding that female students major in departments with a greater number of female faculty members, it is possible that these departments have always had a greater number of female majors and any change in the increased ratio of female faculty members to female students has occurred by way of an increase in the number of female faculty members in those departments and not due to an increase in female majors in search of female role models. With regard to higher degree expectations for females identifying a female role model than for those who did not identify a role model, this finding lends more support for the importance of role models than for having a female role model. Finally, with regard to differential treatment of female students, contradictory findings indicate that male and female students do not experience differential treatment.

Sex role models in the workplace are also referred to as mentors or sponsors. Speizer (1981) notes that researchers in this area report that those people who cannot identify a mentor or sponsor are less successful and less happy in their careers. She reports that these studies have primarily been done using white male respondents, which makes her question the popular notion that for maximum achievement, females and minorities need same-sex or same-race or same-ethnic role models, respectively.

Several criticisms are noted in the literature on roles, including problems with the role concept, role theory, and role modeling. Researchers and other authors continue to differ over definitions of the role concept (Biddle 1986), and the definitions that are produced are often vague and insufficient (Borgatta 1960). Biddle (1986) reports that there is also disagreement with regard to the assumptions that can be made about roles, as well as differences of opinion with regard to explanations for role phenomena.

It is not surprising, then, that given the differences with regard to the role concept, assumptions about roles, and the explanations for role phenomena, Biddle (1986) reports that role theorists often work at cross purposes, which, in turn, prevents formal development of role theory. He also describes the current state of role theory as suffering from "confusion and malintegration."

Research on role modeling also suffers due to the lack of conceptual clarity with regard to the notion of role or roles. This is especially apparent in the literature on sex roles. In addition to conceptual problems, several methodological problems plague the work on role modeling. In general, role modeling is a process that is taken for granted. Researchers rely on retrospective accounts identifying an actor's role model as proof of the existence of role models (Jung 1986; Speizer 1981). Jung (1986) notes that without an experimental design, including pre- and postobservation and controls, the results are subject to alternative explanations.

Speizer (1981) notes that role modeling research has often used small, highly selective, atypical samples from which results are generated. In addition, she notes that researchers have sometimes used cross-sectional information as though the data were collected longitudinally.

One of the most important directions for future work is in clarifying the conceptual definition of role or roles. This is important for role theory as well as for role modeling. Role theorists should focus on integrating their ideas and eliminating the confusion that surrounds the theory or theories. Biddle (1986) claims that role theory will prosper only to the extent that it develops its own theoretical orientation.

Additional directions for future work on role modeling should include ascertaining whether role models do indeed exist and the extent to which role models facilitate or impede the learning process, especially as modified by gender and racial differences between the model and the learner.

(SEE ALSO: *Gender; Role Theory; Socialization; Symbolic Interaction Theory*)

REFERENCES

Angrist, Shirley S. 1969 "The Study of Sex Roles." *Journal of Social Issues* 25:215–232.

Bandura, Albert 1962 "Social Learning Through Imitation." In Marshall Jones, ed., *Nebraska Symposium on Motivation.* Lincoln: University of Nebraska Press.

———, and Richard H. Walters 1963 *Social Learning and Personality Development.* New York: Holt, Rinehart, and Winston.

Biddle, B. J. 1986 "Recent Developments in Role Theory." *Annual Review of Sociology* 12:67–92.

Borgatta, Edgar F. 1960 "Role and Reference Group Theory." In Leonard S. Kogan, ed., *Social Science Theory and Social Work Research.* New York: National Association of Social Workers.

Farmer, Yvette M., Lynn M. Ries, and David G. Nickinovich 1990 "Evaluations of Academic Training." Unpublished manuscript.

Hochschild, Arlie Russell 1973 "A Review of Sex Role Research." In Joan Huber, ed., *Changing Women in a Changing Society.* Chicago: University of Chicago Press.

Jung, John 1986 "How Useful Is the Concept of Role Model?: A Critical Analysis." *Journal of Social Behavior and Personality* 1:525–536.

Kemper, Theodore D. 1968 "Reference Groups, Socialization and Achievement." *American Sociological Review* 33:31–45.

Lipman-Blumen, Jean, and Ann R. Tickamyer 1975 "Sex Roles in Transition: A Ten-Year Perspective." *Annual Review of Sociology* 1:297–337.

Merton, Robert 1957 *Social Theory and Social Structure.* New York: Free Press.

Sarbin, Theodore R. 1954 "Role Theory." In Gardner Lindsay, ed., *Handbook of Social Psychology.* Reading, Mass.: Addison-Wesley.

Speizer, Jeanne J. 1981 "Role Models, Mentors, and Sponsors: The Elusive Concepts." *Signs* 6:692–712.

Thomas, Edwin, and Bruce Biddle 1966 "The Nature and History of Role Theory." In Bruce Biddle and Edwin Thomas, eds., *Role Theory: Concepts and Research.* New York: Wiley.

YVETTE FARMER

ROLE THEORY

ROLE THEORY Role theory concerns the tendency of human behaviors to form characteristic patterns that may be predicted if one knows the social context in which those behaviors appear. It explains those behavior patterns (or *roles*) by assuming that persons within a context appear as members of recognized social identities (or *positions*) and that they and others hold ideas (*expectations*) about behaviors in that setting. Its vocabulary and concerns are popular among both social scientists and practitioners, and role concepts have generated both theory and a good deal of research. Nevertheless, conflicts have arisen about the use of role terms and the focus of role theory, and different versions of the theory have appeared among groups of authors who seem to be unaware of alternative versions. As well, role theory has been weakened by association with controversial theories in sociology.

HISTORY, DIFFERENTIATION, AND CONFUSION

Role theory arose when social scientists took seriously the insight that social life could be compared with the theater, in which actors play assigned "rôles." This insight was pursued independently by three major contributors in the early 1930s with somewhat different agendas. For Ralph Linton, role theory was a means for analyzing social systems, and roles were conceived as "the dynamic aspects" of societally recognized social positions (or "statuses"). In contrast, George Herbert Mead viewed roles as the coping strategies that individuals evolve as they interact with other persons and spoke of the need for understanding others' perspectives ("role taking") as a requisite for effective social interaction.

And Jacob Moreno saw roles as the habitual, sometimes harmful, tactics that are adopted by persons within primary relationships and argued that imitative behavior ("role playing") was a useful strategy for learning new roles.

Moreover, additional insights for role theory were generated by other early authors, particularly Muzafer Sherif's studies of the effects of social norms; Talcott Parsons's functionalist theory, which stressed the importance of norms, consensus, sanctioning, and socialization; Robert Merton's analyses of role structures and processes; the works of Neal Gross, Robert Kahn, and their colleagues, who discussed role conflict and applied role concepts to organizations; Everett Hughes's papers on occupational roles; Theodore Newcomb's text for social psychology, which made extensive use of role concepts; and (in Europe) the seminal monographs of Michael Banton, Anne-Marie Rocheblave, and Ragnar Rommetveit, as well as Ralf Dahrendorf's essay "Homo Sociologicus."

The contrasting insights of these early contributors affected many subsequent writers, and various traditions of role theory have since appeared. Unfortunately, advocates for (or critics of) these differing traditions often write as if they are unaware of other versions. In addition, advocates may propose inconsistent uses for terms, or contrasting definitions for concepts, that are basic in role theory. To illustrate, for some authors the term *role* refers only to the concept of social position, for others it designates the behaviors characteristic of social position members, and for still others it denotes shared expectations held for the behaviors of position members. Such inconsistent uses pose problems for the unwary reader.

Also, role theorists may disagree about substantive issues. For example, some authors use role concepts to describe the social system, whereas others apply it to the conduct of the individual. Again, some writers assume that roles are always tied to functions, whereas others conceive roles as behaviors that conform to expectations, that are directed toward others in the system, that are volitional, that validate the actor's status, or that project a self-image. Such differences in stance have reflected both accidents of intellectual history and the fact that role theorists have wrestled with differing social system forms.

Despite these differences, role theorists tend to share a basic vocabulary, interest in the fact that human behavior is contextually differentiated and is associated with the social position of the actor, and the assumption that behavior is generated (in part) by expectations that are held by the actor and others. This means that much of role theory presumes a thoughtful, phenomenally aware participant, and role researchers tend to adopt methods that call for the observing of roles and for asking respondents to report about their own or others' expectations. Moreover, it also means that role theory may be contrasted with alternative theoretical positions that give stronger emphasis to unconscious motives or behavior-inducing forces of which the actor may be unaware (such as unobvious mechanisms that serve to maintain structured inequalities of power, wealth, or status).

FUNCTIONALIST ROLE THEORY

One early perspective in role theory reflected functionalism. Functionalist thought arose from the contributions of Talcott Parsons and was, at one time, the dominant orientation in American sociology. This theory made use of role concepts, and some authors continue to write as if role theory was or is largely an attempt to formalize functionalism.

Functionalist theory was concerned with the problem of explaining social order. Stable but differentiated behaviors were thought to persist within social systems because they accomplished functions and because actors in those systems shared expectations for behaviors. Such consensual expectations (or "roles") constituted norms for conduct, and actor conformity to norms was induced either because others in the system imposed sanctions on the actor or because the actor internalized them. In addition, those in the system were thought to be aware of the norms they held and could be counted on to teach them to (i.e., to socialize) neophytes as the latter entered the system.

Functionalist thought has been under attack since the 1950s, and many of its basic assumptions have been challenged. Critics have pointed out that persisting behaviors may or may not be functional for social systems, that norms for conduct are often in conflict, that actor conformity need not be generated by norms alone but can also reflect other modes of thought (such as beliefs or preferences), that norms might or might not be supported by explicit sanctions, that norms that are internalized by the actor may be at odds with those that are supported by external forces, and that processes of socialization are problematic. Above all, critics have noted that social systems are not the static entities that functionalist thought portrayed and that human conduct often responds to power and conflicts of interest in ways that were ignored by functionalists. As a result of these attacks, interest in functionalist role theory has declined, although it is still possible to find writers who advocate (e.g., Bates and Harvey 1975) or denounce (Connell 1979) role theory as if it were merely a gloss for functionalism.

ROLE CONFLICT AND ORGANIZATIONAL ANALYSIS

Interest in organizational role theory began with the works of Neal Gross, Robert Kahn, and their associates, who questioned the assumption that consensual norms were required for social stability. Instead, they suggested that formal organizations were often characterized by *role conflict* (i.e., opposing norms that were held for actors by powerful others), that such conflicts posed problems for both the actors and the organizations in which they appeared, and that strategies for coping with or "resolving" role conflict could be studied. These insights stimulated both texts that applied role concepts to organizational analysis and many studies of role conflict and role conflict resolution in organizational contexts (see, for example, van de Vliert 1979; Van Sell, Brief, and Schuler 1981; Fisher and Gitelson 1983).

In addition, the concept of role conflict has proven attractive to scholars who wanted to conceptualize or study problems that are faced by disempowered persons, particularly married women who must cope with the opposing demands of the work place, home maintenance, and support for their husbands (Stryker and Macke 1978; Lopata 1980; Skinner 1980). Unfortunately (for the argument), evidence suggests that role conflicts are not always shunned by disempowered persons (see Sales, Shore, and Bolitho 1980) and that "resolving" those conflicts does not necessarily lead to empowerment.

Despite these latter problems, research on role conflict within the organization continues actively, and some proponents of the organizational perspective have recently turned their attention to the events of role transition, that is, phenomena associated with entry into or departure from a role (see Allen and van de Vliert 1984; Ebaugh 1988).

THE STRUCTURAL PERSPECTIVE

Another use of role concepts has appeared among structuralists and network theorists. This third perspective reflects the early contributions of anthropologists such as S. F. Nadel and Michael Banton, sociologists such as Marion Levy, and social psychologists ranging from Dorwin Cartwright and Frank Harary to Oscar Oeser. As a rule, structuralists concern themselves with the logical implications of ways for organizing social systems (conceived as social positions and roles) and eschew any discussion of norms or other expectation concepts.

To date, much of the work in structural role theory has been expressed in formal, mathematical terms (see Burt 1982; Winship and Mandel 1983). This means that it has had greater appeal for scholars who are mathematically trained. It also constitutes one form of network analysis (although other network perspectives have appeared that do not use role concepts).

ROLE THEORY AMONG SYMBOLIC INTERACTIONISTS

Interest in role theory has also appeared among symbolic interactionists who were influenced not only by George Herbert Mead but also by Everett Hughes, Erving Goffman, and other influential figures. In general, symbolic interactionists think of a role as a line of action that is pursued by the individual within a given context. Roles are affected by various forces including preexisting norms applying to the social position of the actor, beliefs and attitudes that the actor holds, the actor's conception and portrayal of self, and the "definition of the situation" that evolves as the actor and others interact. Roles need not have common elements, but they are likely to become quite similar among actors who face common problems in similar circumstances.

These concepts have been applied by symbolic interactionists to a host of interesting concerns (see, for example, Scheibe 1979; Gordon and Gordon 1982; Ickes and Knowles 1982; Stryker and Serpe 1982; Zurcher 1983; Hare 1985), and a continuing and useful contribution has flowed from Ralph Turner's interest in the internal dynamics of roles and the fact that roles tend to evolve over time (Turner 1979, 1990).

Unfortunately, some persons within this perspective have also been guilty of tunnel vision and have produced reviews in which role theory is portrayed largely as an extension of symbolic interactionist thought (see Heiss 1981; Stryker and Statham 1985). In addition, symbolic interactionism has attracted its share of criticism—among other things, for its tendencies to use fuzzy definitions, recite cant, and ignore structural constraints that affect behaviors—and some of these criticisms have tended to rub off on role theory.

COGNITIVE PERSPECTIVES IN ROLE THEORY

Empirical research in role theory has been carried out by cognitive social psychologists representing several traditions (see Biddle 1986 for a general review). Some of this work has focused on role playing, some of it has concerned the impact of group norms, some of it has studied the effects of anticipatory role expectations, and some of it has examined role taking.

In addition, cognitive social psychologists have studied conformity to many forms of expectations including instrumental norms, moral norms, norms attributed to others, self-fulfilling prophecies, beliefs about the self (such as those induced by altercasting or labeling), beliefs about others, and preferences or "attitudes." These latter studies suggest that roles are often generated by two or more modes of expectational thought, and several models have also appeared from cognitive theorists reflecting this insight (see, for example, Bank et al. 1985).

Unfortunately, much of this effort ignores expectations for social positions and concentrates, instead, on expectations for individual actors. Cognitive role theory also tends to ignore the implications of its findings for structural analysis and thus appears to be atheoretical from a sociological perspective. However, Biddle (1979) has authored a monograph for role theory that uses information from cognitive research to build models for social system analysis.

ROLE THEORY AND THE FUTURE

Role theory is currently weakened by confusion, diffuse effort, and the narrow visions of some of its protagonists. Nevertheless, role theory concerns central issues for sociology, and assumptions about social positions, role behaviors, and expectations for human conduct appear widely in current social thought. Role theory will prosper as ways are found to discuss these issues with clarity, consistency, and breadth of vision.

(SEE ALSO: *Identity Theory; Role Conflict; Role Models; Social Psychology; Symbolic Interaction Theory*)

REFERENCES

Allen, Vernon L., and Evert van de Vliert (eds.) 1984 *Role Transitions: Explorations and Explanations.* New York: Plenum Press.

Bank, Barbara J., Bruce J. Biddle, Don S. Anderson, Ragnar Hauge, Daphne M. Keats, John A. Keats,

Marjorie M. Marlin, and Simone Valantin 1985 "Comparative Research on the Social Determinants of Adolescent Drinking." *Social Psychology Quarterly* 48:164–177.

Bates, Frederick L., and Clyde C. Harvey 1975 *The Structure of Social Systems.* New York: Wiley.

Biddle, Bruce J. 1979 *Role Theory: Expectations, Identities, and Behaviors.* New York: Academic Press.

———1986 "Recent Developments in Role Theory." In R. H. Turner, ed., *Annual Review of Sociology.* Vol. 12. Palo Alto, Calif.: Annual Reviews, Inc.

Burt, Ronald S. 1982 *Toward a Structural Theory of Action: Network Models of Social Structure, Perception, and Action.* New York: Academic Press.

Connell, Robert W. 1979 "The Concept of 'Role' and What to Do with It." *Australian and New Zealand Journal of Sociology* 15:7–17. (Reprinted in R. W. Connell, *Which Way Is Up? Essays on Sex, Class, and Culture.* Sydney: Allen and Unwin, 1983.)

Ebaugh, Helen Rose Fuchs 1988 *Becoming an EX: The Process of Role Exit.* Chicago: University of Chicago Press.

Fisher, Cynthia D., and Richard Gitelson 1983 "A Meta-Analysis of the Correlates of Role Conflict and Ambiguity." *Journal of Applied Psychology* 68:320–333.

Gordon, Chad, and Paddy Gordon 1982 "Changing Roles, Goals, and Self-Conceptions: Process and Results in a Program for Women's Employment." In W. Ickes and E. S. Knowles, eds., *Personality, Roles, and Social Behavior.* New York: Springer-Verlag.

Hare, A. Paul 1985 *Social Interaction as Drama: Applications from Conflict Resolution.* Beverly Hills, Calif.: Sage Publications.

Heiss, Jerrold 1981 "Social Roles." In M. Rosenberg and R. H. Turner, eds., *Social Psychology: Sociological Perspectives.* New York: Basic Books.

Ickes, William, and Eric S. Knowles, eds. 1982 *Personality, Roles, and Social Behavior.* New York: Springer-Verlag.

Lopata, Helena (ed.) 1980 *Research in the Interweave of Social Roles: Women and Men—A Research Annual.* Vol. 3. Greenwich, Conn.: JAI Press.

Sales, Esther, Barbara K. Shore, and Floyd Bolitho 1980 "When Mothers Return to School: A Study of Women Completing an MSW Program." *Journal of Education for Social Work* 16:57–65.

Scheibe, Karl E. 1979 *Mirrors, Masks, Lies, and Secrets: The Limits of Human Predictability.* New York: Praeger.

Skinner, Denise A. 1980 "Dual-Career Family Stress and Coping: A Literature Review." *Family Relations* 29:473–481.

Stryker, Sheldon, and Anne Statham Macke 1978 "Status Inconsistency and Role Conflict." In R. Turner, J. Coleman, and R. Fox, eds., *Annual Review of Sociology.* Vol. 4. Palo Alto, Calif.: Annual Reviews, Inc.

Stryker, Sheldon, and Richard T. Serpe 1982 "Commitment, Identity Salience, and Role Behavior: Theory and Research Example." In W. Ickes and E. S. Knowles, eds., *Personality, Roles, and Social Behavior.* New York: Springer-Verlag.

Stryker, Sheldon, and Anne Statham 1985 "Symbolic Interaction and Role Theory." In G. Lindzey and E. Aronson, eds., *Handbook of Social Psychology.* 3d. ed. New York: Random.

Turner, Ralph 1979 "Strategy for Developing an Integrated Role Theory." *Humboldt Journal of Social Relations* 7:123–139.

———1990 "Role Change." In W. R. Scott, ed., *Annual Review of Sociology.* Vol. 16. Palo Alto, Calif.: Annual Reviews, Inc.

van de Vliert, Evert 1979 "Gedrag in Rolkonfliktsituaties: 20 Jaar Onderzoek rond een Theorie." *Nederlands Tijdschrift voor de Psychologie* 34:125–145.

Van Sell, Mary, Arthur P. Brief, and Randall S. Schuler 1981 "Role Conflict and Role Ambiguity: Integration of the Literature and Directions for Future Research." *Human Relations* 34:43–71.

Winship, Christopher, and M. Mandel 1983 "Roles and Positions: A Critique and Extension of the Blockmodeling Approach." In S. Leinhardt, ed., *Sociological Methodology 1983–1984.* San Francisco: Jossey-Bass.

Zurcher, Louis A., Jr. 1983 *Social Roles: Conformity, Conflict, and Creativity.* Beverly Hills, Calif.: Sage.

BRUCE J. BIDDLE

RURAL SOCIOLOGY Rural sociology is the study of social organization and social processes that are characteristic of geographical localities where population size is relatively small and density is low (Warner 1974). Thus, rural sociology can be defined as the sociology of rural society. Since rural societies do not exist in isolation, rural sociology also addresses the relation of rural society to the larger society. Therefore, it deals also with spatial organization and the processes that produce spatial allocations of population and human activities (Newby 1980; Newby and Buttel 1980).

There is a temptation to equate rural sociology with American rural sociology because the latter is most thoroughly institutionalized and there are more practitioners in the United States than anywhere else in the world. While rural sociology, in its institutionalized form, originated in America, it has flourished in other regions of the world, especially since the end of World War II. No doubt this is due in large part to the "modernization" efforts in the many nations that gained independence since 1950. Outside North America, sociological investigations of rural society often are referred to as peasant studies, development studies, or village studies rather than rural sociology (Newby 1980). Moreover, some aspects of rural sociological analysis are closely related to other social science disciplines, such as settlement patterns with human geography, family and kinship systems with social anthropology, and land tenure and farming systems with agricultural economics.

ROOTS IN SOCIAL THOUGHT

Although the subject matter of rural sociology has been of keen interest to social thinkers for centuries, its treatment by the major nineteenth-century classical theorists led to a polarization that continues today (Duncan 1954; Hofstee 1963; LeFebvre 1953; Mendras 1969). Two points of view, both deeply embedded in the social thought and literature of Western culture and quite limiting if not erroneous, have predominated. The first tradition, an image drawn from the Arcadia of Greek mythology, has been the glorification of village life for the supposed pastoral innocence of its people. The second tradition has been that of the Enlightenment and modern Western rationalism, which viewed the technological and organizational character of urban industrial forces as being superior to the alleged backwardness of rural areas.

These two traditions were ultimately embraced in major nineteenth-century social theories (Nisbet 1966). Some theorists, typified by Durkheim, and Marx to a lesser extent, viewed the urban industrial complex as the center of a new civilization emerging from the social transformations of the industrial revolution. Rural society, in this perspective, was regarded as a residual of preindustrial society and increasingly to be relegated to a secondary status. Other theorists, such as Toennies (1957, original 1887) and early-twentieth-century interpreters of Toennies (e.g., Sorokin and Zimmerman 1929) viewed the emergent cities of industrial capitalism as monuments to the degradation of civilization. Both points of view are deeply imbedded in the social thought of Western culture and continue to shape the perspectives of rural sociology as a scientific enterprise.

RURAL SOCIOLOGY IN AMERICA

The roots of rural sociology in America lie in the social and political turmoil associated with America's version of the Industrial Revolution, which followed the Civil War. As industrial capitalism made its great surge, urban America was on the move, quickly surpassing earlier achievements of European nations. Yet in the midst of obviously rising affluence there existed a paradoxical injustice of poverty and inequality, especially in rural areas (Goodwyn 1978). William Jennings Bryan was defeated in 1896 as the Populist Party candidate for president, but the political unrest in the countryside continued to be a source of concern to urban industrialists, who depended on farmers to provide a stable supply of cheap food for the growing army of industrial workers.

The Country Life Movement emerged at the turn of the century as an urban-sponsored alternative to the radical economic proposals of the rural Populists (Bowers 1974; Danbom 1979; Swanson 1972). It was a social, cultural, and moral reform movement that adopted the view that rural society was backward, lagging behind the evolution of an advanced urban society. The problems of rural people were viewed as stemming from a lack of organization, failures of rural social institutions, inadequate infrastructures, and technological backwardness, rather than from the failures of the industrial capitalist system, as the Populists claimed.

In 1908 President Theodore Roosevelt gave legitimacy to the reform movement by appointing the Commission on Country Life. Spurred by the president's commission and the Country Life Movement, Congress in 1914 passed the Smith-Lever Act, which created the Cooperative Extension Service to modernize rural America (Hooks and Flinn 1981). In 1925 Congress passed the Purnell Act, which provided colleges of agriculture and agricultural experiment stations with funds to support rural sociological research. Shortly thereafter departments of rural sociology began to emerge within universities, often separated from departments of sociology (Sewell 1965). The institutionalization of rural sociology was given further impetus in 1936, when rural sociologists established their own journal, *Rural Sociology,* and during the following year, when they divorced themselves from the American Sociological Society (now the American Sociological Association) by forming the Rural Sociological Society. During the Depression rural sociology received substantial support for research regarding the socioeconomic status of farm families and the effectiveness of various New Deal federal programs.

Because of its historical roots, rural sociology has been an active participant in two conflicting social policies derived from the opposing views of rural society in social thought. The institutional separation of rural sociology from sociology, its organizational location in colleges of agriculture, and its functional integration with cooperative extension have given American rural sociology a strong attachment to technologically driven modernization. For many of its institutional sponsors, whose primary goal has been the technological advancement of agriculture, the predominant justification for supporting rural sociological research has been its presumed ability to enhance the process of modernization of rural society.

Two important consequences have followed from this sponsorship. First, the research agenda of rural sociology has been significantly influenced by politicians and administrators of colleges of agriculture and agricultural experiment stations. Thus, American rural sociological research has tended to be driven primarily by the need to be "useful" in solving practical problems involved in transforming rural society. Second, theoretical development within rural sociology has atrophied. Theoretical work that may contradict the prevailing social policy dogma and thereby threaten its financial and institutional support has been particularly uncommon. Thus, the practice of American rural sociology has been part of an explicit social policy of transforming rural society (Newby 1980).

The opposing cultural theme portrays rural society as a way of life that is superior to existence in the cities and threatened by urban industrial capitalism (Sorokin and Zimmerman 1929). It has protagonists within rural sociology and in society for whom the problem is how to preserve the wholesome qualities of rural society against the encroachments of urban industrial capitalism (e.g., how to avoid community disintegration, loss of local autonomy, the collapse of the family farm, the decline of the traditional rural way of life, degradation of the rural landscape, and depletion of nonrenewable natural resources). These Jeffersonian values of community, individualism, family entrepreneurship, and grass-roots democracy inspire private and public sponsorship of many rural sociological endeavors (Gilbert 1982).

Thus, American rural sociology has been significantly involved in two explicit and conflicting social policies. It has contributed to positivistic social science by providing the basic descriptive information about rural populations, institutions, and social processes that have guided the development of programs to transform rural society. And it has served those committed to preserving selected elements of rural society, a practice that often is perceived by agricultural administrators and proponents of technological innovations as creating barriers to progress.

MAJOR RESEARCH TOPICS

Within the context of these conflicting and vacillating social policy orientations, rural sociology in America has generated a substantial body of research. Some research topics have emerged principally in response to the social policy of transforming rural society and have followed the paradigm of positivism. Other topics are associated more clearly with the preservationist policy orientation and the paradigm of critical sociology. While the alignment of social policy and scientific paradigms is not perfect, there is a clear pattern of association. Both sets of orientations have existed within rural sociology since its inception, with the modernization-positivism orientation clearly dominating the research enterprise until recently.

Modernization-Positivism-Oriented Research. One of the primary concerns of the Commission on Country Life was the lack of complete and accurate information about the conditions of life in rural America. Thus, study of the rural population was one of the first research topics to emerge (Brunner 1957). Initially research was devoted primarily to description of the rural population, not only in an effort to provide more accurate counts of people but also to report on their characteristics in greater detail and to describe demographic processes more accurately. Population studies continue to be extremely important in providing the basic descriptive information about the rural population that is needed to guide the development of programs to transform rural society (Fuguitt, Brown, and Beale 1989).

To the extent that rural population studies depart from purely demographic analyses and venture into sociological investigations, they are usually guided by the systemic perspective of human ecology (Hawley 1950, 1986). In this more sophisticated systems model, population size and density are treated as interdependent with the environment, the level of technology, and the social organization of a locality. It is presumed that population size and density will expand to the maximum possible within the constraints imposed by the other components of the system, especially the technology of transportation and communication. While the perspective offers promise of merging social and spatial analysis, the results have been only partially successful. Rural population studies *cum* human ecology have yet to integrate the social and spatial levels of reality.

As more information about rural populations became available, comparisons with urban populations became possible, and there followed a prolific production of research to examine the belief that population size and density set the conditions of social action and social organization. This was a fundamental premise of the romanticists among the classical sociological writers noted earlier, and which became translated sociologically into the "rural-urban continuum" of Sorokin and Zimmerman (1929) and later the "folk-urban continuum" of Redfield (1947). The evidence that there are universal differences in the cultural and social characteristics that may be derived from differences in population size and density has not been convincing (Pahl 1966). Thus, while comparisons are drawn between rural and urban populations, the causality argument associated with the rural-urban continuum has been discarded by most rural sociologists.

Rural sociologists have conducted hundreds of community studies that serve as a major source of information for the design of community development programs (Bell and Newby 1972; Summers 1986, Luloff and Swanson 1990; Wilkinson 1991). From Galpin's pioneering study in 1915 until the mid-1960s, the study of community was almost synonymous with rural sociology in the United States. By that time the rural-urban continuum, which was the chief frame of reference for many investigators, was falling into disrepute (Pahl 1966). Their studies were being criticized for their impressionistic methodologies and their excessively descriptive nature (Bell and Newby 1972). Moreover, proponents of the mass-society thesis argued that communities had been eclipsed by the forces of urbanization, bureaucratization, and centralization (Stein 1964; Vidich and Bensman 1958; Warren 1963). Community was alleged to be no longer a meaningful locus of social decision making. It was presumed that the increased presence of extralocal forces in the community (vertical integration) had destroyed the horizontal integration of communities and rendered small rural communities powerless in the face of broad and powerful forces of mass society.

Although the tradition of holistic community studies has not returned to its former status, evidence clearly supports the argument that increased vertical integration does not necessarily destroy horizontal integration (Richards 1978; Summers 1986). Rather it is more consistent with the empirical data to view local autonomy as a variable, and the impact of changes in vertical integration as varying according to a complex matrix of variables characterizing the external agent and the community.

In 1897, W.E.B. DuBois began a series of analyses of economic conditions among rural black groups and their relation to agriculture (DuBois 1898, 1901, 1904). Thus, from the turn of the century rural sociologists have been studying the "sociology of agriculture," although that expression did not come into use until the 1970s (Buttel, Larson, and Gillespie 1990). Land tenure and types of farming enterprises were studied to understand the relations of farming and agriculturally based businesses to the conditions of rural living. The methodology of these studies was often that of the community survey, and consequently there was much overlap with population and community studies. Most of these studies were descriptive in nature and generated taxonomies of farming enterprises, which provided further refinements of farm family and farming community characteristics. The resulting social maps of farming communities provided detailed information to guide modernization programs, especially those of the Cooperative Extension Service, with its offices in virtually every rural county in the United States.

Although technological innovations have been occurring in agriculture for centuries, technological change was revolutionized with the introduction of hybrid corn (Ryan and Gross 1943). With this innovation, adoption and diffusion research became a new research field led by rural sociology. The first research focused on identifying which farmers had the highest rates of adoption of hybrid corn and how the adoption process was diffused to other farmers. Soon the research encompassed other innovations and spread to other countries with the modernization era at the end of World War II (Rogers 1983). The basic processes of adoption and diffusion are now reasonably well understood, and training programs based on this knowledge are being implemented worldwide in areas of human behavior that reach well beyond farming practices to include health and nutrition, resource conservation, business management, and many other areas.

Preservationst-Critically Oriented Research. By the 1960s there was a strong and growing disillusionment with the societal consequences of positivistic social science and the absence of a structuralist perspective (Newby and Buttel 1980). It was claimed that theory and research had become uncoupled, with theory being excessively abstract and research exhibiting a mindless empiricism. Several rural sociologists involved in international development research offered challenges to the Western development orthodoxy by claiming that modernization was serving the interests of the powerful and wealthy rather than improving the social and economic well-being of peasants and poor people (Havens 1972; Havens and Flinn 1975; Thiesenhusen 1978). In North America and Europe similar claims were being expressed in the environmental, civil rights, and other social justice movements of the late 1960s. The emerging research topics in rural sociology manifest the intellectual ferment of a more critical perspective on existing public policies, especially in relation to established institutions of agricultural and rural research and programs claiming to improve rural communities and institutions.

The emergent critical perspective incorporates a diversity of theoretical views that recognize the active role of the state in public policy and argue that it is subject to the influences within society of powerful interest groups that often are formed along the lines of class, race, ethnicity, or gender. Thus, the contemporary theoretical debates within rural sociology draw heavily on neo-Marxist and neo-Weberian orientations, with the result that rural sociology and sociology are closer intellectual partners today than at any time in the past fifty years. Although virtually all facets of rural social organization and processes are subjected to the emergent critical perspective, some areas have received more attention than others.

Perhaps the most distinctive feature of the new political economy of agriculture is the prominence of Marxist and neo-Marxist interpretations of the social differentiation of agriculture (Friedland, Barton, and Thomas 1981; Friedmann 1982; Havens et al. 1986; Mooney 1988; Mann 1990). There is clear evidence of growth of large-scale capitalist agriculture accompanied by the persistence of the small-scale family farm. Efforts to understand this duality of agricultural structure has led to sharp debates about the barriers to capitalist transformation of agriculture, the role of small-scale and part-time farms in a functionally integrated capitalist industrial and agricultural system, and the role of the state in promoting capitalist agriculture. Inevitably, the research apparatus of the land grant university system itself has come under critical scrutiny because of its role as a creator and provider of new agricultural technologies that are alleged to contribute to the growth of large-scale capitalist agriculture (Busch and Lacy 1983; Kloppenburg 1988).

Until the late 1960s and early 1970s rural sociology's contribution to the sociology of development was confined largely to adoption-diffusion research related to new agricultural technologies in Third World countries (Hoogvelt 1978; Toye 1987; Webster 1990). Shortly thereafter, following on the growing disillusion with adoption-diffusion research, development-related inquiry in rural sociology shifted dramatically.

Much of the impetus behind criticism of the adoption-diffusion approach came from rural social scientists who did Third World research and who became acutely aware of its shortcomings as a vehicle for understanding agricultural change in the developing countries (Havens and Flinn 1975; George 1976; Lipton 1977; Flora 1990). The theoretical ferment in rural sociology in the 1970s and 1980s was to a large extent derived from debates in the sociology of development, such as the "development of underdevelopment," "dependent development," "core-periphery relations," and "roads of agricultural development."

The "postdiffusion" phase of the sociology of development has led to a far more diversified program of rural sociological research on development processes in the Third World. Although rural sociologists who do sociology of development research tend, not surprisingly, to give particular stress to agricultural development and its environmental implications, increasingly rural sociologists in the United States and other advanced countries do research on development processes that is often indistinguishable from that conducted by scholars who are not identified as rural sociologists. Also, as noted earlier, in many developing countries rural sociology is virtually synonymous with sociology of development, development studies, peasant studies, village studies, and so on.

To a certain extent this emerging research area overlaps the political economy of agriculture with its emphasis on technological change and its effects of distribution of ownership and control of resources, as well as equity in the distribution of benefits of new technologies (Field and Burch 1988). There is the additional concern with the depletion and pollution of nonrenewable resources (Schnaiberg 1980). Social and economic impact assessment has emerged as a research activity that often is characterized by its critical perspective (Freudenburg 1986). A comprehensive theory has not yet emerged that links technological change in natural resource industries to the full range of its ramifications for the environment, its socioeconomic impacts, and its associations with industrial structures. However, the magnitude of its potential impacts and the associated public concern suggests that this area of research has a viable future.

Since the 1920s agriculture and natural-resource-based industries have been declining as sources of employment; the rate of decline accelerated dramatically after World War II. For a brief period during the 1970s manufacturing was a major source of employment growth in rural areas as industries sought cheaper land, lower taxes, and a nonunion labor force willing to work for lower wages and fewer benefits. Although this process continues, service industries have emerged as the major source of employment growth (Brown et al. 1988).

These shifting labor demands have been accompanied by high unemployment in rural areas and a growth of temporary and part-time work, with resulting loss of wages and increasing levels of poverty. Rural labor market analysis has emerged as a new research area in rural sociology as a consequence (Summers, Horton, and Gringeri 1990).

Much of the research is devoted to describing more precisely the nature and extent of rural unemployment and underemployment. However, the theoretical interpretations generally are sensitive to the linkages of rural labor markets to broader issues of economic restructuring. While labor demand-oriented and human capital explanations persist, there are attempts to understand the functioning of rural labor markets within the context of capitalist market institutions in a manner that is reminiscent of institutional labor economics.

Gender studies are not new to rural sociology; the role of women in farming has been a subject of research for at least a quarter century (Haney and Knowles 1988). However, the past decade has witnessed the emergence of theoretical and empirical studies that attempt to explain how the institutions of capitalism, patriarchy, and the domestic ideology influence the work roles of men and women. A major focus of these recent studies has been the nature and extent of farm women's involvement in farm, household, and off-farm work. The rich descriptive detail of gender-based allocations of labor is being integrated into more comprehensive theoretical interpretations of structural changes in both agricultural and nonagricultural industries (Beneria 1985; Leon and Deere 1987; Sachs 1984).

For the past twenty-five years the United States has pursued a variety of programs and policies intended to alleviate poverty (Sanderfur and Tienda 1988; Snipp 1989; Wilson 1987). In spite of these efforts, poverty persists at rates that are higher in rural areas than in urban areas, and the difference is increasing. Moreover, rural poverty is disproportionally concentrated in minority populations. Within the critical perspective it is argued that past and present institutional barriers limit the access of minority populations to the means of economic well-being. Persons of working age are disproportionally handicapped by deficiencies of human capital and discriminatory practices in the labor market. Moreover, these failures have produced a generation of elderly persons who are denied access to important public insurance programs such as Social Security because they were excluded from the labor market in years past or employed in industries that were not covered by such programs. Thus, the state is called into question for its poor performance in developing and implementing adequate public policies, a failure that is alleged to benefit the interests of the wealthy and powerful classes of society (Summers forthcoming).

CONCLUSION

These emergent research topics have not displaced those of an earlier period of rural sociology; they coexist. In doing so, rural sociology continues to serve two conflicting social policy agendas that reflect divergent views of rural society. The field has not escaped its origins in the social thought of nineteenth-century Europe. It does appear to be renewing its intellectual kinship with sociological theory.

The future of rural sociology as a research domain and as an intellectual endeavor appears to be very promising. Only a decade ago some observers were predicting its demise on the grounds that agriculture was declining as a source of employment and urbanization was continuing on a worldwide scale. However, predictions of the death of rural sociology seem to have been premature. The majority of the world population still lives in rural areas, and agriculture dominates the economy of most nations of the world. The ending of the Cold War and the opening of the Eastern Bloc to greater scientific and intellectual exchanges create a vast new market for rural sociology, since all of these nations are predominately rural in composition. Finally, rural sociologists are expanding the scope of their work to include a much broader array of social phenomena and accepting the challenge of building the theoretical and empirical bridges between rural and urban aspects of society.

The growth of rural sociology professional associations is further evidence of its good health. In addition to the Rural Sociological Society, which was created in 1937, there now is the International Rural Sociological Association and independent associations in all the world's regions. Membership in all these associations is increasing; the Rural Sociological Society reported nearly eleven hundred members in 1990, and the attendance at its 1990 annual meeting (over 500) was the largest in its fifty-three-year history.

(SEE ALSO: *Agricultural Innovation; Community; Human Ecology and the Environment; Population*)

REFERENCES

Bell, Colin, and Howard Newby 1972 *Community Studies: An Introduction to the Sociology of the Local Community.* New York: Praeger.

Beneria, Lourdes 1985 *Women and Development: Sexual Division of Labor in Rural Societies.* New York: Praeger.

Bowers, W. L. 1974 *The Country Life Movement in America, 1900–1920.* Port Washington, NY: Kennikat.

Brown, David L., et al. (eds.) 1988 *Rural Economic Development in the 1980s.* Rural Development Research Report No. 69. Washington, DC: USDA, Economic Research Service.

Brunner, Edmund deS. 1957 *The Growth of a Science: A Half-Century of Rural Sociological Research in the United States.* New York: Harper and Row.

Busch, Lawrence, and William B. Lacy 1983 *Science, Agriculture, and the Politics of Research.* Boulder, Colo.: Westview Press.

Buttel, Frederick H., Olaf F. Larson, and Gilbert W. Gillespie, Jr. 1990 *The Sociology of Agriculture.* Westport, Conn.: Greenwood Press.

Danbom, D. B. 1979 *The Resisted Revolution: Urban America and the Industrialization of Agriculture, 1900–1930.* Ames: Iowa State University Press.

DuBois, W.E.B. 1898 "The Negroes of Farmville, Virginia: A Social Study." *Bulletin of the Department of Labor* 3 (14):1–38.

——— 1901 "The Negro Landholders of Georgia." *Bulletin of the Department of Labor* 6 (35):647–777.

——— 1904 "The Negro Farmer." Pp. 69–98 in U.S. Bureau of the Census, *Negroes in the United States.* Washington, D.C.: U.S. Government Printing Office.

Duncan, Otis Durant 1954 "Rural Sociology Coming of Age." *Rural Sociology* 19 (1):1–12.

Field, Donald R., and William R. Burch, Jr. 1988 *Rural Sociology and the Environment.* Westport, Conn.: Greenwood Press.

Flora, Cornelia Butler 1990 "Rural Peoples in a Global Economy." *Rural Sociology* 55 (Summer):157–177.

Freudenburg, William R. 1986 "Social Impact Assessment." *Annual Review of Sociology* 12:451–478.

Friedland, William H., Amy Barton, and Robert J. Thomas 1981 *Manufacturing Green Gold.* New York: Cambridge University Press.

Friedmann, Harriet 1982 "The Political Economy of Food: The Rise and Fall of the Postwar International Food Order." *American Journal of Sociology* 88 (Supplement):S248–S286.

Fuguitt, Glenn V., David L. Brown, and Calvin L. Beale 1989 *Rural and Small-Town America.* New York: Russell Sage Foundation.

Galpin, Charles J. 1915 *The Social Anatomy of an Agricultural Community.* Madison: Wisconsin Agricultural Experiment Station.

George, Susan 1976 *How the Other Half Dies.* New York: Penguin.

Gilbert, Jess 1982 "Rural Theory: The Grounding of Rural Sociology." *Rural Sociology* 47 (Winter):609–633.

Goodwyn, Lawrence 1978 *The Populist Movement: A Short History of the Agrarian Revolt in America.* New York: Oxford University Press.

Haney, Wava G., and Jane B. Knowles (eds.) 1988 *Women and Farming: Changing Roles, Changing Structures.* Boulder, Colo.: Westview Press.

Havens, A. Eugene 1972 "Methodological Issues in the Study of Development." *Sociologia Ruralis* 12 (3–4):252–272.

———, and William L. Flinn 1975 "Green Revolution Technology and Community Development: The Limits of Action Programs." *Economic Development and Cultural Change* 23 (April):469–481.

———, Gregory Hooks, Patrick H. Mooney, and Max J. Pfeffer (eds.) 1986 *Studies in the Transformation of U.S. Agriculture.* Boulder, Colo.: Westview Press.

Hawley, Amos H. 1950 *Human Ecology.* New York: Ronald Press.

———1986 *Human Ecology: A Theoretical Essay.* Chicago: University of Chicago Press.

Hofstee, E. W. 1963 "Rural Sociology in Europe." *Rural Sociology* 28 (3):329–341.

Hoogvelt, Ankie M. M. 1978 *The Sociology of Developing Societies,* 2nd ed. London: Macmillan.

Hooks, Gregory M., and William L. Flinn 1981 "The Country Life Commission and Early Rural Sociology." *The Rural Sociologist* 1 (March):95–100.

Kloppenburg, Jack, Jr. 1988 *First the Seed.* New York: Cambridge University Press.

LeFebvre, Henry 1953 "Perspectives de la Sociologie Rurale." *Cahiers Internationaux de Sociologie* 14:122–140.

Leon, Magdalena, and Carmen Diana Deere (eds.) 1987 *Women and Rural Policy: Feminist Perspectives.* Boulder, Colo.: Westview Press.

Lipton, Michael 1977 *Why Poor People Stay Poor.* London: Temple Smith.

Luloff, A. E., and Louis E. Swanson (eds.) 1990 *American Rural Communities.* Boulder, Colo: Westview Press.

Mann, Susan Archer 1990 *Agrarian Capitalism in Theory and Practice.* Chapel Hill: University of North Carolina Press.

Mendras, Henri 1969 *Rural Sociology in France.* Paris: Mouton.

Mooney, Patrick H. 1988 *My Own Boss.* Boulder, Colo.: Westview Press.

Newby, Howard 1980 "Rural Sociology—A Trend Report." *Current Sociology* 28 (1):1–141.

———, and Frederick H. Buttel 1980 "Toward a Critical Rural Sociology." In F. H. Buttel and H. Newby, eds., *The Rural Sociology of the Advanced Societies.* Montclair, N.J.: Allanheld, Osmun.

Nisbet, Robert 1966 *The Sociological Tradition.*

Pahl, Ray E. 1966 "The Rural-Urban Continuum." *Sociologia Ruralis* 6 (3–4):299–327. Reprinted in Pahl, R. E., ed., 1970 *Readings in Urban Sociology.* Oxford: Pergamon Press.

Redfield, Robert 1947. "The Folk Society." *American Journal of Sociology* 52 (3):293–308.

Richards, R. O. 1978 "Urbanization of Rural Areas." In David Street and Associates, eds., *Handbook of Contemporary Urban Life.* San Francisco: Jossey-Bass.

Rogers, Everett M. 1983 *Diffusion of Innovations.* New York: The Free Press.

Ryan, Bryce, and Neal C. Gross 1943 "The Diffusion of Hybrid Seed Corn in Two Iowa Communities." *Rural Sociology* 8:15–24.

Sachs, Carolyn 1984 *The Invisible Farmers: Women in Agricultural Production.* Totowa, N.J.: Rowman & Allanheld.

Sandefur, Gary D., and Marta Tienda (eds.) 1988 *Divided Opportunities: Minorities, Poverty and Social Policy.* New York: Plenum.

Schnaiberg, Allan 1980 *The Environment: From Surplus to Scarcity.* New York: Oxford University Press.

Sewell, William H. 1965 "Rural Sociological Research, 1936–1965." *Rural Sociology* 30 (Dec.):428–451.

Snipp, C. Matthew 1989 *American Indians: The First of This Land.* New York: Russell Sage Foundation.

Sorokin, P. A., and Carl C. Zimmerman 1929 *Principles of Rural-Urban Sociology.* New York: Henry Holt.

Stein, Maurice 1964 *The Eclipse of Community.* New York: Harper and Row.

Summers, Gene F. 1986 "Rural Community Development." *Annual Review of Sociology* 12:347–371.

——— (Forthcoming) "Minorities in Rural Society." *Rural Sociology.*

———, Francine Horton, and Christina Gringeri 1990 "Rural Labour-Market Changes in the United States." In Terry Marsden, Philip Lowe, and Sarah Whatmore, eds., *Rural Restructuring: Global Processes and Their Responses.* London: David Fulton.

Swanson, R. M. 1972 "The Country Life Movement, 1900–1940." Ph.D. diss., University of Minnesota.

Thiesenhusen, William C. 1978 "Reaching the Rural Poor and Poorest: A Goal Unmet." In H. Newby, ed., *International Perspectives in Rural Sociology.* New York: Wiley.

Toennies, Ferdinand (1887) 1957 *Community and Society: Gemeinschaft und Gesellschaft.* New York: Harper and Row.

Toye, John 1987 *Dilemmas of Development.* New York: Basil Blackwell.

Vidich, Arthur J., and Joseph Bensman 1958 *Small Town in Mass Society: Class, Power and Religion in a Rural Community.* Princeton, N.J.: Princeton University Press.

Warner, W. Keith 1974 "Rural Society in a Post-Industrial Age." *Rural Sociology* 39 (3):306–317.

Warren, Roland 1963 *The Community in America.* Chicago: Rand McNally.

Webster, Andrew 1990 *Introduction to the Sociology of Development,* 2nd ed. Atlantic Highlands, N.J.: Humanities Press International.

Wilkinson, Kenneth 1991 *The Community in Rural Society.* Westport, Conn.: Greenwood Press.

Wilson, William Julius 1987 *The Truly Disadvantaged: The Inner City, the Underclass, and Public Policy.* Chicago: University of Chicago Press.

GENE F. SUMMERS